THE MARK TWAIN PAPERS

Mark Twain's Letters
Volume 3: 1869

THE MARK TWAIN PAPERS AND WORKS OF MARK TWAIN
is a comprehensive edition for scholars of the private papers
and published works of Mark Twain (Samuel L. Clemens).

THE MARK TWAIN LIBRARY
is a selected edition reprinted from the Papers and Works for
students and the general reader. Both series of books are published
by the University of California Press and edited by members of the

MARK TWAIN PROJECT
with headquarters in The Bancroft Library,
University of California, Berkeley.

Editorial work for all volumes is jointly supported by grants from the

NATIONAL ENDOWMENT FOR THE HUMANITIES,
an independent federal agency,
and by public and private donations,
matched equally by the Endowment, to

THE FRIENDS OF THE BANCROFT LIBRARY

The following volumes have been published to date
by the members of the Mark Twain Project:

THE MARK TWAIN PAPERS

Letters to His Publishers, 1867–1894
Edited with an Introduction by Hamlin Hill
1967

Satires & Burlesques
Edited with an Introduction by Franklin R. Rogers
1967

Which Was the Dream? and Other Symbolic
Writings of the Later Years
Edited with an Introduction by John S. Tuckey
1967

Hannibal, Huck & Tom
Edited with an Introduction by Walter Blair
1969

Mysterious Stranger Manuscripts
Edited with an Introduction by William M. Gibson
1969

Correspondence with Henry Huttleston Rogers, 1893–1909
Edited with an Introduction by Lewis Leary
1969

Fables of Man
Edited with an Introduction by John S. Tuckey
Text established by Kenneth M. Sanderson and Bernard L. Stein
Series Editor, Frederick Anderson
1972

Notebooks & Journals, Volume I (1855–1873)
Edited by Frederick Anderson, Michael B. Frank,
and Kenneth M. Sanderson
1975

Notebooks & Journals, Volume II (1877–1883)
Edited by Frederick Anderson, Lin Salamo, and Bernard L. Stein
1975

Notebooks & Journals, Volume III (1883–1891)
Edited by Robert Pack Browning, Michael B. Frank, and Lin Salamo
General Editor, Frederick Anderson
1979

Letters, Volume 1: 1853–1866
Editors: Edgar Marquess Branch, Michael B. Frank,
and Kenneth M. Sanderson
Associate Editors: Harriet Elinor Smith,
Lin Salamo, and Richard Bucci
1988

Letters, Volume 2: 1867–1868
Editors: Harriet Elinor Smith and Richard Bucci
Associate Editor: Lin Salamo
1990

Letters, Volume 3: 1869
Editors: Victor Fischer and Michael B. Frank
Associate Editor: Dahlia Armon

THE WORKS OF MARK TWAIN
Roughing It
Edited by Franklin R. Rogers and Paul Baender
1972

What Is Man? and Other Philosophical Writings
Edited by Paul Baender
1973

A Connecticut Yankee in King Arthur's Court
Edited by Bernard L. Stein,
with an Introduction by Henry Nash Smith
1979

The Prince and the Pauper
Edited by Victor Fischer and Lin Salamo,
with the assistance of Mary Jane Jones
1979

Early Tales & Sketches, Volume 1 (1851–1864)
Edited by Edgar Marquess Branch and Robert H. Hirst,
with the assistance of Harriet Elinor Smith
1979

The Adventures of Tom Sawyer · *Tom Sawyer Abroad*
Tom Sawyer, Detective
Edited by John C. Gerber, Paul Baender, and Terry Firkins
1980

Early Tales & Sketches, Volume 2 (1864–1865)
Edited by Edgar Marquess Branch and Robert H. Hirst,
with the assistance of Harriet Elinor Smith
1981

Adventures of Huckleberry Finn
Edited by Walter Blair and Victor Fischer,
with the assistance of Dahlia Armon and Harriet Elinor Smith
1988

THE MARK TWAIN LIBRARY

No. 44, The Mysterious Stranger
Edited by John S. Tuckey and William M. Gibson
1982

The Adventures of Tom Sawyer
Edited by John C. Gerber and Paul Baender
1982

Tom Sawyer Abroad · *Tom Sawyer, Detective*
Edited by John C. Gerber and Terry Firkins
1982

The Prince and the Pauper
Edited by Victor Fischer and Michael B. Frank
1983

A Connecticut Yankee in King Arthur's Court
Edited by Bernard L. Stein
1983

Adventures of Huckleberry Finn
Edited by Walter Blair and Victor Fischer
1985

Huck Finn and Tom Sawyer among the Indians, and Other Unfinished Stories
Foreword and Notes by Dahlia Armon and Walter Blair
Texts established by Dahlia Armon, Paul Baender, Walter Blair, William M.
Gibson, and Franklin R. Rogers
1989

OTHER MARK TWAIN PROJECT
PUBLICATIONS

The Devil's Race-Track: Mark Twain's Great Dark Writings
The Best from Which Was the Dream? *and* Fables of Man
Edited by John S. Tuckey
1980

Union Catalog of Clemens Letters
Edited by Paul Machlis
1986

Samuel L. Clemens and Olivia L. Langdon in 1869.
Mark Twain Papers, The Bancroft Library (CU-MARK).

THE MARK TWAIN PAPERS

General Editor, ROBERT H. HIRST

Contributing Editors for this Volume
BETH BERNSTEIN
ROBERT PACK BROWNING
RICHARD BUCCI
LIN SALAMO
KENNETH M. SANDERSON
HARRIET ELINOR SMITH

A Publication of the Mark Twain Project
of The Bancroft Library

MARK TWAIN'S
LETTERS
VOLUME 3 ✿ 1869

Editors
VICTOR FISCHER
MICHAEL B. FRANK

Associate Editor
DAHLIA ARMON

Mark Twain

UNIVERSITY OF CALIFORNIA PRESS
Berkeley · Los Angeles · London
1992

Publication of this volume was assisted by
a grant from the

PUBLICATION SUBVENTION PROGRAM, DIVISION OF RESEARCH PROGRAMS, NATIONAL ENDOWMENT FOR THE HUMANITIES, an independent federal agency.

University of California Press
Berkeley and Los Angeles, California

University of California Press, Ltd.
Oxford, England

Manufactured in the United States of America

Library of Congress Cataloging-in-Publication Data

(Revised for vol. 3)

Twain, Mark, 1835–1910.
Mark Twain's letters.

(The Mark Twain papers)
Vol. 3: editors, Victor Fischer, Michael B. Frank; associate editor, Dahlia Armon.
Includes bibliographical references and indexes.
Contents: — v. 2. 1867–1868 — v. 3. 1869.
1. Twain, Mark, 1835–1910—Correspondence.
2. Authors, American—19th century—Correspondence.
3. Humorist, American—19th century—Correspondence.
I. Branch, Edgar Marquess, 1913–   .   II. Frank, Michael B.
III. Sanderson, Kenneth M.   IV. Title.
V. Title: Letters.   VI. Series: Twain, Mark, 1835–1910.   Mark Twain papers.
PS1331.A4   1987   818'.409 [B]   87-5963
ISBN 0-520-03669-7 (v. 2 : alk. paper)   ISBN 0-520-03670-0 (v. 3 : alk. paper)

In memory of

PHILIP E. ALLEN

founder of
THE PARETO FUND
whose generous gift to
The Friends of The Bancroft Library,
together with grants from the
NATIONAL ENDOWMENT FOR THE HUMANITIES,
has made possible the publication of this volume.

Contents

Acknowledgments xvii

Introduction xxv

Editorial Signs xxix

LETTERS: 1869 1

Appendix A: Genealogies of the Clemens and
Langdon Families 447

Appendix B: Enclosures with the Letters 453

Appendix C: Calendar of Courtship Letters, 1868–1870 . . 473

Appendix D: Lecture Schedule, 1868–1870 481

Appendix E: Advertising Circulars 487

Appendix F: Photographs and Manuscript Facsimiles . . 501

Guide to Editorial Practice 551

Textual Commentaries 579

References 675

Index 705

Acknowledgments

Editorial work on this volume was made possible by the generous support of the American taxpayer, and by the professional encouragement of scholars who recommended funding for successive grants to the Mark Twain Project from the National Endowment for the Humanities, an independent federal agency. The University of California Press was likewise assisted in meeting production costs by a grant from the Endowment. We are grateful for this intellectual and material support, part of which the Endowment was able to grant by matching, dollar for dollar, a major contribution to The Friends of The Bancroft Library from the Pareto Fund.

Many individuals and institutions have contributed funds which the Endowment has also matched. We are grateful for the generosity of the following donors to The Friends of The Bancroft Library: the late Violet Appert; Betty G. Austin; Paul Berkowitz; The House of Bernstein, Inc.; J. Dennis Bonney; Harold I. and Beula Blair Boucher; Edmund G. and Bernice Layne Brown; Chevron Corporation; Dow Chemical Company; Launce E. Gamble; Dr. Orville J. Golub; James C. Greene; Constance Crowley Hart and James D. Hart; the William Randolph Hearst Foundation; the Hedco Foundation; Janet S. Hermann; Kenneth E. Hill; R. N. and Elinore Kauffman; the Koret Foundation; Daniel E. Koshland, Jr.; the Mark Twain Foundation; Jane Newhall; James E. O'Brien; the Peninsula Community Foundation; Mrs. John H. Raleigh; Reader's Digest Foundation; John W. and Barbara Rosston; John R. Shuman; the L. J. Skaggs and Mary C. Skaggs Foundation; Marion B. and Willis S. Slusser; the Henry Nash Smith Memorial Fund; the Marshall Steel, Sr., Foundation; Mrs. J. Tourtouret; the estate of John Russell Wagner; Mrs. Paul L. Wattis; and Laurel A. and Jeffrey S. Wruble.

The Mark Twain Committee of the Council of The Friends of The Bancroft Library is chiefly responsible for encouraging these and other donors to lend their support to the ongoing editorial work. Our heartfelt thanks go to the present and former members of this committee: Lawrence W. Jordan, Jr., and Thomas B. Worth, co-chairmen; Henry K. Evers, Stephen G. Herrick, David J. McDaniel, John W. Rosston, and Willis S. Slusser, former chairmen; Cindy Arnot Barber, William P. Barlow, Jr., Barbara Boucke, Henry M. Bowles, June A. Cheit, Launce E. Gamble, Marion S. Goodin, James C. Greene, Constance Crowley Hart, James D. Hart, Peter E. Hanff, William M. Hassebrock, Janet S. Hermann, Roger W. Heyns, Kenneth E. Hill, Nion T. McEvoy, James E. O'Brien, Joseph A. Rosenthal, John R. Shuman, Herbert E. Stansbury, Jr., Norman H. Strouse, and Katharine Wallace, as well as Kimberly L. Massingale, secretary to the Council.

We are indebted to the generations of scholars who have done pioneering work in locating, collecting, and publishing Mark Twain's letters, particularly to Albert Bigelow Paine and his successors as Editor of the Mark Twain Papers: Bernard DeVoto, Dixon Wecter, Henry Nash Smith, and Frederick Anderson. Paine's *Mark Twain: A Biography* (1912) and *Mark Twain's Letters* (1917) are indispensable to the present undertaking, and are the sole source now known for some letters collected here. Wecter's *Mark Twain to Mrs. Fairbanks* (1949) and *The Love Letters of Mark Twain* (1949) were the first to publish Mark Twain's letters in accord with contemporary scholarly standards, in both their annotation and their transcription of the letters themselves. Henry Nash Smith and William M. Gibson's *Mark Twain–Howells Letters* (1960) likewise established a new and higher standard for publication of letters. Anderson assisted Smith and Gibson on that publication and, until his death in 1979, was responsible for the Mark Twain Papers series, which included among its first volumes Hamlin Hill's *Mark Twain's Letters to His Publishers, 1867–1894*. We have profited from these pioneering efforts in ways too numerous to bear mention in the notes.

The ongoing research for the documentation of Mark Twain's letters has required continuing assistance. For valuable aid over many years we are grateful to the staff of The Bancroft Library, especially Brenda J. Bailey, Anthony S. Bliss, Peter E. Hanff, Irene M. Moran, and William M. Roberts. Special thanks go to the staff of the Interlibrary Borrowing Service in the Main Library: particularly Robert Heyer, Leon Megrian, Jo Lynn Milardovich, Kathleen Messer, Helen Ram, and former staff member Rhio Barnhart. Their efforts located many rare and valuable resources that have notably enriched the annotation. We are similarly indebted to Philip Hoehn of the Map Room and to Daniel L. Johnston and Marnie Jacobsen of the Photographic Service in the Main Library.

The Mark Twain Papers in The Bancroft Library is the archive of more than half of the original letters published in this volume; this collection of Mark Twain's own private papers was brought to the University of California in 1949 through the persuasive powers of Dixon Wecter and the generosity of Clara Clemens Samossoud. We are grateful to Violet Appert, Mrs. Eugene Lada-Mocarski, Jervis Langdon, Jr., Mrs. Robert S. Pennock, and Mrs. Bayard Schieffelin, all of whom donated to the Papers manuscripts of letters which appear here. The other primary source of manuscript letters in this volume is the Henry E. Huntington Library, San Marino, California, where we received timely and expert assistance from Sara S. Hodson, Brita F. Mack, Aldo R. Perdomo, Virginia Renner, and Mary Wright. Several letters published here are in the Jean Webster McKinney Family Papers in the Vassar College Library, where Barbara LaMont, Nancy S. MacKechnie, and Eleanor Rogers provided repeated access to Mark Twain materials and supporting documentation. We are grateful as well to Patricia Middleton, Kate Sharp, and Patricia C. Willis of the Beinecke Rare Book and Manuscript Library at Yale University, and for the unfailing cooperation of all the other libraries that own letters published in this volume. We are likewise grateful to Todd M. Axelrod, Jack F. Cooper, Chester L. Davis, Chester L. Davis, Jr., Victor and Irene Murr Jacobs, Theodore H. Koundakjian, and Daphne B. Sears, who generously made accessible to us the letters in their collections; to Charles S. Underhill, who made available a photograph in his collection; and to Nick Karanovich, who provided information and documents which contributed to the annotation.

In the course of transcribing, annotating, and tracing the provenance of these letters we were aided by a great number of people. We have benefitted from the extraordinary generosity and helpfulness of Gretchen Sharlow, Herbert A. Wisbey, Jr., Mark Woodhouse, and Jan Kather of the Mark Twain Archives and Center for Mark Twain Studies at Quarry Farm, Elmira College; Marianne J. Curling, Laura Vassell, and Beverly J. Zell of the Mark Twain Memorial in Hartford; Diana Royce of the Stowe-Day Library in Hartford; William H. Loos of the Buffalo and Erie County Public Library in Buffalo; and Patricia Virgil of the Buffalo and

Erie County Historical Society in Buffalo. We also received invaluable
assistance from: Lisa Backman of the Library of the Boston Athenaeum;
Professor William Baker of Wright State University; Cathy A. Barlow of
the Holyoke (Massachusetts) *Transcript-Telegram;* Joan E. Barney of the
New Bedford (Massachusetts) Free Public Library; Laura J. Berk of the
Illinois State Historical Library in Springfield; Christopher P. Bickford,
Diana E. Mackiewicz, Paige A. Savery, Alesandra M. Schmidt, and
Martha H. Smart of the Connecticut Historical Society in Hartford; Per-
sis E. Boyesen of the Ogdensburg (New York) Public Library; Louise
A. Brackman of the Naperville (Illinois) Heritage Society; Mary B.
Bowling, Lisa Browar, Wayne Furman, Frank Mattson, and Radames
Suarez of the New York Public Library; Matthew C. Bruccoli and Susan
Heath of Bruccoli, Clark, Layman, in Columbia, South Carolina; Ron
D. Bryant of the Kentucky Historical Society in Frankfort; Judith Bush-
nell and David W. Parish of the College Libraries at the State University
of New York in Geneseo; Frank J. Carroll and James H. Hutson of the
Library of Congress; Robert Collins of the Chelsea (Massachusetts)
Public Library; John D. Cushing of the Massachusetts Historical Soci-
ety in Boston; Kevin Danielson of the New Castle (Pennsylvania) Public
Library; Carolyn A. Davis of the George Arents Research Library at
Syracuse University; Timothy L. Decker of the Chemung County His-
torical Society in Elmira; Mary E. Devies of the Marlboro Township
Historical Society in Alliance, Ohio; Kathleen C. Eustis of the California
State Library in Sacramento; Marie Booth Ferré of Dickinson College
in Carlisle, Pennsylvania; James W. Fry of the Library of Michigan in
Lansing; Dorothy T. Frye of the University Archives and Historical Col-
lections at Michigan State University; Kevin J. Gallagher of the Adri-
ance Memorial Library in Poughkeepsie, New York; Myrta Garrett of
Roberts Library at Southwestern Baptist Theological Seminary in Fort
Worth, Texas; Professor William H. Gerdts of the City University of
New York; Margaret Grier of the Otis Library in Norwich, Connecticut;
James L. Hanson of the Batavia (Illinois) Historical Society; Greer
Hardwicke of the Dedham (Massachusetts) Historical Society; Margaret
Humberston of the Connecticut Valley Historical Museum in Spring-
field, Massachusetts; Mary M. Huth of the Rush Rees Library at the
University of Rochester; Amanda C. Jones of the Ulster County Histor-
ical Society in Kingston, New York; Edmund Kenealy of the Canton
(Massachusetts) Public Library; Ernestine A. Kyle of the Ravenna

(Ohio) Heritage Association; Dennis R. Laurie of the American Antiquarian Society in Worcester, Massachusetts; Karen Lightner and DianeJude L. McDowell of the Free Library of Philadelphia; Daniel Lombardo of the Jones Library in Amherst, Massachusetts; Charles S. Longley of the Boston Public Library; Jan J. Losi of the Niagara County Historical Society in Lockport, New York; Ann M. Loyd and Lucille A. Tomko of the Carnegie Library of Pittsburgh; Robert A. McCown of the University Libraries at the University of Iowa; Julie McElroy of the Portage County Historical Society in Ravenna, Ohio; Kathleen McFadden of the Senate House State Historic Site in Kingston, New York; Ruth C. Main of Kent State University; Peter Mehlin of the Brooklyn Public Library; Paul Mercer and Cindy Stark of the New York State Library in Albany; Jay N. Miller; Eric N. Moody of the Nevada Historical Society in Reno; Virginia Moskowitz of the Landmark and Historical Society of Mt. Vernon, New York; Frank Murtha of the Society of the Founders of Norwich in Norwich, Connecticut; Irene R. Norton of the Essex Institute in Salem, Massachusetts; Martha Oaks and William Presson of the Cape Ann Historical Association in Gloucester, Massachusetts; Beverly H. Osborn of the Worcester (Massachusetts) Historical Museum; Arlene C. Palmer of the New Britain (Connecticut) Public Library; Linda Perry of the University Library at the University of Nevada-Reno; Barbara Pickell of the Holyoke (Massachusetts) Public Library; Michael Plunkett of the University of Virginia Library in Charlottesville; Jennie Rathbun and Melanie Wisner of the Houghton Library at Harvard University; Lewis F. Rauco of the State Library of Pennsylvania in Harrisburg; Helen M. Ray of the Franklin (Pennsylvania) Public Library; I. Richard Reed of the Niagara County Department of History in Lockport, New York; Richard W. Reeves of the Free Public Library in Trenton, New Jersey; Professor Tom Reigstad of State University of New York, College at Buffalo; David J. Roarty of the Wyoming Historical and Geological Society in Wilkes-Barre, Pennsylvania; Anne M. Rogers of the Paris-Bourbon County Library in Paris, Kentucky; M. Patricia Schaap of the Livingston County History Research Office in Geneseo, New York; Howard T. Senzel of the Rhode Island Historical Society in Providence; Deborah L. Sisum of the National Portrait Gallery of the Smithsonian Institution; David J. Sleasman of the University of Pittsburgh Libraries; Diana Speis of the Mahoning Valley Historical Society in Youngstown, Ohio; Edward Swovelan of the Kansas State Historical Society in Topeka; John K. Thiele of the Malden (Massachusetts) Public Library; Brian Walsh of the Pawtucket (Rhode Island) Public Library; Betty J. Widger of Ravenna, Ohio; Carla R. Wilson of the Youngstown State University Library; Theodore O. Wohlsen, Jr., of the Connecticut State Library in Hartford; and H. Scott Wolfe of the Historical Collections of the Galena (Illinois) Public Library District.

Throughout the process of design and typesetting for this volume we have had expert assistance from several people at the University of California Press: Fran Mitchell, who patiently guided the book through the production process; Albert Burkhardt, who developed the design of the book; and Sandy Drooker, who created the dust jacket. Our typesetters, Wilsted & Taylor Publishing Services, Oakland, California, provided knowledgeable help in developing and applying the typographical aspect of the transcription system used to represent the texts of Mark Twain's letters. In addition to LeRoy Wilsted and Christine Taylor, we are indebted, for his continuing advice and assistance, to Burwell Davis, and, for their meticulous care and remarkable accuracy in setting the book into type, to Nancy Evans, Sharilyn Hovind, Melody Lacina, Rosemary Northcraft, Jan Seymour-Ford, Janet Stephens, and Kim Zetter. Allen McKinney, Webster Holliday, and Ken Mack of Graphic Impressions, Emeryville, California, provided excellent photographs for the illustrations and manuscript reproductions.

We would like to thank Steven Mailloux of the English Department of Syracuse University for reading a transcription against the original manuscript at Syracuse. And we are grateful to Michael Millgate, who provided many helpful suggestions during the course of an insightful inspection of the volume for the Modern Language Association's Committee on Scholarly Editions, which granted its seal of approval in 1991.

Finally, we wish to thank our associates in the Mark Twain Project for their many willing contributions, not only in their areas of special expertise about Mark Twain, but also in all of the painstaking efforts of checking, collating, and proofreading. Robert Pack Browning provided careful readings of transcriptions of letters at a number of far-flung collections, both public and private. Richard Bucci made available his research concerning the surviving photographs of Olivia L. Langdon and the provenance of Mark Twain's letters. Lin Salamo prepared the volume's index. Kenneth M. Sanderson brought his fine eye for detail and his expertise with Mark Twain's handwriting to bear on the establishment of letter texts and also was instrumental in gaining access to several letters in private collections. Harriet Elinor Smith offered helpful and informed advice at every stage of the preparation of the printer's copy and throughout the production process. As always, the *Union Catalog of Clemens Letters* (1986), edited by our former colleague Paul Machlis, was indispensable to the orderly preparation of this volume. Janice Braun, another former colleague, provided careful readings of transcriptions of letters owned by Yale University. Beth Bernstein carried out a range of research assignments, including the checking of a substantial portion of the annotation. Several other students—Kandi Arndt, Scott Bean, Shawna Fleming, Carol Kramer, Jane Murray, Deborah Ann Turner, and William R. Winn—assisted with a variety of clerical and editorial tasks, greatly facilitating our work. Dorothy ("Sunny") Gottberg, our tireless administrative assistant, handled office business with her accustomed enthusiasm and dispatch. For the efforts of all of these colleagues and friends, we are especially grateful.

V. F.　M. B. F.　D. A.

Introduction

THIS VOLUME opens precisely where the previous one left off—on 1 January 1869, with Clemens at the Cleveland home of Mary Mason Fairbanks, enjoying a brief holiday respite from the lecture tour he had begun some six weeks earlier. The 188 letters included here, the majority of them published for the first time, are all that are known to survive from 1869. They document the continuation of the drive toward security, respectability, and literary recognition that Clemens had begun in 1868, a mission whose specific goals were: marriage to Olivia L. Langdon; the acquisition of a partnership in a thriving urban newspaper; and the publication of *The Innocents Abroad*.

Of these three compelling purposes the first, marriage to Olivia, was predominant, giving focus to the restless pursuit of means and vocation that had engaged Clemens since adolescence. Nearly half of the courtship letters he wrote to Olivia between September 1868, when she refused his initial proposal, and February 1870, when they were married, have been lost. Those that survive from 1869 are the longest letters Clemens ever wrote, constituting the bulk of his extant correspondence for the year. In them, although he and Olivia had been informally engaged since November 1868, Clemens continued his often anxious campaign to assure her, and her family and friends, of his Christian worthiness and dependability. The effort proved successful when the engagement was formalized on 4 February 1869, allowing him to boast to his sister, with the confidence of hindsight: "She said she never could or would love me—but she set herself the task of making a Christian of me. I said she would succeed, but that in the meantime she would unwittingly dig a matrimonial pit & end by tumbling into it—& lo! the prophecy is fulfilled" (p. 85). Yet even after this triumph, Clemens, separated from Olivia for long intervals, felt pressed to bolster her commitment to him with a nearly unbroken stream of daily letters. Frequently he joked with her and chatted about family matters, but more than once he reported fearful dreams of their estrangement, and, to counter her lingering doubts, besieged her with idyllic images of their future home life. He subordinated himself to her "higher wisdom" and called her "my best friend, my wise helpmeet, my teacher of the Better Way" (pp. 153, 163), devotion indeed coming from a man of his long and varied experience of the world to a woman ten years his junior with virtually no experience of life outside her household. For despite the conventional, almost formulaic, aspect of his persistent, and inevitably confining, idealization of Olivia, the depth and sincerity of his feelings are beyond doubt. Intending theirs to be a full partnership, he implored her to give him her complete trust and to let him share her "*every* grief . . . every disturbing thought," and he invited her to become his most intimate advisor, literary as well as personal: "So, just read whatever you please, Livy darling, & make yourself entirely at home—plunge your dainty fingers into my affairs just as much as you want to" (pp. 61, 172).

Clemens's affairs are manifest everywhere here. In letters to his family and associates, as in those to Olivia, he captures the hardships of the lecture circuit—grueling travel, sleepless nights, poor accommodations, immovable audiences—but also the triumphs, for example, his rousing success in Toledo, Ohio, the home of a respected rival lecturer and soon-to-be friend, Petroleum V. Nasby. His own reports of his lectures and the responses of local newspaper reviewers, some of which he clipped and enclosed, demonstrate how, in the course of his 1868–69 tour of the East and Midwest with his "American Vandal Abroad" lecture and his 1869–70 tour of New England with "Our Fellow Savages of the Sandwich Islands," he emerged as the standard by which other humorous lecturers were judged.

Clemens's letters during the first tour and before the beginning of the second show him seeking an alternative to the "lingering eternity" of lecture engagements (p. 62) in attempts, ultimately fruitless, to acquire an interest in the Cleveland *Herald* or the Hartford *Courant*. Meanwhile he was suffering even greater frustration in regard to the publication of *The Innocents Abroad*. Having submitted the manuscript to the American Publishing Company of Hartford in August 1868, he had initially expected publication that fall and then had agreed to a postponement until the following March. But production was delayed and in March 1869 Clemens was just beginning the process of revising and proofreading, drudgery when he was working at his publisher's offices in Hartford, but a delight when he had Olivia's assistance in Elmira. As the proofreading ended and spring turned to summer, his impatience with what seemed to be an ever-receding publication date grew and finally exploded in an accusing letter of 22 July to Elisha Bliss, the shrewd secretary of the American Publishing Company, with whom he was to have a checkered relationship for more than a decade. The two men made their peace, however, and *The Innocents Abroad* issued at the end of July, quickly ringing up large sales and winning nearly universal praise. When in mid-August, with the counsel and financial backing of Olivia's father, Clemens became the managing editor and one-third owner of the Buffalo *Express*, he did so knowing that his expanding reputation as an author would enhance the appeal and influence of the paper.

By the last quarter of 1869, then, Clemens could feel comfortably certain that his rootlessness, his "foolish life *made up* of apprenticeships" (p. 298), was at last behind him. As the year drew to a close, only his marriage to Olivia remained to be accomplished and that was imminent. In a Christmas Day letter, toward the end of the lecture tour he hoped would be his last, he reminded her jubilantly that soon "we shall close our long correspondence, & *tell* each other what our minds suggest, by word of mouth. Speed the day!" (p. 435).

V. F. M. B. F.

Editorial Signs

THE EDITORIAL conventions used to transcribe Mark Twain's letters were designed, in part, to enable anyone to read the letters without having to memorize a list. The following is therefore offered less as a necessary preliminary than as a convenient way to look up the meaning of any convention which, in spite of this design, turns out to be less than self-explanatory. Only the editorial conventions used in this volume are given here, since each new volume will require a slightly different list. New or newly modified conventions are identified by an asterisk (*). Not included are the typographical equivalents used to transcribe Mark Twain's own signs and symbols in manuscript. For those equivalents, and for a more discursive explanation of editorial principles, see the Guide to Editorial Practice on pp. 551–78.

EDITORIAL HEADING

From . . .	Clemens is named in the heading only when he wrote jointly with someone else.
. . . with a note to . . .	Used when two persons are addressed in the same letter, but Clemens intended the second to read *only* the briefer part, or "note."
per . . .	Precedes the name or identity of the amanuensis or agent who inscribed the document sent or received.
2? May	On this day—give or take a day.
1–3 May	On any day (or days) within this span.
1 and 2 May	On both days.

(MS)   The source document is the original letter, almost invariably Clemens's holograph manuscript.

(*damage emended*)   The source document has sustained significant damage, and the transcription therefore includes, without brackets, emendation to restore the affected text.

(MS facsimile)   The source document is a photographic facsimile of the MS, not the MS itself.

(*Paraphrase*)   The source document preserves some of the *words* of the original letter, but is manifestly not a deliberate transcription of it.

(Transcript)   The source document is a printed, handwritten, or typed (TS) transcription of the letter, not necessarily made at first hand.

LETTER TEXT

NEW-YORK   Extra-small small capitals with no initial capitals signify printed text *not* originated by Clemens, such as letterhead or the postmark.

(F)   *Italicized* extra-small small capitals within an oval border transcribe monograms or initials printed or embossed on personal stationery.*

Feb. 13,   Text above a dotted underscore was inscribed in a printed blank in the original document.

. . . .   Editorial ellipsis points (always centered in an otherwise blank line) signify that an unknown amount of the original letter is judged to be missing.

                     Ruled borders are an editorial device to represent the edge of a document, usually printed or partly printed, such as a telegram blank or newspaper clipping.

A two cance-   Cancellation is signified by slashes for single characters
deletions,   (and underscores), rules for two or more characters.

Well, *I* ~~pass.~~ A hairline rule signifies a mock, or pretended, cancellation: words lightly and distinctively crossed out, easily read, and often still necessary to the sense.

marking it ^up^ Insertion is signified by a single caret for single characters, two carets for two or more characters.

shaded words Gray background identifies parts of a letter originated and inscribed by someone other than Clemens.

[ ] Author's square brackets are transcribed this way to avoid any confusion with editorial brackets.

[ ] Editorial square brackets enclose [*editorial description*]; words or characters omitted by the writer an[d] now interpolated by [the] editors; and text modified by description, such as [*in margin:* All well].

◇iamond The diamond stands for a character, numeral, or punctuation mark the editors cannot read because it is physically obscured or obliterated. It *never* stands for the space between words.*

double= The hyphen is to be retained. Single hyphens at the ends
hyphen of lines therefore signify division only.

Sam*l* Superscript ell is always italicized to prevent confusion between one (¹) and ell (ˡ). The sign ‿ transcribes the author's paraph.

✉—————— The envelope and full-measure rule signal that everything transcribed below them was written, stamped, or printed on the envelope or on the letter itself at the time of transmission or receipt.

| Signifies the end of a line in the source document.

To Joseph H. Twichell
1 January 1869 • Cleveland, Ohio
(MS: Davis)

Cleveland, New Year's.

Dear J. H.[1]

While they get the carriage ready (for I am with my dear old ~~ad~~ Quaker City adopted mother,)[2]—for we are going out to pay New Year's calls, I will snatch a moment to say I have just received yours. And along with it a handful of dainty letters from that wonderful miracle of humanity, little Miss Livy. She has a most engaging commercial reliability & promptness allied to her stately commercial style of correspondence. I can always depend on an 8-page letter, every day. Never any whining in it, or any nonsense, but wisdom till you can't rest. Never any foolishness—but whenever she *does* miss fire & drop *herself* into her epistle accidentally, it is perfectly gorgeous. She thinks about me all the time, & informs me of it with Miltonic ponderosity of diction. She loves me, & conveys the fact with the awful dignity of an Ambassador construing an article of international law. But in her **sermons** she excels. They are full of a simple trust & confidence, & touched with a natural pathos, that would win a savage. Ours is a funny correspondence, & a mighty satisfactory one, altogether. ~~Mine~~ ‚My letters‚ are an ocean of love in a storm—hers an ocean of love in the majestic repose of a great calm. But the waters are the same—just the same, my boy.[3]

And I have delightful Christmas letters, this morning, from her mother & father—full of love & trust.[4] ~~The~~ ‚Lo! the‚ world is very beautiful—very beautiful—& *there is a God.* I seem to be shaking off the drowsiness of centuries & looking about me half bewildered at the light just bursting above the horizon of an unfamiliar world.

The ~~ɇ~~ carriage waits![5] Good-bye—love ~~yo~~ to you both—God send you a happy New Year that shall continue happy until the year is old again—& forevermore.

Yrs always
Mark.

---

[1] Clemens first met Twichell and his wife, Harmony, in October 1868. Almost immediately they became close friends, and even confidants in his courtship of Olivia Langdon (*L2*, 269 n. 3).

[2]On 28 December Clemens arrived at 221 St. Clair Street in Cleveland, where his "adopted mother," Mary Mason Fairbanks, lived with her husband, Abel Whitmore Fairbanks, and their four children (*L2*, 66–67, 259 n. 1). He remained there through New Year's Day—except for the evening of 30 December, when he delivered his "American Vandal Abroad" lecture in Akron.

[3]Clemens had characterized Olivia's letters in a similar way in a 12 December letter to Twichell (*L2*, 331–32). Only one of her courtship letters—written on 13 and 14 November 1869—is known to survive (10 and 11 Nov 69 to OLL, n. 1).

[4]All that survives of these letters from Olivia's parents is the remark quoted in the next letter (p. 3).

[5]The carriage was brought by Cleveland banker Solon Long Severance who, along with his wife, Emily, had become acquainted with Clemens on the *Quaker City* excursion. On 30 December 1868, Clemens had informed Olivia that "Solon Severance is coming early with a buggy, New Year's, & we are going to make calls all day long. He knows everybody—& we are going as a Temperance Phalanx, to shed a beneficent influence far & wide over this town!" The next day he told her that Severance would "be after me with a buggy promptly at 11 o'clock" (*L2*, 366, 371).

To Olivia L. Langdon
2 January 1869 • Fort Wayne, Ind.
(MS: CU-MARK)

Fort Wayne, Jan. 2/69.

My Dearest Livy—

    I wish I had written you long ago that I was to come here, instead of absurdly forgetting it, for I might have a letter from you to read tonight, just as well as not. I must go without, now, till Monday. How they have abused me in this town*l*, for the last two or three days! But they couldn't get the newspapers to do it. They said there was some mistake, & steadfastly refused—for which I am grateful.[1] The night I *should* have lectured here, the house was crowded, & *p* yet there was not room for all who came. To-night it was rainy, slushy & sloppy, & only two-thirds of a house came. They were very cool, & did not welcome me to the stage. They were still offended, & showed it. But *I* as soon as I saw that, all my distress of mind, all my wavering confidence, all my down-heartedness vanished, & I never felt happier or better satisfied on a stage before. And so, within ten minutes we were splendid friends—they unbent, banished their frowns, & the affair went off gallantly. A really hearty opposition is inspiring, sometimes. The town dignitaries have called with their congratulations & spent an hour with me & have just gone. The ~~Society~~ Association are jolly, now, for after all the trouble, they had a better house than usual. But what a pity it was we hadn't the big house that assembled before.[2]

Now I am sitting up again to write, Livy, in disobedience to ~~your~~ orders, but then I *must*—for if I didn't write you wouldn't answer, & I never, never, never could enjoy that, you know. And besides, I *want* to write, & so I had rather write & be scolded for it than go to bed & have a good sleep. Even if I only wrote nonsense it would still be pleasant, since it would be chatting with you. [*in margin:* No ink, Livy—pardon.][3]

Oh, let me praise you, Livy, & don't take it to heart so. You mustn't deprive me of so harmless a pleasure as that. Even if you prove to me that you *have* the blemishes you think you have, it cannot appal me any, because *with* them you will still be better, & nobler & lovelier than any woman I have known. I *will* help you to weed out your ~~fail~~ faults when they are revealed to me, but don't you be troubled about the matter, for you have a harder task before you, which is the helping me to weed out mine. Think of that, Livy—think of that, & leave the other to time & circumstances. Now please *don't* feel hurt when I praise you, Livy, for I know that in so doing I speak only the truth. At last I grant you one fault—& it$ is *self-depreciation*. And *isn't* it wrong—isn't it showing ingratitude toward the Creator, who has put so little into your nature & your character to find fault with? And yet, after all, it $ your self-depreciation is a virtue & a merit, for it comes of the absence of egotism, which is one of the gravest of faults. {It isn't any use. I no sooner accuse you than I hasten to take it back again. It isn't *in* me to find a fault of any importance in you & believe in it, Livy, & so where is the use in trying? Scold me—scold me hard, dear—& then forgive me.}

I was just delighted with Mr & Mrs Langdon's letters—& I saw what an idiot I had been to hurry & apologize for my Christmas letter before they had found any fault with it. But the apology was already gone, & I couldn't stop it.[4] But never mind—I thank them from my heart; & next time I write them I will be sagacious & put a little apology in with the letter. Mr. Langdon speaks of ~~my gettin~~ the good policy of my ~~getting~~ achieving Mrs. L.'s favor "if I ever get permission to come again." Commence on him *now* Livy! Don't let him get used to harboring such threatening notions as that. Obtain his consent early, & clinch it. If you use proper diligence & enterprise, you can easily make yourself so troublesome that he will be glad to grant it in order to have peace. *I* could. I saw that Mrs. Langdon's hearty invitation had its effect on Mrs. Fairbanks. She notified me to come & take her to Elmira whenever all circumstances should be favorable.[5] [I didn't read *your* letters to her, Livy—but I suppose I ought to have done it.] She sends her love to all of you, & says she is going to describe how impatient I was for Severance to come, New Year's, & how suddenly it died away when your letter came, & how serene I looked, in the rocking-chair, with my feet on the ~~table,~~ ‸mantel-piece,‸ reading it! [I didn't have my feet there, at all—but I looked comfortable, no doubt.]

And you had a delightful philosophy lesson, Livy,—& wished that we might study it together some day.[6] It is the echo of a wish that speaks in my heart many & many a time. I think, sometimes, how pleasant it would be to sit, ~~lon~~ just us two, long winter evenings, & study together, & read favorite authors aloud & comment on them & so imprint them upon our memories. It is so unsatisfactory to read a noble passage & have no one you love, at hand to share the happiness with you. And it is un-satisfactory to read to one's self, *anyhow*—for the uttered voice so heightens the expression. I think you & I would never tire of reading together. At Mrs. Fairbanks's they make selections against my coming, & so I have a great deal of reading aloud to do during my visits.

Scold me all you please, Livy—I love to hear you scold, because you are such an earnest little body. And it does some good, too. But for your scolding I should have written other letters to-night—but now I shall write only this one. You can't imagine ~~how~~ how dreadfully wearing this lecturing is, Livy. I begin to be appalled at the idea of doing it another season. I shall try hard to get into the Herald on such terms as will save me from it.[7] If I were to confess how few hours I *have* slept since I saw you last, you could not easily believe it,‸—[8] But it can't be helped, Livy— it *can not*. I have so many visitors, & *they* don't know the circumstances, you know—& the railway trips are very long & tedious—very seldom less than 8 hours. I feel a thousand years old, sometimes. But it don't make ~~a~~ so very much difference—I recuperate easily. I thought I was going to sleep, sleep, sleep—& rest, rest, rest—~~at~~ for days, at Mrs. F.,'s, & see nobody but the family, & have *such* a peaceful, quiet, homelike sort of a time, & never go out of the house, for I was very tired—but THEY didn't know, & so I found visits & parties already fixed when I arrived, & so I *rushed*, day & night without ceasing & made my fatigue infinitely worse. But when it was all done, I told them, & so hereafter I am to be *at home* there, which is to say I am not to drive out, nor walk out, nor ∉ visit, nor receive company at all, but am to lead a jolly, rejuvenating, restful life in the very heart of the home circle, & forget that there *is* a driving, toiling world outside, ~~if possible.~~ *Then* I can come away a new man—a young giant refreshed with new wine—& plunge into business again with vim & energy. Besides, you know, we can have visits & visiting, *anywhere*—what we want at home is the home folks & nobody else. It will be splendid, won't it, next time?

I thank you for all you say, for *everything* you say, about religion, Livy, & I have as much confidence as yourself that I shall succeed at last, but Oh, it is slow & often discouraging. I am happy in conducting myself rightly—but the emotion, the revealing religious emotion, Livy, *will not* come, it seems to me. I pray for it—it is all I can do. I know not how to *compel* an emotion. And I pray every day that you may not be impatient or lose confidence in my final conversion—I pray that you may keep your courage & be of good heart. And I pray that my poisonous & besetting *apathy* may pass from me. It is hard to be a Christian *in spirit*, Livy, though the ~~let~~ mere letter of the law seems not very difficult as a general thing. I have hope. Send me the Plymouth Pulpits, Livy—I looked for one yesterday, but it did not come.[9]

Good-night & good-bye. Thank you for the kiss, Livy dear. I send you a dozen herewith! [Livy—Livy—the *picture*.][10] I love you, Livy. I love you more than I can tell.

Devotedly,
Saml L. C.

Livy, put Decatur, Ill., (care *Mrs.* H. O. Johns,) *in place of* Bloomington, Ill.[11]

Miss Olivia L. Langdon
Present.
Politeness of Charlie[12]

[*docketed by OLL:*] *20th*

---

[1]Clemens had forgotten both to record his 29 December appointment in Fort Wayne and to tell Olivia to add it to her copy of his itinerary. After he missed the engagement, and before he could explain himself by telegraph, the Fort Wayne

Gazette declined the usual recriminations: "It is one of those unfortunate circumstances where you cannot blame any one, and when there is no use crying over
spilt milk" ("Mark Twain," 30 Dec 68, 4). On Thursday, 31 December, the *Gazette* reported that a "dispatch received from the lecturer, this morning, announces that he mistook the evening, and that he will be here on Saturday next,
positively" ("Mark Twain," 4). That day Clemens also informed Olivia of his
mistake, adding that he had been "requested by telegraph to talk there Jan 2, &
shall do it" (*L2*, 368). But he recognized that even if she received this news on
Saturday, a reply could not reach him before he left Fort Wayne, and he therefore
did not expect to receive her next letter until Monday, 4 January, in Indianapolis.

  ²The Fort Wayne *Democrat* called Clemens's lecture in Hamilton's Hall, for
the local Library and Lecture Association, "one of the finest, of the character,
that it has ever been our pleasure to listen to. The artistic style in which the
lecturer mingled the sublime and the ridiculous, the pathetic and the humorous,
we have never heard excelled. We thank Mr. Clemens, and the Association who
afforded us the opportunity, for the exquisite pleasure we enjoyed in listening to
his faultless entertainment. The entire absence of all vulgarism, which all the
latter day sons of Momus seem to think so indispensable to wit[,] constituted a
marked feature in Mr. Clemens' lecture" ("The Lecture Course," 4 Jan 69, 4).
And the Fort Wayne *Gazette* remarked that the lecture "kept the audience in
alternate states of laughter and close attention. It was a kind of literary hash,
(not in the least like boarding house hash), made up of the very best materials.
. . . It was a string of pearls from which the string had been lost. . . . In any
event it was a very amusing and interesting lecture; containing passages of
great beauty and eloquence, mixed with a spice of wit which was irresistable . . .
and pleasing by its novelty as well as by its intrinsic merit" ("The Lecture,"
4 Jan 69, 4).

  ³The entire letter is written in pencil.

  ⁴Clemens's Christmas morning letter to the Langdons, mailed in Lansing,
Michigan, is not known to survive, but it was evidently high-spirited. His 29
December apology—"no harm was meant, no undue levity, no disrespect, no
lack of reverence"—was part of a letter in which he also apologized for having
inadvertently offended Jervis Langdon with "the harmless overflow of a happy
frame of mind" on a previous occasion (*L2*, 357, 359).

  ⁵The allusion is to the 1 December 1868 letter in which Mrs. Langdon, expressing "utter surprise & almost astonishment" at Clemens's 25 November dec-
laration of love of her daughter, requested Mrs. Fairbanks's "opinion of him as
a *man;* what the kind of man he *has been*, and what the man he now is, or is to
become." Mrs. Langdon had prefaced her request with this wish: "I WOULD
that I could see you for an hour!" And in closing she remarked: "We do feel very
anxious to see you & Mr Fairbanks here & to have a good long visit from you
both, then will it not be delightful to rehearse every thing that interests us all"
(see *L2*, 286–87 n. 3, where the letter is transcribed in full). Perhaps the most
important circumstance affecting such a visit was the health of Jervis Langdon.
He had been suffering for several months with stomach cancer, as yet undi-
agnosed, which caused his death on 6 August 1870. On 15 January, Olivia invited
the Fairbankses to come to Elmira in February as part of a planned *Quaker City*
reunion (see 14 Jan 69 to OLL, n. 8).

  ⁶Olivia was tutored at home, twice a week, by Darius Reynolds Ford (b.

1825), a Baptist minister and professor of physical science, mathematics, and astronomy at Elmira Female College. In October 1869, after Ford set off on a trip around the world as tutor to Olivia's brother, Charles, Clemens described him in the Buffalo *Express* as:

a scholarly man; a man whose attainments cover a vast field of knowledge. His knowledge is singularly accurate, too; what he knows he is *certain* of, and likewise what he knows he has a happy faculty of communicating to others. He is a man of high social standing and unspotted character. He is a warm personal friend of mine—which is to his discredit, perhaps, but would you have a man perfect? He is a minister of the Gospel, and a *live* one— a man whose religion broadens and adorns his nature; not a religion that dates a man back into the last century and saps his charity and makes him a bigot. (SLC 1869ee)

Including Ford, Elmira Female College, founded in 1855, had a faculty of eleven and claimed to be "the first in this country, and, so far as known, the first in the world, that offered to women the same advantages and adopted the same standard for graduation with colleges and universities for the other sex" ("Elmira Female College," Elmira *Saturday Evening Review*, 11 Sept 69, 5; OLL to Alice B. Hooker, 16 Dec 68, 3 Mar 69, CtHSD; Towner 1892, 609–10, 700–701).

[7] Since late 1868 Clemens had been negotiating to buy a share in the Cleveland *Herald*, owned by Abel W. Fairbanks in partnership with father and son George A. and George S. Benedict (*L2*, 284, 298, 360).

[8] Clemens had last seen Olivia, in Elmira, on 18 December (*L2*, 348).

[9] *Plymouth Pulpit*, a weekly pamphlet, published each of Henry Ward Beecher's sermons after he gave it at Plymouth Church, in Brooklyn. In a letter of 27 December, Clemens had told Olivia he would be "glad to receive the Plymouth Pulpit as often as you will send it" (*L2*, 353).

[10] Olivia had first sent Clemens her photograph in September 1868. On 28 November, two days after she accepted his marriage proposal, Clemens appealed to her for a more satisfactory likeness. He repeated the request in most of the letters he sent her in the month of December (*L2*, 250, 283–84, 291, 293–94, 308–64 passim).

[11] Mrs. Johns was evidently a member of the recently formed "library association" in Decatur, which sponsored Clemens's lecture there on the evening of 12 January. According to the Decatur *Republican*, the association had had an uplifting effect:

The literary and intellectual faculties of the people have been developed until the polished and beautiful utterances of ac[c]omplished and eloquent orators are relished in preference to the coarse and stale jests of the "end man" in the burnt cork concert, or the smutty buffoonery of the clown tumbling in the sawdust ring of the circus. For this refining influence and most gratifying result, we are solely indebted to the ladies of Decatur, and we are truly proud to thus acknowledge their services in the cause of literature, christianity and refinement. . . . All honor then, say we once more, to the ladies of the library association. ("Mark Twain," 14 Jan 69, 1)

[12] "Present" and "Politeness of" were conventional terms of address for letters entrusted to a third party—in this case Olivia's brother, Charles. Clemens's practice was to seal his letters to Olivia in envelopes inscribed as this one is, then to send them to Charles enclosed in second envelopes, none of which survive. Clemens followed this stratagem for privacy from late November 1868, just after Olivia accepted his marriage proposal, until early March 1869 (see 8 and 9 Mar 69 to OLL, n. 6). Olivia docketed Clemens's letters by numbering them consec-

utively, usually on the envelope she received, but sometimes on the letter itself. In writing to Clemens she also used the double envelope stratagem, by having her brother address the outer envelopes (see 14 Jan 69 to OLL, p. 38).

To Mary Mason Fairbanks
7 January 1869 • Rockford, Ill.
(MS: CSmH)

Rockford, after midnight.[1] ⎫
ˏJan. 6.   ⎭ˏ

My Dear Mother—

Hoping to see you Jan. 22, I shall merely drop you a line—must write to Livy to-night yet. She wants me to thank you from her heart for proposing to publish that extract from my Christmas letter to you, & she wants a copy of the paper—poor girl, anybody who could convince her that I was not a humorist would secure her eternal gratitude! She thinks a humorist is something perfectly awful. I never put a joke in a letter to her without feeling a pang. Best girl in the world. So please send me that letter if you can find it, & I will fix the extract for publication & return it to you. Anything that will please her, suits *me*, though it exasperate all the world beside.[2]

Tell Miss Allie[3] not to think hard of me for being so stupid & useless at the party New Year's night—I *could* not help it, I was so tired & miserable & felt so out of place among so much sparkle & animation. I will make it all up next time by being just ȸ as attentive & thoughtful of her welfare as ever I can. She knows I would have done better il if I could. Love & the kindest remembrances to all of you there at my pleasant home in Cleveland,— ˏLove to Severance, also, & his "Bevy."ˏ[4]

Yrs always
Mark.

[1] On 6 January, just a few hours before he wrote this letter, Clemens lectured in Brown's Hall, which seated a thousand (Wallace, 7–8). The Rockford *Register* described the performance and its reception:

> We never saw an audience so determined to laugh "out loud," in all our experience, and we confess to having laughed ourselves until our sides fairly ached, and we could see sev-

eral speakers swimming in the tears in our eyes. Mr. Twain's dry humor and inimitable drollery we never saw equalled, and he conducted his hearers from one laugh into another with such rapidity that scarce a breathing spell was afforded between the outbursts which, as a friend remarked after the lecture, followed each other like the reverberations of thunder. Mr. T. also gave his audience several specimens of his descriptive ability. His account of the Sphynx, being our ideal of poetic thought embodied in the choicest language. It was certainly one of the finest bits of description that we have met with in many a day.

We congratulate those who were present, and we feel deep sympathy for those who remained away and missed a grand opportunity of hearing a speaker who, as a humorist and wit, stands unrivaled on the American stage. ("Mark Twain Is Coming," Galena [Ill.] *Gazette*, 26 Jan 69, 3, reprinting the Rockford [Ill.] *Register*, 9 Jan 69)

[2]Olivia "was rich, beautiful and intellectual," according to her cousin and close friend Harriet Lewis, "but she could not see through a joke, or see anything to laugh at in the wittiest sayings unless explained in detail" (Paff, 2). In part to please her Clemens was about to allow the Cleveland *Herald* to present him "favorably to the public, in another role than that of humorist" by publishing the following "charming extracts" from his "private correspondence":

"Christmas is here—eighteen hundred and sixty-nine years ago the stars were shedding a purer lustre above the barren hills of Bethleham, and possibly flowers were being charmed to life in the dismal plains where the shepherds watched their flocks, and the hovering angels were singing, peace on earth, good will to men—for the Savior was come. Don't you naturally turn in fancy now to that crumbling wall and its venerable olives, and to the mouldy domes and turrets of Bethleham? And don't you picture it all out in your mind as we saw it many months ago? And don't the picture mellow in the distance and take to itself again the soft, unreal resemblance that poetry and tradition give to the things they hallow?

And now that the greasy monks and the noisy mob, and the leprous beggars are gone, and all the harsh cold hardness of real stone and unsentimental glare of sunlight are banished from the vision, don't you realize as in other years, that Jesus *was* born there, and that the angels *did* sing in the still air above, and that the wondering shepherds *did* hold their breath and listen as the mysterious music floated by? *I* do. It is more real than ever, and I am glad, a hundred times glad, that I saw Bethlehem, though at the time it seemed that that sight had swept away forever every pleasant fancy and every cherished memory that ever the City of the Nativity had ever stored away in my mind and heart." ("Mark Twain," Cleveland *Herald*, 16 Jan 69, 4)

For Olivia's thoughts on the publication of this passage, see 14 Jan 69 to OLL, n. 8. For an account of the changes Clemens may have imposed on its original version, which was part of his 24 and 25 December letter to Mrs. Fairbanks, see *L2*, 583–86.

[3]Alice Holmes Fairbanks (b. 1847), Mrs. Fairbanks's stepdaughter (*L2*, 132 n. 10).

[4]Solon and Emily Severance's three young children: Julia, the eldest, and twins Allen and Mary Helen (*L2*, 139 n. 5).

To Olivia L. Langdon
7 January 1869 • Rockford, Ill.
(MS: CU-MARK)

ˬJan. 6./69.ˬ
Rockford, Midnight,

My Dearest Livy—

I was just delighted with your letter received to-day. We forgot the
extract, but I have just written to Mrs. Fairbanks, & she will send it to
me to be prepared for publication. Your letter was so natural, Livy, & so
like yourself. I do *wish* I could see you! I scold you as bitterly as I can for
daring to sit up & write after midnight.[1] Now you have it, at last. And I
forgive you & bless you in the same moment! [Oh, you are so *present* to
me at this moment, Livy, that it seems absurd to be *writing* to you when
I almost seem to touch your forehead with my lips.] [*on thinner paper:*] I
thank you with all my heart for your warm New Year wishes—& you
know that you have mine. I naturally thought of you all the day long, that
day—as I do every day—& a dozen times I recalled our New Year at Mr.
Berry's. I remembered it perfectly well, & spoke of it to Mrs. Fairbanks—& the Moorish architecture, too. And I remembered perfectly
well that I didn't rightly know where the charm was, that night, until
you were gone. And I did have such a struggle, the first day I saw you at
the St Nicholas, to keep from loving you with *all* my heart![2] But you
seemed to my bewildered vision, a visiting *Spirit* from the upper air—a
something to *worship*, reverently & at a distance—& *not* a creature of
common human clay, to be profaned by the *love* of such as I. Maybe it
was a little extravagant, Livy, but I am honestly setting down my
thought, just as it flitted through my brain. *Now* you can understand
why I offend so much with praises—for to me you are *still* so far above
all created things that I cannot speak of you in tame commonplace language—I *must* reserve that for tame, commonplace people. Don't scold
me, Livy—let me pay my due homage to your worth; let me honor you
above all women; let me love you with a love that knows no doubt, no
question—for you are my *world*, my life, my pride, my all of earth that
is worth the having. Develop your faults, if you have them—they have
no terrors for me—*nothing* shall tear you out of my heart. Livy, if you

only *knew* how much I love you! But I couldn't make you comprehend it, though I wrote a year. God keep you from suffering & sorrow always, my honored Livy!—& spare you to me till many & many a peaceful New Year shall wax & wane & crown & re-crown us with their blessings.

My heart warms to good old Charlie,[3] whenever I think of him—& more than ever when he crosses my plane of vision, now, doing thoughtful kindnesses for *you*. He loves you, Livy, as very, very few brothers love their sisters. And you deserve it, you dear good girl, if ever sister did in the world.

"People" made you cross? I wonder what they did. Come to the deserted confessional, Livy—what was it?

Ah, I thought I was going to get a *dreadful* scolding!—I began to wish I had risen earlier, latterly—I was commencing to feel twinges of guilt ~~$~~ tugging at my heart—but I turned the page & presto! you ~~wre~~ were a brave defender of the worn & weary instead! You were my Champion, as it were, & not my censurer. And your mother took the same view of the case—& Mr Beecher also, in his miscellany.[4] I felt ever so much better. And I did love your generous indignation against that outrage, Livy! And well I might—for several times, lately, when I have gone to bed completely tired out, I have fallen asleep fancying that I would sleep *late*, & breakfast with *you* alone—a thing so pleasant to think about—& behold, here was tacit permission for some future day when I may come to you wearied out with these wanderings, & longing for rest. But a plague take that fellow, for an idiot!—to put off his marriage for so silly a thing—to put it off at *all*, even for a day, if she is ready & he has his home prepared. What can compensate him for three long years of happiness spurned?—a "splurge?" Verily it *is* a funny world, ~~Livy,~~ even as you say.[5] Make some more pictures of our own wedded happiness, Livy—with the bay window (which you shall have,) & the grate in the living-room—(which you shall have, likewise,) & flowers, & pictures & books (which we will read together,)—pictures of our future home—a home whose patron saint shall be Love—a home with a tranquil "home atmosphere" about it—such ~~an o~~ home as "our hearts & our God shall approve." And Livy, *don't* say at the bottom of it, "How absurd, perhaps wrong, I am to write of these things which are so uncertain." Don't, Livy, it spoils everything—& sounds so chilly. Let us think these things, & believe them—it is no wrong—let us believe that God has destined us for each other, & be happy in the belief—it will be time enough to doubt

it when His hand shall separate us, if it ever does—a calamity, I humbly
& beseechingly pray ⱨ He will spare us in His great mercy. Let us hope
& believe that we shall walk hand in hand down the lengthening highway
of life, one in heart, one in impulse & one in love & worship of Him—
bearing each other's burdens, sharing each other's joys, soothing each
other's griefs—&, so linked together, & so journeying, pass at last the
shadowed boundaries of l̶i̶f̶ Time & stand redeemed & saved, beyond
the threshold & within the light t̶h̶a̶t̶ ̶b̶e̶a̶m̶s̶ of that Land whose Prince
is the Lord of rest eternal. Picture it, Livy—cherish it, think of it. It is
no wrong—we are privileged to do it by the blameless love we bear each
other. God will bless you in it—will b̶e̶ bless us both, I fervently believe.

When I get starved & find that I have a little wife that knows nothing
about cooking, and—Oh, my prophetic soul![6] *you* know anything about
cookery! I would as soon think of your knowing the science of sawing
wood! We shall have some peculiarly & particularly awful dinners, I
make no manner of doubt, but I guess *we* can eat them, & other people
who don't like them need not favor us with their company. That is a fair
& proper way to look at it, I think.

You are such a darling faithful little correspondent, Livy. I can depend on you all the time, & I do enjoy your letters so much. And every
time I come to the last page & find a blank area on it I want to take you
in my arms & kiss you & wheedle you into sitting down & filling it up—
& right away my conscience pricks me for wanting to make you go to
work again when you have already patiently & faithfully wrought more
than I deserve, & until your hand$ is cramped & tired, no doubt, & your
body weary of its one position.

I bless you for your religious counsel, Livy—& more & more every
day, for e̶v̶e̶r̶y̶ with every passing day I understand it better & appreciate
it more. I am "dark" yet—I see I am still depending on my own strength
to lift myself up, & upon my own sense of what is right to guide me in
the Way—but not always, Livy, not always. I see the Savior dimly at
times, & at intervals *very near*—would that the intervals were not so sad
a length apart! Sometimes it is a *pleasure* to me to pray, night & morning,
in cars & everywhere, twenty times a day—& then again the whole spirit
of religion is motionless (not dead) within me from the rising clear to the
setting of the sun. I can only say, Be of good heart, my Livy—I am slow
to move, & I bear upon my head t̶h̶e̶ a deadly weight of sin—a weight
such as you cannot comprehend—*thirty-three years* of ill-doing & wrong-

ful speech—but I have hope—hope—*hope*. It will all be well. Dare I to say ~~it?~~—to say—& why not, since it is the truth? Only this: I ˌ*fear* Iˌ would distrust a religious faith that came upon me suddenly—that came upon me otherwise than deliberately, & *proven*, step by step as it came. You will blame me for this, Livy—but be lenient with me, for you know I grope blindly as yet.[7]

I am all impatience to see the ~~se~~ picture—& I do hope it will be a good one, this time. I want it to be *more* than a painted iron plate[8]—I want it to be *yourself*—your own dainty self, Livy—I want the eyes to tell me what is passing in the heart, & the hair & the vesture & the attitude to bring to me the vivid presentment of the grace that now is only vaguely glimpsed to me in dreams of you at night when I & the world sleep.

I shudder to think what time it may be! All the sounds are such *late* sounds! But though you were *here* to scold me, darling, I would *not* put this pen down till I had written *I* LOVE *you, Livy!*

Good-bye—Lovingly now & forever & forever

Samˌ*l*.ˌ L. C.

P. S. Can't stop to correct the letter, Livy.

✉—————————————————————————

[*letter docketed by OLL:*][9] *22ⁿᵈ* [*and in pencil:*] *22ⁿᵈ*

---

[1]Clemens wished Olivia to avoid taxing her health, which seems to have remained delicate after a two-year-long illness during adolescence (see *L2*, 287–88 n. 6).

[2]Clemens first met Olivia in late December 1867 at the St. Nicholas Hotel, where the Langdons customarily stayed while visiting New York City. (He soon adopted the St. Nicholas as well.) They met again on New Year's Day, 1868, at the home of Thomas S. and Anna E. Berry, friends of the Langdons', whose residence at 115 West Forty-fourth Street was evidently an example of the Moorish Revival style of architecture, "a short-lived eclecticism inspired by the Byzantine," which became especially popular in the 1870s (Tauranac, 251; H. Wilson 1867, 87, 897; H. Wilson 1868, 943). For further details of their initial meetings, see *L2*, 145–46 n. 3.

[3]Charles J. Langdon.

[4]Thomas Kinnicut Beecher (1824–1900), half brother of Henry Ward Beecher, was pastor of Elmira's Park Congregational Church, to which the Langdon family belonged. His "Friday Miscellany," was a weekly column on religious and social issues published in the Elmira *Advertiser*. Clemens probably alludes to Beecher's Christmas Day column, sent by Olivia. In it Beecher discussed "the will of God as to Sunday observances," saying in part: "The day should bring us rest. Obviously, the rest must be *real* rest and not ceremonial merely. The day is

to be adapted to the need of the man who is to rest. Some should sleep long and well on Sunday, but not in church" (Thomas Kinnicut Beecher 1868; "Nook Farm Genealogy," 6–7; Jerome and Wisbey, 20).

[5] The "idiot" may have been John (or Sanford) Greeves, whose engagement to Olivia's friend Emma Sayles was soon broken off: see 9 May 69 to OLL.

[6] *Hamlet*, act 1, scene 5.

[7] A recurrent Biblical image, for example, Isaiah 59:10—"We grope for the wall like the blind, and we grope as if we had no eyes: we stumble at noonday as in the night; we are in desolate places as dead men."

[8] "It was the custom to 'improve' daguerreotype pictures by colouring them. Colours ground extremely fine were used and dusted on dry with a fine camel-hair brush, the process needing great care, as it was almost impossible to remove any of the colour applied. When the colours were on they were breathed upon to make them adhere" (Jones, 159). If Clemens alludes to a specific daguerreotype of Olivia, it has not been found.

[9] The gap in Olivia's numbering indicates that one letter Clemens wrote her on 4 or 5 January, either from Indianapolis or en route to Rockford, Illinois, has been lost.

To Francis E. Bliss
7 January 1869 • Chicago, Ill.
(MS: CtY-BR)

SHERMAN HOUSE,

CHICAGO, Jan. 7 186 9.

Dear Frank[1]—

I am glad to hear that you are progressing well with the book. It will have a great sale in the West—& the East too. Why don't you issue prospectuses & startling advertisements now while I am stirring the bowels of these communities?[2] I have big houses—& more invitations to lecture than I can fill.

Pay for the shaving-paper[3] & keep it till I come. Send me the bill, or keep that till I come, also, just as is most convenient.

Kind regards to all.[4]

Yrs

~~Mark~~ ͏ˌHis || Markˌ Twain

His = Mark. Mark 2—two marks.[5]

✉︎───────────────────────────────────────

[*letter docketed:*] √ au [*and*] Mark Twain | Jan 7/69 | Author

[1] Francis Edgar Bliss (1843–1915), treasurer of the American Publishing Company of Hartford, was the son of Elisha Bliss, Jr. (1821–80), the firm's secretary and chief executive officer (*L2*, 245 n. 3).

[2] Bliss's progress report has not survived, but evidently it did not suggest any departure from the plan to publish Clemens's book in March 1869. Clemens had delivered his manuscript, together with various photographs to be used in illustrating it, to the American Publishing Company in August 1868, expecting publication later that year. But by mid-October, after a second visit to Hartford, he had agreed to a postponement of several months, chiefly in order to provide time to illustrate. His contract with the company was signed on 16 October, and specified that electrotyping—that is, final preparation of the printing plates—was to be completed within six months, by mid-February 1869 (*L2*, 169, 239 n. 2, 421–22). On 10 November 1868, the Hartford *Courant* summarized the situation: "Mark Twain's new book—'New Pilgrim's Progress'—will be issued about the middle of next March. It was the intention to get it out this fall, but in order to more profusely illustrate it, delay was decided upon" ("Our Publishing Houses," 2). The first copies of *The Innocents Abroad* were not, in fact, ready until July 1869.

[3] Used during shaving for wiping soap and whiskers from the razor (Carter).

[4] In addition to Frank—Elisha Bliss's son by his first wife, Lois, who had died in 1855—the Bliss family consisted of Elisha's second wife, Amelia, whom he had married in 1856, and their three children: Walter (1858–1917), Emma (b. 1860), and Almira (b. 1865). Clemens had stayed with the Blisses while in Hartford in August and October 1868 to work on his book (*L2*, 239 n. 2, 245, 257–58 n. 1).

[5] Clemens had canceled "~~Mark~~" with a double line.

To Mary Mason Fairbanks and Others on the Board of Managers of the Cleveland Protestant Orphan Asylum
7 January 1869 • Chicago, Ill.
(Transcript and MS: Cleveland *Herald*,
12 Jan 69, and CSmH)

SHERMAN HOUSE, }
CHICAGO, JAN. 7.

Mesdames:—On several accounts I shall take a genuine pleasure in complying with your request.[1] First, because I shall be glad—& who would not?—to do what in me lies, in aid of so generous a charity as that which you represent. Secondly, because I regard your invitation as a compliment & one to be greatly esteemed. And finally, because it was a Cleveland audience that took the responsibility of launching me upon this section of the world as a lecturer, & I am naturally curious to know if another Cleveland audience can be found to endorse the kind treatment which I received at the hands of the first.[2]

Therefore, hoping the date will meet with your approbation, I appoint the 22d of the present month for the delivery of the lecture. I also beg leave to specify a repetition of "The American Vandal Abroad" as the lecture to be delivered upon that occasion. I have the honor to be, very respectfully,

SAM'L. L. CLEMENS,

("MARK TWAIN.")

To the ladies of the Cleveland Orphan Asylum.

[*new page:*]

There you are, Mother. I got the shirts[3]—but never a letter from Livy. I just know that old Vandal, your honored husband, has been opening her letters & answering them. He said he would.[4]

Go up to my room & take another whiff—it does you good, mother mine—it softens you—it makes you "drop into poetry" like Silas Wegg.[5]

What can *you* say that Livy will enjoy? Why *anything* you say, she will enjoy. If she didn't, I would give her a curtain lecture. You write to her—that's all. I *won't* "be satisfied with anything short of the highest Christian attainment"—is that strong enough?

And don't you be afraid of being considered "officious" in the matter of suggestions, of advice of or the exercise of maternal authority toward me. Suggest—I listen; advise—I heed; command—I obey. For *you* will never suggest, advise or command anything that will not be for my good. I know that well enough.

I wrote you last night, from Rockford. I continue to have good houses & give satisfaction. I *am* tired & used up, Mother, & look for rest when I get back home. I got Mr. Fairbanks' dispatch & replied.[6] Love to all.

Good bye—affectionately

Mark.

[1]Clemens replied to the following invitation, which was the first part of the letter he received on this day from Mary Mason Fairbanks:

CLEVELAND, Jan. 5th, 1869.

MR. SAMUEL L. CLEMENS:

DEAR SIR:—The ladies having in charge the interests of the Cleveland Protestant Orphan Asylum, propose furnishing to the public a series of entertainments, the proceeds of which, it is hoped, will enable them to discharge a debt in which yearly expenses and recent improvements have involved them.

Confident that your wide-spread reputation as a lecturer and a writer would secure a large and remunerative audience, they desire to know whether your sympathies may not be enlisted in this enterprise.

Will you repeat your very acceptable lecture on "The American Vandal Abroad," or such other lecture as you shall decide, for the benefit of an institution, the charitable aim of which will, we are sure, commend it to your generosity.

Should this request meet with your favor, will you inform us at what time it would be practicable for you to address a Cleveland audience?

> Very Respectfully,
> THE BOARD OF MANAGERS.

Both this text and the text of Clemens's formal reply survive only in the Cleveland *Herald*, where Mrs. Fairbanks, a member of the board of managers since 1866, published them on 12 January ("Cleveland Orphan Asylum," 3; Lorch 1936, 453–54). She directed attention to them with the following paragraph (3):

The Orphan Asylum and "Mark Twain."—As will be seen by the correspondence published to-day the managers of the Protestant Orphan Asylum have succeeded in enlisting the assistance of the celebrated humorist and lecturer "Mark Twain," who will address a Cleveland audience on the 22nd instant, for the benefit of the Asylum. When to the acknowledged merits of the lecturer are added the claims of the orphans upon the sympathies of the public, there can be no reasonable ground for doubt as to the utmost capacity of the largest hall in the city being tested for that occasion. The Cleveland public have never been appealed to in vain for this beneficent charity, and in addition to aiding in a good cause, those who attend the lecture get their money's worth in a lecture of more than ordinary merit.

One original page of Fairbanks's 5 January letter also survives: after replying to it here, Clemens enclosed it in the next letter.

[2] Clemens had opened his current tour with a successful lecture in Cleveland's Case Hall on 17 November (*L2*, 280–81). For his report of the lecture he here agreed to give, see 23 Jan 69 to Twichell and family.

[3] Mrs. Fairbanks reported that her husband "sent your shirts to Chicago Monday," 4 January. Clemens presumably left them behind for the Fairbankses' servants to launder or mend when he departed Cleveland for Fort Wayne on 2 January. On the *Quaker City* excursion, he earlier recalled, Mrs. Fairbanks herself had "sewed my buttons on" and "kept my clothes in presentable trim" (*L2*, 130).

[4] Finding that Olivia's letters to him often arrived after he had departed an appointed place, Clemens temporarily changed his instructions to her, asking that she send them instead "to reach Cleveland on the 28th, 29th, 30th, 31st, of Dec., & 1st of Jan.," the period of his recent stay with Mrs. Fairbanks (*L2*, 346). He nevertheless expected that Abel Fairbanks would have to forward some letters from her that arrived after he left.

[5] The wooden-legged, rascally "scholar" of *Our Mutual Friend* (1864–65).

[6] This exchange of telegrams has not been found, but may have concerned Clemens's effort to buy into the Cleveland *Herald*.

To Olivia L. Langdon
7 January 1869 • Chicago, Ill.
(MS: CU-MARK)

Sherman House,
Chicago, Jan. 7.

My Dear dear dear dear dear dear *dear* Livy—(that is the tamest word
that ever I saw—you have to repeat it 6 or 7̸ seven times to make it express anything)—I shall heap some more newspaper abuse on this house
when I get a chance. It does them good. They give me their best room,
now, & treat me like a lord.[1]

I am tired again, Livy. There were many visitors in, during the
afternoon, & I got no chance to lie down & rest. This is the tenth letter
I have written since I finished the lecture to-night. [They want me to
lecture here again.][2] I *have* to write these letters—there isn't any getting
around it—they are answers to letters received. But don't you know, I
was *so* disappointed, when they gave me a batch of letters today & I ran
them over & found not a line from you. No—not *disappointed,* because
exact I had felt just as sure as I could be, that a letter would reach Cleveland after I left, & be re-mailed to Chicago. But bless your old heart, you
are just as good as you can be, & I forgive you. Forgive you, indeed!—I
am all gratitude to you for what you *do* write.

I have a religious experience (Indianapolis) to tell you about, when
I see you—I can't write it, well.[3] Considering that I must get up & start
at 7 in the morning on a 9-hour railway trip, I had bet[t]er be getting to
bed.[4] I was ever so smart, to write last to you, to-night, Livy—otherwise
those other letters never *would* have been written. I wrote you from
Rockford, last night—did you get it? I sent a porter to mail the letter.

You won't need a long letter from me to-night, for I enclose a couple
to make up. Now perhaps I ought not to have begge asked Mrs. Fairbanks to write you, because it is so fatiguing & troublesome to you to
write letters, & you have so much of it to do. But in about a week you
must answer her letter—& you will, *won't* you? She is a noble, good
woman. I am enclo I will spare you *just one day* to write her—no more—
all the other days you must write to *me*, Livy dear. I am going to enclose
her to-days note in this, whether she likes it or not—*I* like it.

Livy, please put Cleveland, Jan. 22, & Norwalk, Ohio, Jan. 21, in the list of lectures I left you.

The other enclosed letter is from a most estimable young lady whose friendship I acquired in St Louis two years ago. She is a thorough Christian. She was a near ne [a] near neighbor of ours, & my mother & sister are very fond of her, & of all her family.[5] The letter won't interest you, but I thought I would send it because it would be such a good hint to you to send me all the letters which young gentlemen may chance to write to you, Livy—[& then I will go & break their necks for them!]

I am going to bed, now, for I am in a hurry to get to Monmouth, where I know I shall get a letter from you. Leaving you in the loving protection of the Savior, & the gentle guardianship of the angels, I bid you good-bye, & kiss you good-night, my darling Livy.

Devotedly & always,

Sam'. L. C.

[*enclosure:*]

ₐ[Preceding this was a formal invitation to lecture for the orphans in Cleveland,.]ₐ[6]

There—Have n't I done that properly? but it is painful this being *parlaiamentary*. It would suit Col. Kinney but not me.[7]

    Mr. Fairbanks sent your shirts to Chicago Monday—We miss you—all of us, but when I feel quite dreary, I go up and open your door to regale my senses with the still lingering perfume of your cigars—

    "You may break, you may miss the vase if you will

    But the scent of the roses will hang round it still."[8]

Touchingly appropriate— ₐ[Isn't that plaintive, Livy?]ₐ

    Allie[9] is quite as inconsolable as *Hattie Lewis*ᵢ, whose comical estimate of your devotion amuses me exceedingly.[10] I shall write to Livy in the morning—but I'm a goose to do it, for what could I say that she [*end of page*]

✉—————————————————————————

[*on back of letter as folded:*]

Miss Olivia L. Langdon

Present.

Politeness of Charlie.

[*docketed by OLL:*] 23ʳᵈ

[1]Clemens had described his recent stay at the Sherman House in a letter published on 15 November 1868 in the San Francisco *Alta California*. The letter, or at least this part of it, was widely reprinted by such newspapers as the New York *Tribune* (17 Dec 68, 8), the Iowa City *State Democratic Press* (6 Jan 69, 1), and the Indianapolis *Journal* (7 Jan 69, 6):

> I will remark, in passing, that the Sherman House is a good hotel, but I have seen better. They gave me a room there, away up, I do not know exactly how high, but water boils up there at 168°. I went up in a dumb waiter which was attached to a balloon. It was not a suitable place for a bedchamber, but it was a promising altitude for an observatory. The furniture consisted of a table, a camp stool, a wash-bowl, a German Dictionary and a patent medicine Almanac for 1842. I do not know whether there was a bed or not—I didn't notice. (SLC 1868k)

The Sherman House was designed in 1861 by "the supreme architect of the Chicago hotel, William Boyington." It "rose up in six stories of finely cut Athens marble, could accommodate 300 guests, and always had an orchestra playing in its grand dining room." The imposing structure had "a frontage of one hundred and eighty feet on Clark Street and one hundred fifty on Randolph Street" and cost, with furnishings, half a million dollars. It was destroyed by fire in 1871 (Lowe, 66, 95, 114; Masters, 111).

[2]Under the auspices of the Young Men's Library Association, Clemens had delivered his "American Vandal Abroad" lecture in Library Hall to an audience the Chicago *Times* called "quite large" and "very select." Noting that Mark Twain had gained "the title of 'The American Humorist,'" the *Times* reviewer nevertheless unsmilingly reported his assurance "that he used the word vandal, not in its harsher meaning, but as representing an individual who was a jolly, good-natured, companionable adventurer, who is at home everywhere, and delivered his opinions with a perfect freedom and innocence." This critic noticed that the

> recital was interspersed with anecdotes, comparisons, and incidents, which were highly interesting, and frequently utterly ridiculous and absurd. At other times the audience were enraptured with the charming oratorical powers of the speaker. . . . The lecture throughout was one of Mark-ed ability, and was listened to by a delighted audience. ("The American Vandal Abroad," Chicago *Times*, 8 Jan 69, 3)

Clemens next lectured in Chicago, on "Roughing It," in December 1871 (Fatout 1960, 166–67).

[3]Nothing has been learned about Clemens's "religious experience." He had lectured in Metropolitan Hall in Indianapolis, under the auspices of the Young Men's Library Association, on 4 January.

[4]On 8 January Clemens traveled from Chicago to Monmouth, Illinois, about 170 miles to the southwest, presumably on the "Day Express and Mail" of the Chicago, Burlington and Quincy Railroad, which departed at 7:30 A.M. He lectured in Monmouth that evening, in Hardin's Hall, under the aegis of the Quaternion Association ("Railroad Time-Table," Chicago *Times*, 8 Jan 69, 3; "Mark Twain," Monmouth *Review*, 8 Jan 69, 2; Wallace, 14–16).

[5]This enclosure does not survive. It was a letter from Louisa (Lou) Conrad, whom Clemens had met in March 1867 while he was in St. Louis visiting his family (*L2*, 18 n. 1, 19 n. 3, 26 n. 6). She evidently was no longer living there (see 14 Jan 69 to PAM).

[6]See 7 Jan 69 to Mary Mason Fairbanks and others, n. 1. The page enclosed

with the present letter is the only part of Mrs. Fairbanks's original 5 January letter known to survive.

[7] Peter Kinney from Portsmouth, Ohio, had been one of the *Quaker City* excursionists. He had served during the Civil War as a colonel in the Fifty-sixth Ohio Infantry (*L2*, 387; Heitman, 2:118).

[8] The concluding lines of one of Thomas Moore's *Irish Melodies:* "Farewell!—But Whenever You Welcome the Hour" (1813). Mrs. Fairbanks wrote "miss" for Moore's "ruin"; Moore himself had ultimately revised "ruin" to "shatter" (Moore: 1820, 131; 1829, 299–300, 302; 1833, 232–33; 1851, 1:43).

[9] Alice Holmes Fairbanks.

[10] While visiting Mrs. Fairbanks in Cleveland, Clemens doubtless had spoken to her about Harriet (Hattie) Lewis's part in his courtship of Olivia—and may even have shown her the letter from Lewis to which he replied on 10 January.

To Harriet Lewis
10 January 1869 • Galesburg, Ill.
(MS: CtY-BR)

Galesburg, Jan. 10.[1]

Miss Harriet Lewis[2]—

[No, that is too cold for a breaking heart—]

Dear Hattie—It cannot but be painful, I may even go f so far as to say harrowing, to me, to say that which I am about to say. And yet the words must be spoken. I feel that it would be criminal to remain longer silent. And yet I come to the task with deep humiliation. I would avoid it if I could. Or if you were an unprotected female. But it must out. I grieve to say there has been a mistake. ~~Af~~ I did not know my own heart. After following you like your shadow for weeks—after sighing at you, driving out with you, looking unutterable things at you—after dreaming about you, night after night, & playing solitary cribbage with you day after day—after rejoicing in your coming & grieving at your going, since all sunshine seemed to go with you—after hungering for you to that degree that for two days I ate nothing at all but you—after longing for you & yearning for you, & taking little delight in any presence but yours—& after writing all those twenty double-postage letters to you, lo! at last I wake up & find it was not you after all! I never was so surprised at anything in all my life. You never will be able to believe that it is Miss Langdon instead of you—& yet upon my word & honor it is. I am not joking with you, my late idol,—I am serious. These words will break your heart—I feel they will—alas! I *know* they will—but if they don't damage your appetite, Mr. Langdon is the one to grieve, not *you*. A broken heart won't set you back any.

Try to bear up under this calamity. O, ~~grieving~~ ˏsadˏ heart, there is a great community of ~~genro~~ generous souls in good Elmira, & you shall not sorrow all in vain. Trot out your ˏ"wasted form" & plead for sympathy. And if this fail, the dining-room is left. Wend thither, weeping mourner, & augment the butcher's bills as in the good old happy time. Bail out your tears & smile again. Don't pass any more sleepy days & nights on my account,—it isn't complimentary to me. And you were **unusually** distraught & sleepy of late, I take it, for you dated your letter "December" ~~ins~~ 4, instead of January. I know what that indicates. If you will look through those twenty letters you will find that I was in a perfectly awful state of mind whenever I dated one of them as insanely as that.

It grieves me to the heart to be compelled to inflict pain, but there is no help for it, & so you will have to go to Mr. Langdon & explain to him frankly what I meant by such conduct as those—& confess to him, for me, that it was the other young lady instead of you. And I wish you would tell *her*, also, for otherwise she will never suspect it, all my conversations with her having been strictly devoted to the weather. Come—move along lively, now!

But do you know, I can't account for Charley's reticence? He used to write to me very faithfully. But ~~do you know~~ ˏreally & trulyˏ he never has answered one of those twenty letters?[3] Never. ~~But~~ ˏHoweverˏ, hard= heartedness does not affect me. I am so forgiving. Many people would feel hurt, & break off the correspondence—but I forgive him—I forgive him, & shall go on writing to him every day just the same. I shall move him after a while, no doubt. If these letters have grown monotonous to Charley & have ceased to interest him, I am grieved, *I*—I am truly grieved—for I do not know any ~~other~~ way to write "Miss Olivia L. Langdon—Present" but just that way. If I *could* write it in any other way so as to thrill him with enthusiasm, I certainly would.

Are you well, my poor Victim? How is your haggard face? What do you take for it? Try "S. T.—1860—X."[4] And have you hollow eyes, too?—or is most of the holler in your mouth? I am sorry for *you*, my wilted geranium.

And next you'll *fade*, I suppose—they all do, that get in your fix— & then you'll pass out, along with Sweet Lily Ł Dale, & Sweet Belle Mahone, & the rest of the tribe[5]—& there'll be some ghastly old sea= sickening sentimental songs ground out ₐaboutₐ you & about the place where you prefer to be planted, & all that sort of bosh. Do be sensible & *don't*.

But deserted & broken-hearted mourner as you are, you are a good girl; & you are with those who love you & would make your life peaceful & happy though your heart were really torn & bleeding, & freighted with griefs that were no counterfeit. You are where you deserve to be—beyond the ~~pale & law~~ reach & lawful jurisdiction of wasting sadnesses & heart aches and where no trouble graver than a passing, fancied ill, is like to come to you. And there I hope to find you when I come again, you well-balanced, pleasant-spirited, excellent girl, whom I love to hold in warm & honest friendship.

Sincerely,

Saml. L. Clemens.

P. S.—This is No. 22.[6] Don't be foolish, now, & silent, merely because I believe that the other young lady is without her peer in all the world, but write again, please. Tell me more of your wretchedness. I can make you *perfectly* miserable, & then you'll feel splendid. I am equal to a good many correspondences.

><

[*on back of page 1, used as a wrapper:*]

Miss Hattie Lewis

Present.

[1]Clemens lectured in Galesburg on Saturday evening, 9 January ("'Mark Twain,'" Peoria *Transcript*, 11 Jan 69, 3; Wallace, 17).

[2]Harriet Lewis (later Paff), Olivia Langdon's first cousin and close contemporary, was the daughter of a brother or half-brother of Olivia Lewis Langdon. She had been visiting the Langdons since the spring of 1868. Clemens's ally in his courtship, during his visits to Elmira she pretended to be the object of his attentions, a ruse intended to help preserve Olivia's privacy. (Lewis enjoyed teasing Clemens and her cousin by feigning desolation at his preference of Olivia over herself: see *L2*, 249 n. 4, 338 n. 9.) In 1897 she recalled that her performance did succeed in deceiving people, much to the amusement of us all. A friend had written me from Chicago asking if the report was true that was in one of the daily papers—that Mr. C— & I were engaged. I read the letter to O— and said I believed I would write M[r.] C— about the reports and the remarks that had been made because of his attentions to me, and how badly I felt that he had already written 20 letters to her and not one to me—that

I was getting pale and emaciated etc—So we wrote the letter and received a reply. (Paff, 5–6)

Their joint effort has not been found. The present letter is Clemens's reply and was still in Lewis's possession as late as 1897.

   [3] See 2 Jan 69 to OLL, n. 12.

   [4] This intriguing slogan lent a mysterious cachet to P. H. Drake's Plantation Bitters, a stomach tonic sold by the quart and consisting largely of "St. Croix Rum." It appeared "on fences, barns, billboards, and rocks, on mountainsides and at Niagara Falls" and was commonly believed to stand for "started trade in 1860 with ten dollars' capital" (Carson, 42). Newspaper advertisements for Plantation Bitters explained:

They act with unerring power, and are taken with the pleasure of a beverage. They perform most wonderful cures on stubborn cases of Dyspepsia, Liver Complaint, Nervous Affections, Loss of Appetite, Intermittent Fevers, Diarrhea, Sour Stomach, Headache, Fever and Ague, Weakness, Mental Despondency, &c. *As a morning appetizer and after-dinner tonic, they should be in every family. They are a delightful exhilerating stimulant without any subsequent stupefying reaction.*

The product's secret ingredient—"a native of Brazil, and as yet unknown to the commerce of the world," but "used with great effect by the Brazilians, Spanish and Peruvian ladies to heighten their color and beauty"—was doubtless responsible for the "cheerfulness to the disposition, vigor to the appetite, and brilliancy to the complexion" that users allegedly experienced ("Plantation Bitters," Cleveland *Herald*, 13 Jan 69, 4).

   [5] "Lilly Dale" (1852), by H. S. Thompson, and "Belle Mahone," by J. H. McNaughton, were popular songs lamenting the untimely deaths of beloved young women (Chapple, 299, 328–29; Mattfeld, 87).

   [6] That is, the twenty-second of Clemens's letters to Olivia. In fact, she docketed his 7 January letter from Rockford as the twenty-second, his 7 January letter from Chicago as the twenty-third, and his 12 January letter from El Paso as the twenty-fifth. His twenty-fourth letter, sent between 8 and 12 January, is now lost, but it may have enclosed this letter to Harriet Lewis, since Olivia was certainly intended to read both.

To Olivia L. Langdon
with a note to Charles J. Langdon
12 January 1869 • El Paso, Ill.
(MS: CU-MARK)

El Paso, Ill., Jan. 12.

My Dearest Livy—

   I talked in Peoria, last night, to a large audience, & one whose intellectual faces surprised as well as pleased me, for I certainly had expected no such experience in Peoria.[1] They want me to come again next season, & I am sure I shall like to do it if I am so unhappy as to be still in the lecture field. That audience reminded me of my Michigan audiences. Do you know, that with the exception, perhaps, of Mrs. Fairbanks', the Michigan reviews of the lecture were the best-written I have seen yet. I received some last night, & have half a mind to send them to you.[2]

I have to stay here half the day—I am on my way to Decatur.[3] They say I shall probably not be able to get to Ottawa & shall have to skip it. This is bothering me a good deal, for I wanted so much to see Mr. Lewis;[4] & besides I was feeling so sure that your letter with the longed-for picture in it would be there. I was so certain I was going to see your dear face there. This will be a hard disappointment to bear. But I shall telegraph for my letters, & get them as quickly as possible.

I wish I **could** have gone with you in the sleigh, but at that time I was taking a long, dreary trip in the cars.

Why bless your darling heart I *do* love to hear you scold!—& rather than have you stop, Livy, I *will* be distressed when you do it. It *does* make an impression, Livy—it makes a deep impression, it does indeed—it makes me just as happy as I can be. Now I *know* you won't stop scolding, since it makes me happy, you precious little philosopher. And besides, whenever it is "something that really troubles you," I will try honestly to listen & behave better, even if I do seem to talk so jestingly about it. But to tell the truth, I love you so well ~~than~~ that I *am* capable of misbehaving, just for the pleasure of hearing you scold. ~~You know~~ I used to surreptitiously provoke Charlie into uttering outrageous speeches simply that I might ~~hear~~ see you look astounded & hear you say "O *Charlie!*" ‚Forgive me, darling.‚

I remember the cribbage right well, & how I used to swindle you into the notion that I had sixteen in my hand when I hadn't a point, you innocent! And I remember how I used to prevent your putting in your pegs at the beginning of the game—& did it merely because it gave me a chance to touch your hand—~~noth~~ & for no other reason in the world. *I* always thought the cribbage was profitable, because I could sit there & look into your eyes all the time—it was much better than reading any *other* book, Livy! I wish I could have a chapter now. But when we are serene & happy old married folk, we will sit together & con other books

all the long pleasant evenings, & let the great world toil & struggle &
nurse its pet ambitions & glorify its poor vanities beyond the boundaries
of our royalty—we will let it lighten & thunder, & blow its gusty wrath
about our windows & our doors, but never cross our sacred threshold.
Only Love & Peace shall inhabit there, with you & I, their willing vas-
sals. And I will read:

> "The splendor falls on castle walls,
>   And snowy summits old in story"—

& worship Tennyson, & you will translate Aurora Leigh & be gentle &
patient with me & do all you can to ~~make~~ help me understand what the
mischief it is all about. And we ʄ will follow the solemn drum-beat of
Milton's stately sentences; & the glittering pageantry of Macaulay's, &
the shuddering phantoms that come & go in the grim march of Poe's
unearthly verses; & bye & bye drift ~~fairly~~ dreamily into fairy-land & with
the magicᶨian laureate & hear "the horns of elfland faintly blowing."[5]
And out of the Book of Life you shall call the wisdom that shall make our
~~life~~ lives an anthem void of discord & our deeds a living worship of the
God that gave them.

Livy, I comprehend, I thoroughly comprehend your method of acquiring the religious emotion, & shall practice it, with full faith in it.
You are worth a dozen preachers to me, & I love to follow your teach-
ings. Every day in my little Testament I track you by your pencil
through your patient search for that wisdom which adorns you so much;
& every marked verse calls to mind some remark of yours & shows me
how deeply the beautiful precept had sunk into your heart & brain.
No unmarked Testament could teach me half as much as this one, & I
am so glad you gave it me, & I thank ˌyouˌ so much for it, my idolized
Livy.[6]

The time will drag, drag, drag, until I see you again—but I am
thankful that your letters come so often. I wish they came *every* day.
They so fill me with pleasure that I have not the heart to harbor an unkind sentiment toward any creature after I have read one of them.

I *want* to write more, but I suppose I ought to lie down a while.
Please give my love to the good household. Good-bye, & happy dreams
to you, Livy, darling,—& a loving kiss, & all thanks for yours.

Always & devotedly

Sam′. L. C.

⊠——

[*on back of letter as folded:*]

ₐYou didn't answer my last dozen, Charlie. Why is this thus?

Sam.

————ⱮⱮ—ₐ

"Miss Olivia L. Langdon,—

Present."

[*docketed by OLL:*] 25th

[1] On 11 January, sponsored by the Mercantile Library Association of Peoria, Clemens lectured to a capacity audience of about twelve hundred in Rouse's Opera House. The *National Democrat* reported that "the house was as full as comfort would allow," and observed that Clemens's "subject, 'The American Vandal Abroad,' suggested something of reproof, but the wit and humor that tempered the speech made every one forget every thing but that. The public owe the lecture committee thanks for providing for them such an entertainment." The *Transcript* gave a full synopsis, remarking that Mark Twain "is unmistakably a man of high natural ability and considerable culture, and could not fail to make his mark in other than his chosen themes. As a satirist and humorist, he places no dependence upon uncouth spelling or local vernacular. He has an easy don't-carative manner and a little of the swagger of the traditional Yankee joker without a single low or ungrammatical phrase" ("Twain's Lecture," Peoria *National Democrat*, 12 Jan 69, 3; "Mark Twain's Lecture," Peoria *Transcript*, 12 Jan 69, 3; Wallace, 17–20).

[2] Mary Mason Fairbanks reviewed Clemens's 17 November 1868 lecture in the Cleveland *Herald* the following day (*L2*, 280 n. 1). Clemens had lectured four times in Michigan: at Detroit, Lansing, Charlotte, and Tecumseh on 22, 23, 25, and 26 December, respectively. He sent the reviews he had just received to Mrs. Fairbanks: see the next letter.

[3] Where Clemens lectured later on 12 January to "a large and respectable audience. Broadcloths and silks were in the ascendant, and the rowdy or 'fast' element congenial to negro minstrel exhibitions was but slimly represented. The intelligence of our city was out in full force, to be entertained as well as instructed, and decency and decorum were the marked characteristics of those assembled to hear Mark Twain's discourse" ("Mark Twain," Decatur *Republican*, 14 Jan 69, 1).

[4] Olivia's maternal uncle, the father of Harriet Lewis. Despite the "extreme inclemency" of the weather, Clemens managed to make the 106-mile trip northward from Decatur to Ottawa and called on the Lewis family ("Lectures," Ottawa [Ill.] *Free Trader*, 16 Jan 69, 1). See 13 and 14 Jan 69 to OLL.

[5] Clemens's quotations are both from one of his favorite poems, the untitled prefatory lyric (known as the "bugle song") to the fourth canto of Tennyson's *The Princess; A Medley*, first included in the third edition, published in 1850 (Tennyson 1987, 2:185–86, 230–31; Gribben, 2:695). One of Olivia's favorite

poems was Elizabeth Barrett Browning's *Aurora Leigh* (1857), which Clemens more than once professed to find incomprehensible (see *L2*, 268).

[6]Olivia had given this Bible to Clemens, perhaps as a Christmas present, during his 17 and 18 December visit to Elmira (*L2*, 334, 348).

To Mary Mason Fairbanks
12 January 1869 • El Paso, Ill.
(MS: CSmH)

El Paso, Ill, Jan. 12.

Dear Mother:

Enclosed are some Michigan notices. They ought to be printed, in order to keep up the excitement. The best one was written by a distinguished college professor. If you do print them, please save me 6 or 8 copies of each—& if you don't, why, please preserve the originals for me. They came in the letter Mr. Fairbanks sent.[1] Big house last night in Peoria—fine success, too.

Did you write to the girl for whose amusement the sun was created? Love to all.

Yrs Affectionately
Mark.

[1]Abel Fairbanks had forwarded a letter from John Morris enclosing three Michigan lecture reviews. Clemens received the letter on 11 January, in turn enclosed the reviews here, and probably sent Morris's letter to Charles J. Langdon. None of the original clippings is known to survive, although two have been identified (see the next letter and Appendix B). The Cleveland *Herald* did not reprint any of the Michigan reviews, but on 18 January, as a "specimen" of the "universal praise" Mark Twain had received, it did reprint a review from the Indianapolis *Journal* of 5 January ("Lecture for the Benefit of the Orphans," Cleveland *Herald*, 18 Jan 69, 1).

To Charles J. Langdon
12 January 1869 • Ottawa, Ill.
(MS: CU-MARK)

. . . .

[enclosure:]
I have heard from Marshall, Mich—been invited to come there.
Sam.[1]

GRAND RIVER VALLEY RAILROAD COMPANY.

Charlotte STATION,

Jan 4th 186 9

S. L. Clemens

In compliance with my pledge at Jackson I herewith enclose you an article from the Lansing Republican one from the Charlotte Argus by Prof. Ingham & another from the Charlotte Republican by some very good judge who styles himself "Brownie."[2]

How have you fared since we dined on partridge? I do not forget that man meal nor the woebegone expression of our colored "brother" as you catechised him concerning the bill of fare in demand.

You may rest assured that your name will find an acceptable place upon our list another winter if we shall survive or escape the strokes of the that professional Reaper thus long.

Have you heard anything from Marshall a nice old town on the Mich Central about 30 miles west of Jackson. They are in need of a lecture to fill one of Anna Dickinson's appointments that she has taken up for some cause. I have reccommended you to one of their committee & he promised to write you at Cleveland direct.[3] They were anxious to hear how your efforts were received here & at Lansing. If you are to come there I might possibly manage to hear your *gentle voice*.

Yours Truly
John Morris

[on back of enclosure as folded:]
This is from a splendid fellow
—a friend I made in Charlotte.[4]

[1] This comment is a gloss on the fourth paragraph of the enclosure, the covering letter for which is lost. For several reasons, it seems likely that Clemens sent John Morris's letter to Langdon on the day after he sent *its* enclosures to Mary Mason Fairbanks (see the previous letter). His signature is consistent with the way he signed himself to Langdon, and to his family in St. Louis, but to few others. (He did not sign himself "Sam" to Olivia until 13 February, and to Mrs. Fairbanks and to Twichell he was more often "Mark.") And on 14 January he told Olivia: "I wrote Charlie from Ottawa—did he get it?" His anxiety is explained by a $150 deposit for 13 January in the cash account Langdon was maintaining for him (the bookkeeper presumably used the date of the check rather than the date of receipt) ("Sam*ᶦ*. L. Clemens Esq In acc with C. J. Langdon," statement dated "Elmira Aug 9ᵗʰ 1869," CU-MARK). Clemens may have reached Ottawa late on the night of 12 January; he lectured there the following evening.

[2] The reviews that appeared in the Charlotte *Republican* and the Lansing *State Republican* (on 30 and 31 December 1868, respectively) are fully transcribed in Appendix B. The review by "Prof. Ingham," who has not been further identified, has not been found.

[3] Anna Elizabeth Dickinson (1842–1932), the fiery lecturer on abolition and women's rights, was one of the stars of the lyceum circuit, earning as much as $200 per lecture, twice Clemens's rate (see *L2*, 337 n. 6). She was also a much-admired friend of the Langdons'. Doubtless Clemens would have expected them to be gratified by his selection to replace her in Marshall, where he performed on 25 January. For Dickinson's opinion of Clemens and his of her, see 22 Jan 69 to OLL, n. 2.

[4] Morris has not been further identified.

To Olivia L. Langdon
13 and 14 January 1869 • Ottawa, Ill.
(MS: CU-MARK)

Ottawa, Ill., Jan. 13.

My Dearest Livy—

Another botch of a lecture!—even worse than Elmira, I think.[1] And it was such a pity—for we had a beautiful church *entirely full* of handsome, well-dressed, intellectual ladies & gentlemen. They say I *didn't* botch it, but I should think *I* ought to know. I closed with a fervent apology for my failure, just as I did in Elmira—& the apology was the only thing in the lecture that had any life or any feeling in it. It cuts me to the very quick to make a failure. I did feel so ashamed of myself. I even distressed the Committee—I touched their hearts with my genuine suffering, & real good fellows as they are, they came up to my room to comfort me. The failure was chiefly owing to an idiot president, who insisted on introducing me while the people were still pouring in,—& they kept on coming in till one-fourth of the lecture had been delivered to an audience who ¢ were ~en~ exclusive[ly] engaged in watching the new-comers to their seats—it seemed that I *never* would get their attention. I grew so exasperated, at last, that I shouted to the door keeper to close the doors & not open them again on *any* account. But my confidence was gone, the church was harder to speak in than any empty barrel would have been, I was angry, wearied to death with travel, & I just hobbled miserably through, apologized, bade the house good-night, & then gave the President a piece of my mind, without any butter or sugar on it. And now I have to pray for forgiveness for these things—& unprepared, Livy, for the bitterness is not all out of my bad, foolish heart yet.[2]

Took tea with Mr. Lewis—like him ever so much. If you remember, he is like Twichell—you are acquainted with him as soon as you take him by the hand. It would take some time to get acquainted with his wife, though.[3]

Lost my baggage somewhere, day-before yesterday—heard of it to-day, but can't get it before I arrive in Toledo[4]—am lecturing in my bob-tail coat & that makes me feel awkward & uncomfortable before an audience.

Livy, dear, I am instructed to appear & lecture in New York City Feb. 15. It is the most aggravating thing. I have to miss the re-union after all, I suppose, for no doubt I shall have to go on lecturing just the same, after that. But you must write me all that the happy re-unionists do & say, & I shall be with you all in spirit, at least, if not in the flesh. And I shall keep a sharp look-out & see if I can't get a day or two to myself between Jan. 22 & Feb. 13, because I do so long to see you, Livy dear. So far there are only five applications in my agent's hands for lectures during that interval, I think.[5] You ~wr~ were right not to send the picture if it slandered you like the other, but it does seem to me sometimes that *any* ˌnewˌ picture of you would be a comfort to me—one that had seen your own face lately. The old photograph is a dear old picture to me, & I love it; but still it isn't as beautiful as you are, Livy, & I want a picture that is. I am not so absurd as to love you simply for your beauty—I trust you know *that* well enough—but I *do* love your beauty, & am naturally proud of it & I ˌ ~want~ don't wan't the picture to mar it.

Poor Lily Hitchcock!—see how they talk about her in print—just as generous & warm-hearted a girl as you ever saw, Livy, & her mother is such a rare gem of a woman. The family are old, old friends of mine & I think ever so much of them. That girl, many & many & many a time, has waited till nearly noon to breakfast with me, when we all lived at the Occidental Hotel & I was on a morning paper & could not go to bed till 2 or 3 in the morning. She is a brilliant talker. They live half of every year in Paris—& the hearts that rascal has broken, on both sides of the water! It always seemed funny to me, that she & I could be friends, but we *were*—I suppose it was because under all her wild & repulsive foolery, that warm heart of hers *would* show. When I saw the family in Paris, Lily had just delivered the mitten to a wealthy Italian Count, at her mother's request (Mrs. H. said Lily loved him,)[6] & then—but ah me,! it was only going from bad to worse to jilt *any*body to marry Howard Coit. *I* know him, a dissipated spendthrift, son of a deceased, wealthy eminent physician, a most worthy man. Howard "went through" the property in an incredibly short time. And this poor little numbscull Lily's last act was to mortgage her property for $50,000 ,$20,000,, gold, & give the money to that calf. He will squander it in six months if he has not mended greatly. [The above was told me in Chicago by a Confidante of Lily's who was simply under promise to keep the matter from her parents.] Until that moment I said the whole affair must be untrue, because, as detestable as some of Lily's freaks were she could not be capable of deceiving her mother & father & marrying secretly.[7] And to tell the plain truth I don't really believe it yet. She is an *awful* girl (the newspaper article is written by somebody who knows whom he is talking about), but she isn't *that* awful. Li She moves in the ∤ best society in San F. Does that horrify you, Livy? But remember, there never was so much as a whisper against her good name. I am so sorry for that girl, & so very, very sorry for her good kind mother. I hold both of them in grateful remembrance because they said in their happy remembrance always—for they were your *brave*, outspoken sort of friends, & just as loyal to you behind your back as before your face.

Well—I simply meant to enclose the slip, with a line of explanation—I think I rather overdid, it.

Tell Miss Lewis that *I* think the answer is "*Considerable∤*." What is her notion? I have told her brother all *I* knew about her, & a mighty sight that I didn't know. I always like to give good measure.

The passage ~~ma~~ from the "exquisite" struck me at the time as a vivid echo of my own sentiments—I *knew* it would be of yours, without your mentioning it, dear Livy.[8] No, you wouldn't ~~rh~~ ask me to go to prayer meeting if you fancied I was tired, & I am sure I would always try to be as thoughtful of you, & as watchful for your happiness. I think ~~the~~ our very chiefest pleasure would (WILL, Livy,) consist in planning & scheming each for the other's happiness. Livy, I cannot conceive of such a thing as my failing in deference to you, either now or when you are my wife, (for I will not think of your being any one else's wife, Livy,) or ever conducting myself toward you, ~~in the world's presence,~~ in a manner unbecoming to your dignity. Why *did* you talk of not sending "this half sheet?" It delighted *me* more than I can tell. I like all you say about marriage, for it shows that you appreciate the tremendous step it is, & are *á* looking at it in all its parts, & *not* to simply seek flaws in it.

After some littŕle delay, I am back & ready to go on answering your letter—but alas! it is I AM, I am tired to death & *so* sleepy—

And so I press this loving kiss upon your lips, my darling Livy & waft you a fond Good-night.

Sam. L. C.

[*enclosure:*]

An Eccentric California Belle.[9]

San Francisco Correspondence of the Providence Journal.

Mrs. Ellet, in her recent book on "Famous American Women," makes mention of a California lady remarkable for her ability to entertain twenty gentlemen at once by her vivacious conversational powers.[10] If this were the only, or chiefly, remarkable thing about Miss Hitchcock, she would be a far less remarkable personage than she is. But she is a character, and such a character as this age cannot and need not duplicate the country over. As Americans, we have long boasted of the versatility of our climate, soil and people. Perhaps Miss Hitchcock was a necessary national production, that the world may be convinced of the truthfulness of this boast. She is a public character—an actress requiring a far broader stage and larger house than other actresses of the time. She is an only daughter, an only child, I believe, of a wealthy and most respectable family, her father, Dr. Hitchcock, having come to this coast as an army surgeon during the Mexican war. He is now a retired physician and among the most substantial and worthy of San Franciscans.[11] His accomplished daughter has long been one of the belles of this city, without whom no social gathering of the *ton* was complete if she was in the country. When a child she was rescued from a burning building by some members of Knickerbocker Engine Company, No. 5, since which time she has never forgotten them—wearing conspicuously, at all times and in all places, a neat gold "5" upon her dress, and at times making the company, of which she is a duly elected member, costly presents, ranging from the cherished "5" to the gold-mounted fire-horn.[12] She is eccentric to an extent that would shock our New England notions of propriety, showing her eccentricity, now by presenting the "Fives" a barrel of brandy, now by staking a thousand on a favorite horse at the races, again by riding on the cowcatcher with the constructing engineer over the entire length of the Napa Valley Railroad, to which ride she challenged said engineer, and still again by some of the noblest deeds of philanthropy and charity. She has upwards of $50,000 in her own right, and of course is expected to inherit the hundreds of thousands of her father's estate. From her own purse she supplies the wants of many needy objects of charity, being generous to the extreme and of noble impulses. She vibrates between San Francisco and Paris, taking New York and London in her way, and astonishing the natives of each of these quiet (?) intermediate cities by what she does and what she does not do. She defies all rules and conventionalities of society, dresses and acts as she pleases everywhere, selects her company from all classes at will, and yet commands the confidence and good-will of all. She is conspicuous at the grand balls of the Empress at the Tuileries,[13] attends annually the Derby in England, where, it is said, she amuses herself by winning or losing a few hundred pounds a day at the hands of the young sprigs of nobility. A few days since she started in company with her parents overland for New York, and thence to Paris. Two days after her marriage notice appeared as evidence of the last of her eccentricities; she in a quiet way, with the personal knowledge of but two human beings besides herself and the fortunate (?) groom, having suddenly experimented in the *role* of bride. Another admirer was with her all the afternoon of that day, until 6 p. m., when she went, as he supposed, to dinner. At 8 p. m. he met her again by appointment and went with her to the theatre, after which he accompanied her and the family as far as Sacramento on her overland journey, quite ignorant of the fact that from 8 p. m. he had been in company with Mrs. Howard Coit instead of Miss Hitchcock.[14]

⊠————————————————————————————————

[*in pencil on wrapper:*]

Miss Olivia L. Langdon

Present.

[*docketed by OLL:*] 26th

[1] Clemens had delivered the "American Vandal Abroad" in Elmira on 23 November 1868, giving less than his best performance before an audience that included Olivia Langdon and her family (*L2*, 285–86 n. 1, 288).

[2] Sponsored by the Ottawa Young Men's Christian Association (whose "idiot president" has not been further identified), Clemens's 13 January lecture in the Methodist Episcopal Church drew only brief reviews. The Ottawa *Free Trader* thought it "certainly most amusing and droll. . . . Mark's stories are [i]nimitable, and when he tries to be eloquent he succeeds beyond almost any speaker we ever heard" ("Lectures," 16 Jan 69, 1). The Ottawa *Republican* reported that members of the "large audience in the M. E. Church" had expressed "various opinions." "One man said it was 'very funny and at times eloquent,' another, equally as well prepared to judge, thought 'the lecture was mostly nonsense and stale at that'" ("On Wednesday evening . . . ," 21 Jan 69, 3). Clemens's experience on this occasion helps account for this 1871 assertion to James Redpath, then his lecture agent: "I *never* made a success of a lecture delivered in a church yet. People are afraid to laugh in a church. They can't be *made* to do it, in any possible way" (10 July 71 to Redpath [2nd of 3], Friedman, in *MTL*, 1:189). Nevertheless, Clemens performed very successfully in at least three churches during the present tour and once in 1871 recommended using a church as a lecture hall. See 29 and 30 Jan 69 to OLL, n. 1; 17 Feb 69 to Goodman, n. 2; 28 Nov 69 to OLL, n. 2; and 3 Dec 69 to the editor of the Brooklyn *Eagle*, n. 2.

[3] Olivia had not yet met Twichell, but Clemens must have earlier characterized him in such a way that she would understand this comparison of him to her uncle. Nothing further has been learned of Lewis's formidable wife.

[4] Where Clemens lectured on 20 January (see 20 and 21 Jan 69 to OLL).

[5] Clemens lectured in Alliance, Ohio, on 15 February, and never lectured at all in New York City during the present tour. His midwestern agent was G. L. Torbert, of Dubuque, Iowa, secretary of the Associated Western Literary Societies, which coordinated requests for lecturers from member societies (*L2*, 62 n. 4, 241 n. 3, 254–55 n. 2). Torbert left a break in Clemens's schedule that permitted him to visit Elmira from 3 to 12 February (see Appendix D). The "reunion," which Olivia was planning for around 18 February at the Langdon home, was to be a gathering of her brother's special *Quaker City* friends: see 14 Jan 69 to OLL, n. 8.

[6] Clemens had become well acquainted with Eliza (Lillie) Wychie Hitchcock (1843–1929), the belle of San Francisco society, and with her parents, Dr. Charles McPhail Hitchcock (1812–85) and Martha Hunter Hitchcock (1818–99), in 1864, when he was a reporter for the San Francisco *Morning Call*. He had last seen the mother and daughter in Paris in July 1867 (*L2*, 72–73; "Deaths," San Francisco *Evening Bulletin*, 4 Apr 85, 3; Green, 1, 2 facing, 32).

[7] Lillie Hitchcock had dismayed her parents with her marriage—on 19 November 1868, at San Francisco's St. James Church—to Benjamin Howard Coit

(1840–85), the son of Benjamin B. Coit (1801–67), a prominent physician who had come to San Francisco from the East Coast in 1849. Howard Coit had grown up in Buffalo, New York, and in Norristown, Pennsylvania, before leaving his mother and journeying to California in 1857. After about three years in Los Angeles, doing telegraphic and clerical work, and about seven years in Arizona, working as a mining superintendent, he settled permanently in San Francisco in 1867. In November of that year he became a member of the San Francisco Stock and Exchange Board, which had been created in 1862 to facilitate the purchase and sale of mining stock. In December 1869, with assistance from his influential father-in-law (see notes 6 and 11), he won election as the board's "caller"—the chairman responsible for calling out the daily list of stocks for bid—a position he held, by annual re-election and at a salary of $1,000 a month, until illness forced his resignation only weeks before his death. An 1878 biographical sketch of Coit noted that "it would be almost impossible to find another man that could exactly fill his place. It is not profound scholarship, great shrewdness as a 'mining sharp,' or knowledge of stock manipulations, nor a good pair of lungs, a handsome, manly form, or imperturbable good humor, or even inflexible integrity that fit a man for the office of caller of the San Francisco Stock Board. Howard Coit has all these and something more, which inspires such respect and confidence that although he has sold more stocks than any other living man, both buyers and sellers—those who have lost and those who have won fortunes through his ministrations—are satisfied with his fairness and impartiality" (*Pacific Coast*, 46–47). That encomium and others like it suggest that Coit "mended greatly" from the profligate whom Clemens describes. He did not reform entirely, however; his philandering led Lillie to separate from him several years before his death ("Married," San Francisco *Examiner*, 27 Nov 68, 3; Green, 27; "Death of Howard Coit," San Francisco *Morning Call*, 15 May 85, 2; "Sudden Death of Dr. B. B. Coit," San Francisco *Alta California*, 17 Apr 67, 1; "Men We Know," *California Mail Bag* 9 [June 76]: 94; Joseph L. King, 4, 6–7, 9, 43–48, 50, 74, 275, 294, 336; Holdredge, 115, 252, 274–76).

[8] The "exquisite" apparently was all or part of Coventry Patmore's *The Angel in the House* (1854–62), an uplifting four-part verse narrative about two pairs of lovers. Clemens and Olivia read the work in late 1868 and discussed it in their correspondence (see *L2*, 274, 310, 313–14, 343, 369).

[9] Although the clipping that Clemens enclosed does not survive and therefore cannot be positively identified, it is apparent that its text derived ultimately from a newspaper letter from the West Coast, signed "Vallejo," published on 28 December 1868 in the Providence (R.I.) *Journal*. The portion of this letter that dealt with Lillie Hitchcock Coit was reprinted in the Chicago *Tribune* on 11 January (4), three days after Clemens left Chicago en route to other Illinois towns. The likelihood is great, therefore, that he took his clipping either from the *Tribune*, or from some recent reprinting of it. The text of the enclosure is reproduced verbatim from the *Tribune*.

[10] "Miss Lillie Hitchcock was celebrated in San Francisco for brilliant accomplishments and personal graces. She would entertain at one time a circle of twenty gentlemen," according to Elizabeth Fries Lummis Ellet, *The Queens of American Society* (New York: Charles Scribner and Company, 1867), 451. Ellet (1812?–77), a poet, essayist, and translator, is best known for her popular his-

tories of American women, particularly *The Women of the American Revolution* (3 vols., 1848–50) and *Pioneer Women of the West* (1852).

[11] During eighteen years as a surgeon in the United States Army, Charles McPhail Hitchcock served at West Point, on the Canadian border, in Indian Territory, and in the Mexican War of 1846–48, before being posted to San Francisco in 1851, with the rank of major, to serve as medical director of the Pacific Division. In 1853 he resigned from the army to go into private practice. Upon his death in 1885 he left an estate valued at $250,000 (Green, 2 facing, 3–4; Heitman, 1:532; "Death of Howard B. Coit," San Francisco *Morning Call*, 15 May 85, 2).

[12] John Boynton, the fireman who rescued Lillie Hitchcock early on 23 December 1851, recalled that afterward Knickerbocker Engine Company No. 5 received "a barrel of brandy, sent to us by Dr. Hitchcock with a thousand dollars toward a new engine. His was a grateful heart for a life saved from destruction. But it was Lillie Hitchcock's heart which throbbed with eternal love for the members of Number Five. From then on she belonged to us as much as we belonged to her" (Holdredge, 66–68; "Fire," "The Fire on Bush Street," San Francisco *Alta California*, 23 Dec 51, 2, 3). Floride Green, a friend of Lillie's, reported:

Knickerbocker Number 5 became so attached to her that they admitted her to honorary membership October 3, 1863, and her certificate of membership was her most prized possession. After this she was expected to go to all fires that occurred in the day. And at night, if her light was not burning until her engine was housed she was fined. . . . She always wore a little gold 5 pinned to her dress, and signed herself Lillie H. Coit 5. She asked that this 5 be left on her at the end. Everything she had, even her linen, was marked—L.C.H.5. Lacemakers even worked it into her monogram on her fans. (Green, 19–20)

[13] The palace in Paris that was the principal residence of Emperor Napoleon III (1808–73) and the Empress Eugénie (1826–1920).

[14] The Chicago *Tribune* omitted about the final third of the Providence *Journal* article, which included these closing remarks about Lillie Hitchcock Coit:

This is the same youth whom she dared to drive down an embankment on the Cliff House road a few years ago, which he did at the small cost of $1200. Her husband is left behind, she not having seen him, it is said, since they left "Saint James' Free Church." Doubtless ere this she has informed her loving pa and dearest ma of her last romantic experiment, and is now enjoying some other innocent amusement.

But while this heroine is thus eccentric and romantic in her composition, and thus reckless in her demeanor, as before remarked, there are in her character many of the noblest traits possessed by any. She speaks evil of no one, but has a kind word and warm heart for all. Were that heart, these talents and her means consecrated to her God, and her life restrained by the religion of Jesus, she would have almost unlimited capacity for usefulness. (Vallejo)

To Olivia L. Langdon
14 January 1869 • Davenport, Iowa
(MS: CU-MARK)

Davenport, Jan. 14.

Livy, darling, I greet you. We did have a splendid house tonight, &
everything went off handsomely.[1] *Now* I begin to fear that I shan't get a
chance to see your loved face between Jan. 22 & Feb. 13 as I was hoping
& longing I should. Because I have just received some new appointments
by telegraph—the ones I expected. Please add them to your list—carefully, & don't make any mistake: Thus:

Marshall, Mich.,	Jan. 25.
Batavia, Ill.,	Jan. 26
Freeport, Ill.,	Jan. 27
Waterloo, Iowa,	Jan. 28
Galena, Ill	Jan. 29
Jacksonville, Ill.,	Feb. 1.

Others are to come, the dispatch says. [Did I tell you I am to lecture in
Norwalk, Ohio, Jan. 21, & in *Cleveland*, Jan. 22? Put those down too,
Livy.[]] If they don't send me the names of the Secretaries of these added
societies, you will have to tell Charlie to direct your letters to my *nom de
plume*, & then the Secretaries will get them anyhow. Will you try to remember that, dear? And now, since misfortune has overtaken me & I am
not to see you for such a long, long time, won't you please write me *every
day?* I wish you would try, Livy. I don't think you can, & I don't expect
it, either, for it is a great labor—but still I do wish you *could*, if it
wouldn't interfere with your duties or pleasures, or tire you too much. I
find it next to impossible to get the opportunity to write to you every day,
though I would most certainly like to do it—& being forced, as I am, to
devote to it simply such time as I can snatch from sleep, my letters can't
naturally be anything more than mere hasty, chatty paragraphs, with
nothing in them, as a general thing. [*in margin:* I wrote Charlie from
Ottawa—did he get it?]

Where was I on Sunday, Jan. 3? In Fort Wayne. Had my breakfast
brought up, & lay in bed till 1 P.M. I did want to go to church, & the
bells sounded very inviting, but it seemed a plain duty to rest all I could.

[Besides, I don't like to see people nudge each other when I enter a church, & call attention to me. Funny things happen sometimes, though. In Tecumseh, Mich., the preacher got to talking about the mysterious grave of Moses—& there was a broad smile all over the house in a moment—they thought of "Moses Who?" The ~~poor~~ preacher was not at the lecture, & could not understand why his well-delivered & ~~w̶ er~~ earnest pathos should provoke mirth.][2]

Yes I lay abed till 1 P.M, & read your Akron & Cleveland letters several times[3]—& read the Testament—& re-read Beecher's sermon on the love of riches being the root of evil[4]—and read ~~G~~ Prof. Goldwin Smith's lecture on Cromwell[5]—& a most entertaining volume containing the Grecian & other Mythologies in a condensed form[6]—& smoked thousands of cigars, & was excessively happy—that is, as happy as I could ~~b~~ well be, without you there to make it complete. Then I got up & ate dinner with some friends—& went to bed again at 4 in the afternoon & read & smoked again—& got up long, long before daylight [*in bottom margin:* [See back of page 3]][7] & took the cars for the endless trip to Indianapolis ~~via~~ & Chicago. That is the history of Jan. 3, Livy dear, & I remember it ever so pleasantly.

I have seen your young gentlemen women-haters often—I know them intimately. They are infallibly & invariably unimportant whelps with ~~vest~~ vast self-conceit & a skull full of oysters, which they take a harmless satisfaction in regarding as brains. They are day-dreamers, & intensely romantic, though they would have the world think otherwise. ~~They~~ Their pet vanity is to be considered "men of the world"—& they generally know about as much of the world as a horse knows about metaphysics. They are powerfully sustained in their woman-hating & kept well up to the mark by the secret chagrin of observing that no woman above mediocrity ever manifests the slightest interest in them—they come without creating a sensation, & go again without anybody seeming to know it. They are coarse, & vulgar, & mean—these people—& they know it. Neither men or women *I* admire them much or love them—& they know that, also. [*in margin:* I *wish* I could see you, Livy.] They thirst for applause—any poor cheap applause of their "eccentricity" is manna in the desert to them—& they suffer in noticing that the world is ~~unc~~ stupidly unconscious of them & exasperatingly indifferent to them. When *sense* dawns upon these creatures, how suddenly they ~~h~~ discover that they have been ~~pitif~~ pitiable fools—but they are full forty years old, then, & they sigh to feel that those years & their pleasures they might have borne, are wasted, & lost to them for all time. I *do* pity a woman= hater with all my heart.—even The spleen he suffers is beyond comprehension.

Why yes, Livy, you ought to have sent me Mother Fairbanks' letter, by all means. Send it now, won't you, please?[8] She's a noble woman. It will be splendid for her to have you & me both to bother about & scold at, some day. W She will make a fine row with me when she sees me coming back on the 22ᵈ with a new lot of baggage after all her trouble convincing me that I needed nothing more than a valise to travel with. I shall find my ₐlost₎ baggage again at Toledo, I think.

The lady you wrote of was singularly unfortunate—judging at a first glance—but considering that it brought such Christianity, & such happy content in doing good, it seems only rare good fortune after all. Ten millions of years from now she will *shudder* to think what a frightful calamity it would have been, not to have lost her wealth.[9] Did it never occur to you what a particularly trifling & insignificant breath of time this *now* long & vastly important earthly existence of ours will seem to us whenever we shall happen accidentally to have it called to our minds *ten awful millions of years* from now? Will not we smile, then, to remember that we used at times to shrink from doing certain duties to God & man because the world might jeer at us?—& were so apt to forget that the world & its trifling opinions would scarce rise to the dignity of a passing memory at that distant day? Brainless husbandmen that we are, we sow for time, seldom comprehending that we are to reap in Eternity. We are all idiots, much as we vaunt our wisdom. Good-bye. I kiss you good-night, darling. I do love you, Livy!

Always Yours,
Sam*ᶦ*. L. C.

✉——————————————————————————————————————

[*on wrapper:*]

Miss Olivia L. Langdon
Present.
Politeness of Hon. Chas. J. Langdon.
Elmira, New York.

[*docketed by OLL:*] 27ᵗʰ

---

[1]Clemens spoke at Burtis Opera House under the auspices of the Davenport Library Association. In announcing the performance, the Davenport *Democrat*

predicted that it would be "a rich feast of mirth to our lecture going people. Twain is witty without the vulgarity [of] Nasby, and is possessed of fine descriptive powers, and is purely original in style and delivery" ("Mark Twain's Lecture," 11 Jan 69, 1). The lecture, before an audience the *Democrat* reviewer called "quite select and the largest that has greeted any lecture of the course," fulfilled these expectations. Mark Twain spoke for "nearly two hours," offering "fine descriptions, interspersed with anecdotes, comparisons and incidents, which were highly interesting, and frequently utterly ridiculous and absurd. The lecture was a success—a thing to be enjoyed, not remembered. It also paid handsomely and everybody were satisfied" (" 'The American Vandal Abroad,' " 15 Jan 69, 1).

[2]Clemens lectured in Tecumseh on Saturday, 26 December 1868, and attended church the next day. The anecdote that discomfited the local cleric figured in the "Vandal" lecture on at least two other occasions. Clemens did not publish it until 1872, as part of chapter 6 in *Roughing It* (*L2*, 299–300 n. 2).

[3]That is, letters from Olivia that were intended to reach Clemens at Cleveland, where he arrived on 28 December, and at Akron, where he lectured two days later. He returned to Cleveland immediately after the Akron lecture and remained until he left for Fort Wayne on 2 January.

[4]Olivia had sent the issue of the *Plymouth Pulpit* that published Henry Ward Beecher's "The Love of Money," delivered at Plymouth Church, on 22 November 1868. (Probably it was the 5 December issue; at least by late December, the *Plymouth Pulpit* was publishing Beecher's sermons thirteen days after delivery.) Beecher said in part:

> We are not to understand that *money* is the root of all evil; but the *love* of it—bestowing that which we have a right to bestow only on undying and immortal qualities, upon God, and angels, and men—bestowing love, idolatrously, upon material gain. It is not true that all evil in the world springs, in some way, directly or indirectly, from money; but it *is* true that there is no evil to which at one time or another love of money has not tempted men. . . .
>
> If God calls you to a way of making wealth, make it; but remember do not *love money*. (Henry Ward Beecher 1869, 171, 179)

[5]Before leaving England for Ithaca, New York, in October 1868, Goldwin Smith (1823–1910), was a professor of law and history at Oxford. He was also a journalist, lecturer, political activist, and prominent champion of liberal causes. In November 1868 he became professor of English history and constitutional history at newly opened Cornell University, an appointment he held until he resigned in 1872. Clemens presumably read Smith's lecture on Oliver Cromwell—first delivered in Manchester, England, on 21 January 1867—in *Three English Statesmen: A Course of Lectures on the Political History of England* (New York: Harper and Brothers, 1867). The book also included talks on John Pym and William Pitt ("Mr. Goldwin Smith on Cromwell," London *Times*, 22 Jan 67, 9; Gribben, 2:649).

[6]Probably Thomas Bulfinch's *The Age of Fable; Or, Beauties of Mythology*, a collection of Greek, Roman, Scandinavian, Celtic, and Oriental myths, first published in 1855. Olivia had had an edition of that work since January 1864 (Gribben, 1:110). Clemens's failure to refer to the book by title—if in fact *The Age of Fable* was the "most entertaining volume"—suggests that he was unaware that she was familiar with it.

[7]Having inadvertently left one side of the second leaf blank, Clemens filled it with page 6. His pagination ultimately ran as follows: 1–2, 3–6, 4–5, 7–8, 9–10.

[8]Fairbanks's letter—presumably written on 6 January (as indicated in her 5

January letter to Clemens: see 7 Jan 69 to OLL from Chicago)—does not survive, although Olivia's reply does (CtHMTH):

(OLL)

                                                Elmira Jan 15ᵗʰ 1869
Dear Mrs Fairbanks
        Your very welcome letter reached me the 9ᵗʰ—I was very glad of the little visit from you which it gave me— Two or three times during the last six weeks, I have been strongly moved to write you, then I did not know quite how to express with pen and paper, the thoughts that were in my ~~heart~~ ˏmindˏ, I longed rather for the opportunity to speak with you face to face, to talk with you as only women can talk together, and as it is the blessed privilege ~~to~~ of a young woman to talk with an older one—
        I felt proud and humble, both at the same time by your letter—proud that you did not consider me unworthy to receive the love of a strong, noble man, (I remember how very slight a knowledge you have of me)—proud that you should feel that I might *help* Mr Clemens— Humble when I remembered how much I must strive to do, as a Christian woman, in order to accomplish what you believe me capable of accomplishing, humbled, even painfully humbled, when I remembered how weak I was, and how utterly and entirely ˏhelplessˏ, unless there comes into my soul a strength from above— Then I was again raised up, remembering the power and willingness of Him in whom ᵱh I put my trust—
        I believe that two people who are to unite their lives should feel as sanguine about their future, as you feel about ours—so I do not think that you are too sanguine— I cannot understand, ˏ~~how,~~ their chief aim in life being the same, a christian walk and conversation, knowing the uncertainty of human effort, the liability to stumble and fall, how it can be otherwise, than that they shall help and strengthen each other—
        I quite envy you the sight that you are to have of Mr Clemens next week, but then a month from now I hope that he will be with us— Mother and I have been wondering whether we could not have the "Quaker City" reunion at that time— Could you and your husband, with Allie and Mr Stillwel come to us about the 18ᵗʰ of next month? Mother will try and write Mrs Severance, regarding it, before many days— We look forward with a great deal of pleasure to that meeting of Charlie's friends—
        I want to thank you for persuading Mr C. to put that extract from your Christmas letter in print, I want the public, who know him now, only as "the wild humorist of the Pacific slope", to know something of his deeper, larger nature— I remember being quite incensed by a ladieys asking, "Is there any thing of Mr Clemens, except his humour", yet as she knew of him it was not an unnatural question—
        Cousin Hattie Lewis, rec'd a letter two or three days ago from Mr Clemens telling her the truth with regard to his feelings, he came out frankly with her and "broke her heart", I think that she will find it a great relief ˏto have it done,ˏ now that she has lived through it—
        We had heard of Mollies accident, and were very glad to learn that she was doing well— Give my love to her please, also to Allie, and kind regards to the rest of your family— Hoping that I shall see you next month, I am lovingly
                                                Your friend Livy L. Langdon
[*in Charles J. Langdon's hand:*] I am well too.

The *Quaker City* reunion, repeatedly postponed, never took place. Olivia may have found the phrase "Wild Humorist of the Pacific Slope" in Charles Henry Webb's prefatory "Advertisement" to Clemens's first book, *The Celebrated Jumping Frog of Calaveras County, And other Sketches* (New York: C. H. Webb, 1867), which, much to Clemens's dismay, she had been reading in December (*L2*, 369–70; for the text of Webb's "Advertisement," see *ET&S1*, 429).

        [9] This fortunate woman, evidently a "sea-Captain's wife," has not been further identified (see 17 Jan 69 to OLL and CJL, p. 46).

To Pamela A. Moffett
14 January 1869 • Davenport, Iowa
(MS: NPV)

Private. }

Davenport, Iowa, }
Jan 14. }

My Dear Sister:

I lectured here to-night—& have lately lectured in several Michigan towns, & in Akron, Ohio, Fort Wayne, Ind., Indianapolis, Rockford, Monmouth, Galesburg, Chicago, Peoria, Decatur, & Ottawa, Ill—& a lecture every night—& now have to talk in Iowa City, Sparta, Wis., Toledo, Ohio, Norwalk, Cleveland, & a lot of places in Illinois, Michigan, & New York City & New York State, & am getting awfully tired of it.[1] I spend about half as much money as I make, I think, though I have managed to save about a thousand dollars, so far—don't think I shall save more than a thousand more.[2]

One of Mrs. Pavey's daughters (she married a doctor & is living in an Illinois town & has sons larger than I am,) was in the audience at Peoria. Had a long talk with her. She came many miles to be there.[3] Saw a nephew of Tom Collins in Decatur.[4]

The Societies all want to engage me to lecture for them next year, but [*end of page*]

[*two-thirds of MS page (about 65 words) missing*]

That is all of the *private.*[5] Had a letter from Miss Lou Conrad the other day—was near where she lives, but had not time to go there.[6]

What do you think of Norwich, N.Y., for a home? I think it will *exactly* suit you. You can run to New York or visit the sea-side whenever you please, from there.[7]

No, you can't board & lodge in New York City in any sort of respectable & comfortable style for less than $25 to $35 a week apiece.

In the spring go yourself, or send Orion[8]—or both of you go—to Norwich, & you will rent or buy a house & be delighted. I only wish I could live there. I am to lecture every night till Feb. 2. Shall be in Cleveland, Ohio, *one day* only—Jan. 22.

Affectionately
Sam.

Love to all.

---

[1] For the dates of Clemens's appearances in these places, see Appendix D.

[2] Between 17 November 1868, when his tour began, and the date of this letter, Clemens's gross earnings were at least $2,300. He earned a fee of $100 for each performance, but evidently paid his own travel, lodging, and meal costs. As befitted a newcomer to the field, his normal fee was half that of some of his competitors, such as Petroleum Vesuvius Nasby (20 and 21 Jan 69 to OLL, n. 1; *L2*, 246, 282, 294).

[3] Jesse H. Pavey (1798?–1853), a brutal Hannibal tavern keeper during Clemens's youth, and his wife, Catharine (b. 1800?), had a large family that included at least seven daughters. Clemens's visitor might have been any one of four of them—Julia, Sarah, Fanny, or Susan. In 1897, in "Villagers of 1840–3," he identified her as "Mrs. Strong." The Paveys had left Hannibal for St. Louis by mid-1850. In 1855, while working in St. Louis as a printer, Clemens boarded with the widowed Catharine Pavey (for his recollections of this family, see *Inds*, 98–99, 340–41).

[4] Thomas K. Collins (1822–85), a dry goods merchant, was one of Hannibal's foremost businessmen (*Inds*, 94, 102, 315). His nephew has not been identified.

[5] Pamela must have torn away the top two-thirds of this page, which presumably contained Clemens's progress report on his courtship, even before passing the letter on to other members of the family in St. Louis. She thereby complied with his November 1868 request for strict confidentiality—"I make no exceptions" (*L2*, 295).

[6] Clemens sent Louisa Conrad's letter to Olivia Langdon (see 7 Jan 69 to OLL from Chicago, n. 5).

[7] Clemens repeated his previous recommendation (of 24 December) that his sister move with her family to Norwich, in Chenango County, New York, approximately 140 miles from New York City (*L2*, 326–27, 348). She now lived with her mother, two children, and the family's German maid, Margaret, at 1312 Chesnut Street in St. Louis, where she also took in boarders. The family remained at that address until May 1869, the first of several moves within St. Louis. In April 1870, they moved to Fredonia, in westernmost New York, close to Lake Erie and about forty miles from Clemens's Buffalo home (11 May 69 to JLC; 1 Apr 70 to Jervis and Olivia Lewis Langdon, TS in CU-MARK; 21 Apr 70 to OC, CU-MARK; Richard Edwards 1868, 537, 953; Richard Edwards 1869, 569; *MTBus*, 47, 103, 112).

[8] Orion and Mollie Clemens apparently lived in St. Louis throughout 1869 (with Mollie sometimes visiting her parents in Keokuk, Iowa). It is not known whether they were currently living with Pamela.

To Olivia L. Langdon
with a note to Charles J. Langdon
17 January 1869 • Chicago, Ill.
(MS: CU-MARK)

SHERMAN HOUSE,

CHICAGO, Sunday, Jan. 16, 186 9.

My Dearest Livy—

I am uncomfortably lame this morning. I slipped on the ice & fell, yesterday, in Iowa City, just as I was stepping into an omnibus. I landed with all my weight on my left hip, & so the joint is rather stiff & sore this morning.

I have just been doing that thing which is sometimes so hard to do—making an apology. Yesterday morning, at the hotel in Iowa City, the landlord called me at 9 o'clock, & it made me so mad I stormed at him with some little violence. I tried for an hour to go to sleep again & couldn't—I wanted that sleep particularly, because I wanted to write a certain thing that would require a clear head & choice language.[1] Finally I thought a cup of coffee might help the matter, & was going to ring for it—no *bell*. I was mad again. When I *did* get the landlord up there at last, by slamming the door till I annoyed everybody on my floor, I showed temper again—*& he didn't*. See the advantage it gave him. His mild replies shamed me into silence, but I was still too obstinate, too proud, to ask his pardon. But last night, in the cars, the more I thought of it the more I repented & the more ashamed I was; & so resolved to make the repentance good by apologizing—which I have done, in the most ample & unmincing form, by letter, this morning. I feel satisfied & jolly, now.[2]

"Sicisiors" don't spell *scissors*, you funny little orthographist. But *I* don't care how you spell, Livy darling—your words are always dear to me, no matter how they are spelt. And *I* if I fancied you were taking pains, or putting yourself to trouble to spell them right, I shouldn't like it at all. If your spelling is never criticised till *I* criticise it, it will never be criticised at all. I do wish I could have been at the birthday dinner.[3] All that, & the paragraphs about your conversations were just as pleasant as they could be—& yet you thought it was foolish to write them. I am glad enough that you didn't mark them out. It was a good, long, pleasant letter, & I thank you ever so much for it. I can easily see that Mr. Beecher was preaching upon a subject that was near his heart.[4] *People can always talk well when they are talking what they* FEEL. ₍This is the secret of *eloquence₎*—I wish you could hear my mother, sometimes.₎ In the cars, the other day I bought a volume of remarkable sermons—they are from the pen & pulpit of Rev. Geo. Collyer, of Chicago. I like them very much. One or two of them will easily explain the Christian history of the sea= Captain's wife of whom you wrote me. These sermon's lack the profundity, the microscopic insight into the ~~hidden~~ secret springs & impulses of the human heart, & the searching analysis of text & subject which distinguish Henry Wards Beecher's wonderful sermons, but ~~they~~ they are more polished, more poetical, more elegant, ₍more rhetorical,₎ & more dainty & felicitous in wording than those. I will send you the book before long.[5]

Now am I not going to get a letter at Norwalk, Ohio, (Jan. 21,) nor Cleveland, (Jan. 22.)? I do hope I wrote you of those appointments, but I am a little afraid I didn't.[6]

Your Iowa City letter came near missing—it arrived in the same train with me.

It was just like Mr. Langdon in his most facetious mood, to say he would kill me if I wasn't good to you—& it was just like you, you dear true girl, to say you'd never tell—for I believe you *would* go bravely on, suffering in secret from ill-treatment, till your great heart broke. But we shall circumvent Mr. Langdon, utterly—he never will have the satisfaction of killing me—because you & I will live together always in closest love & harmony, & I shall be *always* good to you, Livy dear—*always*. And whenever he needs a model married couple to ~~mo~~ copy after, he will only have to come & spend a few weeks at our home & we will educate him. He will see me honor you above all women, & he will also see us love each other to the utmost of human capability. So he can just put up his tomahawk & wash off his war-paint. He won't have to kill me—*will* he, Livy?

So I am to be three days without a letter. I don't like that much. It comes so natural to get a letter from you every two days that I shall feel odd without one this evening. I am so bound up in you, & you are in my thoughts so constantly by day & in my dreams by night, & you have become so completely a part of my life—of my very flesh & blood & bone, as it were—that I shall feel lost, to-day while this temporary interruption of communication lasts,—I shall feel as if the currents of life have ceased to flow in some part of my frame, having been checked in some mysterious way. Oh, I do *love* you, Livy! You are so unspeakably dear to me, Livy.

I am to start for Sparta, Wisconsin, at 4 PM., to-day. And I am to talk in Franklin, Pa., Feb. 14, & in Titusville, (Pa., I suppose,) Feb. 15—the New York appointment is changed.[7]

Give my loving duty to your father & mother,—please, & tender my savage regards to Miss Lewis & Charlie. And I wish that you would remember me most kindly to Mr. & Mrs. Crane when you write. I like Mr. Crane—I never have seen anything whatever about him to dislike— & you know one can't help liking Mrs. Crane.[8]

Have you got a good picture yet, Livy?—because I want it so badly. Good-bye. Reverently & lovingly I kiss your forehead & your lips, my darling Livy, & wish you rest, & peace, & happy dreams.

For all time, devotedly,

Sam*ᶫ*. L. C.

[*on wrapper, front panel:*]

Miss Olivia L. Langdon

Present.

Politeness of ~~R~~ the Right Reverend

Bishop Chas. J. Langdon.

[*on back panel:*]

ₐCharlie, this makes about twenty-five letters I have directed to you— & you have been faithful in answering in the same way—that is, in di-

Miss Olivia L. Langdon.

recting letters to me written by other people—& a little more interesting than if you had written them yourself, my boy.ₓ[9]

[*docketed by OLL:*] 28th

---

[1]Possibly the special conclusion Clemens added to his benefit lecture for the Cleveland Protestant Orphan Asylum on 22 January: see 5 Feb 69 to Fairbanks, n. 4.

[2]S. B. Sanford managed the recently refurbished Clinton House for its owners, E. Clark and Thomas Hill ("The Clinton House," Iowa City *Republican*, 2 Dec and 23 Dec 68, 3). Clemens's letter apologizing to Sanford is not known to

survive. His offending show of temper occurred on 16 January, the morning after he opened the season's lecture course for the Young Men's Christian Association at Iowa City's Metropolitan Hall. The Iowa City *Republican* denounced both performances:

THE VANDAL IN IOWA CITY.—A splendid audience turned out to hear Mark Twain discourse about "The Vandal abroad," and we fear were generally disappointed. As a lecture it was a humbug. As an occasion for laughter on very small capital of wit or ideas it was a suc[c]ess. There were one or two passages of some merit. His apostrophe to the Sphinx was decidedly good, as was also his description of the ruins of the Parthe[n]on, and of Athens by moonlight. Some touches of Venice did very well, but it was impossible to know when he was talking in earnest and when in burlesque. It was amusing and interesting to see such a crowd of people laughing together, even though we knew half of them were ashamed that they were laughing at such very small witticisms. We were very much disappointed that there was so little substance to his lecture. We would not give two cents to hear him again.

But, lest he might not have succeeded with his "Vandal Abroad," he illustrated the character at the Clinton House, where he stopped. The morning after the lecture nothing was seen of him up to nine o'clock, and the landlord, in his kindness, went to his room to see if he might not be in want of something, but received a storm of curses and abuse for disturbing him. Of course the landlord retreated and left him. After a while a terrible racket was heard and unearthly screams, which frightened the women of the house. The landlord rushed to the room and there found a splendid specimen of the vandal and his works. There, before him, was the veritable animal, with his skin on at least, but not much else, and in a towering rage. He had kicked the fastenings from the door, not deigning to open it in the usual way—that would have been too much like other folks. He poured upon the landlord another torrent of curses, impudence and abuse. He demanded to know where the bell-pull was. The landlord told him they were not yet up, as they had not yet got the house fully completed. His kicking the door open and his lung performance were his substitute for a bell. At two o'clock P. M. he had not dressed, and whether he did before he left on the five o'clock train we did not learn. The Y. M. C. A. were wretchedly imposed upon by Mark Twain, and so of course were the audience. He is the only one engaged for the course whose personal character was unknown. (20 Jan 69, 3)

The same newspaper, in another column, reported that "MARK TWAIN netted the Y. M. C. A. $130 and yet they did not re-engage him." The Iowa City *State Democratic Press*, also on 20 January, confined its remarks to his lecture performance, calling it a success and declaring that his humor was "quite original and his sentiment, though mostly borrowed from [Alexander Kinglake's] 'Eothen' a work published in 1845, was yet well rendered. The attendance was good and the Y.M.C.A. realized handsomely" ("Twain's lecture . . . ," 3; Lorch 1929, 513–17). A later review in the monthly *University Reporter*, although generally favorable, concluded: "We came away feeling a satisfaction that we had heard and seen the man whose fun we have read, but *dissatisfied* in this, that we had heard *so much* that we never care to hear again. It is sad to know that so much power and genius as he possesses are not the instruments for accomplishing a holier purpose than is exemplified by the man's life" (1 [Feb 69]: 74).

³For Jervis Langdon's sixtieth birthday, on 11 January.

⁴Olivia must have described a sermon that Thomas K. Beecher had delivered on Sunday, 10 January, but no text for it has been found.

⁵Clemens discussed the "sea-Captain's wife" in his letter of 14 January to Olivia (p. 40). The book was *Nature and Life: Sermons by Robert Collyer* (Boston: Horace B. Fuller, 1867), which had gone through eight editions by this time. Robert Collyer (1823–1912) was an English-born former blacksmith and Methodist lay-preacher who had been ordained a Unitarian minister and served as

pastor of Unity Church, in Chicago, from 1859 until 1879. Clemens soon sent
his book to Olivia (see 26 and 27 Jan 69 to OLL, p. 78).

⁶Clemens had, in fact, mentioned these appointments at least twice: see 7 Jan
69 (from Chicago) and 14 Jan 69, both to OLL.

⁷The New York City lecture for 15 February was canceled and the two Pennsylvania lectures were rescheduled (see Appendix D).

⁸Susan Langdon Crane (1836–1924), Olivia's foster sister, was born Susan
Dean. Her mother, Mary Andrus Dean, died in 1837 and her father, Elijah
Dean, three years later, and Susan and her three siblings were adopted by various families. Susan's husband, Theodore, was one of Jervis Langdon's principal
business associates. In May 1870, when Langdon reorganized his coal firm as J.
Langdon and Company, Crane became one of his partners (Sharlow; "In Memoriam," Elmira *Saturday Evening Review*, 13 Aug 70, 5).

⁹See 2 Jan 69 to OLL, n. 12. Clemens crowded in the note to Charlie, both
above and below Olivia's name, which he had written first, then boxed.

To Olivia L. Langdon
19 January 1869 • Cleveland, Ohio
(MS: CU-MARK)

Ⓕ

                                                             Cleveland, Jan. 19.

I reached here at daylight yesterday morning, Livy dear, pretty well
tired out with railroading¹—& they called me at 8 o'clock, this morning.
It was a great mistake. They ought to have let me sleep longer. I did not
try to get to Sparta, because I found it could not be done. I found a Plymouth Pulpit here da postmarked *Dec. 30*—a sermon on self-culture &
self-denial—& read it through in bed last night. *"Man is a tease."* You
marked that for *me*, you little rascal—what do you mean by such conduct
as those? But I liked the sermon, notwithstanding it was below Mr.
Beecher's average. You found little in it to mark, but what there was, was
Truth, & came home to me.²

I find the family well & happy. But I meet with one disappointment—Mr. Benedict is sick & very low, & so I cannot talk business ⱳ
with him.³ All yesterday afternoon I played cribbage with Miss Allie⁴—
everybody else was gone up town. I worried her considerably, in a good=
natured way. Occasionally I would say, absently, "Well I wish I were in
Elmira"—& she would retort very sharply,—"Indeed? well why don't
you start?—*I*'m not keeping you." And sometimes I would observe, politely, "I wish you were Livy—then I would take more interest in this

game—I *love* to play cribbage with Livy." We had a very pleasant time of it. She beat four games out of eleven. Charlie Stillwell is in Indiana— she says she writes to him every night, the last thing before she goes to bed; & he writes her every day. It is true—& if you had less to fatigue you, & more leisure, Livy darling, I would beg you to write me every day. Still, th if you did, I am afraid you wouldn't write as long a letter as you do now, & so I am not sure I would be better off. I ought to be grateful enough—& am—that you write me every two days.

Although they called me so early this morning, they didn't and ruined my sleep, for good, they didn't get me up till 10 o'clock & after— & so Mr. & Mrs. F. were gone up town. Miss Allie set the table for me & kept me company—& I *did* wish it were your dear little self instead, but I didn't *say* it until I had got my second cup of coffee. She says the servant girls are never good-natured about late breakfasts, except for *me*—& that they say they are glad to hear I am coming, & glad to do anything for me at any time. Isn't that splendid? Because you know when good-will is shown me by servants, it is a patient, much-suffering sincere good-will, for I am a necessarily a nuisance to them with my rascally irregular ways. But you will break up all my irregularities when we are married, & *civilize* me, & make ,of, me a model husband & an ornament to society—*won't* you, you dear matchless little woman? And you'll be the dearest, best little wife in all the world, & we shall be happier than ever any condition of single life can experience. Let May the day come soon!—Amen.

I haven't been shaved for three days—& when Mrs. Fairbanks kissed me this morning, she said I looked like the moss-covered bucket.[5] Livy dear, be sure & tell Charlie that his letter came this morning, & it shall all be just as he says,—& I would write him a line & shake him by the hand if I had a moment of time to spare. But I haven't even the time to write *you* only these 3 or 4 pages (there goes the dinner-bell) & I'll hear from Mrs. F. in a minute. Must go up town right after dinner. We are going to write you all a family dinner.[6]

Good-bye—& take this loving kiss—& this—& this—my darling Livy—& God bless you.

Saml. L. C.

They are hurrying me—Fairbanks called up stairs to know what part of the chicken I wanted—told him to give me the port side, for'rard of the wheel.

Miss Olivia L. Langdon
Present
—ᴧᴧ—
Politeness of Charlie

[*docketed by OLL in pencil:*] 29ᵗʰ [*and in ink:*] mint

¹Clemens was at the home of Abel and Mary Mason Fairbanks, on whose personal stationery he wrote this letter. He remained with the Fairbankses until 25 January, except for the nights of 20 and 21 January, which he spent in Toledo and Norwalk, respectively, after delivering his lecture.

²"Self-Control Possible to All," the sermon Henry Ward Beecher delivered in Plymouth Church on 11 October 1868, was first published in the *Plymouth Pulpit*, probably on 24 October (see 14 Jan 69 to OLL, n. 4). Beecher advocated a life of self-discipline as a means to "become better, sweeter, more divine and noble." He noted that man was "the only universal tease. The hardest thing to bear is men. They annoy you; they try you; they torment you; they vex you. . . . A man that can bear cheerfully his fellow-men has little to learn." But such a spirit of tolerance was only commendable, he warned, if practiced "for a moral end" and not for worldly gain (Henry Ward Beecher 1869, 51–52, 59).

³Clemens had hoped to talk to George A. Benedict, one of Abel Fairbanks's two partners in the Cleveland *Herald*, about the possibility of buying into the paper.

⁴Alice Holmes Fairbanks.

⁵The allusion is to "The Bucket" (1818), by Samuel Woodworth: "The old oaken bucket, the iron-bound bucket, / The moss-covered bucket which hung in the well." See also *L2*, 35–37.

⁶Neither the letter from Charles J. Langdon nor the family "dinner" (i.e., letter) to Olivia are known to survive.

To Olivia L. Langdon
20 and 21 January 1869 • Toledo, Ohio
(MS: CU-MARK)

Toledo, Ð̶ Jan. 20.

My Dearest Livy—

It was splendid, to-night—the great hall was crowded full of the pleasantest & handsomest people, & I did the *very best* I possibly could—& did better than I ever did before—I felt the importance of the occasion, for I knew that, this being Nasby's residence, every person in the audience would be comparing & contrasting me with him—& *I* am satisfied with the performance. The audience were quiet & critical at first but presently they became warmly *enthusiastic*, & remained so to the very close. They applauded the serious passages handsomely. I have carried off the honors on the Rev. Nasby's own ground—you can believe that, Livy.[1] At the close, the people in the front seats came forward & I made a number of pleasant acquaintances of both sexes & several ages. I watched one young lady[2] in the front row a good deal, because she looked so sweet & good & pretty & reminded me all the time of you—& I ~~made~~ almost made up my mind to go down & introduce myself—but she & her party hesitated for some time & finally came forward & were introduced—& I just think I looked some love into that girl's eyes—couldn't help it, she did so much remind me of you. I have forgotten her name, but she was from Providence, R. I., & is visiting some friends in Norwalk, Ohio, where I lecture to-morrow night. I felt ever so kindly toward her for bringing you before me—I could hardly help telling her so. But she would have resented that, I suppose. Oh, *why* ain't you here? Being *reminded* of you isn't enough—I want to see *you*, you darling "sunbeam," as Mrs. Fairbanks calls you—& it just describes you, too, Livy.

I am most handsomely housed here, with friends—John B. Carson & family. Pleasant folks, & their home is most elegantly appointed. They are as bright & happy as they can be. He is 35 & she is 31 & looks 25. They have a son 14 ~~yeas~~ years old & a daughter 13.[3] The editors of the newspapers, & some other gentlemen & ladies have been up to call on me since the lecture, & sat till midnight.[4] They thought it fun[n]y that I would taste neither shampagne nor hot whisky punches with them, but Mrs. Carson said they needn't mind urging me, as she had provided for me—& she had—a pot of excellent coffee & a lot of cigars. This reminds ∅ me of that Chicago newspaper notice. It was exquisitely lubberly & ill-written all the way through, & made me feel absurd at every other sentence—but then it was written in the kindest spirit, Livy, & the reporter had honestly done his very best, & so we must judge him by his good intent, Livy, & not his performance.[5]

And this naturally reminds me of the California letter you speak of (what you had previously said of it—or *them*, if there was more than one,) has gone to Sparta, Wis., I guess, & I haven't received it yet.) I don't mind anything bad those friends have written your father about me, provided it was only true, but I *am* ashamed of the friend whose friendship was so weak & so unworthy that he shrank from coming out openly & above-board & saying *all* he knew about me, good or bad—for there is nothing generous in his grieving insinuation—it is a covert stab, nothing better. We didn't want innuendoes—we wanted the *truth*. And I am honestly sorry he did not come out like a man & *tell* it.[6] I am glad & proud that you resent the innuendo, my noble Livy. It was just like you. It fills me with courage & with confidence. And I know that howsoever black they may have painted me, you will steadfastly believe that I am not so black *now*, & never *will* be, any more. And I know that you are satisfied that whatever honest endeavor can do to make my character what it ought to be, I will faithfully do. The most degraded sinner is accepted & made clean on high when his repentance is sincere—his *past* life is forgiven & forgotten—& men should not pursue a less magnanimous course toward those who honestly struggle to retrieve their past lives & become good. But what I *do* grieve, over, Livy, is that those letters have pained *you*. Oh, when I knew that your kind heart had suffered for two days for what I had done in past years, it cut me more than if *all* my friends had abused me. Livy I can't bear to think of *you* suffering pain— I had rather feel a thousand pangs than that you should suffer one. I am so glad to know that this pain has spent its force & that you are more at peace, now. *Do* try to banish these things from your mind, Livy, please. You are so ready & so generously willing to do whatever will please me— now *this* will please me above all things. Think, Livy darling, how passionately I love you, how I idolize you, & so how distressed I cannot but feel to know that acts of *mine* are causing you pain—think how wretched such a reflection as that *must* make me, & summon back your vanished happiness, Livy. And reflect, in its place, that I *will* be just as good as ever I *can* be, & will never cause you sorrow any more. You *will* do this, won't you, Livy? Oh, Livy, I *dread* the Sparta letter—for I know I shall find in it the evidence of your suffering—a letter, too, which I have watched the mails so closely for. And those California letters made your father & mother unhappy. But I knew they would—I knew they *must*. How wrong & how unfair, it seems, that they should be caused unhappiness for things which I alone should suffer for. I am sorry—I will atone for it, if the leading a blameless life henceforward *can* atone for it. Already the pleasure of my triumph of this evening is passing from me, & seems only trivial, at best, in presence of this graver matter.

Why, Livy dear, you didn't "*wound*" me—you cannot do that, for I don't judge you by your *acts*, but simply by your *intent*—& how could I suppose you would *intend* to wound me? I do not suppose, & *could* not suppose such a thing—& so I was not wounded, Livy—it is *I* that should be sorry that I wrote so heedlessly as to make you think so.

Livy, you didn't write a "miserable, unsatisfactory note" to Mother Fairbanks at all—for I read it saw how it pleased her, & I read it & I know it pleased *me*, ever so much. You didn't know I would see it, but I *meant* to see it, for Saturday, Sunday & Monday had passed since I had seen a line from your dear hand, & I would have taken it away from her by main force if she hadn't relented & given it to me. I was famished for a letter.[7] Ah, I had boundless fun there all Monday & Tuesday. Nobody there but just the family, & I could *relax* & talk just as much nonsense as I pleased. We didn't carry any sober faces about the house. Charlie Stillwell came home last night, & he & I sat there & swapped horrible ghost stories till they were all half afraid to go to bed, & poor Mollie[8] was sick with fright. Poor child, she loves to hear the stories, but then she can't se sleep afterward. Whenever you write any of them again, please say, "It was a *black* cat—two o'clock in the morning."

Oh you dear little stubborn thing, don't I tell you you *must* be literal?—& yet here you come again & say, "How *foolish* I was to take that "week" with *positive* literalness." You precious intractable pupil! But I will forgive you—for a kiss.

Livy, I am mad at myself for my thoughtlessness—making you run to the daguerrean gallery five times, when I know that it is nothing less than punishment to make you sit up & be stared at by those operators—& I don't *want* them staring at you, & propping up your chin, & profaning your head with the touch of their hands—& so, please don't go again, Livy. Never mind the picture, now—wait till you are in New York again. I was too selfish—I thought only of my own gratification & never once of the punishment I was inflicting on you. But bless your heart, Livy, I never *thought* of your going *five* times. Don't you go again, dear—now don't you do it. And just you be the lovely good girl you are, & forgive my stupid thoughtlessness.

I *am* sorry for Mr. Beecher, for he does seem to have great trouble. It is such a pity that people will blindly criticise his *acts*, instead of looking deeper & discerning the noble *intent* that underlies them. *How* can people ever hope to judge correctly when they persist in forgetting that a man's intent is the only thing he should fairly be judged by? But he ought not to grieve so much. God sees his heart—God weighs his intent—He cannot be deceived. I hope his Christian enterprises will succeed, in spite of all obstacles.[9] Yes, Livy, I guess it is right for you to attend the sociables & do what you can, but I fancy *you* introducing yourself to a stranger & opening a conversation calculated to make him feel comfortable & at home! You ~~would~~ couldn't do it—& I am wicked enough to say I am glad of it, too. Let them introduce the strangers to *you*—that is the proper way, & the safest. Some homely woman would be sure to repulse your advances, & I wouldn't blame her—that is just the style of those homely women. And if you made advances to the men, you know perfectly well they would fall in love with you—& if you don't, *I* do—& I couldn't blame *them*, either. *I* can't keep from falling in love with you—& nobody else. Well, I do love you—I do love you, darling, away beyond all expression. ₍Just kiss me once, Livy, please.₎

"Letters shall go to you as often as possible, but I cannot lock myself up to them." Why you blessed little spitfire, you ~~alwa~~ almost got mad, that time, didn't you! But when you say in the next sentence, "with a kiss, lovingly, Livy," I want to take you in my arms & bless you & soothe your impatience all away; & tell you that howsoever foolishly I talk, I love & honor you away down in my heart, & that its every pulse-beat is a prayer for you & my every breath a supplication that all your days may be filled with the ineffable peace of God.

Livy, *don't* talk about my "crying out against long letters." Just write them, dear, & I shall be only too glad to read them. You cannot make them too long, & you *can't* make them uninteresting, for that is simply impossible. Child, I take an interest in even the blots you make! Make them as long as you can, Livy, please.

But it is just *2:30 A.M.* & I breakfast at 8 precisely & take the train for Norwalk. Don't forget the appointments, Livy:

Marshall, Mich. ————————————————— Jan. 25
Batavia, Ill. ————————————————— 26
Freeport, Ill ————————————————— 27
Waterloo (*Iowa*.) ————————————————— 28
Galena, Ill ————————————————— 29
Jacksonville, Ill ————————————————— Feb. 1.

Good-bye, with a loving kiss & a blessing—

For all time,

Sam*ˡ*. L. C.

✉ ——

Miss Olivia L Langdon
Present

[*docketed by OLL:*] 30th

[1]Toledo's resident celebrity was David Ross Locke (1833–88), since 1865 editor, and by 1868 part-owner, of the Toledo *Blade*. In 1862 Locke had begun writing a series of newspaper letters in the guise of the bumptious and bigoted Reverend Petroleum Vesuvius Nasby. Rendering dialect in violently phonetic detail, and making use of the full range of ironic devices, he effectively championed liberal causes by seeming to oppose them. As Nasby he first took to the lyceum circuit with his "Cussed be Canaan," a vitriolic attack on racial prejudice and injustice, which Clemens would soon hear for the first time in Hartford (see 10 Mar 69 to OLL). In late 1868, Locke added an alternate lecture on women's rights, "The Struggles of a Conservative with the Woman Question." He regularly earned $200 to $250 for each appearance, and as much as $400 in larger cities (Harrison, 3, 97–109, 121–23, 181–85, 192–201; Austin, 34–36, 74–98, 111–19; *Toledo Blade History*, 1–2). Locke was on tour himself at this time and therefore did not attend Clemens's lecture in Toledo, although the *Blade* printed an appreciative review of it (see the enclosures to 23 Jan 69 to Twichell and family, Appendix B).

[2]Unidentified.

[3]Carson was the general freight agent for the Toledo, Wabash and Western Railway. He and his family, who have not been further identified, lived at 190 Superior Street in Toledo (Scott 1868, 60, 103, 386). It is not known when Clemens became acquainted with the Carsons.

[4]Clemens's visitors may have included the Reverend Robert McCune, Locke's associate editor on the *Blade*, as well as J. W. Evers of the *Deutsche Zeitung*, and Clark Waggoner (1820–1903) of the *Commercial* (Scott 1870, 240; Rowell, 90).

[5]Clemens had forsworn "spirituous liquors" and "social drinking," but not smoking cigars, to please Olivia (see *L2*, 284, 353, 354). The Carsons' offer of refreshments had apparently recalled to him a well-intentioned but embarrassing passage from the Chicago *Tribune*'s "lubberly & ill-written" review of his lecture: "Next to Grant, he wears the belt for smoking. He smokes tobacco. Drink never crosses the threshold of his humorous mouth" ("Mark Twain," 8 Jan 69, 4). He had probably described the review or enclosed a clipping in his twenty-fourth letter to Olivia, written between 8 and 12 January, but now lost, although she may have independently seen the following excerpt in the Elmira *Advertiser* on 16 January:

> The Chicago *Tribune* says that the real name of Mark Twain is Samuel G. Clemens. Blessed with long legs, he is tall, reaching five feet ten inches in his boots; weight, 167 pounds; body lithe and muscular; head round and well set on considerable neck, and feet of vast size. He smokes tobacco. The eyes are deepset, and twinkle like stars in a dark night. The brow overhangs the eyes, and the head is protected from the weather by dark and curling locks. He looks as if he would make a good husband and a jolly father. ("Brevities By Pen and Scissors," 4)

[6]In late November 1868 Clemens had provided Olivia's parents with the names of "six prominent men, among them two clergymen" in San Francisco to serve as character references for him (*L2*, 358–63; AD, 14 Feb 1906, CU-

MARK, in *MTA*, 2:110). The Langdons had now begun to receive replies from these men. Included was one that Olivia evidently described in the letter she sent to Sparta, Wisconsin, about 15 January, but which Clemens had yet to receive because he had been unable to get there (see 19 Jan 69 to OLL). This "California letter" may have been from James S. Hutchinson, who was not a reference provided by Clemens, but a former employee of Jervis Langdon's, now a bank cashier in San Francisco. Langdon had instructed Hutchinson to solicit opinions from two men whom Clemens *did* give as references because he thought he was on good terms with them—the Reverend Horatio Stebbins, pastor of the First Unitarian Church, and the Reverend Charles Wadsworth, pastor of the Calvary Presbyterian Church (*ET&S2*, 536–37). Hutchinson managed to contact Wadsworth's deacon, James B. Roberts, who was also the superintendent of the Calvary Presbyterian Sabbath School:

Mr. Roberts replied emphatically: "I would rather bury a daughter of mine than have her marry such a fellow."

Later Mr. Hutchinson made a similar inquiry of the late Rev. Dr. Horatio Stebbins. . . . Doctor Stebbins' reply was: "Oh, Mark is rather erratic, but I consider him harmless."

These replies were forwarded to Mr. Langdon, who later responded to the effect that the matter had gone so far that he could not interfere with it, if he would. (Hutchinson, 36)

In 1906 Clemens recalled that "one clergyman (Stebbins) and that ex-Sunday-school superintendent (I wish I could recall his name) added to their black testimony the conviction that I would fill a drunkard's grave" (AD, 14 Feb 1906, in *MTA*, 2:110). For Clemens's recollection of these responses just a few months after they were received, see 25 Aug 69 to Stoddard.

⁷See 14 Jan 69 to OLL, n. 8.

⁸Mary Paine Fairbanks (b. 1856), the family's youngest child (Fairbanks, 552).

⁹For the past year, as a means of spreading the gospel to those who did not normally attend church, the Reverend Thomas K. Beecher had been conducting Sunday evening services at the Elmira Opera House, usually drawing crowds of thirteen hundred or more. The practice had angered some townspeople who thought a theater an unsuitable place of worship and others who felt it was depressing attendance at regular services. Beecher used his first three "Friday Miscellany" columns of 1869, in the Elmira *Advertiser*, to rebut his critics and he distributed fifteen hundred circulars soliciting public opinion on the matter (Thomas Kinnicut Beecher 1869a–c). Then, at his evening service on Sunday, 31 January, he reported that he had received fewer than one hundred fifty responses to his survey: "Of these answers, *two* were boyish, *three* were insulting, and *one* was obscene. *Three* advise the discontinuance of the meetings. *Two* give *conditional* advice to discontinue. The remainder (*over one hundred and thirty*), with various degrees of enthusiasm, ask for their continuance." Repeating previous appeals for the collaboration of other pastors, Beecher announced: "Sunday Meetings at the Opera House will continue from month to month, as long as a Christian minister can be found to lead them and a company of attentive people to listen to Gospel messages, and join in prayer and praise to God" ("Sunday Meetings at the Opera House," Elmira *Advertiser*, 1 Feb 69, 4). On Sunday, 21 February, while in Elmira to visit Olivia Langdon, Clemens attended Beecher's evening gospel meeting, for the Elmira *Advertiser* observed "the pleasant countenance of Mark Twain" among the audience ("City and Neighborhood," 22 Feb 69, 4). See also 9 and 31 Mar 69 to Crane, n. 7.

To Olivia L. Langdon
21 and 22 January 1869 • Norwalk, Ohio
(MS: CU-MARK)

Norwalk, Ohio, Jan. 21.

My Dearest Livy—

I wrote you last night from Toledo, & naturally feel an impulse to
visit with you to-night again, although I do not know that I really have
anything to say, except that I love you, Livy; & it seems to me that I have
said that before. But then I keep on loving you, you little marvel of creation, & so I cannot well keep from thinking about it & *saying* it. If I only
devoted half as much thought to any other noble study, I would soon
become one of the wisest men on earth. I dreamed about you last night,
& thought I was asleep on the sofa & you came & kissed my forehead—
I wish you would repeat it tonight. And night before last I dreamed I was
riding on the cow-catcher of an engine, & you came & ordered me to get
off it, & I obeyed. You did perfectly right—in fact I love to believe that
you are always right, Livy—except that every time you write me some
pleasant chat about yourself, & show me your heart unwittingly, & give
me a morsel of that affection which I so hunger for, you always say it is
nonsense, & half threaten to scratch it out. You are good & honest when
I am *with* you, & don't mind my knowing that you love me, but then you
go & get frightened & half angry at yourself when you betray it in your
letters—& that is very, very naughty, Livy. Why, I would keep your secret, dear—you needn't be afraid to trust me. If you were only here to-
night, what a cosy visit we could have—for I have a fine large ~~room parlo~~
parlor in this hotel, & it is handsomely furnished & a cheerful fire is
burning, & we would never be disturbed. And I would tell you all the
pleasant things I know, & you shouldn't go to bed till about day after to=
morrow. It would be delightful. And I would drive away all your little
haunting doubts & misgivings, & convince you that when we are married
we shall be as happy, as kings—unpretending, substantial members of
society, with no fuss or show or nonsense about us, but with healthful,
wholesome duties to perform, & with an abundance of love in our hearts
to make them pleasures—& so developing all of good & worthy that is
in our natures, walk serenely down the grand avenues of Time, never
sorrowing to see the drifting years dropping away one by one to join the

buried ages, but glad to know that each passing year left its welcome sign that we were drawing nearer & nearer to that home of rest & peace where we shall know & love each other through all the vague tremendous centuries of eternity.

I feel encouraged to hope that at some time between the 1st & 13th of February I may see you, Livy; & I do pray that it may be so. Every dragging day seems an age to me when I am not with you, & when I *am* with you the perverse hours flash away like hurrying minutes. I came so near going straight to Elmira from Chicago the other day! I could have spent twenty-four hours with you—from Monday evening till Tuesday evening—but the long trip thither & the long trip back to Toledo would have about finished me & left me unfit to attack Nasby's fellow citizens, & I wanted to be in good condition there. That was one consideration—another was that that visit would have been unexpected & therefore a surprise, & you know surprises ~~don't always strike~~ are not always enthusiastically received. Taking all things into consideration, ʄ I thought it better to rob myself of that one day's happiness. But I may have been a little mistaken,—for I would have arrived in tolerably good time to persuade & cheer you out of the distress & dispondency those California letters plunged you into—although on Saturday you were already feeling more restful & satisfied again. But I am so tortured with the dread that you have been in pain, & low-spirited again since then, Livy darling— *please* say it is not so, if you can, Livy. O, be happy always!—you do not deserve to feel one pang of this world's ills, no taint or touch of its desolating sorrows. And *I* am the cause of all the distress you *have* suffered for many weeks. This thought comes down upon me with a heavy hand—it hurts me more than any other. For Livy, we would give pleasure, always, to those we love, not pain. And that you, my brave, true, darling girl, should suffer through me, saddens many a moment for me during these past two days. Send me those California letters, please, Livy—let me see what it is. As you say, ~~Livy,~~ those things are of the past,—& with a brave love that has the true ring, you stand by me now with a loyalty that makes me unspeakably proud of you—but I have a curiosity to know which of those friends has been man enough to come out frankly & worthily & tell the truth, & which ~~have~~ has basely shirked the duty—I would know which to respect & which to despise.

Livy, don't worry with the ferrotype any more, but do something which I wanted to ask you to do when I was there last, but lacked the courage—& that is (now you will, won't you Livy?) let me have that porcelaintype of yours?[1] Do, please, please, *please*, Livy, & you will make me as happy as a lord. *Do*, Livy, & I'll just do anything you say. *I* know all about that picture—& what an idiot I was for not persuading you to let me have it when I was there. And Livy, dear, you have got a guilty conscience, & you know it, about that porcelaintype—for you half suspected, that day, that I knew of its existence, but thinking maybe I didn't, you let it remain a secret—kept a secret from *me*, Livy, & you know you oughtn't to have done it. You ought not to have secrets from me, dear. You ought to have mentioned the porcelaintype, & said "Take it." Now, Livy—my own dear Livy—my precious, peerless Livy—my revered, my honored Livy—*please* give me that picture. I want it all the more because you never would give it to anybody else. You give away photographs to especial friends, but you ha hide that away from all eyes, & refuse to give it to any one—& therefore, Livy dear, that it is the very reason I want it. Now won't you, Livy, please? I love you with *all* my heart, Livy—& I want that picture so much. Now, *won't* you, Livy? I kiss you my thanks, my darling—because I just *know* you are saying yes.

And now it is ten minutes after midnight, & so it is time for you to go to bed. Don't stand on ceremony, & don't stop to argue the question, but just ~~trot along~~ move right along,—I'll carry you up stairs myself.

And my bedtime having arrived also, I will pray, as ~~co~~ customary, for light & guidance, for faith & love, for patience & strength—praying also, that the peace of God may rest in your heart & His Spirit compass you about, shielding you from all harm.

Devotedly
Sam L. C

Miss Olivia L. Langdon
Present.
Politeness of His Holiness Chas. J. Langdon.
[*docketed by OLL:*] 31st

[1] A ferrotype (or tintype) was a positive photograph produced by the standard wet collodion process on a sheet of enameled (usually black) iron or tin. A porcelaintype—like the one Clemens had coveted on 17–18 December 1868—was a photograph reproduced on porcelain, usually by direct transfer (Jones, 240, 426; *L2*, 348).

To Olivia L. Langdon
22 January 1869 • Cleveland, Ohio
(MS: CU-MARK)

Cleveland, Jan. 22.

Oh, Livy darling, I could just worship that picture, it is so beautiful. I am a hundred thousand times obliged to you for it.[1] I think I would perish before I would part with it. But its beauty startles me Livy—it somehow makes me afraid.—+ It makes ˏmeˏ feel a sort of awe—it affects me like a superstition. For it is more than human, Livy—it a̶n̶ is an angel⸗ beauty—something not of earth—something above the earth & its grossness. There is that deep spiritual look in the eyes—that far-away look that I have noted before when I wondered in my secret heart if you were not communing with the inhabitants of another sphere, a grander, a nobler world than ours. This is when I look at the picture a little way off. And it makes me so s̶a̶i̶d̶ sad & so down-hearted, too, because I seem to see in the placid face the signs of a world of unspoken distress, of hidden sorrow, patiently borne, but wearing and exhausting—pain that *I* have caused you, & which you are keeping from me because you would not have me suffer also. And it instantly recalls a remark of yours which t̶r̶o̶u̶b̶l̶e̶d̶ ˏstruckˏ me when you wrote it—that you had determined when I was there last n̶h̶ not to write me of your troubles, ˏthenceforward,ˏ but to say only cheerful things. *Now* my fears are aroused for you, & I exclaim against this, Livy. What I want is, that you should not **experience** doubts & misgivings, & distressful thoughts—but O̶h̶,̶ Livy, when you *do* experience them, I charge you, I beg of you, to let me share them with you. What! you suffer alone, to save *me* sorrow! No, no, Livy, I could n̶e̶v̶e̶r̶ ˏnotˏ me be so selfish, n̶o̶ so unmanly, as to wish that. And in my heedlessness I have allowed you to think me capable of such a thing. Oh, no, Livy—tell me of *every* grief, of every disturbing thought that comes to trouble you. Shared with another, these things are ʎ easier to bear— & there is no one to whom you can unbosom yourself so entirely as to me—for there can be no one in such close & such direct sympathy with you in these particular griefs as I. Give me all your trust, Livy, all your confidence—tell me *everything*, & let me help to give you rest & peace. If I could only pillow your dear head upon my shoulder, now, & put my sheltering arms about you, I *know* I could so talk to you, & so reason with you that these harassing thoughts that are eating away your peace of mind would vanish away & leave you happy & at rest. Oh, it breaks my very heart to think of you suffering, even for an hour. You see I am wrought up, Livy—in fact I am in more distress than words can easily tell—& I find myself fettered hand-&-foot by this lingering eternity of engagements. If I thought this letter would find you still harassed & troubled, I would cancel these engagements & go t by telegraph & go to you. What a driveling idiot I was that I did not go straight to Elmira from Chicago, & let "surprises" & the fatigue of travel take care of themselves. Be sure & tell me, if you are still troubled & ill at ease, Livy—& if you are not, I'll buy myself free of these engagements & go to you—for I *know* I can explain away every haunting spectre that distresses your thoughts.

But when I hold the picture close, Livy, & look at it, most of the *sadness* disappears, & in its place is a tranquil sweetness, & thoughtful ˏa dreamyˏ repose that are as ˏsoˏ enchanting that it seems strange that only a human being sat for the picture. I do think it is the loveliest thing in the whole world—it & it is just exactly like you, Livy. It is precisely like you, as I saw you last. I am so sorry you had to sit so many times & have so much trouble with the ferrotypes. You must have thought I was a selfish, exacting sort of lunatic—but upon my word, Livy, I was so busy clattering around the country that I did not think seriously of how much trouble I was putting you to. This picture pleases me *entirely*—& when you send me a kiss I can take it right from these exquisite features.

Ah, I *wish* I knew what was in the Sparta letter. It *may* come to-morrow—they enclosed a business letter to me from there to-day, & I wonder yours did not come. Somehow I cannot help dreading that letter—& yet when I take out your Toledo letter & read it I feel consoled & satisfied, for that was written *after* the Sparta letter, & you say in it that you are feeling more at rest, & that things look brighter to you. God grant they may continue to grow brighter! There is no use in my trying to be cheerful to-night—for I *am* down-hearted & distressed, & even the worshipped picture is hardly able to lift me up. For myself I care nothing about the California letters,—being conscious that if they have said any permanent or important blemish rests upon either my private character or publicsh reputation they have simply stated that which is *false*—but the thought of their causing you distress, will *not* let me rest—& I have *no* peace. It is the first thing I think of in the morning, & the last that tortures me when the ni long day's fatigues & vexations are over. I have sinned, in the dead past—& now my punishment is come—but *you* should not suffer, my idol—*that* is what drives me frantic.

It blesses me to see by your letter that you think of me & are sorry I must undergo so many tiresome journeys—& in turn I bless *you*, Livy, for this. When you say "*I was sorry*," it means all I could say with my overflowing adjectives, I think.

But Oh, Livy dear, how little you appreciate yourself! You are a living, breathing sermon; a blessing delivered straight from the hand of God; a messenger, that, speaking or silent, carries refreshment to the weary, hope to the despondent, sunshine to the darkened way of all that come & go about you. I **feel** this, in every fibre of my being. And the sound, real good conferred upon the world by the model & example of such a woman as you, is not to be estimated at all. It makes no fuss, no show, but if the good deeds of men are recorded in Heaven, your name is in that book, & set as high as any there, according to your sphere of action. *Don't* grieve, Livy, that you cannot march up & down the troubled ways of life *fighting* wrong & unfettering right, with strong fierce words & dazzling actions, for *that* work is set apart for women of a different formation to do, & being designed for that work, God, who always knows hi His affairs & how to appoint His instruments, has *qualified* them for the work—& He has qualified you for *your* work, & nobly are you performing it. Therefore, be content. Do that which God has given you to do, & do not seek to improve upon His judgment. You cannot do Anna Dickinson's work, & I can freely stake my life upon it, she cannot do yours. Livy, you might as well reproach yourself with for not being able to win bloody victories in battle, like Joan of Arc. In your sphere you are as great, & as noble, & as efficient as any Joan of Arc as ,that, ever lived. Be content with the strength that God has given you, & the station He has given into your charge—& don't be discouraged & unsettled by Anna Dickinson's incendiary words. I like Anna Dickinson, & admire her grand character, & have often & over again made her detractors feel ashamed of themselves; but I am thankful that you are not the sort of woman that is her ideal, & grateful that you never *can* be, Livy, darling.[2]

Livy, the lady you speak of—can it be *possible* that she gives her husband her full confidence?, & that he Can *Could* he, then, see her laden with unrest & not hasten to soothe her & drive away her troubles? Why I could be just as guilty as he is—thoughtlessly, you know—but the faintest whisper from you would set me in a fever to undo the wrong. Livy, dear, *don't* measure me with all the mean husbands in the world; for I'm *not* mean, & heartless & unloving—I am not, indeed, Livy—as truly as I live, I am not the counterpart of that man you speak of. Oh, I *wish* I could think of something that would cheer you up, Livy, & make you feel glad & happy, but somehow it seems that tonight I cannot. Something weighs upon me—a vague foreboding that the illness I have been struggling against for a week is about to come upon me at last. If it *is* to come, I hope it will strike me before I leave this safe haven of mine to-morrow.

Now *that* is cheerful, *isn't* it? But Livy, I don't write you many saddening letters, & so you must giv forgive me this time. *Everything* seems against me to-night. I believe I should be completely & perfectly miserable if I hadn't the picture. But every now & then I look at it, & then for a time I forget all discordant thoughts & am satisfied & happy—& so unspeakably grateful to God for bringing our paths together. The manifest hand of Providence was in it.

I suppose I ought to go to bed, now, since I have neglected the fire & let the room cool down too much. But Livy, I didn't really expect ,you, to take my request that you would write daily, into very serious consideration. I am too thankful for the three or four letters a week, not to feel satisfied & happy. I suppose, though, that I urged you with consuming fervency to write every day—it would be just like me to do it[3]—but if any thoughtful person had said, "Now have you really the heart to place such a burden as that upon her, when you know that her time & her energies are already taxed five times as much as they ought to be, & that she hardly gets any really quieting, comforting rest at all?"—I would have said "*No!*"—& would have felt injured by the insinuation, perhaps. No, no, Livy, every two days is a boon, & a noble one; I thank you & bless you for it, & will not be ungrateful enough to ask you to do more.

I like Mr. Lewis's letter—I couldn't well help that—& I thank him right cordially. I noted your interlineations, Livy—& they told the truth, too. I liked Mr. Lewis.[4]

No, N no, Livy, you need not write Mrs. Fairbanks of the postponement of the re-union[5]—I will tell her. Oh, when *shall* I get to see you! In yesterday's letter I gave a guess about it—but alas! more invitations to lecture have come to-day. I am sorry enough to see them.

How I *love* you, Livy! I kiss the beautiful picture, & send another winging its way down the night wind to seek you out & set you wondering in your dreams who touched your lips—& now, Good-night, my loved & honored Livy, & may the peace of God descend upon you, & His love soothe your good heart to rest.

Always, Devotedly,
Saml. L. C.

[*on back of page 1:*] They all think the picture is marvellously beautiful, & just like you, Livy.

Miss Olivia L. Langdon
Present.

———

Care of Charlie.

[*docketed by OLL:*] 32nd

[1] Olivia evidently anticipated Clemens's request for a porcelaintype. Housed in a purple velvet case, her gift arrived in Cleveland on the evening of 22 January,

Porcelaintype of Olivia L. Langdon, 1869. Mark Twain Papers, The Bancroft Library (CU-MARK). See note 1.

some hours after Clemens returned from Norwalk. It reproduced a new photograph, however, not the one he had requested in the previous letter. (This porcelaintype is misdated 1868 in *L2*, 440.)

[2] The Langdons presumably attended Dickinson's lecture at the Elmira Opera House on 19 January. " 'A Struggle for Life,' a plea for Woman's labor" was an impassioned exhortation to women to train themselves for work and avoid the "invalidism" that came of enforced idleness (Elmira *Advertiser:* "Amusements," 19 Jan 69, 4; "Opera House," 20 Jan 69, 4; *L2*, 337–38 n. 6). In February 1867, after Clemens first heard Dickinson lecture, he sent the San Francisco *Alta California* an admiring report of her technique, saying in part:

> Her sarcasm bites. I do not know but that it is her best card. She will make a right venomous old maid some day, I am afraid. She said that she was arguing upon her favorite subject with a self-sufficient youth one day, and she silenced his guns one after another till at last he staked his all upon one powerful proposition: "Would you have *all* women strong-minded?" "No!" she thundered, "God forbid that the millions of men of your calibre that cumber the earth should be doomed to travel its weary ways unmated!" (SLC 1867b)

That experience perhaps accounts for Clemens's gingerly ambivalence toward Dickinson, which was more than matched by her private opinion of him. In an 1873 letter to her sister, she noted that every time she saw the Langdons she wondered again

> how the flower of their house, Olivia, as frail in body as she is clear of mind & lovely of soul ever married the vulgar boor to whom she gave herself.—I hear of him all about the country at wine suppers, & late orgies,—dirty, smoking, drinking—with brains no doubt, but—
>
> Which is another cause of offence to me.—Just think that John Hay's beautiful "Castilian Days" never paid him but $350,—that Charlie Warner made, all told, from his jolly "Summer in a Garden" less than $1000,—that Whittier for years scarcely earned enough to keep him in bread & butter, & that this man's stuff, "Innocents Abroad" & "Roughing It," have paid him not short of $200.000.—
>
> 'Tis enough to disgust one with one's kind.— (Dickinson to Mary E. Dickinson, 14 Mar 73, Dickinson Papers, DLC)

[3] See 14 Jan 69 to OLL.

[4] Olivia's uncle in Ottawa, Illinois: see 13 and 14 Jan 69 to OLL.

[5] The gathering of *Quaker City* friends planned for around 18 February (see 14 Jan 69 to OLL, n. 8).

To Joseph H. Twichell and Family
23 January 1869 • Cleveland, Ohio
(MS: Davis)

Cleveland, Jan. 23, 1869.

Dear J. H. & Tribe—

Hurrah!—because you *do* rise to the dignity of a Tribe, now, since this last accident. I am *glad* to hear it—don't see why I should be glad, but I *am*—I should actually be ~~dis~~ appalled if *I* were to have a ~~babby~~ baby.[1] But I know *you* are glad, & so I go it blind. That you are glad, is enough for me—count me in. I am *mighty* glad, Twichell. I am, indeed. It must be awful—I mean it must be splendid—but then the whole subject is a little confusing & bewildering to me, ~~be~~ & I don't really know whether this ecstasy of mine is gratitude or consternation—because— well, *you* know how it is with us fellows who have never had any experience—we *mean* well, but then we are so dreadfully off soundings in *these* waters. But I *am* glad, if I bust. And I'll stick to it & take ¢ the chances.

I'll scratch out a suggestive sentence or two & send your letter to Livy—maybe she can raise a hurrah, & have sense enough to know what she means by it—[*torn in order to cancel:*] thou[◊h] I [d◊◊]'t [k◊]ow— I'[◊◊]

[*five lines (about 25 words) torn away*][2]

She must learn to rejoice when we rejoice, whether she knows what she is rejoicing about or not; because we can't have any member of the family hanging fire & interrupting the grand salute merely because they *don't know.* By *George*, I'm mighty glad. I wish there'd been six or seven. Wouldn't we have had a time, though? You hear *me.*

Elmira? Why it just goes on like clock-work. Every other day, without fail, & sometimes *every* day, comes one of those darling 8-page commercial miracles; & I bless the girl, & bow my grateful head before the throne of God & let the unspoken thanks *flow* out that never human speech could fetter into words.

If you could only see her picture! It came last night. She sat ~~five~~ ͺsixͺ times for a ~~mel~~[3] ferrotype—taking 3 weeks to it—& every picture was a slander, & I gently said so—very gently—& at last she tried a porcelain-type—& ~~presto!~~ when I opened the ¢ little velvet case last night, lo! a messenger-angel out of upper Heaven was roosting there! I give you ͺmyͺ word of honor that it is a very marvel of beauty—the expression is sweet, & patient, & *so* far-away & dreamy. What respect, what reverent honor it compels! *Any* man's unconscious impulse would be to take his hat off in its presence. And if he had not the impulse, I would give it him.

I have lectured about 30 times, so far, & from the way the invitations keep coming in, I believe I could stay in the West & never miss a night during the entire season. But I *must* close with the West Feb. 13 & go forward to fill eastern engagements.[4] I *repeated* here, last night & cleared for the Orphan Asylum 807⁰⁰, over á & above everything. That is as far as heard from—it *may* reach $1,000.[5]

Shall be in Hartford about March—& then make a flying trip to California. I swept Nasby's dung hill (Toledo,) like a Besom of Destruction—don't know what a Besom of Destruction is, but it is a noble sort of expression.[6] Came off with flying colors. Print the notices for me.[7] Love to all four of you.

Yrs, always,

Mark.

[1] On 9 January a second child, Julia Curtis, was born to Twichell and his wife, Harmony. Their first child, Edward Carrington, had been born in August 1867 (not 1868, as reported in *L2*, 269 n. 3). The Twichell tribe ultimately included nine children ("Hartford Residents," Twichell Family, 1).

[2] Evidently Clemens removed a suggestive remark aimed at Olivia's innocence about procreation. The first five words of the excised passage were probably "though I don't know—I'll."

[3] Clemens began to write "melainotype," an early name for ferrotype.

[4] Since beginning his tour on 17 November, Clemens is known to have lectured twenty-seven times. He did not "close with the West" until 15 February (see Appendix D).

[5] On the day of this letter the Cleveland *Herald* noted that the Cleveland Protestant Orphan Asylum "netted a liberal sum . . . as every dollar that was received went into the funds of the Asylum, the services of the lecturer, the hall rent, and all the incidental expenses having been generously donated by those concerned." On 17 February, the paper reported $564 as the amount realized, according to the asylum's board of managers ("Mark Twain and the Orphans," 23 Jan 69, 3, clipping in Scrapbook 26:8, CU-MARK; "Cleveland Orphan Asylum," 17 Feb 69, 3).

[6] "I will also make it a possession for the bittern, and pools of water: and I will sweep it with the besom of destruction, saith the Lord of hosts" (Isaiah 14:23).

[7] The lecture reviews that Clemens enclosed do not survive, nor did Twichell succeed in having them reprinted—at least not in the Hartford *Courant* or the Hartford *Times*. (The city's other daily, the *Evening Post*, was unavailable for search.) It seems likely, however, that the enclosures included reviews clipped from the Toledo *Blade* and the Toledo *Commercial*, both of 21 January (see Appendix B).

To Olivia L. Langdon
23 and 24 January 1869 • Cleveland, Ohio
(MS: CU-MARK)

Cleveland, Jan. 23.

Now, you dear little human angel, I will see if I can't write you a letter & still get to bed so early that you will say I have done well & you approve me. I am willing to acknowledge that I scribbled at you to a pretty late hour last night. It would be such a luxury if I hadn't anything to do but write letters to you, Livy.

I had so much calculated upon talking business to Mr. Benedict of the Herald, this time, but it can't be. He is lying very ill—dangerously so—& I must wait.[1] It is aggravating & offensive that he should choose this particular time for getting ill, but it cannot be helped, & I must ~~h~~ not hold him to personal account for it. Still, I cannot ˌbutˌ regard such conduct as ~~those, as infamous.~~ an outrage. He forgets that I am a stranger. I am at least entitled to common courtesy. [Now Livy, I can see your eyes growing larger & larger & the blood forsaking your cheeks, for you are taking all that literally & fancying I have become an absolute *savage*. No, I don't see anything of the kind, dear—I only see you sorry that the unfortunate man is so ill, & hoping with your bravest hope that God will restore him—*that* is what I see.] [*in margin:* Will you make my reverence to Mr. & Mrs. Langdon & ~~g~~ tender to them my love?]

Your last Plymouth Pulpit arrived to-day, & I am saving it to read in bed, presently. But I could not resist the desire to be with *you* a moment—that is, to hunt out your pencil-marks & see where your dear hand had been. And I was *so* delighted to read your unconscious confession in the margin: !

"True—although I want you to know my faults, yet I should be pained if you proved & brought them to light. We want people to think better of us than we think of ourselves, & we feel touched & *not humble* when they dissect us & tell our faults."[2]

Come to my arms, Livy! for, bless your darling heart, you *are* human, after all! Oh, I am so *glad* you said that, Livy; for do you know I was so harassed & bewildered when you used to seem determined that I should discover a fault in you, while, upon the honor of a man I *could not*

find one—& I couldn't understand *why* you should require such a thing
of me—& I sometimes said Surely this girl is deceiving *herself*—she
don't *know* ~~what~~ that this is a thing she could not like. But you were
relentless—you drove me to it—& I remember how I lay for two long
hours, one night, moving you under the microscope, & was absolutely
delighted, at ~~le~~ last, when I thought I had discovered *two* grave faults—
& I hastened to write you—& felt like an idiot ~~the very nex~~ within 24
hours when my cooler, uncrazed judgment tore those two prized faults
to shreds & they vanished into thin air! And then I was distressed! I
wondered how I was going to account to you for those ~~miss~~ boasted
faults, missing already. But what inexpressible relief I ~~fell~~ felt when I
seemed to see by your very next letter that you were about half mad &
~~altogether as~~ *entirely* astounded, that there *was* a fault discernible in you!
Oh you innocent!—how I do love you, Livy![3] And the next letter after
that, almost confirmed this happy seeming, & when I *saw* you last,[4] ~~i~~ one
of your earliest remarks *did* confirm it! I wanted to exult, but I didn't
dare to do it. You spoke of the faults, & said in the *naivest* way imagin-
able, "*Father said he wondered where you found them!*" Well, the man who
could keep from loving *you*, Livy, would simply be more than human.
And in my secret heart *I* wondered where I or any other man would look
for a fault in the blemishless creation that was standing before me at that
same moment. And I ~~fee~~ felt *safe*, safe & happy—for ~~I~~ it was revealed to
me that you were *human* & belonged on this perishable earth like the rest
of us; & so it was no profanity to love you & honor you, & live & labor
for you, & be blessed & rewarded by you, & no wrong to be utterly unable to detect any sign or shadow of a fault in you with merely human
eyes. Ah, Livy dear, I feel perfectly contented & happy, now—I do indeed—for you have shown just that human ~~spirit~~ ˌtraitˌ which I did hope
& believe was in you but which you never have betrayed into words before. And now I can love you & praise you as extravagantly as I please &
you will have to bow your dear head meekly & take it, Livy. Just read
the quoted passage again, you ~~little~~ persecutor of the faithful, & *see* if I
haven't good strong cause to feel thankful to you for writing it? Livy, it
is the greatest consolation & the greatest comfort to me, to firmly &
steadfastly believe that you have not your equal in the whole world, &
now you *will* not go & take it away from me again, will you? Let me be
as proud of you as I want to, Livy—I am sure I have reason enough. All
my belief in you is *honest*, & so you know you ought not to try to mar it.

Don't try to impair my boundless faith in you, Livy—for I so prize it; it is of such inestimable value to me; it so lifts me up, so refines me, so weeds out my grossness, so stamps my aims with worthiness, so invests my ambitions with nobility. What shall our wedded life be, if I lose this, Livy? No—let it *grow*—let it grow—never diminish. Let us hope to say, all our days, to the end:

"OUR echoes roll from soul to soul,
And GROW!—*forever & forever!*"[5]

So that at last, when our work is done, & the evening of life is closing around us, & we are folding our hands to rest, & all loved scenes & familiar sounds are fainting on our ears & fading on our vision, we may know & feel that when the morning breaks we shall take up the old *f* refrain in a Better Land & pulse its music in our hearts

"Forever and *forever!*"

Don't let what I said about your spelling "scissors" disturb you, Livy.[6] I *never* pay any attention to your spelling, but somehow you seem to think it is dreadful not to spell right. I keep thinking of what I said, & wishing I had not said it; though I know that coming from me you will know it was only loving badinage & never intended to carry a sting with it. If I thought I had grieved you in the least degree I would not forgive myself for it.

Twichell is wild with delight over the birth of his little girl, & has sent to me for congratulations. I have sent them, for I *am* glad, as long as he is so delighted. I must enclose a part of his letter & Mrs. Twichell's—because, since you are held lovingly in their hearts & remembered in their prayers, you will not be indifferent to their happiness. I wrote them that I would send their letter to you, & that I knew you would help me hurrah for them. [*in margin:* That "commercial* style"—I wrote T. once, that you never put any nonsense in your letters, but wrote with great gravity in a stately, smooth-flowing commercial style.][7] If I had the naming of that young screech-owl, (provided it is good & pretty,) I would name it after you, Livy. But if it isn't good & pretty, it don't deserve such honor. I don't see what in the mischief anybody should be so glad over a baby for, but we *must* be glad, Livy, otherwise they will think we are hard-hearted people—& I guess we are not that, are we? [*in margin:* I have ~~fet~~ felt rather better, to-day than I have for some little time.]

Of course I had to write them about *you*—I couldn't help it—& I tried to make it just as mild as possible, but the adjectives would leak

out. And *now*, if I don't tell you *what* I said, you will think it was something dreadful. But it wasn't—this was all—or rather, nearly all:

"IF you could only see her picture! It came last night. She sat five
times for a ferrotype, & every picture was a slander; & at last she tried
a porcelaintype—& when I opened its velvet case last night, lo! a
messenger-angel out of Paradise was in it! I give you my word of honor
that it is a very marvel of beauty—the expression is sweet, & patient, &
so far-away & dreamy. And what respect, what reverent honor it compels! *Any* man's unconscious impulse would be to bare his head in its
presence. And if he hadn't the impulse, I would give it him*l*."

It is surely the loveliest picture in the world, Livy—& so I must
thank you again. ~~Oh, the mischief,~~ ˄And now, after all,˄ it is one o'clock,
& I have to get up & go to church in the morning. I must go to bed &
read my Plymouth Church, now, & worship my picture. You must clear
out to bed, too, Livy—it is time.

Don't let anything that is in this wild letter offend you, Livy—I
don't *mean* to hurt you, & you know that. With a kiss & a grateful God
bless you, darling,

Always & devotedly
Sam*ˡ*. L. C.

The lecture cleared $807⁰⁰ for the Orphans, as far as heard from—it *may*
reach $1,000.

———————————————————————————————

Miss Olivia L. Langdon
Present.

Politeness of Archbishop Chas. J. Langdon.

[*docketed by OLL:*] 33ʳᵈ | Congratulations

---

[1] The Cleveland *Herald* reported on 23 January that "Mr. George A. Benedict
is still confined to his house by sickness. Though improving, the probabilities
are against his being out for several days, at least" ("Personal," 3). Even so, Benedict may have managed to get some word to Clemens about the business at
hand: see 5 Feb 69 to JLC and family, n. 2.

[2] Olivia evidently had sent the *Plymouth Pulpit* (probably the 17 October 1868
issue) that published Henry Ward Beecher's "The Nobility of Confession," delivered at Plymouth Church on 4 October. The copy she marked has not been
found, but Beecher's discussion of the impediments to confession included the
following likely provocation for her marginal note:

Then there is that protean influence of vanity. When men have done wrong, they instantly say, "Does any body know it?" If it is not known, they are not much disturbed;

but if men do know it, the question is, "What do they think? What is the impression on the community? What do my friends think?" Vanity teaches men to be more thoughtful of the opinions of their fellow-men than of the opinions of God himself. And there is a lack of confession in many persons whose conscience would lead them to confess, and whose reason would perhaps help them to confess, because there stands vanity, which is wounded so easily, and by so many imaginary things, that they are utterly unwilling to have that which is imperfect in them supposed to be imperfect by others, and are forever resorting to guises and deceits to hide their faults. (Henry Ward Beecher 1869, 39)

[3] See *L2*, 316 and 330.
[4] On 17 and 18 December, in Elmira.
[5] From the final stanza of Tennyson's "bugle song" (see 12 Jan 69 to OLL and CJL, n. 5).
[6] See 17 Jan 69 to OLL.
[7] See 1 Jan 69 to Twichell for the characterization of Olivia's style, to which Twichell, in the enclosure (now lost), evidently referred.

To Olivia L. Langdon
24 January 1869 • Cleveland, Ohio
(MS: CU-MARK)

Cleveland, Jan. 24.

My Dearest Livy—

It has come at last—the Sparta letter.[1] And like all ˄most˄ hidden terrors, I find myself com reassured, ˄as soon as *I* it is uncurtained,˄ & ready to cope with it. I sought eagerly for just one thing—if I could find that, I was safe. I did find it—*you still have faith in me,*. That was enough—it is all I ask. While you stand by me, no task ˄that is set me˄ will be too ˄so˄ hard but that my heart & hands & brain will perform it— slowly, maybe, & discouragingly to your *sometimes* impetuous nature, but *surely*. By your two later letters I saw that you had faith in my me, & that you wrote them was evidence that you still love me—but what I yearned for at this particular moment was the evidence that your faith remained at its post when the storm swept over your heart. I believed I should find that evidence, for I did not think that your faith was á ˄the˄ child of a passing fancy, a creature of the sunshine & destined to perish with it. The belief was well grounded, & I am satisfied. I have been, in times past, that which would be hateful in your eyes, provided you sim- ply viewed me from a distance, without knowing my secret heart—but I have lived that life, & it is of the past. ˄I do not live backwards.˄ God

does not ask of the returning sinner what he *has* been, but what he *is* &
what he *will* be. And this is what you ask of me. If I must show what I
am & prove what I *shall* be, I am content. As far as what I *have* been is
concerned, I am only sorry that I did not tell all ˏofˏ that, in full & relentless detail, to your father & your mother, & to *you*, Livy—for it
would be all the better that you knew it also. I would not seem to have
been that which I was not. If I am speaking carelessly or untruly now, I
am doing a fearful thing, for before I began this letter I offered up that
prayer which has passed my lips many & many a time ~~sin~~ during these
latter months: that I might be guarded from even unconsciously or unwittingly saying anything to you which you might misconstrue & be
thereby *deceived*—& that I might not be guilty of any taint or shadow of
hypocrisy, however refined, in my dealings with you—that I might be
wholly true & frank & open with you, even though it cost me your priceless love, & the life that is now so inestimably valuable to me become in
that moment a blank & hated captivity. Wherefore I now speak to you
standing in the presence of God. And I say that what I have been I am
not now; that I am striving & shall still strive to reach the highest altitude
of worth, the highest ~~ex~~ Christian excellence; that I know of *nothing* in
my past career that I would conceal from your parents, howsoever I
might blush to speak the words; & that it is my *strong conviction* that,
married to you, I would never desire to roam again while I lived. The
circumstances under which I say these things, make the statements as
grave & weighty as if I endorsed them with an oath.

Your father & mother are overlooking one thing, Livy—that I have
been a wanderer from necessity, ~~four-fif~~ three-fourths of my time—a
wanderer from choice only one-fourth. During these later years my
profession (of correspondent,) made wandering a necessity—& *all* men
know that few things that are done from necessity have much fascination
about them. Wandering is not a *habit* with me—for that word implies an
enslaved fondness for the thing. And I could most freely take an oath
that all fondness for roaming is dead within me. I could take that oath
with an undisturbed conscience before any ~~maj~~ magistrate in the land.
Why, a year ago, in Washington, when Mr. Conness, one of our Senators,
~~urged~~ ˏcounseledˏ me to take the post of United States Minister to China,
when Mr. Burlingame resigned (the place was chiefly in Mr. C.'s gift,) I
said that even if I ~~felt~~ ˏcould feelˏ thoroughly fitted for the place, I had at
last become able to make a living at home & ~~had no d~~ wished to settle
down—& that if I roamed more, it must be in pursuit of my regular call-

ing & to further my advancement in my legitimate ~~calling~~ profession. And then ~~at his~~ I went at 11 at night & pledged our delegations to support me for Postmaster of San Francisco, but gave up *that* scheme as soon as I found that the place, honorably conducted, was only worth $4,000 a year & was ⚡ too confining to allow me much time to write for newspapers. [My office-seeking instincts were born & murdered all in one night, & I hope they will never be resurrected again,—a winter spent in Washington is calculated to make a man *above* mere ordinary office=holding.][2]

Wandering is *not* my habit, nor my proclivity. Does a man, five years a galley-slave, get in a habit of it & yearn to be a galley-slave always? Does a horse in a tread-mill get infatuated with his profession & long to continue in it? Does the sewing-girl, building shirts at sixpence apiece grow fascinated with the habit of it at last & find it impossible to break herself without signing the pledge? And being pushed from pillar to post & compelled so long to roam, against my will, is it reasonable to think that I am really fond of it & wedded to it? I think not.

I am very tired & drowsy, & *must* lie down. If I could only *see* you, love, I could satisfy you—satisfy you that I am earnest in my determination ~~th~~ to be *everything* you would have me be—& that I bring to this resolve the consciousness of that faith & strength & steady purpose which has enabled me to cast off so many slavish habits & utterly lose all taste or desire for them—some of them dating back ten years now.[3] Once a Christian, & invested with *that* strength, what should I fear? I pray you be patient with me a little while, till I see you—& hold fast your faith in me & let your dear love still be mine. The Sparta letter was a blessing to me, not a trouble.

With a loving kiss, dear Livy,

Always.
Saml.

Miss Olivia L. Langdon
Present.

[*across envelope end:*] Had concluded to write more, but Dr Sales' son has come.[4] [*docketed by OLL:*] 34th

[1] See 20 and 21 Jan 69 to OLL, n. 6.
[2] See *L2*, 176–77, 178–79. Senator John Conness—a Republican from California and a member of the Senate Committee on Post Offices and Post Roads,

which reported on presidential nominations to postmasterships—controlled the appointment of the San Francisco postmaster. Conness did not automatically have the same influence over the selection of Anson Burlingame's successor as minister to China, since he was not a member of the Committee on Foreign Relations, which reported on ministerial nominations. But he did interest himself in that appointment, and early in 1868 the post went to a Californian: travel writer J. Ross Browne (Senate 1868, 1, 2; Senate 1887, 156, 194; *Congressional Globe* 1868, 1:471). Clemens accepted, then declined, Browne's offer of a "nice sinecure in his Embassy" (*L2*, 223).

³Among these cast-off habits was tobacco chewing. On 2 December 1867 Clemens told Mary Mason Fairbanks that he was "permanently" cured of it (*L2*, 122). Coupled with his present assertion, the following 1907 report by Isabel V. Lyon, then Clemens's secretary, places the reform in 1859, sometime before 9 April, when he completed his steamboat apprenticeship and received his pilot's license: "He was speaking of the power of breaking away from a habit & said that when he was a cub pilot he made up his mind not to chew tobacco any longer. He had the plug in his pocket—& he didn't throw it away & so burn his bridges behind him—No,—he kept the plug in his pocket until it was in a powder, & he never chewed again. He said probably some outside influence was the cause of his reform" (IVL, 238). In a letter of 13 January 1870 to Olivia Langdon, Clemens identified the outside influence: "I stopped chewing tobacco because it was a mean habit, partly, & partly because my mother desired it" (CU-MARK, in *LLMT*, 136).

⁴Dr. Henry Sayles (1811–77) and his wife, the former Emma Halsey (1819–99), neighbors of the Langdons', had four children: Henry (1845–83), Charles (1848–87), Guy (1856–1907), and Olivia's close friend Emma (1844–1916) (Record of Interments, Lot 13, Section H, Woodlawn Cemetery, Elmira, N.Y., annotated by Herbert A. Wisbey, Jr., PH in CU-MARK). It is not known which of the sons Clemens alludes to here.

To Olivia L. Langdon
26 and 27 January 1869 • Batavia, Ill.
(MS: CU-MARK)

Batavia, Ill., Jan. 26.

Livy, darling, I never supposed, before, that a picture could be so much company—& in fact one of those blank, soulless photographs *are* not—*they* don't come out of the case & meet you ~~hav~~ half way, & talk to you with their eyes, like one of ~~tho~~ these porcelaintypes. I have made a pleasant discovery about this picture, & now it is almost like having you with me—*it has sympathies.* Its expression takes the color of whatever mood I chance to be in, & smiles, or is sad, or grave, or tranquilly happy, just as I happen to be myself from time to time. This is true as truth itself,

Livy. The other day when I was so troubled & depressed, it looked as if its dear old heart was breaking; last night, when your Marshall letter[1] filled me with the wildest & happiest spirits, it smiled, & beamed a world of good-nature from its eyes, & tried its very best to speak;—Tto-day this sad-looking village makes me feel ever so friendless & dreáry, & behold, the picture is so overflowing with friendliness, & tries so hard to come out of the case to me, that I grow contented & glad again, in spite of the sad village & its solemn surroundings.[2] I wouldn't part with the picture for the world. But you ought to see how placidly it takes a kiss! It don't object—it don't solicit it—it don't respond. It simply looks good, & no-ble, & calm, & as it if it were satisfied ther that there was all re[s]pect, & homage & reverence in the kiss, as well as passionate love; & that there-fore these kisses cannot ∅ profane it. And I am sure they cannot. How I do *love* ˌLOVEˌ you, Livy!

That Marshall letter was the very happiest & the pleasantest you ever wrote. And of course you threatened not to send itˌ, you little ag-gravation. It made me so jolly & so lively that I felt thoroughly & com-pletely well & hearty in a moment. You see it is much it is because I am much more concerned about *your* state of mind & *your* circumstances than my own—& so when you write a very grave letter I feel dreadfully, because I know you were not happy at the time—but ˌwhenˌ you write what you think is nonsense—little chatty personal matters, home talk & that sort of thing,—I am delighted, because I know you could not do it unless you were feeling cheery & happy-hearted. You can't always feel so, Livy dear, but when you *do*, write me at once, & *don't threaten to tear up* the *letter*—I won't have such conduct as those. And when you feel down-hearted, be SURE to write me—& tell me all—tell me ɣ everything that troubles that dear hea[r]t that is more to me than all the world be-side—for you *must* let me share your troubles,ˌˌ darling. I would have you cheerful & happy all the time—but when you *are* troubled I would not have you put off writing till the feeling is gone, in order that you may not make me sad. No, Livy, when you are heavy-hearted, write at once; & let me put my arms about you, darling, & comfort you, & charm away your griefs with kindly, reassuring words—for this is the true office of love, Livy. Don't keep your sorrows from me, love, but come to me with them always—come to me with them trustingly & confidently, as know-ing that whatever grieves you grieves me also, & therefore I am worthy to help bear the burthen.

I am so glad you wear the ribbon, Li on your hair, Livy—for you

never look so dear, & so dainty & so bewitching—so surpassingly & destructively lovely—as when you wear the blue dress & the blue ribbon—
I mean the dress you wore in the library toward evening, Nov. 27, when
I was about to go away—& I think you were wearing it, too, one afternoon, a short time ago, in the ~~afternoon~~ library, when I bent down over
the back of your chair & kissed you—remember?[3] You often wear it to
dinner. And blue is just the color for you to wear, Livy, because its language is Purity. {I can't write—except by fits & starts—for thinking of
you & longing for you.} I told Mrs. Fairbanks that it was a blue ribbon
that is on your hair in the picture, & that the dress was the particular
blue silk dress I have been speaking about. Was I right? You always look
lovely, & you are always beautiful, my peerless Livy, no matter how you
dress or in what colors (for you *always* dress in ~~utterly faul~~ the most exquisite good taste,) but you are loveliest in blue, I think,,—& next in
solid, unmitigated black—unmitigated save by a red ribbon on your
hair—& a white collar, &c.

    Your criticism on the "Nature & Life" sermons is ~~superb.~~ ,concen-
trated excellence., They *are* cold—cold as ice—& there is little depth to
them, too—but they glitter. They are gracefully worded. One or two of
them are excellent, though, in nearly every way.[4]

    Why, Livy dear, I was so delighted, for I thought you were going to
find a fault in yourself for me—for I knew very well that *I* couldn't—&
behold, you failed, *failed*, FAILED, darling, & found a virtue instead! You
never never will make me believe that coming to the rescue of a man who
is down, with a generous, indignant, outspoken protest, was a fault. Oh,
no, no, my loved & honored Livy, my leal & loyal Livy, my best & truest
Livy in all the world, *Magnanimity* was *always* a Virtue since God created
the ~~H~~ heavens & the earth, & always WILL be! Don't deceive yourself
into the notion that your angry speech was something unworthy, simply
because it rode down opposing opinions careless of consequences.—
Why, if your father was present, he was just as proud of you as he could
be. What a ,"fault",-finder you are, Livy! The more "faults" like *that* you
can find, the more I shall love you & honor you. Try it again, my poor
little discouraged darling. *I* don't see any fault in you—& I *won't!*
There.,~~now.~~

    When am I coming? Why, Livy, I begin to have a vague sort of no-
tion that I *may* get there right after Jacksonville,[5] but it is *very* vague—
not much encouragement about, it. Don't I *wish* I might, though! But I

feel *sure* I shall see you twenty-five days from now. [It sounds like twenty-five years—& *seems* like it, too.] It exasperates me every time I think of the time I wasted in New York doing nothing—would like to have it *now*,—in Elmira.[6]

Ɠ They have come for me—good ni bye, my own darling—with a loving kiss.

Sam[l]. L. C

After the Lecture—This letter was all folded up, sealed & directed, but I *would* pull it open again to kiss you, Livy, & hope you are well & happy, & hope also that if you are writing me, at this moment, you are lovingly but not "stupidly" Livy. [It is all very well for *you* to call yourself names, but I won't allow anybody else to do it.] But whether you are stupid or not stupid, go on & write, anyhow, for I had rather read your most miraculous & extravagant stupidity than anybody else's wisdom.

"I must do it, I must do it, Livy." That reminds me of what I told Mother Fairbanks long ago, when she was trying to comfort me. I said, "She don't love me, & she says she is perfectly aware that she never *can* love me—& so the case looks hopeless—but still, I will keep on hoping & striving, & still asking her—& after she has refused me twelve times, I will be right back there & at it again, just as lovingly, & hopefully & persistently as ever!" Oh, I *could* not do without your love, Livy, ~~darling~~ & I knew it perfectly well. I *had* to persecute you into loving me—there was no help for it—it had to be done. And fervently I pray God to bless you always, Livy, for yielding at last. What a stay & a support you have been to me! No matter how dreary & wretched I may feel when I enter one of these sad, n homeless-looking towns, I soon retreat to the shelter of your love, my Livy, & all is bright & cheerful again. And then I pray that God will bear me up with His strength to do the task that is set before me, feeling in all such cases that my own can be of little avail—~~ev~~ & every time I do that Ɩ the lecture is infallibly a success. It was so to-night. I did feel so heart-broken when I arrived here to-day!—& I feel so perfectly satisfied now—& so do all these people. I kiss you, Livy.[7]

Speaking of Mr. Day & Miss Alice reminds me that the Secretary of this Society here tells me that Nasby is in love with Miss Anna Dickinson, & is paying his attentions to her. I thought you would like to hear, ‸it.‸ I can't give you any particulars, because the matter did not seem to be any business of mine & so I did not ask any questions.[8]

Livy, you must not leave your letters open "till next day" if there is danger that you won't send them. You must send me every line you write—don't leave out *any* of it. I want *every* line that you write. And now do you know that the best time for answering a letter is *immediately after reading it?* It is—one is sure to write frankly & freely & naturally then. And so I want you to promise that every time you receive a letter from me you will put it in your pocket & not read a line of it until you have time to sit down & answer it. Then you won't have a bit of trouble writing, Livy—language & ideas will come freely & easily & naturally. I never get a chance to do that with your letters, though I *want* to—I try not to read them, sometimes, until I can answer them, but I can't do it— can't resist the~~m~~ temptation to ~~answer~~ ˏreadˎ them immediately.

But as usual, I am writing when I ought to be in bed, inasmuch as I must start early in the morning—to Freeport, where I shall get a letter from the dearest girl in all the world, the ~~first letter of the~~ three first letters of whose name is Livy.[9] And so I kiss you good-night again, my precious little sweetheart, & wish you pleasant dreams, & the companionship of the angels, & the ineffable peace of God.

Devotedly & always

Sam*ˡ* L. C.

✉️———————————————————————————————————

Miss Olivia L. Langdon

Present.

Care of His Royal Highness the Grand Mogul.

[*docketed by OLL:*] 35ᵗʰ

[1]Probably written around 21 or 22 January, it had reached Clemens in Marshall, Michigan, where he lectured on 25 January.

[2]First settled in 1833, Batavia had a population of 3,018 by 1870 (Gustafson and Schielke, 59). In 1867, when many states were actively encouraging emigration, the *Kane County Gazetteer* promoted Batavia:

> This large village is beautifully situated on both sides of the Fox River, and on the line of the Chicago, Burlington and Quincy Railroad,—two and a half miles below Geneva, and thirty-five miles distant from Chicago. . . . Improvements on an extensive scale have been made, and many large and substantial buildings erected for business and for residences, which will compare with any other location in the West, of its size. The surrounding district is not only beautiful, but well adapted for the successful operation of any manufacturing purposes, requiring water power for propelling machinery. Here are also inexhaustible quarries of the best limestone, and abundant supplies of valuable timber from the Big Woods, which must tend to render this location permanent and flourishing. . . . The improvements . . . attest the enterprise and activity of its citizens; which, together with its manufactories, foundries, etc., tend to make all that should be asked, for a live and rapidly growing town. (Bailey, 127)

3 Clemens was understandably certain of what Olivia had been wearing on the evening of 27 November 1868, when he first departed Elmira as her fiancé. The moment in the library must have come on 17 or 18 December.

4 See 17 Jan 69 to OLL and CJL, n. 5.

5 Where Clemens was to lecture on 1 February.

6 After leaving Elmira on 27 November 1868 Clemens had gone to New York City, where he remained (except for lectures in Rondout, New York, and Newark, New Jersey, and an evening in Hartford with Joseph H. Twichell) until 10 December. While in New York he investigated opportunities of becoming a newspaper publisher or editor, attended to lecture business, and wrote longingly to Olivia (see *L2*, 297–325).

7 The Batavia correspondent of the *Beacon*, in neighboring Aurora, Illinois, noted on 2 February that " 'Mark Twain' lectured here last Tuesday evening to a crowded house. Our lectures so far have proved a success pecuniarily and otherwise" (Ben). No other account of Clemens's Batavia success has been found.

8 Olivia had evidently mentioned her Hartford friend Alice Beecher Hooker (1847–1928) and Alice's fiancé, John Calvin Day (1835–99), an attorney and businessman. Clemens and the Langdons (except Charles) attended Alice's wedding in Hartford on 17 June 1869. The secretary of the Batavia Laconian Literary Society has not been identified, nor has his report of Dickinson's courtship by Nasby (David Ross Locke) been confirmed. Locke had been married since 1855 to the former Martha H. Bodine, of Plymouth, Ohio, with whom he had three sons. Dickinson never married ("Nook Farm Genealogy," 16; "Married," Hartford *Times*, 18 June 69, 3; Burpee, 1:501; Andrews, 22; Johnson, 3; Harrison, 29–30).

9 The meaning of this remark has not been explained. Clemens was probably writing at least the last part of this letter sometime after midnight, hence in the early hours of 27 January. Later that day he lectured in Fry's Hall, in Freeport, Illinois. The next letter he sent to Olivia (docket number 36) has been lost. He probably wrote it either from Freeport or from Waterloo, Iowa, where on 28 January he attracted a large audience, despite a heavy rain storm ("Mark Twain, the great humorist . . . ," Freeport *Bulletin*, 28 Jan 69, 4; "Mark Twain," Waterloo *Courier*, 4 Feb 69, no page).

To Olivia L. Langdon
29 and 30 January 1869 • Galena, Ill.
(MS: CU-MARK)

Galena, Jan. 29, 1869.

Livy darling, I have received your letter, & am perfectly delighted with it. I have finished my lecture tonight, the people are satisfied, your kiss *has* comforted me, & I am as happy & contented as anybody in the world to-night.[1] And I am not sick yet, & even believe I shall not be—

though for many days I have believed that only the *will* to finish my allotted task was really keeping me up, *& &*—& have felt sometimes that
if I were delivering the last lecture of the list, & *knew* all responsibility
was at last removed, that with the passing away of the tense strain, I
would surely drop to the floor without strength enough to rise again for
weeks. But last night's good rest & your cheery letter have made me
strong, & I feel lively & hearty now. And in the morning I shall send a
telegram to New York notifying Mr. Brooks that I shall start for Elmira
next Wednesday morning (or Tuesday night,) *without fail*, God willing,
so that he can ship my honored Livy straight home *at once*[2]—for I notified the Dubuque man[3] several days ago not to make any more appointments for me in the West. I think I shall reach Elmira very early in the
morning Thursday (at the *furthest*—maybe sooner) & then I shall make
a racket in the closet of my room at your house, & you must get up *immediately,!* Livy, & dress suddenly & come out & give me the Good-
morning kiss I shall have traveled a thousand miles to get—*won't* you,
Livy? And if I get there at any other hour of the day, you must meet me
in the hall or the drawing-room—please, Livy—because I want to see
you & I *can't* sit an hour or two in the library first. Now remember, Livy
dear.

I almost *wanted* to be dangerously ill, because I knew you would
come, & I wouldn't care so very much for being sick provided it brought
me a sight of *you*. You are a good girl, Livy—you are the best & the truest
girl that *I* know. Bless your heart, too, for sending me "The Hidden
Christ" sermon.[4] I see it is marked, by the hand I so love, & the fact that
it is midnight now & I must take the cars at 4 oclock in the morning shall
not deter me from ~~wri~~ reading it before I sleep, I don't care if you *do*
scold. I read—I *devour* religious literature, now, with a genuine interest
& pleasure that I am *so* glad to see growing—& I hope it may *always*
grow—& I do believe it will.

This is the last letter I shall write before I see you, my best beloved,
my most honored Livy, & I am sorry it must be so short—but then I *must*
read the sermon, & I *must* sleep a little. And so, with a loving kiss I bid
you good night & wish you peace & contentment & a happy spirit, you
core of my heart, Livy!

Always, devotedly
Sam*l*. L. C.

P.S. Shan't read it over—*you* must correct it.

✉ ──

Miss Olivia L. Langdon

Present.

Care of the Infant Prodigy.

[*docketed by OLL:*] 37th

[1] Clemens lectured in Galena's Bench Street Methodist Church. He was a late substitute for William Henry Milburn (1823–1903), the blind Methodist Episcopal and Protestant Episcopal preacher and former chaplain of the United States Congress (1845, 1853), who had gone to Berlin for an eye operation ("W. H. Milburn . . . ," Muscatine [Iowa] *Courier*, 11 Feb 69, 2). In announcing the substitution, the Galena *Gazette* of 26 January called "the change of programme a good one, as it is well to have one humorist" ("The Lectures," 3). And on 2 February the paper expressed its satisfaction with the result:

> "Mark Twain" lectured to the largest audience of the course, in this city, Friday evening. He was introduced in a few neat and appropriate remarks by Mr. A. S. Campbell. The Lecturer held his audience for an hour and a half vibrating between hysterical fits of laughter, occasioned by his inimitable drolleries[,] and feelings of admiration produced by his wonderful descriptive powers. We were agreeably surprised in the lecture delivered by "Mark Twain." It has become the fashion of late for men whose names have become familiar to the people to present themselves before the public as lecturers[.] Perhaps they have walked a thousand miles in a thousand consecutive hours, or it may be they have gained the sympathies of the public by their just and conscientious administrative abilities. Such men, however much they may have distinguished themselves in their respective callings, are in the lecture field what quacks are to the medical fraternity: "Mark Twain" *does not* belong to this class. His ability as a lecturer is not excelled by his fame as a writer. ("The Lecture," 3)

[2] Probably on 26 or 27 January Olivia had begun a visit with the Langdons' friends Fidele Brooks and her husband Henry, a leather merchant, who lived at 675 Fifth Avenue in New York City (*L2*, 276 n. 10, 278 n. 2). She returned to Elmira no later than Wednesday, 3 February, the day before she and Clemens became formally engaged.

[3] G. L. Torbert, Clemens's lecture agent.

[4] Olivia must have sent the 23 January 1869 issue of the *Plymouth Pulpit*, which first published Henry Ward Beecher's sermon, delivered at Plymouth Church on 10 January. Beecher expanded upon "two thoughts, . . . *first*, The Lord's presence in unperceived ways in the daily wants of his people; and *second*, The full privilege of the soul in God's presence and providence discerned when the gift is vanishing away" (Henry Ward Beecher 1869, 277).

To Francis E. Bliss
1 February 1869 • Jacksonville, Ill.
(MS: NN-B)

Jacksonville, Ill, Feb. 1.

Dear Frank—

I shall be in Elmira, New York, from Feb. 3 till Feb. 11. Send proofs there if you have any ready.[1] I want to leave for California on a lecturing trip the middle of March.

I have now lectured thirty-five or forty times & am fagged out with travel. Have to begin again Feb. 12, though.~,~& My last lecture will be March 16—won't talk any after that, for *any*body.[2]

Yr friend

Sam*l*. L. Clemens

[letter docketed:] √ author [*and*] Mark Twain | Feb 1/69 | Author

[1] Clemens was answering a request (now lost) for an address to which proofs of his book, still tentatively called "The New Pilgrim's Progress," could be sent. He in fact saw no proofs until early March, when he reached Hartford.

[2] If he wrote this letter after his Jacksonville performance, Clemens had lectured thirty-four times since 17 November 1868. His tour did not end until 20 March, in Sharon, Pennsylvania (see Appendix D).

To Jane Lampton Clemens and Family
5 February 1869 • Elmira, N.Y.
(MS facsimile and *paraphrase:* Davis and CU-MARK)

Elmira, N.Y., ⎫
Feb. 5, 1869. ⎭ .

My Dear Mother & Brother
    & Sisters & Nephew
    & Niece, & Margaret:

This is to inform you that on yesterday, the 4th of February, I was duly & solemnly & irrevocably engaged to be married to Miss Olivia

L. Langdon, aged 23½, only daughter of Jervis and Olivia Langdon, of Elmira, New York. *Amen.* She is the best girl in all the world, & the most sensible, & I am just as proud of her as I can be.[1]

It may be a good while before we are married, for I am not rich enough to give her a comfortable home right away, & I don't want *anybody's* help. I can get an eighth of the Cleveland Herald for $25,000, & have it so arranged that I can pay for it as I earn the money with my unaided hands. I shall look around a little more, & if I can do no better elsewhere, I shall take it.[2]

I am not worrying about whether you will love my future wife or not—if you know her twenty-four hours & then don't love her, you will accomplish what nobody else has ever succeeded in doing since she was born. She just naturally drops into everybody's affections that comes across her. My prophecy was correct. She said she never could or would love me—but she set herself the task of making a Christian of me. I said she would succeed, but that in the meantime she would unwittingly dig a matrimonial pit & end by tumbling into it—& lo! the prophecy is fulfilled. She was in New York a day or two ago, & George Wiley & his wife & Clara know her now. Pump *them*, if you want, to.[3] You shall see her before VERY long. Love to all.

Affec'ly
Sam.

P.S. Shall be here a week.

✉

[paraphrase: S.L.C. to Mrs. Moffett, his sister. Addressed to St. Louis. Postmarked Feb. 6. Return Address: J. Langdon, Elmira on env.][4]

---

[1] In addition to his mother and brother, Clemens addressed both his sister Pamela and his sister-in-law Mollie Clemens, as well as Pamela's children, Annie and Samuel, and the Moffetts' maid, Margaret. All were living in St. Louis, although Orion and Mollie may have been at a separate address (see 14 Jan 69 to PAM, nn. 7 and 8). Clemens had previously informed only Pamela of his love of Olivia, instructing her to "not even *hint* it, to *any* one—I make no exceptions" (*L2*, 295).

[2] Before leaving Cleveland on 25 January, Clemens may have received assurances that George A. Benedict, who had been too ill to meet with him, was nonetheless prepared to sell him part of his and his son's shares in the *Herald*.

[3] George and Elmira Wiley, their daughter Clara, and their four sons had been friends of the Clemenses' in Hannibal and St. Louis. They subsequently moved to New York City, where they became acquainted with the Langdons' friends Henry and Fidele Brooks. Olivia Langdon doubtless had been introduced to the

Wileys during her recent visit with the Brookses, although the Wileys had
known of Clemens's interest in her since early November 1868 (*L2*, 278–79 n. 2).

[4]Only this description of the envelope has been found, mistakenly included
in a transcription made for Dixon Wecter of 29? Nov 68 to PAM (*L2*, 294–95).
In writing to his family in St. Louis, Clemens typically addressed the envelope
to Pamela or to Orion, even when the letter was intended for his mother as well.

To Mary Mason Fairbanks
5 February 1869 • Elmira, N.Y.
(MS: CSmH)

                                                        Elmira, Feb. 5.
My Dear Mother—
    Your blessing! It is accomplished. We are engaged to be married,,
& the date of it is Feb. 4, 1869. Livy wants the date engraved in the ring.
I perceive, now, that she has no finger large enough for the ring we selected. So she will lend me one of her rings to be guided by, & I will hand
it to you on the 12th inst. The one we got will answer for a bracelet,
though,—or a necklace. She is small. There isn't much of her, but what
there is, assays as high as any bullion that ever I saw. All we need, now,
is your blessing, Mother, & I think you will not be likely to withhold it.
It is my wish that Mr. Fairbanks continue to answer all letters that arrive
there from Livy for me.[1]
    I have heard nothing from Alliance—suppose they don't want a lec-
ture. Got the invitation from Columbus, but know of no day I can give
them.[2] My warm love to all the household.
    A Cleveland young man told me all about the fire.[3] Lively times for
you, wasn't it? He said you were out at the Asylum washing orphans
when it happened.[4] I am sorry for the disaster, for no amount of insurance can compensate for the chaos & general upsetting of things a fire
occasions. I am afraid Mollie wasn't there to pray, else the disaster would
have been prevented.[5]
    I owe Sandy[6] a dollar. I enclose it. Please hand it to him, with
thanks. The shirts were in most excellent order, & I shall not neglect to
put them on at very short intervals, & do honor to your thoughtful care
by looking as destructively fascinating as I possibly can.

Good-bye, & God bless you. I am not too stuck up to say that, if I *am* engaged to be married.

Your Knighted & Ennobled Cub,

Your Crowned & Sceptred Scrub,

Mark.

✉—————————————————————————————

Mrs. A.W. Fairbanks | Care "Herald" | Cleveland | Ohio. [*return address:*] RETURN TO J. LANGDON, ELMIRA, N. Y., IF NOT DELIVERED WITHIN 10 DAYS. [*postmarked:*] ELMIRA N.Y. FEB 6

[1] A running joke: see 7 Jan 69 to Fairbanks and others.

[2] Clemens did not perform in Columbus, Ohio, although he had been trying to schedule a lecture there since October 1868 and had even enlisted Abel Fairbanks in the effort (*L2*, 258–59). His continuing difficulties in scheduling a lecture in Alliance, Ohio, are described in the next few letters.

[3] Clemens's young Cleveland acquaintance has not been identified. The Cleveland *Herald* reported the event on Tuesday, 2 February (3):

Fire.—About 11 o'clock on Monday forenoon a fire broke out in the two story frame building at 221 St. Clair street, owned and occupied by A. W. Fairbanks, Esq., and before it could be quenched a loss of about $2,500 ensued. The fire was first discovered by a servant girl who started from the kitchen to attend the front door bell. On opening the door which communicated with the hall, she found the room full of smoke, and immediately gave the alarm. The engines were promptly on hand, and by admirable manag[e]ment the flames were quenched in short order. The fire caught immediately under the hall floor, near the furnace flue and just under the stairway leading to the upper story. It was very fortunate that the fire occurred in the day-time, else, it is quite probable, the whole house would have been burned. As it is several of the carpets and much of the furniture is ruined by fire, water, and breakage, and the principal loss results from this. The alarm came from box 14. The loss is fully covered by insurance.

[4] In concluding his 22 January lecture on behalf of the Cleveland Protestant Orphan Asylum, Clemens made the following remarks, reported (evidently in full) by the Cleveland *Leader:*

Ladies and gentlemen: I am well aware of the fact that it would be a most gigantic fraud for you to pay a dollar each to hear my lecture. But you pay your dollar to the orphan asylum and have the lecture thrown in! So if it is not worth anything it does not cost you anything! [Laughter.] There is no expense connected with this lecture. Everything is done gratuitously and you have the satisfaction of knowing that all you have paid goes for the benefit of the orphans. I understand that there are to be other entertainments given week after next for the same object, the asylum being several thousand dollars in debt, and I earnestly recommend you all to attend them and not let your benevolence stop with this lecture[.] There will be eating to be done. Go there and eat, and eat, and keep on eating and *pay as you go.* [Great laughter.] The proprietors of the skating rink have generously offered to donate to the asylum the proceeds of one evening, to the amount of a thousand dollars, and when that evening comes, go and skate. I do not know whether you can all skate or not, but go and try! If you break your necks it will be no matter; it will be to help the orphans.

Don't be afraid of giving too much to the orphans, for however much you give you have the easiest end of the bargain. Some persons have to take care of those sixty orphans and they have to *wash* them. [Prolonged laughter.] Orphans have to be washed! And it[']s no small job either for they have only one wash tub and it's slow business[!] They can't wash but one orphan at a time! They have to be washed in the most elaborate detail, and by the time they get through with the sixty, the original orphan has to be washed again. Orphans won't stay washed! I've been an orphan myself for twenty-five years and I know this to be true[.] [Great laughter.] There is a suspicion of impurity and imposition about many ostensibly benevolent enterprises, but there is no taint of reproach upon this for the benefit of these little waifs upon the sea of life and I hope your benevolence will not stop here. In conclusion I thank you for the patience and fortitude with which you have listened to me. ("Mark Twain," 23 Jan 69, 4)

The Cleveland *Herald* did not publish this text, but noted that "Mr. Clemens closed with a highly humorous but effective appeal for the orphans that was immensely enjoyed by those present" ("Mark Twain and the Orphans," 23 Jan 69, 3, clipping in Scrapbook 26:8, CU-MARK).

⁵Twelve-year-old Mary Paine Fairbanks evidently was as pious as she was magnanimous (see *L2*, 355).

⁶Clearly a Fairbanks family servant.

To Olivia L. Langdon
13 February 1869 • Cleveland, Ohio
(MS: CU-MARK)

ALL KINDS JOB PRINTING	TERMS.—DAILY, $10; TRI-WEEKLY, $5; WEEKLY, $2 PER YEAR;
AND BOOK BINDING.	FRACTIONS OF A YEAR IN THE SAME PROPORTION.

GEO. A. BENEDICT,	OFFICE CLEVELAND DAILY HERALD 130 & 132 BANK STREET.
GEO. S. BENEDICT,	FAIRBANKS, BENEDICT & CO., PROPRIETORS.
A. W. FAIRBANKS.	

CLEVELAND, O. Feb. 13, 186 9.

Livy, darling, (10 AM.) I have been here two hours in a splendid state of exasperation. I went to bed in the cars at half past nine, last night & slept like a log until 7 this morning, & woke up *thoroughly* refreshed. The first thing Mrs. Fairbanks said was, "where were you last night?—a telegram came from Alliance at 8 o'clock, saying "Splendid audience assembled—where is Mark Twain?—somebody will be responsible for this."

I said "Alliance?—never heard of it!"

And she said Mr. Fairbanks made the appointment for me, & would have telegraphed me but *didn't know where* to telegraph—didn't know but that I had left Elmira—& as my letter from there (received last Monday), said I would reach here on the 12ᵗʰ, he didn't think it necessary to telegraph me anyhow. What abominable absurdity! I said, "Will you *never* learn anything? Are you going to be the same astonishing old aggregation of nonsense all the days of your life? Didn't you *know* I would stay in Elmira to the very last moment?—& didn't you *know* that Livy would be certain to know where I was, & that a telegram to Charley[1] would find me?"—& so on, till she threatened to take the broomstick to me. So you see, I must foot those Alliance bills—it would be dishonorable to do otherwise—& I must make a long trip west in the Spring & deliver that lecture free of charge—as nearly as I can come at it the failure to expend a dollar on a telegram will result in costing me two hundred dollars, four days lost time & five hundred miles of travel—& yet Fairbanks' letter to me, which should have gone to Jacksonville or Galena *by telegraph*, is still chasing around the country somewhere. I have *begged* him, & those ~~hated~~ execrable agents of mine ~~all~~ *always* to use the telegraph, but I can't get them to do it. The U.S. Mail has cost me some fifteen hundred dollars this season, & I would heartily wish it sunk to the bottom of the sea, only that it is so useful to me in hearing from *you*, Livy. So we will let the U.S. Mail still live, my darling—I can't possibly do without it.

Now I am in a good humor again, & all the Alliances in the world can't get me out of it again. I have given Mrs. Fairbanks the little ring, & she will have the engagement ring made. It seems unnatural not to see you this morning, you precious girl—& it seems odd not to find Mrs Langdon's ~~face~~ among the faces about me, or hear ~~that~~ the pleasant cackle of that absurd cousin of yours[2]—I send her my very kindest regards. Give Mr. Langdon my love, please—he is at home by this time.[3]

With a fervent blessing, & a prayer for you, & many & many a kiss, my dear Livy,

Sam.[.]

Miss Olivia L. Langdon
Politeness of the Reformed Pirate.

[*return address:*] FAIRBANKS, BENEDICT & CO. PUBLISHERS OF THE HERALD, BOOK AND JOB PRINTERS, BANK ST., CLEVELAND, O.   P. M. IF NOT CALLED FOR WITHIN TEN DAYS RETURN. [*docketed by OLL:*] 38th

[1] This hypothetical telegram was to be addressed to Charles J. Langdon, in keeping with the continuing effort to divert attention from Clemens's interest in Olivia.

² Harriet Lewis.

³ Jervis Langdon doubtless had been in Elmira for his daughter's formal engagement on 4 February. His reason for being away from home after that date has not been discovered.

⁴ Clemens's elaborate revision of his usual signature to Olivia was in playful recognition of their official engagement. He signed himself "Sam" on all subsequent letters to her.

To Olivia Lewis (Mrs. Jervis) Langdon
13 February 1869 • Ravenna, Ohio
(MS: CU-MARK)

GILLETTE HOUSE,

RAVENNA, OHIO, Feb. 13, 186 9.

Dear Mrs. Langdon—

It is not altogether an easy thing for me to write bravely to you, in view of the fact that I am going to bring upon you such a calamity as the taking away from you your daughter, the nearest & dearest of all your household gods.¹ You might well ask, "Who are you that presumes to do this?" And it would be an hard question to answer. I could refer you to fifty friends, but they could only tell you (& very vaguely, too,) what I *have* been—just as a forester might talk learnedly of a bush he had ₐonceₓ known well, unwitting that it had stretched its branches upward & become a tree, since *he* saw it. It is a bold figure, but not altogether an unapt one. For those friends of mine, who certainly knew little enough of me in the years that are gone, know nothing of me *now*. For instance, they knew me as a profane swearer; as a man of p convivial ways & not averse to social drinking; as a man without a religion; in a word, as a "wild" young man—though never as a dishonorable one, in the trite acceptation of that term. But now I never swear; I never taste wine or spirits upon *any* occasion whatsoever; I am orderly, & my conduct is above reproach in a worldly sense; & finally, I now claim that I am a Christian. I claim it, & it only remains to be seen if my bearing shall show that I am justly entitled to it. so name myself.

I beg, with justice, that you will make due allowance for the fact that I am in some sense a *public* man, in considering my character. You are aware that public men get ample credit for all the sins they commit,

& for a multitude of other sins they never were guilty of. A private citizen escapes public scrutiny, & ~~stands~~ fares all the better for it—but my private character is hacked, ~~& scorched~~ & dissected, & mixed up with my public one, & both suffer the more in consequence. Every man in California could tell you something about me, but not five men in the whole community have really any right to speak *authoritatively* of my *private* character, for I have not *close* friendships with more than that number there, perhaps. I can state as an absolute *truth*, that only one person in all the world really *knows* me, & that is Miss Langdon. To her I must refer you. My own mother & sister do not know me half so well as she does. I never have been in entire sympathy with any one but her (except with a brother, now dead,)[2]—I never have given thorough & perfect trust & confidence to any one in these latter years but her, & so there has always been a secret chamber or so in my being which no friend has entered before. But I have no secrets from her—no locked closets, no hidden places, ⫰ no disguised phases of character or disposition. And so, only she, really knows me.

I do not wish to marry ⫰ Miss Langdon for her wealth, & she knows that perfectly well. As far as I am concerned, Mr. Langdon can cut her off with a shilling—or the half of it. To use a homely phrase, I have paddled my own canoe,[3] since I was thirteen, *wholly* without encouragement or ~~fr~~ assistance from ~~any~~ ₐany₍ₐ₎ one, & am fully competent to ~~pad~~ so paddle it the rest of the voyage, & take a passenger along, beside. While I have health & strength, & the high hope & confidence that God gave me in my nature, I will look to it that we always have a comfortable living, & that is all ₐ(of a purely worldly nature,)₍ₐ₎ that either of us will care a great deal about. Neither of us are much afflicted with a mania for money-getting, I fancy. She thinks we *might* live on two thousand a year (& you know she is an able & experienced housekeeper & has a sound judgment in such matters,) but if I thought I could n't earn more than that, I would not be depraved enough to ask her to marry me yet awhile. No, we can make the canoe go, & we shall not care a straw for the world's opinion about it if the world chooses to think otherwise. This is *our* funeral, & we are proud enough & independent enough to think we can take care of it ~~ourselves.~~ ₐright.₍ₐ₎ If we get in trouble we will sell our point lace & eat our shucks in a foreign land,[4] ⫰ & *fight it out*, but we won't come back & billet ourselves on the old home, & have Charley charging us for board "on the ⫰ European plan" as he is always threatening to do with me when I linger there a few days. There's a shot for Charley! I propose to earn money enough some way or other, to buy a remunerative share ¢ in a newspaper of high standing, & then instruct & elevate & civilize the public through its columns, & my wife (to be,) will superintend the domestic economy, furnish ideas & sense, erase improprieties from the manuscript, & read proof. That is all she will have to do. Mere pastime for a person of her calibre.

Now if anybody wants to ask questions, you can read them any or all of the above & say with perfect confidence, that it is the *truth*. I don't know whether it is what you wanted or not, but I judged that the best way, after all, to write the letter, was to do exactly as I do when I wish to write a newspaper article—that is, sit down & let it *write itself*. This letter has written itself—& you have the result. There is no restraint in it, no expediency, no policy, no diplomacy. It simply means what it says— nothing more, & nothing less.

I tender my loving duty to you & to Mr. Langdon, & wish you ~~all~~ ‚all possible‚ happiness & content, most cordially—& likewise the cheerfulness & peace of mind which were yours before your proud & happy prospective son came to disturb it.[5]

Sincerely—
Saml. L. Clemens.

◄►————————————————————————————

[*on back of page 1, used as a wrapper:*]
Mrs. J. Langdon
Care of Charley.

{ Valentine. }

Mrs. J. Langdon

———

[*on envelope:*] Mrs. J. Langdon | Elmira | New York. [*return address:*] ETNA HOUSE, (LATE GILLETTE HOUSE,) S. W. COR. MAIN ST. & PUB. SQUARE, RAVENNA, O. C.A. PEASE & CO., PROP'RS. [*postmarked:*] RAVENNA O. FEB 13

---

[1] Prompted by the recent disturbing communications from California (see 20 and 21 Jan 69 to OLL, n. 6), Mrs. Langdon had asked Clemens to prepare a statement about his character and intentions that might be read or shown to the Langdons' circle of friends and acquaintances. The present letter was his at-

tempt to comply, but he soon had misgivings about it (see 15 Feb 69 to OLL).
A general sense of Mrs. Langdon's concerns is preserved in her 1 December
1868 letter to Mary Mason Fairbanks (see *L2*, 286–87 n. 3).

[2] Henry Clemens, who died in 1858 (*L1*, 80–82).

[3] The phrase was already proverbial in 1828 (*OED*, 11:53; Mathews, 2:1185).
In about 1858 it became the title of a popular American song, written by Harry
Clifton and arranged by M. Hobson.

[4] "And not many days after the younger son gathered all together, and took his
journey into a far country, and there wasted his substance with riotous living."
"And he would fain have filled his belly with the husks that the swine did eat:
and no man gave unto him" (Luke 15:13 and 15:16).

[5] Before 6 March Clemens had ceased to threaten Mrs. Langdon's "cheerfulness & peace of mind," for on that date she wrote to Mary Mason Fairbanks, in
part:

. . . I feel oppressed (not painfully) with the constant reminder of the more than friend
you have been to my *child elect*, Mr. Clemens—Of him what shall I say?—I cannot express
to you a description of the strange, new element that has entered into, and radiated our
family circle. I cannot tell you what a wealth we feel has been added to us, I cannot tell you
how precious that addition is to us, neither can I describe to you the restful, yea beautiful
background his mind & heart have already made to my husband's & my future life.—I
cannot tell you all these, nor have I need to, for *you* can imagine it all, and I know how
heartily your heart enters into our lives in the matter.—Almost as a matter of course, Mr.
Clemens & Livia's engagement as far as known, has excited much surprise, but I am comforted with the assurance that a kind Heavenly Father has led them in all the way that has
brought them together, *therefore it is as we would have it*. Their love is very beautiful to
look at, and may it grow more & more perfect as they shall travel together toward immortality. (*MTMF*, 82 n. 1)

To Mary Mason Fairbanks
13 February 1869 • Ravenna, Ohio
(MS: CSmH)

GILLETTE HOUSE,

RAVENNA, OHIO, Feb. 13, 186 9.

Dear Mother—

The lecture ~~ton~~ to-night was a handsome success.[1] I shall lecture in
Alliance tomorrow night—this will stop the publication of that article I
wrote for the Alliance paper, & take the blame off Mr. Fairbanks' shoulders, & I am mighty glad of it. He could stand it, I know, because he can
stand *anything* when he chooses to put his philosophy on its mettle, but
then we don't *want* to worry him, do we?[2]

I talk in Titusville Tuesday—in Franklin Wednesday—in Geneseo Thursday—in Auburn Friday[3]—& I lecture Livy Saturday & Sunday. Is all that satisfactory to my venerable & honored mother?

Give my love to all the household, & beli∕eve me the most loving & dutiful cub you have got.

Sam.

P. S. ₍"E-uck!"₎ I just hove a "sigh."

[1] The Ravenna *Portage County Democrat* of 17 February called Clemens's lecture "a success viewed either from a humorous or financial standpoint. The audience was the largest of the season, and without being a witness of the fact it would have been impossible to believe that so much fun could have been compressed into an hour. No one need ever attempt to be funny before a Ravenna audience, unless perfectly sure that he is a funnier man than 'Mark Twain'" ("'Mark Twain,'" 3). And the next day the Ravenna *Democratic Press* reported that Mark Twain's "quaint style, his quiet but yet sparking wit, met the hearty applause, while his eloquent description thrilled, a delighted audience" (TS in CU-MARK, courtesy of William Baker).

[2] Clemens's explanation of how he came to miss his 12 February lecture in Alliance has not been found and, as he indicates, may never have been published. He lectured in Alliance on 15 (not 14) February. His reference here to "tomorrow night" (a Sunday) is probably a simple error, rather than a sign that he was writing on Sunday ("after Saturday midnight," according to *MTMF*, 72). He probably retired before midnight on Saturday, after completing only the first part of the next letter to Olivia Langdon.

[3] Clemens kept his engagements in Titusville and Franklin, Pennsylvania, on 16 and 17 February, respectively. The lecture scheduled for Geneseo, New York, on 18 February was postponed until 1 March; the lecture scheduled for Auburn, New York, on 19 February was canceled.

To Olivia L. Langdon
13 and 14 February 1869 • Ravenna, Ohio
(MS: CU-MARK)

GILLETTE HOUSE,

RAVENNA, OHIO, Feb. 13 186 9
10 P.M.

I am able to inform the blessedest girl in all the world that the lecture to‿night was a *complete* success—& they said, as usual, that it was the largest audience of the season, a thing that necessarily gratifies me, for you know one naturally likes to be popular. And it is Saturday night, too—think of it!—& I need not hide to-morrow, but can go to church morning & evening. Somehow I don't often make a Saturday success.

Now wasn't it rascally to badger Fairbanks so much for not telegraphing me about the Alliance lecture, when I was cordially GLAD, ~~all the time~~ ,when I thought it over,, that he didn't? Because if he had done it we could not have knelt in the presence of God & bound ourselves together that night, my Livy.[1] I didn't badger him *much*, though, & showed no ill humor.

~~L~~ I *love* you, Livy,—indeed I *do* love you, Livy Good-night—I love you beyond all expression, Livy—it is strange I never thought to tell you before. But I *do* love you, darling. [*remainder in ink:*]

Sunday—It rained this morning, & was muddy. I attended the Congregational church—Rev. Mr. Mason. He is florid & flowery, & full of talk, & very disjointed & incoherent. I never made out what he was driving at.[2] *You* could have done it, just as unerringly as you unravel the marvelous ravings of old Mother Browning—now I beg pardon, Livy, with a kiss—you *know* I am learning to love Browning, but I can't altogether help poking fun at her a little. I shall always have an affection for Browning because she exhibits your brains so well. It always makes me proud of you when you assault one of her impenetrable sentences & tear off its shell & bring its sense to light.[3] Well, as I was saying, Mr. Mason talked, & talked, & talked, without rhyme or reason—but a[t] last he said something. He showed how trifling all the plans & thoughts & deeds of this summer-day's life of ours were, & of how little real use, unless they were woven into a ladder to scale the heavens with—& how worse than frivolous it is to live only for this world & its blessings. That started a train of thought—or rather it resurrected a train of thought which has been dwelling in my mind for many weeks, & growing more & more comprehensible & more & more tangible day by day. So the sermon was not lost. I don't know whether I shall go to church ~~again~~ to-night or not. This is my ninth letter, & I have some more to write.[4]

I am about *written out*—but then this is St. Valentine's Day, & I *must* give the greetings of the occasion to the darling little woman who has lifted the clouds from my firmament & made it glad with sunshine. I *must* lay at her feet a life which she has reclaimed from its waste & its worthlessness & made valuable; I *must* consecrate to her the worldly ambitions which were aimless till she gave them ~~ob~~ an object, a direction, a goal to be attained; I *must* offer a prayer for the dear heart that first taught my lips to pray; I *must* beseech Jesus to bless her who has so blessed me; I *must* take my noble Livy to my arms, & this day, of all days in the year, & swear to love, honor & cherish her, through joy & sorrow, through pleasure & pain, through sun & storm, & toil & scheme & labor for her, with hand & brain, by day & by night, all the years of my life, till the shadows of that evening whose sun rises only in eternity, shall close around me,, & thicken into the long night of death. God shield you, & love you & bless you always, my darling!

You will see by the enclosed note from Gen. Hawley, that he w does not wish to say anything of a definite nature until he can consult with his partner, Mr. Warner.[5] I look more & more favorably upon the idea of living in Hartford, & feel less & less inclined to wed my fortunes to a trimming, time-serving, policy-shifte~~d~~ing, popularity-hunting, money=grasping paper like the Cleveland Herald. It would change its politics in a minute, in order to be on the popular side, I think, & do a great many things for money which I wouldn't do.[6] These are hard things to say about a newspaper, but still I *think* them, & of course I am justified in saying things to you which it would not be right to say to anybody else. I would much rather have a mere comfortable living, in a high-principled paper like the *Courant*, than a handsome income from a paper of a lower standard, & so would you, Livy. Well, I shall reach Hartford during the last week in this month, no doubt, & then I will talk the matter all over with Gen. Hawley.

Oh, bother! I'm going to bed. I am not doing anything but *thinking* of you—& I can't write about other things & think of *you* all the time, Livy. I could write *about* you, easy—quires & reams—& *never* get done; but to write *to* you, with only one subject in my head & that subject *yourself*, is impossible. I have the little picture on the table, & it looks on quietly, & never says a word, & don't smile, or laugh, or offer me a kiss—but it is very pleasant, & comforting & companionable, for all that. It keeps my mind off my work, but I can see that it takes an interest in what I am doing, & so I love it & like to have it about. And better than all, I can never think an impure thought with that honored face before me—

I would have to close the case before I could do that. It is my little guardian angel.

I take you to my loving arms ~~in~~ and kiss you fond good-night, my Livy.

Sam[7]

[1] Clemens and Olivia must have "knelt in the presence of God" in Elmira on the evening of 12 February—just before his departure and at about the time he should have been lecturing in Alliance.

[2] The Reverend Edward B. Mason (b. 1837 or 1838) was pastor of the First Congregational Church in Ravenna from 1863 to 1873. Mason was something of a lecturer himself and had been giving a series of highly praised talks in Ravenna, the most recent on 10 February, about a European tour he made in 1868 (McClelland, Riddle, and Kertscher, 11; various reports about Mason, Ravenna *Portage County Democrat*, 1 Apr 68–10 Feb 69, transcriptions supplied by Julie McElroy; personal communication, Betty J. Widger).

[3] See 12 Jan 69 to OLL and CJL, n. 5.

[4] Any of the next three letters may have been among the eight that preceded the Sunday portion of this one.

[5] The enclosure, Joseph Roswell Hawley's letter of 10 February, does not survive, but its import is clear from Clemens's reply to it, and from his next letter to Twichell (both dated 14 February). Clemens was trying to secure a position on the Hartford *Courant*, of which Hawley (1826–1905)—lawyer, anti-slavery crusader, founder of the Connecticut Republican party, distinguished Civil War veteran (retired as a brevet major-general), and former governor of Connecticut (1866)—was editor in chief. In 1857 Hawley had established the Hartford *Evening Press*, where he was joined three years later by associate editor Charles Dudley Warner (1829–1900). In 1867 he, Warner, and their *Evening Press* associate Stephen A. Hubbard (d. 1890), merged that paper with the Hartford *Courant*, also a Republican journal, then owned by William H. Goodrich and his silent partner, Thomas M. Day. On the new *Courant* Warner was again associate editor (acting as editor in chief during Hawley's frequent absences), Goodrich was business manager, and Hubbard had editorial responsibilities and served as business manager when Goodrich retired at the end of 1868. Goodrich's retirement lasted only a year, but it, along with Hawley's political activities during the 1868 presidential campaign, and Warner's six-month absence in Europe, may have created a need for help that Clemens now hoped to satisfy (*BDUSC*, 1157; McNulty, 70–71, 85, 87–91, 100, 131; Rowell, 13; Lounsbery, x–xii; Trumbull, 1:170, 606).

[6] The particular reasons, if any, for these charges have not been determined.

[7] Olivia's docket number for this letter does not survive, probably because she wrote it on the envelope, now lost. It was letter number thirty-nine.

To Elisha Bliss, Jr.
14 February 1869 • Ravenna, Ohio,
(MS: PPiU)

GILLETTE HOUSE,

RAVENNA, OHIO, Feb. 14 186 9.

E. Bliss, Jr.

Dear Sir:

I got your letter in Elmira the other day, & was glad to hear you are getting along so well. I am glad of the pictures—the more we have, the better the book will sell. I shall arrive in Hartford during the last week of this month, & shall be able to stay two or three weeks.

Had a splendid audience here & a splendid success every way. I believe I could get engagements for every night at a hundred dollars, here in the West, as long as I would take them. It *pays* them to hire me, because we are bound to have a good house, whether the weather is good or bad.

When I get to Hartford I will read such proofs as are ready, & will critically revise the MSS of the rest, but I don't much like to entrust even slight alterations to other hands. It isn't a judicious thing to do, exactly. We'll talk it over when I get there.[1]

> Yrs Truly
> Sam*l*. L. Clemens

✉—————————————————————————————————

[*letter docketed:*] √ auth [*and*] Mark Twain | Feb 14/69 | Author

[1]Clemens was responding to the following letter from Bliss (CU-MARK), who had had his manuscript since the previous August:

AMERICAN PUBLISHING CO., PUBLISHERS OF STANDARD WORKS, SOLD BY SUBSCRIPTION ONLY. NOW IN PRESS RICHARDSON'S NEW WORKS, PERSONAL HISTORY OF U. S. GRANT, BEYOND THE MISSISSIPPI. HISTORY OF THE BIBLE, ILLUSTRATED. AGENTS WANTED.

S. DRAKE, PRES'T.   OFFICE AMERICAN PUBLISHING COMPANY,
E. BLISS, JR., SEC'Y.   148 ASYLUM STREET.
F. E. BLISS, TREAS.
                                          HARTFORD, CONN., Feby. 10 186 9.
Sam J. Clemens Esq.

Dear friend, Your favor to Frank recd. I thought as our correspondence has not been extensive, I would write you. Hope you are well & fully recovered from the joint attack of that *boil & cold*. We are glad to hear of your success West, & of your *popularity*. (We glean this from the reports of the press) We presume you have had a very busy trip.

Hope you are enjoying yourself now at Elmira. Now about the *Book*. Would say, that we have no proofs as yet to send. We are pushing things now very rapidly however. We are about ready to begin to electrotype. We are *filling* IT WITH ENGRAVINGS. We had an artist from N. York here 2 or 3 weeks reading Mss & drawing sketches. They are now in hands, of engravers, & we receive *first batch of them* this week when we can push the *electrotyping*, rapidly. We think you will be very much pleased with the style ‚in‚ which we are getting it up   We are inserting a copy of enclosed in every book we send out & are spreading the report of the Book in all circulars &c &c   We anticipate a good sale for it & think we will *disappoint* you *some* in the result, *we hope agreeably*. There will be about *200* engravings in the Book we think, we have 150 now in ready. We have a lot from Beach & use some of yours also. We shall hurry the thing up rapidly as soon as we begin to get engravings, as above.

How long do you propose to be gone to California? And about proofs. It is going to be very hard to get at you with them for the next month. Shall you be here before you go? W̶h̶ Will it be necessary for you to read the proofs.? What do you say to our getting a good *grammarian* & proof *reader here* to revise, that is read & correct proofs? With a permission on your part, to cut out a line or an *unimportant paragraph* where needed to make them come out right on pges, we can get along comfortably, as you will not probably want to alter the Mss. By giving your permission to this arrangement, we can expedite business, & be able by time you sale to give you proofs of a *good deal of the Book*̸. We shall set agents at work as soon as we can see through & shall devote all our energies to its sale. We have never had a book look better for us, & its author, & we trust you will see that the spring arrangement, has been a good one for you. We are spending a good deal of money on it, more than on any book we ever got out except perhaps Miss, which this will very much resemble. Should be pleased to have you come up & spend a week or two if, you can do so. Write again soon & keep us posted as we very likely shall need to ask you questions, about Mss, frequently, as we electrotype. Also write at once if, you accede to our arrangement as to proof reading &c.

All send respects &c

Truly Yours
E Bliss Jr Sy

[*enclosure:*]

PUBLISHERS' ANNOUNCEMENT.

Subscribers for "THE GREAT METROPOLIS" can hardly fail to observe that the volume contains 700 pages instead of 600 as promised in the Prospectus. The number of the engravings is also increased. We universally make our books larger and better than we represent them to be. We trust this fact will be noticed and add to the public confidence in our future promises.

We have now in preparation, and shall issue early in the Spring, through our Agents, "THE NEW PILGRIM'S PROGRESS," by "MARK TWAIN," the well known "Moralist of the Main," and world renowned humorist. We bespeak for it a hearty welcome.

This guileful letter told Clemens just where his book stood in the production process, even as it avoided saying that it was several months behind schedule and could not possibly "issue early in the Spring." Bliss succeeded in loosening Clemens's already shaky grasp of the situation. Even though his contract of 16 October 1868 specified that the book was to be typeset and plated, ready for printing, "during the next 4 months" (within a week of Bliss's letter), no proofs were ready because no type had been set, and no type had been set because (as

Bliss acknowledged) not even the first one hundred fifty illustrations had been electrotyped, the process that necessarily preceded the typesetter's inserting them in the type. The typesetters would not *begin* until enough of the electroplated engravings were at hand to allow their work to proceed uninterrupted. Bliss also tried to minimize at least one source of possible future delay: the author's taking seriously his contractual commitment to "give all neccessary time & attention to the reading of proofs & corre[c]ting the same if necessary." But Clemens was more alert to this ploy, at least in part because of his 1867 experience with the *Jumping Frog* book, for which he had allowed Charles Henry Webb not only to read the proof but to make alterations—with unfortunate results. Clemens reached Hartford on 5 March, later than expected, and only then did he see his first proofs (*L2*, 39–40, 421–22; Hirst, 197–99; Elisha Bliss, Jr., to SLC, 12 July 69, and Francis E. Bliss to SLC, 17 July 69, both in CU-MARK).

To Joseph R. Hawley
14 February 1869 • Ravenna, Ohio
(MS: CtHi)

GILLETTE HOUSE,

RAVENNA, OHIO, Feb. 15— 186 9.

Gen. Jos. R. Hawley
    Dear Sir—
       Your letter of the 10th is received.[1] As the illustrations for my book are progressing so well that the electrotyping may be shortly begun, I suppose I may safely calculate upon a call to ~~Har~~ come to Hartford & begin to read proof, within a fortnight. I shall probably remain there several weeks & shall be glad to talk with you. I think it very likely that it will turn out to be just as well to take the California trip before making permanent business arrangements.

With great Respect—
Mark Twain.

[1] The letter that Clemens enclosed in his own of 13 and 14 February to Olivia, just after writing this misdated reply to Hawley.

To Joseph H. Twichell and Family
14 February 1869 • Ravenna, Ohio
(MS: Davis)

GILLETTE HOUSE,

RAVENNA, OHIO, St. Valentine's 186 9.

Dear J. H & Tribe—

I greet you all with the great accession of love that naturally comes to one ѵ on the feast-day of St Valentine. And you can just rise up & blow your horn, too, & blow it *loud*—because the subscriber is *engaged to be married!*—hip, hip, hip – – [*now*, AL‚L#‚together!] On bended knees, in the presence of God only, we devoted our lives to each other & to the service of God. And let this writing be a witness of it, to you.

And so, as soon as I am permanently settled in life, we shall be married. [I don't sigh, & groan & howl so much, now, as I used to—no, I feel‚ serene, & arrogant, & stuck-up—& I feel such pity for the world & everybody in it but just us two.) I have suddenly grown to be prodigiously important to the world's welfare, somehow—though it didn't use to seem to me that my existence was such a very extraordinary matter.

I do wish you knew Miss Livy. She already knows & loves you both—loves you *all*, I should have said—on my account.

I have received & answered Gen. Hawley's letter. He suggests that I make my California trip first, & then Warner will be home & we can talk business. I think the General would rather *employ* me than sell me an interest—but that won't *begin* to answer, you know. I can buy into plenty of paying newspapers, but my future wife wants me to be surrounded by a good moral & religious atmosphere (for I shall unite with the church as soon as I am located,) & so she likes the idea of living in Hartford. We could make more money elsewhere, but neither of us are much fired with a mania for money-getting. That is a matter of second=rate, even third-rate importance with us.

I shall reach Hartford during the last week of this month, & remain *several* weeks. I shall spend Saturday & Sunday, Feb. 20th & 21st, in Elmira.

Good-bye & God-bless you.

Always yrs
Mark.

To Olivia L. Langdon
15 February 1869 • Ravenna, Ohio
(MS: CU-MARK)

ₐI love you, Livy—Livy dear—Livy love—I *love* you Livy—

=======

I kiss you, Livy—on forehead, cheek & lips.
I love you, Livy.   GILLETTE HOUSE,
I love only Livy—nobody but Livy.ₐ   RAVENNA, OHIO, Feb. ~~16~~ 15 186 9.

Livy, darling, how are you this morning? For it *is* morning, I guess, inasmuch as it is only half past 9, & I have not got up yet. I only awoke a little while ago, & naturally thought of you the first thing. I don't intend to get up till noon.

I wrote to our Mother,—if she will allow me to call her so—& the letter is gone.[1] If I had it back I would write it over again. I see that in letting the letter "write itself" it took entirely too unconventional a form. I forgot, ~~that~~ occasionally, ₐthe factₐ that I was really writing to the PUBLIC, instead of to her. And so I elaborated what needed no elaboration, & merely touched upon matters which should have been treated more fully. But don't you see?—if I had kept the *public* in my mind, the sense of being questioned & cross-questioned by outsiders, upon matters ~~entire~~ essentially private & personal, would have been so oppressive that I could not have written at all. It is hard to know that what you are writing (confessing) about your most delicate & private affairs is to be read by strangers and unlovingly criticised & commented on at tea-tables & among miscellaneous groups who would often rather say a *smart* thing than a kind one. So I think that maybe, after all, there may have been a little natural impulse to *hold back*, instead of speaking out freelyₜ, though I was not really conscious of such an impulse. I do not think I am more sensitive than others would be under like circumstances.

I told Mrs. Fairbanks to have the ring made, & then express it to me at Elmira so that it would reach there about the 20ᵗʰ. And so you see I can put it on your finger myself, my precious little wife.

I wrote Twichell a short note yesterday to thank him for his kind efforts in forwarding our affairs. I told him we meant to lead a useful, ¢ unostentatious & earnest religious life, & that I should unite with the church as soon as I was settled; & that both of us, on these accounts, would prefer the quiet, moral atmosphere of Hartford to the driving, ambitious ways of Cleveland. I wanted him to understand that what we want is a *home*—we are done with the shows & vanities of life & are ready to enter upon its realities—~~that~~ we are tired of chasing its phantoms & shadows, & are ready to grasp its substance. At least *I* am—& ‸"I"‸ means both of us, & ‸"both of us" means I of course—for are not we Twain one flesh?[2]

I read a great deal in the Testament last night—why didn't we read the Testament more, instead of carrying loads of books into the drawing-room which we never read? I thought of it ~~lay~~ Several times=

Clouding up again—well, is it never going to clear off? I will go to sleep again. Take this loving kiss & go to bed yourself, my idol.

Sam.[3]

[1] See 13 Feb 69 to Olivia Lewis (Mrs. Jervis) Langdon.
[2] Matthew 19:4–6:

And he answered and said unto them, Have ye not read, that he which made them at the beginning made them male and female,

And said, For this cause shall a man leave father and mother, and shall cleave to his wife: and they twain shall be one flesh?

Wherefore they are no more twain, but one flesh. What therefore God hath joined together, let not man put asunder.

[3] Olivia's docket number for this letter does not survive, probably because she wrote it on the envelope, now lost. It was letter number forty.

To Olivia L. Langdon
17 February 1869 • Titusville, Pa.
(MS: CU-MARK)

CRITTENDEN HOUSE, TITUSVILLE, PA.   E. H. CRITTENDEN,
E. Z. WILLIAMS, - - - - PROPRIETORS.

TITUSVILLE, PA., Feb. 17 186 9.

Livy dear, I don't feel a bit well this morning, & so I cannot write. I left‸ Ravenna about noon, Monday, for Alliance—lectured there that night—sat up till 2 in the morning (because no porter at hotel to call me,) & returned on a coal train to Ravenna—got to the Ravenna hotel just at 4 o'clock in the morning—went to bed for one hour & a half & then got up half asleep & started in the early train for this Titusville section of country—had to wait from 1 P.M. till 5, at Corry, Pa., & so I found an excellent hotel & went to bed—but several merchants of the place (I use the *nom de plume* on hotel registers when I am a stranger & want a choice room,) ~~same~~ ˌsawˌ my name on the register & called to see me (it was business, not idle curiosity—they wanted to get me to lecture,) & when they were gone I was feverish & restless & couldn't sleep. And at 5 I got up & soon started for this place, arriving just in fair time to open the lecture. I have slept late, this morning, but still I feel stupiefied & idiotic. Good audience, & highly gratified with the lecture.[1]

I *can't* write—about a million odds & ends of things I want to say to you, are whirling through my brain, but I ~~st~~ sit ~~si~~ & look on at this hurricane of whizzing fragments, bewildered—bewildered & helpless. Bewildered & idea-less—that is it. But never mind—I have your letter, & you say in it that you are happy, ~~&~~ & therefore I am content. *I* am happy—happy that I have your love; happy that you can sign yourself "*Your* Livy;" happy to feel & know that you ARE *my* Livy, forever & ever—my Livy & my *wife;* happy in the belief that we shall spend our joined lives in the sincere & earnest service of God. [*in margin:* I read & marked "A Life for a Life" in the cars yesterday—I like it right well.][2]

[~~Mou~~ My tongue & my pen hesitate to use the language of religion—they only gradually surrender consent to use it at all. This is a matter that ~~dis~~ has disturbed me a little—but since reading your letter last night, it don't. When you say of my name, "*Sam*"—

"It does not even now come quite easily from either tongue or pen, but it is sacred to me, & I shall soon grow familiar with it"—

When you say that, I understand my own ~~cau~~ case without another word. I *know* you love me—& yet I see that the peculiar & especial language of this love seems awkward to your unaccustomed tongue. Thank you, Livy.

I am not going to lecture in ~~Ab~~ Auburn on the 19th—& so I shall see you *on that day*—

Until which time, with earnest kisses of love & honor, Good-bye, my darling Livy.

Sam.

✉———————————————————————————————

[*on wrapper:*]

Miss Olivia L. Langdon

Politeness of Mrs. Fair-⎫   Present

banks's youngest pup. ⎭

[*docketed by OLL:*] 41st

¹The Titusville *Morning Herald* reported that Clemens's 16 February lecture in Corinthian Hall drew

> one of the largest and most select audiences of the season. . . . The subject, "The American Vandal Abroad," afforded an excellent field for the versatile genius of "Mark Twain," for rare poetic description, as well as keen and racy bits. The lecturer held the audience in a state of subdued mirthful enjoyment for nearly two hours, occasionally exciting their up-roar[i]ous laughter, or lifting them in his eloquent flights, as he apostrophized the Sphynx, or depicted the glories of Venice or Athens. ("Mark Twain's Lecture," 17 Feb 69, 3)

²On 5 December 1868, Clemens had promised Olivia that he would read this 1859 novel, by Dinah Maria Mulock Craik, about a courtship conducted chiefly through a high-minded correspondence (*L2*, 314).

To Joseph T. Goodman
17 February 1869 • Titusville, Pa.
(*Paraphrase:* Virginia City
Territorial Enterprise, 26 Mar 69)

MARK TWAIN TO BE MARRIED.—We have received a letter from that wise and holy pilgrim, "Mark Twain," dated Titusville, Pennsylvania, February 17,¹ in which he says: "I have pretty thoroughly lectured New York, New Jersey, Pennsylvania, Ohio, Indiana, Illinois, Iowa and Michigan, and am now doing this Pennsylvania oil region. Half a dozen more lectures, I hope, will finish this long, wearisome winter's siege—a dozen anyhow—and then I shall have a holiday. Whoop! you old fool!" He then goes on to say that he could get appointments at $100 per night for four or five months next season in case he should feel inclined to accept, but that he don't know whether or not he will again enter the field, as he is going to get married and so will want to settle down. We are not at liberty to give names, but may be allowed to say that the young lady who has captivated the gushing Mark resides in the town of Elmira, New York, is an only daughter, rich, handsome, and in every respect a suitable companion for an orphan like Mark. If Mark takes his father-in-law's advice he will probably give up lecturing and go to work in one of the old man's coal mines—in short, become a coal-heaver. In concluding his letter Mark says: "I shall lecture in San Francisco in April or May. Come down, boys. I can't go to Virginia, having killed myself there twice already in the lecture business."[2] We should think he might stand a little more of the same kind of "killing," and even tackle once more the terrible footpads of the Divide, though those now infesting that vicinity are of the genuine order—not make-believes, like those who "went through" him on the occasion of his first appearance in this city as a lecturer.[3]

---

[1] The original document has not been found, but it was doubtless written on the same letterhead as the previous and next letters and addressed to Goodman, proprietor and chief editor of the Virginia City *Territorial Enterprise*, who published this report of it there. He had been Clemens's employer in the early and mid-1860s, and more recently had been among the ten indisputably friendly references Clemens volunteered to Jervis Langdon in December 1868, even before the "six prominent men" he named earlier could reply (*L1*, 232–325 passim, especially 242 n. 2; *L2*, 358).

[2] Clemens had performed three times in Virginia City, delivering his Sandwich Islands lecture on 31 October 1866 and his lecture on "Pilgrim Life" on 27 and 28 April 1868. The 1866 performance filled Maguire's Opera House with an audience of some eight hundred, at one dollar apiece—a clear financial success. The two 1868 performances were evidently less lucrative. On 28 April, the Virginia City *Trespass* reported "a very large and fashionable audience of ladies and gentlemen"; the Gold Hill *Evening News* said the lecture was "well attended, and the dress circle fashionably and satisfactorily filled"; and the *Enterprise* noted a "crowded an[d] delighted audience" ("Mark Twain," 3; "'Mark Twain's' Lectures," 3; "Opera House—Mark Twain's Lecture," 3). Such reports were evidently professional courtesy toward a former colleague. Clemens's friend Alfred R. Doten (1829–1903), an experienced newspaperman then working for the Gold Hill *Evening News*, attended both lectures, noting privately on 27 April: "Not very full house – Lecture humorous, very, as well as pleasing & instructive – Much applauded – lasted about an hour." And on 28 April he remarked:

"Mark Twain's" lecture . . . about same audience as last night – Same lecture – at 8½ oclock a piano was heard in behind the curtain – as it went up, Mark was discovered playing rudely on it, & singing "There was an old 'hoss & his name was Jerusalem" etc – He came forward, & apologized for so introducing things on the ground that if any of them had been waiting behind the curtain as long as he had, they would appreciate some relief of the kind – then he went on with his lecture, & I came home – (Doten, 2:996, 997)

Recalling this experience early in 1871, Clemens advised James Redpath of the Boston Lyceum Bureau to schedule temperance lecturer John Bartholomew

Gough for only "1 night (or possibly 2,) in Virginia City Nevada (provided you can get a church—for they *won't* go to that nasty theatre.)" (22 Jan 71 to Redpath, NN-B, in Will M. Clemens, 27).
    [3] See *L1*, 366–67 n. 4.

To Mary Mason Fairbanks
17 February 1869 • Titusville, Pa.
(MS: CSmH)

CRITTENDEN HOUSE, TITUSVILLE, PA.   E. H. CRITTENDEN,
E. Z. WILLIAMS, - - - - PROPRIETORS.

TITUSVILLE, PA., Feb. 17. 186 9.

Dear Mother—

It is all right. By staying up thirty-six hours with only one hour's sleep, I have made the several connections. I talked in Alliance Monday night, docking my wages $20 by way of damages. I talked here last night (saw Mr. & Mrs. Severance & they are well,)[1] & am within two hours' journey of Franklin, where I talk to-night. I shall have to pay the Franklin Ma Society $25 or $30 for putting off the lecture after it was already advertized, & then I shall be all right.[2] And so nobody can say a word against Mr. Fairbanks & me, *now*—for we have fulfilled our contracts & done our duty. Shake hands with him for me.

I haven't ,got, nothing more to write, I believe, because there ain't no topics of interest here to write about, except that Beech was here & the angel of the coal mine went down in an oil well.[3] No damage to either. Oils well that ends well.

By a letter from Charley I am overwhelmed with gratitude to learn that up to *two hours* after I left Elmira, Livy was still well. I send you your youngest pup's letter, to let you see for yourself.[4]

Your affectionate *old* pup,

Mark.

[1] Why the Severances were in Titusville, some one hundred miles from Cleveland, has not been explained.
[2] The Franklin lecture was originally scheduled for Monday, 15 February

("Lecture by Mark Twain," Franklin *Venango Spectator*, 12 Feb 69, 3, TS in CU-MARK).

[3] Beech, the "angel," and the oil well are unidentified. In 1859, the drilling of "the first spouting petroleum well in history" near Titusville had transformed that "drowsy village" into "a boom town of shady characters, hard life, easy philosophy, and rough democracy." By the time of Clemens's lecture, the town boasted itself "the great commercial centre" of the Pennsylvania oil region (*Pennsylvania*, 76, 582; "Mark Twain at Corinthian Hall Tonight," Titusville *Morning Herald*, 16 Feb 69, 3).

[4] The enclosure, Charles Langdon's 12 February letter to Clemens, has not been found.

To Mary Mason Fairbanks
17 February 1869 • Franklin, Pa.
(MS: CSmH)

Livy, Feb. 32, 1946.

Dear ~~Livy~~ Mother—

You are mistaken. I hardly ever think of Livy. I hope I am not a school-boy. I should think I ought to be able to contain my feelings at my time of life. I don't see why ˌyouˌ should think love "simplifies" a man—because it does seem to me sometimes that ˌitˌ don't do anything but *complicate* him. You ought to see how it gets *me* tangled up now & then.

My Livy came to hand all right ˌon Monday,ˌ & I am ever so much obliged to you.[1] You see I *should* have lectured at Livy Monday night, but was persuaded to go to Livy instead, because, you know I ~~di~~ wasn't advertised to talk at Livy till the 18th anyhow, & so I thought I could make it. It begins to look a little shaky, now, though, for it is a long trip.[2] I talked here, to a crammed house, to-night, & gave the very best satisfaction—better than last night, I think, for a drunken man annoyed me a little there.[3] On the 19th I shall reach Elmira—the lecture appointed for that night is postponed—& I shall say a few words to Livy, on general topics, until the evening of the 22d, when I shall sail for Trenton, N. J., if the wind is fair. Bless you for a blessed good mother, both to Livy &

me. Good bye. After Trenton, comes Stuyvesant, N. Y., 25th—& then Hartford for 2 or 3 weeks.[4] Love to all.

> Your happy scrub
> Sam.

[1]Clemens probably refers to the ring borrowed from Olivia to facilitate the sizing of her engagement ring. Mrs. Fairbanks later sent the engagement ring itself directly to Elmira (see 5 Feb 69 and 27 Feb 69, both to Fairbanks).

[2]Clemens lectured in Alliance, Ohio, on Monday, 15 February, instead of in New York City as originally planned. He was scheduled to lecture at Geneseo, New York, on 18 February, the appointment he was now unsure he could keep.

[3]No reviews of Clemens's 17 February lecture in Franklin have been located. The previous evening, in Titusville, his performance had been disrupted by an unseemly disturbance in the rear of the hall, which was equally annoying to the audience and the speaker. A policeman was present, and was in duty bound to eject the blackguard summarily, instead of doing which, as he was directed, he only parleyed with him, and the noise and confusion were kept up with impunity. ("Mark Twain's Lecture Last Evening," Titusville *Morning Herald*, 17 Feb 69, 3)

[4]Clemens's 19 February lecture, which was not rescheduled, was to have been in Auburn, New York. For the remaining engagements of the present tour, both before and after his Hartford stay (5–13 March, not "2 or 3 weeks"), see Appendix D.

To the Young Men's Association of Geneseo Academy, *per* Telegraph Operator 18 February 1869 • Franklin, Pa.

(*Paraphrase:* Geneseo [N.Y.] *Genesee Valley Herald*, 24 Feb 69)

The Y. M. A. had nearly completed arrangements for his lecture, and were still at work, about 10 o'clock on Thursday forenoon, when a telegram was received saying that he was "unavoidably detained," and could not reach here that evening. Telegrams were sent him, and all possible means employed to get him here that evening, if possible, but, of course they were of no avail. He having said that he would be in Elmira until the 22d inst., telegrams and letters were sent him there,[1]

[1]According to the Rochester (N.Y.) *Chronicle*, Clemens sent a dispatch to Geneseo "to say that he had been delayed somewhere in Pennsylvania and

missed the train" ("'Mark Twain' disappointed . . . ," 20 Feb 69, 3, TS in CU-MARK). He later implied that he telegraphed from Franklin: "while I could have made Geneseo easily enough from Titusville, I couldn't do it from Franklin. So I telegraphed them to stop the lecture & send my bill, which they did. I paid it—$22.25" (27 Feb 69 to Fairbanks). The *Genesee Valley Herald*, whose account of Clemens's communications is preserved verbatim in this and the next three letter texts, called his "non-arrival" a "sore disappointment, not only to the Young Men's Association, but to many in this and surrounding towns" ("Mark Twain's Lecture," 3). The Young Men's Association of Geneseo Academy sponsored various extracurricular programs, chief of which was "engaging prominent lecturers of the time to speak in Geneseo" (LaVigne, 1). Geneseo Academy (originally called Temple Hill Academy) was erected in 1826 and was an affiliate of the Buffalo Synod of the Presbyterian church (French, 141–42, 383 n. 9). For Clemens's own account of his experience with the Young Men's Association, see 2 Mar 69 to OLL.

To the Young Men's Association of
Geneseo Academy, *per* Telegraph Operator
21–22 February 1869 • (1st of 3) • Elmira, N.Y.
(Paraphrase: Geneseo [N.Y.] *Genesee Valley Herald*, 24 Feb 69)

and on Monday the cheering intelligence was received that he would *positively* lecture here on Monday evening next, March 1st.

To the Young Men's Association of
Geneseo Academy, *per* Telegraph Operator
21–22 February 1869 • (2nd of 3) • Elmira, N.Y.
(Paraphrase: Geneseo [N.Y.] *Genesee Valley Herald*, 24 Feb 69)

In answer to a telegram, inquiring if he should be advertised immediately, he says: "Advertise liberally and *without fear.*"[1]

[1] Since it seems naive of the Young Men's Association to ask whether to advertise "immediately" a lecture date that Clemens had just confirmed for seven

days hence, the possibility remains that he may have sent only one telegram, on Sunday (21 February) or Monday (22 February), in which he both confirmed the date and answered their question about advertising. On the other hand, these young sponsors certainly *were* naive, and Clemens himself was being both apologetic and, by his own admission, somewhat muddled. He wrote to Olivia on 2 March that he had been "so bewitched" by her from 19 to 22 February that he "could think of nothing connectedly & collectedly *but* you."

To the Young Men's Association of
Geneseo Academy
21–22 February 1869 • (3rd of 3) • Elmira, N.Y.
(Paraphrase: Geneseo [N.Y.] *Genesee
Valley Herald,* 24 Feb 69)

And in a letter subsequently received he expresses himself as being exceedingly sorry that he had caused the disappointment, and desirous of lecturing before the people of Geneseo at a future date, which he fixed at March 1st, and which the Association accepted.[1]

[1]Clemens probably wrote this letter on the same day he sent the preceding telegram. Apparently in a later letter—written between 23 and 25 February, while he was in New York before and after lecturing in Trenton, New Jersey— he asked the Young Men's Association to hold his mail until he arrived in Geneseo (see 2 Mar 69 to OLL).

To Olivia L. Langdon
26 February 1869 • Stuyvesant, N.Y.
(MS: CU-MARK)

Stuyvesant, Feb. 26. ⎫
1 A.M. ⎬

My Darling Livy, it is *too bad.* I had promised myself the happiness of a long letter to you yesterday—but it took them all day to get me a room at the St Nicholas, & so *that* failed. Your father & I called to see Mrs. Brooks in the evening—she was out—& after that I had to go to bed—

tired out. But I left New York early, to-day, purposely that I might get a chance to write, here, this afternoon—but it was no use:[1] they brought me here to be the guest of the Rev. Mr. Nevius, & they kept me in the parlor talking till almost dark (I had your letter in my hand all the time,) & then I had to beg them to let me retire a moment & read it,—I *had* to read it—I couldn't stand it any longer. Just as I finished it they called me to tea—several young ladies present—then talk, talk, talk, till lecture-time.[2] After the lecture they had much company, & the talk continued till almost midnight. *Then* I thought I would get a chance to write, but was fooled again. Three of the young ladies are staying all night—~~ther~~ their room is just across the hall from mine, & they *wouldn't* go to bed, but have kept on chattering at me for more than an hour, asking questions. Finally I started into their room, promising to stop their clatter, & that ended the trouble—for they were undressed, & they barred me out. They are quiet, now.

But it is too late—too late. The night is more than half gone, & I take the train at 9 in the morning. You don't allow me to sit up late to write, you idolized little tyrant, & therefore I must just quit & go to bed. My stove smokes, & I am enveloped in a fog of it, & my eyes smart, although the doors are open & I am very cold. I am tired, & sleepy, & disappointed, & angry, & yet I am trying to write to *Livy*. I ought í not to approach such a presence save in a tranquil spirit,—& with the deference which is your due. Am I *never* going to get a chance to write? Oh, forgive me, darling, & pity me—for I do so *long* to write. I *will* have the time in Lockport, in spite of everybody—& then I'll "let myself out!" [Slang—I'm sorry, Livy, dear.]

This smoke is outrageous. Livy, I *can't* keep my eyes open. And this is such a pitiable return for *your* letter, which made me as happy as a king, you precious, you matchless girl! I *love* you, Livy. I love you with *all* my heart—with every fibre of it. Pray for me, Livy darling—I can pray with only half a heart—I am so disappointed.

I take the comma & the semicolon from the little picture (thank you, "MY Livy"—you ~~sigh~~ sign yourself rightly, my life, my love,) & send in return, *all* the punctuation marks[3]—on brow & lip & eyes—& the grateful homage of a most blest & loving heart. Good-night—& good-bye, for a little season.

                                                    Yours, *always*
                                                    Sam.

[*enclosure:*]

GURNEY & SON,   FIFTH AVE. N Y.

[*on the back:*]   G&S
I HAVE CHAINED THE SUN TO SERVE ME
GURNEY.
FIFTH AVENUE, COR 16TH ST. N. Y.

Miss Olivia L. Langdon
Present.
Care of the best boy in the family.
[*docketed by OLL:*] 43rd

[1]Clemens dated his letter 26 February in strict accord with the early hour, even though when he referred to "to-day" and "yesterday" in the body of the letter, he meant 25 and 24 February, respectively. He had left Elmira on 22 Feb-

ruary, bound for Trenton, New Jersey, by way of New York City, which he probably reached early on 23 February. He lectured in Trenton that evening. (The
letter he probably wrote to Olivia on 23 February, docket number 42, is missing.)
On 24 February he returned to New York and waited "all day" for a room at the
St. Nicholas Hotel, where he joined Olivia's father, who was himself in the city
on business. In the evening they tried and failed to visit Fidele Brooks, and early
on the next day, 25 February, Clemens took the train 125 miles north to Stuyvesant. He lectured in Stuyvesant on the evening of 25 February ("City Items,"
Trenton [N.J.] *State Gazette*, 23 Feb 69, 3; Lane; "Morning Arrivals," New York
Evening Express, 24 Feb 69, 3; "Personal Intelligence," New York *Evening Telegram*, 25 Feb 69, 4; "Home News," New York *Tribune*, 25 Feb 69, 8).

   [2]The Reverend Elbert Nevius (1808–97) had been pastor of the Reformed
Church of Stuyvesant since 1846. He and his wife, the former Maria Louisa Condict (1808–86), had eight children, four of whom were still living at this time,
including Abigail Gertrude (b. 1842), who was probably among the young
women Clemens met (Honeyman, 290–91, 293).

   [3]That is, the kisses borne on the photograph that Clemens enclosed. The "little picture" that Olivia sent, presumably a photograph of herself, has not been
found.

To Olivia L. Langdon
27 February 1869 • Lockport, N.Y.
(MS: CU-MARK)

                                                            Lockport, Feb. 27.
   Livy dear, it does seem that I am doomed never to get a satisfactory
chance to write you again. They gave me no opportunity at Mr. Nevius's,
& so I traveled all night last night, purposely that I might have plenty of
time to-day.[1] But now the day is nearly gone & I have only just gotten rid
of an old California friend or two & the inevitable "committee."[2] And I
have raced my feet off in the storm trying to find the villain (of the "committee") who has got your letter—but of course I have failed, so far. If it
were not wicked, I could cordially wish his funeral might occur tomorrow. However, I have bribed a man to find & bring me his body, dead or
alive—& that letter. I *know* it is from you—there is no question about
that.
   We did not see Mrs. Brooks, my love. As I wrote you from Stuyvesant, she was out. We drove out there in the evening. I was not so very

sorry she was absent, because I preferred to talk to Mr. Langdon, anyhow—for I love him, & I only *like* Mrs. Brooks. Having made the call,
my conscience was clear, because my Livy's orders had been obeyed—
& without orders from you, & *only* you of all people in the world, I
wouldn't have gone—for you know I wouldn't be likely to forget that
neither she nor her husband invited me to come back when I was there
last.[3] But I would go there fifty times if you desired it. Mr. Langdon acted
very badly—& that was one reason why I didn't grieve when we found
her absent. He *persisted* in getting shaved before starting, & for no other
reason ˌthanˌ that he wanted to "show off." He wanted to appear better
looking than me. That was pure vanity. I cannot approve of such conduct
as those.

I could not get much of Mr. Langdon's company (except his Coal
company.) I hardly like to tell on him,—but ˌLˌivy you ought to have seen
what sort of characters he was associating with. He had his room full of
them all the time. He had two abandoned coal-heavers there from Scranton, & two or three suspicious looking pirates from other districts, & that
dissolute Mr. Frisbie from Elmira, & ~~the~~ ˌaˌ notorious character by the
name of Slee, from Buffalo.[4] But it was pleasant. The subject of coal is
very thrilling. I listened to it for an hour—till my blood curdled in my
veins, I may say. And what do you suppose they are going to do? Why
they are going to take the Captain's case into consideration. The Captain
lives at Buffalo, you know. The Captain is all very well, but he don't suit
~~me.~~ ˌthe Company.ˌ He wants his salary raised to three thousand. He says
he can't live on less. Simply because he has a large family to support—
as if the coal company ~~is~~ ˌwasˌ responsible for his family—or any of his
other crimes, for that matter.[5] No—the captain will find that the large-
family dodge won't answer. It is too old. We want something fresh. He
lives in a twelve thousand-dollar house, you know, & ~~they~~ his lease is
about out, & they are going to raise the rent on him from $500 to $800 a
year—& just on that pretense he wants his wages advanced $600ˌ,ˌ per
annum. [*torn in order to cancel:*] I [j◇◇◇] ros[◇ ◇p] &

[*seven lines (between 6 and 40 words) torn away*][6]

The Captain is all very well, you know, but he is altogether too valuable.
He not only transacts all the duties that belong in his departments, but
he transacts a little of everything that comes along. And maybe you won't
b[e]lieve it, but he has actually been selling hundreds of dollars worth of

coal on *tickets*—(hence the term "on tick.") He sold a lot ˏof ɨt demurrage & other stuffˏ on tickets to a Canadian mining company years ago, & they have got that ~~coal~~ ˏplunderˏ yet. Think of selling coal for *tickets*, Livy— when *you* know, & *I* know, that tickets are not good for anything but bread, & to travel on railroads with. But hereafter the notorious Slee will have to take charge of everythingˏ ˏin Buffaloˏ himself—& the Head Centre (I mean the Head Salesman)[7] will hire & discharge the men under him to suit himself, & be personally responsibleˏ ˏto Mr. Sleeˏ —& the Captain will have to keep his fingers out of that pie, & go remarkably slow on the Ticket system, too. And his wages will not be raised, either, unless Mr. Slee thinks fit. ~~But~~ The Captain's ~~family~~ salary *isn't* high enough, according to the size of his family as it now stands, & so it is plain enough to *any* noodle that that family has got to be reconstructed. Therefore, the salary will remain just as it is, & Mr. Slee will proceed to cut ˏdownˏ the Captain's family ~~down~~ to fit it. Business is business, you know. [*in margin:* Mr. Slee gave me a very cordial invitation to visit his home in Buffalo, & I shall do it, some day. I like him first-rate.][8]

[Livy, they spell Plymouth without the u—take courage, my darling.][9]

Mr. Langdon thought of going up to Hartford about to-day, to see the Hookers;[10] & you may well be glad of it, for he would wear himself out with business in New York in another week. He was at it all the time. However, he was in good spirits, & apparently in excellent health.

When I read your Stuyvesant letter I was inclined to be angry with Bement, at first, for writing you a note that made you down-hearted, but upon reflection I felt more charitable. He *couldn't* write you a cordial letter, dear—it wouldn't be human nature—for he loves you himself. Don't talk back, Livy! He *does* love you—& so how *could* he rejoice that you are lost to him?[11]

I am glad I marked those books for you, since the marking gives you pleasure, but I remember that the pencilings are very meagre—for which I am sorry. I have marked many a book for you, in the cars—& thrown them away afterward, not appreciating that I was taking a pleasure of any great moment from you. I will do better hereafter, my precious little wife.

And so *you* have been having visions of our future home, too, Livy? I have such visions every day of my life, now. And they always take one favorite shape—peace, & quiet—rest, & seclusion from the rush & roar

& discord of the world,—You & I apart from the jangling elements of the outside world, reading & studying together when the day's duties are done—in our own castle, by our own fireside, blessed in each other's unwavering love & confidence. But it makes me ever so restive, Livy!— & impatient to throw off these wandering duties that thrall me now, & take you to my arms, never to miss your dear presence again. Speed the day! How I dread the California trip. Three awful months without seeing Livy once—it weakens my resolution to think of it. It is not a week since I saw you, & yet it seems already an age, & I would walk twenty miles through this snow-storm to kiss you, Livy. How will three months seem to me? A century.

Livy, darling, I see by your letter that you are not sleeping enough. Do you want to break this old heart of mine? But I was ever so glad to hear that when your father left, that morning, at 9 o'clock, you were still in bed. What I do *long* to hear, Livy, is that you lie abed *late* in the morning—that you don't get up until your dear eyes *refuse* to stay shut any longer. For it is the *morning* sleep that is so strengthening, Livy. An hour of it is worth any other *three* hours. *Please* sleep later, Livy. I have talked it over with your father, & *he* is ready to le miss the blessing of your presence at breakfast in order that you may become more than ever a blessing to him by building up your strength through late sleeping. I want to see you looking strong and healthy when I take you in my arms on the 17th of March, Livy—& I *can* see you so, if you will only listen to my pleadings & sleep till ten o'clock every morning. Please, Livy darling.

Your new letter is come! No, Livy, Livy, Livy, I *can't* see that you are in constant danger of pursuing your own tastes & pleasures instead of giving up your life for others. What I *do* see, though, is that you are always sacrificing yourself for other peoples' benefit. I *know* it, Livy. You are doing enough. You are doing *all* that God has given you strength to do, & I tremble every time I detect a disposition in you to tax that strength further. Livy, the sweet spirit that goes out from you carries a constant blessing to the every member of the little circle you inhabit. You bless *many* persons by your beautiful life, while w most per people bless only one or two or three, by theirs—& therefore, why not be content? No, no, darling, it makes me uneasy, these thinkings, these longings & aspirings after a broader field of usefulness.[12] It is because such thoughts & such broodings have their effect upon your physical strength—they waste it, they burn it out—& I so long to see you have a strength-restoring season of calm, of contentment, of tranquillity, both of mind & body—for then I *know* you would grow strong, & cheery & happy. *Then* you could think of others' weal as much as you wished, Livy, & I would gladly help you scheme & plan & execute. Don't be hurt at my solicitude, & my anxiety about your health, darling, for it is born of my strong, deep, deathless love for you, my worshipped idol.

I will send Hattie a photograph of the old pattern, & when I sit again, I will send her a new, one.[13] [I talk of sitting, as complacently as if I were an old hen, & used to it.] And this reminds me that I told Mrs. Fairbanks you would sit for a large photograph for her, (like mine that hangs in the library,) as a companion to the one I gave her. She said she wanted her son & her daughter *both*, where she could look at them when she pleased,. But you needn't hurry, Livy—in the spring will do. I will take you to the photographer's & "fix" you,, to suit myself.

The ring continuing to be "the largest piece of furniture in the house" is a burst of humor worthy of your affianced husband, Livy,, you dear little Gravity. How I envy you your multiplicity of cousins!—for I can hardly claim a relative in the world outside our own family. I suppose it *will* be hard to write that letter to the Chicago cousin, under the circumstances, but then you are the brave girl that can do it.[14]

I did not try to get the porcelain picture taken in New York because I would have no chance to examine "proofs" of it, having only half a day to spare there—but I will sit for it in Hartford.[15] Which reminds me, honey, that you must direct your letters henceforward to "Saml. L. Clemens, 148 Asylum st., Hartford,"[16] & thus oblige the man who loves, *loves*, LOVES you, Livy!

I kiss you, my own darling, on lip & cheek & brow, & bid you good=night, & pray that the ministering spirits of God will have you in their keeping & shield you from all harm.

Tell your mother that her eldest son is well, & sends his love.

Thine, until Death doth us part,
Saml.

 —————————————————————————————————————

Miss Olivia L. Langdon
Present.

Care of Charlie.

[*docketed by OLL:*] 44th

[1] If Clemens left Stuyvesant at 9:00 A.M. on 26 February, as planned (see the previous letter), he must have traveled all day as well as all night to reach Lockport, which was approximately 250 miles to the northwest, near Lake Ontario.

[2] Neither the California friends nor any members of the committee have been identified. The latter group represented Clemens's Lockport sponsor—the local post of the Grand Army of the Republic, the organization of Civil War veterans created in 1866 to help families of Union men killed in battle, and to lobby for improved government benefits for surviving veterans ("New Advertisements," Lockport *Journal*, 2 Mar 69, 2, TS in CU-MARK).

[3] Clemens apparently was "there last"—that is, at the Fifth Avenue and 53rd Street home of Fidele and Henry Brooks—on 3 November 1868, several weeks before Olivia accepted his marriage proposal. Then his "Honored Sister," she had insisted that he introduce himself to the Brookses (*L2*, 278 n. 2).

[4] Two of the "characters" Jervis Langdon consorted with have been identified. Eaton N. Frisbie (1833–93), mayor of Elmira in 1868, was president of the Pittston and Elmira Coal Company. John De La Fletcher Slee (1837–1901) was an 1862 graduate of Genesee College, at Lima, New York, and valedictorian of his class. In 1866 he had left a post as professor of Greek and German at Fally Seminary, in Fulton, New York, to go to Buffalo as western sales manager for Jervis Langdon's coal firm. In 1869 he was "the authorized business agent," "general salesman," and "highest officer" of the Anthracite Coal Association of Buffalo, which was formed in 1861 and included the Delaware, Lackawanna and Western Railroad Company as well as Frisbie's and Langdon's firms. When Langdon reorganized his business in May 1870 as J. Langdon and Company, Slee became one of his partners, along with Charles J. Langdon and Theodore W. Crane. Slee had been married since 1862 to the former Emma Virginia Underhill, with whom he had four children ("Coal & Wood," Elmira *Advertiser*, 27 Feb 69, 2; Towner 1892, 351; Gretchen Sharlow and Herbert A. Wisbey, Jr., personal communication; Chemung County Historical Society Biographical File, information courtesy of Timothy L. Decker and Nick Karanovich; SLC 1869m; "Late J. D. F. Slee," Elmira *Gazette*, 10 June 1901, 5; Smith, 2:201; "In Memoriam," Elmira *Saturday Evening Review*, 13 Aug 70, 5).

[5] George Dakin (1815–82), formerly a steamboat captain on Seneca Lake, an independent coal dealer, and a farmer, had gone to Buffalo in 1861 to establish coal yards and supervise coal shipments for the Delaware, Lackawanna and Western Railroad Company. He became known as "practically the founder of the coal business of Buffalo" and the "foremost coal merchant of the city." Dakin and his wife, the former Charlotte Brown, had three sons and four daughters (obituary, Buffalo *Courier*, 2 May 82, 2, TS in CU-MARK).

[6] Clemens tore away the bottom third of the manuscript page. The excised passage probably began: "I just rose up &".

[7] Unidentified.

[8] Clemens and Slee remained good friends for more than thirty years, with Slee occasionally providing assistance in business and personal matters (see Reigstad 1989, 1, 3, 4–5, for details of the friendship).

[9] This teasing aside has not been explained. It may refer to William Bradford's *History of Plimoth Plantation*, written between 1620 and 1647 but not published until 1856 (White, 62), which was conceivably among the books Clemens said he had marked for Olivia (see his seventh paragraph).

[10] John and Isabella Beecher Hooker.

[11] Edward P. Bement evidently worked for Jervis Langdon. Clemens had been persuaded for some time that he was a disappointed suitor of Olivia's (see 6 Mar 69 to OLL and CJL [1st of 2], p. 139, and *L2*, 321 and 369).

[12] Clemens had previously counseled Olivia against a life of active "usefulness" in his letter of 22 January.

[13] For an example of "a photograph of the old pattern," see the previous letter. It is not known whether Clemens ever made good his promise to Harriet Lewis.

[14] Possibly Andrew Atwater, a cousin of Olivia's who seems also to have been a suitor (see 8 and 9 Mar 69 to OLL, p. 154).

[15] See 12–13 Mar 69 to OLL.

[16] The address of the American Publishing Company.

To Jane Lampton Clemens and Family
27 February 1869 • Lockport, N.Y.
(MS, *damage emended:* NPV)

Lockport, N. Y., Feb. 27.

Dear Folks—

I enclose $20 for Ma (No. 10,.) I thought I was getting a little ahead of her little assessment of $35 a month, but find I am falling be-hindhand instead, & have let her go without money.[1] Well, I did not mean to do it. But you see when people have been getting ready for months, in a quiet way to get married, they are bound to grow stingy, & go to saving up money against the awful day when it is sure to be needed. I am particularly anxious to place myself in a position where I can carry on my married life in good shape *on my own hook*, because I have paddled my own canoe so long that I could not be satisfied, now, to let anybody help me—& my proposed father-in-law is naturally so liberal that it would be just like him to want to give us a start in life. But I don't want it that way. I can start myself. I don't want any help. I can run the insti-tution without any outside assistance; & I shall have a wife who will stand by me like a soldier through thick & thin, & never complain. She is only a little body, but she hasn't her peer in Christendom. I gave her only a plain gold engagement ring, when fashion imperatively demands a two-hundred dollar diamond one—& told her it was typical of her future lot—namely, that she would have to flourish on substantials rather than luxuries. [But you see I *know* the girl—she don't care anything about luxuries, for ˌandˌ although she has a respectable fortune in jewels, she wears none of any consequence. One seldom sees a diamond about her.] She is a splendid girl. She spends no money but her usual year's allowance, & she spends nearly every cent of that on other people. She will be a good sensible little wife, without any airs about her. I don't make intercession for her beforehand & ask you to love her, for there isn't any use in that—you couldn't help it if you were to try. In fact, you had better, in self-defence, take warning by Mrs. Brooks & all of Livy's other friends, & try to learn to *hate* her—for I warn you that whosoever comes within the fatal influence of her beautiful nature is her willing slave forevermore. I take my affidavit on that statement. Her father & mother & brother embrace her & kiss her & pet her constantly, precisely as if she were a *sweetheart*, instead of a blood relation. She has unlimited power over her father, & yet she never uses it except to make him help people who stand in need of help, & lavishes

[*seven lines (about 40 words) missing*][2]

allowance.

But if I get fairly started on the subject of my bride, I never shall get through—& so I will quit right here. I went to Elmira a little over a week ago, & staid four days & then had to go to New York on business. Now Lockport wants a lecture—shall talk to-night & Monday night,[3] & then I shall go to Hartford, avoiding New York city if possible so as to save time. I will

[*thirteen lines (about 75 words) missing*][4]

[1] Since March 1868 Clemens had been sending his mother an average of forty dollars per month, slightly more than she had requested, and therefore he was in fact "a little ahead" on his commitment to her. Since early December 1868 he had sent the money in twenty-dollar increments, which she recorded and numbered consecutively on the blank pages of one of his old piloting notebooks. Most of the letters enclosing these payments have not survived, but her record, kept in Clemens's 1860–61 notebook, shows that she received twenty dollars from Clemens on 18 and 26 January 1869 (payments she numbered 7 and 8), on 3 February (numbered 9), and on 3, 6, and 30 March (numbered 10, 11, and 12) (JLC, 4).

[2] If, as seems likely, the missing passage included some further remarks about Olivia which Clemens asked be kept private, it was probably excised by his immediate family before the remaining text was passed on to other, less intimate, relatives and friends. Whatever the motive, Clemens's family were much the

most likely persons to have removed both this and the later passage as well, for by the time Albert Bigelow Paine first published the letter (*MTB*, 1:378–79), the damage had already been done.

[3] That is, Saturday, 27 February, in Lockport, and Monday, 1 March, in Geneseo, New York—but the Lockport lecture had to be postponed (see 28 Feb 69 to OLL).

[4] Although paper sufficient for only thirteen lines is demonstrably missing (the bottom two-thirds of manuscript page number 6), it is likely that more of the original letter was destroyed or removed. For on the evening of 28 February, Clemens told Olivia that he had written "quite á long letters home & to Mrs. Fairbanks last night & this morning." If he had concluded this letter home at the bottom of page 6, it would have been only two-thirds as long as the letter to Fairbanks.

To Mary Mason Fairbanks
27 and 28 February 1869 • Lockport, N.Y.
(MS: CSmH)

Lockport, N.Y., Feb. 27.

Dear Mother—

I would have written you long ago, but about all of that "long ago" was spent in Elmira, & somehow I never could find time to write letters while there. All the time was exhausted in talking with Livy about the weather. The ring came safely to hand—& to us it will be a perpetual reminder of your goodness & your love, since your memory will always be pleasantly associated with it—it came safely to hand, & ƗLivy is manacled with it now, a hapless prisoner for life. She writes, "The ring continues to be the largest piece of furniture in the house, & so in company I am oppressively conscious of it." She disposes ~~her~~ that hand in such awkward & unnatural positions that Hattie, always ready for any cussedness that offers, whispered the question in company, "if her shoulder was dislocated?",—& ~~Livy~~ the conscious Livy blushed. I shall scalp Hattie yet, if she don't go mighty slow. I forgot to tell Livy, but I have written her, that I promised you a large photograph to hang up in your library as a companion to mine—but I told her to hold on till I come, & I will "sit" her myself. In fact she ought to hold on till some time when she is in New York, for she has amply proved by sitting five times for a photograph for me that they *can't* take even passable photographs in Elmira. I want her to look her best, because she isn't as comely as she was a year ago. But she is just as *lovely*—she is every bit as good & lovely as Mrs. Severance,—which, I take it, is saying a good deal.[1]

You remark:

"I am lovely in the midst of confusion. Allie & my husband are gone, & I am reveling in dust & paint."[2]

Why you are *always* lovely, Mother dear. I don't say but what you are *peculiarly* lovely when you are in the midst of dust & confusion, but what I do maintain is, that *in* confusion or *out* of it you are *always* lovely. There, now—don't that cheer you up?

Considering all things, I came out well enough with my appointments, notwithstanding my entanglements gave a power of dissatisfaction. I was in honor *bound* to go to Alliance from Ravenna, because in dismissing the Alliance audience the night I failed to appear, they had *held on to the money*, and had *promised* that the lecture should come off within a week. So I telegraphed Franklin that I would not be there till Wednesday. I pai I paid Alliance their extra expenses, amounting to $20; I paid Franklin *their* extra expenses, amounting to $10—& then found that while I could have made Geneseo easily enough from Titusville, I couldn't do it from Franklin. So I telegraphed them to stop the lecture & send my bill, which they did. I paid it—$22.5 $22.25. So that out of those extras cost me $52 altogether, & over thirty ˏseveralˏ dollars extra traveling expenses, & four or five valuable days' time—for I have to go to Geneseo at last, to satisfy those people. Alliance cost me much more than a hundred dollars, & only paid me eighty. But don't you know that the hand of Providence is in it somewhere? You can depend upon it. I never yet had what seemed at the time to be a particularly aggravating streak of bad luck but that it revealed itself to me later as a royal piece of royal good-fortune. Who am I, mother, that I should take it upon myself to determine what is good fortune & what is evil? For about a week, Providence headed me off at every turn. The real object of it, & the real result, may not transpire till you & I are old, & these days are forgotten— & therefore is it not premature, now, to call it bad luck? We *can't tell*, yet. You ought to have heard me rave & storm at a piece of "bad luck" wi which befel me a year ago—& yet it was the very individual means of introducing me to Livy![3]—& behold, now am I become a philosopher who, when sober reflection comes, hesitateth to rail at what seemeth to feeble finite vision ill luck, conscious that "the end is not yet."[4]

Yes I did receive your letter at Franklin—& answered it, too,[5]—
notwithstanding you think ˬthat possiblyˬ I have "soared beyond the
reach of human sympathy at its need." And I *don't* forget, "in all my
bright hours & in all my happiness" that you are my "faithful friend &
Mother." I should be a faithless ingrate to do such a thing. So far am I
from it, that I remember you & recall you *without effort, without exercise
of will;*—that is, by *natural impulse*, undictated by a sense of duty, or of
obligation. And that, I take it, is the only sort of remembering ~~worth~~
ˬworth theˬ having. When we think of friends, & call their faces out of
the shadowsy & their voices out of the echoes that faint along the corridors of memory, & do it without knowing *why*, ~~but~~ save that we *love* to
do it, we may content ~~out~~ ourselves that that friendship is a Reality, &
not a Fancy—that it is builded upon a rock, & not upon the sands that
dissolve away with the ᶁ ebbing tides & carry their monuments with
them.[6]

I shall reach Hartford about the 5[th] of March & go to work on the
book again—My address will be "*148 Asylum street, Hartford*"—& on the
17[th], if nothing happens, I shall arrive in Elmira again, to stay a week
[*torn in order to cancel:*] [or] t[w]o[,] n[◊ do◊◊◊◊] A[nd]

[*two lines (about 15 words) torn away*][7]

I ought not to say anything about staying a week or two, either—for ~~their~~
there is a possibility that business will so hurry me that I may not even
be able to stay a day or two. Whatever time I spend there will have to be
taken from my visits in Cleveland & St. Louis on my way to Califor[a.], &
my time is so cut down, now, ~~the~~ that there is scarcely *any* of it left. I had
hoped to be in San Francisco by the end of March.

Remember me to all the home folks, & receive thoug the love & the
blessing of thy eldest son—

Sam

Did you see my Vanderbilt letter in the last issue of Packard's
Monthly?[8]

[1] For a photograph of Emily A. Severance, see *L2*, 433.
[2] Mrs. Fairbanks was supervising repairs to the family's Cleveland home,
damaged by fire on 1 February (see 5 Feb 69 to Fairbanks, n. 3). "Lovely" was
possibly Clemens's mischievous misreading of "lonely," but this cannot be confirmed since Fairbanks's letter is now lost.

[3]Clemens's reference cannot be to the first time he was literally introduced to Olivia, since that occurred two months *before* the "bad luck" that struck him just "a year ago." The bad luck he had in mind was probably a crisis that developed between 22 February and 8 March 1868, and that seemed for a while to imperil his plans for a book about the *Quaker City* excursion. In those two weeks, the proprietors of the San Francisco *Alta California* firmly declined to give him permission to reuse the newspaper letters that he had written, and they had published, about the excursion. Their refusal forced him to sail for San Francisco on 11 March, where he soon resolved the problem, and proceeded to finish his manuscript. Shortly after delivering his manuscript to his Hartford publisher, in August 1868, Clemens visited the Langdons in Elmira, where he was introduced to Olivia in the sense that is meant here (*L2*, 198–200, 242–43, 247; compare *MTMF*, 79–80 n. 1).

[4]Matthew 24:6: "And ye shall hear of wars and rumours of wars: see that ye be not troubled: for all these things must come to pass, but the end is not yet."

[5]See 17 Feb 69 to Fairbanks from Franklin, Pennsylvania.

[6]Compare Luke 6:48–49:

He is like a man which built a house, and digged deep, and laid the foundation on a rock: and when the flood arose, the stream beat vehemently upon that house, and could not shake it; for it was founded upon a rock.

But he that heareth, and doeth not, is like a man that without a foundation built a house upon the earth; against which the stream did beat vehemently, and immediately it fell; and the ruin of that house was great.

[7]Clemens tore off all but a few words of the last three lines on the page. The excised passage probably began: "or two, no doubt. And". It may have been at this point that Clemens returned to his letter and revised it on the morning of 28 February.

[8]"Open Letter to Com. Vanderbilt" was a sarcastic attack on steamship and railroad tycoon Cornelius Vanderbilt, written in reaction to the uncritical admiration his shrewd practices usually received from the press. It was published in the March issue of *Packard's Monthly: The Young Men's Magazine*, which appeared about the middle of February. Begun in May 1868, *Packard's Monthly* predicted that its circulation by the end of 1869 would be 100,000, and boasted of grappling "with the evils of the day" and presenting them "as they are, without mitigation or remorse" ("The Magazine" and advertisement, *Packard's Monthly* 2 [Jan 69]: 31 and back cover). It was founded, edited, and published by Silas Sadler Packard (1826–98), who was also the founder and principal of Packard's Business College in New York, as well as the author and publisher of numerous books on penmanship, bookkeeping, and other business skills. On 22 October 1868 Clemens wrote to the San Francisco *Alta California* that he had met Packard while "coming down the street in New York the other day"—a meeting very likely engineered, on about 1 October, by Clemens's *Quaker City* friend and cabin mate, Daniel Slote, whose firm published Packard's "school copy books" (SLC 1868k; advertisement, *Packard's Monthly* 2 [Mar 69]: inside front cover). "Open Letter to Com. Vanderbilt" was the first of Clemens's three contributions to *Packard's Monthly* in 1869 (SLC 1869b, 1869g, 1869i). Clemens never reprinted it, although he did take steps to preserve it: see 13 May 69 to OLL.

To Olivia L. Langdon
28 February 1869 • Rochester, N.Y.
(MS: CU-MARK)

Rochester, N.Y., Feb. 28.

I haven't anything to write, Livy, but then I love you so much that I must find some sort of escape for it or perish. It is an old story to keep telling you I love you, Livy, but then I *do* love you, Livy, & I *must* say it, & so you must put up with it my darling. But you are a patient little martyr to everybody, & you can bear it.

For the first time, I had to dismiss an audience last night without lecturing. It was a fearful storm, & the people could not get out. Not more than a hundred were present. Perhaps I ought to have gone on & lectured, but then the gentlemen of the Grand Army of the Republic had treated me so well (& besides there was a much-prized old California friend or so among them,)[1] that I hated to see them lose money ~~throu~~— & so I said I would foot the expense-bills & dismiss the house—but they wouldn't permit me to pay anything, or depart without my regular salary—& *I* rebelled against that. So we compromised—that is, I ~~am dis~~ talked to the audience a minute or two about the weather & got them to laughing, & so dismissed them in a good humor & invited them to come back Wednesday night & hear "the rest of the discourse"—an invitation which nearly ~~of~~ all of them accepted, for they took their tickets back, as they went out, instead of their money. So you see I am to be in Lockport Wednesday night—& on Friday, if all goes well, I shall be in Hartford, & my labors at an end. I am now on my way to Geneseo—had to leave Lockport this afternoon in order to make it. ~~Those are fine fellows in Lockport, but they stole a march on me. I entertained about fifteen~~

[*That* is the way to scratch it out, my precious little Solemnity, when you find you have written what you didn't mean to write. Don't you see how neat it is—& how impenetrable? Kiss me, Livy—please.][2]

Bless you, darling. [That was only a thought—or maybe a feeling, or an emotion—anyway, it ~~involuntarily~~ swept through heart & brain, making its way warm as it went, & I thought I would set it down—for blessings on *you*, my Livy, like a motions to adjourn, are "always in order."] Why there is material there for a very magnificent conundrum—

which Charlie can't guess, unless he is familiar with the laws that govern parliamentary bodies. For instance: Why is Livy's room like a motion to adjourn? *Answer*—Because it is always in order.

> "A little nonsense now & then
> Is relished by the best of Livys"[3]—

Don't get mad, Livy—I am shut up in a strange hotel for the night, & I must keep up my spirits. And I can't keep up my spirits in any better way than by teasing you, Livy. So you see you are very, very useful to me. Useful to me. Useful to me. *Imperatively necessary to me*—that is the phrase. Necessary to my thought, when I lie down at night & the mystery of the darkness palls the world; necessary to me my dreams, when they are of the pure & the beautiful; necessary to my moments of doubting the promises of God, as showing a hope & a blessing realized; necessary to my day, to add *gladness* to the ~~blank~~ meaningless brightness of the sun; necessary to my hands, to cheer their labor—to my feet, to calm their restlessness—to my brain, to point it to a ~~worthy~~ goal for its ambitions— & necessary, forever & ever necessary, to my *heart*, for God knows it would break without you!

I wrote quite a long letters home & to Mrs. Fairbanks last night & this morning. I told Mrs. F. I would be in Elmira on the 17th, but I said nothing about the re-union, because when I come to count it up on my fingers, my time seems pretty short, if I am going to California. And I do assure you, Livy, that I couldn't spare *you* to the re-unionists many moments at a time if I only had a few days to stay—you can depend upon that, my love. You must just have the re-union while I am in California, Livy. Never mind "Hamlet."[4]

Livy, I have a commission for you to execute. I wish you ,to, cut out every article of mine you see in print, from this time forward, always— & put them away—don't *paste* them into a book, but just put them away where we can use them some day. You can cut the Horace Greeley article out of Mr Langdon's Railway Guide—you remember I showed it to you in there.[5] Now will you do all this for me, Livy darling?

Hattie must not plague you about your arm. Ain't you ashamed of yourself, anyhow, Hattie, for pestering your cousin Livy in this way when she is in company?[6] You are always doing something like that—& you ~~do it~~ just do it out of pure cussedness, too. I won't have Livy ~~teased~~

abused by anybody but me, young woman. Now go & ~~tell your grandmother on me & get me in trouble~~—*more* ~~cus~~ — —[7]

But this wont do—~~the subscriber~~ I must go to bed. And will, in a moment—but I must kiss you first, Livy. And this kiss that I set adrift above the wastes of snow that lie between us, ~~Livy,~~ is freighted with honor, & reverence, & a tender, yearning love that shall never die.

Good-night, *my* Livy.

Forever Yours

Sam

Miss Olivia L. Langdon
Present.

Suavity of Charlie.
[*docketed by OLL:*][8] ~~42~~ 45th | counsel | councel | ~~cons~~ counsel

[1] See 27 Feb 69 to OLL, n. 2.

[2] Clemens used one of his standard techniques for rendering a canceled word or passage unusually difficult to read: in addition to his usual looping deletion mark, he superimposed on the original words several random characters with readily visible, and therefore misleading, ascenders and descenders.

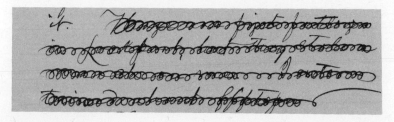

Clemens's "impenetrable" cancellation. Mark Twain Papers, The Bancroft Library (CU-MARK).

[3] A play upon the nursery rhyme: "A little nonsense now and then / Is relished by the wisest men" (Stevenson, 1409).

[4] In 1949, Dixon Wecter speculated that Olivia may have written Clemens that a reunion of the *Quaker City* excursionists without *him* "would be *Hamlet* lacking the Prince" (*LLMT*, 50).

[5] "Private Habits of Horace Greeley," in which Mark Twain poked fun at the eccentric founder and editor of the New York *Tribune*, was first published in the New York weekly *Spirit of the Times* on 7 November 1868 (SLC 1868j). Like much of Clemens's journalism of this period, it was widely reprinted by newspapers and by commercial publications such as the unidentified "Railway Guide."

[6] See the previous letter.

[7] Clemens knew Olivia's paternal grandmother, Mrs. Eunice King Ford, who lived with the Langdons at this time. He probably canceled these remarks when he remembered that she was not also Hattie Lewis's grandmother. The two cousins had never known the grandmother they may have had in common, Olive Barnard Lewis (1772?–1812), first wife of their grandfather, Edward Lewis (1768–1840) (Gretchen Sharlow and Herbert A. Wisbey, Jr., personal communication).

[8] Olivia corrected her docket number immediately, and therefore the revision is not evidence that this letter arrived before the letter Clemens wrote from Trenton on 23 February, now lost, which was actually number 42.

To Olivia L. Langdon
2 March 1869 • Rochester, N.Y.
(MS: CU-MARK)

~~Lockp~~

Rochester, March 1.[1]

I love you, Livy. That is not what I sat down especially to say; if it were, I might continue to write, now that I am at it, & never stop again. No—I wished to say, *particularly*, Be sure & send my first Geneseo letter (I mean the one *you* first wrote me, to that point,) to Hartford. Do I make myself understood? Don't you see, Livy, I was so bewitched by you, there in Elmira, that I could think of nothing connectedly & collectedly *but* you, & so I forgot to telegraph those Geneseo folks to retain your letter till I came,—& I wrote them from New York, too late—& so *of course* they had no better sense than to send the letter back to Elmira, directed to Mr Langdon. Now Livy, please don't tear it up, but forward it to me at Hartford, there's a darling.[2]

And the next thing I wish to say, is, please tell Charlie to ~~say~~ tell those tailors to make my coat nearly or full three-quarters of an inch higher in the back of the neck than this one. This one gives me the lock-jaw every time I look in the glass. The collar is an unmitigated atrocity. I want the collar of the new coat to be five inches higher than the collar of this one. Tell Charlie, please.[3]

In Geneseo yesterday I got your letter of the 25th. And so you are writing me every day? That is right, you dear ~~L~~ little Livy—only, don't you write me or anybody else when you are tired or ~~have~~ are hurried by company. I shall write you every chance I get, just the same; & any time that a letter ~~seems~~ is due from you & ⫫ it don't come, I shall feel satisfied that you needed rest, or something interfered, & so I shall be content. I am at rest & peace in you now, ⫦ my Livy, & I know perfectly well that when no obstacles intervene, you will be sure to write me regularly—but not a great many weeks ago, the failure of one of your letters to arrive when it was expected, would have terrified me.

You have been writing every day, & I only every other day. But my reason was that I had no opportunity to write oftener. I was in Geneseo ~~twenty-four~~ ˏthirtyˏ hours, & *ought* to have been permitted to write from there, but wasn't. Half a dozen young gentlemen, ~~of Charlie's~~ 20 to 25 years of age, received me at the depot with a handsome open sleigh, & drove me to the hotel in style—& then *took possession of my room*, & invited a dozen more in, & ordered cigars, & made themselves entirely happy & contented.[4] But they were hard to entertain, for they took me for a lion, & ~~were ludicrously~~ I had to carry the bulk of the conversation myself, which is a thing that presently grows wearisome. At dinner I begged off from going sleigh-riding, & said I wanted to go to bed in about an hour. After dinner they came up again. Pretty soon I spoke once more of retiring. It produced no effect. Then I rose & said, "Boys, I shall have to bid you a good-afternoon, for I am stupid & sleepy—& you must pardon my bluntness, but I *must* go to bed." Poor fellows, they were stricken speechless—they looked mortified, & went blundering out like a flock of sheep, treading on each other's heels in their confusion. I undressed & went to bed, & *tried* to go to sleep—but again & again my conscience smote me—again & again I saw that picture of their exodus from the room—again & again I thought of how mean & how shameful a return I had made for their well-meant & whole-hearted friendliness to me a stranger within their gates[5]—& how puppyish it was in me to be angered instead of gladdened by ~~the~~ that gushing cordiality of youth, a thing which ought to have won me by its very *naivete* & its rare honesty. And then I said to myself, I'll make amends for this—& so got up & dressed & gave the boys *all* of my time till midnight—& ˏalsoˏ from this noon till I left aˏt four this afternoon. And so, if any man is thoroughly popular with the young people of Geneseo to-day, it is I. We had a full house last night, & a fine success. I just *love* boys of their age with all my heart—& I don't see how I ever could have treated them discourteously. [Yes I do, too. I know the secret of it. I *wanted to read your let-*

ter—& if they had only just allowed me an hour of privacy for that, I would have been with them heart & hand from that time forth.] Some of those boys came fourteen miles, from a college at Lima, & were splendid young scalawags.[6] The whole tribe came to the hotel after the lecture, & entertained me with vocal & piano ~~mush~~ music in the parlor, & with cider & whole worlds of tobacco smoke—but *they* drank a little of everything, & made music which you might have heard a mile. I played sedate old gentleman, but never reproved them once, for I couldn't help saying to myself, You'll be all the better men for sowing your wild oats while you are *young*—*I*'ll go your security. They assembled in the street before the hotel, shortly after I had retired, & gave me three terrific cheers—which was rather more honor than I desired. Of course I *half* promised to lecture in Geneseo *&* *in the middle of August*, at which time they propose to give me a ball & a concert—& I also *half*-promised to spend my summer vacation there—& I have made that *half*-promise in a good many places, (but always with the thought in my mind, "It will depend entirely upon where *Livy* is going to spend her vacation"—for I don't propose to be very far from *you*, my dear, when *vacations* fall to my good fortune.]

Now if you have kept up your letter a day, I ought to find a perfect feast awaiting me at Hartford—& I do hope it is the case. Remember, "148 Asylum street," Livy dear. But since you have a house full of company to entertain, I am a little afraid you won't have time to write, except after your bed-time,—& you must not do that, Livy. If either of us must suffer, let it be me.

Bless you I am glad to be in your apple sauce—or even in your soup, Livy—for it is a sign that I am in your thoughts, & therefore in your heart, the daintiest mansion that *I* ever *I* inhabited, my darling. And I pray that its doors may never be closed against me until one or the other of us shall go forth forever from among the living. You were brave, Livy—it was like you to come out & acknowledge ~~that you~~ what was in your mind, ~~wh~~ without adopting one of those false little subterfuges usual in such circumstances & commonly regarded as permissable.

I still look among the faces in my audiences for one like yours—for one that shall give token of a nature like yours—& I still look in vain. And so I grow prouder & prouder of you day by day, *&* as each new evidence comes that there is none like you in all the world. If ever a man had reason to be grateful to Divine Providence, it is I. And often & often again I sit & think of the wonder, the curious mystery, the *strangeness* of it, that there should be only *one* woman among the hundreds & hundreds of thousands whose features I have critically scanned, & whose characters I have read in ~~ther~~ their faces—only *one* woman among them all ~~that~~ ₐwhomₐ I could love with all my whole heart, & that it should be my amazing good fortune to secure that woman's love. And more, that it should be revealed to me in a single *instant* of time, when I ⫻ first saw you, that you were that woman.[7] It passes my comprehension. I have stated the case truly—& I can swear to it as I have stated it. I have known many, very many estimable & lovely women, but they all betrayed one or more unpleasant qualities—& all this time, twelve long years, I have been ⫰ growing naturally more & more critical & hard to please, as is the way of old bachelors—but behold, I have found you at last, & in you I can discover *no* ~~bles~~ blemish.[8] It is strange, it is very strange. The hand of Providence is in it. When I cease to be grateful, deeply grateful to you for your priceless love, my honored Livy, I shall be—dead. Never before, Livy—never before.

I have been reading—I *am* reading—Gulliver's Travels₍, & am much more charmed with it than I was when I read it last, in boyhood—for now I can see what a scathing satire it is upon the English government₍;; whereas, before, I only gloated over its prodigies & its marvels. Poor̂ Swift—under the placid surface of this simply-worded book flows the full tide of his venom—the turbid sea of his matchless hate. You would not like the volume, Livy—that is, a part of it. Some of it you would. If you would like to read it, though, I will mark it & tear ⫻ it until it is fit for your eyes—for portions of it are very coarse & indelicate. I am sorry enough that I didn't ask you to let me prepare Don Quixote for your perusal, in the same way. It pains me to think of your reading that book just ~~it~~ as it stands. I have thought of it with regret, time & again. If you haven't finished it, Livy, don't do it. You are as pure as snow, & I would have you always so—untainted, untouched even by the impure thoughts of others. You are the purest woman that ever I knew—& your purity is your most uncommon & most precious ornament. Preserve it, Livy. Read nothing that is not *perfectly* pure. I had rather you read fifty "Jumping Frogs" than one Don Quixote.[9] Don Quixote is one of the most exquisite books that was ever written, & to lose it from the world's literature would be as the ~~pass~~ wresting of a constellation from the symmetry & perfection of the firmament—but neither it nor Shakspeare are proper books for virgins to read until some hand has culled them of their grossness. No gross speech is ever harmless. "A man cannot handle pitch & escape defilement," saith the proverb.[10] I did not mean to write a sermon, but still I have done it. However, it is good sense, & it was a matter that lay near my heart; & so I am not sorry that it is written.

It is high time you were in bed, Livy—& so if you will put your arms about my neck & kiss me, while I look for a moment into the eyes that are dearer to me than the light that streams out of the Heavens, you may go. And take you these two kisses & place them as I would if I were there—& so Goodnight, & God bless you always, my own darling.

Till death,

Sam

Miss Olivia L. Langdon
Present.
Politeness of the Hardware Cub.[11]

[*docketed by OLL:*] 46th

[1] The date was Tuesday, 2 March. After lecturing in Geneseo the previous evening, Clemens was again in Rochester, bound for Lockport, where he had rescheduled his lecture for Wednesday, 3 March.

[2] If Olivia followed Clemens's previous instruction to "give letters 4 days in which to reach any point in the list" (*L2*, 341), she would have sent her letter on 14 or 15 February, in time to reach Clemens at Geneseo (about seventy miles northwest of Elmira) by 18 February, the date on which he was originally supposed to lecture.

[3] Clemens's tailor was Cyrus W. Fay in Elmira. Charles's record of his cash account with Clemens shows a payment of $145 for clothing from Fay on 1 March (Boyd and Boyd, 106; "Sam*l*. L. Clemens Esq In acc with C. J. Langdon," statement dated "Elmira Aug 9th 1869," CU-MARK).

[4] Some of Clemens's guests belonged to the Young Men's Association of Geneseo Academy, his sponsor in Geneseo (see 18 Feb 69 and 21–22 Feb 69 [three letters], all to the Young Men's Association). Others evidently did not: see note 6.

[5] A recurrent phrase in the Bible, for example: "But the seventh day is the sabbath of the Lord thy God: in it thou shalt not do any work, thou, nor thy son, nor thy daughter, thy manservant, nor thy maidservant, nor thy cattle, nor thy stranger that is within thy gates" (Exodus 20:10).

[6] Genesee College, founded in 1849, was part of Genesee Wesleyan Seminary, founded at Lima, New York, in 1830 by the Methodist Episcopal church. The college closed in 1871, and was succeeded that year by Syracuse University (Cummings, 156–57, 163–64, 166, 167, 427, 429; French, 384 n. 6; Bickel).

[7] Clemens first saw Olivia in late December 1867, although in September of

that year, aboard the *Quaker City*, he had seen her brother Charles's photograph of her (*L2*, 145–46 n. 3).

[8] In dating the beginning of his romantic interest in women from about 1857 or 1858, when he was in his early twenties, Clemens excludes several young women with whom he had earlier been on friendly terms: Ann Virginia Ruffner, Ann Elizabeth Taylor (or her two sisters, Mary Jane and Esther), Ella Creel, and Ella Patterson. Rather he seems to have had in mind one or more of his clearly romantic attachments: Nancy Miriam (Myra) Robbins, whom he knew in St. Louis during his years as a pilot (1857–61) and about whom he still dreamed as late as 1867; Emma Comfort Roe, "that sweetheart of mine you say got married," as he described her to his mother in mid-1863; or Laura M. Wright, whom he met in May 1858 and about whom he evidently dreamed occasionally for the rest of his life (*ET&S1*, 120–25; *L1*, 114 n. 7, 116 n. 14, 248; *L2*, 54).

[9] Clemens's comparison was prompted in part by what he had previously said about his own first book: "*Don't* read a word in that Jumping Frog book, Livy—*don't*. I hate to hear that infamous volume mentioned. I would be glad to know that every copy of it was burned, & gone forever. I'll never write another like it" (*L2*, 369–70).

[10] "He that toucheth pitch shall be defiled therewith" (Ecclesiasticus 13:1).
[11] The epithet is explained in *L2*, 341–42 n. 3.

To Olivia L. Langdon
4 March 1869 • Lockport, N.Y.
(MS: CU-MARK)

Lockport, March 4.

I am not going to write you, this morning, my little darling—I simply want to say I love you, Livy. I have not got up, yet, & shall not till after noon. My *last* lecture (for some time, at least,) is delivered, & I am so glad that I *must* fly to you (on paper,) & make you help me hurrah.[1] The long siege is over, & I may rest at last. I feel like a captive set free. Kiss me, Livy—you whom I love better [than] life—you core of my very heart—you whom I almost absolutely worship—you noblest, purest, dearest heart that ever brought balm & blessing to a weary life.

It is all over, & I am unspeakably glad. If I could only see *you*, now, I would be completely happy.

Rev. Mr. Bennett called on me last night, whose church & Sunday school I used to attend every Sunday twenty years ago. My mother & sister belonged to his church.[2] I did not know his face, not having seen him for more than nineteen years, but I recognized his voice & knew the name that belonged to it. Our family will be glad to hear of him. His visit has filled my brain with trooping phantoms of the past—of dead faces & forgotten forms—of scenes that are faded—of old familiar voices that are silent forever, & old songs that are only a memory now.

I'll go to bed again, having said Good morning to you, my precious little Livy, & wished you a pleasant day. Go you to bed also, & rest. With a kiss & a God-bless you darling, I am Yours & your o[n]ly, forever

Sam

Forgot to ask Mr Langdon to make Mr. Twichell's a̶c̶k̶ acquaintance in Hartford—it is too bad.[3]

Write me at Hartford henceforward, honey.

Miss Olivia L. Langdon

Present

Care of Charlie

[*docketed by OLL:*] 47[th]

[1] Clemens next lectured in Newtown, New York, on 16 March.

[2] The Reverend Joseph L. Bennett (b. 1823 or 1824), now evidently a resident of Lockport, was called to the pastorate of the First Presbyterian Church of Hannibal on 10 June 1848. Installed as the church's regular pastor exactly four months later, he remained in that post until the spring of 1852. Jane Lampton Clemens and Pamela Moffett had joined the church in 1841 (*Hannibal Census*, 319; Sweets, 6, 7, 17, 44; Fotheringham, 14; "The Presbytery of Northern Missouri . . . ," Hannibal *Missouri Courier*, 29 Apr 52, no page).

[3] Jervis Langdon had gone to Hartford, as planned, to call on John and Isabella Beecher Hooker (see 27 Feb 69 to OLL, p. 116). Clemens's 5 March letter to Olivia suggests that, at least in part, the visit was prompted by the Hookers' initial response to the news of her engagement. Twichell could have been counted on to rebut any criticisms of Clemens that they offered—but, as it turned out, they spoke approvingly of him to Langdon: see 12 Mar 69 to OLL.

To George W. Elliott
5–10 March 1869 • Hartford, Conn.
(*Paraphrase:* APC 1869a, 1)

From the Mohawk Valley, N. Y., Register.
By a private note from "Mark Twain," we learn that he is about to issue his new book, "The New Pilgrim's Progress," and then transform himself into a pilgrim again and start for California.[1]

[1]Neither the original letter, nor Elliott's paraphrase of it in his newspaper, the Fort Plain (N.Y.) *Mohawk Valley Register*, has been found. That paraphrase survives only as it was reprinted in advertisements for *The Innocents Abroad*, first produced in early July. Although Clemens might have written this "private note" at almost any time in February or early March, when he still expected both to publish his book and to be in California by the end of March, he most likely would have waited until he had seen tangible progress towards publication. This letter therefore may be assigned to the initial period of his 5–13 March stay in Hartford, after he first saw such progress, in the form of early proofs of the illustrations, but before he learned that his book was in fact *not* "about to issue," and that he needed to find a different title for it. Associate editor of the *Mohawk Valley Register*, Elliott had been Clemens's host, and had praised him lavishly in print, when he lectured in Fort Plain the previous December (*L2*, 335). In 1869 Elliott continued this obsequious treatment, notwithstanding Clemens soon tired of it (see 21 Aug 69 to OLL, n. 6).

To Olivia L. Langdon
5 March 1869 • Hartford, Conn.
(MS: CU-MARK)

Hartford, March 5.

What a darling little goose it is! ~~To~~ Not to know any better than to send Mrs Brooks' letter to me without reading it!—when it was left *unsealed* purposely that the dearest eyes in all the world might enjoy its first perusal. What a —. But *I* won't abuse my darling—I will leave that to somebody who don't love ~~her, as I Wh~~ the very ground she walks on, as I do. Why ~~bel~~ bless your heart, Livy, you *did* have a "right" to read it— & you needn't have been so ~~char~~ diffident about "claiming" your rights. But I must not forget to re-inclose it to you, for it is written in Mrs. B.'s happiest ~~style,~~ diction, & is fired with the enthusiasm & gilded with the graces that distinguish her conversation. I like her all the better, now, because when anybody praises *you* it unbars the gates of my heart & straightway they ~~swing~~ ₓopenₓ wide to give honor & welcome to the devotee. I get all the cuffs & you all the compliments from these congratulating friends of yours, Livy dear, (*vide* this letter of Mrs. Brooks' & the Hooker letter to Mr. Langdon), but bless you *I* can stand it—I don't mind it—I *like* it—because it shows that they have a just appreciation of you.[1] And then I know that the reason why *I* appear so shabbily in their eyes ~~in~~ is that they place me in contrast with you, you flaming sun, you ineffable princess of fairy-land. And so I don't have any sort of a show. But let them just ~~loost me~~ average me along with that vain, ill-natured, overbearing Hattie Lewis, for instance, & then they would see me shine. I expect I would just dazzle their critical eyes out. ⅄ Upon my word they are refreshing, these felicitating letters!

"Livy was such a delicate little flower, just in the soil where she grew, nurtured under such genial skies, & blossoming into a lily as pure as that which St. Cecilia, &c &c—"

⸁And now you have come & dug her up, & she will necessarily wilt & go to destruction—

That is the general idea of it, you know, but she switched off before she said, ‸it,‸ dear good woman.

These folks all say, in effect, "Poor Livy!" I begin to feel like a criminal again. I begin to feel like a "thief" once more. And I *am*. I have stolen away the brightest jewel that ever adorned an earthly home, the sweetest face that ever made it beautiful, the purest heart that ever pulsed in a sinful world. God give me grace to love & honor, to cheer & shelter it all the days of my life till I die! And when any harm shall threaten it, any pain, or sorrow or affliction brood in the air above it, Heaven give me heart to say, Lord let the blow fall on me—not her.

Keep Mrs. Brooks' letter for me, Livy dear. How my heart used to sink down, down, down, with a hopeless longing, to hear her talk like this about you, & so make you seem so unapproachable, so unattainable—so far away beyond the reach of my supplicating hands, my beseeching lips![2] But praise & thanks unto God, whose servant I am, you are all mine, now, darling, & the light of your eyes will never be turned from me nor your dear heart closed against me any more. Let them cuff me & compliment you to their hearts' content—I just glory in it. I ẃ have looked all through Mrs. B.'s letter for a sort of a crumb of a compliment to *me*—but no, there isn't anything but a beautiful Christian spirit of forgiveness toward me for going & doing as I have done, & a disposition to shake hands on *that*, & say Let by-gones be by-gones. Well, all right— I will write her a good hearty letter, & shake hands, & offer right cordially a "warm nook" by our fireside—& when she comes, Livy, I'll make it about the warmest nook that ever *she* got into, to pay for this!

But you know *me*, Livy, darling, & my "talk"—& you know that as long as she says loving, appreciative words about *you*, it will not be *me* that will ever fail to give her a royal welcome to our home. Whoever loves you is my friend—with the free privilege of "cuffing" me as much as they want to.

This letter isn't *begun* yet—but I have to go to Twichell's—promised I would. With many a kiss, Good-bye, my precious little Louise.[3]

Forever yours
Sam

Miss Olivia L. Langdon
Present

Care Charley.
[*docketed by OLL:*][4] 47th 48th

[1]Olivia presumably had shown the Hookers' letter to Clemens during his February visit to Elmira. Neither it nor the letter from Fidele Brooks is known to survive.

[2]Clemens seems to imply here that he had visited Mrs. Brooks on more than one occasion, although only one visit has been documented (see 27 Feb 69 to OLL, n. 3).

[3]Olivia's middle name.

[4]Olivia's revision of the docket numbers on this and the next letter suggests that she received them before Clemens's 4 March letter.

To Olivia L. Langdon
with a note to Charles J. Langdon
6 March 1869 • (1st of 2) • Hartford, Conn.
(MS: CU-MARK)

Hartford, March 6.

Livy my darling, when I arrived here yesterday it had been *seven* days since I had seen a line from you, & it seemed that never anything in the world looked so good to me as your letter when they handed it to me. I can very easily appreciate how you felt when my letters failed so long. And it was singular, wasn't it? I wrote almost every day—& as I write slowly, I was up very late at night writing, sometimes⸺. ‚Got a letter to=day.‚ I have only received five letters from you since I saw you, twelve days ago. Can it be possible that I have written fewer than you? If I had only had sense enough to think of it I could have written a letter in the St. Nicholas reading-room that day in New York instead of waiting all day for a room,—but that was the only ,really *good*, opportunity of writing to you that I lost while I was gone.[1] I am too fond of writing to you to, let ever let chances slip heedlessly. Why, Livy dear, when I begged you to write me three times a month (& you wouldn't, you know,) I used to write to you every day, just the same—but I didn't send them![2] *Where* is that first Geneseo letter? It *must* be at the office. Do send down & see, Livy. If I catch Ed Bement reading that, I'll tomahawk him. It was addressed to Mr Langdon.[3]

I like the pictures (for the book) ever so much. Only a dozen or two of them are finished, but they are very artistically engraved. Some of the little Cathedral views are very fine.[4] Many of the pictures are simply illustrative of incidents. They were drawn by a young artist of considerable talent.[5] I have asked for copies to send to you. There is one of me "on the war-path," which is *good*.[6] Ever since I got up today I have been re-reading the old MS, but I find little to alter. It will take me several days to get through, & in the meantime the proofs will begin to come in. So I shall need you, my little wife. However, most of the proofs will come to me at Elmira, & *then* I can make use of you. Bless you, I long to see you, Livy.

I cut yesterdays letter short last night & went up to see the Twichells (who send their love & blessing to you—baby[7] & all), but my head was so full of you & the letter cut short which I so wanted to write, that I was fidgety & unhappy, & so I came away at half past eleven. They insisted on my making my home at their house while I stay, but I feared to be in the way, & so refused. [It is funny that I am so willing to be in the way at *your* house—isn't it Livy? But then I have always felt perfectly comfortable there, & never once suspected that you so regretted my concluding to stay a fortnight that first time I visited Elmira—why it even touches my pride yet to think of it!—what did you want to go & tell me that, for, you dear little persecutor?][8]

I was just savage for I while yesterday, Livy—all through the agents, as usual. After traveling one whole night & more than half a day, I arrived here only to find that I must turn right around & *go back* to fill two appointments fifty or a hundred miles *southwest* of Lockport! They had *written* me at Lockport, as usual, in violation of my oft-repeated appeal

to them to *always telegraph* me. I finally sent word that I wouldn't go—
that I would pay all expenses the societies have incurred, & come on or
after March 20, if they still wanted me—& I fervently hope they won't.[9]
It does seem as if I never am going to get a week with you undisturbed
by the ghost of some villainous forthcoming lecture. If I had made that
long trip I would be in a nice condition, now, to lecture.

After I came home last night I wrote quite a letter to Mrs Brooks,
& accepted her "right hand of fellowship" & guaranteed her a "warm
nook by our fireside"—& I tir tried to quiet any misgivings she may have
about our future happiness. I *know* we shall be happy—I don't bother
anything at all about it. I shan't have any aim or object or ambition of an
earthly nature but just to cherish you, & honor you, & love you, & help
you, & fill all your days with rest, & peace, & happiness—& as concerns
what you will do for me, I never have had a misgiving about that, & never
shall. Your phantoms of mismated marriages, you must enjoy all to yourself my Livy—they never scare me. You are my very ideal of a wife,
"healthy" or not healthy, & I know of nothing that could make you more
absorbingly lovable than you are—& so I am well content. I know, that
I am not your ideal of what a husband should be, though, & so your
occasional doubts & misgivings are just & natural—but I *shall* be what
you would have me, yet, Livy—never fear. I am improving. I shall do all
I possibly can to be worthy of you—& my assurance of it is that I never
for one moment cease to be grateful for the dear love you have given me.
God grant I may live to prove my gratitude.

I comprehend Mr. Beecher's sermon as you have synopsized it,
Livy, & I recognize in it hope for me.[10] I had a long talk with Mr. Twichell
upon religion last night, but, as I told you, I was thinking of you, &
besides I was repentant & down-hearted for having allowed myself to get
ʄ so angry at the agent in the afternoon, & so I was not in a fit frame of
mind to converse upon so hallowed a subject—I did not & *could* not feel
worthy.

Since you speak of it, I propose to call on the Hookers to-night—
not *the* Hookers exactly, but the Burton branch,[11] & then if the original
branch invite me, I will visit there also. I am afraid I never shall feel right
in that house, though. I let my trust & confidence go out to them as I
seldom do with new acquaintances, & they responded by misunderstanding me. If I had given them *all* of my trust & confidence, they never

could have humiliated me by any ordinary slight, because then, not expecting such things, I would have been stupidly blind to them—[it just occurs to me that maybe Mrs. Fairbanks has slighted me fifty times, but I never thought of it before—I suppose she would have to knock me down to make me understand it—& even then I guess I wouldn't give her up till she told me *why*]—But it is different with the Hookers. I like them pretty well, but I believe it is more because you like them than for any other reason. And for the same reason I shall choke down my gorge & do the *very best* I can to like them well—always provided, that they will give me a chance—can't *seek* it, though, Livy darling.[12]

You see I don't care much about *acquaintances*. When I can come & go, & not be misunderstood, & can be at liberty & unweighed, uncriticised, unsuspected, a part of the very household, as at your house & Mrs. Fairbanks' my "friendship" (as we term it) really comes nearer being *worship* than anything ˌelseˌ I can liken it to—but to be a ceremonious visitor; a person of set hours & seasons; a foreigner in the household, without naturalization papers; an alien from whose ears the language of the fireside is withheld; an effigy to poke *p o l i t e n e s s e s* at & offend with affabilities that are hollow, invitations that are not meant, & complimentary lies that are as thin & perishable as the air they are made of—*this* is Acquaintanceship, & a very little of it goes a great way with *me*.

But I must go & call on my friends (or acquaintances?) the Hookers, & learn to like them with all my might for your sake—if they will let me.

And so good night, my own darling, & God & the sinless angels guard you. Please take this kiss, Louise.

Ȧ Forever Yours

Sam

✉——————————————————————————

☞ Please deliver this letter, Charlie—How are you, Cub?

———————

Miss Olivia L. Langdon

Present.

[*docketed by OLL:*] 48th 49th

---

[1] Inasmuch as Clemens received a letter from Olivia on 1 March (as he reported to her the following day) and another on 5 March, it only *seemed* like seven days

since he had last heard from her. He himself had written seven letters in the eleven days since 24 February, the day he spent waiting at the St. Nicholas Hotel.

[2] These unsent letters must have preceded 30 October, by which time Olivia had granted Clemens the "privilege of writing as much as I please" (*L2*, 274).

[3] Bement, Olivia's former suitor, soon left Jervis Langdon's employ. On 24 April 1869 he became the new proprietor of the Bazaar, on Water Street in Elmira, "a popular place for the purchase of fancy goods, toys, &c." ("The Bazaar," "Bazaar," Elmira *Advertiser*, 24 Apr 69, 4).

[4] One full-page and five "little" cathedral views appeared in *The Innocents Abroad* (chapters 18 and 22). The list of illustrations in the front of the book numbered them 58, 59, 60, 62, 63, and 79 which, together with other evidence, suggests that Clemens certainly saw more than "a dozen or two" illustrations at this time. His report that only that number had been "finished" must therefore mean electroplated and sent to the typesetter—presumably those that would be needed soonest: twenty-one illustrations for chapters 1–9, numbered 3 through 23 in the list of illustrations. Probably the only form of the illustrations Clemens saw at this time were the artist's, or engraver's, proofs, taken directly from the woodblock. Notably, he gives no sign that he was troubled by how few illustrations were "finished," even though a month earlier Bliss assured him that the American Publishing Company was about to receive the "*first batch*" of electros that week, and could thereafter "push the *electrotyping*, rapidly" (14 Feb 69 to Bliss, n. 1).

[5] True W. Williams, the principal illustrator for *The Innocents Abroad*, was employed at this time by the New York firm of Fay and Cox, which had contracted with Bliss to provide the 234 wood engravings for the book. Williams later contributed illustrations to *Roughing It* (1872), *The Gilded Age* (1874), and *A Tramp Abroad* (1880), and he was the principal illustrator for *Sketches, New and Old* (1875) and *The Adventures of Tom Sawyer* (1876). He also helped illustrate, for the American Publishing Company and other Hartford publishers, a number of works by other authors (*MTB*, 1:366; Hirst, 198–99, 207; Sinclair Hamilton 1958, 116, 155, 223–24; Sinclair Hamilton 1968, 100, 151).

[6] This illustration (numbered 40 in the list of illustrations) was probably drawn by Williams. Appearing in chapter 13, it was captioned "Return in War-Paint" and accompanies the following passage:

The guides deceive and defraud every American who goes to Paris for the first time and sees its sights alone or in company with others as little experienced as himself. I shall visit Paris again some day, and then let the guides beware! I shall go in my war-paint—and I shall carry my tomahawk along.

The same illustration was later used to embellish advertising circulars and wall posters for the book (see, for example, Advertising Circular for *The Innocents Abroad*, Appendix E).

[7] Two-month-old Julia Curtis Twichell.

[8] Clemens's initial visit with the Langdons lasted from 21 August through 8 September 1868 (*L2*, 242–44, 247–49).

[9] Only one of these two unidentified societies appears to have accepted Clemens's offer. On 20 March he lectured at Sharon, Pennsylvania, about 160 miles southwest of Lockport, New York ("Mark Twain," Sharon *Times*, 24 Mar 69, or Sharon *Herald*, 27 Mar 69, reprinted in Advertising Circular for *The Innocents Abroad*, Appendix E).

[10] It is not known which of the recent sermons by Thomas K. Beecher or Henry Ward Beecher Olivia had "synopsized."

[11] In 1866, Hartford attorney Henry Eugene Burton (1840–1904) had married Mary Hooker (1845–86), the eldest daughter of John and Isabella Beecher Hooker ("Nook Farm Genealogy," Beecher Addenda, iv; Geer 1869, 70).

[12] From 22 to 25 January 1868, while on his first visit to Hartford, Clemens had stayed with the "original branch" Hookers in their home on Forest Street. Exactly how they misunderstood and humiliated him is not known, but whatever occurred was the more memorable to Clemens because it followed upon an illusion of acceptance which lasted at least until 24 January, when he wrote his family that he was having "a tip-top time" (*L2*, 161). His determination to like John and Isabella Hooker at any cost was especially prompted by Olivia's warm friendship with their second daughter, Alice, and also by Mrs. Langdon's intimacy with Isabella ("Nook Farm Genealogy," Beecher Addenda, iv; Van Why, 4–5, 9).

To Olivia L. Langdon
with a note to Charles J. Langdon
6 March 1869 • (2nd of 2) • Hartford, Conn.
(MS: CU-MARK)

Hartford, March 6. ⎫
9 PM. ⎭

Livy dear, I have already mailed to-days letter, but I am so proud of my privilege of writing the dearest girl in the world whenever I please, that I must add a few lines, if only to say *I love you, Livy*. For I *do* love you, Livy—as the dew loves the flowers; as the birds love the sunshine; as the wavelets love the breeze; as mothers love their first-born; as memory loves old faces; as the yearning tides love the moon; as the angels love the pure in heart. I so love you that if you were taken from me it seems as if all my love would follow after you & leave my heart a dull & vacant ruin forever & forever. And so loving you I do also honor you, as never vassal, leal & true, honored sceptred king since this good world of ours began. And now that is honest, & I think you ought to reach up & give me a kiss, Livy. [Or I will stoop down to your dainty little altitude, very willingly, for such a guerdon.]

I suppose I have been foolish, Livy dear, but ~~bless you~~ I couldn't help it. I have walked all the way out to Nook Farm from this hotel, (the Allyn House,) this bitter-cold stormy night—& then concluded I would call on the Hookers **another time.**[1] Now hold on, Livy dear—don't ruffle your feathers too soon—don't "fly off the handle," as we say in Paris— but hear me out. I was going to call on the Burtons, you know. Well, it's an awful night outside—& breasting the blinding gusts of snow (for the wind was lifting it out of the streets & blowing it in clouds that made the gas ~~lap~~ lamps loom vaguely, as in a fog,) it took me half an hour to ~~g~~ walk there, & then—why *then*, the depraved & unreliable Burtons were *not at home.* Johnny (I think that is Mr. Hooker's boy's name,)[2] was there, & said *his* folks were all at home & he thought they would be glad to see me—& that there was a young lady there from somewhere—& so forth & so on. But I was justly incensed at the unaccountable conduct of those Burtons in being out on such a night; & I—I—I—I—I—

Well, I thought I had a splendid excuse to give you, & so escape a scolding, but I don't know what the mischief has become of it. There wasn't fire enough to get right warm by, & I thought I had better get back into the cold quick, while I was used to it—so I left my card, & said that as it was nearly 9 o'clock & consequently too late for visiting, in this land of steady habits, I would not go to Mr. Hooker's now, but would come again at a more proper time—& then went away, thinking to my- self, "What a ~~perfect~~ *mercy* it is that I am alone—if Livy were here I should "catch it" for just such conduct as these." I struggled against it, Livy, but I couldn't help it—I COULDN'T *help* it. Scold away, you darling little ~~rascal~~ sweetheart—because I just *know* you will. And I expect I deserve it, maybe. [But I wanted to come back & go on writing to you, Livy dear, I guess *that* was the reason—now *can't* you let that appease you?₌ ~~honey?~~—there's a dear, sweet, precious, good Livy. I'm *bound* to call on the Hooker's! E pluribus Unum! ~~(Don't~~ ‸(I do not‸ know what E pluribus Unum means, but it is a good word, anyway.) ~~Let's~~ ‸Now we will‸ kiss & make friends, Livy.]

~~You little ras darling,~~ ‸[How's this?]‸[3] ~~y~~You MUSTN'T ~~p~~ enclose other people's letters in yours—put them in another envelop. Here I thought I had a good long letter from you to-day, & behold, half of it was from my sister. What do you want to disappoint me so, for?

She has read the *l*Letter to Vanderbilt in a Western paper, & says— however, it is too much trouble to copy the passage—I will send the whole letter—there are no secrets in it, & besides it refers to my princess in one place, anyhow. She naturally feels drawn toward you, & has asked, in her diffident way, about the propriety of writing a line to you. ~~I am~~

~~not going~~ I guess ~~I'll~~ ₐI will, tell her to bang away. [Because, you know, you like to write to strangers, & it will just be fine for you to acknowledge the receipt of her letter & say a pleasant word in reply.] All that ever you will need to say will be to tell her that I am earnestly seeking a Christian life, & no letter that ever fell under her eye will seem so beautiful, ₐto her.ₐ My sister is a good woman, familiar with grief, though bearing it bravely & giving no sign upon the surface; & she is kind-hearted, void of folly or vanity, perfectly unacquainted with deceit or dissimulation, diffident about her own faults, & slow to discover those of others. She isn't such a gem as you, ~~by a long shot,~~ & neither is any other woman, but then she is ₐa very, very ~~go~~ excellent woman anyway₍,₎ ~~Livy.~~[4] You'll like her, Livy—she don't seem to spell worth a cent. You see she spells cow with a k. And she has spelled "tripped" with only one p, & she puts only one t in "delighted," & only two s's in "expression." I can stand those little blunders well enough, but I do hate to see anybody spell John with a G. I look upon that as perfectly awful. I notice that you always spell John with a G. [Now forgive me, Livy darling—you *know* I wouldn't poke fun at you to save a man's life if I thought it would wound you. *I* don't care a straw *how* you spell, Livy dear—I hardly ever notice when you make a mistake—& bless you I am just as proud of you as if you could beat the Unabridged Dictionary spelling. It would be a pity indeed if *I* presumed to criticise your spelling—I who am sown as thick with faults as you are with merits, & shining virtues, & beautiful traits of character; & yet you have found it in your heart to take me just as I am & lift me up & bless me with your priceless love—*I* never can be *your* critic, my loved & honored Livy.]

I called at the Courant office yesterday, but Gov. Hawley was absent in Washington. They said he would arrive in town tonight & call on me at the hotel.[5]

George Francis Train is here, lecturing to-night at Allyn Hall, about Ireland. I have not called on the distinguished jail-bird—I don't like him. He may have some little reason to dislike me, but none to like me. I blackguarded him like everything in a newspaper letter once, which was pretty widely copied. I would like to trot him out again, ever so well—[excuse that slangy language, Livy—I am on a slangy subject.] He is lecturing to the Irish, to-night, & lying like all possessed, I make no manner of doubt—[excuse *that*, too, Livy—I guess I had better get off of this subject.][6]

Yes, Livy, as you say, I suspect that if you write me every second day it will be as much as I ought to expect of you—& as much as your various taxes upon your time, & your frequent company-interruptions, will allow you to do. I must ~~bef~~ beware how I run the risk of being a burden to you, in either great or small things, instead of a help. Therefore, make sunshine for me—make me glad & happy, & generous toward the world & its ills, with one of those prized little missives signed "Your Livy" only when you have plenty of time at hand or when desire prompts you. [You compel yourself to write sometimes when you simply feel that you *ought* to write—& then it is a hardship to you.] Never mind me—see that you make yourself contented & happy—for that is what *I* want to see, my dear.

Well, some things *can't* be done as well as others,[7] do you know that? I have been trying my very best, for two days, to answer your letters received yesterday & to-day—& the first letter I wrote, yesterday, I laid yours on the table by me & got ready—but I wrote about twenty pages of stuff & *never* got to it. This evening I laid your *two* letters by me & began again—& wrote fifteen or sixteen pages of rubbish, & never once got to *them*. And now to-night I placed them by me once more, determined to answer them this time, anyway—& here I am. The fact is, I think to myself, every time, "Now I will just chat a little with Livy about one thing or another, & then after that I will read her letters over again & answer them." But then I chat *too long*—& so the answering has to be deferred. I guess I'll accomplish it tomorrow, Livy—be patient, my little treasure. To think that ~~in~~ within the last twenty-four hours I should have written fifty mortal pages of manuscript to you, & yet am obliged at last to beg further time wherein to answer your two letters.[8] I am acting a good deal like a "Committee of the Whole" in one of these one-horse State Legislatures, early in the session when they keep sounding the lobby's financial pulse on certain bills, by "reporting progress" ~~&~~ and "asking leave to sit again" till the lobby grows frantic & disgusted.

Goodnight & God bless you, my darling. Take my kiss & my benediction, & try to be reconciled to the fact that I am

YOURS, forever & always,

Sam

P. S.—I have read this letter over & it is flippant, & foolish & puppyish. I wish I had gone to bed when I got back, without writing. You said I must never tear up a letter after writing it to you—& so I send it. Burn it, Livy—I did not think I was writing so clownishly & shabbily. I was in much too good a humor for sensible letter writing.

———————————————————————————

Miss Olivia L. Langdon

Present.

Cart it home, Charlie,, please.

[*docketed by OLL:*] 50th

[1] The Hookers' house was about a mile and a quarter west of the Allyn House, which was at 80 Asylum Street (Geer 1869, map facing 29, 29, 40). In 1853 John Hooker had been one of the original purchasers of Nook Farm, a 140-acre plot of land in Hartford.

This acreage was bounded on the north by Farmington Avenue; the north branch of the Park River formed the western boundary. The south branch of and then the main Park River made the southern boundary as far as the eastern limit of Sigourney Street. In this same year John Hooker opened Forest Street and built his imposing brick Gothic home at the northeast corner of that street and Hawthorn Street. . . . During the years between 1853 and 1873 a community of relatives and friends grew at Nook Farm. Their activities and interests ranged from politics to journalism to the woman suffrage movement and literature. (Van Why, 7)

[2] Actually Edward Beecher Hooker (1855–1927), known as Ned ("Nook Farm Genealogy," 16, Beecher Addenda, iv).

[3] This teasing insertion invited Olivia to inspect the especially thorough way Clemens had canceled the preceding phrase. Although his initial impulse was to cancel "ras" in a way that was clearly intended to be read (as he had already canceled "~~rascal~~" in the preceding paragraph), he ended by heavily canceling the whole phrase, adding a few false leads for good measure (crossing the first letter of "little," for instance). He used the same heavy method to cancel two words in the previous paragraph ("~~perfect~~" and "~~honey?~~") and one phrase in the paragraph following ("~~by a long shot~~").

[4] Pamela A. Moffett was nearly thirty-eight when her husband, William, died in 1865 at the age of forty-nine, leaving her with two children, aged thirteen and four. Pamela had long been keenly interested in her brother's salvation. In a letter of 6 March 1864, for example, she wrote to him:

My dear brother, you talk of pursuing happiness, but never overtaking it. This may be, and doubtless is true, of him whose hopes ‚of happiness‚ all centre in this world, but it is not, and never can be true, of the genuine christian. He sees in every trial, in every bereavement, in every seeming misfortune, the hand of God interposed for his good.
He may grieve, for he is still human, indeed he must grieve, for by sorrow the heart is ʃ softened, the mind purified and refined, and thus he becomes susceptible of higher and purer joys than he coold ever otherwise know.
My dear Brother, let me implore you, if not for your own sake, for the sake of all who love you in this world, let not this admonition pass unheeded. "Turn ye, turn ye, for why will ye die saith the Lord." Let the Spirit of God, which has been knocking at the door of your heart for years, now come in, and make you a new man in Christ Jesus.

All the family but you, have given evidence of an interest in religion, and will you stand alone, and be separated from the rest, not only in this world, but in the world to come? No no it cannot be; I cannot bear to think of it. I wish you would read at least one chapter in your Testament every day, and think seriously upon it; and I will send you papers from time to time, which I hope you will read care carefully. (CU-MARK)

⁵Hawley was in Washington to attend the presidential inauguration of Ulysses S. Grant on 4 March. Clemens still wanted to discuss purchasing a share of Hawley's Hartford *Courant* (see 13 and 14 Feb 69 to OLL, p. 96).

⁶The widely reprinted letter was "Information Wanted," addressed to the editor of and published in the New York *Tribune* on 22 January 1868 (SLC 1868c). It burlesqued Train (1829–1904), the flamboyant shipping and railroad promoter, world traveler, pamphleteer, lecturer, political agitator, and Fenian. According to Train's own account, by the time of his Hartford lecture he had been jailed on thirteen occasions. "My prison experience has been more varied than that of the most confirmed and hardened criminal; and yet I have never committed a crime, cheated a human being, or told a lie" (Train, 314–25, 329). The Hartford *Courant*, in reviewing the lecture that had been announced as "Ireland's Persecutions and Ireland's Future Prosperity," observed that Train's actual subject

> was Train. Titles to his discourses are always purely ornamental; he discards them entirely in his speeches. The persecutions of Ireland were the persecutions of Train *in* Ireland, the future prosperity of Ireland, was the future of Train, depending upon Irishmen to place him in the White House in 1872[.] . . . His speech, however, was greatly enjoyed by all present; its scattering shots hit everybody and everything, and made fun enough for half a dozen lectures. The assurance of the man, his pluck, his sublime "cheek," and withal his keen satire, made him an attraction, for there is not his equal in this country. ("George Francis Train," 8 Mar 69, 2)

⁷The daredevil Sam Patch's motto, reversed: see *L2*, 254 n. 1.

⁸The three letters to Olivia written "within the last twenty-four hours" fill forty-one manuscript pages.

To Olivia L. Langdon
with a note to Charles J. Langdon
8 March 1869 • Hartford, Conn.
(MS: CU-MARK)

Hartford, 8ᵗʰ—

Livy dear, I am only going to ʄ write a page,—simply to *be* talking to you though it be for only a moment. I have been hard at work all day. I do wish I had you here to help me, sweetheart. I wrote a long newspaper article last night, & it kept me hard at it till 11 o'clock. It was Sunday & I ought not to have been at work—had resolutely foreborne to glance at page or proof of the book—but then *this* was one of those that must be written instantly, while the fever is on, for it can never be resurrected again.[1] I went to bed, then, & read the Testament now & then, & now & then the Autocrat of the Breakfast Table, till 3 in the morning[2]—but the excitement of writing so furiously (26 pages in a very few hours) & so interestedly, had made me *permanently* wide-awake, & I couldn't conjure up the faintest shadow of sleepiness. Then I turned down the gas, & for two hours I lay still & thought—thought of —. Well, you know the subject of my thoughts as well as I do. But do you know, I found that you were just as sleepless a subject as any other, & I *couldn't* [have any] success. But finally, about daylight I dropped off, & never woke again till 9.30, when I got up & have been at work ever since. [*in top margin:* .ɘɔnɘɔulƨnɒɿT][3] When I went out ~~to~~ after breakfast to see if there was a letter from you (none, my love, but I was not really expecting one, from what you had said, though inwardly wishing that I might be pleasantly disappointed,) I ~~met~~ ˏsawˏ Mrs. Burton[4]—was approaching her from behind, & arrived just in time to receive her in my arms as she lost her balance & fell backwards when climbing into her carriage. She was surprised to find it was not a stranger. She invited me to come up to dinner at 6, & now in the course of 5 minutes I am going to start. ~~Saw M~~ And I'll call on the Hookers or die. Saw Mr. Hooker a moment after I left Mrs. B. He was the very man I *wanted* to see. Because I *like* him, in spite of prejudice & everything else.

With a kiss & blessing, Good-bye, Livy darling.

ˏFor all time,ˏ ˏYrs,ˏ Sam

✉︎————————————————————————————————

[*uncanceled three-cent stamp*][5]

ˏCharlie, please tell those tailors[6] to make me a vest & pants like those they have made for me before. The rest of this letter is for Livy.

Sam

Miss Olivia L. Langdon.

Elmira

New York.

[*docketed by OLL:*] 51ˢᵗ

[1] See the next letter, n. 2.

[2] At Olivia's request, Clemens annotated a copy of Oliver Wendell Holmes's well-known collection of humorous essays (Boston: Phillips, Sampson and Com-

pany, 1858), making it their "courting book" (see 30 Sept 69 to Holmes). Clemens's marginalia are preserved on microfilm in the Mark Twain Papers and have been transcribed and published in Booth, 459–63; the present location of the original annotated volume is not known.

[3] Evidently in order to demonstrate translucence in the paper he was using, Clemens wrote the word on the back of his third page, then added the period on the front, so that both are readily visible from either side, but only close examination reveals where each was inscribed.

[4] Mary Hooker Burton.

[5] Clemens explained this stamped but unpostmarked envelope in his letter of 10 March to Olivia and Charles (see also 8 and 9 Mar 69 to OLL, n. 6).

[6] Cyrus Fay's establishment in Elmira.

To John Russell Young
8–10 March 1869 • Hartford, Conn.
(MS: DLC)

Private.—

Jno Russell Young Esq[1]

    Dear Sir—

        This is a very able article—but still you may not need it, for all that. So, if you should not, won't you let your Secretary mail it back to me at Hartford, (148 Asylum st.,) so that I can gouge some other journal with it?[2]

        My book, "The New Pilgrim's Progress," is will issue in about 3 or 4 weeks—the 200 engravings are tip-top. I like them.[3]

                    Yrs Truly

                    Saml. L. Clemens.

◼—————————————————————————————————————

[*letter docketed:*] File. | Ans. | JRY

[1] Only twenty-eight, Young had been the managing editor of Horace Greeley's New York *Tribune* since mid-1866. He would be forced to resign on 19 May, under much publicized charges of misconduct (Broderick, 127–28). In 1867 Young had arranged for Clemens to write letters to the *Tribune* from the *Quaker City* excursion. When Clemens subsequently took up his temporary post as secretary to Senator William M. Stewart in Washington, he became an "occasional" contributor to the *Tribune*, publishing five articles there in 1868 (SLC 1868c, 1868e, 1868g, 1868i, and 1868*l*). His normal rate of pay was forty dollars per column and he usually dealt personally with Young and his private secretary, Daniel Church McEwen (1843–1909), formerly secretary to Secretary of State William

H. Seward (*L2*, 54–55, 60–61, 108–9, 113–14, 117–18; "Personal," New York *World*, 24 Oct 67, 4; "Daniel Church McEwen," New York *Times*, 2 Nov 1909, 9).

[2] The enclosure has not survived, but it was most likely the manuscript of "The White House Funeral," evidently the "long newspaper article" Clemens wrote on Sunday evening, 7 March. This article, to which Clemens assigned the fictional dateline, "*Washington*, March 4, 1869," was a bitterly scornful, mock report of President Johnson's final cabinet meeting on that, Grant's inaugural, day. Clemens may have been prompted to the subject by Joseph Hawley, due back from the inauguration and pledged to call on him Saturday evening, 6 March (see 6 Mar 69 to OLL and CJL [2nd of 2], p. 145). The *Tribune*, under Young's influence, had been very outspoken in calling for Johnson's impeachment, and was therefore a logical place to publish "The White House Funeral." The text survives only in a set of *Tribune* galley proofs now in the Mark Twain Papers. Preserved at the very end of the proofs, following the end of Clemens's text, is the headline for someone else's letter, published on 27 March, but "The White House Funeral" was not published then or at any other time. The existence of proofs shows that the decision to kill the article came at the last moment, perhaps when Clemens saw the following in the Elmira *Advertiser* for 26 March:

DISPATCHES from Washington yesterday inform us that Ex-President JOHNSON lies dangerously ill at his home in Greenville, Tennessee. Dr. BASIL NORRIS has been summoned by telegraph, and left Washington yesterday for Greenville.

—A rumor was circulated in New York last evening that Mr. JOHNSON was dead. But no intelligence to that effect had been received from any authentic source, and it is therefore to be received only as a rumor without reliable foundation. (1)

"The White House Funeral" is published for the first time in Appendix B.

[3] The span of dates estimated for this letter is based chiefly on the assumption that Clemens finished the article and mailed it to Young soon after he began it— probably before 10 March. Certainly by 13 March he would not have given his book's title as "The New Pilgrim's Progress," or indicated that publication would occur in "3 or 4 weeks" (see 13 Mar 69 to Fairbanks, n. 5). And although he had actually seen only eighty engravings by 13 March, he invokes the round number of "200 engravings," which Elisha Bliss had used in his letter of 10 February, to let Young know how many illustrations were projected (see 14 Feb 69 to Bliss, n. 1). Many of the 234 engravings eventually included in *The Innocents Abroad* were still unfinished.

To Olivia L. Langdon
8 and 9 March 1869 • Hartford, Conn.
(MS: CU-MARK)

[*in top margin:* ·xu⅄ɥdS ǝɥʇ ǝsoʃɔuǝ I ·S˙d][1]

Hartford 8th.

How this precious little wife of mine does tantalize me! Here we have been married ever since the 4th of February, as it were, & she tells me *half* an incident, & then magnifies her misdemeanor by leaving out the names! Bow your naughty head & receive your scolding, you most lovely & lovable of all creatures that be upon the earth. Tell me *who* you were irritated with, & what it was about, Louise). Every single little thing that concerns you has a great, broad, measureless interest to me, & now you have given me only *half* of your confidence, Livy. I want it, all, dear. Trust me Livy, won't you?—in little matters at as well as great ones. Don't have any reserve—any weighings—any questionings about the propriety of things, Livy. Tell anything & everything, with the absolute *knowledge* that it will interest me & be honored & respected. You will—*won't* you, Livy? Except, of course, it be a matter which I have manifestly *no business* to know, or a thing which it would be unpleasant to you to tell. In such cases of course I would have you be silent—for it would ill become me to pry into them. But you understand me, my princess.

It was a happy, generous letter, Mrs. Crane's, & I thank her ever so much for it. She means that she & I shall be friends, & I mean it too,— & what you don't approve in her note, young woman, is what pleases me most. Do you suppose I could listen with any patience or any friendly feeling to a body who ventured to point out a flaw in my Livy? I wouldn't speak to my own brother if he did it, until he took it back again. To hear people praise you is music to me, & I could listen to it always—but I can't allow *anybody* to disparage you. I couldn't like Mrs. Crane if she were to do that.[2] Bless your good old heart, I love you past all power of language to tell.

Now it's a darling Livy![3] That is right. When I can know that you are sleeping late at last—the later the better—I shall be as happy as a king. Mr. Langdon will keep his promise, & from the day you begin you will grow stronger, & more happy-spirited & beautiful,—though sooth to say, there isn't much room for you to grow more beautiful than you are. Commence *now*, Livy—right away.

You *will* talk back, will you?, you obstinate thing? SILENCE! He *does* love you! You had better be careful, now. If you don't walk pretty straight I will kiss you when I come. You are a good, noble girl, Livy— & if you won't give up your opinion, why—I'll give up mine.

I was going to sit for my picture to-day, but hard work to-day & a sleepless night last night had damaged my beauty too much. I hope to do it tomorrow, though, if I can get the fagged look out of my countenance. And then I'll send it to you right away, & bring the original very shortly afterward. Only nine more days between me & happiness! But how they do drag.

Yes, the re-union will easily keep till I return from Cal. I can't talk about Cal—I dread the trip so much—not the trip, but the long separation. Unless Charlie telegraphed me every now & then, it would just be insupportable. I mean to arrange that with him.

No, Livy, I yield in the matter of sowing the wild oats. I have thought it over—& I have also talked it over with Twichell the other night, & I fear me I have been in the wrong. Twichell says, "Don't *sow* wild oats, but *burn* them." I was *right*, as far as I went,—for I only thought of sowing them being the surest way to ~~fit the~~ make the future man a steady, reliable, *wise* man, thoroughly fitted for this life, equal to its emergencies, & triple-armed against its wiles & frauds & follies. But there is a deeper question—whether it be advisable or justifiable to trample the laws of God under foot at *any* time in our lives? I had not considered that. Through your higher wisdom I now & then catch glimpses of my own shallowness, my idol, my darling. God keep you always free from taint of my misshapen, narrow, worldly fancies—& keep me always pliant to your sweet influence. You must lead, till the films are cleansed from my eyes & I see the light. Thenceforward we will journey hand-in-hand,. Hand in hand till we emerge from the twilight of Time into the fadeless lustre of Eternity.

Do I dislike to have you write of those past experiences? Why, *no* Livy. To tell of them draws their sting, relieves their pain—& who should joy to help you, to ~~shoo~~ bear you up, to soothe your troubled heart to rest & peace, if not I? Who can feel for you as I do? Who has such absolute part & ownership in all that touches you as I have? With whom can you experience such close, ~~in~~ peculiar, interior communion as with me? Whom can you open your secret heart to so unreservedly as to me? No, my Livy, you can have no grief, no burden, but that half of it, by divine right of the hopes, the loves, the lives we have blended together for ever & ever, is *mine*. Tell me all that grieves you, my other self,—give me all trust & confidence.

I am sorry that this trial came upon you, Livy, but glad that your love for me proved so sound, so strong, so sufficient. I am glad, a thousand times glad—glad, & proud, & grateful. It is a love that cannot perish.

Do you mean your cousin Andrew Atwater? *Whoever* it is, I wish to hold him in grateful remembrance if he did that which made it possible for you & me to—⊢ ˌbecome all in all to each other.ˌ[4] Oh, Livy! The clock has just struck 3! Another night without sleep! I am terrified. With kisses & blessings, good-bye my own darling.

Forever

Sam

March 9—*Noon*—Have just awakened out of such a delicious dream of you, Livy—thought you slept late, & I marched uninvited into your room & thanked you & kissed you for doing it!—a preposterous thing, which I certainly could have no excuse for doing, *except* in a dream. It was very delightful, but I thought you did not entirely appreciate being woke up to be felicitated, & ˌyouˌ turned over & went immediately to sleep again! But it was plainly & distinctly the dear old face that I so love, & the memory of it is with me yet. I hope you *did* sleep late.

Read this part of the Miscellany again, Livy, & tell me truly if youʃ ever saw a text so misconstrued, so utterly misinterpreted in all your life before—see if you ever saw a sermon wander so prodigiously wide of its proposition. And then imagine yourself to have been the utterer of the text, & see if you would acknowledge any man's right to deliberately make you appear to have said what you never had any idea of saying. Mr. Greeley has always argued simply against a poor, unmanly, mean⸗spirited *dependence* of a man upon his friends for his bread—& behold how Mr. Beecher has distorted his intent. It is not right. I say nothing against the sermon *as* a sermon, but I do say that it ought never to have been placed after that text. You can damn *any* text if you can have the privilege of placing it in an utterly false light. "Thoug shalt not bear false witness against thy neighbor."[5]

Yes indeed, Livy dear, I will furnish articles for you to cut out. You are the very little help-meet I have needed so long in this regard. Thank you.

Now you can turn over & go to sleep again,—but with a kiss first. Good-bye, my darling.

Sam.

[*enclosures:*]

PYRAMIDS AND SPHYNX.

FRIDAY MISCELLANY.

BY T. K. B.

These homes may be rude and humble; the inmates may be compelled for years to work hard and live coarsely; *but then toil will be sweetened by a proud consciousness that they no longer owe their livelihood to man's favor.* —Horace Greeley in Independent.

This sentiment, which we italicise is a favorite one with Mr. GREELEY. It appears often in his writings. It may be read always in his counsel to young men and to depressed classes. It is the "moral" of his autobiography. Ask no favors—help yourself—rely on your own energy—hold up your head—work your way—be a man!

To this style of sentiment and exhortation we reply:—

All grace, mercy and charity are effectually shut out from any society made up of struggling, determined, self-asserting atoms. The fish in the sea that eat and are eaten; cats, tigers and birds of prey that devour their palpitating victims; and great trees that rob the grass of sunshine and the earth of moisture, forbidding little ones to grow—such lower forms of life obey nature's law, (might makes right) and their laborious victories are inspired with a "proud consciousness that they owe their livelihood to no favor."

But we cannot consent that man comes by his fairest and noblest dimension in any such struggle for existence or race for preference. Gratitude for favors received; a cheerful contented dependence of weakness upon strength; a Godlike sense of care and responsibility nobly freighting the rich, the powerful and the wise, a willingness to grant favors and a willingness to receive favors thankfully;—these and similar graces of spirit and conduct seem to us far more desirable than the hard and merciless competitions which Mr. GREELEY has so courageously challenged and so famously out[-]run.

Every right-spirited man will long to support himself and be burdensome to no one. Every loving child will early wish to bring in something to the family treasury. Not for the sake of a proud consciousness of independence, pride has nothing to do with it. It is love that prompts. The loving are never too proud to ask help from the loving! The humble would rather ask and receive, than demand and exact!

The society of men should not be a great, pushing, scrambling crowd in which the strong and the cunning get ahead, and never say thank you. Society should be a great family, in which the strong bear the weak, and please not themselves, while the weak do their best and say "thank you sir."

We cease to be sons of GOD and brethren of JESUS whenever we begin our races or determine to hew our own path to prosperity. Let every man please his neighbor *unto edification.*

We would rather die in the countyhouse, an unnamed pauper having led a life of gentleness and industry, than by strivings for masteries to have gained place and renown among men and a "proud consciousness of independence." Because all good and perfect gifts come from above, we believe in looking up and asking. We believe and teach that dependence, humble dependence is the social law of CHRIST's kingdom. And they who must be independent, and must have that "proud consciousness" are as the prodigal son who took his

> goods and went to a far country and found
> loneliness and rags. Like him still, may
> all such find also seasonable repentance.

✉—————————————————————————————————

Miss Olivia L. Langdon | Elmira | New York. [*postmarked:*][6] HARTFORD
CONN. MAR 10 [*docketed by OLL:*][7] ♭ 52nd

[1] Clemens added this postscript on 9 March, enclosing a proof of the wood
engraving for a full-page illustration that eventually appeared in chapter 58 of
The Innocents Abroad. The proof he enclosed has not been found: it has been
simulated by reproducing the printed illustration (at 67 percent of actual size).

[2] Susan Crane's letter, probably written in late February and received in Elmira about 4 March, has not been found. It was evidently addressed to her family, among whom she now ceremoniously and cordially included Clemens. Jervis
Langdon replied to her as follows:

> DEAR SUE,—I received your letter yesterday with a great deal of pleasure, but the letter
> has gone in pursuit of one S. L. Clemens, who has been giving us a great deal of trouble
> lately. We cannot have a joy in our family without a feeling, on the part of the little incor-
> rigible in our family, that this wanderer must share it, so, as soon as read, into her poc-
> ket and off upstairs goes your letter, and in the next two minutes into the mail, so it is
> impossible for me now to refer to it, or by reading it over gain an inspiration in writing
> you. . . . (*MTB*, 1:379)

For Clemens's synopsis of Crane's letter, insofar as it concerned him, see 9 and
31 Mar 69 to Crane.

[3] In this paragraph and the next four, Clemens addresses Olivia's responses to
matters he discussed in his letters of 27 February, 28 February, and 2 March, in
particular: Jervis Langdon's endorsement of his campaign for "late sleeping";
rejected suitor Edward Bement; the planned reunion of *Quaker City* friends; and
his advice to his Geneseo hosts about sowing wild oats.

[4] That is, by withdrawing some prior claim on Olivia's affections, possibly in
response to a recent letter from her (see 27 Feb 69 to OLL, p. 118).

[5] Clemens must have enclosed the first section (about one-fourth) of the two-
column article that Olivia had originally sent him on Friday, 5 March, or the
following day: the Elmira *Advertiser*'s latest "Friday Miscellany" by the Reverend Thomas K. Beecher (Beecher 1869d). Horace Greeley had made the remarks
that provoked Beecher in a thoughtful essay in the New York *Independent* of 25
February, "The Future of the Blacks in America," in which he suggested that
they improve their lot by forming self-sufficient communities where they could
have employment, land, and homes independent of the antagonistic white society (Greeley). The original enclosure has not been found: it is simulated here
in a line for line resetting.

[6] Although Clemens addressed to Olivia, and even stamped, the envelope of
his 8 March letter, this is the first letter that he actually mailed directly to her
since their informal engagement on 26 November 1868 (see 2 Jan 69 to OLL, n.
12).

[7] Olivia seems to have experimented with a monogram for herself, which she
then canceled by writing her docket number over it.

To Olivia L. and Charles J. Langdon
10 March 1869 • Hartford, Conn.
(MS: CU-MARK)

Hartford, March 10.

I suppose my darling ~~Lou~~ Livy is well, to-night. I am sure I fervently hope so, at any rate. I am venturing on a dangerous experiment,
now—sitting down here ∮ to try to write half a page to you & ∮ then stop.
It isn't so easy to stop as it is to determine to do it. And I ought to be in
bed—for Nasby called at my room at 10 last night & we sat up & talked
until 5 minutes past 6 this morning. [In fancy I am getting a scolding,
now, & I know perfectly well that I deserve it. And I can't take any revenge, either—for at this distance I can't very well kiss the scolder & so
close her lips.] But Livy, I took a strong liking to this fellow, who has
some very noble qualities I do assure you, & I did *want* to talk. I won't
behave so any more, Livy dear. So you forgive me for just this once, *don't*
you, Livy?—the blessedest darling that ever did live. And Livy, it may
seem strange to you, but honestly I was perfectly fascinated with Nasby's
lecture, & find no flaw in it—yet I went there purposely to criticise, &
was not made acquainted with the lecturer until after the speech was
finished.[1]

It is another stormy night—raining & blowing great guns. I went
out to Mrs Hooker's at ∮ 7 PM, & got pretty well soaked through. [The
fact is, I met her accidentally yesterday & she gave me a good honest
invitation to come to-night—Twichell & I are to sup there on Friday.] It
is 10 PM, & I have just returned. Had a pleasant time. Little Miss Baker
was there—very pretty girl—& we played whist, Mrs H. & I against
Baker & Miss Alice. Mr. Day ~~could~~ didn't come out, on account of the
storm,—or, they thought maybe he had gone to a lecture. So I didn't see
him.[2] They pressed me very pleasantly to stay all night, & smoke as
much as I pleased in my bedroom—& urged that you would desire me
to remain & not go out in the storm ~~+~~ again, if you were here. But bless
you, you *warn't* there, loveliest of your sex, else I wouldn't be here at this
Allyn House at this moment, I promise you.

Had a negative taken yesterday, & expect to send you the picture tomorrow. Too cloudy to print a specimen to-day. The negative seems excellent,—so I look for no delay.[3]

Mrs. Hooker compares you to a dainty little wax-flower—how is that? *I* like it, Miss, if you don't. I like *any* figure that people use when they mean to speak lovingly & praisefully of my Livy. You miracle!

Nasby's visit interrupted my letter to the "little woman," Mrs. Crane, so it isn't finished yet. Must do it to-morrow.[4] [¶] Na Nasby wants to get me on his paper. Nix.[5]

To Charlie—darling scrub—Bother the account! Let the tailor look out for it himself. I'll pay him when I come. I am glad to hear of Ida ‸(concerning her age,)‸—& glad to hear you are overtaking her so fast.[6]

To Livy again—darling girl—Yes, Charlie & you are right. I did send you a letter in your own name yesterday, & stamped one the day before, intending to do the same, but had to open it to add something to Charlie on the envelop, & so had to use two envelops as usual.[7]

I am working so hard & so unremittingly that there is no life in me now—so don't look for any im in my letters, dear. I am afraid I shan't have time to finish revising the MS.

Do you know, I found there was hardly a button on the shirts I brought away with me? Wish I had got you to use your sensible eyes in examining them, instead of trusting to my awkward ones.

Must not try to answer your pleasant letter to-night, my darling little Lou Livy (*I* like Livy ever so much the best—simply used Louise because I couldn't help loving it *because* it was your name.] Go to Good night—go to bed, my pet. With a warm kiss, *eloquent* of love & honor,

Yrs always—

Sam.

✉——————————————

Miss Olivia L. Langdon | Elmira | New York. [*postmarked:*] HARTFORD CONN. MAR 12 [*docketed by OLL:*] 53rd

[1] Petroleum V. Nasby delivered "Cussed be Canaan" in Hartford on 9 March. The Hartford *Courant* reported that he "gave great satisfaction," but the rival *Times* disagreed: "Those who have not yet got enough of the American citizen of African descent, had an opportunity at Nasby's lecture, last night, (subject 'cursed be Canaan') to get a belly-full. It was a dismal failure, so far as any fun or wit was concerned, and was all 'nig, nig, nigger;' and the Republicans in that audience felt like changing the title of that lecture, to 'Cussed be Nasby'" ("Nas-

by's Lecture," Hartford *Courant*, 10 Mar 69, 2; "Nasby's Lecture, Last Evening," Hartford *Times*, 10 Mar 69, 2). Several months later Clemens himself described the performance for his San Francisco *Alta California* readers:

It is a very unvarnished narrative of the negro's career, from the flood to the present day, and bristles with satire. For instance, the interpolating of the word white in State Constitutions existing under a great general Constitution which declares all men to be equal, is neatly touched by a recommendation that the Scriptures be so altered, at the same time, as to make them pleasantly conform to men's notions—thus: "Suffer little white children to come unto me, and forbid them not!" The lecture is a fair and logical argument against slavery, and is the pleasantest to listen to I have ever heard upon that novel and interesting subject. It is necessarily severe upon the Democracy, but not more so than one would expect from Nasby. . . . Well, Nasby is a good fellow, and companionable, and we sat up till daylight reading Bret Harte's Condensed Novels and talking over Western lecturing experiences. But lecturing experiences, deliciously toothsome and interesting as they are, must be recounted only in secret session, with closed doors. Otherwise, what a telling magazine article one could make out of them. (SLC 1869h)

Clemens never published an article about his lecture experiences. In 1898, however, he discussed them in an autobiographical sketch that included an account of Nasby's Hartford lecture. Recalling Nasby's "petrified" posture and "roaring" and "ruthless" technique, he concluded that the lecturer's success, "was due to his matter, not his manner; for his delivery was destitute of art, unless a tremendous & inspiring earnestness & energy may be called by that name" (SLC 1898, 3–5).

[2] Miss Baker has not been identified. John Day was Alice Hooker's fiancé.

[3] See 12–13 Mar 69 to OLL.

[4] See 9 and 31 Mar 69 to Crane.

[5] Clemens's dismissal of Nasby's offer was less final than it appears here: see 26? Mar 69 to Jane Lampton Clemens and family. The daily edition of the Toledo *Blade* had a circulation of only 3,000. But the weekly edition, to which Nasby gave his particular attention, had a circulation of 75,000 and claimed a readership of 500,000 (Rowell, 90, 295). The *Blade* had been "one of the North's strongest pro-Lincoln publications," during the Civil War, and afterward it "agitated for the end of racial discrimination and for the amelioration of its consequences," achieving its greatest success between 1865 and 1888, while Nasby was editor and part owner (*Toledo Blade History*, 1–3).

[6] Charles's record of his cash account with Clemens shows that Clemens did indeed pay an additional bill of $23 to tailor Cyrus Fay on 31 March, two weeks after he arrived back in Elmira ("Sam'. L. Clemens Esq In acc with C. J. Langdon," statement dated "Elmira Aug 9th 1869," CU-MARK; see 2 Mar 69 to OLL, n. 3). Ida B. Clark, Charles's fiancée, had turned twenty on 7 March. He would not be twenty until 13 August. They married at the age of twenty-one, on 12 October 1870.

[7] The date of the postmark (March 10) on the previous letter, which was sent directly to Olivia, shows that she could scarcely have received it, let alone replied to it, when Clemens wrote this paragraph. Despite appearances, therefore, the paragraph was his effort to anticipate her reaction and to mollify her, if necessary—even as he repeated the deed with the present letter. If Olivia was alarmed, she gave no indication of it that has survived. In fact, by the end of March, the newly founded Elmira *Saturday Evening Review Devoted to Literature, Science,*

Arts, News &c. had received a reasonably authoritative report of their engagement:

> —Madame Rumor says that S. C. CLEMENS, a quondam California miner, who is now quite extensively known as a humorous sketch writer and lecturer, sporting the *nom de plume* of MARK TWAIN, has won the heart and hand of one of Elmira's fairest daughters. ("Local Jottings," 27 Mar 69, 8)

To Olivia L. Langdon
12 March 1869 • Hartford, Conn.
(MS: CU-MARK)

Hartford, March 12.

My Darling!—Your letter of the 8ᵗʰ & 9ᵗʰ is just come, & is the dearest, happiest letter that ever I received in all my life. *I* Why, it was like a grand, awakening, unexpected sunburst through a sky that had for many, many days *seemed* bright, ~~after a fashion~~ albeit its brightness was marred by airy mists scarce noted,—but whose lustre is all at once discovered to have been vague & dim, ~~con~~ when thus suddenly contrasted with the fervent splendors that are flaming out of the Heavens. Bless your heart I would walk twenty miles for such a letter any time, my darling little wife. There isn't a sad word in all your letter; nor a doubt; ∅ nor a misgiving; nor a shade or shadow of unrest; nor of melancholy or dejection; nor of a passive love. But it is all life, & action; strong feeling; buoyancy; cheerfulness; hope, trust, confidence, belief; and a love that is not passive, but grows, ~~exp~~—expands—*reaches forward*. And so the clouds are gone, & my Livy is *happy*. It does me more good to think of it than I can tell in words—it so lifts me up & fills all my being with a great contentment, that all my petty vexations fade away & are lost to sight. With all my heart & all my soul I bless you, Livy.

If I had not already been to Mrs. Hooker's, I surely would drop everything (but my letter to my little sweetheart,) & start this moment. But don't you see, Livy—I *only* wanted to be certain I would be treading on safe ground—that was all. My remembrances of my last visit there were still fresh, & were not entirely encouraging. And so I would rather have staid away always than have taken any chances. Under the same circumstances I would have intruded on *you*, I make no doubt—but then you have been *necessary* to me, just about ever since I saw you first, but the Hookers are not. And so, with them, I could afford to feel my way. *I* didn't know how they had talked to Mr. Langdon, you unreasonable little thing![1] Livy, darling, you don't know anything of the toiling, struggling, uncharitable outside world, & you can't readily put yourself in my place. Why, in former years I have been pointedly snubbed & slighted many & many a time—& don't you know, the necessary effect of that was to beget a habit of *caution?* Of course—it couldn't be otherwise.

But when once a body's *confidence* is secured, the whole thing if is different—slights are not expected, then, & seldom discovered. I remember that in a dream, last night, even *you* snubbed me in the most cruel way—but in my simplicity it seemed perfectly proper & right. I thought I arrived at the side gate in a carriage, & walked around to the front of the house, by the pathway, & as I neared the front door I saw you run tw toward the drawing-room window, making gestures with your hands which I took to be gestures of gladness & welcome—for I was expecting the same! But alas,! they were ẃ to warn me not to enter yet, because the phy- philosophy lette lesson was going on. I burst into the drawing-room door—but Mary stopped me & sent me to the library, & said you would come after a while. And as I went away I heard yours & professor Ford's voices discussing the properties of light, & heat, & bugs.[2] But upon my word I was only disappointed—not hurt, not offended. Why do you treat people that way in dreams, I want to know? Why can't you behave yourself?

No, my own Livy, it was unpardonable thoughtlessness in *me*, to tell you that what you revealed about my first visit had touched me.[3] It simply brought back to me my desperate temerity in venturing to locate myself for two weeks in a house where I was a stranger—& in what strong anxiety & dread I was sometimes, lest ,that, some humiliation might ẃ visit me in my defenceless position. But *you* were the magnet, & I could not depart from the influence. It seems impossible that even the faintest slight could have escaped me my notice during that forn fortnight—& yet notwithstanding on I must have annoyed *all* of you pretty often, I have no remembrance of ever having seen in it in any of your faces or your manner. So don't you bother about that first visit, Livy dear. But for that remark of yours, I would always have fancied I was quite a pleasant addition to the family circle at that time! And but for *my* stupid remark *about* your remark, my own precious Livy would have been spared her temporary distress of mind on her first page. So *I* apologize, Livy—*you* are not to do it. You close with a remark, though, that comes home to us both—the *results* of that visit. I am so glad I made it that there are not words enough in the whole language to express it. I will make it my business to forget that it ever caused you ~~um~~ uneasiness, & remember only that it gave me my darting,[4] my matchless, my beautiful Livy,—my best friend, my wise helpmeet, my teacher of the Better Way—my wife.

Livy, Livy, Livy dear, I did *write* the letters—but how could I dare hope, then, that you would ever care to read them? And so they are destroyed. ₌And I am very, very sorry, Livy, since you are.₌ I was ~~ide~~ idle ~~pa~~ every ~~day~~ ₌night₌ & part of every day, then, & could write you to my heart's content—yet ever since I have been privileged to *send* letters to you after they are written, I get *no* time, scarcely. It is well for *you*, my dear, that it is so—for I guess I would just flood you with letters₌, if I had a chance. Mrs. Hooker said I must not let you write me oftener than about ϕ twice a week, because writing was such confining & tiresome work—& ϕ I said I would most willingly have it so, if it would save you from labor & weariness, but that I must be allowed to hold ~~to my~~ jealously to my privilege of writing you *every time* I had a chance.

I *do* like "Grandmarṁ," but it is hard to talk to her, because sometimes she don't hear—& it is not easy to find subjects that she takes a lively interest in—& moreover, ~~that~~ after ~~you say~~ ₌one says₌ ₌you say₌ something to her, ~~there is~~ such an awful season of suspense ensues before you can tell whether your shot took effect or not. But ~~sh~~ we shall get better acquainted.[5] It isn't any hardship to talk to any *other* member of the family, I am precious certain of that—even that splendid cub of a Charlie, whom I think all the world of.

I am so sorry Hattie Lewis is gone. When is she coming back? I will bring her trunk from the depôt myself.

The printers are so slow about those pictures, that I shall have to *bring* them, I expect. I have only read thirty pages of proof, so far, & shall read fifty or sixty today or to-morrow (& then leave town). So you see, you'll have to help read some five or six hundred pages. Oh, *I'll* make you useful! You are just as ornamental as ever you can be—all you need is to be useful.

I am not all afraid of the Hookers, now—dine there to-night. *Woe!* WOE! WOE! you blessed little rascal!

How I do *love* you, Livy! You engaging little scold! I drove you to

it at last—& I do *love* to hear you ¢ scold! But they *shan't* pity my *I* Livy—
I won't have it. I'll cultivate them with all my might. I'll *fascinate* them—
I'll absolutely fascinate them! They shall honor you always.

Of course they abused me for taking you away from them—every-
body does *that*. But I ~~glory~~ like it—I glory in it. I wouldn't *want* people
to say: "Well, thank goodness, he has taken *her* out of the way!" No—I
like to be envied—just as the groups of men used to when I drove you
out in the buggy, & the vision of your faultless face rose upon them.
Happy dog I was! For I was & am so proud of you, my Livy!

Only five days after this, & I shall clasp my darling in my arms! How
I do LOVE you, Livy!

Good-bye—with a kiss of reverent honor & another of deathless affection—and—Hebrews XIII—20, 21.[6]

Yours forever—

Sam.

ₐExcuse mistakes, Livy—no time to read this over.ₐ

P. S.—I go to Boston to-morrow, at Nasby's request, to spend two
days with him & the literary lions of the "Hub."[7] Monday night I leave
there for New York—lecture Tuesday in Newtown, & *the*—very—
next—evening, I spurn the U. S. Mail & bring my kisses to my darling
myself!

✉—————————————————————————————

Miss Olivia L. Langdon | Elmira | New York. [*postmarked:*] HARTFORD
CONN. MAR 13 [*docketed by OLL:*] 54th

[1] Olivia must have countered Clemens's ill feeling toward the Hookers with
the news that they had recently spoken well of him to her father (see 4 Mar 69 to
OLL, n. 3, and 6 Mar 69 to OLL and CJL [1st of 2], n. 12).

[2] Darius Ford was Olivia's tutor (see 2 Jan 69 to OLL, n. 6). Mary may have
been either Mary Crossey or Mary Greene—both domestics in the Langdon
household (OLC to Jervis and Olivia Lewis Langdon, 6 Feb 70, CtHMTH; Boyd
and Boyd, 117).

[3] See 6 Mar 69 to OLL and CJL (1st of 2), p. 139.

[4] Clemens inadvertently crossed the ell in "darling."

[5] Olivia's thrice-widowed paternal grandmother, Mrs. Eunice K. Ford (no relation to Darius Ford), had turned eighty-seven on 11 March. Since 1867 or
1868, she had been in a state of "almost helplessness," according to the Reverend
Thomas K. Beecher's 1873 eulogy of her. Beecher observed that her personality
had been shaped by her having lived her formative years at a time "when getting
a living meant *incessant work*. She got her style of character at a time when every-

body if they stopped work suffered." Out of sympathy with a younger generation born to the relative luxury of the nineteenth century, she had

never been able, therefore, to make herself a composite part of this or any family. One generation cometh, another goeth. It is very high praise to say that this, which she could not approve, but which could not be changed, she bore and sometimes criticised with a humor that was almost a pleasure. Power and progress swept on, and she stood as by a river side declaring that things were slipping from under her,—not saying it unkindly, but in a way that amused them about her. (Thomas Kinnicut Beecher 1873, 1, 6–10)

6 "Now the God of peace, that brought again from the dead our Lord Jesus, that great Shepherd of the sheep, through the blood of the everlasting covenant,/ Make you perfect in every good work to do his will, working in you that which is well pleasing in his sight, through Jesus Christ; to whom be glory for ever and ever. Amen."

7 Among the literary lions Clemens soon visited with Nasby was Oliver Wendell Holmes (1804–94), who received them at his Boston home.

To Olivia L. Langdon
12–13 March 1869 • Hartford, Conn.
(MS: CU-MARK)

· · · ·

[*enclosure:*]

[inside case, under porcelaintype:]

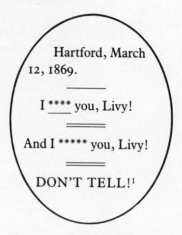

Hartford, March
12, 1869.

———

I **** you, Livy!

═══

And I ***** you, Livy!

═══

DON'T TELL![1]

[1] With its purple velvet case, Clemens's porcelaintype formed a matched pair with the porcelaintype that Olivia had sent him in January (see 22 Jan 69 to OLL). It reproduced a photograph taken by Edwin P. Kellogg, whose studio at 279 Main Street, in Hartford, Clemens had visited on 9 March. Afterward he promised Olivia that he would "send you the picture tomorrow" (10 Mar 69 to OLL), but he did not write until 12 March, and he apparently did not then enclose it. Olivia's docket numbers and his own testimony establish that at noon on 13 March he mailed her another letter from Hartford (number 55), which is now lost. He enclosed a recent letter from Mary Mason Fairbanks, as well as "half a dozen or so" illustrations cut from the proofs of his book (13 Mar 69 to OLL). Those enclosures, also lost, would surely have afforded adequate padding for this porcelaintype, with its message penciled on the case-lining.

To Horatio C. King and John R. Howard
13 March 1869 • Hartford, Conn.
(MS: PCarlD)

Hartford, March 13.

Gentlemen—

Yours of *Feb. 15*, has only just reached me. I am sorry it came so late, for I would have liked to lecture for you.

It is too late for both parties, now, however, as your season is over, & I must make ready for a short visit to California.

   You will easily excuse my delay in replying, considering the reason
for the same.

Very Truly &c.

Sam*ˡ*. L. Clemens.

Horatio C. King ⎱
Jno. R. Howard ⎰Com*ᵉ*.[1]

✉—————————————————————————————————

Horatio C. King, | 38 Wall st | New York.[2] [*postmarked:*] HARTFORD CONN.
MAR 14 [*docketed by King:*] Mark Twain[3]

[1] The 15 February invitation to which Clemens replied does not survive, but
it clearly came from a committee representing the Young People's Association of
Henry Ward Beecher's Plymouth Church. Late in 1869 that association again
tried to schedule a lecture by Clemens (see 6 Dec 69 to Redpath). Both Horatio
Collins King (1837–1918) and John Raymond Howard (1837–1926) were members of Plymouth Church—King since 1866, Howard since 1857. King, a New
York lawyer, was married to Howard's sister, Esther. Their brother Edward Tasker Howard (1844–1918) had met Clemens in Hawaii in 1866 (see *L1*, 346 n. 10,
where, however, he is misidentified as an Englishman). John Howard, formerly
an editorial writer for the New York *Times* and other papers, since early 1868
had been a member of the New York subscription house of J. B. Ford and Company, which published Horace Greeley and Henry Ward Beecher, among others.
In the early 1870s King and Howard both worked with Beecher on the *Christian
Union*, and Howard later wrote *Henry Ward Beecher: A Study of His Personality,
Career, and Influence in Public Affairs* (1891) and edited numerous anthologies of
essays, orations, and poetry (Howard and Jervis, 1:294; "Edward Tasker Howard," New York *Times*, 9 Aug 1918, 11; Noyes L. Thompson, 243, 244; "A New
Publishing House," New York *Evening Post*, 8 Jan 68, 2; Mott 1957, 422–23,
425).

[2] King's business address. His home address was 150 Hicks Street, Brooklyn
(Wilson 1868, 591).

[3] King further adorned the envelope with a sketch of a house beneath an in-
verted pyramid of ditto marks and dashes.

To Mary Mason Fairbanks
13 March 1869 • Hartford, Conn.
(MS, *damage emended:* CSmH)

Hartford, March 13.

Dear Mother—

What a time of it you do have with your fires! It was too bad—
too bad that after all your pains, all your hard work refitting & furnishing
the house after the other calamity, this new one should come and spoil it
all. Still, you do not seem cast down by it, & I hope cheerfulness will
continue to abide with you. ~~Only~~ Six o'clock in the morning! Only to
think—if I had been there, I would have been so drenched with water,
& so vexed with smoke, & so annoyed with the rushing & shouting of
the firemen all about me, that I would have had to cover up my head with
the bedclothes, & ‸even then‸ I doubt if I could have slept at all. By
George, I would have had to got up mighty early. It is dreadful to think
of.[1]

No—I would have got up at the first alarm, & *helped*—that is what
I would have done—& you know it.

I sent your whole letter to Livy, just as it was.[2] Formerly, I would
have had to cut it, but now she takes an interest in everything that I do.
Wonderful girl—I just *like* her. She is just counting the minutes till I
come again, I expect. [Well, she *is*—you needn't laugh.] I shall be there
next Wednesday evening, & stay till she & I read 500 or 600 pages of
proof together—two or three weeks. Think of it! Splendid girl. *She*'ll
take to you, easy enough. Don't be afraid about that.[3] So you see I *am*
publishing a book—but don't ask any more dog-goned questions about
it! You ought to see the pictures—they are *very* gay—& they are ingeniously drawn & daintily engraved, too. I have examined proofs of
eighty of them, so far, and like them all. I would have sent you some if
your letter had come two hours sooner—but I only could keep a dozen
(cut them out of the pages while reading proof,)—mailed them to Livy
at noon. The others I cannot get yet. They want to put a ~~stell~~ steel portrait of me in, for a frontispiece, but I refused—I hate the effrontery of
shoving the pictures of nobodies under people'‸s‸ noses in that way, after
the fashion of ~~paten~~ quacks & negro minstrels. Told them to make a
handsome *wood* engraving of the Quaker City in a storm, instead. We'll

have Dan in (copied neatly from his photo.)—& Jack with his buckskin patch—& far-fetched imaginary ~~cuts~~ portraits of old Andrews, Cutter & Greer*,*, the "Interrogation Point." There are some imaginary "Old Masters" that are good*,*—rich, I *should* ~~sh~~ say. Because I am down on them fellers.[4] What shall I *call* the book? I want a name that is **striking, comprehensive, & out of the common order**—something not worn & hackneyed, & not commonplace. I had chosen "The New Pilgrims' Progress," but it is thought that many dull people will shudder at that, as at least taking the name of a consecrated book in vain, & perhaps burlesquing it, within. I have thought of *ʄ* "The Irruption of the Jonathans— *Or,* the Modern Pilgrim's Progress"—you see the second title can remain, if I only precede it with something that will *let it down easy.* Give me a name, please.[5]

Nasby called on me the other night, & we sat up talking all night. Like him first rate—liked his lecture, too—think it is a lecture to be proud of. I go to Boston to-night to have a bit of a time with him & the literary nobs—he promises a good time. But shall be in Elmira Wednesday.

No, ma'am—I *won't* make Cleveland only a way station for Elmira— I mean to come there & stay just as long as I *can*, when I start to California. Because I want to see you, the worst kind.

What do *you* think of Livy? Makes me feel awful to think of that first letter she wrote me—remember it?[6] And that poem in the Atlantic—representing her out of reach—

> "And all my life shall lift its hands
> In earnest longing toward thy face"[7]—

I wasn't going to regard her at *that* distance.

I send my love to all the good old household.

Good-bye

Dutifully & Lovingly

Mark.

---

[1] On Saturday, 6 March, the Cleveland *Herald* reported that a fire had broken out in the attic of the Fairbanks home "at six o'clock, on Friday night."

Owing to the secluded position of the fire a hole had to be cut through the roof before the water could be brought to bear upon it, but once when this was done the firemen made short work with their natural enemy. Everything was admirably managed, not an article was removed from the house or lost, though the furniture and ceiling suffered a good deal from the water. . . . The loss cannot yet be estimate[d], though it is considerable. The building and its contents were fully insured. This is the second fire at the same place within a few weeks. ("Fire," 3)

The previous fire occurred on 1 February (see 5 Feb 69 to Fairbanks, n. 3).

2 See 12–13 Mar 69 to OLL.

3 Mrs. Fairbanks and three of her children had met Olivia in 1868, when they spent the week of 10–16 June with the Langdons in Elmira—well before Clemens's momentous visit that August. Although the two women had since exchanged letters, they did not meet again until Olivia's wedding in February 1870 (*L2*, 231 n. 9, 351 n. 2).

4 The book eventually had a double frontispiece: "The Quaker City in a Storm" at Clemens's suggestion, and "The Pilgrim's Vision" at Bliss's (see 20 Apr 69 to Bliss, n. 2). Daniel Slote's portrait ("Dan"), obviously drawn from a photograph, appeared in chapter 27; John A. ("Jack") Van Nostrand was depicted in chapter 57 wearing buckskin-seated trousers ("Rear Elevation of Jack"). The ostensible portraits of the other *Quaker City* passengers mentioned were indeed "far-fetched" and "imaginary": Dr. Edward Andrews ("The Oracle") was caricatured in chapter 7; a picture of Bloodgood Haviland Cutter ("Poet Lariat") in chapter 10 was a recognizable likeness of Clemens himself; and the illustration of Frederick H. Greer ("Interrogation Point") in chapter 7 looked suspiciously like Charles J. Langdon. Five imaginary "Old Masters," sketches of "monks and martyrs," appeared in chapter 23 (Hirst, 210–13).

5 Fairbanks's reply to this request survives only in Clemens's response: see 24 Mar 69 to Fairbanks. His search for a title to replace the one he had chosen in the fall of 1868 may have been prompted by a confrontation with the president of the American Publishing Company, Sidney Drake, sometime during the week Clemens had just spent in Hartford (*L2*, 275 n. 1; Geer 1869, 495). In 1906 Clemens recalled that as soon as he had gotten "free of the lecture field," he hastened to Hartford, only to find his book at a standstill:

Bliss said that the fault was not his; that he wanted to publish the book but the directors of his Company were staid old fossils and were afraid of it. They had examined the book, and the majority of them were of the opinion that there were places in it of a humorous character. Bliss said the house had never published a book that had a suspicion like that attaching to it, and that the directors were afraid that a departure of this kind could seriously injure the house's reputation; that he was tied hand and foot, and was not permitted to carry out his contract. One of the directors, a Mr. Drake—at least he was the remains of what had once been a Mr. Drake—invited me to take a ride with him in his buggy, and I went along. He was a pathetic old relic, and his ways and his talk were also pathetic. He had a delicate purpose in view and it took him some time to hearten himself sufficiently to carry it out, but at last he accomplished it. He explained the house's difficulty and distress, as Bliss had already explained it. Then he frankly threw himself and the house upon my mercy and begged me to take away "The Innocents Abroad" and release the concern from the contract. I said I wouldn't—and so ended the interview and the buggy excursion. Then I warned Bliss that he must get to work or I should make trouble. He acted upon the warning, and set up the book and I read the proofs. (AD, 21 May 1906, CU-MARK, in *MTE*, 147, and *AMT*, 158–59)

Charles Dudley Warner, later Clemens's Hartford neighbor and his collaborator on *The Gilded Age*, recalled that Bliss secured permission to proceed only after addressing the company's board of directors, as follows:

"Well, gentlemen," he said, "you have all had an opportunity to express your opinion as to whether or not our company should publish this work, and your collective decision, based upon your individual views, seems to be decidedly against the publication of it. Now that you have had your opportunity to publish this book, and have rejected it, I want to say to you that I shall immediately enter into negotiations with Mark Twain for the purpose of publishing the book on my own personal account. The humor of it is new, I'll admit, but I am positive that it will be cordially welcomed by the American people for this reason, if for no other. To me the reading of the manuscript has been a delight. I am willing to risk a considerable amount of my personal means to publish it, for I am satisfied that it will prove a most profitable venture for me. That is all, gentlemen." (E. J. Edwards, 8)

   6 Olivia's initial rejection of Clemens's proposal of marriage, no longer extant. For his reply to it, see *L2*, 247–49.

   7 From William Winter's "Love's Queen," published in the *Atlantic Monthly* for October 1868:

> But all my life shall reach its hands
> Of lofty longing toward thy face. (22:475)

The poem's speaker expressed enraptured contentment with his loved one's sun-like inaccessibility.

To Olivia L. Langdon
13 March 1869 • Hartford, Conn.
(MS: CU-MARK)

Hartford, March 13.

It lacks something of midnight, yet—& so there is time at least to say— I *love* you, Livy, bless your dear old heart.

> "And all my life shall lift its hands
> In earnest longing toward thy face"[1]—

The sweetest face that ever turned the cares of life to trifles & its ills to blessings—& the dearest girl, withal, that ever made man look back upon his life & say "Of what use was this blank?—what was the object of it?—was ~~this~~ that person that lived that life, & this that lives this new, ampler, grander, happier life, the *same* person?" It looks so preposterous. How *did* I ever live without you, Livy? You darling!

   I have just answered Mother Fairbanks' letter, and tried to comfort her in her new misfortune. It seems *too* bad that after all her trouble & bother & labor in reinstating her household gods & restoring her pleasant home, this new calamity should come, & lay waste the work of her hands.

   Why didn't you put in just a word in Charlie's letter, you precious Livy? But you *would* have done it if you had known I was not to hear from you for four whole days—I *know* you would. If I had only had sense enough to ~~write~~ tell you to write me at the ~~Everett~~ ˌAstorˌ House in New

York, I could have got it on ~~Monday~~ Tuesday.[2] Never mind, though—
you have been a dear, faithful, generous little correspondent, & are entitled to a rest. But what a vexatious darling it is!—to send me a Beecher
sermon, with never a pencil mark in it.[3] That isn't any way to do, honey.
I tore off the envelop & looked all the way through it, hunting for some
sign or footprint of Livy—but not a mark was there, & I was so disappointed. But I forgive you—I could forgive you *any*thing. Just so you
love me, that is sufficient. If it *had* been marked, I would have dropped
my work & read it at once—couldn't have finished my work in time,
then—couldn't have gone to Boston. Did you have a premonition of
that, I wonder? It is all the better, though, as it is. To-morrow will be
Sunday, & then I can read it. It is a good girl.

I have examined proofs of some eighty engravings, so far, & like all
of them but one. I sent you half a dozen or so this morning—would have
sent them all if they would let me. Several of the little views are handsome. Some proof sheets will doubtless reach Elmira before I do. Open
the package if you choose, little Curiosity, for you have just as much authority to do it as I have, & I want you to *feel* that way, & know it—but
don't show them to anybody else, ˄till I come,˄ because to acknowledge
the plain truth, I am fully as sensitive about having an article of mine
seen *in proof*, as I could be to have my ordinary ~~m~~ friendly letters in
Manuscript read by strangers. But with *you* it is different—I haven't the
slightest possible sensitiveness on that score with you—you are *part of*
me—you are *myself*—& I would no more be troubled by *your* looking
over my shoulder than it would embarrass me to look over my *own* shoulder. So, just read whatever you please, Livy darling, & make yourself
entirely at home—plunge your dainty fingers into my affaŕirs just as
much as you want to—& the more you do it the more you'll delightt me
(with *two* t's, you mutineer). They ~~m~~ wanted to make a portrait of me—
steel engraving—for a frontispiece; but I naturally objected—refused,
rather; that is a sort of impertinent intrusion upon the public that ~~suits~~
~~should~~ be left to the patent-medicine gentry.

Charlie writes that he has bought a horse that *I can't drive*. Well! I'd
like to *see* the horse that I can't drive. ~~I~~ But if I can't really drive that
horse, what are we going to do, Livy? I don't like to ask Charlie to do
such a thing, but then I don't see any other way—so when we ride out
he will have to walk, & lead the horse. I know it is hard, but it is his own
fault, for buying such a beast.[4]

Had a really pleasant time at Mrs. Hooker's last night, Twichell &

I. I *do* LIKE Mr. Jno. Hooker—he is splendid,—& I think a good deal of Mrs & Miss Hooker, too. I showed them the little picture,, & the first thing Miss Alice said, was: "Why she has a *ribbon* on her hair—I thought she never wore them." I said "it was a fancy you had acquired lately, & I thought it a very comely one." And indeed it is. My darling hardly seems in full dress, now, without her ribbon.[5]

Mrs. Hooker advanced some theology which startled me—but it did more than that with Twichell—it *troubled* him, exceedingly. It was a reference to some vague expression in Peter which Mrs. H. construed to mean that Christ preached, & still preaches to the souls in purgatory[6]— & in it she found authority for believing that those that die suddenly, & all of us, in fact, have another opportunity, hereafter, of compassing salvation. She quoted also the remark to the thief on the cross, about supping with him in "Paradise" (one of whose meanings is equivalent to our term "purgatory.")[7]

Twichell was so distressed about it that he was at my bedside soon this morning, & remained a long time urging me to search the Scriptures for myself, & not let one or two vague speeches of the Apostles lift themselves up & overshadow the ~~vol~~ vast array of evidence which the Testament offers plainly, forcibly & directly in opposition to the doctrines which they *seem* to promulgate.

I satisfied him that I was not given to taking firm & final hold of things without due deliberation, & that what Mrs. H. had said was not likely to leave a permanent & damaging impression. Good fellow, Twichell is, & faithful & true,—whole-hearted—magnificent. I love him. I gave him all your loving messages to himself & his household idols, & received fervent ones to you in return. He wants us to spend the summer vacation with him & Mrs. T. in the Adirondacks. Said we would, if Mr. & Mrs. Langdon would go, & you were willing. He has been there—last summer—& is perfectly infatuated with the place.

And here I talk, talk, talk—because I *can't* let my Livy go ~~when~~— want to talk to her *all* the time—& the first thing I know, that train[8] will waltz along & leave me.

Time's nearly up—take my kiss & my blessing, you worshipped darling, whom I so love & honor.

Always Yours

Sam.

P. S. I *love* you Livy. I love you will all my might. And next Wednesday[9] I shall *see* you—hasten the day!

✉—————————————————————————————————————

Miss Olivia L. Langdon | Elmira | New York. [*postmarked:*] HARTFORD
CONN. MAR 14 [*docketed by OLL:*] ⌀[10] 56th

[1] Identified in 13 Mar 69 to Fairbanks, n. 7.
[2] Clemens was to be in New York City on Tuesday, 16 March, bound for Newtown, on Long Island, where he lectured that evening. The letter he had received
from Charles J. Langdon has not been found.
[3] An unidentified issue of the *Plymouth Pulpit*.
[4] See 9 and 31 Mar 69 to Crane, n. 3.
[5] The porcelaintype that Clemens received on 22 January. See 22 Jan 69 to
OLL, n. 1, and 26 and 27 Jan 69 to OLL.
[6] Possibly "By which also he went and preached unto the spirits in prison" (1
Peter 3:19).
[7] "And Jesus said unto him, Verily I say unto thee, To day shalt thou be with
me in paradise" (Luke 23:43).
[8] To Boston.
[9] 17 March.
[10] See 8 and 9 Mar 69 to OLL, n. 7.

NO LETTERS are known to survive for the next ten days. Four letters
that Clemens sent to Olivia before 21 March (docket numbers 57–60)
are among the missing documents. Even without the details they would
provide, however, the general outline of his activities during most of the
period can be established. Following his 14–15 March visit to Boston
with Petroleum V. Nasby, at which time he met Oliver Wendell Holmes,
Clemens went to New York City on the night of 15 March. The next day,
before lecturing in Newtown, on Long Island, he probably stopped in
at the offices of the New York *Tribune* to confer with John Russell Young,
to whom he had recently offered "The White House Funeral," about
further contributions to the paper. On 17 March Young sent him an "extract" from a San Francisco *Evening Bulletin* article on the importation
and sale of Chinese women as prostitutes, inviting him to write something about that "singular social question." Clemens's response has not
been found, but he presumably declined within a day or two, for on 20
March Young instead addressed the issue by reprinting part of the *Bulletin* article and accompanying it with a *Tribune* editorial (Young to SLC,
17 Mar 69, DLC; "The Importation of Chinese Women," San Francisco
Evening Bulletin, 25 Feb 69, 3; "The Traffic in Chinese Women," "Love-

liness by the Cargo," New York *Tribune*, 20 Mar 69, 4, 6). Meanwhile, Clemens left New York for Elmira, arriving in the evening on 17 March. Although the next batch of proofs of his book, consisting of chapters 10–14 (pages 90–138), must have been awaiting him, other commitments surely forestalled any sustained proofreading for four or five days. On 18 March, for example, Clemens helped the Langdons entertain a prominent guest: Wendell Phillips (1811–84), the social reformer and former abolitionist, spent the day at their home receiving callers, including the Reverend Thomas K. Beecher. Later, in the margin of the copy of Holmes's *Autocrat of the Breakfast-Table* that he was marking for Olivia, Clemens apologized for embarrassing her on that occasion: "I ought not to have said what I did in Wendell Phillips' presence 3 days ago, & which produced a blush which touches me yet with its distress—& will, for many days to come" (PH in CU-MARK, in Booth, 460). Despite this incident, it is likely that on the evening of 18 March Clemens and Olivia, along with her parents, attended Phillips's lecture on Daniel O'Connell, the Irish political leader, in the Elmira Opera House (Thomas K. Beecher to Ella L. Wolcott, 18 Mar 69, CtHSD; "City and Neighborhood," "Opera House. Lecture of Wendell Phillips," Elmira *Advertiser*, 19 Mar 69, 4). Either on 19 March or the day after, Clemens traveled to Sharon, Pennsylvania, where he concluded his lecture season with a "grand success" on 20 March. By that date he had decided on a new title for his book, for the Sharon reviewer reported: "He is about to issue a work of some six hundred pages, 'The Innocents Abroad, or the New Pilgrim's Progress'" ("Mark Twain," Sharon *Times*, 24 Mar 69, or Sharon *Herald*, 27 Mar 69, reprinted in Advertising Circular for *The Innocents Abroad*, Appendix E). And in his *Autocrat of the Breakfast-Table*, Clemens affirmed the decision: "'The Innocents Abroad—Or, The New Pilgrim's Progress.' [Sharon, Mch 21." (PH in CU-MARK, in Booth, 459, with the date mistranscribed "Mch 31."). Probably on 21 March he returned to Elmira, where he resumed proofreading and wrote the next sequence of letters.

To Mary Mason Fairbanks
24 March 1869 • Elmira, N.Y.
(MS: CSmH)

J. LANGDON, MINER & DEALER IN ANTHRACITE &
BITUMINOUS COAL   OFFICE NO. 6 BALDWIN STREET

ELMIRA, N.Y. March 24 186 9.

Dear Mother—

Why in the world didn't Mr. Fairbanks & my dear sister Allie wait a little? I arrived the day after they left. Wanted to see both of them. I can see that they were just as fascinating as ever, by the way they all talk at the house.

Why, it don't astonish *me* that Mr. Fairbanks liked Livy. How could he have helped it, I would like to know? No—it don't astonish me—it only gratifies me.

Did you see "J. B.'s" able bosh in reply to me, in the last Packard? I hate to talk back at such small fry, but *how* can I resist the opportunity of saying something deliciously mean & vicious it offers me?[1]

The idea that I don't love Mrs. Severance! I never heard such a preposterous thing in my life. I won't entertain such nonsense. I *do* think the world of her—all that she will let me, *I* know.

Don't you worry about the proofs. Livy & I will read them backwards, & every other way,—but principally backwards I guess. I think of calling the book "The Innocents Abroad—Or, The New Pilgrim's Progress." Isn't that better than "Alonzo & Melissa" & that other rubbish you propose?[2] And how could it be "The Loves of the Angels," when there's only *one* angel—only one that's fledged, anyway?

I am glad about the fire—glad they put it out, I mean. And glad they saved the shirts—though I wasn't particular—got some of Dan's yet.[3] Well, I hope you won't have any more distress with fires.

Have just about decided to go to California by sea. I am very sorry about that, because in that case I'll not see you for months, you know—& I want to see you badly. If it warn't for Livy, I would be in Cleveland now. Livy has about half a mind to forbid the California journey altogether. She is a small tyrant, physically, but a powerful one when she chooses to let herself out. Well, I guess I'm needed up at the house, now,

& I'll close this. The Princess is well, & would send her love to you all if she were here—so I send it for her, along with mine.

Faithfully, lovingly & dutifully, your cub,

Sam.

[1] "J.B." had published "An Open Letter to Mark Twain" in the April number of *Packard's Monthly* (2:120–21), which appeared on 20 March ("New Publications," New York *Tribune*, 20 Mar 69, 5). Answering Clemens's "Open Letter to Com. Vanderbilt" in the previous number, "J.B." argued at length that Vanderbilt's money had been "honestly earned" through "financial genius" and that his fortune and his various enterprises afforded jobs "to thousands of men directly employed thereon." Clemens is not known to have rebutted this "able bosh" in print.

[2] *Alonzo and Melissa; or, the Unfeeling Father* was Daniel Jackson's title for the gothic romance he plagiarized from Isaac Mitchell in 1811. Mitchell had serialized the story in 1804, and published it in book form as *The Asylum; or, Alonzo and Melissa* in 1811, but it was under Jackson's title that it achieved great popularity, going through numerous editions during the first three-quarters of the nineteenth century (Hart 1983, 42, 498).

[3] On 28 May 1867, Clemens had informed his San Francisco *Alta California* readers that Daniel Slote would be a satisfactory cabin mate aboard the *Quaker City* because he "has got many shirts, and a History of the Holy Land, a cribbage-board and three thousand cigars. I will not have to carry any baggage at all" (SLC 1867d). His own "saved" shirts were some he had left with Mrs. Fairbanks for laundering, his customary practice, when he stopped at her Cleveland home on 13 February, between the two fires there (see 7 Jan 69 to Fairbanks and others, and 5 Feb 69 and 13 Mar 69 to Fairbanks).

To Jane Lampton Clemens and Family
26? March 1869 • Elmira, N.Y.

(MS facsimile: Davis)

[*first six MS pages (about 750 words) missing*]

of it, for you know it is not good judgment,) ˄Orion on the same paper,˄ & then we could be all come-atable.[1]

My head is so busted up with endeavors to get my own⸝ plans straight, that I am hardly in a condition to fix up anybody else's. ~~Livy &~~ ~~I sit for hours~~—I don't know whether I am going to California in May— I don't know whether I want to lecture next season or not—I don't know whether I want to yield to Nasby's persuasions & go with him on the

Toledo Blade—I don't know *any*thing.[2] I am too happy & comfortable
& sleepy, now, to know anything. And I don't care a dam. [I mean a mill
dam, of course—for I have not been a profane man for 2 years—(but
between you & I, I put that "don't care a dam" in, solely for Livy's benefit, for I knew perfectly well that she had crept up behind me at that
moment & was looking over my shoulders—but you bet you she's gone
off, now!) I ought not to tease her & "sell" her so much, but I can't easily
help it, & she is as long-suffering ~~as any Job~~ & patient as any Job. She is
almost perfection—I solemnly swear to that. I never have discovered a
fault in her yet, or any sign or shadow of a blemish.[3] And I must inform
you that I sing her praises in a weaker key than any other friend she has.
Good-bye. Love to you all.

Affectionately

Sam.

[1] Someone in Clemens's family had evidently suggested that his brother Orion
could get a job on whatever newspaper Clemens joined. Orion was presently
living in St. Louis (see 14 Jan 69 to PAM, n. 8), but it is not known if or where
he was employed.

[2] Two weeks earlier, Clemens had been determined to refuse Nasby's offer: see
10 Mar 69 to OLL and CJL, p. 159. Although the date of this letter remains
uncertain, it was written on the same stationery used in the next letter, to Elisha
Bliss, the only other letter in this period to use it. In addition, Clemens clearly
wrote to his mother on or about 26 March, for her notebook record of payments
from him lists payment number 12 ($20) as received on 30 March (JLC, 4).

[3] But see 23 and 24 Jan 69 to OLL.

To Elisha Bliss, Jr.
30 March 1869 • Elmira, N.Y.
(MS: CU-MARK)

Elmira, March 30.

Friend Bliss—

I sent the proofs to-day. I could have sent them sooner, but was lazy.
I will not delay you next time. I was glad Frank telegraphed.[1]

I have concluded that if you will print the following titles on slips
you will like one or the other of them:

$$\left\{ \begin{array}{c} \text{``The Innocents Abroad;} \\ \text{or,} \\ \text{The Modern }_\wedge(New)_\wedge \text{ Pilgrim's Progress.''} \end{array} \right.$$

Or this:

$$\left\{ \begin{array}{c} \text{``The Exodus of the Innocents;} \\ \text{or,} \\ \text{The New Pilgrim's Progress.''} \end{array} \right.$$

I like "The Innocents Abroad" rather the best.

Trot your proofs along, as fast as you please—& the sooner the book is out, the better for us, no doubt.

Yrs Truly

Mark.

[*letter docketed:*] √ [*and*] Mark Twain | March 30/69

[1] Before leaving Hartford for Boston, late on the night of 13 March, Clemens had read ninety pages of proof for *The Innocents Abroad:* from his preface, list of illustrations, and detailed table of contents, up through the end of chapter 9 (page 89) (see 12 Mar 69 to OLL, p. 163). He went to Elmira on the evening of 17 March, but probably could not begin reading the next batch of proofs there for another four or five days (see p. 175). Once he did begin, the major cause of delay undoubtedly was his desire to prolong the pleasure of reading with Olivia, whom, moreover, he had given the "prerogative" to "scratch out all that don't suit her" (9 and 31 Mar 69 to Crane, p. 181).

To Susan L. Crane
9 and 31 March 1869 • Hartford, Conn.,
and Elmira, N.Y.
(MS: CU-MARK)

Hartford, March 9, 1869.

Mrs Crane—

Dear Friend—

You must let me thank you with all my heart for your cordial words,; for your praises of Livy; for your kindly prepossession toward

me; for your welcome to the family circle & its altar; for the high position
you assign me there; and for the generous interest you manifest in *our*
future, whose slowly-lifting curtain is already revealing soft-tinted visions of the mysterious land we are approaching. I thank you & Mr.
Crane most kindly for all your ~~w~~ good words & good wishes.

Elmira, March 31.

{ The difference in the color of the ink ~~will si~~ must signify an interval of
about 3 weeks.[1] I had ~~w~~ just finished that first paragraph at 10 oclock one
night, in Hartford, when Rev. Petroleum V. Nasby came in & introduced
himself, & we sat up & talked a while—until 5 minutes after 6 in the
morning, in fact. Press of business prevented my finishing my letter after that.

Livy told you that secret, after all? I hoped she would. I had a vague
sort of idea that she would—& so, after a fashion, I was a prophet. And
I further prophecied that you would reveal it to me—& therein, also,
was my judgment correct. Now that the revelation has been made by
you, & endorsed by Livy, I am entirely satisfied & happy. And now,
being a member of the family by brevet, *I* & gladly & cheerfully accept-
ing the responsibilities of the position, I am doing the best I can to fill
your place & Mr. Crane's while you are absent[2]—& not succeeding very
well, I can tell you, for they sigh for you & long for you with a frequency
& a fervency that is in the last degree discouraging to me, considering
the efforts I am making. And now Mr Langdon is gone, & ~~I am of cou~~ of
course I am trying to fill *his* place, too—but I didn't know, before, how
much room he took up. I am a failure. That is apparent enough. So you
& Mr. Crane may come back by the next train (regardless of any previous
orders you may have received,) & I will telegraph for Mr. Langdon. I
will subside, & take care of Livy—I am equal to *that* position, anyhow.

Charley's new horse is lame.[3] The bird-cages hang in the conservatory & the ~~br~~ birds make music during meals. Mark & Jep are well &
cheerful—Jep is going to be sold, or given away, or executed—I do not
know his crime. Julia is gone—went to-day. Mary is back—came yesterday. George the coachman has a wife—had her before, likely, but I did
not know it until to-day.[4] He is sociable—calls Miss Langdon "Livy."
Hattie Lewis grows more & more outrageous every day—& so everybody likes her better & better. Two milliners ‸have‸ been in the house
for a week, making up things for Livy & me. They have n't begun on me

yet, but I suppose they will. I occupy your rooms, & smoke in them occasionally, but *ever* so gently—& with the windows wide open. It is cool, but comfortable. I will get away before you come, & then you cannot scold. Livy & I read a Testament lesson in your parlor every afternoon. Your clock is running, your exquisite little picture of a sunset view in the country hangs in its place in the corner over the desk; everything is just as you left it—except, somehow, it seems to me that the engraving of "Shakspere's Courtship"[5] did not always hang with its face to the wall. However, I may be mistaken. Livy & the Spaulding girls are taking chemistry lessons, & we are all afraid to stay in the house from 11 till noon, because they are always cooking up some new-fangled gas or other & blowing everything endways with their experiments.[6] It is dreadful to think of having a wife who will be always inventing new chemical horrors & experimenting on me with them. However, if Livy likes it, I shan't mind being shot through the roof occasionally & scattered around among the neighbors. I shall get rich on ~~acci~~ extra-hazardous accident= policies. The family has got to be supported **some** way or other. [Livy will probably read this before she sends it, & then she'll scratch out all that don't suit her.] It is a prerogative she has. She acquired it helping me read "proof" for my book. Mr. Beecher has gone off on a week's holiday.[7] The river is up, & flooding things.[8] It is supper time, now. I must get an early start & clear out,;—for ~~those~~ the Spaulding girls are coming right away after supper to help Livy finish blowing out the starboard side of the house with ~~what~~ a rascally new gas that didn't go good to-day. They expect me to hold the retort while they touch it off—they always expect me to do that—*they* never get in danger themselves—but I am not going to do it——I am going down town. My eye-winkers are all singed off, *now*.

I have told you all the news that the others would not be likely to tell you (except that we play euchre every night, & sing "Geer," which is Livy's favorite, & "Even Me," which is mine, & a dozen other hymns—favorites of the other members)[9]—& although this news sounds trifling, & it still mentions *names* you love to hear, & ~~THINGS~~ *things* that are familiar to your memory, —& those features of a letter were what I always liked best when in exile in the lands beyond the Rocky Mountains,—so I offer no apologies.[10] [And you know they never would have told you about that chemistry diabolism—you never would have gotten the straight of it from anybody but me.]

I shake hands cordially with you both, & wish you well, & hope I
may yet have the happiness of seeing you before I sail for California.

Sincerely Yours

$\left.\begin{array}{l}\text{,A True Copy.}^{11}\\ \text{Witness:}\\ \text{LIVY.}\end{array}\right\}_\wedge$ Saml. L. Clemens.

[1] Clemens wrote the first part of this letter in black ink, now faded to brown.
Beginning with "wishes" (180.5), he completed it in purple, except for two
words ("Now" and "I" at 180.16 and 180.25), which are in brown. The change
to purple ink signaled the passage of time; the two changes back to brown ink,
whether intentional or accidental, have not been explained.

[2] The Cranes were spending the winter in the South, mostly in Florida, hoping
that the climate would help remedy Susan's throat ailment. Theodore returned
to Elmira on 17 April, Susan about two weeks later, following a stay in Richmond, Virginia (OLL to Alice B. Hooker, 16 Dec 68, CtHSD; "City and Neighborhood," Elmira *Advertiser*, 19 Apr 69, 3).

[3] This horse, if it recovered sufficiently to be serviceable, may have been the
one later noticed by the Elmira *Saturday Evening Review*: "CHARLES LANGDON
has a stepper, Hambletonian brown mare" ("Horse Flesh," 21 Aug 69, 8).

[4] Jep, presumably a dog, had committed the crime of "landscape gardening"
(17 and 18 May 69 to OLL, p. 242). The departing visitor may have been
Olivia's cousin and contemporary, Julia Langdon, the daughter of Jervis Langdon's brother John (1806–61). "Mary" has not been certainly identified, but
see 12 Mar 69 to OLL, n. 2. "George" and his wife are likewise unidentified
("Langdon Line," TS genealogy in CU-MARK; "Personal Record of Andrew
Langdon," NBuHi; Gretchen Sharlow and Herbert A. Wisbey, Jr., personal
communication).

[5] Unidentified.

[6] Olivia's interest in chemistry may have been stimulated by a 12 March meeting of the local Academy of Sciences in the Langdon home. "About fifty Aca-
demicians and their invited guests were present, and were elegantly entertained
by their generous host and hostess." In his inaugural address that evening, President William H. Gregg emphasized the importance of chemistry, which, "more
than either of the other sciences, develops our resources and adds to our national
wealth, by the introduction of new and cheap processes for the utilization of the
raw and waste materials of our large manufacturing interests" ("Academy of Sciences," Elmira *Saturday Evening Review*, 13 Mar 69, 5, and 20 Mar 69, 7). Joining Olivia for instruction by Darius Ford were Clara L. Spaulding (1849–1935)
and her older sister Alice (d. 1935), daughters of Henry Clinton Spaulding, a
prosperous Elmira lumber merchant, and his wife, the former Clara Wisner. In
1906 Clemens described Clara Spaulding as "my wife's playmate and schoolmate
from the earliest times, and she was about my wife's age, or two or three years
younger—mentally, morally, spiritually, and in all ways, a superior and lovable
personality" (AD, 26 Feb 1906, CU-MARK, in *MTA*, 2:140). Spaulding, who

married lawyer John Barry Stanchfield (1855–1921) in 1886, became Clemens's trusted friend as well as Olivia's, and was regarded as an aunt by their children (OLL to Alice B. Hooker, 3 Mar 69, CtHSD; Salsbury, 433; "Matrimonial Mentions," Elmira *Morning Telegram*, 5 Sept 86, 8; "Stanchfield Funeral to Be Held Tuesday," Elmira *Star Gazette*, 1 July 1935, 10; Towner 1892, 128; Herbert A. Wisbey, Jr., personal communication).

[7] The Reverend Thomas K. Beecher, the Langdons' pastor, had left Elmira for Pittsburgh probably on 25 or 26 March. The Reverend James Chaplin Beecher (1828–86), of Owego, New York, Thomas's younger brother, substituted for him on Easter Sunday, 28 March, both at the morning service in Park Congregational Church and at the Elmira Opera House that evening. Beecher returned in time to publish his regular "Friday Miscellany" in the Elmira *Advertiser* on 2 April, the first part of which described his recent trip. Shortly after his return there were new developments in the controversy over his Opera House services (see 20 and 21 Jan 69 to OLL, n. 9). The New York *Evangelist* announced on 1 April:

> The MINISTERIAL UNION OF ELMIRA, N. Y., at a recent meeting, passed resolutions disapproving the teachings of Rev. T. K. Beecher, declining to cooperate with him in his Sunday evening services at the Opera House, and requesting him to withdraw from their Monday morning meeting. This has resulted in his withdrawal, and thus the pastors are relieved from further responsibility as to his action. ("Ministers and Churches," 4)

On 7 April, Jervis Langdon wrote a letter supporting Beecher to the Elmira *Advertiser*, which published it the next day as "Mr. Beecher and the Clergy." Reproducing the *Evangelist* notice, Langdon asked sarcastically that "all orthodox sectarian papers" copy it because he thought it "very unfair that the clergymen of Elmira should be held responsible by any one for Mr. Beecher's action and teaching in the Opera House" (Langdon). Langdon also "headed a movement to buy shares in the Opera House to ensure the future of this outrage" (Max Eastman, 624–25). Clemens himself was soon drawn into the effort on Beecher's behalf, writing "Mr. Beecher and the Clergy" (SLC 1869d), signed "Cheerfully, S'CAT," and published in the *Advertiser* on 10 April ("Nook Farm Genealogy," Beecher Addenda, iv; Elmira *Advertiser:* "Services To-morrow," 27 Mar 69, 4; "City and Neighborhood," 29 Mar 69, 4; "Friday Miscellany," 2 Apr 69, 3).

[8] Melting snow and recent heavy rains had swelled the Chemung River, but the danger of a flood, initially thought serious, proved "not so imminent as to excite serious apprehensions" ("City and Neighborhood," Elmira *Advertiser*, 31 Mar 69, 4).

[9] "Geer" probably was the "common meter tune . . . composed by Henry Wellington Greatorex in 1849" (Ensor, 21). Among the hymns sung to it were three included in the *Plymouth Collection of Hymns and Tunes* (originally published in 1855), a volume familiar to Clemens from the *Quaker City* excursion and probably used by the Park Congregational Church in Elmira: "While Thee I seek, protecting Power," by Helen Maria Williams (1762–1827); "O God of Bethel! by whose hand," the version by John Logan (1748–88) of a hymn by Philip Doddridge (1702–51); and "How deep and tranquil is the joy," by Andrew Reed (1787–1862) (Henry Ward Beecher 1864, 218). It is not known which, if any, of these was Olivia's favorite. "Even me" was the refrain to "Lord, I hear of showers of blessing," an 1860 hymn by Elizabeth Codner (1824–1919) not

included in the *Plymouth Collection*. Its tune, also known as "Even Me," was composed by William B. Bradbury in 1862. In his and Olivia's copy of Holmes's *Autocrat of the Breakfast-Table*, Clemens wrote: "Midnight March 25, 1869—I wish 'Even Me' to be sung at my funeral" (PH in CU-MARK, in Booth, 461). The hymn was not performed at his memorial service in New York City on 23 April 1910, or at his funeral in Elmira the following day (Julian, 1:187–88, 305, 690, 831, 2:953–54, 1281; Frost, 495, 544; Dawson, 551; Leonard Woolsey Bacon, 201; New York *Times:* "Last Glimpse Here of Mark Twain," 24 Apr 1910, part 2, 3; "Mark Twain At Rest; Buried Beside Wife," 25 Apr 1910, 9).

[10] Writing from Virginia City on 18 March 1864, Clemens reproached his sister Pamela for failing to be particular about such details in her letters to him: "An item is of no use unless it speaks of some *person*, & not then, unless that person's *name* is distinctly mentioned. The most interesting letter one can write to an absent friend, is one that treats of *persons* he has been acquainted with, rather than the public events of the day" (*L1*, 274). Clemens addressed the same advice, "and with asperity, to every man, woman, and child east of the Rocky Mountains" when he published "An Open Letter to the American People" in February 1866 (SLC 1866).

[11] No fair copy of this letter has been found. The document transcribed here was almost certainly the one sent, and remained in the Langdon family until 1972. The witness's signature was probably written by Clemens, in imitation of Olivia's handwriting.

From Samuel L. Clemens and Olivia L. Langdon
to Mary Mason Fairbanks
31 March and 1 April 1869 • Elmira, N.Y.
(MS: CSmH)

J. LANGDON, MINER & DEALER IN ANTHRACITE &
BITUMINOUS COAL   OFFICE NO. 6 BALDWIN STREET

ELMIRA, N.Y. March 31—[1] 186 9.

Dear Mother—

Bless you *I* don't want to go to California at all—& really I have not by any means determined to go, as yet. I know very well that I *ought* to go, but I haven't the slightest inclination to do it. Indeed, indeed, indeed I DO want to go & see you first, but if I do that I shall have to go to St. Louis also, & I just hate the idea of that. I don't think April a good month to take Livy to Cleveland in, do you? The grass & flowers & foliage will not be out, then; & wherever Livy goes, Nature ought to have self-respect enough to do look her level best, you know.

We have read & re-shipped some fifty pages of proof, & it looks like it is going to take a month to finish it all. I rather hope it will take six.

I am in exile here at the office, for an hour, while the girls take their chemistry lesson. However, I suppose it is about over, now, & so I will return. [Livy will begin to feel anxious.]

I saw M̸ D^r· & Mrs. What you may call him—the Comm[i]ssioner of the US of America to Europe Asia & Africa, at Sharon, Pa., the other day. They came 20 miles to hear me lecture. ~~Lord,~~ They ought to read the *book*—there is where the interest will be, for them. Mrs. G. is grown stout & fat, & absolutely *immense*. She looks as tall & as huge as Pompey's p̸Pillar, & inconceivably vulgar. She cannot weigh less than three hundred pounds. This is honest.[2]

[*on smaller paper:*]

ₐApril 1.ₐ[3]

Livy says—well, I can't get the straight of it—but the *idea* of it, is, that some western friends are to be visited in May, & so maybe she & I & Mrs. Langdon can go out a little in advance, otherwise if it was, & so she could—but if not, then perhaps it would be just as well for ~~bu~~ both of us & certainly as convenient for *you*, especially while Severance is. [Well, that is what *she* says, you know, but ~~blamed if~~ *I* ₐdon'tₐ know what it means.] [She made that correction—I like "blamed."] Well, the general idea is, that maybe we can go out to Cleveland & see you, in advance of the gathering of the clans. Savez? So, therefore, whereas, if we *do* go, Fairbanks & I can talk business[4]—but we are not at all certain that we can go, for Livy has to be bridesmaid for Alice Hooker & both of us have to read proof for a month (because I am publishing a book, you know,) Livy is here (Mrs. Crane's parlor,) & we are writing letters & been two hours writing ~~four~~ ₐtwoₐ pages, & she has only written a page & a half— dinner time, now & we must tell you good-bye how do you like the enclosed portrait of Mr. Cutter which I ~~snaked~~ ₐcutₐ it out of the proofs we have been reading Andrews always distorted the phrase "Poet Laureate" into Poet Lariat if you remember I do love to all good bye[5]

Yr Dutiful Scrub

Mark.

(e-*hic!*) ~~Drat~~ ⌐Those sighs. Mr Clemens wants me to find a word to put in the place of the one erased, but I do not know how to translate the word

[That was a much more ~~bullyer~~ ‚appropriate‚ word than any other I can ever find—but she has marked it out & so it has got to go, you know.]

[There is another word ~~busted~~ ‚scratched‚ out—*Who's* a-writing this letter, anyway, I want to know?] [*We* are.] [She *would* have the last word.]

[*enclosure:*]

"POET LARIAT."

✉ Mrs. A. W. Fairbanks | Care "Herald" | Cleveland | O̲h̲i̲o̲. [*postmarked:*]
ELMIRA N.Y. APR I

[1] Clemens wrote the 31 March portion of this letter in red ink.

[2] Dr. William Gibson and his wife, Susan, were from Jamestown, Pennsylvania, and had been among the passengers on the *Quaker City* excursion. Dr. Gibson, though never mentioned by name, was ridiculed throughout *The Innocents Abroad*—starting with a reference to his title, which he had acquired by offering to collect samples for the Department of Agriculture, and which he was evidently inclined to elaborate. In chapter 2, Mark Twain is found reading over the passenger list before departure when he comes across "a gentleman who had 'COMMISSIONER OF THE UNITED STATES OF AMERICA TO EUROPE, ASIA, AND AFRICA' thundering after his name in one awful blast." On 20 February 1868, Clemens had sent Mrs. Fairbanks a copy of this passage from his manuscript, noting that it "touches D^r. Gibson on a raw place. If he were a man of any appreciation, it would be a royal pleasure to see him waltz around when he reads that. But bless you it will all be lost. That complacent imbecile will take it for a compliment" (*L2*, 189–90). Pompey's Pillar was a large granite monolith in Alexandria, mentioned in chapter 57 of *The Innocents Abroad*, where "One of our

most inveterate relic-hunters" tried and failed to break off a piece, another reference to Gibson (*L2*, 192–93 n. 4).

[3]Clemens wrote the date in black ink, the rest of the letter in purple.

[4]That is, Clemens's possible partnership in the Cleveland *Herald*.

[5]The actual enclosure has been lost. It is simulated here from chapter 10 (page 91) of *The Innocents Abroad*, which was among the proofs (chapters 10–14, pages 90–138) that Clemens had returned to Elisha Bliss on 30 March. Mark Twain never referred by name to Dr. Edward Andrews of Albany, New York, calling him instead "the Oracle" and describing him as "an innocent old ass" who "never uses a one-syllable word when he can think of a longer one, and never by any possible chance knows the meaning of any long word he uses." The prototype for the " 'Poet Laureate,' " also unnamed in *Innocents*, was Bloodgood Haviland Cutter, a wealthy Long Island farmer, who gave "copies of his verses to Consuls, commanders, hotel keepers, Arabs, Dutch,—to any body, in fact," and who began signing his gifts as "the Laureate of the Ship" (chapter 7). In chapter 10, where this illustration (actually a caricature of Mark Twain) occurs, the Oracle addresses the poet as "Poet Lariat."

To Elisha Bliss, Jr.
10? April 1869 • Elmira, N.Y.
(Transcripts: CU-MARK; Davis 1951b;
Parke-Bernet 1938c, lot 37; *MTB*, 1:380)

Elmira, April Something, 1869.[1]

Friend Bliss—

All the names were correct, I think, except Masserano. Jam the Queen of Greece in anywhere. She is the daughter of the Emperor of Russia & can stand it. *No*—put her in the Grecian chapter—that will be better.[2]

You will find *Scylla & Charybdis* mentioned *before* you come to Athens—perhaps the cut you speak of comes in there. (If it is a picture of Acropolis, though, put it in along with the description of the Acropolis in the Chapter on Greece.)[3]

I think the "suppositions" I dealt in about the oyster shells were not funny but foolish—& so, being disgusted I marked them out & was sorry I had ever printed them—so I think it much better to let them stay out. But you are always accommodating & I wish to be accommodating too—so if you prefer it, let the "suppositions" go in. (I don't say that reluctantly, but cordially & heartily, & *meaning* it.)[4]

Your printers are doing well. I will hurry the proofs.

Always, &c.,

Mark.

[1] The date conjectured for this letter depends upon Clemens's first sentence, which alludes to his listing of famous men, including the Prince of Masserano (Carlo Emanuele Ferrero La Marmora, 1788–1854), in chapter 15 (page 140) of *The Innocents Abroad*. Clemens had evidently corrected a misspelling of "Masserano." In response, Bliss appears to have requested confirmation, which the present letter provides, that the other names were correct. Clemens finished his proofreading of chapters 15–17 (pages 139–70) by 3 April (Saturday), for he noted in his copy of Holmes's *Autocrat:* "April 2—midnight—Livy and I read 18 pages of proof—Versailles and Genoa [chapters 16 and 17]" (PH in CU-MARK, in Booth, 459). He probably mailed these chapters back to Bliss on 5 April (Monday). If Bliss received them two days later and replied on the following day (8 April)—enclosing the next batch of proof as well (chapters 18–22, pages 171–227)—then Clemens probably received his letter and wrote this response on Saturday, 10 April. It is unlikely that this exchange took less time, and it cannot have taken more, since it clearly was completed before 12 April, when Clemens replied to yet another question from Bliss about chapter 16.

[2] The former Olga Konstantinovna Romanov (1851–1926) had been the wife of Christian William Ferdinand Adolphus George (1845–1913), King George I of Greece, since 1867. She was the daughter of Grand Duke Konstantin Nikolaevich Romanov (1827–92), the younger brother of Aleksandr Nikolaevich Romanov (1818–81), Tsar Aleksandr II. Her portrait eventually appeared, as Clemens here decided, in chapter 33 (page 355) of *The Innocents Abroad*. Bliss's questions about where to place this and other illustrations do not signify that Clemens had received proofs for these later chapters. The process of inserting electrotyped engravings in the standing type necessarily preceded, by several days, at least, the generation of author's proofs.

[3] "View of the Acropolis, Looking West" appears in chapter 32 of *Innocents*, the first of the two chapters partly devoted to Greece. It follows the "Oracle's" confusion of Scylla and Charybdis with Sodom and Gomorrah and precedes Mark Twain's night visit to the Acropolis.

[4] The "suppositions" accounted comically for the presence of oyster shells in the hills above Smyrna. Probably in early March, when he went over his manuscript for the last time, Clemens "marked them out" in a clipping from the 21 November 1867 San Francisco *Alta California* that he used as part of his printer's copy for chapter 39 (SLC 1867f; Hill, 28; Hirst, 234). The passage was restored to that chapter (pages 414–15), as Bliss requested.

To Pamela A. Moffett
10? April 1869 • Elmira, N.Y.
(MS: Davis)

Elmira, Ap*l*. Something, 1869.[1]

My Dear Sister =

I wrote yesterday, & I surely did not expect to write again today—but Livy is taking a nap & I have an hour to myself. She is wise. We are going out to dinner, & it's a fearful bore, & she is getting up strength for the occasion, through sleep. I have been outraging her feelings again. She is trying to cure me of making "dreadful" speeches as she calls them. In the middle of winter when I was here, we had a "run" on the hot house for a day or ɪɦ two—which is to say, an unusual lot of people died & their friends came to get roses & things to decorate the coffins with, & at the end of a week there was hardly a dozen flowers of any kind left. Charley & I made a good many jokes about it, & thus horrified. But a while ago I came in with a first-rate air of dejection on, & heaved a vast sigh. It trapped Livy into a burst of anxious solicitude, & she wanted to know what the matter was. I said, "I have been in the conservatory, & there is a perfect *world* of flowers in bloom—& we haven't a confounded corpse!" I guess Orion will appreciate that. I don't like to fool Livy this way, & don't do it often, but sometimes th her simplicity is so tempting I can't resist the inclination. I wish you could see that girl—the first time I ever saw her I said she was the most beautiful creature in the world, & I haven't altered my opinion yet. I take as much pride in her brains as I do in her beauty, & as much pride in her happy & equable disposition as I do in her brains.

Haven't got anything to write about, so I will enclose one of Livy's letters—don't read it to anybody but the family & Margaret,[2]—but M. *is* one of the family, I suppose. Livy is a sensible girl, & don't go into any hysterics in her letters—but I do when I write her. Her letter will help you to know her.

Affectionately—

Sam.

ˏMr. &ˏ Mrs. Langdon asks me to send her their regards,—& Livy also.

[1]Clemens most likely wrote this letter on the same day as the previous one to Bliss, as indicated by their nearly identical datelines.
[2]The family's housekeeper in St. Louis. Clemens's enclosure does not survive.

To Mary Mason Fairbanks
12 April 1869 • Elmira, N.Y.
(MS: CSmH)

Elmira, Apl. 12.

Dear Mother—

I One thing I *do* pride myself on—& that is, that I am a dutiful son. Now you always told me, on board the ship, to revere the Old Masters & love them, & speak well of them & appreciatively. It was on that account that I took pains all through the book (for I am publishing a book) to make mention of them & their works. And now I perceive that my engravers have caught my spirit of adulation & are helping me to glorify Titian & those other scrubs. They have made some very beautiful studies from the Old Masters—& I enclose the rough proofs. (They will be handsome when well printed.) Do you know, I think these things unequaled in American art. Notice the cheerful satisfaction that is in St Mark's face—& also the easy confidence of his manner. Could anything be finer? ,², The St Matthew is the noblest work of art I ever saw. There is an amount of feeling about it that you find nowhere else except in the Paul Veronese school. The pleasant *negligé* of the attitude irresistibly suggests Leonardo da Vinchi. The ~~calm thoughtfulness~~ ,dreamy spirituality, of the face ~~at~~ arrests the attention of even the most careless observer.*/* 3.—The Jerome is after Tintoretto. There are touches here & there & dainty little effects, that will bring that great artist to your mind.[1] 4.—Now the tranquil satisfaction with which St Sebastian goes about with a lot of arrows sticking in him, will remind you of St Sebastians by *all* the old masters—every one of them.

We must go to dinner, now ~~els~~—Livy & I[2]—else I would write you more about the old masters. Love to the family. And to Mr & Mrs Severance. Allong &c

Yr Son
Mark.

[*enclosures:*]

ST. SEBASTIAN, BY THE OLD MASTERS.

ST. UNKNOWN, BY THE OLD MASTERS.

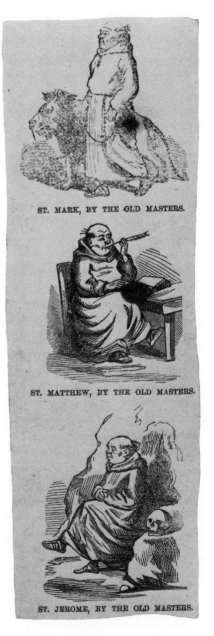

ST. MARK, BY THE OLD MASTERS.

ST. MATTHEW, BY THE OLD MASTERS.

ST. JEROME, BY THE OLD MASTERS.

✉ ——

Mrs. A. W. Fairbanks | Care "Herald" | Cleveland | Ohio. [*postmarked:*]
ELMIRA N.Y. APR 12

[1]Clemens enclosed illustrations from chapter 23 (pages 238–39) of *The Innocents Abroad*, which he had cut from the proofs he probably received on this day. His references here to Tintoretto (Jacopo Robusti, 1518?–94), Paul Veronese (Paolo Caliari, 1528–88), Leonardo da Vinci (1452–1519), and Titian (Tiziano Vecellio, 1488?–1576) are all clearly playful, but do not appear to refer to specific paintings by them, even though Tintoretto and Veronese did paint St. Jerome and St. Matthew, respectively.
[2]The company at dinner may well have included Anna E. Dickinson, who had arrived in Elmira on Saturday, 10 April, to visit with the Langdons ("City and Neighborhood," Elmira *Advertiser*, 12 Apr 69, 4). Apparently Clemens first met Dickinson during this visit, although he had seen her lecture and known of her friendship with the Langdons much earlier.

To Elisha Bliss, Jr.
12 April 1869 • Elmira, N.Y.
(MS: CU-MARK)

Elmira, April 12, 1869.

Friend Bliss—

I think St Mark & the others, "by the Old Masters" are the very funniest pictures I ever saw. I cut them out of the proof to send to Mrs. Fairbanks of Cleveland who always pleaded that the Old Masters might be spared from a blackguarding. I think *all* the engravings are handsome & attractive. I *did* "copper" that fountain, but since it looks like the one you got in Paris (Ky.) yourself, I haven't another word to say. You see *I* thought it looked like a lot ~~or~~ of niggers & horses adrift in a freshet— but I don't say a word, now, Bliss. I guess it will look well when it is neatly printed.[1]

Your idea about the "Echo" diagram is correct—glad it is to be engraved. ˏWhat is become of the beautiful view of Spires (Milan Cathedral)?ˏ

OVER

How is the name business?

The ℰ̶ Crusade of the Innocents—Or, Pil. Prog. &c.

The Innocents Abroad—Or, &cc

The Exodus of the Innocents—Or &c[2]

I'm pushing the proofs. Hereafter, they will return to you by the very next mail after reception.[3]

Yrs

Mark.

✉ ―――

[*letter docketed:*] √ [*and*] Mark Twain | April 12/69

[1]Clemens had "coppered" (questioned) the illustration of a fountain at Versailles in the proofs for chapter 16 (page 154) of *The Innocents Abroad*, which he probably returned on 5 April (see 10? Apr 69 to Bliss, n. 1). It was based on a contemporary photograph of the fountain of Apollo, "with a group of the sun-god in his chariot, environed with tritons, nymphs, and dolphins" (Baedeker, 286; Hirst, 217–18, 220). Within a day of sending Clemens the proofs for chapters 18–22, Bliss must have sent him proofs for chapters 23–27, together with his response to the query about the fountain illustration. Judging by Clemens's reply, Bliss admitted that he too had been skeptical of this illustration, but explained, perhaps facetiously, that he had allayed his concern by comparing it with an imitation of the original fountain in Paris, Kentucky (no confirmation has been found that such an imitation existed). The problem that Clemens had perceived may have been in part the result of the process of pulling proof: since the illustration was of a fountain at night, it was easy to make the ink impression too dark.

[2]The "Echo" diagram was the drawing of Clemens's notebook in chapter 19 (page 197), which evidently had not been included in the proofs, but was still "to be engraved." The "Spires" of the cathedral at Milan eventually appeared in chapter 18 (facing page 172). Clemens's question here shows that he had seen an artist's proof of the engraving while still in Hartford. Bliss responded, and also commented on "the name business," in the following letter (CU-MARK):

AMERICAN PUBLISHING CO., PUBLISHERS OF STANDARD WORKS, SOLD BY SUBSCRIPTION ONLY. NOW IN PRESS RICHARDSON'S NEW WORKS, PERSONAL HISTORY OF U. S. GRANT, BEYOND THE MISSISSIPPI. HISTORY OF THE BIBLE, ILLUSTRATED. AGENTS WANTED.

S. DRAKE, PRES'T.	OFFICE AMERICAN PUBLISHING COMPANY,
E. BLISS, JR., SEC'Y.	148 ASYLUM STREET.
F. E. BLISS, TREAS.	HARTFORD, CONN., April 14 186 9

Friend "Mark. T"

Yours recd. Glad the "*picters*" suit—Have got a *pile more doing*. The *Spires* ~~are~~ is *a full page cut* & not yet done—will appear in due season. Shall have *16. full ˌpageˏ cuts* – – I like "Innocents abroad" & also "Crusade of the Innocents" both are good. Keep up a d—l of a thinking & *may-be* (it is about time for them) you will get something better if not either will do.—

You get my *idea exactly* of the fountain, when I saw it,– (but dont tell any one about that Paris of mine being in (Ky) some may think I have been *Abr-rroad*

The fact is, that fountain is splendid, & *so is a big freshet!* It looked I said like a *whale spout* with Jonas thrown up, in any quantity, all *sea sick* & spouting themselves—nevertheless, it is good, & will do, particularly the *lamps*

No proofs today. Will be some tomorrow.

Printers slower than the d—l – – I wish I was a type setter I^d push it. Never mind the book will appear & the country will *have some pep*— I am sticking in the cuts, in the last chapters now.

Yours
E Bliss Sy

[3]It is likely that Clemens returned proofs of chapters 18–22 (pages 171–227) with this letter. He may already have had the next batch of proofs in hand, but he did not return them for another three days (see the next letter).

To Elisha Bliss, Jr.
15 April 1869 • Elmira, N.Y.
(MS: CtY-BR)

Elmira, Thursday, 1869.

Friend Bliss—

Yes, on page 233 it *ought* to be "forgot *it* in France"—as you suggest.

Sometimes it should be "St Peter" & sometimes "St. Peter's." I have made the correction.[1]

Well, I am sure I hope we *shall* ~~made~~ make a big campaign with the book. It is a *readable* book, I know—because I wrote it myself. And it is going to be a mighty handsome book—as your letter-press & pictures show, plainly enough.

~~I begin to be afraid that I have given you MSS enough for about a million pages.~~

Yrs in a hurry
Mark.

✉———————————————————————————

[letter docketed:] √

[1]Clemens was returning the proofs of chapters 23–27 (pages 228–97), which he had probably received on Monday, 12 April. Bliss had called his attention to the omitted "it" in chapter 23 (page 233), and to a possible inconsistency in chapter 26 (pages 271–75), where he initially referred to the "Church of St. Peter"

but afterward called it simply "St. Peter's." The particular correction is uniden-
tifiable since neither the printer's copy nor the proofs is known to survive.

To Mary Mason Fairbanks
15 April 1869 • Elmira, N.Y.
(MS: CSmH)

"After dinner" ⎫
Elmira, Ap*ᶧ*. 15, 1869. ⎭

My Dear Mother—
    "How much longer is Elmira to contain" me? Well, I can't tell,
yet. We can't figure it out, yet. Livy says, until business obliges me to
go. I feel about that way myself. I'm not in any hurry. I consider it "pol-
itic" to tire them all out *now* if I am ever going to do it—& not wait until
it is everlastingly too late. But you are right—& your head is level—your
head is *always* level on the wisdom of life. No indeed, you are *not* too
"officious"—I want you to understand that your Motherly "officious-
ness" is always welcome, & always *required* of you. But Livy & I have
talked this thing all over, to-day—& the result is, I am going to stay a
while longer,—though, to speak truly, you[r] letter came near making
me pack my trunk.[1]
    Why bless you I almost "abandoned all idea" *l* months ago, when
Mr. Benedict declined to sell an interest, & I knew so well that it would
very much cripple Mr. Fairbanks' strength in the establishment to part
with a share of his half. I did not want to talk to B. again, & I didn't want
Mr. Fairbanks to take me ~~in unless the taking me~~ into the partnership
unless the doing it would help us *both*—not make me & partly unmake
him.[2] So I began looking around. I made proposals to an eastern newspaper firm, & they wrote to one partner to come home from Europe & *l*
see about it. He was to have spent the summer or a part of it abroad, but
they say he will now get back in May.[3] Therefore I am reading proof &
waiting. I wait very patiently, because this thing of settling down for life
is the solemnest ~~thin~~ matter that has ever yet come into my calculations,
& I am not inclined to get in a sweat about it, or make a move without
looking well into it first. I must not make a mistake in this thing. As I do
not quite understand having secrets from you, I will say that the eastern
paper I allude to is the Hartford Courant—though I have a strong

impression that I told you about it or wrote you about it some time ago. But you know, one can't *write* business worth a cent—I'll *tell* you what plans I have now, or may conceive, when I see you—which I hope won't be many weeks hence. I think two or three of us will make you a visit as soon as this proof-reading is over. I would talk more with Livy about it, but that it is a little far away as yet. She will be of the party—the others will doubtless be Mrs. Langdon & myself.

I tell you Mr. Fairbanks' instincts are sound—a man in love *don't* bother about business much, & that is a petrified fact—but bye-&-bye— bye-&-bye.

Every day I expect a call to "come to Hartford" & cut down the MSS. We have read 300 pages of proof & are only to the middle of Rome[4]—at this rate the book will make at least a thousand pages—& so it *must* be cut down by wholesale. What I hate, is, that it will be the best part that will be sacrificed by the scissors.

Please to kiss Mollie[5] for me—& give my love to the rest of the household. I would write more, & write interestingly, too, but supper is ready & Livy is suffering for my presence. She has changed her notions, some, since that first letter of hers which I read to you last fall—for which I am profoundly thankful. [Supper bell.] [Second gong.] [Mary.][6]

"Coming!" [I mean "adieu."]

> Yr affectionate
> & dutiful son
> Mark.

[1] Mrs. Fairbanks had presumably advised Clemens to leave Elmira because of the attention that his engagement was receiving in the press. In fact, on the morning of 15 April, the Elmira *Advertiser* remarked:

> —We come across the following, or a similar paragraph, in nearly all of our exchanges about these days: "It is credibly rumored that MARK TWAIN, the truest humorist this country has produced, genial and refined, is about to wed an Elmira lady, admired of all and settle down there." ("City and Neighborhood," 4)

[2] In his letter of 13 and 14 February to Olivia, Clemens first expressed his growing dissatisfaction with the Cleveland *Herald* and his interest in looking elsewhere. Mrs. Fairbanks's letter (not extant) doubtless urged him to pursue negotiations with Benedict in Cleveland.

[3] The absent partner was Charles Dudley Warner, who finally returned from Europe in June (see 21 June 69 to OLL, n. 3).

[4] That is, to the end of chapter 27 (page 297) of *The Innocents Abroad*.

[5] Twelve-year-old Mary Paine Fairbanks.

[6] See 12 Mar 69 to OLL, n. 2.

To Elisha Bliss, Jr.
20 April 1869 • Elmira, N.Y.
(MS: CU-MARK)

                                             Elmira, Apl. 20.
Friend Bliss—
   I wish you would have MY revises revised again & look over them
yourself & see that my marks have been corrected. A proof-reader who
persists in making *two* words ˄(& sometimes even *compound* words)˄ of
"anywhere" and "everything;" & who spells villainy "vill*i*any" & liq-
uefies "liqu*i*fies" &c, &c, is ~~not three removes from an idiot,—~~ ˄infer-
nally unreliable—˄ & so I don't like to trust your man. He never yet has
acceded to a request of mine made in the margin, in the matter of spelling & punctuation, as I know of. He shows spite—don't trust him, but
revise my revises yourself. I have long ago given up trying to get him to
spell those first-mentioned words properly. ~~He is an idiot—& like all
idiots, is self-conceited.~~[1]
   I begin to be afraid there is too much MSS. It don't seem to me that
I ought to be only just getting to ~~Herculaneum~~ Pompeii at the 326th
page—ought to be a heap further along than that, I should think. Half
of the book is finished, now, but I feel almost sure that ~~we~~ it is going to
crowd things to get the rest of the MSS into 326 pages more. Please run
over & measure the remaining MSS & see how much more it is going to
make than what you want. I shall hate like everything to leave here,
(**even for forty minutes**—tell Mrs. Bliss that) but still, if the MSS **must**
be cut down, & it *can't* be helped, telegraph me & I will dart for Hartford
instantaneously˄ ~~at once immediately.~~
                      "The Innocents Abroad;
                                  or
              The M~~o~~d New Pilgrim's Progress"
seems to be the neatest & the easiest understood—by farmers & everybody—suppose we adopt it—& *you* suggest to the artist an idea for a
~~frontispiece~~ ˄il title-page˄—you are good at it—remember your idea
about it before?—What they *expected* to see—& what they *did* see?[2]
                                             Yrs—
                                             Mark.

I think my next proof will include the chapter on *Pompeii*=please send me TWO copies of that chapter. Instruct your foreman about it, now while you think of it.[3]

[1] Clemens was returning his proofs ("revises") for chapters 28–30 (pages 298–326) of *The Innocents Abroad*, which he had probably received from Bliss the previous day, or at the earliest, on Saturday, 17 April. (He was not reading *revised* proof, but rather was asking Bliss to do so.) All of the words referred to here had appeared in those pages at least once, but "any where" and "every thing" survived into print uncorrected, there and throughout the book. Bliss's proofreader has not been identified.

[2] The cover and spine of *The Innocents Abroad* reproduced the title as Mark Twain wrote it here. "Pilgrim's" became "Pilgrims'" on the title page, however, almost certainly at the instigation of the proofreader or publisher. This change created grammatical agreement with "Innocents," but obscured the original contrast of Mark Twain with the hero of John Bunyan's classic (Hirst, 229–30). Bliss followed up his own earlier suggestion, and "The Pilgrim's Vision" appeared facing "The Quaker City in a Storm" as a double frontispiece.

[3] Bliss's foreman has not been identified, nor has Clemens's purpose in requesting the duplicate set of proofs been explained.

THE PILGRIM'S VISION.

Dual frontispiece for *The Innocents Abroad*, reproduced from the first edition. See note 2.

To James Redpath
20 April 1869 • Elmira, N.Y.
(Merwin-Clayton, 14 and 15 May 1906)

Apl. 20, 1869.

. . . .

Nasby & I hunted for you in Boston lately, unsuccessfully—it will be some time before I know *positively* whether I can lecture at all[1]

. . . .

Samuel L. Clemens
Mark Twain.

[1]Clemens and Petroleum V. Nasby were in Boston together on 14 and 15 March. James Clark Redpath (1833–91), author, journalist, abolitionist, social reformer, and educator, founded the Boston Lyceum Bureau (later the Redpath Lyceum Bureau) in 1868, in partnership with George L. Fall (d. 1874 or 1875), to supply the need for a central booking agency for lecturers. The date of this letter fragment establishes the beginning of Clemens's long, congenial association, both personal and professional, with Redpath, who replied on 24 April (see 10 May 69 to Redpath, n. 1). The Lyceum Bureau also represented many of the other leading speakers of the day, including, by 1870 at least, Nasby (Eubank, 84, 89–99, 103–6, 114, 295–98; Horner, 141–55, 175, 180–81).

To Elisha Bliss, Jr.
29 April 1869 • Elmira, N.Y.
(MS: CU-MARK, NN-B,
and CtY-BR)

Elmira, Ap*l*. 29.
Friend Bliss—
    All right. I hope there won't be a necessity to cut much, but when you say you are only to the 800 or 900th page you don't comfort me so entirely, because so much of the 400 or 500 pages still left are reprint, & so will string out ~~like~~ a heap.[1]
    Certainly—snatch out *Sampson*—it ~~t~~ isn't even necessary to mention him. Yes, snatch out the *Jaffa Colony*, too. Also, snatch out my *Temperance Society experience. ~~Also, if you choose, you can snatch~~——[I will

re-inclose your letter, so that you can see in detail what you have suggested—then just follow your own written suggestions—they suit me.]²

I suppose I ~~pub~~ put Ab (Ab del Kader) in by mistake among the
pictures. I don't mention him anywhere. I simply bought his photograph
in Constantinople because his father & mine were about of an age &
might ~~even~~ have been twins if they had had the same mother. Of course
this ~~ref~~ thought touched me, & made Ab seem near & dear to me—made
him seem a sort of jack-legged uncle to me, as I may say—& so I bought
his picture, with many tears. I wish to have it buried with me. Preserve
it. But if you have got a picture of the old Agitator made, don't waste it—
put it in, & call it "Specimen of how the Innocents usually appeared, in
the Orient"—or *some*thing, no matter what. ‸You can add the above as
explanatory foot-note.‸³

As to the rest of your letter, Good, good, good.

Tell me just about when our proofs will reach ~~the Jaffa (end of Palestine).~~ the beginning of Egypt.⁴ It is time I was thinking about packing
my trunk.

Yrs Truly

Mark Twain

[*enclosures:*]

‸Abd-el-Kader.‸

ABDULLAH FRÈRES
PHOTOGRAPHES DE SA MAJESTÉ IMPÉRIALE
LE SULTAN
—
PERA
CONSTANTINOPLE.

Who the d—l is this & where
do you mention him. I dont get
him somehow

ABDULLAH FRÈRES. PHOT.

~~This is the Sultan of Turkey's official signature~~

ABDULLAH FRÈRES
PHOTOGRAPHES DE SA MAJESTÉ IMPÉRIALE
LE SULTAN

PERA
CONSTANTINOPLE.

Is this Viceroy of Egypt?
Yes.

Sultan of Turkey—belongs with Napoleon III in early chapters about Paris. But jam him in ANYwhere you please.

ABDULLAH FRÈRES
PHOTOGRAPHES DE SA MAJESTÉ IMPÉRIALE
LE SULTAN

PERA
CONSTANTINOPLE.

Is this sultan of Turkey? who you saw with Napoleon?
Yes.

⊠——

[*letter docketed:*] √ [*and*] Mark Twain | April 29/69

[1] With his most recent letter (now lost), Bliss had probably sent proofs for chapters 35–39 (pages 381–417, equivalent to printer's copy pages 800–880). He also confirmed what Clemens had suspected as early as 15 April: the printer's copy was too long, and would need to be cut in the portion that was not yet set in type. Clemens was concerned at least in part because, compared with the first eight or nine hundred pages, which were largely in manuscript, the last four or five hundred pages made heavy use of clippings ("reprint") from his letters to the San Francisco *Alta California*, New York *Tribune*, and New York *Herald*. Although the printer's copy is now lost, it is clear that Clemens pasted these clippings to blank sheets, revising them in the margins. It is also clear that he thought a page of copy made from clippings contained two or three times the number of words in a page of his own handwriting. As he neared the end of composition, on 17 June 1868, he told Mary Mason Fairbanks that he was then writing "page No. 1,843. ‚2,343.‚"—even though the actual number of pages never exceeded 1,400 and was probably closer to 1,300 (well within the total estimated in the present letter). Clemens's 1,843 and 2,343, not previously understood (*L2*, 222 and 230 n. 4), each included his adjustment for 500 pages made from clippings: the first figure counted them twice—843 + (500×2)—the second counted them three times—843+(500×3)—giving, in effect, the number of pages there would have been had the entire printer's copy been in his handwriting.

[2] Bliss's letter must have made a number of suggestions for shortening the part of the printer's copy that had not yet been typeset. The three mentioned by Clemens all applied to chapters 56–58 (pages 604–34, equivalent to printer's copy pages 1,200–1,300). The passage about Samson that Bliss removed doubtless followed a remark that he let stand in chapter 56 (page 605): "we rode through a piece of country which we were told once knew Samson as a citizen." The deleted matter may have been a version of the "Biography of Samson" that Clemens had planned to send to the New York *Tribune* in the fall of 1867 (*N&J1*, 414). Bliss did not remove Clemens's account of the Jaffa Colony in chapter 57 (pages 613–14), nor did he shorten it in any way now detectable. He did remove the "*Temperance Society experience*," probably from chapter 58, following the reminiscence of "Holliday's Hill" (page 628). This may have been a version of another Hannibal story, which Clemens had told in April 1867 in an *Alta California* letter written from New York:

And they started militia companies, and Sons of Temperance and Cadets of Temperance. Hannibal always had a weakness for the Temperance cause. I joined the Cadets myself, although they didn't allow a boy to smoke, or drink or swear, but I thought I never could be truly happy till I wore one of those stunning red scarfs and walked in procession when a distinguished citizen died. I stood it four months, but never an infernal distinguished citizen died during the whole time; and when they finally pronounced old Dr. Norton convalescent (a man I had been depending on for seven or eight weeks,) I just drew out. I drew out in disgust, and pretty much all the distinguished citizens in the camp died within the next three weeks. (SLC 1867c)

[3] Bliss had written three questions about illustrations on the backs of *cartes de visite* that Clemens here re-enclosed with his answers, amplifying the first re-

VICEROY OF EGYPT.   ABDUL AZIZ.

Ismail Pasha, viceroy of Egypt, and Abdul Aziz, sultan of Turkey, reproduced from the first edition of *The Innocents Abroad*, pages 612 and 126. See pp. 202–3 n. 3.

sponse in this paragraph. Clemens originally submitted these photographs (reproduced here at 80 percent of actual size) with his printer's copy, identifying the subject and the relevant page number on the front (in pencil). In the first case, even though Bliss could tell generally where the illustration was to go, he could not connect the penciled identification ("Abd-el-Kader | Page 1228") with any reference in the text. Clemens wrote "over" on the front and repeated the identification on the back, both in the same purple ink he used for this letter. Although the Algerian hero Abd-el-Kader (1807?–83) is never mentioned, Bliss placed him just after the Viceroy of Egypt in chapter 57 (page 614) above the caption "Eastern Monarch." In the second and third cases, Clemens had originally written "Viceroy of Egypt & son | Page 1228" and "Sultan of Turkey | & | Napoleons Photograph | page 296" in pencil on the front. He added "over" in purple ink on the front of each, before responding, also in purple, to Bliss's questions on the back. Bliss's problem here was that the two men looked so much alike, as Clemens himself acknowledged independently (see *N&J1*, 396). Their similarity was especially true of the engravings based on these photographs, which were published in chapter 57 (page 612) and chapter 13 (page 126).

   [4] That is, the beginning of chapter 57 (page 609).

To Olivia L. Langdon
8 May 1869 • New York, N.Y.
(MS: CU-MARK)

S^T. NICHOLAS HOTEL   NEW YORK

N. Y. 8th.—

It has been a long, long time since I saw you, little darling. When they handed Charley a letter last night, my heart gave a great bound, for some instinct suggested that it might be from you & contain a postscript for me,—but it was not so. It was only a hardware letter, I suppose—at any rate it was not from Livy, & did not even mention murmur the music of her name.[1] But tonight at 9 oclock I shall hear from the darling, in Hartford—& as the Bliss's will have gone home to supper for the night by that time, I mean to telegraph them, presently, to send my letters to the hotel,[2] so that they may be there when I arrive.

(I *love* you, Livy.) Charley got up at the usual hour & went to his doctor's, but I lay abed till 12 (it is 20 minutes *after* 12, now,) & I feel pretty brisk this morning & shall feel still brisker when I shall have had my breakfast. Charley & I went to Booth's, last night, to see Othello, the great miscegenationist. The acting was good, of course, Edwin Adams playing Othello, Booth Iago, & Booth's affianced, Miss McVicker, Desdemona. And I never saw such noble scenery in my life before—the sunsets & sunrises behind the hills, with little shreds of tinted & silvered cloud floating in the dreamy mid-air, counterfeited nature rarely. As I have said, the acting was good.[3] I think less of Othello, now, than I ever did before. I wouldn't be jealous of *my* wife. And I cannot approve of his friend Iago. I begin to think Iago was a villain. I am sure that much of his conduct was questionable, & some little of it open to the grave suspicion. I believe Desdemona to have been foully murdered. They have added a good deal to the interest, as well as the naturalness of this play by having a jury sit on Desdemona & return a *f* Verdict that she "came to her death from woul wounds inflicted by some blunt instrument, supposed to have been a pillow, in the hands of a party by the name of Othello, husband of the deceased." And with this the play closed.[4]

My dearie, you will scold, maybe, but we didn't get to Mrs. Brooks' yesterday, as we had intended to do. We were at Dan's store & the Tribune office till 2 P.M., & then it seemed useless to go all the way to 53^d street when the chances were we would find her absent driving in the park.[5] And we didn't go to Beecher's church[6] for several reasons, about the strongest of which was, that other things intervened.

I am stupid. I am hungry (but not much.) I will to breakfast. I kiss my darling & bless her.

Good-bye
Sam

Miss Olivia L. Langdon | Elmira | New York [*return address:*] s^t. nicholas hotel broadway new york [*hotel stamp:*] st. nicholas hotel, new york. may 8 [*postmarked:*] new york may 8 4 p.m. [*docketed by OLL:*] 61st

[1] Accompanied by Charles Langdon, Clemens left Elmira for New York City on 5 May. Both men checked into the St. Nicholas Hotel on the following day ("Personal," New York *Evening Mail*, 7 May 69, 3; "Morning Arrivals," New York *Evening Express*, 7 May 69, 3). Langdon, a partner in the Elmira hardware firm of Ayrault, Rose and Company, was in New York to receive medical treatment for an unidentified ailment (*L2*, 342 n. 3). Clemens ended his seven-week stay in Elmira partly to work on his book in Hartford, and partly because Mary Mason Fairbanks, Mrs. Langdon, and even his own mother had questioned the propriety of his staying under the same roof with his fiancée (see 15 Apr 69 and 10 May 69, both to Fairbanks).

[2] The Allyn House.

[3] Booth's Theatre, at Twenty-third Street, between Fifth and Sixth avenues, was opened by renowned actor Edwin Booth (1833–93) on 3 February 1869. It boasted luxurious seating for seventeen hundred (with standing room for three hundred more), elaborate studios for creating the kind of stage scenery Clemens described, and complex machinery for changing sets during a performance, including a thirty-two-foot-deep pit into which an entire set could be lowered out of sight. Called "the stateliest, the handsomest, and the best appointed structure of its class that can now be found on the American continent," the theater remained under Booth's control until his financial reverses during the panic of 1873 forced him to relinquish it ("The Drama," New York *Tribune*, 18 Nov 68, 5, 4 Feb 69, 5). The production of *Othello* that Clemens saw on 7 May had opened on 26 April to mixed reviews. The New York *Tribune* pronounced it "the best representation of a Shakespearean play that has been given here for years," with Booth himself a "triumphant success," Edwin Adams (1834–77) a "true work of art," and Mary McVicker (d. 1881), whom Booth married on 7 June, "sweet and charming." The New York *Herald* disagreed, dismissing it as "not a striking performance" and finding Booth perfunctory, Adams "common place," and McVicker "no Desdemona at all" ("The Drama," New York *Tribune*, 28 Apr 69, 5; "Amusements," New York *Herald*, 27 Apr 69, 9).

[4] This spurious conclusion was Clemens's "snapper" to his deadpan account

of the plot. No such addition was reported by the reviewers, either of this production or of the one immediately preceding it, with Booth as Othello and Adams as Iago. On the contrary, the New York *Tribune* remarked that "Mr. Booth's restorations of the text of 'Othello' are numerous and commendable" ("The Drama," 13 Apr 69, 5).

[5] Slote, Woodman and Company, the blank-book and stationery manufacturing firm co-owned by Daniel Slote, was located at 119 and 121 William Street, at the tip of Manhattan, only a short distance from the New York *Tribune* offices at 154 Nassau Street. The Brookses' home—at 675 Fifth Avenue, on the corner of Fifty-third Street, a few blocks from Central Park—was an inconvenient distance from both (H. Wilson 1869, 821, 1023). While at the *Tribune* office, Clemens probably read proof of the "squib" he published in the paper on 8 May (see the next letter, n. 2).

[6] Henry Ward Beecher's Plymouth Church, in Brooklyn, where the regular Friday evening prayer meeting was held on 7 May (Noyes L. Thompson, 299).

To Olivia L. Langdon
8 May 1869 • Hartford, Conn.
(MS: CU-MARK)

Hartford, 8th May.

Patience! Fortitude! These are rare virtues. I possess them, little darling—for it is now exactly 9 PM & for nearly an hour & a half I have had your precious letter in my pocket, yet behold, even at this very moment the seal is unbroken! I am suffering to know what is in it, but I am determined to enjoy the luxury of reading it in bed, with the added delight of a cigar. I tell you, dearie, it is a hard task to carry one of your letters an hour & a half without opening it. But then the pleasure I shall have will repay all my patience. I am writing now, because I cannot consent to rob myself of the solace of writing you *every* day; & you see, ever so many things may occur tomorrow to lose me that pleasure. Bless your dear little heart, my own darling! The more I think of you the better I love you & the more bitter this see separation seems. Livy, you are so interwoven with the very fibres of my being that if I were to lose you it seems to me that to lose memory & reason at the same time would be a blessing to me. God preserve you, my little jewel. I felt very thankful this morning when "our" good mother's letter to Charley said your cold was growing better, albeit a little impatient that it was only growing better "slowly."

Charley drove up to the depot with me & I left him in good spirits—
& forgot to retain the carriage & send him back in it. I never thought of
it until this moment, & now I am so ashamed of myself that the pleasure
of reading your letter is going to be marred by my upbraiding conscience. I will write him & apologize. Oh, this is *too* bad. I would give
anything if this had not occurred. Charley ~~don't like to walk~~ is all kindness & thoughtfulness, & I am all stupidity & carelessness. He never
would have been so inconsiderate of my comfort as to serve me such a
scurvy trick as this. I won't add another line to this until I have asked his
pardon.

    *   *   *   *   *   *   *

Well, I have written Uncle Cholley a most humble letter, & I begin
to feel better already.

Livy, one of those New York papers said "Mark Twain is at the St
Nicholas, & we have seen him & he is only *one.*"—a play upon **Twain** &
our reported marriage. How's *thim?*[1]

That squib I wrote about the Wilson murder case was in the New
York Tribune this morning. Did my little business manager cut it out &
preserve it? It isn't important, but then it comes under the head of the ⌀
especial duty I assign you, & so you must attend to it, honey.[2]

I have seen Mr. Twichell just a moment, & he wants me to spend a
week with him. His wife is going away Monday. Told him I didn't know.
⌀ Am to spend the evening with him tomorrow & talk about it.

I am satisfied there is another letter in the post office from you by
this time, & I do *wish* I had it.

I am writing on a marble-top table, & if I don't quit right away I
shall get a scolding from the dearest girl in the world—therefore, with
worlds of love, & a kiss & a blessing, I am your devoted,

                                         Sam

———————————————————————————

Miss Olivia L. Langdon | Elmira | New York [*return address:*] ALLYN
HOUSE, HARTFORD, CONN.   R. J. ALLYN.[3] [*postmarked:*] HARTFORD CONN. MAY
9 [*docketed by OLL:*] 62nd

[1] A search of the available files of more than two dozen New York newspapers
failed to identify the source of this quotation, which may or may not have been
a reference to Clemens's forthcoming marriage.
[2] The "squib" was:

REMARKABLE MURDER TRIAL.

To the Editor of The Tribune.

SIR: The Wilson trial came to an end yesterday. In some respects this was the most remarkable case that has ever had a place upon the criminal records of the country. It excited great interest in this part of the State, and, during the last ten days, the court-room has been pretty generally crowded with eager listeners. The facts in the Wilson case were simply these: On the 17th of February last, George L. Roderick provoked a quarrel with Dr. R. Wilson, in front of the Union Hotel in this place. Wilson put up with a good deal of abuse before he even showed temper. He even tried to pacify Roderick, but to no purpose. Roderick called him a thief, a liar, a swindler; yet Wilson bore it all calmly. Roderick grew more excited, and heaped one opprobrious epithet after another upon Wilson, and finally called him a member of the New-York Legislature. At this, Wilson sprang to his feet, and remarking to Roderick that he would not take that from any man, shot him dead with an axe-handle. Such was the evidence elicited upon the trial. The Court acquitted Wilson, upon the ground that the provocation was sufficient.   MARK TWAIN.

Elmira, N.Y., April 29.

(New York *Tribune*, 8 May 69, 4)

The events and persons alluded to were entirely fictitious: no Wilson murder occurred in Elmira, nor was there any such trial, nor even any "Union Hotel." The New York *Evening Telegram* recognized Mark Twain's purpose, noting that he "has grown so satirical of late as to awaken the enmity of several pugnacious politicians whose courage he has ventured to doubt. They threaten to *toe* the Mark in proof of their pluck" (8 May 69, 2). The objects of his ridicule were Republican Senators William Sprague (1830–1915) of Rhode Island and Joseph C. Abbott (1825–81) of North Carolina. In a Senate speech on 22 April Sprague had referred to two political opponents as "a large mastiff and a mongrel puppy." Abbott assumed he was the puppy (making the mastiff Clemens's old acquaintance, James W. Nye, a Republican senator from Nevada), and replied to Sprague, threatening him with "physical castigation," and demanding a retraction or, by implication, satisfaction on the field of honor. But on 26 April, despite what the New York *Times* described as "the most ferocious face-makings, and terrific threats ever witnessed," the two men were reconciled in a mild exchange of letters (New York *Times*: "Washington," "United States Senate," 23 Apr 69, 1; "Washington," 27 Apr 69, 5; "Sprague and Company," 28 Apr 69, 6). The Elmira *Advertiser* reported this story in two brief reports that Mark Twain must have read, and it reprinted his *Tribune* letter, without comment, one week after it appeared ("News By Telegraph," 23 Apr 69, 1; "The Abbott-Sprague Quarrel Settled," 27 Apr 69, 1; "Remarkable Murder Trial," 15 May 69, 4). On 22 May, however, aspiring local author and lecturer James Ausburn Towner (1836–1909) also reprinted Mark Twain's letter as part of "Ishmael's Corner" in the Elmira *Saturday Evening Review*, disparaging its humor as unsubtle and interlarding his own sarcastic remarks ("There's richness for you; there's fatness; there is such an air of fresh unctious humor about it") while evidently failing to recognize that any satire was intended (Towner 1869b; "Ishmael," Elmira *Saturday Evening Review*, 14 Aug 69, 8).

[3] Richard J. Allyn, proprietor of the Allyn House (Geer 1869, 40).

To Olivia L. Langdon
9 May 1869 • Hartford, Conn.
(MS: CU-MARK)

Hartford, 9th.

Break *our* engagement, darling? I would *infinitely* rather die. No, Livy, if note is taken of the deeds of men, our troth is writ in the eternal records of Heaven. We were created for each other, & can no more wilfully separate than can the forces of nature defy the God that created them. For all time wWe are bound together ˏeach otherˏ by viewless chains that are strong as the granite ribs that link the mountains together, & more enduring than the Pyramids that mock at the perishable vanities of men—for these chains are of eternity itself, & cannot know death.

You are right when you say we shall not break our engagement. My life thenceforward would be only a vain & foolish sort of existence, for I know by every instinct that is in me that I am not capable of loving any other woman as I love you. And life is but a dull, eventless captivity without love.

To say that I am sorry for Emma, but ill expresses it—for I can, after a fashion, divine what my torture would be if I were in her place.[1] That I can divine one-half the magnitude of the terrible calamity, though, I do not pretend. It suggests graves, madness, winding-sheets & death!—in a word, all nameless horrors that can befall the unfortunate. In presence of the thought, I feel as if I want to put my arms about you & clasp you close to my breast, & know & feel that you are my darling yet, that I have not lost you.

I am more than sorry for Emma—I feel more kindly toward her than I ever did before—& my rebuking conscience iterates & reiterates to me that all the time that I would have stood between you & her & bolted the sheltering doors against her, she was beseeching seeking restful words for a troubled spirit & balm for a sore heart.

All the ill news comes at once. A friend of Twichell's is in misfortune—a young minister whom I met, with his wife,[2] at Twichell's house several times heretofore. He loved her to idolatry, & now she is taken from him. She had a miscarriage two years ago, & cam what with her bodily sufferings & grief for the loss of the child, she came near dying.

Last week she had another miscarriage, & did not survive it. The young widower is well nigh beside himself with despair. Death is for us both, my Livy, but not broken engagements. Our marriage—for marriage it is—is for time & eternity.

"Livy, Livy, Livy" (I love the name,) I am *so* sorry, but we can't have proofs to send you. The publisher & the ~~proof-reader a~~ electrotyper are at daggers' points, & as the latter is not *obliged* by custom or contract to furnish duplicate proofs, Bliss has little hope of getting them. He will try, but expects a refusal. And I have put so much "poetry in the margin" that it seems hardly worth while for me to make an attempt, especially as Bliss says he is a crusty, ill-natured Englishman[3]—still, I mean to make the attempt anyhow. I have read ₍over₎ fifty pages of proofs this morning—dull, stupid, aggravating, tiresome drudgery it was. It seems incredible to me that these are the very same kind of proofs I used to *love* to read with my darling & string out as long as possible. But this time I *galloped* through them & was perfectly delighted when I got through. It took me about two hours—or even less. I haven't even made a *start* toward answering your dear good letters (7th & 8th received to-day,) & yet I must stop writing now, for at 3 or 3.30 oclock I must be at Mrs. Hooker's, & it is considerably after 2, now & I am not yet shaved.

Hat's gone, now, I suppose, & I am most sincerely sorry, for if she isn't a blessing to a household, all my judgments are gone astray. And she was such company & such a help to you, that I feel a grateful ~~gr~~ glow around about my heart every time I think of her. Anybody that is good to Livy can command my love & ~~reg~~ respect. I shall write her, to Lisbon, Ill.[4]

Livy dear, you must deliver my love unto your father & mother (& in no stinted measure or in frozen parliamentary pomp & circumstance, I warn you,) & unto your sister Sue & Theodore as well. I love all those parties.

Confound it, I forgot to give Hattie the mocking-bird.

The peace of God be with you, my own darling, & His angels keep you.

Sam

Miss Olivia L. Langdon | Elmira | New York [*return address:*] ALLYN HOUSE, HARTFORD, CONN.   R. J. ALLYN. [*postmarked:*] HARTFORD CONN   MAY 11 [*docketed by OLL:*][5] 64th

[1] Emma Sayles's engagement to John (or Sanford) Greeves, now broken, had interested Clemens since 1868 (see *L2*, 369). Sayles eventually married William A. McAtee (1838–1902), a presbyterian clergyman (Record of Interments, Lot 13, Section H, Woodlawn Cemetery, Elmira, N.Y., annotated by Herbert A. Wisbey, Jr., PH in CU-MARK).

[2] Both remain unidentified.

[3] Unidentified.

[4] Evidently Olivia had advised Clemens to write to Harriet Lewis at Lisbon, Illinois, rather than at her home in Ottawa, about twenty miles to the southwest, which he had visited in January (see 13 and 14 Jan to OLL).

[5] Since the postmark follows the date of this letter by two days, the envelope transcribed here may well belong to a letter now missing, written on 10 May (see 10 May 69 to Redpath, n. 2). If so, the present letter would have been docketed 63, presumably on its envelope, now lost. Two subsequent letters in the sequence are also missing: docket numbers 65 and 66, probably written on 11 or 12 May.

To Mary Mason Fairbanks
10 May 1869 • Hartford, Conn.
(MS: CSmH)

148 Asylum st. $\left.\right\}$
Hartford, 10th

Dear Mother—

I *wrote* you some ten days ago, but I discover, now, that I failed to mail the letter. I judge that that is the reason why you have been so dilatory about replying to it. I confess that I have felt a little hurt about it, & said as much to Livy—but I do not feel so much injured, now.

You drove me away from Elmira at last. Your first shot staggered me, & your second "fetched" me. You made me feel meaner & meaner, & finally I absolutely couldn't stand it—& so I surprised them all by suddenly packing my trunk. Livy spoke right out, & said that to leave was unnecessary, uncalled-for, absurd, & utterly exasperating & foolish—but I smoothed her feathers down at last by insisting that your ~~jug~~ judgment in this matter, just as usual, was solid good sense—I smoothed her plumage down but I never convinced her. ~~However, when~~ And I never convinced Mr. Langdon, or Mr. or Mrs. Crane, or Hattie Lewis— but when Livy fancied that her mother did not coincide with the others quite cordially enough, her pride took fire & she spiked her guns & said Go‚!——and come back in fourteen days by the watch! Such are her or-

ders. So you see what you have done, Mother. You have filled with sor-
row two loving hearts. [Now you weep—& by geeminy you ought to.]
But if it will comfort you, I will say that my other mother, there in St
Louis, kept writing me to vamos the Langdon ranche, too.

ʃ So I *have* vamosed it,—& if it were to do over again I wouldn't.
And now that I am away, I am afraid I shall disobey Livy's orders & not
return on the 19ᵗʰ· She was in dead earnest about it, & so was her
mother—but I will write & say I *will* return if ~~she~~ they will pack up &
go to Cleveland with me—provided you want us—I believe it is a good
while since you said you did.

Have read 500 pages of proof—only about 200 more to read—& so
the thing *is* nearly done. It is gotten up regardless of expense, & the pictures *are* good, if I do say it myself. There is a multitude of them—
among them *good* portraits of Dan, Duncan, Beach, Sultan of Turkey,
Viceroy of Egypt, Napoleon (I think,) & a poor picture of Queen of
Greece—& above all, a rear view of Jack & his half-soled pantaloons.[1]
Dan's & Duncan's portraits are *very* good. I was sorry they put Beach in,
simply because the letter-press did not seem to call for it—but then he
was at a deal of trouble making house-room for the artists while they
sketched his foreign pictures, & so *they* wanted his photograph in. So it
is all right.[2]

I wrote Mr. Fairbanks tonight, after many days' delay. I had hoped
that Livy & I would nestle under your wing, some day & have you teach
us how to scratch for worms, but fate seems determined that we shall
roost elsewhere. I am sorry. But you know, I want to *start* right—it is the
safe way. I want to be permanent. I must feel ~~thou~~ thoroughly & completely *satisfied* when I anchor "for good & all." Is it not what you would
desire of any other son of yours?[3]

I have no news to tell you, except that Livy is no stronger than she
was six months ago—& it seems hard, & grieves me to have to say it. I
cannot talk about it with her, though, for she is as sensitive about it as I
am about my drawling speech & stammerers of *their* infirmity. She turns
crimson when it is mentioned, & it hurts her worse than a blow.

Mrs. Crane *seems* better from her southern life, but *is* not. The doctors cut her throat again the other day. [*paragraph indention deleted*]
Charley says, (I do not know his authority,) that her days are numbered,
& are few.[4] Charley is just arrived at the St Nicholas to stay a month &
be doctored, & Hattie Lewis was to leave to-day for her home in Illinois.
Livy, Hattie, Charley & I, all gone within 5 days of each other[5]—don't

you suppose the house seems a little bit solemn after just *such* a cleaning out? Mr. Langdon says he ain't going to ~~say~~ stay in any such a place. Livy's letters are not absolutely *gay*. Good-bye, & write me. Peace unto you & your household.

Yr loving son
Sam.

[1]Clemens had probably read proof of *The Innocents Abroad* through chapter 47 (page 502), leaving 13 chapters (148 pages) yet to read. Some of the portraits he mentions here had been prepared for that final segment of the book. Sultan of Turkey Abdul Aziz (1830–76) and Emperor of France Napoleon III (Charles Louis Napoleon Bonaparte, 1808–73) appear in chapter 13. Daniel Slote appears in chapter 27. Queen Olga of Greece appears in chapter 33. Viceroy of Egypt Ismail Pasha (1830–95), Moses S. Beach, and John A. ("Jack") Van Nostrand in "half-soled pantaloons" appear in chapter 57. *Quaker City* Captain Charles C. Duncan appears in chapter 60. All but the portrait of Van Nostrand were based on *carte de visite* sized photographs collected by Clemens (Hirst, 199, 205, 210–16).

[2]Moses S. Beach had advanced the $1,250 passage money of William E. James, the professional photographer who accompanied the *Quaker City* excur-

REAR ELEVATION OF JACK.

Jack Van Nostrand, reproduced from the first edition of *The Innocents Abroad*, page 610. See note 1.

sion. James made dozens of stereoscopic photographs during the journey, later offering them for sale to the excursionists and to the general public. Beach allowed illustrators from the New York firm of Fay and Cox to stay at his Brooklyn home while using a set of James's photographs to prepare sketches of foreign sites for *Innocents* (for a discussion of James's role in the excursion, as well as a selection of his photographs, see Hirst and Rowles, 15–33). Beach also made available the collection of picture cards, similar to modern postcards, that he himself had assembled. He is mentioned in "the letter-press," in chapter 57, only as the benefactor of the refugees from the troubled Jaffa Colony.

³Clemens's letter to Abel Fairbanks, which does not survive, evidently renounced his interest in the Cleveland *Herald*. Nevertheless, Fairbanks still hoped to attract him (see 4 June 69 to JLC and family).

⁴See 9 and 31 Mar 69 to Crane, n. 2. The authority for Charles J. Langdon's gloomy prognosis may have been Thaddeus S. Up de Graff (1839–85), the Elmira eye, ear, and throat surgeon treating Susan Crane (*MTMF*, 97 n. 2; Towner 1892, 313–14). She survived both Langdon and Clemens, however, dying in 1924 at the age of eighty-eight. Langdon's own infirmity has not been identified.

⁵Olivia may have been spending a day or two on an excursion with her friend Ella J. Corey: see 17 and 18 May 69 to OLL.

To James Redpath
10 May 1869 • Hartford, Conn.
(Transcripts, MS, and MS facsimile: various sources)

> 148 Asylum Street
> American Publishing Co.
> Hartford, May 10

Jas. Redpath, Esq.

Dear Sir:

I have been slow about answering but then I have been very busy & besides I wanted to consider a little.¹

1. Very well. Please go on, as you propose, & use my name "from the 1st of November."

2. As to terms. Say we let the customary price be $100, & increase or diminish it according to circumstances—decreasing it, if you see fit, where several appointments, in one neighborhood can be clubbed together & secured by so doing. As to making it more than $100 in any case, be the judge yourself, I shall not complain if you never do it. I talked all around through the West last winter, & always charged $100,

but then the distances were grand, gloomy & peculiar and I wouldn't go over the same ground again for the same money, by any means. I hate long journeys, & so does everybody.

(There need be no "condition" about California. I shall be back before Nov. 1, if I go.)

I seldom save anything I write, or any notices of lectures. But the young lady whom I think most of, does, & I have written her.[2] Whatever stock of this kind she may have on hand I will mail to you. I remember she has an article on Vanderbilt from Packard's Monthly—makes a column. Do you want it? [*in margin:* Until I hear from *her* the enclosed is all I can put my hands on & they don't signify.][3] I like the Du Chaillu dodge of circularizing the lyceums *tolerably*, & only tolerably. It is calculated to make one feel rather like a "celebrated" corn-doctor. But maybe it is for the best & therefore I will presently collect and send material for circular whereby to delude secretaries.

(Mem.—Mr. Bridgman (I think I have the name right) Secretary of the Something ("Institute," I think,) called this morning to talk business.[4] I told him you would attend to his case whenever his mind is made up. Please don't charge him less than $100—& I don't think it would be just to charge more. However, that is your business, not mine.)

. . . I am here reading the proofs of my book, which will issue from the press of the "American Publishing Co." . . . It is a sort of stunning narrative of the renowned Pleasure Excursions of Capt. Duncan's Quaker City steamer to Europe, Egypt, Palestine, & pretty nearly everywhere else, two years ago. (The one Beecher & Gen. Sherman were to have gone in).[5] It will contain about 700 pages octavo, . . . over 200 artistic engravings built expressly for it. Some 26 . . . are full page. . . . The pictures have cost $5,000 . . . it is no slouch of a book. . . . the New England journals.[6] The book is published only by subscription.

If I go to California I shall write a dozen letters to the N. Y. *Tribune*, & if you can have them copied wholly or in part, it will be well—especially as the title of next winters lecture will be *"Curiosities of California."* Haven't written it yet, but it is mapped out, & suits me very well. [*Mem.* Nearly all the societies wanted a Cal. lecture last year, & of course it will be all the better, now, when the completion of the Pacific RR has turned so much attention in that direction.[7] There is *scope* to the subject, for the country is a curiosity; do. the fluctuations of fortune in the mines, where men grow rich in a day & poor in another; do. *the people*—for you have

been in new countries & understand ⸗ that;[8] do. the Lake Tahoe, whose
wonders are little known & less appreciated here; ditto the *never=
mentioned* strange Dead Sea of California;[9] & ditto a passing mention,
maybe, of the Big Trees & Yo Semite.

But I did not intend to write you to death.

But a word more. A New York agent writes: "Stick to New England
if you are resolved to do it, but let me make, say ten engagements for you
in near places in New York & Penn. Select any month you please and
any price (125.—$150 &c) but let me have your name for that number of
engagements."[10]

What shall I say? I almost promised to open the courses next season
in Newark, N. J. Pittsburgh, Pa. & I *think* Cleveland, O. provided I lectured at all. Now I *would* like to talk in Newark, Brooklyn & New York,
but I don't want to go further away, & I don't know of *ten* places around
there that I want to talk in. Make a suggestion, please.

I would like very much to talk in about *five* small places first, to *get
the hang* of my lecture, & then talk for one of the two big lecture societies
of Boston. You know one *corrects* & *amends* portions of his lecture th all
the time, the first five or six nights, & he *never is* satisfied with it till about
the sixth delivery. Will you make a note? Well, I believe I have answered
it all of your letter

Yrs. Truly

Sam. L. Clemens.

I don't try to use two lectures during the same season. And I don't like
an old one.

---

[1]Clemens was answering the following letter from Redpath, itself a reply to
Clemens's letter of 20 April:

Boston, Ap. 24/69

S. L. Clemens, Esq

Dear Sir—I was very sorry that I failed to see you when in Boston; but next time I hope
to have better luck.

Now, about lecturing. Let me use your name, say for—"from the 1st of November,"
conditional on your return from California;—tell ‸me‸ your terms; send me the titles of your
lectures; and I will work you up during the summer   Send me regularly all *your short
humorous pieces* so that I may get them republished, and so keep up & increase your reputation in N. E. I think you wᵈ do well in this section; altho' you are not so widely known
here as in the Middle & Western States. However by sending me a lot of your newspaper
scraps that can be remedied.

What I propose to do for lecturers is to advertise my whole list in leading papers,
send circulars to every "Post," (GAR)   Y. M. C. A. & Lyceum, & newspaper editor in
N.Y; and when the lecturer furnishes me with special circulars scatter them at my own
expense

Now, this I w^d like to do for you

I enclose the two last that have come to hand for me. Can't you get up something similar & let me have 500 copies.

Some lecturers prefer also to spend some money (in my name) in special advertisements. Du Chaillu did it & it paid. Whatever am't (if any) you choose to send for this purpose, I will expend judiciously.

Circulars, however, you ought to have.

Finally, don't think that I'm half such a dandy as this Notepaper w^d seem to imply—I have nothing else & it is my daughters!

> Yours truly
> Jas Redpath

P.S. My final list for the season won't be issued till the middle of August. But a Spring list is necessary, as a sort of opening medicine to the body Lyceumic. (PH in CU-MARK, courtesy of Nick Karanovich)

Redpath's enclosures do not survive with his letter. One of them may have been a circular advertising Paul Belloni Du Chaillu (1835–1903), the French-born African explorer and author.

[2]Clemens made his request of Olivia in a 10 May letter, now lost (see 9 May 69 to OLL, n. 5). Her reply, enclosing reviews, reached him on 14 May.

[3]The enclosures have not been located, but may have included some of the "American Vandal Abroad" reviews that Redpath later used in "circularizing the lyceums" for the 1869–70 lecture season (see Boston Lyceum Bureau Advertising Circular, Appendix E).

[4]William S. Bridgman (or Bridgeman), assistant cashier at the Hartford National Bank, was vice president of the Hartford Young Men's Institute. Organized in 1838 to foster "literary culture" and to take advantage of "the lectures then being delivered before lyceums the country round," the institute maintained a reading room and a library that had grown to over 20,000 volumes by 1869 (Burpee, 1:381; Geer 1869, 61, 489, 505).

[5]For Henry Ward Beecher's and William Tecumseh Sherman's reasons for withdrawing from the *Quaker City* excursion, see *L2*, 24–25 n. 3, and 50–51 n. 1.

[6]In the missing passage preceding this phrase Clemens evidently suggested that reviews of *The Innocents Abroad* appearing in New England newspapers would prove useful in publicizing his lecture tour.

[7]The spike-driving ceremony at Promontory, Utah, celebrating the meeting of the tracks of the Central Pacific and Union Pacific railroads, and hence the completion of the transcontinental line, took place on the day Clemens wrote this letter (Hart 1987, 191). That morning the Hartford *Courant* advised its readers that the event was set for "about 2:35 p.m., Hartford time":

Arrangements have been made with the Western Union Telegraph company, so that each stroke of the hammer on the last spike driven shall be reported simultaneously at New York and San Francisco. The operator will accompany each blow of the hammer with a tap of the finger upon the key. A conversation with the New York office last evening assured us that the blow can be repeated at Hartford as well, and moreover, it could be struck upon the great fire bell. Why not? Who will attend to it? Let us hear upon the bell the strokes of the hammer that puts down the connecting rail twenty-five hundred miles away. ("The Pacific Railroad," 2)

[8]In the mid- and late 1850s, Redpath, then a journalist crusading for abolition, had made several visits to recently created Kansas Territory, the site of contention between pro- and anti-slavery forces. In an Autobiographical Dictation of 11 October 1906 Clemens commented on Redpath's activities there:

The chief ingredients of Redpath's make-up were honesty, sincerity, kindliness, and pluck. He wasn't afraid. He was one of Ossawattomie Brown's right-hand men in the bleeding Kansas days; he was all through that struggle. He carried his life in his hands, and from one day to another it wasn't worth the price of a night's lodging. He had a small body of daring men under him, and they were constantly being hunted by the "jayhawkers," who were pro-slavery Missourians, guerrillas, modern free lances— (CU-MARK, in SLC 1907b, 330)

Subsequently Redpath traveled to Haiti, which he regarded as a suitable haven for Southern blacks. At the request of the Haitian government he established bureaus for black emigration in Boston and New York and in 1861 and 1862 he served as "Commercial agent of Hayti for Philadelphia, Joint commissioner plenipotentiary of Hayti to the government of the U.S., & General agent of emigration to Hayti for the U.S. & Canada" (Redpath). He was influential in securing United States recognition of Haitian independence, wrote *A Guide to Hayti* (1860), and published John Relly Beard's *Toussaint L'Ouverture: A Biography and Autobiography* (1863).

[9] Mono Lake, about fifteen miles east of Yosemite, "so alkaline that only one kind of brine shrimp and one kind of fly can live in it" (Hart 1987, 327). On 27 June Clemens began writing his lecture on California, the only surviving fragment of which contains a detailed description of Lake Tahoe (see 26 June 69 to JLC and PAM, n. 5).

[10] Probably James K. Medbery (see 21 Sept 69 to Crane, n. 2).

To Jane Lampton Clemens
11 May 1869 • Hartford, Conn.
(MS: CU-MARK)

148 Asylum st. ⎫
Hartford, May 10.[1] ⎭

Dear Mother—

Well, I *did* manage to leave Elmira, but I had to promise that I would return in fourteen days. Mr. Langdon said it was useless & foolish to go away at all—let the world talk, if it wanted to.

I have read 500 pages of proofs—have less than 200 more to read. It will be out in a few weeks, now. They have spent $5,000 on the engravings. It will be a stylish volume.

I am very glad you are going to live by yourselves, for I have felt for a long time that ˎthe care ofˎ keeping boardersˎing was just undermining your health & Pamelas—now I am sure both will improve. And besides, a boarding-house was no place for Annie. Boarders, as a rule, are a bad lot—though you had an exceptionally good lot, with one or two exceptions—you remember to whom I refer, no doubt. I am grateful to Pamela for promising me a bed when I come—have some hope of getting there before many months.

I don't know the date of the last money I sent,—but it seems a good while ago. If you require some, let me know—I am economising because I am at a perfectly ruinous expense here—but I do not mean to economise at *your* expense—so speak out, if you want it.[2]

Yes, Annie *could* come to the wedding if we *had* one, & freely—but there won't be any—only the family & a couple of witnesses will be present, & it will take place in Mr Langdon's house.[3]

It is 2 o'clock in the morning. Good-night. Love to Orion & Mollie & all.

ₐI don't know your address.ₐ[4]

Lovingly
Sam.

[1] Actually 11 May. When writing after midnight, as the penultimate paragraph shows he was doing, Clemens normally carried over the previous day's date.

[2] Jane Clemens had last received money from her son, $20, on 30 March, the twelfth such payment he had sent since December 1868. She next received $30 from him, on 29 May (JLC, 4). For Clemens's own accounting of his contributions to her support, as well as his personal expenses, see 23 June 69 to PAM.

[3] Pamela Moffett and her daughter, Annie, did attend Clemens's wedding, on 2 February 1870, in the parlors of the Langdon house. The Buffalo *Express* reported: "Only the immediate friends of the bride and bridegroom were present, forming quite a large company, however, and including many from a distance" ("Personal," 3 Feb 70, 4). And Albert Bigelow Paine, presumably repeating information received from Clemens, noted: "The guests were not numerous, not more than a hundred at most" (*MTB*, 1:394).

[4] That is, the *new* address in St. Louis—203 South 16th Street—to which Jane Lampton Clemens and the Moffett family had moved, or were about to move, from 1312 Chesnut Street.

To Olivia L. Langdon
12 May 1869 • Hartford, Conn.
(MS: CU-MARK)

W̵ Hartford, May ₐ12thₐ ⎫
Wednesday Eve.[1] ⎭

Was there *ever* such a darling as Livy? I *know* there never was. She fills *my* ideal of what a woman should be in order to be enchantingly lovable. And so, what wonder is it that I love her so? And what wonder is th it that I am deeply grateful for permission to love her? Oh you are such an exquisite little concentration of loveliness, Livy! I am not saying these things because I am stricken in a new place, dearie—no, they are simply the things that are always in my mind—only they are demanding expression more imperiously than usual, maybe, because (9:30 P. M.,) I am just in from one of those prodigious walks I am so fond of taking in these solemn & silent streets by night, & these pilgrimages are pretty thoroughly devoted to thinking of you, my dainty little idol.

How *could* I walk these sombre avenues at night *without* thinking of you? For their very associations would invoke you—every flagstone for many a mile is overlaid thick with ‚an‚ invisible fabric of thoughts of you—longings & yearnings & vain caressings of the empty air for you when you were sleeping peacefully & dreaming of other things than *me*, darling. And so now, & always hereafter, when I tread these stones, these sad phantoms of a time that is gone, (thank God!) will rise about me to claim kinship with these new *living* thoughts of you that are all radiant with hope, & requited love, & happiness. God bless & keep you always, my Livy!

I am in the same house (but not in the same room—thanks!) where I spent three awful weeks last ⌠ fall, worshipping you, & writing letters to you, some of which I mailed in the waste-paper basket & the others never passed from brain to paper.[2] But I don't like to think of those days, or speak of them.

Now that I am well again, dearie, I am not afraid to tell you that I have been sick for a day or two. It was of no particular consequence (I worked nearly all the time,) & it was useless to make you uneasy. This morning I felt almost persuaded that I was going to have a severe attack—but it is all well, now, gone, now, & I am well & cheery, & am enjoying the warm night & writing you in my night-clothes for comfort—& smoking. The good God that is above us all is merciful to me, —from Whom came your precious love—from Whom cometh all good gifts[3]—& I am grateful.

[Lucky I am, now, to be able to write with *two* pictures of you before me—& one of dear old Hat. (tie.)[4]] Give me a kiss, please.

I guess I'll have to have a letter every day, dearie. Except, of course, when it would be too much of a hardship. I did not hear from you to-day, & I confess & do assure [you] I *wanted* to. However, this is

all pure selfishness & I will not be guilty of it. Write every other day—
that is work enough for such a dear little body as you.

I expect to scribble very meagre letters to you, because I confess
that I use you as a sort of prize for good behavior—that is, when I trans-
act all my duties, my abundant & ample reward is the luxury of writing
to you—& when I fail to finish up my duties, Jack must go without
his supper which is to say, I must lose the luxury of writing you. But
the other night I did a vast deal of work, ⱨ keeping myself to it with
the encouraging assurance that I might talk to Livy when it was all
done—& so at last I worried through—but alas for my reward, I could
hardly sit up, & so I had to go to bed & lose all I had worked for so well.
Now I have reached my goal for to-day, for I finished my work before
supper.

[The picture of you with Hattie strikes me a little better, now, but
it still looks a little thin, & I am haunted with the fear that you are not
as well as usual. Am I right? Excuse this solicitude—ɏ for you are very
dear to me, Livy—dearer than all things else on earth combined.]

Walking, to-night, I heard the voices of ten million frogs warbling
their melancholy dirge on the still air. I wished Mrs. Langdon were there
to enjoy the plaintive concert. I mean to ~~cath~~ catch two or three hundred
of them & take them home to Elmira. We can keep ₐsome ofₐ them in the
cage with the mocking-bird, & colonize the rest in the conservatory.
They made good music, to-night, especially when it was very still &
lonely & a ~~s⌀~~ long-drawn dog-howl swelled up out of the far distance &
blended with it. The shadows seemed to grow more sombre, then, & the
stillness more solemn, & the whispering foliage more spiritual, & the
mysterious murmur of the night-wind more freighted with ₐtheₐ moan-
ings of shrouded wanderers from the ~~grave~~ tombs. The "voices of the
night"[5] are always eloquent.

I suppose you are having summer weather, now. We are—& it is
perfectly magnificent. I do *love* the hot summer weather. If I had had my
darling here to-day, & Jim & "our" buggy, we would have had a royal
drive. The town is budding out, now—the grass & foliage are, at least—
& again Hartford is becoming the pleasantest city, to the eye, that America can show. The park & the little river look beautiful—& yesterday as
the sun went down, & flung long shafts of golden light athwart its grassy
slopes & among ~~is~~ its shrubs & ~~elms~~ stately elms & bridges, & gilded the
graceful church spires beyond, it was a feast to look upon.[6] But it was

only a half-way sort of feast, after all, without ~~liv~~ Livy—a ~~din~~ banquet of one cover, & as one might say.

Oh you darling little speller!—you spell "terrible" right, this time. And I won't have it—it is un-Livy-ish. Spell it wrong, next time, for I love everything that is like Livy. Maybe it is wrong for me to put a premium on bad spelling, but I can't help it if it is. Somehow I love it in you—I have grown used to it,—+ accustomed to expect it, & I honestly believe that if, all of a sudden, you fell to spelling every word right, I should feel a/ pain, as if something very dear to me had ,been, mysteriously spirited away & lost to me. I am not poking fun at you, little sweetheart.

Livy, you must not let Mr. Beecher beat you more than one game in five—you must do credit to your teacher. But you did everlastingly slaughter him on the first game, & *that* was doing credit to your teacher. It was about the way I beat *you*, my love.[7]

From the stillness that reigns in the house, I fancy that I must be the only person up, though I know it is not late. However, the very dearest girl in the wide world has given me strict orders to go to bed early & take care of myself, & I will obey, though I had rather write to her than sleep—for, writing to her, it is as if I were *talking* to her—& to talk to her so, is in fancy to ~~look~~ hold her tiny hand, & look into her dear eyes, & hear her voice that is sweet as an answered prayer to me, & clasp her pigmy foot, & hold her dainty form in my arms, & kiss her lips, & cheeks, & hair, & eyes, for love, & her ſ ~~sac~~ ,sacred, forehead in honor, in reverent respect, in gratitude & blessing. Out of the depths of my happy heart wells a great tide of love & prayer for this priceless treasure that is confided to my life-long keeping. You cannot see its intangible waves as they flow toward you, darling, but in these lines you ~~may~~ will hear, as it were, the distant beating of its surf.

I leave you withou the ministering spirits that are in the air about you always. Good-night, with a kiss & a blessing, Livy darling.

Sam

⬛—————————————————————————————

Miss Olivia L. Langdon | Elmira | New York. [*postmarked:*] HARTFORD CONN. MAY 13 [*docketed by OLL:*] 67th

[1] Olivia inserted the number in Clemens's dateline.
[2] Clemens was staying at the home of Elisha Bliss, at 273 Asylum Street, a few

blocks from the American Publishing Company offices at 148 Asylum Street. He had also stayed with Bliss while working on the printer's copy of *The Innocents Abroad* in October 1868, shortly after Olivia rejected his initial proposal of marriage (Geer 1869, 55, 495; *L2*, 247–49, 257–58 n. 1).

³"Every good gift and every perfect gift is from above, and cometh down from the Father of lights, with whom is no variableness, neither shadow of turning" (James 1:17).

⁴Clemens evidently alludes to *three* photographs: the porcelaintype he received in January (see 22 Jan 69 to OLL, n. 1), a porcelaintype reproduction of a picture he had had since 1868 (see 15 May 69 to OLL [2nd of 2], n. 2), and the picture of Harriet Lewis with Olivia that he refers to more explicitly later in this letter (reproduced on page 504).

⁵The title of Henry Wadsworth Longfellow's first collection of poems (1839).

⁶Clemens describes a forty-six acre tract, bounded on three sides by Park River, in central Hartford, a short distance from the Bliss home. Known at this time simply as "the park," in 1876 it was named for Horace Bushnell (1802–76), the Congregational clergyman who was instrumental in its creation (Trumbull, 1:390, 447–49; Geer 1869, map facing 29, 452).

⁷Olivia and the Reverend Thomas K. Beecher had been playing cribbage, which Clemens had taught her (see also 12 Jan 69 to OLL and CJL).

To Olivia L. Langdon
13 May 1869 • Hartford, Conn.
(MS: CU-MARK)

Hartford, Thursday.

Why, you little rascal! to throw such a handful ‚of‚ sarcasms at me. Bless your dear heart, that joke would have been "lost" if I hadn't explained it, & yet here you are letting on that you would have seen through it without any assistance.¹ But it isn't any use to try to get around it in this way. "I'm crushed"—that is all there is about it. I am more than crushed—I am *withered!* Don't you do me so again, or I shall have to box your ears when I see you—or kiss you, at any rate. Now you just cipher out those puns in the Autocrat² yourself, Miss, since you are grown so dreadfully ingenious as to discover a joke after it? is pointed out to you. [How's thim?]

Livy darling, if you have two copies of Vanderbilt, send one of them to me—tear it out & enclose it in your letter. But if you haven't two, I don't want it.³

Those wintergreens were deliciously fragrant, & I thank Mrs. Sue very much for them,—"Sister Crane," I mean.

Indeed I wish somebody would wake me up at midnight & give me one of *your* letters—I think I would enjoy the surprise. As it is, I get them in the middle of the day, & have to walk about a mile to get to a place where I can read them in solitude & uninterrupted. If I could only have fortitude enough to keep them until I had gone to bed, they would be worth double as much to me. I am sorry, now, that I did not write you a good long letter upon that occasion, since it was to be so honored.

Little sweetheart, I had a scary dream about you last night. I thought you came to me crying, & said "Farewell"—& I knew by some instinct that you meant it for a final farewell, & that we were never to see each other & never to be anything to each other any more. It ṁ made me feel as if the world had dropped from under my feet! And so, through a simple dream, it was revealed to me the sensation I had vainly tried in waking ∅ hours to imagine when thinking of Emma Sayles.[4] I pray Heaven I may never know the reality, if for the anguish of this vision has shown me what torturing myser misery it would be. I dreamt that I put my arms about you & soothed away your grief a little, & persuaded you to sit down—& then I talked to you, & bye & bye your tears ceased & your eyes brightened, & your hand sought mine & nestled in it, & the old loving trust that is so beautiful to see came back into your face,—& Livy was *mine* again! Forever & forever. But the instant I awoke I looked for all around, in a bewildered way, & half doubting, & when I saw that you were nowhere in sight, all that hev heavy distress swept back upon me like a flood & I thought the *reconciliation* had been the dream, & that the farewell was *reality*—& then I felt O, so unspeakably desolate. But presently, when it flashed upon me that I had *written* you before I went to bed—& that I had received letters from you within a day or two—& then saw your pictures lying almost within reach, I could have jumped out of the window for joy! And I have been jolly all day—& have mentioned to myself, many, many times, that it was all a hideous dream & she is *my* darling yet. If anybody were to tell me now that a dream is able to turn the hair gray in a single night, I would believe it. I sorrow for John Greeves, & for Emma Sayles. I comprehend their case now. I did not, before.

I *think* this is Thursday, but I don't know. Yes, it *is* Thursday—I remember, now. But the days drag so—it *ought* to be Friday. I look for "Uncle Cholley" Saturday. He said he would come, when I left him in New York. I wrote him last night to telegraph me & say what train he would be in, so that I could meet him. We shall have to call on his friend Alice Hooker.[5]

When I began writing this letter I had just finished going over the last of the Book MSS. & scratching out for the last time. No proofs have come in since Monday ‚or Tuesday‚ —none will come in for a day or two yet. When they do, Bliss will try to get duplicates to send to you—thinks he can get them if anybody can. Well, I should think he could—there is no use in being ridden over by an old—old—Englishman like that Electrotyper. If he don't behave himself I shall have to call on him yet, & kill him. He is only 60 years old, & may be is too young to die.

I *love* you, Livy. I love you better & better every day, my little darling. And it will take more than dreams to separate us, *won't* it? Indeed it will.

I have read Victor Hugo's new story—all that has been published so far. It is wild, wierd—& half the time incomprehensible.[6]

Livy dear, you must take the Bagster Bible once more, & transcribe the next section of sequences in the life of Christ & send to me—won't you. Do it some time when you have nothing important on hand. If I were there we would take the references right from the printed tables themselves, & so save the trouble—but as I am away off here, I must ask you to follow the old plan again.[7]

Now I ~~havn~~ have nothing henceforth to do but write newspaper letters, read proof, & scribble letters to Livy—the two former irksome duties, the latter a very dear & happy privilege.[8] Being obliged to go through all the old proofs yesterday, nearly every purple ink correction brought my Livy before me, with her work, in Mrs. Crane's little parlor—& often a remembered mark reminded me of just what you were doing & how you were looking when it was made. I would give much to own those rusty old bundles of paper—I would keep them carefully always, & hoard them as treasures above gold & silver & precious stones.[9]

And now that my work is become easy, I would call on Gen. Hawley once more, but he is not in town.[10] I want to get located in life. *I want to be married*, bless your dear little heart.

But I must stop. If this were written in my usual hand it would make sixteen pages.[11] I must not forget that I inflicted ten or twelve pages on you last night. However, you like it, dearie, as much as I like a long letter from you, & so I only said that in fun. I waft you a ~~low~~ loving kiss, a warm embrace & a fervent blessing, my own darling.

Sam

✉━━

Miss Olivia L. Langdon | Elmira | New York. [*postmarked:*] HARTFORD CONN. MAY 14 [*docketed by OLL:*] 68th

[1] The joke evidently was the "play upon **Twain** & our reported marriage" that Clemens glossed in his letter of 8 May to Olivia from Hartford.

[2] Holmes's *Autocrat of the Breakfast-Table.*

[3] The extra copy of "Open Letter to Com. Vanderbilt" (SLC 1869b) was for James Redpath, who did not, however, use the article in advertising Mark Twain for the 1869–70 lecture season (see 10 May 69 to Redpath and Boston Lyceum Bureau Advertising Circular, Appendix E).

[4] See 9 May 69 to OLL, n. 1.

[5] Charles J. Langdon regarded Hooker as his confidante and one of his "best & most respected friends" (*L2*, 324 n. 8). Neither Clemens's letter nor Langdon's telegram is known to survive.

[6] William Young's translation of Hugo's *L'Homme qui rit* (*The Man Who Laughs; Or, By the King's Command*) appeared in weekly installments in *Appletons' Journal of Literature, Science, and Art* from 3 April through 4 September 1869. In the fall of the year Clemens wrote, but did not publish, a burlesque of the novel (see *S&B*, 40–48).

[7] A copy of *The Holy Bible* (London: S. Bagster and Sons, 1846) owned by Clemens survives in the Mark Twain Library, in Redding, Connecticut (Gribben, 1:65). Replete with reference materials, including explanatory notes, chronological tables, and a subject index, it may well have been the volume that Olivia used in instructing him.

[8] Clemens's next known newspaper letter appeared in the San Francisco *Alta California*, but not until 25 July (SLC 1869h). And although he wrote a sketch on 13 May and another two days later, only the second of these became part of a newspaper letter, also published in the *Alta*, on 1 August (see 14 May 69 to OLL, n. 3, and 15 and 16 May 69 to OLL, n. 5).

[9] Although Clemens and Olivia both used her purple ink when in Elmira, the reference here is almost certainly to Olivia's own marks on the proofs for *The Innocents Abroad*—the result of her "prerogative" to "scratch out all that don't suit her" (9 and 31 Mar 69 to Crane, p. 181). If Clemens did in fact save the proofs for his book, they have not been found.

[10] Clemens again wished to confer with Hawley about a partnership in the Hartford *Courant.*

[11] This letter, more meticulously inscribed than some, is eight pages long.

To James Redpath
14 and 17 May 1869 • Hartford, Conn.
(Swann, lot 299, and Merwin-Clayton, lot 129)

Hartford, Friday, May 14.[1]

.   .   .   .

The newspaper notices . . . do not seem to amount to anything, & so I give up trying to make a circular out of them. I have never taken any pains to preserve notices . . . I wish you would have your office boy get up the circular the way you want it—& have them printed & send me a copy or two & the bill . . . I haven't had any experience like this & you have . . . I haven't any photographs, but I have a negative . . . & will order some & send one . . .

Clemens

.   .   .   .

Upon second thought, I have made an attempt. Maybe . . . it will do.[2]

[1]Clemens probably began this letter shortly after receiving some lecture reviews from Olivia Langdon on the morning of 14 May, then held it for completion until Monday, 17 May, pending receipt of at least one additional review (see the next letter).

[2]Neither Clemens's "attempt" at an advertising circular nor any of the lecture reviews he enclosed with it are known to survive. Even discounting these enclosures, as much as half of the letter text may be missing.

To Olivia L. Langdon
14 May 1869 • Hartford, Conn.
(MS: CU-MARK)

Hartford, Friday.

A natural impulse siezes me to write to my darling, every opportunity I get. I suppose I ought to be writing a newspaper letter, but the mood is not with me & I would only fail. But if I fail with Livy, she won't mind it.

You are the faithfullest little wife that ever a man had. I hardly dared to hope for a letter when I went down town this morning, but there it was—& I felt so grateful to you, dearie. I adjourned to the shade of an elm in the park (glorious, *isn't* it, that we seek shade, once more, instead of warm places to shield us from hideous winter?)[1] Bless ~~her~~ you, I can see you in the big black chair as distinctly as if I were there. I wish I could *touch* you. (That word touch is your handwriting—maybe "Sister Crane" was not so far wrong when she fancied a resemblance in our hands,—if there is, I have unconsciously adopted yours.) Take the pen & write "touch,," with your eyes shut.[2]

Uncle Cholley isn't coming—have just received a telegram. He says he will write & explain.

I wrote an article last night on the "Private Habits of the Siamese Twins,," & I put a lot of obscure jokes in it on purpose to tangle my little sweetheart.[3] I am not going to explain them, either, you little rascal, because ~~th~~ you threw that sarcasm at me. "So there, now."

Twichell & I, & another preacher or two, & the editor of the "~~p~~ Post" are to take tea—with Mr. Henry Clay Trumbull, this evening, but *you* can't go, on account of that sarcasm.[4]

The printing of the book is let ~~two~~ to two different houses, both large concerns, (so I suppose we are to have more than one set of electrotype plates,) & ~~each is~~ ,they are, to print 10,000 copies each, right away. One paper mill has contracted to make paper for ~~this~~ Mr. Bliss *only* all the summer, & drop everything else. The main part of this paper is for my book, & the remainder is for a final edition of Richardson's "Beyond the Mississippi"—they think the opening of the Pacific R.R. will warrant the effort to sell a new edition.[5]

Bother the California trip!—I can't hear from the boys in Washington when they propose that we shall start. I *must* hear within a day or two, though, I suppose, & then I'll tell Livy. It is *splendid* to have somebody to tell things to who will take an interest in them. Heretofore, when I was going to California, I told my *landlord*—& he sent in his bill. That was all *he* cared about it. Now there is somebody who will care to know *when*, & *how*, & all about it,, bless her heart.

I was writing in the *supposition* that I had written about this before, but I don't really believe I have. *I* can't remember. Anyway, Riley & Young ~~wrote~~ ("New York Tribune"—*not* J. R. Y., but his brother—& "Alta California")[6] wrote me from Washington that they are going across the Plains early in June, & wanted me to go with them instead of by sea. I said I liked it & I guessed I would (for they are splendid good jolly company—much better than I would have at sea.) So I told them to appoint the exact day for leaving, & let me know, & the chances were a hundred to one that I would go.

You see, I can't talk business to the Courant, for Warner is not home yet.[7] I don't want to talk to the Post people till I am done with the Courant (for cou nothing could be done, inasmuch as I have passed my word that I would not close a bargain with another party without first seeing Hawley again.) But chiefly, the book will possibly make me better known in New England & consequently more valuable to a newspaper—& so that will be good capital to trade on after a little. And *finally*, I do not want to be idle all the summer—& so, what *can* I do but go to Cal⁼? I am writing very cheerfully about it, but I do wish something would turn up to make that fearful trip entirely useless & unnecessary. For I do *not* want to make it—however, you know that, yourself.

I am ever so much obliged for the notices, my pet. You are the most valuable girl in the world. I *never* could have kept those things, & yet just now it *n* is very necessary to have them for the Boston lecture agent. I knew I could trust you to scare up some of them; but I was surprised & glad you had so many. This is Friday—I will wait till Monday, (time for your return letter,) & in the meantime, dearie, won't you look again for that N. Y. Tribune notice? I sent it you in a letter dated at New York the 28th of last November. If you can find that letter, maybe it is in it yet. However, there is no use in looking for dates—*shake up* all the letters of mine you can find, & if it is in any one of them I guess it will fall out.[8]

But here! this won't do. While I am writing to the concentrated sun, moon & stars, the time to go to Trumbull's is almost at hand. Good⁼ bye—& blessings on my Livy darling.

Sam

 Miss Olivia L. Langdon | Elmira | New York. [*postmarked:*] HARTFORD CONN. MAY 15 [*docketed by OLL:*] 69th | touch

[1] "For never-resting time leads summer on / To hideous winter and confounds him there" (Shakespeare, Sonnet V, "Those hours that with gentle work did frame").

[2] Olivia experimented on the envelope. The result is reproduced here, along with Clemens's inscription:

SLC: *[signature]*   OLL: *[signature]*

[3]On 18 May Silas S. Packard paid Clemens $25 for "Personal Habits of the Siamese Twins," which he published in *Packard's Monthly* in August ("Mr S. L. Clemens in a/c & Interest a/c with Slote Woodman & Co to August 15. 1869," CU-MARK; SLC 1869i). Clemens reprinted the sketch several times before finally collecting it in *Mark Twain's Sketches, New and Old* (1875).

[4]The editor of the Hartford *Evening Post* was Isaac Hill Bromley (see 21 June 69 to OLL, n. 4). The Reverend Henry Clay Trumbull (1830–1903), a resident of Hartford and brother of local historian James Hammond Trumbull (1821–97), was the New England secretary of the American Sunday-School Union, founded in 1817 to promote biblical instruction (Trumbull, 1:171).

[5]The success of the first edition of Albert Deane Richardson's *Beyond the Mississippi* (Hartford: American Publishing Company, 1867) helped persuade Clemens to publish his own book by subscription (*L2*, 119–21, 125–26, 160). The 1869 "final" edition incorporated new chapters on the history of the transcontinental railroad, which had just been completed (see 10 May 69 to Redpath, n. 7).

[6]John Henry Riley (1823–72), Washington correspondent for the San Francisco *Alta California*, shared rooms with Clemens in the capital during the winter of 1867–68. James Rankin Young (1847–1924) was head of the New York *Tribune*'s Washington bureau. His brother, John Russell Young (1840–99), was within five days of resigning as managing editor of the *Tribune*, the result of alleged misconduct ("Death of Col. J. Henry Riley," Philadelphia *Inquirer*, 23 Sept 72, 2; *L2*, 110 n. 6, 196 n. 1; Broderick, 127–28; Duncan, 38–39).

[7]Charles Dudley Warner, co-editor of the Hartford *Courant*, did not return from Europe until June (see 21 June 69 to OLL, n. 3).

[8]On 28 November 1868 Clemens had sent Olivia a letter enclosing notices of his 6 May 1867 Sandwich Islands lecture in New York City, preserved for him by his agent, Frank Fuller. (This letter was memorable to Clemens not only for its enclosures, but because it was the first he wrote to Olivia after their informal engagement.) Among the reviews was "Mark Twain as a Lecturer" (New York *Tribune*, 11 May 67, 2; in *L2*, 417–19), by Edward H. House, whom Clemens identified as "the most eminent dramatic critic in the Union" (*L2*, 291). Clemens must have requested the *Tribune* review in the letter (now lost) he wrote to Olivia on 10 May (see 10 May 69 to Redpath, n. 2). She may never have located this notice; at least James Redpath ("the Boston lecture agent") did not use it in his advertising circular (see Boston Lyceum Bureau Advertising Circular, Appendix E).

To Olivia L. Langdon
15 May 1869 • (1st of 2) • Hartford, Conn.
(MS: CU-MARK)

[*in top margin:* 'Go to bed, Livy.']

Thursday, Midnight.[1]

I have already written to you once or twice to-day, & so I am not going to write you now—but I can't resist the temptation to simply say Good-night, & that I love you, darling—because I *do* love you, Livy—you *know* I do—you know it perfectly well you little rascal. Just back from Rev. Mr. Trumbull's—nobody was there but Twichell & Gov. Hawley & me—Post man[2] was obliged to be absent. We have had a ~~y~~ royal time. I have laughed till I feel all tired out. You never heard so many stories told in one evening. There was only one drawback. Mrs. Trumbull kept her little ~~cheer~~ children present all the evening, & of course they were fidgetty (the youngest was, at ~~lest~~ least, & kept everybody uneasy for fear it would break its neck climbing around.[3] [*in top margin:* Those Livy—Livy?—Livy!] Now I *did* say to myself, five or six times, during the evening, "I *can't* keep a diary, & yet I'll want to run a paragraph into an article, some day, about the ~~abomination~~ inappropriateness & general disagreeableness of mixing infants into grown people's entertainments, & I shall want it [to] read vividly & fresh, & so of course it must be written *now*, while it is *hot*, & laid away for use—& so I'll inflict ~~is~~ it all on poor Livy as soon as ever I get home, & set it forth in all its malignity & its virulence, & ask her to ~~s~~ lay that page by somewhere so that I can call for it when I want it— [*in top margin:* What a darling it is!] & so, by making Livy my diary, I can secure two valuable birds with one stone, viz., I can write the things necessary without its being irksome, because they will be written for the dearest little body in the universe; & 2[d], I shall have a diary who will always know where to put her hand on the document entrusted to her, which is a thing *I* never could do, &c, &c, &c,"— [*in margin:* Livy, Livy, Livy.]

But now the spirit of it is all gone—& I feel only ~~kindness~~liness toward the pleasant mother & charity toward the young blockheads that were a nuisance without knowing it—& so there is nothing for the diary, Livy dear. [*in top margin:* Livy, I *love* you.] But on the contrary I have said just exactly enough to entitle me to a scolding, & I'm morally bound to get it. But the reproof will come from such dear lips that I shall not know it is a reproof, thinking it a blessing. ˄(How's *thim?*)˄ [You know it is wasting time to scold *me*, Livy, because I love everything you say, rebukes, abuse, & compliments alike.) [*in margin:* I *love* you, Livy.]

There are two hundred & twenty-four illustrations in the book, Livy.[4] As I told you, the first edition ˄of the book˄ will be 20,000 copies, & it will take the whole force of the paper mill ~~four weeks to make~~ a good while (maybe longer—the man don't know, yet,) to make that amount of paper—for the weight of the same is over *thirty tons*.

Must go to bed—but ain't sleepy—simply obeying Livy's orders. God bless my own little darling.

Sam.

Livy dear, please send me that mutilated copy of the Jumping Frog of mine, if it is there[5]—send by express, not mail. It has writing in it & would require letter postage,—& it is considered improper to break the law. When you mark the Beecher sermons, you must always put 2 or 3 stamps on them.[6]

[*on back of page 1:*] Oh dear me suz! how I do *love* you, Livy!

⊠————————————————————————————————

Miss Olivia L. Langdon | Elmira | New York. [*postmarked:*] HARTFORD CONN. MAY 15 [*docketed by OLL:*] 70ᵗʰ

[1] In fact, it was 12 A.M. on Saturday, 15 May. As the preceding letter establishes, the visit to the Trumbull home that Clemens goes on to describe here took place on the evening of Friday, 14 May.

[2] Isaac Bromley.

[3] The former Alice Cogswell Gallaudet (1834–91) had been married to the Reverend Henry Clay Trumbull since 1854. She was the daughter of the Reverend Thomas Hopkins Gallaudet, who in 1817 founded the American Asylum in Hartford, the first free American school for the deaf (see *L2*, 275 n. 3). The Trumbulls had three children at this time, Sophia Gallaudet, Mary Prime, and Alice Gallaudet, aged twelve, nine, and two, respectively (Martha H. Smart, personal communication).

[4] Actually there were 234, including the dual frontispiece.

[5] For Clemens's revisions in an 1869 copy of his *Celebrated Jumping Frog of Calaveras County*, see *ET&S1*, 556–57.

[6] Olivia was continuing to send Clemens the sermons of Henry Ward Beecher, as printed in the weekly *Plymouth Pulpit*. In 1869, as now, postal regulations required additional postage when any writing or personal message was included with printed materials (Senate 1876, 19).

To Olivia L. Langdon
15 May 1869 • (2nd of 2) • Hartford, Conn.
(MS: CU-MARK)

Hartford, Saturday.

It is a darling good girl to write so regularly & so frequently, & I do thank her with all my heart for it. It makes a spoiled child of me, too—for now that I am used to it I could hardly manage to get along *without* a letter from my darling every day. It is cruel to exact it, & I *don't*, except in longing for it.

Oh don't you be afraid, dearie, that I can paint you too highly to the Twichells or anybody else. You are *not* a commonplace, ordinary mortal. I won't *have* such language. *They* will see you with loving eyes, & although they nor any one else can love you as madly as I do, they still have sense & reason & they will see in you a girl that is without a peer among all the girls they ever saw before. I am just as well satisfied of that as I am of my own existence. Therefore don't you be the least bit afraid. And *they* are not diffident like Ida.[1] They are full of vim & heartiness & will put you so at ease in ten minutes that you will forget all your self= consciousness & be at home.

Livy, what darling fat cheeks you had when that profile was taken. You shall have them again, yet, & be your dear old self again. You must take a good walk *twice* a day—do you hear? If one walk does you good, two will do you more.

Now *I* didn't do anything naughty in showing that picture—because it was *just the same* as the one I showed them before, only it is porcelain.[2] 'Tisn't as beautiful as you, anyhow. And I *wouldn't* show your picture to any but a very particular friend, because I regard it as too sacred. I wish I had a hundred pictures of you. I do want to *see* you so badly. Pictures are delightful to have, but they are not *Livy*.

Let Emma read "Introspection" in that little book of Arnold's poems. It will break ~~heart~~ her heart.[3] She is sad & restless & don't sleep? Why don't ~~John~~ ˌDr.ˌ Greeves go to her *anyhow*, in defiance of her edict of banishment? *I* would. I would override a hundred thousand edicts of banishment. I would go to *you* over stacks of such edicts as high as the moon. I would go to you through hunger & thirst, disease, insult, death—*everything*. I would not stop for all the edicts that ever were penned. I would find you even though you hid in the caves of the earth, & I would *have* you, though the Arch Fiend himself stood watch over you. Greeves not come *yet?* Why what is the matter with the man? He will waste precious time until she has fought her battle out & conquered herself, & then she won't have him at all. Do you suppose he means to give it up? If he does, then I will say, for one, that she served him just right. I wouldn't *have* such a man.

I hasten [to] reassure you, darling. I haven't mentioned Emma's secret to any soul—which means that I haven't even remotely hinted at *anybody's* broken engagement or anybody's private affairs of any kind. But I fully understand & appreciate your solicitude, my Livy, remembering that you imposed no secresy upon me—& if the news had come from anybody but you I might have been just thoughtless enough to mention it when I spent the afternoon at the Hooker's,[4] inasmuch as it was then so fresh in my mind & taking up so large a share of my thoughts—~~be~~ but I knew it was no business of mine to ~~tell~~ repeat things you tell me without finding out, first, whether they ~~were~~ ˌareˌ secrets or not. For you & I have no secrets from each other, & I have no right to suppose a thing is not a secret simply because you have told it me without making a reservation. No, I shan't mention it to any one, little dearie.

Livy dear, the onus of Alice's request is not upon *you.* All you have to do is simply ˌtoˌ *make* it, to Emma—that is all. Ask Emma what reply you shall make to Alice, & send that reply *to* Alice, without any circumlocution. The *openest*, frankest, straightest road, in pretty much all cases, is the best. You will find that other courses are beset, as a general thing, with ~~secresies,~~ concealments, misunderstandings & ~~various sorts of~~ suspicions. Don't you see, dear?—all you want is *Emma's* answer— *you* don't have to account to Alice for any whys & wherefores—your course is plain & easy.[5] I am ~~adv~~ advising with a good deal of effrontery, but then it is *good* advice, darling, & well meant. [*in margin:* I *love* you, Livy.]

"Don't feel that you must write every day if it is a tax to you." A tax, Livy? It is a luxury. I would not part with it for anything. I never have an idle moment but instantly the impulse siezes me to write you. I often want to write you three or four times a day. Once or twice a week (*if I am not well,*) I sit & drag along & *can't* write, but bless you I love to *try*, & so where is the "tax?" Don't distress yourself a bit about this sort of a tax. It is a real, living, & genuine *pleasure* to me to write you *every* day, & I would feel that in a large sense a day was *lost* wherein I was cheated out of this most happy privilege. I am too eager & too willing to commune with you to ever find a hardship in it. Livy, Livy, Livy! *how* did you ever come to bless me with the imperial riches of your love? It is all a mystery all to me—an splendid vision—an intoxicating dream. It does seem too exquisite a fortune, too beautiful a possession to be real, sometimes. But glad am I, in my heart of hearts, to know that it *is* real, & that this most holy thing the earth can give me is mine for time & eternity.

Livy dear, it is raining again. It rains pretty much all the time, now. "Showers the thirsty land refreshing,"[6] fall day & night. I would like to hear you sing it. Maybe your singing wouldn't attract attention in a crowd, but *I* love it. It is a little voice, but very dear to me—& very sweet, too.

Good-bye again, my beloved, my honored, my darling Livy. (I am sorry I am done.)

Sam.

What, Livy, think you are presumptuous in advising me about expunging infelicities from the book? Not a bit of it, darling. I am glad & proud to have you do it. And any suggestion you make about *anything* shall be honored.

---

[1] Ida Clark, who was engaged to Charles J. Langdon.

[2] This porcelaintype, apparently made from the same negative as the "fat cheeks" profile Clemens received in 1868, is reproduced in *L2*, 440, where the date of the original print ("1866 or 1867") is given.

[3] Matthew Arnold is not known to have published a poem entitled "Introspection." The editions of his poetry that had issued by 1869 included many introspective poems, however, some of them concerned with parted lovers. Any of these might have affected Emma Sayles, who had recently broken her engagement. The particular edition of Arnold's poems that Olivia Langdon owned has not been identified (Arnold, passim; Gribben, 1:28).

[4] The visit that had cut short Clemens's 9 May letter to Olivia.

[5] Having learned of Emma Sayles's broken engagement, Alice Hooker was hesitant about inviting Sayles to Hartford to attend her 17 June wedding to John Day. On 24 May, Olivia wrote to Hooker: "I suppose that you will have had a letter from Emma Sayles before this reaches you, she was to send one out on Saturday evening [22 May]—She had decided to go to Hartford with us as of course she wrote you" (CtHMTH).

[6] From the first stanza of "Even Me," the hymn Clemens had earlier called his favorite (see 9 and 31 Mar 69 to Crane, n. 9).

To Olivia L. Langdon
15 and 16 May 1869 • Hartford, Conn.
(MS: CU-MARK)

Hartford, Saturday Night.

Livy dear, only let me say Good-night—that is all. Just as I expected, & just as I said in your mother's letter, Mr. Bliss forgot to mail
that letter to you, & I ~~foun~~ discovered the fact an hour after supper &
took it & cleared out for the post office—it was raining like sixty. I
grabbed a seedy old umbrella in the hall & hurried. But that umbrella
appeared to go up too much & sloped the wrong way—it was like a funnel—& Livy, would you believe it, before I had walked three blocks it
had conveyed more than eighteen tons of rain-water down the back of
my neck. ~~If~~ Why, I was ringing wet. And I had my thin shoes on, & I
began to *soak up*, you know. Barrel/s & barrels I soaked up—& that
water rose in me, & rose in me, higher & higher, till it issued from my
mouth, & then from my nose, & ~~per~~ presently I began to cry—part from
grief & part from overflow—because I thought I was ɏ going to be
drowned, you know—& I said I was a *fool* to go out without a life=
preserver, which Livy always told me never to do it, & now what would
become of *her?*

Well, you know I live half way from Hooker's to the post office, &
it is six miles by the watch, & I only got there just in the nick of time to
mail my letter three hours & a half before the mail closed, & I tell *you* I
was glad, & felt smart[1]—& then I bought 4 new numbers of Appleton's
~~month~~ Journal[2] & went up town & called on Billy Gross a minute,[3] &
went away from there & left my Appletons,—& went down to ₍the₎ pho-
tographers & ordered a lot of pictures from the negative of the porcelain
I gave you,[4] & came away from there & forgot my umbrella—& then
rushed back to ~~Appletons~~ Gross's & got my Appleton's—& crossed over
& started home & got about 3 miles & a half & recollected the umbrella,
& said "All right, never had a se[e]ming misfortune yet that wasn't a
blessing in disguise," & so, turned & tramped back again, damp but
cheerful—twice three & a half is nine miles—& *got* my umbrella, &
started out & a fellow said, "Oh, good, it's you, is it?—you've got my
umbrella—funny I should find you *here*." And it *was* funny. We had un-

consciously swapped umbrellas at the post office, or up a tree, or some-where, & here, ever so long afterward, & ever so far away, I find him standing unwittingly by his own umbrella looking at those pictures, with my old funnel in his hand. But the moment I picked his property up he recognized it—splendid umbrella, ~~chronome~~ magic case, chronometer balance—he paid a thousand dollars for it in Paris—& it was unques-tionably ~~by~~ my umbrella that he had, because ~~his~~ what was left of his paper collar was washed down around the small of his back & he had come just in an ace of ~~gettin~~ being drowned before he noticed the little peculiarity of my property—& you know he had made a pass at that da-guerrean shop & climbed in there just in time to save his life,—& *he* was wet, Livy, you better believe. He was very glad to see me. And I went away cheerful, & said "I *never* had a seeming misfortune yet ~~but~~ that wasn't a blessing in disguise—& it holds good yet, & it was a blessing this time, too—for that other fellow." And then I came home, you know. And since then I have written a beautiful little romance about a nigger which was stolen out of Africa which was a prince—& sold into Ameri-can slavery, & discovered, 30 years afterward & purchased of his master by the American public & sent home to Timbuctoo—& it is a *true* ~~roman~~ story, too, & Rev. Trumbull told me all about it—& his father had seen this poor devil with his own eyes—& T. showed me his majesty's portrait (original) *painted by Inman.* And if you were here you ‸could‸ *read* this stirring romance, darling, & mark out all the marginal poetry—& mark out all the jokes you didn't understand—& all the—well *everything*— you should mark it *all* out, if you wanted to, for if Livy didn't like it nobody else should have a *chance* to like it[5]—& since then—it is just "‸midnight—& All's well!"

A thousand blessings on your honored head & kisses on your pre-cious lips, my own darling. Good-night.

Sam.

Miss Olivia L. Langdon | Elmira | New York. [*postmarked:*] HARTFORD CONN. MAY 17 [*docketed by OLL:*] 72nd

---

[1] Elisha Bliss's home, at 273 Asylum Street, where Clemens was staying, was about a mile west of the Hartford post office (which remained open until 9 P.M.), at 252 Main Street. John and Isabella Beecher Hooker's home, at the corner of Forest and Hawthorn streets, was about half a mile further west (Geer 1869, map facing 29, 29, 33, 36, 55, 220; Van Why, 7).

[2]Clemens was reading a translation of Victor Hugo's *L'Homme qui rit*, which was running serially in *Appletons'* (see 13 May 69 to OLL, n. 6).

[3]William H. Gross was co-owner, with Flavius A. Brown, of Brown and Gross, booksellers, at 313 Main Street, "up town" from the post office (Geer 1869, 63, 64, 137).

[4]Clemens had given this porcelaintype to Olivia in mid-March (see 12–13 Mar 69 to OLL). See 19 and 20 May 69 to OLL for a reproduction of the print he had now ordered from Edwin P. Kellogg, at 279 Main Street (Geer 1869, 166).

[5]"Romance in Real Life," Mark Twain's account of Abduhl Rahhahman, became part of a letter he published in the San Francisco *Alta California* on 1 August 1869. "The story I have told is a neat little romance and is *true*," he concluded. "I have ornamented it, and furbished it up a little, here and there, but I have not marred or misstated any of the main facts" (SLC 1869j). The present whereabouts of the painting by Henry Inman (1801–46), the well-known portrait and genre artist, which Henry Clay Trumbull had shown to Clemens, is not

Abduhl Rahhahman. Engraving by Thomas Illman of the painting by Henry Inman. Print Collection, Miriam and Ira D. Wallach Division of Art, Prints and Photographs, The New York Public Library, Astor, Lenox and Tilden Foundations (NN). See note 5.

known. An engraving of it by Thomas Illman (d. 1859 or 1860) is reproduced here ("The African Prince . . . ," Oxford [Ohio] *Literary Register*, 15 Sept 28, 252–53; Bolton, 411; Groce and Wallace, 339).

To Olivia L. Langdon
17 and 18 May 1869 • Hartford, Conn.
(MS: CU-MARK)

Hartford, Monday Night.

I can't resist the temptation to write you a line or two, even though I sneeze myself to death before I get through with it. What a bewitching little darling you are, Livy. You were going to come. It seems almost a misfortune that ~~it~~ I *wasn't* dangerously sick, so that I might see the dear face again. I used to think of sickness with dread—for I always had visions of dreary hospitals—solitude—shut out from friends & the ~~wor~~ great world—dragging, uneventful minutes, hours, weeks—hated faces of hired nurses and harsh physicians—& then an unmourned death, a dog's burial, and—dissection by the doctors![1] But with *you* at the bedside—it seems to me that sickness would be luxury! You *are* a noble, true-hearted little darling, Livy. And I *love* you.

The printing is proceeding, & the bright, clean pages look handsome. I sent you ˏto-dayˏ a duplicate of the only proofs I have had since those I read when I first arrived here (except one little trifle of a few pages.)

No, I haven't seen Mr. Beecher.[2] As I passed up the street yesterday, John Day bowed to me from the Allyn House steps, & I returned his salutation, though I did not remember who he was, at first.[3] I didn't feel like crossing over, & he didn't, either, & so we both of us didn't cross ~~of us~~ over at allˏ, neither of us which. Somehow that sentence don't sound right, but I guess you can make it out. Colds always make me stupid & blundersome.

"The little throat trouble that you have is nothing at all serious." Oh, *Livy!* You are not doing anything at all for that throat. Now why *will* you distress me so? That dreaded disease. Livy, do please doctor it until it is *entirely* cured, just to please me. It is not a trifling sore throat that lasts *two weeks*. It is the first foot-hold of that awful disease that lasts *for life*. I lay this thing up against Mrs. Corey & I never *will* forgive her for it, if one sign or symptom of it is left four days after you get this.[4] It can be cured in that time, with care & attention, if it is not that frightful permanent disease. Up to this time I have prayed night & day like a hypocrite & a liar—for I have thought of that trip every day, & always with a spasm of anger against that woman. I wish she had been in Jericho before she took it into her head to drag you out to that dismal valley & leave you to stare at vacancy & freeze yourself to death for an hour & a quarter while she cavorted through the woods, never caring two cents *how* you put in the dreary time. Livy, I am *angry* ʌ(but not at *you*, my precious)ʌ. You are all good, & true, & generous & forgiving & unselfish—all things that are a glory to womanhood find meet & blend themselves together in the matchless mosaic of your character—& a single day's health to you is ʄh worth more than the eternal salvation of—— I am just running away with myself. Livy, your inoffensive sore throat is nothing to you, & you can afford to be indifferent about it—but it is *misery & death* to *me*—& so, *won't* you make a sacrifice for me & doctor it night & day faithfully & without shirking, till it is entirely cured, so that I can breathe again & be at rest? Livy, if you knew how this spectre goads, me, tortures me, you would not be so thoughtless as to be indifferent to it. There—have I hurt her? God forbid that I should ever, by word or deed, hurt you Livy, my beautiful, my pride, my darling. But I am distressed. I never, never will leave you again when you are not well. My conscience upbraided me cruelly when I *did* leave you so. But you said it was nothing—& you thought it, else you would not have said it; & I believed it, because I would believe your simple word against the oaths of the world. But my mind was full of bodings.

Later in the Evening.—If I can kep keep that torturing subject out of my mind, I shall remain in the good humor I am now in. Theodore was just *right* in that fight, & I am glad he won. We cannot have Mrs. Sue running around town acting Florence Nightingale in a hospital for decayed carpets.[5] [Except it be at the request of Mrs. Corey.]

Mr. Beecher robs himself of the best happiness of his life when he enjoys a pl his pleasures in solitude. What is a splendid sunset worth when there is nobody to see it with you—no sympathetic ear to pour your raptures into? And what is *any* joy (except the miser's,) without companionship? And then the glaring *wrong* of the thing: for Mrs. Beecher shares his sorrows, & this earns the *right* to share his pleasures.

But it seems that when the two are done carrying all the *burdens* of the day, he has no more use for her—she may sit down in sadness & weariness, while he loses the memory of the drudgery in the happy relief of pleasure. It ~~don't suit~~ is selfish—though, superbly gifted as he is, let us charitably try to fancy that he don't know₎ ₍it.₎ Only, my dear, I will suggest that his heart & his brain would not have been so dull in these matters *with his first wife*. I think he possesses a very ~~fr~~ good *brotherly* love for his ₎present₎ wife—& you furnish me ample proofs that he possesses nothing more. Therefore, with such a love, let us not expect of ~~his~~ him the noble things that are born only of a far higher & sublimer passion. It is the native *instinct* of *our* love to have no secrets, no concealments— therefore it is no merit in us to avoid this misfortune of his—we never will have to *reason* ourselves into doing a thing that necessarily comes natural to us. We shan't be able to *comprehend* this thing of having secrets. But the brotherly instinct is to conceal more things than it reveals—nothing but the cold, dismal *reasoning faculty* can enable Mr. Beecher to change this—& then he will have the *corpse* of the marital love,—but with no pulse in its temples, no light in its eyes, no tenderness in its heart.[6]

You little rascal, you *slurred over* Noyes's name$, because you knew very well you didn't know how to spell it! Never mind, Livy darling, you know your spelling is perfectly safe in my "deluded" eyes, because I love everything you do, whether it be good, bad, or indifferent. Let Mrs. Sue be troubled no more about her memoir.~~rial~~ *I* will write it—(with pleasure, I came near saying, but it seems like rather a doubtful compliment, & so I withhold the words.) I will write it, & I will ~~do it~~ do it with such grace & such felicity that the ghost of the late William Lord Noyes shall tear its filmy garments with envy & chagrin.[7] I will put in tasty congratulations from each member of the family, & from all the admirals & brigadier generals, & even from the President, the Emperor of the French, & Queen Victoria—for *both* of you—both of you in the same volume— & I will write all these felicitations myself—every *one* of them—so that I shall know that ₎they₎ are just exactly as they ought to be. ~~I.~~ And I'll have some poetry in—some of those sublime conundrums from Young's Night Thoughts[8] which only Livy can ~~guess the~~ cipher out the meaning of, & some dark & bloody mystery out of the Widow Browning[9]—& ~~some~~ also some poetry of my own ~~composition—~~ ₎construction—₎& between the three I guess we'll "hive" the gentle reader. And I shall have

in a lot of smart remarks made by both of you when you were teething
(after the "load of hay" pattern) & I shall get up these remarks myself,
so as to be sure that they are not insipid like the late W^m· L.'s, (which I
regard as altogether "too thin.") And I will put speeches into your ma-
turer mouths which shall astonish the nations,—profound remarks
upon agriculture, commerce, diplomacy, war, chemistry, afghans for ba-
bies at $15 a day,[10] ~~geog~~ geology, theology, cut-throat,[11] painting, sculp-
ture, niggers, poetry, politics,—*everything* that erudition loves & intel-
lectuality revels in. And there shall be a picture of ~~both of~~ you two & Jim
for a frontispiece, with your autographs underneath, which I will write
myself, so that people can *read* them. And I will have pictures of the
Spaulding girls (together with *their* regrets,) & pictures of Mr. & Mr[s].
Langdon ,& Hattie, & the mocking-bird in a group, & a portrait of the
late Jep engaged in his favorite study (landscape gardening,)—& toward
the end a handsome likeness of your grandmother, along with *her* letter
announcing her exasperation at the sad news. And away over at the extreme back-end of the book I shall wind up with a ,weeping & disconsolate, picture of Theodore's friend, ~~going for the eternal flying~~ with a
basket, going for flying arbutus—& "HOOFING IT," as Charley says.[12]

There you are. *I*'m no compiler of Wm Lord Noyes bosh. When *I*
~~gr~~ get up memoirs I make the deceased get up too—at least turn over.
How many copies do you want issued, young women?

But my dears, it is my fervent hope that I shall be ~~dust~~ spared the
sad office I have so banteringly assumed, by being already dust & ashes
when "memoirs" of you shall have become possible & proper.

"Lovingly YOUR Livy"—the very dearest words to me that ever
illuminated paper & gave it a glory as of a vision. How the words seem
to *nestle up* to me!—& put arms about me, & a loved head upon my shoulder, & the hymning of the angels in my heart! You *are* my Livy—& ~~you~~
I am grateful that it is so, beyond all power of ~~lan~~ speech to express—&
I pray God you may remain my Livy *always*.

I secured the rooms for you—& felt all the time that I was doing a
thing that somehow would prevent my seeing you. And so I was not
cheerful over it. But I *must* see you. There are only one or two suits of
rooms on the second floor (all stores on first, you know,) & those are
occupied by permanent families; but they will dig out a family, or, failing that, give you their best on the 3^d floor.[13]

I haven't half finished my letter, darling, but I suppose I ń ought to quit for tonight & snort & sneeze a while.

Give my love to all the household gods & goddesses. Good-night, little darling—blessings, & kisses & pleasant dreams.

Saml.

[*on back of page 1:*] Livy, I LOVE you! And I've got a perfectly *awful* cold. Took to my bed in pure desperation to-day. ~~Would~~ I was afraid to stay there, though—had to get up & attend to business, anyhow. I not going to take the slightest care of this cold till your throat is *well*. So there now! I shall take off my underclothes to-night; & tomorrow I shall not wear any socks. I will *not* get well till you do. So there now, again![14]

I LOVE you, Livy.

Miss Olivia L. Langdon | Elmira | New York. [*postmarked:*] HARTFORD CONN. MAY 18 [*docketed by OLL:*] 73rd [*and in pencil:*] The removal rendered unnecesary

---

[1] A disturbing prospect indeed for someone who, at the age of eleven, had witnessed the autopsy performed on his father (see *Inds*, 105, 286).

[2] Apparently Olivia had advised Clemens that the Reverend Thomas K. Beecher was, or was about to be, in Hartford.

[3] See 26 and 27 Jan 69 to OLL, n. 8.

[4] The "awful disease" was diphtheria, which threatened Olivia more than once in later years. Mrs. Corey probably was Ella J. Corey, who first met Olivia in 1858 and remained her lifelong friend (Ella J. Corey to SLC, 23 Oct 1904, CU-MARK).

[5] Nothing is known of the enterprise, presumably charitable, which seemed threatening to Susan Crane's health.

[6] Thomas K. Beecher's first wife, Olivia Day (1826–53), died less than two years after their marriage. In 1857 Beecher married her cousin and closest friend, Julia Jones (1826–1905). The Reverend Annis Ford Eastman, one of Beecher's associate pastors at Park Congregational Church recalled: " 'We were made one,' Mr. Beecher said long afterward, 'first in love of Livy, and then in grief for her.' " But, Eastman observed:

It was a strange marriage for the girl who had been sought by so many others of high character and unusual gifts, strange also for the man who all his life long frankly declared that in Livy's death he died to this world. A common sorrow at first, then a common work for the world, drew these two in a union which, through forty-three years, blessed the world as few of the most auspicious marriages have done. The home of these two became a school of virtue, a living illustration of the power of true religion to harmonize warring temperaments, to make the peace of God rule where many of the natural conditions of concord were lacking. Nothing was greater in the lives of these two intense and contradictory natures than their triumphant struggle to keep the unity of the spirit; their success was due to the inherent unselfishness of both. None of those "disobediences" on Mrs. Beecher's part, which she used to bewail even while she held to their necessity, were for selfish ends; none were prompted by a woman's petty vanity or pique, all were in the service of some moral ideal. And on Mr. Beecher's part, though he used humorously to say that he was as well as a man could be who had been hitched to a steam engine for so many years, there was always the most generous appreciation of her share in all that he had done and become. (Annis Ford Eastman, 16, 35–36)

("Nook Farm Genealogy," 7, 12; Max Eastman, 620; Jerome and Wisbey, 116.)

[7]Noyes (1846–66), of Corning, New York, about ten miles from Elmira, had died suddenly of "congestion of the brain" just before his twentieth birthday. His grandfather, Thomas, and his father, Henry Babcock Noyes, were partners of Sylvester G. Andrus and Jervis Langdon in the Elmira lumber firm of Andrus, Langdon and Company, which was founded in 1845 and dissolved in 1855 (Corning *Journal:* "Died," 15 Mar 66, no page; "Henry B. Noyes . . . ," 1 Aug 89, 3; Elmira *Saturday Evening Review:* "In Memoriam," 13 Aug 70, 5). Susan Crane, who like Olivia had known Noyes as a child, had evidently seen a memoir of him that moved her to wonder how her own memorial might read, prompting Clemens's facetious promise to write it. Olivia's note on the envelope of this letter suggests that Noyes's family was contemplating reinterment at this time.

[8]Edward Young's lengthy poem *The Complaint, or Night Thoughts on Life, Death, and Immortality*, originally published 1742–45.

[9]Elizabeth Barrett Browning was never a widow; Robert Browning, who died in 1889, outlived her by twenty-eight years. Clemens liked to pretend that he found Mrs. Browning's poetry mystifying (see 12 Jan 69 to OLL and CJL, p. 26).

[10]Possibly another allusion to Susan Crane's charitable work with "decayed carpets."

[11]A name applied to a number of games of chance, but especially, at this time, to forms of poker and euchre (*OED*, 4:182–83).

[12]In addition to Mr. and Mrs. Jervis Langdon, the identifiable individuals mentioned in this passage are: Clara and Alice Spaulding, Harriet Lewis, Theodore Crane, and Charles Langdon. Jep, evidently banished for destroying the Langdon garden, seems to have been a dog, whereas Jim was a horse (see 12 May 69 to OLL, p. 221).

[13]The Langdons had asked Clemens to reserve rooms for them in Hartford for their June visit to attend the wedding of Alice Hooker. Since he here indicates that the arrangements might keep him from seeing Olivia, it is likely that the family had decided, for decorum's sake, that he should not stay at the same hotel with them.

[14]Clemens must have added these closing remarks on 18 May, probably just before mailing the letter, since enough time had evidently passed for his "Monday Night" anxiety about Olivia to become mere playful concern.

To Olivia L. Langdon
19 and 20 May 1869 • Hartford, Conn.
(MS: CU-MARK)

~~Tuesday~~ Wednesday Afternoon.

Livy dear, I *think* it is ~~Tues~~Wednesday, & yet I feel almost certain that it is as much as *Thursday*—though lying in bed the last day or two being a thing I have never been used to,—& being alone, also, & the rain seeming never to cease its dreary dirges day or night—the time has so dragged, dragged, *dragged*, that when the lagging sun goes down at last it seems as if I cannot *remember* when it rose, it was such an age ago. So I try to *think* it is only Wednesday, though a *month* has surely drifted by in these long-drawn hours. I am tired of fretting & chafing. I will leave this bed tomorrow, sick or well. I am *not* sick enough to deem it imprudent, else I would not make so decided a determination.

If I am writing a foolish low-spirited letter, remember it is to you *only*, & you will not betray me—you will not reveal its contents. Otherwise I would deny myself the relief of writing, while I am in such a depressed state. I expected to be in Elmira to-day (or is it to-morrow?) but the first mention you made of my intended return was a little discouraging, & so I did not know what to say, & said nothing, ~~in~~ meaning to judge by subsequent events whether— Well, somehow I can't get my thoughts straight—I am all confused & blundering—I only know that in your last letter there seems an intimation that I am not to see you before I go to California—& yet I was counting so entirely upon the reverse of this. Why Livy, I *can't* go away without seeing you. I am only flesh & blood—I cannot do impossibilities. Livy dear, do not be conventional with *me*—I am not with you. You manifest reserve. Don't do that. Tell me whatever is in your mind, freely—& let it be in your mind, above all things, that I am to see you before I go. Livy, I am not prying into your secrets—I know you would not accuse me of that—but it *did* seem uncharacteristic of you to imply that I was coming, & yet never once say "Come!" So ~~I knew~~ I thought upon the matter, & put myself in your place, & fancied whether I would use decided language or not—& I knew I *would!* Wherefore it seemed plain that Livy had something to say to me which she did not say—& it was naughty, Livy darling, very naughty. I thought when I first left that the same ~~pol~~ reasons which made it proper & best for me to go would hold good longer than an absence of two weeks; but still, in my selfish disregard of expediency & my longing to see you, I would have marched back at the end of the fortnight, but that there was such an appalling ~~non-com~~ lack of heartiness in your subsequent references to that matter! Forgive me, Livy, if I hurt you—for you hurt *me* dreadfully. And we must give & take, dearie. ~~An~~ Only I want to have the most of the taking to do. But bless you, darling, I knew you had reasons, & ~~never~~ I ~~just~~ accepted my fate with a fair degree of cheerfulness, *because* of that full confidence & trust which I had & shall always have in you. But I said, "She might *tell* me—for I am sure I can bear Livy's decrees handsomely if she will only *trust* me." But this last one I don't get over so easily. This thing of my going to California without seeing you, goes clear beyond my capabilities. *Entirely.* I honored your other implied wish—& it was no small sacrifice, either—but this time, Livy, *what* am I to do? I surely thought I would be *rewarded* for this fortitude of mine, & I know I *deserve* it—but instead of rewarding me, / you just as good as threaten me with a greater punishment! "Be good, sweet child"—remove this ~~mysterious~~ disability—tell me I may see you—& tell me *when*—for if I see California before I see you, I will see it not a day earlier than the millennium. There, now!

Don't scold me, Livy dear. I am weak, & savage, & foolish by turns—& I chafe like any prisoner—& it is night, at last, & there is the eternal miserere of the rain. I'll get up & march down town tomorrow *sure*—for I *must* have somebody to talk to—I'm *full* of talk. I never wanted to hear Bliss talk till to-day—for he is worse than a clatter-mill when he gets started. But he brought my tea up himself a while ago, (*tea*—that spoon/-victuals for infants,) & I thought I could listen to him forever. And now *he* is gone, sorrow catch him, & left me only the sad melancholy music of the rain. You will laugh at all this, Livy, but I am not used to confinement, & it seems to make a baby of me. If my memory serves me I have been bedridden only ~~once~~ ‸twice‸ before in 23 years— cholera in St Louis 16 years ago—& 20 ¥ hours in Damascus 2 years ago.[1] But I'll be out of this tomorrow, I'm pretty sure,—I am *sure*. I would not be here now, but that I have achieved such a ghastly accession to my cold every time I have ventured out. Well, *I* never had such a cold before— & in strict confidence, between you & me, I never want another one like it. I haven't done anything for it, because Bliss isn't worth ₰ a cent for a nurse, & his wife is away on a visit, ~~& won't be home~~ But when she comes home, in a day or two I—shall be well by that time.

Livy, in one of the first violences of this distemper, I abused Mrs Corey in a letter to you, & now I beg your pardon for it—& I beg it in *earnest*, too. I ought to have been too thoughtful of your feelings to say harsh things to you about your friends—for it is a beautiful trait in your character that you love them so & stand up for them so loyally; & it seems strange to me that I who am so proud of you for it am yet capable of wounding you through that very trait. I am a brute. I am very, very sorry, Livy, to have shown you this lack of respect, this want of deference. It has been in my mind very often, since. It is a pity that I cannot think harsh things of people without saying them to you, & so offending a heart that I would so much rather fill with happiness. Forgive me, Livy darling.

You see I am not trying to answer your letters (3 yesterday & to=day, thank you with all my heart, Livy,)—I have no ability to write. You will let me wait till this exasperation of trying to scribble on a book in bed is no longer necessary—I know you will.

But here—this is all wrong. And ‸from‸ this moment I will not chafe any more—not *once*. I will accept the situation, & in the spirit of the sermon you sent me, say, "God's will be done."[2] An easy thing to say, about such a trifle—but could I say it about things of real moment? I hope so. I do not know. One cannot tell till he is tried.

Good-night, Livy. I am glad I ~~to~~ warned you to keep this foolish screed to yourself, dearie. It has been better than medicine to me to write it—& the reason I don't tear it up is because I think we know each other well enough to not misunderstand each other dreadfully; & love each other well enough to bear with weaknesses & foolishnesses, & even wickednesses (of mine.) [I could not apply those harsh terms to *you*, be-cause ~~I~~ ‸it‸ did not seem natural—& so my sentence broke down awk-wardly.] [But I *do* love you well enough to bear with those things in you, if I saw them.]

And without any misgivings I mail this letter, which I would tear up if it were written to anybody else. You will not scoff, or get angry at any-thing my disordered head has framed among its half-coherencies. Thanks for the book, the sermon & the Bible notes.

Good-night. God & his good angels keep you, darling.

Sam

[*on separate sheet around the enclosure:*]

                                                        Morning.
I am up—& shall go down town ~~before I go back to bed—shall stay up~~
My cold is worse. Never mind—it will break today, maybe.

                                                        Sam

[*enclosure:*][3]

✉———————————————————————————————

Miss Olivia L. Langdon | Elmira | New York. [*postmarked:*] HARTFORD
CONN. MAY 20 [*docketed by OLL:*] 75th

    [1]Clemens visited St. Louis for two months in the summer of 1853 and after-
ward lived there for about a year, from the summer of 1854 to the summer of
1855. No letters survive from the first period and the few that survive from the

second make no mention of cholera (see *L1*, 1–3, 46–58). In an autobiographical note made long afterward, however, Clemens tentatively dated an incidence of the disease that he at least witnessed: "Watching cholera funerals '54?" (PP†). No significant cholera outbreaks in 1853 or 1854 have been documented, but "there was a slight outbreak . . . in 1855" (Scharf, 2:1580). In chapter 47 of *The Innocents Abroad* Clemens identified his illness in Damascus, which occurred in mid-September 1867, as cholera (*L2*, 132 n. 6, 395).

²The unidentified sermon probably was by the Reverend Henry Ward Beecher, whose sermons Olivia regularly sent to Clemens.

³The enclosure does not survive with the letter, but must have been a copy of the photograph reproduced here, one of the prints Clemens had recently ordered (see 15 and 16 May 69 to OLL).

To Olivia L. Langdon
with a note to Jervis and Olivia Lewis Langdon
24 May 1869 • South Windsor, Conn.
(MS: CU-MARK)

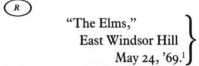

"The Elms,"
East Windsor Hill
May 24, '69.¹

My precious little darling, my heart does yearn for you this morning! If you were only here what a visit we would have, all to ourselves. This place where I am writing is a little framed & plastered smoking-cottage down among the grassy meadows & shrubbery 100 yards from the house; it consists of just *one* room, about four times as large as the closet you hang your dresses in; it is shaded by apple-trees in full bloom, & giant elms; it has a large window in each of three sides, & a door in the other— so that there is a world of light, & no matter which direction the breeze comes from ~~in~~ it can pass freely through. It is carpeted, & has a lounge, two desks, two tables & two chairs in it, & pictures on the walls, & is so retired & still, & *so* cosy & comfortable. The place is vocal with the music of birds & fragrant with the breath of flowers—& out of one window, through openings between the elms, I ~~cath~~ catch a glimpse, of far-reaching vistas of rolling meadows & purple hills all draped in the regal panoply of spring. It is such a *love* of a place! And to think ~~this~~ that this Sabbath-repose is undisturbed by *any* sound but the rejoicings of the

birds! Cosy! why your bedstead would almost entirely fill the apartment.
If you were only here, Paradise would have come again, indeed! And we
would sit on that lounge & so give ourselves up to happiness that the
flight of time would never be heeded.

I have enjoyed this visit to this quaint old-fashioned country house
of Mr. Roe's. He is 71 years old, & his wife is as good & motherly as any
old soul you ever saw. We sat last night till late, & talked, & young Roe
(my old Nevada & California friend—the son & heir of Roe, senior,)
played on the piano & sang till, with the full & fervent enjoyment of the
time I was so filled with loving memories of you & thoughts about you
that I seemed more touched with gratitude to God than ever before, for
this priceless love of yours that He has poured out upon my life to make
it beautiful & blessed.[2] I asked them to find a Plymouth Collection & sing
"Geer,"[3] & then my darling you seemed almost present in the flesh. And
as the rich chords floated up, the air seemed filled with a mysterious
presence, & I fancied it was the soul of Livy wandering abroad on the
invisible wings of a dream while the sweet body slee slept. Oh you visit
me, even when you do not know it yourself. We had family prayers, &
beautiful & earnest & touching they were, too—& when the kneeling
patriarch pleaded for "our dear ones," it was as if I uttered the words
myself, they so truly voiced the supplication that was in my heart. And
when I went to bed, my busy brain was so thronged with images of you
that it seemed for two hours that I never *would* be able to banish the
worshipped little visitor & calm myself to sleep. How you haunted me!
What a variegated & ceaseless pantomime of appearing & re-appearing
you did keep up!—& how you did tantalize me with becoming *almost*
tangible & kissable, & then turning to the lovely impalpableness of a
dream-spirit in the twinkling of an eye, before I could lay my longing
hands upon you! *You* little bundle of aggravation! And so she was—but
it ever so easy to love her, anyhow. Oh, your dear sweet face looks up so
placidly & contentedly from the little picture, here in the midst of this
woodland Sabbath-tranquillity. She is such a bewitching little nun, in
that picture. I carry this with me yet, & leave the other at home, because,
although in one or two respects the other is the more beautiful face, *this*
one loves me, while the other does not know me & so does not care for
me,—it carries in its face the interests & memories of a time when I had
not yet been born into the beautiful revelation that there was a Livy in
all the world—& most surely I had not yet dreamed that there was *such*

a Livy—a ~~lo~~ Livy without whose love I would now hold life the saddest, saddest gift that God could condemn me to go on possessing.[4] For *you* are the life-principle in me—*you* are the only part of me that is worth the sustaining—& so if you, the crystal fountain, were taken from me, of what worth were the scarred & unsentient rock any more? Would the mosses grow about it, & the flowers adorn it, & the foliage chant above it, as before? Or would these wither & die, & desolation come? Would a heart that you had made rich with your love, ever see anything but poverty & rags in any other? Never, in my sincere belief, so help me God.

Mr. A. S. Roe, the elder, is the author of numerous novels, & has the author-instinct to seek the fellowship of scribblers—& so has sent frequent cordial invitations to me to visit at his house, & now, for many reasons, I am glad I am come. I like the family, & have enjoyed myself— & besides, this health-giving air has filled me with a glad new life, & a snap & a vigor that are [more] pronounced than what I felt even before I was sick. I feel about restored to health. I suppose I shall return to Hartford this evening.

But Livy darling, the matter that lies closest to my heart, is to urge you, to beg you, to [*remainder on larger paper:*] beseech you to come down to New York right away with your father & mother—for Charley writes me they are coming. *Do*, Livy dear, please. Now you know it is only two weeks & a half till you will be in Hartford,[5] & couldn't you spend that very jolly in New York? *Do*, Livy dear, Livy darling—I would go down immediately, & we would read all the rest of the proof there together,— all the *vital* part of the Holy Land—& we would go everywhere that you wanted to go, & do everything you wanted to do. Now Livy dear, life is short & uncertain (I had dreadful dreams last night), & do let us be together all we can. We do not know at what moment Death may invade our Eden & banish one or the other & make it desolate. And if you positively *can't* come now, (Oh *do*, please, Livy,) come the 1st—or the 2d— or the 3d—but *don't* put it away off till the 10th. It seems a century. I am so *hungry* to see you. I would be in Elmira *now* if there were n't such delays in getting the proofs back & forth—but in New York they can come down at night & go back in the morning—just the length of time I bestow on them here. [*in margin:* Flowers for you & Mrs. Sue.][6]

To *Mr. & Mrs. Langdon*—Please won't you bring Livy down to New York with you, *right now*. There are *awful* things in the proofs which she needs to scratch out, & I am putting in more & more awful ones every

day & making it perfectly horrible because I am a helpless orphan & have
no one to keep me from doing it, but I wouldn't do it if Livy were by—
& it takes so long now for proofs to get to Elmira that some of the pages
get hurried into stereotype before her corrections can get back. *And my
goodness gracious, how I do want to see her!* (ẁ Please, WON'T you bring
her with you?[7]

Lovingly

Sam*l*.

Livy, Livy, Livy darling, it is such a happiness, such a pleasure,
such a luxury, to write you, that I don't know when to stop. Oh, you *must*
come down right away with your father & mother. I would be the most
delighted man on the whole earth. I would just almost fly away with ecstasy. Please, little woman, little darling, come.

It punishes *you*, does it, for me to make a "fr prize for industry" of
you? Well it does my heart good to hear you say it, darling, & I won't do
so any more. I will write Livy *first*, & then work—& I fancy I shall work
the better for it, likely. But *your* suggestion is depravity itself, darling!
it is monstrous! it is an outrage on all charity! Leave your letters unread
till I have finished my work for the day. Oh, *Livy!* what impossibilities
your little busy head does conceive! Why, child, I will not do anything
of the kind. You might as well tell me to sit & toil in Mrs. Sue's little
parlor, through hours of labor, with your radiant presence by me making
all the place pure & holy & glad & beautiful, & never kiss the dear lips
till my task was done! Oh, *would* I? Trust me for it, I *never* would. Oh
darling, darling, darling, I do so *love* you—I am so proud of you—I am
so blessed in you—I so worship you! Rest the dear old head on my shoulder & let me look into the happy eyes again, O sacred head to me, & eyes
that are to me of as beacons of hope & love & peace, looking out over the
troubled waters & telling me of the haven that is at hand, upon whose
protecting reefs the storms of life shall beat in vain till Death at last shall
open wide the way!

Good-bye princess—darling—idol.

Sam.

Miss Olivia L. Langdon | Elmira | New York. [*on the flap:*] Ⓡ
[*postmarked:*] WAREHOUSE POINT CT.[8] MAY 20 [*docketed by OLL:*] 81st

[1] Olivia's docket number for this letter establishes that five letters, now lost, preceded it.

[2] Azel Stevens Roe (1798–1886) was a wine merchant in New York City before relocating to his farm on East Windsor Hill, about eight miles northeast of Hartford. (East Windsor Hill became part of South Windsor when East Windsor was divided in 1845.) There, beginning in 1850, he wrote a series of novels that enjoyed large sales in the United States and England. His son, Azel Stevens Roe, Jr., was a tutor of the deaf at the State Deaf and Dumb and Blind Institution in San Francisco in 1863, and by late 1865 was a music teacher in that city. In 1867 he was a resident of Virginia City, Nevada, where he taught vocal and instrumental music. No details of his acquaintance with Clemens in the West have been recovered, nor is it known if he had seen Clemens since, but following the present reunion the two men stayed in touch for a time. After Clemens settled in Hartford in 1871, Roe "spent some pleasant nights with him" there and Clemens "paid a visit to the elder Roes" (Samuel Chalmers Thompson, 76). It was probably the May 1869 visit that Roe recalled in 1906 as one of the highlights of their friendship:

I have been away in the Far West for fifteen years, but am now living at the dear old home, where in the little summer house at the foot of the garden, you wrote your name on the window at my mother's request.

It is still there & recalls to my mind when I see it those past happy hours. (Roe to SLC, 3 Jan 1906, CU-MARK)

("Death of Azel S. Roe," Hartford *Courant*, 4 Jan 86, 2; Trumbull, 1:169, 2:124–25, 129; Burpee, 2:983, 987–88; Langley 1863, 22, 119, 309, 509; Langley 1865, 378; "A. S. Roe, Jr.," Virginia City *Territorial Enterprise*, 12 Dec 67, 2.)

[3] Olivia's favorite hymn (see 9 and 31 Mar 69 to Crane, n. 9).

[4] For the "more beautiful" photograph, see 22 Jan 69 to OLL, n. 1. The "bewitching" photograph, evidently not the "fat cheeks" profile Clemens mentioned in his second letter of 15 May to Olivia, has not been identified.

[5] That is, a week before the 17 June wedding of Alice Hooker.

[6] A residue of the flowers Clemens enclosed remains on the manuscript page.

[7] Apparently Clemens had just been in New York City himself, for the record of the cash account Charles J. Langdon was keeping for him indicates that he received fifty dollars there on 23 May ("Sam[l]. L. Clemens Esq In acc with C. J. Langdon," statement dated "Elmira Aug 9th 1869," CU-MARK). No evidence has been found that the Langdons went to New York at this time, with or without Olivia. Clemens rejoined her in Elmira before the end of May.

[8] Warehouse Point, "on the main line of the New York, New Haven & Hartford railroad . . . was a busy shipping center" in East Windsor, and also the site of one of the town's post offices (Burpee, 2:990–91).

To Olivia L. Langdon
29 May 1869 • Elmira, N.Y.
(MS: CU-MARK)

Saturday Night.[1]

Livy darling, precious little Comforter, you have cast out the devil that possessed me for the present, & all is well. I have kept the promises & obeyed the instructions. All *is* well—all *will* be well. I am grateful beyond all power of speech to express, for such a patient, wise, gentle, loving darling to lift me above myself & give me peace. You are the only person that is always master & conqueror of all my moods—& you are this through a persistence that never flags, a patience that never tires & never is disheartened, & a love that is invincible. Sleep in peace, darling—& blessings rest upon you.

Sam.

✉————————————————————————————————————

Livy | Present.

[1] The tone and content of this letter, which was hand delivered to Olivia in Elmira, suggest 29 May 1869 as the most likely date of composition.

To John J. Murphy
1 June 1869 • Elmira, N.Y.
(MS: MoSW)

J. LANGDON, MINER & DEALER IN ANTHRACITE &
BITUMINOUS COAL   OFFICE NO. 6 BALDWIN STREET

ELMIRA, N.Y. June 1, 186 9.

Friend John—

I got your letter some little time ago, but I am so addicted to putting off till next week what should be done today, that up to this time it is unanswered.[1] I have read proof ever since I saw you—read, & read, & read—interminably. I am sick & tired of it—& still there are several chapters to read yet. I *never n* knew anything to drag as this thing does.

Blame it, I want to go to California, & I *don't* want to go—the latter is the more vociferous & well defined of the two inclinations.

Well, I'm going to dinner, now, if they don't quit ringing for me. I will go *any*how. Good bye, my boy. The paper comes regularly, & I am much obliged to you for it.

Faithfully your friend

Sam*ⁱ*. L. Clemens.

[1] The letter from Murphy, New York business agent of the San Francisco *Alta California*, does not survive. In July, he wrote again, promising to assist Clemens with arrangements for his planned California trip (see 9 July to Redpath, n. 1).

To Silas S. Packard and Other Members of the New York Press Club
1 June 1869 • Elmira, N.Y.
(MS, *damage emended:* ViU)

Friend Packard—

Can't come—enclose letter & speech to be read in meeting—best I can do under the circumstances. If these & your other proceedings are published, should like to have a copy or two secured for my scrapbook—will you?—for I am pleasantly employed & don't look at newspapers.[1]

Shall be at St Nicholas Hotel from 11ᵗʰ to 15ᵗʰ.

Good-bye.

Sam*ⁱ*. Clemens

The punctuation & names are *exactly* as they should be ("fought, bled & lied" should have no itali[c]s & no marked emphasis.[2]

[*on smaller paper:*]

Hartford, June 1, 1869.[3]

GENTLEMEN OF THE N.Y. PRESS CLUB:

I thank you kindly for your invitation to be present at the Press Club dinner[4] & take part in the general destruction of provisions & rhetoric. I sincerely regret that I shall not be able to attend. I had felt so sure of being present that I constructed a toast & speech for the occasion, & sat up ~~several~~ ₍two₎ nights memorizing them. And now that I am all ~~fixed,~~ ₍set,₎ I can't go. Still, I cannot consent that this thunder shall be wasted, & therefore I beg to append my toast & speech, just as I would have expelled them from my system had it been my fortune to assist at the dinner. As follows:

"MR. PRESIDENT[5] & GENTLEMEN—I thank you most heartily—I, that is, I—I am happy in being considered worthy to—to—in truth, gentlemen, I am unprepared to make a speech—this call is entirely unexpected, I assure you—I did not expect it—that is, I did not expect to be called upon—if I had expected to be called upon I would have prepared myself, but not ex—being, as I may say, entirely unprepared & not expecting it, it is entirely unexpected to me, & I am entirely unprepared. But I thank you very kindly, I assure you. However, at this moment a thought occurs to me. I will offer a sentiment, & preface it with a few subsequent remarks which I hope to be able to make in the interim, if the theme shall chance to suggest to me anything to say. I beg that you will fill your ~~horns~~

(*Private memorandum*—To recollect to take notice, at this point, whether these fellows are drinking out of gourds, goblets, jugs, or what they *are* drinking out of, & so not make any stupid blunder, & spoil the effect of the speech,) and join me in a toast:—

"To One whose eminent services in time of great national peril we gratefully acknowledge—whose memory we revere—whose death we deplore—the journalist's truest friend, the late 'RELIABLE CONTRABAND.'[6]

"MR. PRESIDENT & GENTLEMEN—It is my painful duty to mar these festivities with the announcement of the death of one who was dear to us all—our tried & noble friend, the 'Reliable Contraband.' To the world at large this event will bring no sorrow, for the world never comprehended him, never knew him as we did, never had such cause to love him—but unto *us* the calamity brings unutterable anguish, for it heralds the loss of one whose great heart beat for us alone, whose tireless tongue vibrated in our interest only, whose fervent fancy wrought its miracles solely for our enrichment & renown.

"In his time, what did he not do for us? When marvels languished & sensation dispatches grew tame, who was it that laid down the shovel & the hoe & came with healing on his wings? The Reliable Contraband. When armies fled in panic & dismay, & the great cause seemed lost beyond all hope of succor, who was it that turned the tide of war & gave victory to the Vanquished? The Reliable Contraband. When despair hung its shadows about the hearts of the people & sorrow sat upon every face, who was it that braved every danger to bring cheering & incomprehensible news from the front? The Reliable Contraband. Who took Richmond the first time? The Reliable Contraband. Who took it the second time? The Reliable Contraband. Who took it *every* time until the last, & then th felt the bitterness of hearing a nation applaud the man more who took it once[7] than that greater man who had taken it six times, before? The Reliable Contraband. When we needed a bloodless victory, whom did we look to to win it? The Reliable Contraband. When we needed news to make the people's bowels yearn & their knotted & combinéd locks to stand on end like quills upon the fretful porcupine,[8] whom did we look to to fetch it? The Reliable Contraband. When we needed *any* sort or description of news, upon *any* sort or description of subject, who was it that stood always ready to steal a horse & bring that news along? The Reliable Contraband.

"My friends, he was the faithfullest vassal that ever fought, bled & lied in the glorious ranks of journalism. Thunder & lightning never stopped him—annihilated railroads never delayed him—the telegraph never overtook him—military secresy never cru crippled his ḥ knowledge—strategic feints never confused his judgment—cannon balls couldn't kill him—clairvoyance couldn't find him—Satan himself couldn't catch him! His information comprised all knowledge, possible & impossible—his imagination was utterly boundless—his capacity to make mighty statements & so back them up as to make an inch of truth cover an acre of ground without appearing to stretch or tear, was a thing that appalled even the most unimpressible with its awful grandeur.

"The Reliable Contraband is no more. Born of the war, & a necessity of the war & of the war only, he watched its progress, took note of its successes & reverses, manufactured & recorded the most thrilling features of its daily history, & then when it died his great mission was fulfilled, his occupation gone, & he died likewise. No journalist here present can lay his hand upon his heart & say he had not cause to love this faithful creature over whose unsentient form we drop these unavailing tears—for no journalist among us all can lay his hand upon his heart & say he ever lied with such pathos, such unction, such exquisite symmetry, such sublimity of conception & such felicity of execution as when he did it through & by the inspiration of this regally gifted

marvel of mendacity, the lamented 'RELIABLE CONTRABAND.' Peace to
his ashes!"

Respectfully, ~~Subm~~
Mark Twain

[*letter docketed:*] Mark Twain

[1] Clemens's employment was the proofreading of *The Innocents Abroad*, pleasant now since once again it was shared by his fiancée.

[2] Packard followed the instructions for this phrase exactly when he published
Clemens's speech as "Mark Twain's Eulogy on the 'Reliable Contraband'" in
Packard's Monthly for July (SLC 1869g).

[3] "Hartford" presumably was a subterfuge by which Clemens hoped to avoid
published comment on his reason for being in Elmira, which was well known to
members of the Press Club (see the postscript to 4 June 69 to JLC and family).
Above this dateline, Packard noted: "To follow Ed. Remarks." When he printed
the letter, however, he omitted Clemens's dateline, salutation, and first two paragraphs, replacing them with this introduction:

Our estimable contributor, Mark Twain, is at present busy at Hartford, crowding his new
book, "The New Pilgrim's Progress," through the press. *How* busy, will be apparent in
the fact that he could not find time to eat a Delmonico Dinner with the members of the
New York Press Club. With his usual sagacity, however, he saw the advantage of being
represented; and so, when he found it impossible to go, he sent on his speech, to be orated
by another—the very identical speech, he writes, which he should *extemporaneously* have
"expelled from his system" had he been present. As the proceedings of the Press Club are
never made public, this document, like other as brilliant lucubrations of the evening,
would have been doomed to the darkness of silence but for the timely aid of that ubiquitous
"Reliable Contraband," who, though dead enough for an eulogy and an epitaph, is sufficiently alive to serve his old friends when he knows them. So this *morceau* was rescued
from oblivion and the hands of the reporters for exclusive publication in PACKARD'S
MONTHLY. (SLC 1869g, 220)

[4] Held on 5 June.

[5] Unidentified.

[6] During the Civil War, slaves who lived in areas captured by Union forces or
fled behind Union lines were generally considered "contraband of war." Hence
"contraband" became synonymous with "Negro" or "slave." As Clemens makes
clear, reporters sometimes attributed rumors and other dubious news items to
such individuals. Having read Clemens's speech in *Packard's Monthly*, David
Ross Locke (Petroleum V. Nasby) ironically seconded his lament at the demise
of the "Reliable Contraband":

You know that that lemon, our African brother, juicy as he was in his day, has been
squeezed dry. . . . You see friend Twain the 15th Amendment busted Cussed be Canaan. I
howled feelingly on the subject while it was a living issue for I felt all that I said and a great
deal more, but now that we have won our fight, why dance frantically on the dead corpse
of our enemy? . . . The Reliable Contraband (by the way that thing of yours *is* good) is
contraband no more, but a citizen of the United States and I speak of him no more. (Locke
to SLC, 14 July 69, CU-MARK; published with omissions in *MTB*, 1:385–86)

[7] Ulysses S. Grant, whose forces captured Richmond, the Confederate capital, in early April 1865, after a protracted siege, and a few days later brought the Civil War to an end at Appomattox.

[8] *Hamlet*, act 1, scene 5. Also Genesis 43:30 ("And Joseph made haste; for his bowels did yearn upon his brother . . . ") and I Kings 3:26 ("Then spake the woman whose the living child was unto the king, for her bowels yearned upon her son . . .").

To Jane Lampton Clemens and Family
4 June 1869 • Elmira, N.Y.
(MS: NPV)

Elmira, June 4.

Dear Folks—

Livy sends you her love & loving good wishes, & I send you mine. The last 3 chapters of the book came to-night—we shall read it in the morning & then, thank goodness, we are *done*.

In twelve months (or rather I believe it is fourteen,) I have earned just *eighty dollars* by my pen—~~three~~ two little magazine squibs & one newspaper letter—altogether the idlest, laziest 14 months I ever spent in my life.[1] And in that time my *absolute* & *necessary* expenses have been scorchingly heavy—for I have now less than three thousand six hundred dollars in bank out of the eight or nine thousand I have made during those months, lecturing. My expenses were something frightful during the winter.[2] I feel ashamed of my idleness, & yet I have had really *no* inclination to [do] anything but court Livy. I haven't any other inclination *yet*. I have determined not to work as hard traveling, any more, as I did last winter, & so I have resolved not to lecture outside of the 6 New England States next winter. My western course would easily amount to $10,000 next winter, but I would rather make 2 or 3 thousand in New England than submit again to so much wearing travel. [I *have* promised to talk ten ~~times for~~ nights for a thousand dollars in the State of New York, provided the places are close together.] But after all, if I get located in a newspaper in a way to suit me, in the meantime, I don't want to lecture *at all* next winter, & probably shan't. I most cordially hate the lecture-field. And, after all, I shudder to think I may never get out of it. In all conversations with Gough, & Anna Dickinson, Nasby, Oliver

Wendell Holmes, Wendell Phillips & the other old stagers, I could not observe that *they* ever expected or hoped to get out of the business.[3] *I* don't want to get wedded to it as they are. Livy thinks we can live on a very moderate sum & that we'll not need to lecture. I know very well that *she* can live on a small allowance, but I am not so sure about myself. I can't scare her by reminding her that her father's family expenses are forty thousand dollars a year,[4] because she produces the documents at once to show that precious little of this outlay is on *her* account. But I must not commence writing about Livy, else I shall never stop. There isn't such another little piece of perfection in the world as she is.

My time is become so short, now, that I doubt if I get to California this summer. If I manage to buy into a paper, I think I will visit you a while & not go to Cal at all. I shall know something about it after my next trip to Hartford. We all go there on the 10th—the whole family—to attend a wedding,, on the 17th.[5] I am offered an interest [in] a Cleveland paper which would pay me $2,300 to $2,500 a year, & a salary added of $3,000. The salary is fair enough, but the interest is not large enough, & so I must look a little further. The Cleveland folks say they *can* be induced to do a little better by me, & urge me to come out & talk business. But it don't strike me—I feel little or no inclination to go.[6]

I believe I haven't anything else to write, & it is bed-time. I want to write to Orion, but I keep putting it off—I keep putting *every*thing off. Day after day Livy & I are together all day long & until 10 at night, & then I feel dreadfully sleepy. If Orion will bear with me & forgive me I will square up with him yet. I will even let him kiss Livy.

My love to Mollie & Annie & Sammie & Margaret & all. Good-bye.

> Affectionately,
>
> Sam.

~~I see~~

[*new page:*]

P.S. I see that the toast I am ~~respond~~ appointed to respond to at the New York Press Club dinner to-morrow night is, "When I, twain, shall become one flesh—the future husband the husband of the future." Pretty pointed—& pretty suggestive. But I shan't be there—& as I am only an invited guest & a sort of honorary member (for I never have joined,) I have used my privilege of proposing my own toast & making my own speech upon it in my own way—& have forwarded the manuscript.[7]

¹Clemens had in fact written and published at least fifteen newspaper and magazine pieces since April 1868. He had also produced several manuscripts he did not publish (see SLC 1869b–e; 15 and 16 May 69 to OLL, n. 5; and, in *L2*, SLC 1868ww, SLC 1868xx, SLC 1868zz, and SLC 1868aaa–rrr).

²The "eight or nine thousand" included profits from ten lectures Clemens gave in California and Nevada in the spring and summer of 1868 (an eleventh was a benefit performance). Receipts then were sometimes disappointing, but on the whole the brief tour was remunerative: the first of three San Francisco performances alone earned Clemens about $1,600. Although his total western earnings cannot be known, any reasonable estimate, added to the hundred-dollar fees of his November 1868–March 1869 tour—at least forty-two lectures, but with expenses that consumed as much as half his gross earnings (see 14 Jan 69 to PAM)—makes the approximate figures he gave here quite plausible (17 Feb 69 to Goodman, n. 2; *L2*, 205–10, 212, 213 n. 4, 216, 217, 233–35).

³Clemens discussed lecturing with Nasby in Hartford on 9 and 10 March, and with him and Holmes in Boston on 14 or 15 March. He talked with Wendell Phillips on 18 March at the Langdon home, and with Anna Dickinson after she arrived there on 10 April. It is not known when he had last spoken with John Bartholomew Gough.

⁴Jervis Langdon's taxable income for 1868 was $43,500, an amount exceeded by only one other Elmira resident. (The average income of the 305 Elmirans who paid taxes—on incomes ranging from $1.00 to $58,503—was about $1,600.) Langdon paid an income tax of $2,175 ("Incomes," Elmira *Advertiser*, 24 Apr 69, 1).

⁵While in Hartford for the wedding of Alice Hooker and John Day, Clemens investigated the possibility of becoming a partner in the Hartford *Courant* (see 21 June 69 to OLL, n. 3).

⁶Nevertheless, Clemens did meet with the Cleveland *Herald* owners in Cleveland in mid-July, a month before he bought a share in the Buffalo *Express* (see 5 July 69 to Fairbanks, n. 4).

⁷Clemens probably received word of his appointed toast in a letter from the New York Press Club, after he mailed his letter of 1 June. The toast would not have been published, since the proceedings of the club were confidential (see 1 June 69 to Packard and others, n. 3).

To Mary Mason Fairbanks
4 June 1869 • Elmira, N.Y.
(MS: CSmH)

Elmira, June 4.

Dear Mother—

I have been in bed, reading & smoking, two or three hours, but I do not yet discover any inclination to go to sleep. I suppose it is because

I am waiting for the morning to come, so that I can see Livy. Don't know what else. I am in love with Livy. I think considerable of her. I had a dreadful time making this conquest, but that is all over, you know, & now I have to set up nights trying to think what I'll do next. I believe I will commence & rehearse it all over again. I like it.

To-day the *last* chapters of the proof came, & to-morrow we shall finish reading & be done with the tiresome book forever. I am ever so glad of it, & I do not want another task like it shortly. I lost very nearly all my interest in it, long ago. It makes just about 650 or ~~65~~ 660 pages, & so is not too bulky, after all.

We have all given you scissors[1] for not stopping here, & I warn you that you will catch it livelier still if you go by again. Mr. Langdon sticks to his fell threat to follow you to Cleveland & stay 3 weeks if you repeat this iniquity—he does *more* than stick to it—

. . . .

[1] "A severe scolding" (Mathews, 2:1473).

To Olivia L. Langdon
8 June 1869 • Elmira, N.Y.
(MS: CU-MARK)

In Bed, June 8—10 P.M.

It *is* the sweetest face in all the world, Livy. To-day in the drawing-room, & to-night on the sofa when Miss Mary[1] was playing—& afterward when you were sewing lace & I saw you from the front yard, through the window—these several times to-day this face has *amazed* ͵me͵ with its sweetness, & I have felt so thankful that God has given into my charge the dear office of chasing the shadows away & coaxing the sunshine to play about it always. It is such a darling face, Livy!—& such a darling little girlish figure—& such a dainty baby-hand! And to think that with all this exquisite comeliness should be joined such rare & beautiful qualities of mind & heart, is a thing that is utterly incomprehensible. Livy, you are as kind, & good, & sweet & unselfish, & just, & truthful, & sensible *and* intellectual as the homeliest woman I ever saw (for you know that ~~all~~ these qualities ~~never existed before in any but~~ belong peculiarly to homely women.) I have so *longed* for these qualities in my wife, & have so grieved because she would have to be necessarily a marvel of ugliness—I who do so worship beauty. But with a good fortune which is a very miracle, I have secured all these things in my little wife— *and* beauty—beauty beyond any beauty that I ever saw in a face before. And not mere statuesque, mathematically proportioned beauty of feature, but pure *loveliness*. For you are just as lovely & lovable as it is possible for any human being to be, O peerless Livy! If it be possible for one to go crazy with love, Livy, I am doomed to pine in a madhouse yet. And how you do bear with all my faults & foibles, & shame my littleness with the grand nobility of your nature. Heaven knows that I honor you, Livy, with a most true & reverent honor—& that the homage I pay to your virtues is the most unsullied sentiment that emanates from my heart.

You will think, sometimes, of the sad possibility we were speaking of to-night, & fortify yourself against its pernicious effects, my Livy. ~~Pa~~ Misfortunes are not hard to bear if we only get ready for them in time. Part of the afternoon I was thinking this matter over, & I had a great dread of the suffering it might cost you to see your father & mother in misfortune. I even thought it might kill you, because any sorrow of theirs would so weigh upon you. But I am not distressed any more, now. I believe you would rise up to the emergency, & put forth a strength which would comfort them & bravely bear them up. We would not let them be melancholy, would we, Livy? We would make them happy or perish in the attempt—wouldn't we? Indeed we would, my precious little jewel.[2]

Livy, I lost full two hours of your society this afternoon, & I grieve over it yet. It is gone forever & forever. I can never get it back. Those two hours were so blank & useless & tiresome—& they might have been so perfectly happy. I lived 33 years without you, Livy—lost time, every hour of it. I can't live without you any more. You Ninth Statue![3] You little miracle! You darling! I would not part with you for all the kingdoms of the earth & the glory thereof. And I pray that when you die, my widowed heart may break & its pulses cease forever. For what would existence be without you? There would never be joy in the sunshine any more; nor melody in music; nor gladness in the summer air; nor splendor in the expiring day; nor sublimity in the sea; nor beauty in the rainbow; nor worship in the grateful incense of the flowers. For wherewithal wu would ye delight a heart that was dead, & eyes that saw only a memory, & arms that could never know again the little form they so loved to clasp?

Good-night, my sacred idol—& good angels weave the spells of dreamland about you & bless you with their sinless presence.

Sam.

Livy—

Present.

[*docketed by OLL:*] 82nd | Found under my door in the morning—

¹Unidentified.
²Clemens and Olivia had evidently discussed the danger currently looming over one of her father's large investments: see the next letter, n. 2.
³The allusion has not been explained.

To Whitelaw Reid
15 June 1869 • New York, N.Y.
(MS: DLC)

St Nicholas Hotel, 15th.

Whitelaw Reed, Esq¹
    Dear Sir =
        I am ~~very~~ exceedingly & particularly obliged to you for that paragraph this morning about Memphis. The old gentleman is highly gratified.² I hope to be able to do a favor for you some time in case you will do me the honor to ask one.

Very Truly Yours,
Mark Twain

[1] After becoming nationally known for his Civil War dispatches to the Cincinnati *Gazette*, Reid (1837–1912) joined the staff of the New York *Tribune* in September 1868 as Horace Greeley's assistant and chief editorial writer, assuming the duties of managing editor in mid-May 1869, when John Russell Young resigned (Duncan, 18–19, 36–39; Cortissoz, 1:148–49; Baehr, 71–72).

[2] The gratified individual was Jervis Langdon, who arrived at the St. Nicholas with his wife, daughter, and Clemens on 10 June, en route to Hartford for the 17 June wedding of Alice Hooker and John Day. Langdon was owed five hundred thousand dollars by Memphis, Tennessee, the result of his investment in the northern firm of Brown and Company, which had contracted to pave the city's streets. When payment for the work was not promptly forthcoming, Clemens used his influence with the New York *Tribune* to bring public pressure on Memphis. The *Tribune* editorialized on 15 June (4):

> We see from the newspapers of Memphis that they are claiming theirs as the best paved city in the South. From the same papers we see that the contractors [Northern men] who put down the pavements are ill-esteemed because they want to get their pay. We see also in the same journals earnest appeals to Northern capitalists to make investments in the South, and exhibits of the inducements offered for Northern capital. Are we to understand that this Memphis business is a sample of the inducements they offer?

For Memphis's response, see 26 June 69 to Reid, n. 1 ("Morning Arrivals," New York *Evening Express*, 11 June 69, 3; hotel arrivals, New York *Tribune*, 11 June 69, 8, 12 June 69, 5; 23 June 69 to PAM).

To Olivia L. Langdon
21 June 1869 • Hartford, Conn.
(MS: CU-MARK)

Hartford, June 21.

By the almanac, darling, this is the longest day in the year—& since you are gone from me I would know it to be the longest day without having to refer to the almanac. For I do miss you so much. "Old" Bliss says you are the prettiest girl he has seen for 2 years—& thinks he could venture to say longer, but he can't ~~depen~~ recollect further back than that. Young Bliss says it is his usual luck—when he finds a girl he wants, somebody else has already got her.[1] He thinks there can't be any more like you—& I *know* it. You are the Ninth Statue—the Jim of the Ocean[2]— you are the dearest, & the loveliest, & the *best* girl in all the world.

I don't think I shall accomplish anything by tarrying here, & so I shall be in New York tomorrow evening. Warner says he wishes he could effect a copartnership with me, but he doubts the possibility of doing it—will write me if anything turns up.[3] Bromley of the Post says the 5 owners of that paper are so well satisfied with the progress the paper is making that they would be loo loth to sell.[4] He wants to talk with me again to-morrow morning. However, I am not anxious, for the Post is ₰ not quite as desirable property in my eyes as it₰ is in theirs.

P. S. However, I believe I'll run out now & fill an appointment. Good-bye—in haste, my darling

Sam

✉—————————————————————————————

[*in ink:*] Miss Olivia L. Langdon | 675 Fifth Avenue | New York.[5] [*return address:*] ALLYN HOUSE, HARTFORD, CONN.   R. J. ALLYN. [*postmarked:*] HARTFORD CONN. JUN 22 [*docketed by OLL:*] 83rd

[1]Clemens probably went to Hartford from New York, for the Hooker-Day wedding, on 16 June, a few days after the Langdons. He introduced Elisha and Frank Bliss to Olivia sometime before 21 June, when she and her parents left Hartford for New York City.

[2]"Columbia, the Gem of the Ocean," or "The Red, White, and Blue," was introduced to American theater audiences in 1843. It was evidently written by songwriter Thomas à Becket, although it has often been attributed to singer David T. Shaw, who first performed it (Elson, 226–32; Cable Company, 6; Luther, 109–10; de Charms and Breed, 8; Sears, 104; Mattfeld, 63).

[3]Charles Dudley Warner (1829–1900), associate editor and part-owner of the Hartford *Courant*, had been in his youth a typesetter, postal clerk, railway surveyor, and an occasional contributor to magazines. After receiving a law degree in 1858 and practicing for two years, in 1860 he became associate editor to his friend Joseph R. Hawley on the Hartford *Evening Press*, which they merged with the *Courant* in 1867 (see 13 and 14 Feb 69 to OLL, n. 5). Warner had returned to Hartford from Europe on 16 June after nearly a year's sojourn. On 17 June he attended the Hooker-Day wedding, where he surely first met Clemens, who was to become a life-long friend and his collaborator on *The Gilded Age* (1874). Probably on 21 June they had the discussion about a "copartnership" in the *Courant* summarized here—a conversation Clemens had been anticipating since February. In his 27 December 1869 letter to Olivia, he characterized the *Courant* management's response to his proposal as "contemptuous indifference" (Lounsbury, v, vii–xii; Hawley, 10; Hartford *Courant*: "Brief Mention," 16 June 69, 2; "A Wedding in Hartford," 19 June 69, 2; "Mr. Warner's Death," 22 Oct 1900, 7).

[4]Isaac Hill Bromley (1833–98), lawyer, founder of the Norwich (Conn.) *Morning Bulletin*, and former member of the Connecticut General Assembly, became editor and part-owner of the Hartford *Evening Post* in 1868. Three of his partners in the paper have been identified: H. T. Sperry, Ezra Hall, and Marshall Jewell (for the latter, see also 23 June 69 to Olivia Lewis Langdon, n. 4). The *Post*, like the *Courant*, was a Republican paper. It claimed "the largest circula-

tion of any evening paper in New England outside of Boston," compared to the *Courant*'s "daily 4,000 and weekly 9,000" (Rowell, 13; "Isaac H. Bromley Dead," New York *Tribune*, 12 Aug 98, 7; Trumbull, 1:611).

[5] The address of Henry and Fidele Brooks. Evidently on 22 June Olivia and her parents checked out of the St. Nicholas Hotel, where they had spent the previous night. Olivia then began a three-day visit with the Brookses, while her parents returned to Elmira ("Morning Arrivals," New York *Evening Express*, 22 June 69, 3).

To Samuel Bowles
22 June 1869 • Hartford, Conn.
(Transcript and *paraphrase:* Libbie, lot 372)

Hartford, June 22.

[*paraphrase: To Samuel Bowles, editor of the Springfield Republican, asking if he will sell him a part interest in the paper.*][1] Since I have some reputation for joking, it is the part of wisdom to state that I am not joking this time—I am simply in search of a home. I must come to anchor

. . . . .

---

[1] Samuel Bowles (1826–78) had been editor, reporter, and part-owner of the Springfield (Mass.) *Daily Republican* for most of the twenty-five years since its inception in 1844, and of the *Weekly Republican* for most of the eighteen years since the death of its founder, his father, Samuel Bowles (1797–1851). During the late 1850s, the *Republican* became nationally known for its support of a constitutional end to slavery, for its endorsement of the new Republican party, and for the quality and breadth of its news reporting. The New York *Tribune* called it "the best and ablest country journal ever published on this continent" (*DAB*, 2:515). The combined circulation figures of the *Daily*, *Weekly*, and *Semi-Weekly Republican* were nearly 25,000 in 1869. Bowles and Clemens could have met in California in August 1865 (see 24 and 25 Nov 69 to OLL, n. 6). They certainly met in October 1868, for on the twenty-second of that month Clemens informed the *Alta California:* "I saw Mr. Sam Bowles in Springfield yesterday. He is just back from his trip to the Mountains. He says his interest in the Pacific Coast remains unabated" (SLC 1868k). The *Republican*'s city editor, Herbert L. Bridgman, recalled that meeting: "I'll never forget how, in the dusk of one autumn evening, I heard 'Joe' Hawley's cheery voice as he strode along through the outer offices to Mr. Bowles's private room. . . . 'Sam, I want you to know this here man with me. He calls himself Mr. Clemens, but his real name is Mark Twain'" (Hooker, 125; "Obituary: Samuel Bowles, Journalist," New York *Times*, 17 Jan 78, 4; Rowell, 48).

To Olivia Lewis (Mrs. Jervis) Langdon
23 June 1869 • New York, N.Y.
(MS: NPV)

Everett House[1]
New York, 23^{d}

Dear Mrs Langdon—

It is 7.30 P.M., & I have not seen Livy since 2. The amount of fortitude necessary to enable me to endure this separation is just about the amount required to enable a martyr to endure burning at the stake. Maybe martyrs enjoy this sort of heroism—I *don't*. However, I believe Livy thinks one visit a day to Mrs. Brooks's (with an apostrophe & an extra s,) is enough, & so I submit. I arrived here at 5 PM yesterday, & went up to Mrs. B.'s & staid till 10, leaving promptly at that hour. I was there to-day from 11 till 2, & I am not to go again till to-morrow.

Livy is thoroughly enjoying herself, & it does me good to see how those two children nestle respectfully about her, & gaze at her, & hang upon her words, & worship her.[2] But it only gratifies me—it does not surprise me. It would surprise me if they did otherwise. Remsen is somewhat jealous of me—& he looked so sorrowful when I took possession of Livy to help her up & down stairs (a felicity which he had been enjoying,) that I was not distressed at all when she declined my assistance & accepted his. Still, if this infant becomes too pointed in his attentions, I shall have him for breakfast some morning.

Livy was a little homesick after you departed, she says, & half wished she had gone with you. At first I was sorry she ~~had~~ ‚did‚ not go, & so save herself from that depression of spirits, but I soon felt otherwise—for I saw that she was happy & contented, & moreover that she was recuperating fast & looking stronger & brighter, & I felt that a ten-hour rail-trip added right on to the fatigues she had been undergoing, could not have been good for her. It would have worn the poor child out. I am going to start home with her Saturday morning, (she having canvassed the matter of her own accord with Mrs Brooks & satisfied herself that there ~~w~~ can be no impropriety in it,) & then we will all go out immediately & see Mrs. Fairbanks[3]—for there is nothing much to be gained by getting into the Hartford *Post* (though further of that with Mr. Langdon.) ~~The Governor Jewell told me~~[4] We looked for Charley this morning, but I have just come from his hotel & *they* are not expecting him.

Sanford Greeves was at Mrs Brooks's's last night—a good, well-behaved, gentle-natured, fair & honorable ~~& very~~ young man, of little force & very harmless. It is well his good angel saved him from matrimony. ~~Emma~~ Figuratively speaking, Emma would have made him climb a tree in less than six months. How she *would* have lorded it over him! Why they were utterly unfitted for each other, & I cannot ₐsee₄ what ever ~~pro~~ bred their love. He is so meek, & she so—so—so *otherwise* as you might say. They got ready for mating, several centuries too soon, as nearly as I can make it out, after ciphering all through the Book of Revelations. Now if they *could* only have been patient, & waited for the Millennium,—when "the lion & the lamb shall lie down together."[5] It would have been all right, *then*—but not in the nineteenth century.

I wanted to take Greeves by the hand, & throw myself on his bosom & weep down the back of his neck, & congratulate him, but I didn't dare to do it. Because Livy was there—& you know I have to walk mighty straight when she is around. She isn't very strong, but she can make *me* behave.

Pray give my love to Mr. Langdon, & to Theodore & Mrs. Sue—& permit me to subscribe myself

Lovingly & dutifully
Sam*ˡ*. L. Clemens.

[1] The Everett House, located on the north side of Union Square at Fourth Avenue and Seventeenth Street, was, according to an 1866 guidebook, "a convenient and delightful place for visitors, being not only in the fashionable part of the city, but also contiguous to the cars, stages, &c." (James Miller, 69).

[2] The children were Fidele Brooks's son, Remsen, and her younger sister, Josephine Griffiths Polhemus, who was living with her while attending school in New York City (*L2*, 278–79 n. 2).

[3] In Cleveland, as Clemens indicates in the next letter.

[4] Marshall Jewell (1825–83), part-owner of the Hartford *Post* and recently elected governor of Connecticut, had been one of the guests at Alice Hooker Day's wedding. He and his family were to become friends of the Clemenses in the 1870s (Sobel and Raimo, 1:180; "A Wedding in Hartford," Hartford *Courant*, 19 June 69, 2).

[5] The "lion" was Livy's friend Emma Sayles, until recently engaged to Sanford

(or John) Greeves (see 9 May 69 to OLL). The phrase in quotation marks is a rather free extrapolation from Isaiah 11:6, "The wolf also shall dwell with the lamb, and the leopard shall lie down with the kid; and the calf and the young lion and the fatling together; and a little child shall lead them."

To Pamela A. Moffett
23 June 1869 • New York, N.Y.
(MS: CU-MARK)

Everett House, }
New York, 23^d

My Dear Sister:

  We have all been to Hartford, for the last ten days, attending the wedding of a niece of Henry Ward Beecher.[1] Mr. Beecher congratulated me very cordially on my engagement. He thinks Livy is a gem of a girl. I concur.

  Mr. & Mrs. Langdon went home day before yesterday,[2] but as I had some business to attend to, Livy waited for me, & is stopping with some friends in Fifth Avenue,, where I go to see her every day. These friends are great favorites with the Langdons, & will spend the month of August at his house. They are Mr. & Mrs. Brooks & son, & a young sister of Mrs. B. I never saw anybody absolutely worshipped as they worship Livy. I think Brooks would give half his fortune to have us take up our permanent residence in his family. They think ever so much of George Wiley & his wife, too. George was very kind to Livy the last time she was here, & so I am commanded to go & call on him to-morrow.[3]

  I mean to go to Cleveland in a few days, to see what sort of an arrangement I can make with the Herald people. If they will take sixty thousand dollars for a one-third of the paper, I know Mr. Langdon will buy it for me. This is strictly private—don't mention my affairs to ANYbody.

  The first edition of the book—20,000 copies—is being printed.

  Mr. Langdon thinks it is very unfortunate if you have contracted to part with the land at $1 per acre—especially if the other party is empowered to sell at any figure he pleases. But if you get $30,000 cash out of it, *I* shall be satisfied. The rest of us might afford to hold on for higher prices, but Ma can't—she is growing old, & I do wish I could see her in liberal circumstances. I should not think Mr. Langdon would have much patience with any sort of Tennessee matters, for the city of Memphis owes him five hundred thousand dollars, & he is having a lively time getting it. I tell him he never *will* get it, but I don't find it easy to discourage him. His agent there is a pretty live man, & if he hadn't his hands so af awfully full I would touch him up on Tennessee land through Mr. Langdon. However, if your present contract is binding it would not be worth while.[4]

I will go down town tomorrow & get some money to send to Ma. For a week or two I have been away from my base of supplies & could not make a remittance. I am economising as well as I can, but I am not making a cent. However, I don't wish to economise at Ma's expense. I am afraid I shall be in a poor condition to marry in the winter, but I *shall* marry, nevertheless, if I get settled. If I go into the Cleveland Herald I mean to make my *salary* support me, (if I have only an eighth or tenth interest,) without touching the profits. Livy will be well suited with that arrangement.

She wants to see you all—but I guess she must wait awhile. She is a staunch friend of Orion's, & I fancy she is about half in love with him.[5]

Don't you worry about my "taking away the only daughter" when they are so anxious to have us remain in Elmira. I will engage that they *follow* that daughter within twelve months. They couldn't stay away from her. And they think about as much of me as they do of her[6]—& so with both of us away, I fancy they will pack up & come along bye & bye. And Mr. Langdon has his prodigious coal business so well in hand that he could sit down in Cleveland & manage it about as well as in Elmira.

You seem to think that I spend money *foolishly*—but I don't. My *absolute* expenses are $50 a week, just for food, lodging & washing, & it is not possible to live for less. My other expenses are not very heavy, but still unavoidable, & not *very* light. Then add large & constant railroad expenses, & you see it foots up. I have not run behindhand with Ma. She only asked $35 a month, ~~& I have paid her a~~ ($400 a year,) & I have paid her as much as $500 in the last thirteen months.[7] I ought to have done better, I know (& one $50 bill I believe she said she didn't receive, & so I have not counted it,) but then you must give me the little credit that is due me, you know. If ever I get settled, I can supply her easily—could now if I were only located instead of moving constantly from one expensive hotel to another.

Send me the land agent's prospectus—to Elmira. Livy will forward it to me, in case I am not in St Louis by that time. I will pay my ~~exp~~ share of the taxes & things—I would do pretty much anything to "get shut" of that land.[8] And Pamela, I will gladly repay you for the expenses you incur on Ma's account, only give me a little time. You bear with my shortcomings as patiently as a saint.

I must go. Good-bye. Love to all, & all good fortune attend you.

~~Afe~~ Affectionat[e]ly

Sam.

✉️ ————————————————————————————————————

Mrs. W. A. Moffett | 203 South 16th st[9] | St. Louis | Mo. [*return address:*] ~~S. Clemens~~ EVERETT HOUSE   W. B. BORROWS,[10] NEW-YORK. [*hotel stamp:*] EVERETT HOUSE   UNION SQUARE, N.Y.   JUN 23 1869 [*postage stamp and postmark torn away*]

[1] Alice Hooker Day's mother, Isabella Beecher Hooker, was Henry Ward Beecher's half-sister ("Nook Farm Genealogy," Beecher Addenda, ii–iv).

[2] In fact, the Langdons seem to have left New York on 22 June (see 21 June 69 to OLL, n. 5).

[3] Olivia had met George and Elmira Wiley sometime between 26 January and 3 February 1869 (see 29 and 30 Jan 69 to OLL, n. 2, and 5 Feb 69 to JLC and family, n. 3).

[4] Orion Clemens had given land agents J. E. Merriman and Company of St. Louis an exclusive option until April 1870 to sell the Clemens family's land in Fentress County, Tennessee, at a base price of one dollar per acre. (Orion had surveyed the land in 1858, deciding then that title could be established to thirty thousand acres—possibly less than half of his father's original purchase, which in 1870 Samuel Clemens estimated as about seventy-five thousand acres.) Orion explained his agreement with the St. Louis agents in a letter to his brother in late June, since lost, and then repeated the essentials in a letter to him on 7 July (see 26 June 69 to JLC and PAM and 3? July 69 to OC, n. 1). Pamela clearly had anticipated Orion, advising Clemens in a letter written around mid-June, also lost, in which she asked for Jervis Langdon's opinion of the arrangement with Merriman and Company, probably because she and her mother distrusted Orion's estimate of the land's value. Langdon's Memphis agent has not been identified (Richard Edwards 1869, 1088; OC to MEC, 28 May 58, CU-MARK; SLC 1870a, 1; *L1*, 326).

[5] For an instance of Olivia's friendly feeling for Orion, see 10 and 11 Nov 69 to OLL, n. 1.

[6] "It is just a twelve-month tomorrow since Mr Clemens first talked with me of his love for Livia, now he seems so incorporated into our whole being that I seem hardly to remember when it was not so. . . . We are all increasingly attached to Mr Clemens, every time he leaves us loving him better than when

he came" (Olivia Lewis Langdon to Mary Mason Fairbanks, 25 Nov 69, CtHMTH).

[7] Jane Clemens's financial record shows that she "received of Sam" a total of $470 between 5 May 1868 and 29 May 1869 (JLC, 4).

[8] On 28 January 1869 Jane Clemens noted that she "paid Ten, Taxes $17,50 for Sam and me" and on 8 March 1869 she recorded an additional payment of $7.35 for "Tenn land" (JLC, 9).

[9] The address to which Pamela moved in May. She moved again, to 1511 Pine Street, by early September (see 3? July 69 to OC, n. 2).

[10] William B. Borrows, presumably the manager of the Everett House (Wilson 1869, 114).

To Olivia L. Langdon
23 June 1869 • New York, N.Y.
(MS: CU-MARK)

> Everett House, }
> 10 o'clock Tuesday Eve.[1] }

Little saint,—dear, *good* little girl—generous, unselfish Livy darling—my other self—I keep thinking of your remaining here more on my account than your own—*altogether* to gratify me, I almost think you said—& while I continually bless you for it, & love you, love you dearly for it, I as continually supplicate that your comfort & happiness may be such that you will not regret it for a single moment, & that you will not feel sad & homesick again, as you did when your mother & father went away. These thoughts have formed the ceas[e]less undercurrent of my meditations ~~for~~ during the two hours that I have been sitting here writing, & so it is but natural to give them relief at last on paper. It is a darling good girl, & it rests me to write to her. And bless you it will not be in any wise a wearisome ~~wa~~ journey to me to post off to 675 5th ave., presently & thrust this under the door. I do hope you are asleep, now, Livy, & that you won't wake up till 9 in the morning. It *grieves* me so to hear that you have not rested well. And I am afraid you neglect your afternoon nap at Mrs. B.'s. Don't do that, Livy, please. Brighten yourself up, dearie, & recuperate from your long fatigue. I have written six pages to our good mother to-night, & told her you were looking rested, & happy, & strong & bright—& that I would bring you home Saturday none the worse for your sojourn here. And I have written a long letter to my mother & sister in St Louis, also.

I have spent many & many a long, lonesome hour since I saw you, & have regretted that I went up stairs so soon to-day.

I am afraid Remsen isn't tall enough or strong enough to help you much, & those stairways are very long, & steep, & fatiguing,—but I hadn't the heart to insist on taking you up myself, to-day, when I saw how my proposal to do it distressed him. He is jealous of me, anyhow, & I didn't want to provoke him to violence. Still, my dear, please don't traverse those stairs much with such inefficient assistance, for it hurts me to think of it. It would hurt Remsen to know how I am slandering his generous & certainly well-meant efforts, I know, but nevertheless I have more confidence in the strong arms of his father or his mother than in his. Politeness demanded that I should allow this pleasure to Remsen, but it was a politeness that I yielded with many misgivings. (Now I ought *not* to have written any of this, but it *would* be written, in spite of me, for it has lain heavily on my mind.)

I ~~went~~ walked down to the St Nicholas Hotel at 6.30 this evening, but Charley hadn't come, nor had he telegraphed for a room. And so, whether he comes to-night or not, I am going shopping with you to‑morrow. If he comes, all right—we will both go with you. I have thought it all over, this afternoon—therefore, dearie, make up your mind to put up with it. And also make up your mind to shop just as much as you please, for you will not be able to tire *my* patience in the slightest possible degree. You shan't take Charley along, & let him leave you as soon as shopping grows irksome to him. I couldn't have a moment's peace if I knew you were driving about these streets alone. You are too precious to be risked carelessly like common clay.

I spent two hours in the Academy of Design, this afternoon, & I would have enjoyed it *a* rarely if I had had company. If you had been staying at a hotel you would have been with me*,*, & then I would have been comfortable. If we have an opportunity, we must drop in there to‑morrow. There is a portrait there which reminds me ever so strongly of some one we both know, & I wondered & wondered how it came there. I also wondered whether the resemblance was real, or only a creation of my own imagination. So I thought I would like to turn you loose in the Academy & see if you could find the picture without a hint from me.[2]

It is a quarter after eleven, & I must hurry up to Mrs. Brooks's's with this. I shall call on you at 10 in the morning, or just as soon as possible thereafter, & shall be very sick if my dearie is not at home. Good night, darling, & angels as pure as your own thoughts & sinless as your own heart minister to you, & God in his goodness bless you & keep you.

Sam.¹

——

Miss Olivia L. Langdon
Present.

[*docketed by OLL:*] 84th | Under the door at Mrs Brooks

---

¹ Since Clemens says in his first paragraph that he had written the two previous letters "to-night," this letter must also have been written on Wednesday evening, 23 June.

² The National Academy of Design, at the northwest corner of Twenty-third Street and Fourth Avenue, was six blocks from Clemens's hotel. Its annual spring exhibition had opened in mid-April. Among the portraits, one reviewer noted the following:

Very grateful and very subtly charming is No. 181, by Mr. H. P. Gray, the "Portrait of a Young Lady." There is nothing brilliant, nothing rich; no superb shawl, no luminous jewel. All is quiet, simple, truthful, tasteful. In the oneness of tone there is a prevalence of lead-color, half-relieved, and somewhat oddly, by a bit of blue ribbon in the hair. Let this be contrasted with its *vis-à-vis*, No. 254, also a young lady's "Portrait," by Mr. G. A. Baker, which is all dash and sparkle and gay animation. The latter will catch the many admirers; the former will hold the few. It is the old difference between the popular and the good. ("National Academy of Design," *Appletons' Journal of Literature, Science, and Art* 1 [5 June 69]: 308)

The first portrait, with its "bit of blue ribbon," reminded Clemens of Olivia (see 26 and 27 Jan 69 and 13 Mar 69, both to OLL). The artist, Henry Peters Gray (1819–77), was a prolific painter of contemporary and classical subjects and a regular exhibitor at the Academy of Design (Disturnell, 102; Moses King 1893, 308; "Table-Talk," *Appletons' Journal of Literature, Science, and Art* 1 [8 May 69]:186; Naylor, 1:355–57; Tuckerman, 442–45).

~~To Orion Clemens~~
To Jane Lampton Clemens and Pamela A. Moffett
26 June 1869 • Elmira, N.Y.
(MS: CU-MARK)

Elmira, June 26.

My Dear ~~Br~~Mother & Sister

I shipped my old trunk & valise to you day before yesterday while in New York, intending to follow them in the course of a week or more. I shall probably go to Cleveland tomorrow or next day, but I doubt if I enter into any arrangement with the Herald, for Livy does not much like the Herald people & rather dislikes the idea of my being associated with them in business—& besides, they will ~~hardl~~ not like to part with as much as a third of the paper, & Mr. Langdon thinks—(as I do,) that a small interest is not just the thing.[1]

We have all been to Hartford on a villainously expensive trip to attend Alice Hooker's ~~wee~~ wedding. My expenses were ten to twelve dollars a day, & Mr. Langdon's ~~about~~ ˄over˄ fifty. We were gone fifteen days.[2] I wanted to stay a day or so in New York, & so Livy visited with friends there & waited for me. I brought her home yesterday. She stood the trip right well.

I told Slote to send Ma $150;—a check for it, on John Daly or some book firm. Daly's firm was "Daly & Boas," I think—look in the Directory.[3] If I come to St Louis I want to shut myself up in the house & not see anybody.[4] I must write next winter's lecture. Livy thinks I ~~can~~ ought to be able to write it here, but I doubt it. I'll give it a trial tomorrow morning, but I don't think it will work.[5]

Got a good letter from Orion today˄,˄ for which I am much obliged.[6] I guess I won't have time to answer it to-day.

Affectionately,

Sam.

[1] Since writing to Pamela Moffett on 23 June, mentioning a plan to offer $60,000 for a one-third interest in the Cleveland *Herald*, Clemens seems to have received a discouraging letter from Abel Fairbanks. Although Olivia Langdon was aware of Clemens's personal reservations about Fairbanks and knew of Fairbanks's mishandling of Clemens's lecture arrangements in February (see *L2*,

301, and 13 Feb 69 to OLL), her dislike of the "Herald people" was most probably a response to their foot-dragging, since late 1868, over her fiancé's business propositions. Not only were Fairbanks and his partners, George A. and George S. Benedict, reluctant to part with a satisfactory share of the *Herald*, the "small interest" they were about to offer carried a price higher than Clemens was willing to pay (see 5 July 69 to Fairbanks, n. 4).

[2] Clemens traveled with the Langdons from Elmira to New York on 10 June, left for Hartford on 16 June, stopped again in New York on 22 June, and returned to Elmira on 25 June. The record of his cash account with Slote, Woodman and Company shows that he withdrew $200 on 11 June ("Mʳ S. L. Clemens in a/c & Interest a/c with Slote Woodman & Co to August 15. 1869," CU-MARK).

[3] The record of Clemens's account with Slote, Woodman and Company shows a withdrawal of $200 on 25 June. Presumably Clemens kept $50 for himself, and had the remainder sent to his mother, who recorded receipt of a check for "$100 50" on 29 June (JLC, 4). The firm of John J. Daly and John R. Boas, wholesale stationers, was listed in the St. Louis directory at 321 North Main Street (Richard Edwards 1869, 179, 259).

[4] When a month later Clemens still had not arrived in St. Louis, Jane Clemens sent him the following letter (CU-MARK):

> St Louis July 25
>
> My dear son
>
> I have been waiting, waiting, for you, your trunks have been here more than a month. Suppose I send you my trunks and a letter telling you I will be along in a week or so, and then I stay over four weeks what would you think of me especially if I had not been to see you for six or seven ~~times~~ ₐyears, but one time—would you conclude I was weaned from you and cared but little for you and how would you feel to think I had forgotten my own child. seven years ago all the people I know could not have made me believe that one of my children would not think worth while to come and see me. There is no excuse for a child not to go and see his old mother when it is in his power. I met Bixby yesterday he asked me where you was and what you was doing, I was sorry I could not tell him what you are doing, we have not heard from you lately.
>
> I did not tell you I recivd the check the money and all right, because we have looked anxously ever since the trunks came for you. If a carrige or omnibus comes near the gate we are shure it is Sam. You can immagine the rest. To my dear son.
>
> Your mother

Horace Bixby was Clemens's old piloting mentor (*L1*, 70–71).

[5] The lecture was "Curiosities of California," which Clemens "mapped out" by 10 May and substantially drafted by 5 July. He abandoned it sometime before 27 September in favor of "Our Fellow Savages of the Sandwich Islands," with which he opened the 1869–70 lecture season on 1 November in Pittsburgh (10 May 69 to Redpath; 5 July 69 to Fairbanks; 27 Sept 69 to Bliss). Part of the California lecture, entitled "Scenery" and describing Lake Tahoe, survives in the Mark Twain Papers (SLC 1869f).

[6] Orion's "good letter" presumably described his plan to dispose of the Clemenses' Tennessee land. He, like Pamela Moffett, had probably asked Clemens to obtain Jervis Langdon's opinion of the arrangements (see 23 June 69 to PAM, n. 4).

To Whitelaw Reid
26 June 1869 • Elmira, N.Y.
(MS: DLC)

J. LANGDON, MINER & DEALER IN ANTHRACITE &
BITUMINOUS COAL   OFFICE NO. 6 BALDWIN STREET

ELMIRA, N.Y. June 26th 186 9.

Mr. Reid—Dear Sir:

I got your note of 24th, just before leaving New York, & was glad to see the Appeal acknowledge your several propositions in such a docile & un-bloodthirsty manner. A dozen lines in the Tribune seem to move their bowels more than all the supplications of the sorrowful pavement= contractors. We thank you again. The correction under the "General Notice" head, which you mention, has been crowded out by press of matter, no doubt, as Mr. Langdon & I are unable to find it in the Tribune or of yesterday or the day before. But we are still on the lookout for it.[1] Mr. Langdon's patience, even with Memphis Aldermen, was hard to wear out, but it *is* worn out at last, & he has instructed Brown & Co. to "go for them" in the U. S. courts, without further temporizing. He is the easiest & most generous-hearted creditor, with all sorts of people, I ever saw, but I guess he is pretty hard to manage when he gets mad once.

I hope your little family are well, & enjoying themselves, up there among the pleasant nutmeggers.[2]

Yrs. Truly
Sam'. L. Clemens.

[1] Reid's note is not known to survive. The Memphis *Appeal* had responded to the New York *Tribune* of 15 June (see 15 June 69 to Reid, n. 2) with assurances that northern capitalists were, in fact, favorably regarded by the South:

The contractors are not ill-esteemed; on the contrary, they are favorably regarded by press and people. The refusal of the City Council to consent to a reconsideration of the contract with BROWN & Co., and to make new terms at their request, does not argue that they are ill-esteemed. . . . We do appeal to Northern capitalists to make investments in the South, . . . and what is more, we have the best reason to believe that our appeals will not be in vain, notwithstanding the evident effort . . . to make it appear that Memphis and its people are characterised by unfairness and dishonesty. Will the *Tribune* be good enough to make a correction in accordance with the facts? ("We copy the following . . . ," 20 June 69, 2)

The "correction" promised by Reid, and awaited by Clemens and Langdon, finally appeared in the *Tribune* on 28 June (5):

> The *Memphis Appeal* assents to everything THE TRIBUNE has had to say concerning the Nicolson Pavement, and their difficulties with the Northern contractors, and their anxiety to get other Northern capitalists to make investments at the South. But it asks us to deny that they have any ill opinion of the contractors. We hasten to make the correction.

Nicolson pavement, patented by Samuel Nicolson (1791–1868) in 1854 and popular in American cities of the 1860s, was made up of a bed of sand upon which were laid one-inch-thick boards, a coat of asphalt, wooden blocks fixed in place with board strips and coal and pebbles, hot tar to fill all chinks, and a final covering of coarse sand or pebbles (Lester; Leggett, 2:1022).

[2] Reid, who was unmarried and without a "little family," was presumably vacationing in Connecticut, "the nutmeg state."

To Orion Clemens
3? July 1869 • Elmira, N.Y.
(*Paraphrase:* OC to MEC, 7 July 69, CU-MARK)

I have been writing at some length to Sam, in answer to one received yesterday, in which he said Mr. Langdon offered $20,000 ͺcashͺ and $10,000 canal stock for our land.[1] . . . Sam wrote that he wanted a quiet place to write his next winter's lecture[2]

[1] Orion responded to his brother on 7 July:

> I am much pleased with Mr. Langdon's offer; but as you suggest, he must not buy blindfold, or until he sends his Memphis agent there to examine. Neither you nor Ma nor Pamela know anything about the land. . . . I have laboriously investigated the titles, localities and qualities, and I would put its present value at about five thousand dollars, though Ma and Pamela would not be willing to take that. . . . The difficulties are that Tennessee grants the same land over and over again to different parties if they apply for it, leaving them to fight out among themselves questions of priority of entry and compliances with the provisions of the laws, and will then give it with a better title than all of them to some stranger with seven years possession under a deed from some person having himself absolutely no shadow or pretense of title.

Orion proposed trying to perfect the family's title by leasing the land in "160 acre tracts and settling immigrants on them with seven or eight years' leases. . . . How would it do to propose to Mr. Langdon an equal copartnership—we to furnish the land and he the means to colonize?—Provided we make no other disposition of the land before next April, as, until that time, it is locked up in the hands of Merriman & Co." And he closed by reiterating the terms of his agreement with the St. Louis land agents, which Jervis Langdon had found questionable: "If Merriman & Co. sell for a dollar an acre, we give them 5 pr ct. If they sell for over a dollar we give them half of all over, provided their commission shall not be less than 5 pr ct." (CU-MARK). Langdon's response to Orion's "equal copartnership" proposal is not known. In November 1869, Clemens declined to involve him in any sort of purchase, although he agreed to approach him about mining the coal on the land (see 9 Nov 69 to PAM).

 [2] In his 7 July letter, Orion promised his brother: "We can fix you a nice, quiet place to write your lecture. A friend, Mr. Woodward, having gone with his family to spend the summer in the North, Mollie and I have taken the house till they come back, about the first of September. It is a three story brick." On the same day, he wrote Mollie that in offering the room, "I did not say where, meaning to leave that to you. The 2 Second story rooms are Miss Brackett's" (CU-MARK). The house of Calvin M. Woodward, a professor of geometry and drawing at Washington University, was at 1501 Chesnut Street, where Orion and Mollie stayed until early September, when they moved to Pamela Moffett's house at 1511 Pine. "Miss Brackett" was probably Anna C. Brackett, a public school teacher (Richard Edwards 1868, 187; Richard Edwards 1869, 87, 829; Richard Edwards 1870, 71, 940; William Stotts to OC and MEC, 5 Sept 69, CU-MARK).

To Mary Mason Fairbanks
5 July 1869 • Elmira, N.Y.
(MS: CSmH)

Elmira, Monday, July 4⎫
(Which is the 5ᵗʰ⎭ .[1]

Dear Mother =

I haven't got up yet. It is an hour or two to breakfast. But I hate sluggards. I prefer to devote those precious hours to reading & study which some parties *í* waste in repose. All the bummers in town are busting fire-crackers & otherwise glorifying ₲ Him to whom, above all others, we owe this precious Washington's Birth-Day. And so I couldn't sleep if I were to try.

I had expected to be with you before this—several days before this—but as I came booming along in innocent mirth, I unexpectedly got aground here. And so I have been "sparring off" ever since.[2] They left Livy in New York,,—up to Mrs. Brooks's—,& I brought her along, as I was coming this way ,ᵢ,, ~~anyhow~~., She helps me spar. Been at it a week. But it is slow ~~effort~~ work, because I like sparring off better than *going* off—& besides, I am writing next winter's lecture. It takes me every day to do it, & it isn't finished yet. I write up on top of the house, where it is cool & solitary.[3] I have written more than enough for a lecture, but it must be still *l* added to & then cut down. I shall have it ready for your inspection [*in margin:* over] in almost no time, maybe less, & then I shall advance out there & read it to you. I shall telegraph you first, so you can*l* be out if not receiving company that day.

I pray you remember me to Mr. Fairbanks, whose last note I did not answer because I intended to answer it in person before this date.[4] Unto all my brother & sister cubs[5] I send greeting, & great love. And Livy, the new cub—your cub-in-law, so to speak—adds *her* love.

Good-bye—

Lovingly Yr delinquent son

Sam.

[1] Because the Fourth of July fell on a Sunday in 1869, most celebrations in Elmira were postponed until Monday (Elmira *Advertiser:* "City and Neighborhood," 3 July, 5 July 69, 4; "No Paper To-Morrow," 5 July 69, 1).

[2] A riverboat term meaning to aid a vessel over a shallow bar by the use of long, stout poles, or spars, and tackles (Whitney and Smith, 9:5795).

[3] Clemens was working on "Curiosities of California," which he eventually decided not to use, in the cupola of the Langdon home (see the illustration, p. 505).

[4] Clemens had received Abel Fairbanks's latest word concerning the Cleveland *Herald* between 23 and 26 June (see 26 June 69 to JLC and PAM, n. 1). At Jervis Langdon's suggestion, before going to Cleveland he spent 13 and 14 July in Buffalo, presumably investigating the possibility of a partnership in the Buffalo *Express*. While there, staying at the Tifft House, he also toured the city. On 15 July he at last went to Cleveland, where he doubtless stayed as usual with the Fairbankses. It was during this visit that Abel Fairbanks "astonished" and "disheartened" him by proposing that he assume the role of *Herald* political editor, and by asking $62,500 for the one-third interest he wanted, a price Fairbanks in effect *raised* with his next offer (see 1 Aug 69 to Bliss, n. 2, and 14 Aug 69 to the Fairbankses) ("Personal," Buffalo *Express*, 14 July 69, 4; "City Notes," Buffalo *Express*, 15 July 69, 5; "Personal," Cleveland *Herald*, 16 July 69, 3; 19 Aug 69 to OLL).

[5] Charles Mason Fairbanks (1855–1924), Alice Holmes Fairbanks, and Mary Paine Fairbanks, the latter two previously identified (Fairbanks, 552; "Charles M. Fairbanks, Newspaper Man, Dies," New York *Times*, 30 May 1924, 15).

To James Redpath
9 July 1869 • Elmira, N.Y.
(Transcripts: CU-MARK and Merwin-Clayton, lot 125)

J. LANGDON, MINER & DEALER IN ANTHRACITE &
BITUMINOUS COAL   OFFICE NO. 6 BALDWIN STREET

ELMIRA, N.Y. July 9, 186 9

Dear Sir:

I failed to get the letter you speak of. Yes, put me down for the Boston lecture you speak of, by all means. Put me down for any time & place without consulting me—for without doubt I shall leave for California about 1st August. I go partly to advertise myself for in New England by newspaper letters.[1] What Boston paper shall—what newspaper big gun—had I better write for? Will you speak to me of them about it? No matter about the price—let them pay what they think is fair.

Yrs—in haste—

Sam'. L. Clemens

[1]Redpath's letter does not survive. Clemens was preparing for his long-contemplated trip to California. Evidently he had asked John J. Murphy, the San Francisco *Alta California*'s New York business agent, who had expedited his *Quaker City* assignment in 1867 (see *L2*, 22–24), for assistance. Murphy replied on 12 July: "I have been waiting to see Huntington [Collis P. Huntington, one of the proprietors of the Central Pacific Railroad] for some time. . . . It is more than probable that I can get you a pass on the Central, but improbabl[e] that I can do any more. . . . You can write for the Alta whenever you have time and inclination and it will be all right" (CU-MARK). About this time Clemens also wrote to Petroleum V. Nasby, inviting him along to give his "Cussed be Canaan" lecture. On 14 July Nasby responded:

My good friend Clemens:—your letter came duly to hand   As I had no idea of going to the Pacific this season your proposition takes my breath away. If I had my new lecture completed I wouldn't hesitate a minute, but really isn't "Cussed be Canaan" too old? . . .
    Give me a week to think of your proposition. If I can jerk a lecture in time I will go with you. The Lord knows I would like to. I will give you a definite answer yes or no within a week   (CU-MARK; published with omissions in *MTB*, 1:385–86)

Ultimately neither man made the trip west. (For Clemens's opinion of "Cussed be Canaan," see 10 Mar 69 to OLL and CJL, n. 1.)

To Elisha Bliss, Jr.
12 July 1869 • Elmira, N.Y.
(MS facsimile: Sears)

J. LANGDON, MINER & DEALER IN ANTHRACITE &
BITUMINOUS COAL   OFFICE NO. 6 BALDWIN STREET

ELMIRA, N.Y. July 12— 186 9

Friend Bliss—

The circular for the Book is nice—it is tip-top—it is handsome.
I wish you would send me half a dozen more—& if you have plenty to
spare, send a few dozen or a few hundred to my agent, James Redpath,
20 Bromfield street, Boston.[1]

In a hurry

Yrs Truly
Sam*l*. L. Clemens.

✉————————————————————————————

[*letter docketed:*] √ [*and*] Mark Twain | July 12/69

[1]On 17 July Frank Bliss replied for his father: "We send via mail a very few
of the circulars all that we have today, shall have plenty in 2 or 3 days as soon as
some corrections are made in the plates, we send a few to Redpath, & will send
him more in a short time, if you wish more of them let us know, have all you
want" (CU-MARK). The corrected circular, with a redesigned final page, was
most likely the one distributed, at least on occasion, at Clemens's lectures during
the fall of 1869. It was incorporated into the canvasser's prospectus for *The Innocents Abroad*, which was ready on 13 July ("Mark Twain's New Book," Boston
Journal, 10 Nov 69, 4; Hirst, 256, 258). Both the original circular and the redesigned final page are reproduced in Appendix E. See also 10 May 69 to Redpath,
n. 1.

To Elisha Bliss, Jr.
22 July 1869 • Elmira, N.Y.
(MS, *damage emended*, and transcript:
Cooper and CtY-BR)

Elmira, July 22.
Mr Bliss, are you not making a mistake about publishing this year?
The book was to have been ready peremptorily just a year ago, exactly.
Then, as it was necessary to make room & a market for Grant's biography, it was judged much better to delay this book of mine a month or
two. Then, to ~~harass~~ ₐbe up with₎ a rival publisher ~~& damage~~ ₐ& make
capital out of₎ a rival book, it was thought best to make a *spring* book of
mine, in order to give the "Metropolis" a chance. And *then*, in order once
more to fight a rival book & a rival house, it was considered best to make
mine a *summer* book & give the "Mississippi" a fresh boost. And now
that the further delay of my book will encourage agents to continue to
labor for the "Mississippi" (I only just barely suppose this from hearing
you tell a new agent he could have my book when issued *if* he would
work on the "Mississippi" *until* that vague & uncertain event transpired,) it is deemed best ₐto₎ hold it back & make a *fall* book of it.
    Do not misunderstand. I am not complaining. I am not contending
that there is any ⱥ occasion for you to comply with that portion of a contract which stipulates that the book shall be issued "early in the spring."
I am not pretending that there is a *community* of interest here which
would make it improper for you to take the liberty & the responsibility
of departing from the letter of a contract in order to subserve your interest, without first inquiring, for form's sake whether it will be satisfactory
all round—or whether it will be equally profitable all round. I am not
contending that I am hurt unto death simply because the delay for
"Grant" damaged my interests₎; or ~~that~~ ₐbecause₎ the delay for the "Me-
tropolis₎," damaged my interests likewise; or because the delay necessary to make me a spring vegetable damaged my interests; or because
the delay in order [to] open up the "Mississippi" again damaged my interests; or because the further delay to bail the "Mississippi["] dry is *still*
damaging my interests. *No*. All *I* want to know is,—viz:—to-wit—as
follows:

After it is done being a fall book, upon what argument shall you perceive that it will be best to make a winter book of it? And—

After it is done being a winter book, upon what argument shall you perceive that it will be best to make another spring book of it again? And—

When it is done being another spring book again, upon what argument shall you perceive that it will be best to—to—to—[1]

Are you going to publish it *before* Junius Henri Brown's ~~entir~~ ƒTravels in Italy & Germany, or after?[2]

All I desire is to be informed from time to time what future season of the year the publication is postponed to, & why—so that I can go on informing my friends intelligently—I mean that infatuated baker's dozen of them who, faithful unto death, still believe that I *am* going to publish a book.

But seriously, I object to any further delay, & hereby enter my protest against it. These delays are too one-sided. Every one of them has had for its object the furthering of the Am. Pub. Co.'s interest, & to compass this, *my* interests have been entirely disregarded. We both know what figure the sales were expected to reach if due & proper diligence were exerted in behalf of the publication. If that result is not achieved shall you be prepared to show that your tardiness was not the cause?— & ~~sh~~ failing this, shall you be prepared to recompense me for the damage sustained? These are grave questions. I have ceased to expect a large sale for a book whose success depended in a great measure upon its publication while the public were as yet interested in its subject,[3] but I shall feel entirely justified in holding the Publishing Company responsible in case the sales fall short ˌorˌ reasonably short of what we originally expected them to reach.

I think you will do me the justice to say that I have borne these annoying & damaging delays as patiently as any man with bread & butter & reputation at stake could have borne them. I cannot think I have been treated just right.

Yrs Truly
Saml. L. Clemens.

P. S. I am sorry to add to your woes—I know you have your full complement, anyhow—but ~~consider that~~ remember that my share may be cut short, or even threatened by the delays.[4]

[*letter docketed:*] Samuel Clemens

[1] This letter was prompted by the following response (CU-MARK) to a Clemens inquiry, no longer extant, about exactly when *The Innocents Abroad* would be published:

AGENTS WANTED FOR STANDARD WORKS.	OFFICE AMERICAN PUBLISHING COMPANY,
S. DRAKE, PRES'T.	NO. 149 ASYLUM STREET,
E. BLISS, JR., SEC'Y.	
F E BLISS, TREAS.	HARTFORD, CONN., July ~~11~~ 12th 186 9

Friend Twain,
    Yours rec'd. Our Pros will be out in 2 or 3 days   We are binding books also. We have deemed it best not to open our batteries right in the heat of *haying*
    We shall commence in course of a week or so. We shall ship Books to *California* on the steamer of *24th* inst—Prospectus will go on 16th so you see the Books will be there by the *time you are*—We shall do all in our power to make a big thing out of this. Unfortunately we have been delayed too long to make a summer Book of it—but *unavoidably*   We propose to make a fall book of it with every advantage of full preparation & an early start—
                                                    Truly
                                                    E Bliss Jr Scy

After completing three months of proofreading on 5 June, and having acquiesced in previous postponements, Clemens expected to promptly receive bound copies of his book. The announcement that its publication was again delayed therefore struck him as just another in a series of deliberate obstructions, including Bliss's 1868 publication of Albert Deane Richardson's *A Personal History of Ulysses S. Grant* and his 1869 publication of Richardson's *Beyond the Mississippi* (revised edition) and Junius Henri Browne's *The Great Metropolis: A Mirror of New York* (14 May 69 to OLL; 4 June 69 to Fairbanks; *L2*, 163 n. 5, 169–70, 217, 239 n. 2, 257, 421–22). For Bliss's responses to Clemens's charges, see 1 Aug 69 and 12 Aug 69 to Bliss, nn. 1.

[2] Apparently the working title for Browne's *Sights and Sensations in Europe*, not published by the American Publishing Company until July 1871 (APC 1866–79, 70).

[3] As a result of Clemens's 1868–69 "American Vandal Abroad" lecture tour.

[4] Clemens's postscript has been partly obliterated by damage to the manuscript page. Approximately half of the present reading has been supplied conjecturally (see the textual commentary).

To Elisha Bliss, Jr.
1 August 1869 • Elmira, N.Y.
(Transcript: CU-MARK)

Elmira Aug. 1

Friend Bliss—
    I had some notion of running up to Hartford, but I believe I shall not be able to do it. I suppose you are right about sending the books to

the newspapers the first thing,—you are old in the business & ought to know best—though I thought maybe it would have been better to get all your machinery in trim first.[1] However, after so long a time to get ready in, you must surely be about as ready as it is possible to be in *this* world, anyhow. I wrote you a wicked letter, & was sorry afterward that I did it, for it occurred to me that perhaps you had very good reasons for delaying the book till fall which I did not know anything about. But you didn't state any reasons, you know—& I have been out of humor for a week. I had a bargain about concluded for the purchase of an interest in a daily paper & when everything seemed to be going smoothly, the owner *raised* on me. I *think* I have got it all straightened up again, now, & therefore am in a reasonably good humor again.[2] If I made you mad, I forgive you.

The 3 books you speak of have not come. How did you direct them?—to Twain or Clemens?—& by what express did you send them?

I have received a jolly good letter from Henry Clay Trumbull, which I enclose. You had better go & tell him *this* is a plenty good enough notice, if he will let it be printed with his name signed to it.[3]

Yrs Truly,
Saml L. Clemens.

[1] Clemens had received this icy rejoinder, dictated around 30 July (CU-MARK), to his 22 July letter:

AGENTS WANTED FOR STANDARD WORKS.   OFFICE AMERICAN PUBLISHING COMPANY,
S. DRAKE, PRES'T.   NO. 149 ASYLUM STREET,
E. BLISS, JR., SEC'Y.
F E BLISS, TREAS.   HARTFORD, CONN., July 186 9
Mr Clemens

   Your communication is rec'd. I cannot to day reply to it as I wish, I will do so in a day or two. In meantime I have the honor to send you 3 Vols of *"The Innocents,"* one for yourself, & one each for the 2 papers in *Elmira* which please deliver with the extra sheets also—   We did not propose to send to the press until next month for valid reasons, but we shall send at once, hoping that the effects may not all be lost by the notices appearing at a most inauspicious time when most people are busy or away from home—
Any notices of the press that may come to your eye please send me with name of paper
Very Truly
E Bliss Jr. Secy

Bliss registered the copyright for *Innocents* on 28 July, probably just before sending this brief note (Copyright). For his full reply to Clemens's 22 July outburst, see 12 Aug 69 to Bliss, n. 1. For the Elmira newspapers' responses to *Innocents*, see 14 Aug 69 to Bliss, nn. 1, 4, and 15 Aug 69 to Bliss, n. 1.

[2] Sometime between 16 and 22 July, Clemens had returned from Cleveland to Elmira irritated with Abel Fairbanks's revised terms for a share of the Cleveland *Herald* (see 5 July 69 to Mary Mason Fairbanks, n. 4). But he evidently made an effort to reconcile himself, writing Fairbanks on 26 July to inquire about the paper's assets and the increase in Fairbanks's asking price. On 27 July, Fairbanks

replied in some haste, apparently trying to mollify Clemens both with explanations and an adjusted price (CU-MARK):

> You were misled as to our profits decreasing from year to year— . . .
>
> I have had an offer, of $100.000 for one half of the concern, and since that time we have added $10.000 to $15.000, and the business has increased largely, but you know it is almost impossible to set an absolute correct valuation upon an institution of this kind.
>
> In the first offer I made you, I then felt & do now, that it was a fair one, however, I may be mistaken—
>
> I have great confidence in the ability of the office to make money, with the proper effort—it is like land, left idle would produce nothing, but with judicious management & tilling, would abundantly reward the effort—
>
> I should have been glad to [have] had Mr. L & yourself here, and let you examine more closely & I explain more fully, all that you might wish to know—
>
> Let me make a proposition, that I will take $50.000 for one quarter of the office—as it stands, assuring you there are no debts against it, & you become interested in all that is due it—
>
> Let me hear from you. My people are all well—
>
> > Yours truly
> > A. W. Fairbanks

Clemens probably received this letter no earlier than 1 August, when he and the Langdons returned from three days at Niagara Falls. If he read it before writing to Bliss, he apparently did so without perceiving what he would soon understand—that the new offer in effect raised the price again, from $62,500 for the one-third share he wanted to $50,000 for an insufficient one-fourth. And this offer, too little and too costly, was also too late. For Clemens had already received and was considering an offer of a one-third share of the Buffalo *Express* (see 14 Aug 69 to the Fairbankses).

[3] The enclosure has not been found. Trumbull's position as a well-known Congregational minister, member of a socially prominent Hartford family, and New England secretary of the American Sunday-School Union, would have made his endorsement of *The Innocents Abroad* reassuring to readers worried that the book was subversive or irreverent. After conferring with Trumbull, however, Bliss decided to use the letter "*privately not publicly*" (see 12 Aug 69 to Bliss, n. 1). In 1870, after *Innocents* had achieved a large sale in spite of such fears, Bliss observed: "Even the ministers throughout the land who at first predicted, from its title and its subject it would prove sacrilegious, have found it very far from it, and now recommend it to their friends in high glee. . . . Sunday school libraries are adding it to their lists, and Sunday school teachers turn to it for information when they want to talk of the Holy Land" (Bliss).

To Olivia L. Langdon
8 August 1869 • Buffalo, N.Y.
(MS: CU-MARK)

Buffalo, Sunday.[1]
Livy darling, often during this lonesome day I have found myself saying unconsciously, "I will never make her unhappy any more." That is
an emanation of a guilty conscience. I did not think I was acting so badly.
But I *must* have been, else why this accusing repetition of that promise?
It is not a new thing, though. Always, as soon as we are separated, I begin
to think of how many things I ought to have done which I did not do, &
how many things I *did* do which I ought *not* to have done,[2] & so have
failed to give you happiness that it lay in my power to give you. And I
keep on accusing until I hate myself. I wish I could be *myself* again for a
little while, so that I could gladly do everything that would please you,
& ri resist every provocation to make you unhappy. My darling, I hurt
you yesterday, I know it perfectly well. The reason you staid in your
room so long when I was waiting was be to quiet your feelings down &
keep from crying. I tried to look into your eyes when you came out, but
discovered no trace of tears. ‚(You avoided my scrutiny.)‚ But my heart
smote me all the same. Livy, Livy, Livy, I do hate myself at this moment—I do despise myself, to think that all your precious love, and all
your patient‚ gentleness & your beautiful nature were not puissant
enough to curb my little peevish spirit & bridle my irreverent tongue. I
was not fit to stand in such a presence in such a mood. I have made you
suffer, Livy, & now I am suffering in expiation of it. And I hope I shall
suffer a million fold more, if ever word or deed of mine shall hurt you
again.

*   *   *   *   *   *   *

9 *P.M.*—I have just come in from church. I don't know what
church it was, or the name of the preacher. They sang pPresbyterian
hymns & there was a sort of Presbyterian frozen-solemnity and stony
unfeelingness about church & congregation which cheered me greatly,—
& brought to me peace & hap satisfaction. The sermon impressed me,
in spite of its sing-song delivery, & I feel encouraged to pray for a kindlier

spirit to take possession of my heart now that ~~these~~ this long season of harassment is drawing to a close.[3] His text was: "Son, remember." (Luke XVI., 24.)[4] The idea of the discourse was that each day's words & deeds are silently, secretly, & inexorably written down by our memories— nothing omitted, nothing slurred over—nothing palliated, nothing excused, *nothing rubbed out*—& in the hereafter this appalling book will be opened before us & we confronted with its pitiless testimony—~~& all through this~~ So it behoves us to take critical care of each day's doings, & see that its record balances blamelessly at night—not content ourselves with a "trial-balance" once a month & a grand footing-up once a year, —let *all* the pages of this dread journal be clean at the last day, & not be content that only a part of them are so.

Livy dear, I need you, ~~I long~~ to-night—I wish you were here. I love you, love you, *love* you, Livy, with all my whole heart, my darling, & before I lie down I will pray that I may yet be truly worthy of you & be enabled to entirely comprehend & appreciate the exquisite refinements of your nature, & so comprehending be withheld from rudely touching them & giving you pain.

Good-night, Livy dear. I owe your father many, very many thanks, ⟨for my obligations to him almost overshadow my obligations to Charley, now⟩[5] & I will ask you to express them for me—for if there is one thing you can do with a happier grace than another, it is to express gratitude to your father.

I enclose Mrs. Langdon's pencil—I ought to be ashamed of myself, but I *couldn't* recollect it, at least I couldn't *spare* it sooner. I *love* you, Livy. With a kiss & a blessing

                                                            Sam

✉ ————————————————————————————

[*in ink:*] Miss Olivia L. Langdon | Elmira | N. Y. [*postmarked:*] BUFFALO N.Y. AUG 9 [*docketed by OLL:*] 90th

---

[1] Five letters to Olivia immediately preceding the present letter (docket numbers 85–89) are now lost. Clemens probably wrote some of these in mid-July, when he traveled first to Buffalo, and then to Cleveland. Others he probably wrote during the first week of August, after his and the Langdons' visit to Niagara, while he was shuttling between Elmira and Buffalo, enduring the "bore of wading through the books & getting up balance sheets" for the Buffalo *Express* (14 Aug 69 to the Fairbankses). Following the present letter ten letters to Olivia (docket numbers 91–100), probably written daily from 9 through 18 August, are lost.

[2] "We have left undone those things which we ought to have done; And we have done those things which we ought not to have done" (from "A General Confession," *Book of Common Prayer*, 25). The *Book of Common Prayer*, containing the Church of England's prescribed forms of worship, was created in 1549. It had been adopted, in somewhat modified form, by the Protestant Episcopal church of the United States in 1789 (Blunt, xx–xxx, xliv–xlv, 3).

[3] Clemens alludes both to his recent spat with Elisha Bliss, and to his frustrated efforts to reach an agreement with the Cleveland *Herald*.

[4] Actually Luke 16:25: "But Abraham said, Son, remember that thou in thy lifetime receivedst thy good things, and likewise Lazarus evil things: but now he is comforted, and thou art tormented." Neither the preacher nor his church has been conclusively identified. Although it has been suggested that Clemens heard the Reverend Grosvenor Williams Heacock at the Lafayette Street Presbyterian Church, several other Presbyterian churches were within easy walking distance of the boarding house where he was presumably staying at this time (see Reigstad 1990, 1, and 21 Aug 69 to OLL, n. 3).

[5] Clemens was obliged to Olivia's brother for having introduced him to her, via her photograph, in 1867 (see *L2*, 145 n. 3). His obligations to Olivia's father were more material: by the time he wrote this letter, Jervis Langdon must have promised to advance him half the $25,000 purchase price for a one-third share of the Buffalo *Express* and to stand as his guarantor for the balance (12 Aug 69 to Bliss, n. 2; 20 and 21 Aug 69 to PAM, p. 311).

To Elisha Bliss, Jr.
12 August 1869 • Buffalo, N.Y.
(MS: CU-MARK)

"Daily Express" Office,
Buffalo, Aug. 12.

Friend Bliss—

Your splendid letter has arrived, & I confess I owe you one. I was in an awful sweat when I wrote you, for everything seemed going wrong end foremost with me. I had just got mad with the Cleveland Herald folks & broken off all further negotiations for a purchase, & so I let you & some others have the benefit of my ill nature. But that is all gone by, & now we will ƀ smoke the pipe of peace & bury the hatchet.[1] I have bought one-third of the Buffalo "Express,"[2] & it is an exceedingly thriving newspaper.[3] We propose to make it more so. I expect I shall have to buckle right down to it & give up lecturing until next year.

I was at Elmira yesterday & saw the book, & my faith in it has all come back again. It is the very handsomest book of the season & you ought to be proud of your work. It will sell. Between us we will *make* it sell. Miss Langdon has a very flattering letter about it from young Mrs. Perkins of Hartford. I will get a copy & send to you. They live in that big place at the foot of the street that starts from the front of the Episcopal church.[4] Send Henry Ward Beecher a copy. However, I believe I put his name in that list. I will send you the Elmira notices when they appear. I gave that handsome gilt-edged copy to my sweetheart[5]—I wish you would send one like it to Charley J. Langdon, Elmira, & one to my mother, Mrs. Jane Clemens, 203 South 16th street, St. Louis, Mo. I have no copy myself, but I can get along without, ~~have~~ having already perused it. I think it would be a good idea to send both bound & unbound copies to the Buffalo *Express*, the Buffalo *Courier*, & the Buffalo *Commercial*, but that is for you to judge of.[6]

Well, I believe I haven't anything more to say, except that I like the circulars,[7] I like the book, I like you & your style & your business vim, & believe the chebang will be a success.

Heartily & sincerely
Sam*l*. L. Clemens.

"Buffalo Express" is my address hereafter—shall marry & come to anchor here during the winter.

[*letter docketed:*] √ *Clemens* [*and*] √ [*and*] Mark Twain | Aug 12/69

[1] Bliss's "splendid letter" (CU-MARK) was the detailed response he had promised to Clemens's 22 July accusations:

AGENTS WANTED FOR STANDARD WORKS.
E. G. HASTINGS, PRES'T.
E. BLISS, JR., SEC'Y.
F. E. BLISS, TREAS.

OFFICE AMERICAN PUBLISHING COMPANY,
NO. 149 ASYLUM STREET,

HARTFORD, CONN., Aug. 4 186 9

Friend Clemens

Yours of 1st is at hand, enclosing comments from Trumbull. That is all O.K. He has been in to see me 2 or 3 times. We shall use the letter in a very quiet way occasionally—*privately not publicly*, but where it will do, to show a part of it—& get a good effect from it—I enclose you a few of our Circulars &c—& you will see we have got our machinery in operation We have just commenced in town here & as far as we can see or hear the thing takes first rate—We believe the Book will be a success & will disappoint you, if, as you said in your last you had lost all hopes of its meeting with a large sale—I have been intending to reply fully to your last letter—but must say, that I could not get myself into the right humor for it. I felt very much annoyed & hurt, at what was therein written, as I had not dreamed such a construction was placed upon what I was doing. I do not wish to go over the ground unless it is necessary—I know not where you got the idea we was to make

a late fall Book of it. I have never sd so   I only proposed delaying the opening of the Ball for a week or two until haying & harvesting was over. The [*i.e.*, To] show you how absolutely dull July is I will add that we shipd but *1300 Books* all told last month—I will only refer to one ~~subject~~ ˌstatementˌ in yours which was that the Book was to be out peremptorily on the *1ˢᵗ of Aug. 1868*—Now you will recollect you arrived in N.Y from Cal. on the 25ᵗʰ of July, & only placed the Mss. in our hands sometime *in Aug.* & therefore you could not certainly expect the Book to be published before we had the Mss! The first delay, was in order to give us time to *illustrate it* not to give room for *Grant* as that book would be past by time we could possibly have got out yours. The *Metropolis* was got out not to work against a rival house or to make business out of their capital but to fill in ~~som~~ between Grant & your Book in the Spring, while we were lying still as it were—
   The delay this spring, has been by the great quantity of illustrations put in & other causes. You must know that I tried hard to get it out early as possible—I did *not sham it*—Failing to get it early in the season—I held to my sentiments always believed in that the first of the season is the best time to bring out a book—therefore for the past 2 months I have held back as it were on it—rather than pressed it, in order to take the *flood tide* for the Book—
   It has been done solely with a view to the interest of the Book, on which *I* personally have risked almost my ~~sagacity~~ reputation for judgment & sagacity for knowing what will sell—Nothing has been before it in my mind, & I did not suppose you dreamed there was. Everything looks prosperous now & the cold water bath you gave me in your last has perhaps been *refreshing* after all—so I dont lay up anything, you said—only hope you will hereafter, if you want to say such things to me again, just come out plain & call me a d—d cheat & scoundrel—which will really it seems to me cover the whole ground & be a great deal more brief. Now lets let the thing drop & *sell the Book*—Thats what we want to do. We propose now to send out from 1 to 2,000 copies to Editors at once, with advts. without limit & hope if, you have a shot in your locker ˌto spareˌ, you will now pour on a broadside—& lets put the thing through sharply. Please write me often & send me all the notices you see in papers &c—The Books to Elmira were sent by Ex. from here to N.Y. then by same Ex. to "*Mark Twain*" Esq   Have you got them yet. I mail you some slips also to day   look for them

truly
Bliss

Despite Clemens's eagerness to make peace with Bliss and his apparent acceptance of Bliss's explanation, he persisted in his mistaken belief that the publication delay was thirteen months (from July 1868). In 1876 he told William Wright (Dan De Quille): "I have been through that mill (of 'When is your book going to be out?') so often that it long ago ceased to have any power to annoy me—though when the 'Innocents' was in press I confess I wished a million times that I had never written a book. . . . Bliss never yet came within 4 months of getting a book out at the time he said he would. On the Innocents he ~~fell short~~ overstepped his word & his contract *13 months*—& I suffered questioning all that time" (SLC to Wright, 28 Jan 76, Evans Morris†). And in 1903, he asserted: "In August of that year [1869], the Company having during 13 months tried all kinds of ways to get out of publishing 'The Innocents Abroad,' (the late Mr. [Sidney] Drake begging me, as a charity, to take the book away, because it was not serious enough and could finish the destruction of the Company), I telegraphed from Elmira that I would bring suit if the book was not on sale in 24 hours. So it was issued, without a canvasser under engagement, a year after the subject of it had passed out of public interest, and had to be revived—if possible—by the book itself" (SLC 1903, 1–2). Actually, however, Clemens was misremembering his March ultimatum (see 13 Mar 69 to Fairbanks, n. 5). As the present letter and

Clemens's 1 August letter to Bliss make clear, no August confrontation took place. Nor has any record of the threatening telegram Clemens recalled been found.

2 The purchase, for $25,000, was not yet complete. On 13 August John D. F. Slee, business agent and salesman for the Anthracite Coal Association in Buffalo, wrote Clemens: "In response to my letter of yesterday I have Telegram from Mr. Langdon saying he will send check to-day for $7500#—This will doubtless reach us by tomorrow mornings mail—I will give you check for $5000# makeing the $12,500— . . . will it not be well for you and Mr. Kennett to call and execute those papers this afternoon, leaving them in trust with Mr. Rogers until Mr. Kennet has his money—Say to him I expect to be ready with the funds tomorrow morning" (CU-MARK). To this loan from Jervis Langdon, Clemens added $2,500 of his own to complete the down payment—drawing $2,445 of it on 20 August from his cash account with Slote, Woodman and Company in New York ("Mr S. L. Clemens in a/c and Interest a/c to Jany 1st 1870 with Slote Woodman & Co.," CU-MARK). The seller, Thomas Aiguier Kennett (1843–1911), a graduate of Yale and an experienced newspaperman, had bought his interest in the *Express* in 1866, becoming vice-president of the Express Printing Company. After selling out to Clemens, he joined a firm of stockbrokers in New York, and then, from 1873 until the end of his life, he edited trade journals such as the *Carpet and Upholstery Trade Review* and the *Decorator and Furnisher*. The Buffalo law firm of Dennis Bowen and Sherman S. Rogers handled the financial transaction between Kennett and Clemens and may have drawn up the new *Express* partnership agreement as well (Frank H. Severance, 334; "Editor Kennett Dead," New York *Times*, 30 June 1911, 9; *Buffalo Directory*, 234).

3 The Buffalo *Express*, according to its masthead "the official paper of the city," was a Republican daily and weekly (issuing Thursdays) established in 1846 by Almon M. Clapp (1811–99). When the Express Printing Company was formed in 1866, Clapp's partners were his son, Harry H. Clapp, Josephus N. Larned, George H. Selkirk, and Thomas A. Kennett. The Clapps sold their interest to the remaining partners in April 1869, four months before Clemens bought Kennett's share. Although the *Express* did not publish circulation figures, its distribution, which reached Toronto and parts of Pennsylvania and Ohio, suggests that it was indeed "thriving" (Frank H. Severance, 224–25; Rowell, 66; Gregory, 445; *Buffalo Directory*, 252; "Valedictory," Buffalo *Express*, 3 Apr 69, 2; "The Express," Buffalo *Express*, 23 Apr 69, 2).

4 Lucy Maria (Adams) Perkins (1833–93) was the wife of Charles Enoch Perkins (1832–1917), a cousin of Olivia's friend Alice Hooker Day. Her flattering letter has not been found. The Perkins house, on Woodland Street, was at the foot of Niles Street; Trinity Episcopal Church, on Sigourney Street, was at the head. In the 1870s, after Clemens and Olivia settled in Hartford, Charles Perkins was their lawyer (Geer 1869, map facing 29, 214, 264, 477; "Nook Farm Genealogy," 22, Beecher Addenda, ii–iv; "Hartford Residents," Adams Family, 3).

5 Clemens signed the flyleaf the following month: "To Miss Livy Langdon | From Saml. L. Clemens. | Sept., 1869." In 1906, he appended a note, which said in part, "This was doubtless the first copy issued from the press" (Christie 1988b, lot 1166).

6 For the Buffalo press's response to *Innocents*, see 27 Sept 69 to Bliss, n. 4.

7 The revised version of the advertising circular that Clemens had acknowledged a month before: see 12 July 69 to Bliss, n. 1.

To Elisha Bliss, Jr.
14 August 1869 • Buffalo, N.Y.
(MS: NBuHi)

Buffalo Express
Aug. 14.

Friend Bliss—

I enclose the Elmira Gazettes report—the only one that has come to hand thus far.[1]

I entered upon possession to-day & made the first payment ($15,000.)[2]

I met all the Buffalo press at a press dinner this evening, & I guess they will do the book up properly when it comes to hand.[3]

Yrs Truly
Clemens.

[*enclosure:*][4]

.   .   .   .   .

Twain is some thing beside a wit—he is oft times a dealer in the purest of imagery. While he writes with an assured and certain humor, his wit sparkles brighter by a sudden seriousness unexpectedly met; it makes the humor more reliable by contrast; while the grace and beauty of the moralization charms and pleases.

Twain can write seriously as well as wittily, and though his sober thoughts are not solemnly sermon-tinged, yet their earnest grotesqueness impresses one quite as deeply and points the moral even as surely, though the standpoint of observation be not the same.

Mr. Clemens' book is all the more relishable on this account.

He writes purely—not grossly. It is comparatively easy to be naughtily funny. Vulgarity is too often mistaken for wit. A sharp, sacrilegious expression, a startling play upon subjects, which by their very nature should be exempt from touch, are often, especially in a conversational sense, taken as evidences of acuteness. Twain has proven himself above such. His points are not objectionable—and his wit, even if it be deep some times, is creamy and rich, and does not pall. We like it because of its refinement.

Lieutenant Dale has commenced canvassing this city.[5] Sold only by subscription.

✉——————————————————————————————

[*letter docketed:*] √ [*and*] Mark ~~Twin~~ Twain | Aug 14/69

[1]Clemens had not seen a brief notice in the Elmira *Advertiser* of 13 August (4):

The Innocents Abroad.

We are indebted to the Hartford Publishing Company for a copy of MARK TWAIN's new work, bearing the above title. Written in the easy and pleasing style of that distinguished humorist, the book is an exception to most traveller's journals, being not only graphic in its descriptions and reliable in its statements, but in every way eminently readable. Humor is there in no unstinted measure, and pathos is not wanting. We shall refer to the work at greater length in a few days. Sold only by subscription.

A second, somewhat longer, review appeared in the *Advertiser*, but not until 17 September. The reviewer explained his delay in reading the "corpulent volume," which he pronounced "one of the most delightful books, ever published": "We should have completed this pleasing task some time since, but for the fact that we were obliged to take our chance with half dozen others of the family" ("The Innocents Abroad," 1). The Elmira *Saturday Evening Review* also was to publish two notices (see 15 Aug 69 to Bliss, n. 1).

[2]Reportedly Clemens actively assumed his post as managing editor of the Buffalo *Express* on 15 August (see *MTB*, 1:387). John Harrison Mills (1842–1916), an artist who was on the editorial staff of the paper in 1869, later wrote: "I cannot remember that there was any delay in getting down to his work. I think within five minutes the new editor had assumed the easy look of one entirely at home, pencil in hand and a clutch of paper before him, with an air of preoccupation, as of one intent on a task delayed" (Mills). Earl D. Berry (1851–1919), then an *Express* reporter and subsequently city editor, recalled Clemens's advent more dramatically:

"Is this the editorial room of The Buffalo Express?"

"It is," responded a chorus of voices.

"Are you sure that this is the editorial room of The Buffalo Express?"

"Certainly, what can we do for you?"—and one or two chair occupants made inviting gestures for the stranger to enter the room.

There was a brief pause and then Samuel L. Clemens stepped across the threshold, and with cold and biting emphasis drawled: "Well, if this is the editorial room of The Buffalo Express I think that I ought to have a seat, for I am the editor."

Of course, the enlightened politicians were effusive in their greetings and each one tried to express his appreciation of "Mark Twain's little joke," but the new editor frowned them down and made no bones of letting them know that the nature of his work made it desirable that he be alone. Mark Twain and the politicians never affiliated.

In the many years that Postmaster Almon M. Clapp controlled The Buffalo Express, the counting room and editorial room had become headquarters—or rather lounging places—for local Republican politicians. Each evening would find some of these politicians in the editorial room. Mr. Clapp did not object to their assembling there and the editorial writers bore with them patiently although they often must have interfered with work. Mr. Clemens had not met any of the politicians and not one of them had seen him up to the time of his self-introduction to them on the first evening that he undertook to do editorial work. On that occasion he found every chair in the room occupied and not one familiar face. A general smoke-fest was in progress and nobody paid any attention to the stranger who stood in the doorway. (Berry)

Clapp, founder of the *Express*, was twice appointed postmaster of Buffalo by Abraham Lincoln (1861, 1865), but did not hold the office in 1869. After selling his share of the *Express* in April of that year, he moved to Washington to accept the post of congressional printer ("John Harrison Mills," Buffalo *Enquirer*, 24 Oct 1916, 2; "Earl D. Berry Dead," New York *Times*, 23 Dec 1919, 9; *Buffalo Directory*, 44, 227; "The Government Printer," Buffalo *Express*, 29 Apr 69, 2).

³ The host of the dinner was Elam R. Jewett (1810–87), former publisher of the Buffalo *Commercial Advertiser*, which printed the following report on 16 August (3):

A PLEASANT REUNION.—On Saturday last a pleasant company partook of the hospitalities of Mr. E. R. JEWETT, at his elegant country residence, located on what used to be known as the "Buffalo Plains," but which is now far inside our city boundaries, and adjoining the proposed new Park. The company was largely composed of representatives of the Press of our city—of which the host is a founder—and the hours were passed in viewing the beauties of the scenery, in pleasant converse, and in partaking of an elegant repast. There are few so delightful spots about Buffalo, and none where hospitality is more gracefully dispensed.

Clemens recalled this dinner again in his letter of 3 September 1869 to Olivia Langdon ("A Veteran Journalist's Death," New York *Times*, 11 Jan 87, 5; Smith, 2:36–40).

⁴ The enclosure no longer survives. Its text is taken from the Buffalo *Express* of 9 October 1869 ("Advertising Supplement," 1), which in part reprinted the Elmira *Gazette* review of about 12 August 1869.

⁵ George W. Dale was an Elmira book agent ("Book Agent's Notice," Elmira *Gazette*, 25 Nov 69, 4).

To James Redpath
14 August 1869 • Buffalo, N.Y.
(Merwin-Clayton, lot 127)

Aug. 14, 1869

. . . .

I feel compelled to beg off & withdraw from the lecture field entirely for this season, certain unforeseen events having conspired to change all my plans. To wit: I have just purchased one-third of the Buffalo Express & gone pretty largely in debt to accomplish it. . . . Moreover, the party of the second part & myself have decided to be married about the close of December, & I am informed by parties of large experience that one requires two months to get ready to marry & three more to get used to it. This just about covers the entire lecture season & rules me out[1]

.   .   .   .

[1]Clemens repeated his withdrawal request in a second, now missing, letter to Redpath (see 21 Aug 69 to Crane and 21 Aug 69 to OLL).

To Mary Mason and Abel W. Fairbanks
14 August 1869 • Buffalo, N.Y.
(MS: CSmH)

Buffalo, Aug 14.

Dear Mother—

Before either your letter or that of Mr. Fairbanks arrived, I had received a proposition from one of the owners of the Buffalo Express who had taken a sudden notion to sell, & I have been busy in the matter ever since—always intending to write to both of you, & always writing to Livy instead.[1] I had but little trouble in coming to an understanding with the Buffalo man, but then the bore of wading through the books & getting up balance sheets; & the other bore of taking a tedious invoice, & getting everything intelligible & ship-shape & according to the canons of business, were the things that made the delay. As soon as Mr. Langdon saw the books of the concern he was satisfied.

I was satisfied before. I was not particular whether it made more or less money than the Herald, not being as covetous now as I was when I was a young man, but I *was* growing particular about the ¢ routine of duties I was going to launch myself into for life. The more I thought of trying to transform myself into a political editor, the more incongruous & the more hazardous the thing looked. I always did hate politics, & the prospect of becoming its servant at last, & especially when there was no necessity for doing it, was anything but attractive. It just offered *another* apprenticeship—another one, to be tacked on to the tail end of a foolish life *made up* of apprenticeships. I believe I have been apprentice to pretty much everything—& just as I was about to graduate as a journeyman I ₐalwaysₓ had to go apprentice to something else. *No* sir, I said, I'll prostitute my talents to something else. I am capable of slaving over an editorial desk without rest from noon till Midnight, & keep it up without losing a day for 3 years on a stretch, as I am abundantly able to prove, but I am sure it is has to be at agreeable work. I shall have to work hard in this Express office, & do a little of everything—but we have a political editor,[2] & so I need never write any politics unless I want to—& I am just exactly as likely to want to as you are to want to write slang & profanity. My Your aversion to the latter is no stronger than mine to the former. I was astonished—& disheartened, too—when Mr. Fairbanks proposed it—& many a pleasant dream vanished away in that moment—but still, for the sake of being with you & on the Herald, I was ready to accept the issue. The Express proposition just arrived in time to k stop me from going to Cleveland to be a politician. Well—I don't know—I don't know—under your just & firm guidance I might have succeeded—but *I* would I ever have felt at home & fitted to my place? Might not doubts, & questionings, & possibly regrets, have come when it was too late? One cannot teach an old dog new tricks, & I guess it has fallen out mainly as Providence intended it should. But although we are to remain separate in property & person mother, I hope we shall disᵒᵒ no suffer no separation in love—& I neither fear it or expect it.

I am writing this letter to you & Mr Fairbanks both, because I owe him one & you must write read this to him instead. We came very near being associated in business together, & I went home mighty sorry about that $62,500 raise.

Livy & I are to be married the last of December or the first week in January—& therefore I have canceled all of next winter's lecture engagements. We shall come here & go to housekeeping at once.

We got up a nice *surprise* for you at Niagara, & lo & behold you wasn't there. What kind of conduct is those? You *said* you would be there with Charley.[3] Ida was already there, & Charley went, & our entire tribe, including Dʳ & Mrs. Sayles—& we had just got comfortably housed there in our hotel when Mrs Brooks & *her* entire tribe happened in from New York & surprised *us*. We meant to stay several days, but we only staid two or three.[4] We hunted high & low for you, & in both hemispheres—under the American Eagle & likewise the Canadian lion. But you were not. You were like Rachel's children—*they* were not. She refused to be comforted. Such was our gait.[5]

But this will never do. It is bedtime. My cordial love to all the family & my benison upon thee, & upon thy house, & upon all thy possessions whatsoever.ever.

Lovingly Yr Son

Sam*ˡ*.

[1] Abel Fairbanks's letter of 27 July survives in the Mark Twain Papers (see 1 Aug 69 to Bliss, n. 2, for a partial transcription). Mrs. Fairbanks's letter has not been found.

[2] Josephus Nelson Larned (1836–1913), both political editor and editor in chief of the Buffalo *Express* in 1869. Born in Chatham, Ontario, Larned was educated in the public schools of Buffalo and, after working as a bookkeeper and then a clerk, got his first newspaper job at the Buffalo *Republic* in 1857. Two years later he joined the staff of the *Express*, becoming associate editor in 1860 and part owner in 1866. After leaving the paper in 1872, Larned served as Buffalo superintendent of education, was responsible for the development of what became the local public library, was active in several civic organizations, and wrote a number of well-regarded histories and history textbooks. He and Clemens remained lifelong friends. Among the other staff members of the *Express* when Clemens took possession were: Chester A. Wilcox, city editor; Francis Wardell, circulation manager; and Wardell's nephew, James (Jimmie) Brennan, office boy (Olmsted, 4, 6, 9, 10, 11, 15–17, 19–21, 28; Frank H. Severance, 224; Berry; *Buffalo Directory*, 486, 495; "Twain Success Puzzle to His Old Office Boy," Buffalo *Courier-Express*, 24 Feb 1929, sec. S, 8).

[3] Fourteen-year-old Charles Mason Fairbanks.

[4] The visit to Niagara Falls probably occupied the last three days in July. The sole documentary evidence for those dates is found in the record of the cash account Charles Langdon kept for Clemens: a 1 August charge (most likely made at the end of the trip) of $15.40 for "Expenses at Niagara," broken down into "Hotel Bill 10.50" and "Fare to Elmira 4.90" ("Saml. L. Clemens Esq In acc with C. J. Langdon," statement dated "Elmira Aug 9th 1869," CU-MARK). Joining Clemens and the Langdon family were: Ida Clark, Charles Langdon's fiancée, perhaps accompanied by her parents, Jefferson B. and Julia Clark; Elmira neighbors Dr. and Mrs. Henry Sayles; and Fidele Brooks of New York City, whose party most likely included her husband, son, and sister—Henry Brooks, Remsen G. Brooks, and Josephine Griffiths Polhemus. Jervis Langdon probably combined his visit to the falls with an inspection of the Buffalo *Express*'s financial records in nearby Buffalo. The Niagara excursion provided Clemens with material for his first two Saturday contributions to the *Express:* "A Day at Niagara" and "English Festivities. And Minor Matters" (SLC 1869n, 1869s), which he later revised into a single sketch, "Niagara," and collected in *Mark Twain's Sketches, New and Old* (1875).

[5] "Thus saith the Lord; A voice was heard in Ramah, lamentation, and bitter weeping; Rachel weeping for her children refused to be comforted for her children, because they were not" (Jeremiah 31:15).

To Elisha Bliss, Jr.
15 August 1869 • Buffalo, N.Y.
(Transcripts: WU; Chicago 1936, lot 124;
and CU-MARK)

Buffalo, Aug. 15.

Friend Bliss—

There is a literary weekly of trifling circulation & influence in Elmira called the *Saturday Review*—I mention it so that you can send it a
book if you think it worth while. Don't send it through me, because I
have reasons.[1] The Review is handsome & right well edited, I am obliged
to say that.[2]

I enclose letters to Reed of the Tribune and *Wm. H. Chase* of the
Herald, to be sent with the books. Maybe you had better envelop & mark
them "Personal," & deliver them through your agent.[3]

I can't write to the Boston men, for I am not *well* acquainted with
any of them, & moreover I have forgotten their names. Redfield[4] would
be just the man to attend to it handsomely—but then a while ago I con-
ceived that the book was going to issue too late to give me a large lecture
list in New England, and so I canceled my engagements & withdrew
from the field. Their courses are pretty much filled, now.

Since purchasing here I have shut off all my engagements outside of
N. England & withdrawn from the talking ring wholly for this season.
You know when I got to counting up the irons I had in the fire (marriage,
editing a newspaper & lecturing) I said it was most too many for the
subscriber.

I like the "puffs."[5] I will attend to the Buffalo books for the press—
send them along as soon as you please—did I tell you that I took dinner
with the whole press gang, yesterday?—Good fellows they are, too.

Yrs in haste

Clemens

[1] Clemens wanted the Elmira *Saturday Evening Review* to notice his book, but
did not want to appear to be asking a favor of a fledgling journal (first issued on
13 March 1869) which had previously treated him unsympathetically, both directly and by implication. On 24 April, *Review* columnist Ausburn Towner (Ishmael) had denounced American vernacular humorists in general, comparing
them to "ugly jack-lanterns" and concluding:

It is not the want of an international copy-right alone, that keeps down the standard and
the worth of American books; it is because these night-prowlers, these whisky-drinkers,

these self-styled "humorists" (alas! that humor should be fallen so low,) by their incessant howling so fill the papers, the lecture stands and the ears of our countrymen, that they are forced to be taken as the general representatives of our culture and our literature. (Towner 1869a)

And on 22 May Towner had launched a broadly sarcastic attack on Mark Twain in particular, belittling his "Remarkable Murder Trial" (see 8 May 69 to OLL from Hartford, n. 2). Bliss evidently did send *Innocents* to the *Review*, which gave it two notices. On 21 August, remarking that the book had acquired "some local importance" because the author "has spent so mu[ch] time in Elmira, and his face has become so familiar that he seems almost as one of us," Towner first offered praise: "I don't know of a book of travels, and I have read cartloads of them, that contain anything so full of wit, wisdom, satire and beautiful writing." But then he raised issues which had earlier troubled the American Publishing Company's directors:

> To many minds, alas! for what human work can be perfect, this book has one blot that I fear will mar its sale—its apparent irreverence, its playful allusions to matters that a large portion of mankind have been taught to regard as sacred. It is dangerous in the extreme for one depending upon the people of Christian lands for his success in life, to rub up violently or pleasantly, and even with no evil intent, against religious prejudices.
>
> I am sure the author means no harm, either in the additional title to his book, or in his mixing up the scenes of a land to which all Christian hearts turn with an awe, and a reverence, with stories of baulky horses, paraphrases of Bible incidents, and flippant suggestions that the present aspect of the country and its inhabitants give rise to. These are only matters that would naturally present themselves to the mind of a nimble-witted man, who was struck by the contrast of things as they are, to their appearance as shown in pictures. (Towner 1869c)

The regular book reviewer had no such reservations, however, writing on 2 October 1869:

> This is the latest venture of the prince of American humorists, MARK TWAIN. . . . It is full of unexpectedly bright sayings, which take the reader by sudden surprise; the veriest old blue stocking cannot read it without laughing at its rare and strange combinations of facts and incidents.—It is probably one of the best specimens of quaint and characteristic American humor. . . . There is health about it, and it beams with a cheerful, hopeful, religious vein. ("Book Notices," 5)

[2] The *Review*, edited and published by local printers Orrin H. Wheeler and Robert M. Watts, "was an idea of Robert Watts, the junior member of the firm named, who infused into job printing a dainty delicacy and taste never surpassed in that line in Elmira. His newspaper . . . was like him, the best of book paper, the cleanest cut and clearest of type" (Towner 1892, 398–99; Rowell, 67; Boyd and Boyd, 214, 216).

[3] The letter to Whitelaw Reid follows. The letter to William H. Chase, the New York *Herald* art critic who occasionally wrote book reviews and dramatic notices, has not been found. Clemens had known Chase at least since 1867 (see *L2*, 107 n. 2, 298). For Clemens's reaction to the unsigned *Herald* review, which appeared on 31 August 1869, see his 3 September letter to Bliss. Bliss's New York City agent has not been identified.

[4] Clemens meant James Redpath, his Boston lecture agent.

[5] Another *Innocents Abroad* advertising circular. It probably came in a 14 August letter from Bliss that Clemens forwarded to Pamela Moffett (see the postscript to 20 and 21 Aug 69 to PAM). This leaflet combined an American Publishing Company letter to newspaper editors with samples of early reviews. The strategy was successful, for some of the "puffs" were later reprinted in local newspapers (see Appendix E, and Hirst, 265–66).

To Whitelaw Reid
15 August 1869 • Buffalo, N.Y.
(MS: DLC)

Hartford, Aug. 15.

Whitelaw Reed Esq
Dear Sir:

To-day my new book will be sent to the *Tribune*—& this is to ask you if you won't get your reviewer to praise the bad passages & feeble places in it for me. They are the only ones I am worrying about, you know—the meritorious parts can get along themselves, of course.

I date this at Hartford, so that there shall not appear to be any collusion between my publisher & me, or that he has suggested this note,—but in reality I am ~~rea in reality~~ in the "Express" office at Buffalo, & have not been near Hartford lately.[1]

Heartily Yrs
Sam[l]. L. Clemens.

[1] This letter may have accompanied a review copy. The New York *Tribune*'s long and complimentary notice appeared on 27 August 1869. For Clemens's reaction to it, see his letter of 7 September to Reid.

To Olivia L. Langdon
19 August 1869 • Buffalo, N.Y.
(MS: CU-MARK)

Office, 7.30 AM. ⎫
Thursday. ⎭

My child, I ~~w~~ believe you'll have to be obeyed at last—I don't see any easy way around it without having your fingers in my hair. And so ~~this~~ at this moment I slash from this morning's paper everything of mine that is in it. Of course it don't take ten or twelve hours to write those twenty or thirty pages of MS., dearie, but it ~~tak~~ takes a deal of time to skim through a large pile of exchanges, because one gets interested every now & then & stops to read a while if the article looks as if it might be a good thing to copy.[1] And then one is interrupted a good deal by visiters—& there is proof-reading to do, & a great many little things that use up

time—but it is an easy, pleasant, *delightful* situation, & I never liked anything better.[2] I am grateful to Mr. Langdon for thinking of Buffalo with
his cool head when we couldn't think of any place but Cleveland with
our hot ones. [Before I forget it, tell [him] I got his dispatch yesterday,
but of course I never could have needed it, for I think Slee would not
dare to write & print articles over his name, and I am particularly sure *I*
wouldn't.][3] So you see, with all my work I do very little that is visible to
the naked eye, & certainly not enough, visible or invisible, to hurt me.
I am simply ~~running~~ working late at night in these first days until I get
the reporters accustomed & habituated to doing things my way,—after
that, a very little watching will keep them up to the mark. I simply want
to educate them to modify the adjectives, ~~cut~~ curtail their philosophical
reflections & leave out the slang. I have been consulting with the foreman of the news room for two days, & getting *him* drilled as to how I
want the type-setting done—& this morning he has got my plan into full
operation, & the paper is vastly improved in appearance. I have annihilated all the glaring thunder-&-lightning headings over the telegraphic
news & made that department look quiet & respectable.[4] Once in two
months, hereafter, when anything astounding *does* happen, a grand display of headings will attract immediate attention to it—but where one
uses them *every day*, they soon cease to have any force. We are not astonished to hear a drunken rowdy swear, because he does it on great &
trivial occasions alike—but when we hear a staid clergyman rip out an
oath, we know it *means* something.

My own little darling, I clear forgot to write with a pen—forgive me
this time & I will be more careful hereafter—I will, Livy.

Tell Charlie I am ä very grateful for his cordial family invitation to
come, from the head even unto the tail of it—but I cannot tell, until to=
morrow, whether I can do it or not.[5]

Your little head is *always* right, honey. I *do* find it nearly impossible
to keep my newspaper thoughts still on Sunday. But I will try to do better, darling.

I still don't know whether you get the paper or not—but I know it
is sent. I have instructed them to send the Weekly to Hattie Lewis, also.

Good bye, my darling Livy, whom I love with all my whole heart,
& whose spirit presence is never absent from my thoughts, but is the
dear companion of my communings morning, noon & night. Peace &
blessings & kisses, little sweetheart.

Sam

[*enclosure:*]⁶

INSPIRED HUMOR.

The New York *World* is not generally regarded as a humorous paper, but once in a while the arid solemnity with which it projects a comical idea into the body of one of its heaviest editorials would make Artemus Ward turn in his grave. For example, observe this, in Tuesday's leader: "The Democracy of New York this year must "elect a Democratic Legislature, *an* "*honest and incorruptible Democratic* "*Legislature; an able and experienced* "*Democratic Legislature.*" And again: "The Democratic party has for its task "to completely redeem the State and "the nation from Republican corrup-"tion, extravagance, and misrule." The humor of those two sentences rises to sublimity. And the manner of their expression has all that seemingly dense unconsciousness about it which is the soul of all true humor. Two better things than those remarks have not been said this year, even in Mr. Schuyler's "Personal" column. The bare idea of an incorruptible Democratic New York Legislature is a burst of humor so grand, so enormous in its proportions, so supernatural in its conception, and withal so solemn and awe-imposing, that the provincial mind contemplates it with humbled posture and reverent head uncovered, feeling that the ground is holy and that the Presence that speaks is the dread and mighty Momus his very self. *awe-inspiring*

The other joke, of loading down the astounded Democracy with such a task as the redeeming anything or anybody from corruption, extravagance and misrule, is fully as colossal as its brother. There is a volcanic magnificence about these two jests that fascinates while it terrifies the beholder. The pair should be placed on record together among the precious archives of the nation, and sent down to posterity as the most stupendous achievement which the world of humor gave birth to in the eventful nineteenth century. But with notes attached, explaining that this severely virtuous Democracy is the Democracy whose devotees plunged the nation into a monstrous civil war; burned colored orphan asylums; conducted the Andersonville prison; respected Andrew Johnson; removed Mr. Lincoln in an abrupt and peculiarly Democratic way; instituted the Ku-Klux-Klan; ran for Vice President the melancholy frag-ment which whisky had left of what was once Francis P. Blair; sapped the public Treasury under Johnson by all the devices known to fraud; voted early and always for repudiation; and whose party's crowning work is its government of New York city; a party whose religion is to war against all moral and material progress, and who never were known to divert to the erection of a school house moneys that would suffice to build a distillery. The explanatory notes should go with the jokes, by all means.

✉——————————————————————————————————

[*in ink:*] Miss Olivia L. Langdon | Elmira | N. Y. [*return address:*] IF NOT
DELIVERED WITHIN 10 DAYS, TO BE RETURNED TO [*postmarked:*] BUFFALO N.Y.
AUG 19 [*docketed by OLL:*] 101st

[1] Signed articles by Mark Twain did not begin appearing in the Buffalo *Express*
until 21 August (see 26 and 27 Sept 69 to Fairbanks, n. 1). His contributions to
the 19 August issue of the paper therefore cannot all be identified. Nevertheless,
his remarks here suggest that he assembled the "People and Things" column,
mining the *Express*'s exchanges for items and supplying a few of his own. Probably he also wrote "Inspired Humor" (see note 6).

[2] *Express* reporter Earl D. Berry recalled Clemens's first summer in the editorial offices of the newspaper:

The Express occupied the whole of a four story, ramshackle brick building. . . . The editorial room was on the third floor front and the city editor's room was just above it. Each
room was unpainted and unadorned—except by cobwebs. The only furniture consisted of
cheap wooden tables and chairs and a crude row of bookshelves built against a side wall.
In cold weather heat was furnished by old-fashioned coal stoves of the baseburner type. A
long table in the center of the editorial room was the only desk accommodation.
    Mr. Clemens was a believer in personal comfort while at work. On hot days in particular
he cast aside formalities—and a considerable portion of his clothing as well. At the outset
he bought a comfortable lounging chair with a writing board hinged on to the arm, and it
was no infrequent sight during the summer to find him nestled cosily in that chair, a pipe
in his mouth and only a negligee shirt, trousers and socks in evidence as costume. His collar
and shoes would most likely be in a waste basket and his hat, coat and waistcoat wherever
they chanced to land when he cast them off. (Berry)

[3] Langdon's dispatch must have asked that his name not be signed to, or in-
voked in, any Buffalo *Express* articles about the current controversy over coal
prices. Prompted by the belief that the Anthracite Coal Association (comprising
three companies, including Langdon's—see 27 Feb 69 to OLL, n. 4) was responsible for the high price of coal in Buffalo, residents began in early August
to form the Citizen's Mutual Coal Mining, Purchasing and Sale Company—a
cooperative designed to circumvent the alleged "monopoly." Langdon was evidently less disturbed by this economic threat than by the personal criticisms of
him published in newspaper reports of the cooperative movement. The *Express*,
which had not reported these criticisms but had been sympathetic to the citizens'
cause, was about to modify its position: on 20 August Clemens published "The
'Monopoly' Speaks," an editorial noting that "up to the present time we have
heard only the people's side of the coal question, though there could be no doubt
that the coal men had a side also." He directed his readers to a letter, in that day's
issue, from a "gentleman of unimpeachable character," John D. F. Slee, the "authorized business agent and general salesman of . . . 'the Anthracite Coal Association,' . . . the highest officer in their employ in Buffalo" (SLC 1869m). In
his letter Slee urged the *Express* to reprint a lengthy article from the New York
Evening Post which, he said, indicated "how utterly groundless is the charge of
'extortion' brought against the so-called monopolists." (The *Express* of course
complied, also on 20 August.) Slee attributed high prices to the "unreasonable
demands of the miners," who were striking for improved wages and working
conditions, demands the Association was resisting "well nigh alone." He re-

jected reports that "Mr. Langdon controls most of the coal sent to this market"; denied allegations that Langdon sought to control canals and railroads serving Buffalo; and concluded with a defense of Langdon's character: "Mr. Langdon needs no encomiums from me, but no man knows him but ranks him as one of the most liberal-minded and high-toned business gentlemen in the State" (Slee). The change in the *Express*'s views drew pointed comment from a source well aware of the new editor's personal ties (see 3 Sept 69 to OLL, pp. 333–34). Langdon, for his part, was aware of the public relations value of "liberal-minded" gestures. Exactly a week after publishing Slee's letter, the *Express* was able to report:

We learn with sincere gratification that Mr. James [i.e., Jervis] Langdon, of Elmira, has made a voluntary donation of fifty tons of hard coal to the Buffalo General Hospital. Mr. Langdon is a large dealer in coal and ships largely to this city. Although he is wealthy and a member of a corporation, he has a soul of *his own* and his liberality is not confined to the city in which he resides. This liberal donation so graciously tendered will gladden the hearts of the inmates of the Hospital as the cold Winter comes, and cause them to bless the giver, and the citizens of Buffalo will honor the man who has honored the cause of charity in this city. ("A Liberal Gift to the General Hospital," 27 Aug 69, 4)

(Buffalo *Express:* "Cheap Coal," 4 Aug 69, 4; "Coal," 12 Aug 69, 4; "The Anthracite Coal Mines," 20 Aug 69, 2, reprinting the New York *Evening Post*, 14 Aug 69, 1.)

⁴See the illustrations comparing the front pages of 18 and 19 August.

⁵Charles Langdon's "family" invitation, probably asking Clemens to Elmira for the weekend of 21–22 August, could have come directly or in a letter from Olivia; no letter from either survives.

⁶None of Clemens's enclosures from the Buffalo *Express* of 19 August survive with the letter. The clipping of "Inspired Humor" (SLC 1869k), found separately among the Mark Twain Papers and reproduced here at 61 percent of actual size, may have been one of them, however. Clemens corrected "awe-imposing" to "awe-inspiring" in pencil. Probably also enclosed were at least the final two or three paragraphs of the "People and Things" column (SLC 1869*l*): see Appendix B.

Detail of the front page of the Buffalo *Express* of 18 August 1869, before Clemens redesigned the paper's typography. Reproduced from the microfilm edition in the Buffalo and Erie County Public Library, Buffalo, New York (NBu). See p. 304.

Detail of the front page of the Buffalo *Express* of 19 August 1869, after Clemens redesigned the paper's typography. Reproduced from the microfilm edition in the Buffalo and Erie County Public Library, Buffalo, New York (NBu).

To Pamela A. Moffett
20 and 21 August 1869 • Buffalo, N.Y.
(MS and MS facsimile: NPV and Davis)

Buffalo, Aug. 20.

My Dear Sister—

I have only time to write a line. I got your letter this morning &
mailed it to Livy.[1] She will be expecting me to-night & I am sorry to
disappoint her so, but then I could not well get away. I will go next
Saturday.

I have bundled up Livy's picture & will try & recollect to mail it to=
morrow. It is a porcelaintype & I think you will like it.[2]

I am sorry I never got to St Louis, because I may be too busy to go
for a long time. But I have been busy all the time & St Louis is clear out
of the way, & remote from the world & all ordinary routes of travel.[3] It
You must not place too much weight upon this idea of moving the capital
from Washington. St. Louis is in some respects a better place for it than
Washington though there isn't more than a toss-up between the two after
all. One is dead & the other in a trance. But Washington *is* in the centre
of population & business, while St Louis is far removed from both. And
you know there *is* no *geographical* centre any more. The railroads ʌ& tele-
graphsʌ have done away with all that. It is no longer a matter of sufficient
importanɟce to be gravely considered by thinking men. The only *centres*,
now, are narrowed down to those of intelligence, capital & population.
As I said before Washington is the nearest to those—& you don't have
to paddle across a river on ferry boats of a pattern popular in the dark
ages to get to it, nor have to clamber up vilely paved hills in ~~nasty~~ rascally
omnibuses along with a herd of all sorts of people after you are there.
Secondly, The removal of the capital is one of those old, regular, reliable
dodges that are the bread & meat of back country congressmen. It is
agitated *every* year. It always has been, it always will be. ~~Thirdly~~ It is not
new in any respect. *Thirdly,* The Capitol ʌhasʌ cost $40,000,000 already
& lacks a good deal of being finished, yet. There are single stones in the
Treasury building (& a good many of them,) that cost twenty-seven
thousand dollars apiece—& millions were spent in the construction of

that & the Patent Office & the other great government buildings. To move to St Louis the country must throw away a hundred millions of capital invested in these buildings, & go right to work to spend a hundred millions on new buildings in St Louis. Shall we ever have a Congress a *majority* of whose members are hopelessly insane? Probably not. But it is possible—unquestionably such a thing is possible. Only I don't believe it will happen in our time, & I am satisfied the capital will not be moved until it *does* happen. But if St. Louis would donate the ground *& the buildings*, it would be a different matter. It [would] take the "helft" of St Louis to be worth the money, though. No, Pamela, I don't see any good reason to believe you or I will ever see the capital moved.[4]

I have twice instructed the publishers to send Ma a book—it was the first thing I did—long before the proofs were finished. Write me if it is not yet done.

Livy says we *must* have you all at our marriage,—& I say we can't. It will be at Christmas or New Years, when such a trip across the country would be equivalent to murder & arson & everything else. And it would cost five hundred dollars—an amount of money she don't know the value of now, but will before a year is gone. She grieves over it, poor little rascal, but *I* it can't be helped. She must wait awhile, till I am firmly on my legs, & then she shall see you. She says her father & mother will *invite* you just as soon as the wedding date is definitely fixed, *any*way—& she thinks that's *bound* to settle it.[5] But the ice & snow, & the long hard journey, & the injudiciousness of laying out any money except what we are *obliged* to part with while we are so much in debt, settles the case differently. For it *is* a debt. Mr. Langdon is just as good as bound for $25,000 for me, & has already ₱ advanced half of it in cash. I wrote & asked whether I had better send him my note, or a due-bill, or how he would prefer to have the indebtedness made of record—& he answered every *other* topic in the letter pleasantly but never replied to that at all. Still, I shall give my note into the hands of his business agent here,[6] & pay him the interest as it falls due. We must "go slow." We are not in the Cleveland Herald. We are a hundred thousand times better off, but there isn't so much money in it. I have partners I have ~~the~~ a strong liking & the highest respect for. I am well satisfied.

Do you receive the paper? Have ordered it sent to you.

I enclose the key of the trunk, & Mollie is welcome to all the shirts she can find in it or in the valise—but I do not think there are any. I do not want any of the clothing, Pamela, except the summer clothing—I mean the white linen vests & pants & coats (for if they ain't there *I* don't know what has become of them. I had to buy a ~~lot~~ new lot of vests this summer.) Lay the ~~♦♦~~ summer clothing to one side till next summer.

Don't tumble the manuscripts any more than you can help—but search out & send me my account of the Deluge (it is a diary kept by Shem). There are 70 or 80 pages of it. It is no account now, but I shall *make* it so before I am done with it—there is substance there for a telling article.[7]

The family all seem to know & like Orion particularly well, & want to see him. They naturally want to see *all* of you. Livy has an adopted sister (Mrs. Crane,) who is the counterpart of Livy in purity of heart, goodness, unselfishness & thorough loveliness of character. I suppose, some day, you will do as everybody else does, *worship* Susie Crane. From morning till night that little woman is busy—& always for somebody else: making bouquets for the ~~poo~~ church, or a corp[s]e—visiting the poor & relieving them—nursing the sick—*hunting up* the needy & the suffering—thieving Livy's work clandestinely & doing it for her—decking the house with flowers when I am coming, or at least managing to gouge more than half the labor out of Livy's hands—forever doing *some*-thing for somebody, & withal so quietly, & so daintily & secretly, that you only detect ~~her late presence~~ that she has been about ̶w̶ by a sort of nameless exquisite grace that ~~in~~ her handiwork leaves in the ordering & arrangement of inanimate things—a charm, a something that is suggestive of a fragrance still haunting a spot where a bouquet has been. Twenty-three years those girls have lived together without a bitter thought or a harsh word toward each other, & yet no blood relationship existing between them.

But I *must* go to bed. I always get up at 7 now, & breakfast at half-past. It is toward 2 in the morning at this moment. Give my love to all the household, & tell Margaret I didn't mean to disappoint her & behave so badly, but I got bothered & delayed.

Affectionately

Sam

[*new page, in ink:*]

MORNING EXPRESS $10 PER ANNUM.   OFFICE OF THE EXPRESS PRINTING COMPANY
EVENING EXPRESS $8 PER ANNUM.   NO. 14 EAST SWAN STREET.
WEEKLY EXPRESS $1.50 PER ANNUM.
BUFFALO, Aug. 21 186 9.

P. S.—

† I forgot that this letter of my publisher a week ago, explains where you are to get that book if Hutchinson has not already sent it to you. Show Hutchinson this note from Bliss.[8]

Sam.

[1] Pamela's letter has not been found. Clemens must have enclosed it in one of two letters to Olivia, docket numbers 102 and 103, now lost.

[2] Probably a copy of one of the porcelaintypes Clemens had received earlier in the year (see 22 Jan 69 to OLL, n. 1, and 15 May 69 to OLL [2nd of 2], n. 2). The likeness was to be his family's introduction to Olivia, a reenactment of his own first glimpse of her (see *L2*, 145 n. 3).

[3] Clemens had sent his baggage to St. Louis on 24 June, expecting to follow shortly (see 26 June 69 to JLC and PAM).

[4] On 5 July the Chicago *Tribune* had begun, in concert with other midwestern newspapers and local politicians, to urge the removal of the capital, not to Chicago, but to St. Louis, exciting the hopes of residents there. By 13 August supporters of the move had called for a national convention in St. Louis on 20 October. Two of the matters under general discussion were the value of existing government buildings and the cost of removal. Clemens evidently got his estimates from the Buffalo *Express*'s newspaper exchanges. He concluded here that it would take the "Hälfte," or half, of St. Louis to make the move financially feasible. The day after Clemens wrote this portion of his letter, the *Express* published an editorial probably written by him, perhaps in collaboration with Josephus Larned (see 21 Aug 69 to OLL), that echoed these remarks to his sister:

The "question" of removing the national capital (together with its seventy-five millions of dollars' worth of national buildings, of course,) is again being discussed by some of the country papers in the back settlements, incited to it by the St. Louis papers. There is nothing to be alarmed about in this thing. The question of removing the capital of the nation out in the woods somewhere comes up regularly once a year, and will continue to do so until the final judgment. (SLC 1869o)

(Chicago *Tribune:* "Removal of the Capital," 5 July 69, 2; "The National Capital," 11 Aug 69, 2; "The National Capital Movement," 13 Aug 69, 1; Buffalo *Express:* "Removal of the Capital," 17 Aug 69, 2.)

[5] Within a day, however, Clemens named a wedding date (though, as it turned out, not the actual one) in his letter to Henry Abbey. It seems likely that he here intentionally withheld it from his family.

[6] John D. F. Slee.

[7] In late July 1866, Clemens recorded in his notebook his earliest known plan for a "Deluge" piece, a project he returned to recurrently throughout his life: "Conversation between the carpenters of Noah's Ark, laughing at him for an old visionary—his money as good as anybody's though going to bust himself on this

crazy enterprise" (*N&J1*, 147). This letter is the first evidence of his having written a substantial portion of the narrative. Pamela evidently complied with his request for the manuscript and within five months Clemens decided he had the material for more than just a "telling article": "I mean to take plenty of time & pains with the Noah's Ark book—maybe it will be several years before it is *all* written—but it will be a perfect lightning-striker when it **is** done" (22 Jan 70 to Elisha Bliss, Jr., CU-MARK, in *MTLP*, 29). In late 1870 he included a part of the manuscript, known only as "Pre-flood show," in the printer's copy for a sketchbook he wanted Bliss to publish but later abandoned (*ET&S1*, 574–75, 584–85). Seventeen years later he described as still "unfinished" a narrative, all of whose action "takes place in Noah's ark," which he then thought had occupied him for "sixteen years" (14 May 87 to Jeannette Gilder, unmailed letter, CU-MARK, in *MTL*, 2:486–87), and in 1909 he recalled, again somewhat inaccurately: "As to that 'Noah's Ark' book, I began it in Edinburgh in 1873; I don't know where the manuscript is, now. It was a Diary, which professed to be the work of Shem, but wasn't. I began it again several months ago, but only for recreation; I hadn't any intention of carrying it to a finish—or even to the end of the first chapter, in fact" (SLC 1909, 6–7). Fragments of this long-germinating book survive in the Mark Twain Papers and portions were included by Bernard DeVoto in "Papers of the Adam Family" (*LE*, 57–114).

   [8] The enclosed letter from Bliss, evidently written on 14 August, does not survive. Francis A. Hutchinson of F. A. Hutchinson and Company, subscription book publishers, handled sales of *The Innocents Abroad* in St. Louis ("The Innocents Abroad," St. Louis *Central Baptist*, 19 Aug 69, 1; Richard Edwards 1869, 431; Richard Edwards 1870, 461, 1066).

To Henry Abbey
21 August 1869 • Buffalo, N.Y.
(MS: Axelrod)

MORNING EXPRESS $10 PER ANNUM.   OFFICE OF THE EXPRESS PRINTING COMPANY
EVENING EXPRESS $8 PER ANNUM.   NO. 14 EAST SWAN STREET.
WEEKLY EXPRESS $1.50 PER ANNUM.
                                                  BUFFALO, Aug 21 186 9.

Henry Abbey Esq

   Dear Sir—Yes, I have a pleasant remembrance of our ride, & would like to repeat it. And I remember promising to lecture for you, too, in case I lectured any of any consequence next winter—at least I suppose I remember it—& I ~~know~~ believe I promised Crane to lecture for him under the same conditions, though I am not sure about that, for it would have been absurd to make two engagements so close together as your two towns.[1]

But circumstances have altered things greatly. I was under contract to make a ~~w~~ New England tour next winter, but I have been obliged to write there & ask to be excused. I have bought into this paper, & business will compel me to stick to my post. If my promise was a positive one I hope you will be merciful to a fellow journalistic sinner & let me off for this time.

I see you had a notion to ~~le~~ have me lecture on my wedding day! (Jan. 10,,)—but this is strictly *private* & you must not mention it.

Ys Sincerely
Sam*ˡ*. L. Clemens.

[1] Henry Abbey (1842–1911) of Kingston, New York, a former journalist, was a flour and grain merchant and by 1869 had published the first three of his dozen volumes of poetry (Clearwater, 545–46). Clemens must have met him in late 1868, when he met Henry M. Crane, of nearby Rondout, which eventually was incorporated into Kingston (see the next letter).

To Henry M. Crane
21 August 1869 • Buffalo, N.Y.
(MS: ViU)

MORNING EXPRESS $10 PER ANNUM.   OFFICE OF THE EXPRESS PRINTING COMPANY
EVENING EXPRESS $8 PER ANNUM.   NO. 14 EAST SWAN STREET.
WEEKLY EXPRESS $1.50 PER ANNUM.

BUFFALO, Aug. 21 186 9.

My Dear Crane—

I *did* hope to lecture for you, but I can't.[1] I am sorry, but the thing can't be helped. I have already taken a newspaper & am going to take a wife—& that ~~ȿ~~ is enough to look after for the present. I am under contract to lecture in New England, but have written to-day to ask to be ~~exp~~ excused, & no doubt I shall be.[2]

Have heard from Kingston,[3] but cannot talk there either.

Sincerely
Sam*ˡ*. L. Clemens.

[1] Crane (1838–1927), a bookkeeper, had been (and probably still was) secretary of the Lincoln Literary Association, of Rondout, New York, for which Clemens had delivered his "American Vandal Abroad" lecture on 2 December

1868 (*Ulster County Directory*, 239; Crane family monument, Montrepose Cemetery, Kingston, N.Y., information courtesy of Amanda C. Jones; *L2*, 47–48, 247 n. 3, 262).

[2] Clemens had already written James Redpath on 14 August to "beg off." Redpath's response, now lost, must have urged him to reconsider. Clemens's letter of 21 August, doubtless more emphatic, is not known to survive.

[3] See the previous letter.

To Olivia L. Langdon
21 August 1869 • Buffalo, N.Y.
(MS: CU-MARK)

MORNING EXPRESS $10 PER ANNUM.	OFFICE OF THE EXPRESS PRINTING COMPANY
EVENING EXPRESS $8 PER ANNUM.	NO. 14 EAST SWAN STREET.
WEEKLY EXPRESS $1.50 PER ANNUM.	

BUFFALO, Aug. 21, P.M. 186 9.

Darling, it is 9 o'clock, now, & you are aware that there are no kisses for us to-night.[1] I feel more than half sorry I ~~do~~ did not go to you, for I have not succeeded in doing the mass of work I had laid out for myself, for sitting up so late last night has kept me stup/efied all day. It is the last time I shall be out of bed at midnight. And this night I mean to catch up. I shall be in bed, Puss, before your dainty little figure is tucked between your sheets, this evening. Bless your precious heart, I wish I could see you. I am afraid this is going to be a pretty long week, without a glimpse of my darling. But then (D. V.,) I shall put my arms about you next Friday evening & stay till Monday morning. You see I ought to be at my post by 8 o'clock every morning, & *fresh*—~~which I wouldnt~~ so I would have to return on Saturday night—& that was partly why I put off my visit this week. But Larned says don't bother about that—he will do the work of both of us from ~~3~~ ~~3~~ 3 P.M. ~~Satu~~ Friday till Monday noon whenever I want to go to Elmira—which is equivalent to getting out two editions of the paper alone.[2] He is not a very bad fellow.

McWilliams & I went down to the Lake after supper & had a row. I needed the exercise.

His wife sorts out my soiled linen, takes a list of it, delivers it to the washerwoman in my absence, returns it again & attends to the settlement of the bill—& Mac tells me she will cheerfully ~~do me~~ do any mending I may need. She is a very excellent ~~little~~ young lady, & I like her very much.[3] Thanks to my darling's busy fingers, however, I haven't any mending to do,, at present.

Among the books sent us to review was one called "Wedlock," which I siezed & read, intending to mark it & take it to you, but it ,was, nothing but a mass of threadbare old platitudes & maudlin advice shoveled together without rhyme or reason, & so I threw it away & told Larned to embody that opinion in his notice (he was reviewing the books.)[4]

I wrote Redpath to-day, asking him to let me off entirely from lecturing in New England ne this season, for if I would rather scribble, now, while I take a genuine interest in it, & it I am *so* tired of wandering, & want to be still & rest.

That thief that wrote about the dead canary & sends me so much execrable music[5] has found me out & is writing publishing extravagant puffs of me & mailing the papers to me, duly marked, as usual.[6] I shall offer a bounty for his scalp, yet. He is one of the most persistent & exasperating acquaintances I was ever afflicted with.[7]

Larned & I sit upon opposite sides of the same table & it is exceedingly convenient—for if you will remember, you sometimes write till you reach the middle of a subject & then run hard aground—you know what you *want* to say, but for the life of you you can't say—your ideas & your words get thick & sluggish & you are vanquished. So occasionally, after biting our nails & scratching our heads awhile, we ∮ just reach over & *swap manuscript*—& then we scribble away without the least trouble, he finishing my article & I his. Some of our patch-work editorials are of this kind are all the better for the new life they get by crossing the breed.

Little dearie, little darling, in a few minutes, after I ,shall, have read a Testament lesson & prayed for us both, as usual, I shall be in bed. And I shall dream, both before & after I go to sleep, of the little flower that ,has, sprung up in the desert beside me & shed its fragrance over my life & made its ways attractive with its beauty and turned its weariness to contentment with its sweet spirit. And I shall bless you, my darling, out of the fulness of a heart that knows your worth beyond the ken of any, even those that have been with you always; & out of the depths of a gratitude that owes to you the knowledge of what light is, where darkness was, & peace where turbulence reigned, & the beauty & majesty of love where a loveliness soul sat in its rags before & held out its unheeded hand for charity. Better than ot all others I understand you & appreciate you, for this ˏitˏ is the prerogative of love to attain to alone, & therefore better than all others I can love you, & *do* love you, & *shall* love you, always, my Livy.

Good night darling—& peaceful slumbers refresh you & ministering angels attend you.

Sam.

✉ ——

Miss Olivia L. Langdon | Elmira | N. Y. [*return address:*] IF NOT DELIVERED WITHIN 10 DAYS, TO BE RETURNED TO [*postmark, hand corrected at post office:*] BUFFALO N.Y. AUG ~~23~~ 22 [*docketed by OLL:*] 104ᵗʰ | E | Express | Es E Ex | Express | Express | Espress

[1] Presumably Clemens had written, or telegraphed, Olivia on Friday, 20 August—two missing letters, docket numbers 102 and 103, might have been written that day—to tell her that, work permitting, he would arrive in Elmira on Saturday evening, but not to expect him if he were not there by 9:00 P.M. (He had already disappointed her by not arriving on Friday: see 20 and 21 Aug 69 to PAM.)

[2] The Saturday and Monday editions. The *Express* did not publish on Sunday (Rowell, 66).

[3] John James McWilliams (1842–1912), of Cornwall on Hudson, New York, was a graduate of the State Normal College at Albany. In 1860 he had moved to Elmira, where he worked in the First National Bank and then for J. Langdon and Company. Recently he had transferred to Langdon's Buffalo office, where he was a bookkeeper. McWilliams and his wife, Esther ("Essie") Keeler Norton McWilliams, of Elmira, were newlyweds, having married in Elmira on 24 June 1869. (Later they had a son and a daughter, Shirrell and Mary.) Like Clemens, the McWilliamses lived at the boarding house maintained by Mrs. J. C. Randall at 39 Swan Street, within two blocks of the Buffalo *Express* offices at 14 East Swan Street. Clemens gave their name to the fictional couple—based principally on himself and Olivia—whom he first portrayed in "The Experience of the Mc-Williamses with Membranous Croup," in *Mark Twain's Sketches, New and Old* (1875) (Reigstad 1989, 3–4; "Mentions," "Married," Elmira *Advertiser*, 25 June 69, 4; "J. J. M'Williams's Busy Life Ended by Pneumonia," Buffalo *Courier*, 12 June 1912, 7; *Buffalo Directory*, 170, 381, 513; Reese).

[4] *Wedlock; or, The Right Relations of the Sexes: Disclosing the Laws of Conjugal Selection, and Showing Who May, and Who May Not Marry* was written and published in 1869 by Samuel Roberts Wells, editor and publisher of the *American Phrenological Journal*. Larned wrote: "Its contents are about one-third good sense, one-third bosh, and the other third dead wood stuff for filling out the volume. The sensible portion, moreover, is as old in the knowledge of mankind as Adam and Eve. On the whole, we are afraid we can't speak highly of the work" (Larned 1869a).

[5] "The Dead Canary," by George W. Elliott (see 5–10 Mar 69 to Elliott), was

a lyric about a bird named Lillie who expires from sorrow after her two eggs are "crushed" by "sad mishap" and "mysterious fate." Widely reprinted (for example, in the Elmira *Advertiser*, on 21 May 1869, 4), its final verse ran:

> Ye murderers, unawed by fear,
> Who bend at Herod's crimson shrine!—
> Turn once a scaleless vision here,
> And view this lifeless bird of mine:
> Then in your hell-born purpose pause!
> Forsake the path so reckless trod;
> Lest, while ye scoff at Nature's laws,
> Ye feel the withering curse of God!
>   (Elliott 1869a)

Elliott had been sending Clemens copies of his lyrics, including his latest, "The Blush Rose," which he had published, along with a complete list of his songs (all set to music by others), on 6 August in the Fort Plain (N.Y.) *Mohawk Valley Register*. Clemens may have thought Elliott a "thief" because several of the listed titles seemed suspiciously derivative: "Banks of the Genessee," "Columbia, Queen of the Land," "Carrie, with the Golden Hair," "Allie, the Blue-Eyed Blonde," and "The Sweet Good Night" (Elliott 1869b).

[6]Elliott published two "extravagant puffs" in the 20 August *Mohawk Valley Register:*

—SAML. L. CLEMENS ("Mark Twain") has bought an interest in the Buffalo *Express*. We welcome "Mark Twain" to our ranks as a needed accession to journalistic jollity; but it is to be regretted that he did not have a little more time for preparation. His personal safety would have been subserved by the erection of an iron building, thoroughly braced and girded, for an office. Now, his life will remain in perpetual peril, because the constant cachinnatory explosions inside and outside the establishment, from those whose sense of propriety and humanity will be lost in their risible overflow, will cause the very walls of the building to topple till they fall! (Elliott 1869c)

When "Mark Twain" announced his intention to finish his book and leave for California, we feared that his fair fame would be forever blasted. It seemed as though he were apprehensive of the disastrous consequences of his book; and like experienced railroad men who, hearing a short, sharp whistle from the locomotive, prepare for some impending danger, he was anxious to seek a place of safety, remote from the scene of ruin he had wrought. We had personally seen the almost fatal effects of his "Jumping Frog." We once read a sketch from it to a circle of friends, and before we had finished, their eyes looked as though they had been weeping over the loss of all they had in the world. They held their sides and groaned aloud with pain. We read another sketch, and it finished them for the time, as completely as though they had all been stricken down with paralysis. The result was, they each had to be carefully carried home on a furlough by their friends!

We knew that the present work would be voluminous, and we trembled for the result. Happily the publishers hit upon a plan of letting the book out gradually, through an army of agents, who were to be instructed to caution people of delicate consti[t]utions in regard to its powerful effect. Finally, the business of distribution was so admirably arranged, that "Mark Twain" concluded to settle down on the Buffalo *Express;* to remain and stand the consequences, be they what they might—even though the book should be the substantial building of his fortune and his fame!

For us to even name the varied contents of "The Innocents Abroad," would be to throw our readers into a violent *qui vive*, from which they would, perhaps, never recover! The work will not be for sale at the bookstores, because it would be dangerous to people to have it lying around loose. It can be obtained only of the regularly appointed agents, and should be read sparingly, at first. It will cause the lean to grow fat, the weak to wax strong, the blind to open their eyes, and the dolefully delirious to dance with joy! Buy it, by all means! Have the necessary sum awaiting in your wallet, stowed securely away in your *porte monnaies*, or carefully concealed in the corners of your handkerchiefs. Buy it, and you will bless "Mark Twain" to the end of your existence. Its mirthful memories will shed a halo of happiness around your pathway and over your declining years, like the mellow hues of a golden sunset around the rock-ribbed, snow-capped, cloud-enveloped Sierras of the West! (Elliott 1869d)

Clemens and Bliss repeatedly quoted only the penultimate sentence from the second "puff" in their advertising materials for *Innocents* ("Advertising Supplement," Buffalo *Express*, 9 Oct 69, 2; APC 1869b, [2], and 1870, [2]).

[7]On 26 August Clemens attempted, unsuccessfully, to placate his persecutor with a noncommittal paragraph in the Buffalo *Express*. Around the same time he also sent him a not entirely complimentary letter (see 6 and 7 Sept 69 to OLL, nn. 2 and 6).

To Charles Warren Stoddard
25 August 1869 • Buffalo, N.Y.
(Transcript and *paraphrase:* Freeman 1936, lot 68)

Buffalo, August 25th

Dear Charlie—

    .   .   .   .

I have written Bret that we must have the "Overland," see that he sends it, will you?[1] You speak of Mr. Stebbins. He came within an ace of breaking off my marriage by saying to the gentleman instructed by "her" father to call on him & inquire into my character, that "Clemens is a humbug—shallow & superficial—a man who has talent, no doubt, but will make a trivial & possibly a worse use of it—a man whose life promised little & has accomplished less—a humbug, Sir, a humbug"[2] . . . The friends that I had referred to in California said with one accord that I got drunk oftener than was necessary & that I was wild & Godless, idle, lecherous & a discontented & unsettled rover & they could not recommend any girl of high character & social position to marry me—but as I had already said all that about myself beforehand there was nothing shocking or surprising about it to the family.[3] [*paraphrase: He continues regarding a lecture program and mentions his lecture on the Sandwich Island[s], etc.*][4]

. . . .

[1] Stoddard, who had known Clemens since 1864 or 1865, was a frequent contributor of poetry and prose to the San Francisco *Overland Monthly*, edited since its inception in the summer of 1868 by Bret Harte (*L2*, 30–31, 232–33, nn. 1). Clemens's letter to Harte has not been recovered, but his high regard for the *Overland Monthly* is clear from a report he sent to the San Francisco *Alta California* in July 1869:

The Eastern press are unanimous in their commendation of your new magazine. Every paper and every periodical has something to say about it, and they lavish compliments upon it with a heartiness that is proof that they mean what they say. Even the *Nation*, that is seldom satisfied with anything, takes frequent occasion to demonst[r]ate that it is sati[s]fied with the *Overland*. And every now and then, it and the other critical reviews of acknowledged authority, take occasion to say that Bret Harte's sketch of the "Luck of Roaring Camp" is the best prose magazine article that has seen the light for many months on either side of the ocean. They never mention who wrote the sketch, of course (and I only guess at it), for they do not know. The *Overland* keeps its contributors' names in the dark. Harte's name would be very familiar in the land but for this. However, the magazine itself is well known in high literary circles. I have heard it handsomely praised by some of the most ponderous of America's literary chiefs; and they displayed a complimentary and appreciative familiarity with Harte's articles, and those of [Noah] Brooks, Sam. Williams, [William Chauncey] Bartlett, etc. (SLC 1869j)

Harte evidently did arrange for the magazine to be sent to the Buffalo *Express:* on 13 September the paper reprinted most of his incisive comments on Elizabeth Stuart Phelps's *The Gates Ajar* (1868) from the current issue (Harte 1869a, 293–94). It was likely Clemens himself who observed that the "book notices of the *Overland Monthly*, of San Francisco, have achieved a celebrity which is great in America and still greater in England, as models of piquancy, critical analysis and felicitous English" (SLC 1869x).

[2] For other accounts of the remarks by San Francisco clergyman Horatio Stebbins, see 20 and 21 Jan 69 to OLL, n. 6.

[3] Clemens exaggerates his candor. In his letter of 24 January 1869 to Olivia Langdon he conceded that he had not revealed his past "in full & relentless detail" to her or her parents.

[4] Probably Clemens here recalled one or both of his 1866 Sandwich Islands lectures in San Francisco: his 2 October debut performance or his equally successful farewell appearance on 10 December (see *L1*, 361, 372–73). The dealer's catalog that supplies the text for this letter describes it as an "A.L.S., 5 pp., folio." Clemens's words-per-page rate on apparently similar stationery—for example, his 1 September 1869 letter to Olivia Langdon—suggests that the present text is about one-fourth of the complete letter to Stoddard.

To Olivia L. Langdon
25 and 26 August 1869 • Buffalo, N.Y.
(MS: CU-MARK)

ₐI love you, Livy.

————ₐ *

ₐWill Livy enclose the enclosed book notices to Bliss, 147 Asylum?ₐ[1]

Buffalo, Wednes⁻ Night.

My Livy, my faithful little wife, this is the last letter I shall write before
I see you—& I use the pencil because I am in bed & cannot well use ink.[2]
[*in margin:* You little rat, there is no letter for me this morning {Thurs-
day.}] Larned, & a Mr. Johnson[3] & I, took a small row-boat, to-night, &
went out into the Lake, & around a jutting stone breakwater, intending
to reach a sandy beach beyond, & go in bathing—but the wind rose & a
heavy sea came on & pitched the poor little shell about in the wildest
way—& the spray came over the ~~size~~ side, & a capsize was imminent.
Think of poor Larned in such a sea, far from shore, in water a hundred
feet deep & he not able to swim. I tell you I felt a good deal more concern
for him than I "let on." And then both of them wanted to land (I was
steering,) but I knew that would never do, in such a surf—such a poor
little boat wouldn't have lived a quarter of a second—& so I headed her
out in the Lake again & they had to fight those great waves all the way
back again—& I tell you the planning of how to take hold of a drowning
man without letting him get hold of *me*, (those people who can't swim
always get frightened & do that,) was a[s] tangled a question as I have
had on my mind lately—but we seemed bound to go over presently. We
didn't, though, darling, because I *do* know how to handle a boat—& we
weathered that breakwater in safety. And to this moment I cannot think
of any safe way of taking hold of a drowning man. If it were *you*, I
wouldn't feel any concern—because I would say, "Place your hands on
my shoulders, Livy, & kick out when I do with your legs & you are just
as safe here for the next hour or two as you could be anywhere"—& you
would ~~do that~~ trust me & do it, & it would be all right & the little rascal
wouldn't be afraid. But I felt ever so much more comfortable when we
got in the smooth water again inside the breakwater.

Honey, I shall start home at 3 P.M. Friday (I think that is the hour,) & arrive about 8 I guess[4]—I don't expect to telegraph—& I hope you will let me kiss you when I come—I have almost forgotten my what a kiss is like—I wonder how people can go off on long voyages of y months & years & leave their wives at home. They are not Livies or they couldn't.

I am reading the sermon, & I like it. I have already read all the places the dainty little fingers marked, & have gone back to start at the beginning. I see ʃ enough to know I shall like the sermon.[5] Bless your darling heart—*nobody* has such a dear, good, precious, priceless, darling little sweetheart as I have, & I do *love,* you Livy, with all my whole heart—& I love you more & more every day & am so satisfied, & restful & peaceful in your love, & can never be tossed on the sea of life again.

[no signature]

✉──────────────────────────────────────

[in ink:] Miss Olivia L. Langdon | Elmira | N. Y. *[return address:]* OFFICE OF THE BUFFALO EXPRESS   14 EAST SWAN ST., BUFFALO, N. Y. *[postmarked:]* BUFFALO N.Y. AUG 26 *[docketed by OLL:]* 108th

[1] The enclosures, notices of *The Innocents Abroad* gleaned from the Buffalo *Express*'s exchanges, have not survived. Almost without exception, reviews were enthusiastic in their praise, and Bliss used extracts in a variety of advertising matter, including a supplement to the canvasser's prospectus that included twenty-eight different newspaper notices published before the end of August (APC 1869b, [1–4]). Since assuming his post on the *Express* in mid-August, Clemens could have seen (and might have enclosed) at least the following reviews, all of which Bliss used in his supplement: "Literary," New York *Evening Express*, 14 Aug 69, 2; "Mark Twain's New Book," New York *Leader*, 14 Aug 69, 5; "Literary," Newark *Advertiser*, 14 Aug 69, 1; "The Innocents Abroad," New York *Evening Post*, 16 Aug 69, 1; "Mark Twain's New Book," New York *Sun*, 16 Aug 69, 2; "'Mark Twain' . . . ," New York *World*, 16 Aug 69, 5; "Mark Twain as a Pilgrim," Salem (N.J.) *National Standard*, 18 Aug 69, 2; "Mark Twain's Travels," Springfield (Mass.) *Republican*, 18 Aug 69, 2; "'Mark Twain' . . . ," Providence *Journal*, 19 Aug 69, 2; "From the numerous extracts . . . ," Providence *Morning Herald*, 20 Aug 69, 2; "The Innocents Abroad," New York *Liberal Christian*, 21 Aug 69, 3; "New Publications," New York *Times*, 23 Aug 69, 2; "Recent Publications," Paterson (N.J.) *Guardian*, 23 Aug 69, 2.

[2] Clemens planned to go to Elmira on the afternoon of Friday, 27 August, for the weekend visit he had postponed the week before (see 21 Aug 69 to OLL).

[3] Probably William H. Johnson, head bookkeeper at the Buffalo *Express* (*Buffalo Directory*, 345; "Twain Success Puzzle to His Old Office Boy," Buffalo *Courier-Express*, 24 Feb 1929, sec. S, 8).

⁴The Erie Railway's "Lightning Express" boarded daily in Buffalo at 2:50 P.M., arriving in Elmira at 8:23 ("Travelers Guide," Buffalo *Express*, 26 Aug 69, 2).

⁵Doubtless by the Reverend Henry Ward Beecher. Olivia continued to send Clemens copies of Beecher's published sermons.

To A. Miner Griswold (Fat Contributor)
1 September 1869 • Buffalo, N.Y.
(MS: CLjC)

MORNING EXPRESS $10 PER ANNUM.   OFFICE OF THE EXPRESS PRINTING COMPANY
EVENING EXPRESS $8 PER ANNUM.   NO. 14 EAST SWAN STREET.
WEEKLY EXPRESS $1.50 PER ANNUM.
                                        BUFFALO, Sept 1. 186 9.

Dear F. C.—

We accept, & exchange with pleasure. If I had received your letter a week sooner, I would have remained in the lecture field & helped you talk. I was to have opened in Boston Nov. 10, but did not intend to go out of New England. But the other day I wrote Redpath, drawing out altogether. If he says it is all right, I am out of the field entirely for this season—& I hope this will be the case, for I had rather stay in one place a while, now, just for the novelty of it.[1]

Across these sweltering intervening States I stretch my longing & lengthening hand for a friendly shake, & with it goeth my blessing.

Cordially Yours

Mark Twain

[1] Since 1858, under the pseudonym "Fat Contributor," Alphonso Miner Griswold (1834–91) had been publishing humorous sketches while serving on the editorial staffs of the Buffalo *Republic and Times*, the Detroit *Advertiser*, the Cleveland *Plain-Dealer*, and the Cincinnati *Times*, of which he was now city editor. (Clemens here agrees to add the *Times* to the *Express*'s exchanges.) Well known as a lecturer in the Midwest, Griswold was engaged to make his New England debut, in James Redpath's Boston Lyceum Course, on 24 November 1869 ("'The Fat Contributor,'" Boston *Advertiser*, 23 Nov 69, 1). His lecture that evening in Boston's Music Hall, on "Indian Antiquities—humorously considered," suffered by comparison with the performance Clemens himself gave there on 10 November. The Boston *Advertiser* called Griswold "a rather colorless copy of Mark Twain, or rather like a little of Mark Twain and a little water mixed together" ("Mr. A. Miner Griswold on 'Injun Meal,'" 25 Nov 69, 1).

To Olivia L. Langdon
1 September 1869 • Buffalo, N.Y.
(MS: CU-MARK)

Buffalo, Sept. 2.[1]

Yes, my little darling, I *am* bothered somewhat about that housekeeping business. Even if everything else about it was perfectly delightful I couldn't bear the idea of your sitting or working *alone* all day while I was at the office, & you won't consent to have Hattie Lewis or anybody with you for company. No, sir, as I came out from supper last night, I said to myself (I had just been away up stairs visiting), "It seems to me that Mac & his wife[2] are happy & happily situated in their two unpretending rooms—& suppose Livy & I were keeping house out where Larned is, & Livy at home all by herself half the time—& so worried, & tired out, & sick & dej discouraged that she would be a moving object to look upon—*no* sir, we must n't think of it for just one year.[3] We must board (not in this caravansery, but in a house where there are no other boarders, & where the girl can have somebody to go & speak to when she is lonely.) We must board one year—& *then* we'll *both* be consumingly anxious to keep house—as it is, it would be a great undertaking, right in the middle of a Buffalo winter for two novices like Livy & me." We'll talk this over next time I run home, darling, for if you think over it & are still in favor of housekeeping right from the start, why we *will* keep house right from the start.

I enclose a letter from my sister.[4] I really wish I *could* have her & Annie at our marriage. I'll think about it.

Remember, Puss, if we can get the Spauldingses & Prof Ford to live with us as you propose, we will keep house, by *all* means.[5] And remember, too, my darling, that your wishes shall be obeyed as to how we are to live, but I only desire that you will think the matter over right carefully, examining it at all points before you decide. It is a dear good little girl to give up her cherished dreams to please me—we'll talk it all over, Livy—prepare yourself.

Thank you for your mother's letter—I perceive that they are all enjoying themselves & improving in health, & I am particularly & exceedingly glad of it—& being "one of the dear ones" I have a right to be, haven't I, sweetheart?[6]

I grieve every time I think of my tube-roses never worn, that she gathered for me.[7] But this grieving two or three days brings back no opportunity. I'll *learn* to like button-hole flowers because Livy does.—tThere *shall* be something we both love, dearie. If it be not some author, some dainty office of a flower, some manner of living, or other fleeting & unessential thing, then it shall be God.

Yes, dearie, think over all the plans, so that when "— — — —" we can proceed understandingly.

What printed matter written by me have you got stowed away, Livy?[8]

Iń am in a hurry, now, & so I kiss my darling good morning & good-day & good-night, & get to work.   Sam.

✉—————————————————————————————————

Miss Olivia L. Langdon | Elmira | N. Y. [*return address:*] OFFICE OF THE BUFFALO EXPRESS   14 EAST SWAN ST., BUFFALO, N. Y. [*postmarked:*] BUFFALO N.Y. SEP 1 [*docketed by OLL:*] 110th

[1]Clemens wrote and mailed this letter on 1 September, just after working on the *Express* for the following day. The envelope is postmarked 1 September, a date that would have allowed time for Olivia to receive the letter and respond to Clemens's remarks about the "button-hole flowers" (paragraph five)—and for Clemens to have her response before he wrote to her on 3 September.

[2]John and Esther McWilliams (see 21 Aug 69 to OLL, n. 3).

[3]Larned and his wife—the former Frances Anne Kemble McCrea (1838–1915) of Chatham, Ontario, whom he had married on 29 April 1861—lived at 40 Eleventh Street, about a mile and a half from the *Express* office. They had at least one child, Mary (1864–1940), at this time. Eventually they had a second daughter, Anne (1872–1951), and a son, Sherwood (dates unknown) (Olmsted, 11; "Obituary: Mrs. J. N. Larned," Buffalo *Morning Express*, 28 Nov 1915, sec. 6, 45; *Buffalo Directory*, 364; Reese; Buffalo *Evening News:* "Miss Mary Larned," 2 July 1940, 4; obituary of Anne Larned, 15 Mar 1951, 48).

[4]Pamela Moffett's letter is not known to survive.

[5]Neither Darius Ford nor Clara and Alice Spaulding, whom Ford had tutored along with Olivia, ever were part of the Clemens household in Buffalo (see 9 and 31 Mar 69 to Crane, n. 6).

[6]"Mr. and Mrs. J. LANGDON went to Spencer Springs in their own conveyance on Thursday [26 August]," joining Dr. and Mrs. Henry Sayles (their neighbors) and many other Elmirans at the popular summer resort ("Local Happenings," Elmira *Saturday Evening Review*, 28 Aug 69, 8). Located about twenty miles northeast of Elmira, the establishment had a "new three-story hotel, one hundred feet long, and a large dormitory," provided "good saddle horses, and horses

and carriages" and an "attending physician" for its guests, as well as "a series of bath rooms, got up with all the modern conveniences. . . . Invalids can avail themselves, thereby, of the healing waters, both externally and internally" ("Spencer Springs," Elmira *Saturday Evening Review*, 15 May 69, 8, and 21 Aug 69, 8).

[7] During Clemens's 27–30 August visit with Olivia.

[8] Earlier in the year, Clemens had given Olivia a "commission" to clip and save his published articles for future use (see 28 Feb 69 to OLL).

To Elisha Bliss, Jr.
2 September 1869 • Buffalo, N.Y.
(MS: CU-MARK)

MORNING EXPRESS $10 PER ANNUM.   OFFICE OF THE EXPRESS PRINTING COMPANY
EVENING EXPRESS $8 PER ANNUM.   NO. 14 EAST SWAN STREET.
WEEKLY EXPRESS $1.50 PER ANNUM.

    BUFFALO, Sept 2 186 9.

Friend Bliss—

Have you an agent here?

We are going to get out a supplement, (with perhaps a little reading matter in it,) containing "Notices of the Press" on my accepssion ᷉to the editorship᷉. Would it be a good idea for you to send me a lot of ᷉newspaper᷉ notices of the *book* to add afterwa them, with the card of the publishing house attached? We could circulate several thousand, & we could send you a lot to Hartford to be distributed through your agents & agencies. Is the idea good? Is it worth the trouble? How many could you use? What do you think of it, anyhow?[1]

I wish you would send me a copy of the book—never have had a good chance to look at it yet. I suppose it would not be wo good policy to send the Buffalo papers copies until an agent is here ready to take advantage of the notices.

I enclose a letter from Packard, of the *Monthly*—I thought maybe you might be able to use a paragraph—but as it is a private letter do not do more than hint at him—don't use his name.[2]

        Yrs
        Clemens

Hurry & send that complimentary book to Dan Slote, 121 William street. Don't delay.

✉———————————————————————————————————————

[letter docketed:] √ *[and]* Mark Twain | Sep 2/69

¹Bliss, whose reply to this letter has not been found, did not have agents in Buffalo until late September (see 27 Sept 69 to Bliss). Clemens waited until 9 October to publish the Buffalo *Express* advertising supplement. Under the heading "Complimentary," it reprinted thirty-nine "Press Greetings" to the new editor, most of them undated. (The greetings from the Buffalo *Commercial Advertiser*, the Buffalo *Courier*, and the Buffalo *Post* were misdated 4 August, although the first two and probably the last had appeared on 16 August, two days after Clemens purchased one-third of the *Express*.) In addition, under the heading "Opinions of the Press," the *Express* supplement printed forty-six extracts from "some twelve hundred complimentary notices of the book which have appeared in the several sections of the Union" ("Advertising Supplement," Buffalo *Express*, 9 Oct 69, 1–2). Clemens may have incorporated some new clippings from Bliss, but he probably relied for Bliss's contribution on the press extracts already in place in the canvasser's prospectus for *The Innocents Abroad* (APC 1869b, [1–4]). It is not known if Bliss distributed copies of the *Express* advertising supplement.

²Silas Packard's letter does not survive, nor has any excerpt from it been identified in Bliss's promotional materials for *Innocents*. *Packard's Monthly* reviewed the book in its October number, which issued about 20 September, and Clemens extracted the review for the *Express*'s "Opinions of the Press" ("Books and Things," *Packard's Monthly* 2 [Oct 69]: 318–19; "Advertising Supplement," Buffalo *Express*, 9 Oct 69, 1). Bliss later included an excerpt from the notice in his revised supplement to the canvasser's prospectus (APC 1870, [5]).

To Stephen C. Massett (Jeems Pipes)
2 September 1869 • Buffalo, N.Y.
(MS: CtHMTH)

MORNING EXPRESS $10 PER ANNUM.   OFFICE OF THE EXPRESS PRINTING COMPANY
EVENING EXPRESS $8 PER ANNUM.   NO. 14 EAST SWAN STREET.
WEEKLY EXPRESS $1.50 PER ANNUM.
                                        BUFFALO, ~~Aug~~ Sept. 2 186 9.

Friend Massett
            Got it—thank you.¹
        In a desperate hurry

                                        Yrs &c
                                        Clemens

¹Massett (Jeems Pipes of Pipesville), the veteran comic journalist, songwriter, and entertainer whom Clemens had met in the offices of the San Francisco

Call in May or June 1868, was living in New York City at the St. Denis Hotel, when not traveling as a correspondent for the New York *Evening Telegram* and as a lecturer (*L2*, 231 n. 12; "The Lecture Season," New York *Evening Telegram*, 7 Aug 69, 2). Ten days before the present letter, Clemens had reprinted in the *Express* this sardonic squib from the Brooklyn *Eagle:* "On Sunday morning last at the Episcopal Church (St. Marys) at Peekskill, Mr. Stephen Massett delivered a sermon from the text 'Nothing but Leaves,' for the benefit of the funds of the church. If Massett's sermons are only as serious as his comic lectures they must be quite edifying" (SLC 1869q). The item Clemens acknowledges here probably was a clipping from the New York *Evening Telegram* of 30 August, calling Massett "one of our most successful lecturers" and crediting him with "a vein of thoughtfulness running through his composition" ("Journalistic Jottings," 2, reprinting the White Plains [N.Y.] *Eastern State Journal* of 27 August; Rowell, 82). This was the sort of praise that Clemens was himself accustomed to receiving (see, for example, 6 and 7 Sept 69 to OLL, n. 8).

To Elisha Bliss, Jr.
3 September 1869 • Buffalo, N.Y.
(MS: CU-MARK)

MORNING EXPRESS $10 PER ANNUM.   OFFICE OF THE EXPRESS PRINTING COMPANY
EVENING EXPRESS $8 PER ANNUM.   NO. 14 EAST SWAN STREET.
WEEKLY EXPRESS $1.50 PER ANNUM.
                  BUFFALO, Sept. 3. 186 9.

Friend Bliss—

I "cave." You are right, & I was not. But I am only impatient about things once or twice a day—& then I sit down & write letters. The rest of the time I am serene.[1]

Yes the Herald's is a good notice & will help the book along. The irreverence of the volume appears to be a tip-top good feature of it, ~~financially~~ ‸diplomatically‸ speaking, though I wish with all my heart there wasn't an irreverent passage in it.[2]

~~The books have probably come—they have been to~~
The books will arrive today, no doubt, ~~& as soon you have an agent in this region~~ & we'll turn the papers loose on them at once, if you say so, ‸(or would you rather we waited till you have an agent here?[3]

                      Ys Truly
                      Clemens

[*letter docketed:*] √ [*and*] Mark Twain | Sep 3/69

[1] Neither Clemens's impatient letter, probably written around 31 August, nor Bliss's reply is known to survive.

[2] The New York *Herald* reviewed the book favorably on 31 August. About the "pilgrimage to the Holy Land," it commented:

This part of the work some over-pious and fastidious critics have condemned because, as they urge, of its levity. We cannot find anything so very irreverent in his account. . . . We recognize as legitimate humor the grave statement that the party "looked everywhere as we passed along, but never saw grain or crystal of Lot's wife," although to some this sentence might seem somewhat irreverent. Here and there we find passages which might have been left out without injury to the work. The author, however, evidently has no respect for tradition—not even for Bible tradition. After swallowing all the free-thinking and rationalistic emanations of the day, we shall not strain over a few paragraphs, which, if not marked by austere piety, need not, necessarily, be regarded as sacrilege. If the Holy Land did not inspire the author with enthusiastic emotions, we have no doubt it was because the Holy Land has been persistently lied about by nearly all other authors. ("Literature," 8)

Clemens omitted this and other references to his supposed "irreverence" when he reprinted the review in the Buffalo *Express* of 9 October ("Advertising Supplement," 1).

[3] Bliss responded, within four days, with copies of *Innocents* for the Buffalo papers and, apparently, with a suggestion that advertising and reviews be coordinated for late September or the first part of October (see 7 Sept 69 [2nd of 2], and 27 Sept 69, both to Bliss).

To Henry M. Crane
3 September 1869 • Buffalo, N.Y.
(MS: CtHMTH)

MORNING EXPRESS $10 PER ANNUM.   OFFICE OF THE EXPRESS PRINTING COMPANY
EVENING EXPRESS $8 PER ANNUM.   NO. 14 EAST SWAN STREET.
WEEKLY EXPRESS $1.50 PER ANNUM.

                                                    BUFFALO, Sept 3 186 9.

Friend Crane—

  I would do it in a minute (especially as I find it impossible to cancel all my appointments & therefore have to go into the field after all), but it will not do, because Mr. ~~Abbott~~ ˏAbbeyˏ says I promised to talk in Kingston, & I think I did, though I am not sure of it. I was afraid to promise you, you remember, & so I don't [know] what I could have been thinking of when I made the other promise. But you see how it is—I only use one lecture at a time, & therefore cannot talk it to two towns so close together.—̸ If I talked in either, you see yourself it would have to be for ~~Abbott~~ Abbey in Kingston, & so I'll keep on undebatable ground & steer clear of both places. I'm sorry, Crane, but if you were in my shoes you would do just as I am doing.[1]

Yrs Truly

Sam[1]. L. Clemens.

P. S. You have paid for & will receive our Weekly fourteen months— up to Jan. 1, 1871.

[1] A similar apology and explanation may have gone to Henry Abbey about this time. Despite the present refusal and the previous one of 21 August, Crane repeated his request to Clemens within the week.

To Olivia L. Langdon
3 September 1869 • Buffalo, N.Y.
(MS: CU-MARK)

MORNING EXPRESS $10 PER ANNUM.	OFFICE OF THE EXPRESS PRINTING COMPANY
EVENING EXPRESS $8 PER ANNUM.	NO. 14 EAST SWAN STREET.
WEEKLY EXPRESS $1.50 PER ANNUM.	BUFFALO, Friday Eve[g] 186 9.

Oh no, my darling, you are making a wild mistake—I *do* love to wear a button-hole bouquet, Livy, about the house, especially & particularly when you make it for me.[1] I like them well I do not think I ever wore one until you taught me to like them, but now, I under your instructions I have learned to like them well enough to make them for myself when I get a chance & you are not by to do it for me. At the Press Dinner out at Mr Jewels's a fortnight ago[2] I decorated myself with a delicate & beautiful panzy or two, & first one admired & followed suit & then another, until presently every individual present had flowers in his button-hole, & we wore them all the afternoon. And seeing how our tastes ran, Mr. J. set a his gardener quietly to work, & when we were ready to leave, at night we were each presented with an elaborate bouquet. No, dearie, I have such an invincible repulgnance to show or display in a man's dress, or anything that has a snobbish air about it, that I can't wear flowers in the street yet, but what I meant you to understand, was, that I would break down my prejudice & *learn* to do it because to please *you*, dearie. That was all. Livy, in all my experience I never saw an American in the street with flowers in his button-hole but he happened to be a fellow who had a weak spot about his head somewhere. Now you know, dearie, that that *will* give a man a ~~pej~~ prejudice, bye-&-bye. It always brings San Francisco to my mind, & Geo. Ensign & Emperor Norton, who have just about monopolized bouquet wearing in that city. If my memory serves me ~~you~~ I did what I could to paint ~~Eng~~ Ensign's portrait in my book— maybe as "M'sieu Gor-r-dong," but I am not sure. Anyway, it closes by saying he does all he can to inspire the idea that he looks like Napoleon "& with an amount of gratitude entirely disproportioned to the favor done him, he *thanks* his Maker that he is *as* he is, & goes on enjoying his little life just the same as if ~~the~~ he *had* really been deliberately designed & erected by the great Architect of the Universe!" That is meant for Geo. Ensign—& when I uttered [it] in a lecture on Venice in San Francisco there was a perceptible flutter all over the house, because they recognized the ~~poo~~ portrait—& poor George was present, though I didn't know he was there—only thought it likely he *would* be. He never appears anywhere, in the house or out of it, without his buttonhole bouquet—& so other people eschew them, to a great extent.[3] Now darling, there are good,, & great men, no doubt, who wears these flowers publicly, like George, but the awful majority are insufferable snobs. And there are good & great men, no doubt, who put an initial for their first name & spell their second out in full—but the awful majority of men who do that, will lie, & swindle & steal, just from a natural instinct. Livy dear, I am writing all this because it is *important*—it is not a ~~ti~~ trivial matter, in my eyes, that you should do anything for me & see me receive it tranquilly,, or possibly shrinkingly, when my natural impulse ought to be to receive it with warm delight & gratitude, as another token of your love for me. I should not seem unenthusiastic at such a time without being able to give you a most ample & convincing reason for it. And many a time I have remembered ~~m~~ remorsefully how ~~your~~ the knot of tube-roses ~~w~~ which your loving fingers formed for me lay neglected ~~in~~ on the library table simply because I had a silly prejudice against wearing them in the street—& I have been angry at myself & wished I could have the opportunity over again. My darling, I love the flowers as bouquets on the table, & am proud when I arrive at home & fancy they were put there for me, though I would never dare to *say* a ~~world~~ word or seem to notice them lest I might discover to my chagrin that my vanity had led me astray & attributed to me an honor not intended for me. And I love the button-hole bouquets in the house, honestly—better than in the street, you will readily believe, by this time. Livy dear, you will hurt me if you neglect to decorate my button-hole hereafter—& I will do penance & wear a sunflower down street if you say so.

I am so disappointed. Redpath says he *can't* get me free from Boston & 2 or 3 other places—& so I submit, & have written him to let me out to lyceums far & near, & for half the winter or all of it—do with me as he chooses while the lecture season lasts. There was no way that was better. It isn't worth the bother of getting well familiarized with a lecture & then deliver it only half a dozen times. I considered the matter well, & concluded that I ought to have some money to commence married life with, & if I tried to take it out of the office I might fail to be able to pay the first note that falls due next August.[4] And yet the distress of it is, that the paper will suffer by my absence, & at the very time that it ought to keep up its best gait & not lose the start we have just given ˌitˎ & have the long, hard pull of giving it a *new* start after a while. I ~~am~~ feel sure that the money I make lecturing, the paper will lose while I am gone—but you see how I am situated. When I once start in lecturing I might as well consent to be banged about from town to town while the lecture season lasts ⸝, for it would take that shape anyhow.

But our marriage! That is where the shoe pinches *hard*, dearie. It will just suit *you* to put it off till spring, but it don't suit me. ~~Suppose we we~~ However, I don't really think I shall have to talk any to speak of after the first of February, & so I shan't be delayed ~~over~~ more than a month, after all. Last year I hadn't a great many appointments in February, & if the same is to be the case this time I won't talk *at all* in that month. I shall know about this matter shortly, through Redpath. Livy dear, have I done wisely, or foolishly? Two things demand that the season shall stop as early as possible—my desire to bring you home as my wife; & the interest of the paper. Both touch me as being urgent. Tell me all you think, Livy darling.

Another of those anti-monopoly thieves sent in a long *gratuitous* advertisement to-night, about coal "for the people" at $5.50 a ton—& I have deposited it under the table. The effrontery of these people transcends everything I ever heard of. Do they suppose we print a paper for the fun of it? This man Deuther sent in just such a thing the other day, & I left *that* out. The other papers insert both of them for nothing. Day before yesterday there was a sneaking little communication in one of the other papers wondering why the Express had become so docile & quiet about the great coal monopoly question. If Mr Deuther don't go mighty slow I will let off a blast at him some day that will lift the hair off his head & loosen some of his teeth.⁵ Good-bye little sweetheart—I've lost my temper, now.

Sam.

✉—————————————————————————————

Miss Olivia L. Langdon | Elmira | N. Y. [*postmarked:*] BUFFALO N.Y. SEP 4 [*docketed by OLL:*] 113ᵗʰ

¹See 1 Sept 69 to OLL.

²That is, the dinner given by Elam R. Jewett (see 14 Aug 69 to Bliss, n. 3).

³Joshua Abraham Norton (1818–80) was the famous San Francisco eccentric who declared himself "Norton I, Emperor of the United States" and during more than two decades prowled the city in quasi-military dress and a plumed top hat (*L1*, 324–25 n. 2; Hart 1987, 354–55). George H. Ensign (1822–71), a San Francisco real estate broker and a founder of the Spring Valley Water Works, which supplied San Francisco with drinking water, was known as "the Beau Brummel of the town" (Woods, 128; "Died," San Francisco *Morning Call*, 4 Oct 71, 4; Langley 1868, 204; Wheat, 283; Pisani, 354–55). The passage Clemens quotes, evidently from memory, appears in chapter 23 of *The Innocents Abroad*. He had used it in his San Francisco lecture of 2 July 1868, "The Oldest of the Republics, VENICE, Past and Present," drawn from the then recently completed manuscript of *Innocents*. In October 1868 he had identified the prototype of "M'sieu Gor-r-dong" not as George Ensign, but as one of Mary Mason Fairbanks's friends (*L2*, 233–35, 263).

⁴Probably a payment on the $10,000 Clemens owed Thomas A. Kennett rather than the interest on his $12,500 indebtedness to Jervis Langdon, which he was planning to pay to John D. F. Slee "as it falls due" (see 12 Aug 69 to Bliss, n. 2; and 20 and 21 Aug to PAM, p. 311). Clemens's letter to James Redpath is not known to survive. He himself announced his decision to lecture (see 9 Sept 69 to the Lyceums).

⁵One of the more vigorous organizers of the Citizen's Mutual Coal Mining, Purchasing and Sale Company—a cooperative intended to undercut the Anthracite Coal Association, whose price per ton of coal was $10.50—was George A. Deuther, a Buffalo dealer in "Mouldings, Window and Looking Glass Plates at wholesale, and a complete stock of Artists' Materials" ("Be Wise . . . ," Buffalo *Commercial Advertiser*, 18 Sept 69, 2). Although the *Express* had given detailed coverage to the public meetings that led up to the formation of the cooperative, articles on the "coal question" virtually ceased after Clemens's editorial, "The Monopoly Speaks" (see 19 Aug 69 to OLL, n. 3), a fact noted by the Buffalo *Courier* on 1 September:

> A change seems to have come over the tone of the *Express* in reference to the coal monopoly. A very short time ago, it was engaged in an honorable rivalry with us to be foremost in the effort to confer the benefit of cheap coal on the people, and bring down the present high prices of fuel. Is the change merely temporary and accidental? Or may we look for an unfavorable reverse of the politics of that journal on this and kindred topics? The recent silence seems ominous. What is the reason for it? ("Change in the Express," 1)

The *Courier* and the Buffalo *Commercial Advertiser*, both sympathetic to the anti-monopolists, regularly printed submissions from Deuther. On 4 September, both papers published his latest notice, which the editors of the *Advertiser* said would be "read with pleasure by all interested in the procurement of cheap coal" ("Samples of Cheap Coal.—Card from Mr. Deuther," 3):

> Pursuant to my recent public promises through the press, I now announce that the promised coal for samples has arrived, the delay of which will, perhaps, be explained through our courts, as some evil spirit has tampered with two consignments to me . . .
>
> On the 6th, 7th, 8th and 9th days of this month the distribution of the above coal will take place in samples from ten to twenty-five pounds or more, in front of my store, No. 184 Washington street . . .
>
> From September 6th up to the 13th—seven days only (Sundays excepted)—I will devote to taking orders, free of all commission, from such anti-monopoly coal citizens as may wish to buy the coal at $5 50 per ton . . .
>
> On the 14th of September I would ask to be considered as discharged from my voluntary gratuitous services in this matter, although this is not to say that I shall stop to "pitch into" the coal monopoly in another way, which at present would not be proper to make public.
>
> N. B.—No orders will be taken from coal dealers on this occasion. With due respect,
> > GEO. A. DEUTHER.

(Buffalo *Express:* "Notes from the People," 6 Aug 69, 4; Buffalo *Courier:* "Anti-Monopoly Coal Business—Notice," 19 Aug 69, 2; Buffalo *Commercial Advertiser:* "Cheap Coal—Card from Mr. Deuther," 20 Aug 69, 3; "Cheap Coal," 18 Sept 69, 3.)

To Olivia L. Langdon
6 and 7 September 1869 • Buffalo, N.Y.
(MS: CU-MARK)

In Bed ⎫
Monday Night ⎭ .

Livy darling, I got your letter this evening, though I looked for it this morning—I had forgotten that you told me to expect the letters in the evening hereafter. Yes, dearie, I will leave this letter unsealed until I get a Salutatory to send to you in the morning.[1]

I have got an answer from the Dead Canary, which he says requires no answer.[2] He is torn with anger, & impugns my veracity in saying I know nothing about poetry—& to ~~th~~ prove the falsity of my word, does me the compliment to refer me to my remarks about Galilee, where I have *written* it.[3] Fool, not to see that I meant I ~~kn~~ was not a capable judge of *his kind* of poetry. But wasn't it rich & unconscious egotism in him to think I merely wished to avoid *saying* how beautiful his poetry was. And he says he asked me for a sarcasm & *got* it!—the shrewdest sarcasm I ever penned! That is the rankest egotism I ever ~~penned~~ heard of,, & the ~~sim~~ most innocent. I meant it for a solemn *truth* when I said his poetry was bad, but he *cannot* believe it. I do so long to drop him a line that would give him exquisite anguish—but I can't waste powder on such small game as that. He threatens to destroy me ~~with a~~ by means of a withering review of my book in his little one-horse ~~weekly~~ paper which a couple of hundred Mohawk Dutchmen spell their way through once a week. This fellow's idea of his importance trenches upon the sublime. In all my life I never saw anything like it. It is the calmest, serenest, ~~asinine~~ iron-clad, asinine complacency the world has ever produced.[4] Do you know, that creature is ~~oz~~ oozing his poetical drivel from his system all the time. No ~~how~~ subject, however trivial, escapes him. And he dotes upon—he worships—he passionately admires, every sick rhyme his putrid brain throws up in its convulsions of literary nausea. He cuts it out of the paper—he prints it on dainty strips of fine white paper, along with the reminder that "It will be remembered that Mr. Elliott is the author of Bonnie Eloise," "the Dead Canary," "The Disconsolate Sow"[5] &c &c.—& he prints it again on a large sheet of white satin, & gilds it, & puts it in a gold frame & hangs it up in his parlor, with the date when the abortion was produced, attached. And behold, he invites strangers to his house under pretense of treating them to a pleasant dinner, but in reality to bore them with this awful bosh, this accumulation of inspired imbecility, this chaos of jibbering idiocy ~~wro~~ tortured into rhyme. He is the funniest ass that brays in metre this year of our Lord 1869.

I am rid of him now—but Livy, he did follow me up with amazing diligence. He wrote 3 times for an opinion of the Dead Canary, you remember—& several times about that whining summer-complaint of a song about some Mohawk wench's golden hair—& some four or five times concerning that ~~wail~~ long-metre wail about a Blush Rose.[6] I have suffered all this / from that man, & yet he is going to swoop down on me with the Fort Plain Register & gobble me off the face of the earth. The unkindness of this person is more than I can bear, I am afraid. Still, I can bear his unkindness better than I can his poetry. Though sooth to say, it is equal to anything I have everý seen in the death column of the Philadelphia Ledger.[7] (*Why* didn't I think of that sooner, & publish it in answer to his request for a sarcasm? That one would have been recognized as exquisitely felicitous.] Poor wretch, he wanted a compliment so badly—& I had the heart to refuse him. But he didn't *say* he did—he only shows *now* that he did.

But honey, I have used up all my paper again. The Cincinnati, Toledo & other western papers speak as highly of the books as do the New York & Philadelphia papers.[8]

But I must kiss my darling good night, now, & hope to touch her dear lips in reality within 4 or 5 days. The peace of God be & abide with you now & always, my angel-revelation of the Better Land.

Sam.

[*in ink:*][9]

Erie Dispatch

Sp Spiders

Medbury—(6,701.)(?)

Redpath

Pittsburgh Lec. Com.

Write Fairbanks

[*in pencil:*] Livy dear, I am ~~hav~~ exercising an influence ~~of~~ on Larned I think—he is writing his best, & does it better & better—his article "Found Drowned," in ~~yester~~today's paper, is a rare gem—simply needs a trifl~~ine~~ of polishing in one or two places.[10]

[*in margin of page 1:*] Send this letter back to me, little sweetheart—I'll have use for it.

 [*in ink:*] Miss Olivia L. Langdon | Elmira | N. Y. [*postmarked:*] BUFFALO N.Y. SEP 7 [*docketed by OLL:*] 115½ | "Bonnie Eloise"

[1] Almost certainly Clemens did wait until the morning of 7 September in order to enclose a clipping of his "Salutatory" from the Buffalo *Express* of 21 August. The original enclosure has not been found, but its text is transcribed from the *Express* in Appendix B.

[2] Clemens must have written to George W. Elliott (author of "The Dead Canary") sometime after 21 August, when he last complained about him in a letter to Olivia. No correspondence between the two men is known to survive.

[3] In chapter 48 of *The Innocents Abroad*, Clemens devoted over six pages to Galilee in an effort to show it stripped of "the paint and the ribbons and the flowers" that other writers had deceptively added. Elisha Bliss reprinted a portion of Clemens's account in his advertising pamphlet of late August or early September, *Stray Leaves from Mark Twain's New Book* (APC 1869c, [13]), and it was also widely excerpted or mentioned by reviewers. Elliott printed part of its conclusion in the Fort Plain (N.Y.) *Mohawk Valley Register* of 10 September (2):

ELOQUENT EXTRACT.

When, during his pilgrimage through the Holy Land "MARK TWAIN" sat outside the tent, one night, alone under the star-lit vault of heaven and framed the beautiful metaphors in the following paragraph—extracted from his "Innocents Abroad"—he "builded better than he knew:"

"Night is the time to see Galilee. Genessaret under these lustrous stars, has nothing repulsive about it. Genessaret with the glittering reflections of the constellations flecking its surface, almost makes me regret that I ever saw the rude glare of day upon it. Its history and its associations are its chiefest charm, in any eyes, and the spells they weave are feeble in the searching light of the sun. *Then*, we scarcely feel the fetters. Our thoughts wander constantly to the practical concerns of life, and refuse to dwell upon things that seem vague and unreal. But when the day is done, even the most unimpressible must yield to the dreamy influences of this tranquil starlight. The old traditions of the place steal upon his memory and haunt his reveries, and then his fancy clothes all sights and sounds with the supernatural. In the lapping of the waves upon the beach, he hears the dip of ghostly oars; in the secret noises of the night he hears spirit voices; in the soft sweep of the breeze, the rush of the invisible wings. Phantom ships are on the sea, the dead of twenty centuries come forth from the tombs, and in the dirges of the night-wind the songs of old forgotten ages find utterance again."

[4] Elliott did not publish a "withering review" of *Innocents* in the *Mohawk Valley Register*. On the contrary, during the last five months of 1869, despite Clemens's sarcastic letter of late August or early September, he persistently excerpted and advertised the book while reprinting articles by Mark Twain and publishing items about him. In addition to "Eloquent Extract," the following have been identified: "Buying Gloves in Gibraltar," "His Duty," 27 Aug, 1, 2; "Agents Can Now Get . . . ," 3 Sept, 4, and 24 Sept, 3; "Eulogy on Women," 17 Sept, 1; "Rev. H. W. Beecher—His Private Habits," 29 Oct, 1; "Mark Twain," 5 Nov, 1; "New Advertisements," 5, 12, 19, and 26 Nov, 4; "A Good Letter," 26 Nov, 1; "Editorial Brevities," 17 Dec, 2.

[5] "The Disconsolate Sow" was not one of Elliott's published titles (see 21 Aug 69 to OLL, n. 5).

[6] Elliott's latest lyric, which he had published on 6 August and subsequently sent to Clemens. Its first verse and chorus are:

> Let wayward fortune hide her smile,
>   Come sorrows when they will;
> We've always something left beside
>   To make us happy still;
> For deep within the heart's recess—
>   Through all its joys and woes—
> There blooms, in charming loveliness,
>   The modest hued blush rose!
>
> CHORUS:
>   The tender thoughts of one alone,
>   That in its blossoms dwell,
>   I could reveal; but yet, but yet,
>   I do not care to tell!
>
>   (Elliott 1869b)

Clemens had remarked upon this "long-metre wail" in the Buffalo *Express* of 26 August: "We acknowledge the receipt of a song entitled, 'The Blush Rose,' from the author, Mr. George W. Elliott, associate editor of the Fort Plain *Register*. He predicts that it will have a popularity second to none in his list of published songs. Mr. Elliott is the author of 'Bonnie Eloise,' and several other melodies of similar character, which have been widely known in their day" (SLC 1869r).

[7] The obituary column of the Philadelphia *Public Ledger*, which frequently accompanied death notices with "a little verse or two of comforting poetry," was one of Clemens's favorite targets (see *L1*, 39 n. 4).

[8] Clemens could have seen reviews in the Toledo *Commercial*, the Cincinnati *Commercial*, and the Cincinnati *Gazette*, the first two of which he later extracted for the 9 October *Express*. The Toledo paper observed that Mark Twain combined humor with "a deeper vein of sense and of feeling" while the *Commercial* of Cincinnati noted that he combined humor with "sketches of men and manners as graphic and clear as any thing one will find in works of travel or personal reminiscence" ("Literary Matters," Toledo *Commercial*, 3 Sept 69, 2; Cincinnati *Commercial*, 4 Sept 69, 4; Cincinnati *Gazette*, 31 Aug 69, 1; "Advertising Supplement," Buffalo *Express*, 9 Oct 69, 1, 2). There were closely held subsidiaries of the American Publishing Company in both cities, R. W. Bliss and Company in Toledo, and Nettleton and Company in Cincinnati ("Hartford Residents," Bliss Family, 2; Hill, 16).

[9] Clemens wrote this list for his own use, on an otherwise blank leaf, probably before he began his letter. When he used that leaf for the fifth and sixth pages of the letter, he began on the blank side and continued on the verso, so that the list appeared upside down at the bottom of the sixth (and final) page. No letters to the Fairbankses around this time have been found. Nor is any letter extant to the Pittsburgh lecture committee, for whom Clemens was to lecture on 1 November. James Redpath and James K. Medbery were competing to represent him in the lecture field (see 21 Sept 69 to Crane, n. 2). The Erie (Pa.) *Dispatch* was a Republican daily and weekly paper (Rowell, 94). "Spiders" and "6,701" have not been explained.

[10] Larned did not sign this long, mawkish obituary of Guy H. Salisbury, a Buffalo newspaperman who, in spite of "heavy troubles that crushed him down," had been known for his "inextinguishable cheerfulness and kindly geniality" and for "the natural sweetness of his gentle and generous disposition" (Larned 1869b). Clemens probably did not enclose a clipping of "Found Drowned," since the Langdons were by this time receiving the *Express* daily.

To Elisha Bliss, Jr.
7 September 1869 • (1st of 2) • Buffalo, N.Y.
(MS: TxEU)

MORNING EXPRESS $10 PER ANNUM.
EVENING EXPRESS $8 PER ANNUM.
WEEKLY EXPRESS $1.50 PER ANNUM.

OFFICE OF THE EXPRESS PRINTING COMPANY
NO. 14 EAST SWAN STREET.

BUFFALO, Sept. 7, 186 9.

Friend Bliss—

Mrs. W^m. Barstow, of Fredericksburg, Va., who applies to you for the Virginia agency of the book, is an old & valued friend of mine, and I want ~~to~~ you to manage to comply with her request, ~~no matter~~ if it can possibly be done. If you will make the appointment & send her all the books she wants & she fails to sell a book or pay a cent, I will be responsible & foot the bill out of my own pocket—for which promise this note may be retained as my guaranty. I have every confidence in her.[1]

> Yrs Truly,
> Sam*ˡ*. L. Clemens.

[letter docketed:] √ *[and]* Mark Twain | Sep 7/69

[1] As the next letter makes clear, Bliss received this letter from Kate D. Barstow herself, to whom Clemens had sent it, presumably enclosed in a cover letter, now lost.

To Elisha Bliss, Jr.
7 September 1869 • (2nd of 2) • Buffalo, N.Y.
(MS: CU-MARK)

Friend Bliss—

I guess Mr. Wilder ought to have a book—I think he ought,— don't you? Will you send him one—& drop him a line, or do something?[1]

Our books have come, & they are splendid. We'll come out in the papers with notices at the times specified, & will mention the Rochester agent.[2]

A most excellent old friend of mine, Mrs. Wm H. Barstow, ~~of~~ has written me from Fredericksburg, Va., asking for ~~the~~ a Virginia agency for the book, & I have written her a letter to be sent to you, seconding her request. She is out of luck & among strangers, with 3 small children to look after, & as I ~~sl~~ knew her in her better days, before she acquired a worthless husband, I want her to have an agency. She is an educated, cultivated lady, & has a deal of vim & enterprise in her, if trouble hasn't broken her spirit. I know her well enough to ~~be personal~~ be willing to let you send books to her without any cash in advance & be personally & ~~responsible~~ financially responsible for those books myself. You will hear from her shortly, no doubt.[3]

> Yrs
> Clemens

✉───

[*lett. ᵈocketed:*] √ [*and*] Mark Twain | Sep 9/69

¹Clemens evidently enclosed a request, now missing, from the unidentified Mr. Wilder.

²Two of the Buffalo newspapers reviewed *The Innocents Abroad* on 16 October, evidently around the "time specified" by Bliss. Neither mentioned his Rochester agent, who was identified in advertisements for the book (see 27 Sept 69 to Bliss, nn. 3, 4).

³Clemens ultimately had to make good on his guarantee to Bliss when Kate D. Barstow was unable to pay for all of the copies of *Innocents* sent to her. Barstow had been trained as a school teacher before going to Nevada Territory. She married William H. Barstow there, possibly in 1863 when he was one of the school trustees for Storey County (their eldest child was born early in 1864). Clemens knew both of the Barstows before their marriage. He first met William in the fall of 1861, when Barstow was assistant secretary of the Council of the first Nevada Territorial Legislature. In 1862 Barstow was partly responsible for offering him a regular position on the Virginia City *Territorial Enterprise*. During much of the 1870s, Barstow was without work, as he apparently was at the time Clemens wrote this letter (*L1*, 201 n. 8, 231; in CU-MARK: Elisha Bliss, Jr., to SLC, 15 Feb 70; SLC to Elisha Bliss, Jr., 23 Feb 70, in *MTLP*, 32–33; Kate Barstow to SLC, 16 Oct 81).

To John H. Gourlie, Jr.
7 September 1869 • Buffalo, N.Y.
(MS: CtHMTH)

MORNING EXPRESS $10 PER ANNUM.	OFFICE OF THE EXPRESS PRINTING COMPANY
EVENING EXPRESS $8 PER ANNUM.	NO. 14 EAST SWAN STREET.
WEEKLY EXPRESS $1.50 PER ANNUM.	BUFFALO, Sept. 7 1869.

With pleasure

Yrs Truly

Sam⁺. L. Clemens

"Mark Twain"

Jno. H. Gourlie, Esq.¹

¹It was probably John Hamilton Gourlie, Jr. (1853–1904), who had requested Clemens's autograph. Gourlie, named after an uncle who was a founder of the Century Club of New York, later wrote *General Average* (1881), about the laws and customs of the United States and other countries, and by the end of his life was "a recognized authority on insurance matters" ("John H. Gourlie Dead," New York *Times*, 21 Feb 1904, 7).

To Whitelaw Reid
7 September 1869 • Buffalo, N.Y.
(MS: DLC)

MORNING EXPRESS $10 PER ANNUM.   OFFICE OF THE EXPRESS PRINTING COMPANY
EVENING EXPRESS $8 PER ANNUM.   NO. 14 EAST SWAN STREET.
WEEKLY EXPRESS $1.50 PER ANNUM.
                                        BUFFALO, Sept 7 186 89.

Dear Mr. Reid—

I was away from town when the *Tribune* notice of the book arrived, & I have had a time of it, since, to get hold of it—but I have succeeded. I am ever so much obliged to you for that notice, & I confess that
I felt a deal relieved when I read it, for I was afraid from the start that I
might "catch it" disagreeably & caustically in the *Tribune*, & yet I
would not & could not write seriously and try to get you to be a traitor
to your own judgment & say kind things of the volume ~~when you~~ if you
couldn't feel them, though the publisher thought that would be a proper
enough thing to do.[1] I didn't mind asking you to touch up those Memphis
pavement-sharps,[2] because I was able to swear to the right & wrong of
that matter, but *I* it was different with the book. I am very much obliged,
& I will reciprocate if I ever get a chance. The book is selling furiously,
& the publisher says he is driving ahead night & day trying to keep up.
Certainly & surely ~~the~~ it is n't every adventurer's maiden experiment
that fares so kindly at the hands of the press as mine has, & so if it don't
~~sell~~ sell a prodigious edition, after all the compliments & the publicity it
has received, ~~it will~~ the fault will lie elsewhere than with the press.[3]

Thank you for the invitation—& I shall be glad to have my headquarters at the Tribune, which is the only ~~on~~ office I have been much
acquainted & at home in*/*, there.[4] I could not get rid of some few of my
lectures *at* engagements *at all*, & so now I am trying to get back those I
canceled & enough more to employ me in the east for about two
months—& that just puts my marriage off indefinitely—which is about
the first of Feb. no doubt. I'll not talk in the west [at] all if I can help it.
I would give nearly anything to get clear out of talking at all this winter.

When you happen to be at Buffalo or Elmira, you must come & see
me—half of me is at Mr. Langdon's in Elmira, you know, & so I am really

writing ~~of~~ over a fraudulent & assumed name when I sign myself Twain. No—that is wrong—I mean I am *not* writing over, &c &c. Wishing you all comfort, peace & prosperity—I am—

> Sincerely Yours
>
> Sam*ᶥ*. L. Clemens.

[1]Clemens had requested a sympathetic review of *The Innocents Abroad* in his letter of 15 August to Reid. The New York *Tribune*'s evenhanded review, which included liberal extracts from the book, appeared on Friday, 27 August, the day Clemens left Buffalo for a weekend in Elmira:

Mark Twain, as the readers of THE TRIBUNE at any rate must remember, was one of the confiding band who in 1867 sailed from New-York in the Quaker City on a sort of wholesale Sunday-school excursion round the world. They were to go everywhere and see everything, and have no great trouble about it either, for their leader decided what they ought to see and showed them just how to see it. . . . Mark Twain occasionally during the voyage contributed to THE TRIBUNE his impressions of foreign lands and people, and a narrative of some of the incidents of the trip. Here, however, we have a complete history of the voyage, copiously illustrated. Mr. Clemens has an abominable irreverence for traditions and authority,—which sometimes unfortunately degenerates into an offensive irreverence for things which other men hold sacred,—and makes not the slightest hesitation at expressing his opinions in the very plainest possible language, no matter how unorthodox they may be. There is nothing which he fears to laugh at, and though some people may wish that he had been a little more tender of the romance of travel, it is certainly refreshing to find a tourist who does not care what other tourists have said before him. The greater part of his book is pure fun, and considering how much of it there is, the freshness is wonderfully well sustained. ("Mark Twain's Book," 6)

Clemens published a long excerpt from the review—omitting the remarks about irreverence, however—in the 9 October Buffalo *Express* ("Advertising Supplement," 1).

[2]See 15 June 69 and 26 June 69, both to Reid.

[3]By the end of August, six weeks after the American Publishing Company received the first 403 copies of *Innocents*, over 5,800 volumes had been ordered from the bindery to meet the sales demand (APC 1866–79, 46–47, 93).

[4]In a letter no longer extant, Reid had formally invited Clemens to renew the association he had enjoyed with the *Tribune* while it was under John Russell Young's management.

To Olivia L. Langdon
7 September 1869 • Buffalo, N.Y.
(MS: CU-MARK)

MORNING EXPRESS $10 PER ANNUM.   OFFICE OF THE EXPRESS PRINTING COMPANY
EVENING EXPRESS $8 PER ANNUM.   NO. 14 EAST SWAN STREET.
WEEKLY EXPRESS $1.50 PER ANNUM.
                                                 10 P.M.
                                BUFFALO, Sept. 7 186 9.

I know a little rascal that I wish was in my arms now. It is raining, &
Larned is gone home & is comfortably housed, & can listen to the storm
& have somebody he loves best to help him g̶r̶ feel grateful for shelter
from it & from the toiling & moiling, the sordid & selfish struggling of
the great world outside—somebody to talk to—somebody to kiss—
somebody's eyes to look into & worship. But I shall have to go to a solemn, silent room, presently, & if the speechless furniture welcomes me,
well & good—if the dumb emptiness has a word for me, well & good
again—otherwise they day will have passed & the night waned apace
without a sentence of conversation, for both of us have sat still & busy
since breakfast. Bless me, how I am drawn toward you at such times! It
seems a crime not to have broken my word & banished lecturing forever,
so that I might have my little wife at the earliest moment. I wish you were
in my arms, Livy dear, & then I wouldn't care for anything.

But I have your letters, darling. I haven't yet got over a secret thrill
of vanity when I see the dear old familiar hand on a letter for me, & I
doubt if I ever shall. I always feel proud. And a year ago, I *was* so proud
to get a letter from you in Cleveland, with a picture in it, notwithstanding t̶h̶e̶i̶r̶ there was sorrow enough in the w̶o̶r̶d̶i̶n̶g̶ tidings it brought.
And I was proud of the few letters I got in Hartford[1]—& *now*, why I
can hardly comprehend that it is actually *I* that get a letter *every day*
from Livy—& she is *mine*—my own Livy for time & eternity—never
to be taken from me by any hand but that of the arch Destroyer to
whose edict all must bow. You are unspeakably precious to me my darling—a blessing before which all other earthly treasures are dross &
worthless.

I have got the sermon, dearie, but have not yet broken the seal—it
has a double stamp on it, & so I ʄ know m̶y̶ the little hand has been mark-

ing something, & I shall have the pleasure of reading it as soon as I go to bed,—bless her dear old heart.[2]

I have been preparing some newspaper notices of the book to publish in a supplement, but ~~thre~~ they threaten to make a page of the paper.[3] I suppose I shall have to cut them down some, though I had hoped to bore you with them in full & let you preserve them for me, as the Dead Canary[4] does. I find I have lost some of the best. I may have forgotten to file them.

Sweetheart, I think I sent you the Salutatory this morning—I know I hunted one up, intending to do it. You must have it, because you will have to edit my "Works" when I am gone. I ~~wis~~ meant to cut out a column of those "People & Things," occasionally, for they are excellent, as texts to string out a sketch from, but as usual I have neglected it.[5]

Puss, I shall bid you good night, now, for I lay reading altogether too late, last night, & disobeyed my little princess's commands, & of course I feel stupid in consequence today. I must obey better. Never mind—after a while when we are together, you will have me where you can say "It is time for you to go to sleep, now"—& then I shall obey promptly. Because then I shall have had your company instead of having to read musty books, & I shall be cheerfully willing to obey.

Go to bed, now, little sweetheart, whom I love, & honor, & bless, reverently & with my whole heart.

Sam.

Do you remember young Mrs. Barstow whom I told you about? That unfortunate (or worthless) husband of hers is not improving, it seems. She wants to try to earn a living for herself, poor girl—she wants an agency for the book. She is in Fredericksburg, Va., with her husband, & is out of money. I have written Bliss to send her all the books she wants & I would pay the bill if she failed to do it. She seems to have found a large-hearted & courageous friend, ,in a Southern lady, a quaint, outspoken one,, even in her adversity—for she is a good girl.[6]

Miss Olivia L. Langdon | Elmira | N. Y. [*postmarked:*] BUFFALO N.Y. SEP 8 [*docketed by OLL:*] 116th | 116th

[1] Olivia's first letter after she had refused Clemens's initial proposal of marriage, written about the middle of September 1868, had enclosed a picture.

Clemens had received two letters from her in Hartford, one on 16 October 1868, and the other by 30 October (see *L2*, 250–51, 266, 271).

²Olivia had undoubtedly sent a *Plymouth Pulpit*, containing one of Henry Ward Beecher's sermons, not now identifiable.

³The newspaper reviews of *The Innocents Abroad*, in conjunction with the "Press Greetings" to Clemens, filled one and one-third pages of the Buffalo *Express* of 9 October (see 2 Sept 69 to Bliss, n. 1).

⁴George W. Elliott.

⁵Clemens had probably "cut out" portions of at least one "People and Things" for Olivia to save (see 19 Aug 69 to OLL, nn. 1, 6).

⁶Barstow's friend, who may have written to Clemens on her behalf, remains unidentified (see 7 Sept 69 to Bliss [two letters]).

To Henry M. Crane
8 September 1869 • Buffalo, N.Y.
(MS: ViU)

MORNING EXPRESS $10 PER ANNUM.	OFFICE OF THE EXPRESS PRINTING COMPANY
EVENING EXPRESS $8 PER ANNUM.	NO. 14 EAST SWAN STREET.
WEEKLY EXPRESS $1.50 PER ANNUM.	BUFFALO, Sept 8, 186 9.

Friend Crane—

I have already written Abbey that as I was so mixed about it I would keep on the safe side & not lecture in either town.¹ Of course I can't go deliberately & talk in Rondout after that. If you have me on your memorandum book, it is a mistake—for I can easily swear I didn't promise you—the only trouble is I can't swear I *didn't* promise Abbey, though I can't see ~~why~~ what I could have been thinking of to promise him when I was asked twenty times in different cities last winter to put my name down for this year & *positively refused in every instance*. So you see how I am situated. Abbey's word is as good as mine, & he says I promised him—I don't deny it—I simply don't remember it. And not denying it, of course I can't talk for you in the face of that fact.

I would like ~~might~~ to be fixed so that I could talk for one or the other of you, & if I were there I would pitch pennies with both of you—but I ain't, you see, & we'll have to let those two communities pass unpersecuted with my lecture for this winter. Submit this to Mrs. Crane,² & she will say again that I am right.

No, your "persistence" don't annoy me a bit—it is complimentary to me.[3] I am only going to lecture till the middle of January, anyhow. My marriage was booked for Jan. 10, but had to be postponed till the first week in February on account of ~~th~~ some lecture engagements which I could not get canceled. But it won't be postponed again., ~~unless for the~~ I accept your congratulations upon that forthcoming event, & thank you right cordially.

Sincerely Yrs.

Sam*ᶥ*. L. Clemens.

(Over)

It won't do for me to book myself for 1870–71, because I hope to get out of the lecture-field forever before that time, & so I must make no promises. But you'll receive early notice ~~of who my~~ from my advertisements if I *do* enter the field that year, for I never intend to begin late again. I'll start early—only, I am almost willing to promise that I'll not be in the field at all that year. Make a note of this, & see if I don't come pretty near being a prophet. I mean to make this newspaper support me hereafter.[4]

Mark.

✉———————————————————————————————

Personal. | Henry M. Crane Esq | Rondout | N. Y. [*postmarked:*] BUFFALO N.Y. SEP 9 [*docketed by Crane:*] Twain | ans^d sep 11 [*and*] 95.13 | 142 | 142 | 200

  60

  42

[1]Clemens did not *explicitly* convey this message in his 21 August letter to Henry Abbey, which suggests that he was alluding here to a letter written since then, no longer extant. Possibly he wrote such a letter on 3 September, the same day he last corresponded with Crane.

[2]Martha Powley Crane (1840–1934) (Crane family monument, Montrepose Cemetery, Kingston, N.Y., information courtesy of Amanda C. Jones).

[3]The persistence was effective: see 21 Sept 69 to Crane, n. 1.

[4]After avoiding the lecture platform in 1870–71, Clemens returned to the circuit the following season.

To Olivia L. Langdon
8 and 9 September 1869 • Buffalo, N.Y.
(MS: CU-MARK)

Buffalo, Sept. 8, 1869.

Livy, my precious little darling, I am as happy as a king, now that it is settled & I can count the exact number of days that are to intervene before we are married. I am full of thankfulness, & the world looks bright & happy ahead. On the fourth day of February, one year after the date of our engagement, we shall step together out into the broad world to tread its devious paths together ~~the~~ till the journey of life is done & the great peace of eternity descends upon us like a benediction.[1] We shall never be separated on earth, Livy; & let us pray that we may not in Heaven. This 4th of February will be the mightiest day in the history of our lives, the holiest, & the most generous toward us both—for it makes of two fractional lives a whole;~~,~~ & it gives to two purposeless lives a work, & doubles the strength of each ~~to do it~~ whereby to perform it; it gives to two questioning natures a reason for living, & something to live for; it will give a new gladness to the sunshine, a new fragrance to the flowers, a new beauty to the earth, a new mystery to life; & Livy it will give a new revelation to love, a new depth to sorrow, a new impulse to worship. In that day the scales will fall from our eyes & we shall look upon a new world.[2] Speed it!

I have written to Redpath that my lecture-tour must come to a permanent close a week or ten days before the end of January, & when I hear from him, if he has made no appointments after Jan. 15, I will not let him make any. I ought to have the whole month, if I can get it. I am booked for Newark, N. J., Dec. 29.

It seems a dreadfully long time till Feb. 4, dearie, but I am glad we are to have that day, for it will always be pleasant to keep our engagement & wedding anniversaries together. I would rather have that day than any in the whole 365, for it will be doubly dear to me, & be always looked forward to as one peculiarly & sacredly blessed—the day about which the most precious memories of my life have been concentrated. We can always prepare for it weeks ahead & keep it in state.

Livy darling, I ought not to have told you about Charlie's trip, maybe, & yet after all, I ought, for we *must* begin to do something for that boy.[3] It is nearly time for him to have finished his wild oats (though he will *not* cease to sow them for six or eight years yet unless he gets married sooner.) If he is to be married a year hence there is no great need of solicitude, but still there is some need. There is only one uncomfortable feature about him, & that is his disposition to ~~do~~ dishonor his father's wishes under shelter of absence. Most boys do that, & so he is not worse ~~that~~ than his race—but most boys *shouldn't* do it, for it is a bad foundation to build upon. I suspect that the most promising course will be to set Ida[4] to reforming him. Judging by my experience, you ~~re~~ energetic & persistent little task-mistress, if ~~anything~~ anybody can change his style of conduct, it is the darling that has her nest in his heart. I gave Charlie a scorching lecture on this fault of his, two months ago, & he ~~so~~ seriously promised reform—but he needs ~~a lecture~~ a reminder every day, or else he is sure to drift backward.[5] I am sorry I made my darling sad about it. Don't be sad, dearie, Charlie will come out all right, yet. It would be an unnatural marvel if Charlie were a better boy than he is. Let us not expect extravagant things of the fellow. He is another sort better & manlier than ninety-nine out of a hundred boys in his situation in life. Now if you ~~b~~ knew boys as well as I do, sweetheart, you would know that as well as I do. Let us do the rascal justice, Livy. I suppose *I* was a better boy at his age, but then you know I—well I was an exception, you understand—my kind don't turn up every day. We are very rare. We are a sort of human century plant, & ~~b~~ we don't blossom in everybody's front yard.[6]

* * * * . Since I wrote that last line I have read column after column of proof, & now it is so late that I must stop talking with Livy & go home to bed. It has rained all day & I suppose is raining yet, & I told Jo. Larned to stay at home after supper & be a comfort to his wife & I would sit up & do the work for both—though there wasn't a great deal to do, for that fellow works straight along all day, day in & a day out, like an honest old treadmill horse. I tell him I wish I had his industry & he had my sense.

Good-night my darling little wife, idol of my homage & my worship, & the peace of the innocent abide with you.

Sam

[*in pencil:*]

In the morning—(got your letter)—O the darling little ~~goose~~ ˄traducer!˄ when I said "the country," I meant *America*. But it was natural for you to ~~m~~ think I was malicious, but I wasn't, honey—I bear Ishmael not the least malice—certainly none that I would express in an undignified way. Now I kiss you & tell you ~~you~~ the mistake you made was perfectly natural to one who knew Ishmael had abused me in print.[7]

Darling, I propose to start to Elmira Friday night at 11—& start back at same hour on Monday night. Is my sweetheart answered. I kiss my darling good-bye, now, till Saturday morning.

✉———————————————————————————

[*in ink:*] Miss Olivia L. Langdon | Elmira | N. Y. [*postmarked:*] BUFFALO N.Y. SEP 9 [*docketed by OLL:*] 117th

[1] In fact the wedding took place on 2 February 1870.

[2] Acts 9:18: "And immediately there fell from his eyes as it had been scales: and he received sight forthwith, and arose, and was baptized."

[3] On 4 October 1869 Charles Langdon—accompanied by Elmira College professor Darius Ford, previously Olivia's tutor—was to begin a lengthy study tour of the world. The family had not told Olivia about the trip, probably because they knew she would be upset to learn that Charles would not be on hand for her wedding. As she later remarked: "We all dislike very much to have Charlie absent when I am married, but if he waited six months, it would bring him into the Southern countries in the wrong time of year, and a year he did not want to wait, as he desired to get back to Ida before that time. So there seemed no other way but for him to go this Fall" (OLL to Alice Hooker Day, 1 Nov 69, CtHSD). For further details of the world trip, see 26 and 27 Sept 69 to Fairbanks, n. 5, and 9 Oct 69 to Colfax, nn. 2, 5.

[4] Ida Clark, Charles's fiancée.

[5] According to Langdon family tradition, Charles's heavy drinking, which continued through most of his life, was the "fault" that his parents hoped he would reform while under Darius Ford's tutelage.

[6] On 23 August 1869 the Buffalo *Express* had reported on a century plant that had bloomed in Rochester, becoming such a public attraction that it was to be placed on exhibit in Chicago ("The Century Plant on Its Travels," 4). The Langdons were not yet receiving the *Express*, but Clemens might well have enclosed a clipping in a letter to Olivia on or soon after the twenty-third. Three letters written around then (docket numbers 105, 106, and 107) are missing.

[7] Clemens here acknowledged writing "More Byron Scandal," an editorial in the Buffalo *Express* of 7 September. The editorial excerpted the Elmira *Advertiser*'s 3 September "Friday Miscellany," in which the Reverend Thomas K. Beecher rebuked Ausburn Towner (Ishmael) for his 28 August column in the Elmira *Saturday Evening Review*. There, Beecher charged, Towner had directed "coarse words of discourtesy" at Harriet Beecher Stowe for "The True Story of Lady Byron's Life," her recent *Atlantic Monthly* article accusing Lord Byron of

incest with his half-sister, Augusta Leigh. In the 4 September *Review* Towner conceded the justice of Beecher's rebuke. Three days later, probably without having seen Towner's admission, Clemens endorsed Beecher's remarks: "What Mr. Beecher says to 'Ishmael' will apply equally well to many another writer in the country who has deemed the flinging of inelegant personalities at Mrs. Stowe legitimate 'argument,' where materials for refuting her testimony were not to be had" (SLC 1869v; Thomas Kinnicut Beecher 1869e; Towner 1869d–e; Stowe). In a letter of 8 September (now lost), Olivia evidently assumed that Clemens intended to ridicule Towner for his provincialism, in revenge for Towner's previous "abuse" of him (see 8 May 69 to OLL from Hartford, n. 2, and 15 Aug 69 to Bliss, n. 1). Clemens abandoned at least one attempt to satirize "the Byron business" (see 7 Oct 69 to Unidentified), although he may have written about it more than once for the *Express*. For an argument that he wrote and published six editorials on the subject, including "More Byron Scandal," between 24 August and 17 September, see Baender; for an account of the furor caused by Stowe's charges, see Lentricchia.

To the Lyceums
9 September 1869 • Buffalo, N.Y.
(Buffalo *Express*, 11 Sept 69)

PERSONAL.

This is to inform lyceums that, after recently withdrawing from the lecture field for next Winter, I have entered it again (until Jan. 10), because I was not able to cancel all my appointments, it being too late, now, to find lecturers to fill them. This is also to request that invitations for me be addressed to Mr. JAMES REDPATH, 20 Bromfield street, Boston, my lecture agent (instead of to me as heretofore), and thus some delay and inconvenience will be avoided.

Mark Twain.

OFFICE BUFFALO EXPRESS, Sept. 9, 1869.[1]

[1] On 24 September, the Elmira *Advertiser* reported: "Mark Twain announces that, having been unable to arrange for substitutes, he will lecture until January 16th" ("Neighborhood and News Items," 4).

To Ausburn Towner (Ishmael)
17 September 1869 • Elmira, N.Y.
(MS, *not sent:* CU-MARK)

Elmira, Sept. 17.

My Dear Insect:

With more than the solicitude of a mother I have watched your little ambitions develop, one by one, & with more than the grief of such a parent have seen them, one by one take their places among the world's unnoticed failures.

When you started out to make a literary notoriety for yourself, & chose a nom de plume ("Ishmael,") playfully at variance with your disposition, which is rather that of the pretty, gambolling lamb than the bloodthirsty man of war,[1]

[remainder of page blank]

[1] See 8 and 9 Sept 69 to OLL, n. 7. Clemens may have found fresh cause for irritation in Towner's most recent column, in the 11 September Elmira *Saturday Evening Review*. Towner there denied that "the influence of woman in any matter of public notoriety is softening or refining," claiming that women writers routinely depicted "lewdness" and "sin," that Harriet Beecher Stowe "hesitates not to go beyond them all in her exposition of the weakness of human nature," and that "the influence of this kind of writing permeates society to an extent that is appalling" (Towner 1869f). Clemens wrote in black ink, now faded to brown. Intermittent patches of purple, also faded, may have been the result of re-dissolved purple residue in the pen itself.

To Henry M. Crane
21 September 1869 • Buffalo, N.Y.
(MS: ViU)

MORNING EXPRESS $10 PER ANNUM.   OFFICE OF THE EXPRESS PRINTING COMPANY,
EVENING EXPRESS $8 PER ANNUM.   NO. 14 EAST SWAN STREET.
WEEKLY EXPRESS $1.50 PER ANNUM.
BUFFALO, Sept 21 18 69.

Friend Crane—

Now you have got the thing straight & pleasant—therefore I have enclosed your letter to my Boston agent, ~~Red~~ & he will reply to you.[1] He & Medbery appear to be in a tangle, somehow, ~~& so~~ but I guess they will get straightened out shortly.[2]

Yrs Truly
Clemens.

📨—————————————————————————————————

[*letter docketed:*] Mark Twain | 1869

[1] Crane and Henry Abbey had apparently ended their competition to schedule a lecture by Clemens (see 21 Aug 69 to Abbey, and 21 Aug 69, 3 Sept 69, and 8 Sept 69 to Crane). Clemens lectured in Rondout, New York, for Crane, on 12 January 1870.

[2] James Knowles Medbery (1838–73) was a New York journalist who worked on the *Round Table*, the *Evening Mail*, the *Evening Post*, and from 1869 to 1871 was the literary editor of the *Christian Union*. "In 1866 he established the [American] Literary Bureau at New York. *This comprised the first lecture bureau, in this country, which combined the promotion of literary lecturers with the examining and editing of various publications*—articles for magazines, etc." (MacKaye, 1:113, 114). In fact, the bureau's "Authors' Department" functioned as a complete literary agency, soliciting manuscripts, negotiating contracts, and supervising publication (American Literary Bureau, 12). Medbery evidently was the agent who approached Clemens in the spring of 1869 (see 10 May 69 to Redpath, p. 216). Presumably his "tangle" with James Redpath, Clemens's Boston-based agent, was the result of the American Literary Bureau's claim to represent Clemens. As late as 20 November 1869, the bureau was advertising itself to "Lecture Committees throughout the country" as Mark Twain's agent ("Lectures and Meetings," New York *Tribune*, 20 Nov 69, 5).

To George E. Barnes
21 September 1869 • Buffalo, N.Y.
(MS facsimile: MHi)

Buffalo, Sept. 21.

Friend Barnes:[1]

I have been absent ~~so~~ several days, but I am ready to say I wish you well, now. Now I *could* have sent you our weekly paper at a dollar & a half a year—but did you ever know me to do anything mean? No, sir. I told them to send you the *daily*, which will cost ten dollars a year in greenbacks.[2] See the confidence I repose in you! Put ∅ us in the Schedule in Bankruptcy. Nothing would afford me such high gratification as to seem to have credit enough to procure me a place among that honored class who are able to contract debts.

I hope to get out there some day & go with you & Mr. Swain's folks to another pic-nic again. We had a deal of fun, that time, without the fatigue of traveling.[3]

May I introduce a couple of friends of mine—Prof. Ford & Chas. J. Langdon? They are on a leisurely voyage around the world,[4] & will sail for China in November. I'll give them a note to you. Langdon is to be my brother-in-law, & is of course a very particular friend.

Cordially,

Mark Twain

[1]George Eustace Barnes (d. 1897) was the editor and co-owner of the San Francisco *Morning Call* who had hired and, without acrimony, fired Clemens as a local reporter in 1864 (*L1*, 317–18 n. 3; *CofC*, 9–10, 15, 283).

[2]In 1864 a greenback in San Francisco had been worth less than half its face value in gold. Clemens had addressed this inequity more than once in the columns of the *Morning Call*, a fact he expected Barnes to remember (*L1*, 314 n. 4; *CofC*, 227–31). Federal legislation enacted in March 1869 called for an early redemption of the notes in coin, but it was a decade before the gold standard was resumed. Meanwhile, the greenback continued to be a devalued currency: in September 1869 a one-dollar greenback was worth, on the average, seventy-three cents in gold (Barrett, 171, 205–28; Mitchell, 8).

[3]While living in San Francisco in the mid-1860s, Clemens had become acquainted with Robert Bunker Swain, superintendent of the local United States branch mint. The "pic-nic" with Swain, his wife, Clara, and their son, as well as Barnes, probably took place in the spring or early summer of 1868, however. The following invitation was written as early as Friday, 10 April 1868, a week

after Clemens's return to San Francisco from the East Coast, but no later than Friday, 3 July 1868, three days before he departed again (CU-MARK):

> Friday P M
>
> Dear Clemens,
>
> I have been hoping to see you all the week to ask you [to] dine with me on Sunday. I would be most happy to have you, and so would Mrs Swain. We generally dine at 4½ o'clock, & on Sundays, when there can [be] no business standing in the way, we try to have a good time
>
> Please say amen, & oblige
>
> > Yours cordially
> > R B Swain
>
> Sam⟨*⟩. L Clemens Esq

On the envelope, which was hand delivered, Clemens jotted directions to the Swains' home at 814 Powell Street—"Bet Cal & Sac on Powell on east side—centre block—best looking house—door plate."—and later added a reminder that the invitation was for "Sunday, 4½ PM." In December 1868 Clemens included Swain among the character references he gave to Jervis Langdon (Langley 1867, 462; *L2*, 205, 234, 359).

⁴Actually they did not leave Elmira until 4 October.

To Elisha Bliss, Jr.
21 September 1869 • Buffalo, N.Y.
(Parke-Bernet 1938b, lot 72)

Buffalo, Sept. 21, 1869.

Friend Bliss.

The Editor of the Overland Monthly writes as enclosed. Isn't Bancroft doing rather meanly in this matter? Will you answer the enclosed postmaster & the Pittsburgh man & oblige yrs.[1]

Clemens

[1]None of Clemens's three enclosures survives. The letter from Bret Harte, editor of the *Overland Monthly*, protested the refusal of Hubert H. Bancroft, the San Francisco book dealer who was West Coast agent for *The Innocents Abroad*, to provide a review copy. Harte's reaction to the manuscript of *Innocents*, which he read and helped revise in June 1868 (see *L2*, 232–33 n. 1), had made Clemens particularly anxious for him to write a review:

He praised the book so highly that I wanted him to review it *early* for the Overland, ~~so that I could~~ & help the sale out there. I told ~~the~~ my publisher. He ordered Bancroft to send Harte a couple of books before anybody else. Bancroft declined! I wrote ~~a not~~ Harte & enclosed an order on Bancroft for 2 book[s] & directing that the bill be ~~sent~~ deducted from my publishers returns or sent to me. Mr. Bancroft *"preferred the money."* Good, wasn't it? [He wrote me the other day, asking me to help get him agency for my new book for Pacific

& the Orient—which I *didn't.*] Well, sir, Harte wrote me the *most daintily contemptuous &*
insulting letter you ever read—& what I want to know, is, where *I* was to blame? (26 Nov 70
to Charles Henry Webb, ViU†)

Harte's long and complimentary review appeared in the *Overland Monthly* in
January 1870. He characterized *Innocents* as "six hundred and fifty pages of open
and declared fun" and said that it confirmed his belief "that Mr. Clemens deserves to rank foremost among Western humorists" (Harte 1870, 100, 101).

To Silas S. Packard
21 September 1869 • Buffalo, N.Y.
(Packard, 110)

Buffalo, Sept. 21.

Friend Packard—
 'Taint any use—it can't be done[1]

. . . .

Yrs as Ever
Clemens.

[1]Clemens was probably declining to write yet another article for *Packard's
Monthly*, to which he had already made three contributions between March and
August 1869 (SLC 1869b, 1869g, 1869i).

To William P. Carpenter
23 September 1869 • Buffalo, N.Y.
(MS: NNC)

Buffalo, Sept. 23.

Dear Sir—
 I have forwarded your note to my Boston agent, Mr. Redpath, &
he will fix a date & reply to you.[1]
 With thanks—

Yrs Truly
Sam*l*. L. Clemens.

[1]William Penn Carpenter represented the Utica (N.Y.) Mechanics' Association, for which Clemens lectured on 14 January 1870. He was a bookkeeper for J. S. and M. Peckham, a Utica stove company ("Mark Twain," Utica *Observer*, 14 Jan 70, 3; *Utica Directory*, front flyleaf, 46). This letter survives in the papers of his son, philologist and educator William Henry Carpenter.

To Mathew B. Cox
24 September 1869 • Buffalo, N.Y.
(Transcript and *paraphrase:* Argus)

MORNING EXPRESS $10 PER ANNUM.	OFFICE OF THE EXPRESS PRINTING COMPANY
EVENING EXPRESS $8 PER ANNUM.	NO. 14 EAST SWAN STREET.
WEEKLY EXPRESS $1.50 PER ANNUM.	

BUFFALO, Sept. 24, 186 9.

[*paraphrase: to Capt. M. B. Cox, San Francisco, introducing to him Prof. Ford and Charles J. Langdon, of Elmira, New York,*] who are bound around the globe on a pleasure trip . . . Don't tell them how you used to mix the cocktails at 7 bells, & give mine to me in my berth, like the very best old rascal in the world, as you are. And don't tell them about Mrs. Sherwood & those other ladies putting flour on my pillow the night of the 1st April[1] . . . & do you remember the night of the "Equinoctial storm" which I put into poetry?[2] I can't think of that long, bewitching exquisite voyage without going into ecstacies of pleasurable feeling.

·   ·   ·   ·

Yours for a thousand years,
Mark Twain.

[1] Mathew Bold Cox, superintendent of the Pacific Mail Steamship Company's docks in San Francisco, was Clemens's companion and cabin mate during his voyage from New York to San Francisco in the spring of 1868. Mrs. Sherwood, along with her two children and a nurse, was also among the passengers. Her practical joke on the night of 1 April, the final night of the journey, occurred aboard the Pacific Mail Steamship Company's *Sacramento*, which made the Panama to San Francisco leg of the trip (*L2*, 235–36; "Passengers Sailed," New York *Tribune*, 12 Mar 68, 3; "Arrival of the Sacramento," San Francisco *Times*, 3 Apr 68, 1).

[2] "Ye Equinoctial Storm," Clemens's poem about a night of revelry aboard the *Sacramento*, remained unpublished until 1884, when it appeared in the San Francisco *Wasp* (SLC 1884).

To Mary Mason Fairbanks
26 and 27 September 1869 • Buffalo, N.Y.
(MS: CSmH)

MORNING EXPRESS $10 PER ANNUM.   OFFICE OF THE EXPRESS PRINTING COMPANY
EVENING EXPRESS $8 PER ANNUM.   NO. 14 EAST SWAN STREET.
WEEKLY EXPRESS $1.50 PER ANNUM.
                                     BUFFALO, Sept 27 186 9.

My Dear Mammy—

I'll love you, & reverence you, both. And I will try & be as dutiful
& tractable a "child" as any you have got in your collection. I don't wonder you are a trifle uneasy about the Saturday articles, for *I* am. You see,
I am worried about getting ready to lecture, & so I fidget & fume &
sweat, & I can't write serenely. Therefore I don't write Saturday articles
that are satisfactory to me.[1] I'm not ∤ *settled* yet. My partners wanted me
to lecture some this winter, though, & it seemed necessary anyhow, since
I could not get all my engagements canceled.

You have about made me give up the "pictures." I hate pictures like
these, myself. But as they cost nothing, my partners thought we might
as well have them. I am to leave, next week, to begin to cook up my
lecture, & so we'll not have any more, I guess.[2]

Me "getting cross over your talk?" No—bang away—I l̶i̶ enjoy it.
No, I don't mean that—I mean I don't mind it—or rather, I mean that
I *like* it. Now I have got it. I like your criticisms, because they nearly
always convince me—always, I guess, is nearer the truth. And because
I love you, I would like the criticisms, even if they *didn't* convince me.

Well, I'll let Death alone. I will, mother—honest—i̶f̶ I won't bother
him if he don't bother me. No, but really, I *will* be more reverential, if
you want me to, though I tell you it don't jibe with my principles. There
is a fascination about meddling with forbidden things.[3]

I can't come to see you till spring,̸, b̶e̶c̶a̶u̶s̶e̶ on account of lecturing
& such things—but if Livy invites you you will come to our wedding,
won't you? I think she'll either invite both of my n̶o̶t̶ mothers[4]—I would
invite hers, if she had a million. And *then* we'll get a chance to see you.
Feb. 4 is the wedding-day—the anniversary of the engagement. I chose
that date on the score of economy—shan't have to buy another ring—
shall simply p̶u̶t̶ add "Feb. 4, 1870" on the inside of the engagement

ring. No—that is Livy's idea, & I think it is good, & neat, & sensible. The lecturing caused the postponement. Can't tell yet, whether we are going to keep house, but I have made up my mind that it has got to be one or the other. *I*'m not particular. Suppose we shall board till spring.

Did Charley write you that he is going around the globe? Prof. Ford is sent along with him as tutor & traveling companion. They start next Thursday & go overland to California & Denver & Salt Lake & Nevada mines & Big Trees & Yo Semite,—then a 25-day voyage to Japan—then China—then India,—Egypt & away up the Nile—the Holy Land all over again—Russia & the Emperor all over again—& we are all to meet them in Paris 12 ~~or 13 months~~ months hence & make the tour of England, Germany, &c., with them. They are to travel leisurely, & take the world easy. [I feel a sort of itching in my feet, mother—& if my life were as aimless as of old, my trunk would be packed, now.][5]

But really & truly I must write to that girl to-night before ever I go to bed—& in order to do it I must cut this note short. Goodbye. I embrace the household.

> Lovingly,
> Your Eldest,
> Sam

[*on different paper:*]
　P S.
　Dear Mother—

In writing you last night,[6] I forgot to ask you to thank the *Herald* reviewer for his handsome notice of my book, & Frank or Mr Fairbanks for sending me copies. They just came in good time, for I was compiling a few notices to make up into an advertising supplement.[7]

We had Prince Arthur in town a little while this afternoon, but he never called on me, & so I threw myself back on my dignity & never called on *him*. He is too stuck-up, altogether. I am on too familiar terms with his betters in Russia to go browsing around after mere princes. I let him shin around town as long as he wanted to, & shin out ~~of~~ again when he got ready. But I wrote him up.[8]

> Lovingly
> Sam.

[1]The only Buffalo *Express* articles that Clemens regularly signed "Mark Twain" appeared on Saturdays. To date he had published six such pieces: "A Day

at Niagara," "English Festivities. And Minor Matters," "Journalism in Tennessee," "The Last Words of Great Men," "The 'Wild Man.' 'Interviewed,'" and "Rev. H. W. Beecher. His Private Habits." The record of Clemens's cash account with the Express Printing Company indicates that the paper paid him $25 for each of these (SLC 1869n, 1869s, 1869u, 1869w, 1869y, 1869aa; "Statement of S. L. Clemen[s]'s a/c from Aug 9' 1869 to Jany 1st 1870," CU-MARK).

[2]Of the first six Saturday articles only the fourth and sixth were published without crudely drawn and printed illustrations. "I am obliged to leave out the illustrations, this time," Mark Twain explained on 11 September. "The artist finds it impossible to make pictures of people's last words" (SLC 1869w). The drawings presumably "cost nothing" because they were prepared by John Harrison Mills, the Buffalo artist who was on the staff of the *Express*. All subsequent sketches were unillustrated.

[3]Mrs. Fairbanks had objected to the irreverent treatment of death in "The Last Words of Great Men": "A distinguished man should be as particular about his last words as he is about his last breath. He should write them out on a slip of paper and take the judgment of his friends on them. He should never leave such a thing to the last hour of his life, and trust to an intellectual spurt at the last moment to enable him to say something smart with his latest gasp and launch into eternity with grandeur" (SLC 1869w).

[4]Clemens apparently neglected to cancel "either" when he changed the direction of his sentence.

[5]Repeated reports in the Elmira press suggest that Clemens let it be understood that he would go with Ford and Langdon, at least to California. The day before he wrote this letter the Elmira *Saturday Evening Review* said: "MARK TWAIN will accompany the round the world travelers, Prof. D. R. FORD and CHARLES J. LANGDON, as far as San Francisco." Two days before Ford and Langdon actually left it said: "Prof. FORD, MARK TWAIN, and C. J. LANGDON leave for westward ho! on Monday" ("Local Happenings," 25 Sept, 2 Oct 69, 8). And on Monday, 4 October, the Elmira *Advertiser* reported: "Prof. FORD and Mr. C. J. LANGDON leave this city to-day at 12:20 by the Northern Central line for their trip around the world. At Rochester they will take a Pullman Sleeping Coach for Chicago, and thence by the Pacific Road for California. They will be accompanied on their journey as far as San Francisco by MARK TWAIN" ("The College Reunion," 4). Although Clemens had abandoned his own plans for a California trip in mid-August, when he purchased his interest in the Buffalo *Express*, he may have considered accompanying Langdon and Ford. But by 27 September he decided to stay in the East to prepare a replacement for the "Curiosities of California" lecture he had planned to use on his 1869–70 tour (see 27 Sept 69 to Bliss, n. 2). Whether or not he planted the reports in the Elmira papers, he soon determined how to turn them to good use. On 13, 14, and 15 October the Buffalo *Express* carried the following advertisement on its front and back pages:

MARK TWAIN
IN
SATURDAY'S EXPRESS.
A VOYAGE
AROUND THE WORLD,
BY PROXY.
FIRST OF A SERIES OF LETTERS.

The initial letter, published on 16 October, began with a note to the reader dated "NEW YORK, October 10," in which Clemens said in part: "I am just starting on a pleasure trip around the globe, *by proxy*. That is to say, Professor D. R. FORD, of Elmira College, is now making the journey for me, and will write the newspaper account of his (our) trip. No, not that exactly—but he will travel and write letters, and I shall stay at home and add a dozen pages each to each of his letters. One of us will furnish the fancy and the jokes, and the other will furnish the facts. I am equal to either department, though statistics are my best hold" (SLC 1869ee). Eight such letters, all written entirely by Mark Twain, were published in the *Express* between 16 October 1869 and 29 January 1870: their subjects were nearly identical to what Clemens had earlier told James Redpath he would cover in "Curiosities of California." Ford published two letters, both initialed by him, on 12 February and 5 March 1870 (10 May 69 to Redpath; SLC 1869ee–ff, 1869hh, 1869kk–*ll*, 1870c, 1870e–f; Ford 1870a–b). Langdon and Ford were called home in late June 1870, when Jervis Langdon's stomach cancer became critical, so that the planned family meeting in Paris never occurred.

[6]Clemens misdated the first part of his letter by one day. The events discussed in the next paragraph occurred on 27 September.

[7]Clemens included a long excerpt from the Cleveland *Herald* review, published on 23 September ("The Innocents Abroad," 1), in his 9 October Buffalo *Express* "Advertising Supplement" (1). The unidentified reviewer emphasized that Mark Twain was not "a mere buffoon or professional joke maker. He has eyes to see and a mind to appreciate the beautiful and the sublime as well as the absurd, and when his deeper feelings overmaster his jesting mood he can describe what he saw and felt in eloquent and earnest words." Frank was Abel Fairbanks's twenty-four-year-old son from his first marriage (Fairbanks, 552).

[8]Prince Arthur William Patrick Albert (1850–1942)—seventh child and third son of Queen Victoria and later Duke of Connaught and Strathearn and Earl of Essex—who was stationed with the British army in Montreal, was briefly in Buffalo on 27 September. Of his visit, Clemens said in part:

He made no remarks to us; did not ask us to dinner; walked right by us just the same as if he didn't see us; never inquired our opinion about any subject under the sun; and when his luncheon was over got into his carriage and drove off in the coolest way in the world without ever saying a word—and yet he could not know but that that was the last time he might ever see us. But if he can stand it, we can.

Prince Arthur looks pleasant and agreeable, however. He has a good, reliable, tenacious appetite, of about two-king capacity. He was the last man to lay down his knife and fork.

This is absolutely all that England's princely son did in Buffalo—absolutely all! We shall go on and make all the parade we can about it, but none of his acts in Buffalo were noisy enough for future historical record. It was *Veni, Vidi, Vici*, with him. He came—he saw that lunch—he conquered it. (SLC 1869cc)

In fact, after lunching at the Tifft House, Arthur made a quick tour of the city. Among his stops was the local headquarters of the Fenians. The Irish revolutionary movement had launched one abortive invasion of Canada in 1866 and was to launch another, which the prince helped repel, in 1870 ("Prince Arthur," Buffalo *Commercial Advertiser*, 28 Sept 69, 3; *DNB*, 16–17). For Clemens's acquaintance with Arthur's "betters in Russia," see *L2*, 80–85.

To Elisha Bliss, Jr.
27 September 1869 • Buffalo, N.Y.
(MS: CU-MARK)

MORNING EXPRESS $10 PER ANNUM.   OFFICE OF THE EXPRESS PRINTING COMPANY
EVENING EXPRESS $8 PER ANNUM.   NO. 14 EAST SWAN STREET.
WEEKLY EXPRESS $1.50 PER ANNUM.
                                   BUFFALO, Sept 27 186 9.

Friend Bliss—

Arnold called on me two days ago, & introduced his two Buffalo canvassers. I don't know anything about him. He said he was going to rush things right along. I told him we were going to publish a supplement of notices of the book next Saturday,[1] & he a (a page or more) & he asked that the type be kept standing till Saturday afternoon, when he would arrive & see if he could make a trade for 5 or 10,000 copies for distribution. I told I gave him to understand that we would furnish them at cost, or even less. He said nothing about advertising in the Buffalo papers.

I like newspapering very well, as far as I have got—but I leave adjourn, a week hence, to commence preparing my lecture, & shall not be here again till the middle of February. After a few days, now, you I shall be *in Elmira till Nov. 1. Recollect.*[2]

Yes, our paper is a good one to advertise in, & so is the "Commercial-Advertiser" & the "Courier." (Latter is Democratic.) Democratic, but good boys.)[3]

None of us have noticed the book yet—shall, this week, maybe.[4] Regards to Mrs. B. & the longest half of Frank.

Yrs
Clemens.

I think the book is making more stir than other people's books, & I guess you are pushing it to for all it is worth.

[*letter docketed:*]

these books were all ordered to be delivered, & I wrote to each party informing them of the fact[5]

Bliss
Sep 30th/69

[1] The Buffalo *Express* "Advertising Supplement" appeared on Saturday, 9 October.

[2] Clemens left Buffalo for Elmira on the evening of 30 September. There he wrote the Sandwich Islands lecture he used on the tour he began on 1 November, instead of the "Curiosities of California" talk he had previously drafted ("'Mark Twain,'" Buffalo *Courier*, 1 Oct 69, 2; 10 May 69 to Redpath; 26 June 69 to JLC and PAM; 5 July 69 to Fairbanks).

[3] The Buffalo *Commercial Advertiser*, established in 1820, was a Republican evening daily and tri-weekly published by James N. Matthews and James D. Warren. The Buffalo *Courier*, established in 1835, was a Democratic morning daily and weekly published by Joseph Warren, James M. Johnson, Ethan H. Howard, and Milo Stevens. Among the "good boys" on the *Courier* was its co-editor, poet David Gray (1836–88), who became one of Clemens's closest Buffalo friends (Rowell, 66; *Buffalo Directory*, 55, 169, 171–72, 311, 337, 386). The American Publishing Company's advertisement for *The Innocents Abroad* ran daily in the Buffalo *Express*, beginning 1 October (4):

"The Innocents Abroad."

MARK TWAIN'S new book, bearing the above title, has just been issued by the American Publishing Company. GEORGE H. ARNOLD, 32 Reynold's Arcade, Rochester, is the General Agent for this section of the State. He has appointed Messrs. George B. Briggs and George M. Hewitt to act as canvassers for Buffalo.

Persons desiring the book can leave their addresses in the counting-room of this office, and the canvassers will call upon them.

The *Courier* and the *Commercial Advertiser* did not carry any advertising for the book.

[4] The Buffalo *Express*, which had published a brief complimentary notice of *Innocents* on 18 August ("Mark Twain's New Book," 4, reprinting the New York *World*, 16 Aug 69, 5), printed its full review, presumably by Josephus Larned, on 16 October (2):

NEW BOOKS.

If any book of late years has so generally interested the press of the country and received so extensive and favorable an introduction to the public as has Mark Twain's "Innocents Abroad," since its appearance, we fail to remember the instance. We gave to our readers last week, in a supplementary sheet, some specimens of the notices we have found in our exchanges. Numerous as were the excerpts there collected, they represent but a fraction of what have fallen under our observation, and the notable fact is, that, instead of the mere mention so commonly accorded to a new book, almost every journal has given it an unusually elaborate review, written, not in a simple spirit of courtesy, but evidently with an inspiration of interest excited by reading the work. The truth is, we believe, that no one of an ordinary disposition of mind can dip into the volume without being snared by a curious fascination. It is so different from any narrative of travel that ever was written before. The mere tickle of an ever pervading humor is not all that makes it delightful, but that humor is like an atmosphere, in which the old world scenes that so many tourists and travelers have led us into, take on a new and altogether novel appearance, so that we follow our droll excursionist from place to place as eagerly as though we had never been carried to them by any narrative before. It would be a great mistake to suppose that the book is just a big package of Mark Twain's jokes, to be read with laughter, and for the sake of laughter. It is the panorama of Europe and the Holy Land as they were seen by one who went abroad with no illusions; who carried about with him a shrewd pair of American eyes, and used them to get his own impressions of things, as they actually presented themselves, not as he has been taught to expect them; who bore with him, moreover, as acute an appreciation of sham and humbug as his sense of the humorous and ludicrous was keen. What he saw he tells, and we believe there is more true description in his book than in any other of the kind that we have read. What is to be told soberly he tells soberly, and with all the admiration or reverence that is due to the subject. But he does like to wash off false colors, to scrape away putty and varnish, to stick a pin into venerable moss grown shams—and it is a perpetual delight to his reader to see him do it in his droll, dry way. We have yet to find the person who could open the book and willingly lay it down again; for, certainly, it is not often that more or livelier entertainment can be had in the same compass. The work has been published by the American Publishing Company, at Hartford, and is sold by agents who canvass for subscriptions.

Also on 16 October, the Buffalo *Commercial Advertiser* (3) printed its review:

"MARK TWAIN'S" NEW BOOK.—We have received from the American Publishing Company, of Hartford, a copy of "Mark Twain's" (SAMUEL L. CLEMENS) new book entitled "The Innocents Abroad, or the new Pilgrims' Progress;" being some account of the steamship *Quaker City's* pleasure excursion to Europe and the Holy Land; with descriptions of countries, nations, incidents and adventures, as they appeared to the author. It makes a volume of over 650 pages, 8vo, with 234 illustrations, and is handsomely gotten up, so far as mechanical execution is concerned.

The text is marked throughout with the author's irresistable humor, which, blended with a conscientious narrative of facts, makes the volume peculiarly attractive. Unlike most attempts to be funny, (and especially at such length) Mr. CLEMENS's book is a success. In ninety-nine cases in a hundred, a fat octavo joke is sure to pall the taste of an average reader. It is much like living for a week or two on sweetmeats. In his "Innocents Abroad," Mr. CLEMENS seems most successfully to have blended facts with fancy, humor with instruction; and to have produced a pleasant, piquant and really enjoyable book.

We learn that it will be sold exclusively by agents, like all the publications of the American Publishing Company, and that agents are now canvassing this city and county for subscriptions. Our readers will be called upon by them in due time, and we can assure them that the book is worthy of their favor.

David Gray published a long and laudatory review in the Buffalo *Courier*, but not until 19 March 1870; the reason for the delay is not known (Gray).

[5]Presumably Bliss had informed the Buffalo newspapers that he had sent their review copies of *Innocents* in care of Clemens, who received them by 7 September (see 7 Sept 69 to Bliss [2nd of 2]).

To Oliver Wendell Holmes
30 September 1869 • Buffalo, N.Y.
(MS: DLC)

EDITORIAL ROOMS OF "THE EXPRESS,"

BUFFALO, Sept. 30 18 69.

Dear Mr. Holmes—

If I can get my pen to go along over this new-fangled cobble-stone paper without kicking up behind, (which I wish I had the author of it here,) I will acknowledge the receipt of your note & thank you heartily for your good words.[1]

Since you would like to know what excuse I had for sending you so large a book, Mr Holmes, I can easily furnish a good one. I ~~have~~ had read the "Autocrat of the Breakfast Table" two or three times already, when a superior young lady requested me a short time ago to read it again & *mark* it & marginal-note it all the way through for her,, (Young ladies like that sort of thing)—~~they are the parties that damage the library books~~—& I did. Then I said in my secret soul, I have got a chance at this gentleman who writes Autocrats of Breakfast Tables & gives me extra work to do, & I will hurl my six hundred & fifty pages at him ~~if I "fetch" the State~~ if I miss him & "fetch" the State house! [N. B.—Elsie Venner is waiting to be marked—commission from the same party.][2]

But speaking seriously, I so enjoyed reading the Autocrat the third time that I ~~gave~~ imposed the pleasant task upon myself of ~~redin red~~ reading it again & marking it without a suggestion from anybody. [Mem.— Am in the habit of marking books for the party mentioned a while ago.] I hadn't any real "excuse," but I sent the book just as a sort of unobtrusive "Thank-you" for having given me so much pleasure often & over again. That is honest, as sure as

> I am
> Yours Most Truly
> Sam[l]. L. Clemens

---

[1] Clemens was responding to the following letter:

Boston Sept. 26[h] 1869.

Dear Mr. Clemens,

I don't see what excuse you had for sending me such a great big book, which would have cost me ever so many dollars, but I assure you it was very welcome in spite of that— more welcome than you could have guessed it would be, for independently of the pleasure I have had from your other writings, and the agreeable recollection of your visit to my house in company with Mr Locke, some parts of your travels had a very special interest for me. I may mention especially your visits to Palestine and Egypt. You looked at these two countries in a somewhat different way it is true, from D[r] Robinson, or Lepsius, but I always like to hear what one of my fellow-countrymen who is not a Hebrew scholar or a reader of hieroglyphics, but a good humored traveller with a pair of sharp twinkling Yankee (in the broader sense) eyes in his head, has to say about the things that learned travellers often make unintelligible and sentimental ones ridiculous or absurd. Not long ago I read Hepworth Dixon's book about the Holy Land and since that Lady Herbert's. What a different way they had of looking at things to be sure. I am tolerably familiar with other books on the East and I have a large collection of stereographs of Egypt and Palestine— one of the largest I think that anybody has about here. So you can imagine with what curiosity I followed you through scenes that were in a certain sense familiar to me and read your familiar descriptions and frequently quaint and amusing comments, from such an entirely distinct and characteristic point of view.

I was rather surprised and much pleased to find how well your ship's company got on together. I had an idea they got sick of each other. I once crossed the ocean with another human being occupying the same stateroom—a German, who was well enough, I don't doubt—but didn't I loathe the sight and smell of him before our forty two days passage was over!

Well, I hope your booksellers will sell a hundred thousand copies of your Travels— don't let them get hold of this letter for the rascals always print everything to puff their books—private or not—which is odious but take my word for it your book is very entertaining and will give a great deal of pleasure.

> Yours very truly
> O W Holmes

Holmes alluded to: Edward Robinson (1794–1863), American philologist, geographer, and biblical scholar, author of *Biblical Researches in Palestine, Mount Sinai and Arabia Petraea* (1841); Karl Richard Lepsius (1810–84), German explorer and philologist, author of a number of books on Egypt; William Hepworth Dixon (1821–79), English historian, author of *The Holy Land* (1865); and Mary Elizabeth Herbert (1822–1911), Baroness Herbert of Lea, translator, novelist, travel writer, and religious biographer, author of *Cradle Lands* (1867), an account of travels in Egypt and the Holy Land. Clemens and David Ross Locke had visited Holmes in Boston on 14 or 15 March 1869.

[2]*Elsie Venner: A Romance of Destiny* (1861) was Holmes's first novel.

To Unidentified
7 October 1869 • Elmira, N.Y.
(MS: CU-MARK)

Elmira, N. Y. Oct. 7.

Dear Sir—

Well I like the Stowe article, too, for it is good. But see how tastes run—I think the Humboldt one ever so much better. "Humboldt's Extract of Buchu" is gorgeous. Yes, I like them both, but I stick to Humboldt. I like Humboldt the best. Maybe it is because I am prejudiced against the Byron business—because I tried to burlesque it, & had my labor for my pains—our stove got the article.[1]

I thank you very much for your offer of newspaper help, & also I thank you for your friendly feeling toward a newspaper man. I find a deal of it among the boys, but one cannot have too much of it. It never palls on the appetite.

I lecture in Pittsburgh Nov. 1, & then go straight to New England

& lecture there till Jan. 15, when I am obliged to close for the season[2]—
but I am as grateful for your tender of newspaper favors as if I were going
to lecture in the West & could take advantage of them.

I am "setting" on my lecture diligently, & will hatch it & leave here
early next week.

Cordially Yours,
Mark Twain

[1]One of the articles sent by Clemens's correspondent, evidently a western
journalist, clearly was a humorous sketch about Baron Alexander von Humboldt
(1769–1859), the German naturalist and explorer, whose birth centennial had
been widely celebrated in the United States on 14 September. "Humboldt's Extract of Buchu" was a punning reference to the patent medicine, formulated in
part from the buchu plant (source of a commonly prescribed diuretic), that
Henry T. Helmbold had been promoting as a cure for bladder and kidney ail-
ments, as well as venereal disease, since 1850 ("Humboldt," New York *Times*,
15 Sept 69, 1, 8; Young, 113–14; Helmbold). The other article must have been
a satire of the "Byron scandal" evoked by Harriet Beecher Stowe (see 8 and 9
Sept to OLL, n. 7). Clemens apparently consigned his own burlesque to his files,
not to his stove. Among his surviving manuscripts is an unfinished letter from
Lord Byron in Hell, which reads in part:

> Mr. MARK TWAIN—*Dear Sir:* I have been a good deal interested in the Byron
> Scandal lately stirred up on earth by Mrs. Harriet Beecher Stowe—for the Under-World
> takes the papers & is always posted. . . . the plain truth is, I *did* do all that wickedness I
> am charged withal. I did that, & more. I am the Wickedest Man in—in this region. My
> conscience tortures me night & day. Nothing will relieve me but a confession. The recent
> revelation gave me some relief, but only a little—only a little. It only revealed one of my
> crimes—one of my mildest. What I need is a full exposé. Let me whisper in your ear: I
> had nine children by the late Mrs. Leigh. I devoured them. I destroyed my maternal
> grandfather with a pitchfork—not in a spirit of revenge, but simply as an experiment, to
> see if one's grandfather *could* be destroyed with a pitchfork. I threw my paternal grand-
> father out of the fifth story window, just to see what he would say. He never ~~se~~ said any-
> thing. I flayed my brother John alive, merely to annoy him. I ~~have~~ committed all the crimes
> known t[o] the law. I ~~have~~ robbed, & burned, & betrayed, & assassinated. (SLC 1869t, 1,
> 3–5)

In July 1870, in one of his "Memoranda" columns for the *Galaxy* magazine,
Clemens wrote:

> There are some things which cannot be burlesqued, for the simple reason that in them-
> selves they are so extravagant and grotesque that nothing is left for burlesque to take hold
> of. For instance, all attempts to burlesque the "Byron Scandal" were failures because the
> central feature of it, incest, was a "situation" so tremendous and so imposing that the hap-
> piest available resources of burlesque seemed tame and cheap in its presence. (SLC 1870h,
> 137)

[2]In fact Clemens's tour was extended to 21 January 1870 (see Appendix D).

To Schuyler Colfax
9 October 1869 • Elmira, N.Y.
(MS: MH-H)

J. LANGDON, MINER & DEALER IN ANTHRACITE &
BITUMINOUS COAL   OFFICE NO. 6 BALDWIN STREET
Private.
ELMIRA, N.Y. Oct. 9. 186 9.

Dear Mr. Colfax—

I write now, in the hope of catching you just as you reach home—
the telegraph says you left Salt Lake yesterday.[1]

Just this side of Salt Lake you must have met ~~the~~ a train containing
two especial friends of mine—young CHAS. J. LANGDON (whose sister I
am to marry during the coming winter,) & his tutor & traveling companion PROF. D. R. FORD, of Elmira College. Mr. Langdon has shipped
them off on a ‚pleasure‚ tour round the globe, with orders to take their
time & ransack it thoroughly.[2]

They have special letters from ~~the~~ Gov. Hoffman, Simon Cameron
& others, to friends in Europe, & I have given them ~~letters~~ all the letters
they need for California.[3] Now can't you & won't you sit down & write a
line of *general* introduction to—to—well, to *anybody*—Ministers & Consuls, say—just the grandeur of the thing is what I am looking at—for *any*
hotel-keeper will know that parties can be trusted who carry letters from
Vice Presidents. I have no compunctions about asking this favor, for you
know Prof. Ford a little, & Mr. Langdon senior, also, I believe—& the
Langdons knew your first wife well, both here at the water-cure & in
Washington some 7 years ago. This almost makes you kin.[4]

Yrs Cordially

Mark Twain.

P. S.—If you write it you can send it either to me, here, or to Prof.
Ford, Occidental Hotel, San F. They do not sail from San F. till about
Nov. 1, for Japan. Six weeks ago I sent you my new book ("Inno-
cents")—sent it to Washington.[5]

[1]Vice-President Schuyler Colfax (1823–85) was returning to Washington,
D.C., after a two-month tour of the Pacific states. His visit to Salt Lake City on
5 October and his departure for the East the following day (not on 8 October)

were reported in the Elmira *Advertiser*'s "News by Telegraph" summary on 9 October ("Vice President Colfax at Salt Lake City," 1; Hollister, 342).

[2] Olivia Langdon emphasized the educational goals of the world trip in a letter of 1 November 1869 to Alice Hooker Day:

> Father wanted to compensate Charley as much as he could for his inability to study, he was obliged to gain information in some other way than from books—Father felt that if he could get Prof. Ford to go as Charlies companion, he would be just the right man, when they were on ship board, Charlie would be able to study with him some, and when traveling on land, Prof. Ford could give him all the history of the place, also the Geology and Botany of the country—They intended to take up Astronomy while on the ocean— (CtHSD)

The Langdons hoped that Ford would teach Charles moderation as well (see 8 and 9 Sept 69 to OLL, n. 5).

[3] The letters of introduction from John Thompson Hoffman (1828–88), former Democratic mayor of New York City (1865–68) and incumbent governor of New York State (1869–72), and Simon Cameron (1799–1889), Republican (formerly Democratic) senator from Pennsylvania (1845–49, 1857–61, 1867–77), presumably were secured by Jervis Langdon, who may have become acquainted with both men as a result of his extensive coal business in New York and Pennsylvania. Clemens gave Langdon and Ford letters to at least two San Franciscans, George E. Barnes and Mathew B. Cox. And either at Clemens's request or Cox's, Richard B. Irwin, an agent for the Pacific Mail Steamship Company in San Francisco, assisted the travelers (21 Sept 69 to Barnes; 24 Sept 69 to Cox; 8 July 70 to OLC, CU-MARK, in *LLMT*, 154; Sobel and Raimo, 3:1085–86; *BDUSC*, 732; Langley 1869, 329).

[4] Colfax and his first wife, Evelyn Clark, whom he married in 1844, had gone to Washington, D.C., in 1855, when he began his initial term in the House of Representatives as a Republican from Indiana. Evelyn Colfax, an invalid for several years before her death in 1863, had received treatment at the Elmira Water Cure, a health resort on East Hill, not far from the Langdon home. Nothing is known of the Langdons' association with her there or in Washington. Colfax had been married to his second wife, Ellen W. Wade, niece of Benjamin F. Wade, former Republican senator from Ohio, for almost a year (Hollister, 208, 210; Jerome and Wisbey, 36, 116; Boyd and Boyd, 114).

[5] Colfax, an admirer of Clemens's work at least since early 1868, provided the requested introduction (see *L2*, 155, and 10 or 11 Dec 69 to Colfax). Langdon and Ford had left by rail for California on 4 October, planning, according to Olivia Langdon, to visit "Salt Lake City, and other places of interest. (silver mines &c) on the way." They sailed from San Francisco for Japan on 4 November aboard the Pacific Mail Steamship Company's *America*, and then were to proceed "through China and India, visiting Palestine, then into Egypt, going up the Nile. They will spend the hottest months of next Summer in the Northern countries of Europe—Russia, Germany, England, Scotland &c.—From there to France, Switzerland and Italy in the Fall—they expect to be gone from a year to eighteen months" (OLL to Alice Hooker Day, 1 Nov 69, CtHSD; "Passengers for China and Japan," San Francisco *Morning Call*, 5 Nov 69, 2).

To the California Pioneers
11 October 1869 • Elmira, N.Y.
(New York *Tribune*, 14 Oct 69)

ELMIRA, Oct. 11, 1869.

To the California Pioneers.[1]

GENTLEMEN: Circumstances render it out of my power to take advantage of the invitation extended to me through Mr. Simonton, & be present at your dinner in New York.[2] I regret this very much, for there are several among you whom I would have a right to join hands with on the score of old friendship,[3] & I suppose I would have a sublime general right to shake hands with the rest of you on the score of kinship in Californian ups & downs in search of fortune. If I were to tell some of my experiences, you would recognize Californian blood in me, I fancy. The old, old story would sound familiar, no doubt. I have the usual stock of reminiscences. For instance: I went to Esmeralda early. I purchased largely in the "Wide West," the "Winnemucca," & other fine claims, & was very wealthy.[4] I fared sumptuously on bread when flour was $200 a barrel, & had beans every Sunday when none but bloated aristocrats could afford such grandeur. But I finished by feeding batteries in a quartz-mill at $15 a week, & wishing I was a battery myself & had somebody to feed *me.*[5] My claims in Esmeralda are there yet. I suppose I could be persuaded to sell. I went to the Humboldt District when it was new. I became largely interested in the "Alba Nueva," & other claims with gorgeous names, & was rich again—in prospect. I owned a vast mining property there. I would not have sold out for less than $400,000, at that time—but I will now. Finally I walked home—some 200 miles—partly for exercise & partly because stage fares were expensive.[6] Next I entered upon an affluent career in Virginia City, & by a judicious investment of labor & the capital of friends, became the owner of about all the worthless wildcat mines there were in that part of the country. Assessments did the business for me there. There were 117 assessments to one dividend, & the proportion of income to outlay was a little against me. My financial thermometer went down to 32 Farenheit, & the subscriber was frozen out. I took up extension[s] on the main lead—extensions that reached to British America in one direction & to the Isthmus of Panama in the other—& I verily believe I would have been a rich man if I had ever found those infernal extensions. But I did n't. I ran tunnels till I tapped the Arctic Ocean, & I sunk shafts till I broke through the roof of perdition, but those extensions turned up missing every time. I am willing to sell all that property, & throw in the improvements. Perhaps you remember the celebrated "North Ophir?" I bought that mine. It was very rich in pure silver. You could take it out in lumps as large as a filbert. But when it was discovered that those lumps were melted half-dollars, & hardly melted at that, a painful case of "saltin" was apparent, & the undersigned adjourned to the poor-house again.[7] I paid assessments on "Hale & Norcross" till they sold me out, & I had to take in washing for a living—& the next month that infamous stock went up to $7,000 a foot.[8] I own millions & millions of feet of affluent silver leads in Nevada—in fact I own the entire undercrust of that country, nearly, & if Congress would move that State off my property so that I could get at it, I would be wealthy yet. But no, there she squats—& here am I. Failing health persuades me to sell. If you know of any one desiring a permanent investment, I can furnish him one that will have the virtue of being eternal.

I have been through the Californian mill, with all its "dips, spurs, & angles, variations, & sinuosities."[9] I have worked there at all the different trades & professions known to the catalogue. I have been everything, from a newspaper editor[10] down to cowcatcher on a locomotive, & I am encouraged to believe that if there had been a few more occupations to experiment on, I might have made a dazzling success at last, & found out what mysterious design Providence had in view in creating me.

But you perceive that although I am not a pioneer, I have had a sufficiently variegated time of it to enable me to talk pioneer like a native, & feel like a Forty-Niner. Therefore, I cordially welcome you to your old remembered homes & your long-deserted firesides, & close this screed with the sincere hope that your visit here will be a happy one, & unembittered by the sorrowful surprises that absence & lapse of years are wont to prepare for wanderers; surprises which come in the form of old friends missed from their places; silence where familiar voices should be; the young grown old; change & decay everywhere; home a delusion

& a disappointment; strangers at the hearth-stone; sorrow where gladness was; tears for laughter; the melancholy pomp of death where the
grace of life had been!

With all good wishes for the Returned Prodigals, & regrets that I
cannot partake of a small piece of the fatted calf (rare & no gravy),[11] I am,
yours cordially,

Mark Twain.

[1]Approximately two hundred members of the Society of California Pioneers
(individuals who emigrated to California before the end of 1849) arrived in New
York City by overland railway on 23 September, having departed Sacramento
one week before ("Home Again," New York *Times*, 23 Sept 69, 2). On 22 September and again on 27 September, Clemens had reported on their trip in his
"People and Things" column in the Buffalo *Express:* "The California Pioneers
are on their way to the Atlantic States"; "The Pioneers have arrived in New
York" (SLC 1869z, 1869bb). And he published the following item in the *Express*
on 29 September:

THE CALIFORNIA PIONEERS.

These gentlemen, being an association of persons who went to California with the first
gold excitement, hold an anniversary meeting on each 9th of September, and over their
champagne recount the stirring deeds of the "Early days." Apropos of the excursion party
of a hundred of them, which reached New York overland, a day or two ago, we drop in this
gently sarcastic paragraph from the *Overland Monthly:*
  One can not but admire, on the whole, the heroic manner in which the Society of California Pioneers grapple with the Past, Present and Future of the State annually on the
ninth day of September. The prospect of yearly going over the same field of retrospect—
not in itself very wide or very long—would, we think, deter any but really very courageous
or very self devoted men from the task. This year they got through it very creditably, with
the usual prophecy of a brilliant future, and the usual bland indorsement of every thing
and every body connected with the State.
  Of course these anniversaries are stimulating to patriotism and local pride; but we have
yet to learn that California patriotism and local pride require any stimulating, and are
doubtful whether a Society for the Suppression of Local Pride would not, on the whole,
be more truly beneficial to a State whose natives think nothing of seriously asking strangers
"if this is not the most wonderful country on the globe?"—and who write indignant and
provincial letters to the newspapers when lecturers do not flatter them. And we confess to
indulging in a fond and foolish dream of the future—based not so much upon the Pioneers'
oration as upon the Pioneers' projected excursion over the Pacific Railroad to their old
Eastern homes—when California Pioneers shall be able to see that the world has not stood
still, outside of California, for the last twenty years; that there are cities as large as San
Francisco much more cleanly in aspect and tasteful in exterior; that there are communities
as young as ours in which there is a greater proportion of public spirited and generous men,
and public spirited and generous works; that there are cities of half our wealth that, boast-
ing less and doing more, would be ashamed to keep their public library for twelve months
before the world in the attitude of bankruptcy, and that there are countries less self-
heralded for their generosity and charity that would not dare to invite immigration to their
doors without a public hospital to take care of their sick and suffering. (SLC 1869dd)

The *two* "gently sarcastic" paragraphs, by Bret Harte, had appeared in the *Overland Monthly* for October 1869 (Harte 1869b, 383; Thomas, 1:114, 143–44).

[2] On the evening of 13 October about one-fourth of the party of pioneers attended an elaborate banquet, at Lorenzo Delmonico's restaurant at Fifth Avenue and Fourteenth Street, given by some seventy to one hundred New York residents formerly of California. James William Simonton (1823–82), who read Clemens's letter at the banquet, had become a proprietor of the New York *Times* soon after its founding in 1851 and then served as its Washington correspondent until he went to California, where in 1859 he became a co-owner of the San Francisco *Evening Bulletin*. In 1867, while retaining his interest in the *Bulletin*, he returned to New York to become general agent of the Associated Press, a position he held for fourteen years. Late in 1869 Simonton also became a co-owner of the San Francisco *Morning Call* ("The California Pioneers," New York *Times*, 14 Oct 69, 7; "The California Pioneers," New York *Tribune*, 14 Oct 69, 5; Lloyd Morris, 28; Gody, Harvey, and Reed, 200, 206; Mott 1950, 278; "General Telegraphic News," New York *Tribune*, 7 Dec 69, 7).

[3] Clemens had probably seen the New York *Times* article of 23 September that identified the excursionists ("Home Again," 2), including at least four whom he knew personally: Sacramento lawyer James W. Coffroth and, from San Francisco, undertaker Atkins Massey, physician Stephen R. Harris, and policeman Henry H. Ellis (*L1*, 313; *CofC*, 234, 273; Branch 1959, 143).

[4] The celebrated Wide West and Winnemucca mines were located in the Esmeralda mining district, an area claimed by both Esmeralda County, Nevada Territory, and Mono County, California, when Clemens was there in September 1861 and then from April to September 1862. He and his brother Orion purchased feet nominally worth $5,000 in at least thirty different ledges in the region, including an extension of the Winnemucca. There is no record of his having "purchased largely," if at all, in the Wide West. Ultimately, the fabulous riches he anticipated from his Esmeralda claims eluded him (*L1*, 187 n. 2, 217 nn. 2, 3; mining deeds in CU-MARK; Branch 1985).

[5] For a week in June 1862, Clemens worked at Clayton's Mill, near Aurora, in the Esmeralda district, in hopes of learning the process for reducing silver ore developed by its proprietor, Joshua E. Clayton. In chapter 36 of *Roughing It*, he described the "tedious and laborious" routine of the mill (*L1*, 188 n. 9, 193, 216, 219, 225).

[6] Clemens explored the mining area of Humboldt County, Nevada Territory, in the winter of 1861–62. He and Orion eventually owned feet in at least fifteen mining claims there, including the Alba Nueva. For his accounts of his Humboldt experiences, which did not include a walk "home" to Carson City, see his letter of 30 January 1862 to his mother (*L1*, 146–52) and chapters 27–33 of *Roughing It* (*L1*, 167 n. 2, 190, 191 n. 5; mining deeds in CU-MARK).

[7] Clemens alluded to this incident of "salting" in a letter to the Chicago *Republican* in May 1868 (SLC 1868h). Four years later he told about it again in chapter 44 of *Roughing It*. There is no record that he actually purchased an interest in the North Ophir, which was near Virginia City, but in July 1863 he received five feet in that mine, evidently in exchange for "puffing" it in the Virginia City *Territorial Enterprise* (*L1*, 260).

[8] The Hale and Norcross Silver Mining Company frequently assessed its shareholders in order to raise capital to work its claim near Virginia City. In the mid-1860s Clemens had difficulty meeting assessments of $25, and sometimes

$50, per share every two months: in October 1864 four shares he had put in his brother's name were advertised as delinquent before he managed to pay the assessed $100 himself, and in May 1865 two shares in his own name evidently were auctioned to pay off a delinquent $50. Nevertheless, he may have realized something from his Hale and Norcross investment, for when he left San Francisco temporarily in December 1864 he had $300 that possibly came from sale of that stock. And in May 1868 he told the Chicago *Republican:* "Hale & Norcross, whereof I sold six feet at three hundred dollars a foot, is worth two thousand, now, and was up to seven thousand during the winter" (SLC 1868h; *L1*, 300–301 n. 4, 309 n. 5, 316 n. 5, 319 n. 5, 320).

[9]The formulaic language used in recording a mining claim (see *Roughing It*, chapter 29), and also in deeds to claims.

[10]Clemens was local reporter, or editor, of the San Francisco *Morning Call* from June to October 1864 (*CofC*, 1–2).

[11]The Prodigal Son "took his journey into a far country, and there wasted his substance with riotous living," but returned to his father's house, where he was forgiven and was fed on "the fatted calf" (Luke 15:11–32).

To Emily A. Severance
27 October 1869 • Elmira, N.Y.
(MS: OClWhi)

Elmira, Oct 27.

Dear Mrs Severance—

I thank you most kindly for your good words & your friendly regard, & shall do all I can to honor them. I am glad you like the book, & not in the least surprised that you find things in it that should have been left out—I can find such myself without the least trouble—& you will believe me when I say they grieve me indeed. I find there are more of them than I thought there were. The book fairly bristled with them at first, & it ẃ is well I weeded it as much as I did. But for you & Mrs. Fairbanks it would have been a very sorry affair. I shall always remember both of you gratefully for the training you gave me in—you in your mild, persuasive way, & she in her efficient tyrannical, overbearing fashion.

I expected to be in Cleveland tomorrow on my way to Pittsburgh, but find I shall have to take another route.[1]

We shall expect you & Solon, & the Fairbanks household, to drop be at our wedding in February, without fail—so you must stand by to drop everything at the tap of the gong, & start.

No, Charley isn't dodging his engagement—he & Ida are to be married as soon as he gets back. It is all arranged, & all parties are happy & satisfied.[2]

With loving regards to you & Solon, I am as always,

Yr friend

Sam[l]. L. Clemens.

Mrs Langdon & Livy ask to be remembered.

[1]Clemens's travel plans were affected by a derailment on the evening of 26 October:

As the Fast Express train coming West, (No. 1,) on the Erie Railway, was running at the rate of thirty-five miles an hour, it encountered a broken rail when going around a curve in the road about a mile east of Susquehanna, and all the five passenger cars (including the Palace Car,) together with one baggage car, were thrown from the track. No one was seriously hurt. . . . All the five passenger coaches were crowded with passengers, and it is a miracle that many of them were not seriously injured. The rail which caused the accident was broken in five pieces. ("Railroad Accident," Elmira *Advertiser*, 27 Oct 69, 1)

The break in the track, about 65 miles east of Elmira, may have prevented the timely arrival of the train Clemens had been expecting to take west to Cleveland. In his 19 November letter to Mrs. Fairbanks, he ascribed his failure to visit her to "distress about those Railways."

[2]Charles J. Langdon married Ida Clark on 12 October 1870, three and a half months after the premature end of his world tour.

To Olivia L. Langdon
30, 31 October, and 1 November 1869 • Pittsburgh, Pa.
(MS: CU-MARK)

II. P.M.

Pittsburgh Oct. 30

Diary[1]

Livy Darling—

~~We~~ I have just this moment returned & gone to bed.

We had a pleasant time of it. They came for me at 7.30, & we went to a private room in a restaurant & had an oyster supper in a quiet, comfortable, sensible way—no wine, no toasts, no speeches—nothing but conversation. (Though it *was* appalling to have 30 newspaper men lay down their napkins with the last course & gather their chairs together in front of me, a *silence* following—for that silence naturally had the effect of suggesting that I was expected to do the talking—a thing which was not meant at all. Still, it was a little startling.)[2]

During the evening, a dry, sensible genius, a Mr. Smythe, told his experiences as a lecturer. He said:

"A year ago, I was ass enough to go to Europe. When I came back I was ass enough to think I was stocked with knowledge about Europe that the public would like to hear. I expected they would be calling on me for a lecture, & so hurried to get ready. I wrote my lecture in the third story of a printing office in the intervals between calls for "copy," & I judged it was a pretty creditable effort. I said to myself, I can do this sort of thing just as well as Mark Twain did—& if I had his house to hear me, I could show them. Then I waited for the flood—the freshet of calls from the lyceums. It was a good opportunity to wait—a singularly good one—it never has ceased to be,,—to I am still waiting. I did not get any calls. I could not understand it. But I knew the people were suffering for the lecture, & so I quit bothering about calls, & went & took the Academy on my own hook. At the appointed time I was on hand, & so were eleven other people. At half past 8, observing that the rush had ceased & that the audience were unquestionably assembled, I stepped on to the stage with my MSS, & for an hour & a half I instructed those 11 people. I was "out" $75 on the experiment. A friend met me a day or two afterward & said he had heard I had been out lecturing. I said Yes, I was out yet,.

I waited again for calls. They did not come. I then cast my eye upon East Liberty, a suburb of Pittsburgh. I knew they were aching to have me there but dare n't invite me. And so I went *there* on my own hook. I paid $35 for the use of the theatre. At half past 7 I took a retired stand opposite & watched. At 8 or a little after, the first great wave of relief se swept over my soul—I saw a man enter the hall. I went into a saloon & drank to him. Bye & bye I saw two men go in at once. I took a drink to them. After a little a carriage drove up & the estimable Mrs. Swisshelm, of whom you may have heard, went in.[3] I drank to her. At 8.30, nobody else having come, I drank to the absent.

Then I went over & read my MSS. drearily, & was absolutely happy, even cheerful, once—when I got through.

Then I rested for a while & at length determined to go up to Steubenville, O., & give those people a taste of my quality. When I got there

I looked wistfully about the street corners for my posters, but I did not see any. I hunted up the bill poster, & he explained ~~he~~ that it had been rainy, & he had refrained from posting the bills because they would not stick. I went to the village newspaper man who had been advertising me, & he encouraged me to believe there would be a slim attendance. He was a man of very good judgment. At 8.30 nobody had come, & for the sake of economy I discharged the doorkeeper, & went off with the journalist to take a drink. I could not get rid of him, somehow—on account of one of us being in the other's ~~dist~~ debt, ~~pe~~ I thought. At 9 we went back & found one man in the house. I felt a little cheered, for this was nearly as large an audience as I had ever had. I began my lecture, but when I was half through a thought occurred to me & I asked that man who he was. He said he was the janitor. "Then I suppose you do not pay?"

"No."

So I closed the lecture at that point.

Subsequently I received my first invitation. This began to look like business. It was to go to Greensburg & lecture for the benefit of the Methodist Mite Society—$25 & expenses.[4] I went with a light heart. Some newspaper friends volunteered to go with me—& they are a class of people who are given to drink. They were companionable, but expensive.

We arrived in a rain storm—& very dark. The Rev. Mr. Noble received me in considerable state & walked me to the Court House. At 8.30 an audience of nearly 13 persons had assembled—it seemed a sort of ovation—I was not accustomed to these multitudinous manifestations of popular favor. The Rev. Noble introduced me in a right pretty speech, & then I delivered my lecture. It was complimented a good deal, & the Rev. Noble was so kind as to say they might want me again in case the Society survived this ordeal. The Secretary then came forward & said there had not been as large an attendance as he had hoped for & so the finances were correspondingly ~~$~~ meagre, but if five dollars would be any object to me, ~~the~~ a draft for that amount——

I begged him to let the whole sum go into the coffers of the Mite Society, & I hope[d] that in its sudden acquisition of wealth it would not grow proud, but would sometimes think of its benefactor.

Since then I have thought seriously of forsaking the lecture field, & will remark that my lecture, unmutilated, & with all the places for applause legibly marked in it, is for sale."[5]

Pittsburgh, Oct. 31.

I walked all around town this morning with a young Mr. Dean, a cousin of Wm D. Howells, editor of the *Atlantic Monthly*. He kindly offered to give me a letter of introduction to Mr. Howells, but I thanked him sincerely & declined, saying I had a sort of delicacy about using letters of introduction, ~~not~~ simply because the[y] place the other party in the position of being obliged to take the stranger by the hand whether or no & show him civilities which he may not feel like showing him, or at least may not feel like it at that particular time. He may have engagements—business—the headache—twenty circumstances may conspire to make the entertainment of a guest a hardship. I prefer to be casually introduced, or to call ceremoniously with a friend—then the afflicted party is perfectly free to treat me precisely as he chooses, & no harm done.[6]

———

Many gentlemen have called on me to-day. Mr. E. B. Coolidge, formerly of the Navy—met him once when I was visiting Admiral Thatcher ~~in San Francisco, on~~ on board his flagship, at San Francisco. W. A. Taylor, of the *Post;* Asa L. Waugaman (~~ke~~ knew him in Nevada); A H Lane, Jno. G. Holmes, W^m. L. Chalfant, W^m. C. Smythe of the *Dispatch;* W. W. Thompson; W^m. N. Howard; Geo. W. Dean; O. T. Bennett of the *Commercial;* & ~~ten or more~~ a number of gentlemen ~~whose~~ came with one or another of the above & sent no cards.[7] So they have dropped in one after another all day long & have made the time busy & pleasant. I am to go to church to-night with Mr. Chalfant.

Waugaman made me go to his house to see his wife,. ~~I st~~ I knew her in Nevada, too. I staid 15 minutes, & would have remained to supper, for the table looked tempting, but their young boy of 7 is one of your petted smarties whose entire mind is given to climbing around & getting where he can intercept your vision & attract your attention—industriously watching your eye & changing position so as to intercept it again if you change the direction of your glance—a child with a feverish desire to do something surprising & win the notice of the stranger—a creature that parades its toys & asks its mother questions concerning them which it is plain are merely asked to compel the stranger's attention to them & gouge a remark out of him—a soiled & ~~stubb~~ nasty imp that sings nursery stuff in ~~the~~ a loud & still louder & louder key as the conversation rises to meet the emergency, & does it all to win coveted admiration—a small ~~wit~~ ˯whelp˯ that says those ineffably ~~stupid~~ flat things which mothers treasure up & repeat, & regard as "smart" things, purring & smiling blandly the while—a little pug-nosed, mop-headed, sore-toed, candy= smeared beast that paws after things at table, & spills its coffee, & eats mashed potatoes with its fingers, & points & clamors for "some of that"—a sinful, tiresome, homely, ~~ha~~ hateful, execrable NUISANCE at all times & in all places whatsoever!

I may be a brute. Doubtless I am. But such is my opinion of this breed of children, nevertheless. The "four-year-old" department of Harper's Monthly is written in vain for *me*.[8]

Well, Livy dear, I was afraid that brat would be at supper—mothers who rear such prodigies always like to have them on exhibition—& so I first started to *ask*, & then, recognizing that that would not be strictly polite, I simply declined supp & returned to the hotel.

———————

One of the newspaper gentlemen who called today was Mr. Bennett of the *Commercial*, a good fellow, modest & pleasant. He wants to make a synopsis of my lecture to-morrow night, or report it in full. I told him a synopsis of a humorous lecture holds up all the jokes, in a crippled condition for the world to remember & so remembering them hate them if ever they hear that lecturer repeat them in solemn & excruciating succession one after the other.

And I said to take the points out of a humorous lecture was the same as taking the raisins out of a fruit cake—it left it but a *pretense* of a something it was *not*, for such as came after.

And further, the charm of a humorous remark or still more, an elaborate succession of humorous remarks, *cannot* be put upon paper—& whosoever reports a humorous lecture *verbatim*, & necessarily leaves the *soul* out of it, & no more presents that lecture to the reader than ~~does a man bring a woman's husband to her~~ a person presents a *man* to you when he ships you a corpse.

I said synopses injure—they do harm, because they ȼ travel ahead of the lecturer & give people a despicable opinion of him & his production.

I said my lecture was my property, & no man had a right to take it from me & print it, any more than he would have a right to take away any other property of mine. I said "I showed you what time it was by my watch a while ago, & it never occurred to me that you might pull the hands off it so that it would be only a stupid blank to the next man that wanted the time—but yet I see you meditate pulling the hands off my lecture with your synopsis & making it a blank to future audiences. You see me sitting here perfectly serene although I know you could walk off with my valise while I am talking with these other gentlemen—but won't steal my valise because it is property—my property. Now *do* take the valise & let the lecture alone. I own both of them—I *alone.* P̶ Take the valise—it is only worth a hundred dollars—the lecture is worth ten thousand."

This was all perfectly friendly & good-natured, of course. I was trying to show ~~how~~ him how in the wrong he was—I had no desire to offend him, & I didn't.

But Livy if his chief orders him to report the lecture he can't help himself[9]—for although the law protects rigidly the property a shoemaker contrives with his hands, it will not protect the property I create with my brain.[10]

———

I went to church & heard a man from a distance preach, a sermon without notes—which was well—but in a frozen, monotonous, precise & inflectionless way that showed that his discoursed was a carefully memorized production. There was something exceedingly funny about this bald pretense of delivering an off-hand speech—& something exceedingly funny, too in a full-grown man "speaking a piece" after the manner of a little schoolboy. His gestures were timid—never could finish one—always got scared & left it half made. He evidently had the places marked, & knew how he wanted to make them, but he didn't dare.

Oh, the music was royal! It was superb! It was the very ecstasy of harmony! With the first grand explosion of rich sounds, I started from my reverie & thought, Heavens! What a choir we've got here! And I looked up, & there were only 4 singers! But how their voices did match,—~~& blend—& wind in & out,~~ ‚& blend together—‚ & how they did peal out at times—& then languish & die—& then swell upward ‚again‚ & reel away ~~drun~~ through the charmed atmosphere in a drunken ecstasy of melody!

My! what a soprano singer! When I thought the very hair would stand up straight with delight, & looked again & wondered if that grand flood of mellow sound *did* issue from so small a constitution—& how it could come with such utter absence of effort.

And when they sang "O'er the Dark Waves of Galilee" I didn't feel as if I *could* sit still. What worship was in the music! ~~And h~~ How it preached, how it pleaded! And how earthy & merely human seemed the clergyman's poor vapid declamation! *He* couldn't make us comprehend Christ desolate & forsaken, but the music did.[11]

Oh, wouldn't Hattie Lewis have stood on her head if she had been there! Livy I never heard anything like it in all my life.

And do you know there are some people whose complacency *nothing* can subdue. In the midst of the beautiful music a skinny old cat sitting next me tuned her pipe & began to yowl. Well I came as near as anything to banging her over the head with a pew. Now *was* there ever such effrontery as that woman's.

The second tune was a little too complicated for her & I had a rest. On the third, I waited in pure torture all through the first verse, & felt ~~re~~ happy, satisfied, safe—but on the second the venerable screech-owl came to the rescue again & filed her saw all through the hymn.

The young man who went with me got tired of the sermon early. He evidently was not used to going to church, though he talked as if he was. Toward the last he got ~~his~~ himself down till he was resting on the end of his backbone; & then he propped his 2 knees high against the pew in front of him; he stroked his thighs reflectively with his palms; he yawned; he started twice to stretch, ‚but‚ cut it short & looked dejected & regretful; ~~in~~ he looked at his watch 3 times; & at last he got to belching.* I then threw him out of the window. [1 PM.[12] Good night & God bless & preserve you, my own darling.]

Sam.

*'Tisn't elegant, but there isn't any other, Livy.

✉️——————————————————————————

[*in ink:*] Miss Olivia L. Langdon | Elmira | N. Y. [*postmarked:*] PITTS-BURGH PA. NOV 1 [*and*] PHILADA. P.O. RECEIVED NOV 2   10 AM [*docketed by* OLL:] ~~128~~ 128th

[1] Evidently Clemens considered writing his lecture tour letters to Olivia in the form of a diary. Of the sixteen letters to her that survive from the last nine weeks of 1869, he in fact wrote eight in his notebook, but never attempted to preserve

them as a unit, instead tearing each out upon completion for immediate mailing. The present letter is the first of the eight. The others are his letters of 10 November, 10 and 11 November, 15 and 16 November, 14 December, 15 and 16 December, 18 and 19 December, and 27 December. Clemens also wrote his letters of 15 December to Jane Lampton Clemens and family and 17 December to Pamela A. Moffett on notebook pages. The notebook itself does not survive.

[2] Clemens arrived in Pittsburgh on the afternoon of Saturday, 30 October. That evening he was the guest of honor at a banquet, at "McGinley's dining saloon, on Wood street," hosted by the lecture committee of the Mercantile Library Association, whose annual course of lectures he opened at the Academy of Music on 1 November. In addition to the committee, the dinner was attended by a few other members of the association and by representatives of the city press. "The occasion was marked by a total absence of formality and stiffness. . . . Mr. Clemens made two or three dozen warm personal friends during the evening; friends who will long remember pleasantly the two hours spent in his quaint, genial society" ("Sociability with Mark Twain," Pittsburgh *Evening Chronicle*, 1 Nov 69, 3).

[3] Jane Grey Cannon Swisshelm (1815–84), the journalist, antislavery reformer, and women's rights advocate. In 1847 she founded the Pittsburgh *Saturday Visiter*, a political weekly that she edited for ten years, producing the caustic editorials denouncing slavery that made the paper one of the best known of the abolitionist journals.

[4] The object of a "mite society" was to collect funds for charitable purposes (Mathews, 2:1066). The term alludes to the widow's "two mites, which make a farthing" of Mark 12:42–44—a small contribution willingly given and all that the giver could afford. Greensburg was about twenty-five miles southeast of Pittsburgh.

[5] This tale of frustrated ambition, told by William C. Smythe of the Pittsburgh *Dispatch*, was noted by a reporter for the Pittsburgh *Commercial*—undoubtedly Oliver T. Bennett (both men were among the callers Clemens mentions later in this letter)—who remarked that after the meal "an hour was spent in social conversation. Mr. Clemens gave a humorous account of his railway experience in coming to Pittsburgh, and also gave an interesting and humorous description of his first lecture in San Francisco. A member of the press who was present related his experience as a lecturer, and although his efforts had not been so successful as Mark Twain's, his account of the difficulties he encountered was an excellent one" ("Compliment to Mark Twain—The Lecture To-night," 1 Nov 69, 4).

[6] Clemens's guide was George W. Dean, Pittsburgh agent of the Enterprise Insurance Company of Philadelphia. His father, William, a former Ohio River steamboat pilot and now the general agent and a director of the Allegheny Insurance Company of Pittsburgh, was William Dean Howells's maternal uncle. Clemens soon managed his own introduction to Howells (1837–1920), who since 1866 had been assistant to *Atlantic Monthly* editor James T. Fields and was in charge of the magazine's "Reviews and Literary Notices." In reviewing *The Innocents Abroad* at length in the December 1869 issue (published by mid-November), Howells praised Clemens's "good-humored humor" and "ironical drollery" and pronounced him worthy of "something better than the uncertain standing of a popular favorite" (Howells 1869, 765, 766). Pleased, Clemens paid a visit to the *Atlantic* editorial office at 124 Tremont Street, Boston, later in No-

vember or in December, to express his appreciation to Fields—whereupon he met the review's author (Cushing, 559–60; Thurston 1869, 121, 143, 26 [back advertising section]; Gould, 633–37; Anderson, Gibson, and Smith, 430; Howells 1910, 3; *MTHL*, 1:6).

[7]Clemens must have met E. B. Coolidge, now working as a clerk in Pittsburgh, in May or June 1868, the only time they and Rear Admiral Henry Knox Thatcher (1806–80), commander of the North Pacific Squadron, were all in San Francisco together. The San Francisco directory for 1868–69 lists Coolidge, but does not confirm a connection with the United States Navy or otherwise identify his occupation. No details of Clemens's meeting with Thatcher aboard his flagship *Pensacola* have been found. Asa Lobeus Waugaman (b. 1830 or 1831), a native of Pennsylvania and now owner of a saloon, name undetermined, at 44 Smithfield Street in Pittsburgh, had been one of the proprietors of the El Dorado Saloon and Chop House in Virginia City from 1862 (possibly earlier) until no later than November 1866, by which time he was operating Asa's, a San Francisco saloon. Of Clemens's other callers, four were members of the Pittsburgh Mercantile Library Association's lecture committee: Augustus H. Lane (d. 1896), a partner in B. Wolff, Jr., and Company, a hardware firm; John Grier Holmes (1849–1904), who in 1869 joined his family's banking house, N. Holmes and Sons; William Lusk Chalfant (1843–95), a lawyer; and William Neill Howard (b. 1834), the chairman of the lecture committee, who was connected with local manufacturing and mining firms. The remaining visitors were editor William A. Taylor of the Pittsburgh *Post*, attorney William W. Thomson (d. 1899), and reporters William C. Smythe, of the Pittsburgh *Dispatch*, and Oliver T. Bennett, of the Pittsburgh *Commercial* (Langley 1868, 154; San Francisco City and County, s.v. "Wangaman [i.e., Waugaman], Asa Lobeus"; Thurston 1869, 59, 106, 254, 433, 467, 511, 63 [back advertising section]; Thurston 1870, 437, 458, 480; *Bench and Bar*, 2:883, 901–2; *Encyclopedia of Pennsylvania*, 1:427–29; San Francisco *Alta California*: "Visiting the 'Pensacola,'" 5 May 68, 1; "Gone North," 25 June 68, 1; Virginia City *Territorial Enterprise*: "El Dorado Saloon . . . ," 10 Jan 63, 4; "Local Matters," 24 Nov 66, 3; "Asa's," 24 Nov 66, 2; Pittsburgh *Post*: "Academy of Music," 30 Oct 69, 4; Pittsburgh *Gazette*: "Death Notices," 24 Jan 96, 5).

[8]The "Editor's Drawer" of *Harper's New Monthly Magazine* often printed the "smart" comments of children. Clemens's impatience with the Waugamans' son recalls his similar irritation at the home of Henry Clay Trumbull (see 15 May 69 to OLL [1st of 2]).

[9]Bennett contented himself, and presumably his "chief," with a two-sentence summary of "Our Fellow Savages of the Sandwich Islands," preceded by a paraphrase of Clemens's opening remarks:

> Mr. Howard, Chairman of the Lecture Committee, introduced Mr. Clemens, who said he could not recommend the lecture he was going to deliver, because he was not familiar with it himself. He had delivered it before the pupils of a deaf and dumb asylum and they said it was as good a lecture as they ever heard; he had also delivered it before the inmates of an insane asylum, and they were enthusiastic; he had also experimented a little with it on a sick man and it was very successful—poor fellow he was gone now. Nothing could reconcile him to his approaching doom; but when the third portion of the lecture was being delivered he went off as smoothly and serenely as a bombshell. The subject of the lecture was then discussed at considerable length, the speaker alluding to the geographical position of the islands, and describing the habits of the people, the climate, and the volcanoes.

The lecture was intersper[s]ed with humorous passages that kept the audience in the best humor, and they appeared highly entertained, and also had an opportunity of acquiring a great deal of valuable information. ("The Lecture Season," Pittsburgh *Commercial*, 2 Nov 69, 4)

The Pittsburgh *Gazette*, seconding reports by Bennett and the Pittsburgh *Post*, noted that Clemens attracted to the Academy of Music "the very largest audience we have ever seen assembled to greet a lecturer." When all twenty-five hundred seats were occupied, additional chairs were placed on stage for the lecture committee and the local press, while another five hundred spectators had to stand during the performance. The *Gazette* deemed it "an able and brilliant effort in keeping with the high reputation of its author. There were just enough fun-provoking passages introduced to lighten up the burdensome task of properly describing a region about which most people think little and care much less." And the Pittsburgh *Evening Chronicle* commented: "Perhaps the lecture was not so thoroughly delightful as that on the 'American Vandal,' but it was very delightful, notwithstanding. . . . Rarely has the closest student of geography or ethnology obtained so much information so delightfully about the Hawai[i]ans and their homes as last night. The lecture had one grave fault—it was not long enough" ("Mark Twain Last Night," Pittsburgh *Gazette*, 2 Nov 69, 4; "Academy of Music—Mark Twain's Lecture," Pittsburgh *Post*, 2 Nov 69, 1; "The Lecture Season," Pittsburgh *Evening Chronicle*, 2 Nov 69, 3). The $120 that Clemens received in Pittsburgh was, as far as can be determined from the partial records that survive, the highest fee of his 1869–70 tour. Usually he received either $75 or $100 (Erasmus Wilson, 886; George L. Fall to SLC, 27 Oct 69, 7 Dec 69, James Redpath Letterpress Book, 26, 632, IaU).

[10] The copyright law of 1831, still in effect in 1869, permitted a twenty-eight-year copyright with renewal for an additional fourteen years. Throughout his career, Clemens protested the inadequacy of such protection, sometimes in language that echoed his present complaint to Olivia. For example, in an interview with New York *Times* reporter Robert Donald in December 1889, he remarked: "Every one ought to get value for his labor, whether he makes boots or manuscripts" (Donald). And on 7 December 1906, testifying before the joint Congressional Committee on Patents, which was considering new copyright legislation, he argued that a book, although consisting "solely of ideas, from the base to the summit," was "like any other property, and should not be put under the ban of any restriction." Rather, it was the possession of its author and his heirs "forever and ever, just as a butcher shop would be, or—I don't care—anything, I don't care what it is. It all has the same basis. The law should recognize the right of perpetuity in this and every other kind of property" (SLC 1906, 119).

[11] "O'er the Dark Wave of Galilee" was by William Russell (1798–1873), a Glasgow-born educator who settled in the United States in 1817 (Julian, 982). Set to the long-meter tune "Warner," it was included in the *Plymouth Collection of Hymns and Tunes*, familiar to Clemens and probably used by Olivia and her family:

> O'er the dark wave of Galilee
> The gloom of twilight gathers fast,
> And on the waters drearily
> Descends the fitful evening blast.
> The weary bird hath left the air,
> And sunk into his sheltered nest;

The wandering beast has sought his lair,
   And laid him down to welcome rest.
Still near the lake, with weary tread,
   Lingers a form of human kind;
And on His lone, unsheltered head,
   Flows the chill night-damp of the wind.
Why seeks He not a home of rest?
   Why seeks He not a pillowed bed?
Beasts have their dens, the bird its nest;
   He hath not where to lay His head.
Such was the lot He freely chose,
   To bless, to save the human race;
And through His poverty there flows
   A rich, full stream of heavenly grace.
       (Henry Ward Beecher 1864, 72)

[12] Actually 1 A.M. on Monday, 1 November.

NO LETTERS have been found for the week of 2–8 November. According to the itinerary that George L. Fall had sent Clemens on 27 October, his 1 November Pittsburgh lecture was to be followed the next day by a performance in Sharon, Pennsylvania, after which he was not to lecture again until 8 November, in Worcester, Massachusetts. On 28 October James Redpath had urged him to "stay at Elmira all the time between Sharon & Worcester" and on 1 November Redpath confirmed that "we have nothing between second and eighth" (Fall to SLC, 27 Oct 69; Redpath to SLC, 28 Oct 69, 1 Nov 69; all in Redpath Letterpress Book, 26, 51, 94, IaU). Nevertheless, a late substitution for Sharon and an addition may have been made, for the Pittsburgh *Gazette* of 2 November reported that Mark Twain "goes to Brookville [Pennsylvania] to-day and will stop at Johnstown [Pennsylvania] to lecture at the Opera House to-morrow evening. Great preparations are being made at both places to accord him that welcome he so richly deserves from an appreciative people" ("Mark Twain Last Night," 4). No confirmation of this report has been found, but Clemens's subsequent stop possibly was Hartford, on 4 or 5 November, in response to Elisha Bliss's bulletin about royalties from the first three months' sale of *The Innocents Abroad:* "We want to *pay up.* Shall we forward statement & check to you at Elmira or await your arrival here?" (Bliss to SLC, 1 Nov 69, CU-MARK). (Clemens's first royalty check, on sales of some 15,500 books, but reduced by an 1868 advance of $1,000 and by $250 for copies sent to reviewers, probably came to around

$1,845.) By the evening of Saturday, 6 November, Clemens was in Boston, attending the annual dinner of the Boston Press Club and accompanying his dinner companions to Selwyn's Theatre to see *Lady Audley's Secret*, a sensational melodrama based on Mary Elizabeth Braddon's popular novel (1862). Boston then remained his base throughout November, while he was lecturing in New England. His 8 November Worcester lecture appears to have been canceled, however. Local papers did not advertise or review it, and the 1869–70 season program of the Worcester Lyceum and Natural History Association did not include it (copy in CU-MARK, courtesy of Dennis Laurie, American Antiquarian Society, Worcester; Boston *Evening Transcript:* "Amusements," "Mark Twain . . . ," 6 Nov 69, 2; "Press Dinner," 8 Nov 69, 4; Boston *Evening Gazette:* "Saturday Notes," 7 Nov 69, 3, TS in CU-MARK; Hirst, 314; Hart 1950, 122).

To Pamela A. Moffett
· 9 November 1869 • Boston, Mass.
(*MTL*, 1:167–9, and Paine, 946)

Boston, Nov. 9, 1869.

My dear Sister:

Three or four letters just received from home. My first impulse was to send Orion a check on my publisher for the money he wants, but a sober second thought suggested that if he has not defrauded the government out of money, why pay, simply because the government chooses to consider him in its debt? No. Right is right. The idea don't suit me. Let him write the Treasury the state of the case, & tell them he has no money. *If* they make his sureties pay, *then* I will make the sureties whole, but I won't pay a cent of an unjust claim. You talk of disgrace. To my mind it would be just as disgraceful to allow one's self to be bullied into paying that which is unjust.[1]

Ma thinks it is hard that Orion's share of the land should be swept away just as it is right on the point (as it always *has* been) of becoming valuable. Let her rest easy on that point. This letter is his ample authority to sell *my* share of the land *immediately* & appropriate the proceeds—giving no account to *me*, but repaying the amount to Ma first, or in case of her death, to you or your heirs, whenever in the future he shall be able to do it. Now, I want no hesitation in this matter. I renounce my ownership from this date, *for this purpose*, provided it is sold just as suddenly as he can sell it.

In the next place—Mr. Langdon is old, & is trying hard to withdraw from business & seek repose. I will not burden him with a purchase—but I will ask him to take full possession of a coal tract of the land without paying a cent, simply conditioning that he shall mine & throw the coal into market at his own cost, & pay to you & all of you what he thinks is a fair portion of the profits accruing—you can do as you please with the rest of the land. Therefore, send me (to Elmira,) information about the coal deposits so framed that he can comprehend the matter & can intelligently instruct an agent how to find it & go to work.[2]

To-morrow night I appear for the first time before a Boston audience—4,000 critics—& on the success of this matter depends my future success in New England.[3] But I am not distressed. Nasby is in the same boat. To-night decides the fate of his brand-new lecture. He has just left my room—been reading his lecture to me—was greatly depressed. I have convinced him that he has little to fear.[4]

I get just about five hundred more applications to lecture than I can possibly fill—& in the West they say "Charge all you please, but *come*." I shan't go West at all. I stop lecturing the 22d of January, *sure*. But I shall talk every night up to that time. They flood me with high-priced invitations to write for magazines & papers, & publishers besiege me to write books. Can't do *any* of these things.

I am twenty-two thousand dollars in debt, & shall earn the money & pay it within two years—& therefore I am not spending any money except when it is *necessary*.[5]

I had my life insured for $10,000 yesterday (what ever became of Mr. Moffett's life insurance?) "for the benefit of my natural heirs"—the same being my mother, for Livy wouldn't claim it, you may be sure of that. This has taken $200 out of my pocket which I was going to send to Ma.[6] But I will send her some, soon. Tell Orion to keep a stiff upper lip—when the worst comes to the worst I will come forward. Must talk in

Providence, R. I., tonight. Must leave now. I thank Mollie & Orion & the rest for your letters, but you see how I am pushed—ought to have 6 clerks.

Affectionately,

Sam.

[1]Orion Clemens was being dunned by R. W. Taylor, comptroller of the United States Treasury Department. At issue were disbursements of government funds that Orion, as secretary of Nevada Territory, had made between 1 July 1863 and 31 October 1864 for the printing of the laws and documents of the territorial legislature. On 9 June 1869 Taylor wrote Orion two letters, demanding reimbursement totaling $1,330.08: $954.43 in disallowed payments to printers; and $375.65 for the "Balance due the United States per your last a/c" (CU-MARK). Taylor's letters did not reach Orion immediately because they were mistakenly sent to Carson City. Although he received them in St. Louis by August, he did not reply until 4 October. In his letter to Taylor that day, Orion reported that he was requesting the printers to "send me forthwith the money overpaid them." Doubtful that they would be able to do so, he respectfully protested that it was "rather severe to require me to refund to the United States out of my own pocket all the profit those printers ever got." He explained that after converting the government's greenbacks to coin, "which alone was used as currency" in Nevada, at the rate of "40 cents on the dollar or less," and after paying their compositors, the printers had received only "FIVE CENTS per 1000 ems for profit, presswork, binding, paper, ink, delivery, &c! Even if I paid them more, were they not justly entitled to a fair profit?" (rough draft in CU-MARK). On 30 October Taylor responded, informing Orion that allowance of a previously disallowed payment of $375 would be "considered" as soon as he deposited "to the credit of the U.S. Nine hundred and fifty five dollars and eight cents" (CU-MARK). Orion had been bonded for $10,000 before assuming his post in 1861—the "sureties" to which Clemens alludes—but he was apparently too intimidated to remind Taylor of that fact and had instead appealed to Clemens for help in meeting the Treasury Department's demand. Clemens referred the matter to his old Virginia City acquaintance Thomas Fitch, who in early 1869 had taken office as a Republican congressman from Nevada. Writing to Pamela Moffett on 14 January 1870, he enclosed "a note from Tom Fitch by which Orion will see that Tom is moving in the matter. Let Orion drop him simply a line, thanking him" (NPV†). Fitch's note does not survive; at present nothing is known of his assistance to Orion or of the resolution of the government's claim (William C. Miller, 1; *L1*, 319 n. 4).

[2]Jervis Langdon had offered to buy the Tennessee land outright in late June or early July 1869, but Orion had declined to sell (see 3? July 69 to OC). Presumably the demand from the Treasury Department had now made him reconsider. In a letter to Olivia Langdon—probably written on 9 November (docket number 132, now missing)—Clemens did propose that her father mine the land for coal; Jervis Langdon's failure to respond frustrated that plan (see 10 and 11 Nov 69 to OLL, n. 1). Subsequently Orion exercised the authority over the property that his brother granted him in the present letter. Writing to Clemens On 4 November 1880, he remembered making an unprofitable trade in which "the mass of

the Tennessee land was swept away," but noted that "Ma has some of the Tennessee land left." And he confessed: "I deeply regret that I did not send you a deed for all the Tennessee land when you had a chance to trade with Mr. Langdon. But I feared you would unconsciously cheat your prospective father-in-law" (CU-MARK).

[3] In 1898 Clemens recalled the importance of a Boston debut and described the preparations for it managed by the Boston Lyceum Bureau:

We had to bring out a new lecture every season, now, ‚(Nasby with the rest‚)‚ & expose it in the "Star Course," Boston, for a first verdict, before an audience of 2500 in the old Music Hall; for it was by that verdict that all the lyceums in the country determined the lecture's commercial value. The campaign did not really *begin* in Boston, but in the towns around; we did not appear in Boston until we had rehearsed about a month in those towns, & made & all the necessary corrections & revisings.

This system gathered the whole tribe together in the city early in October, & we had a lazy & sociable time there for several weeks. We lived at Young's hotel; we spent the days in Redpath's bureau, smoking & talking shop; & early in the evenings we scattered out amongst the towns & made them indicate the good & poor things in the new lectures. (SLC 1898, 7–8)

Clemens's first Boston appearance was in the Boston Lyceum Course, organized by Redpath "as a relief to the earnest, stately and solemn programmes of the other courses," and offering a "bright, brilliant and sunny series of Lectures and Entertainments, which will be given in Music Hall on successive Wednesday evenings" ("Boston Lyceum Course," Boston *Advertiser*, 22 Sept 69, 1). Built in 1852 and acclaimed for its fine acoustic properties, Music Hall seated about 2,600, not 4,000 (Moses King 1885, 252; Edwin M. Bacon, 304).

[4] Entitled "The Struggles of a Conservative on the Woman Question," Nasby's new lecture was a satirical attack on the opponents of women's rights. He delivered it in the Parker Fraternity Course (Redpath did not represent him until the 1870–71 season). The Boston *Evening Transcript* remarked that the lecture afforded "much amusement to a large audience in Music Hall last evening. They (the struggles) were well spiced with humor, and the serious passages were well received by Mr. Locke's hearers" ("Rev. Petroleum V. Nasby's Conservative . . . ," 10 Nov 69, 4). The Boston *Advertiser* called the performance "one of Nasby's peculiar efforts in the serio-comic line,—in which he represents himself as holding certain opinions for the purpose of making those opinions ridiculous." Although critical of Nasby's rapid and monotonous speaking style, and unpersuaded that his serious message would have effect, the paper took note of the audience's "applause and laughter . . . in unstinted measure" and predicted that "Mr. Locke's native shrewdness and good sense and his funny sayings will win a reasonable degree of favor for this lecture wherever it is delivered" ("Nasby on 'The Woman Question,'" 10 Nov 69, 1; Redpath and Fall, 3, 17; Eubank, 295, 297).

[5] Clemens had borrowed $12,500 from Jervis Langdon in order to make a $15,000 down payment to Thomas Kennett for a share of the Express Printing Company, and still owed Kennett $10,000 for the balance of the purchase price.

[6] Presumably Pamela had collected the life insurance left by her husband, William, when he died in 1865. Clemens purchased policy number 11439 from the Continental Life Insurance Company of Hartford, through Lyman Beecher, a nephew of the Reverends Thomas K. and Henry Ward Beecher. In partnership with James S. Parsons and Arthur S. Winchester, Lyman Beecher represented

Continental Life in Boston. An 1877 letter to Clemens from Beecher's brother, Robert, then the secretary of Continental, reveals that Clemens allowed his policy to lapse after making two premium payments. The record of Clemens's cash account with the Express Printing Company indicates that he paid the second of these, $187.60, to Lyman Beecher on 7 November 1870 (18 and 19 Dec 69 to OLL; "Nook Farm Genealogy," Beecher Addenda, ii–iii; *Boston Directory*, 76, 480, 653, 921; Robert E. Beecher to SLC, 16 June 77, CU-MARK; "Statement of S. L. Clemen[s]'s acc't from Sept 25/70 to Feb 20/71," CU-MARK).

To Olivia L. Langdon
10 November 1869 • Boston, Mass.
(MS: CU-MARK)

Boston, Nov. 10.

Livy Darling—

I shall spend New Year's day at home, if spared—& then I'll see the dear old face again.[1]

Got your letter of 7th today—thank you with all my heart, dearie. Just see how Theodore threatens an orphan.[2]

Talked last night in Providence, R.I., to 1800 people in a house which has regular seats for only 1500. Gave good satisfaction.[3] But tonight, my darling—tonight is the rub. Can't possibly tell how I shall come out.

They want me to talk again in Providence this season—told them had no spare time.

Must hurry, sweetheart, & so, God bless & keep you. Good-bye.

Sam.

Bless your dear heart, my worshipped Livy, I was too much "crowded" to write, during that four days' hiatus (hiatus is a good word.)[4]

[*enclosure:*]

Brother Clemens

If you dont write me oftner (for Livie), I'll have you "for breakfast" and give her the breast—and use your feathers to reseat her Rocking Chair.

Yours in greif—Theodore.

Nov 7. 2 PM.

✉️———————————————————————————————————

[*in ink:*] Miss Olivia L. Langdon | Elmira | N. Y. [*postmarked:*] BOSTON
MASS. NOV 10   2 P.M. [*docketed by OLL:*] 133rd

[1]Clemens was spared a lecture engagement on 1 January 1870. After an appearance in Williamsport, Pennsylvania, on New Year's Eve, he traveled to Elmira where, except for a 4 January lecture in Owego, New York, about thirty
miles to the east, he remained until the evening of 5 January, when he resumed
his tour.
[2]Clemens alludes to his enclosure, from Theodore Crane.
[3]See the Providence review enclosed in Clemens's next letter to Olivia.
[4]The hiatus, which Olivia had questioned in her 7 November letter, was 2–5
November. For a reconstruction of the events that "crowded" Clemens then, see
pp. 385–86. The four letters he wrote to Olivia between 6 and 9 November
(docket numbers 129–32) are lost.

To Olivia L. Langdon
10 and 11 November 1869 • Boston, Mass.
(MS: CU-MARK)

Boston, Nov. 10.

Darling, it is midnight. House full—I made a handsome success—*I*
know that, no matter whether the papers say so in the morning or not. I
am dreadfully tired, & will go to bed, now—had company here till this
moment.

Livy dear, (Nov. 11.) have bought full wedding outfit to-day
(haven't got a cent left,) & occasionally ~~an~~ the packages will arrive by
express directed simply to "J. Langdon, Elmira." Now your mother
must unpack them & put them away for me & be sure not to let Mr.
Langdon go wearing them around. I tell you, they are starchy.

Kisses & blessing on my little darling

Sam[1]

[*enclosures:*][2]

Mark Twain on "The Sandwich Islands."

Boston had a very novel, if not a very startling, sensation last evening in the shape of a lecture from Mr. Samuel L. Clemens, who is known to fame as the humorist Mark Twain. Known to fame, we say, for who that breathes the vital-air in America has not heard of the jumping frog of Calaveras County, California? and who has not read of the "new specimen" which Mark Twain made by combining a hawk and a crow in "one neat job?" A company, even greater than that which usually attends the Bureau lectures, assembled in the Music Hall last night with faces primed for merriment, and punctually to the hour Mr. Clemens and Mr. Redpath appeared upon the platform. This was of course, and it was also of course that for fifteen minutes afterwards the speaker's voice should be made inaudible by the rustling and creaking and tramping of the regular crowd of the tardy.

Mark Twain is a very good looking man. He is of medium height and moderately slender build, has light brown hair, a reddish brown moustache, regular features and a fresh complexion; and he has a queer way of wrinkling up his nose and half closing his eyes when he speaks. The expression of his face is as calm and imperturbable as that of the sphinx. Looking at him you feel it to be an impossibility that he should ever hurry or ever be out of temper, and you might suppose him to be incapable of a joke, if it were not for the peculiar twinkle in his merry eyes. His voice is remarkably light and remarkably dry,—like some German wines,—and it seems to be modulated to only two keys. His style of speaking is unique to the last degree. It is all of a piece with the quality of his humor, and fits him like a glove. He delivers his sentences without haste, and in a tone of utter indifference, marking the highest waves of his thought only by a strong flavor of nasality, and knowing for the most part only the rising inflection at the beginning, middle and end of his sentences. The rising inflection is not native here, nor is it born in the manner of any of our own speakers. Mr. Dickens first taught us how it might be used to advantage, and Mark Twain, doubtless without borrowing a leaf from Mr. Dickens's note-book, has found out for himself how effective an adjunct it is to humorous speech. In short, the platform manner of Mr. Clemens is the exact reflection in speech of his peculiar style of composition. The fun of both is genuine enough; but the perception of the fun is unmeasurably heightened by the apparently serious intention of the general discourse, and at times by an air of half seriousness in the joke itself. The audience gets into a queer state after a while. It knows not what to trust; for while much is meant to be seriously taken, the fun is felt to be the real life of the thing; and yet they never know where the fun will come in. Even when Mr. Clemens has made a really fine period, or introduced a brilliant descriptive passage, he takes pains to turn the affair into a joke at the end. As, for instance, after a very graphic and well written description of the great volcanic eruption in the Sandwich Islands, delivered with perfect indifference and almost as if with an effort—he paused for just an an instant, and then said in the same passionless tone: "There! I'm glad I've got that volcano off my mind." The manner is a direct resultant of the matter; and the manner of his speech does a great deal for the substance of his discourse. The story of "Our Fellow-Savages in the Sandwich Islands" would not be nearly so funny to read as it is to hear from Mark Twain's lips;—though we do not mean to deny that there is a great deal of genuine and irresistible humor in the texture of the discourse. Indeed, we mean to say, distinctly, that the contrary was the fact, and that Mr. Clemens showed himself last night in the character of a very quaint, peculiar, and eminently original humorist. America has produced, at least, a quintette of genuine humorists, whose productions have many of the *indicia* of genius, if they are not wholly inspired by it.

At one point in his lecture, namely, in the midst of a discussion of cannibalism, Mark Twain paused and said with an indescribable look: "At this point I usually illustrate cannibalism before the audience; but I am a stranger here, and feel diffident about asking favors." However, he said, if there is any one present who is willing to contribute a baby for the purposes of the lecture, I should be glad to know it now. I am aware, though, that children have become scarce and high of late, having been thinned out by neglect and ill treatment since the woman movement began.

But we must leave the rest to the imagination of our readers, only saying that Mr. Clemens told two of the funniest of exaggerated stories in the most irresistible fashion, and concluded his lecture with a few graceful words of thanks to the audience for their attention. Perhaps he is not a great humorist, but he is a genuine humorist. The man who can say that the Islanders' dish of plain dog "is only our cherished American sausage with the mystery removed" is one whose reputation fame will not suffer to die; and if Mr. Clemens can please everywhere as he pleased in Boston last night, he will be sure to make his fortune if he does not become a standard author.

Parade and Dinner of the Independent

[*on a small scrap of paper:*]

All between where I have torn it in two was devoted to one of those infamous synopses of the lecture. But I like this notice first-rate—it is all namby-pamby praise.[3]

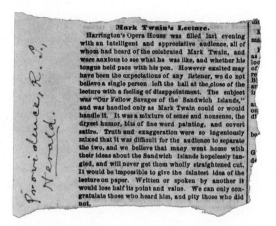

Mark Twain's Lecture.

Harrington's Opera House was filled last evening with an intelligent and appreciative audience, all of whom had heard of the celebrated Mark Twain, and were anxious to see what he was like, and whether his tongue held pace with his pen. However exalted may have been the expectations of any listener, we do not believe a single person left the hall at the close of the lecture with a feeling of disappointment. The subject was "Our Fellow Savages of the Sandwich Islands," and was handled only as Mark Twain could or would handle it. It was a mixture of sense and nonsense, the dryest humor, bits of fine word painting, and covert satire. Truth and exaggeration were so ingeniously mixed that it was difficult for the audience to separate the two, and we believe that many went home with their ideas about the Sandwich Islands hopelessly tangled, and will never get them wholly straightened out. It would be impossible to give the faintest idea of the lecture on paper. Written or spoken by another it would lose half its point and value. We can only congratulate those who heard him, and pity those who did not.

Providence, R. I., Herald.

✉

[*in ink:*] Miss Olivia L. Langdon | Elmira | N. Y. [*return address:*] YOUNG'S HOTEL, COURT AVENUE, BOSTON, MASS.[4] [*postmarked:*] BOSTON MASS. NOV. 11 3.P.M. [*docketed by OLL:*] 134th

[1] Olivia's 13 and 14 November letter—mailed to Danvers, Massachusetts, where Clemens lectured on 17 November—was in part a reply to the present letter. It is the only one of her courtship letters known to survive (CU-MARK):

Nov. 13th 1869—Elmira

My dear, I am sorry that there has gone no letter to you today, but it has been a very busy day and I could not find the time to write, and now I must send you only a few lines, as it is rather late—

Sunday morning—

I was too stupid to write last night after I had commenced, so I put by the letter and went to bed—

I read Father what you wrote about the Tennesee land, he said, it was too bad for your brother to be such a drag to you, he did not make any remark about his working the land, and I did not like to press the matter because I know that he has a good deal on his hands—more than he ought to have, but if you think that I better bring it before him again, I will do so—

I am very sorry that your brother is troubled, and very thankful that you are prospspered, glad on your account and glad because you can help others—God gives diversities of gifts, he has not given to your brother money making wisdom, but, from what you say, he has given y̶ him a beautiful spirit nevertheless—as g̶o God prospers us, we will not, w̶e will not forget ɦHim, and allow ourselves to blame those who seem to use less judgement in getting on in this world, but will help just as many people to lift their burdens as we are able—   You are a good youth to say what you have to your brother about helping him to the money when he cannot get along longer without it, because I know that while you are in debt you do not know very well how to spare money, but it is the gifts that really cost us something that are most valuable in Gods sight—We will be the more economical in our way of living, I will look out that I get few dresses and gloves and the like, and we shall be able to help them on—I am glad that your work is doing so well, for two very obvious reasons——

I am so happy, so perfectly at rest in you, so proud of the true nobility of your nature—
it makes the whole world look so bright to me, that I cannot but have a great desire to do
all I can to lift the burdens from those who are carrying a heavy load—I feel so that I have
no burden, that I am so richly cared for, that I cannot but have a tender yearning for those
whose backs seem almost broken with the heavy load under which it is bent—we are happy,
my dear, therefore we are the better able and must be the more ready to help others—and
I know that you are,

I wakened this morning, and looked out on the winter landscape, which I so dearly
love, felt the comfort and beauty of my home, felt the love of those here and yours which
I know to be true and steady even when sa sepirated from me, and I felt like dancing, that
seemed the most natural way to express it—I believe dancing and singing was ˌis‚ a true
way to give *praise* to God—our whole natures seem to enter in then——

It snowed nearly all night last night, and this morning the ground and dresse ɖ trees were
beautifully arrayed in their white garments—

We are all delighted that you are to be with us on New Year's day, I trust that no adversity
may come to you—

I was indeed proud and happy that you succeeded so well in Boston—

Don't let your sister stay away from our wedding because she fancies her clothes are not
fine enough—   We want *her*, and her daughter here we don't mind about her ‚their‚
clothing.

I had a perfectly delightful letter yesterday from Mrs Brooks, she is as lovely and charming as ever—

I would like to write on but I must elost close this and get ready for Sunday school—

Now and always lovingly Livy

[2]Clemens tore the enclosures from page one of the Boston *Advertiser* of 11
November and page two of the Providence *Morning Herald* of 10 November.
They are reproduced at 75 percent of actual size.

[3]Clemens wrote these two sentences on a strip he tore from the bottom of a
leaf of the *Eclectic Magazine* for November 1869 (n.s., 10:625–26). The offending synopsis read as follows:

We are obliged to say again, as we said in the cases of Nasby and Josh Billings, that there
is little use in trying to write a sketch of the discourse. But we must attempt to give our
readers a little taste of the speaker's quality. Mr. Clemens devoted the first ten minutes of
his lecture to a painfully accurate description of a person afflicted with the most loathsome
form of Oriental leprosy; and then he gave five minutes to the narration of a boyish adventure which ended in his seeing the horrible face of a dead man in the moonlight. And all
this mass of horror for what? Simply that he might say that his memory was full of unpleasant things so linked together that when he thought of one he inevitably thought of another,
and so on through the entire series; and starting with leprosy and dead faces in the moonlight his mind necessarily ran through other unpleasant things until it brought him to the
Sandwich Islands and his lecture. The position of the islands he gave geographically; but
why they were placed so far away from everything and in such an inconvenient space, he
declined to consider. The man who would have discovered the islands but did not, he said,
was diverted from his course by a manuscript found in a bottle; and this, said Mark Twain,
is not the only case in which a man has been turned from the true path by suggestions
drawn from a bottle. The European nations brought into the islands their own diseases,
together with civilization, education and other calamities. The effect of this had been to
diminish the native population:—education in particular causing a frightful mortality as
the facilities for learning were multiplied. But fifty thousand natives are now left upon the
islands, and it is proposed to start a few more seminaries to finish them. The country
people of the islands, the women, he said, wear a single garment made of one piece: "and
the men don't." But when the weather is inclement the men wear cotton in their ears. The
hospitality of the people he declared to be of a very high and generous order. A stranger

might enter any house and straightway his host would set before him raw fresh fish with the scales on, baked dogs, fricas[s]eed cats, and all the luxuries of the season. But in trade they were exceedingly sharp and deceitful,—lying invariably from one end of the transaction to the other; not descending to common lies either, but indulging in lies that are "gorgeously imposing and that awe you by their grandeur." The fondness of the islanders for dogs he declared to be intense. Dogs had the best of everything and were the close companions of the men. "They fondle and caress the dog until he is a full grown dog, and then they eat him." "I couldn't do that," said Mr. Clemens, in one of his dryest and funniest passages: "I'd rather go hungry two days than eat an old personal friend in that way."

Clemens apparently sent another *Advertiser* clipping to the Buffalo *Express*, for on 13 November the paper reprinted it, without the synopsis ("Mark Twain in Boston," 2). The other Boston papers seconded the *Advertiser*'s "namby-pamby praise." Typical was the *Herald*, the city's leading daily, whose review concluded: "The whole lecture was a rare treat, and all who were fortunate enough to hear it will remember its rich and racy points as long as they live" ("Mark Twain at Music Hall," 11 Nov 69, 2; see also "Mark Twain 'At Home,'" Boston *Post*, 11 Nov 69, 3; "Local Intelligence," Boston *Evening Transcript*, 11 Nov 69, 4; "Mark Twain's Lecture," Boston *Evening Journal*, 11 Nov 69, 4).

⁴This hotel, established in 1845 by George Young, still its proprietor, was "a small and cosey hostelry, hidden from the main thoroughfares by the tall buildings in front and on either side of it. It was famous for its good beds, its solid comforts, and its choice table . . . and its patronage came chiefly from businessmen" (Edwin M. Bacon, 514–15; *Boston Directory*, 663, 775).

To Olivia L. Langdon
15 and 16 November 1869 • Clinton and Holyoke, Mass.
(MS: CU-MARK)

Clinton, Mass, Nov. 15.

Livy Darling—

I had to submit to the customary & exasperating drive around town in a freezing open buggy this morning (at Norwich) to see the wonders of the village.¹

[Mem.—They always consist of the Mayor's house; the ex-mayor's house; the house of a State Senator; house of an ex-governor; house of a former Member of Congress; the public school with its infernal architecture; the female seminary; paper mill or factory of some kind or other; the cemetery; the Court house; the plaza; the place where the park is going to be—& I must sit & shiver & stare at a melancholy grove of skeleton trees & listen while my friend gushes enthusiastic statistics &

dimensions. All towns are alike—all have their same stupid trivialities to show, & all demand an impossible interest at the suffering stranger's hands. Why *won't* these insane persecutors believe me when I protest pleadingly that I *don't* care two cents for all the thrilling wonders the village can boast.

[How I gloat in secret when one of these people regrets that I cannot "remain over" & see his accursed village! And how unblushingly I repeat the threadbare lie that I am sorry!

[After the natural wonders are all visited, then we have to call on other inanimate wonders with dull faces, but with legs to them that show them to be human: the mayor; the richest man; the wag of the village (who instantly assails me with old stale jokes & humorous profanity); the village editor—& a lot more of people I take no possible interest in & don't want to see. And when by some divine accident one of them isn't at home, what a fervent prayer of thankfulness rises up in my heart!]

I only have to submit to these inflictions when I am the guest of somebody & cannot refuse to suffer in return for his hospitality. When I am paying my own bills, at a hotel, I talk out & say No *Sir*—not any village wonders for the subscriber, if you please.

Here I am in a hotel—the Clinton House—& a villainous one it is— shabby bed, shabby room, shabby furniture, dim lights—everything shabby & disagreeable.

Holyoke, Mass, 16

Livy Darling—

I got your little letter a while ago & am therefore glad & happy— happier & more & more grateful for your love with every day that goes over my head. I would not know what to do or whither to turn to give life a value if I were to lose my darling now. I am so wrapped up in you, I so live in you, that it to lose you would be equivalent to losing life itself.

I left Boston without baggage, thinking I would go back there from Norwich the same night—but the trains left at such inconvenient hours that I went from there to Clinton—found a similar state of things & came straight here. But as I am clear out of shirts (wore this one yesterday) I shall take an early train to Boston tomorrow before I go to Danvers.[2]

Loving kisses, darling.

Sam.

P. S.—The photograph was Josh Billings.[3]

This is the way to spell a certain word, little sweetheart—*"pretty"*—do you see, honey? I have not looked to see whether any others are misspelt or not, because I don't care whether they are or not—but that one just happened to fall under my eye at this moment.

I am so dead stupid, from getting up so early this morning, that I fairly dread going on that ~~state~~ stage to-night. Come, my darling, ~~stam~~ check that cold *immediately*, & look out for the sore throat—don't you dare to go out with only one shawl.

I cured my cold with two long & severe Turkish baths taken in immediate succession, with cold shower baths between[4]—next morning I was entirely well.

Sam

▣──────────────────────────────────

[*in ink:*] Miss Olivia L. Langdon | Elmira | N. Y. [*postmarked:*] HOLYOKE MASS. NOV 17 [*docketed by OLL:*] 138ᵗʰ | S S | P. S

[1] Clemens had lectured in Norwich, Connecticut, on 13 November.

[2] Norwich was about 80 miles southwest of Boston. From there Clemens had traveled about 65 miles northeast to Clinton, to lecture on 15 November. Holyoke, where he performed the following evening, was about 50 miles southwest of Clinton and about 80 miles west of Boston. Danvers, Massachusetts, the site of his 17 November lecture, was 15 miles north of Boston.

[3] Josh Billings (Henry Wheeler Shaw, 1818–85) had been a farmer, real estate salesman, Ohio River steamboat owner, and auctioneer before, in the late 1850s, he began contributing to newspapers the steady stream of aphorisms, short essays, and sketches that made him a popular cracker-barrel philosopher. His third book, *Josh Billings' Farmer's Allminax* (New York: G. W. Carleton), the first of a series of ten comic annuals, was published in October 1869 and reportedly sold 30,000 copies in its first week and over 90,000 within three months. Also popular as a humorous lecturer, Billings had appeared in Boston's Music Hall on 27 October, two weeks before Mark Twain, speaking on "Milk and Natral History" in James Redpath's Boston Lyceum Course (Kesterson, 20–24; "Neighborhood and News Items," Elmira *Advertiser*, 2 Dec 69, 4; Cyril Clemens, 115; "Special Notices," Boston *Evening Transcript*, 27 Oct 69, 4). The photograph of Billings has not been identified, but he must have given it to Clemens in the second week of November, around the time the two men were photographed with Petroleum V. Nasby (see 24 and 25 Nov 69 to OLL, n. 10). Clemens probably enclosed it in one of three letters he wrote to Olivia between 11 and 15 November (docket numbers 135–37), now lost.

[4] A variant of the "water cure" therapy that became popular in the United States in the 1840s and 1850s in treating everything from nosebleeds to cancer (see *Inds*, 267).

To Mary Mason Fairbanks
19 November 1869 • Boston, Mass.
(MS: CSmH)

Boston, Nov. 19.

My Dear Mother—

Why mercy,! were you expecting me? Do you know, I just *thought*
you would be looking for me—but bless you, I couldn't help it. If it were
only Livy's fault—but there isn't anybody to saddle it on—I guess it was
my distress about those Railways—which is funny, because formerly I
would just as soon have been smashed up on one of those railroads as any
other way.[1] But my life has grown very precious—to Livy. Well, I'm
coming right along, now, in the spring—I am indeed,—/— & I shall bring
my wife. Then you can scold us both, & all of us will enjoy it the more.

I have an easy time of it this year—talk nearly altogether in New
England, & shall close during the last week in January. I can't ~~talk~~ take
near all the engagements that offer, but I take one for every night of the
season (except Saturdays & Sundays, which I reserve to "loaf" in.) It is
jolly. I shall sleep in Boston a good deal of the time. I have been lecturing
ₓalmostₓ every night for some two weeks, & have retained my handsome
room in this hotel all the time. Shall give it up for a while, next Tuesday,
& go into Vermont & Connecticut. But I shall talk many times in Mass.,
yet, this winter.

Goodbye & love to you all—for I have many business letters to answer yet, this afternoon, & a lecture to deliver to-night in a neighboring
city. Hurry's the word! ₓ(Found it in an old dictionary—didn't see it
before.)ₓ

Always Lovingly
Sam*l.*

Got lots more baggage—bought another satchell the other day.

✉———————————————————————————————

Mrs. A. W. Fairbanks | Care "Herald" | Cleveland | Ohio. [*return ad-
dress:*] YOUNG'S HOTEL, COURT AVENUE, BOSTON, MASS. [*postmarked:*] BOSTON
MASS. NOV. 20. 9 P.M.

[1]A railroad accident in late October had influenced Clemens's decision not to visit Mrs. Fairbanks then (see 27 Oct 69 to Severance, n. 1).

To Olivia L. Langdon
19 November 1869 • Boston, Mass.
(MS: CU-MARK)

[*on the back:*][1]
Boston, 19th—Livy dear, I believe I am to talk in one corner of Brooklyn Dec. 1, & repeat in Plymouth Church Dec. 4. Have a call from New York for Dec. 3, but don't know yet whether we shall take it or not. I am indifferent—just as soon not.[2] I have no paper up here, & in a few minutes I start out to talk in ~~the~~ a suburban city (Jamaica Plains.) It is now 6 P.M.—lecture begins at 7.45.[3]

                                        Sam.

✉️——

[*in ink:*] Miss Olivia L. Langdon | Elmira | N. Y. [*across end:*] Note enclosed. [*return address:*] YOUNG'S HOTEL, COURT AVENUE, BOSTON, MASS. [*postmarked:*] BOSTON MASS. NOV 19   8.P.M. [*docketed by OLL:*] 141ˢᵗ

¹Clemens wrote this note around the imprint—"BLACK, 163 WASHINGTON ST., BOSTON"—of photographer James Wallace Black (*Boston Directory*, 83). He then wrapped the *carte de visite* (reproduced here at 82 percent of actual size) in a scrap torn from the first leaf of the *Eclectic Magazine* for November 1869 (n.s., 10:513–14).
²On 3 December Clemens lectured in Poughkeepsie, New York. He canceled the second of his Brooklyn lectures, actually scheduled for 6 December (see 3 Dec 69 to the Editor of the Brooklyn *Eagle*, and 4 Dec 69 and 6 Dec 69, both to Redpath).
³The lecture in the Town Hall of Jamaica Plain, a wealthy suburb of Boston, was a benefit for "a Benevolent Educational Enterprise" ("Unique Entertainment by Mark Twain," Boston *Evening Transcript*, 13 Nov 69, 1; Edwin M. Bacon, 259).

To James K. Medbery
20 November 1869 • Boston, Mass.
(MS facsimile: MacKaye, 1:plate 21)

                                                    Boston, Nov. 20.
Friend Medbery—
        You *must* excuse this delay, but I couldn't get time to answer sooner.
        No, I can't write the Christmas book at any price, because I shall be traveling every day & lecturing every night till that time & beyond. Much obliged to you, though.¹
        Shall be in New York, Nov. 30, & talk in Brooklyn Dec. 1 & Dec. 4. Can't you call on a fellow?
                                                    Faithfully yrs
                                                    Mark Twain.

¹Medbery had solicited the holiday book for the "Authors' Department" of his American Literary Bureau (see 21 Sept 69 to Crane, n. 2).

To George H. Selkirk
20–28 November 1869 • Boston, Mass.,
or Hartford, Conn.
(MS: CU-MARK)

OFFICE OF OAKLAND DAILY TRANSCRIPT.

OAKLAND, Nov 9 1869.

Sam*ˡ* Clemens, Esq
    Dear Sir:
        I send you a copy of the *Transcript*, and will hereafter send it to the *Express*. Can you send us an exchange, as I wish to publish your matter first-hand if possible

                Yours
                Henry George[1]

Give him a Weekly exchange, Col.[2]

                Mark

---

[1] Henry George (1839–97)—later renowned for his writings on political economy—was at this time the editor of the Oakland (Calif.) *Transcript*. A native of Philadelphia, he had migrated to California in 1858, where, after his marriage in 1861, he experienced years of poverty while supporting his family as a typesetter, mining speculator, door-to-door salesman, and newspaper contributor before serving as managing editor of the San Francisco *Times* and then of the San Francisco *Chronicle* in 1867–68. He edited the *Transcript* for only a few months, from September 1869 to February 1870, and then became managing editor of the Sacramento *Reporter*. George and Clemens might have met in San Francisco in the spring of 1865, when both men were contributors to the *Californian*, or in Sacramento the following year. According to George's son, while his father was a struggling printer in the state capital and "ready to turn his hand to whatever would bring him a living. . . . a young newspaper man named Samuel L. Clemens, who, under the *nom de plume* of 'Mark Twain,' had won a reputation on the Coast as a humourist of a dry and original quality, came to Sacramento to lecture. Another newspaper man, Denis E. McCarthy, acting as manager, hired Henry George to take tickets at the door" (Henry George, Jr., 138). Although George's son assigned the occasion to 1862, it in fact must have been Clemens's lecture of 11 October 1866, at which time, as in 1862, George was a Sacramento printer (Henry George, Jr., 175–76, 197, 208, 211; Henry George; Barker, 58–63, 67, 72, 74–76, 91, 101, 105, 110, 113, 124, 131, 138, 144; *L1*, 362).

[2] George H. Selkirk, one of Clemens's partners, was business manager of the

Buffalo *Express* and president of the Express Printing Company. He had been a lieutenant colonel in the Forty-ninth New York Infantry during the Civil War. The dating of Clemens's directive to him remains uncertain. The postmarks on the envelope of Henry George's letter indicate that it left Oakland on 8 November and arrived in Buffalo ten days later. After delivery to the *Express* office, it was forwarded to Elmira and may have arrived at the Langdon home as early as 19 November. If Olivia immediately enclosed it in a letter addressed to Boston, Clemens could have received it there and responded as early as 20 November. If instead she forwarded it to his next known lecture stop, he would not have received it until 23 November, in Hartford. And if it was among the November letters from her that were delayed in reaching him, he might not have received it until the twenty-eighth of the month. The weekly edition of the *Express*, which Clemens here authorizes for Henry George, issued on Thursdays and presumably included Clemens's "matter" from the daily paper. Between 1 November 1869 and 21 January 1870, the period of his lecture tour, his contributions to the daily *Express* consisted of "Around the World" letters 3–6 as well as: "A Good Letter," two "Browsing Around" letters, "Ye Cuban Patriot," "An Awful—Terrible Medieval Romance," and "A Ghost Story" (SLC 1869gg–mm, 1870b–d; Berry; "Twain Success Puzzle to His Old Office Boy," Buffalo *Courier-Express*, 24 Feb 1929, sec. S, 8; Frank H. Severance, 334; Heitman, 2:145; Rowell, 66; 25 Nov 69 and 28 Nov 69, both to OLL).

To Hiram J. Ramsdell
23 November 1869 • Boston, Mass.
(Transcript and *paraphrase:* Charles Hamilton 1964, lot 32)

Boston, Nov. 23, 1869.

Dear Ramsdell—

[*paraphrase: Mark Twain explains that his lecture agent, Redpath, opens most of his letters, thus creating discrepancies.*] Confound it, I would a heap rather have lectured for the boys, of course—have always been laying for a chance to do it . . . my lecture list hasn't a single unoccupied night in it—therefore, you old rip, how can your servant lecture for the boys?[1] . . . But you better not write me down, you freebooters, & you better not tear down my bills, either, unless you want to stand a small trial for incest, or arson, or whatever the technical term for such a crime may be. Go slow!

No, my boy, write me up—that is the way to achieve the affection & reverence of your country. Protect my bills (pay them, for instance,)

& uphold mine honor & my reputation. That is the way to bring down your gray hairs with satisfaction to the grave . . .

Thine ever,
Sam*.* L. Clemens.

[1]Hiram J. Ramsdell (1839–87)—Washington correspondent for the New York *Tribune* and the Cincinnati *Commercial* and one of the newspapermen Clemens had known in the capital in the winter of 1867–68—evidently had requested a lecture before the Washington Correspondents' Club. Founded in 1867 "for the cultivation of fraternal sentiment," the club had as its chief function "an annual dinner where their friends were entertained" (Bryan, 2:586). Clemens had spoken in response to a toast at the first such dinner, in January 1868, but had not kept a promise to give a benefit lecture for the club around that time (see *L2*, 130, 131–32 n. 5, 155–58, 196 n. 1). His current tour included an 8 December lecture in Washington, in the Grand Army of the Republic Course ("Death of Mr. Ramsdell," Washington *Critic*, 26 May 87, 1; *Congressional Globe* 1871, 2:847, 848).

To Olivia L. Langdon
24 and 25 November 1869 • Hartford, Conn., and Boston, Mass.
(MS: CU-MARK)

Late P.M.
Hartford Nov. 24/69

I *am* perplexed—for I wonder where my darling is. She keeps writing me indefinitely about going to New York, this week, but I can't make out what part of this week she means.[1] She is a dear little—rascal. But I love her—I love her with a stronger, prouder & profounder affection every day as the time goes by. One year ago, lacking a day, my life was glorified with the gladdest surprise that had ever burst upon it—& since that moment my Livy has been all in all to me. I have now known almost ten months of restful happiness,[2] a satisfied tranquillƴity, a broadening charity, a more generous view of men & motives, an unaccustomed stirring within me of religious impulses, not grand and strong, it is true, but steady & hopeful—the subdued & far-off cadences of approaching music, as it were. A new, strange, beautiful life these ten months have given me; a broadening & aspiring life, a life worth ages of the desert existence that went before it. And therefore how can I help loving the noble woman who has made this paradise for me & ~~beautified~~ adorned it with ~~the~~ her enduring love & the gentle graces of her nature? I *do* love you, darling, with all ˏtheˏ energy of a heart starved for love these many & many years. And its passion-torrents are left behind, its rocks & shoals are passed, its restless rivulets are united, & so, in one stately river of p̸Peace it holds its unvexed course to that sea whose further tides break upon the shores of Eternity.

We have had a pleasant day & a pleasant evening, child. I called at Mr Hooker's a moment & saw him—then went over to Warner's & visited with him & his wife an hour. She sent a world of love & loving messages to you which I ship to you in bulk to save port dues. I like her.[3]

Warner soon talked himself into such a glow with the prospect of what we could do with the Courant now that I have achieved such a sudden & sweeping popularity in New England, that he forgot we had not yet come to any terms, & fell to appointing the work I should do on the paper. The same way this evening at Twichell's, in another long private conversation. I told him I would not leave the Express unless the boys were willing, & I felt sure they would not be—& that I would not ask them to give me as much for my interest as I gave for it, for they should not say I left without benefiting them by leaving—further, by his own showing, the only Courant fifth I could get they had foolishly bought from a partner & paid $4,000 more for it than they considered it worth, in order to get rid of him, & borrowed the money to do it with; (unpaid yet—a hungry debt of $ near $30,000).[4] I said it would be paying the Express ~~$3,000~~ $5,000 to let me go, & paying the Courant $29,000 for $25,000-interest to take me in—$9,000 altogether to get hold of an interest far less valuable & lucrative than my Express interest—& all I should get for it would be, the pleasure of living in Hartford among a most delightful society, & one in which you & I both would be supremely satisfied in. I said if I were absolutely worth $35,000 I would pay $9,000 in a moment for the sake of getting ourselves comfortably situated, but unfortunately I wasn't worth any such sumˏ. I said I would do nothing till I talked with you. He wanted me to talk with Mr. Langdon & write the result, & I said I would.[5]

Three times I have met Sam Bowles, of the Springfield Republican, & notwithstanding he wrote me a note saying I must always sit at his table when in Springfield, I was ashamed to find myself calling him ∂ in my secret heart a born & bred *cur*, every time. And notwithstanding my shame, I could not help comforting myself with the reflection that my judgment of men was oftener right than wrong. The other day we met him, & afterward I said, "Nasby, I never have heard anybody say a word against Sam. Bowles, & he always treats me politely, but I cannot get rid of the conviction that he is a dog"—& Nasby said a very great many people had very convincing proofs that Mr. Bowles was exactly that. Then I remembered his treatment of Richardson, a circumstance I had forgotten,, since Bliss told me the other day. And now it came ab out, confidentially, from Twichell, to-night, that last June both Hawley & Warner were full of the idea of having me on the Courant, but ran to consult Bowles the great journalistic oracle, & he advised them not to do it—& in their simplicity they took in good faith the word of a man who had just come from California & knew what a card I was there & consequently what a trump I could make myself here.[6] Livy darling I guess we couldn't pull loose all the Buffalo anchors easily, & so we may as well give up Hartford—but my gracious, wouldn't I like to tilt that Courant against the complacent Springfield Republican & make that journal sick? I think so.

My pet, I had to give up Mrs Perkins.[7] I slopped out there in the mud today (it rained like all possessed, yesterday, but held up & did not interfere with my audience at night.)[8] When I reached her house she had been gone to the city about fifteen minutes. I was very sorry, but it couldn't be helped.

Didn't see Alice Day—am afraid I didn't right thoroughly want to, though maybe I might have been mistaken.

I have ordered Twichell to stand by & assist Mr. Beecher to marry us, & I told him you wanted it so.[9] It's powerful expensive, but then we'll charge him for his board while he is there.

Bless your old heart I wish I could see you. Rather see you than anybody in the world. I *would*, Livy, old sweetheart. I would, indeed. Because I love you. I love you with *all* my heart, Livy darling.

Good-bye, & the peace of God be rest upon you now & always, darling.

Sam.

[*enclosure:*]¹⁰

Josh Billings.   Mark Twain.   Petroleum V. Nasby.
THE AMERICAN HUMORISTS.
Published by G. M. Baker, 149 Washington St., Boston.

[*on the back:*]   H. G. SMITH,
                                    STUDIO BUILDING,
                                         BOSTON.

Miss Olivia L. Langdon | ~~Elmira~~ | ~~N. Y.~~ ˌSt. Nicholas Hotel | New York.ˌ
[*return address:*] BOSTON LYCEUM BUREAU, NO. 20 BROMFIELD ST. BOSTON. [*post-marked:*] BOSTON MASS. NOV. 25. 8.P.M. [*docketed by OLL:*] 147ᵗʰ

¹On 22 November Olivia and Jervis Langdon had gone to New York City, where they registered at the St. Nicholas Hotel. Assisted by Susan Crane, who had preceded them by a week, and by John D. F. Slee and his wife, Emma, father and daughter spent the next few days making wedding preparations and purchasing furnishings for the house in Buffalo that was to be Jervis Langdon's wedding gift. "Mr L. & Sue will return from New York this week," Olivia's mother wrote Mary Mason Fairbanks on 25 November, "& next week I expect to join Livia there to remain 2 or 3 weeks" (Olivia Lewis Langdon to Fairbanks, 25 Nov 69, CtHMTH; "Morning Arrivals," New York *Evening Express*, 24 Nov 69, 3; "Personal," New York *Tribune*, 24 Nov 69, 5).

[2] It was on 25 November 1868 that Olivia admitted "over & over & over again" that she loved Clemens (*L2*, 294); they became formally engaged on 4 February 1869.

[3] John Hooker's home at Forest and Hawthorn streets, was near Charles Dudley Warner's, on Hawthorn. Warner's wife, the former Susan Lee (1838?–1921), of New York City, whom he had married in 1856, was known for her warm hospitality and her talent as a pianist. She and Olivia became close friends after the Clemenses settled in Hartford (Van Why, 4, 5, 7, 42, 44–45, 51; "Nook Farm Genealogy," 30).

[4] The available "Courant fifth" was the share that William H. Goodrich had relinquished at the end of 1868. Goodrich returned to the paper on 31 December 1869 by purchasing, instead of his former share, the "fractional pecuniary interest" that belonged to silent partner Thomas M. Day ("Partnership Changes," "A Card," Hartford *Courant*, 1 Jan 70, 2). Before becoming co-owner of the Buffalo *Express*, Clemens had been interested in buying into the *Courant*.

[5] Such a letter to Warner, if ever written, is not known to survive.

[6] Clemens's and Nasby's encounter with Samuel Bowles must have come during the second week of November 1869, when both lecturers were in Boston. Bowles might have first met Clemens in San Francisco in August 1865, while on a trip west with Schuyler Colfax and Albert D. Richardson. (If so, his 1868 meeting with Clemens would have been their second encounter: see 22 June 69 to Bowles, n. 1). Both Bowles and Richardson published books about the trip— Bowles's *Across the Continent* (Springfield, Mass.: S. Bowles and Company, 1865) and Richardson's *Beyond the Mississippi* (Hartford: American Publishing Company, 1867, 1869 [revised edition]). Bowles, whose mistreatment of Richardson has not been explained, was well known for his abrasiveness. Wendell Phillips, for example, called him "a veteran" in the "fine art" of "abuse and insolence," lavished from "his coward's castle, on every true man for the last fifteen years" (Hudson, 584). Richardson's life was about to come to a sudden end. On 25 November 1869 he was fatally wounded by Daniel McFarland, the divorced husband of his fiancée, Abby Sage McFarland, and he died a week later.

[7] Lucy Perkins (see 12 Aug 69 to Bliss, n. 4).

[8] The Hartford *Courant*'s thoughtful review, probably written by Charles Dudley Warner, analyzed "the uncommon success with the audience" of Clemens's 23 November lecture at Allyn Hall:

> The hall has not been so crowded, on any occasion, for a long time. And the vast audience sat for over an hour in a state of positive enjoyment, in a condition of hardly suppressed "giggle" and expectancy of giggle, with now and then a burst of hearty, unrestrained laughter. The laughter was never forced; people laughed because they could not help it. And what was it all about?
>
> Mr. Clemens, a self-possessed gentleman, with a good head and a face that led one to expect humor, with an unembarrassed but rather nonchalant manner, was walking about the stage, talking about the Sandwich Islands; talking, and not repeating what seemed to be a written lecture. It was a conversational performance. His stories, his jokes, his illustrations, were told in a conversational way, and not "delivered." With a half lingering hesitation in his speech, and a rising inflection of voice, he talked exactly as he does in private; and the same peculiarities that make him to the parlor a capital narrator, ensured him success before this audience.
>
> The thing seems very simple, and yet there was a good deal of art in it. Perhaps we can find in the cyclopedia more than he told us about the Sandwich Islands, more and a good

deal less. But we do not find Mark Twain in the cyclopedia account, nor his peculiar manner of looking at things. The art of the lecture consisted in the curious mingling of grave narration and description with the most comical associations, and with occasional flashes of genuine wit. And the whole was leavened by a manner that would make the fortune of a comedian. Mr. Dickens's greatest success was in comedy, and even his finest passages of humor owed their best effect to the manner of the artist. In the humorous lecture or reading it is impossible to separate the person from what he says or reads.

Mr. Clemens made as decided a hit with his audience in Hartford as he did in Boston. And we do not doubt that it was a genuine success. We did not go expecting him to expound political economy or the philosophy of Kant, but to have an hour of healthy laughter; and we thanked fortune that we had it, and that there is left a genuine humorist who can give it to us. And when we went away we did not care to make an inventory of our "information." For ourselves, we reckon among our benefactors those who can make us laugh, innocently. Humor has its office. ("The Humorous Lecture—Mark Twain," 25 Nov 69, 2)

[9] Joseph H. Twichell in fact assisted Thomas K. Beecher with Clemens's and Olivia's "simple and impressive" marriage ceremony in Elmira on 2 February 1870 ("Personal," Buffalo *Express*, 3 Feb 70, 4).

[10] As Clemens's revisions on the envelope show, he held on to this letter until 25 November, when he returned to Boston, hoping for a note from Olivia informing him of her whereabouts. Probably that evening he enclosed the photograph (reproduced here at 82 percent of actual size), just before he decided to mail the letter to New York City—although he still had no confirmation that she was there (see the next letter). It and the similar photograph that he sent to Olivia two days later were taken during the week of 7–13 November: "Mark Twain, Josh Billings and Petroleum V. Nasby were photographed together last week. When shall these three meet again!" (Boston *Saturday Evening Gazette* ["Sunday Morning Edition"], 14 Nov 69, 2, TS in CU-MARK). George M. Baker, a friend of James Redpath's, evidently had contracted with photographer Horatio G. Smith and with "The American Humorists" for the sale of these photographs ("Presentations," Boston *Advertiser*, 27 Dec 69, 1; *Boston Directory*, 62, 563).

To Olivia L. Langdon
25 November 1869 • Boston, Mass.
(MS: CU-MARK)

Boston, 25th, 12 PM

Well! here I am, with only the little picture to kiss when I could just as well have had the blessed original in my arms at this moment as any other way.[1] Nasby broke down & closed out the Rutland, Vt., Society, & that relieved me & the rest of going there[2]—& that gave me two idle days following Hartford, which I'd ‚I could‚ have spent in New York if I had known you would be there, but somehow I had gathered the impression that you wouldn't be there till the *latter part* of the week. I do not really believe you are ther in New York *yet*—for I telegraphed your father today & got no reply. But I suppose you *will* be there shortly.

I got a letter from you in Jamaica Plains—isn't that the one? I have written them at Rutland to forward my letters here. If I had only known anything about the may map, there never would have been any necessity of your writing me anywhere but Boston, up to this time. I turn up here every day or two. Don't know how it will be in the future—will send you the new list to-morrow.

I don't see how I ever could have been so stupid as not to telegraph Elmira from Hartford—only, I hadn't the remotest possible idea that you were going down the first of the week. I am just as grieved as if I had lost a month right out of the middle of my life. Even though I live to see you day & night for many years, I still have suffered loss, for I cannot get back those two days—& I might have been with my darling. Well, let's be cheerful, anyway, old sweetheart, you precious darling, you blessed dream & blessed reality—let us find no fault with circumstances that may have been ordered by Providence—how can we know.

It is midnight—Billings has just gone—had a quiet, pleasant, conversational evening. Showed me his photographs—has two enchanting daughters, both married & mothers.[3]

BED! That is the idea *now*. Bless you sweetheart you are so lovely in the little picture tonight. I shall have to take it to bed with me so that I can look at it the first thing in the morning. I kiss you, darling & bless you.

Sam.

⊠──

Miss Olivia L. Langdon | St. Nicholas Hotel | New York. | [*flourish*] [*return address:*] BOSTON LYCEUM BUREAU, NO. 20 BROMFIELD ST. BOSTON. [*postmarked:*] BOSTON MASS. NOV. 26. 2 P.M. [*docketed:*] ST. NICHOLAS HOTEL NEW YORK NOV 27 1869 [*docketed by OLL:*] 148th

¹The "little picture" was probably a small, oval porcelaintype in a velvet- and gold-lined wooden case. On the inside of the case, beneath the picture, is inscribed "Oct. 29 1869" in an unknown hand (see p. 504).

²That is, Nasby had made a concession to Redpath's other lecturers in consenting to be the last speaker in the Rutland course. He lectured on "The Struggles of a Conservative on the Woman Question" in the Rutland Opera House on 17 November, "to the evident satisfaction of his hearers"—the local chapter of the Grand Army of the Republic ("Nasby's Lecture," Rutland *Weekly Herald*, 18 Nov 69, 8). Clemens evidently had been scheduled to lecture in Rutland on 24 or 25 November.

³Henry Wheeler Shaw (Josh Billings) had been married to the former Zilpha E. Bradford since 1845. Their daughter Kate Alice had two children, Henry Shaw and Rosa Grace, with her husband, Jose Ventura Santana, of Caracas, Venezuela. Their daughter Grace Ann had one child, Bradford, with her husband, William H. Duff, of New York City (Cyril Clemens, 31, 45, 145, 152, 179).

To Olivia L. Langdon
27 November 1869 • Boston, Mass.
(MS: CU-MARK)

Boston, Saturday.

Oh, you little rascal! I can't keep the run of you to save me. You speak as if you are going to Mrs. Brooks's, but you don't say precisely *when*, & so I don't know just how to direct my letter. However, I will send it to 675 5th ave., & take the chances.¹ It can't matter greatly, if it fails to reach you, for I am only going to write a line to say I am well, & then go to bed.

Had a big house last night, as usual,. Didn't make a brilliant success otherwise, though.² Good-bye little darling, will write tomorrow.

Sam.

[*enclosures:*]

Josh Billings.   Mark Twain.   Petroleum V. Nasby.
THE AMERICAN HUMORISTS.
Published by G. M. Baker, 149 Washington St., Boston.

[*on the backs:*]

BLACK,

163 WASHINGTON ST., BOSTON.[3]

H. G. SMITH,

STUDIO BUILDING,

BOSTON.

Miss Olivia L. Langdon | 675 Fifth avenue | New York. [*return address:*]
YOUNG'S HOTEL, COURT AVENUE, BOSTON, MASS. [*postmarked:*] BOSTON MASS.
NOV. 27   8.P.M. [*docketed by OLL:*] 149th

[1] Apparently upon her father's departure for Elmira, Olivia was to move from
the St. Nicholas Hotel to the home of Fidele Brooks, to await her mother. If
Jervis Langdon in fact left as scheduled at the end of November, he soon returned to New York to be with his wife and daughter (see the next letter, n. 1).

[2] The site of this indifferent performance has not been identified.

[3] The following note was written in pencil across this imprint, possibly by
photographer James Wallace Black: "Twain 12 | N Y Some done Friday night."
Both enclosures are reproduced here at 82 percent of actual size.

To Olivia L. Langdon
28 November 1869 • Boston, Mass.
(MS: CU-MARK)

Boston, Sunday M.

Livy darling, I thank dear Mrs Susie very much for helping to get you ready to come to me. Anybody that helps in that is my good friend, & I in turn his humble servant. The day approaches, old fellow! Only nine weeks, & then —! Hurrah! Speed the day!

You are with Mrs. Brooks today, I suppose, & consequently happy. Tomorrow morning I shall telegraph her to know where you will be on Wednesday. If at her house, I shall stop at the Everett (or maybe at the Albemarle,) & run up & see you till noon, & then bid you good-bye until next day, for you would all be in bed by the time I got back from Brooklyn. But if you are at the St. Nicholas I shall stop there till 2 PM., & then you shall sit up & wait till I return from Brooklyn.[1]

Tomorrow evening at 6.30 I must run out to Newtonville, half an hour's journey by rail, & lecture, returning here at 10 P.M.[2] ~~Tus~~ Tuesday I shall run down to Thompsonville & talk till half past 8, & then trot along about ~~an hour~~ half an hour & sit up with Twichell at Hartford till after midnight, & then take a sleeping car for New York, arriving at 5 o'clock Wednesday morning.

This is your birthday darling, & you are 24.[3] May you treble your age, in happiness & peace, & I be with you to love you & cherish you all the long procession of years! I have kept this day & honored this anniversary alone, in solitary state—the anniversary of an event which was happening when I was a giddy school-boy a thousand miles away, & played heedlessly all that day & slept heedlessly all that night unconscious that it was the mightiest day that had ever ⸚ winged its viewless hours over my head—unconscious that on that day, two journeys were begun, wide as the poles apart, two paths marked out, which, wandering & wandering, now far & now near, were still narrowing, always narrowing toward one point & one blessed consummation, & these the goal of twenty-four years' marching!—unconscious I was, in that day of my heedless boyhood, that an event had just transpired, so tremendous that without it all my future life had been a sullen pilgrimage, but with it ⸚

that same future was saved!—a sun had just peered above the horizon which should rise & shine out of the zenith upon those coming years & fill them with light & warmth, with peace & blessedness₁, for all time.

I have kept the day alone, my darling—we will keep it together hereafter, God willing. My own birthday's comes Tuesday, & I must keep that alone also, but it don't matter—I have had considerable experience in that.

~~Th~~ Twichell gave me one of Kingsley's most tiresomest books— "Hypatia"—& I have tried to read it & can't. I'll try no more. But he recommended Chas. Reade's "Hearth & Cloister" & I bought it & am enchanted. You shall have it if you have not read it.[4] I read with a pencil by me, sweetheart, but the book is so uniformly good that I find nothing to mark. I simply have the inclination to scribble "I love you, Livy" in the margin, & keep on writing & re-writing "I love you Livy—I love my Livy—I worship my darling"—& bless your dear heart I *do* love you, love you, *love* you, Livy darling, Livy mine—but it won't do to write it in books where unsanctified eyes may profane it—& so, you see, sweetheart, there is nothing to mark.

Livy my precious sweetheart, I have received all your letters & my uneasiness is gone—got 4 in one day, & what a blessed feast it was! I was glad that it had happened so, since it brought so ample a pleasure.

I remember Miss Bateman—she was a gentle-looking little school girl of 12 or 13 when I used to see her in her front yard playing, every day.[5]

And now, if my child is ~~tr~~ tired reading this—which I am proud to say I don't believe she is,—I will write some other letters. Thank goodness I shall kiss you, Wednesday, right on your blessed little mouth. And so good-bye, my own loved & honored Livy.

Sam^{*l*}.

Miss Olivia L. Langdon | 675 Fifth avenue | New York. [*postmarked:*] BOSTON MASS. NOV. 29. 5 A.M. [*docketed by OLL:*] 150th

[1] Clemens planned to reach New York City on Wednesday morning, 1 December, so as to have time with Olivia before lecturing that evening in Brooklyn. Upon arriving, he registered at the Westminster Hotel and then, evidently on 2 December, moved to the St. Nicholas, presumably because Olivia was there ("Personal," New York *Tribune*, 2 Dec 69, 5; "Morning Arrivals," New York *Evening Express*, 3 Dec 69, 3). Olivia was now accompanied by her mother and,

possibly, by her father, who was certainly there by the following week. Two of Clemens's December letters indicate that he saw Jervis Langdon in New York during the first ten or eleven days of the month (see 10 or 11 Dec 69 to Colfax and 15 Dec 69 to JLC and family). In any event, Clemens was able to visit with Olivia before leaving for his 3 December lecture in Poughkeepsie and, after returning to New York City that night or the next morning, until he left for Philadelphia, where he lectured on 7 December. Jervis Langdon, if he already was in New York, probably made a brief trip home, to receive a prominent family friend: Anna E. Dickinson arrived in Elmira on the afternoon of 10 December, lectured that evening at the Opera House, and "as usual, during her stay in this city . . . was a guest of JERVIS LANGDON, Esq." (Elmira *Advertiser:* "City and Neighborhood," 10 Dec 69, 4, 11 Dec 69, 4; "Anna Dickinson on 'The Mormons,'" 11 Dec 69, 4).

²Clemens lectured on 29 November in the Congregational Church in Newtonville, Massachusetts. Although a church could be an inhospitable setting for a humorous lecture (see 13 and 14 Jan 69 to OLL, n. 2), that was not the case in Newtonville. There Clemens "elicited shouts of laughter. Three divines of the town were noticed as present, apparently in a most enjoyable frame of mind" ("Lectures," Newton *Journal*, 4 Dec 69, 2).

³Olivia's birthday was 27 November.

⁴Clemens's library included both Charles Kingsley's *Hypatia; or, New Foes with an Old Face* (Boston: Crosby and Nichols, 1862), about fifth-century Alexandria, and Charles Reade's *The Cloister and the Hearth: A Tale of the Middle Ages* (Chicago: M. A. Donahue and Company, n.d.). These novels were originally published in 1853 and 1861, respectively (Gribben, 1:373, 2:571).

⁵Olivia must have attended one of the final New York performances of British playwright Tom Taylor's *Mary Warner*, with Kate Josephine Bateman (1843–1917) in the title role. On 27 November the melodrama, about a wife who confesses to a theft she believes her husband has committed, closed a run of six weeks at Booth's Theatre. Bateman and her sister Ellen were already famous as child actors when their father, Hezekiah, brought them to St. Louis in 1855, where he managed the Pine Street Theatre until 1859. Clemens lived in St. Louis for the first six months of 1855. During that period he could have seen Kate Bateman, then almost twelve, "every day" while calling on his sister Pamela and her husband William A. Moffett, who were living on Pine Street between Fifth and Sixth streets—near the theater, on Pine between Third and Fourth, and probably near the Bateman residence as well. The 1855 St. Louis directory does not provide an address for Hezekiah Bateman and no directory was published the following year, but the 1857 directory lists him on Fifth Street, where he and his family also may have been living in 1855 ("Amusements," New York *Times*, 19 Oct 69, 5, 7, 26 Nov 69, 5; *L1*, 46, 58; Ludlow, 526–27, 709; Knox, 133; Kennedy 1857, 20, 156).

To Olivia L. Langdon
29 November 1869 • Boston, Mass.
(MS: CU-MARK)

[*on back of itinerary as folded:*]
Don't know whether you've got a copy of this or not, Livy darling.

———∿∿∿———

All well, sweetheart—I *do* love you, Livy—Livy I love you, honey.

BOSTON LYCEUM BUREAU, NO. 20 BROMFIELD ST.
JAMES REDPATH. GEORGE L. FALL.[1]

BOSTON, Nov. 29th 18 69.

Memo of Engagements   Sam'l L. Clemens. from Dec 1. 1869.

1869.

Dec.	1.	Brooklyn	N.Y.	Brooklyn Lib. Asso'n—90 South St. G. W. Frost.
	3.	Poughkeepsie	"	John Grubb.
	6.	Brooklyn	"	Miss S. E. Wason N° 70 Orange St.
	7.	Philadelphia.	Pa	T. B. Pugh.
	8.	Washington	D.C.	J. O. P. Burnside. 2[d] Ass't P. M. Gen'l office.
	9.	Germantown.	Pa.	L. R. Hamersly. "Chronicle"
	10.	M[t]. Vernon.	N.Y.	John Marsellus. No. 58 White St. N. York
	11.	West Meriden.	Conn:	Cha's H. Shaw.
	13.	New, Britain	"	J. Warren Tuck.
	14.	Warren.	Mass.	J. W. Hastings.
	15.	Pawtucket.	R.I.	Tho[s] P. Barnefield.
	16.	Waltham	Mass.	G. A. Bates.
	17.	Abington	"	Henry B. Pearce.
	20.	Canton	"	E. L. Abbott.
	21.	Hudson.	"	Rev. H. G. Gay.
	22.	Portland	Me.	H. F. Furbish.
	23.	Rockport	Mass	Rev. G. H. Vibbert.

24.	Salem	"	John W. Berry.
27.	New Haven.	Conn:	R. P. Cowles.
28.	Trenton.	N.J.	John Taylor.
29.	Newark.	"	G. L. Hutchins.
30.	Wilkes-Barre.	Pa.	H. W. Palmer.
31.	Williamsport	"	J. A. Beeber.

₁*1870.*₁

Jan.				
	4.	Owego	N.Y.	Ira F. Hart. Elmira N.Y.
	6.	Amenia	"	Joel Benton "Times"
	7.	Cohoes	"	Silas Owen
	10.	Albany	"	Rob. W. C. Mitchell.
	11.	West Troy	"	G. R. Meneely.
	12.	Rondout	"	H. M. Crane.
	13.	Cambridge	"	A. H. Comstock.
	14.	Utica	"	W. P. Carpenter.
	17.	Baldwinsville	"	W. F. Morris.

⊠——————————————————————————————

Miss Olivia L. Langdon | 675 Fifth Avenue | New York. | [*flourish*]
[*return address:*] YOUNG'S HOTEL, COURT AVENUE, BOSTON, MASS. [*postmarked:*]
BOSTON MASS. NOV. 29. 8.P.M.

[1] The memo is in Fall's hand. Among Clemens's contacts at his various lecture stops were: S. E. Wasson, a Brooklyn teacher (see 4 Dec 69 and 6 Dec 69, both to Redpath); T. B. Pugh, a Philadelphia impresario, whose popular "Star Course of Lectures" featured the leading performers of the day; James Oliver Perry Burnside (b. 1828); Lewis Randolph Hamersly (1847–1910), who later compiled several directories of military biography; John Marsellus (1846–1941), a clerk at the hosiery firm of William H. and Leonard C. Thorne, at 58 White Street, New York, and afterward a casket manufacturer; Thomas Pierce Barnefield (1844–99), a Rhode Island supreme-court reporter; the Reverend George H. Vibbert, a crusader for prohibition; Henry Wilbur Palmer (1839–1913), a Wilkes-Barre attorney and later a four-time Republican congressman from Pennsylvania; Ira F. Hart, an Elmira physician; poet Joel Benton (1832–1911), who managed the Amenia, New York, lecture course and was to be reached through the weekly Amenia *Times*, which he had edited from 1851 to 1856; George Rodney Meneely, proprietor of a bell foundry in West Troy, New York; Henry M. Crane; and William Penn Carpenter (see 8 Sept 69 and 21 Sept 69 to Crane and 23 Sept 69 to Carpenter).

To the Editor of the Brooklyn *Eagle*
3 December 1869 • Brooklyn, N.Y.
(Brooklyn *Eagle*, 4 Dec 69)

To the Editor of the Brooklyn Eagle:[1]

I was to have lectured in Brooklyn on Monday, Dec. 6th, but a misunderstanding has intervened, and I take this method of informing the public that I have canceled the engagement, and will not be present upon that occasion.[2]

MARK TWAIN.

BROOKLYN, Dec. 3d.

---

[1] Thomas Kinsella (1832–84), a native of Ireland, was hired by the Brooklyn *Eagle* as a typesetter in 1858, became a law reporter, and in 1861 assumed the editorship, which he retained until his death. Under Kinsella's direction, the *Eagle* became Brooklyn's leading journal and claimed "the largest circulation of any evening paper in the United States" (Rowell, 65).

[2] The misunderstanding is explained by the next two letters, to James Redpath. Clemens had delivered the first of his scheduled Brooklyn lectures on the evening of 1 December, at the Bedford Avenue Reformed Church, for the Brooklyn Library Association, also called the Williamsburgh Library Association. The Brooklyn *Times* reported that the performance "gave delight" and evoked "ever recurring peals of laughter." And the Brooklyn *Eagle* remarked upon "the frequent interruptions of the audience whose senses of appreciation were unmistakeably tickled in the right spot" ("The Sandwich Islands," Brooklyn *Times*, 2 Dec 69, 2; "Williamsburgh Library Association Lecture," Brooklyn *Eagle*, 2 Dec 69, 3; Lain, 68).

To James Redpath
per Telegraph Operator
4 December 1869 • New York, N.Y.
(MS, copy received: Jacobs)

THE WESTERN UNION TELEGRAPH COMPANY.

DATED   New York   Dec 4   186 9

RECEIVED AT

TO   James Redpath

20 Bromfield st[1]

Yes I did I will never suggest again this is no regular course it is an
infernal mite society[2] a pure charity speculation what the mischief did
they come boring me with their offensive letters *for* any how. Read
her letter once more that I sent you She has not been civil at all first
or last[3]

Clemens

58/15 126
Z A

✉

[docketed by George Fall:] N.Y. | Saml *[and in unidentified hand:]* S. L.
Clemens | New York   Dec. 4 '69

[1] The address of Redpath's Boston Lyceum Bureau.
[2] See 30, 31 Oct, and 1 Nov 69 to OLL, n. 4.
[3] Clemens apparently was responding to the following telegram, sent to the
home of Henry and Fidele Brooks:

Samuel L. Clemens, Six hundred Seventy five Fifth Avenue, New York,—
Please see Miss Wason, Brooklyn.
Not speculators but regular Course. This engagement was made at your own written
request.

James Redpath.
(undated copy, James Redpath Letterpress Book, 600, IaU)

S. E. Wasson kept a private school at 70 Orange Street, in Brooklyn (Lain, 686,
813). Her "pure charity speculation" has not been identified; the letter from her
that Clemens forwarded to Redpath is not known to survive.

To James Redpath
6 December 1869 • New York, N.Y.
(MS: ViU)

New York, Dec 6th 1869.

Mr. Sam'l L. Clemens,

    Dear Sir,

       As you will perhaps remember, the lecture committee of the "Plymouth Young People's Association" desired to secure your services, for a lecture to be delivered, during the present month, in Plymouth Church, Brooklyn. Your agent in Boston wrote us some two weeks ago, that you were to lecture in Brooklyn, Dec. 1st and again Dec 6th, and would prefer not to engage yourself for a third time. Seeing your card, however, in the Brooklyn evening papers of Saturday last, we thought you might, perhaps, be induced to change your answer previously given us.

       If you can lecture for us any night of this or next week, we would be pleased to have you communicate with either of us, as below.

             Yours truly,

              Wm. F. West

                 31 Mercer St, near Grand

              Horatio C. King   } Committee.[1]

                 38 Wall St.

              Lorin Palmer

                 170 Water St.

[*in available space:*]

Dear Redpath—

    I talked with Horatio C. King about this but I didn't want to lecture in Brooklyn any more, & so I told him I had no night open.

    This is the very society I thought that infernal woman was representing. This is the Society I have long been wanting to talk for & King & I have often tried to fix a date & never could before.[2]

    But I've got enough. I never *will* lecture outside of New England again—& I never will lecture in Brooklyn at all. I'm just beat out with that most ~~infernal~~ ˎinfernal˯ Mite Society. I published a card in the Brooklyn papers saying I would not be present at the Brooklyn Athe-

neum to-night.³ I am to blame from the very start—& NOBODY ELSE. I
have done all this on my own responsibility—I shoulder it *all*.

Mark.

Suspend judgment, Redpath, till you see me. We were both mistaken about that Miss Wason's Mite Society. If she writes complainingly
to you, tell her *I* you are authorized by me to pay the expense she has
been at if it is not over fifty dollars—& that is all the reparation you know
how to make. [She did no advertising, & that was one thing I was ˌsoˌ
outrageously mad about. She put in one square (marked eod ˱e ie.
"every other day") in the least circulated Brooklyn paper, & not a line
in any other—& th̶ she made *that* ad. read as if *I* was talking on my own
hook & for no society—a public independent mountebank in an unused
barn of a theatre up a back street.] Excuse *me* from talking in any such
place.⁴

Mark

Snowing & blowing—this is the worst night you ever saw—I am glad I
just saved myself.

¹ The lecture invitation, including the signatures, is in a single hand, probably
William F. West's. West and Lorin Palmer, like Horatio C. King, were members
of Henry Ward Beecher's Plymouth Church—since 1865 and 1859, respectively.
The addresses given here were business locations. Palmer was a New York to-
bacconist, in partnership with Amasa H. Scoville; West was a New York im-
porter, in partnership with William S. Field (Noyes L. Thompson, 246, 250;
Wilson 1869, 353, 858, 859, 994, 1167).

² One such attempt had come early in 1869 (see 13 Mar 69 to King and Howard). A lecture itinerary prepared for Clemens on 25 November 1869 by George
L. Fall—"Mark Twain's Engagements from Dec 1ˢᵗ 1869" (James Redpath Letterpress Book, 481, IaU)—had included a 6 December lecture at Plymouth
Church. In requesting to speak for S. E. Wasson on that date (see the preceding
letter, n. 3), Clemens had mistakenly assumed that she represented the Plymouth Young People's Association. Therefore when he received Fall's 29 November revised itinerary, which replaced the Plymouth Church engagement with the
lecture for Wasson, he was unaware that anything was amiss (see 29 Nov 69 to
OLL).

³ The only version of Clemens's "card" that has been recovered is his 3 December letter to the editor of the Brooklyn *Eagle*.

⁴ The Brooklyn Atheneum, on the corner of Atlantic and Clinton streets, reportedly was "a literary institution, containing a fine library, reading-room,
lecture-room, &c. . . . It is a handsome brick building, with stone facings"
(James Miller, 112–13). The offending advertisement of Clemens's scheduled
lecture there has not been identified, but it was not the only notice that S. E.
Wasson placed. The Brooklyn *Eagle*, the borough's most influential paper, carried at least one advertisement ("Lectures," 2 Dec 69, 1). And the Brooklyn

Union, which also had a large circulation, printed at least one announcement ("Amusements," 4 Dec 69, 2). Neither paper identified the organization that Wasson represented, however (Rowell, 65).

To Schuyler Colfax
10 or 11 December 1869 • New York, N.Y.
(MS: NSyU)

[*one-third MS page (about 9 words) missing*]

Away at this late day I come forward to thank you cordially & sincerely for the letter you furnished to Charley Langdon & Prof. Ford. ₍I have been lecturing every night since,₎₎ It was exactly the thing they needed, & will admit them into all doors like another "Open Sesame." I wouldn't have bothered you ~~with it~~ ₍about it,₎₎ knowing how busy you are, but then I didn't know those kings over there, & I *had* to do it. If they ₍boys₎ get into ~~trouble,~~ ₍any close places₎ now, they will not have any trouble in the matter of getting our Ministers & Consuls to give attention to their case. And so I thank you again. I wanted to ~~tha~~ do this by word of mouth, but I had only one night in Washington—not an hour of daylight.[1] THE young lady who occupies the most of the universe,—₎& also her father & mother—send their kindest remembrances.

Sincerely Yours—

Sam*ˡ*. L. Clemens.

[1] See 9 Oct 69 to Colfax. Clemens may here be answering a letter from Colfax that had sought him in Elmira, at the Boston Lyceum Bureau, or at one or more of his lecture stops. Possibly, however, he had learned of Colfax's " 'Open Sesame' " in a letter from Langdon or Ford, or through Olivia or her parents. In any case, he clearly wrote this "thank you" soon after 8 December, when he lectured in Washington but failed to see Colfax. Most likely he did so in New York City, either on 10 December, before or after his lecture in Mount Vernon, New York, or the following day before he lectured in West Meriden, Connecticut ("Morning Arrivals," New York *Evening Express*, 11 Dec 69, 3).

To James Redpath
13 December 1869 • Springfield, Mass.
(Merwin-Clayton, lot 128)

128. CLEMENS (SAMUEL L.) A. L. S. (*Mark*), 1 page, 8vo, Dec.
13, 1869,[1] directing a change in the advertisement of his lecture.
"About twice a week I have to make an annoying apology to the
audience."[2]

[1] After his 13 December lecture in New Britain, Connecticut, Clemens left by
train for Springfield, Massachusetts, about twenty-five miles north, where he
spent the night. Although he might have written to Redpath before departing or
en route, it is more probable that he did so after his arrival in Springfield.

[2] Pursuant to Clemens's letter of 10 May 1869, Redpath had distributed a circular to lyceums announcing that " 'Mark Twain's' only lecture for the season of
1869–70 will be entitled 'The Curiosities of California' " (see Boston Lyceum
Bureau Advertising Circular, Appendix E). Clemens had remained committed
to such a lecture at least into early summer, then abandoned it by 27 September,
five weeks before the beginning of his tour (see 5 July 69 to Fairbanks and 27
September 69 to Bliss). Redpath must have adjusted his publicity promptly, perhaps with an amended circular, for newspaper advertisements in host cities generally reported the new topic—"Our Fellow Savages of the Sandwich Islands."
Nevertheless, Clemens sometimes had to explain the substitution at the last moment: his 10 December audience in Mount Vernon, New York, for example, had
expected to hear him talk about California ("On Friday evening . . . ," Mount
Vernon *Chronicle*, 18 Dec 69, 2). Presumably in the missing portion of the present letter he requested measures to eliminate remaining confusion—possibly
through the placement of "special advertisements" such as Redpath had proposed on 24 April (see 10 May 69 to Redpath, n. 1). Advertisements in the
weekly Jamestown, New York, *Journal* indicate that late corrections were indeed
made. On 24 December, the paper announced the title of Mark Twain's Jamestown lecture, scheduled for 21 January 1870, as "Curiosities of California," but
the following week corrected it to "Our Fellow Savages of the Sandwich Islands"
("Y.M.C.A. Lecture Course for 1869 and 1870," 8).

To Olivia L. Langdon
14 December 1869 • Springfield, Mass.
(MS: CU-MARK)

Springfield, Dec. 14.

Livy my peerless, I had a packed house in New Britain last night, & although I forgot & left out a~~ll~~ *l* considerable portion of the lecture the audience were none the wiser, & the ~~talk~~ discourse was plenty long enough. The other night at Meriden I struck upon an entirely new *manner* of telling a favorite anecdote of mine,[1]—& now, without altering a single word, it shortly becomes so absurd that I have to laugh, myself. Last night I got to one particular point in it 3 different times before I could get by it & go on. Every time I lifted my hand aloft & took up the thread of the narrative in the same old place the audience exploded again & so did I. But I got through at last, & it was very funny. This teaches me that a man might tell that Jumping Frog story fifty times without learning *how* to tell it—but between you & I, privately, Livy dear, it is the best humorous sketch America has produced, yet, & I must read it ~~p~~ in public some day, in order that people may know what there is in it.[2]

I lay abed till 11 this morning, for I found that sleeping beside an open window had given me a cold in the head.

And honey, I had such a vivid, *vivid* dream! I thought you had discarded me, & that you avoided me so carefully that for several days although we were under the same roof & [I] often caught momentary glimpses of you or your dress, I could not get speech with you. And to add to my misery, I always had a glimpse of a rival when I had one of you. He was *always* with you, & I seemed to understand that he was an old rejected lover of yours (but not W.,)[3] who had patiently waited, knowing that he could regain his place in your love if he could but get with you in my absence. Once I thought I was going to catch you alone, for I saw you hasten into a private room. I ran to it, but only to see you with glad face & beaming eyes throw yourself into a seat close to that hated rival—whose perfectly imbecile face I then saw for the first time, & from that moment merely despised instead of hating him.

Well, that very afternoon I caught you alone for a few moments, & ah, yours ~~were~~ was the saddest, saddest face that ever was. But you were in the toils of that man & could not escape. Your face said that there was

no more *true* happiness for you on earth—nothing but a feverish fascination, & then a vapid, vacant existence, then Death. It broke my heart
to see this fearful thing in the darling old face I was still worshipping. I
pleaded with you—supplicated you—beseeched you—but you put me
gently aside, & said you knew you were drifting to certain wreck, but it
could not be helped—it was too late—if ~~tha~~ this man had *only* been kept
out of the way but a month or two longer ~~you~~ ‚all‚ would have been well—
but henceforth you & I must travel different paths in life, & from this
moment these paths must diverge & never come together any more forever. ~~You would think of a~~ You would "‚think of me sometimes, & hold
me in regard as an esteemed acquaintance‚.", ~~, as a pleasant humorist."~~
I siezed your hand, & said, "O, Livy, I loved you with such infinite
tenderness!"

Then the tears sprang to your eyes & you threw your arms about
my neck,‚—~~but on~~ But only for an instant. Then you sprang up & said
"No!—it is over for all time!" And you fled away & left me prostrate
upon the floor.

Livy, for an hour after I awoke, this morning (but had not yet
opened my eyes,) I lay in unspeakable misery, grieving over my sad
mischance & going patiently over each incident & each circumstance
vainly trying to discover how the awful calamity had been brought upon
me. And such exquisite suffering it was! And how perfectly matchless
seemed the gem I had lost! And I comprehended that in losing you the
very universe had gone from me & black chaos was come again.

And then I opened my eyes. The apartment was strange to me!
Presently it flashed upon me—it was only a hideous dream! God knows
that the bliss, the ecstasy of that moment falls to a man's lot no second
time in the long span of his human life. You mine again—my own, my
darling—& I so longed to put my arms about you & *feel* & know that the
ghastly dream was gone forever. I want no more such dreams, my Livy.

I shall be in Warren[4] tonight & in Boston to-morrow.

Peace & happiness & all contentment abide with you, my precious
darling.

Sam.[5]

---

[1] Apparently Clemens's tale about an "Incorporated Company of Mean Men,"
later used in chapter 77 of *Roughing It* ("Mark Twain's Lecture," Meriden
[Conn.] *Republican*, 13 Dec 69, 2). The Meriden lecture took place on 11
December.

[2] On 15 March 1870 Clemens carried out this plan. That evening he shared a

stage in Buffalo with English elocutionist Henry Nichols, who read from Shake-speare, Dickens, Thackeray, and others:

"Mark Twain" appeared twice during the evening and read, "The Jumping Frog of Cala-veras County," and, also, the chapter on European Guides from "The Innocents Abroad," in both of which he gave the audience a touch of originality that was pronounced decidedly refreshing. His style of elocution is peculiarly his own, and the manner in which he delin-eated the humor of his sketches was irresistably funny. The audience was kept in the best possible humor during his recitations, and at the end called loudly for a repetition by Mark, who coolly informed the assemblage that his "contract" had been fulfilled, etc., etc., therefore no *encore* was obtained. ("The Readings Last Evening," Buffalo *Express,* 16 Mar 70, 4)

[3] Unidentified.

[4] Warren, Massachusetts.

[5] The envelope to this letter, presumably bearing Olivia's docket, is missing. Since she docketed Clemens's next letter "156th," the present one almost cer-tainly was 155.

To Jane Lampton Clemens and Family
15 December 1869 • Boston, Mass.
(MS: NPV)

₂20 Bromfield st.,₁
Boston, Dec. 15. }

My Dear Folks—

    I arrived here late last night after lecturing in Warren, & shall leave at dusk to lecture in Pawtucket Rhode Island. I shall be talking every night in the neighboring cities at night for the next 2 or 3 weeks, & spending my days in Boston.

    I got your letter, Pamela, & am much obliged, but I will not try to answer it, for I have caught a severe cold, & do not feel very well.

    I left Livy & the folks at the St. Nicholas, where they will remain a week or so buying Livy's "trowsers" (trousseau) as Mr. Langdon calls it.

    I sent you my share of the Tennessee money—however, I believe I wrote you about that. I enclose $25 for Ma.[2]

In haste affc^ty
Sam.

[1] Clemens was at the Boston Lyceum Bureau.

[2] Jane Lampton Clemens recorded the receipt of this amount on 18 December. By her own reckoning, she received a total of $415 from Clemens during 1869. On 8 December, he had withdrawn $250 from his cash account with Slote,

Woodman and Company of New York, all or part of which may have gone toward his share of "the Tennessee money"—undoubtedly a tax payment on the family property, which Orion Clemens was attempting to sell. No record of receipt of Clemens's contribution has been identified, nor has his letter about it been located (JLC, 4; 23 June 69 to PAM, n. 4; 3? July 69 to OC, n. 1; "Mʳ S. L. Clemens in a/c and Interest a/c to Jany 1ˢᵗ 1870 with Slote Woodman & Co.," CU-MARK).

To Olivia L. Langdon
15 and 16 December 1869 • Pawtucket, R.I., and
Boston, Mass.
(MS: CU-MARK)

Pawtucket, R.I, 14ᵗʰ.

My child, I was thunderstruck at getting no letter from you in Boston to-day. It seemed to me that I had neither seen nor heard from you for many a day—but now that I come to count up I am astonished to find that I saw you, touched you, held you in my arms, kissed you, only four days ago.[1] This will give you an idea of how immensely long a lecture season seems. A 3-month season seems a year ordinarily—& when you come to add absence from one's sweetheart, it becomes a sort of lifetime.

Had a talk with Fred Douglas, to-day, who seemed exceedingly glad to see me—& I certainly was glad to see *him*, for I do so admire his "spunk."[2] He told the history of his child's expulsion from Miss Tracy's school, & his simple language was very effective. Miss Tracy said the pupils did not want a colored child among them—which he did not believe, & challenged the proof. She put it at once to a vote of the school, and asked "How many of you are willing to have this colored child be with you?" And they *all* held up their hands! Douglas added: "The children's hearts were right." There was pathos in the way he said it. I would like to hear him make a speech. Has a grand face.[3]

I have such a cold that I did not thoroughly please myself to-night though the audience seemed to like it.[4] I am writing in bed, now—which you

[at least two MS pages (about 130 words) missing][5]

write a breakfast. Take all the sleep you can, little rascal, it will do you more good than harm.

I did not write you to-day—my cold reduced me to a spiritless state. I wouldn't be writing you now, only I love you so, Livy, that I can't help it. I *have* to commune with you, even if it be in simply a few sentences scratched with a vile, blunt pencil. I was afraid something was the matter, but I am content, now that I have heard from my darling.

I bless you & kiss you, my precious Livy, & have prayed that God would fill your soul with peace & shelter you from harm.

Sam.

[✉]

[*in ink:*] Miss Olivia L. Langdon | St. Nicholas Hotel | New York. | Room 242. [*return address:*] BOSTON LYCEUM BUREAU, NO. 20 BROMFIELD ST. BOSTON. [*postmarked:*] BOSTON MASS. DEC. 16 8.P.M. [*docketed:*] ST. NICHOLAS HOTEL NEW-YORK DEC 17 1869 [*docketed by OLL:*] ~~Dec 14~~th | 156th [*and in pencil:*][6]

```
              12    6   52
               1        6
120               312
144        
264        25         12
360        12          30
624        50         360
  2        25
           300


7        12              20 25
         10                52
         120               50
         24               125
         12              1300
         1560
Servants 700                      20
Horse    300                       4
Living   1300<                    80
         2300                    150
                                4500
                                  80

  4000
  2300                         12500
  1700
```

[1] Clemens's lecture itinerary had permitted him to spend most of 1–6 December and part of 10–11 December with Olivia in New York City. As his third paragraph here indicates, he was writing on 15 December, following his Pawtucket lecture.

[2] Clemens probably spoke with Frederick Douglass (1817?–95), the former slave who had achieved fame as an abolitionist and journalist, in Boston, before leaving for Pawtucket. Douglass was himself on a month-long lecture tour of New England—he had spoken on "Our Composite Nationality" in Boston's Music Hall, in the Parker Fraternity Course, on 7 December—and, like Clemens, may have been making Boston his headquarters (Boston *Evening Transcript:* "Special Notices," 7 Dec 69, 2; "Local Intelligence," 8 Dec 69, 4; New York *Tribune:* "Boston," 11 Dec 69, 2). Olivia's parents had known Douglass since September 1838 when, while living in Millport, New York, they abetted his escape from slavery in Maryland. Douglass recalled the assistance in a letter to Mrs. Langdon three months after her husband's death (CtHMTH):

Rochester: Nov 9th 1870

Dear Mrs Langdon:

Pardon the Liberty, but as one who nearly thirty years ago, learned something of the noble character of your lamented Husband, I beg you to allow me to enroll myself among the many who to day hold his name and history in grateful memory. If I had never seen nor heard of Mr Langdon since the days that you and himself made me welcome under your roof in Millport, I should never have forgotten either of you. Those were times of inefface[a]ble memories with me, and I have carried the name of Jervis Langdon with me ever since. The record of his life as given in the address of his Pastor has touched me deeply—and hence these few words. Please give my thanks to your Dear son for sending me a copy of that address.

Very truly with great Respect yours
Frederick Douglass

[3] Douglass had declined to send his nine-year-old daughter, Rosetta, to one of the segregated schools that Rochester, New York, had established for black children. Instead he enrolled her in the city's oldest female academy, the all-white Seward Seminary, headed by principal Lucilia Tracy (Blassingame et al., 534 n. 14; McKelvey, 345). The September 1848 incident he recalled for Clemens did not end with the children's unanimous vote of acceptance. As Douglass reported at the time:

Each scholar was then told by the principal, that the question must be submitted to their parents, and that if one parent objected, the child would not be received into the school. The next morning my child went to school as usual, but returned with her books and other materials, saying that one person objected, and that she was therefore excluded from the Seminary.

This account was part of the indignant open letter to the objecting parent— H. G. Warner, editor of the Rochester *Courier*—that Douglass published in his own paper, the weekly Rochester *North Star*, on 22 September 1848. In concluding his protest, Douglass wrote:

I am also glad to inform you that you have not succeeded as you hoped to do, in depriving my child of the means of a decent education, or the privilege of going to an excellent school. She had not been excluded from Seward Seminary for five hours, before she was gladly welcomed into another quite as respectable, and *equally* christian to the one from which she was excluded. She now sits in a school among children as pure, and as white as you or yours, and no one is offended. (Douglass)

[4]The reviewers were unimpressed, however. The Providence *Journal* observed: "The lecturer labored under considerable indisposition of body, and his voice was made dry and husky by a severe cold, all of which had an unfavorable effect upon the evening's entertainment" ("Pawtucket," 17 Dec 69, 1). And the Pawtucket *Gazette and Chronicle* of 17 December (3) remarked:

"MARK TWAIN" delivered the opening lecture of the Young Men's Christian Association Course, on Wednesday evening last, in Armory Hall. He was introduced by himself, and his lecture was "intensely interesting to those who were intensely interested." We are of the opinion of our young friend Crowninshield, at No. 3 Almy's Block, who is the sole agent for North Providence for "Mark's" new book, that "he is a *fair* lecturer, but he writes much better than he talks."

[5]Clemens wrote the following portion of this letter on 16 December, after returning to Boston. The surviving leaves show that he tore both the 15 and 16 December segments from his notebook at the same time. The missing matter almost certainly included a dateline for the continuation.

[6]Olivia canceled "Dec 14th" when she realized that Clemens's dating of this letter was incorrect. The calculations that follow were her attempt to project her future household budget. Identifiable costs are: living expenses of $25 a week, or $1,300 a year; care of a horse at $25 a month, or $300 a year; and wages for servants—apparently including one at $10, one at $12, and one at $30 per month—totaling $624 a year, which Olivia rounded upward to $700. The total potential expenses came to $2,300 of an anticipated annual income of $4,000.

To Pamela A. Moffett
17 December 1869 • Boston, Mass.
(MS: CU-MARK)

Boston, ₫ Dec. 17.

My Dear Sister—

Yours of 10th is received. I know Mrs. Langdon wants you & Annie to get there several days before the wedding, because their might be little chance to visit, later. We have about persuaded her to give us a perfectly private wedding, but we can't tell how it will be, yet. Livy has written delightedly to say you are likely to come. Her heart is thoroughly set upon it$_{/}$, & I don't like to have the child disappointed.

Purchase no outfit. Come as you are.[1]

I examined my pocket a moment ago, to see if I had $500 to send to Ma, but I only found $300. I have been paying out a few more hundreds within a few days, & must work two or three days longer before I can forward the $500. But it shall be forthcoming.[2]

I am killed up with a cold, & shall not lecture to-night—so *there* goes a few weeks' board.[3]

~~We~~ No—we are not to be married in the evening, but about noon. Then if we *must* have a reception, that will take place in the evening. The idea of *our* starting on a bridal "trip," is funny. Neither of us are fond of traveling, & you may be sure we shall not go a mile that we are not obliged to go.

We shall go to Buffalo the day after the marriage & never stir another peg till we are compelled to do it.

I cordially accept Annie's & Sammy's explanations—& there is good hard sense & candor enough in Sammy's to compensate for fifty lost presents. I fully appreciate Annie's, too, for if there is one thing I cordially hate more than another, it is the bore of selecting a present. I have already told Livy that I shall deliberately violate the custom to giving the bride a wedding present—& by a sing~~le~~ular coincidence I used both ~~an~~ Annies & Sammy's reason's in explanation of my conduct.[4]

I am sorry Ma's health remains so bad—St Louis is not the climate to improve it, I am afraid.

In haste,

> Affectionately
>
> Sam.

---

[1] An echo of Olivia's 13 and 14 November letter to Clemens (see 10 and 11 Nov 69 to OLL, n. 1).

[2] The "few more hundreds" may have included, in addition to lecturing expenses, an interest payment on Clemens's indebtedness to Jervis Langdon (see 12 Aug 69 to Bliss, n. 2, and 20 and 21 Aug 69 to PAM, p. 311). Since Clemens's lecture fee during the present tour was generally either $75 or $100, he was capable of completing the $500 for his mother within a few days. Nevertheless, he did not send her a check for that amount until early January 1870. She recorded its receipt on the sixth of the month (JLC, 4). Clemens intended her to use at least some of this money to come to Elmira for his 2 February 1870 wedding (see 21 Dec 69 to OLL). Jane Clemens did not make the trip (Dixon Wecter was mistaken in reporting that she did: see *MTMF*, 115 n. 2). Pamela and Annie Moffett were able to attend, however, afterward spending part of February with the newlyweds in Buffalo and visiting for a week with the Langdons in Elmira. They also explored Fredonia, New York, renting the house to which they and Jane Clemens would move in the spring (*MTMF*, 122; *MTBus*, 107, 112).

[3] The canceled lecture was to have been in Abington, Massachusetts. There is no indication that it was rescheduled.

[4] No letters from Annie and Samuel Moffett have been found. Pamela may have simply passed on their explanations in her letter of 10 December, also now lost.

To Olivia L. Langdon
18 and 19 December 1869 • Boston, Mass.
(MS: CU-MARK)

Boston, Dec. 18 PM

Sweetheart, I wrote you this morning, & dated the letter *yesterday*. So you must never pay any attention to my *dates*—they are hardly ever right.[1]

I have a letter from Mrs. Barstow in which she says Joe Goodman has gone to New York & will go from there to Elmira. *She* does not mention Joe's wife—& so Mrs. G. is not with him. I am glad.

I have no doubt Joe has already gone to Elmira, but I do not know whether he has or not, & so I hardly know how to get an invitation to him to send his card to your home. I must think up some way of managing it.[2]

And right away I will write to the Alta for those two letters for my darling. I will not neglect it longer, Livy dear.[3]

19th—I haven't anything to write, to-day, except that I *love* you Livy—nothing to write but that——except that my breast is better, nearly well, in fact, the soreness in my throat is gone, & amounted to nothing in the first place—I have staid in my room all day long & think I shall be entirely ready for the stump again to-morrow night.

Last night I went to bed at 8 o'clock, & Gov. Hawley came in shortly after (we were at the "Burd dinner" during the afternoon)[4] & sat reading till a late hour, & ~~them~~ then Lyman Beecher came in & I made him stay till 1 o'clock, for I had gone to bed to rest & read, not sleep. Lyman's mother is at the point of death.[5]

Kittie Barstow wants me to write to some of the Senators to get a place in the Treasury clerkships for her well-meaning but useless husband—& I shall do it, though it is fearfully disagreeable to help to make one's government a poorhouse for idle & worthless people like Billy Barstow. I shall ask the favor as a kindness to his wife, & not as a recognition of any sort of merit in *him*.[6]

Goodbye, my idol, & God bless you & protect you. I shall see you once more, twelve days from now.

Sam.

✉

[*in ink:*] Miss Olivia L. Langdon | Elmira | N. Y. [*postmarked:*] BOSTON
MASS. DEC. 20. 3 A.M. [*docketed by OLL:*] ~~158th~~ | 159th 18th Dec[7]

[1]Presumably Olivia had remarked, in a 17 December letter, on Clemens's er-
roneous dating of his letter of 15 and 16 December. His misdated morning letter
of 18 December was the second of two missing at this point (docket numbers 157
and 158). The other probably was a letter of 17 December.

[2]Goodman had left California by overland rail on 1 December, bound for
Washington, D.C., New York, and then Europe for several months. Arriving in
Washington by 8 or 9 December, he evidently visited his and Clemens's old Nevada friends, Kate D. Barstow and her husband, William, at their home in Fredericksburg, Virginia, near the capital. Although the Langdons would be meeting
Goodman for the first time, they may have corresponded with him after Clemens
offered him as a character reference in December 1868 (*L2*, 358). Goodman and
Clemens were about to see each other as well—possibly in New York in late December or in New York or Elmira in early January 1870—as indicated by the
following commentary on Goodman's relationship with his wife, Ellen (1837?–
93), which Clemens sent to Olivia shortly afterward:

I plainly see, now, why Joe Goodman gradually lost all interest in his poetry (he was a born
poet) & finally lost all ambition in that direction & ceased to write. The one whose applause
would have been dearer to him & more potent than that of all the world beside, could not
help him, or encourage him or spur him, because she was far below his intellectual level &
could not appreciate the work of his brain or feel an interest in it. When I told him you
took care of my sketches for me & listened with a lively interest to any manuscript of mine
before it was printed, he dropped an unconscious remark that was so full of pathos—so
fraught with "It might have been"—that my heart ached for him. He *could* have been so
honored of men, & so loved by all ~~who~~ for whom poetry has a charm, but for the dead
weight ∅ & clog ~~of a wife~~ upon his winged genius, of a wife whose soul could have no
companionship save with the things of the dull earth. (10 Jan 70 to OLL [2nd of 2], CU-
MARK, published in part in *MFMT*, 209–10)

("For Europe," Virginia City *Territorial Enterprise*, 2 Dec 69, 2; 21 Dec 69 to
OLL; Goodman, 5.)

[3]In pursuing her "commission" to collect and save articles by Clemens (see 28
Feb 69 to OLL), Olivia had asked for his two 1869 letters to the San Francisco
Alta California. Published on 25 July and 1 August, they are his last known contributions to the paper (SLC 1869h, 1869j). In January 1870, in response to
prompting from Olivia, Clemens again promised to provide her with the second
of them (10 Jan 70 to OLL [2nd of 2], CU-MARK, published in part in *MFMT*,
209–10). The fragment of it that survives in the Mark Twain Papers may have
been from the clipping that she eventually received.

[4]The dinner Clemens attended with Joseph R. Hawley, former governor of
Connecticut, was in honor of "the Sage of Walpole," Francis W. Bird (1809–94).
A Republican with a strong anti-slavery record, Bird had been denied re-election
to the Massachusetts legislature on 2 November as a result of "a split in the republican ranks on prohibition and local issues." He had opposed absolute prohibition because, as he told the Lyceum Association of East Walpole on 15 December: "He must be very blind to the signs of the times who believes it possible

to sustain and enforce the present Prohibitory Law" ("The State Election," Boston *Advertiser*, 4 Nov 69, 1; "Walpole," Boston *Evening Transcript*, 16 Dec 69, 4; "Francis W. Bird," New York *Times*, 24 May 94, 4).

[5] Katherine Edes Beecher, mother of Lyman Beecher (see 9 Nov 69 to PAM, n. 6), died in 1870.

[6] Clemens had already done a kindness for Kate D. Barstow and soon wrote at least one letter on behalf of her husband (see 7 Sept 69 to Bliss [two letters] and 25 Dec 69 to OLL).

[7] Clemens's morning letter of 18 December, no longer extant, must have reached Olivia after the present one, occasioning her revision of this docket number.

To Olivia L. Langdon
21 December 1869 • Boston, Mass.
(MS: CU-MARK)

BOSTON LYCEUM BUREAU, NO. 20 BROMFIELD ST.
JAMES REDPATH. GEORGE L. FALL.

BOSTON, Dec. 21 18 69.

Little sweetheart, I have the advantage of you at last. Often & over again your letters for me have been accumulating at some point distant from me while I have been fidgetting & doing without. But now for a day or two I have been forwarding my remarks to Elmira while my darling has been still vegetating in New York. And this one goes to Elmira, too. But I sent your father a telegram a little while ago to let you know that Joe Goodman & Mr. Seeley are in New York on their way to Elmira. Seeley is after the comfortable, berth of U. S. District Judge for the District of Nevada—an old friend of mine.[1]

I do hope Joe won't get tight while he is here in the States, but I wouldn't be surprised if he did. But he is a splendid fellow, anyhow.

I have written my sister in such a way that she will be almost sure to come to our wedding. I have promised to send my mother $500⁻ in a short time—& I will pay my sister's expenses too.

I talked last night in Canton, & had the hospitalities of Mr. Ames, (son of Oakes Ames the P.R.R. Mogul) inflicted on me—& it is the last time I will stop in a New England private house. Their idea of hospitality is to make *themselves* comfortable *first*, & leave the guest to get along *if*

he can. No smoking allowed on the premises. The next New Englander that
receives me into his house will take me as I *am*, not as I ought to be. To
curtail a guest's liberties & demand that he shall come up to the host's
peculiar self-righteous ideas of virtue, is simply pitiful & contemptible.
I hate Mr. Ames with all my heart.[2] I had no sleep last night, & must seek
some rest, little sweetheart.[3] Bless you my own darling, whom I love better & better & more & more tenderly every day.

Sam.

✉

Miss Olivia L. Langdon | Elmira | N. Y. [*return address:*] BOSTON LYCEUM
BUREAU, NO. 20 BROMFIELD ST. BOSTON. [*postmarked:*] BOSTON MASS. DEC. 21.
8.P.M. [*docketed by OLL:*] Dec 21st 160th

[1] Jonas Seely (1832?–83), a lawyer in Carson City and Virginia City in the early
1860s, and currently an acting United States district attorney in Nevada, had
accompanied Goodman to Washington. Seely was seeking the post that had been
held for four years by a close Nevada friend of Clemens's, Alexander W.
("Sandy") Baldwin (1840–69), who was killed in a California train accident on
14 November. (Goodman and Seely had been pallbearers at Baldwin's funeral in
Oakland two days later and Clemens had memorialized him in "A Fair Career
Closed," in the Buffalo *Express* of 27 November, as "a shining example of how
generous Fortune can be, and how fickle" [SLC 1869ii].) Seely was one of two
principal contenders for the appointment, which carried an annual salary of
$3,500—considered inadequate but reportedly about to increase to $6,000. The
other was Edgar W. Hillyer (d. 1882), the prosecuting attorney for Storey
County, Nevada, who was "backed by Senator [William M.] Stewart and certain
commanding influences" ("The U.S. District Judgeship," Virginia City *Territorial Enterprise*, 11 Dec 69, 2). Unknown to Clemens, Hillyer had been appointed on 15 December. He was confirmed by the Senate by 23 December
(Kelly 1862, 88; Kelly 1863, 279; "Died," San Francisco *Morning Call*, 16 June
83, 4; "Obsequies of the Late Judge Baldwin of Nevada," San Francisco *Evening
Bulletin*, 17 Nov 69, 3; *L1*, 280 n. 11; Chase et al., 124; Virginia City *Territorial
Enterprise*: "For Europe," 2 Dec 69, 2; "Confirmed," 23 Dec 69, 2).
[2] Oakes Ames (1804–73)—the wealthy manufacturer and capitalist, member
of Congress since 1862, and principal figure in the Crédit Mobilier corporation
through which he corruptly financed the recently completed Union Pacific Railway—had four sons: Oakes Angier (1829–99), Oliver (1831–95), Frank (1833–
98), and Henry. Oakes Angier and Oliver both lived in North Easton, Massachusetts, about eight miles south of Canton, while Frank lived in Canton itself,
making him the most likely to have been Clemens's inhospitable host (nothing
is known of Henry). Frank Ames had been educated at the Leicester and An-
dover Academies before entering his family's lucrative shovel-manufacturing
business. At present he was a chief owner of the Kinsley Iron and Machine Company in Canton, had extensive business interests elsewhere, particularly in railroads, and was active in Republican politics ("Address of the Republican State
Committee," Boston *Advertiser*, 26 Oct 69, 4; "Hon. Frank M. Ames," Boston
Evening Transcript, 25 Aug 98, 5).
[3] Clemens wished to be rested for his lecture in Hudson, Massachusetts, on

the evening of 21 December (no reviews have been located). His sponsor there was the Reverend H. G. Gay. An incident Clemens recalled in 1907 must have occurred in Gay's home, although Clemens's account disguised the actual time and place:

> Once I was a hero. I can never forget it. It was forty years ago, when I was a bashful young bachelor of thirty-two. I lectured in the village of Hudson, New York, & was the guest of the village parson, there being no hotel in the place. In the morning I was summoned to the parlor for family worship. It began with a chapter from the Old Testament,. Seated elbow to elbow around the walls were the aged clergyman's family of young folks, along with twenty-one maidens & youths from neighboring homes. I was pleasantly wedged between two young girls—sweet & modest & diffident lassies. The preacher read the first verse; a youth at his left read the second; a girl at the youth's left read the third— & so on down, toward me. I ran my finger down to my verse, purposing to familiarize myself with it, & so that I could read it acceptably when my turn came ,should, come. I got a shock! It was one of those verses which would make a graven image blush. I did not believe I could read it aloud in such a company, & I resolved that I would not try. Then I noticed that the poor girl at my left had put her finger on that same verse & was showing signs of distress. Was it her verse? Had I miscounted? I counted again, & found it really was her verse, & not mine. By this time it was my turn was come. I saw my chance to be a hero, & I rose to the occasion: I braced up & read my verse & hers too! I was proud of myself, for it was as fine & grand as saving her from drowning. (SLC 1907a, 4–6†)

Entries in an 1879 notebook of Clemens's indicate that the embarrassing biblical verse was 2 Kings 18:27—"But Rab-shakeh said unto them, Hath my master sent me to thy master, and to thee, to speak these words? hath he not sent me to the men which sit on the wall, that they may eat their own dung, and drink their own piss with you?" (*N&J2*, 302–3).

To Olivia L. Langdon
25 December 1869 • Boston, Mass.
(MS: CU-MARK)

Boston, Dec. 25, 1869.

A ṁ happy Christmas to my darling, & to all that are dear to her! You are at home, now, Livy, & all your labors & vexations are over for a while. Poor child, I am afraid you are pretty well worn out. But you must be quiet, for a few days & recruit your strength, & then I shall find you restored & well when I see you a week hence.

I did not write you yesterday, sweetheart, & I suppose it was mutual, for you could have had no opportunity to write me.[1] I called at Redpath's a while ago when I arrived in town, thinking I might hear from you, but I did not. I shall expect a letter in the loved & familiar hand in New Haven day after tomorrow, though—& a month after that, & a litt we shall close our long correspondence, & *tell* each other what our minds suggest, by word of mouth. Speed the day!

It is just a year today since I quit drinking all manner of tabooed beverages, & I cannot see but that I have fared considerably better in consequence, than I did formerly—& certainly I have not upon my soul the sin of leading others to dissipate. But all that goes to *your* credit, not mine. I did not originate the idea.[2]

I had a delightful time of it last night, with the lecture (in Slatersville—the place was changed,) & was *really* hospitably entertained in a private family—a rare thing in New England.[3] The night before, the dog at whose house I staid took advantage of his hospitality (I was undressing & could not leave) to ask me to abate ten dollars on my lecture price,—asked it as a *charity* to his society. I told him I wouldn't—that I hated the dishonored name of charity in the questionable shape it usually comes in. He said they had liked the lecture, & they wanted to keep the society all alive so that they could hear me next winter. I said that when I jammed their hall full of people & then they had the cheek to ask me to abate my price, they hadn't money enough to hire me to talk in such a place again. In the morning he called me to breakfast, but I said it as it was only 7 o'clock I would manage to do without breakfast until I could get it in some other town. And when I went down stairs I said, "Doctor Sanborn, here are ten dollars for my night's lodging." He said he was much obliged, & would hand it to the committee. I said he would do nothing of the kind—I would not abate one cent on my price, & he must accept ten the ten dollars for his New England hospitality, or not take it at all. He took it with a world of servile thanks. (He was the chief physician of Rockport & a very prominent citizen.)[4]

Honey, I got the Jamaica Plains letter, & it did w just as well as a new one would have done. It was from *you*, my darling, & that makes a letter always fresh & full of interest.[5]

Mrs. Barstow has been trying to get a clerkship for her husband in the Treasury Department at Washington, so that he could support her & the children & let her get the rest & recreation her ill health demands, but she couldn't accomplish it right away. She did not want to bother me, she said, but it was no bother—I wrote to Senator Stewart, & he said he would put Barstow into a clerkship right away. So *that* is all right.[6] I may write again, to-day, sweetheart, but just at present I will close & run down to breakfast.[7] God's peace be with you my darling little wife.

Sam.

[*enclosures:*][8]

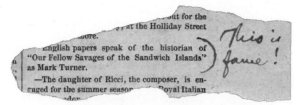

...ut for the
...at the Holliday Street
...ore.
...nglish papers speak of the historian of
"Our Fellow Savages of the Sandwich Islands"
as Mark Turner.

—The daughter of Ricci, the composer, is engaged for the summer seaso... ...oyal Italian
...der

This is fame!

Mark Twain's Savages.

Everybody went to Lincoln Hall to laugh
last night, and everybody did so, partly because they came with that intent and partly
because they couldn't help it. At 8 10 P. M.
the lecturer made his appearance on the
stage, accompanied by Colonel Burnside, of
the Grand Army of the Republic, and was
greeted with applause from some portions of
the hall, the majority of those present seeming to be in doubt as to whether the tall,
slight individual with the Colonel was Mark or
somebody else. All doubts were resolved in a
few moments, however, when the party referred to walked forward, with a slight stoop, to
the stand, and in a very deliberate manner
proceeded to introduce, with many highly
complimentary allusions, Mr. Samuel L.
Clemens, otherwise "Mark Twain",—otherwise
himself. He stated that Colonel Burnside had
kindly offered to introduce him, but as he
(Colonel Burnside) knew him only by his *nom
de plume*, and as he (Mark Twain) knew considerably more about himself than anybody
else, he thought he was better qualified to perform that ceremony. He had studied the
usual form, and he thought he had finally
mastered it. After considerable humorous
circumlocution the lecturer got at his subject,
"Our Fellow-savages, the Sandwich Islanders," and for an hour and a half kept the
unfaltering attention of his audience by a
serio-comic description of the islands and their
inhabitants.

Miss Olivia L. Langdon | Elmira | N. Y. [*return address:*] YOUNG'S HOTEL,
COURT AVENUE, BOSTON, MASS. [*postmarked:*] BOSTON MASS. DEC. 25. 6.P.M.
[*docketed by OLL:*] 163rd

[1] Presumably because Olivia was returning to Elmira from New York City,
her wedding preparations there now completed. The letters Clemens evidently

wrote to her on 21 and 22 December (docket numbers 161 and 162) are now lost.

[2] On 26 November 1868, the day of his informal engagement to Olivia, Clemens decided to give up alcohol, but it was a month before he announced the decision to her (see *L2*, 284, 354).

[3] Clemens's hosts in Slatersville, Rhode Island, have not been identified. He had been scheduled to lecture in Salem, Massachusetts, on Christmas Eve, but instead substituted in Slatersville for his friend Josh Billings, who was ill ("Slatersville," Woonsocket [R.I.] *Patriot and Rhode Island State Register*, 24 Dec 69, 2; Henry Wheeler Shaw [Josh Billings] to James Redpath and George L. Fall, 18 Dec 69, CtHMTH).

[4] In Rockport, Massachusetts, Clemens "was housed at the home of temperate Dr. [John E.] Sanborn on Broadway, next to the town hall. Despite the packed auditorium [eight to twelve hundred people at twenty-five cents a ticket], the committee asked Twain to cut his fee by ten dollars. His refusal to do so and his brusque manner, especially at being called for breakfast too early, so angered his hosts that the children of the family were forbidden to read later Twain books, however diverting they were" (Swan, 190). According to a local reviewer, Clemens's 23 December lecture also made an unfavorable impression:

Mark Twain perpetrated his talk here last Friday [actually Thursday] evening. His performance was according to appointment, and still it was a disappointment. A good many of the ticket holders wanted a humorous lecture, and they all know now just what a humorous lecture is, and the Rockport market is supplied with that style of goods for the present. The regular lectures are not always weekly; but this one was very weakly. He is accused of being a humorist, but his hearers here will generally vote for a verdict of not guilty of the charge. He showed at least exceeding ingenuity, for he contrived to conceal his wit and humor so adroitly, that his audience found it very difficult to detect it. In short, his lecture was remarkably satisfactory, only with an emphatic dis- before it. ("Rockport," Gloucester [Mass.] *Cape Ann Advertiser*, 31 Dec 69, 2, TS in CU-MARK)

[5] This letter had been pursuing Clemens since 19 November, when he lectured in Jamaica Plain.

[6] Clemens's letter to Senator William M. Stewart of Nevada, his former employer, on behalf of William H. Barstow, is not known to survive.

[7] Probably Clemens did write again on Christmas Day, but that letter and one he almost certainly wrote on 26 December (docket numbers 164 and 165) have not been found.

[8] The first enclosure was from the Boston *Advertiser* ("In General," 25 Dec 69, 1). The second was from the review of Clemens's 8 December Washington lecture that had appeared in the Washington *Morning Chronicle* (9 Dec 69, 4). (Both are reproduced here at 85 percent of actual size.) An identical clipping from the *Chronicle* survives in a family scrapbook (Scrapbook 8:65, CU-MARK). The portion of the review that Clemens declined to save or pass on to Olivia read:

Many of his facts are new and interesting, but it is a pity that most of his really good stories are familiar to his audience before he tells them from having already been printed in connection with his lecture. To many, Mark fell rather below the estimate which had been formed of him from his humorous writings. It would be doing an injustice to the memory of poor A. Ward to say that the droll Mark was his equal in point of genuine wit and humor. That he approaches him there can be no doubt, but in that genial, modest, and sparkling flow of fun which Artemus used so happily, the latter was by far his superior.

We do not desire to unduly depreciate the abilities of Mark, for he is very funny, and eminently satisfactory to his audience. It is by comparison, however, that we determine merit, and, no one, we believe, can object to the method, for it is the same as that [by] which men, as well as things, are measured and their values ascertained.

Other Washington papers of 9 December expressed no such reservations. In its review, preserved on the same page in the scrapbook, the *Evening Star* remarked approvingly on Mark Twain's similarity to Artemus Ward while refraining from printing any "fine things" or "funny things" from his lecture "for they are his property, to be used a good many times in the course of the winter, and he has suffered already by newspaper depredations" ("Washington News and Gossip," 1). The *National Intelligencer and Express* commented that "the lecture abounded in fresh and sparkling witticisms, which were rendered in Mark's usual happy vein. The audience were greatly pleased with the entertainment" ("Amusements," 2). And the *National Republican* reported that Mark Twain "convulsed his hearers with laughter" and achieved "a success of the most decided character" ("Mark Twain's Lecture Last Night," 4).

To Olivia L. Langdon
27 December 1869 • New Haven, Conn.
(MS: CU-MARK)

New Haven, Dec. 27.

Sweetheart, it is after supper, & I shall have a few minutes to spare before the committee come for me, I suppose.

I forgot to thank the man with the umbrella for assisting you to the streetcar, but I thank him now, sincerely₎, Livy darling.

I stopped two hours in Hartford today & Twichell & I bummed around together—(I had telegraphed him to be at the depot.) I told him he must come a day or two *before* the wedding, & he said he would arrive Tuesday evening, Feb. 1ˢᵗ, with Mrs. T. (leaving the children behind. I said we would have him at the *house* if we had any room—otherwise he would have to go to the hotel (which he said he would probably have to go there because we would be sure to be crowded.) I said I meant to write you about it anyhow, before the house party should be permanently decided on.

You & I & the Twichells leave for the Adirondacks, old fellow, the first day of August (D.V.)—& if all the folks will go, so much the better. We spend the month there.[1]

Twelve thousand copies of the book sold *this month*. This is perfectly enormous. Nothing like it since Uncle Tom's Cabin, I guess.[2]

To-day we came upon a democrat wagon in Hartford with a cargo in it composed of Mrs. Hooker & Alice (who looks as handsome as she ever did in her life,) Mrs. Warner & another lady. They all assailed me violently on the Courant matter & said it had ceased to be a private desire that we take an ownership in that paper, & had become a public demand. Mrs. H. said Warner & Hawley would do anything to get me in there (this in presence of Mrs. W. who did not deny ~~but~~ it by any means,) & Mrs. H. said she had been writing to ~~Mrs.~~ Mr. Langdon to make us sell out in Buffalo & come here. (It afforded me a malicious satisfaction to hear all this & contrast it with the insultingly contemptuous indifference with which the very same matter was treated last June, (by *every one of them*.)[3]

Revenge is wicked, & unchristian & in every way unbecoming, & I am not the man to countenance it or show it any favor. (But it is powerful sweet, anyway.)

I have read several books, lately, but none worth marking, & so I have not marked any. I started to mark the Story of a Bad Boy, but for the life of me I could not admire the volume much.[4] I am now reading Gil Blas, but am not marking it. If you have not read it you need not. It would sadly offend your delicacy, & I prefer not to have that dulled in you. It is a woman's chief ornament.[5]

Well, these people are a long time coming. The audience must be assembling by this time—in Boston three-fourths of them would be in the house at this hour.

Good-bye my loved & honored Livy, & peace be with you.

Sam.

 ──

[*in ink:*] Miss Olivia L. Langdon | Elmira | N. Y. [*postmarked:*] NEW HAVEN CT. DEC 27 [*docketed by OLL:*] 166th

[1] These plans were not realized. On 1 August 1870 Clemens and Olivia, then pregnant, were in Elmira, at the bedside of Jervis Langdon, who died from stomach cancer five days later. Soon after, the Clemenses returned to Buffalo, where Olivia was slow to recover from the loss of her father.

[2] While in Hartford Clemens had gotten a sales report on *The Innocents Abroad* from Elisha Bliss. The December 1869 figures, representing gross receipts of about $50,000 and an author's royalty of about $2,500, proved to be the best

monthly result in the book's spectacular sales history. Nevertheless, even with the 15,500 volumes sold during the first quarter and the 6,204 ordered from the bindery in November, the first five months' sales of *Innocents* did not approach the 100,000 volumes that Harriet Beecher Stowe's novel sold in a comparable span in 1852 (*MTMF*, 114; *L2*, 421; Hirst, 313–16; APC 1866–79, 50, 93; Hart 1950, 110–11).

[3] See 21 June 69 and 24 and 25 Nov 69, both to OLL.

[4] *The Story of a Bad Boy* by Thomas Bailey Aldrich (1836–1907) was serialized in monthly installments in *Our Young Folks* throughout 1869 and issued in book form in December. Fields, Osgood and Company of Boston published both the journal and the book, as well as *Every Saturday*, the weekly journal edited by Aldrich ("New Publications," New York *Tribune*, 14 Dec 69, 6; Mott 1957, 175, 357). Clemens first corresponded with Aldrich, who became a close friend, in January 1871.

[5] Probably Clemens read Alain René Le Sage's picaresque romance (originally published 1715–35) in an 1868 reprint of Tobias Smollett's 1749 translation from the French, *The Adventures of Gil Blas of Santillane*—either the volume published in New York by D. Appleton or the one issued in Philadephia by J. B. Lippincott and Company (Gribben, 1:407). Le Sage's tale became the standard by which Clemens judged his own first novel about a "bad boy." On 5 July 1875, after finishing *The Adventures of Tom Sawyer*, he wrote William Dean Howells that he "didn't take the chap beyond boyhood. I believe it would be fatal to do it in any shape but autobiographically—like Gil Blas. I perhaps made a mistake in not writing it in the first person" (*MTHL*, 1:91). *Adventures of Huckleberry Finn* adopted the autobiographical mode.

To Joseph H. Twichell
28 December 1869 • New York, N.Y.
(MS: CtY-BR)

New York, Dec. 28

Dear J. H.—

I hasten to enclose to you my R R ticket from New Haven to New York, before I forget to recollect it. You see, when I found, last night, that there was a *boat* at 11 P.M., & that a man would have to get up as early as day before yesterday to catsh any train that would leave before noon, I of course sent down & engaged a stateroom—& as I haven't any earthly use for this R R ticket, my soul swells with a boundless generosity, & I send it to you.[1] If it shall be the means of making one ~~year~~ small year of ~~your sad this~~ ˏyourˏ sad earthly pilgrimage seem happier, & brighter, & bullyer, it is all I ask. Pax Vobiscum! (I don't know what Pax

Vobiscum means, but it is the correct thing to say in the way of a bene-diction, I believe.) Good-bye. Great love to the wife & the boys.

Yrs always

~~Sam~~ Mark.

I wrote Livy about your coming Feb. 1—& to be ready for the woods the first of August—& what Mrs. Hooker said to us—& everything, —Hello, I didn't see that blank page on the other side.[2]

[1] Clemens had taken one of the coastal steamers that made daily trips between New Haven and New York City ("Steamboats," New York *Times*, 27 Dec 69, 7). He was on his way to keep a 28 December lecture engagement in Trenton, New Jersey, where he was "invited to be the guest of Mr Alfred Reed" and was prom-ised "a big house & cordial welcome both publicly & in private: also, the fee here has increased to $100" (James Redpath to SLC, 30 Nov 69, Redpath Letterpress Book, 531, IaU).

[2] Clemens squeezed his postscript into the left margin before noticing the blank verso.

To Elisha Bliss, Jr.
28 December 1869 • New York, N.Y.
(MS: Axelrod)

New York, Dec. 28.

Friend Bliss—

My room-mate in the Quaker City, Dan. Slote, 121 William street, has sold about 200 copies of the book to his ˌpersonalˌ friends (the agent[1] here lets him have them at 20 per cent. off,) & he has given ~~wa~~ away 12 or 15 copies at his own expense. I suggest to him that he keep a lot in his own office to supply his friends with, & tell him you will not object to let him have them at canvassers' rates (which is 40 per cent off, I believe.) This cannot interfere in the least with canvassers or general agents, & will only pick up odd chances that they could not come at. So, if you are willing, you may send Dan 50 copies ~~of~~ (cloth,) & half a dozen half-Turkey, ˌat canvassers rates.ˌ It is Dan's picture in the book that attracts his friends.[2] He knows everybody in New York. ~~Dan~~

You need not charge Dan anything in advance—let him pay for the books after he sells them—(charge them to *me* if they must be charged to anybody—I will be responsible. I want Dan to get even on the copies he has given away. He will not sell a copy to a bookseller or to anybody but personal friends. I shall be glad if you will let him have all the books he wants at canvassers' price—to be paid for after the books are sold. I know Dan Slote pretty well, after traveling 6 months with him.

Yrs

Mark.

[*on back of letter as folded:*]
Dan knows *every body*, & thinks he could have sold 500 copies by this time if he had had them.

He knows the agent here, well, & has got his books from him, heretofore.

Write Dan, if you choose.

[*letter docketed:*] √ auth [*and*] Mark Twain | Dec 28/69

[1] Unidentified.
[2] Slote's picture ("Dan") appears in chapter 27 of *The Innocents Abroad*.

Appendixes

Appendix A

Genealogies of the Clemens and Langdon Families

THESE GENEALOGIES are documented in *Mark Twain's Letters, Volume 1: 1853–1866* (379–81) and *Volume 2: 1867–1868* (375), respectively, where they were originally published. Pamela Clemens's first name is given here as before, in accord with her preferred usage, although in fact she was named for her paternal grandmother, Pamelia Goggin, and occasionally signed herself Pamelia (*MTBus*, 4–5; quit-claim deed from Pamelia A. Moffett to Charles L. Webster, 17 Oct 81, NPV).

Clemens Family

John Marshall Clemens
 b. 11 Aug 1798
 d. 24 Mar 1847

m. 6 May 1823 ——————

Jane Lampton
 b. 18 June 1803
 d. 27 Oct 1890

Orion Clemens
 b. 17 July 1825
 d. 11 Dec 1897

m. 19 Dec 1854 ——————————

Mary Eleanor (Mollie) Stotts
 b. 4 Apr 1834
 d. 15 Jan 1904

Pamela Ann Clemens
 b. 13 Sept 1827
 d. 31 Aug 1904

m. 20 Sept 1851 ——————

William Anderson Moffett
 b. 13 July 1816
 d. 4 Aug 1865

Pleasant Hannibal Clemens
 b. 1828 or 1829
 d. aged 3 months

Margaret L. Clemens
 b. 31 May 1830
 d. 17 Aug 1839

Benjamin L. Clemens
 b. 8 June 1832
 d. 12 May 1842

SAMUEL LANGHORNE CLEMENS
 b. 30 Nov 1835
 d. 21 Apr 1910

m. 2 Feb 1870 ——————

Olivia Louise (Livy) Langdon
 b. 27 Nov 1845
 d. 5 June 1904

Henry Clemens
 b. 13 July 1838
 d. 21 June 1858

Jennie Clemens
b. 14 Sept 1855
d. 1 Feb 1864

Annie E. Moffett
b. 1 July 1852
d. 24 Mar 1950

m. 28 Sept 1875

Charles Luther Webster
b. 24 Sept 1851
d. 26 Apr 1891

Samuel Erasmus Moffett
b. 5 Nov 1860
d. 1 Aug 1908

m. 13 Apr 1887

Mary Emily Mantz
b. 19 Aug 1863
d. 2 Oct 1940

Langdon Clemens
b. 7 Nov 1870
d. 2 June 1872

Olivia Susan (Susy) Clemens
b. 19 Mar 1872
d. 18 Aug 1896

Clara Langdon Clemens
b. 8 June 1874
d. 19 Nov 1962

m. 6 Oct 1909

1) Ossip Gabrilowitsch
b. 7 Feb 1878
d. 14 Sept 1936

m. 11 May 1944

2) Jacques Alexander Samossoud
b. 8 Sept 1894
d. 13 June 1966

Jane Lampton (Jean) Clemens
b. 26 July 1880
d. 24 Dec 1909

Alice Jane (Jean) Webster
b. 24 July 1876
d. 11 June 1916

m. 7 Sept 1915 ——————— [1 child]

Glenn Ford McKinney
b. 15 Feb 1869
d. 15 Feb 1934

William Luther Webster
b. 15 Oct 1878
d. ? Mar 1945

Samuel Charles Webster
b. 8 July 1884
d. 24 Mar 1962

m. 1920?

Doris Webb
b. ?
d. 9 July 1967

Anita Moffett
b. 4 Feb 1891
d. 26 Mar 1952

Francis Clemens Moffett
b. 1 Oct 1895
d. 4 Mar 1927

Nina Gabrilowitsch
b. 18 Aug 1910
d. 16 Jan 1966

Langdon Family

Jervis Langdon
  b. 11 Jan 1809
  d. 6 Aug 1870

    m. 23 July 1832

Olivia Lewis
  b. 19 Aug 1810
  d. 28 Nov 1890

Susan Langdon (adopted)
  b. 18 Feb 1836
  d. 29 Aug 1924

    m. 7 Dec 1858

Theodore W. Crane
  b. 26 Sept 1831
  d. 3 July 1889

Olivia Louise (Livy) Langdon
  b. 27 Nov 1845
  d. 5 June 1904

    m. 2 Feb 1870

SAMUEL LANGHORNE CLEMENS
  b. 30 Nov 1835
  d. 21 Apr 1910

Charles Jervis Langdon
  b. 13 Aug 1849
  d. 19 Nov 1916

    m. 12 Oct 1870

Ida B. Clark
  b. 7 Mar 1849
  d. 17 Dec 1934

[see Clemens genealogy]

Julia Olivia (Julie) Langdon
    b. 21 Nov 1871
    d. 15 July 1948

      m. 29 Nov 1902 ———————— [2 children]

Edward Eugene Loomis
    b. 2 Apr 1864
    d. 11 July 1937

Jervis Langdon
    b. 26 Jan 1875
    d. 16 Dec 1952

      m. 2 Oct 1902 ———————— [2 children]

Eleanor Sayles
    b. 10 Feb 1878
    d. 15 June 1971

Ida Langdon
    b. 15 Oct 1880
    d. 9 Oct 1964

Appendix B

Enclosures with the Letters

ENCLOSURES ARE transcribed here when they are too long to be presented conveniently with the letters themselves. Textual commentaries for these enclosures appear following the commentaries for the letters.

Enclosures with 12 January 1869
To Mary Mason Fairbanks • El Paso, Ill.
(Charlotte *Republican*, 30 Dec 68, and
Lansing *State Republican*, 31 Dec 68)

THE LECTURE.

On Christmas evening we listened to a lecture by Mark Twain, the humorist. His subject, the American Vandal Abroad, gave him full opportunity to indulge in his rich vein of mirth provoking wit, while yet there was under all a foundation of good sense; but both humor and sense served as a setting for earnest word pictures of places and scenes and works of art, in Europe, Egypt and Palestine, which made the lecture much more than a mere piece of amusing drollery. In a few simple sentences he would bring before the imagination clear and brilliant pictures which are next to, and perhaps more impressive, than the real scene. For Artists and Poets always see more in Nature to love and admire than ordinary observers. Such lectures convince me that far more satisfactory and enduring imagery can be impressed upon the mind by words, tone and gesture, than by painting or engraving. A picture, for instance, can give us an idea of a city as a whole, only by a dim and distant view, which seldom interests; while description will bring before us the sky, not only as seen from the distance, but as though we were moving through it.

After holding the audience spell bound, for a while, before the Sphinx, with its melancholy gaze over the past ages, or after contemplating some beautiful scene like Venice, its silent palaces[,] its bridges and gondolas; or Athens looked down upon by bright moonlight from the Acropolis, he would leave dry land and take to his native element of quaint humor. Then came in his laughable, matter-of-fact Vandalisms, which, while enjoyed, also served to heighten the previous enjoyment. He mingled in a little of the grotesque and just enough of the terrible to heighten the glow of his humorous descriptions, while these, in turn, served, by contrast, to enrich the splendor of his great pictures. It was this artistic changing of the excitement for different faculties and the different sides of our nature, that so completely entertained, and rested, and kept the attention of the audience constantly fixed. This is all art, the very highest kind; that consummate art which conceals itself under the perfect simplicity and naturalness of its own production; which, in choosing language, gives us a medium of such chrystaline clearness that language, by the hearer, is never thought of.—The art that prunes, rejects, condenses, polishes and elaborates sentences, imagery and thought.

This Artist seems intentionally to avoid all effort at sublimity and pathos. For there was not a particle of either of these great powers in his lecture. This, too, the Artist learns—to know where he might fall and where he can safely venture.

In wit, of the keen, cold, sparkling kind, he might, doubtless, have given us enough; but good taste and that sympathy which is the source of all genial humor, taught him to refrain. Cutting wit, unless for the tough hide of vice or bigotry, ought not to be cultivated or indulged in. Readers and hearers all relish something else much better than sarcasm; and yet, if cutting becomes necessary, all prefer to see the operation performed kindly, with a good sharp instrument, and not with an old saw.

In this lecture there was not an unkind cut for man or beast; not even a kick for the Grecian bend.[1] There was not a word to disturb any one's belief, religious or political. In such a lecture anything offensive would be much out of place. But when Theodore Tilton comes we shall probably all of us get disturbed. Among our old and cherished opinions we

---

[1] "A mode of walking with a slight stoop forward, at one time affected by some women" (Whitney and Smith, 1:522).

can then expect, earthquakes and volcanic eruptions[.] We will then learn the difference between the Humorist and the Reformer.[2]

The Winter Lecture Course seems to have become an established institution throughout the country. It gives the public a good opportunity to meet face to face with the distinguished writers and speakers; to see them in their best moments, when animated with intellectual effort. It gives us the rich result of years of labor and culture, not only as the product of the pen, but the thought aided by the elocution of the thinker. It will tend to improve public speaking and writing, by teaching the public to appreciate true oratory and to discriminate between the crude and diffuse and the polished and condensed in literature; between the affected and trifling, and the manly and substantial in thought. It teaches us our mother tongue, its true pronunciation, and the great power and beauty of language when properly used.

BROWNIE.[3]

The Lecture of Mark Twain.

Last Wednesday evening Mead's Hall was well filled to hear Mark Twain discourse on the American Vandal abroad. He is a young man, little over thirty years of age, and looks as though he had never been a drawing room pet, but had been used to the rough and tumble, the ups and downs of life. His wit was eminently dry, and the force of his manner, which is natural, and not affected, made it still more striking. He talked easily, walking up and down the stage at a pace that slowly marked the time of his words. His delightful description of Venice by moonlight, the Sphinx, the Acropolis at Athens, were as fine specimens of word painting as can be drawn by any other lecturer. Each of these telling passages would be followed by some humorous comment that would convulse the house with laughter. The lecture was intended to amuse, as well as to instruct, and the object was fully attained. A lecturer tells his own

------

[2] Since 1863, Theodore Tilton (1835–1907), the poet and social reformer, had been editor of the weekly New York *Independent*, using its columns to campaign on behalf of abolition and women's suffrage. Tilton was touring with a lecture on "The American Woman" and appeared in Charlotte on 28 January 1869 (Mott 1938, 367, 371–74; "Theodore Tilton . . . ," Charlotte *Republican*, 30 Dec 68, 1; "To the Lecture Going People of Iowa City," Iowa City *Republican*, 6 Jan 69, 3).

[3] Unidentified.

jokes best, and we will not repeat them. Those who heard appreciated
the fun, and those who failed to hear, had no business to be somewhere
else. The Vandal, who yet disgraces the national name in the classic cities
of the old world, was drawn to the life.

The real name of Mark Twain is S. L. Clemens, and he was for several
years city editor of a paper in Virginia City, Nevada, and first attracted
the attention of the reading public by contributions to California papers.
He is a special correspondent of the New York *Tribune*, and every thing
he writes adds to his reputation as an American humorist. His manner
is judged by many to be affected on the stage, which is untrue, his manner being the same in personal conversation, and an infirmity which, as
he says, was honestly inherited.

As a humorous lecturer we have no hesitation in giving Mark Twain a
decided preference over the renowned and lamented Artemus Ward. If
Nasby, by the will of Lowell, becomes his successor as a humorist, we
think Twain is destined to more than make good the place formerly filled
by Ward.[4] He is sure to provoke the hearty laugh that shakes the cobwebs
from the brain and the hypochondria from the ribs. And as laughter is
no sin, if it takes the proper time to come in, we hope Twain will make
his calling and election sure, and continue to amuse as well as instruct
the grave, austere, American nation.

Enclosures with 23 January 1869
To Joseph H. Twichell and Family • Cleveland, Ohio
(Toledo *Blade* and Toledo *Commercial*, 21 Jan 69)

MARK TWAIN'S LECTURE.—White's Hall was filled from cellar to garret, last night, by one of the best tickled audiences that ever assembled
there to hear a lecture or see the speaker. Mark Twain tickled them. And
he did it so easily and almost constantly, that they didn't know what they

---

[4] Artemus Ward (Charles Farrar Browne) died of tuberculosis in Southhamp-
ton, England, on 6 March 1867 (*L2*, 9 n. 2). The vernacular political and social
satire of Petroleum Vesuvius Nasby (David Ross Locke), in his lectures and his
widely reprinted Toledo *Blade* letters, made him seem a logical successor to
James Russell Lowell, whose *Biglow Papers*, dialect verse in a similar vein, appeared serially before being collected in 1848 and 1867. Lowell, at this time
Smith Professor of French and Spanish at Harvard, was devoting himself to literary criticism.

were laughing at more than half the time. Twain is witty, and his wit comes from his own fertile brain. His style is original; and his manner of speaking is not after the manner of men generally. His serious face and long drawn words are, of themselves, sufficient to make one laugh, even if there were not in every sentence expressed a sparkling gem of humor, and original idea. His anecdotes, with which the lecture is replete, are rich, and, as he tells them, irresistibly funny. In some of his descriptions of European places and characters the lecturer delivers, at times, most eloquent passages, brilliant in thought and word.

That MARK TWAIN is a success as a lecturer, as well as writer, we think no one who heard "The American Vandal Abroad," last night, will dispute.[1]

> **Mark Twain.**—White's Hall was crowded ith a very intelligent and appreciative audience last night, to hear MARK TWAIN's "American Vandal Abroad," and a more delighted audience never occupied those seats. There is an originality and pungency to his wit, and a purity of tone and expression which gives it a relish to the most cultivated minds. There is nothing gross and course in his utterances—no appeals to the baser passions and prejudices—but an easy flow of humor which will make the muscles of the face ache from constant contraction. But then, his lecture is not all wit. It is dotted all over with most beautiful word pictures, and its humor is so interwoven with facts and incidents collected by many weary months of travel in the East that the wit serves to drive the truths deeper into the mind. It is seldom that our people have such an intellectual feast set before them, and we were pleased to see so large a number present to enjoy it.

[1] Elisha Bliss later included the *Blade* review in his advertising circular for *The Innocents Abroad;* James Redpath used the *Commercial* notice in his Boston Lyceum Bureau advertising circular for the 1869–70 lecture season (see Appendix E for both circulars).

Enclosure with 8–10 March 1869
To John Russell Young • Hartford, Conn.

(New York *Tribune* galley proof)

THE WHITE HOUSE FUNERAL.

A LETTER FROM MARK TWAIN.[1]

To the Editor of The Tribune.

SIR: I can truly say that this has been the most melancholy day of my life. When I arose this morning & reflected that on this day it was to be given me to see that noble band of patriots, the President & his Cabinet, delivered over to the cold charities of a thankless nation, my heart was ready to break.[2] My brain was flooded with tender memories of blessings brought to me by this paternal administration that was now dying—memories of clerkships which I had held & salaries I had received for work which was never required of me; memories of the franking privilege enjoyed by me, along with all the cooks, & barbers, & Congressmen, & correspondents in Washington;[3] of building-stone which I had been allowed to sell from the Capitol grounds & pocket the money, owing to my acquaintance with certain officials of the Senate; of sums I

---

[1] Since Clemens formally submitted this letter as an article, he may well have supplied the title and even the subtitle.

[2] The members of Andrew Johnson's cabinet, three of whom had also served under Lincoln, were: William H. Seward (1801–72), secretary of state since 1861; Hugh McCulloch (1808–95), secretary of the treasury since 1865; John M. Schofield (1831–1906), secretary of war since 1868; William M. Evarts (1818–1901), attorney general since 1868; Alexander W. Randall (1819–72), postmaster general since 1866; Gideon Welles (1802–78), secretary of the navy since 1861; and Orville H. Browning (1806–81), secretary of the interior since 1866 (*White's Conspectus*, 5–11).

[3] Between 25 November and 2 December 1867, while serving as private secretary to Senator William M. Stewart of Nevada, Clemens evidently also was, at least informally, clerk to one of the four Senate committees Stewart served on: Judiciary, Public Lands, Pacific Railroad, and Mines and Mining. In 1891, Stewart recalled: "I made him a clerk to my committee in the Senate, which paid him six dollars per day, then I hired a man for $100 per month to do the work" ("Mark Twain's Revenge," New York *Recorder*, 5 Apr 91, no page, clipping enclosed in Robert W. Carl to SLC, 5 Apr 91, CU-MARK; see also *L2*, 78, 109 n. 2, 112–13, 139 n. 4). Although Clemens criticized the "franking privilege," he did "enjoy" it himself, more than once using Stewart's signature to post his own mail (see *L2*, 128–29, 152).

had clandestinely amassed by procuring & selling to the Associated Press the President's several Messages before they were transmitted to Congress[4]—these, & a thousand touching recollections of a like nature came thronging in sad procession down the corridors of my memory, & I bowed my head & wept.

I proceeded to the White House at 10 o'clock to be present at the closing Cabinet meeting of Mr. Johnson's administration, but was stopped by one McKeever,[5] who would not let me in until I had satisfied him that I had been Clerk of the Senate Committee on Conchology, & consequently was an ex-officio member of the Cabinet.[6] I did not know what ex-officio meant, & neither did he; & so he had no recourse but to give me the benefit of the doubt & permit me to enter. Mr. Seward was upon the floor, about to make his farewell remarks. He & all the others were in tears. Mr. Seward said:

"Brethren, it is a sad day for us all. It is a sad day for the country. We are about to retire from the exalted stations which we have held so long & be lost for all time in the nothingness of utter obscurity. Within the short compass of a single day we shall be forgotten—we shall be as the dead. At such a time as this, nothing can have power to make glad our heavy hearts. All we need attempt to do will be to seek a balm that shall relieve, in some degree, the griefs that burden them. I can point you to only one medicine that may accomplish this, & that is the recalling to your memories the services you have conferred upon your country, the noble deeds you have done in her behalf, the inspired efforts you have made to build up her glory, & the amounts you have collected for it. It is good to me to look back upon my own labors in these regards. I have nothing to regret. I have always done my duty by my country when it seemed best. I have always been consistent. I have always stood by the party in power. I was always the first to desert it when it lost its prestige.[7]

[4] Clemens had remarked at length upon such "dreadful leaks somewhere in the old Ship of State" in a 17 December 1867 letter from Washington to the San Francisco *Alta California* (SLC 1868d).

[5] Johnson's cabinet met for the last time on Tuesday, 2 March 1869 ("Dispatches to the Associated Press," New York *Times*, 3 Mar 69, 1). McKeever has not been identified.

[6] Clemens made the same facetious identification of his clerkship in "The Facts Concerning the Recent Resignation," in the New York *Tribune* of 27 December 1867 (SLC 1867h).

[7] Seward was a Whig stalwart from the 1830s until that party merged with the new Republican party in 1855. He served a Republican administration under Lincoln, then stayed on to play a central role under Johnson, a Democrat.

I would have been ready to join hands with this new Administration, in accordance with my custom, & weep upon its neck, but that that notorious & underhanded reticence which distinguishes it rendered it impossible for me to find out what its politics were going to be. Wherefore this bitter day, a broken-hearted old man, I totter into my political grave, unhonored & unsung. No drop of Logan's blood will flow in the veins of a solitary official of this new race, for behold my son dies with me.[8] Woe is me! But I have a record. I have a record that shall be my comfort & my solace. With Mr. Lincoln I stood by the Republicans with unswerving tenacity, & with Mr. Johnson I have stood by the Democrats. I have been always ready & willing to embrace Christianity, infidelity, or paganism, according to which held the most trumps. I have been always ready to eat horse with the Frenchmen, dog with the Hawaiians, or missionary with the Fejees, on the same general basis.[9] I have always been ready to blow hot, or blow cold, or not blow at all, just as my best official interests seemed to dictate. I have usually smelt pretty loud in the people's nostrils, but I never have cared how I smelt, so long as my fragrance emanated from an office. My record is satisfactory to me. I have done some things for my country which will not be soon forgotten. I have filled the foreign world with a Falstaffian army of the jack-leggedest consuls that ever flaunted ignorance & imbecility on foreign soil since the world began—vagrants, & pot-house politicians, & poor relations of Congressmen, & village doctors who don't know a purge from a poultice, & country lawyers who made a living God knows how on this side the water, &

[8] Frederick W. Seward (1830–1915) was assistant secretary of state under his father. Mingo Indian chief Tahgahjute (1725?–80), known as James (sometimes John) Logan, was famous for remarks he reputedly made reproaching whites after a 1774 massacre in which members of his family were killed. The attributed statement, including the words "There runs not a drop of my blood in the veins of any living creature," was widely published in newspapers of the day. Quoted by Thomas Jefferson in *Notes, on the State of Virginia* (1800), it became a school declamation exercise.

[9] Allusions to controversial elements of Seward's foreign policy during the 1860s, namely: his cautious dealings with France in regard to its support for the Confederacy and its incursions into Mexico; his efforts to extend American influence to the Hawaiian Islands, including an abortive reciprocity treaty that Clemens had supported in a 10 December 1867 letter from Washington to the *Alta California* (SLC 1868a); and his possible interest in the Fiji Islands, three of which were reportedly to be given to the United States as "compensation for American sailors eaten by the king's subjects" (Van Deusen, 363, 368–69, 532–34).

make it now on the other side by acting as fences to foreign shopkeepers & peddling gimcracks to traveling Americans on commission—a scurvy lot, *I* can tell you. Government pays them just exactly enough to keep them from starving to death, so as to keep out respectable men; & when there is anything over, Government seizes it—when it can.[10] And I set a spy on the elegant Mr. Motley, & the first time his precious affectation of originality betrayed him into exploiting an opinion which was not furnished him in his instructions, I suggested to him that it was time for him to pack his carpet-sack & come home. The good people raved somewhat over this indignity offered to a great historian they seemed to be foolishly proud of, but they put up with it, you know, because they had to.[11] And it was I that added to America's list of foreign Ministers that great & inscrutable diplomat, Reverdy Johnson—that man who has so exalted us in the eyes of Great Britain—that noble heart whose loving instincts fondle all the world; whose charitable tears fall upon the just & the unjust alike, involving pirates & princes in one common deluge of forgiveness; who taketh his meals out, & saveth his salary. I sent that noble son of Maryland there, & mark my words, he will settle this Alabama matter forever & forever, when he has finished his dinner.[12] And moreover, gentlemen, during my term as Secretary of Real Estate, I have bought all the icebergs & volcanoes that were for sale on earth, & I would have bought all the outside universe if the money had held out. Brethren, bless you, bless you all. I have done. Let us mingle our tears together. I now resign all pomp & state of office forever, & retire to my country seats which I provided in the day of my prosperity for my refuge in the hour

[10] Clemens had previously criticized the consular service, and the "cheap pothouse politicians" its low salaries attracted, in a 14 December 1867 letter from Washington to the *Alta California* (SLC 1868b).

[11] Historian John Lothrop Motley (1814–77) was minister to Austria from 1861 until 1867, when he was forced to resign, more by Johnson than Seward, after allegations reached Washington that he had denounced the administration.

[12] Reverdy Johnson (1796–1876) was appointed minister to Great Britain in 1868. One of his chief assignments was to settle claims for damages done during the Civil War by the *Alabama* and other vessels built in Great Britain for the Confederacy. In February 1869, the Senate Committee on Foreign Relations voted to reject the treaties he negotiated, however, and the *Alabama* matter remained unsettled until 1872. Johnson was personally criticized for servility and for fraternizing, particularly at public banquets, with enemies of the United States, among them John Laird, builder of the *Alabama* (Steiner, 243–45, 248–51).

of adversity. Henceforth I shall Summer in Alaska & Winter in St. Thomas.[13] Adieu, my brethren."

For a few minutes no sound disturbed the solemn stillness save the melancholy drip, drip, dripping of the tears, & the suppressed snuffling of the mourners. Then Gideon, that noble old tar, arose, & took his quid out of his mouth & laid it on the table; & took his trowsers by the waistband, & gave them a brisk hitch upward, lifting his right leg at the same time; then he shied his tarpaulin gaily across the room, & making a speaking trumpet of his hands, he shouted in a voice that seemed to come out of the midst of stormy winds & lashing seas:

"Shipmets, ahoy! Shiver my timbers, but—"

Here the tears came again, his lips twitched convulsively, & he broke down. Presently he was able to go on, but with only a broken & feeble articulation:

"Shipmets, it ain't any use. It is a sorrowful day for us all. The good old craft we've sailed so long has changed owners & shipped another crew. When it was 'bout ship with us or take the breakers, I thought it was all right with Seymour at the hellum & Blair to stand by to hand the tacks & sheets. But Lord bless you, when it was time to luff & bring her to the wind, Seymour was asleep, & when he did fetch her to it by-&-bye, she was all quivering & ready to fall off, that there Blair was making trouble with the watch below with his eternal gab,[14] & so she missed stays & broached to & shipped a sea that washed her clean as a capstan-bar from rudder-pintel to flyingjiboom. It wasn't no use to bother, *then*. The weather-braces came home by the run, the lee-scuppers fouled the futtock shrouds, & the r'yals & skys'ls split to ribbons, the maintogallans'l parted & shook the reefs out of the dead-lights, & douse my glim if the

[13] Seward purchased Alaska from Russia, for $7,200,000, in March 1867. In November 1867 he purchased the islands of St. Thomas and St. John, in the Danish West Indies, for $7,500,000, but the acquisition ultimately failed to win Senate approval. Clemens wrote scornfully of these "territorial speculations" in his 14 December 1867 Washington letter to the *Alta California* and in "Information Wanted" in the New York *Tribune* of 18 December 1867 (Van Deusen, 526–29, 540–49; New York *Times:* "Denmark," 4 Nov 67, 1; "Our New Possessions," 5 Nov 67, 4; SLC 1868b, 1867g).

[14] Gideon Welles, a long-time Democrat before helping to found the Republican party, had supported Horatio Seymour (1810–86) and Francis Preston Blair (1821–75), Democratic candidates for president and vice-president, respectively, in their losing campaign against the Republican ticket of Ulysses S. Grant and Schuyler Colfax. Seymour was a reluctant candidate who was unable to offset the damaging effects of Blair's inflammatory rhetoric.

clew-garnets of the starboard galley didn't fetch away, & carry the gas-kets of the poop-deck & the whole cussed top-hamper of the booby-hatch with them! Awful? It's no name for it, messmets. Well, well, it's all over—& I'm sure *I* never done anything. I stood my watch regular, & there ain't any man that can point to anything that ever *I* done. It's sad times for us, boys, it's sad times—because it's all up with *us*. Well, well, well—our cable's hove short, & we'll stand by to cat the anchor—yo-o-heave-yo!

> 'And he *was* a galliant sailior lad,
> He *was* a galliant sailior lad,
> Oh, he *was* a galliant sailior lad,
> All when he sailed the seas.' " [15]

And then the weather-beaten old son of the ocean hitched up his trowsers & put his quid in his mouth again, & sat down. And very, very soon his rollicking jollity (which was really only a fitful reminiscence, as it were, of his old devil-may-care sailor life on the Erie Canal),[16] faded & fainted from his face & his voice, & again the unbidden tears welled from his eyes & rippled softly through the tufts of hair upon his nose.

The other members of the Cabinet then gave in their experience, with the exception of Gen. Schofield & myself;[17] & presently Andrew Johnson, that grand old second Washington, that resurrected Moses, rose & said:

"My children, when I came before the American people four years

[15] The source, if any, for this chanty has not been identified. The preceding passage employs accurate nautical terminology throughout, but sometimes in intentionally nonsensical combination. For example, the "booby hatch," an opening into a ship's below deck area, has no "top hamper," that is, the masts, sails, rigging, and all other above deck gear. Likewise, the galley has no "clew garnets," which are ropes and tackle used to haul up main sails, and the "dead lights," metal shutters over portholes, have no "reefs," actually the folded portions of sails (Blackburn; Palmer). Despite these burlesque elements, however, Clemens effectively conveys an image of a foundering vessel.

[16] Welles—originally from Connecticut, and a former owner and editor of the Hartford *Times* and a founder of and political writer for the Hartford *Evening Press*—had never been a sailor on the Erie Canal or anywhere else. He had been chief of the Bureau of Provisions and Clothing for the Navy (1846–49), however, and as navy secretary ran an efficent and even innovative department. Clemens had also poked fun at him, calling him a "staunch old salt," in "Concerning Gideon's Band," published in the Washington *Morning Chronicle* on 27 February 1868 (SLC 1868f).

[17] An 1853 graduate of West Point, John M. Schofield achieved the rank of brevet major-general during the Civil War.

ago to deliver my inaugural, I was too full for utterance. [Emphatic assenting sobs from the Cabinet.][18] My emotions at this moment are no less profound, albeit they may be in some sense different in their nature. In quitting my high office, I am able to look back upon my administration of its duties without regret. By diligently violating my oath; by stultifying myself upon every occasion; by being stubborn in the wrong, & feeble & faithless toward the right; by obstructing the laws; by nursing anarchy & rebellion, & by deliberate treachery to the party that made me & trusted me, I have wiped away the contempt in which, because of my obscure origin & humble occupation, my own loved section of the country did formerly hold me, & brought it to regard me with reverence & honor.[19] My great deeds speak for themselves. I vetoed the Reconstruction acts; I vetoed the Freedmen's Bureau; I vetoed civil liberty; I vetoed Stanton; I vetoed everything & everybody that the malignant Northern hordes approved; I hugged traitors to my bosom; I pardoned them by regiments & brigades; I was the friend & protector of assassins & perjurers; I smiled upon the Ku-Klux; I delivered the Union men of the South & their belongings over to murder, robbery, & arson; I filled the Government offices all over this whole land with the vilest scum that could be scraped from the political gutters & the ranks of the Union-haters; I gave the collection of the Nation's revenues into the hands of convicted thieves, & when they were convicted again, I gave them free pardon. I hanged a woman for complicity in a crime, & let men more guilty than she, go unwhipped of justice; I have made the name of office-holder equivalent to that of rogue; born & reared 'poor white trash,' I have clung to my native instincts, & done every small, mean thing my eager hands could find to do. And when my term began to draw to a close, & I saw that but little time remained wherein to defeat justice, to further exasperate the people, & to complete my unique & unprece-

---

[18]Although drunk at his inauguration as Lincoln's vice president on 4 March 1865, Johnson did speak, delivering a "harangue" that scandalized those in attendance, including members of the cabinet whose titles or names he forgot (Trefousse, 189–90).

[19]Johnson was born in 1808 in a log cabin in Raleigh, North Carolina. His father, Jacob, was illiterate and worked as a bank porter, constable, and town bell-ringer. His mother, the former Mary McDonough, was a seamstress and laundress. Possibly at the age of ten, but certainly by the age of thirteen, Johnson was apprenticed to a tailor. He practiced that trade successfully until the late 1830s (Trefousse, 18–40).

dented record, I fell to & gathered up the odds & ends, & made it perfect—swept it clean; for I pardoned Jeff Davis; I pardoned every creature that had ever lifted his hand against the hated flag of the Union; I appointed the historian of the Confederacy to office in the Customs; I resurrected Wirtz; I rescued the bones of the patriot martyr, Booth, from the mystery & oblivion to which malignity had consigned them, & gave them sepulchre where I & many a generation of sorrowing worshipers may go & do honor to the brave heart that did not fear to strike a tyrant, even when his back was turned; I have swept the floors clean; my work is done; I die content."[20]

There was not a dry eye in the house; neither was there a sore heart. These inspiring words had driven all grief away. It was now after 12 o'clock. No time must be lost. Gideon produced a deck of cards, & we

[20] Among Johnson's "great deeds" were: vetoes of Reconstruction acts on 2 March, 23 March, and 19 July 1867, all of them immediately overridden by Congress; a 19 February 1866 veto of a bill extending the life of the Freedmen's Bureau, sustained by Congress; a 27 March 1866 civil rights bill veto, overridden by Congress early that April; the 21 February 1867 dismissal of Edwin M. Stanton as secretary of war (Johnson had suspended Stanton in August), essentially for insubordination and disloyalty, which precipitated impeachment proceedings against Johnson; the failure to stop the 7 July 1865 hanging of Mary Surratt, at whose Washington boardinghouse John Wilkes Booth had plotted Lincoln's assassination, but who was not proved to be implicated in Booth's crime; the pardoning on 11 February 1869 of Dr. Samuel A. Mudd (1833–83), convicted, evidently unjustly, of helping Booth escape; the pardoning on 2 March 1869 of Edward Spangler, also convicted of helping Booth escape, and Samuel Arnold, an accomplice in Booth's prior plan to abduct Lincoln; the February 1869 release for private burial of Booth's remains and those of Henry Wirz, former commander of the Confederate prison at Andersonville, Georgia, who was executed in November 1865 for murder and conspiracy; proclamations of amnesty for former Southern rebels on 29 May 1865, 7 September 1867, 4 July 1868, and 25 December 1868, the last a general amnesty that included Confederate president Jefferson Davis; and the appointment in late 1868 of Edward A. Pollard (1831–72), editor of the Richmond (Va.) *Examiner* from 1861 to 1867 and author of numerous works supporting the Confederacy, to a clerkship in the New York Custom House, which, after public outcry, Pollard was forced to resign shortly before the end of the year (Castel, 25, 26, 34–35, 64–68, 70–71, 111, 115, 129–37, 150–77; Trefousse, 211, 216–17, 227, 287–88, 337, 346–47, 376; Mudd, 24, 318–20, 326; New York *Times:* "Mr. E. A. POLLARD . . . ," 6 Dec 68, 6; "Edward A. Pollard," 9 Dec 68, 11; "The Amnesty Proclamation," 19 Jan 69, 1; "E. A. Pollard and Collector Smythe," 28 Jan 69, 5; "E. A. Pollard," "Collector Smythe and Mr. Pollard," 29 Jan 69, 2, 4; "The Pardon of Dr. Mudd," 12 Feb 69, 3; "John Wilkes Booth," 17 Feb 69, 1; "The Remains of Henry Wirz," 25 Feb 69, 1; "Spangler and Arnold Pardoned," 4 Mar 69, 1).

played seven-up for the furniture. Gideon won the deal. [He previously knew where the Jack was.] A. J. won the jug. McCullough won the desks & chairs. Other members won the carpets & pictures. Browning won the stove, & a relative carried it out while it was still hot. Randall didn't win anything at all, except a map of Washington that had all the roads represented as leading out of the city & none leading in. However, it fitted his requirements to a dot. Seward won everything worth having, because, being an old hand at State craft, he carried the thing they call a cold deck.

About this time we heard music, & beheld the Usurper Grant & his minions approaching. Then, bedewed with tears, & loaded with furniture, we went forth from the pleasant shelter of the White House forever.

Washington, March 4, 1869.   MARK TWAIN.

═══════════

Enclosure with 19 August 1869
To Olivia L. Langdon • Buffalo, N.Y.
(Buffalo *Express*, 19 Aug 69)

PEOPLE AND THINGS.

—The complaint of the coal mines—colliery.—*Boston Post.*

—The reception of the Governor-General of Canada at Prince Edward Island was very cordial.[1]

—The Aldermen and members of the Board of Health, of Milwaukee, have had a sort of family swimming-match. The doctors won—the Al[d]ermen got aground.

—Philadelphia is almost out of water to drink, because of the exceeding low stage of the Schuylkill river. Considerable distress has resulted.

—Redpath's Lyceum Bureau, Boston, has on its list one hundred and

---

[1] Sir John Young (1807–76) was appointed governor-general of Canada and governor of Prince Edward Island (not part of Canada until 1873) in January 1869, retaining the posts for three and one half years. This item is among those Clemens reprinted without embellishment from the *Express*'s exchanges. His hand is clear in several of the succeeding ones, however.

fifty lecturers and readers, whose services are available for the forthcoming season.

—Sir Hildebrand, of Missouri, has emigrated. He had thinned out the population until further amusement was too difficult to obtain to make it worth a man's while.[2]

—Frederick Wermicke, a soldier of the First Empire, aged 87 years, was arrested in Madison county, Missouri, recently for some offense against the revenue laws. The old gentleman's eldest son is 60 years of age and his youngest two.

—One of those venerable parties, a pre-Adamite man, has been dug up from a depth of ninety-eight feet, in Alabama. He was of prodigious stature, and is supposed by savans to have existed twelve thousand years ago. Life was entirely extinct when they got him out.[3]

—Another Colfax party has gone to the Pacific, viz: Geo. Mathews and wife, the mother and step-father of the Vice-President,[4] their daughter Carrie and James M. Mathews, brother of George, his wife and daughter, Lucy. They expect to be absent about three months.

—Miss Carrie A. Benning, a young lady of Harris county, Georgia, who was reduced by the war from wealth to poverty, has in cultivation a five acre field of cotton, which is said to be the best in the neighborhood. She planted and worked it herself, with no assistance except in one plowing.

—Lord Taunton, better known formerly as Henry Labouchere, paid back £100,000 compensation money which the Bristol and Exeter Rail-

[2] Samuel Hilderbrand (or Hildebrand), a bandit and former Confederate marauder said to have killed at least eighty men, was hunted by Missouri officials throughout the summer of 1869. On 6 August, in a taunting letter written from Memphis, Tennessee, to the editor of the St. Louis *Missouri Republican*, he announced that he was "going into business in this section of the country," but promised to return to Missouri to avenge himself on his pursuers. Hilderbrand's letter was reprinted in the New York *Times* and probably elsewhere (New York *Times:* "A Missouri Desperado," 18 June 69, 5; "The Missouri Desperado," 20 June 69, 5; "Sam Hildebrand," 3 July 69, 5; "Sam Hildebrand," 5 Aug 69, 5; "Hilderbrand, the Missouri Outlaw—A Letter to His Pursuers," 15 Aug 69, 3).

[3] Clemens had previously poked fun at such discoveries in "Petrified Man," published in the Virginia City *Territorial Enterprise* in October 1862 (see *ET&S1*, 155–59).

[4] In 1822, about five months before Schuyler Colfax's birth, his father (also Schuyler) died. In 1834 his mother, the former Hannah Stryker of New York, married George W. Matthews of Baltimore.

road Company had paid his father for cutting through his lands. He saw that his estates were enhanced in value by far more than the ordinary price of the land taken from him.[5]

—An Alexandria (Egypt) merchant, ruined by the Viceroy's heavy taxes, recently sold his son to a slave dealer to obtain yet another 900 piastres for the tax gatherer. It would have been far better to have sold him short for double the amount, and then run off before he was worth it.

—*Figaro* says "while London raised a monument to the wealthy American, Mr. Peabody, the Pope has ordered a bust to the Yankee so universally honored. On his voyage to Rome Mr. Peabody presented to the treasury of Pope Pius IX., for his poor, $1,000,000. A fact curious to note is that Mr. Peabody is a Protestant."[6]

—A man in Maine has been digging for Captain Kidd's treasures for a year past, under the guidance of the spirits. He is very enviably fixed, because, from present appearances, his job will afford him steady employment as long as he may want it. There would also seem to be work enough to even justify him in hiring some outsiders to help him.

—The Newport lady with the ring "cut out of a solid diamond" is still going the rounds of the press with undiminished ferocity. Those things are common in Pennsylvania. The species is the "black" diamond, and this Newport lady's experiment has lately raised its price several dollars a ton, and brought sorrow to many a struggling family. Let her have her share of the abuse.

—Kalloch, of Kansas, and formerly of Boston, is summering in Maine. His talents are unimpaired.[7]

[5] Labouchere (1798–1869), created Baron Taunton of Taunton in the county of Somerset in 1859, was a respected official in several British administrations. He had died on 13 July.

[6] Merchant and financier George Peabody (1795–1869), originally from Massachusetts, was renowned for his philanthropy, both in the United States and abroad. In London, where he settled permanently in 1837, he was particularly revered for his donation, between 1862 and 1868, of $1,750,000 for the construction of workers' housing (his will increased the amount by $750,000). The city unveiled a bronze statue of him in July 1869, less than four months before his death. Peabody made his contribution to Pius IX in early 1868 "for the hospital of San Spirito and some of the Vatican's other charities" (Parker, 171, 202).

[7] Isaac Smith Kalloch (1831–87), a Baptist minister, had moved from Boston to Kansas, after being tried, but not convicted, of adultery. In Kansas he became involved in questionable land and railroad speculations. Later he was a controversial mayor of San Francisco (1879–81) and then a lawyer in Washington Territory (Hart 1987, 254).

—Choy-Chow and Sing-Man, the distinguished Chinamen, have started on their return to California:

> California's dull,
> For she's lost her Moguls,
>   And don't know where for to find them;
> But let them alone
> And they'll waggle home,
>   And carry their tails behind them.

—The Hartford's *Post's* inextinguishable "old man" has turned up again. He is only sixty-five, this time, but makes up for it in the liveliness of his experiences and the amount of things he can do. He is Cornelius Snyder, of Spencer, Ky., upon this occasion, and has "been twice married—eighteen children by his first wife. He has walked fifty-four miles in seven hours, and is to-day, perhaps, one of the best walkers of the State." Weston is young yet—let him be encouraged. There is no telling what he may be able to do when he has had sixty-five years' practice.[8]

—The Brown family are assembling in convention at Simpson's Corners, R. I., to form a plan of action with regard to their immense estates in England. So the telegram is worded. This is bad enough as it is—but will it stop here? Those Smiths will be at it next. It would be more generous in these two families to club themselves together in a joint convention and hire one of those ample western deserts to hold it in, and not be discommoding a helpless little State like Rhode Island which has never done them any harm.

—A correspondent of the Cleveland *Herald* reports that a Mrs. Birney, 62 years of age, living near Tippecanoe, Harrison county, Ohio, has for twenty years been in the habit of falling into a state of unconsciousness at about ten o'clock on Sunday mornings, during which she delivers ungrammatical religious discourses. Of course, when a woman does anything remarkable, it must be published far and wide, but acres and acres of poor clergymen can go on doing such things all their lives and a subsidized press takes no notice of it. A mean partiality ill becomes journalism.[9]

—"For many years the most wonderful comet the world has ever seen"

---

[8] Edward Payson Weston (1839–1929) was a well-known long-distance walker.

[9] The Cleveland *Herald* published a long, unsigned letter about Nancy Birney on 11 August 1869 ("A Strange Phenomenon," 4). Clemens accurately reported the germ of it in the first sentence here, but the concluding remarks were entirely his own.

has been advertised to appear and remain visible during the months of July and August and September of this year, and grow constantly brighter until it has finished its engagement, when it will depart in the direction of Saturn to play an engagement in the provinces. The journalists of Wisconsin are observing it now, though why a comet should visit Wisconsin before it visits New York is another of those astronomical mysteries. It appears after eleven at night, and is thenceforth visible until nearly daylight. It is described as being "many thousand times larger than the earth, and is a solid mass of fire with a tail that would reach around the earth more than a hundred times." We feel compelled to throw cold water on this comet—not in the hope of putting it out, but simply because comets, as a general rule, ought not to be encouraged, and more especially because Wisconsin journalists are too far from good points of observation to see correctly and have no business meddling with astronomy anyhow. Their comet bears marks of human manipulation, for Providence never makes these sort[s] of things out of "solid masses of fire." We do not approve of criticising comets, especially with asperity, but this one has too short a tail for the amount of style it appears to be putting on. We never had any opinion of short-tailed comets.[10]

Enclosure with 6 and 7 September 1869
To Olivia L. Langdon • Buffalo, N.Y.
(Buffalo *Express*, 21 Aug 69)

"SALUTATORY."

Being a stranger, it would be immodest and unbecoming in me to suddenly and violently assume the associate editorship of the BUFFALO EXPRESS without a single explanatory word of comfort or encouragement to the unoffending patrons of the paper, who are about to be exposed to constant attacks of my wisdom and learning. But this explanatory word shall be as brief as possible. I only wish to assure parties having a friendly interest in the prosperity of the journal, that I am not going to hurt the paper deliberately and intentionally at any time. I am not going to introduce any startling reforms, or in any way attempt to make trouble. I am

[10] The Wisconsin newspaper that Clemens quoted has not been identified.

simply going to do my plain, unpretending duty, when I cannot get out of it; I shall work diligently and honestly and faithfully at all times and upon all occasions, when privation and want shall compel me to do it; in writing, I shall always confine myself strictly to the truth, except when it is attended with inconvenience; I shall witheringly rebuke all forms of crime and misconduct, except when committed by the party inhabiting my own vest; I shall not make use of slang or vulgarity upon any occasion or under any circumstances, and shall never use profanity except in discussing house-rent and taxes. Indeed, upon second thought, I will not even use it then, for it is unchristian, inelegant and degrading—though to speak truly I do not see how house-rent and taxes are going to be discussed worth a cent without it. I shall not often meddle with politics, because we have a political editor who is already excellent, and only needs to serve a term in the penitentiary in order to be perfect.[1] I shall not write any poetry, unless I conceive a spite against the subscribers.

Such is my platform. I do not see any earthly use in it, but custom is law, and custom must be obeyed, no matter how much violence it may do to one's feelings. And this custom which I am slavishly following now, is surely one of the least necessary that ever came into vogue. In private life a man does not go and trumpet his crime before he commits it, but your new editor is such an important personage that he feels called upon to write a "salutatory'['] at once, and he puts into it all that he knows, and all that he don't know, and some things he thinks he knows but isn't certain of. And he parades his list of wonders which he is going to perform; of reforms which he is going to introduce, and public evils which he is going to exterminate; and public blessings which he is going to create; and public nuisances which he is going to abate. He spreads this all out with oppressive solemnity over a column and a half of large print, and feels that the country is saved. His satisfaction over it [is] something enormous. He then settles down to his miracles and inflicts profound platitudes and impenetrable wisdom upon a helpless public as long as they can stand it, and then they send him off Consul to some savage island in the Pacific in the vague hope that the cannibals will like him well enough to eat him. And with an inhumanity which is but a fitting climax to his career of persecution, instead of packing his trunk at once he lingers to inflict upon his benefactors a "Valedictory." If there is anything

[1] Josephus N. Larned.

more uncalled for than a "Salutatory," it is one of those tearful, blub-
bering, long-winded "Valedictories"—wherein a man who has been annoying the public for ten years cannot take leave of them without sitting
down to cry a column and a half. Still, it is the custom to write Valedictories, and custom should be respected. In my secret heart I admire my
predecessor[2] for declining to print a Valedictory, though in public I say
and shall continue to say sternly, it is custom and he ought to have
printed one. People never read them any more than they do the "Salu-
tatories," but nevertheless he ought to have honored the old fossil—he
ought to have printed a Valedictory. I said as much to him, and he
replied:

"I have resigned my place—I have departed this life—I am journal-
istically dead, at present, ain't I?"

"Yes."

"Well, wouldn't you consider it disgraceful in a corpse to sit up and
comment on the funeral?"

I record it here, and preserve it from oblivion, as the briefest and best
"Valedictory" that has yet come under my notice.   MARK TWAIN.

P. S.—I am grateful for the kindly way in which the press of the land
have taken notice of my irruption into regular journalistic life, tele-
graphically or editorially, and am happy in this place to express the
feeling.[3]

[2] Thomas A. Kennett.
[3] In the Buffalo *Express* of 9 October 1869, Clemens reprinted thirty-nine editorial "Press Greetings" ("Advertising Supplement," 1).

Appendix C

Calendar of Courtship Letters: 1868–1870

THIS CALENDAR, spanning volumes 2–4 of *Mark Twain's Letters*, lists every letter Clemens is believed to have sent Olivia Langdon—whether or not any text for it has survived—between 7 September 1868 and 20 January 1870, shortly before their marriage on 2 February. Nearly half the courtship letters are now lost. Nevertheless, missing letters have been assigned specific dates and places, or at least a specific range of dates and places, as the evidence warrants. The docket numbers of missing letters (Olivia usually numbered each envelope) have been inferred from the letters that do survive and are supplied within square brackets. Bracketed numbers are also supplied whenever an envelope is missing and no docket appears on the letter, and, in one case [81½], when Olivia may not have numbered a letter at all.

DOCKET	DATE	PLACE
1	7 and 8 Sept 68	Elmira
2	21 Sept 68	St. Louis
[3]	4–5 Oct 68	Hartford
4	18 Oct 68	Hartford
5	30 Oct 68	Hartford
6	28 Nov 68	New York
[7]	*missing, 28 Nov–3 Dec 68*	New York
8	4 Dec 68 (1st of 2)	New York
9	4 Dec 68 (2nd of 2)	New York
10	5 and 7 Dec 68	New York
11	9 and 10 Dec 68	New York
12	12 Dec 68	Norwich, N.Y.
13	19 and 20 Dec 68	Fort Plain, N.Y.
14	21 and 23 Dec 68	Detroit
15	23 and 24 Dec 68	Lansing, Mich.
16	25 Dec 68	Lansing

DOCKET	DATE	PLACE
17	27 Dec 68	Tecumseh, Mich.
18	30 Dec 68	Cleveland
19	31 Dec 68	Cleveland
20	2 Jan 69	Fort Wayne, Ind.
[21]	*missing, 4 or 5 Jan 69*[1]	Indianapolis or Chicago
22	7 Jan 69	Rockford, Ill.
23	7 Jan 69	Chicago
[24]	*missing, 10 Jan 69*[2]	Galesburg, Ill.
25	12 Jan 69	El Paso, Ill.
26	13 and 14 Jan 69	Ottawa, Ill.
27	14 Jan 69	Davenport, Iowa
28	17 Jan 69	Chicago
29	19 Jan 69	Cleveland
30	20 and 21 Jan 69	Toledo
31	21 and 22 Jan 69	Norwalk, Ohio
32	22 Jan 69	Cleveland
33	23 and 24 Jan 69	Cleveland
34	24 Jan 69	Cleveland
35	26 and 27 Jan 69	Batavia, Ill.
[36]	*missing, 27? or 28? Jan 69*	Freeport, Ill., or Waterloo, Iowa
37	29 and 30 Jan 69	Galena, Ill.
38	13 Feb 69	Cleveland
[39]	13 and 14 Feb 69	Ravenna, Ohio
[40]	15 Feb 69	Ravenna
41	17 Feb 69	Titusville, Pa.
[42]	*missing, 23 Feb 69*[3]	Trenton, N.J.
43	26 Feb 69	Stuyvesant, N.Y.
44	27 Feb 69	Lockport, N.Y.
42 45	28 Feb 69	Rochester
46	2 Mar 69	Rochester

[1] Clemens evidently did not write on 3 January from Fort Wayne (see 14 Jan 69 to OLL), nor on 6 January from Rockford until past midnight (letter 22). He lectured in Indianapolis on 4 January and the following day may have stopped in Chicago en route to Rockford.

[2] Very likely Clemens wrote to Olivia on 10 January from Galesburg, the same day he wrote to Harriet Lewis, enclosing both letters in an envelope addressed to Charles J. Langdon (see 10 Jan 69 to Lewis, n. 6).

[3] Because Clemens was in Elmira from 19 through 22 February, and did not write on either 24 or 25 February, this letter was almost certainly written on 23 February from Trenton (17 Feb 69 to Fairbanks, 26 Feb 69 to OLL).

DOCKET	DATE	PLACE
47	4 Mar 69	Lockport
4̶7̶ 48	5 Mar 69	Hartford
4̶8̶ 49	6 Mar 69 (1st of 2)[4]	Hartford
50	6 Mar 69 (2nd of 2)	Hartford
51	8 Mar 69	Hartford
52	8 and 9 Mar 69	Hartford
53	10 Mar 69	Hartford
54	12 Mar 69	Hartford
[55]	12–13 Mar 69	Hartford
56	13 Mar 69	Hartford
[57]	*missing*	
[58]	*missing* *13–16 Mar 69*	Boston; New York; Newtown, N.Y.
[59]	*missing* *19–20 Mar 69*[5]	Sharon, Pa.
[60]	*missing*	
61	8 May 69	New York
62	8 May 69	Hartford
[63]	*missing, 9? May 69*	Hartford
64	9 May 69[6]	Hartford
[65]	*missing, 10 May 69*	Hartford
[66]	*missing, 10–12 May 69*	Hartford
67	12 May 69	Hartford
68	13 May 69	Hartford
69	14 May 69	Hartford
70	15 May 69 (1st of 2)	Hartford
[71]	15 May 69 (2nd of 2)	Hartford
72	15 and 16 May 69	Hartford
73	17 and 18 May 69	Hartford
[74]	*missing, 18? May 69*	Hartford
75	19 and 20 May 69	Hartford

[4]Whereas Olivia renumbered Clemens's 28 February letter to correct a miswriting, she presumably renumbered these two letters after the late arrival of his letter of 4 March.

[5]Clemens could have written these letters during two intervals when he was absent from Elmira: 13–16 March and 19–20 March. He was in Elmira on 17, 18, and possibly 19 March, and again from about 21 March through early May (see p. 175).

[6]The envelope published with the 9 May letter (docket number 64) may actually belong to a missing letter of 10 May (see 10 May 69 to Redpath, n. 2), which would make the 9 May letter number 63, the 10 May letter number 64, and two letters written 10–12 May numbers 65 and 66 (9 May 69 to OLL, n. 5).

DOCKET	DATE		PLACE
[76]	*missing*		
[77]	*missing*		
[78]	*missing*	*20–23 May 69*[7]	Hartford and New York?
[79]	*missing*		
[80]	*missing*		
81	24 May 69		So. Windsor, Conn.
[81½]	29 May 69[8]		Elmira
82	8 June 69		Elmira
83	21 June 69		Hartford
84	23 June 69		New York
[85]	*missing*		
[86]	*missing*		
[87]	*missing*	*12–22 July 69*	Buffalo and Cleveland
[88]	*missing*	*1–7 Aug 69*[9]	Buffalo
[89]	*missing*		
90	8 Aug 69		Buffalo
[91]	*missing, 9? Aug 69*		Buffalo
[92]	*missing, 10? Aug 69*		Buffalo
[93]	*missing, 11? Aug 69*		Buffalo
[94]	*missing, 12? Aug 69*		Buffalo
[95]	*missing, 13? Aug 69*		Buffalo
[96]	*missing, 14? Aug 69*		Buffalo
[97]	*missing, 15? Aug 69*		Buffalo
[98]	*missing, 16? Aug 69*		Buffalo
[99]	*missing, 17? Aug 69*		Buffalo
[100]	*missing, 18? Aug 69*		Buffalo
101	19 Aug 69		Buffalo
[102]	*missing, 19 or 20 Aug 69*		Buffalo

[7] It is not possible to assign these letters to specific days or places. Presumably Clemens sent some of them from Hartford. He was in New York City by 23 May, however, and may have written one or more there before his arrival in South Windsor, Connecticut, by that evening. He did not write from South Windsor until the next day.

[8] Since no docket number is missing between 81 and 82, this undated note, if written on 29 May as its content suggests, was either not assigned a number by Olivia, or, like Clemens's letter of 6 and 7 September, was assigned the "½" number conjectured here.

[9] Except for his visits to Cleveland in mid-July and Buffalo in early August, Clemens spent most of the time between 23 June and 8 August with Olivia in Hartford, Elmira, and Niagara Falls (26 June 69 to JLC and PAM; 1 Aug 69 to Bliss, n. 2; 8 Aug 69 to OLL, n. 1).

DOCKET	DATE	PLACE
[103]	*missing, 20 Aug 69*[10]	Buffalo
104	21 Aug 69	Buffalo
[105]	*missing, 22? Aug 69*	Buffalo
[106]	*missing, 23? Aug 69*	Buffalo
[107]	*missing, 24? Aug 69*	Buffalo
108	25 and 26 Aug 69	Buffalo
[109]	*missing, 30 or 31 Aug or 1 Sept 69*[11]	Buffalo
110	1 Sept 69	Buffalo
[111]	*missing, 2? Sept 69*	Buffalo
[112]	*missing, 3? Sept 69*	Buffalo
113	3 Sept 69	Buffalo
[114]	*missing, 4? Sept 69*	Buffalo
[115]	*missing, 5? Sept 69*	Buffalo
115½	6 and 7 Sept 69[12]	Buffalo
116	7 Sept 69	Buffalo
117	8 and 9 Sept 69	Buffalo
[118]	*missing*	
[119]	*missing*	
[120]	*missing*	
[121]	*missing*	
[122]	*missing* — *14–29 Sept 69*	Buffalo
[123]	*missing*	
[124]	*missing*	
[125]	*missing*	
[126]	*missing*	
[127]	*missing, 28? or 29? Oct 69*[13]	en route to Pittsburgh?

[10] It must have been in this letter or the preceding one that Clemens enclosed the letter he received on 20 August from Pamela Moffett (see 20 and 21 Aug 69 to PAM).

[11] Clemens went to Elmira on Friday, 27 August, and probably returned to Buffalo on Monday, 30 August.

[12] Olivia used Clemens's standard method of interpolating a number by adding "½," indicating that she received or docketed this letter after letter 116.

[13] Clemens spent most of the time between 3 and 30 September in Buffalo, with at least one weekend trip to Elmira (from 10 to 13 September). On 30 September, he went to Elmira and remained there for almost a month, until the beginning of his lecture tour. It is therefore probable that he wrote letters 118 through 127 in Buffalo between 14 and 29 September (one of them on the night of 26 September), although he may have written the last of the sequence en route to Pittsburgh, his first lecture stop, on 28 or 29 October (8 and 9 Sept 69 to OLL; 26 and 27 Sept 69 to Fairbanks; 27 Sept 69 to Bliss, n. 2; 27 Oct 69 to Severance).

DOCKET	DATE	PLACE
128	30, 31 Oct, 1 Nov 69	Pittsburgh
[129]	*missing, 6? Nov 69*	Boston
[130]	*missing, 7? Nov 69*	Boston?
[131]	*missing, 8? Nov 69*	Worcester? or Boston, Mass.
[132]	*missing, 9? Nov 69*[14]	Boston or Providence, R.I.
133	10 Nov 69	Boston
134	10 and 11 Nov 69	Boston
[135]	*missing, 12? Nov 69*	Boston?
[136]	*missing, 13? Nov 69*	Norwich, Conn.
[137]	*missing, 14? Nov 69*[15]	Norwich, Conn.
138	15 and 16 Nov 69	Clinton and Holyoke, Mass.
[139]	*missing, 17? Nov 69*	Danvers or Boston, Mass.
[140]	*missing, 18? Nov 69*	Boston?
141	19 Nov 69	Boston
[142]	*missing, 20? Nov 69*	Boston
[143]	*missing, 21? Nov 69*	Boston
[144]	*missing, 22? Nov 69*	Boston
[145]	*missing, 23? Nov 69*	Boston or Hartford
[146]	*missing, 24? Nov 69*	Hartford
147	24 and 25 Nov 69	Hartford and Boston
148	25 Nov 69	Boston
149	27 Nov 69	Boston
150	28 Nov 69	Boston
[151]	29 Nov 69	Boston
[152]	*missing* ⎤	Philadelphia; Washington,
[153]	*missing* ⎬ *7–13 Dec 69*[16]	D.C.; Germantown, Pa.; West
[154]	*missing* ⎦	Meriden, Conn.; New Britain, Conn.; or Springfield, Mass.

[14] In his letter of 10 November 69 to Olivia, Clemens confessed to a "four days' hiatus"—probably 2–5 November—during which he wrote no letters. It is therefore likely that he wrote letters 129–32 during the next four days. His whereabouts in the first part of November remain somewhat uncertain (see pp. 385–86).

[15] In one of these three missing letters, Clemens evidently enclosed a photograph of Josh Billings (see 15 and 16 Nov 69 to OLL, n. 3).

[16] Clemens probably did not write to Olivia on 30 November since he expected to see her early the next day in New York City. He spent the week of 1–7 December with her there, except for a trip to Poughkeepsie to lecture on 3 December. Therefore he probably wrote letters 152–54 after he left New York on 7 December. Of the places where he lectured or stayed between 7 and 14 December, only Mt. Vernon, New York, on 10 December, was an unlikely site for a letter since Clemens evidently saw Olivia in New York City on the day of that performance and again on 11 December (15 and 16 Dec 69 to OLL, n. 1).

DOCKET	DATE	PLACE
[155]	14 Dec 69	Springfield, Mass.
156	15 and 16 Dec 69	Pawtucket, R.I., and Boston
[157]	*missing, 17 Dec 69*	Boston
[158]	*missing, 18 Dec 69*[17]	Boston
~~158~~ 159	18 and 19 Dec 69[18]	Boston
160	21 Dec 69	Boston
[161]	*missing, 21? Dec 69*	Hudson, Mass.
[162]	*missing, 22? Dec 69*[19]	Portland, Me.
163	25 Dec 69	Boston
[164]	*missing, 25? Dec 69*[20]	Boston
[165]	*missing, 26? Dec 69*	Boston
166	27 Dec 69	New Haven
[167]	*missing, 27–31 Dec 69*[21]	New Haven; Trenton, N.J.; Newark; Wilkes-Barre, Pa.; or Williamsport, Pa.
168	6 Jan 70	New York
169	8 Jan 70 (1st of 2)	Troy, N.Y.
170	8 Jan 70 (2nd of 2)	Troy
[171]	*missing, 9? Jan 70*	Troy
172	10 Jan 70 (1st of 2)	Albany
173	10 Jan 70 (2nd of 2)	Albany
[174]	*missing, 11? Jan 70*[22]	West Troy, Troy, or Albany, N.Y.
[175]	*missing, 12? Jan 70*	Rondout, N.Y.
176	13 Jan 70	Cambridge, N.Y.
177	14 Jan 70	Troy
178	14 Jan 70	Utica, N.Y.

[17] Clemens wrote this letter on the morning of 18 December, misdating it 17 December. Since he had been too ill to write a complete letter on 16 December, he must have written letter 157 on 17 December.

[18] Olivia revised the docket of this letter after she belatedly received or docketed Clemens's letter of 18 December.

[19] Clemens probably wrote letter 161 in Hudson, Massachusetts, where, after lecturing, he seems to have spent the night of 21 December (see 21 Dec 69 to OLL, n. 3). He probably wrote letter 162 the following night, after lecturing in Portland. Since it wasn't until Christmas Day that he wrote Olivia of the imposition he suffered in Rockport, Massachusetts, on 23 December, he presumably did not write to her then. He definitely wrote no letter on 24 December.

[20] In letter 163 Clemens anticipated writing Olivia another letter that day.

[21] Clemens must have written this letter before going to Elmira, where he "spent Jan. 1, 2, 3 & 5" of 1870 (6 Jan 70 to Fairbanks, CSmH, in *MTMF*, 112).

[22] After lecturing in West Troy on 11 January 1870, Clemens may have spent the night there or, conceivably, returned to his former lodgings in nearby Troy or Albany.

DOCKET	DATE	PLACE
[179]	*missing, 15? Jan 70*	Oswego, N.Y.
[180]	*missing, 16? Jan 70*	Oswego?
[181]	*missing, 17? Jan 70*	Baldwinsville, N.Y.
[182]	*missing, 18? Jan 70*[23]	Syracuse or Ogdensburg, N.Y.?
[183]	*missing, 19? Jan 70*[24]	Buffalo?
184	20 Jan 70	Hornellsville, N.Y.

[23] Clemens registered at a Syracuse hotel on 18 January before he went on to Ogdensburg for his evening lecture ("City Items," Syracuse *Standard*, 19 Jan 70, 3).

[24] Clemens lectured in Fredonia, New York, on the evening of 19 January, but it is unlikely that he wrote to Olivia then since his letter of the following day from Hornellsville contains his report of the Fredonia performance. He may, however, have written a 19 January letter from Buffalo, where he spent part of the day, probably visiting his office at the *Express*, before going to Fredonia.

Appendix D

Lecture Schedule, 1868–1870

THIS SCHEDULE, spanning volumes 2–4 of *Mark Twain's Letters*, lists Mark Twain's known lecture appearances during two tours: 17 November 1868–20 March 1869 and 1 November 1869–21 January 1870. The first was managed in the Midwest by G. L. Torbert, of Dubuque, Iowa, secretary of the Associated Western Literary Societies, and in the East by Clemens himself, with partial assistance from James K. Medbery's American Literary Bureau in New York (*L2*, 241 n. 3, 254–55 n. 2). The second, an exclusively eastern tour, was managed by James Redpath and George L. Fall of the Boston Lyceum Bureau. The primary sources consulted in recreating Clemens's itineraries were his surviving letters, Fall's letters of 27 October and 7 December 1869 to him (Redpath Letterpress Book, 26, 632, IaU), and Fall's 29 November 1869 "Memo of Engagements" (enclosed in 29 Nov 69 to OLL). In some instances, these documents have provided the only evidence of the date and place of a lecture. In most cases, however, information in them has been confirmed by announcements, reviews, or reports in local newspapers (unless otherwise indicated, a cited newspaper was published in the town or city where Clemens lectured).

1868–1869 Tour

DATE	PLACE	SOURCE
17 Nov 68	Cleveland, Ohio	*Herald*, *Leader*, and *Plain Dealer* (18 Nov 68)
19 Nov 68	Pittsburgh, Pa.	*Gazette* (20 Nov 68)
23 Nov 68	Elmira, N.Y.	*Advertiser* (24 Nov 68)
2 Dec 68	Rondout, N.Y.	2 Dec 68 to Langdon (*L2*, 298)
9 Dec 68	Newark, N.J.	*Advertiser* (10 Dec 68)
11 Dec 68	Norwich, N.Y.	5 and 7 Dec 68 to OLL (*L2*, 315)

DATE	PLACE	SOURCE
16 Dec 68	Scranton, Pa.	5 and 7 Dec 68 to OLL (*L2*, 315)
19 Dec 68	Fort Plain, N.Y.	*Mohawk Valley Register* (25 Dec 68)
22 Dec 68	Detroit, Mich.	*Advertiser and Tribune* and *Free Press* (23 Dec 68)
23 Dec 68	Lansing, Mich.	*State Republican* (31 Dec 68)
25 Dec 68	Charlotte, Mich.	*Republican* (30 Dec 68)
26 Dec 68	Tecumseh, Mich.	14 Jan 69 to OLL
30 Dec 68	Akron, Ohio	29 Dec 68 to Langdon (*L2*, 360); Cleveland *Leader* (1 Jan 69)[1]
2 Jan 69	Fort Wayne, Ind.	*Democrat* and *Gazette* (4 Jan 69)
4 Jan 69	Indianapolis, Ind.	*Journal* (5 Jan 69)
6 Jan 69	Rockford, Ill.	Galena (Ill.) *Gazette* (26 Jan 69), reprinting Rockford *Register* (9 Jan 69)
7 Jan 69	Chicago, Ill.	*Tribune, Times, Republican,* and others (8 Jan 69)
8 Jan 69	Monmouth, Ill.	*Atlas* and *Review* (8 Jan 69)[2]
9 Jan 69	Galesburg, Ill.	Peoria (Ill.) *Transcript* (11 Jan 69)
11 Jan 69	Peoria, Ill.	*Transcript* and *National Democrat* (12 Jan 69)
12 Jan 69[3]	Decatur, Ill.	*Republican* (14 Jan 69)
13 Jan 69	Ottawa, Ill.	*Free Trader* (16 Jan 69) and *Republican* (21 Jan 69)[4]
14 Jan 69	Davenport, Iowa	*Democrat* (15 Jan 69)
15 Jan 69	Iowa City, Iowa	*Republican* (6 and 20 Jan 69)
20 Jan 69[5]	Toledo, Ohio	*Commercial* and *Blade* (21 Jan 69)
21 Jan 69	Norwalk, Ohio	*Reflector* (26 Jan 69)
22 Jan 69[6]	Cleveland, Ohio	*Herald, Leader,* and *Plain Dealer* (23 Jan 69)

[1] The *Leader* mistakenly reported that Clemens lectured in Akron on Thursday, 31 December. He had canceled 14 and 31 December lectures in New York City and Dayton, Ohio, respectively; missed a 15 December engagement in Buffalo; and "broke a lecture engagement" in an unidentified town to be in Elmira with Olivia Langdon "from 7 p.m. 17th to 7 p.m. 18th" (*L2*, 308, 340, 348, 368).

[2] Notices in these and other Illinois newspapers cited in this calendar are reprinted or summarized in Wallace.

[3] Originally Clemens was scheduled to appear in Bloomington, Illinois, on this date (2 Jan 69 to OLL).

[4] The *Free Trader* mistakenly reported that Clemens lectured on Tuesday, 12 January.

[5] Clemens was unable to reach Sparta, Wisconsin, for a scheduled 18 January lecture (14 Jan 69 to PAM; 17 Jan 69 and 19 Jan 69, both to OLL).

[6] A benefit for the Cleveland Protestant Orphan Asylum (7 Jan 69 to Fairbanks and others).

DATE	PLACE	SOURCE
25 Jan 69	Marshall, Mich.	*Statesman* (28 Jan 69)
26 Jan 69	Batavia, Ill.	Aurora (Ill.) *Beacon* (4 Feb 69)
27 Jan 69	Freeport, Ill.	*Bulletin* (28 Jan 69) and *Journal* (3 Feb 69)
28 Jan 69	Waterloo, Iowa	*Courier* (4 Feb 69)[7]
29 Jan 69	Galena, Ill.	*Gazette* (2 Feb 69)
1 Feb 69	Jacksonville, Ill.	*Journal* (2 Feb 69) and *Sentinel* (5 Feb 69)
13 Feb 69	Ravenna, Ohio	*Portage County Democrat* (17 Feb 69) and *Democratic Press* (18 Feb 69)[8]
15 Feb 69[9]	Alliance, Ohio	17 Feb 69 to OLL
16 Feb 69	Titusville, Pa.	*Morning Herald* (17 Feb 69)
17 Feb 69[10]	Franklin, Pa.	17 Feb 69 to Fairbanks (two letters)
23 Feb 69	Trenton, N.J.	*True American* (17–23 Feb 69) and *State Gazette* (23 Feb 69)
25 Feb 69	Stuyvesant, N.Y.	Hudson (N.Y.) *Columbia Republican* (16 Feb 69)
1 Mar 69	Geneseo, N.Y.	*Genesee Valley Herald* (24 Feb 69)
3 Mar 69[11]	Lockport, N.Y.	*Journal* (4 Mar 69)
16 Mar 69	Newtown, N.Y.	12 Mar 69 to OLL
20 Mar 69	Sharon, Pa.	*Times* (24 Mar 69) or *Herald* (27 Mar 69)

1869–1870 Tour

1 Nov 69	Pittsburgh, Pa.	*Commercial, Gazette, Post* (2 Nov 69), and others

[7] The *Courier* mistakenly reported that Clemens lectured on Friday, 29 January.

[8] The *Democratic Press* mistakenly reported that Clemens lectured on Sunday, 14 February.

[9] Clemens originally expected to lecture in New York City on 15 February. Subsequently that date was reassigned to Titusville, then to Franklin, and finally to Alliance, where he had missed an engagement on 12 February. The Titusville and Franklin lectures were moved to 16 and 17 February, respectively (13 and 14 Jan 69, 17 Jan 69, and 13 Feb 69, all to OLL; 13 Feb 69 to Fairbanks, n. 2; 17 Feb 69 to Fairbanks from Titusville).

[10] Clemens postponed an 18 February lecture in Geneseo, New York, until 1 March and canceled a 19 February lecture in Auburn, New York (17 Feb 69 to Fairbanks from Franklin, nn. 2, 4; 18 Feb 69 and 21–22 Feb 69 [three letters], all to the Young Men's Association of Geneseo Academy).

[11] A storm had forced Clemens to reschedule this lecture from 27 February (27 Feb 69 and 28 Feb 69, both to OLL).

DATE	PLACE	SOURCE
2 Nov 69	Sharon, Pa.? or	Fall to SLC, 27 Oct 69
	Brookville, Pa.?	Pittsburgh *Gazette* (2 Nov 69)
3 Nov 69	Johnstown, Pa.?	Pittsburgh *Gazette* (2 Nov 69)
8 Nov 69[12]	Worcester, Mass.?	Fall to SLC, 27 Oct 69
9 Nov 69	Providence, R.I.	*Evening Press, Journal,* and *Morning Herald* (10 Nov 69)
10 Nov 69	Boston, Mass.	*Advertiser, Herald, Post* (11 Nov 69), and others
11 Nov 69	Charlestown, Mass.	*Advertiser* (13 Nov 69)
13 Nov 69	Norwich, Conn.	*Advertiser* (15 Nov 69, cited in Lorch 1968, 359 n. 5)[13]
15 Nov 69	Clinton, Mass.	*Courant* (20 Nov 69)
16 Nov 69	Holyoke, Mass.	Springfield (Mass.) *Republican* (16 Nov 69)
17 Nov 69	Danvers, Mass.	*Monitor* (24 Nov 69)
19 Nov 69	Jamaica Plain, Mass.	Boston *Post* and Boston *Journal* (11 Nov 69), Boston *Evening Transcript* (13 Nov 69)
23 Nov 69[14]	Hartford, Conn.	*Courant* (24 Nov 69) and *Times* (25 Nov 69)
26 Nov 69	Unidentified site	27 Nov 69 to OLL
29 Nov 69	Newtonville, Mass.	Newton *Journal* (4 Dec 69)
30 Nov 69	Thompsonville, Conn.	Springfield (Mass.) *Republican* (2 Dec 69)
1 Dec 69[15]	Brooklyn, N.Y.	*Times* and *Eagle* (2 Dec 69)
3 Dec 69	Poughkeepsie, N.Y.	*Eagle* and *Press* (4 Dec 69)

[12] The Brookville and Johnstown lectures, although announced by the Pittsburgh *Gazette*, are not on the 1–10 November itinerary in Fall's 27 October letter to Clemens and are not mentioned in Clemens's surviving letters or by local reviewers. They therefore remain doubtful—as do the Sharon and Worcester appointments, which *are* on Fall's list, but may not have been kept (see pp. 385–86).

[13] The *Advertiser*, which doubtless reported the date of the Norwich lecture, was not available for examination. This performance almost certainly was on Saturday, 13 November, rather than the previous night, for which no lecture has been identified. Clemens spent all of Sunday, 14 November, as well as the morning of Monday, 15 November, in Norwich, which he was unlikely to have done had he lectured there on Friday, 12 November (15 and 16 Nov 69 to OLL).

[14] An engagement in Rutland, Vermont, on 24 or 25 November, apparently was canceled (25 Nov 69 to OLL).

[15] As a result of a misunderstanding, Clemens canceled a second Brooklyn lecture, scheduled for 6 December (4 Dec 69 and 6 Dec 69, both to James Redpath).

DATE	PLACE	SOURCE
7 Dec 69	Philadelphia, Pa.	*Evening Bulletin, Inquirer* (8 Dec 69), *Sunday Mercury* (12 Dec 69), and others
8 Dec 69	Washington, D.C.	*Evening Star, Morning Chronicle, National Republican* (9 Dec 69), and others
9 Dec 69	Germantown, Pa.	29 Nov 69 to OLL
10 Dec 69	Mount Vernon, N.Y.	*Chronicle* (18 Dec 69)
11 Dec 69	West Meriden, Conn.	Meriden *Republican* (13 Dec 69)
13 Dec 69	New Britain, Conn.	*Record* (26 Nov, 17 Dec 69)
14 Dec 69	Warren, Mass.	29 Nov 69 to OLL
15 Dec 69	Pawtucket, R.I.	*Gazette and Chronicle* and Providence *Journal* (17 Dec 69)
16 Dec 69[16]	Waltham, Mass.	*Free Press* and *Sentinel* (17 Dec 69)
20 Dec 69	Canton, Mass.	Dedham (Mass.) *Gazette* (18 and 25 Dec 69)
21 Dec 69	Hudson, Mass.	29 Nov 69 to OLL
22 Dec 69	Portland, Me.	*Eastern Argus* and *Press* (23 Dec 69), *Transcript* (1 Jan 70), and others
23 Dec 69	Rockport, Mass.	Gloucester (Mass.) *Cape Ann Advertiser* (31 Dec 69)[17]
24 Dec 69[18]	Slatersville, R.I.	Woonsocket (R.I.) *Patriot and Rhode Island State Register* (24 Dec 69)
27 Dec 69	New Haven, Conn.	*Morning Journal and Courier* and *Palladium* (28 Dec 69)
28 Dec 69	Trenton, N.J.	*State Gazette* (29 and 30 Dec 69) and *True American* (29 and 30 Dec 69)
29 Dec 69	Newark, N.J.	*Advertiser* and *Journal* (30 Dec 69)
30 Dec 69	Wilkes-Barre, Pa.	29 Nov 69 to OLL
31 Dec 69	Williamsport, Pa.	*Gazette and Bulletin* (1 Jan 70)
4 Jan 70	Owego, N.Y.	*Gazette* and *Times* (6 Jan 70)

[16] Lectures scheduled for 17 and 18 December in Abington and Lynn, Massachusetts, respectively, were canceled because Clemens was ill (29 Nov 69, 18 and 19 Dec 69, both to OLL; 17 Dec 69 to PAM; Fall to SLC, 7 Dec 69, Redpath Letterpress Book, 632, IaU). The Boston weekly *Flag of Our Union* reported on 18 December that "Mr. Mark Twain lectures to-night in Boston with engagements to fulfil the subsequent nights in Charlestown, Chelsea, Roxbury, and other adjacent places" (808), but none of the specifics of this report are confirmed by Clemens or Fall or by local newspapers.

[17] The *Advertiser* mistakenly reported that Clemens lectured on Friday, 24 December.

[18] Originally scheduled to lecture in Salem, Massachusetts, on 24 December, Clemens was a late substitute in Slatersville for Josh Billings.

DATE	PLACE	SOURCE
6 Jan 70	Amenia, N.Y.	29 Nov 69 and 6 Jan 70 (CU-MARK), both to OLL
7 Jan 70	Cohoes, N.Y.	*Cataract* (8 and 15 Jan 70)
10 Jan 70	Albany, N.Y.	*Argus, Evening Journal,* and *Express* (11 Jan 70)
11 Jan 70	West Troy, N.Y.	Troy *Times* and Troy *Whig* (12 Jan 70)
12 Jan 70	Rondout, N.Y.	29 Nov 69 and 10 Jan 70 (2nd of 2, CU-MARK), both to OLL
13 Jan 70	Cambridge, N.Y.	*Washington County Post* (14 Jan 70)
14 Jan 70	Utica, N.Y.	*Observer* (15 Jan 70)
15 Jan 70	Oswego, N.Y.	*Commercial Advertiser and Times* (17 Jan 70)
17 Jan 70	Baldwinsville, N.Y.	29 Nov 69 and 10 Jan 70 (2nd of 2, CU-MARK), both to OLL
18 Jan 70	Ogdensburg, N.Y.	Cleveland *Herald* (20 Jan 70)[19]
19 Jan 70	Fredonia, N.Y.	*Censor* (26 Jan 70)
20 Jan 70	Hornellsville, N.Y.	*Tribune* (2 Dec 69, 28 Jan 70)
21 Jan 70	Jamestown, N.Y.	*Journal* (22 and 28 Jan 70)

[19] The *Herald*, evidently drawing on one of its newspaper exchanges, reported that Mark Twain lectured in Ogdensburg "a day or two since." This engagement, neither advertised nor reviewed in the Ogdensburg *Journal*, must have been a late addition: Clemens did not include it in the 11–21 January itinerary he sent to Olivia Langdon (10 Jan 70 to OLL [2nd of 2], CU-MARK).

Appendix E

Advertising Circulars

THREE CIRCULARS from 1869, the first distributed by the Boston Lyceum Bureau and the others by the American Publishing Company, are reproduced here in facsimile. Clemens collaborated in the preparation of all of them and discussed them in his correspondence with James Redpath and Elisha Bliss.

Boston Lyceum Bureau Advertising Circular

Prepared by James Redpath during May and June of 1869, this circular was intended to attract lecture engagements for Mark Twain during the 1869–70 season. It was in large part made up of press notices from the previous season's tour. Redpath, who solicited copies of reviews from Clemens on 24 April 1869 (see 10 May 69 and 14 and 17 May 69, both to Redpath), eventually included eight extracts from seven newspapers: the Cleveland *Herald* ("Mark Twain and the Orphans," 23 Jan 69, 3, and "Library Association—Lecture of 'Mark Twain,'" 18 Nov 68, 8, the latter by Mary Mason Fairbanks [identified in the circular as "Another Cleveland journalist"]); the Newark (N.J.) *Courier* (probably 10 Dec 68); the Chicago *Times* ("The American Vandal Abroad," 8 Jan 69, 3; misidentified as the *Tribune*); the Brooklyn *Eagle* ("Mark Twain on the Sandwich Islands," 11 May 67, 3); the Detroit *Advertiser and Tribune* ("Mark Twain's Lecture," 23 Dec 68, no page; misidentified as the *Republican*); the Toledo *Commercial* ("Mark Twain," 21 Jan 69, no page); and the Chicago *Tribune* ("Mark Twain," 8 Jan 69, 4; misidentified as the *Republican*). The circular is reproduced here actual size.

THE BOSTON LYCEUM BUREAU

IS PREPARED TO MAKE ENGAGEMENTS FOR

"MARK TWAIN,"

[SAMUEL L. CLEMENS.]

MARK TWAIN is widely known as one of the most humorous writers in the country. He has made very successful lecturing tours in the West, but has never, we believe, appeared before in a New England Lyceum. His lecture on the " American Vandal Abroad " was everywhere spoken of by the Press, in the highest terms of commendation.

From a large number of flattering notices, we extract a few sentences only, in order to show that his fame as a writer does not suffer by his appearance as a lecturer

THE *Cleveland Herald* says : " No written description can do justice to the lecture. It must be heard to be fully appreciated. After hearing it the second time we do not wonder that "The Vandal " met with the unbounded enthusiasm that has attended it at every place where it has been heard. The humor of the lecture is peculiar and irresistible, the descriptive portions brilliant and eloquent, and the whole tone humanitarian and elevating."

Another Cleveland journalist says : — " The course of lectures before the Library Association was inaugurated last evening by the brilliant entertainment of the humorist, " Mark Twain." Notwithstanding the unpropitious weather, and strong counter attractions in the way of amusements, Case Hall was early filled with an assembly who were prepared to criticise closely this new candidate for their favor. A few moments sufficed to put him and his audience on the best of terms, and to warm him up with the pleasant consciousness of their approval. For nearly two hours he held them by the magnetism of his varied talent.

" We shall attempt no transcript of his lecture, lest with unskilful hands we mar its beauty, for beauty and poetry it certainly possessed, though the production of a professed humorist.

" We know not which most to commend, the quaint utterances, the funny incidents, the good-natured recital of the characteristics of his harmless " Vandal," or the gems of beautiful descriptions which sparkled all through his lecture. We expected to be amused, but we were taken by surprise when he carried us on the wings of his redundant fancy, away to the ruins, the cathedrals, and the monuments of the Old World. There are some passages of gorgeous word-painting which haunt us like a remembered picture.

" We congratulate Mr. Twain upon having taken the tide of public favor " at the flood " in the lecture field, and having conclusively proved that a man may be a humorist without being a clown. He has elevated the profession by his graceful delivery and by recognizing in his audience something higher than merely a desire to laugh. We can assure the cities who are awaiting his coming, that a rich feast is in store for them, and Cleveland is proud to offer him the first laurel leaf in his *role* as lecturer, this side the " Rocky slope."

Boston Lyceum Bureau circular, page 1 of a four-page folder. Mark Twain Papers, The Bancroft Library (CU-MARK).

THE *Newark Courier* says: —"The second lecture in the Clayonian course was delivered by Mr. Samuel Clemens, ("Mark Twain") at the Opera House last evening, before a large and intelligent audience,—a Gough audience in size, and Emersonian in intelligence. It being the first appearance of Mr. Clemens in Newark, it is just possible that curiosity to see the singular writer who has given currency to many of the drollest things in our literature, was one of the incentives which literally packed the house last evening. No higher compliment could have been paid the lecturer than this assembly of our best citizens and their families, many of whom rarely attend lectures of any kind. Mr. Clemens met with a very flattering reception at the hands of his auditors, and left a very favorable impression of his merits on the minds of all. We trust the acquaintance thus auspiciously begun may be renewed by future engagements in this city.

" It would be impossible to do " Mark Twain " justice in the brief space allotted to a sketch of his lecture on " The Vandal Abroad." He is one of the few who must be reported *verbatim* in order to give any intelligible idea of his matter and manner. In him quaint humor and eloquent and powerful description are very happily blended ; and the facility with which he glides from one to the other is most enjoyable. His quick perceptions of the ludicrous side of life are only equalled by his shrewd observation and poetic insight—passing from grave to gay with a recklessness absolutely side-splitting. We are at a loss which to admire most, his mirth or his seriousness. Both are admirable in themselves, and the combination of the two produces a wonderfully pleasant effect.

" The lecture occupied about an hour and a half in delivery and was listened to with the closest attention throughout."

THE *Chicago Tribune* in the course of a long notice said : " the attendance was quite large and the audience very select. The recital was interspersed with anecdotes, comparisons, and incidents, which were utterly ridiculous and absurb, At other times the audience were enraptured with the charming oratorical powers of the speaker. The lecture throughout was one of Mark-ed ability, and was listened to by a delighted audience."

THE *Brooklyn Eagle* said of his Sandwich Islands lecture : —" A choice audience assembled last evening to hear Mark Twain, the California humorist, discourse upon the life and habits of the Sandwich Islanders. It would be manifestly unfair to report this most acceptable lecture, and no type could do justice to the cool, self-possession of the lecturer. His style is quaint and taking, and commends itself to an audience before they are aware of it, and is entirely original. To those who may think that the modern style of manner is put on, it is only necessary to say that Mr. Twain in every day life is as staid and circumspect as he is before the public. He is a man who will wear ; he has a new subject, dresses it up in a new attire and presents facts and comicalities in a style entirely his own. The lecture occupies over an hour and affords the public a treat they should hear, and having done so will not soon forget. In California Mr. Twain is well known, and draws like a poultice, but among us he is a stranger. Notwithstanding this he will soon win his way to public favor, as shown by the very flattering reception given him in New York at the Cooper Institute, and last night at the Atheneum. He should be heard by every person who appreciates humor, as presented in its very drollest features."

THE *Detroit Republican* said : " Last evening at Young Men's Hall, Mr. Clemens—otherwise known as " Mark Twain,"—his newspaper *nom de plume*, lectured before the Young Men's Society, to a very large audience,, his subject being " The American Vandal Abroad." The lecturer depicts the American character in its most strongly developed forms, as seen in the citizens of the United States, who, without

Boston Lyceum Bureau circular, page 2.

489

education or cultivation, visit Europe and the East, and surprise the inhabitants of those regions by his peculiar views of things abroad.

"The lecturer possesses a very peculiar manner, having an expressive countenance, little gesture, but what little there is, is very expressive, and walking up and down the stage in a familiar way that at once attracts the attention and interest of an audience.

"Mr. Clemens is not a mere humorist, as his description of the Egyptian Sphinx last evening conclusively shows. The wonderful age of this creation of man's work, the grand scenes which it has witnessed, the strange changes it has seen, the story which its silent, patient face tells, were admirably depicted, and received a burst of genuine and hearty applause.

"His joking is immense, his stories being intensely funny and his manner being inimitable, something entirely new to audiences, at least of this country, and which we think is entirely new on the lecture stage. His delivery is slow and measured and extremely dry and funny.

"One of the richest things in the lecture was the description of the American Vandal in Paris. The Vandal in Italy was also depicted very funnily.

"The story of the affixing the skin of a man to the door of one of the churches in Italy, and the dreams and suggestions to which the account of the story had given rise in his mind were graphically and very funnily described, causing the audience intense excitement.

"Venice was beautifully described in a few lines, her palaces, canals, sculptures, pictures, cathedrals, and other monuments of her glory. Mr. Clemens branched off upon the song of a gondolier, which he represented in a very ludicrous light. The movements of the gondolas, however their silence, their mystery, their air of being abroad upon some secret errand born of no good, were very handsomely portrayed.

"A moonlight view of Athens, with its cold, yet beautiful statues, its buildings of historic fame, its histories of former glory, and the shadows which the spectacle brought up before him, were beautifully given. The memories which Athens calls up are among the most wonderful that are suggested by any city of the world, and as depicted in the vivid, burning, beautiful language of Mr. Clemmens, they were brought before the listener with a brilliancy and perfection of coloring very rarely seen, even in the writings of the best American or English authors.

"The visit which the Vandal of the Quaker City, Mr. Clemens, paid to the Czar of Russia, was detailed very graphically, the vast power of Alexander II. being portrayed in vivid language and giving a truthful, though somewhat grotesque, idea of the influence and dignity of the Emperors of Russia. Much that was very funny in connection with the interview was also detailed. The Czar was described as the friend of America, as a man of modesty and extreme courtesy and an unusually agreeable person to know.

"The lecture closed with a funny story listened to by a delighted audience.

The Toledo Commercial said :—" White's Hall was crowded with a very intelligent and appreciative audience last night, to hear Mark Twain's " American Vandal Abroad," and a more delighted audience never occupied those seats. There is an originality and pungency to his wit, and a purity of tone and expression which gives it a relish to the most cultivated minds. There is nothing gross and coarse in his utterance—no appeals to the baser passions and prejudices—but an easy flow of humor which will make the muscle of the face ache from constant contraction. But then, his lecture is not all wit. It is dotted all over with most beautiful word pictures, and its humor is so interwoven with facts and incidents collected by many weary months of travel in the East that the wit serves to drive the truths deeper into the mind. It

Boston Lyceum Bureau circular, page 3.

is seldom that our people have such an intellectual feast set before them, and we were pleased to see so large a number present to enjoy it."

The *Chicago Republican* thus described the lecturer: — "Blessed with long legs, he is tall, reaching five feet ten inches in his boots; weight, 167 pounds; body lithe and muscular; head round and well set on considerable neck, and feet of no size within the ken of a shoemaker; so he gets his boots and stockings always made to order. Next to Grant he hears the belt for smoking. He smokes tobacco. Drink never crosses the threshold of his humorous mouth. Fun lurks in the corners of it. The eyes are deep set and shine like stars in a dark night. The brow overhangs the eyes, and the head is protected from the weather by dark and curling locks. The face is eminently a good one, a laughing face, beaming with humor and genuine good nature. He looks as if he would make a good husband and a jolly father. As a humorous lecturer, he is a success. His manner is peculiar; he hangs round loose, leaning on the desk, or flirting round the corners of it; then marching and countermarching in the rear of it, marking off ground by the yard with his tremendous boots. He would laugh at his own jokes, but that his doing so would detract from the fun of his hearers, so he contents himself by refusing to explode, and swallows his risibility until the lecture is over, when he feels easier and blows off steam. His voice is a long, monotonous crawl, well adapted to his style of speaking. The fun invariably comes in at the end of a sentence, after a pause. When the audience least expects it, some dry remark drops and tickles the ribs, and endangers the waist buttons of the "laughists." During the evening, as if to prove that there was something besides humor in him, he branched out into quite eloquent passages, which were applauded. The lecture was good and the attendance ——large."

"Mark Twain's" only lecture for the season of 1869-70 will be entitled "The Curiosities of California," of which State he has been a resident for a number of years.

———⧓———

For Terms, and to make arrangements, address,

JAMES REDPATH,

No. 20 Bromfield Street,

BOSTON.

Boston Lyceum Bureau circular, page 4.

491

Advertising Circular for The Innocents Abroad

In early July 1869, before publication of *The Innocents Abroad*, the American Publishing Company prepared a four-page circular to advertise the book, in part from reviews of Clemens's 1868–69 lecture tour. The first page of the circular, entitled "Opinions of the Press," published reviews from the Cleveland *Herald* (Mary Mason Fairbanks, "Library Association—Lecture of 'Mark Twain,'" 18 Nov 68, 1), the Toledo *Blade* ("Mark Twain's Lecture," 21 Jan 69, 4), the Sharon (Pa.) *Times* or *Herald* (24 or 27 Mar 69), and an unidentified Chicago newspaper (8? Jan 69). It also quoted the Elmira *Gazette* (27? Apr 69), which had praised *The Innocents Abroad* on the basis of "advance sheets," and the Fort Plain (N.Y.) *Mohawk Valley Register* (9 Apr? 69). Several days after Clemens received a sample copy of the circular, however, Frank Bliss of the American Publishing Company wrote that they were making corrections "in the plates" (see 12 July 69 to Elisha Bliss, n. 1). The corrections consisted of a revised and redesigned page 2 and several minor alterations to page 3. The first printing is reproduced here actual size, except for page 4, shown at 89 percent. A reproduction of the revised page 2 follows. The revised circular was later incorporated into the sales prospectuses for *Innocents*, preceded by collected reviews of the book (APC 1869b and 1870).

OPINIONS OF THE PRESS.

The author of this work during the past winter delivered in scores of cities in the West, his popular lecture termed "The American Vandal Abroad," to large and delighted audiences. The material for that lecture was drawn from this book, and is a fair specimen of its style and quality. The lecture is spoken of in the following manner by the press:

At Cleveland, Ohio.

LIBRARY ASSOCIATION—LECTURE OF "MARK TWAIN."—We shall attempt no transcript of this lecture, lest with unskillful hands we mar its beauty, for beauty and poetry it certainly possessed, though the production of a professed humorist.

We know not which most to commend, the quaint utterances, the funny incidents, the good-natured recital of the characteristics of his harmless "Vandal," or the gems of beautiful description which sparkled all through his lecture. We expected to be amused, but we were taken by surprise when he carried us on the wings of his redundant fancy, away to the ruins, the cathedrals, and the monuments of the old world. There are some passages of gorgeous word-painting which haunt us like a remembered picture. We congratulate Mr. Twain upon having taken the tide of public favor "at the flood" in the lecture field, and having conclusively proved that a man may be a humorist without being a clown. He has elevated the profession by his graceful delivery and by recognizing in his audience something higher than merely a desire to laugh. We can assure the cities who are awaiting his coming, that a rich feast is in store for them, and Cleveland is proud to offer him the first laurel leaf in his role as lecturer, this side the "Rocky slope."

At Toledo, Ohio.

MARK TWAIN'S LECTURE.—White's Hall was filled from cellar to garret, last night, by one of the best tickled audiences that ever assembled there to hear a lecture or see the speaker. Mark Twain tickled them. And he did it so easily and almost constantly, that they didn't know what they were laughing at more than half the time. Twain is witty, and his wit comes from his own fertile brain. His style is original; and his manner of speaking is not after the manner of men generally. His serious face and long drawn words are, of themselves, sufficient to make one laugh, even if there were not in every sentence expressed a sparkling gem of humor and original idea His anecdotes, with which the lecture is replete, are rich, and, as he tells them, irresistibly funny. In some of his descriptions of European places and characters the lecturer delivers, at times, most eloquent passages, brilliant in thought and word. That Mark Twain is a success as a lecturer, as well as writer, we think no one who heard "The American Vandal Abroad," last night, will dispute.

At Sharon, Penn.

MARK TWAIN.—This combination of letters spells a name and designates a man for whom we have the most intense veneration. We had the privilege and pleasure of hearing his quaint and instructive lecture, the "American Vandal Abroad," on Saturday evening last. A large and appreciative audience greeted him, all anxious to hear and see the man who had placed himself so high in their esteem by the many brilliant witticisms from time to time seized with avidity by the public press, and through it placed before the world. Mr. Twain was heard and admired. New and warm friends were added to his list and the old ones retained. Such a deep interest was manifested in the lecture that at the close a general dissatisfaction was apparent that he did not speak longer. It seemed too short, but upon consulting the time it was discovered to the great surprise of all that he had talked one hour and a half. A sermon of the same dimensions to the self-same audience would have found many dozing, and at the hour of high noon! The lecture was a grand success. Everybody was pleased. He is about to issue a work of some six hundred pages, "The Innocents Abroad, or the New Pilgrim's Progress." We long to see it, and predict for it an extensive sale.

At Chicago.

"MARK TWAIN" ON THE SPHYNX.—Among the gems of fine description in the lecture of Mark Twain, Tuesday evening, that of the mysterious Sphynx thrilled his audience with admiration.

From the Elmira, N. Y., Daily Gazette.

MARK TWAIN'S NEW BOOK, "THE INNOCENTS ABROAD, OR THE NEW PILGRIM'S PROGRESS."—Advance sheets of the new work have incidentally come under our notice—and from them we are prepared to speak highly of Mr. Clemens' prospective book. It has for its foundation a description of the sights and scenes of famous places abroad, while they are treated in that peculiarly attractive vein of power and genuine humor, which has made him widely famous, and placed him at the head of the witty writers of America. Mr. Clemens, however, is something besides a literary humorist. There occurs in his writing a blending of sentiment and thought as fine and striking as they are beautiful and sparkling—ideas as clear and penetrating as his humor is fresh. From what we have seen of his new book we are led to believe that it will do much towards advancing his reputation, and establish it on an enduring basis. That it will be a success is already assured.

From the Mohawk Valley, N. Y., Register.

By a private note from "Mark Twain," we learn that he is about to issue his new book, "The New Pilgrim's Progress," and then transform himself into a pilgrim again and start for California. The first part of the information we hail with the utmost satisfaction, but we regret that he is soon to leave the Atlantic coast. However, as many people will kill themselves with laughter over his book, he might be subject to the annoyance of frequent arrests for being accessory before the fact to numerous cases of manslaughter. In California he would be safe among his earlier friends, who know him better, and would let him off more easily.

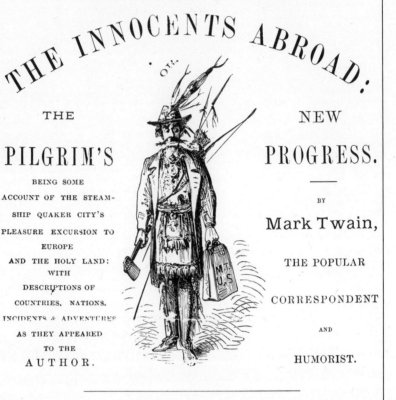

☞ The Most Unique and Spicy Volume in Existence.

THE INNOCENTS ABROAD:

OR,

THE

PILGRIM'S

BEING SOME
ACCOUNT OF THE STEAM-
SHIP QUAKER CITY'S
PLEASURE EXCURSION TO
EUROPE
AND THE HOLY LAND:
WITH
DESCRIPTIONS OF
COUNTRIES, NATIONS,
INCIDENTS & ADVENTURES
AS THEY APPEARED
TO THE
AUTHOR.

NEW

PROGRESS.

BY

Mark Twain,

THE POPULAR

CORRESPONDENT

AND

HUMORIST.

ONE LARGE AND EXCEEDINGLY HANDSOME VOLUME

OF

Over 650 Octavo Pages,

PROFUSELY ADORNED

WITH 334 BEAUTIFUL, SPIRITED, AND APPROPRIATE ENGRAVINGS,

EXECUTED BY SOME OF THE MOST NOTED ARTISTS IN THE LAND; FULLY ILLUS-
TRATING THE DESCRIPTIONS GIVEN OF COUNTRIES, NATIONS, INCIDENTS,
ADVENTURES, CHARACTERS, ETC., MET WITH BY THE PARTY WHOSE
(TO THEM) MOST REMARKABLE PILGRIMAGE THE AUTHOR IN
THESE PAGES HAS CHARACTERISTICALLY RECORDED.

Advertising circular for *The Innocents Abroad*, page 2.

This work is not one of an ordinary nature, traveling over paths trodden by hundreds of others, treading with greatest care and caution in their very footsteps, and seeing only what they saw, praising only what they praised, and condemning only what they condemned, but the author has here given a new and entirely original view of persons, places and things abroad, describing them as they appeared to him. New and quaint ideas of old yet interesting subjects, humorous and witty delineations of men and character, vivid and sparkling descriptions of scenes and incidents—fresh and amusing anecdotes, and a laughable relation of adventures, experiences, and ludicrous every day occurrences and mishaps of this party, will we are confident, make this volume one of the most enjoyable to be found.

The trip of the "Quaker City," which is the ground work of this Book, was an original and unique affair. Persons, differing in temperament, ideas, character, and habits, were brought intimately together for months, and mingled (as far as it was possible for elements so directly opposite to mingle) in one mass, engaging in the same pursuits and amusements, yet each endeavoring to carry out his own views and plans.

Thousands of miles were passed over, Europe, Asia, and Africa visited by the party. Fortunately, among the group was one whose ready and facetious pen has been able to do something like justice to the thousands of queer and ludicrous incidents which must have occurred, and to the many adventures that must have been encountered in these travels by sea and land; one who had the forethought to secure his memorandums upon the spot, and who relates things as they occurred, without fear or favor, and describes places and things as they really are, without prejudice or bias.

While running over with wit and humor, and sharp with satire upon many of the customs and follies of the age, it still teems with glowing descriptions, and with elegant and classical allusions. The scholar will find pleasure in its perusal as well as others. No one will rise from its reading without having a better and clearer knowledge of the countries it describes than ever before, and more ability to judge between truth and fiction in what he may read respecting them in the future.

Advertising circular for *The Innocents Abroad*, page 3.

CONDITIONS:

The work is printed from new clear type, on fine extra calendered paper, in

One Large Octavo Volume of Over 650 Pages,

BEAUTIFULLY ILLUSTRATED WITH

234 ENGRAVINGS,

From original Photographs, and sketches from the pencils of some of the most eminent artists. These engravings have been prepared with the utmost care, and, in beauty, of liveness, and humor, will equal those of any other work in the country. No expense or pains have been spared to make this Book one of real merit and value—creditable to the Author the Artists, and the Publishers.

IT IS SOLD EXCLUSIVELY BY AUTHORIZED AGENTS, AND CAN BE OBTAINED FROM NO OTHER SOURCE.

It will be delivered to subscribers at the following prices:

Beautifully Bound in Fine Cloth, Sprinkled Edge, - - - - - $3.50
    do.   *Gilt Edge,* - - - - - 4.00
    do.   *Leather, Library Style, Sprinkled Edge,* - - 4.00
    do.   *Half Calf or Morocco,* - - - - - 5.00

☞ *Payment to be made upon the receipt of the Work.*

Persons giving their signatures to these conditions, will be considered subscribers for the Work. But no obligation will rest upon any subscriber to receive the book unless it equals, in every respect, description given and sample shown.

Advertising circular for *The Innocents Abroad*, page 4.

Advertising circular for *The Innocents Abroad*, revised page 2.

497

Advertising Mailer for The Innocents Abroad

Before the middle of August 1869, the American Publishing Company produced a second circular to advertise *The Innocents Abroad*. Formulated as a letter to newspaper editors, it reprinted extracts from six early, favorable reviews, edited by Elisha Bliss to remove any allusions to coarseness or irreverence. The six uncredited notices were all later reprinted and identified (or misidentified) by Bliss in a gathering of reviews for the prospectus and in other advertising materials (APC 1869b, 1869c, and 1870). They were from the Hartford *Courant* ("The New Pilgrim's Progress," 31 July 69, 1); an unidentified newspaper ("Mark Twain as a Pilgrim," which Bliss subsequently confused with a reprint in the Salem [N.J.] *National Standard*, 18 Aug 69, 2); the Elizabeth (N.J.) *Journal* ("The Innocents Abroad," no date, no page); the Hartford *Times* ("New Book by 'Mark Twain,'" 28 July 69, 2); and, entitled "Mark Twain" in the circular, a conflation of reviews from two newspapers, the Meriden (Conn.) *Republican* (2 Aug 69, 2, source for all but the third paragraph) and the Bridgeport (Conn.) *Standard* (no date, no page, third paragraph only). This copy of the circular is dated 10 August and inscribed "Bliss & Co | 137 Market St," the name and address of the Newark, New Jersey, subsidiary of the American Publishing Company. It is reproduced below at 50 percent of actual size.

Advertising mailer for *The Innocents Abroad*, top half. Henry W. and Albert A. Berg Collection, The New York Public Library, Astor, Lenox and Tilden Foundations, New York City (NN-B).

the whole book is dashed, here and there, in unexpected places with the most extravagant humor. The author is not straining to be funny ; he is not trying to make a joke book ; and there is nothing in it of that painfully unnatural sort of wit that is so wearisome. *Very few will be able to read it without laughing at least half the time.* It may be absurd, but it certainly is funny. In the midst of the most serious passages, some quaint observation is dropped that has a good deal of the quality of the best humor.

To attempt anything like a criticism of Mark Twain's peculiar humor, or to try to explain why it is that he is able to make people laugh in spite of themselves, is unnecessary now. We will rather quote a little from the book itself, premising, however, that it is full of bright things, shrewd observations, that lurk here and there, and must be read with the context to be appreciated. And what we quote loses some of its point from the absence of the drawings, many of which are capital. We do as well as we can, however, and select something, on the principle, as Mr. Twain says, that somebody has to hang in France in case of a railway accident, because "it is better that one innocent man should suffer than five hundred ;" we take one or two characteristic things and leave out a thousand.

Mark Twain as a Pilgrim.

The raciest book we have met with for many a day, is one just published by the American Publishing Company of Hartford, Conn., who have our thanks for the copy sent us. It is called the "Innocents Abroad, or The New Pilgrim's Progress," by "Mark Twain," whose name alone is a guarantee of a good Book. Much as we had expected to be pleased, we must truthfully say that we had no idea so much humor, wit, geniality, fine description and good sense, could be contained within the covers of any one book. It is a splendid book in every meaning of the word. It is readable, enjoyable, laughable ; it is instructive, original, and fascinating ; it is open, frank and truthful ; it is keen, satirical, comical, and funny ; its descriptions are beautiful, and its style is unique, and not of a common stamp ; its morals are of a high tone, and cannot be impeached ; it will give the reader a new view of the countries and people that it describes, showing them upon a side never before exposed. It is not a book filled with caricature and stale jokes, but a clear, well written volume upon most interesting subjects, yet viewing them from an entirely new stand-point and portraying them in an original and characteristic manner.

We turned over the pages, without selection of pieces, and commenced reading, and invariably in less than two minutes we were boiling over with laughter. Our sides ache, and we lay aside the volume to rest, and to advise our friends and readers, one and all, to buy the book at the first opportunity, and read it through. It is full of excellent illustrations, in fact, taken all in all, is the jolliest, pleasantest, most fascinating, and handsomest volume we know of.

It has six hundred and fifty pages and two hundred and thirty-four engravings. It is sold only by subscription, and is certain to have a large sale, and become more popular than any book out.

tions, and issued by the American Publishing Company—a successful Hartford house whose ventures are distinguished for their shrewd and judicious taste in hitting the popular mark. "Mark Twain," (Mr. Samuel L. Clemens) was one of the pleasure excursion party who went from New York to Europe and Palestine, on the steamer "Quaker City," in the summer of 1867. He gives us, in this attractive volume, a decidedly original collection of pictures of travel, executed both with the pen and the pencil ; and the illustrations are by no means the least valuable part of the work. It is a lively, laughter-exciting book, such as one rarely meets among volumes of travels ; yet the fun is not the only feature of the book. It abounds in interesting information, conveyed in a wide range of facts, adventures and personal experiences. For the "Quaker City" party visited some of the most interesting parts of the world ; and, though it was a well traveled route, familiar to readers of books of travel, Mr. Clemens contrives to give us new views of old scenes, many new facts and decidedly new impressions. It is a book for any leisure hour, and especially for those to take with them who are going on a summer trip to the sea-side, the country, or the mountains ; it is fresh, racy and sparkling as a glass of iced champagne, and a good deal better for the health and digestion. Seated under a shady tree with this instructive picture book before him, one can in most moods be better entertained than with a living companion. It gives us living scenes and pictures of life and experience in far distant lands, so graphically portrayed that the book will make an attractive addition to the treasures of the library and the drawing-table, for the benefit of one's self or friends in a winter evening. Everybody should buy and read it.

Mark Twain.

We hope our readers will purchase one new book just as soon as the Agent for this place shall put in an appearance. We refer to Mark Twain's new book entitled the "New Pilgrim's Progress." We read the proof-sheets, and we have just completed the published book, and sometime hence we expect to read it again.

Mark Twain, always interesting, in this book has outrivaled himself. It is instructive, humorous, racy, full of quaint expressions that make you laugh unexpectedly, and before you are quite ready ; critical, sometimes caustic, but always good natured ; never prosy or wearisome. You begin the book and do not want to leave it till the last line is reached. Mark never describes a place, or sees a sight as others do. He is intensely original ; and for us there is where the charm lies.

It is a work permanently adapted for home reading aloud, and will invariably call up around the fireside a spirit of mirth and congeniality. No one can read its pages without feeling there is still beauty and sunshine in the world.

If there is not an immense sale for this book we shall be greatly disappointed. Published by that enterprising house, the American Publishing Company, Hartford, Conn. We shall give our readers, in a few days, extended extracts from the book.

Advertising mailer for *The Innocents Abroad*, bottom half.

Appendix F

Photographs and Manuscript Facsimiles

REPRODUCED HERE are thirty-eight contemporary images of Samuel Clemens's and Olivia Langdon's families, friends, and associates during the period of these letters, many of them never before published. Immediately following these documents is a representative selection of seven letters in Clemens's holograph, reproduced in photofacsimile. We provide these documents partly for their inherent interest, and partly to afford readers a chance to see for themselves what details of the manuscript the transcription includes, as well as what it omits. Because of the imperfect nature of these facsimiles, close comparison with the transcription may turn up apparent discrepancies between the two.

MARK TWAIN·

Samuel L. Clemens, 1869. One of several poses from a sitting photographed by
Gurney and Son, New York (see p. 113 for another). Copy in the Mark Twain
Papers, The Bancroft Library (CU-MARK), courtesy of John L. Feldman.

Olivia L. Langdon and Harriet Lewis, 1869. Tintype. Mark Twain Papers, The Bancroft Library (CU-MARK).

Olivia L. Langdon. Dated "Oct 29 1869" inside the case in an unidentified hand. Porcelaintype. Mark Twain Papers, The Bancroft Library (CU-MARK).

Langdon house, Elmira, 1870s. Mark Twain Papers, The Bancroft Library (CU-MARK).

Julia Jones Beecher and her Congregational Church (later Park Church) Sunday School class, 1858–60. Olivia Langdon is at the top and her friend Emma Nye at the bottom. The composite photograph may also include Alice and Clara Spaulding, Fidelia Bridges, Ella (later Corey), Emma Sayles, and Mary Nye, most of whom remained in Beecher's class for up to seven years (Wolcott, 6–7; Julia Jones Beecher, 13; Wisbey, 1–2).

Theodore W. Crane, c. 1869. Mark
Twain Archives, Center for Mark
Twain Studies at Quarry Farm,
Elmira College (NElmC).

Ida B. Clark, c. 1869. Mark Twain
Memorial, Hartford, Connecticut
(CtHMTH).

Thomas K. Beecher, c. 1870.
Stowe-Day Foundation, Hartford,
Connecticut (CtHSD).

Alice Spaulding, 1860–61. Mark
Twain Archives, Center for Mark
Twain Studies at Quarry Farm,
Elmira College (NElmC).

Clara L. Spaulding, early 1870s.
Mark Twain Memorial, Hartford,
Connecticut (CtHMTH).

Darius R. Ford, c. 1865. Mark
Twain Archives, Center for Mark
Twain Studies at Quarry Farm,
Elmira College (NElmC).

Ella J. Corey and child, c. 1866.
Mark Twain Archives, Center for
Mark Twain Studies at Quarry
Farm, Elmira College (NElmC).

Samuel E. Moffett, c. 1866.
Courtesy of Vassar College Library
(NPV).

Annie E. Moffett, c. 1869.
Courtesy of Vassar College Library
(NPV).

Mary Mason Fairbanks, 1868.
Mark Twain Memorial, Hartford,
Connecticut (CtHMTH).

Abel W. Fairbanks, 1880s
(Fairbanks, facing 551).

Isabella Beecher Hooker, c. 1872. Stowe-Day Foundation, Hartford, Connecticut (CtHSD).

John Hooker, c. 1869. Stowe-Day Foundation, Hartford, Connecticut (CtHSD).

Edward B. Hooker, c. 1867. Stowe-Day Foundation, Hartford, Connecticut (CtHSD).

Alice B. Hooker, 1868. Stowe-Day Foundation, Hartford, Connecticut (CtHSD).

Harriet Beecher Stowe, c. 1870.
Stowe-Day Foundation, Hartford,
Connecticut (CtHSD).

Henry Clay Trumbull, c. 1864, as
chaplain of the Tenth Regiment
Connecticut Volunteers. Connecticut
Historical Society, Hartford (CtHi).

John C. Day, 1861–65. Stowe-Day
Foundation, Hartford, Connecticut
(CtHSD).

Anna E. Dickinson, 1860. Stowe-
Day Foundation, Hartford, Connecticut (CtHSD).

Oliver Wendell Holmes, 1868.
Huntington Library, San Marino,
California (CSmH).

James C. Redpath, c. 1870
(Pond, 533).

James K. Medbery, c. 1869,
from a portrait by Frank B.
Carpenter (Mackaye, 1:
plate 21).

Frederick Douglass, 1860s.
Huntington Library, San Marino,
California (CSmH).

Charles Dudley Warner, 1870s.
Stowe-Day Foundation, Hartford,
Connecticut (CtHSD).

Whitelaw Reid, 1861–65. Huntington Library, San Marino, California
(CSmH).

Samuel Bowles, c. 1869 (Bowles,
frontispiece).

Joseph R. Hawley, 1861–65. Stowe-
Day Foundation, Hartford,
Connecticut (CtHSD).

Henry George, 1865 (Walker, facing 302).

Stephen Massett, 1877. California State Library (C).

Lillie Hitchcock, 1862. The Bancroft Library (CU-BANC).

John D. F. Slee, 1870s. Courtesy of
Charles S. Underhill.

Schuyler Colfax, c. 1869.
Library of Congress (DLC).

Josephus N. Larned, 1880s. Buffalo
and Erie County Historical Society
(NBuHi).

Sherman House,
Chicago, Jan. 7.

My dear dear dear dear dear dear dear Livy — (That is the tamest word that ever I saw — you have to repeat it 6 or seven times to make it express anything) — I shall heap some more newspaper abuse on this house when I get a chance. It does them good. They give me their best room, now, & treat me like a lord.

I am tired again, Livy. There were many visitors in, during the afternoon, & I got no chance to lie down & rest. This is the tenth letter I have written since I finished the lecture to-night. [They want me to

Clemens to Olivia L. Langdon, 7 January 1869, Chicago, Ill. Mark Twain Papers, The Bancroft Library (CU-MARK). The first five pages of the letter are written on the rectos of five leaves torn from folders; the sixth page is on the recto of an enclosed leaf written to Clemens by Mary Mason Fairbanks; the verso of the enclosure served as a wrapper for the letter. Transcribed on pp. 18–19; reproduced at 80 percent of actual size.

2

lecture here again. 7 —
I have to write these letters
— there isn't any getting a-
round it — They are an-
swers to letters received.
But don't you know, I was
so disappointed, when they
gave me a batch of letters
to day & I ran them over
& found not a line from
you. ~~xxxxxxxxxxxx~~
~~xxxxxxxxxxxxxx~~
I had felt just as sure
as I could be, that a letter would reach Cleveland
~~after~~ I left, & be re-mailed
to Chicago. But bless
your old heart, you are just
as good as you can be, &
I forgive you. Forgive
you, indeed! — I am all
gratitude to you for what
you _do_ write.

Manuscript page 2, to Olivia L. Langdon, 7 January 1869. Recto of the second
leaf.

I have a religious experience (Indianapolis) to tell you about, when I see you — I can't write it, well. Considering that I must get up & start at 7 in the morning on a 9-hour railway trip, I had better be getting to bed. I was ever so smart, to write last to you, to-night, Livy — otherwise those other letters never would have been written. I wrote you from Rockford, last night — did you get it? I sent a porter to mail the letter.

You won't need a long letter from me to-night, for I enclose a couple to make up. Now perhaps I ought not to have ~~asked~~ asked Mrs. Fairbanks to write you, because it is so

Manuscript page 3, to Olivia L. Langdon, 7 January 1869. Recto of the third leaf.

4

fatiguing & troublesome
to you to write letters &
you have so much of it
to do. But in about a week
you must answer her let-
ter — & you will, won't you?
She is a noble, good woman.
~~I am unable~~ I will spare
you just one day to write
her — no more — all the
other days you must write
to me, Livy dear. I am
going to enclose her to-days
note in this, whether she likes
it or not — I like it.

Livy, please put Cleveland
Jan. 22, & Norwalk, Ohio, Jan. 21,
in the list of lectures I left you.

The other enclosed letter
is from a most estimable
young lady whose friend-
ship I acquired in St Louis
two years ago. She is a thorough Christian. She was

Manuscript page 4, to Olivia L. Langdon, 7 January 1869. Recto of the fourth
leaf.

5

near neighbor of ours, & my
mother & sister are very
fond of her, & of all her family.   The letter won't interest you,
but I thought I would send it
because it would be such a
good hint to you to send me
all the letters which young
gentlemen may chance to
write to you, Livy — { & then
I will go & break their necks
for them! }

I am going to bed, now,
for I am in a hurry to get
to Monmouth, where I know
I shall get a letter from you.
Leaving you in the loving protection of the Savior, & the gentle
guardianship of the angels,
I bid you good-bye, & kiss you
good-night, my darling Livy.
                Devotedly & always
                    Saml. L. C.

Manuscript page 5, to Olivia L. Langdon, 7 January 1869. Recto of the fifth leaf.

[Preceding this was a formal invitation to lecture for the orphans in Cleveland.]

There —— Haven't I done that properly? but it is painful this being parliamentary. It would suit Col. Binney but not me.

Mr. Fairbanks sent your shirts to Chicago Monday —— We miss you — all of us, but when I feel quite dreary, I go up and open your door to regale my senses with the still lingering perfume of your cigars —
"You may break, you may ruin the vase if you will,
But the scent of the roses will hang round it still."
Touchingly appropriate —— [Isn't that plaintive, Livy?]

Allie is quite as inconsolable as Hattie Lewis, whose comical estimate of your devotion pleases me exceedingly. I shall write to Livy in the morning — but I'm a goose to do it, for what could I say that she

Manuscript page 6, enclosure to Olivia L. Langdon, 7 January 1869. Recto of the sixth leaf.

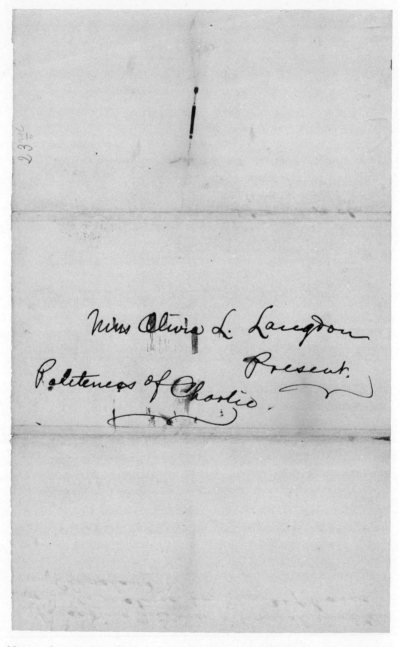

Manuscript page 7, to Olivia L. Langdon, 7 January 1869. Verso of the sixth leaf, which Clemens used as a wrapper. It bears Olivia Langdon's contemporary endorsement ("23rd") and a fragment of rubber band later used in storing the letter.

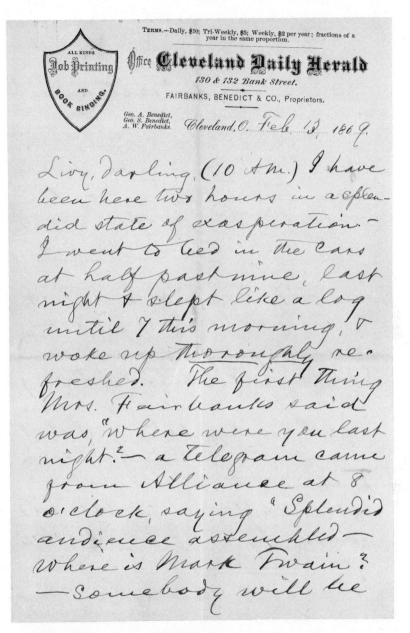

Clemens to Olivia L. Langdon, 13 February 1869, Cleveland, Ohio. Mark Twain Papers, The Bancroft Library (CU-MARK). The six-page letter is written on the rectos and versos of three leaves. Transcribed on pp. 88–89; reproduced at 74 percent of actual size.

responsible for this."

I said "Alliance? —never heard of it!"

And she said Mr. Fairbanks made the appointment for me, & would have telegraphed me but didn't <u>know</u> <u>where</u> to telegraph — didn't know but that I had left Elmira — & as my letter from there (received last Monday) said I would reach here on the 12th, he didn't think it necessary to telegraph me anyhow. What abominable absurdity! I said, "Will you <u>never</u> learn anything? Are you going

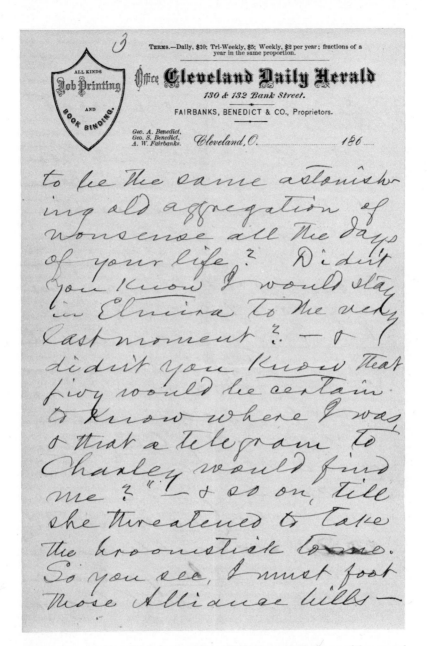

TERMS.—Daily, $10; Tri-Weekly, $5; Weekly, $2 per year; fractions of a year in the same proportion.

ALL KINDS
Job Printing
AND
BOOK BINDING

Office Cleveland Daily Herald

130 & 132 Bank Street.

FAIRBANKS, BENEDICT & CO., Proprietors.

Geo. A. Benedict,
Geo. S. Benedict,
A. W. Fairbanks.

Cleveland, O. _____ 186_

to be the same astonish-
ing old aggregation of
nonsense all the days
of your life? Didn't
you know I would stay
in Elmira to the very
last moment? — & /
didn't you know that
Livy would be certain
to know where I was
& that a telegram to
Charley would find
me?" — & so on, till
she threatened to take
the broomstick to ~~me~~.
So you see, I must foot
those Alliance bills —

Manuscript page 3, to Olivia L. Langdon, 13 February 1869. Recto of the second leaf.

it would be dishonorable to do otherwise — & I must make a long trip west in the Spring & deliver that lecture free of charge — as nearly as I can come at it The failure to expend a dollar on a telegram will result in costing me two hundred dollars, four days lost time & five hundred miles of travel — & yet Fairbanks' letter to me, which should have gone to Jacksonville or Galena by _telegraph_ is still chasing around the country somewhere. I have _begged_ him, & these ~~other~~ wearable agents of mine _always_ to use the telegraph, but I can't

Manuscript page 4, to Olivia L. Langdon, 13 February 1869. Verso of the second leaf.

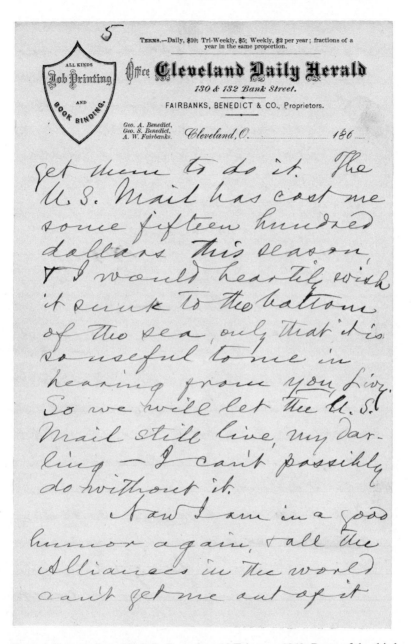

get them to do it. The
U. S. Mail has cost me
some fifteen hundred
dollars this season,
& I would heartily wish
it sunk to the bottom
of the sea, only that it is
so useful to me in
hearing from you, Livy.
So we will let the U. S.
Mail still live, my dar-
ling — I can't possibly
do without it.

Now I am in a good
humor again, & all the
Alliances in the world
can't get me out of it

Manuscript page 5, to Olivia L. Langdon, 13 February 1869. Recto of the third leaf.

again. — I have given Mrs. Fairbanks the little ring, & she will have the engagement ring made. It seems unnatural not to see you this morning, you precious girl — & it seems odd not to find Mrs Langdon's ~~face~~ among the faces about me, or hear ~~that~~ pleasant cackle of that absurd Cousin of yours — I send her my very kindest regards. Give Mr. Langdon my love, please — he is at home by this time.

With a fervent blessing, & a prayer for you, & many & many a kiss, my dear Livy.

Sam. L. C.

Manuscript page 6, to Olivia L. Langdon, 13 February 1869. Verso of the third leaf.

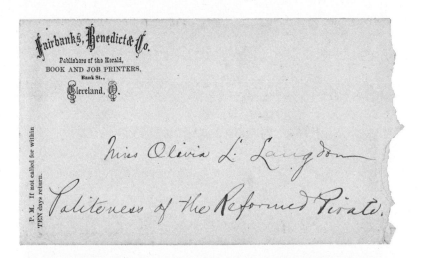

The envelope, addressed to Olivia L. Langdon, 13 February 1869, transmitted via Charles J. Langdon. Reproduced at 78 percent of actual size. The back of the envelope bears Olivia's contemporary endorsement ("38th") as well as Clara Clemens's later annotation, "missed lecture."

Elmira, March 30.

Friend Bliss—

I sent the proofs to-day. I could have sent them sooner, but was lazy. I will not delay you next time. I was glad Frank telegraphed.

I have concluded that if you will print the following titles on slips you will like one or the other of them:

"The Innocents Abroad;
or,
The (New) Modern Pilgrim's Progress."

Or This:

Clemens to Elisha Bliss, Jr., 30 March 1869, Elmira, N.Y. Mark Twain Papers, The Bancroft Library (CU-MARK). The two-page letter is written on both sides of a single leaf, embossed with the initial "L," torn from a folder. Both pages bear contemporary endorsements written at the American Publishing Company. Transcribed on pp. 178–79; reproduced actual size.

"The Exodus of the Innocents;
The New Pilgrim's Progress."
or

I like "The Innocents
Abroad" rather the best.

Trot your proofs along
as fast as you please —
& the sooner the book is out,
the better for us, no doubt.
Yrs Truly
Mark.

Mark. of Geneva.
March 30/69

Manuscript page 2, Clemens to Elisha Bliss, Jr., 30 March 1869. Verso, showing a strip of paper along the right margin added by a later owner for tipping the letter into a book.

148 Asylum st.
Hartford, May 10.

Dear Mother —

Well, I *did* manage to leave Elmira, but I had to promise that I would return in fourteen days. Mr. Langdon said it was useless & foolish to go away at all — let the world talk, if it wanted to.

I have read 500 pages of proofs — have less than 200 more to read. It will be out in a few weeks, now. They have spent $5,000 on the engravings. It will be a stylish volume.

Clemens to Jane Lampton Clemens, 11 May 1869, Hartford, Conn. Mark Twain Papers, The Bancroft Library (CU-MARK). The letter is written on three sides of two leaves torn from a folder. Transcribed on pp. 218–19; reproduced at 86 percent of actual size.

I am very glad you are going to live by your-selves, for I have felt for a long time that the care of keeping boardering was just under-mining your health & Pamelas — now I am sure both will improve. And besides, a boarding-house was no place for Annie. Boarders, as a rule, are a bad lot — though you had an exceptionally good lot, with one or two excep-tions — you remember to whom I refer, no doubt. I am grateful to Pamela for promising me a bed when I come — have some hope of getting there before many months!

I don't know the date of the last money

3

I sent — but it seems a good while ago. If you require some, let me know — I am economising because I am at a perfectly ruinous expense here — but I do not mean to economise at your expense — so speak out, if you want it.

Yes, Annie could come to the wedding if we had one, & freely — but there won't be any — only the family & a couple of witnesses will be present, & it will take place in Mr Langdon's house. It is 2 o'clock in the morning. Good-night. Love to Orion & Mollie & all. I don't know your address. Lovingly Sam.

Manuscript page 3, to Jane Lampton Clemens, 11 May 1869. Recto of the second leaf.

534

Clemens to Olivia L. Langdon, 15 May 1869 (1st of 2), Hartford, Conn. Mark Twain Papers, The Bancroft Library (CU-MARK). This five-page letter with several marginal interpolations is written on the rectos of four leaves torn from folded sheets, with a marginal addition on the verso of the first leaf showing through the left margin of the first page. Transcribed on pp. 231–32; reproduced at 80 percent of actual size.

least, & kept everybody uneasy for fear it would break its neck climbing around. Now I did say to myself, five or six times, during the evening, "I can't keep a diary, & yet I'll want to run a paragraph into an article, some day, about the ~~observation~~ inappropriateness & general disagreeableness of mixing infants into grown people's entertainments, & I shall want it read vividly & fresh, & so of course it must be written now, while it is hot, & laid away for use — & so I'll inflict it all on poor Livy as soon as ever I get home, & set it forth in all its malignity & its virulence, & ask her to lay that page by somewhere so

Manuscript page 2, to Olivia L. Langdon, 15 May 1869 (1st of 2). Recto of the second leaf.

536

that I can call for it when I want it — & so, by making Livy my diary, I can secure two valuable birds with one stone, viz; I can write the things necessary without its being irksome, because they will be written for the dearest little body in the universe; & 2ᵈ, I shall have a diary who will always know where to put her hand on the document entrusted to her, which is a thing I never could do, &c, &c, &c, " —

But now the spirit of it is all gone — & I feel only kindliness toward the pleasant mother & charity toward the young blockheads that were a nuisance without knowing it — & so there is nothing for the diary, Livy dear.

Manuscript page 3, to Olivia L. Langdon, 15 May 1869 (1st of 2). Recto of the third leaf.

4   Livy, I love you.

But on the contrary I have said just exactly enough to entitle me to a scalding, & I'm morally bound to get it. But the reproof will come from such dear lips that I shall not know it is a re-proof, thinking it a blessing. — (How's *thim*?) [You know it is wasting time to scold *me*, Livy, because I love everything you say, rebukes, abuse, & compliments alike.)

There are two hundred & twenty-four illustrations in the book, Livy. As I told you, the first edition of the book will be 20,000 copies, & it will take the whole force of the paper mill ~~~~~~~~~~~~~~ a good while (maybe longer — the man don't know, yet) to make that a-mount of paper — for the weight of the same is over thirty tons.

obeying Livy's orders. Must go to bed — but aint sleepy — simply God bless my own little darling.
                                                            Sam.

Manuscript page 4, to Olivia L. Langdon, 15 May 1869 (1st of 2). Recto of the fourth leaf.

Manuscript page 5, to Olivia L. Langdon, 15 May 1869 (1st of 2). Verso of the first leaf.

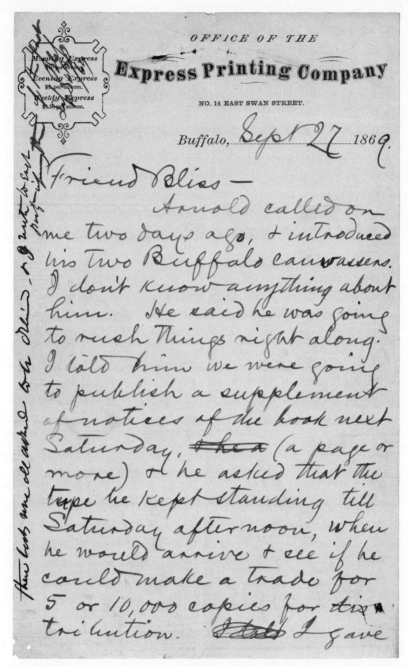

OFFICE OF THE

Express Printing Company

NO. 14 EAST SWAN STREET.

Buffalo, Sept 27 1869.

Friend Bliss —

Arnold called on me two days ago, & introduced his Two Buffalo canvassers. I don't know anything about him. He said he was going to rush things right along. I told him we were going to publish a supplement of notices of the book next Saturday, ~~the~~ (a page or more) & he asked that the type be kept standing till Saturday afternoon, when he would arrive & see if he could make a trade for 5 or 10,000 copies for dis~~tri~~ tribution. ~~State~~ I gave

These books are all ordered to be deliv ~~d~~, & I wrote to each party informing them of the fact

Clemens to Elisha Bliss, Jr., 27 September 1869, Buffalo, N.Y. Mark Twain Papers, The Bancroft Library (CU-MARK). The letter is written on both sides of a single leaf. Page 1 bears Bliss's contemporary endorsement, "these books were all ordered to be delivered, & I wrote to each party informing them of the fact | Bliss | Sep 30th/69." Transcribed on p. 362; reproduced at 85 percent of actual size.

him to understand
that we would furnish
them at cost, or even less.
We said nothing about ad-
vertising in the Buffalo
papers.

I like newspapering very
well, as far as I have got —
but I ~~have~~ adjourn, a
week hence, to commence
preparing my lecture, &
shall not be here again
till the middle of February.
After a few days, now, ~~you~~
I shall be in <u>Elmira</u> till
Nov. 1. <u>Recollect.</u>

Yes, our paper is a
good one to advertise in & so
is the "Commercial-Advertiser"
& the "Courier." (Latter is ~~[illegible]~~
Democratic, but good boys.)

None of us have noticed the book
yet — shall, this week, maybe. Regards
to Mrs. B. & the longest half of Frank.
Yrs Clemens.

[left margin, vertical] I think the book is making more stir than other peoples' books, & gives you are pushing it for all it is worth.

Manuscript page 2, to Elisha Bliss, Jr., 27 September 1869. Verso.

Boston, Dec. 17.

My Dear Sister —

Yours of 10th is received. I know Mrs. Langdon wants you & Annie to get there several days before the wedding, because their might be little chance to visit, later. We have about persuaded her to give us a perfectly private wedding, but we can't tell how it will be, yet. Livy has written delightedly to say you are

Clemens to Pamela A. Moffett, 17 December 1869, Boston, Mass. Mark Twain Papers, The Bancroft Library (CU-MARK). This six-page letter is written on the rectos and versos of three leaves torn from the notebook in which Clemens wrote his "Diary" letters to Olivia Langdon (see pp. 381–82 n. 1). Transcribed on pp. 429–30; reproduced actual size.

likely to come. Her
heart is thoroughly
set upon it, & I don't
like to have the
child disappointed.

Purchase no
outfit. Come as
you are.

I examined my
pocket a moment
ago, to see if I had
$500 to send to Ma
but I only found
$300. I have been
paying out a few
more hundreds
within a few days,
& must work two
or three days longer

Manuscript page 2, to Pamela A. Moffett, 17 December 1869. Verso of the first
leaf.

before I can for-
ward the $500. But
it shall be forthcom-
ing.

I am killed up
with a cold, & shall
not lecture to-
night — so there
goes a few weeks'
board.

~~The~~ No — we
are not to be mar-
ried in the evening,
but about noon.
Then if we *must*
have a reception,
that will take
place in the eve-
ning. The idea

Manuscript page 3, to Pamela A. Moffett, 17 December 1869. Recto of the second leaf.

of our starting
on a bridal "trip,"
is funny. Neither
of us are fond of
traveling, & you
may be sure we
shall not go a
mile that we are
not obliged to go.
We shall go to
Buffalo the day af-
ter the marriage
& never stir another
peg till we are com-
pelled to do it.
I cordially ac-
cept Annie's & Sam-
my's explanations
— & there is good

Manuscript page 4, to Pamela A. Moffett, 17 December 1869. Verso of the second leaf.

545

hand sense & can-
dor enough in
Sammy's to com-
pensate for fifty-
cent presents. I
fully appreciate
Annie's, too, for if
there is one thing I
cordially hate more
than another, it is
the bore of selecting
a present. I have
already told Livy.
that I shall de-
liberately violate
the custom to giving
the bride a wedding
present — + by a
singular coinci-

Manuscript page 5, to Pamela A. Moffett, 17 December 1869. Recto of the third
leaf.

dence. I used both
~~Mollie's~~ & Sammy's
reasons in expla-
nation of my con-
duct.

I am sorry Ma's
health remains so
bad — St Louis is
not the climate to
improve it, I am
afraid.

In haste,
Affectionately
Sam.

Manuscript page 6, to Pamela A. Moffett, 17 December 1869. Verso of the third leaf.

Editorial Apparatus

Guide to Editorial Practice

THE AIM OF *Mark Twain's Letters* is to publish, in chronological order, the most reliable and the most legible text possible for every personal and business letter written by (or for) Samuel L. Clemens, and to publish the letters he received, selectively, as a part of the annotation. The editorial aim for that annotation is to explain whatever requires explanation, either in notes appended to the letters, or in editorial narrative between them, with cross-references and reidentifications accomplished (as necessary) largely through the index. Three further matters, about which it is useful to be informed only as the need arises, are treated in the textual commentaries at the back of the volume: (a) when and where a letter has been previously published, if at all; (b) where and by whom the original documents have been preserved, or not, as the case may be; and (c) how and on what evidence the text of each letter has been established for this edition.

Fundamentally, the text of any letter is a matter of historical fact, determined for all time by the original act of sending it. Its text therefore includes everything that was originally sent, from the envelope to the enclosures: all nonverbal elements, all words and word fragments, numerals, punctuation, and formal signs—whether canceled or standing, inscribed or adopted, written or stamped by others during the time of original transmission and receipt. There is no necessary or obvious hypothetical limit on which of these elements may be significant. We must begin, in fact, with the assumption that almost any aspect of an original letter might be significant, either to the writer or the recipient, or both— not to mention those for whom the letters are now being published. In principle, therefore, the text of any letter properly excludes only such additions, revisions, and corrections as were made in the documents after the original transmission and receipt—even if such changes were made by the writer or the original recipient, or someone acting on their behalf.

But while there are few limits on what properly constitutes the text of a letter, there are many limits on what constitutes a satisfactory transcription of it. Most of Clemens's letters that survive in the original holograph, for example, lack the original envelope. Some lack one or more of the enclosures, or have been deliberately censored with the scissors, and not a few have been accidentally damaged and partly lost in one way or another, subsequent to their original transmission. All such accidents, however, limit only how much of the letter may be said to survive in its original documents, not how much of it ought to be, or even can be, transcribed. It is commonplace for a letter to survive partly in its original documents, and partly in a copy of originals otherwise missing or lost: any transcription that did not rely on *both* could scarcely be called complete, let alone reliable. The real question is not how transcriptions may be limited because parts of a letter no longer survive, but how much of the text that does survive a transcription may *leave out* and still function as intended.

We assume that the purpose of publishing letters is to make them easier to read than they are in the original documents. On that assumption, a successful transcription must include enough of the text to enable someone to rely on *it*, rather than the original, and it must exclude enough to make the transcribed text easier to read (or at least not more difficult to read) than the original. Thus, when the documents originally sent are intact and available, we transcribe them as fully and precisely as is compatible with a highly inclusive *critical text*—not a literal, or all-inclusive one, but a typographical transcription that is optimally legible and, at the same time, maximally faithful to the text that Clemens himself transmitted.[1] Original documents are therefore emended (changed) *as little as possible*, which means only in order to alter, simplify, or omit what would otherwise threaten to make the transcription unreadable, or less than fully intelligible in its own right. When, however, the original

[1] The transcription is not a *literal text*, even though it is probably as inclusive as most texts for which that claim is made, nor is it a *noncritical text*, as defined by G. Thomas Tanselle, since even though it "aims at reproducing a given earlier text [i.e., the original letter] as exactly as possible," the editor essentially defines what *is* possible by deciding what can be transcribed legibly. The editor is therefore "making decisions about how the new text will differ from the text in the document," with the result that the transcription necessarily "becomes a critical text" ("Textual Scholarship" in *Introduction to Scholarship in Modern Languages and Literatures*, edited by Joseph Gibaldi [New York: Modern Language Association, 1981], 32, 47).

documents are lost, we necessarily rely on the most authoritative *copy* of them. Since copies by their nature contain errors, nonoriginal documents are emended *as much as necessary*, partly for the reasons we emend originals, but chiefly to restore the text of the lost original, insofar as the evidence permits. The only exceptions (each discussed below) are letters which survive (a) only in the author's draft, (b) only in someone else's paraphrase of the original, (c) only in damaged originals or unique nonoriginals, and (d) in originals that, wholly or in part, can be faithfully reproduced only in photographic facsimile. But whether or not a letter survives in its original documents, every departure from the text of the documents used (designated the copy-text) is recorded as an emendation in the textual commentary for that letter, barring only the most trivial kinds of change, which are instead categorized and described here.

Mark Twain's Letters, Volume 1 (1988), first applied this basic rationale for emendation while also deploying a new system of manuscript notation. We called the result "plain text," partly to distinguish it from the alternative methods still used most frequently to publish letters, so-called "clear text" and "genetic text."[2] We require two things of every transcription in plain text: (a) it must be sufficiently faithful to the text of the letter to serve as the most *reliable substitute* now possible for it; and

[2] According to Fredson Bowers, "General methods of transcription divide neatly in two," which is to say (a) *clear texts*, with supplementary apparatus containing all details of revision, and (b) *genetic texts*, without supplementary apparatus because the text itself contains all such details. A clear text transcribes the revised form of a manuscript "diplomatically," meaning that the "transcription exactly follows the forms of the manuscript in spelling, punctuation, word-division, italics (for underlining), and capitalization, but not in matters of spacing or in line-division, nor is a facsimile visual presentation of alterations attempted." A genetic text, on the other hand, includes authorial alterations in the text "by means of a number of arbitrary symbols like pointed brackets to the left or right, arrows, bars, and so on," with the common result that it is often "difficult to read the original text consecutively" and "impossible to read the revised text at all in a coherent sequence" ("Transcription of Manuscripts: The Record of Variants," *Studies in Bibliography* 29 [1976]: 213–14, 248). *Plain text*, however, descends from a kind of transcription not mentioned by Bowers, in which the myriad details of a manuscript (particularly the author's alterations to it) are systematically divided between the text and its apparatus, precisely in order to make the text as complete and informative as possible without destroying its legibility (see *N&J1*, 575–84). The practical result of this division is radically improved by adopting a less obtrusive and more readable system of notation than has been used in the past: plain text manages simultaneously to increase both overall legibility *and* the amount of detail that can be included in the transcription.

(b) it must be *easier to read* than the original letter, so long as its reliability is preserved intact. To the extent that maximum fidelity and maximum legibility come into conflict, this way of linking them ensures that neither goal is maximized at undue expense to the other. The linkage works well for Clemens's letters, in part because they (like many people's letters) were intended to be read in manuscript, and his manuscripts are typically very legible to begin with. But in no small part, the linkage succeeds because the new system of notation is able to make legible in transcription many aspects of manuscript which would otherwise pose the necessity of choosing between maximum fidelity and maximum legibility. The consequence is that a typical letter transcription in plain text, though obviously not a replacement for the original, can still be read, relied on, and quoted from, as if it were the original.

While the notation system is admittedly new, it makes as much use as possible of editorial conventions that are familiar, traditional, and old. We have, for instance, deliberately kept the number of new conventions to a minimum, modifying or adding to them only very gradually, and only as the letters themselves demand it. When editorial conventions are new, they often adapt familiar conventions of both handwriting and typography. New conventions are in general called for by the effort to include, or at least to include more legibly, what has tended to be problematic, or simply ignored, in earlier methods of transcription. Two examples here will suffice. To transcribe printed letterhead in a way that is practical, inclusive, and fully intelligible, plain text uses EXTRA-SMALL SMALL CAPITALS for the printed words and a dotted underscore below whatever the writer put in the printed blanks, such as the date and place. Likewise, to transcribe all cancellations and identify all insertions (even of single characters) where they occur in the text, but without making the result illegible, plain text uses ~~line-through~~ cross-out rules, ⸔ slashes, and ˏinferiorˏ carets.

Most of these devices can now be produced with the type itself, making them economical both to set and to print. And many can fairly be characterized as type-identical with their handwritten counterparts. A line or a slash through type, crossing it out, needs no interpretation: it simply *means* canceled, just as it would in manuscript. The overall effect therefore contrasts favorably with the effect of arbitrary symbols, such as ⟨pointed⟩ brackets to the left ⟨a⟩ or right, ↑ arrows, ↓ | bars ↑ , ↓ and so on—editorial conventions that today will seem both new and numerous, that will almost certainly mean something different from one edition to the next, and that in any case must be consciously construed at each occurrence.

A related risk of type-identical signs, on the other hand, is that their editorial function as *signs* will be forgotten—that they will be seen to picture, rather than to transcribe (re-encode), the original manuscript. It thus bears repeating that plain text, despite its greater visual resemblance to the handwritten originals, is emphatically not a type facsimile of them. Like all diplomatic transcription *except* type facsimile, plain text does not reproduce, simulate, or report the original lineation, pagination, or any other formal aspect of the manuscript, save where the writer intended it to bear meaning and that meaning is transcribable— which is exactly why it does reproduce or simulate many formal elements, such as various kinds of indention and purposeful lineation. In fact, it is usually the case that these formal (nonverbal) aspects of manuscript already have more or less exact *equivalents* in nineteenth-century typographical conventions.

Clemens's letters lend themselves to such treatment in part because his training as a printer (1847–53) began a lifelong fascination with all typographical matters, and in part because he lived at a time when the equivalents between handwriting and type were probably more fully developed and more widely accepted than they had ever been before (or are likely ever to be again). The consequence for his handwritten letters was that, while he clearly never intended them to be set in type, he still used the handwritten forms of a great many typographical conventions as consistently and precisely in them, as he did in literary manuscripts that were intended for publication. This habitual practice makes it possible to transcribe his letters very much as if they were intended for type—to use, in other words, the system of equivalents employed by nineteenth-century writers to tell the typesetter how the manuscript should appear in type—but in reverse, to tell those who rely on the typographical transcription just how the letter manuscript appears. In short, Clemens's typographical expertise makes his letters easier to transcribe fully and precisely, as well as easier to read in transcription, than they otherwise would be, assuming that we understand the meaning of his signs and the code for their typographical equivalents exactly as he did—an assumption that cannot always be taken as granted.

1. The Author's Signs

A few of the typographical signs in these letters may seem a bit unfamiliar, if not wholly exotic. Others may seem familiar, even though they in fact no longer have the precise and accepted meaning they had when Clemens used them. Especially because some signs have fallen into disuse and (partly for that reason) been adapted by modern editors for their own purposes, it is the more necessary to emphasize that here they bear only the meaning given them by Clemens and his contemporaries. Purely editorial signs in the transcription are identified on pages xxix–xxxi above, and since they sometimes adapt typographical conventions, they must not be confused with authorial signs. They have, in fact, been designed to avoid such confusion, and especially to avoid usurping the normal, typographical equivalents for authorial signs.

Still, authorial signs present two related but distinct problems for successful transcription: (a) how to explicate those signs whose authorial meaning differed from the modern meaning, but can still be recovered, at least in part; and (b) how to represent authorial signs whose earlier typographical equivalent, if any, remains unknown—at least to the editors. The glossary of SPECIAL SORTS and table of EMPHASIS EQUIVALENTS which follow here are intended to solve these problems—to alert the reader to those changes in meaning which we can identify, and to describe the handwritten forms for which the typographical forms are taken to be equivalent—or, in a few cases, for which they have been *made* equivalent because we lack a better alternative.

The glossary includes signs that do not appear in every volume of *Mark Twain's Letters*, much less in every letter, and it omits some signs that will only be added as they become relevant in subsequent volumes. Like the glossary, the table provides some information that was, and often still is, regarded as common knowledge, which may explain why the contemporary equivalent for some authorial signs has proved so elusive. That no table of comparable detail or completeness has so far been found in any grammar, printer's handbook, dictionary, or encyclopedia, would appear to indicate that the system of emphasis was almost completely taken for granted, hence rarely made fully explicit or published, even by those who relied upon it. The particular meaning for Clemens of all such equivalents between manuscript and type, at any rate, has had to be deduced or inferred from the letters themselves, and from his numerous literary manuscripts, with his instructions for the typist and typesetter (sometimes with the further evidence of how they responded to his instructions), as well as from the consistent but usually partial evidence in a variety of printer's handbooks, encyclopedias, manuals of forms, and other documents bearing on what we take to be the system of equivalents between handwriting and type (*L1*, xlvi n. 3).

SPECIAL SORTS

asterisks * * * Always called "stars" by Clemens and by printers generally, asterisks appear in his manuscript as simple "Xs" or crosses (X), or in a somewhat more elaborate variant of the cross (✳), often when used singly. In letters (and elsewhere) he used the asterisk as a standard reference mark, either to signal his occasional footnotes, or to refer the reader from one part of a text to another part. (The conventional order of the standard reference marks was as follows: *, †, ‡, §, ‖, ¶, and, by the end of the century, ☞.) He also used asterisks for a kind of ellipsis that was then standard and is still recognizable, and for one now virtually obsolete—the "line of stars"—in which evenly spaced asterisks occupy a line by themselves to indicate a major omission of text, or—for Clemens, at any rate—the passage of time not otherwise represented in a narrative. For the standard ellipsis, we duplicate the number of asterisks in the source, thus: * * * * (see also *ellipsis*, below). In transcribing the line of stars, however, the exact number of asterisks in the original becomes irrelevant, since the device is intended to fill the line, which is rarely the same length in manuscript as it is in the transcription. The line of stars in the original is thus always transcribed by seven asterisks, evenly separated and indented from both margins, thus:

*   *   *   *   *   *   *

braces } Clemens drew the brace as a wavy vertical line that did not much resemble the brace in type, except that it clearly grouped two or three lines of text together. He drew braces intended for three or more lines as straight (nonwavy) lines with squared corners, like a large bracket, usually in the margin. He occasionally used the two- and three-line braces in pairs, vertically and horizontally, to box or partly enclose one or more words, often on a single line. The one-line brace ({ }) was evidently not known to him, and would probably have seemed a contradiction in terms. It appears to be a modern invention, but has sometimes proved useful in the transcription when the original lineation could not be reproduced or readily simulated (see *L1*, 219). Otherwise, the transcription always prints a brace and preserves, or at least simulates, the original lineation.

dashes – — Clemens used the dash in all four of its most common
——— ——— typographical forms (en, em, two-em, and three-em), as
= = well as a parallel dash, usually but not invariably shorter than an em dash. The parallel dash appears to be used interchangeably with the much more frequently used em dash, but almost always at the end of a line (often a short line, such as the greeting). Its special meaning, if any, remains unknown. Clemens occasionally used dashes visibly longer than his em dash, presumably to indicate a longer pause: these are transcribed as two-, three-, or (more)-em dashes, by relying on the length of em dashes in the manuscript as the basic unit. That Clemens thought in terms of ems at all is suggested by his occasional sign for a dash that he has interlined as a correction or revision (⊢⊣), which was then the standard proofreader's mark for an em dash. Clemens used the dash as *terminal* punctuation only to indicate abrupt cessation or suspension, almost never combining it with a terminal period. Exceptions do occur (see p. 78), but most departures from this rule are only apparent or inadvertent. For instance, Clemens frequently used period and dash together in the standard typographical method for connecting sideheads with their proper text ('P.S.—They have'), a recognized decorative use of period-dash that does not indicate a pause. The em, two-em and, more rarely, the en and the parallel dash were also used for various kinds of ellipsis: contraction ('d—n'); suspension ('Wash = '); and ellipsis of a full word or more ('until ——.'). Despite some appearance to the contrary, terminal punctuation here again consists solely in the period. On the other hand, Clemens often did use the period and dash combined when the sentence period fell at the end of a slightly short line in his manuscript ("period.— | New line"), a practice derived from the typographical practice of justifying short lines with an em dash. These dashes likewise do not indicate a pause and, because their function at line ends cannot be reproduced in the transcription, are always emended, never transcribed. Clemens used en dashes in their familiar role with numerals to signify "through" ('Matt. xxv, 44–45'). And he used both the em dash and varying lengths and thicknesses of *plain*

rule—in lists, to signify "ditto" or "the same" for the name or word above, and in tables to express a blank. See also *ellipsis* and *rules*, below.

ellipsis ----- Nineteenth-century typography recognized an enviably
...... **** large variety of ellipses (or leaders, depending on the use
------- to which the device was being put). Clemens himself de-
— — — — monstrably used hyphens, periods, asterisks, en dashes, and em dashes to form ellipses or leaders, in his letters and literary manuscripts. The ellipsis using a dash of an em or more is also called a "blank" and may stand for characters ('Mr. C—'s bones') or a full word left unexpressed. In the second case, the dash is always separated by normal word space from the next word on *both* sides ('by — Reilly'), thereby distinguishing it from the dash used as punctuation ('now— Next'), which is closed up with the word on at least one side, and usually on both ('evening—or'). When any of these marks are used as leaders, the transcription does not necessarily duplicate the number in the manuscript, using instead only what is needed to connect the two elements linked by the leaders. But for any kind of ellipsis except the "line of stars" (see *asterisks*), the transcription duplicates exactly the number of characters used in the original.

fist ☞ Clemens used the "fist," as it was called by printers (also
☜ "hand," "index," "index-mark," "mutton-fist," and doubtless other names), not as the seventh of the standard reference marks, but for its much commoner purpose of calling special attention to some point in a text. As late as 1871 the *American Encyclopaedia of Printing* characterized the device as used "chiefly in handbills, posters, direction placards, and in newspaper work,"[3] but Clemens used it often—and without apology—in his letters. We transcribe it by a standard typographical device, either right- or left-pointing, as appropriate, except in special circumstances. The following case, for instance, requires facsimile of the original, since Clemens clearly meant to play upon the term "fist" by drawing the device as a distinctly *open hand:*

"Put it *there*, Charlie!" (*L2*, 331)

---

[3] *American Encyclopaedia of Printing*, edited by J. Luther Ringwalt (Philadelphia: Menamim and Ringwalt, J. B. Lippincott and Co., 1871), 217.

paragraph   ¶   The paragraph sign is both a mark of emphasis and the
sixth of the reference marks. It is actually "P" reversed
(left for right, and white for black) to distinguish it from that character.
Clemens, however, commonly miswrote it as a "P," drawing the hollow
stem with large, flat feet, but not the left/right or white/black reversal
in the loop. Whenever the sign is used in a letter, we transcribe it by the
standard typographical device, with a record of emendation when it has
been misdrawn. Clemens used the paragraph sign as a reference mark
and as shorthand for the word "paragraph," but most commonly in letters to indicate a change of subject within a passage, one of its original
meanings. When he inserted the paragraph sign in text intended for a
typesetter, he was doubtless specifying paragraph indention. But when
he used it in a letter, he was usually invoking that original meaning. The
transcription always prints the sign itself, even when it was inserted (¶)
or was manifestly an instruction to a typesetter. In the textual commentary, however, the paragraph sign in brackets [¶] is *editorial* shorthand
for "paragraph indention."

rules   Double rules (a), *parallel rules* (b), and *plain rules* (c), or
═══ (a) ═══ rule dashes, in manuscript are usually, but not invaria-
═══ (b) ═══ bly, centered on a line by themselves, serving to separate
──── (c) ──── sections of the text. When used within a line of text, they
are positioned like an ordinary em dash and may serve
as a common form of ellipsis, or to mean "ditto," or simply to fill blank
space in a line. This last function may be compared with the original
purpose of the eighteenth-century flourish, namely to prevent forged additions in otherwise blank space. But as with the flourish, this function
had in Clemens's day long since dissolved into a mainly decorative one.
Rules appear in Clemens's manuscript in three distinguishable species,
each with two variant forms. We construe wavy lines in manuscript as
"thick" rules, and straight lines as "thin" rules, regularizing length as
necessary. (a) *Double rules* appear in manuscript as two parallel lines, one
wavy and the other straight, in either order. (b) *Parallel rules* appear in
manuscript as two parallel lines, either both wavy or both straight (thick
or thin). (c) *Plain rules* appear as single lines, either wavy or straight
(thick or thin).

EMPHASIS EQUIVALENTS

Clemens used the standard nineteenth-century system of underscoring
to indicate emphasis, both within and between words. He indubitably

understood the equivalents in type for the various kinds of underscore, but even if he had not, they could probably be relied on for the transcription of his underscored words, simply because the handwritten and the typographical systems were mutually translatable. Although we may not understand this system as well as Clemens apparently did, it is still clear that he used it habitually and consistently, and that anomalies are much more likely to result from our, rather than his, ignorance or error.

Occasionally Clemens used what appear to be two variations of a single underscore—a broken underscore (*not* prompted by descenders from the underscored word) and a wavy underscore (more distinctly wavy than normally occurs with any hand-drawn line). If these are in fact variations of a single underscore, they evidently indicate a more deliberate, or a slightly greater, emphasis than single underscore would imply. They have been transcribed in *l e t t e r s p a c e d   i t a l i c* and **boldface** type, respectively, even though we do not know what, if any, typographical equivalent existed for them (both are marked * in the table). Clemens occasionally used letterspacing, with or without hyphens, as an a-l-t-e-r-n-a-t-i-v-e to italic, but he seems not to have combined it with italic, so that this editorial combination may always signify broken underscore. Wavy underscore in manuscript prepared for a printer did mean boldface, or some other fullface type, at least by 1900, but it is not clear for how long this convention had been in place. And in any case, boldface would now ordinarily be used for a level of emphasis higher than CAPITALS or *ITALIC CAPITALS*, so that the use of boldface type to represent wavy underscore is necessarily an editorial convention.

Clemens also sometimes emphasized capital letters and numerals in ways that appear to exceed the normal limits of the typographical system as we know it. For instance, when in manuscript the pronoun 'I̲' has been underscored twice, and is not part of an underscored phrase, we do not know what typographical equivalent, if any, existed for it. Since the intention is clearly to give greater emphasis than single underscore, rendering the word in small capitals (ɪ) would probably be a mistake, for that would indicate *less* emphasis than the absence of any underscore at all (I). In such cases (also marked * in the table), we extend the fundamental logic of the underscoring system and simulate one underscore for each manuscript underscore that exceeds the highest known typographical convention. 'I̲' in manuscript is therefore transcribed as an italic capital with one underscore (*I̲*). Otherwise, underscores in the original documents are simulated only (a) when Clemens included in his letter

MANUSCRIPT	TYPE
lowercase	roman lowercase
Capitals and Lowercase	Roman Capitals and Lowercase
<u>lowercase</u>	*italic lowercase*
<u>Capitals and Lowercase</u>	*Italic Capitals and Lowercase*
*<u>Capitals and Lowercase</u>	**Italic Letterspaced*
*Capitals and Lowercase	**Boldface Capitals and Lowercase*
<u>lowercase</u>	ROMAN SMALL CAPITALS
<u>Capitals and Lowercase</u>	ROMAN CAPITALS AND SMALL CAPITALS
CAPITALS or <u>lowercase</u>	ROMAN CAPITALS
<u>CAPITALS</u> or <u>lowercase</u>	*ITALIC CAPITALS*
*<u>CAPITALS</u>	**ITALIC CAPITALS*
*<u>1</u>, <u>2</u>, <u>3</u>, <u>4</u>, <u>5</u>	**<u>1</u>, <u>2</u>, <u>3</u>, <u>4</u>, <u>5</u>*

something he intended to have set in type, in which case his instructions to the typesetter must be reproduced, not construed, if they are to be intelligibly transcribed; and (b) when he deleted his underscore, in which case the transcription simulates it by using the standard manuscript convention for deleting an underscore.

Since underscores in manuscript may be revisions (added as an afterthought, even if not demonstrably so), one virtue of the system of equivalents is that it allows the transcription to encode exactly how the manuscript was marked without resorting to simulation. There are, however, some ambiguities in thus reversing the code: for example, a word inscribed initially as 'Knight' or 'knight' and then underscored three times would in either case appear in type as 'KNIGHT'. Clemens also sometimes used block or noncursive capitals or small capitals, simulating 'KNIGHT' or 'KNIGHT', rather than signaling them with underscores. Ambiguities of this kind do not affect the final form in the text, but whenever Clemens used block or noncursive letters, or when other uncertainties about the form in the manuscript arise, they are noted or clarified in the record of emendations.

2. Revisions and Self-Corrections

The transcription always represents authorial *revisions* where they occur in the text, just as it does all but the most ephemeral kinds of *self-correction*. Either kind of change is wholly given in the transcription, except when giving all details of an individual occurrence or all cases of a particular phenomenon would destroy the legibility of the transcription. For *revisions*, the transcription always includes at least the initial and the final reading, with intermediate stages (if any) described in the record of emendations. But in letters, revisions are rarely so complicated as to require this supplemental report.

Self-corrections are sometimes omitted by emendation, and are more frequently simplified by emendation than are revisions, chiefly because if fully transcribed in place they often could not be distinguished from revisions, except by consulting the textual commentary—even though the distinction is perfectly intelligible in the original letter. This limitation comes about in part because causal evidence of errors, such as a line ending ("misspel- | ling") or a physical defect in the pen or paper, cannot be represented in the text without adding a heavy burden of arbitrary editorial signs. Thus a word miswritten, then canceled and reinscribed because of such a defect would, in the transcription, look like a revision, or at least like hesitation in the choice of words. In part, however, the problem with transcribing self-corrections lies in the sheer number that typically occur in manuscript. Self-corrections internal to a word, for example, are so frequent that more than one kind of emendation has had to be invoked to bring their presence in the transcription within manageable, which is to say readable, limits.

Another limitation of the present system is that the transcription does not distinguish between *simple deletions*, which may have been made either before or after writing further, and *deletions by superimposition*, in which the writer deleted one word by writing another on top of it, hence certainly before writing further. Because we have no way to make this distinction legible in the transcription, we represent all deletions as simple deletions. In the first volume, we supplemented the transcription in this respect by recording as emendations "each instance of deletion by superimposition" (*L1*, xxxiv), thereby enabling anyone to ascertain the method of cancellation used, since deletions by superimposition were always described ('x' *over* 'y'), whereas simple deletions were not. The advantage of this procedure was that, while clumsy and expensive, it meant the transcription with its apparatus could always be relied on to indicate the method of cancellation, whether or not the editors thought this information was useful in any given case. Its great disadvantage was that it caused the record of emendations to be nearly overwhelmed by reports of superimposition, only a small percentage of which were of any interest.

Pending the invention of an affordable, reliable way to signal this distinction in the transcription, subsequent volumes record deletion by superimposition *only* when it is judged to be useful information—chiefly where the timing of a cancellation can be established as immediate from this evidence in the manuscript, although in the transcription the timing appears indeterminate. For example, where the transcription reads 'Dont you', the manuscript might show either (a) that 'you' followed 'Dont' (a simple deletion, hence indeterminate), or (b) that 'you' was superimposed on 'nt' (deletion by superimposition, hence certainly immediate). Since the record of emendation gives *only* those cases where cancellation by superimposition establishes the immediate timing of a change, and only where this fact is deemed relevant, readers are entitled to infer from the *absence* of an entry for two such words ('& at', for example) that simple deletion has occurred. Where it is deemed irrelevant ('in order that so that'), the method of deletion is neither transcribed, nor recorded as an emendation.

All transcribed deletions are, with minor exceptions, fully legible to the editors, and were therefore arguably so to the original recipient of the letter. But Clemens clearly did make some deletions easier or more difficult to read than others. His occasional addition of false ascenders and descenders to his normal deletion marks, for instance, has the intended effect of making it quite difficult to read what was canceled, at least so long as the presence of these false clues remains undetected. Such cases show, in fact, that Clemens must have known that his normal methods of cancellation did not prevent most readers from reading what he crossed out. Indeed, we know from letters in this volume that he enjoyed teasing his fiancée about her practice of reading his cancellations— even going so far as to challenge her to read a deletion he made "impenetrable" (see p. 126).

It is clear that Clemens experimented with a wide variety of cancellations more or less actively *intended* to be read, but even apart from these deliberate and relatively rare cases, his methods of cancellation in letters ranged across a full spectrum of difficulty. The transcription does not, however, attempt routinely to discriminate among these, simply because we lack any conventional means for representing the differences legibly. Cancellations thus actively intended to be read—or not, as the case may be—are identified in the notes when their special character is not otherwise apparent from the transcription. But deletions accomplished by unusual methods *are* simulated whenever possible, for the methods themselves often convey some such intention (see, for example, p. 337). And in letters included in this volume, Clemens used two methods of cancellation which occupy opposite ends of the spectrum of difficulty, and which the transcription therefore simulates.

Mock, or pretended, cancellations are words crossed out so lightly that they are easily read, visibly distinct from normal deletions, as well as being (for the most part) deletions of words still necessary to the sense. Clemens used various methods for creating mock cancellations, but the transcription renders them uniformly as struck through by a hairline rule, which is visibly thinner and rides higher on the x-height than the half-point rule used for normal deletions. (Compare 'Well, *I* ~~pass.~~' with 'Well, *I* ~~pass.~~'). Clemens also deleted parts of some letters by tearing away portions of the manuscript page, which he then sent, visibly mutilated. By their very nature, such deletions are unlikely to be read by anyone, but occasionally Clemens left enough evidence in the torn page to permit as much as the first or last line of the suppressed passage to be reconstructed. Yet even if the entire excision somehow survived, it would not be included in the transcription, simply because it was not part of the letter he sent. When text canceled in this fashion can be reconstructed, therefore, it is transcribed with wholly missing characters as diamonds and partly missing characters as normal alphabetical characters, bracketed as *interpolations:* 'I [j◇◇◇] ros[◇ ◇p] &' (p. 115). The result is not, in the ordinary sense, readable—any more than the original manuscript at this point was, except where one or two characters or words left standing could still be read, out of context. The fully legible reconstructed reading is, therefore, given only in the notes.

It may be added here that some deletions in manuscript, especially of punctuation, were indicated there only by methods not themselves transcribable. For instance, when Clemens added a word or more to a sentence already completed, he rarely struck out the original period. Instead, he signaled his intention simply by leaving only the usual word space between the original last word and the first word of his addition, rather than the larger space always left following a sentence period. Whenever someone reading the manuscript would have *understood* something as canceled, even though it was not literally struck out, the transcription represents it as if it had been deleted in the normal fashion, and the record of emendations reports the fact as an *implied deletion*.

DELETIONS

■ Single characters and underscores are deleted by slash marks—occasionally even when the deletion is internal to the final form of the word ('privile*d*ge'). Single characters include the symbol for illegible character (∅) and, more rarely, Clemens's own deleted caret (ʌ), when that alone testifies to his having begun a change.

■ Two or more characters are deleted by a horizontal rule ('~~have written~~') —occasionally even when they are internal to the word ('examin~~ed~~ation').

■ Separate, successive deletions of two or more characters are signified by gaps in the horizontal rule ('~~that dwell in~~ all ~~the hearts~~'). These gaps *never* coincide with line ends in the transcription. Thus, horizontal rules that continue from the end of one line to the next ('~~it by any wilful act of her own~~') *always* signify a single, continuous deletion, never separate ones.

■ Deletions *within* deletions are shown by combining the horizontal rule with the slash mark for single characters ('~~thought~~'), or two horizontal rules for two or more characters ('~~I was sail~~'). The earlier of the two deletions is always represented by the shorter line: to read the first stage, mentally *peel away* the longer line, which undeletes the second stage.

INSERTIONS

■ Insertions are defined as text that has been placed between two previously inscribed words or characters, or between such a word or character and a previously fixed point (such as the top of the page), thus written *later than* the text on either side of it. Insertions may be interlined (with or without a caret), squeezed in, or superimposed on deleted characters—methods not distinguished in the transcription and not recorded as emendations except when pertinent. .

■ Single characters (including punctuation marks) are shown inserted by a caret immediately beneath them ('& I desire').

■ Two or more characters are shown inserted, either between words or within a word, by a pair of carets ('into').

INSERTIONS WITH DELETIONS

■ Insertions may be combined with deletions of one or more words, and in various sequences:

'worth knowing, the King included, I believe.'
'Eighteen months A short time, ago'
'intended to say, Aunt Betsey, that,'

■ Insertions may be combined with deletions within a word:

'Malcolmb'
'mMay-tree'
'wishesing'

In the last two cases here, the carets indicating insertion designate characters that have been superimposed on the characters they delete. Superimposition is, in such cases, a kind of insertion designed to place new characters next to older, standing characters. Clemens might have achieved much the same thing, albeit with greater trouble, by crossing out the old and literally interlining the new characters. The timing of insertions combined with deletions internal to a word must, in any case, be understood as pertaining only to the sequence of change to that word, not as later than any other part of the text.

With the one class of exceptions noted at the end of this paragraph, alterations within a word are transcribed in the text only (a) if the rejected form was a complete word, even though not a possible word in context, or (b) if it was a recognizable start on, or misspelling of, a word possible in context. Thus the reader will find 'literafture' in the text because it contains the beginning of 'literary', which was possible in context, but will not find 'excursinon' except in the report of emendations because it contains no other word or part of a word possible in context, nor is it a genuine misspelling. This rule of thumb has been devised partly because the notation for internally altered words is unconventional, and partly because such internal self-corrections occur very frequently in manuscript, so that if always transcribed they would introduce a large number of trivial puzzles throughout the text, threatening if not destroying its legibility. In fact, to reduce the impediment further, the editors may simplify internally altered words, (c) whether or not the original form was a word, or start of a word possible in context, *whenever Clemens reused three or fewer characters* (counting quotation marks, parentheses, dollar signs, and the like). In such cases the transcription gives the canceled and the final form in succession, just as if they had been separately inscribed. Thus we transcribe 'and any' for what could be accurately, but not as legibly, transcribed as 'anyd' or 'andy'—forms which are used to record the emendation. Altered numerals of more than one digit must always be simplified in this way, even if the writer reused more than three characters.

To quote the letters without including the author's alterations, omit carets and crossed-out matter, closing up the space left by their omission. Compound words divided at the end of a line in this edition use the double hyphen (⸗) if and only if the hyphen should be retained.

3. Emendation of the Copy-Text

We emend original documents as little as possible, and nonoriginal documents as much as necessary, but we emend both kinds of copy-text for two fundamental reasons: to avoid including an error, ambiguity, or puzzle that (a) is *not in* the original, or (b) *is* in the original, but cannot be intelligibly transcribed without altering, correcting, resolving, or simplifying it.

Errors made by the writer are not emended if they can be intelligibly transcribed. Some few errors may be corrected by *interpolation*—supplying an omitted character or word within editorial square brackets—but only if the editor is confident that the writer has inadvertently omitted what is thus supplied. Interpolated corrections may be necessary to construe the text at all, let alone to read it easily, and would therefore be supplied by any reader if not supplied by the editor. Permitting interpolated corrections in the text is thus a logical extension of transcribing errors when, and only when, they can be intelligibly transcribed. Interpolated corrections, at any rate, do not conceal the existence of error in the original, and are therefore not *emendations* of it: like editorial description, or superscript numbers for the notes, they are always recognizably editorial, even when they enclose a conjecture for what the writer meant to but did not, for whatever reason, include in the letter sent. Interpolations are therefore not normally recorded in the textual commentaries. Interpolations are not always supplied, even if what is missing seems beyond serious doubt, nor could they be used to correct all authorial errors of omission: mistaken 'is' for 'it', for example, or a missing close parenthesis that must remain missing because it might belong equally well in either of two places.

Most errors in a *nonoriginal* copy-text, such as a contemporary newspaper, are attributable not to the writer, but to the typesetter, and are therefore emended. Yet even here, certain grammatical errors and misspellings may be recognizably authorial, and therefore not emended. On the whole, however, Clemens's precise and meticulous habits, which were well known in editorial offices even before he left the West, make it more rather than less likely that errors in such a printing are the typesetter's—especially because editors and typesetters were typically committed by their professions not to a literal transcription, but to a "correct" form of any document they published. Typesetting errors are self-evident in such things as transposition ('strated' for 'started'), wrong font ('carriEd'), and some kinds of misspelling ('pouud'). In addition, we know that by 1867 Clemens consistently wrote '&' for 'and' in his letters—except where the word needed to be capitalized, or the occasion was somewhat more formal than usual (for example, see *L2*, 35–37). In any nonoriginal copy-text, therefore, 'and' is sure to be a form imposed by the typesetter, who had good professional reasons for excluding '&' as an unacceptable abbreviation. The word is therefore always emended as an error in nonoriginal copy-texts.

But if authorial errors are preserved uncorrected, it may well be asked why it is ever necessary to emend *originals* to avoid including them, not to mention how this can be done without changing the meaning of the original letter, and therefore the reliability of the transcription.[4] The general answer to these questions is that in a transcription which does not reproduce the text line for line with the original, some forms in the original must *be* changed if they are not to assume a different meaning

[4]G. Thomas Tanselle, "Historicism and Critical Editing," *Studies in Bibliography* 39 (1986): 8 n. 15.

in the transcription—in other words, if they are not to become errors in it. Clemens's characteristic period-dash combination at the end of a line is a classic example of something that must be emended because it would become an error if literally transcribed. The period-dash apparently combined as terminal punctuation in Clemens's manuscripts virtually always occurs at a line end, at least until about the mid-1880s, when he seems to have trained himself not to use the dash there, probably because contemporary typesetters so often misinterpreted his manuscript by including it in the type, where it would appear as an intralinear dash between sentences. The typographical origin of this device was probably as an inexpensive way to justify a line of type (especially in narrow measure, as for a newspaper), but Clemens would certainly have agreed with the majority view, which frowned upon the practice.[5] As already suggested (p. 558), when Clemens used a dash following his period, he indicated simply that the slightly short line was nevertheless full, and did not portend a new paragraph. The device may owe something to the eighteenth-century flourish used to prevent forged additions in otherwise blank space, since it sometimes occurs at the end of short lines that are followed by a new paragraph. At any rate, he never intended these dashes to be construed as punctuation. Yet that is precisely what happens if the typesetter or the reader does not recognize the convention and reads it as a pause. Any dash following terminal punctuation at the end of a line is therefore not transcribed, but emended. When "period.— | New line" occurs in a newspaper or other printing of a lost letter, it doubtless reflects the typesetter's own use of this method for right justification, and is necessarily emended. And when "period.— Dash" occurs within a line in such a printing, it is almost certainly the result of the typesetter's misunderstanding the convention in Clemens's manuscript, and is likewise emended.

Ambiguities left by the writer are also not emended if they can be intelligibly transcribed. But both original and nonoriginal copy-texts will inevitably contain ambiguous forms that, because the transcription is not line for line, must be resolved, not literally copied. Am-

---

[5] The dash "is totally inadmissible as something to fill out a line, when that ends with a period and there is hardly enough matter" ([Wesley Washington Pasko], *American Dictionary of Printing and Bookmaking* [New York: Howard Lockwood and Co., 1894; facsimile edition, Detroit: Gale Research Company, 1967], 132).

biguously hyphenated compounds ("water-|wheel"), for example, cannot be transcribed literally: they must be transcribed unambiguously ("waterwheel" *or* "water-wheel"), since their division at a line end cannot be duplicated. Using the editorial rule (|) to show line end would introduce a very large number of editorial signs into the text, since consistency would oblige the editor to use the symbol wherever line endings affected the form in the transcription. Even noncompound words divided at the end of a line may sometimes be ambiguous in ways that cannot be legibly preserved in the transcription: "*wit-*|ness" in the copy-text must be either "*witness*" or "*wit*ness." Dittography (of words as well as punctuation) likewise occurs most frequently at line ends—physical evidence that makes it readily intelligible as an error in the source, but that is lost in a transcription which abandons the original lineation. Dittography becomes more difficult to construe readily when it is simply copied, because the result is at least momentarily ambiguous. It is therefore emended, even in intralinear cases, in order not to give a distorted impression of this overall class of error. The general category of manuscript forms affected by their original position at line ends, however, is even larger than can be indicated here.

Puzzles created by the writer are likewise preserved if they can be intelligibly transcribed. On the other hand, we have already described several aspects of the author's alterations in manuscript which would, if transcribed, introduce puzzles in the transcription: the method of cancellation, errors with a physical cause, implied deletions, self-corrections that would masquerade as revisions, and changes internal to a word which the editor may simplify. These alone show that holograph manuscripts invariably contain many small details which we simply have no adequate means to transcribe. But with the system of notation used in plain text, it is technically feasible to include many more of these details in the transcription than we do. For instance, when Clemens wrote the words 'yourself about' in an 1853 letter, he actually made and immediately corrected two small errors: 'yourse*f*lf abo*f*ut'. The transcription, following the rules of thumb already described, omits both self-corrections, recording them as emendations: the first because the rejected form ('yoursef') is not a complete word, nor does it begin a possible word in context, nor is it a genuine misspelling; the second because the rejected form ('abot') does not begin any possible word, in or out of context.

The question posed by such details is not simply whether including them would make the text more reliable or more complete (it would), but whether they *can* be intelligibly and consistently included without creating a series of trivial puzzles, destroying legibility, while not adding significantly to information about the writer's choice of words or ability to spell. There are, in fact, a nearly infinite variety of manuscript occurrences which, if transcribed, would simply present the reader with a puzzle that has no existence in the original. For instance, a carelessly placed caret, inserting a phrase to the left instead of the right of the intended word, is readily understood in the original, but can be transcribed literally only at the cost of complete confusion. And when Clemens writes off the right edge of the page and must then reinsert words he has just deleted on the right, but now in the left margin, literal transcription which did not also represent the cause of the changes would create a puzzle where there simply is none in the original.

Exceptional Copy-Texts. When the original documents are lost, and the text is therefore based on a nonoriginal transcription of one kind or another, the normal rules of evidence for copy-text editing apply. When, however, two transcriptions descend independently from a common source (not necessarily the lost original itself, but a single document nearer to the original than any other document in the line of descent from it), each might preserve readings from the original which are not preserved in the other, and these cannot be properly excluded from any text that attempts the fullest possible fidelity to the original. In such cases, no copy-text is designated; all texts judged to have derived independently from the lost original are identified; and the text is established by selecting the most persuasively authorial readings from among all variants, substantive and accidental. Before this alternative method is followed, however, we require that the independence of the variant texts be demonstrated by at least one persuasively authorial variant occurring uniquely in each, thereby excluding the possibility that either text actually derives from the other. If independent descent is suspected, even likely but not demonstrable in this way, the fact is made clear, but whichever text has the preponderance of persuasively authorial readings is designated copy-text, and the others are treated *as if* they simply derived from it, whether or not their variants are published.

Damaged texts (usually, but not necessarily, the original letters) are emended as much as possible to restore the original, though now invisible, parts of the text that was in fact sent. This treatment of an original document may seem to be an exception to the general rule about emending originals as little as possible, but a damaged manuscript is perhaps best thought of in this context as an imperfect copy of the original. And despite some appearance to the contrary, emendation in such cases is still based on documentary evidence: sometimes a copy of the original made before it was damaged, or damaged to its present extent—more commonly, evidence still in the original documents but requiring interpretation, such as fragments of the original characters, the size and shape of the missing pieces, the regularity of inscribed characters (or type) and of margin formation, the grammar and syntax of a partly missing sentence, and, more generally, Clemens's documented habits of spelling, punctuation, and diction. This kind of evidence cannot establish beyond a reasonable doubt how the text originally read. Its strength lies instead in its ability to *rule out* possible readings, often doing this so successfully and completely that any conjecture which survives may warrant some confidence. At any rate, we undertake such emendations even though they are inevitably conjectural, in part because the alternative is to render the text even less complete and more puzzling than it is in the damaged original (since sentence fragments are unintelligible without some conjecture, however tentative), and in part because only a specific, albeit uncertain, conjecture is likely to elicit any effort to improve upon what the editors have been able to perform. For this same reason, a facsimile of any seriously damaged document is always provided, either in an appendix with other manuscript facsimiles or in the textual commentary for that letter.

Letters and, more frequently, parts of letters that survive in the original but cannot be successfully transcribed constitute another exception and will be published in facsimile. For example, two letters that Clemens typed in 1874 (joking the while about his difficulties with the typewriter) clearly exceed the capacity of transcription to capture all their significant details, particularly the typing errors to which he alludes in them. Partly because they were typed, however, the original documents are relatively easy to read and therefore can be published in photographic facsimile, which preserves most of their details without at the same time making them any harder to read than the originals. These are true exceptions in the sense that most of Clemens's typed letters can and will be transcribed. But it is generally the case that facsimile cannot provide an optimally reliable and readable text, even of Clemens's very legible holograph letters, which comprise at least eight thousand of the approximately ten thousand known letters.

Yet by the same principles which justify transcription of most letters into type, facsimile should serve to represent within a transcription most elements of a manuscript which would (a) not be rendered more clearly, or (b) not be rendered as faithfully by being transcribed (newspaper clippings, for instance)—or that simply cannot be faithfully transcribed, redrawn, or simulated (drawings, maps, rebuses, to name just a few of the possibilities). It follows that if an original newspaper clipping enclosed with a letter cannot, for any reason, be reproduced in legible facsimile, it will be transcribed line for line in what approximates a type facsimile of the original typesetting. If the text of an enclosed clipping survives, but no example of the original printing is known, it is transcribed without simulating the newspaper format. And long or otherwise unwieldy, or doubtful, enclosures may be reproduced in an appendix, rather than immediately following the letter.

Letters which survive only in the author's draft, or in someone else's paraphrase of the original, are also exceptions. In the first case, the source line of the editorial heading always alerts the reader that the text is a draft. In such cases, emendation is confined to those adjustments required for any original manuscript, and is not designed to recover the text of the document actually sent, but to reproduce the draft faithfully as a draft. Likewise, if a letter survives only in a paraphrase, summary, or description, it is included in the volume only if the nonoriginal source is judged to preserve at least some words of the original. And like the author's draft, it is not necessarily emended to approximate the original letter text more closely, since its nonauthorial words usually provide a necessary context for the authorial words it has, in part, preserved. When it is necessary to interlard paraphrase with transcription, the paraphrase appears in italic type and within editorial brackets, labeled as a paraphrase, in order to guarantee that there will be no confusion between text which transcribes the letter and text which does not pretend to. When nonoriginal sources use typographical conventions that are never found in Clemens's manuscripts—word space on both sides of the em dash, for instance, or italic type for roman and vice versa—the normal forms of the lost manuscript are silently restored.

Silent Emendations. In addition to the method of cancellation, which is usually omitted from the transcription and the record of emendations, several other matters may involve at least an element of unitemized, which is to say silent, change. To save space, we transcribe only routine addresses on envelopes by using the vertical rule (|) to signify line end; nonroutine text on envelopes is transcribed by the same principles used elsewhere. The text of preprinted letterhead is reproduced in EXTRA-SMALL SMALL CAPITALS, usually in its entirety, but as fully as possible even when unusually verbose, and never to an extent less than what Clemens may be said to adopt or refer to ("I'm down here at the office"). Only substantive omissions from letterhead are reported as emendations, since the decorative variations of job type are literally indescribable. Postmarks are also transcribed in EXTRA-SMALL SMALL CAPITALS, but only unusual postage stamps are transcribed or described. Whenever Clemens used any of the following typographical conventions in his original letter (hence also whenever they occur in nonoriginal copy-texts and are deemed authorial), the transcription reproduces or simulates them, even when it is necessary to narrow the measure of the line temporarily, which is done silently: diagonal indention; hanging indention; half-diamond indention; squared indention; the flush-left paragraph and the half line of extra space, which is its collateral convention; text centered on a line, positioned flush right, or flush left; and quotations set off by quotation marks, indention, reduced space between lines (reduced leading in type), extra space above or below (or both), smaller characters in manuscript (smaller type in nonoriginals), or any combination of these conventions.

In this volume, as in the previous two, normal paragraph indention is standardized at two ems, with variations of one em and three ems often occurring in the same letter. We silently eliminate minor, presumably unintended variation in the size of all indentions, and we place datelines, complimentary closings, and signatures in a default position, unless this position is contradicted by the manuscript, as when extra space below the closing and signature show that Clemens intended them to appear on the same line. But unmistakably large variation in the size of indention is treated as deliberate, or as an error, and reproduced or simulated, not corrected or made uniform. Notes which Clemens specifically did *not* insert within the letter text but wrote instead in its margin are nevertheless transcribed at the most appropriate place within the text, and identified by editorial description: '[*in margin:*] All well', or '[*in bottom margin:* over]'. The editorial brackets in these cases may enclose just the editorial description, or both the description and the text described, depending on which conveys the original most economically. The only alternative to transcribing these notes where they are deemed "appropriate" is to transcribe them in a *completely* arbitrary location, such as the end of the letter. We likewise transcribe postscripts in the order they occur, even if this differs from the order they were intended to be read, so long as the intended order remains clear. Thus a marginal 'P.P.S.' can intelligibly precede a 'P.S.', just as a 'P.S.' inserted at the top of a letter can precede the letter proper, whether or not it was actually intended to be read first. But if, for example, a postscript inserted at the top is written across or at right angles to the main text—a sign it was *not* intended to be read before or with the text it crosses—the intended order must prevail over the physical order, and the postscript is therefore moved to the end of the letter. Only *changes* in writing media are noted where they occur in the text, as in '[*postscript in pencil:*]', from which it may also be reliably inferred that all preceding text was in ink. Line endings, page endings, and page numbers are silently omitted from the transcription, but where they affect the text or its emendation, they are given in the record of emendation.

4. Textual Commentaries

The textual commentaries each contain five (or at most six) sections or parts. ■ The *headings*, which repeat the editorial headings of the letters themselves, but give the date first, and add the record numbers from the *Union Catalog of Clemens Letters* (*UCCL*) at the end, are designed to serve as a calendar of letters for the volume. ■ *Copy-text* identifies the document or documents that serve as the basis for the transcription, and from which the editor departs only in the specific ways listed as emendations. ■ *Previous publication* cites, in chronological order, and may also briefly characterize, known forms of publication before this one. This section does not attempt a complete record of previous publication, but only suggests roughly how and when the letter was first made public and therefore accessible to scholarship. Publications to which frequent reference is made may be described in the first of two prefatory sections, called Description of Texts. ■ *Provenance* likewise gives what is known about the history of ownership of the original letter. It makes frequent reference to the second of two prefatory sections, called Description of

Provenance. ■*Emendations and textual notes* records, in a list keyed by page and line number to the edited text, all deliberate departures from the copy-text (barring changes categorized here as *silent emendations*), and may include (a) editorial *refusals* to emend, identified by *"sic,"* only when readings are deemed especially at risk of being mistaken for typographical errors in the edited text, and (b) *textual notes*, which are always italicized and within square brackets, to explain the reasoning behind any particular emendation of, or refusal to emend, the copy-text. When no copy-text has been designated because two or more documents descend independently from the lost original, *all variants* are recorded and identified by abbreviations defined under the heading *Copy-text*, and this section is renamed *Emendations, adopted readings, and textual notes*, to signify that no preferred text, or copy-text, exists for that letter. ■*Historical collation* appears in the commentaries only rarely and is used to list variants between nonoriginal documents that may have descended independently from a common source, but have not been drawn upon for the text.

All entries in these lists begin with a page and line cue (for example, 120.3, meaning page 120, line 3), followed by the word or passage to be documented, exactly as it stands in the transcription, except where indention [¶], line ending (|), or abbreviation ('Write . . . is') is necessary. As far as possible, entries are confined to the words and punctuation being documented. Line numbers include every line of letter text on a page, even when the page contains text for more than one letter, including all *rules*, all enclosures, and all lines that are wholly editorial, such as '[*about one page (150 words) missing*]', '[*in pencil*]', the editorial ellipsis (. . . .), or the full-measure envelope rule. Line numbers *exclude* all editorial matter in the letter headings and in the notes. Each reading is separated by a centered bullet (•) from the corresponding reading of the copy-text, *transcribed* without change or emendation, insofar as our notation permits, or *described* within brackets and in italic type, as necessary.

EDITORIAL SIGNS AND TERMS

[¶]	Paragraph indention.
~	A word identical to that on the left of the bullet (hyphenated compounds are defined as one word).
∧	Punctuation absent from text to the right of the bullet.

‖	End of a line at the end of a page.
[t◊◊t wi]thin brackets	Text within brackets is missing from, or obscured in, a damaged copy-text, and therefore can be identified only conjecturally. Diamonds stand for missing and invisible characters; normal characters stand for partly visible characters; and word space is conjectural, not actually visible. Thus the following notation shows which characters have been emended into the copy-text, and how they must have been configured in the *un*damaged original *if and only if* the conjecture is correct.

120.5–6   did not mean • di[◊ ◊◊◊ ◊◊◊◊] [*torn*]

Alternative conjectures are almost always possible, and may be more or less plausible, insofar as they too are consistent with the physical and syntactical evidence.

above	Interlined or written in the space above something else. Compare '*over*' and '*across*'.
across	Written over and at an angle to previously inscribed text.
conflated	Sharing an element, usually a minim.
false start	Start anticipated, requiring a new beginning, as in a race.
implied	Understood as intended, even though not literally or completely inscribed.
miswritten	Malformed, misshapen—*not* mistaken in any other sense.
over	Superimposed on something, thereby deleting it. Compare '*above*' and '*across*'.
partly formed	Not completed, hence conjectural.

R. H. H.
Revised, June 1991

Textual Commentaries

THE CONTENT and purpose of the textual commentaries, as well as the special symbols and terms used in them, are described in the last part of the Guide to Editorial Practice, pp. 551–78. In what follows here we summarize information about prior publication and provenance which would otherwise have to be frequently repeated in the commentaries for letters in this volume.

1. Description of Texts

Individual commentaries may designate as copy-text one or both of the following publications. When the information given here is pertinent for any reason, the reader is specifically referred to it.

MTB   *Mark Twain: A Biography. The Personal and Literary Life of Samuel Langhorne Clemens by Albert Bigelow Paine, with Letters, Comments and Incidental Writings Hitherto Unpublished; Also New Episodes, Anecdotes, etc.* 3 vols. New York and London: Harper and Brothers, 1912. *BAL*, p. 251. *Copy used:* copy #1, CU-MARK. Where *MTB* has served as copy-text, copy #1 (publisher's code H-M on the copyright page of volume 1, signifying the first impression, ordered in August 1912) has been collated against copy #2 (code K-K, signifying an impression ordered in October 1935, which is the latest impression located). In 1935 Paine made a few corrections in the plates, but no variants in the texts of the letters collected in the present volume have been found.

    MTB was first issued in three volumes, then in four and later in two, all with the same pagination. Paine said that he had "obtained his data from direct and positive sources: letters, diaries, account-books, or other immediate memoranda" (*MTB*, 1:xv). His industry in this respect was such that several letters he published have not since been found in their original form and are therefore known only from his transcriptions (or occasional facsimiles) in *MTB* and *MTL*. Although the printer's copy for *MTB* has not been found, it is known that Paine's general method of acquiring letter texts was to borrow the original whenever possible, presumably transcribe it himself, probably on a typewriter, and then return the manuscript to its owner. He presumably had full access both to the documents (now in the Mark Twain Papers) that Clemens himself defined and set aside for his official biography, and to those now in the McKinney Family Papers. He also had access to at least some of the letters in the Moffett Collection, but it is not known whether these were ever fully in his hands or transcribed for him. Although he published many of the letters now in the McKinney Family Papers, he published relatively few of those in the Moffett Collection. *MTB* is copy-text for a few letters not republished in *MTL*. But letter texts in *MTB* are generally excerpts and, judging from collation with letters that are still extant in manuscript, they were more freely edited than the corresponding passages published in *MTL*. Excerpts from *MTB* appeared in *Harper's Monthly Magazine* in thirteen installments, running from November 1911 through November 1912, hence, largely before *MTB* appeared in September 1912. Collation shows that when the book and the magazine both include text for a letter, they sometimes contain evidence of having each derived independently from a common source (very likely a typescript and its carbon copy), even though each has been separately copy-edited. Whenever persuasively authorial variants are found uniquely in both texts, the transcription is based on both. When such variants cannot be found, *MTB* is designated copy-text and the magazine, which was generally edited more heavily than the book, is treated as if it simply derived from *MTB* instead of their common source.

MTL   *Mark Twain's Letters, Arranged with Comment by Albert Bigelow Paine*. 2 vols. New York and London: Harper and Brothers Publishers, 1917. *BAL* 3525. *Copy used:* copy #1, CU-MARK. As indicated under *MTB*, the letters published in *MTL* are generally more complete as well as more reliable than those extracted or published in full in *MTB*. Because printer's copy for *MTL* has likewise not been found, it is not always clear what relation it bore to the printer's copy for *MTB*. Transcriptions are based on both *MTL* and *MTB* only when persuasively authorial variants occur uniquely in both, thus establishing their independent derivation from the lost manuscripts. Otherwise, if a letter appears both in *MTL* and *MTB*, *MTL* is chosen as copytext and *MTB* treated as if it simply derived from *MTL* instead of their common source.

Most of the letters published in *MTL* survive as original manuscripts. Collation of these documents with their transcriptions in *MTL* shows, in addition to the expected errors and omissions, that the *MTL* transcription always spelled out ampersands, and always imposed a uniform style on the dateline, greeting, complimentary closing, and signature lines. The uniformity of this house styling is established by a very large body of letter manuscript, and Clemens's consistency in using certain forms is likewise established by an even larger body of evidence. When the copy-text is *MTL*, this evidence is considered sufficient to permit the conjectural restoration of the likely forms in the original letter, at least in these uniformly styled elements. All emendations to remove this nonauthorial styling in *MTL* are, of course, published.

2. Description of Provenance

Brownell   The George H. Brownell Collection is housed in the
Collection   Rare Book Department of the Memorial Library of the
University of Wisconsin (WU). George H. Brownell (1875–1950) was a midwestern newspaperman who eventually became a full-time Mark Twain scholar, devoted especially to the task of obtaining photocopies (or originals) of Clemens's uncollected journalism and letters. In 1935 he helped found the Mark Twain Society of Chicago and, in 1941, the Mark Twain Association of America. In January 1939 he became the first editor of the *Twainian*, a position he held until his death. In October 1936, Brownell acquired an unusual collection of Clemens material from a Mark Twain collector, Irving S. Underhill (who died in 1937, in Buffalo). According to Brownell,

the aged, bed-ridden Irving S. Underhill had begun his preparations for death by shipping the more valuable items in his Twain collection to a New York auction concern. To me, at that time, he shipped two large cartons of miscellaneous Twainiana of no sale value, but having for me an almost inestimable bibliographical value.

Contained in one of those cartons was a box of Mark Twain letters—not the originals, but copies of the originals made by typewriter, pen and pencil. I never learned from Mr. Underhill how he acquired this strange collection of fully 200 Twain letters. My guess is that the copies were made by some dealer, long ago, at a time when the originals were passing through his hands to the purchaser. Mr. Underhill might then have bought or traded something to the dealer for the copies. (Brownell 1943, 2)

Brownell's conjecture was correct. The copies had been made by Dana S. Ayer of Worcester, Massachusetts, a book and manuscript dealer who had been a salesman (as of the late 1890s) for the American Publishing Company (*BAL* 3521; Second Life Books, lot 764; Samuel R. Morrill to Clifton W. Barrett, 24 Apr 1957, ViU). Brownell compiled a list of Underhill's documents, which included 158 Ayer transcriptions of Clemens letters (Brownell 1941). None of these letters was written earlier than 1867, when Clemens first corresponded with Elisha Bliss of the American Publishing Company. More than half of them were addressed to Bliss or to his son, Francis E. Bliss, who were both officers of the American Publishing Company. Most of the remaining letter transcriptions were addressed to Frank Fuller, Clemens's business agent from the spring of 1867 until sometime in 1868, when Clemens presumably placed Bliss in charge of past as well as his then current business correspondence (Brownell 1941). In the fall of 1942, Brownell loaned the Ayer transcriptions to Bernard DeVoto, who in turn had the majority of them retranscribed, depositing these retranscriptions in the Mark Twain Papers (described below). Brownell ultimately bequeathed the documents to the University of Wisconsin, where they now reside.

The original manuscripts for most of the letter transcriptions in the Brownell Collection have been found and are accessible to the editors, but a few letters are known only by the copy Ayer made of the original. By assessing the overall accuracy of Ayer's transcriptions and identifying the kinds of errors he introduced into them, it is possible to emend the texts of those few letters or parts of letters for which no manuscript survives, in order to restore the likely reading of the lost original. Two letters in the present volume derive in part from Ayer transcriptions: 10? April 1869 and 15 August 1869, both to Elisha Bliss.

Huntington   Henry E. Huntington (1850–1927), financier, railway
Library   executive, and heir to Collis Potter Huntington's rail-
                    road fortune, bequeathed his San Marino, California, estate as an endowed public museum and art gallery for his enormous collection of rare books, manuscripts, and paintings. The Clemens ma-

terial at the Huntington Library includes literary manuscripts and nearly two hundred autograph letters. Over half of these letters are addressed to Mary Mason Fairbanks, and were bought by Henry Huntington from the Fairbanks family in 1918 (Thomas Nast Fairbanks to Dixon Wecter, 4 Dec 1947, and Wecter to Fairbanks, 6 Dec 1947, CU-MARK). Nineteen letters in this volume belong to the Huntington Library: seventeen to Mary Mason Fairbanks, part of a letter to her and the other managers of the Cleveland Protestant Orphan Asylum, and one letter to her and Abel W. Fairbanks.

McKinney   The Jean Webster McKinney Family Papers, housed in
Family Papers   the Francis Fitz Randolph Rare Book Room, Helen D.
       Lockwood Library, Vassar College, Poughkeepsie, New York (NPV). This collection was given to Vassar in 1977 by Jean and Ralph Connor, of Tymor Farm, LaGrangeville, New York. Jean Connor inherited the papers from her mother, Jean Webster McKinney, who had in turn inherited them from her mother, Annie Moffett Webster, Clemens's niece and the wife of Charles L. Webster, his business partner from 1884 to 1888. The letters and other Clemens materials in the collection represent one of the three principal caches of family letters, which passed from Clemens to his mother, Jane Lampton Clemens (d. 1890), his brother Orion (d. 1897) and sister-in-law Mollie Clemens (d. January 1904), and ultimately to his sister, Pamela A. Moffett (d. August 1904). Some of these documents went eventually to Pamela's son, Samuel E. Moffett (see Moffett Collection, below), and some to her daughter, Annie Moffett Webster. Not surprisingly, therefore, several manuscript letters are now found partly in the McKinney Family Papers and partly in the Moffett Collection.

Mollie Clemens wrote her nephew Samuel Moffett on 31 July 1899, "We never destroyed Sams letters—*excepting* by his request, or a few no one should see" (CU-MARK). At least one partly destroyed (censored) letter survives in this collection (see *L1*, 347–49), but by far the larger toll was probably taken by accidental physical damage or loss, and by the deliberate destruction, following Mollie Clemens's death, of most of Clemens's letters to his mother. As early as 1881, Orion Clemens had assembled a number of his brother's letters written between about 1853 and 1865 as part of a sprawling manuscript for his own never-published autobiography, finding even then that not all the letters had been preserved intact. On 6 October 1899, Pamela Moffett sent an unknown number of original letters to her son, Samuel Moffett, then a journalist in California, saying in part that she "was sorry to see that parts of some of the letters were missing" (CU-MARK). He tried to publish at least a few of these letters in biographical sketches of Clemens, but was eventually told to preserve them for publication after Clemens's death. Some, if not all, of these letters must eventually have become part of the Moffett Collection.

But in 1904, according to a 1935 Associated Press story in an unidentified newspaper clipping, Mollie Clemens's executor, John R. Carpenter, burned "almost four trunks" of Clemens's letters to his mother, "as requested by the famous humorist." Carpenter confided his story, according to this report, to Dr. G. Walter Barr of Keokuk, who gave this account:

> When Mrs. Clemens died [in 1890], . . . her carefully preserved personal and family treasures went into the possession of her son, Orion. When Orion died, his wife had the succession and kept it inviolate until her own death in 1904.
>
> John R. Carpenter was administrator of Orion's wife's estate and the treasured archives of Mother Clemens were delivered to him. One item was a collection of letters from Mark Twain to his mother, running through many decades, from youth to worldwide fame.
>
> But with those three or four trunks of letters was an admonition. Mark Twain had enjoined his mother that she always burn his letters to her. She had not done so, but had passed on the mandamus to Orion and to the wife of the latter, and Carpenter was familiar with it.
>
> He had a treasure of incalculable value and an imperative order to destroy it.
>
> Carpenter realized fully the value of the material he was about to burn in his library grate. When I exclaimed that to destroy all those letters was a monstrous crime against biography, history and the record of a man who belonged to the whole world, he answered that he agreed with me—but what could be done under the circumstances?
>
> Mark Twain had written those letters to his mother in perfect candor—and about the whole sum of his candid writing was in them—intending and believing that nobody else would ever see them, and had ordered them burned.
>
> And so Carpenter burned every one. It took him several long evenings to complete the job thoroughly. ("Mark Twain Letters to Mother Burned at Direction of Author," unidentified clipping, datelined 14 Dec [1935], PH in CU-MARK; the New York *Times* also published an abbreviated version of this story on 15 Dec 1935, 2)

That this story was not a fiction is suggested by the postscript of Clemens's 14 February 1904 letter to Carpenter, the original draft of which survives in the Mark Twain Papers: "If there are any letters of mine, I beg that you will destroy them."

The McKinney Family Papers consist of Clemens documents typically left by him, at various times, with his sister. They include his earliest surviving notebook (probably written in 1855; see *N&J1*, 11–39); half a dozen literary manuscripts, incomplete and unpublished, written principally between 1859 and 1868 (see *ET&S1–3*); more than six hundred letters and telegrams from Clemens to various members of his family, and to business associates like Webster, as well as family photographs and mementoes, and letters and documents by other family members and close associates (Simpson, 6–14). Six letters in this volume belong to the McKinney Family Papers: 14 January 1869, and part of 20 and 21 August 1869, both to Pamela A. Moffett; 27 February 1869, 4 June 1869, and 15 December 1869, all to Jane Lampton Clemens and family; and 23 June 1869 to Olivia Lewis (Mrs. Jervis) Langdon.

Mark Twain   The Mark Twain Papers, The Bancroft Library, Univer-
Papers   sity of California, Berkeley (CU-MARK). The core of
                this collection consists of the original documents that
Clemens made available to Albert Bigelow Paine for the official biography Paine was to produce, and from which (in part) Paine eventually published his selected editions of letters, notebooks, and the autobiography. Since Clemens's death in 1910, these papers were successively in the care of Paine (1910–37); Bernard DeVoto at Harvard (1938–46); Dixon Wecter at the Huntington Library, San Marino, California, and later at the University of California in Berkeley (1946–50); Henry Nash Smith (1953–63); and Frederick Anderson (1963–79), both of the latter at the University of California in Berkeley, and both successors to Paine, DeVoto, and Wecter as the official literary executor of the Clemens estate. Upon the death of Clara Clemens Samossoud in 1962, the papers were bequeathed to the University of California, and in 1971 they became part of The Bancroft Library, where they now reside.

The original collection segregated by Clemens for Paine included forty-five of the approximately fifty extant notebooks kept between 1855 and 1910; approximately seventeen thousand letters received by Clemens or his family; an estimated six hundred literary manuscripts, most of them unpublished, including the autobiographical dictations; as well as photographs, clippings, contracts, and a variety of other documents originally owned by Clemens. Four letters in this volume are definitely

from this original collection:12 January 1869 to Charles J. Langdon, 5–
10 March 1869 to George W. Elliott, 17 September 1869 to Ausburn
Towner, and 20–28 November 1869 to George H. Selkirk. One letter
may belong either to it or to the Moffett Collection (see below): 23 June
1869 to Pamela A. Moffett. Since Paine's tenure, primary and secondary
documents have been added in various ways to the Papers—ranging
from gifts of both photocopied and original manuscripts and documents, to large purchases and bequests comprising many hundreds of
documents, to the systematic compilation of a secondary archive of photocopies, collected from institutions and private owners of original documents around the world, for the specific purpose of publishing a comprehensive scholarly edition of Mark Twain's Works and Papers.

Samossoud Collection (1952), The Mark Twain Papers. Among the documents in Clemens's possession at the time of his death, but not included
in the Mark Twain Papers or made wholly available to Paine, were the
letters written to his fiancée and wife, Olivia L. Langdon, and later to
their daughters, Susie, Clara, and Jean. Dixon Wecter was permitted to
transcribe most of these letters, as well as some others that were still
owned and separately housed by Clara. He used these transcriptions as
the basis for his selected edition, *The Love Letters of Mark Twain*
(*LLMT*), published in 1949, and ultimately deposited all of them in the
Mark Twain Papers. On 21 March 1952, however, the University of California purchased from Clara's husband Jacques Samossoud (d. 1966)
approximately five hundred original letters written to Olivia between
September 1868 and her death in 1904. Other parts of the large cache of
family letters still held by Clara and her husband were sold or given at
various times between 1949 and 1962 to other persons and institutions,
not all of which have yet been identified. (See, for example, Doheny Collection, above. Clara likewise gave Chester L. Davis, Sr., and the Mark
Twain Research Foundation of Perry, Missouri, a number of Clemens's
letters, as well as some of Olivia's.) This volume contains seventy-four
letters in the Samossoud Collection, all to Olivia (a few of them with
notes to her brother or parents as well).

Moffett Collection (1954), The Mark Twain Papers. This collection represents the portion of Pamela Moffett's papers which passed to her son,
Samuel, instead of her daughter, Annie (see McKinney Family Papers,
above). The collection became the property of Samuel Moffett's daughter Anita Moffett (d. 1952), either upon his death in 1908, or upon the
death of Anita's younger brother, Francis Clemens Moffett, in 1927. The

papers were discovered in 1953 by Paul P. Appel, a Mamaroneck, New York, book dealer (not in 1954 by Jacob Zeitlin, as reported in *L2*, 516), in a warehouse sale that included some of Anita Moffett's effects: sixteen hundred letters by Clemens, his family, and associates (including Pamela's letters to her son and daughter); ten scrapbooks of newspaper clippings for the period 1858–98, evidently compiled by Orion and Mollie Clemens, and containing original printings of Clemens's (and Orion's) western journalism, which had been largely unknown to Paine and all subsequent scholars (see *MTEnt*); deeds to 1860s Nevada mining claims owned by Clemens or his brother; family photographs; and a family Bible. The collection was purchased for the University of California in 1954 by a group of anonymous donors. The inventory of Clemens letters made at the time is not always specific enough to enable the editors to be certain whether some letters were part of the Moffett acquisition or were already part of the Mark Twain Papers in 1954. Four letters in this volume definitely belong to the Moffett Collection: 11 May 1869 to Jane Lampton Clemens, 26 June 1869 to Jane Lampton Clemens and Pamela A. Moffett, 3? July 1869 to Orion Clemens, and 17 December 1869 to Pamela A. Moffett. One letter may belong either to it or to the Mark Twain Papers Collection (see above): 23 June 1869 to Pamela A. Moffett.

Mendoza Collection (1957), The Mark Twain Papers. In January 1957 the University of California purchased a collection of one hundred sixteen Clemens letters written between 1867 and 1905 (all but one of them to Elisha Bliss or Henry H. Rogers), as well as eleven other miscellaneous items. This collection was offered for sale to the University by Aaron Mendoza of the Isaac Mendoza Book Company, New York City. The letters came from the collection of C. Warren Force (1880–1959), who had bought the letters to the Blisses in 1938 at the sale of the collection of George C. Smith, Jr. (Parke-Bernet 1938a, lot 126). In 1939 Force had given Bernard DeVoto transcripts of the letters to the Blisses. The Mark Twain Papers now contain about eighty-five letters to Rogers (or members of his family) and forty-nine original letters to Elisha Bliss or Francis E. Bliss. Of the total, all but roughly twenty letters were part of the Mendoza Collection, which contributes eight letters to this volume, all to Elisha Bliss: 30 March 1869, 12 April 1869, 20 April 1869, 29 April 1869, 12 August 1869, 3 September 1869, 7 September 1869 (2nd of 2), and 27 September 1869. See also Brownell Collection, above.

Tufts Collection (1971), The Mark Twain Papers. The James and John

M. Tufts Collection was assembled chiefly by James Tufts, an acquaintance of Clemens's and, for more than forty years (1892–1935), a prominent San Francisco journalist who at various times was an editor for the *Call*, the *Chronicle*, and the *Examiner*. The collection was purchased in 1971 from Tufts's son, Dr. John M. Tufts of Kentfield, California. It includes twenty-three original letters by Clemens to various correspondents, literary manuscripts, first printings of his sketches, first editions of his books, and photographs. Two letters in this volume belong to the Tufts Collection: 17 February 1869 to Joseph T. Goodman and 2 September 1869 to Elisha Bliss.

Appert Collection (1973 and 1977), The Mark Twain Papers. The gift of Mr. and Mrs. Kurt E. Appert of Pebble Beach, California, this collection includes more than fifty letters by Clemens to various correspondents, literary manuscripts, photographs, letters from various hands to Clemens, first editions of his works, and books from his library. One letter in this volume belongs to the Appert Collection: 7 October 1869 to Unidentified.

■ 1 January 1869 · To Joseph H. Twichell · Cleveland, Ohio · *UCCL* 00216

■*Copy-text:* MS, collection of Chester L. Davis, Jr. ■*Previous publication: LLMT*, 41–42. ■*Provenance:* This letter, like those of 23 January and 14 February 1869, was evidently later returned to Clemens or his daughter Clara by Twichell or Twichell's heirs. It survived in the Samossoud Collection at least until 1947: sometime between then and 1949 Dixon Wecter saw it there and had a typescript made. Chester L. Davis, Sr. (1903–87), afterwards acquired the MS directly from Clara Clemens Samossoud (see Samossoud Collection, p. 586). In 1991 it was sold to an unknown purchaser (Christie 1991, lot 83). ■*Emendations and textual notes:*

1.7	Livy. She · ~.—|~
1.22	trust. ~~The~~ · ~.—|~
1.26	~~yo~~ to · y̸to

■ 2 January 1869 · To Olivia L. Langdon · Fort Wayne, Ind. · *UCCL* 00217

■*Copy-text:* MS, Mark Twain Papers, The Bancroft Library, University of California, Berkeley (CU-MARK). ■*Previous publication: MFMT*, 21–22, brief excerpt; *LLMT*, 356, brief paraphrase; *MTMF*, 61, brief quotation; Harnsberger, 58, brief excerpt. ■*Provenance:* see Samossoud Collection, p. 586. ■*Emendations and textual notes:*

3.1	sometimes. The • ~.—|~
3.28–29	trying? Scold • ~?—|~
4.26	one. You • ~.—|~
4.30	it.⫟ But • ~.⫟ —| ~ [*period over dash*]
4.35	Mrs. F.,'s, • [*sic*]
4.36	homelike • home-|like
5.2	worse. But • ~.—|~

■ 7 January 1869 · To Mary Mason Fairbanks · Rockford, Ill. · *UCCL* 00219

■*Copy-text:* MS, Huntington Library, San Marino, Calif. (CSmH, call no. HM 14236). ■*Previous publication:* Wecter 1947b, 66, and *LLMT*, 12, brief quotation; *MTMF*, 63–64. ■*Provenance:* see Huntington Library, pp. 582–83. ■*Emendations and textual notes:*

8.10	world. So • ~.—|~
8.11	letter • ₦ letter [*corrected miswriting*]
8.18	₦ if • i∦f
8.20	Cleveland﹐ • [*deletion implied*]

■ 7 January 1869 · To Olivia L. Langdon · Rockford, Ill. · *UCCL* 00220

■*Copy-text:* MS, Mark Twain Papers, The Bancroft Library, University of California, Berkeley (CU-MARK). ■*Previous publication:* Wecter 1947a, 37, with omissions; *LLMT*, 42–46; *MTMF*, 63, brief quotation. ■*Provenance:* see Samossoud Collection, p. 586. ■*Emendations and textual notes:*

10.6	publication. Your • ~.—|~
10.7	yourself. I • ~.—|~
10.27	commonplace • common-|place
11.26	prepared. What • ~.—|~
11.27	~~Livy,~~ • [*false ascenders/descenders*]
11.32	whose patron saint shall • whose patron saint ‖ ~~whose patron saint shall~~ | shall
11.33	it • it ~~it~~
12.2	He • ~~He~~ He [*rewritten for clarity*]
12.3	highway • high-‖way

12.11	~~be~~ bless • bϕless
13.2	~~it?~~ • [*question mark partly formed*]
13.10	vesture • [*doubtful 'ϕ vesture'; 'ϕ' partly formed*]

■ 7 January 1869 · To Francis E. Bliss · Chicago, Ill. · *UCCL* 00221

■*Copy-text:* MS, Willard S. Morse Collection, Collection of American Literature, Beinecke Rare Book and Manuscript Library, Yale University (CtY-BR). ■*Previous publication: MTLP*, 17. ■*Provenance:* donated to CtY in 1942 by Walter F. Frear. ■*Emendations and textual notes:*

14.9	shaving-paper • shaving-|paper

■ 7 January 1869 · To Mary Mason Fairbanks and Others on the Board of Managers of the Cleveland Protestant Orphan Asylum · Chicago, Ill. · *UCCL* 00222 (formerly 00223 and 00222).

■*Copy-text:* "Cleveland Orphan Asylum," Cleveland *Herald*, 12 Jan 69, 3, is copy-text for 'SHERMAN . . . Asylum.' (15.1–16.13); and MS, pages 3–4, Huntington Library, San Marino, Calif. (CSmH, call no. HM 14237), is copy-text for the remainder. The MS consists of two torn half-sheets of blue-lined off-white wove paper, 4$^{15}/_{16}$ by 8 inches, and inscribed on the rectos only in black ink. ■*Previous publication: MTMF*, 67, brief quotation of *Herald* text, and 65–66, MS text. ■*Provenance:* Pages 1 and 2 of MS are not known to survive; for pages 3 and 4, see Huntington Library, pp. 582–83. ■*Emendations and textual notes:*

[*Herald is copy-text for* 'SHERMAN . . . Asylum.' *(15.1–16.13)*)]

15.3	*Mesdames:* • ~:
15.4	& • and [*also at 16.1, 3*]
	[*MS is copy-text for* 'There . . . Mark.' *(16.15–34)*]
16.20	enjoy? Why • ~?—|~
16.22	all. I • ~.—|~
16.33	affectionately • ['ly' *conflated*]

■ 7 January 1869 · To Olivia L. Langdon · Chicago, Ill. · *UCCL* 00224

■*Copy-text:* MS, Mark Twain Papers, The Bancroft Library, University of California, Berkeley (CU-MARK). A photographic facsimile of the letter is on pp. 516–22. Clemens's MS consists of five leaves (torn from folders) of blue-lined onionskin, approximately 5$^{1}/_{8}$ by 8$^{1}/_{16}$ inches, inscribed on the rectos only in black ink. His enclosure, from Mary Mason Fairbanks's 5 January 1869 letter to him, consists of one sheet (torn from a folder) of blue-lined off-white wove paper, 5 1/16 by 8 1/8 inches, inscribed by Fairbanks on the recto in purple ink and by Clemens on the recto and verso in black ink. ■*Previous publication: LLMT*, 356, brief paraphrase; *MTMF*, 64, brief excerpt. ■*Provenance:* see Samossoud Collection, p. 586. ■*Emendations and textual notes:*

18.3	word • wor[d] word [*written off edge of page onto next page following* 'received.' *at 18.12; blotted*]
18.4	∱ • [*badly formed*]
18.11	again.] I • ~.]—|~
18.20	& • [*doubtful* '∤ &']
18.21	railway • rail-|way
19.5	a near ne [a] near neighbors • a near ne ‖ near neighbors ['a near ne' *written off edge of page onto next page preceding signature*]
19.18	Cleveland, • [*deletion implied*]

■ 10 January 1869 · To Harriet Lewis · Galesburg, Ill. · *UCCL* 00226

■*Copy-text:* MS, Collection of American Literature, Beinecke Rare Book and Manuscript Library, Yale University (CtY-BR). ■*Previous publication: LLMT*, 46–49. ■*Provenance:* donated to CtY in 1949 by Richard A. Wheeler and Ruth Wilcox Wheeler, niece of Harriet Lewis Paff. ■*Emendations and textual notes:*

21.4	∱ • [*partly formed*]
21.6	spoken. • [*doubtful* 'spoken.+'; *period followed by inkblot*]
21.20	is. I • ~.—|~
22.2	heart—I • ~—‖—~
22.5	grieving • [*false ascenders/descenders*]
22.6	genro generous • genroerous
22.8	dining-room • dining-|room
22.24	retiᶠcence • reti-|ᶠcence
22.38	geranium • [◊]eranium [*torn*]
23.7	broken-hearted • broken-|hearted
23.8	make • mak make [*rewritten for clarity*]
23.12	and • a[n]d [*torn*]
23.12	graver than a • grave[r t]ha[n ◊] [*torn and faded*]
23.16	Sincerely • [Si]ncerely [*torn*]
23.17	Saml. • [S]aml. [*torn*]
23.18	be • [*doubtful* '∱ be'; 'f' *partly formed*]
23.20	Tell • [Te◊l] [*torn*]

■ 12 January 1869 · To Olivia L. Langdon with a note to Charles J. Langdon · El Paso, Ill. · *UCCL* 00227

■*Copy-text:* MS, Mark Twain Papers, The Bancroft Library, University of California, Berkeley (CU-MARK). ■*Previous publication:* Wecter 1947a, 37–38, with omissions. ▪*Provenance:* see Samossoud Collection, p. 586. ▪*Emendations and textual notes:*

25.23–24	it. But • ~.—|~
25.24	~~than~~ that • tha*n*t
26.15	magic*i*ian • ['*i*' *partly formed*]
26.17	~~life~~ lives • lif*e*ves

▪ 12 January 1869 · To Mary Mason Fairbanks · El Paso, Ill. · *UCCL* 00229

▪*Copy-text:* MS, Huntington Library, San Marino, Calif. (CSmH, call no. HM 14238). A separate commentary for two enclosures (Appendix B), which do not survive with the letter, appears on p. 672. ▪*Previous publication: MTMF*, 66. ▪*Provenance:* see Huntington Library, pp. 582–83. ▪*Emendations and textual notes:* none.

▪ 12 January 1869 · To Charles J. Langdon · Ottawa, Ill. · *UCCL* 00230

▪*Copy-text:* MS, Mark Twain Papers, The Bancroft Library, University of California, Berkeley (CU-MARK). ▪*Previous publication: MTMF*, 66, brief quotations. ▪*Provenance:* see Mark Twain Papers, pp. 585–86. ▪*Emendations and textual notes:*

29.14	~~man~~ meal • ma*n*eal
29.17	~~the~~ that • th*e*at
29.22	reccommended • [*sic*]

▪ 13 and 14 January 1869 · To Olivia L. Langdon · Ottawa, Ill. · *UCCL* 00231

▪*Copy-text:* MS, Mark Twain Papers, The Bancroft Library, University of California, Berkeley (CU-MARK), is copy-text for the letter. The original enclosure, which does not survive, was most likely a clipping from the Chicago *Tribune* ("An Eccentric California Belle," 11 Jan 69, 4). Copy-text is a microfilm edition of the newspaper in the Newspaper and Microcopy Division, University of California, Berkeley (CU-NEWS). ▪*Previous publication: LLMT*, 49–52, without the enclosure. ▪*Provenance:* see Samossoud Collection, p. 586. ▪*Emendations and textual notes:*

[*MS is copy-text for* 'Ottawa . . . Sam. L. C.' (*30.1–33.19*)]

31.5	~~en~~ exclusive[ly] • e*n*xclusive

31.5	new-comers • new-|comers
31.9	an~~y~~ • ['y' *partly formed; possibly* 'amn']
31.15	much. If • ~.—|~
31.31	~~wr~~ were • w~~r~~ere ['r' *partly formed*]
32.7	morning. She • ~.—|~
32.18	~~$50,000~~ ˏ$20,000ˌ • $~~$~~20,000
32.32	outspoken • out-|spoken
32.38	know. I • ~.—|~
33.1	~~ma~~ • ['a' *partly formed*]
33.3	~~rh~~ • [*partly formed; possibly* 'w']
33.12	tell. I • ~.—|~
	[*Tribune* is copy-text for 'An . . . Hitchcock.' *(33.21–34.38)*]
34.10	the • [◊]he [*badly inked*]
34.16	father's • fa[◊]her's [*badly inked*]
34.21	defies • defie[s] [*badly inked*]
34.25	attends • att[◊]nds [*badly inked*]

■ 14 January 1869 · To Olivia L. Langdon · Davenport, Iowa · *UCCL* 00232

■*Copy-text:* MS, Mark Twain Papers, The Bancroft Library, University of California, Berkeley (CU-MARK). ■*Previous publication: LLMT*, 357, brief paraphrase; *MTMF*, 66, brief quotation. ■*Provenance:* see Samossoud Collection, p. 586. ■*Emendations and textual notes:*

39.5	~~poor~~ • [*false ascenders/descenders*]
39.6–7	~~er~~ earnest • e~~r~~arnest
39.10	~~G~~ • [*partly formed*]
39.14	~~b~~ • [*partly formed*]
39.22	~~vest~~ vast • v~~e~~ast
39.27	woman-hating • [*doubtful* 'wom~~e~~an-hating']
39.33	thirst • ~~thirst~~ thirst [*rewritten for clarity*]
40.1	thei~~r~~ • ['r' *partly formed*]
40.8	~~W~~ • [*partly formed*]
40.22	us?—& • ~?—|—~
40.23	rise • ris~~e~~e

■ 14 January 1869 · To Pamela A. Moffett · Davenport, Iowa · *UCCL* 00233

■*Copy-text:* MS, Jean Webster McKinney Family Papers, Vassar College Library (NPV). The surviving MS consists of three and one-third leaves, inscribed on the rectos only. Pages 1, 2, and 4 survive intact, but the top two-thirds of page 3 was cut off, doubtless by Pamela Moffett, and does not survive. No characters or portions of characters from the excised portion remain on the surviving third. ■*Previous publication: MTBus*, 103–4, with omission. ■*Provenance:* see McKinney Family Papers, pp. 583–85. ■*Emendations and textual notes:*

43.5	to-night • to-|night
43.8	&̸ a • ['a' *over* '&']
44.1	there. I • ~.—|~

■ 17 January 1869 · To Olivia L. Langdon with a note to Charles J. Langdon · Chicago, Ill. · *UCCL* 00234

■*Copy-text:* MS, Mark Twain Papers, The Bancroft Library, University of California, Berkeley (CU-MARK). ■*Previous publication:* Wecter 1947a, 38, with omissions; *LLMT*, 52–55. ■*Provenance:* see Samossoud Collection, p. 586. ■*Emendations and textual notes:*

45.25	I̸ • [*partly formed*]
46.5	eloquence, • [*deletion implied*]
46.7	pulpit • pulp̶u̶tit
46.9	sermon's • [*sic*]
46.28	a • a̸ a [*rewritten for clarity*]
47.2	lasts, • [*deletion implied*]
47.7	14 • [*doubtful* '1̸4̸'; '5' *partly formed*]

■ 19 January 1869 · To Olivia L. Langdon · Cleveland, Ohio · *UCCL* 00235

■*Copy-text:* MS, Mark Twain Papers, The Bancroft Library, University of California, Berkeley (CU-MARK). ■*Previous publication: LLMT*, 55–56; *MTMF*, 67, brief quotations. ■*Provenance:* see Samossoud Collection, p. 586. ■*Emendations and textual notes:*

50.6	t̶h̶ • [*partly formed*]
50.28	says, • [*deletion implied*]

■ 20 and 21 January 1869 · To Olivia L. Langdon · Toledo, Ohio · *UCCL* 00236

■*Copy-text:* MS, Mark Twain Papers, The Bancroft Library, University of California, Berkeley (CU-MARK). ■*Previous publication:* Wecter 1947a, 38–39, with omissions; *MTMF*, 67, brief quotation. ■*Provenance:* see Samossoud Collection, p. 586. ■*Emendations and textual notes:*

51.10	to-night • to-|night
52.15	to-morrow • to-|morrow
52.23	~~yeas~~ years • yea$rs
52.24	newspapers • news-|papers
52.29	notice. It • ~.—|~
52.35–36	one,) . . . yet.) • [*first closing parenthesis left undeleted*]
53.12	sincere—his • ~—|—~
54.7	much. You • ~.—|~
54.17	~~se~~ sleep • s¢leep
54.21	pupil! But • ~!—|~
54.36	*How* • ~~How~~ | *How* [*corrected miswriting*]
55.5	a conversation • a ‖ a conversation
55.8	safest. Some • ~.—|~
55.16	~~alwa~~ almost • alwamost [*canceled* 'a' *partly formed*]
55.18	want • [*doubtful* 'want$'; 't' *followed by inkblot*]
55.31	Ill. • [*possibly* 'Ill.,'; *ink splattered*]

■ 21 and 22 January 1869 · To Olivia L. Langdon · Norwalk, Ohio · *UCCL* 00237

■*Copy-text:* MS, Mark Twain Papers, The Bancroft Library, University of California, Berkeley (CU-MARK). ■*Previous publication: LLMT*, 357, brief paraphrase. ■*Provenance:* see Samossoud Collection, p. 586. ■*Emendations and textual notes:*

58.8	I • *I* I [*rewritten for clarity*]
59.16	received. Taking • ~.—|~
59.16	*t* • [*partly formed*]
59.18–19	persuade • persu$ade ['$' *partly formed*]
59.19	dispondency • [*sic*]
59.31	~~Livy,~~ • [*false ascenders/descenders*]
59.32	past,—& • ~,—|—~
59.35	~~have~~ has • ha~~ve~~s ['e' *partly formed*]
59.39–60.1	porcelaintype • porcelain-|type
60.13	~~ha~~ hide • h$ide ['a' *partly formed; possibly* 'o']
60.14	~~it~~ is • i$s
60.16	much • ~~much~~ much [*rewritten for clarity*]
60.21	~~co~~ customary • c¢ustomary

■ 22 January 1869 · To Olivia L. Langdon · Cleveland, Ohio · *UCCL* 00238

■*Copy-text:* MS, Mark Twain Papers, The Bancroft Library, University of California, Berkeley (CU-MARK). ■*Previous publication: MFMT*, 19–20, brief excerpt; *LLMT*, 58, 357, brief excerpts and paraphrase. ▪*Provenance:* see Samossoud Collection, p. 586. ▪*Emendations and textual notes:*

61.5	afraid.⅄ It • ~.⅄|~
61.12	s̶a̶i̶d̶ sad • saíd
61.16–17	t̶r̶o̶u̶b̶l̶e̶d̶ • [*false ascenders/descenders*]
61.21	O̶h̶,̶ • [*heavily canceled; false ascenders/descenders*]
61.23	you. What • ~.—|~
61.24	n̶o̶ so • ńso
61.27	ḍ • [*partly formed*]
61.30	your trust • your	your trust
62.13	if you are • if you i̶f̶ ̶y̶o̶u̶ are
62.18	t̶h̶o̶u̶g̶h̶t̶f̶u̶l̶ • [*false ascenders/descenders*]
62.35	down-hearted • down-|hearted
63.4	over. I • ~.—|~
63.6	m̶y̶ ̶i̶d̶o̶l̶ • [*false ascenders/descenders*]
63.10	overflowing • over-|flowing
63.29	yours. Livy • ~.—|~
64.2	C̶a̶n̶ Could • C̶a̶n̶ould [*underscored after revision*]
64.17	to-night • to-|night
65.4	Livy! I • ~!—|~

▪ 23 January 1869 · To Joseph H. Twichell and Family · Cleveland, Ohio · *UCCL* 00240

▪*Copy-text:* MS, collection of Chester L. Davis, Jr. A typed transcription (TS), made for Dixon Wecter from the original MS, and checked and annotated by him, is in the Mark Twain Papers, The Bancroft Library, University of California, Berkeley (CU-MARK). Where the MS has sustained minor damage, the TS reading is given in the table below. A separate commentary for two enclosures (Appendix B), which do not survive with the letter, appears on p. 672. ▪*Previous publication: LLMT*, 57–58, and *MTMF*, 68, brief quotations. ▪*Provenance:* The letter was evidently returned to Clemens or his daughter Clara by Twichell or Twichell's heirs. It survived in the Samossoud Collection at least until 1947: sometime between then and 1949 Wecter saw it there and had the TS made. Chester L. Davis, Sr., afterwards acquired the MS directly from Clara Clemens Samossoud (see Samossoud Collection, p. 586). In 1991 it was sold to an unknown purchaser (Christie 1991, lot 84). ▪*Emendations and textual notes:* The bottom fifth of page 2 was torn away by Clemens, although portions of a few characters remain (67.13–14). At some later date, Albert Bigelow Paine or Twichell wrote "Mark tore this" on a strip of brown paper pasted to the left margin verso; and the left margin of page 4 was trimmed.

67.1–2   ~~babby~~ baby • ba~~bb~~yy

67.13–15   [*torn . . . away*] • [*Although the bottom fifth of MS page 2 was torn away by Clemens, presumably as the most complete method of cancellation, portions of some characters remain visible. For the reconstructed reading, see the illustration below (taken from the MS facsimile in CU-MARK, reproducing the original at approximately 70 percent of actual size) and p. 68, n. 2.*]

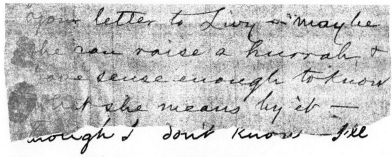

67.32   respect (TS) • [◊]espect [*trimmed*]

67.33   compels (TS) • [c]ompels [*trimmed*]

67.33   unconscious (TS) • uncon-|[◊]cious [*trimmed*]

67.35   far, (TS) • far[◊] [*torn*]

68.4   Shall be in Hartford (TS) • Shal[l] be in [Ha◊]tford [*torn*]

68.4   make (TS) • [ma◊◊] [*torn*]

68.5   California. (TS) • Californi[◊◊] [*torn*]

68.5   (Toledo,) (TS) • ([◊◊]ledo,) [*torn*]

■ 23 and 24 January 1869 · To Olivia L. Langdon · Cleveland, Ohio · *UCCL* 00239

■*Copy-text:* MS, Mark Twain Papers, The Bancroft Library, University of California, Berkeley (CU-MARK). ■*Previous publication: LLMT*, 357, brief paraphrase; *MTMF*, 68, brief quotation. ■*Provenance:* see Samossoud Collection, p. 586. ■*Emendations and textual notes:*

69.10   ʏ • [*partly formed*]

70.6   ~~le~~ last • l*é*ast

70.10   ~~miss~~ • miss-|

70.11   ~~fell~~ felt • fel*f*t

70.14   Livy! And • ~!—|~

70.15   *ɑ* • [*possibly 'u' or partly formed 'w'*]

70.22   ~~fee~~ felt • fe*f*lt

71.2   such • ~~such~~ such [*rewritten for clarity*]

71.12   f • [*partly formed*]
71.31   screech-owl • screech-|owl
71.35   hard-hearted • hard-||hearted
71.36   ~~fet~~ felt • fe/lt

■ 24 January 1869 · To Olivia L. Langdon · Cleveland, Ohio · *UCCL*
00241

■ *Copy-text:* MS, Mark Twain Papers, The Bancroft Library, University of California, Berkeley (CU-MARK). ■ *Previous publication: LLMT*, 59–61. ■ *Provenance:* see Samossoud Collection, p. 586. ■ *Emendations and textual notes:*

73.10   ~~my~~ me • m/e
74.19   ~~ex~~ Christian • ['C' *over* 'ex']
74.33   ~~maj~~ magistrate • ma/gistrate
74.35   ~~urged~~ • [*false ascenders/descenders*]
75.3   Postmaster • Post-|master
75.7   again, • [*deletion implied*]

■ 26 and 27 January 1869 · To Olivia L. Langdon · Batavia, Ill. ·
UCCL 00242

■ *Copy-text:* MS, Mark Twain Papers, The Bancroft Library, University of California, Berkeley (CU-MARK). ■ *Previous publication: LLMT*, 357, brief paraphrase. ■ *Provenance:* see Samossoud Collection, p. 586. ■ *Emendations and textual notes:*

76.5   ~~the~~ these • th∅ese
77.5   sad-looking • sad-|looking
77.11   ~~it~~ if • i/f
77.11   ~~ther~~ that • the~~r~~at
77.11   re[s]pect • re-|pect
77.14   ~~love~~ ˏLOVEˏ • [*one underscore altered to three*]
77.24   happy-hearted • happy-|hearted
77.27   ɏ • [*possibly partly formed* 'w']
77.29   ~~darling~~ • [*false ascenders/descenders; heavily canceled*]
78.11   about. Was • ~.—|~
78.13   ~~utterly faul~~ • [*false ascenders/descenders; very heavily canceled*]
78.17   ~~superb~~ • [*false ascenders/descenders*]
78.28   ╟ • [*partly formed*]
78.38   about, • [*deletion implied*]

79.4–5	Elmira. [¶] ~~G~~ • ~.—| [¶] ~
79.6	kiss. • ~~kiss~~ ˏkiss.ˏ [*rewritten for clarity*]
79.21	~~darling~~ • [*false ascenders/descenders; heavily canceled*]
79.24	last. What • ~.—|~
79.29	~~ev~~ • ['v' *partly formed*]
79.31	heart-broken • heart-|broken
79.31	to-day • to-|day
80.11	theɱ • ['m' *partly formed*]
80.14	~~the~~ three • thŕee

■ **29 and 30 January 1869 · To Olivia L. Langdon · Galena, Ill. · UCCL 00243**

■*Copy-text:* MS, Mark Twain Papers, The Bancroft Library, University of California, Berkeley (CU-MARK). ■*Previous publication: LLMT*, 357, brief paraphrase. ■*Provenance:* see Samossoud Collection, p. 586. ■*Emendations and textual notes:*

81.5	to-night. And • ~.—|~
82.17	other • ['o' *malformed; possibly mended from partly formed 'h' or 't'*]

■ **1 February 1869 · To Francis E. Bliss · Jacksonville, Ill. · UCCL 02446**

■*Copy-text:* MS, Henry W. and Albert A. Berg Collection, The New York Public Library, Astor, Lenox and Tilden Foundations, New York City (NN-B). ■*Previous publication: MTB*, 1:377, brief paraphrase; AAA/Anderson 1934, lot 123, brief excerpt; *MTMF*, 68, with omissions, and 87, brief excerpt. ■*Provenance:* An Ayer transcription and a Brownell typescript of this letter are at WU; see Brownell Collection, pp. 581–82. ■*Emendations and textual notes:* none.

■ **5 February 1869 · To Jane Lampton Clemens and Family · Elmira, N.Y. · UCCL 00245**

■*Copy-text:* MS facsimile serves as copy-text for the letter. The editors have not seen the MS, but in 1982 Chester L. Davis, Sr., then executive secretary of the Mark Twain Research Foundation in Perry, Mo., provided a photocopy to the Mark Twain Papers. Copy-text for the envelope paraphrase is a typescript, made for Dixon Wecter, Mark Twain Papers, The Bancroft Library, University of California, Berkeley (CU-MARK). ■*Previous publication: LLMT*, 64; *MTMF*, 69, brief quotation. ■*Provenance:* The letter and envelope were returned to Clemens, presumably by Pamela Moffett, for they both survived in the Samossoud

Collection at least until 1947: sometime between then and 1949 Wecter saw the MS there and had the letter transcribed and the envelope paraphrase made. The envelope had evidently become separated from the letter, for the paraphrase of its text was mistakenly typed with the transcription of a letter to Pamela Moffett, now dated 29? November 1868 (*L2*, 294–96). Davis acquired the MS of the letter and the envelope directly from Clara Clemens Samossoud after 1947 (see Samossoud Collection, p. 586). ■*Emendations and textual notes:*

84.17	Margaret • ['M' *possibly written over a partly formed, uppercase character*]
85.19	want₁ • [*deletion implied*]

■ 5 February 1869 · To Mary Mason Fairbanks · Elmira, N.Y. · *UCCL* 00246

■*Copy-text:* MS, Huntington Library, San Marino, Calif. (CSmH, call no. HM 14239). ■*Previous publication: MTMF*, 69–70; Harnsberger, 55, brief quotation. ■*Provenance:* see Huntington Library, pp. 582–83. ■*Emendations and textual notes:*

86.4	date of • datɖe of
86.8	though₁ • [*deletion implied*]
86.11	Fairbanks • Fairbam̶knks
86.11	continue • ['e' *over miswritten* 'u']
87.8	ELMIRA • E[LM◇RA] [*badly inked*]

■ 13 February 1869 · To Olivia L. Langdon · Cleveland, Ohio · *UCCL* 00247

■*Copy-text:* MS, Mark Twain Papers, The Bancroft Library, University of California, Berkeley (CU-MARK). A photographic facsimile of the letter is on pp. 523–29. The MS consists of three leaves of blue-lined off-white wove paper, approximately 5⁹⁄₁₆ by 8½ inches, inscribed on all six sides in black ink, now faded to brown. ■*Previous publication: LLMT*, 357, brief paraphrase; *MTMF*, 70–71, with omissions. ■*Provenance:* see Samossoud Collection, p. 586. ■*Emendations and textual notes:*

88.8	exasperation. I • ~.—|~
88.10–12	"where . . . "Splendid . . . this." • [*sic*]
89.12	a̶l̶l̶ always • al̸ways [*underscored after revision*]
89.22	t̶h̶a̶t̶ the • thate
89.24	Langdon • [*doubtful* 'Langdons'; 's' *partly formed*]

■ 13 February 1869 · To Olivia Lewis (Mrs. Jervis) Langdon · Ravenna, Ohio · *UCCL* 00249

■ *Copy-text:* MS, Mark Twain Papers, The Bancroft Library, University of California, Berkeley (CU-MARK). ■ *Previous publication: LLMT*, 65–67. ■ *Provenance:* donated to CU-MARK in 1972 by Mrs. Eugene Lada-Mocarski, Jervis Langdon, Jr., Mrs. Robert S. Pennock, and Mrs. Bayard Schieffelin, great-grandchildren of Olivia Lewis Langdon. ■ *Emendations and textual notes:*

90.7	gods. You •	~.—|~
90.8	aṉ •	['n' *partly formed*]
91.11	sympathy •	symatpathy
91.13	& so •	ⱥ & so [*corrected miswriting*]
91.16	ȧ •	[*partly formed; possibly* 'o' *or* 'c']
91.28	money-getting •	money-|getting
91.38	ẉ •	[*possibly partly formed* 'w']
92.3	newspaper •	news-|paper
92.12	newspaper •	news-|paper
92.12	*itself.* This •	~.—|~
92.31	O. FEB 13 •	[O◊ FEB 13] [*badly inked; possibly* 'O. FEB 15']

■ 13 February 1869 · To Mary Mason Fairbanks · Ravenna, Ohio · *UCCL* 00248

■ *Copy-text:* MS, Huntington Library, San Marino, Calif. (CSmH, call no. HM 14241). ■ *Previous publication: MTMF*, 72. ■ *Provenance:* see Huntington Library, pp. 582–83. ■ *Emendations and textual notes:*

93.4	~~ton~~ to-night •	toṉ-night ['ṉ' *partly formed*]

■ 13 and 14 February 1869 · To Olivia L. Langdon · Ravenna, Ohio · *UCCL* 00250

■ *Copy-text:* MS, Mark Twain Papers, The Bancroft Library, University of California, Berkeley (CU-MARK). ■ *Previous publication: LLMT*, 357, brief paraphrase; *MTMF*, 71, 73, brief quotations. ■ *Provenance:* see Samossoud Collection, p. 586. ■ *Emendations and textual notes:*

94.11	able •	abl~~el~~e [*corrected miswriting*]
94.11–12	to-night •	to-|night
95.3	to-morrow •	to-|morrow
95.6–7	~~all the time~~ •	[*heavily canceled*]
95.11	Ḻ •	[*partly formed*]

95.11   Livy$_i$— • ~.—|— [*deletion of period implied*]
95.11   Livy   Good-night • Livy | Good-night
95.28   blessings. That • ~.—|~
96.2   o̶b̶ • ['b' *partly formed*]
96.12   ẇ • [*partly formed*]
97.3   good-night • good-|night

■ 14 February 1869 · To Elisha Bliss, Jr. · Ravenna, Ohio · *UCCL* 00251

■*Copy-text:* MS, University of Pittsburgh, Pittsburgh, Pa. (PPiU). ■*Previous publication:* none known. ■*Provenance:* This letter, presumably kept in the American Publishing Company files after receipt, was tipped into volume 1 of *The Innocents Abroad*, the first volume of a special " 'Manuscript' Set" of the Autograph Edition of *The Writings of Mark Twain* published by the American Publishing Company in 1899. Later sold by a Philadelphia bookseller, Charles Sessler, the set, designated "No. 163" of a limited issue of 512 copies, was eventually purchased by Mrs. Pitt O. Heasley, who donated it to PPiU. ■*Emendations and textual notes:* The MS shows a number of inkblots, evidently from ink splattered at the American Publishing Company after receipt of the letter.

98.4   Sir • S[i]r [*covered by inkblot*]
98.5   your • [y◊◊r] [*covered by inkblot*]

■ 14 February 1869 · To Joseph R. Hawley · Ravenna, Ohio · *UCCL* 00253

■*Copy-text:* MS, Joseph R. Hawley Papers, Connecticut Historical Society, Hartford (CtHi). ■*Previous publication:* none known. ■*Provenance:* This letter may have been donated to CtHi at the time of Hawley's death in 1905. ■*Emendations and textual notes:* none.

■ 14 February 1869 · To Joseph H. Twichell and Family · Ravenna, Ohio · *UCCL* 00252

■*Copy-text:* MS, collection of Chester L. Davis, Jr. ■*Previous publication:* *MTMF*, 74, excerpt; Davis 1976, 1. ■*Provenance:* The MS was evidently returned to Clemens or his daughter Clara by Twichell or Twichell's heirs. It survived in the Samossoud Collection at least until 1947: sometime between then and 1949 Dixon Wecter saw it there and had a typescript made (which is no longer extant). Chester L. Davis, Sr., afterwards acquired the MS directly from

Clara Clemens Samossoud (see Samossoud Collection, p. 586). In 1991 it was sold to an unknown purchaser (Christie 1991, lot 85). ▪*Emendations and textual notes:*

101.11–13   [I . . . two.) • [*sic*]
101.27   third-rate • third-|rate

▪ 15 February 1869 · To Olivia L. Langdon · Ravenna, Ohio · *UCCL* 00254

▪*Copy-text:* MS, Mark Twain Papers, The Bancroft Library, University of California, Berkeley (CU-MARK). ▪*Previous publication:* Wecter 1947b, 66–67; *LLMT*, 357, brief quotation; *MTMF*, 71 (misdated 13 February) and 73, brief quotations. ▪*Provenance:* see Samossoud Collection, p. 586. ▪*Emendations and textual notes:*

102.5   ~~16~~ 15 • 1~~6~~5 ['6' *partly formed*]

▪ 17 February 1869 · To Olivia L. Langdon · Titusville, Pa. · *UCCL* 00255

▪*Copy-text:* MS, Mark Twain Papers, The Bancroft Library, University of California, Berkeley (CU-MARK). ▪*Previous publication:* *LLMT*, 14, 357, brief quotation and paraphrase. ▪*Provenance:* see Samossoud Collection, p. 586. ▪*Emendations and textual notes:*

104.15   ~~st~~ sit • s~~i~~t
104.15   ~~si~~ • ['i' *partly formed; possibly* 'so']
104.24   ~~Mou~~ My • M~~ou~~y ['u' *possibly* 'n']
104.30   ~~cau~~ case • ca~~u~~se
104.34   ~~Ab~~ Auburn • A~~b~~uburn ['b' *partly formed*]
104.36   Good-bye • Good-|bye

▪ 17 February 1869 · To Joseph T. Goodman · Titusville, Pa. · *UCCL* 00256

▪*Copy-text:* Paraphrase, "Mark Twain to be Married," Virginia City *Territorial Enterprise*, 26 Mar 69, 3, PH in Mark Twain Papers, The Bancroft Library, University of California, Berkeley (CU-MARK). The article was probably written by Goodman, although it has also been attributed to William Wright (Dan De Quille) (Loomis, 341). ▪*Previous publication:* none known except the copy-text. ▪*Provenance:* see Tufts Collection, pp. 587–88. ▪*Emendations and textual notes:*

106.3   coal-heaver • coal-|heaver

■ 17 February 1869 · To Mary Mason Fairbanks · Titusville, Pa. ·
    UCCL 00257

■*Copy-text:* MS, Huntington Library, San Marino, Calif. (CSmH, call no. HM
14242). ■*Previous publication: MTMF*, 75; Davis 1979, with omission. ■*Provenance:* see Huntington Library, pp. 582–83. ■*Emendations and textual notes:*

107.10   putting • ['g' *over miswritten* 'n']
107.11   word • woreed
107.16–17   either. Oils • ~.—|~

■ 17 February 1869 · To Mary Mason Fairbanks · Franklin, Pa. ·
    UCCL 00258

■*Copy-text:* MS, Huntington Library, San Marino, Calif. (CSmH, call no. HM
14245). ■*Previous publication: MTMF*, 76–77. ■*Provenance:* see Huntington Library, pp. 582–83. ■*Emendations and textual notes:*

108.4   school-boy • school-|boy
108.6   doń • ['n' *partly formed*]
108.11   di • ['i' *partly formed; possibly* 'de']
108.16   there. On • ~.—|~
108.17   a few • af few [*false start;* 'f' *partly formed*]

■ 18 February 1869 · To the Young Men's Association of Geneseo Academy, *per* Telegraph Operator · Franklin, Pa. · *UCCL* 04736

■*Copy-text:* Paraphrase, "Mark Twain's Lecture," Geneseo (N.Y.) *Genessee Valley Herald*, 24 Feb 69, 3, PH of newsprint in the History Research Office, County
of Livingston, Geneseo, N.Y. ■*Previous publication:* see *Copy-text;* LaVigne, 6,
paraphrase. ■*Provenance:* The original telegram is not known to survive. ■*Emendations and textual notes:* none.

■ 21–22 February 1869 · To the Young Men's Association of Geneseo
    Academy, *per* Telegraph Operator · (1st of 3) · Elmira, N.Y. · *UCCL*
    11696

■*Copy-text:* Paraphrase, "Mark Twain's Lecture," Geneseo (N.Y.) *Genessee Valley Herald*, 24 Feb 69, 3, PH of newsprint in the History Research Office, County
of Livingston, Geneseo, N.Y. ■*Previous publication:* see *Copy-text;* LaVigne, 6,
paraphrase. ■*Provenance:* The original telegram is not known to survive. ■*Emendations and textual notes:* none.

■ 21–22 February 1869 · To the Young Men's Association of Geneseo Academy, *per* Telegraph Operator · (2nd of 3) · Elmira, N.Y. · *UCCL* 05164

■*Copy-text:* Paraphrase, "Mark Twain's Lecture," Geneseo (N.Y.) *Genessee Valley Herald*, 24 Feb 69, 3, PH of newsprint in the History Research Office, County of Livingston, Geneseo, N.Y. ■*Previous publication:* see *Copy-text;* LaVigne, 6, paraphrase. ■*Provenance:* The original telegram is not known to survive. ■*Emendations and textual notes:* none.

■ 21–22 February 1869 · To the Young Men's Association of Geneseo Academy · (3rd of 3) · Elmira, N.Y. · *UCCL* 11536

■*Copy-text:* Paraphrase, "Mark Twain's Lecture," Geneseo (N.Y.) *Genessee Valley Herald*, 24 Feb 69, 3, PH of newsprint in the History Research Office, County of Livingston, Geneseo, N.Y. ■*Previous publication:* see *Copy-text;* LaVigne, 6, paraphrase. ■*Provenance:* Clemens's MS is not known to survive. ■*Emendations and textual notes:* none.

■ 26 February 1869 · To Olivia L. Langdon · Stuyvesant, N.Y. · *UCCL* 00259

■*Copy-text:* MS and enclosed photograph, Mark Twain Papers, The Bancroft Library, University of California, Berkeley (CU-MARK). ■*Previous publication:* *LLMT*, 357, brief paraphrase. ■*Provenance:* see Samossoud Collection, p. 586. ■*Emendations and textual notes:*

112.10–11	~~ther~~ their • the/ir
112.25	"let • ⸤ "~ [*corrected miswriting*]
112.26	Livy/ • [*deletion implied*]
112.33	~~sigh~~ sign • sig/n ['h' *partly formed*]
112.36	little • li[t]tle [*torn before inscription*]

■ 27 February 1869 · To Olivia L. Langdon · Lockport, N.Y. · *UCCL* 00260

■*Copy-text:* MS, Mark Twain Papers, The Bancroft Library, University of California, Berkeley (CU-MARK). ■*Previous publication:* Wecter 1947b, 66, brief quotation; *LLMT*, 67–72; Davis 1977b, 4, excerpt. ■*Provenance:* see Samossoud Collection, p. 586. ■*Emendations and textual notes:*

114.5	to-day • to-|day
115.16	coal-heavers • coal-||heavers
115.29	thousand-dollar • thousand|-dollar

Letter of 27 February 1869 to Olivia L. Langdon. Surviving portion of MS page 5, with part of the first line Clemens tore away from it editorially reconstructed; reproduced at 78 percent of actual size (CU-MARK).

115.32	[j◊◊◊] ros[◊ ◊p] & • [*The conjectured first line of this suppressed passage (see p. 119, n. 6) is based on the hypothetical reconstruction of the torn MS reproduced above.*]
116.1	tick.") He • ~.")—|~
116.25	down-hearted • down-|hearted
117.1	world⸝⸍ You • [*deletion implied*]
117.19	le • ['e' *partly formed*]
117.28	peoples' • [*sic*]
117.33	~~per~~ people • pe⸍ople
118.8	new⸝ • [*deletion implied*]
118.12	daughter • [*doubtful* 'daughte⸍r']

■ 27 February 1869 · To Jane Lampton Clemens and Family · Lockport, N.Y. · *UCCL* 00262

■*Copy-text:* MS, *damage emended,* Jean Webster McKinney Family Papers, Vassar College Library (NPV). ■*Previous publication: MTB,* 1:378–79, excerpts; *MTL,* 156–57, with omissions; *MTMF,* 101, brief quotations; Harnsberger, 56, excerpts. ■*Provenance:* see McKinney Family Papers, pp. 583–85. ■*Emendations and textual notes:* The letter was written on six half-sheets of flimsy paper that has badly deteriorated. Several words, characters, and punctuation marks are wholly or partly missing from pages 1, 2, 4, 5, and 6, but most are readily conjectured from the context. Two substantial passages are missing from pages 5 and 6. The manuscript has been mounted on backing sheets; upon the backing sheet of page 1 Albert Bigelow Paine has supplied several missing words, but his conjectures are not completely sound, although some may have been based on the manuscript when it was in a less damaged state. Readings in the present text that were first supplied by Paine on the manuscript backing sheet are followed in the table below by '(ABP)'; readings first supplied by Paine in *MTL* are followed by '(*MTL*)'; the remaining readings are conjectures by the present editors. See below for illustrations of damaged pages 1, 5, and 6, editorially reconstructed and reproduced at 78 percent of actual size.

120.4	but find (ABP) • but [◊i◊◊] [*torn*]
120.4–5	behindhand instead • behindh[◊◊◊ ◊◊◊]|stead [*torn*]; behind with her in-|stead (ABP); behind with her instead (*MTL*) [*Paine altered Clemens's 'h' to a 'w'*]
120.5	her go without (ABP) • her [◊◊ ◊◊◊◊◊◊◊] [*torn*]
120.5–6	did not mean (ABP) • di[d ◊◊◊ ◊◊◊◊] [*torn*]
120.6	see when (ABP) • s[◊◊ ◊◊◊◊] [*torn*]
120.6	getting ready (ABP) • g[◊◊◊◊◊◊ ◊◊◊◊◊] [*torn*]
120.7	quiet way to (ABP) • qui[◊◊ ◊◊◊ ◊◊] [*torn*]
120.9	position • po-|sit[◊]on [*torn*]
120.16	soldier • soldie[r] [*torn*]
121.6	sensible • s[e◊]sible [*torn*]
121.8	try. In • ~.—|~
121.13	embrace • em[◊]|brace [*torn*]
121.13	pet her • pet h[◊◊] [*torn*]
121.13	she • s[h◊] [*torn*]
121.14	*sweetheart,* instead of • *sweetheart,* [◊◊]ste[◊◊ ◊◊] [*torn*]
121.14	has unlimited • has [◊◊◊]|limited [*torn*]
121.15	father, • fath[◊◊◊] [*torn*]
121.15	except • exc[◊◊◊] [*torn*]
121.16	who • w[h◊] [*torn*]
121.16	lavishes • lavi[◊◊◊◊] [*torn*]
121.18	allowance. • a[llo]wa[nce◊] [*torn*]
121.19	started • s[t◊◊t]ed [*torn*]
121.20	quit • ~~quit~~ quit [*corrected miswriting*]

Lockport, N.Y., Feb. 27.

Dear Folks—

[1]   I enclose $20 for Ma
(No. 10.)   I thought I was getting
a little ahead of her little assess-
ment of $35 a month, but find
I am falling behindhand instead, & have let her go without
money. Well, I did not mean
to do it. But you see when
people have been getting ready
for months, in a quiet way to
get married, they are bound
to grow stingy, & go to saving
up money against the awful
day when it is sure to be
needed. I am particularly anxious to place myself in a po-

Letter of 27 February 1869 to Jane Lampton Clemens and family. Surviving portion of MS page 1, with missing words editorially reconstructed; reproduced at 78 percent of actual size (CU-MARK).

Letter of 27 February 1869 to Jane Lampton Clemens and family. Surviving portion of MS page 5, with missing words editorially reconstructed; reproduced at 78 percent of actual size (CU-MARK).

121.22   Now Lockport wants a • Now [L◇◇◇◇◇◇◇ ◇◇◇◇◇ ◇] [*torn; follows*
             'X' *in pencil in an unidentified hand*]
121.22   shall talk to-night & • shall [t◇◇◇ ◇◇◇◇◇◇◇◇ ◇] [*torn*]
121.22–23   & then I shall go • & [◇◇◇◇ ◇ ◇◇◇◇◇ ◇◇] [*torn*]
121.23   avoiding New • avoi[◇◇◇◇ ◇◇◇] [*torn*]
121.23   possible so as to • possi[◇◇◇ ◇◇ ◇◇ ◇◇] [*torn*]

■ 27 and 28 February 1869 · To Mary Mason Fairbanks · Lockport,
N.Y. · *UCCL* 00261

■*Copy-text:* MS, Huntington Library, San Marino, Calif. (CSmH, call no. HM
14244). ■*Previous publication: MTMF,* 77–81; LaVigne, 6, brief excerpt.
■*Provenance:* see Huntington Library, pp. 582–83. ■*Emendations and textual
notes:*

123.17   Wednesday. I̶ p̶a̶i̶ • ~.—|~ ~
123.21 $̶2̶2̶.̶5̶ $22.25 • $22.ƒ25
123.35   w̶i̶ which • w/hich
124.10   out • out ‖ out
124.12   o̶u̶t̶ ourselves • ou/rselves
124.19   [or] t[w]o[,] n[◇ do◇◇◇◇] A[nd] • [*The conjectured first line of this
             suppressed passage (see p. 125, n. 7) is based on the hypothetical re-
             construction of the torn MS reproduced on p. 611.*]
124.21–22   t̶h̶e̶i̶r̶ there • thei̶rre
124.24   Califor^a·, • [*possibly* 'Califor^a;']
124.25   t̶h̶e̶ that • th/at
124.27   the home • [◇]he home [*torn*]

8

out of the shadows, & their voices out of the echoes that faint along the corridors of memory, & do it without knowing why, but save that we love to do it, we may content ourselves that that friendship is a Reality, & not a Fancy — That it is builded upon a rock, & not upon the sands that dissolve away with the ebbing tides & carry their monuments with them.

I shall reach Hartford about the 5th of March & go to work on the book again — My address will be "148 Asylum street, Hartford" — & on the 17th, if nothing happens, I shall arrive in Elmira again, to stay a week or two, no doubt. And

Letter of 27 and 28 February 1869 to Mary Mason Fairbanks. Surviving portion of MS page 8, with part of the first line Clemens tore away from it editorially reconstructed; reproduced at 78 percent of actual size (CSmH).

■ 28 February 1869 · To Olivia L. Langdon · Rochester, N.Y. · *UCCL* 00263

■*Copy-text:* MS, Mark Twain Papers, The Bancroft Library, University of California, Berkeley (CU-MARK). ■*Previous publication: LLMT*, 357, brief paraphrase; *MTMF*, 81, brief quotation. ■*Provenance:* see Samossoud Collection, p. 586. ■*Emendations and textual notes:*

126.19	~~of~~ • ['f' *partly formed*]
126.23–24	~~Those~~ . . . ~~fifteen~~ • [*false ascenders/descenders; see the illustration, p. 128, n. 2*]
126.28	darling. [That • ~.—|[~
126.29	~~involuntarily~~ • [*false ascenders/descenders*]
127.1	govern • goverɳn
127.3–4	order. [*line space*] "A • ~. ‖ "~
127.9	Livy. So • ~.—|~
127.9–10	useful to me. Useful • ~ ~ ~.—|~
127.12	~~me~~ my • mɇy
127.34	arm. Ain't • ~.—|~
128.1–2	~~tell~~ . . . ~~cus——~~ • [*cancellation tightly looped to hinder decipherment; deletion of dashes implied; see the illustration below, reproduced at 80 percent of actual size*]

128.5	~~Livy,~~ • [*very heavily canceled*]
128.14	~~42~~ 45ᵗʰ • 4ɇ5ᵗʰ
128.14	counsel	councel	~~cons~~ counsel • counsel	councel	co~~n~~sunsel [*The order in which Olivia wrote these words is not evident from their placement.*]

■ 2 March 1869 · To Olivia L. Langdon · Rochester, N.Y. · *UCCL* 00264

■*Copy-text:* MS, Mark Twain Papers, The Bancroft Library, University of California, Berkeley (CU-MARK). ■*Previous publication: LLMT*, 72–77; LaVigne, 6, excerpts. ■*Provenance:* see Samossoud Collection, p. 586. ■*Emendations and textual notes:*

129.8	& collectedly • & c[↔l]‖ & collectedly [*blotted and torn; false as-cenders/descenders*]
129.16	one. This • ~.—|~
129.16–17	lockjaw • lock-‖jaw
129.20	25ᵗʰ. And • ~.—|~
129.21	Ľ • [*partly formed*]
130.4	Ľ • [*partly formed*]
130.7–8	me. [¶] You • ~.—| [¶] ~
130.30	~~the~~ that • th¢at
130.35	I. We • ~.══|~
131.4	scalawags • s¢calawags [*miswritten 'ȼ' or doubtful 'ȼ'*]
131.5	~~mush~~ music • mus~~h~~sic
131.15	*half*-promise • *half*-|promise
131.16–19	(but . . . fortune.} • [*sic*]
131.28	Ĭ • [*partly formed*]
131.28	darling. And • ~.—|~
131.31	~~that you~~◊ • [*partly formed character*]
131.32	~~wh~~ without • wh̸ithout ['h̸' *partly formed*]
132.4	~~ther~~ their • the/ir
132.4	among • amon/g
132.12	ῃ • [*partly formed*]
132.14	~~bles~~ blemish • ble/mish
132.24	is • ~~is~~ is [*corrected miswriting; canceled 's' partly formed*]
132.33–34	Livy. Read • ~.—|~
133.4	it. However • ~.—|~

■ 4 March 1869 · To Olivia L. Langdon · Lockport, N.Y. · *UCCL* 00265

■*Copy-text:* MS, Mark Twain Papers, The Bancroft Library, University of California, Berkeley (CU-MARK). ■*Previous publication: LLMT*, 358, brief paraphrase. ■*Provenance:* see Samossoud Collection, p. 586. ■*Emendations and textual notes:*

134.10	could only see *you* • could ‖ ~~only see you~~ ‖ only see *you* [*revised to avoid show-through*]
135.9	~~ack~~ acquaintance • ack̸-|quaintance ['k' *partly formed; possibly* 't']

■ 5–10 March 1869 · To George W. Elliott · Hartford, Conn. · *UCCL* 11599

■*Copy-text:* Paraphrase, advertising circular for *The Innocents Abroad*, first printed in July 1869 (APC 1869a, 1, see Appendix D), Mark Twain Papers, The

Bancroft Library, University of California, Berkeley (CU-MARK). ■*Previous publication:* Fort Plain (N.Y.) *Mohawk Valley Register*, possibly 9 April 1869. A clipping is missing from page 3 of that date's issue in the surviving file of the *Register* in the Fort Plain Library (Sandra Cronkhite, personal communication). ■*Provenance:* see Mark Twain Papers, pp. 585–86. ■*Emendations and textual notes:* none.

■ 5 March 1869 · To Olivia L. Langdon · Hartford, Conn. · *UCCL* 00267

■*Copy-text:* MS, Mark Twain Papers, The Bancroft Library, University of California, Berkeley (CU-MARK). ■*Previous publication: LLMT*, 358, brief paraphrase. ■*Provenance:* see Samossoud Collection, p. 586. ■*Emendations and textual notes:*

136.2	~~To~~ Not • ~~TNot~~ Not [*rewritten for clarity*]
136.5	abuse • [*doubtful 'a͟buse'; 't' partly formed*]
136.7	~~bel~~ bless • ~~belless~~
136.8–9	rights. But • ~.—|~
136.9	re-inclose • re-|inclose
136.10	~~style,~~ • [*heavily canceled; false ascenders/descenders*]
137.3	~~looot me~~ • [~~looot m~~]e [*torn*]
137.3	ill-natured • ill-|natured
137.13	said, • [*deletion implied*]
137.33	Let by-gones • Let by-|gones

■ 6 March 1869 · To Olivia L. Langdon with a note to Charles J. Langdon · (1st of 2) · Hartford, Conn. · *UCCL* 00268

■*Copy-text:* MS, Mark Twain Papers, The Bancroft Library, University of California, Berkeley (CU-MARK). ■*Previous publication:* Wecter 1947b, 67, brief paraphrase; *LLMT*, 78, 84, 358, excerpt, brief quotation, and paraphrase; *MTMF*, 81–82, excerpts. ■*Provenance:* see Samossoud Collection, p. 586. ■*Emendations and textual notes:*

138.17–18	long. And • ~.—|~
138.20	twelve • ~~twe~~ twelve [*corrected miswriting*]
139.1	you? If • ~?—|~
139.4	room, • [*deletion implied*]
139.6	to,~~let~~ • [*deletion of comma implied*]
139.31	fortnight • fort-|night
139.34	I while • [*sic*]
140.9	~~tir~~ tried • ti͟rried [*canceled 'r' partly formed*]

140.28	down-hearted · down-‖hearted
140.29	ł · [*partly formed*]
141.3	maybe · mayb[e] [*written off edge of page onto next page*]
141.3	slighted · slighte[d] [*written off edge of page onto next page*]
141.18	fireside · fire-|side
141.26	Ą · [*partly formed*]

■ 6 March 1869 · To Olivia L. Langdon with a note to Charles J. Langdon · (2nd of 2) · Hartford, Conn. · *UCCL* 00269

■ *Copy-text:* MS, Mark Twain Papers, The Bancroft Library, University of California, Berkeley (CU-MARK). ■ *Previous publication: LLMT,* 79–83. ■ *Provenance:* see Samossoud Collection, p. 586. ■ *Emendations and textual notes:*

143.7	first-born · first-|born
143.16	~~bless you~~ · [*This was the first of several cancellations in this letter; some, like this, were heavily canceled; some, in addition, used false ascenders and descenders; one was lightly canceled, intended to be read; and one was a combination of the various kinds of cancellations, with Clemens's comment on it (see the entries and illustrations below, and p. 147, n. 3).*]
144.1	**time.** Now · ~.—|~
144.6	~~lap~~ lamps · lap̸mps ['p̸' *partly formed*]
144.20	~~perfect~~ · [*false ascenders/descenders*]
144.23	will. And · ~.—|~
144.26	~~, honey?~~ · [*heavily canceled; for this and the following two cancellations, see the illustration*]
144.27	~~(Don't~~ · [*heavily canceled*]
144.28	anyway.) ~~Let's~~ · ~.)—|~ ['Let's' *possibly* 'Lets'; *heavily canceled*]
144.30	~~You little ras darling,~~ · [*Clemens first lightly canceled* 'ras', *intending Olivia to read it; he then heavily canceled all four words, crossed an* 'l' *and used a false ascender to hinder decipherment; see the illustration below.*]

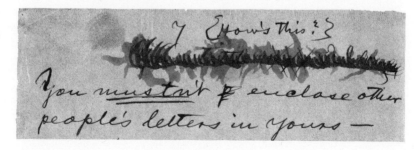

6

but I couldn't help it — I
couldn't help it. Scold a-
way, you darling little ~~Hus-~~
~~band~~ sweetheart — because
I just *know* you will. —
And I expect I deserve it,
maybe. [But I wanted to
come back & go on writing
to you, Livy dear, I guess
that was the reason — now
can't you let that appease
you? ~~xxxxxx~~ — there's a dear,
sweet, precious, good Livy.
I'm *bound* to call on the
Hooker's! E pluribus
Unum! ~~xxxx~~ (I do not
know what
E pluribus Unum means, but
it is a good word, anyway.) —
~~xxxxx~~ (you we will) Kiss & make friends, Livy.]

Letter of 6 March 1869 to Olivia L. Langdon (2nd of 2). MS page 6, showing a cancellation
intended to be read and three unusually heavy cancellations; reproduced at 78 percent of
actual size (CU-MARK).

145.6	with • with ‖ ~~with~~
145.7	kind-hearted • kind-|hearted
145.10	~~by a long shot,~~ • [*heavily canceled*]
145.11	anyway,~~, Livy.~~ • [*heavily canceled*]
145.17	G. [Now • ~.—|[~
145.33	newspaper • news-|paper
146.4	~~bef~~ beware • be*f*ware ['f' *partly formed*]
146.5–6	help. Therefore • ~.—|~
146.15	to-day • to-|day
146.19	to-night • to-|night
146.32	darling. Take • ~.—|~
147.8	50ᵗʰ • ~~50ᵗʰ~~ | 50ᵗʰ [*corrected miswriting*]

■ 8 March 1869 · To Olivia L. Langdon with a note to Charles J. Langdon · Hartford, Conn. · *UCCL* 00271

■ *Copy-text:* MS, Mark Twain Papers, The Bancroft Library, University of California, Berkeley (CU-MARK). ■ *Previous publication: LLMT*, 83, 358, excerpts and brief paraphrase. ■ *Provenance:* see Samossoud Collection, p. 586. ■ *Emendations and textual notes:*

148.3–4	day. I • ~.—|~
148.6	foreborne • [*sic*]
149.4	3 • ~~3~~ 3 [*corrected miswriting*]
149.24	Good-bye • Good-|bye

■ 8–10 March 1869 · To John Russell Young · Hartford, Conn. · *UCCL* 00270

■ *Copy-text:* MS, Papers of John Russell Young, Library of Congress, Washington, D.C. (DLC). ■ *Previous publication:* none known. ■ *Provenance:* donated to DLC in 1924 by May Davids (Mrs. John Russell) Young and Gordon R. Young. ■ *Emendations and textual notes:* The MS is torn along the left margin, removing some characters or portions of characters.

150.6	Hartford • [◊]artford [*torn*]
150.6	so • [◊]o [*torn*]
150.6	other • [◊]ther [*torn*]

150.8	Pilgrim's • Pil-	[◊]rim's [*torn*]
150.8	issue • is-	[◊u]e [*torn*]
150.9	200 • [2]oo [*torn*]

■ 8 and 9 March 1869 · To Olivia L. Langdon · Hartford, Conn. ·
UCCL 00272

■ *Copy-text:* MS, Mark Twain Papers, The Bancroft Library, University of California, Berkeley (CU-MARK), is copy-text for the letter. Neither enclosure survives. Copy-text for the first, a partial clipping of the 5 March "Friday Miscellany" from the Elmira *Advertiser* (Thomas K. Beecher 1869d; see p. 157, n. 5), is a microfilm edition of the newspaper in CU-MARK. Because a fully legible photographic facsimile is not feasible, it is reprinted here line-for-line. Copy-text for the second, a full-page illustration proof for *The Innocents Abroad* ("Pyramids and Sphynx"), is the published illustration facing page 629 in the first issue of the first American edition, reproduced here at 67 percent of actual size from a copy owned by Robert H. Hirst now on deposit in CU-MARK. ■ *Previous publication: LLMT*, 74, 358, brief excerpt and paraphrase. ■ *Provenance:* see Samossoud Collection, p. 586. ■ *Emendations and textual notes:*

152.3	earth. Tell • ~.—	~
152.4	Louise⫽. Every • ~⫽.—	~
152.7	a̶t̶ as • a⫽s
152.9	of • of ‖ o̶f̶
152.32	y̶o̶u̶ ̶o̶b̶s̶t̶i̶n̶a̶t̶e̶ ̶t̶h̶i̶n̶g̶?̶ • [y◊u ◊]b[◊t◊◊◊◊te]̶ ̶t̶h̶i̶n̶g̶?̶ [*torn*]
153.20	misshapen • mis-	shapen
154.33	regard. Thank • ~.—	~

■ 10 March 1869 · To Olivia L. Langdon and Charles J. Langdon ·
Hartford, Conn. · *UCCL* 00274

■ *Copy-text:* MS, Mark Twain Papers, The Bancroft Library, University of California, Berkeley (CU-MARK). ■ *Previous publication: LLMT*, 358, brief paraphrase; *MTMF*, 85, brief excerpts. ■ *Provenance:* see Samossoud Collection, p. 586. ■ *Emendations and textual notes:*

| 158.25 | storm,— • [*possibly* 'storm⸴—', *deletion implied; dash extends above comma*] |
| 158.25 | lecture • le[c]ture [*torn*] |

158.28	storm⊥ • [*dash partly formed*]
159.9	look • ʃ look [*corrected miswriting;* 'ʃ' *partly formed*]
159.11	concerning • ['ni' *conflated*]
159.13	yesterday • yester[da]y [*torn*]
159.17	i̶m̶ in • im̸n
159.18–19	MS. [¶] Do • ~.—| [¶] ~
159.23–24	(*I* . . . name.] • [*sic*]
159.24	G̶o̶ ̶t̶o̶ Good • Good ˄to˄

■ 12 March 1869 · To Olivia L. Langdon · Hartford, Conn. · *UCCL* 00275

■*Copy-text:* MS, Mark Twain Papers, The Bancroft Library, University of California, Berkeley (CU-MARK). ■*Previous publication: LLMT*, 9, 83–84, 358, excerpts and brief paraphrase. ■*Provenance:* see Samossoud Collection, p. 586.
■*Emendations and textual notes:*

161.1	12 • [*doubtful* '1ʃ2'; '3' *partly formed*]
161.3	I • [*partly formed*]
161.6	noted,⁻˄ • [*deletion implied*]
161.14	e̶x̶p̶ • ['p' *partly formed*]
162.9	aʃ • [*partly formed* 'l'; *possibly* 't' *or* 'b']
162.9	i̶f̶ is • iʃs
162.15	t̶w̶ toward • tⱳoward
162.18	p̶h̶y̶- philosophy • p̱hilos-y̶-|ophy
162.18	l̶e̶t̶t̶e̶ lesson • l̶e̶t̶tesson
162.32	m̶e̶ my • mⱷy
162.32	f̶o̶r̶n̶ fortnight • forⱷtnight ['ⱷ' *partly formed*]
162.33	o̶n̶ • ['n' *partly formed*]
162.34	i̶n̶ it • iⱷt ['n' *partly formed*]
163.2	it. You • ~.—|~
163.5	u̶m̶ uneasiness • uⱷnea-|siness
163.6	darting • [*sic*]
163.10	i̶d̶e̶ idle • idⱷle ['ⱷ' *partly formed*]
163.16	ⱷ • [*partly formed, possibly* 'a']
163.17	ⱷ • [*partly formed, possibly* 'a']
163.20	"Grandmaⱷ," • ['ⱷ' *partly formed*]
163.22	y̶o̶u̶ ̶s̶a̶y̶ ˄one says˄ you say˄ • y̶o̶u̶ ˄o̶n̶e̶˄ ˄you˄ sayⱷ
163.24	s̶h̶ • ['h' *partly formed*]
163.36	to-night • to-|night
163.37	WOE • ['Woe' *underscored three times*]

164.5	*that.* But • ~.—|~
164.5	~~glory~~ • ['y' *partly formed*]
164.13	XIII • [*small capitals simulated, not underscored*]
164.17	to-morrow • to-|morrow
164.18	literary • ~~literary~~ literary [*corrected miswriting*]
164.23	HARTFORD • HAR[TFO]RD [*stamped off edge of envelope*]

■ 12–13 March 1869 · To Olivia L. Langdon · Hartford, Conn. ·
UCCL 11634

■ *Copy-text:* MS, Mark Twain Papers, The Bancroft Library, University of California, Berkeley (CU-MARK). ■ *Previous publication:* none known. ■ *Provenance:* see Samossoud Collection, p. 586. ■ *Emendations and textual notes:* none.

■ 13 March 1869 · To Horatio C. King and John R. Howard · Hartford,
Conn. · *UCCL* 11118

■ *Copy-text:* MS, Special Collections, Dickinson College, Carlisle, Pa. (PCarlD).
■ *Previous publication:* none known. ■ *Provenance:* donated to PCarlD by Constance Gray (Mrs. Merwin Kimball) Hart, granddaughter of Horatio C. King.
■ *Emendations and textual notes:*

166.14	over • ov/er
167.8	HARTFORD • H[ARTFOR]D [*badly inked*]

■ 13 March 1869 · To Mary Mason Fairbanks · Hartford, Conn. ·
UCCL 00276

■ *Copy-text:* MS, *damage emended*, Huntington Library, San Marino, Calif.
(CSmH, call no. HM 14246). ■ *Previous publication: MTMF*, 83–86. ■ *Provenance:* see Huntington Library, pp. 582–83. ■ *Emendations and textual notes:* Portions of the MS are torn (the right margin of MS page 1, a lower left portion of page 4, and the left margin of page 6), obliterating some characters or portions of characters. See below for illustrations of damaged pages 1 and 4, editorially reconstructed and reproduced at 78 percent of actual size.

168.5   calamity, • calam[i◊◊] [*torn*]

168.5   and • an[d] [*torn*]

168.6   not • n[◊◊] [*torn*]

168.7   continue • con[◊]|tinue

168.7   ~~Only~~ • O[n]~~ly~~ [*torn*]

168.8   had been • had been̸n

168.11   have • have have

168.29   a • a̸

168.32   ~~paten~~ • ['n' *partly formed*]

169.1   have • [◊a]ve [*torn*]

169.2   far-fetched • far-|fetched

169.4   ~~sh~~ say • s̸h̸ay ['h' *partly formed, possibly* 't']

169.10   t̸ • [*partly formed*]

169.11   title • titlle [*miswritten*]

169.16   of. I • ~.—|~
169.20   to come • [t]o come [*torn*]
169.20   long • [l]ong [*torn*]
169.20–21   California. Because • ~.—|~

■ 13 March 1869 · To Olivia L. Langdon · Hartford, Conn. · *UCCL* 00277

■ *Copy-text:* MS, Mark Twain Papers, The Bancroft Library, University of California, Berkeley (CU-MARK). ■ *Previous publication: LLMT*, 83, 358, brief paraphrases; *MTMF*, 82, brief excerpt. ■ *Provenance:* see Samossoud Collection, p. 586. ■ *Emendations and textual notes:*

171.2   midnight • mid-|night
171.8   blank?— • ~?—|—
171.9   it?— • ~?—|—
171.9   ~~this~~ that • thisat
172.1   ~~Monday~~ • ['y' *partly formed*]
172.3   rest. But • ~.—|~
172.21   ṁ • [*possibly* 'w' *or* 'n']
173.7   startled • [*possibly* 'startdled']
173.19   ~~vol~~ • [*possibly* 'wh' *with* 'h' *partly formed*]
173.25   whole-hearted • whole-|hearted
173.31   ~~when~~ • [*possibly* 'where']
173.38   will • [*sic*]

■ 24 March 1869 · To Mary Mason Fairbanks · Elmira, N.Y. · *UCCL* 00278

■ *Copy-text:* MS, Huntington Library, San Marino, Calif. (CSmH, call no. HM 14247). ■ *Previous publication: MTMF*, 86–88. ■ *Provenance:* see Huntington Library, pp. 582–83. ■ *Emendations and textual notes:*

176.4   Mother— • [*After writing the salutation, Clemens turned the page ninety degrees clockwise and wrote the remainder of the letter perpendicular to the letterhead, dateline, and salutation.*]

■ 26? March 1869 · To Jane Lampton Clemens and Family · Elmira, N.Y. · *UCCL* 00285

■ *Copy-text:* MS facsimile. The editors have not seen the MS, but in 1977 Chester L. Davis, Sr., then executive secretary of the Mark Twain Research Foundation in Perry, Mo., provided a photocopy to the Mark Twain Papers. The surviving MS consists of one leaf, numbered "7" on the recto and unnumbered on the verso. The first three leaves (pages 1–6) are missing. The paper is the same Langdon stationery that Clemens used in his 30 March letter to Elisha Bliss (see the next commentary). The ink (described as "pinkish" by Wecter on the typescript) was probably purple—the same bluish violet shade Clemens used in Elmira throughout 1869 and until mid-1877 in letters and manuscripts (see *P&P*, 455). ■*Previous publication: LLMT*, 85, with omission; Davis 1977a. ■*Provenance:* The MS was evidently returned to Clemens by Pamela Moffett, for it survived in the Samossoud Collection at least until 1947: sometime between then and 1949 Dixon Wecter saw it and had a typescript made. Davis afterwards acquired the MS directly from Clara Clemens Samossoud (see Samossoud Collection, p. 586). ■*Emendations and textual notes:*

177.10	~~hours——~~ •	*[deletion of dash implied]*
178.2	[I •	*[no closing bracket]*

■ 30 March 1869 · To Elisha Bliss, Jr. · Elmira, N.Y. · *UCCL* 00279

■*Copy-text:* MS, Mark Twain Papers, The Bancroft Library, University of California, Berkeley (CU-MARK). A photographic facsimile of the letter is on pp. 530–31. The MS consists of one leaf (torn from a folder) of blue-lined off-white wove paper, 4 by 6 inches, with an embossed "L," inscribed on both sides in black ink. The right margin of the verso is overlaid with a strip of paper applied when the MS was tipped into a book. ■*Previous publication:* Parke-Bernet 1938a, lot 126, excerpt; *MTMF*, 88, brief quotation; *MTLP*, 17–18. ■*Provenance:* see Mendoza Collection, p. 587. ■*Emendations and textual notes:* none.

■ 9 and 31 March 1869 · To Susan L. Crane · Hartford, Conn., and Elmira, N.Y. · *UCCL* 00273

■*Copy-text:* MS, Mark Twain Papers, The Bancroft Library, University of California, Berkeley (CU-MARK). ■*Previous publication:* none known. ■*Provenance:* This letter, evidently the document sent to Susan Crane, remained in the Langdon family until 1972 when it was donated to CU-MARK by Mrs. Eugene Lada-Mocarski, Jervis Langdon, Jr., Mrs. Robert S. Pennock, and Mrs. Bayard Schieffelin. ■*Emendations and textual notes:*

180.4	thank you •	thank̸ you [*false start*]
180.6	Elmira •	Ɇ Elmira [*corrected miswriting*]
180.8	ѡ •	[*partly formed, possibly 'v' or 'u'*]
180.13	secret, •	[*comma in purple ink covered by stray mark in brown ink, not intended as a cancellation*]
180.15	prophecied •	[*sic*]

180.20	Mr. • [*possibly* 'Mr.ş', *deletion of partly formed* 's' *implied*]
180.23	cou • ['u' *partly formed*]
180.30	br birds • bⱼirds
180.33	coachman • coach-|man
181.11	new-fangled • new-|fangled
181.16	extra-hazardous • extra-|hazardous
181.17	**some** • [*possibly* 'some'; *heavy underscore with a pronounced waver traced over*]
181.19	has. She • ~.—|~
181.21	must • musust [*corrected miswriting*]
181.22	outⱼ; • [*possibly* 'outⱼ,', *deletion implied*]
181.22	those the • theose
181.33	& • [*possibly* 'ℓ']
181.33–34	THINGS things • [*two underscores altered to one*]
181.34	familiarⱼ • [*deletion implied*]
181.34	memory,— • [*deletion implied*]
182.7	LIVY. • ['Livy' *underscored three times. The signature was almost certainly written by Clemens, although the handwriting resembles Olivia's (see the illustration reproduced below at 78 percent of actual size). Even if she had signed it, however, it is likely that he would have added the three underscores.*]

■ 31 March and 1 April 1869 · From Samuel L. Clemens and Olivia L. Langdon to Mary Mason Fairbanks · Elmira, N.Y. · *UCCL* 00280

■*Copy-text:* MS, Huntington Library, San Marino, Calif. (CSmH, call no. HM 14248), is copy-text for the letter. The enclosure, an illustration which Clemens cut out of the *Innocents Abroad* proof sheets ("Poet Lariat"), does not survive. Copy-text is the published illustration on page 91 in the first issue of the first American edition, reproduced actual size from a copy owned by Robert H. Hirst now on deposit in CU-MARK. ■*Previous publication: MTMF*, 88–90, without the enclosure. ■*Provenance:* see Huntington Library, pp. 582–83. ■*Emendations and textual notes:*

185.6	Comm[i]ssioner • ['mm' *conflated*]
185.18	~~bu~~ both • b~~/~~oth
185.20	~~blamed if~~ • [*canceled by Olivia Langdon*]
185.30	~~snaked~~ • [*canceled by Olivia Langdon*]
185.35	~~Drat~~ {Those • [*revised by Olivia Langdon*]
186.1	~~bullyer~~ • [*canceled by Olivia Langdon*]
186.1	appropriate • appr[o]priate [*badly inked*]
186.3	~~busted~~ • [*canceled by Olivia Langdon*]
186.10	ELMIRA N.Y. • [E◊◊]IRA [N◊◊]. [*badly inked*]

■ 10? April 1869 · To Elisha Bliss, Jr. · Elmira, N.Y. · *UCCL* 00288

■ *Copy-text:* None. The text is based on four transcripts:

P¹	*MTB*, 1:380
P²	Parke-Bernet 1938c, lot 47
P³	Typescript in CU-MARK
P⁴	Davis 1951b

P¹ may have derived either from the MS or from a handwritten transcription of it (now lost) made by Dana Ayer; P² derived directly from the MS; and P³ and P⁴ each derived independently from Ayer. Albert Bigelow Paine had transcribed the short excerpt that appears in P¹ by 1912 ('Your . . . proofs' [188.3]), the same year he published the identical text, with only an editorial change in the final punctuation, in Paine, 944. If he had seen the MS, rather than the Ayer transcription, it was no longer available five years later (*MTL*, 1:157). P², however, which published the dateline, signature, and three excerpts ('the Queen of Greece' [187.3–4], 'is . . . it' [187.4–5], and 'I think . . . foolish' [187.11–12]), was certainly based on the MS, which had fallen into private hands by 1938 (see *Provenance*). The identical text was republished with no changes in Parke-Bernet 1941, lot 87. P³, a typescript made by Bernard DeVoto from the Ayer transcription, was made in 1942 while the transcription was still in Brownell's possession. P⁴ apparently derived independently from the Ayer transcription after the Brownell Collection had moved to WU. ■ *Previous publication:* see *Copytext; MTLP*, 20–21; McBride, 365, excerpt. ■ *Provenance:* The MS evidently remained among the American Publishing Company's records until it was first sold (and probably at that time was copied by Dana Ayer; see Brownell Collection, pp. 581–82). The MS was eventually acquired by William Randolph Hearst, who sold it in 1938, presumably to Harold Fisher, who in turn sold it in 1941 (Parke-Bernet 1938c and 1941). Its present location is unknown. ■ *Emendations, adopted readings, and textual notes:* Adopted readings followed by '(C)' are editorial emendations of the source readings.

187.1	Elmira, April Something, 1869. (P³,⁴) • Elmira, *April Something*, 1869. [*reported, not quoted*] (P²); [*not in*] (P¹)
187.2–3	Friend . . . Jam (P³,⁴) • [*not in*] (P¹,²)

187.2	Bliss— (C) • ~: (P[4]); ~:— (P[3])
187.3–4	the . . . Greece (P[2,3,4]) • [*not in*] (P[1])
187.4	in anywhere. She (P[3,4]) • [*not in*] (P[1,2])
187.4–5	is . . . it. (P[3,4]) • ~ . . . ~$_\wedge$ (P[2]); [*not in*] (P[1])
187.5	& (P[2]) • and (P[3,4])
187.5–10	*No* . . . Greece.) (C) • ~ . . . ~.$_\wedge$ (P[3]); **No** . . . ~.) (P[4]); [*not in*] (P[1,2])
187.7	*Scylla & Charybdis* (P[3]) • **Scylla and Charybdis** (P[4])
187.7	*before* (P[3]) • **before** (P[4])
187.11–12	I . . . foolish (P[2,3,4]) • [*not in*] (P[1])
187.12	funny (P[2]) • ~, (P[3,4])
187.12–188.2	—& . . . it.) (C) • —and . . . ~., (P[3,4]); [*not in*] (P[1,2]) ['&' *also emended from* 'and' *at 187.12* ('& was'), *14, and 188.2* (*twice*)]
188.2	*meaning* (P[3]) • **meaning** (P[4])
188.3	Your . . . proofs. (P[3,4]) • ~ . . . ~$_\wedge$ (P[1]); [*not in*] (P[2])
188.4	Always, &c., (C) • Always, etc., (P[3,4]); [*not in*] (P[1,2])
188.5	Mark. (P[3,4]) • ~$_\wedge$ [*reported, not quoted*] (P[2]); [*not in*] (P[1])

■ 10? April 1869 · To Pamela A. Moffett · Elmira, N.Y. · *UCCL* 00289

■*Copy-text:* MS, collection of Chester L. Davis, Jr. ■*Previous publication: MFMT*, 14, with omissions; *LLMT*, 85–86. ■*Provenance:* The MS was evidently returned to Clemens by Pamela Moffett, for it survived in the Samossoud Collection at least until 1947: sometime between then and 1949 Dixon Wecter saw it and had a typescript made (now in CU-MARK). Chester L. Davis, Sr., afterwards acquired the MS directly from Clara Clemens Samossoud (see Samossoud Collection, p. 586). In 1991 it was sold to an unknown purchaser (Christie 1991, lot 87). ■*Emendations and textual notes:*

189.4	myself. She • ~.—|~
189.9	m̶ • [*partly formed*]
189.18	t̶h̶ • [*partly formed*]
189.31	h̶e̶r̶ their • their$_{\wedge\wedge}$

■ 12 April 1869 · To Mary Mason Fairbanks · Elmira, N.Y. · *UCCL* 00282

■*Copy-text:* MS and enclosed illustration proofs, Huntington Library, San Marino, Calif. (CSmH, call no. HM 14249). ■*Previous publication: MTMF*, 90–91, without the enclosures. ■*Provenance:* see Huntington Library, pp. 582–83. ■*Emendations and textual notes:*

190.3   ʃ • [*partly formed*]
190.19   3.—The • ~.—|~ ['3.—' *marked to close up to* 'The']

■ 12 April 1869 · To Elisha Bliss, Jr. · Elmira, N.Y. · *UCCL* 00281

■*Copy-text:* MS, Mark Twain Papers, The Bancroft Library, University of California, Berkeley (CU-MARK). ■*Previous publication: MTMF*, 90, brief excerpt; Davis 1951b, with omission; *MTLP*, 18–19; McBride, 365, brief paraphrase. ■*Provenance:* see Mendoza Collection, p. 587. ■*Emendations and textual notes:*

192.12   o̶r̶ of • oɟf
193.2   T̶h̶e̶ E͟ *Crusade of the Innocents* • [*underscored before deletion of* 'The']

■ 15 April 1869 · To Elisha Bliss, Jr. · Elmira, N.Y. · *UCCL* 00283

■*Copy-text:* MS, Willard S. Morse Collection, Collection of American Literature, Beinecke Rare Book and Manuscript Library, Yale University (CtY-BR). ■*Previous publication: MTMF*, 93, brief quotation. ■*Provenance:* donated to CtY in 1942 by Walter F. Frear. ■*Emendations and textual notes:*

194.3   it • [*doubtful* 'iø̸t'; *partly formed letter*]
194.6   m̶a̶d̶e̶ make • maɖke
194.7   book. It • ~.—|~

■ 15 April 1869 · To Mary Mason Fairbanks · Elmira, N.Y. · *UCCL* 00284

■*Copy-text:* MS, Huntington Library, San Marino, Calif. (CSmH, call. no. HM 14250). ■*Previous publication: MTMF*, 91–94. ■*Provenance:* see Huntington Library, pp. 582–83. ■*Emendations and textual notes:*

195.22   ʃ • [*partly formed*]
195.26   t̶h̶i̶n̶ • ['n' *partly formed*]
196.4   hence. I • ~.—|~

■ 20 April 1869 · To Elisha Bliss, Jr. · Elmira, N.Y. · *UCCL* 00286

■*Copy-text:* MS, Mark Twain Papers, The Bancroft Library, University of California, Berkeley (CU-MARK). ■*Previous publication: MTB*, 1:380, brief quotation; Parke-Bernet 1938a, lot 126, brief quotation; *MTMF*, 93, brief excerpts; Davis 1951a; Davis 1959, 1; *MTLP*, 19–20. ■*Provenance:* see Mendoza Collection, p. 587. ■*Emendations and textual notes:*

197.6	villainy • [*second 'i' retraced, possibly for emphasis*]
197.7	liquifies • [*second 'i' retraced and underscored*]
197.7	idiot,— • [*deletion of dash implied*]

■ 20 April 1869 · To James Redpath · Elmira, N.Y. · *UCCL* 00287

■*Copy-text:* Merwin-Clayton, lot 126. ■*Previous publication:* none known except the copy-text. ■*Provenance:* The present location of the MS is not known. ■*Emendations and textual notes:* The Merwin-Clayton catalog does not identify the addressee, describing the letter as an "A. L. S. 1 page, 4to. Apl. 20, 1869." The paper was probably the same as that Clemens used for his letters to Elisha Bliss of 12, 20, and 29 April: white wove, unwatermarked, measuring 10⁹⁄₁₆ by 8¹⁄₁₆ inches, ruled in light blue.

199.1	Apl. 20, 1869. • [*reported, not quoted*]
199.3	& • and
199.4	all • all," etc.
199.6–7	Samuel . . . Twain. • Signed "Samuel L. Clemens;" also "Mark Twain."

■ 29 April 1869 · To Elisha Bliss, Jr. · Elmira, N.Y. · *UCCL* 00290

■*Copy-text:* MS, Mark Twain Papers, The Bancroft Library, University of California, Berkeley (CU-MARK); enclosed photographic *carte de visite* of Abd-el-Kader, Henry W. and Albert A. Berg Collection, The New York Public Library, Astor, Lenox and Tilden Foundations, New York City (NN-B); enclosed *cartes* of the Viceroy of Egypt and Sultan of Turkey, Willard S. Morse Collection, Collection of American Literature, Beinecke Rare Book and Manuscript Library, Yale University (CtY-BR). The rectos of each enclosure are reproduced in facsimile; the versos are transcribed, incorporating a facsimile of the Sultan of Turkey's signature from the originals. Although Clemens does not specifically refer to the second and third enclosures in this letter, it is unlikely that he returned them to Bliss much earlier than this date, and certainly he would not have had them early enough to enclose in his letter of 15 April, with which they were later sold (see *Provenance*). Bliss, who was working consecutively through the book, had probably discovered his question about the second enclosure when he questioned the placement of the first; Clemens had marked them both with the same manuscript page number. Engravings made from these two photographs were published in chapter 57 of *The Innocents Abroad*, on pages 614 and 612. ■*Previous publication:* letter and inscriptions on Abd-el-Kader enclosure: AAA/Anderson 1936, lot 72, brief excerpt; letter only: Davis 1951b, excerpt; *MTLP*, 21–22. ■*Provenance:* Sometime before 1938, the letter was owned by E. E. Moore of Pittsburgh, who lent it to George H. Brownell to transcribe (although Brownell evidently already had an Ayer transcription). In 1938, after having been acquired by George C. Smith, Jr., the MS was sold to C. W. Force. It was acquired in 1957 by CU-MARK (see Mendoza Collection, p. 587). The Abd-el-Kader photograph (NN-B) was sold, along with a transcription of the letter, in the 1936 sale of the collection of Irving S. Underhill. Its provenance from 1936 until its acquisition by NN-B is unknown. The photographs of the Viceroy of Egypt and Sultan of Turkey (CtY-BR), which had been inserted into a first edition of *Innocents* along with Clemens's letter of 15 April 1869 to Bliss and other items, were in 1942 sold as part of the Morse Collection and donated to CtY by Walter F. Frear. ■*Emendations and textual notes:* The MS was written in purple ink and subsequently splashed with black ink, probably upon receipt, since the dockets are also in black ink.

200.3	~~pub~~ put • pu~~b~~t
200.19	Mark Twain • [*Clemens extended his signature with several extra minims and an ornate, looped paraph*]
201.4	jam • ~~jam~~ jam [*corrected miswriting*]

■ 8 May 1869 · To Olivia L. Langdon · New York, N.Y. · *UCCL* 00291

■*Copy-text:* MS, Mark Twain Papers, The Bancroft Library, University of California, Berkeley (CU-MARK). ■*Previous publication:* none known. ■*Provenance:* see Samossoud Collection, p. 586. ■*Emendations and textual notes:*

204.6	me, • [*deletion implied*]
204.9	Bliss's • [*sic*]
204.14	brisk • bris~~h~~k
204.18–19	sunsets • sun-|sets
204.26	added • adde[d] [*torn*]
204.27	t • [*partly formed*]
204.28	~~woul~~ wounds • wou~~l~~nds
205.5	hungry • ['un' *conflated*]
205.10	Langdon • Langdo[n] [*torn*]
205.10	York • Yor[k] [*torn*]
205.12	YORK. MAY 8 • [YO]RK. [M]AY 8 [*badly inked*]
205.12	MAY 8 4 P.M. • MAY [8] [4] P.M[◊] [*badly inked*]

■ 8 May 1869 · To Olivia L. Langdon · Hartford, Conn. · *UCCL* 00292

■*Copy-text:* MS, Mark Twain Papers, The Bancroft Library, University of California, Berkeley (CU-MARK). ■*Previous publication: LLMT*, 358, brief paraphrase. ▪*Provenance:* see Samossoud Collection, p. 586. ▪*Emendations and textual notes:*

206.13	bitter • ~~btt~~ bitter [*corrected miswriting*]
206.13	~~see~~ separation • se¢paration [*doubtful* 'se~~e~~pparation']
206.13	seems. Livy • ~.—|~
207.9	another • ~~an~~ | another [*corrected miswriting*]
207.21	moment, • moment[,] [*written off edge of page*]
207.22	didn't • didn'[t] [*written off edge of page*]
207.23	the • th[e] [*written off edge of page*]
207.31	Langdon • Langdo[n] [*torn*]
207.31	York • Yor[k] [*torn*]

▪ 9 May 1869 · To Olivia L. Langdon · Hartford, Conn. · *UCCL* 00293

▪*Copy-text:* MS, Mark Twain Papers, The Bancroft Library, University of California, Berkeley (CU-MARK). ▪*Previous publication: LLMT*, 358, brief paraphrase. ▪*Provenance:* see Samossoud Collection, p. 586. ▪*Emendations and textual notes:*

210.23	~~gr~~ glow • g⁄low ['r' *partly formed*]
210.24	her. Anybody • ~.—|~
210.25	~~reg~~ respect • re¢spect

▪ 10 May 1869 · To Mary Mason Fairbanks · Hartford, Conn. · *UCCL* 00296

▪*Copy-text:* MS, Huntington Library, San Marino, Calif. (CSmH, call no. HM 14240). ▪*Previous publication: LLMT*, 89, brief excerpt; *MTMF*, 94–98; Harnsberger, 55, brief excerpt. ▪*Provenance:* see Huntington Library, pp. 582–83. ▪*Emendations and textual notes:*

211.13–14	~~jug~~ judgment • ju¢dgment
212.4	ranche • [*sic*]
212.5	I⁄ • [*partly formed*]
212.6	away, • away[,] [*written off edge of page onto next page*]
212.6	disobey • dis-[-]|obey [*hyphen written off edge of page onto next page*]
212.7	about • abou[t] [*written off edge of page onto next page*]

212.8   she they • ₰they

212.12   of • o[f] | of [*written off edge of page onto next page*]

212.15   Viceroy • Vice-|roy

212.16   half-soled • half-|soled

212.26   thou thoroughly • thoṷroughly ['ṷ' *partly formed*]

212.35–36 day. [*paragraph indention deleted*] Charley • ~.—‖ —— ~

212.38   to-day • to-|day

212.39   within • with[-]|in [*written off edge of page onto next page*]

213.2   say stay • saytay [*canceled* 'y' *partly formed*]

■ 10 May 1869 · To James Redpath · Hartford, Conn. · *UCCL* 00298
■ *Copy-text:* This five-leaf, ten-page letter has been reconstructed from four separate sources:

P¹	AAA 1925, lot 107
P²	Typescript in CU-MARK
P³	MS pages 7–8 in CtY-BR
P⁴	PH of MS page 10 (AAA 1925, lot 107)

P¹ and P² derive independently from the MS. Where the MS and an MS facsimile survive, P³ and P⁴ respectively serve as sole copy-text for the letter. The extracts in P¹ were published in AAA 1925, lot 107, when the MS was intact. P², a partial TS in CU-MARK made by Frank Glenn in 1943, was prepared from the MS after two leaves (pages 5–6 and 7–8) had been removed from it. P³, one of those leaves (pages 7–8), survives in the Collection of American Literature, Beinecke Rare Book and Manuscript Library, Yale University (CtY-BR). P⁴, a photofacsimile of MS page 10, was published with the P¹ extracts in AAA 1925, lot 107. ■ *Previous publication:* none known except P.¹ ■ *Provenance:* The MS was intact in 1925, when it was sold as part of the library of William F. Gable (AAA 1925, lot 107). By 1940, two leaves (MS pages 5–6 and 7–8) had been removed from the letter (Parke-Bernet 1940, lot 69), and by 1942 they had been tipped into first edition copies of *The Innocents Abroad* and *Roughing It*, respectively, which were sold as part of the estate of William H. Woodin of New York (Parke-Bernet 1942, lot 129, which mistakenly identifies the recipient of Clemens's letter as "Major Pond, his lecture manager"). The remainder of the letter (MS pages 1–4 and 9–10) was transcribed by Frank Glenn, a Kansas City, Mo., book dealer, with no indication that any text was missing, and the transcription was sent to Bernard DeVoto in 1943. The copy of *Roughing It* containing MS pages 7–8 was donated to CtY in 1943 by George Corey, but the present location of the rest of the MS is not known. ■ *Emendations, adopted readings, and textual notes:* Adopted readings followed by '(C)' are editorial emendations of the source readings.

214.1–215.3   148 . . . everybody. (P[1]) • 114 . . . ~. (P[2]); [*not in*] (P[3,4])

214.1   148 [*reported, not quoted*] (P[1]) • 114 (P[2])

214.2   Co. (P[2]) • Company [*reported, not quoted*] (P[1])

214.3   Hartford, [*reported, not quoted*] (P[1]) • Hartfor. (P[2])

214.3   May 10 (C) • May 10, 1869 [*reported, not quoted*] (P[1]); May 10
              (1869) (P[2])

214.4   Jas. (P[1]) • ~$_\wedge$ (P[2])

214.5–10   Dear . . . 2. (P[2]) • [*not in*] (P[1])

214.8   name "from (C) • ~"~ (P[2])

214.10   & (P[2]) • and (P[1]) [*also at 214.15, 215.1* ('& peculiar'), *3*]

214.11–14   decreasing . . . it. (P[2]) • [*not in*] (P[1])

214.13   secured (C) • securred (P[2])

215.1   grand, (P[2]) • ~$_\wedge$ (P[1])

215.1–2   and . . . means. (P[2]) • [*not in*] (P[1])

215.1   wouldn't (C) • would'nt (P[2])

215.3   journeys, (P[1]) • ~$_\wedge$ (P[2])

215.4–20   (There . . . mine.) (P[2]) • [*not in*] (P[1,3,4])

215.4   "condition" about (C) • $_\wedge$~$_\wedge$ "~(P[2])

215.9   Monthly (C) • Monthlym (P[2])

215.10–11   [*in margin:* Until . . . signify.] (C) • [*The sentence appears without
              indention in* P[2], *as the second paragraph of the postscript at the very
              end of the letter. But* P[4], *the photofacsimile of the last manuscript page,
              shows that the sentence did not in fact appear there. It was probably
              written in the margin of the preceding paragraph* 'I seldom . . . sec-
              retaries.' (215.6–15) *and has been moved to its present position be-
              cause the stressed* 'her' *implies a context in which Olivia Langdon's
              assistance would have been immediately understood.*]

215.17   Institute," (C) • ~", (P[2])

215.21–28   . . . I . . . book. . . . (C) • . . . ~ . . . ~. (P[1]); [*not in*] (P[2,3,4])

215.22   "American Publishing Co." (C) • '~ ~ ~.' (P[1])

215.24   & (C) • and (P[1])

215.28–216.5 the . . . death. (P[3]) • [P[3] *is copy-text*]

215.32   winters • [*sic*]

216.6–13   But . . . Now (P[2]) • [*not in*] (P[1,3,4])

216.7   ten (C) · then (P[2])

216.9   &c (C) • & c (P[2])

216.13–25   I *would* . . . one. (P[4]) • [P[4] *is copy-text*]

216.18   portions (C) • portio[ns] [P[4] *badly inked or MS torn*]

216.19   *never* (C) • [◊]ever [P[4] *badly inked or MS torn*]

■ 11 May 1869 · To Jane Lampton Clemens · Hartford, Conn. · *UCCL* 00294

■ *Copy-text:* MS, Mark Twain Papers, The Bancroft Library, University of California, Berkeley (CU-MARK). A photographic facsimile of the letter is on pp. 532–34. The MS consists of a torn folder (two leaves) of embossed, blue-lined off-white laid paper, approximately 4 13/16 by 7 11/16 inches, inscribed on the first three pages in black ink, now faded to brown. ■ *Previous publication:* none known. ■ *Provenance:* see Moffett Collection, pp. 586–87. ■ *Emendations and textual notes:*

218.12	Pamelas • [*sic*]
219.3	sent, • [*deletion implied*]

■ 12 May 1869 · To Olivia L. Langdon · Hartford, Conn. · *UCCL* 00299

■ *Copy-text:* MS, Mark Twain Papers, The Bancroft Library, University of California, Berkeley (CU-MARK). ■ *Previous publication:* Wecter 1947b, 67, brief quotation; *LLMT*, 87–90; *MTMF*, 97, brief excerpt. ■ *Provenance:* see Samossoud Collection, p. 586. ■ *Emendations and textual notes:*

220.2	th • [*partly formed*]
220.4	stricken • strick-¢[n]|en [*written off edge of page*]
220.37	hardship. I • ~.—|~
221.3	scribble • scribllble [*corrected miswriting*]
221.4–5	transact • tr transact [*corrected miswriting*]
221.16	right? Excuse • ~?═|~
221.20	cath catch • cathch ['h' *partly formed; possibly* 'calltch']
221.24	so • ['s' *followed by* 'l' *or partly formed* 't' *or* 'h']
221.27	night-wind • night-|wind
221.30	now. We • ~.—|~
221.33	drive. The town • ~.—~	~
221.35	show. The • ~.—|~
221.37	is its • its
222.1	liv • ['iv' *partly formed; possibly* 'lu']
222.2	& • [*partly formed*]
222.7	+ accustomed • ['accustomed' *over dash*]
222.21	look • ['k' *partly formed*]
222.22	answered • answeredswere[d] [*written off edge of page*]
222.24	f sac ,sacred, • [f] sac ‖ ,sacred, [*torn*]

222.30   witho̶u̶ • ['u' *partly formed*]
222.34   HARTFORD • HA[R◇◇o]RD [*badly inked*]

■ 13 May 1869 · To Olivia L. Langdon · Hartford, Conn. · *UCCL* 00300

■ *Copy-text:* MS, Mark Twain Papers, The Bancroft Library, University of California, Berkeley (CU-MARK). ■ *Previous publication: LLMT*, 358, brief paraphrase. ■ *Provenance:* see Samossoud Collection, p. 586. ■ *Emendations and textual notes:*

224.13   m̶h̶ • [*partly formed*]
224.18   m̶y̶s̶e̶r̶ misery • m̶y̶s̶e̶r̶isery
224.25   h̶e̶v̶ heavy • hey̶avy
225.1   Friday. I • ~.—|~
225.18   wierd • [*sic*]
225.25   h̶a̶v̶n̶ have • havn̶e ['n' *partly formed*]
226.3   l̶o̶w̶ loving • l̶o̶woving

■ 14 and 17 May 1869 · To James Redpath · Hartford, Conn. · *UCCL* 09755

■ *Copy-text:*

    P¹   Swann, lot 299
    P²   Merwin-Clayton, lot 129

P¹ is sole copy-text for most of the letter. The dateline only is based on P¹ and P², each of which derives independently from the MS. ■ *Previous publication:* none known other than P¹ and P². ■ *Provenance:* The present location of the MS, sold in 1906 by the Merwin-Clayton Sales Company and in 1990 by Swann Galleries, is unknown. ■ *Emendations, adopted readings, and textual notes:* The Merwin-Clayton catalog, which does not identify the addressee, describes the MS as an "A. L. S. 2 pages, 8vo. May 14, 1869. . . . on very thin paper and in poor condition." According to the 1990 Swann catalog, the paper is "browned and slightly light from prior framing; expert tissue restoration and slight loss of text on both leaves." The paper and ink are doubtless the same as those Clemens used in his first letter of 15 May to Olivia Langdon (see p. 635).

227.1   Hartford, Friday, May 14. • Hartford, Friday, 14 May (P¹); May
          14, 1869. (P²) [*both reported, not quoted*]
227.3–12 The . . . do. (P¹) • [*not in*] (P²)
227.10   Clemens • Autographed Letter Signed "Clemens," (P¹)
227.12   Upon • In a postscript, Twain adds, "Upon (P¹)

■ 14 May 1869 · To Olivia L. Langdon · Hartford, Conn. · *UCCL* 00302

■ *Copy-text:* MS, Mark Twain Papers, The Bancroft Library, University of California, Berkeley (CU-MARK). ■ *Previous publication: LLMT*, 358–59, brief paraphrase. ■ *Provenance:* see Samossoud Collection, p. 586. ■ *Emendations and textual notes:*

227.14	siezes • [*sic*]
228.5	winter?) Bless • ~?)—|~
228.10	touch,," • [*possibly* 'touch,̭,"']
228.16	t̶h̶ • [*partly formed*]
229.18	those • those those

■ 15 May 1869 · To Olivia L. Langdon · (1st of 2) · Hartford, Conn. · *UCCL* 00301

■ *Copy-text:* MS, Mark Twain Papers, The Bancroft Library, University of California, Berkeley (CU-MARK). A photographic facsimile of the letter is on pp. 535–39. The MS consists of four leaves (torn from folded sheets) of blue-lined onionskin, 5 3/16 by 8 3/16 inches, inscribed on all four rectos and the verso of the first leaf in black ink, now faded to brown. ■ *Previous publication: LLMT*, 359, brief paraphrase. ■ *Provenance:* see Samossoud Collection, p. 586. ■ *Emendations and textual notes:*

231.1	'pəq • [']pəq [*The comma is written off the torn edge of the page onto the next page, where it appears in the position of an apostrophe between the last two letters of* 'want' *at 231.16.*]
231.11	c̶h̶e̶e̶r̶ children • cheerildren
231.12	l̶e̶s̶t̶ least • lestast
231.13	climbing • climbl̸ing
231.20	i̶s̶ it • iśt
231.29	kindn̶e̶s̶s̶liness • kind-|n̶e̶s̶s̶liness
231.30	blockheads • block-|heads
232.3	*thim?*)ₓ [You • ~?)ₓ —|[~
232.3–5	[You . . . alike.) • [*sic*]
232.17	Beecher • Beeche[◊] [*torn*]

■ 15 May 1869 · To Olivia L. Langdon · (2nd of 2) · Hartford, Conn. · *UCCL* 00303

■ *Copy-text:* MS, Mark Twain Papers, The Bancroft Library, University of California, Berkeley (CU-MARK). ■ *Previous publication: MFMT*, 17, excerpt, printed as part of 8 June letter; *LLMT*, 359, brief paraphrase. ■ *Provenance:* see Samossoud Collection, p. 586. ■ *Emendations and textual notes:*

233.3   for it • for̸ it [*false start; 'i' partly formed*]
234.3   Fiend • Fie̸nd
234.4   *yet?* Why • ~?—|~
234.15   Hooker's • [*sic*]
234.17   b̶e̶ but • b̸ut
234.18   finding out • findo̶u̶ing out [*canceled* 'u' *partly formed*]
234.35   siezes • [*sic*]
235.6   an̸ • ['n' *partly formed*]

■ 15 and 16 May 1869 · To Olivia L. Langdon · Hartford, Conn. ·
UCCL 00304

■*Copy-text:* MS, Mark Twain Papers, The Bancroft Library, University of California, Berkeley (CU-MARK). ■*Previous publication:* Wecter 1947b, 67–68; *LLMT*, 90–92. ■*Provenance:* see Samossoud Collection, p. 586. ■*Emendations and textual notes:*

236.4   f̶o̶u̶n̶ • ['n' *partly formed*]
236.13   p̶e̶r̶ presently • p̶e̶rres-|ently
236.14   y̸ • [*partly formed*]
237.21   T. • [*doubtful* '≴ T.'; 's' *partly formed*]

■ 17 and 18 May 1869 · To Olivia L. Langdon · Hartford, Conn. ·
UCCL 00305

■*Copy-text:* MS, Mark Twain Papers, The Bancroft Library, University of California, Berkeley (CU-MARK). ■*Previous publication:* Wecter 1947b, 68–69, with omissions; *LLMT*, 93–97. ■*Provenance:* see Samossoud Collection, p. 586. ■*Emendations and textual notes:*

239.3   it. What • ~.—|~
239.6   again. I • ~.—|~
239.21   all,̸, • [*possibly* 'all,,'; *comma over wiped-out comma*]
240.28   k̶e̶p̶ keep • kep̸eep
241.7   f̶r̶ • [*possibly* 'fi' *or* 'fo']
241.9   h̶i̶s̶ him • hi̸m
241.37   c̶o̶m̶p̶o̶s̶i̶t̶i̶o̶n̶— • [*false ascenders/descenders; deletion of dash implied*]
242.7   g̶e̶o̶g̶ geology • geo̸logy ['g' *partly formed*]
242.17   back-end • back-|end
242.21   g̶r̶ get • g̸et ['r' *partly formed*]
242.26   YOUR • Your [*underscored three times*]

242.30   l̶a̶n̶ • ['n' *partly formed*]
243.8   I not • [*sic*]

■ 19 and 20 May 1869 · To Olivia L. Langdon · Hartford, Conn.
   UCCL 00306
■ *Copy-text:* MS, Mark Twain Papers, The Bancroft Library, University of California, Berkeley (CU-MARK), is copy-text for the letter. The enclosure, a *carte de visite* print of a photograph of Clemens taken by E. P. Kellogg of Hartford, Conn., does not survive with the letter. It is reproduced in facsimile from another copy in CU-MARK, which in 1870 Clemens enclosed in his wedding invitation to his Hannibal friend, Rebecca Pavey Boas. ■ *Previous publication:* *LLMT*, 97–100, without the enclosure. ■ *Provenance:* see Samossoud Collection, p. 586. ■ *Emendations and textual notes:*

245.2   T̶u̶e̶s̶Wednesday • T̶u̶e̶s̶-Wednes-₍day
245.3   *Thursday* • *Thur₍sday*
245.29   I̶ k̶n̶e̶w̶ • [*heavily canceled*]
246.7   A̶n̶ Only • ₍Only₍
246.9   j̶u̶s̶t̶ • [*heavily canceled*]
246.21   millennium. There • ~.—|~
246.28   spoonf̶-victuals • ['f' *partly formed*]
246.32   twice • t̶w̶i̶ twice [*corrected miswriting*]
246.32–33   years—cholera • ~—‖—~
246.33   y̶ • [*partly formed*]
247.4   it—& • ~—‖—~
247.9   trait. I • ~.—|~
248.9   CONN. • CONN[◊] [*badly inked*]

■ 24 May 1869 · To Olivia L. Langdon with a note to Jervis and Olivia
   Lewis Langdon · South Windsor, Conn. · *UCCL* 00309
■ *Copy-text:* MS, Mark Twain Papers, The Bancroft Library, University of California, Berkeley (CU-MARK). ■ *Previous publication:* Wecter 1947b, 67, brief quotation; *LLMT*, 359, brief paraphrase. ■ *Provenance:* see Samossoud Collection, p. 586. ■ *Emendations and textual notes:*

249.13   i̶n̶ it • it̶
249.17   c̶a̶t̶h̶ catch • catḥch
249.19   t̶h̶i̶s̶ that • thi̶sat
250.1–2   apartment. If • ~.—|~
250.17   s̶l̶e̶e̶ slept • sleṭpt
250.24   worshipped • woṣhrshipped [*canceled* 'h' *partly formed*]

250.29	but • ['t' *over miswritten* 'u']
250.30	it ever • [*sic*]
251.1	lo • ['o' *partly formed*]
251.5	more? Would • ~.—|~
251.24	together, • [*deletion implied*]
251.27	last • l[a]st [*obscured by residue of dried flowers*]
252.14	fr • ['r' *partly formed*]
252.25	so proud • $ so proud [*corrected miswriting; possibly* 'A so proud']
252.36	POINT CT. MAY 2◊ • P[OI]N[◊ ◊◊◊] M[AY 2◊] [*badly inked*]

■ 29 May 1869 · To Olivia L. Langdon · Elmira, N.Y. · *UCCL* 00307

■ *Copy-text:* MS, Mark Twain Papers, The Bancroft Library, University of California, Berkeley (CU-MARK). Clemens wrote this letter on a strip of paper measuring about 3 by 8 ½ inches, torn from the endpaper of a ledger book (ruled on one side only in blue with red dividing rules), that shows evidence of having had ink inscription on the missing portion. ■ *Previous publication: MFMT*, 237. ■ *Provenance:* see Samossoud Collection, p. 586. ■ *Emendations and textual notes:* none.

■ 1 June 1869 · To John J. Murphy · Elmira, N.Y. · *UCCL* 00310

■ *Copy-text:* MS, William K. Bixby Papers, Washington University, St. Louis, Mo. (MoSW). ■ *Previous publication:* none known. ■ *Provenance:* donated to MoSW, possibly in 1931, upon the death of William K. Bixby. ■ *Emendations and textual notes:*

255.1	*don't* want to • *don't* wantø to [*false start*]
255.4	*any*how • [*possibly* '*any* how']

■ 1 June 1869 · To Silas S. Packard and Other Members of the New York Press Club · Elmira, N.Y. · *UCCL* 00311 (formerly 00311 and 00312)

■ *Copy-text:* MS, *damage emended*, Clifton Waller Barrett Library, University of Virginia, Charlottesville (ViU). ■ *Previous publication:* SLC 1869g (Press Club letter only), with omissions. ■ *Provenance:* deposited at ViU by Clifton Waller Barrett on 17 December 1963. ■ *Emendations and textual notes:* The left margin of the letter to Packard, where Clemens wrote instructions for printing his speech, is torn, obliterating characters or portions of characters. The page is reproduced below, showing the curatorial number 'B2-13-6314Q(3).' On the verso of the last page of the speech an unknown hand wrote a series of names ('E Brismard E. Saymore,' etc.), numbers, and decorative curlicues, probably an exercise in penmanship.

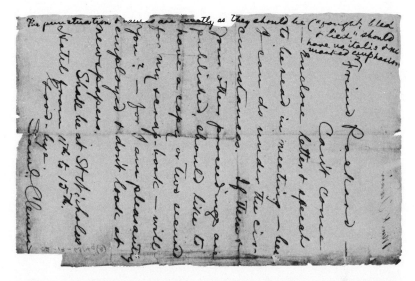

Letter of 1 June 1869 to Silas S. Packard and others. MS page 1, with docket showing through from verso in upper right and with missing words in left margin editorially reconstructed; reproduced at 57 percent of actual size (ViU).

255.17	names • n[◊m]es [*torn*]
255.17	*exactly* as • *exac*[t◊y ◊◊] [*torn*]
255.17–18	("fought . . . emphasis. • [*no closing parenthesis*]
255.24	felt • [*doubtful* 'fe∤lt'; '∤' *partly formed*]
256.18–19	speech,)	and • ~,)——|~
256.22	'RELIABLE • [*possibly* '∤ 'RELIABLE']
257.11	combinéd • [*sic*]
257.19	∤ • [*partly formed*]

■ 4 June 1869 · To Jane Lampton Clemens and Family · Elmira, N.Y.
· *UCCL* 00315

■ *Copy-text:* MS, Jean Webster McKinney Family Papers, Vassar College Library (NPV). ■ *Previous publication: MTB*, 1:379, brief excerpt; *MTL*, 158–59, without postscript; *MTBus*, 106, postscript only; *MTMF*, 100, brief excerpts. ■ *Provenance:* see McKinney Family Papers, pp. 583–85. ■ *Emendations and textual notes:*

260.5–6   myself. I • ~.—|~
260.18   further. The • ~.—|~
260.31   ~~respond~~ • ['d' *partly formed*]

■ 4 June 1869 · To Mary Mason Fairbanks · Elmira, N.Y. · *UCCL* 00313

■ *Copy-text:* MS, Huntington Library, San Marino, Calif. (CSmH, call no. HM 14251). The surviving MS page is a torn half-sheet of beige laid paper, measuring 5 3/16 by 8 1/16 inches, with chain lines 1/4 inch apart (possibly intended as rules), watermarked "LACROIX" in block letters. ■ *Previous publication: MTMF*, 98–99. ■ *Provenance:* see Huntington Library, pp. 582–83. ■ *Emendations and textual notes:*

262.8   shortly. I • ~.—|~
262.9   ~~65~~ 660 • 6⫻60

■ 8 June 1869 · To Olivia L. Langdon · Elmira, N.Y. · *UCCL* 00316

■ *Copy-text:* MS, Mark Twain Papers, The Bancroft Library, University of California, Berkeley (CU-MARK). ■ *Previous publication: MFMT*, 16–17, excerpt. ■ *Provenance:* see Samossoud Collection, p. 586. ■ *Emendations and textual notes:*

264.1   ~~wu~~ would • w⫽ould

■ 15 June 1869 · To Whitelaw Reid · New York, N.Y. · *UCCL* 00317

■ *Copy-text:* MS, Papers of the Reid Family, Library of Congress, Washington, D.C. (DLC). ■ *Previous publication:* none known. ■ *Provenance:* donated to DLC between 1953 and 1973 by Mrs. Helen Rogers Reid and her sons, Whitelaw Reid and Ogden R. Reid. ■ *Emendations and textual notes:* none.

■ 21 June 1869 · To Olivia L. Langdon · Hartford, Conn. · *UCCL* 00318

■ *Copy-text:* MS, Mark Twain Papers, The Bancroft Library, University of California, Berkeley (CU-MARK). ■ *Previous publication: LLMT*, 101. ■ *Provenance:* see Samossoud Collection, p. 586. ■ *Emendations and textual notes:*

266.3   ~~loo~~ loth • lo⫽th
266.4   to-morrow • to-‖morrow
266.5–6   theirs. | [*line space*] | [¶] P. S. • ~.—| [*line space*] | [¶] ~ . ~.

■ 22 June 1869 · To Samuel Bowles · Hartford, Conn. · *UCCL* 09743

■*Copy-text:* Transcript and paraphrase, Libbie, lot 372. ■*Previous publication:* none known except the copy-text. ■*Provenance:* Sometime after receipt, the letter became part of the collection of Franklin B. Sanborn (1831–1917), who was associated with the Springfield (Mass.) *Republican* from 1856 until 1914 (Hart 1983, 665). The MS was sold in 1918 and its present location is not known. ■*Emendations and textual notes:* The Libbie catalog describes the MS as "CLEMENS, Samuel L. ('Mark Twain') *a. l. s.* in pencil, 1 page 12°, Hartford, June 22." The inclusion of the pseudonym in quotation marks is catalog style and probably not indicative of how Clemens signed his name.

267.1	Hartford, June 22. • [*reported, not quoted*]
267.3	[*no* ¶] Since • [¶] "~
267.5	anchor • anchor," etc.

■ 23 June 1869 · To Olivia Lewis (Mrs. Jervis) Langdon · New York, N.Y. · *UCCL* 00319

■*Copy-text:* MS, Jean Webster McKinney Family Papers, Vassar College Library (NPV). ■*Previous publication: MTBus*, 104–6. ■*Provenance:* see McKinney Family Papers, pp. 583–85. ■*Emendations and textual notes:*

268.29	herself • herseflf
268.30	ẃ • [*partly formed*]
269.2	~~The Governor Jewell told me~~ • [*Clemens may have completed* 'The Governor' *before canceling* 'The' *and continuing with* 'Jewell']
269.21–22	behave. [¶] Pray • ~.—| [¶] ~

■ 23 June 1869 · To Pamela A. Moffett · New York, N.Y. · *UCCL* 00320

■*Copy-text:* MS, Mark Twain Papers, The Bancroft Library, University of California, Berkeley (CU-MARK). ■*Previous publication:* none known. ■*Provenance:* Mark Twain Papers or Moffett Collection, see pp. 585–87. ■*Emendations and textual notes:*

270.20	ẚ one-third • ['o' *over* 'a']
270.26	pleases. But • ~.—|~
271.6	~~af~~ awfully • afwfully ['f' *partly formed; possibly* 'l' *or* 'b']
271.15	my *salary* • mysa *salary* [*false start;* 'a' *partly formed*]
271.23	& • & ẋ [*partly formed*]

272.8   A̶f̶e̶ Affectionat[e]ly • Af̶fectionatly
272.12   S̶.̶ ̶C̶l̶e̶m̶e̶n̶s̶ • [*very heavily canceled*]
272.13   HOUSE   UNION   SQUARE,   N.Y. • HOUS[E]   U[NI]ON   [SQUA]RE,
            N.[Y◊] [*badly inked*]
272.13   23 1869 • [2◊ 1]8[69] [*badly inked*]

■ 23 June 1869 · To Olivia L. Langdon · New York, N.Y. · *UCCL*
00321

■*Copy-text:* MS, Mark Twain Papers, The Bancroft Library, University of California, Berkeley (CU-MARK). ■*Previous publication: LLMT*, 359, brief quotation. ■*Provenance:* see Samossoud Collection, p. 586. ■*Emendations and textual notes:*

273.9   homesick • home-|sick
273.12   paper. It • ~.—|~
274.19   room. And • ~.—|~
274.32–33   to-morrow • to-|morrow
275.5   Sam.*¹* • [*sic*]

■ 26 June 1869 · T̶o̶ ̶O̶r̶i̶o̶n̶ ̶C̶l̶e̶m̶e̶n̶s̶ To Jane Lampton Clemens and Pamela A. Moffett · Elmira, N.Y. · *UCCL* 00322

■*Copy-text:* MS, Mark Twain Papers, The Bancroft Library, University of California, Berkeley (CU-MARK). ■*Previous publication:* none known. ■*Provenance:* see Moffett Collection, pp. 586–87. ■*Emendations and textual notes:*

276.2   My Dear B̶r̶Mother & Sister • [*Clemens altered* 'Brother' *to*
            'Mother' *before he added* '& Sister']
276.6   Herald, • [*possibly* 'Herald/,']
276.8   har̶d̶l • ['l' *partly formed*]
276.12   w̶e̶e̶ wedding • we̶dding

■ 26 June 1869 · To Whitelaw Reid · Elmira, N.Y. · *UCCL* 00323

■*Copy-text:* MS, Papers of the Reid Family, Library of Congress, Washington, D.C. (DLC). ■*Previous publication:* none known. ■*Provenance:* donated to DLC between 1953 and 1973 by Mrs. Helen Rogers Reid and her sons, Whitelaw Reid and Ogden R. Reid. ■*Emendations and textual notes:*

278.7   un-bloodthirsty • un-blood-|thi̶rsty
278.12   o̶r̶ of • of̶f

■ 3? July 1869 · To Orion Clemens · Elmira, N.Y. · *UCCL* 11698

■*Copy-text:* Paraphrase in MS, Orion Clemens to Mary E. (Mollie) Clemens, 7 July 1869, Mark Twain Papers, The Bancroft Library, University of California, Berkeley (CU-MARK). ■*Previous publication:* none known. ■*Provenance:* see Moffett Collection, pp. 586–87. Samuel Clemens's original letter may have been destroyed in 1904. ■*Emendations and textual notes:* none.

■ 5 July 1869 · To Mary Mason Fairbanks · Elmira, N.Y. · *UCCL* 00324

■*Copy-text:* MS, Huntington Library, San Marino, Calif. (CSmH, call no. HM 14252). ■*Previous publication: MTMF*, 99–100. ■*Provenance:* see Huntington Library, pp. 582–83. ■*Emendations and textual notes:* Although Clemens used a sheet of Jervis Langdon's business stationery for this letter, he made some effort to avoid emphasizing its letterhead (see 26 June to Reid for a transcription of an identical pre-printed letterhead). He first folded the sheet lengthwise so that the letterhead was positioned inside and not visible. After filling both front and back of the folded sheet, he opened it, turned it over, and, with the letterhead positioned upside-down and at the bottom of the page, completed the letter.

280.7	G •	[*partly formed*]
281.2	I •	[*partly formed*]

■ 9 July 1869 · To James Redpath · Elmira, N.Y. · *UCCL* 00325

■*Copy-text:*

P¹	Transcript, CU-MARK
P²	Merwin-Clayton, lot 125

P¹, a photocopy of a handwritten transcription in an unidentified hand, is sole copy-text for most of the letter (282.1–10 and 282.12–13, 'J. LANGDON . . . it?' and 'Yrs . . . Clemens'), Mark Twain Papers, The Bancroft Library, University of California, Berkeley (CU-MARK). The remainder is based on P¹ and P², each of which derives independently from the original MS. ■*Previous publication:* none known other than P². ■*Provenance:* The location of the MS, which was sold in 1906 by the Merwin-Clayton Sales Company, is not known. The handwritten transcription was once part of the Tufts Collection (see pp. 587–88). From 1977 to 1987 it was in the possession of Theodore H. Koundakjian, who provided a photocopy to CU-MARK. It is now at Iwaki Meisei University, Iwaki, Japan. The transcript is written on a sheet of paper with the letterhead "THE S.F. EXAMINER | SAN FRANCISCO." ■*Emendations, adopted readings, and textual notes:*

282.1–10   J. LANGDON . . . it? (P¹) • [*not in*] (P²)

282.1–3   J. LANGDON . . . July 9, 1869 • J. (or I) Langdon | Miner &
            Dealer In | Anthracite & Bituminous Coal | Office | No 6 Baldwin
            Street | Elmira N.Y. July 9, 1869 (P¹) [*text of letterhead adopted in
            part from 26 June 69 to Reid*]

282.11   fair. (P²) • ~∧ (P¹)

282.12–13   Yrs . . . Clemens (P¹) • [*not in*] (P²)

■ **12 July 1869 · To Elisha Bliss, Jr. · Elmira, N.Y. · *UCCL* 00326**

■ *Copy-text:* MS facsimile. The editors have not seen the MS, which is in the
collection of Daphne B. Sears. ■ *Previous publication:* none known. ■ *Provenance:*
In 1949 the Mark Twain Papers received a transcription from Francis Richmond
Sears, whose father had acquired the letter from Elisha Bliss. In 1981 Sears's
widow, Daphne B. Sears, sent the photograph of the MS that serves as copy-
text. ■ *Emendations and textual notes:*

283.7   dozen$ • [*possibly* 'dozen'; 'n' *followed by inkblot*]

■ **22 July 1869 · To Elisha Bliss, Jr. · Elmira, N.Y. · *UCCL* 00327**

■ *Copy-text:* MS, collection of Jack F. Cooper, serves as copy-text, with damage
emended from a handwritten transcription made by Dana Ayer, Collection of
American Literature, Beinecke Rare Book and Manuscript Library, Yale University (CtY-BR), made when the MS was presumably in somewhat better condition. By 1925, however, it had been damaged and repaired: "Each sheet
backed with transparent silk gauze, and inlaid; a portion of the second and of
the last sheets torn away, damaging some words" (Dawson's Book Shop, lot 112).
■ *Previous publication:* AAA 1924, lot 65, excerpts; *MTLP*, 22–24, with omission. ■ *Provenance:* The MS, accompanied by a typewritten transcript, was sold
in 1924 (AAA 1924, lot 65) and again in 1925 (Dawson's Book Shop, lot 112).
Thereafter, probably during the 1930s, it was acquired by Sadie Lydia Marshall
Cooper, grandmother of the present owner, Jack F. Cooper. Two distinct transcriptions of the letter in Dana Ayer's hand exist, both lacking the postscript.
The first, at CtY-BR, was evidently made directly from the MS. The second,
now at WU, derives from the first, as does a typescript, also at WU. See Brownell
Collection, pp. 581–82. ■ *Emendations and textual notes:* The MS consists of 9
torn half-sheets of flimsy wove paper, inscribed on one side only. Pages 2 and 9
are badly damaged, with several words, characters, and punctuation marks
wholly or partly missing. See below for illustrations of the damaged pages, editorially reconstructed and reproduced at 81 percent of actual size.

284.6   ~~& damage~~ • [*false ascenders/descenders*]

284.14–15   transpired (Ayer) • transp[ir]ed [*torn*]

284.15	hold it back (Ayer) •	h[◇◇◇ ◇◇ ◇◇◇k] [*torn*]
284.15	book of it. (Ayer) •	b[◇◇◇ ◇◇ ◇◇◇] [*torn*]
284.16	misunderstand. (Ayer) •	mi[◇◇◇◇◇◇◇◇◇◇◇◇] [*torn*]
284.19	is •	[i̶s̶] is [*torn during inscription*]
284.25–26	Metropolis̶ •	['ś' *partly formed*]
285.11	the publication •	t̶h̶e̶ the publication [*corrected miswriting*]
285.18	disregarded •	[*doubtful* 'I disregarded']
285.27	short ˏorˏ (Ayer) •	[s◇◇◇◇ ◇◇] [*torn*]
285.27	what (Ayer) •	[w◇◇◇] [*torn*]
285.30	delays •	d̶l̶e̶l̶ delays
285.30	with •	[◇◇th] [*torn*]; whose (Ayer)
285.31	reputation (Ayer) •	repu-|[◇◇ti◇n] [*torn*]
285.31	borne (Ayer) •	[◇◇◇◇◇] [*torn*]
285.31	I have •	[◇ ◇◇◇◇] [*torn*]; that I have (Ayer)
285.35	P. S. I am sorry •	[◇◇ ◇◇ ◇ ◇◇ ◇]orry [*torn*]
285.35	woes—I know •	[◇◇◇◇◇◇ ◇◇◇w] [*torn*]
285.35–36	complement, anyhow •	[◇◇◇◇◇◇◇◇◇◇ ◇n]yhow [*torn*]
285.36	c̶o̶n̶s̶i̶d̶e̶r̶ ̶t̶h̶a̶t̶ remember •	c̶o̶n̶s̶i̶d̶-|[◇◇ ◇◇◇◇ ◇◇◇◇m]ber [*torn*]
285.36–37	may be cut short •	[◇◇◇ ◇◇ ◇◇◇ ◇◇]ort [*torn*]
285.37	by the delays. •	[◇◇ ◇◇◇ ◇◇◇◇◇◇◇] [*torn*]
286.2	Samuel Clemens •	[S]a[muel Clem◇◇s] [*torn*]

■ 1 August 1869 · To Elisha Bliss, Jr. · Elmira, N.Y. · *UCCL* 00328
■ *Copy-text:* TS, Mark Twain Papers, The Bancroft Library, University of California, Berkeley (CU-MARK), courtesy Goodspeed's Book Shop, Boston. ■ *Previous publication: MTMF*, 101, excerpt; *MTLP*, 24–25. ■ *Provenance:* The MS

in case the sales fall short, or
reasonably short of what
we originally expected them
to reach.

I think you will do
me the justice to say that I
have borne these annoying
& damaging delays
as patiently as any man
with bread & butter & reputation at stake could have
borne them.   I cannot think
I have been treated just right.

Yrs Truly

Saml. L. Clemens.

P. S. I am sorry to add to your
woes — I know you have your full
complement anyhow — but consider
the like vein that my share
may be cut short, or even threatened
by the delay.

Letter of 22 July 1869 to Elisha Bliss, Jr. MS page 9, with missing words editorially reconstructed; reproduced at 81 percent of actual size. Courtesy of Jack F. Cooper.

was sold in 1967 by Goodspeed's Book Shop. Its present location is not known.
■ *Emendations and textual notes:*

286.3   Aug. 1 • Aug.1

■ 8 August 1869 · To Olivia L. Langdon · Elmira, N.Y. · *UCCL* 00329
■ *Copy-text:* MS, Mark Twain Papers, The Bancroft Library, University of California, Berkeley (CU-MARK). ■ *Previous publication: LLMT*, 359, brief paraphrase. ■ *Provenance:* see Samossoud Collection, p. 586. ■ *Emendations and textual notes:*

289.12   ri • ['i' *partly formed; possibly* 'e']
289.29   greatly, • ~, [*deletion implied*]
290.1   these this • theseis
290.8   this • ['s' *partly formed*]
290.26   blessing • ['ing' *conflated*]

■ 12 August 1869 · To Elisha Bliss, Jr. · Buffalo, N.Y. · *UCCL* 00330
■ *Copy-text:* MS, Mark Twain Papers, The Bancroft Library, University of California, Berkeley (CU-MARK). ■ *Previous publication: MTMF*, 102, excerpt; *MTLP*, 25–26. ■ *Provenance:* see Mendoza Collection, p. 587. Two typed transcriptions, at WU and ViU, may have been made by George Brownell or Dana Ayer from a lost handwritten transcription by Ayer. See Brownell Collection, pp. 581–82. ■ *Emendations and textual notes:*

291.8   nature. But • ~.—|~
292.2   sell. Between • ~.—|~
292.6   church. Send • ~.—|~
292.11   have having • havɡing

■ 14 August 1869 · To Elisha Bliss, Jr. · Buffalo, N.Y. · *UCCL* 00331
■ *Copy-text:* MS, Buffalo and Erie County Historical Society, Buffalo, N.Y. (NBuHi), is copy-text for the letter. The original enclosure, a review of *The Innocents Abroad* clipped from the Elmira *Gazette*, does not survive with the letter and no copy of the *Gazette* was available to the editors. Copy-text is a partial reprinting in the Buffalo *Express* "Advertising Supplement" (9 Oct 69, 1). It is reprinted here line-for-line from a microfilm edition of the newspaper in the Buffalo and Erie County Public Library, Buffalo, N.Y. (NBu). ■ *Previous publication:* AAA/Anderson 1934, lot 134, brief excerpt; *MTMF*, 102, brief excerpt. ■ *Provenance:* The MS was sold in 1934 as part of the collection of William L. Clements or E. W. Evans, Jr. (AAA/Anderson 1934, lot 134). By 1941, it had

been acquired by Robert W. Bingham, who donated it in 1942 to NBuHi.
■*Emendations and textual notes:*

| 295.4 | Gazettes • [*sic*] |
| 296.4 | ~~Twin~~ Twain • Twi~~n~~ain [*deletion of 'i' implied*] |

■ 14 August 1869 · To James Redpath · Buffalo, N.Y. · *UCCL* 00386

■*Copy-text:* Merwin-Clayton, lot 127. ■*Previous publication:* none known other
than the copy-text. ■*Provenance:* The present location of the MS (sold at auction
in 1906 by the Merwin-Clayton Sales Company) is not known. ■*Emendations and
textual notes:* The auction catalog describes the MS as an "A.L.S., 2 pages, 8vo,
Aug. 14, 1869, to James Redpath."

297.1	Aug. 14, 1869 • [*reported, not quoted*]
297.3	[*no* ¶] I • [¶] "~
297.3	& • and [*also at 297.5, 7, 8; 298.1, 2*]
298.2	out • out," etc.

■ 14 August 1869 · To Mary Mason and Abel W. Fairbanks · Buffalo,
N.Y. · *UCCL* 00332

■*Copy-text:* MS, Huntington Library, San Marino, Calif. (CSmH, call no. HM
14253). ■*Previous publication: MTMF*, 103–5. ■*Provenance:* see Huntington Library, pp. 582–83. ■*Emendations and textual notes:* A few characters or portions
of characters are torn away in the upper right margin of MS page 3 and in the
upper left margin of the verso, page 4.

298.21	more • mor[◊] [*torn*]
298.21	hazardous • haz[◊]|ardous [*torn*]
298.27	apprentice • [a]pprentice [*torn*]
298.30	abundantly • abundab~~l~~ntly [*canceled* 'l' *partly formed*]
299.1	~~at~~ agreeable • a~~t~~greeable ['t' *partly formed; possibly* 'b']
299.4	want to as • want~~t~~ to as [*false start*]
299.9	k̸ • [*partly formed*]
299.12	ȷ̸ • [*partly formed*]
299.16	~~dis◊◊ no~~ • [*heavily canceled; possibly* '~~disco no~~']

■ 15 August 1869 · To Elisha Bliss, Jr. · Buffalo, N.Y. · *UCCL* 00333

■*Copy-text:* None. The text is based on three transcripts, each of which derives
independently from the MS:

P[1]	Handwritten transcription in WU
P[2]	Chicago 1936, lot 124
P[3]	Typescript in CU-MARK

P[1], University of Wisconsin, Madison (WU), was made by Dana Ayer during the late 1890s or after; P[2], a partial transcript, was made in 1936 when the MS sold at auction (Chicago 1936); P[3], Mark Twain Papers, The Bancroft Library, University of California, Berkeley (CU-MARK), was made by Joseph Rosenberg of Chicago in 1943, when he owned the MS. ▪*Previous publication:* see *Copy-text; MTLP*, 27. ▪*Provenance:* The MS evidently remained among the American Publishing Company's files until it was sold (and may have been copied at that time by Dana Ayer; see Brownell Collection, pp. 581–82). Acquired by an unidentified owner, it was sold again in 1936 and by 1943 had been acquired by Joseph Rosenberg. Its present location is not known. The Ayer transcription was in turn copied by a typist and both the handwritten and typed transcriptions are at WU. ▪*Emendations, adopted readings, and textual notes:* P[2] describes the MS as an "A. L. S. 'Clemens.' 3pp., 8vo. Buffalo, Aug. 15. To 'Friend Bliss.' In pencil."

301.1	Aug. 15. (P[2]) • [*reported, not quoted*]; Aug 15/69 (P[1]); Aug. 15, (P[3])
301.2	Bliss— (P[3]) • ~,— (P[1]); ~. (P[2])
301.3–16	There . . . now. (P[1,3]) • [*not in*] (P[2])
301.3	& (P[3]) • and (P[1]) [*also at 301.6, 9, 10, 12, 15; see also 301.18*]
301.4	*Review*—I (P[3]) • ~—∣ [¶] ~ (P[1])
301.5	me, (P[3]) • ~∧ (P[1])
301.8	*Wm.* (P[3]) • ~∧ (P[1])
301.10	agent. (P[3]) • ~∧ (P[1])
301.17	[¶] Since purchasing (P[3]) • [¶] ~~Since purchasing~~ ‖ [¶] Since purchasing (P[1]); [*no ¶*] Since purchasing (P[2])
301.18	& (P[2,3]) • and (P[1]) [*also at 301.20*]
301.19	fire (P[2,3]) • ~, (P[1])
301.20	newspaper (P[2,3]) • ~, (P[1])
301.20	lecturing) (P[2,3]) • ~,) (P[1])
301.21	subscriber. (P[1,3]) • ~∧ (P[2])
301.22–25	I . . . haste (P[1,3]) • [*not in*] (P[2])
301.24	are, (P[3]) • ~∧ (P[1])

▪ 15 August 1869 · To Whitelaw Reid · Buffalo, N.Y. · *UCCL* 00334

▪*Copy-text:* MS, Papers of the Reid Family, Library of Congress, Washington, D.C. (DLC). ▪*Previous publication:* none known. ▪*Provenance:* donated to DLC between 1953 and 1973 by Mrs. Helen Rogers Reid and her sons, Whitelaw Reid and Ogden R. Reid. ▪*Emendations and textual notes:*

303.6	They • T[h◊◊] [*torn*]

▪ 19 August 1869 · To Olivia L. Langdon · Buffalo, N.Y. · *UCCL* 00335

▪*Copy-text:* MS, Mark Twain Papers, The Bancroft Library, University of California, Berkeley (CU-MARK), is copy-text for the letter. Although no enclosures survive with the letter, a clipping from the Buffalo *Express* that Clemens may have enclosed ("Inspired Humor," 19 Aug 69, 2 [SLC 1869k]) survives separately in CU-MARK. It is reproduced here in photographic facsimile. See Appendix B for another possible enclosure. ■*Previous publication: LLMT*, 102–4, without the enclosure; *MTMF*, 102, brief quotation. ■*Provenance:* see Samossoud Collection, p. 586. ■*Emendations and textual notes:*

303.20   t̶a̶k̶ • ['k' *partly formed*]
303.23   visiters • [*sic*]
304.12   c̶u̶t̶ curtail • cuʃrtail
304.15   type-setting • t̶y̶p̶ type-setting [*corrected miswriting*]
304.28–29   to-morrow • to-|morrow
304.34   Weekly • Weeʃkly
306.3   BUFFALO • B[UFFA]LO [*badly inked*]

■ 20 and 21 August 1869 · To Pamela A. Moffett · Buffalo, N.Y. · *UCCL* 00336

■*Copy-text:* MS, pages 1–8 and 13, Jean Webster McKinney Family Papers, Vassar College Library (NPV), is copy-text for 'Buffalo . . . strong' and 'MORN-ING . . . Sam.' (310.1–311.34 and 313.2–10). MS facsimile, pages 9–12, is copy-text for 'liking . . . Sam' (311.34–312.35). The editors have not seen this portion of the MS, but in 1977 Chester L. Davis, Sr., then executive secretary of the Mark Twain Research Foundation in Perry, Mo., provided a photocopy to the Mark Twain Papers. ■*Previous publication: MTB*, 1:386, brief excerpt; *MTL*, 160–62, with omissions; *MTMF*, 102, brief excerpt; Davis 1978, with omission. ■*Provenance:* for MS pages 1–8 and 13, see McKinney Family Papers, pp. 583–85. Pages 9–12 were evidently returned to Clemens by Pamela Moffett, for they survived in the Samossoud Collection at least until 1947: sometime between then and 1949 Dixon Wecter saw them and had a typescript made (now in CU-MARK). Davis afterwards acquired the pages directly from Clara Clemens Samossoud (see Samossoud Collection, p. 586). ■*Emendations and textual notes:*

310.24–25   there. Secondly • ~.—‖~
310.27   be. T̶h̶i̶r̶d̶l̶y̶ • ~.—|~
311.16   New Years • [*sic*]
311.17   equivalent • equʃivalent
311.17   else. And • ~.—|~
311.34   it. I • ~.—|~
312.5   ⊘⊘ • [*possibly* 't̶r̶u̶'; *partly formed* 'u']
312.8   is no • is ₐof₎ no [*insertion not in Clemens's hand*]
312.23   ẃ • [*possibly* 'm' *or* 'in']

■ 21 August 1869 · To Henry Abbey · Buffalo, N.Y. · *UCCL* 00337

■ *Copy-text:* MS, collection of Todd M. Axelrod. ■ *Previous publication:* Freeman 1947, lot 337, brief quotations. ■ *Provenance:* Sold in 1947 by Samuel T. Freeman and Company of Philadelphia (Freeman 1947, lot 337), the MS was acquired before March 1975 by Noel J. Cortés. It was again sold in 1982 by Maurice F. Neville Rare Books, and acquired by Todd M. Axelrod. ■ *Emendations and textual notes:*

315.2   ẇ̶ · [*partly formed*]

■ 21 August 1869 · To Henry M. Crane · Buffalo, N.Y. · *UCCL* 00338

■ *Copy-text:* MS, Clifton Waller Barrett Library, University of Virginia, Charlottesville (ViU). ■ *Previous publication: Collector* (October 1948), lot M 1956, excerpt. ■ *Provenance:* sold by Walter R. Benjamin Autographs in 1948; deposited at ViU by Clifton Waller Barrett on 17 December 1963. ■ *Emendations and textual notes:*

315.19   to-day · to-|day
315.19–20   e̶x̶p̶ excused · exp̸cused

■ 21 August 1869 · To Olivia L. Langdon · Buffalo, N.Y. · *UCCL* 00339

■ *Copy-text:* MS, Mark Twain Papers, The Bancroft Library, University of California, Berkeley (CU-MARK). ■ *Previous publication: LLMT*, 104–6. ■ *Provenance:* see Samossoud Collection, p. 586. ■ *Emendations and textual notes:*

316.6   d̶o̶ did · d̸id
316.9   midnight · mid-|night
316.18   ʃ̸ · [*partly formed*]
316.26   l̶i̶t̶t̶l̶e̶ young · ['young' *over wiped-out* 'little']
317.1   much. Thanks · ~.—|~
317.4   siezed · [*sic*]
317.20   middle · md̸iddle
317.32   its · i̶t̶ its [*corrected miswriting*]
317.37   lovel̶i̶ness · ['ess' *over wiped-out* 'in']
317.38   charity. Better · ~.—|~
317.38   o̶t̶ · ['t' *partly formed*]

■ 25 August 1869 · To Charles Warren Stoddard · Buffalo, N.Y. · *UCCL* 00340

■ *Copy-text:* Transcript and paraphrase, Freeman 1936, lot 68, courtesy of William P. Barlow, Jr. A later, partial publication in *LLMT*, while possibly an independent transcription from the MS, shows no variants other than those of omission. ▪*Previous publication:* see *Copy-text;* and *LLMT*, 58, excerpt. ▪*Provenance:* The present location of the MS, part of the Charles T. Jeffery Collection before its sale in 1936, is not known. ▪*Emendations and textual notes:* The Freeman catalog describes the MS as an "A. L. S., 5 pp., folio, Buffalo, August 25th, N. Y." Single quotation marks in the copy-text are silently emended to double quotation marks.

320.1   Buffalo, August 25th • [*reported, not quoted*]
320.2   Charlie— • ~.
320.7   & • and [*also at 320.8, 9, 10, 12 (twice), 13 ('& a' and '& unsettled')*]

▪ 25 and 26 August 1869 · To Olivia L. Langdon · Buffalo, N.Y. · *UCCL* 00341

▪*Copy-text:* MS, Mark Twain Papers, The Bancroft Library, University of California, Berkeley (CU-MARK). ▪*Previous publication: LLMT*, 359, brief paraphrase. ▪*Provenance:* see Samossoud Collection, p. 586. ▪*Emendations and textual notes:*

322.24   breakwater • break-|water
322.30   afraid. But • ~.—|~
323.4   у́ • [*partly formed*]
323.9   ʈ • [*partly formed*]
323.11   *love,* • [*possibly 'love ,'*]

▪ 1 September 1869 · To A. Miner Griswold (Fat Contributor) · Buffalo, N.Y. · *UCCL* 11538

▪*Copy-text:* MS, James S. Copley Library, La Jolla, Calif. (CLjC). ▪*Previous publication:* Maggs, lot 34, excerpt. ▪*Provenance:* Sold by Maggs Brothers Limited in 1988 to John L. Feldman, who in turn sold it in 1990 to CLjC. ▪*Emendations and textual notes:* none.

▪ 1 September 1869 · To Olivia L. Langdon · Buffalo, N.Y. · *UCCL* 00343

▪*Copy-text:* MS, Mark Twain Papers, The Bancroft Library, University of California, Berkeley (CU-MARK). ▪*Previous publication: LLMT*, 106, 359, brief quotation and paraphrase. A postscript formerly identified by Dixon Wecter as part of this letter has been dated 4–5 October 1868 (*LLMT*, 359; *MTMF*, 106;

L2, 255). ▪*Provenance:* see Samossoud Collection, p. 586. ▪*Emendations and textual notes:*

326.17–18   BUFFALO N.Y. SEP • [BUF]FALO N.Y. [SEP] [*badly inked*]

▪ 2 September 1869 · To Elisha Bliss, Jr. · Buffalo, N.Y. · *UCCL* 00342

▪*Copy-text:* MS, Mark Twain Papers, The Bancroft Library, University of California, Berkeley (CU-MARK). ▪*Previous publication:* none known. ▪*Provenance:* see Tufts Collection, pp. 587–88. ▪*Emendations and textual notes:*

327.8   acceþssion • ['p' *partly formed*]
327.9   editorship,. Would • ~ₐ.—|~
327.10   afterwa • after┊|wa
327.13   It Is • Iŧs
328.2   Mark . . . 69 • [*ink scraped away by unidentified owner or curator of the MS*]

▪ 2 September 1869 · To Stephen C. Massett (Jeems Pipes) · Buffalo, N.Y. · *UCCL* 00218

▪*Copy-text:* MS, Cyril Clemens Collection, Mark Twain Memorial, Hartford, Conn. (CtHMTH). ▪*Previous publication:* none known. ▪*Provenance:* donated to CtHMTH in 1985 by Cyril Clemens. ▪*Emendations and textual notes:* none.

▪ 3 September 1869 · To Elisha Bliss, Jr. · Buffalo, N.Y. · *UCCL* 00344

▪*Copy-text:* MS, Mark Twain Papers, The Bancroft Library, University of California, Berkeley (CU-MARK). ▪*Previous publication: MTMF*, 110, excerpt; *MTLP*, 28. ▪*Provenance:* see Mendoza Collection, p. 587. ▪*Emendations and textual notes:* The MS shows a number of inkblots, evidently from ink splattered at the American Publishing Company after receipt of the letter.

329.6   & • [◇] [*obscured by inkblot*]
329.12   irreverent • irrev-|[e]re[n]t [*obscured by inkblot*]
329.16   (or • [*no closing parenthesis*]

▪ 3 September 1869 · To Henry M. Crane · Buffalo, N.Y. · *UCCL* 00345

▪*Copy-text:* MS, Cyril Clemens Collection, Mark Twain Memorial, Hartford, Conn. (CtHMTH). ▪*Previous publication: Collector* (November 1949), lot I 2269, excerpts. ▪*Provenance:* The MS was sold in 1949 by Walter R. Benjamin Autographs of New York and sold again sometime before 1972 by Paul C. Richards, then of Brookline, Mass. It was eventually acquired by Cyril Clemens, who donated it to CtHMTH in 1985. ▪*Emendations and textual notes:*

330.13   together.⌐ If • ~.—|~ [*deletion implied*]
                      ʌ   ʌ

▪ 3 September 1869 · To Olivia L. Langdon · Buffalo, N.Y. · *UCCL*
  00346

▪*Copy-text:* MS, Mark Twain Papers, The Bancroft Library, University of California, Berkeley (CU-MARK). ▪*Previous publication: LLMT*, 106–9. ▪*Provenance:* see Samossoud Collection, p. 586. ▪*Emendations and textual notes:*

331.12   button-hole • button-|hole
331.16   me. At • ~.—|~
331.18   panzy • [*sic*]
331.23   repul̸gnance • ['l' *partly formed*]
331.28   button-hole • button-|hole
332.5   ~~Eng~~ Ensign's • En̸gsign's
332.14   ~~poo~~ portrait • po̸rtrait
332.23   ~~ti~~ trivial • t̸rivial ['i' *partly formed*]
332.28   it. And • ~.—|~
332.30   ẅ • [*partly formed; possibly* 'y']
332.35   ~~world~~ word • worl̸dd
333.21   ~~we~~ • ['e' *partly formed*]
334.3   sweetheart • sweet-|heart

▪ 6 and 7 September 1869 · To Olivia L. Langdon · Buffalo, N.Y. ·
  UCCL 00347

▪*Copy-text:* MS, Mark Twain Papers, The Bancroft Library, University of California, Berkeley (CU-MARK), is copy-text for the letter. A separate commentary for the enclosure (Appendix B), which does not survive with the letter, appears on p. 673. ▪*Previous publication: LLMT*, 359–60, brief paraphrase. ▪*Provenance:* see Samossoud Collection, p. 586. ▪*Emendations and textual notes:*

335.9   m̸ • [*partly formed*]
336.12   ~~oz~~ oozing • o̸ozing
336.36–38   (*Why* . . . *felicitous.*} • [*sic*]
337.11   d̸s • ['p' *partly formed*]
337.18   ~~yester~~today's • ~~yester-~~|today's
                    ʌ ʌ   ʌ ʌ

■ 7 September 1869 · To Elisha Bliss, Jr. · (1st of 2) · Buffalo, N.Y. · *UCCL* 08611

■*Copy-text:* MS, Special Collections Library, University of Texas at El Paso (TxEU). ■*Previous publication:* Parke-Bernet 1946, lot 120, brief paraphrase. ■*Provenance:* The MS, inherited by Mrs. Robert I. Ingalls, Jr., of Birmingham, Ala., from her father, R. Jay Flick of Lenox, Mass., was sold to an unidentified buyer in 1946 (Parke-Bernet 1946, lot 120) and was eventually acquired by TxEU. ■*Emendations and textual notes:* none.

■ 7 September 1869 · To Elisha Bliss, Jr. · (2nd of 2) · Buffalo, N.Y. · *UCCL* 00348

■*Copy-text:* MS, Mark Twain Papers, The Bancroft Library, University of California, Berkeley (CU-MARK). ■*Previous publication: LLMT*, 131, brief quotation. ■*Provenance:* see Mendoza Collection, p. 587. ■*Emendations and textual notes:*

340.2	J • [*possibly miswritten* 'I']
340.11	s~~l~~ • ['l' *partly formed; possibly* 'h']
340.14	~~personal~~ • ['l' *partly formed*]
340.15–16	personally & ~~responsible~~ financially • personally &	~~responsible~~ & financially

■ 7 September 1869 · To John H. Gourlie, Jr. · Buffalo, N.Y. · *UCCL* 10500

■*Copy-text:* MS, Mark Twain Memorial, Hartford, Conn. (CtHMTH). ■*Previous publication:* McBride, 365. ■*Provenance:* acquired by CtHMTH in 1978. ■*Emendations and textual notes:* none.

■ 7 September 1869 · To Whitelaw Reid · Buffalo, N.Y. · *UCCL* 00350

■*Copy-text:* MS, Papers of the Reid Family, Library of Congress, Washington, D.C. (DLC). ■*Previous publication:* none known. ■*Provenance:* donated to DLC between 1953 and 1973 by Mrs. Helen Rogers Reid and her sons, Whitelaw Reid and Ogden R. Reid. ■*Emendations and textual notes:*

342.24	~~on~~ office • o~~n~~ffice ['n' *partly formed*]

■ 7 September 1869 · To Olivia L. Langdon · Buffalo, N.Y. · *UCCL* 00349

■*Copy-text:* MS, Mark Twain Papers, The Bancroft Library, University of California, Berkeley (CU-MARK). ■*Previous publication: LLMT*, 360, brief paraphrase. ▪*Provenance:* see Samossoud Collection, p. 586. ▪*Emendations and textual notes:*

344.13	they day •	[*sic*]
344.23	~~their~~ there •	thei̶rre [*canceled* 'r' *partly formed*]
345.4	~~thre~~ they •	thr̶eey
345.11	~~wis~~ •	['s' *partly formed*]
345.17	youl̸ •	['l' *partly formed*]
345.33	BUFFALO •	B[U◊◊A]LO [*badly inked*]
345.33	SEP •	[SE]P [*badly inked*]

▪ 8 September 1869 · To Henry M. Crane · Buffalo, N.Y. · *UCCL* 00352

▪*Copy-text:* MS, Clifton Waller Barrett Library, University of Virginia, Charlottesville (ViU). ▪*Previous publication: Collector* (May 1949), lot I 948, excerpts. ▪*Provenance:* sold by Walter R. Benjamin Autographs in 1949; deposited at ViU by Clifton Waller Barrett on 17 December 1963. ▪*Emendations and textual notes:*

346.14	situated. Abbey's •	~.—|~

▪ 8 and 9 September 1869 · To Olivia L. Langdon · Buffalo, N.Y. · *UCCL* 00351

▪*Copy-text:* MS, Mark Twain Papers, The Bancroft Library, University of California, Berkeley (CU-MARK). ▪*Previous publication: MFMT,* 17–18, excerpt; Wecter 1947b, 69; *LLMT,* 109–11. ▪*Provenance:* see Samossoud Collection, p. 586. ▪*Emendations and textual notes:*

348.12	whole;̠,̶&̶ •	[*semicolon mended from comma*]
348.15	sunshine •	sun-|shine
349.7	~~do~~ dishonor •	d̸ishonor
349.9	~~that~~ than •	thaⁱn
349.12	~~anything~~ anybody •	any-|~~thing~~ body
349.14–15	~~so~~ seriously •	s̸eriousₗy
349.25	⌀ •	[*partly formed*]
349.32	& a day •	[*sic*]
350.2	~~goose~~ •	[*heavily canceled*]
350.7	knew •	['w' *malformed; doubtful* 'knews']
350.12	BUFFALO •	[BU◊]F[AL]O [*badly inked*]
350.13	SEP •	[SE]P [*badly inked*]

■ 9 September 1869 · To the Lyceums · Buffalo, N.Y. · *UCCL* 11512

■ *Copy-text:* Buffalo *Express*, 11 Sept 69, 1, from a microfilm edition of the newspaper in the Buffalo and Erie County Public Library, Buffalo, N.Y. (NBu). ■ *Previous publication:* none known other than the copy-text. ■ *Provenance:* The location of the MS is not known. ■ *Emendations and textual notes:*

351.2   withdrawing • with[◊]|drawing [*badly inked*]
351.3   lecture field • l[e]cture fi[e]ld [*badly inked*]
351.5   lecturers • l[◊]ctur[e]rs [*badly inked*]

■ 17 September 1869 · To Ausburn Towner (Ishmael) · Elmira, N.Y. · *UCCL* 08697

■ *Copy-text:* MS, *not sent*, Mark Twain Papers, The Bancroft Library, University of California, Berkeley (CU-MARK). ■ *Previous publication:* none known. ■ *Provenance:* see Mark Twain Papers, pp. 585–86. ■ *Emendations and textual notes:*

352.10   bloodthirsty • blood-|thirsty

■ 21 September 1869 · To Henry M. Crane · Buffalo, N.Y. · *UCCL* 00353

■ *Copy-text:* MS, Clifton Waller Barrett Library, University of Virginia, Charlottesville (ViU). ■ *Previous publication: Collector* (May 1949), lot I 950, excerpt. ■ *Provenance:* sold by Walter R. Benjamin Autographs in 1949; deposited at ViU by Clifton Waller Barrett on 17 December 1963. ■ *Emendations and textual notes:* none.

■ 21 September 1869 · To George E. Barnes · Buffalo, N.Y. · *UCCL* 00354

■ *Copy-text:* MS facsimile. The editors have not seen the MS, but a photocopy was provided in 1981 by the Massachusetts Historical Society, Boston (MHi). ■ *Previous publication:* none known. ■ *Provenance:* The MS, in the Dwight Papers at MHi at least until 1981, could not be located in 1989. ■ *Emendations and textual notes:*

354.3   s̶o̶ several • s◊everal
354.7   ◊ • [*partly formed; possibly* 'a']

■ 21 September 1869 · To Elisha Bliss, Jr. · Buffalo, N.Y. · *UCCL* 00355

■ *Copy-text:* Parke-Bernet 1938b, lot 72. ■ *Previous publication:* none known other than the copy-text. ■ *Provenance:* The MS, presumably kept in the Amer-

ican Publishing Company files after receipt, was in 1899 tipped into volume 1 of
The Innocents Abroad, the first volume of a special issue of one thousand sets of
the "Edition de Luxe" of *The Writings of Mark Twain*. The present location of
the MS, possibly part of either the Ormond G. Smith or George E. Chisolm collection before its sale in 1938, is not known. ■*Emendations and textual notes:* The
Parke-Bernet catalog describes the MS as an "A. L. s. *'Clemens'*. 1 p., small 4to,
Buffalo, September 21, 1869."

355.1	Buffalo, Sept. 21, 1869. • *[reported, not quoted; the month is spelled out in the usual catalog style]*
355.2–3	Bliss. [¶] The • ~. *[no ¶]*~
355.5–6	yrs. | Clemens • ~. ~

■ **21 September 1869 · To Silas S. Packard · Buffalo, N.Y. · *UCCL* 00356**

■*Copy-text:* Packard, 110. ■*Previous publication:* none known other than the
copy-text. ■*Provenance:* The present location of the MS is not known. ■*Emendations and textual notes:* The copy-text, rendered in italics except for the number '21,' is silently emended to roman type.

356.3–5	done | . . . . | Yrs • done, etc. | *[line of stars]* | Yrs

■ **23 September 1869 · To William P. Carpenter · Buffalo, N.Y. · *UCCL* 00357**

■*Copy-text:* MS, William Henry Carpenter Papers, Columbia University, New
York City (NNC). ■*Previous publication:* none known. ■*Provenance:* donated to
NNC with the papers of William Penn Carpenter's son, philologist and educator
William Henry Carpenter (1853–1936). ■*Emendations and textual notes:* none.

■ **24 September 1869 · To Mathew B. Cox · Buffalo, N.Y. · *UCCL* 10990**

■*Copy-text:* Transcript and paraphrase, Argus, at the University of Wisconsin,
Madison (WU). ■*Previous publication:* none known. ■*Provenance:* The Argus
Book Shop offered the MS for sale in a 1939 letter to George Brownell. He evidently did not purchase it, although he kept the letter describing it; see Brownell
Collection, pp. 581–82. The present location of the MS is not known. ■*Emendations and textual notes:* The Argus letter describes the MS as "Three pages,
8vo, closely written. Office of the Express Printing Company, Buffalo, Sept. 24,
1869."

357.1–4	MORNING . . . 1869. • *[reported, not quoted; text of letterhead adopted in part from 26 and 27 Sept 69 to Fairbanks]*

357.6   who • "~
357.8   & • and [*also at 357.10, 11*]
357.11–12 "Equinoctial storm" • '~ ~'
357.13   feeling. • feeling." etc.
357.15–16 Yours . . . Twain. • Subscribed and signed, "Yours for a thousand years, Mark Twain."

■ 26 and 27 September 1869 · To Mary Mason Fairbanks · Buffalo, N.Y. · *UCCL* 00359

■*Copy-text:* MS, Huntington Library, San Marino, Calif. (CSmH, call nos. HM 14254 and HM 14258). ■*Previous publication: MTMF*, 106–9. ■*Provenance:* see Huntington Library, pp. 582–83. ■*Emendations and textual notes:*

358.6   both. And • ~.—|~
358.11   ∲ • [*possibly partly formed* 'w' *or* 'm']
358.17   more • m̸ more [*corrected miswriting*]
358.20   it. Now • ~.—|~
358.29   n̶o̶t̶ mothers • [*possibly miswritten* 'mot'; 't' *partly formed*]
359.11   months • m̶o̶n̶ months [*rewritten for clarity*]
359.11–12 England • E̶n̶ England [*corrected miswriting*]
359.17   household • house-|hold
359.24   writ∤ing • ['t' *partly formed*]

■ 27 September 1869 · To Elisha Bliss, Jr. · Buffalo, N.Y. · *UCCL* 00358

■*Copy-text:* MS, Mark Twain Papers, The Bancroft Library, University of California, Berkeley (CU-MARK). A photographic facsimile of the letter is on pp. 540–41. The MS consists of one leaf of blue-lined off-white wove paper, 4⅞ by 7¹⁵⁄₁₆ inches, inscribed on both sides in black ink. ■*Previous publication: MTLP*, 28–29. ■*Provenance:* see Mendoza Collection, p. 587. ■*Emendations and textual notes:* Pinholes in the top margin of the MS, if not added by a later hand, may indicate that Clemens sent an enclosure, now missing, or that Bliss pinned the letter to his book order. Black ink was splattered along the bottom of both sides of the MS, probably by Elisha Bliss, when he made his marginal note.

362.12   t̶o̶l̶d̶ • ['d' *partly formed*]
362.15   a • ∤ a [*corrected miswriting*]

■ 30 September 1869 · To Oliver Wendell Holmes · Buffalo, N.Y. · *UCCL* 00360

■*Copy-text:* MS, Papers of Oliver Wendell Holmes, Library of Congress, Washington, D.C. (DLC). ■*Previous publication:* none known. ■*Provenance:* it is not known when DLC acquired the MS. ■*Emendations and textual notes:*

365.4   ~~have~~ had • ha~~v~~ed
365.15–16   ~~redin~~ red reading • ~~redin~~ re~~d~~ading [*canceled 'n' partly formed*]
365.19   "Thank-you" • "Thank-|you"

■ 7 October 1869 · To Unidentified · Elmira, N.Y. · *UCCL* 00361
■*Copy-text:* MS, Mark Twain Papers, The Bancroft Library, University of California, Berkeley (CU-MARK). ■*Previous publication:* none known. ■*Provenance:* sold by John Howell Books in 1972 and donated to CU-MARK in 1973; see Appert Collection, p. 588. ■*Emendations and textual notes:*

366.3   good. But • ~.—|~

■ 9 October 1869 · To Schuyler Colfax · Elmira, N.Y. · *UCCL* 00362
■*Copy-text:* MS, Houghton Library, Harvard University (MH-H). ■*Previous publication:* Anderson Galleries, lot 21. ■*Provenance:* sold in 1928 as part of the manuscript collection of Schuyler Colfax; inserted in a copy of *The Innocents Abroad* (1869) from the library of Harold Murcock; donated to Harvard University in 1935. ■*Emendations and textual notes:*

368.28–29   ("Innocents") • [*possibly* '("Innocents")']

■ 11 October 1869 · To the California Pioneers · Elmira, N.Y. · *UCCL* 00363
■*Copy-text:* "The California Pioneers," New York *Tribune*, 14 Oct 69, 5. The *Tribune* was most likely typeset directly from the MS. Another printing in the Buffalo *Express* ("*Mark Twain*. His Greeting to the California Pioneers of 1849," 19 Oct 69, 2) differs from the *Tribune* in ten readings, only one of them substantive ('big' for 'large' at 371.8). While the *Express* might conceivably have had an independent source, perhaps a marked copy of the *Tribune* sent by Clemens himself, the variation between the two printings is slight, and the revisions well within the province of a typesetter or newspaper editor. Collation shows that all other known printings are derivative. ■*Previous publication:* see *Copy-text* and "Mark Twain. His Greeting to the California Pioneers of 1849," (Elmira *Advertiser*, 25 Oct 69, 3); *Mark Twain's Letter to the California Pioneers* (Oakland, Calif.: DeWitt and Snelling, 1911); *MTL*, 1:163–65; Davis 1950. ■*Provenance:* The MS may have been kept by the Society of California Pioneers, San Francisco, but by 1983 it could not be found. ■*Emendations and textual notes:*

370.4   & • and [*also at 370.7, 9, 13 (twice), 15, 17 (twice), 20, 21, 24, 25, 26, 29, 30; 371.1, 2, 4, 6, 10 (twice), 12 (twice), 13, 14, 15, 17, 22 (twice), 23, 25, 27, 31, 32 (twice), 33, 34, 37; 372.1, 4, 5*]

370.5	New York • New-York
371.20	eternal • external

■ 27 October 1869 · To Emily A. Severance · Elmira, N.Y. · *UCCL* 00364

■*Copy-text:* MS, Western Reserve Historical Society, Cleveland, Ohio (OClWHi). ■*Previous publication:* Emily A. Severance, 217–18; *MTMF*, 110, excerpts. ■*Provenance:* Julia Severance Millikin (Emily Severance's daughter) owned the MS at least until the late 1940s, when Dixon Wecter transcribed it on Huntington Library stationery; it was acquired by OClWHi in 1986. ■*Emendations and textual notes:*

374.9	ẅ • [*partly formed*]

■ 30, 31 October, 1 November 1869 · To Olivia L. Langdon · Pittsburgh, Pa. · *UCCL* 00365

■*Copy-text:* MS, Mark Twain Papers, The Bancroft Library, University of California, Berkeley (CU-MARK). This letter, written on twenty-one leaves cut from a pocket notebook, was the first of ten surviving letters (eight of them to Olivia Langdon) written on notebook pages before the end of 1869. The notebook no longer survives (see pp. 381–82, n. 1). ■*Previous publication:* Wecter 1947b, 69–71, with omissions; *LLMT*, 112–18. ■*Provenance:* see Samossoud Collection, p. 586. ■*Emendations and textual notes:*

376.19	hook. At • ~.—|~
376.20	ceased • ce | ceased [*corrected miswriting*]
376.24	yet, • [*deletion implied*]
376.36–37	through. [¶] Then • ~.—| [¶] ~
377.2	hunted • ['un' *conflated*]
377.4	newspaper man • newspaper | man [*doubtful* 'newspaper-|man']
378.15	to-day • to-|day
378.17	flagship • flag-|ship
378.18	ke knew • kénew
378.20	Thompson • [*Clemens completed* 'Thompson' *before canceling* 'p']
378.24	to-night • to-|night
379.5	& spills • & | & spills
379.7	ha hateful • ha | hateful [*possibly rewritten for lack of room*]
379.8	whatsoever • whatsoveever
379.15	supp • [*sic*]
379.19	to-morrow • to-|morrow
379.30	reader • reader | reader [*corrected miswriting*]

379.31   ~~does~~ . . . presents‸ • ['does a' *canceled when* 'a‸ person presents‸'
              revised]
379.35   production • produc-|tion.‸ ||~~tion.~~
380.8   own • own ~~ow~~
380.8   ʸ • [*partly formed*]
380.11   good-natured • good-|natured
380.12   ~~how~~ him • how‸im
380.15–16   shoemaker • shoe-|maker
380.21   discoursed • [*sic*]
380.25   schoolboy • school-||boy
380.28–29   dare. [*line space*] [¶] Oh • ~.—| [*line space*] | [¶] ~
381.5   ~~And h~~ • [*possibly* 'And th'; 't' *partly formed*]
381.13   yowl. Well • ~.—|~
381.18   screech-owl • screech-|owl
381.21   he talked • ~~he~~ he talked [*corrected miswriting*]
381.22   ~~his~~ himself • hisʼmself
381.23   knees • ~~knees~~ | knees [*corrected miswriting*]
381.32–33   PITTSBURGH • PITT[SBU◇]GH [*badly inked*]
381.33   NOV • [NOV] [*badly inked*]
381.33   PHILADA. P.O. • PHIL[ADA. P].O. [*badly inked*]
381.34   ~~128~~ • [*doubtful* '1ʄ28'; *heavily canceled*]

■ 9 November 1869 · To Pamela A. Moffett · Boston, Mass. · *UCCL*
00371
■*Copy-text:*

P¹	*MTL*, 1:167–69
P²	Paine, 946

P¹ is sole copy-text for most of the letter. One paragraph only ('To-morrow . . .
fear.', 387.17–22) is based on P¹ and P², each of which derives independently
from the original MS (*MTB*, 1:389, prints the same paragraph as P² with no
change other than the styling of the ampersand to 'and'). ■*Previous publication:*
see *Copy-text.* ■*Provenance:* The present location of the MS is not known.
■*Emendations and textual notes:* The rationale for emendations to remove *MTL*
styling is given in Description of Texts, pp. 580–81. Adopted readings followed
by '(C)' are editorial emendations of the source readings.

386.1–387.16 Boston . . . work. (P¹) • [*not in*] (P²)
386.1   Boston, Nov. 9, 1869. (C) • BOSTON, *Nov. 9, 1869.* (P¹)
386.2–3   My dear Sister: | [¶] Three (C) • [¶] MY DEAR SISTER,—Three
              (P¹)
386.8   & (C) • and (P¹) [*also at 387.2, 8, 9, 11, 12 (twice), 15, 16; see also
              387.18, 24*]

387.17	To-morrow (P²) • Tomorrow (P¹)
387.18	& (P²) • and (P¹)
387.20	To-night (P²) • Tonight (P¹)
387.23–388.5	I . . . Sam. (P¹) • [*not in*] (P²)
387.24	& (C) • and (P¹) [*also at 387.27 (twice), 29, 30 (twice); 388.1 (twice)*]
388.5	Sam. (C) • SAM. (P¹)

■ 10 November 1869 · To Olivia L. Langdon · Boston, Mass. · *UCCL* 00366

■*Copy-text:* MS, Mark Twain Papers, The Bancroft Library, University of California, Berkeley (CU-MARK); written on three leaves of the same notebook paper as 30, 31 October, 1 November to Olivia Langdon. ■*Previous publication: LLMT*, 360, brief paraphrase. ■*Provenance:* see Samossoud Collection, p. 586. ■*Emendations and textual notes:*

390.4–5	again. [¶] Got • ~.—| [¶] ~
390.5–6	dearie. Just • ~.—|~
390.13	sweetheart • sweet-|heart
391.2–3	BOSTON MASS. NOV. 10 2 P.M. • [◇◇STON M]A[S]S. [NO]V. [◇◇] [2 ◇].M. [*badly inked*]

■ 10 and 11 November 1869 · To Olivia L. Langdon · Boston, Mass. · *UCCL* 00367

■*Copy-text:* MS, Mark Twain Papers, The Bancroft Library, University of California, Berkeley (CU-MARK), is copy-text for the letter. Clemens tore the enclosures from the Boston *Advertiser* ("Mark Twain on 'The Sandwich Islands,'" 11 Nov 69, 1) and the Providence (R.I.) *Morning Herald* ("Mark Twain's Lecture," 10 Nov 69, 2). They survive with the letter and are reproduced in facsimile. Clemens wrote this letter on one leaf of the same notebook paper as 30, 31 October, 1 November to Olivia Langdon. He wrapped the Boston *Advertiser* review in a strip torn from the *Eclectic Magazine*, n.s. 10 (November 1869): 625–26. ■*Previous publication: MFMT*, 18, without the enclosures and with omissions; *LLMT*, 120, 360, brief quotation and paraphrase. ■*Provenance:* see Samossoud Collection, p. 586. ■*Emendations and textual notes:*

391.5	midnight • mid-|night
391.10	left, • [*deletion implied*]
391.14	blessing • ['ing' *conflated*]
393.26	BOSTON MASS. • [BOS]TON [M]ASS. [*badly inked*]

■ 15 and 16 November 1869 · To Olivia L. Langdon · Clinton and Holyoke, Mass. · *UCCL* 00368

■*Copy-text:* MS, Mark Twain Papers, The Bancroft Library, University of California, Berkeley (CU-MARK); written on five leaves of the same notebook paper as 30, 31 October, 1 November to Olivia Langdon. ■*Previous publication:* *LLMT*, 121–22, 360, excerpt and brief paraphrase. ■*Provenance:* see Samossoud Collection, p. 586. ■*Emendations and textual notes:*

396.1	have • have | have
396.1	the̶i̶r̶ • ['r' *partly formed*]
396.5–6	boast. [¶] [How • ~.—| [¶] {~
396.8	threadbare • thread-|bare
397.3–4	misspelt • mis-|spelt
397.7	s̶t̶a̶t̶e̶ stage • sta̶t̶ege
397.7	to-night • to-|night
397.15	Langdon • Langdo[n] [*torn*]
397.15	N. Y. • N. [Y◊] [*torn*]

■ 19 November 1869 · To Mary Mason Fairbanks · Boston, Mass. · *UCCL* 00373

■*Copy-text:* MS, Huntington Library, San Marino, Calif. (CSmH, call no. HM 14255). ■*Previous publication: MTMF*, 111. ■*Provenance:* see Huntington Library, pp. 582–83. ■*Emendations and textual notes:*

398.12	t̶a̶l̶k̶ take • tal̶k̶ke
398.16	̷a̶l̶m̶o̶s̶t̷ • [*heavily canceled*]
398.29–30	BOSTON MASS. NOV. 20. 9 P.M. • [B]OS[TO]N [M◊◊◊◊ ◊◊]V. [20]. [9 ◊◊◊◊] [*badly inked*]

■ 19 November 1869 · To Olivia L. Langdon · Boston, Mass. · *UCCL* 00374

■*Copy-text:* MS, on the back of a *carte de visite* photograph of Clemens, Mark Twain Papers, The Bancroft Library, University of California, Berkeley (CU-MARK). Clemens wrapped the photograph, reproduced in facsimile, in a scrap torn from the *Eclectic Magazine*, n.s. 10 (November 1869): 513–14. ■*Previous publication: LLMT*, 360, brief paraphrase without the photograph. ■*Provenance:* see Samossoud Collection, p. 586. ■*Emendations and textual notes:*

399.3	4. Have • ~.—|~
400.4	BOSTON . . . 8.P.M. • [BO]STON [MA]SS. NOV 1[9] 8.P.M[◊] [*badly inked*]

■ 20 November 1869 · To James K. Medbery · Boston, Mass. · *UCCL* 00375

■*Copy-text:* MS facsimile, MacKaye, 1:plate 21. ■*Previous publication:* none known other than the copy-text. ■*Provenance:* The present location of the MS is not known. ■*Emendations and textual notes:* none.

■ 20–28 November 1869 · To George H. Selkirk · Boston, Mass. · *UCCL* 10552

■*Copy-text:* MS, on a letter from Henry George to Clemens, 9 Nov 69, Mark Twain Papers, The Bancroft Library, University of California, Berkeley (CU-MARK). ■*Previous publication:* none known. ■*Provenance:* presumably returned to Clemens by Selkirk; see Mark Twain Papers, pp. 585–86. ■*Emendations and textual notes:*

401.6   to the • to to the

■ 23 November 1869 · To Hiram J. Ramsdell · Boston, Mass. · *UCCL* 00376

■*Copy-text:* Transcript and paraphrase, Charles Hamilton, lot 32. ■*Previous publication:* none known other than the copy-text. ■*Provenance:* The MS was sold at auction by Charles Hamilton Autographs in 1964; its present location is not known. ■*Emendations and textual notes:* The Hamilton catalog describes the MS as an "A.L.S., 2 pages, 4to, Boston, November 23, 1869."

402.1   Boston, Nov. 23, 1869. • [*reported, not quoted; the month is spelled out in the usual catalog style*]
402.2   Dear Ramsdell— • To "Dear Ramsdell."
403.3–4   Thine . . . Sam*ˡ*. L. Clemens. • The letter concludes with a flourishing, "Thine ever, Saml. L. Clemens."

■ 24 and 25 November 1869 · To Olivia L. Langdon · Hartford, Conn., and Boston, Mass. · *UCCL* 00377

■*Copy-text:* MS and enclosed photograph, Mark Twain Papers, The Bancroft Library, University of California, Berkeley (CU-MARK). The photograph is reproduced in facsimile. ■*Previous publication:* *LLMT*, 122–24, without the enclosure. ■*Provenance:* see Samossoud Collection, p. 586. ■*Emendations and textual notes:*

403.14   tranquill*y*ity • ['*y*' *partly formed*]
404.5   ~~beautified~~ • [*false ascenders/descenders*]
404.28 $ • [*partly formed*]

404.29 $~~3,000~~ $5,000 • $$~~3~~5,000

404.34   satisfied in. • [*altered in pencil, possibly by Clara Clemens Samos-soud or by Dixon Wecter, to* 'satisfied. ~~in.~~'; *see* LLMT, *123*]

405.12   a~~b~~ • ['b' *partly formed*]

405.15   consult • consuℓlt

406.10   BOSTON LYCEUM • [B]OSTON LYCEUM [*torn*]

■ 25 November 1869 · To Olivia L. Langdon · Boston, Mass. · *UCCL* 00378

■*Copy-text:* MS, Mark Twain Papers, The Bancroft Library, University of California, Berkeley (CU-MARK). ■*Previous publication: LLMT*, 360, brief paraphrase. ■*Provenance:* see Samossoud Collection, p. 586. ■*Emendations and textual notes:*

409.6   I~~'d~~ • [*false ascenders/descenders; possibly* 'I'll']

409.13   ~~may~~ map • maýp

409.29   BED • [*block capitals, not underscored*]

410.3   BOSTON LYCEUM • [◊O]STON LYCEUM [*torn*]

410.4   BOSTON MASS. • [B◊◊◊◊]N [◊◊◊◊◊] [*badly inked*]

410.4   NOV. 26. 2 P.M. • [◊◊V]. 26. [2] P[◊]M. [*badly inked*]

410.4   ST. NICHOLAS HOTEL • [◊◊◊ ◊◊◊◊◊◊◊◊ ◊]OTEL [*badly inked*]

410.5   NOV 27 1869 • [◊◊V] 27 186[9] [*badly inked*]

■ 27 November 1869 · To Olivia L. Langdon · Boston, Mass. · *UCCL* 00379

■*Copy-text:* MS and enclosed photographs, Mark Twain Papers, The Bancroft Library, University of California, Berkeley (CU-MARK). The photographs are reproduced in facsimile. ■*Previous publication: LLMT*, 360, brief quotation without the enclosures. ■*Provenance:* see Samossoud Collection, p. 586. ■*Emendations and textual notes:*

410.8   youŕ • ['r' *partly formed*]

410.12   usual, • [*deletion implied*]

411.11   BOSTON MASS. • [◊◊◊◊◊N ◊A]SS. [*badly inked*]

411.12   27 • [27] [*badly inked*]

■ 28 November 1869 · To Olivia L. Langdon · Boston, Mass. · *UCCL* 00380

■*Copy-text:* MS, Mark Twain Papers, The Bancroft Library, University of California, Berkeley (CU-MARK). ■*Previous publication: MFMT*, 18–19, excerpt;

LLMT, 125–27. ▪*Provenance:* see Samossoud Collection, p. 586. ▪*Emendations and textual notes:*

412.14	T̶u̶s̶ Tuesday • Tu/esday
412.19	birthday • birth-|day
413.25	t̶r̶ tired • t/ired
413.32	BOSTON • B[◇◇◇◇N] [*badly inked*]

▪ 29 November 1869 · To Olivia L. Langdon · Boston, Mass. · *UCCL* 00381

▪*Copy-text:* MS, on the back of a two-page lecture itinerary written by George L. Fall of the Boston Lyceum Bureau, in the Mark Twain Papers, The Bancroft Library, University of California, Berkeley (CU-MARK). ▪*Previous publication: LLMT*, 360, brief paraphrase. ▪*Provenance:* see Samossoud Collection, p. 586. ▪*Emendations and textual notes:*

415.4	sweetheart • sweet-|heart
415.11	I. • [*what appears to be a second period follows, probably formed when Fall was rechecking the information; similar marks appear after* '3.', '13.', '14.', '16.', *and* 'Morris.' *(415.13, 24, 25, 27, and 416.16)*]
416.1–2	Berry. | 27. • Berry. ‖ Dec. 27. [*repeat of* 'Dec.' *occasioned by page break in MS*]
416.20	BOSTON MASS. • [◇◇S]TON MAS[◇◇] [*badly inked*]
416.20	29. 8.P.M. • 2[9.] 8.[P.M.] [*badly inked*]

▪ 3 December 1869 · To the Editor of the Brooklyn *Eagle* · Brooklyn, N.Y. · *UCCL* 02283

▪*Copy-text:* "Our Correspondence. Mark Twain's Lecture—A Card," Brooklyn *Eagle*, 4 Dec 69, 2, in a microfilm edition of the newspaper in the Brooklyn Public Library, Brooklyn, N.Y. (NB). ▪*Previous publication:* none known other than the copy-text. ▪*Provenance:* The MS of Clemens's letter is not known to survive. ▪*Emendations and textual notes:*

417.2	Dec. • ~,
417.5–6	occasion. | MARK TWAIN. • ~. [*extra space*] ~~.

▪ 4 December 1869 · To James Redpath · New York, N.Y. · *UCCL* 02445

▪*Copy-text:* MS, copy received, telegram blank filled out in the hand of a telegraph operator, collection of Victor and Irene Murr Jacobs, Roesch Library,

University of Dayton, Dayton, Ohio (ODaW). ▪*Previous publication:* Will M.
Clemens, 27, excerpt; John Anderson, Jr., lot 49, excerpt. ▪*Provenance:* The
telegram, transcribed by Will Clemens before 1900, was one of five telegrams
from Clemens to Redpath sold in three successive sales: in 1903 (John Anderson,
Jr., lot 49); in 1910 in the library of George Bentham (Anderson Auction Company, lot 180); and in 1925 in the library of William F. Gable (AAA 1925, lot
108). In 1973, it was bought as one of four by Victor and Irene Murr Jacobs.
▪*Emendations and textual notes:* The following unexplained numbers, concluding evidently with the Western Union operator's initials, appear in various places
on the telegram blank: 654 | 369 | 9 | 58/15/ 126 | ZA.

418.1   THE . . . COMPANY. • *Blank No. 1.* | THE WESTERN
           UNION TELEGRAPH COMPANY. | [¶] The rules of this
           company require that all messages received for transmission,
           shall be written on the message blanks of the Company, under
           and subject to the conditions printed thereon, which condi-
           tions have been agreed to by the sender of the following mes-
           sage. | THOS. T. ECKERT, Gen'l Sup't, NEW YORK. WIL-
           LIAM ORTON, Pres't, O. H. PALMER, Sec'y, NEW YORK.

▪ 6 December 1869 · To James Redpath · New York, N.Y. · *UCCL*
00383
▪*Copy-text:* MS, on a letter from the lecture committee of the Plymouth Young
People's Association of Plymouth Church, Brooklyn, in the Clifton Waller Barrett Library, University of Virginia, Charlottesville (ViU). ▪*Previous publication:*
Anderson Auction Company, lot 181, excerpts. ▪*Provenance:* deposited at ViU
by Clifton Waller Barrett on 17 December 1963. ▪*Emendations and textual notes:*

419.25   more • ᵐᵒʳ more [*corrected miswriting*]

▪ 10 or 11 December 1869 · To Schuyler Colfax · New York, N.Y. ·
UCCL 00384
▪*Copy-text:* MS, Syracuse University, Syracuse, N.Y. (NSyU). The topmost
portion of the MS page, which probably contained at least Clemens's dateline
and salutation, is cut away, leaving no trace of the missing characters. The letter
was written on a sheet of laid paper, ruled in blue, measuring 6 inches across.
The length now measures 6¼ inches. ▪*Previous publication:* none known.
▪*Provenance:* The MS was pasted into a first edition of *The Innocents Abroad*
sometime before 1928, when Merle Johnson made some descriptive notes about
the letter on an endpaper. The book and MS were donated to NSyU in 1953 by
Adrian Van Sinderen (1887–1963), a trustee of the Library Associates. ▪*Emendations and textual notes:* none.

■ 13 December 1869 · To James Redpath · Springfield, Mass. · *UCCL* 00385

■*Copy-text:* Merwin-Clayton, lot 128. ■*Previous publication:* none known other than the copy-text. ■*Provenance:* The present location of the MS (sold at auction in 1906 by the Merwin-Clayton Sales Company) is not known. ■*Emendations and textual notes:* none.

■ 14 December 1869 · To Olivia L. Langdon · Springfield, Mass. · *UCCL* 00387

■*Copy-text:* MS, Mark Twain Papers, The Bancroft Library, University of California, Berkeley (CU-MARK); written on six leaves of the same notebook paper as 30, 31 October, 1 November to Olivia Langdon. ■*Previous publication:* *MFMT*, 46, excerpt with omissions; *LLMT*, 41, 360, excerpt and brief paraphrase. ■*Provenance:* see Samossoud Collection, p. 586. ■*Emendations and textual notes:*

423.3	a̶l̶ • ['l' *partly formed*]
423.11	I. But • ~.—|~
423.15	p̶ • [*partly formed*]
423.32	~~were~~ was • ~~wer~~eas
424.6	~~tha~~ this • thảis
424.9–10	forever. ~~You~~ • ~.—|~
424.12	siezed • [*sic*]

■ 15 December 1869 · To Jane Lampton Clemens and Family · Boston, Mass. · *UCCL* 00389

■*Copy-text:* MS, Jean Webster McKinney Family Papers, Vassar College Library (NPV); written on one leaf of the same notebook paper as 30, 31 October, 1 November to Olivia Langdon. ■*Previous publication: LLMT*, 127, excerpt. ■*Provenance:* see McKinney Family Papers, pp. 583–85. ■*Emendations and textual notes:*

| 425.1 | Bromfield • Bromfie̶ld |

■ 15 and 16 December 1869 · To Olivia L. Langdon · Pawtucket, R.I., and Boston, Mass. · *UCCL* 00388

■*Copy-text:* MS, Mark Twain Papers, The Bancroft Library, University of California, Berkeley (CU-MARK); written on three leaves of the same notebook paper as 30, 31 October, 1 November to Olivia Langdon. ■*Previous publication: LLMT*, 127–28. ■*Provenance:* see Samossoud Collection, p. 586. ■*Emendations and textual notes:*

426.1   R.I, • [*possibly* 'R.I₁, '; *comma over period*]
426.8   sweetheart • sweet-|heart
426.12   school, • ~,,
426.14   of • ~~of~~ of
427.11   BOSTON LYCEUM • [◊]OSTON LYCEUM [*torn*]
427.12   ST. NICHOLAS HOTEL • ST[◊] NICHOLAS H[o◊◊◊] [*badly inked*]
427.13   NEW-YORK • NEW-YOR[◊] [*badly inked*]
427.23   ~~20~~ 25 • 2φ5

■ 17 December 1869 · To Pamela A. Moffett · Boston, Mass. · *UCCL*
  00390
■ *Copy-text:* MS, Mark Twain Papers, The Bancroft Library, University of California, Berkeley (CU-MARK). A photographic facsimile of the letter is on pp.
542–47. The MS, written on three leaves of the same notebook paper as 30, 31
October, 1 November to Olivia Langdon, consists of three consecutive leaves of
blue-lined and red-columned off-white wove paper, 3½ by 5¹¹⁄₁₆ inches, torn
from Clemens's notebook, inscribed on all six sides in pencil. Page 1 was splattered with black ink. ■ *Previous publication:* none known. ■ *Provenance:* see Moffett Collection, pp. 586–87. ■ *Emendations and textual notes:*

429.1   d • [*partly formed*]
429.4   their • [*sic*]
430.1   to-night • to-|night
430.14–15   custom to giving • [*sic*]
430.16   Annies . . . reason‸'s • [*sic*]

■ 18 and 19 December 1869 · To Olivia L. Langdon · Boston, Mass. ·
  UCCL 00391
■ *Copy-text:* MS, Mark Twain Papers, The Bancroft Library, University of Cal-
ifornia, Berkeley (CU-MARK); written on three leaves of the same notebook
paper as 30, 31 October, 1 November to Olivia Langdon. ■ *Previous publication:*
LLMT, 360, brief paraphrase. ■ *Provenance:* see Samossoud Collection, p. 586.
■ *Emendations and textual notes:*

431.2   *yesterday.* So • ~.—|~
431.21   ~~them~~ then • the‸n
431.27   poorhouse • poor-|house
432.2–3   BOSTON MASS. • [◊]OSTON [MASS]. [*badly inked*]
432.3   20. • [2]o. [*badly inked*]
432.3   ~~158ᵗʰ~~ | 159ᵗʰ • ~~15φ9ᵗʰ~~ | 159ᵗʰ [*revision rewritten for clarity*]

■ 21 December 1869 · To Olivia L. Langdon · Boston, Mass. · *UCCL* 00392

■*Copy-text:* MS, Mark Twain Papers, The Bancroft Library, University of California, Berkeley (CU-MARK). ■*Previous publication: LLMT*, 128–29. ■*Provenance:* see Samossoud Collection, p. 586. ■*Emendations and textual notes:*

434.11   BOSTON MASS. • [BOS◊◊N] MASS[.] [*badly inked*]
434.12   8.P.M. • [8].[P].[M.] [*badly inked*]

■ 25 December 1869 · To Olivia L. Langdon · Boston, Mass. · *UCCL* 00393

■*Copy-text:* MS, Mark Twain Papers, The Bancroft Library, University of California, Berkeley (CU-MARK), is copy-text for the letter. Clemens tore the enclosures from the Boston *Advertiser* ("In General," 25 Dec 69, 1) and the Washington *Morning Chronicle* (9 Dec 69, 4). They survive with the letter and are reproduced in facsimile. ■*Previous publication: LLMT*, 129–30, without the enclosures. ■*Provenance:* see Samossoud Collection, p. 586. ■*Emendations and textual notes:*

436.19   town. And • ~.—|~
436.23   ~~ten~~ the • ten̄he
436.26   ᴡ̶ • [*partly formed; possibly* 'n']
437.48   BOSTON MASS. • [BOS]TON MASS. [*badly inked*]

■ 27 December 1869 · To Olivia L. Langdon · New Haven, Conn. · *UCCL* 00394

■*Copy-text:* MS, Mark Twain Papers, The Bancroft Library, University of California, Berkeley (CU-MARK); written on four leaves of the same notebook paper as 30, 31 October, 1 November to Olivia Langdon. ■*Previous publication: LLMT*, 131–32. ■*Provenance:* see Samossoud Collection, p. 586. ■*Emendations and textual notes:*

439.7   depot.) I • ~.)—|~
440.5   lady. They • ~.—|~
440.7–8   demand. Mrs. • ~.—|~.
440.10   ~~Mrs.~~ Mr. • Mr.ₐs̶.
440.16   not • ~~no~~ not [*corrected miswriting*]
440.20   volume • ~~vo~~ volume [*corrected miswriting*]

■ 28 December 1869 · To Joseph H. Twichell · New York, N.Y. · *UCCL* 00395

■*Copy-text:* MS, Joseph H. Twichell Collection, Beinecke Rare Book and Manuscript Library, Yale University (CtY-BR). ■*Previous publication:* none known.

∎*Provenance:* It is not known when Twichell's papers were deposited at Yale, although it is likely that he bequeathed them to the university upon his death in 1918 (*L2*, 570). ∎*Emendations and textual notes:*

441.6   catsh • [*sic*]

∎ 28 December 1869 · To Elisha Bliss, Jr. · New York, N.Y. · *UCCL* 00396

∎*Copy-text:* MS, collection of Todd M. Axelrod. ∎*Previous publication:* Christie 1981, lot 54, excerpt; Neville, lot 526, excerpt. ∎*Provenance:* The MS, part of the estate of Marjorie Wiggin Prescott, was sold in February 1981 by Christie, Manson & Woods to Maurice F. Neville Rare Books, who in turn sold it in 1983 to Todd M. Axelrod. ∎*Emendations and textual notes:*

442.19   half-Turkeyᵢ • [*deletion implied*]
442.22   (charge • [*no closing parenthesis*]

∎ Appendix B: Enclosures with 12 January 1869 · To Mary Mason Fairbanks · El Paso, Ill.

∎*Copy-text:* Charlotte (Mich.) *Republican*, 30 Dec 68, 1, and Lansing (Mich.) *State Republican*, 31 Dec 68, 3; both from microfilm editions at the Michigan State Library, Lansing (Mi). ∎*Previous publication:* none known other than the copy-text. ∎*Provenance:* Neither of the enclosures survives with the letter. ∎*Emendations and textual notes:* none.

∎ Appendix B: Enclosures with 23 January 1869 · To Joseph H. Twichell and Family · Cleveland, Ohio

∎*Copy-text:* "Mark Twain's Lecture," Toledo *Blade*, 21 Jan 69, 4, and "Mark Twain," Toledo *Commercial*, 21 Jan 69, no page. Copy-text for the first is a microfilm edition at the University of Toledo, Ohio (OTU). Copy-text for the second, reproduced here in photographic facsimile, is a clipping in the Mark Twain Papers, The Bancroft Library, University of California, Berkeley (CU-MARK). ∎*Previous publication:* none known other than the copy-text. ∎*Provenance:* Neither of the enclosures survives with the letter. ∎*Emendations and textual notes:* none.

∎ Appendix B: Enclosure with 8–10 March 1869 · To John Russell Young · Hartford, Conn.

∎*Copy-text:* Galley proof for New York *Tribune*, 27 Mar 69, in the Mark Twain Papers, The Bancroft Library, University of California, Berkeley (CU-MARK).

■*Previous publication:* none. ■*Provenance:* see Mark Twain Papers, pp. 585–86.
■*Emendations and textual notes:*

458.6	& • and [*also at 458.7, 11, 13 (twice), 14, 15; 459.1, 3, 4, 5, 9, 11 (twice), 12, 13, 17, 22, 25; 460.2, 3, 6, 8, 10, 11, 21, 22 (twice), 23 (twice), 24; 461.2, 4, 6, 9, 13, 15, 16, 17, 18, 19, 21 (twice), 24 (twice); 462.1, 4, 5, 6 (twice), 7, 8, 10, 12, 13, 16, 18, 19 (twice), 20 (twice), 21, 22, 23 (twice), 26 (twice), 27 (twice); 463.1, 2, 4, 5, 7, 14 (twice), 16, 17 (twice), 18, 20 (twice), 22; 464.6, 7, 8 (twice), 9, 10, 11, 12, 14, 16 (twice), 17, 18 (twice), 20, 22, 23, 25, 26, 28, 29 (twice); 465.1 (three times), 6 (twice), 7, 8, 13; 466.3 (twice), 4, 6, 10 (twice), 11*]
459.6	the White • ihe White
459.23	memories • memeries
461.20	gentlemen • gentleman
464.1–2	[Emphatic . . . cabinet.] • [~ . . . ~.]
464.24	justice; • [*possibly* 'justice:']
465.10	content." • content "
466.1–2	[He . . . was.] • [~ . . . ~.]

■ Appendix B: Enclosure with 19 August 1869 · To Olivia L. Langdon · Buffalo, N.Y.

■*Copy-text:* "People and Things," Buffalo *Express*, 19 Aug 69, 2 (SLC 1869*l*). Copy-text is a microfilm edition of the newspaper in the Buffalo and Erie County Public Library, Buffalo, N.Y. (NBu). ■*Previous publication:* Clemens borrowed some of the items in "People and Things" verbatim from other newspapers, largely unidentified. No reprint of the entire column is known, but parts of it may have been borrowed in turn. ■*Provenance:* The original clipping that Clemens enclosed is not known to survive. ■*Emendations and textual notes:*

470.8	daylight • day-|light

■ Appendix B: Enclosure with 6 and 7 September 1869 · To Olivia L. Langdon · Buffalo, N.Y.

■*Copy-text:* "Salutatory," Buffalo *Express*, 21 Aug 69, 2 (SLC 1869p). Copy-text is a microfilm edition of the newspaper in the Buffalo and Erie County Public Library, Buffalo, N.Y. (NBu). ■*Previous publication:* in addition to the copy-text, *MTB*, 1:387–88, excerpt. ■*Provenance:* The original clipping that Clemens enclosed is not known to survive. ■*Emendations and textual notes:*

471.35	trunk • truuk
472.20	journalistic life, • ~, ~_∧_

References

THIS LIST defines the abbreviations used in this book and provides full bibliographic information for works cited by the author's name and publication date, or by a short title. Alphabetization is letter-by-letter: i.e., "Vann" precedes "Van Why."

AAA.
> 1914. *Catalogue of the George P. Upton Collection of Autograph Letters of Celebrities*. Sale of 23 April. New York: American Art Association.

> 1924. *Fine Books and Manuscripts of the Greatest Rarity and Interest. Including the Further Property of a Prominent Pennsylvania Collector*. Sale of 1–2 December. New York: American Art Association.

> 1925. *The Renowned Collection of the Late William F. Gable of Altoona, Pennsylvania*. Part 6. Sale of 8–9 January. New York: American Art Association.

AAA/Anderson.
> 1934. *The Fine Library of the Late Mrs. Benjamin Stern, Together with Autograph Letters from the Collection of William L. Clements and E. W. Evans, Jr., and Other Properties*. Sale no. 4111 (9, 10, and 11 May). New York: American Art Association, Anderson Galleries.

> 1936. *The Library of the Late Elbridge L. Adams . . . First Editions and Manuscripts of Works by Samuel L. Clemens, mainly the Collection of Irving S. Underhill, Buffalo, N.Y.* Sale no. 4228 (29 January). New York: American Art Association, Anderson Galleries.

AD   Autobiographical Dictation.

American Literary Bureau.
> 1870. *The Lecture Season*. Vol. 1, June. New York: American Literary Bureau.

AMT
> 1959. *The Autobiography of Mark Twain*. Edited by Charles Neider. New York: Harper and Brothers.

Anderson Auction Company.
> 1910. *Library and Art Collection of George Bentham of New York City*. Part 1. Sale no. 867 (28 and 29 November). New York: Anderson Auction Company.

Anderson, Frederick, and Kenneth M. Sanderson, eds.
  1971. *Mark Twain: The Critical Heritage*. New York: Barnes and Noble.

Anderson, Frederick, William M. Gibson, and Henry Nash Smith, eds.
  1967. *Selected Mark Twain–Howells Letters, 1872–1910*. Cambridge: Belknap Press of Harvard University Press.

Anderson Galleries.
  1928. *Historical Autograph Letters & Documents from the Collection of Schuyler Colfax*. Part 2. Sale no. 2236 (23 February). New York: Anderson Galleries.

Anderson, John, Jr.
  1903. *Catalogue of a Fine Collection of American Historical Autograph Letters*. Sale no. 168 (15 April). New York: John Anderson, Jr.

Andrews, Kenneth R.
  1950. *Nook Farm: Mark Twain's Hartford Circle*. Cambridge: Harvard University Press.

APC (American Publishing Company).
  1866–79. "Books received from the Binderies, Dec 1ˢᵗ *1866* to Dec 31. *1879*," the company's stock ledger, NN-B.

  1869a. "Opinions of the Press." Advertising circular and supplement to the prospectus for *The Innocents Abroad*, [1–4]. Hartford: American Publishing Company. A copy of the earliest impression of the circular and a copy of the revised version bound into the prospectus are in CU-MARK.

  1869b. "Paragraphs from Notices of this Book." Advertising supplement in the prospectus for *The Innocents Abroad*, [1–4]. Hartford: American Publishing Company. Copy in ViU.

  1869c. *Stray Leaves from Mark Twain's New Book*. Hartford: American Publishing Company. Copy in the collection of Nick Karanovich.

  1870. "Paragraphs from Notices of this Book." Advertising supplement in the prospectus for *The Innocents Abroad*, [1–7]. Hartford: American Publishing Company. Copy in CU-MARK.

Argus.
  1939. Letter from Argus Book Shop, Chicago, Ill., to George Hiram Brownell, 24 March (WU).

Arnold, Matthew.
  1979. *The Poems of Matthew Arnold*. Edited by Kenneth Allott and Miriam Allott. 2d ed. London and New York: Longman.

Austin, James C.
  1965. *Petroleum V. Nasby (David Ross Locke)*. Twayne's United States Authors Series, edited by Sylvia E. Bowman, no. 89. New York: Twayne Publishers.

Axelrod   Collection of Todd M. Axelrod.

Bacon, Edwin M.
  1883. *King's Dictionary of Boston*. Cambridge, Mass.: Moses King.

Bacon, Leonard Woolsey, ed.
  1883. *The Church-Book: Hymns and Tunes for the Uses of Christian Worship*. New York: D. Appleton and Co.

Baedeker, Karl.
1884. *Paris and Environs*. 8th rev. ed. Leipzig: Karl Baedeker.

Baehr, Harry W., Jr.
1936. *"The New York Tribune" since the Civil War*. New York: Dodd, Mead and Co.

Baender, Paul.
1959. "Mark Twain and the Byron Scandal." *American Literature* 30 (January): 467–85.

Bailey, John C. W., comp.
1867. *Kane County Gazetteer*. Chicago: John C. W. Bailey.

BAL
1957. *Bibliography of American Literature*. Compiled by Jacob Blanck. Vol. 2. New Haven: Yale University Press.

Barker, Charles Albro.
1955. *Henry George*. New York: Oxford University Press.

Barrett, Don C.
1931. *The Greenbacks and Resumption of Specie Payments, 1862–1879*. Cambridge: Harvard University Press.

BDUSC
1989. *Biographical Directory of the United States Congress, 1774–1989*. Bicentennial Edition. Washington, D.C.: Government Printing Office.

Beecher, Henry Ward.
1864. *Plymouth Collection of Hymns and Tunes; for the Use of Christian Congregations*. New York: Barnes and Burr.
1869. *The Sermons of Henry Ward Beecher, in Plymouth Church, Brooklyn. From Verbatim Reports by T. J. Ellinwood. "Plymouth Pulpit," First Series: September, 1868–March, 1869*. New York: J. B. Ford and Co.

Beecher, Julia Jones.
1896. "I Remember, I Remember." In *Park Church*, 12–15.

Beecher, Thomas Kinnicut.
1868. "Friday Miscellany." Elmira *Advertiser*, 25 December, 3.
1869a. "Friday Miscellany." Elmira *Advertiser*, 1 January, 3.
1869b. "Friday Miscellany." Elmira *Advertiser*, 8 January, 3.
1869c. "Friday Miscellany." Elmira *Advertiser*, 15 January, 3.
1869d. "Friday Miscellany." Elmira *Advertiser*, 5 March, 3.
1869e. "Friday Miscellany." Elmira *Advertiser*, 3 September, 3.
1873. *Memorial Remarks of Rev. Thomas K. Beecher, at the Funeral of Mrs. Eunice K. Ford, Who Died January 14th, 1873*. Elmira: privately published.

Ben [pseud.].
1869. "From Batavia." Letter dated 2 February. Aurora (Ill.) *Beacon*, 4 February, 1.

Bench and Bar
1903. *The Twentieth Century Bench and Bar of Pennsylvania*. 2 vols. Chicago: H. C. Cooper, Jr., Bro. and Co.

Berry, Earl D.
   1917. "Mark Twain As a Newspaper Man." *Illustrated Buffalo Express*, 11 November, sec. 5, 40.

Bickel, Bob.
   1990. "Scholar, Area Historian Revive Twain's Adventure in Geneseo." Rochester (N.Y.) *Democrat and Chronicle*, 30 January, sec. A, 1, 10.

Blackburn, Graham.
   1981. *The Overlook Illustrated Dictionary of Nautical Terms*. Woodstock, N.Y.: Overlook Press.

Blassingame, John W., Richard G. Carlson, Clarence L. Mohr, Julie S. Jones, John R. McKivigan, David R. Roediger, and Jason H. Silverman, eds.
   1982. *The Frederick Douglass Papers. Series One: Speeches, Debates, and Interviews. Volume 2: 1847–54*. New Haven and London: Yale University Press.

Bliss, Elisha, Jr.
   1870. "Mark Twain's Innocents Abroad." *Author's Sketch Book* 1 (November): 3.

Blunt, John Henry, ed.
   1868. *The Annotated Book of Common Prayer: Being An Historical, Ritual, and Theological Commentary on the Devotional System of the Church of England*. 3d ed. London: Rivingtons.

Bolton, Theodore.
   1940. "A Catalogue of the Paintings of Henry Inman." Supplement. *Art Quarterly* 3:401–18.

Book of Common Prayer
   1857. *The Book of Common Prayer, and Administration of the Sacraments; and Other Rites and Ceremonies of the Church, According to the Use of the Protestant Episcopal Church in the United States of America: Together with the Psalter, or Psalms of David*. New York: D. Appleton and Co.

Booth, Bradford.
   1950. "Mark Twain's Comments on Holmes's *Autocrat*." *American Literature* 21 (January): 456–63.

Boston Directory
   1869. *The Boston Directory, Embracing the City Record, A General Directory of the Citizens, and a Business Directory . . . for the Year Commencing July 1, 1869*. Boston: Sampson, Davenport, and Co.

Bowles, Samuel.
   1869. *Our New West. Records of Travel between the Mississippi River and the Pacific Ocean*. Hartford: Hartford Publishing Company.

Boyd, Andrew, and W. Harry Boyd, comps.
   1872. *Boyds' Elmira and Corning Directory: Containing the Names of the Citizens, a Compendium of the Government, and Public and Private Institutions . . . 1872–3*. Elmira: Andrew and W. Harry Boyd.

Branch, Edgar Marquess.
   1950. *The Literary Apprenticeship of Mark Twain*. Urbana: University of Illinois Press.

1985. "Fact and Fiction in the Blind Lead Episode of *Roughing It.*" *Nevada Historical Society Quarterly* 28 (Winter): 234–48.

Broderick, John C.
1976. "John Russell Young: The Internationalist as Librarian." *Quarterly Journal of the Library of Congress* 33 (April): 117–49.

Bryan, Wilhelmus Bogart.
1916. *A History of the National Capital from Its Foundation through the Period of the Adoption of the Organic Act.* 2 vols. New York: Macmillan Company.

Budd, Louis J.
1977. "A Listing of and Selection from Newspaper and Magazine Interviews with Samuel L. Clemens, 1874–1910." *American Literary Realism* 10 (Winter): i–100.

Buffalo Directory
1869. *Buffalo City Directory. Embracing a General Directory of Residents, a Street and Avenue Directory, Climatology of Buffalo, City and County Officers, Societies and Incorporated Companies, Banks, Telegraph and Railroad Companies, Table of Stamp Duties, Rates of Postage, Etc.* Buffalo: Warren, Johnson and Co.

Burpee, Charles W.
1928. *History of Hartford County, Connecticut, 1633–1928.* 3 vols. Chicago, Hartford, Boston: S. J. Clarke Publishing Company.

C   California State Library, Sacramento.

Cable Company.
1951. *The One Hundred and One Best Songs: for Home, School and Meeting.* Chicago: Cable Company.

Carson, Gerald.
1961. *One for a Man, Two for a Horse.* New York: Bramhall House.

Carter, Albert.
1988. "Tonsorial Days." Unrecorded oral reminiscence, 18 November. Witnessed in CU-MARK by Victor Fischer and Michael B. Frank.

Castel, Albert.
1979. *The Presidency of Andrew Johnson.* American Presidency Series, edited by Donald R. McCoy, Clifford S. Griffin, and Homer E. Socolofsky. Lawrence: Regents Press of Kansas.

CCC   Honnold Library, Claremont, California.

Chapple, Joe Mitchell, ed.
1950. *Heartsongs Dear to the American People.* Cleveland and New York: World Publishing Company.

Chase, Harold, Samuel Krislov, Keith O. Boyum, and Jerry N. Clark, comps.
1976. *Biographical Dictionary of the Federal Judiciary.* Detroit: Gale Research Company.

Chicago.
1936. *Library of the Hanna Homestead, Fort Wayne, Ind., with Selections from*

Libraries of Chicago's First Families: Burley, Tyrrel, et al. Sale no. 58 (25 and 26 February). Chicago: Chicago Book and Art Auctions.

Christie.
  1981. *The Prescott Collection: Printed Books and Manuscripts . . . the Property of the Estate of Marjorie Wiggin Prescott.* Sale of 6 February. New York: Christie, Manson and Woods International.

  1988a. *The Estelle Doheny Collection from the Edward Laurence Doheny Memorial Library, St. John's Seminary, Camarillo, California.* Sale of 1 and 2 February (Doheny III). New York: Christie, Manson and Woods International. Annotated copy in CU-MARK.

  1988b. *The Estelle Doheny Collection from the Edward Laurence Doheny Memorial Library, St. John's Seminary, Camarillo, California.* Sale of 17 and 18 October (Doheny IV). New York: Christie, Manson and Woods International. Annotated copy in CU-MARK.

  1991. *Printed Books and Manuscripts, Including Americana: . . . The Estates of Henry Bowen, Chester Davis, William Salloch.* Sale of 17 and 18 May. New York: Christie, Manson and Woods International.

CJL   Charles Jervis Langdon.

Clearwater, Alphonso T., ed.
  1907. *The History of Ulster County, New York.* Kingston, N.Y.: W. J. Van Deusen.

Clemens, Cyril.
  1932. *Josh Billings, Yankee Humorist.* Webster Groves, Mo.: International Mark Twain Society.

Clemens, Samuel L. See SLC.

Clemens, Will M.
  1900. "Mark Twain on the Lecture Platform." *Ainslee's Magazine* 6 (August): 25–32.

CLjC   The James S. Copley Library, La Jolla, California.

CofC
  1969. *Clemens of the "Call": Mark Twain in San Francisco.* Edited by Edgar M. Branch. Berkeley and Los Angeles: University of California Press.

Congressional Globe
  1868. *The Congressional Globe: Containing the Debates and Proceedings of the Second Session Fortieth Congress; Together with an Appendix, Comprising the Laws Passed at that Session; and a Supplement, Embracing the Proceedings in the Trial of Andrew Johnson.* Washington, D.C.: Office of the Congressional Globe.

  1871. *The Congressional Globe: Containing the Debates and Proceedings of the First Session Forty-Second Congress; with an Appendix, Embracing the Laws Passed at that Session; also, Special Session of the Senate.* 2 vols. Washington, D.C.: Office of the Congressional Globe.

Copyright.
  1869. Title page of *The Innocents Abroad.* Deposited for copyright, 28 July 1869. Rare Book and Special Collections Division, DLC.

Cortissoz, Royal.
1921. *The Life of Whitelaw Reid*. 2 vols. New York: Charles Scribner's Sons.

CSmH   Henry E. Huntington Library, San Marino, California.

CtHi   Connecticut Historical Society, Hartford.

CtHMTH   Mark Twain Memorial, Hartford, Connecticut.

CtHSD   Stowe-Day Memorial Library and Historical Foundation, Hartford, Connecticut.

CtY-BR   Beinecke Rare Book and Manuscript Library, Yale University, New Haven, Connecticut.

CU-BANC   The Bancroft Library, University of California, Berkeley.

CU-MARK   Mark Twain Papers, CU-BANC.

Cummings, Anson Watson.
1886. *The Early Schools of Methodism*. New York: Phillips and Hunt; Cincinnati: Cranston and Stowe.

CU-NEWS   Newspaper and Microcopy Division, University of California, Berkeley.

Cushing, Thomas, ed.
1889. *History of Allegheny County, Pennsylvania*. Chicago: A. Warner and Co.

DAH
1940. *Dictionary of American History*. Edited by James Truslow Adams and R. V. Coleman. 5 vols. New York: Charles Scribner's Sons.

Davis   Collection of Chester L. Davis, Sr., Mark Twain Research Foundation, Perry, Missouri, and collection of Chester L. Davis, Jr.

Davis, Chester L., Sr.
1950. "Mark Twain's Letter to the California Pioneers." *Twainian* 9 (November–December): 4.

1951a. "Revising the Revisor." *Twainian* 10 (January–February): 1.

1951b. "More Background on 'Innocents.'" *Twainian* 10 (May–June): 3.

1959. "Mark Twain's Personal Marked Copy of John Bunyan's 'Pilgrim's Progress.'" *Twainian* 18 (May–June): 1–4.

1976. "Mark Twain's Forthcoming Marriage (St. Valentine Letter to Rev. Joe Twichell)." *Twainian* 35 (March–April): 1–2.

1977a. "The Engaged Couple (Incomplete Letter)." *Twainian* 36 (July–August): 1.

1977b. "Family Letters of the 1870's (Mark's Inventions and 'The Gilded Age.')" *Twainian* 36 (September–October): 1–4.

1978. "'Dear Sister' Letter (August 20, 1869)." *Twainian* 37 (January–February): 1–3.

1979. "When we run . . ." *Twainian* 38 (September–October): 4.

Dawson, W. J., ed.
1913. *The American Hymnal*. New York: Century Company.

Dawson's Book Shop.
1925. *A Catalog of Rare Books*. No. 37 (February). Los Angeles: Dawson's Book Shop.

de Charms, Desiree, and Paul F. Breed.
1966. *Songs in Collections: An Index*. Detroit: Information Service.

DeWitt and Snelling.
1911. *Mark Twain's Letter to the California Pioneers*. Oakland, Calif.: DeWitt and Snelling.

Disturnell, John, comp.
1876. *New York As It Was and As It Is*. New York: D. Van Nostrand.

DLC   United States Library of Congress, Washington, D.C.

DNB
1959. *The Dictionary of National Biography, 1941–1950*. Edited by L. G. Wickham Legg and E. T. Williams. London: Oxford University Press.

Donald, Robert.
1889. "Mark Twain and His Book: The Humorist on the Copyright Question." New York *Times*, 10 December, 5. Reprinted in Budd, 43–46.

Doten, Alfred.
1973. *The Journals of Alfred Doten, 1849–1903*. Edited by Walter Van Tilburg Clark. 3 vols. Reno: University of Nevada Press.

Douglass, Frederick.
1848. "H. G. Warner, Esq., (Editor of the Rochester Courier)." Rochester (N.Y.) *North Star*, 22 September, 2. Reprinted in Foner, 1:371–74, misdated 30 March 1849.

Duncan, Bingham.
1975. *Whitelaw Reid: Journalist, Politician, Diplomat*. Athens: University of Georgia Press.

Eastman, Annis Ford.
[1905]. *A Flower of Puritanism: Julia Jones Beecher, 1826–1905*. Elmira: Snyder Brothers.

Eastman, Max.
1938. "Mark Twain's Elmira." *Harper's Monthly Magazine* 177 (May): 620–32. Reprinted in Jerome and Wisbey, 129–47.

Edwards, E. J.
1910. "New News of Yesterday." New York *Evening Mail*, 4 May, 8.

Edwards, Richard.
1868. *Edwards' Tenth Annual Director to the Inhabitants, Institutions, Incorporated Companies, Manufacturing Establishments, Business, Business Firms, etc., etc., in the City of St. Louis, for 1868*. St. Louis: Richard Edwards.

1869. *Edwards' Eleventh Annual Directory to the Inhabitants, Institutions, Incorporated Companies, Manufacturing Establishments, Business, Business Firms, etc., etc., in the City of St. Louis, for 1869*. St. Louis: Charless Publishing and Manufacturing Company.

1870. [*Edwards' Twelfth Annual Director to the . . . City of St. Louis, for 1870*]. St. Louis: Southern Publishing Company.

1871. *Edwards' Thirteenth Annual Director to the Inhabitants, Institutions, Incorporated Companies, Business, Business Firms, Manufacturing Establishments, etc., in the City of St. Louis, for 1871*. St. Louis: Southern Publishing Company.

Elliott, George W.
1869a. "The Dead Canary." Fort Plain (N.Y.) *Mohawk Valley Register*, 5 March, 1.

1869b. "The Blush Rose." Fort Plain (N.Y.) *Mohawk Valley Register*, 6 August, 3.

1869c. "Saml. L. Clemens." Fort Plain (N.Y.) *Mohawk Valley Register*, 20 August, 2.

1869d. " 'Mark Twain's' New Book." Fort Plain (N.Y.) *Mohawk Valley Register*, 20 August, 2.

Elson, Louis C.
1899. *The National Music of America and Its Sources*. Boston: L. C. Page and Co.

Encyclopedia of Pennsylvania
1904. *Encyclopedia of Genealogy and Biography of the State of Pennsylvania, with a Compendium of History*. 2 vols. New York and Chicago: Lewis Publishing Company.

Ensor, Allison R.
1987. "The Favorite Hymns of Sam and Livy Clemens." *Mark Twain Journal* 25 (Fall): 21–22.

ET&S1
1979. *Early Tales & Sketches, Volume 1 (1851–1864)*. Edited by Edgar Marquess Branch and Robert H. Hirst, with the assistance of Harriet Elinor Smith. The Works of Mark Twain. Berkeley, Los Angeles, London: University of California Press.

ET&S2
1981. *Early Tales & Sketches, Volume 2 (1864–1865)*. Edited by Edgar Marquess Branch and Robert H. Hirst, with the assistance of Harriet Elinor Smith. The Works of Mark Twain. Berkeley, Los Angeles, London: University of California Press.

ET&S3
Forthcoming. *Early Tales & Sketches, Volume 3 (1866–1868)*. Edited by Edgar Marquess Branch and Richard Bucci, with the assistance of Harriet Elinor Smith. The Works of Mark Twain. Berkeley, Los Angeles, London: University of California Press.

ET&S4
Forthcoming. *Early Tales & Sketches, Volume 4 (1869–1870)*. Edited by Edgar Marquess Branch and Richard Bucci, with the assistance of Harriet Elinor Smith. The Works of Mark Twain. Berkeley, Los Angeles, London: University of California Press.

Eubank, Marjorie Harrell.
1969. *The Redpath Lyceum Bureau from 1868 to 1901*. Ph.D. diss., University of Michigan, Ann Arbor.

Fairbanks, Lorenzo Sayles.
1897. *Genealogy of the Fairbanks Family in America, 1633–1897*. Boston: American Printing and Engraving Company.

Fatout, Paul.
1960. *Mark Twain on the Lecture Circuit*. Bloomington: Indiana University Press.
1976. *Mark Twain Speaking*. Iowa City: University of Iowa Press.

Feldman   Collection of John L. Feldman.

Fitch, Thomas.
1978. *Western Carpetbagger: The Extraordinary Memoirs of "Senator" Thomas Fitch*. Edited by Eric N. Moody. Reno: University of Nevada Press.

Foner, Philip S.
1950–75. *The Life and Writings of Frederick Douglass*. 5 vols. New York: International Publishers.

Ford, Darius R.
1870a. "Around the World. Letter Number IX." Letter dated 19 November 1869. Buffalo *Express*, 12 February, 2.
1870b. "Around the World. Letter Number X." Letter dated 17 and 24 January. Buffalo *Express*, 5 March, 2.

Fotheringham, H.
1859. *Hannibal City Directory, for 1859–60*. Hannibal: H. Fotheringham.

Freeman.
1936. *Rare Books and Autographs of the Late Charles T. Jeffrey*. Part 1. Sale of 23 March. Philadelphia: Samuel T. Freeman and Co.
1947. *Rare American Historical Autographs . . . The Collection of the Late Frederick S. Peck, Belton Court, Barrington, Rhode Island*. Part 2. Sale of 17 March. Philadelphia: Samuel T. Freeman and Co.

French, John Homer.
1860. *Gazetteer of the State of New York*. Syracuse: R. Pearsall Smith. Citations are to the 1980 reprint edition, Interlaken, N.Y.: Heart of the Lakes Publishing.

Friedman   Collection of Roy J. Friedman.

Frost, Maurice, ed.
1962. *Historical Companion to Hymns Ancient & Modern*. London: Proprietors, Hymns Ancient and Modern.

Geer, Elihu, comp.
1869. *Geer's Hartford City Directory; For 1869–70: Containing Every Kind of Desirable Information for Citizens and Strangers; Together with a Classified Business Directory, and a Newly Engraved Map of the City*. Hartford: Elihu Geer.
1879. *Geer's Hartford City Directory, for the Year Commencing July, 1879; and*

Hartford Illustrated: Containing a Classified Business Directory; New Street Guide, Map, Engravings. Hartford: Elihu Geer.

1882. *Geer's Hartford City Directory and Hartford Illustrated; For the Year Commencing July 1st, 1882: Containing a New Map of the City; New Street Guide; General Directory of Citizens, Corporations, Etc.* Hartford: Elihu Geer.

George, Henry.
1865. "A Plea for the Supernatural." *Californian* 2 (8 April): 9.

George, Henry, Jr.
1900. *The Life of Henry George.* New York: Doubleday and McClure Company.

Gody, Lou, Chester D. Harvey, and James Reed, eds.
1939. *The WPA Guide to New York City: A Comprehensive Guide to the Five Boroughs of the Metropolis . . . Prepared by the Federal Writers' Project of the Works Progress Administration in New York City.* New York: Random House. Citations are to the 1982 reprint edition, New York: Pantheon Books.

Goodman, Caleb.
1946. Record of relocation of Goodman family remains to vault 1023, Cypress Lawn Cemetery, Colma, California. Record dated 16 September. PH in CU-MARK, courtesy of Jay N. Miller.

Gould, Emerson.
1889. *Fifty Years on the Mississippi River; Or, Gould's History of River Navigation.* St. Louis: Nixon-Jones Printing Company.

Gray, David.
1870. "New Publications." Buffalo *Courier*, 19 March, 2.

Greeley, Horace.
1869. "The Future of the Blacks in America." New York *Independent*, 25 February, 1.

Green, Floride.
1935. *Some Personal Recollections of Lillie Hitchcock Coit–5.* San Francisco: Grabhorn Press.

Gregory, Winifred, ed.
1937. *American Newspapers, 1821–1936: A Union List of Files Available in the United States and Canada.* New York: H. W. Wilson Company. Citations are to the 1967 reprint edition, New York: Kraus Reprint Corporation.

Gribben, Alan.
1980. *Mark Twain's Library: A Reconstruction.* 2 vols. Boston: G. K. Hall and Co.

Groce, George C., and David H. Wallace.
1957. *The New-York Historical Society's Dictionary of Artists in America, 1564–1860.* New Haven: Yale University Press.

Gustafson, John A., and Jeffery D. Schielke.
1980. *Historic Batavia, Illinois.* Batavia: Batavia Historical Society.

Hamilton, Charles.
1964. *Charles Hamilton Auction.* Sale no. 4 (21 May). New York: Charles Hamilton Autographs.

1973. *Charles Hamilton Auction.* Sale no. 67 (3 May). New York: Charles Hamilton Autographs.

Hamilton, Sinclair.
1958. *Early American Book Illustrators and Wood Engravers, 1670–1870.* Princeton, N.J.: Princeton University Library.

1968. *Early American Book Illustrators and Wood Engravers, 1670–1870: Volume II, Supplement.* Princeton, N.J.: Princeton University Press.

Hannibal Census
[1850] 1963. "Free Inhabitants in . . . Hannibal." *Population Schedules of the Seventh Census of the United States, 1850. Roll 406. Missouri: Marion, Mercer, Miller, and Mississippi Counties.* National Archives Microfilm Publications, Microcopy no. 432. Washington, D.C.: General Services Administration.

Harnsberger, Caroline Thomas.
1960. *Mark Twain, Family Man.* New York: Citadel Press.

Harrison, John M.
1969. *The Man Who Made Nasby, David Ross Locke.* Chapel Hill: University of North Carolina Press.

Hart, James D.
1950. *The Popular Book: A History of America's Literary Taste.* New York: Oxford University Press.

1983. *The Oxford Companion to American Literature.* 5th ed. New York and Oxford: Oxford University Press.

1987. *A Companion to California.* Rev. ed. Berkeley, Los Angeles, London: University of California Press.

Harte, Bret.
1869a. "Current Literature." *Overland Monthly* 3 (September): 292–96.

1869b. "Etc." *Overland Monthly* 3 (October): 382–88.

1870. "Current Literature." *Overland Monthly* 4 (January): 100–104. Reprinted in Anderson and Sanderson, 32–35.

"Hartford Residents."
1974. "Hartford Residents." TS by anonymous compiler, CtHSD.

Hawley, Joseph R.
1900. "To the Editor of the Courant." Undated letter, probably written 21 October. In "Charles Dudley Warner," Hartford *Courant,* 22 October, 10.

Heitman, Francis B.
1903. *Historical Register and Dictionary of the United States Army, from Its Organization, September 29, 1789, to March 2, 1903.* 2 vols. Washington, D.C.: Government Printing Office.

Helmbold, Henry T.
1868. "Notice to the Public." *Harper's Weekly* 12 (28 March): 207.

HHR
1969. *Mark Twain's Correspondence with Henry Huttleston Rogers, 1893–1909.* Edited by Lewis Leary. The Mark Twain Papers. Berkeley and Los Angeles: University of California Press.

Hill, Hamlin.
1964. *Mark Twain and Elisha Bliss*. Columbia: University of Missouri Press.

Hirst, Robert H.
1975. "The Making of *The Innocents Abroad:* 1867–1872." Ph.D. diss., University of California, Berkeley.

Hirst, Robert H., and Brandt Rowles.
1984. "William E. James's Stereoscopic Views of the *Quaker City* Excursion." *Mark Twain Journal* 22 (Spring): 15–33.

Holdredge, Helen.
1967. *Firebelle Lillie*. New York: Meredith Press.

Hollister, O. J.
1886. *Life of Schuyler Colfax*. New York and London: Funk and Wagnalls.

Holmes, Oliver Wendell.
1858. *The Autocrat of the Breakfast-Table*. Boston: Phillips, Sampson and Co.

Honeyman, A. Van Doren.
1900. *Joannes Nevius, Schepen and Third Secretary of New Amsterdam under the Dutch, First Secretary of New York City under the English, and His Descendants, A. D. 1627–1900*. Plainfield, N.J.: Honeyman and Co.

Hooker, Richard.
1924. *The Story of an Independent Newspaper: One Hundred Years of the "Springfield Republican," 1824–1924*. New York: Macmillan Company.

Horner, Charles F.
1926. *The Life of James Redpath and the Development of the Modern Lyceum*. New York and Newark: Barse and Hopkins.

Howard, Henry W. B., and Arthur N. Jervis, eds.
1893. *The "Eagle" and Brooklyn: The Record of the Progress of the Brooklyn "Daily Eagle." Issued in Commemoration of Its Semicentennial and Occupancy of Its New Building; Together with the History of the City of Brooklyn from Its Settlement to the Present Time*. 2 vols. Brooklyn: Daily Eagle.

Howells, William Dean.
1869. "Reviews and Literary Notices." *Atlantic Monthly* 24 (December): 764–66.
1910. *My Mark Twain: Reminiscences and Criticisms*. New York and London: Harper and Brothers.

Hudson, Frederic.
1873. *Journalism in the United States, from 1690 to 1872*. New York: Harper and Brothers.

Hutchinson, Joseph.
1910. "Two Opinions of Twain." San Francisco *Call*, 24 April, 36.

IaU   University of Iowa, Iowa City.

Inds
1989. *Huck Finn and Tom Sawyer among the Indians, and Other Unfinished Stories*. Foreword and notes by Dahlia Armon and Walter Blair. Texts established by Dahlia Armon, Paul Baender, Walter Blair, William M. Gibson, and

Franklin R. Rogers. The Mark Twain Library. Berkeley, Los Angeles, London: University of California Press.

IVL (Isabel V. Lyon).
1907. "Datebook for 1907." MS notebook of three hundred and sixty-eight pages, CU-MARK.

Jerome, Robert D., and Herbert A. Wisbey, Jr.
1977. *Mark Twain in Elmira*. Elmira: Mark Twain Society.

JLC (Jane Lampton Clemens).
1861–70. Financial record kept in SLC's Notebook 3, CU-MARK. Page references are to a sixteen-page TS in CU-MARK.

Johnson, Miriam H.
n.d. "Batavia Public Library—A History." TS in CU-MARK.

Jones, Bernard E., ed.
1912. *Cassell's Cyclopaedia of Photography*. London: Cassell and Co.

Julian, John, ed.
1907. *A Dictionary of Hymnology*. 2d rev. ed. London: John Murray. Citations are to the 1957 reprint edition. 2 vols. New York: Dover Publications.

Kelly, J. Wells, comp.
1862. *First Directory of Nevada Territory*. San Francisco: Valentine and Co.

1863. *Second Directory of Nevada Territory*. San Francisco: Valentine and Co.

Kennedy, Robert V., comp.
1857. *Kennedy's Saint Louis City Directory for the Year 1857*. St. Louis: R. V. Kennedy.

1859. *St. Louis Directory, 1859*. St. Louis: R. V. Kennedy.

Kesterson, David B.
1973. *Josh Billings (Henry Wheeler Shaw)*. Twayne's United States Authors Series, edited by Sylvia E. Bowman, no. 229. New York: Twayne Publishers.

King, Joseph L.
1910. *History of the San Francisco Stock and Exchange Board*. San Francisco: Jos. L. King.

King, Moses.
1885. *King's Hand-Book of Boston*. 7th ed. Cambridge, Mass.: Moses King.

1893. *King's Handbook of New York City*. 2d ed. Boston: Moses King.

Kiskis, Michael J., ed.
1990. *Mark Twain's Own Autobiography: The Chapters from the "North American Review."* Wisconsin Studies in American Literature, edited by William L. Andrews. Madison: University of Wisconsin Press.

Knox, T. H., comp.
1854. *The St. Louis Directory, for the Years 1854–5*. St. Louis: Chambers and Knapp.

L1
1988. *Mark Twain's Letters, Volume 1: 1853–1866*. Edited by Edgar Marquess Branch, Michael B. Frank, Kenneth M. Sanderson, Harriet Elinor Smith,

Lin Salamo, and Richard Bucci. The Mark Twain Papers. Berkeley, Los Angeles, London: University of California Press.

L2

1990. *Mark Twain's Letters, Volume 2: 1867–1868.* Edited by Harriet Elinor Smith, Richard Bucci, and Lin Salamo. The Mark Twain Papers. Berkeley, Los Angeles, London: University of California Press.

Lain, George T., comp.

1869. *The Brooklyn City and Business Directory for the Year Ending May 1st, 1870.* Brooklyn: Lain and Co.

Lane, Sally.

1984. "Then and Now." Trenton (N.J.) *Sunday Times Magazine*, 8 April, 18.

Langdon, Jervis.

1869. "Mr. Beecher and the Clergy." Elmira *Advertiser*, 8 April, 1.

Langley, Henry G., comp.

1863. *The San Francisco Directory for the Year Commencing October, 1863.* San Francisco: Towne and Bacon.

1865. *The San Francisco Directory for the Year Commencing December, 1865.* San Francisco: Towne and Bacon.

1867. *The San Francisco Directory for the Year Commencing September, 1867.* San Francisco: Henry G. Langley.

1868. *The San Francisco Directory for the Year Commencing October, 1868.* San Francisco: Henry G. Langley.

1869. *The San Francisco Directory for the Year Commencing December, 1869.* San Francisco: Henry G. Langley.

Larned, Josephus Nelson.

1869a. "Current Literature." Buffalo *Express*, 21 August, 2.

1869b. "Found Drowned." Buffalo *Express*, 6 September, 4.

LaVigne, Gary W.

1961. "Mark Twain's Visit to Geneseo." Livingston (N.Y.) *Republican*, 7 September, 1, 6. Reprinted in *Twainian* 20 (November–December): 1–4.

Leggett, Mortimer D., comp.

1874. *Subject-Matter Index of Patents For Inventions Issued by the United States Patent Office from 1790 to 1873, Inclusive.* 3 vols. Washington, D.C.: Government Printing Office.

Lentricchia, Frank, Jr.

1966. "Harriet Beecher Stowe and the Byron Whirlwind." *Bulletin of the New York Public Library* 70 (April): 218–28.

Lester, Lisle.

1863. "The Chicago, or 'Nicholson' Pavement." Undated letter to the editor. *Mining and Scientific Press* 7 (21 December): 4.

Libbie.

1918. *Autographs. Letters and Manuscripts Left by the Late Frank B. Sanborn, Concord, Mass. . . . ; The Collection of James Terry, of Hartford, Conn.* Sale of 23 April. Boston: C. F. Libbie and Co.

LLMT
1949. *The Love Letters of Mark Twain*. Edited by Dixon Wecter. New York: Harper and Brothers.

Loomis, C. Grant.
1946. "Dan De Quille's Mark Twain." *Pacific Historical Review* 15 (October): 336–47.

Lorch, Fred W.
1929. "Lecture Trips and Visits of Mark Twain in Iowa." *Iowa Journal of History and Politics* 27 (October): 507–47.

1936. "Mark Twain's Orphanage Lecture." *American Literature* 7 (January): 453–55.

1968. *The Trouble Begins at Eight: Mark Twain's Lecture Tours*. Ames: Iowa State University Press.

Lounsbury, Thomas R.
1904. "Biographical Sketch." In *The Complete Writings of Charles Dudley Warner*. Vol. 15. Hartford: American Publishing Company.

Lowe, David.
1975. *Lost Chicago*. Boston: Houghton Mifflin. Citations are to the 1985 reprint edition, New York: American Legacy Press.

Ludlow, Noah M.
1880. *Dramatic Life as I Found It*. St. Louis, n.p. Citations are to the 1966 reprint edition, edited by Francis Hodge and Richard Moody, New York: Benjamin Blom.

Luther, Frank.
1942. *Americans and Their Songs*. New York: Harper and Brothers.

McBride, William H., comp.
1984. *Mark Twain: A Bibliography of the Collections of the Mark Twain Memorial and the Stowe-Day Foundation*. Hartford: McBride/Publisher.

McClelland, Sarah K., Maxwell Riddle, and Richard H. Kertscher.
1947. *One Hundred and Twenty-five Years of the First Congregational Church, Ravenna, Ohio, 1822–1947*.

MacKaye, Percy.
1927. *Epoch: The Life of Steele MacKaye, Genius of the Theatre, in Relation to His Times & Contemporaries*. 2 vols. New York: Boni and Liveright.

McKelvey, Blake.
1945. *Rochester, the Water-Power City, 1812–1854*. Cambridge: Harvard University Press.

McNulty, John Bard.
1964. *Older than the Nation: The Story of the Hartford Courant*. Stonington, Conn.: Pequot Press.

Maggs.
1988. *Autograph Letters & Historical Documents*. Catalog no. 1086. London: Maggs Brothers Limited.

Masters, Edgar Lee.
1933. *The Tale of Chicago*. New York: G. P. Putnam's Sons.

Mathews, Mitford M., ed.
1951. *A Dictionary of Americanisms on Historical Principles*. 2 vols. Chicago: University of Chicago Press.

Mattfeld, Julius.
1971. *Variety Music Cavalcade, 1620–1969: A Chronology of Vocal and Instrumental Music Popular in the United States*. 3d ed. Englewood Cliffs, N.J.: Prentice-Hall.

MEC   Mary E. (Mollie) Clemens.

Merwin, Henry Childs.
1911. *The Life of Bret Harte*. Boston and New York: Houghton Mifflin Company.

Merwin-Clayton.
1906. *Catalogue of Rare Autograph Letters, Manuscripts and Documents*. Sale of 14 and 15 May. New York: Merwin-Clayton Sales Company.

MFMT
1931. *My Father, Mark Twain*. By Clara Clemens. New York and London: Harper and Brothers.

MH-H   Houghton Library, Harvard University, Cambridge, Massachusetts.

Miller, James, comp.
1866. *Miller's New York as It Is*. New York: J. Miller. Citations are to the 1975 reprint edition, *The 1866 Guide to New York City*. New York: Schocken Books.

Miller, William C.
1973. "Samuel L. and Orion Clemens vs. Mark Twain and His Biographers (1861–1862)." *Mark Twain Journal* 16 (Summer): 1–9.

Mills, John Harrison.
[1912]. "Reminiscences." Unpublished manuscript excerpted in *MTB*, 1:388.

Mitchell, Wesley C.
1908. *Gold, Prices, and Wages Under the Greenback Standard*. University of California Publications in Economics. Vol. 1. Berkeley: University Press.

Moore, Thomas.
1820. *Irish Melodies and a Melologue upon National Music*. Dublin: William Power.

1829. *The Poetical Works of Thomas Moore, Including His Melodies, Ballads, Etc*. Paris: A. and W. Galignani.

1833. *The Works of Thomas Moore, Esq*. Leipzig: Ernest Fleischer.

1851. *The Poetical Works of Thomas Moore. As Corrected By Himself in 1843*. 2 vols. New York: Robert Martin.

Morris, Evans   Collection of Evans Morris.

Morris, Lloyd.
1951. *Incredible New York: High Life and Low Life of the Last Hundred Years*. New York: Random House.

MoSW   Washington University, St. Louis, Missouri.

Mott, Frank Luther.
　　1938. *A History of American Magazines, 1850–1865*. Cambridge: Harvard University Press.

　　1950. *American Journalism: A History of Newspapers in the United States through 260 Years, 1690 to 1950*. Rev. ed. New York: Macmillan Company.

　　1957. *A History of American Magazines, 1865–1885*. 2d printing [1st printing, 1938]. Cambridge: Belknap Press of Harvard University Press.

MTA
　　1924. *Mark Twain's Autobiography*. Edited by Albert Bigelow Paine. 2 vols. New York: Harper and Brothers.

MTB
　　1912. *Mark Twain: A Biography*. By Albert Bigelow Paine. 3 vols. New York: Harper and Brothers. [*Volume numbers in citations are to this edition; page numbers are the same in all editions.*]

MTBus
　　1946. *Mark Twain, Business Man*. Edited by Samuel Charles Webster. Boston: Little, Brown and Co.

MTE
　　1940. *Mark Twain in Eruption*. Edited by Bernard DeVoto. New York: Harper and Brothers.

MTHL
　　1960. *Mark Twain–Howells Letters*. Edited by Henry Nash Smith and William M. Gibson, with the assistance of Frederick Anderson. 2 vols. Cambridge: Belknap Press of Harvard University Press.

MTL
　　1917. *Mark Twain's Letters*. Edited by Albert Bigelow Paine. 2 vols. New York: Harper and Brothers.

MTLP
　　1967. *Mark Twain's Letters to His Publishers, 1867–1894*. Edited by Hamlin Hill. The Mark Twain Papers. Berkeley and Los Angeles: University of California Press.

MTMF
　　1949. *Mark Twain to Mrs. Fairbanks*. Edited by Dixon Wecter. San Marino, Calif.: Huntington Library.

MTTB
　　1940. *Mark Twain's Travels with Mr. Brown*. Edited by Franklin Walker and G. Ezra Dane. New York: Alfred A. Knopf.

Mudd, Nettie, ed.
　　1906. *The Life of Dr. Samuel A. Mudd*. New York and Washington, D.C.: Neale Publishing Company.

N&J1
　　1975. *Mark Twain's Notebooks & Journals, Volume I (1855–1873)*. Edited by Frederick Anderson, Michael B. Frank, and Kenneth M. Sanderson. The

Mark Twain Papers. Berkeley, Los Angeles, London: University of California Press.

N&J2
1975. *Mark Twain's Notebooks & Journals, Volume II (1877–1883)*. Edited by Frederick Anderson, Lin Salamo, and Bernard L. Stein. The Mark Twain Papers. Berkeley, Los Angeles, London: University of California Press.

Naylor, Maria, ed.
1973. *The National Academy of Design Exhibition Record, 1861–1900*. 2 vols. New York: Kennedy Galleries.

NB   Brooklyn Public Library, Brooklyn, New York.

NBu   Buffalo and Erie County Public Library, Buffalo, New York.

NBuHi   Buffalo and Erie County Historical Society, Buffalo, New York.

NCAB
1898–1984. *The National Cyclopedia of American Biography*. Volumes 1–62 and A–M plus index. New York: James T. White and Co.

NElmC   Mark Twain Archives and Center for Mark Twain Studies at Quarry Farm, Elmira College, Elmira, New York.

Neider, Charles, ed.
1982. *The Selected Letters of Mark Twain*. New York: Harper and Row.

Neville, Maurice F.
1982. *Catalogue Number Eight. Fine First Editions & Literary Autographs*. Santa Barbara: Maurice F. Neville Rare Books.

NN   The New York Public Library, Astor, Lenox and Tilden Foundations, New York City.

NN-B   Henry W. and Albert A. Berg Collection, NN.

NNC   Columbia University, New York City.

"Nook Farm Genealogy."
1974. "Nook Farm Genealogy." TS by anonymous compiler, CtHSD.

NPV   Jean Webster McKinney Family Papers, Francis Fitz Randolph Rare Book Room, Vassar College Library, Poughkeepsie, New York.

NSyU   Syracuse University, Syracuse, New York.

OC   Orion Clemens.

OClWHi   Western Reserve Historical Society, Cleveland, Ohio.

ODaU   Collection of Victor and Irene Murr Jacobs, Roesch Library, University of Dayton, Dayton, Ohio.

OED
1989. *The Oxford English Dictionary*. 2d ed. Prepared by J. A. Simpson and E. S. C. Weiner. 20 vols. Oxford: Clarendon Press.

OLC   Olivia Langdon Clemens.

OLL   Olivia Louise Langdon.

Olmsted, John B.
  1915. "Josephus Nelson Larned." *Publications of the Buffalo Historical Society* 19:3–33.

OTU   University of Toledo, Toledo, Ohio.

Pacific Coast
  1878. *Pacific Coast Annual Mining Review and Stock Ledger.* San Francisco: Francis and Valentine.

Packard, Silas Sadler.
  1885. "Hints on Correspondence." *Packard's Short-Hand Reporter and Amanuensis* 1 (April): 110.

Paff, Harriet Lewis.
  1897. "What I Know about Mark Twain." MS of twelve pages, CtY-BR.

Paine, Albert Bigelow.
  1912. "Mark Twain: Some Chapters from an Extraordinary Life. Seventh Paper." *Harper's Monthly Magazine* 124 (May): 934–47.

Palmer, Joseph, comp.
  1975. *Jane's Dictionary of Naval Terms.* London: Macdonald and Jane's.

PAM   Pamela Ann Moffett.

Park Church
  1896. *The Park Church. 1846–1896.* Elmira: Park Church.

Parke-Bernet.
  1938a. *William Blake . . . Samuel L. Clemens Manuscripts, Autographs, First Editions Including the Manuscript of "Tom Sawyer" from Which the London Edition Was Printed . . . Collected by the Late George C. Smith, Jr., New York, N.Y.* Sale no. 59 (2–3 November). New York: Parke-Bernet Galleries.

  1938b. *Sets of Standard Authors, Colored Plate & Other Illustrated Books . . . Collected by the Late Ormond G. Smith, Wheatley Hills, N.J. . . . the late George E. Chisolm, Morristown, N.J. . . . A Collection of about 2500 Chirographical Specimens from the XIIIth to the XIXth Century Formed by a New York Gentleman, with Properties from Other Owners.* Sale no. 61 (9–10 November). New York: Parke-Bernet Galleries.

  1938c. *Great Events in American History . . . Manuscripts by Famous American Authors . . . The William Randolph Hearst Collection.* Part 1. Sale no. 63 (16–17 November). New York: Parke-Bernet Galleries.

  1940. *Library Sets of Standard Authors . . . from the Collection of Percy R. Pyne, 2nd, Removed from Rivington House, Roslyn, Long Island; First Editions of English and American Authors Collected by Jacques Wallach, New York; . . . Selections from the Libraries of Harold Palmer, Manchester, Massachusetts, N. N. Van Brunt, Longmeadow, Springfield, Mass. . . . and Properties from Other Owners.* Sale no. 160 (10–11 January). New York: Parke-Bernet Galleries.

  1941. *First Editions, Standard Sets, Autograph Letters & Manuscripts . . . Belonging to Harold Fisher . . . with Additions from Other Owners.* Sale no. 248 (15–16 January). New York: Parke-Bernet Galleries.

  1942. *First Editions, Original Drawings, Paintings, Caricatures: The Work of the Great English Illustrators and Authors of the XVII–XIX Centuries*

. . . *Collected by the Late William H. Woodin, New York.* Part 2. Sale no. 331 (6–8 January). New York: Parke-Bernet Galleries.

1946. *Sporting & Color Plate Books . . . First Editions; Standard Authors; the Important Library Collected by the Late R. Jay Flick, Lenox, Mass. Sold by Order of His Daughter Mrs Robert I. Ingalls, Jr, Birmingham, Alabama, the Present Owner.* Sale no. 722 (8–9 January). New York: Parke-Bernet Galleries.

Parker, Franklin.
1971. *George Peabody: A Biography.* Nashville: Vanderbilt University Press.

PCarlD   Dickinson College, Carlisle, Pennsylvania.

Pennsylvania
1940. *Pennsylvania: A Guide to the Keystone State.* Compiled by workers of the Writers' Program of the Works Projects Administration in the State of Pennsylvania. New York: Oxford University Press.

Pisani, Donald J.
1974. "'Why Shouldn't California Have the Grandest Aqueduct in the World?': Alexis Von Schmidt's Lake Tahoe Scheme." *California Historical Quarterly* 53 (Winter): 347–60.

Pond, James B.
1900. *Eccentricities of Genius.* New York: G. W. Dillingham Company.

PP   Free Library of Philadelphia, Philadelphia, Pennsylvania.

PPiU   Special Collections Department, University of Pittsburgh Libraries, Pittsburgh, Pennsylvania.

Redpath, James.
1861–62. "Correspondence of James Redpath, Commercial agent of Hayti for Philadelphia, Joint commissioner plenipotentiary of Hayti to the government of the U.S., & General agent of emigration to Hayti for the U.S. & Canada, December 31, 1861 to May 12, 1862." MS of 470 pages, NN.

Redpath, James, and George L. Fall.
1870. *The Lyceum: Containing a Complete List of Lecturers, Readers, and Musicians for the Season of 1870–71.* Vol. 1, July. Boston: Redpath and Fall.

Reese, George W.
1867. *Geo. W. Reese's New Map of the City of Buffalo.* New York: Clerk's Office of the District Court of the Northern District of New York.

Reigstad, Tom.
1989. "Twain's Langdon-Appointed Guardian Angels in Buffalo: 'Mac,' 'Fletch,' and 'Dombrowski.'" *Mark Twain Society Bulletin* 12 (July): 1, 3–6, 8.
1990. "Twain's Buffalo Clergyman and the Beecher Preacher Exchange." *Mark Twain Society Bulletin* 13 (July): 1–3.

Rose, William Ganson.
1950. *Cleveland: The Making of a City.* Cleveland and New York: World Publishing Company.

Rowell, George P.
1869. *Geo. P. Rowell & Co's American Newspaper Directory.* New York: George P. Rowell and Co.

Salsbury, Edith Colgate, ed.
1965. *Susy and Mark Twain: Family Dialogues*. New York: Harper and Row.

S&B
1967. *Mark Twain's Satires & Burlesques*. Edited with an introduction by Franklin R. Rogers. The Mark Twain Papers. Berkeley and Los Angeles: University of California Press.

San Francisco City and County.
1868. *Supplementary List of Citizens of the United States Resident in the City and County of San Francisco, and Registered in the Great Register of Said City and County, Since the Making Out of the General List, in July, 1867*. San Francisco: Mullin, Mahon and Co.

Scharf, J. Thomas.
1883. *History of Saint Louis City and County, from the Earliest Periods to the Present Day*. 2 vols. Philadelphia: Louis H. Everts and Co.

Scott, Charles I.
1868. *Scott's Annual Toledo City Directory for 1868–69, Embracing a Large Amount of Valuable Information of Local Societies, Incorporated Bodies, &c., Together with a General Business Directory*. Toledo: Charles I. Scott.

1870. *Scott's Annual Toledo City Directory for 1870–71. Embracing a Large Amount of Valuable Information of Local Societies, Incorporated Bodies, &c., Together with a General Business Directory*. Toledo: Charles I. Scott.

Sears, Minnie Earl, ed.
1926. *Song Index: An Index to more than 12000 Songs in 177 Song Collections Comprising 262 Volumes*. New York: H. W. Wilson Company.

Senate.
1868. "List of Committees of the Senate of the United States." In *Miscellaneous Documents of the Senate of the United States for the Second Session of the Fortieth Congress, 1867–'68*. Washington, D.C.: Government Printing Office.

1876. "A Compilation of the Laws of the United States, showing the changes in the 'Domestic rates of postage' and in the 'Franking privilege,' from 1789 until the present time." In *Miscellaneous Documents of the Senate of the United States for the First Session of the Forty-Fourth Congress*. Vol. 1. Washington, D.C.: Government Printing Office.

1887. *Journal of the Executive Proceedings of the Senate of the United States of America*. Vol. 13, *From December 1, 1862, to July 4, 1864, Inclusive*. Vol. 14, Part 2, *From February 13, 1866, to July 28, 1866, Inclusive*. Vol. 15, Part 2, *From March 13, 1867, to November 29, 1867, Inclusive*. Vol. 16, *From December 2, 1867, to March 3, 1869, Inclusive*. Washington, D.C.: Government Printing Office.

Severance, Emily A.
1938. *Journal Letters of Emily A. Severance: "Quaker City" 1867*. Foreword and epilogue by Julia Severance Millikin. Cleveland: Gates Press.

Severance, Frank H., comp.
1915. "Bibliography: The Periodical Press of Buffalo, 1811–1915" and "Editorial Notes." *Publications of the Buffalo Historical Society* 19:177–343.

Sharlow, Gretchen.
1990. "Lost and Found: A Research Note on Susan Crane's Adoption." *Dear Friends: An Occasional Newsletter for Its Friends Published by the Elmira College Center for Mark Twain Studies at Quarry Farm* (November): 2.

Simpson, Alan.
1977. *Mark Twain Goes Back to Vassar: An Introduction to the Jean Webster McKinney Family Papers.* Poughkeepsie, N.Y.: Vassar College.

SLC (Samuel Langhorne Clemens).
1866. "An Open Letter to the American People." New York *Weekly Review* 17 (17 February): 1. Reprinted in *ET&S3*, no. 181.

1867a. *The Celebrated Jumping Frog of Calaveras County, And other Sketches.* Edited by John Paul. New York: C. H. Webb.

1867b. " 'Mark Twain' in New York. Letter Number X." Letter dated 23 February. San Francisco *Alta California*, 5 April, 1. Reprinted in part in *MTTB*, 101–10.

1867c. "Letter from 'Mark Twain.' [No. 14.]" Letter dated 16 April. San Francisco *Alta California*, 26 May, 1. Reprinted in *MTTB*, 141–48.

1867d. "Letter from 'Mark Twain.' [No. 23.]" Letter dated 28 May. San Francisco *Alta California*, 28 July, 1. Reprinted in *MTTB*, 238–48.

1867e. "The American Colony in Palestine." Letter dated 2 October. New York *Tribune*, 2 November, 2. Reprinted in *TIA*, 306–9.

1867f. "The Holy Land Excursion. Letter from 'Mark Twain.' [Number twenty-five.]" Letter dated 6 September. San Francisco *Alta California*, 21 November, 1. Reprinted in *TIA*, 168–72.

1867g. "Information Wanted." Letter dated 10 December. New York *Tribune*, 18 December, 2. Reprinted in *ET&S3*, no. 216.

1867h. "The Facts Concerning the Recent Resignation." New York *Tribune*, 27 December, 2. Reprinted in *ET&S3*, no. 217.

1868a. "Mark Twain in Washington. [Special Correspondence of the Alta California.]" Letter dated 10 December 1867. San Francisco *Alta California*, 15 January, 1.

1868b. "Letter from 'Mark Twain.' [Special Correspondent of the Alta California.]" Letter dated 14 December 1867. San Francisco *Alta California*, 21 January, 2.

1868c. "Information Wanted." Undated letter to the editor. New York *Tribune*, 22 January, 2.

1868d. "Mark Twain in Washington. [Special Correspondent of the Alta California.]" Letter dated 17 December 1867. San Francisco *Alta California*, 28 January, 2.

1868e. "The Facts Concerning the Recent Important Resignation." Letter dated 9 February. New York *Tribune*, 13 February, 2.

1868f. "Concerning Gideon's Band." Undated letter to the editor. Washington (D.C.) *Morning Chronicle*, 27 February, 2.

1868g. "The Chinese Mission." Undated letter to the editor. New York *Tribune*, 11 March, 2.

1868h. "Letter from Mark Twain." Letter dated 2 May. Chicago *Republican*, 31 May, 2.

1868i. "The Treaty with China." New York *Tribune*, 4 August, 1–2.

1868j. "Private Habits of Horace Greeley." *Spirit of the Times*, 7 November, 192.

1868k. "Letter from 'Mark Twain.'" Letter dated 22 October. San Francisco *Alta California*, 15 November, 1.

1868*l*. "Concerning Gen. Grant's Intentions." New York *Tribune*, 12 December, 4.

1869a. *The Innocents Abroad; or, The New Pilgrims' Progress*. Hartford: American Publishing Company.

1869b. "Open Letter to Com. Vanderbilt." *Packard's Monthly* 2 (March): 89–91.

1869c. "The White House Funeral." Written on 7 March for the New York *Tribune*, but never published. One sheet of *Tribune* galley proof, CU-MARK.

1869d. "Mr. Beecher and the Clergy." Elmira *Advertiser*, 10 April, 1. Reprinted in *WIM*, 42–47.

1869e. "Remarkable Murder Trial." Letter to the editor dated 29 April. New York *Tribune*, 8 May, 4.

1869f. "Scenery." MS of eleven pages, written in late June or early July as part of a lecture on "Curiosities of California," CU-MARK. Published in Wecter 1948, 13–17, and in *ET&S4*, no. 236.

1869g. "Mark Twain's Eulogy on the 'Reliable Contraband.'" *Packard's Monthly* 2 (July): 220–21. Reprinted in *ET&S3*, no. 235.

1869h. "Letter from Mark Twain." Letter dated July. San Francisco *Alta California*, 25 July, 1.

1869i. "Personal Habits of the Siamese Twins." *Packard's Monthly* 2 (August): 249–50. Reprinted in *ET&S4*, no. 237.

1869j. "Letter from Mark Twain." Letter dated July. San Francisco *Alta California*, 1 August, 1.

1869k. "Inspired Humor." Buffalo *Express*, 19 August, 2.

1869*l*. "People and Things." Buffalo *Express*, 19 August, 2. Reprinted in part in *ET&S4*, no. 239.

1869m. "The 'Monopoly' Speaks." Buffalo *Express*, 20 August, 2.

1869n. "A Day at Niagara." Buffalo *Express*, 21 August, 1. Reprinted in *ET&S4*, no. 241.

1869o. "Removal of the Capital." Buffalo *Express*, 21 August, 2.

1869p. "Salutatory." Buffalo *Express*, 21 August, 2. Reprinted in part, misdated 18 August, in *MTB*, 1:387–88.

1869q. "People and Things." Buffalo *Express*, 23 August, 2.

1869r. "People and Things." Buffalo *Express*, 26 August, 2.

1869s. "English Festivities. And Minor Matters." Buffalo *Express*, 28 August, 1. Reprinted in *ET&S4*, no. 247.

1869t. Untitled burlesque letter from Lord Byron to Mark Twain, MS of five pages, written ca. September, CU-MARK. Published in Baender, 481–82.

1869u. "Journalism in Tennessee." Buffalo *Express*, 4 September, 1. Reprinted in *ET&S4*, no. 252.

1869v. "More Byron Scandal." Buffalo *Express*, 7 September, 2.

1869w. "The Last Words of Great Men." Buffalo *Express*, 11 September, 1. Reprinted in *ET&S4*, no. 257.

1869x. "The Gates Ajar." Buffalo *Express*, 13 September, 2.

1869y. "The 'Wild Man.' 'Interviewed.' " Buffalo *Express*, 18 September, 1. Reprinted in *ET&S4*, no. 259.

1869z. "People and Things." Buffalo *Express*, 22 September, 2.

1869aa. "Rev. H. W. Beecher. His Private Habits." Buffalo *Express*, 25 September, 1. Reprinted in *ET&S4*, no. 260.

1869bb. "People and Things." Buffalo *Express*, 27 September, 2.

1869cc. "Arthur." Buffalo *Express*, 28 September, 4.

1869dd. "The California Pioneers." Buffalo *Express*, 29 September, 2.

1869ee. "Around the World. Letter No. One." Letter dated 10 October. Buffalo *Express*, 16 October, 1. Reprinted in *ET&S4*, no. 263.

1869ff. "Around the World. Letter No. 2." Letter dated 5 October. Buffalo *Express*, 30 October, 1. Reprinted in *ET&S4*, no. 264.

1869gg. "A Good Letter." Buffalo *Express*, 10 November, 1.

1869hh. "Around the World. Letter No. 3." Undated letter. Buffalo *Express*, 13 November, 1. Reprinted in *ET&S4*, no. 265.

1869ii. "Browsing Around." Letter dated November. Buffalo *Express*, 27 November, 2. "A Fair Career Closed" and "Getting My Fortune Told" reprinted in *ET&S4*, nos. 273 and 274.

1869jj. "Browsing Around." Letter dated November. Buffalo *Express*, 4 December, 2. "Back from 'Yurrup' " reprinted in *ET&S4*, no. 275.

1869kk. "Around the World. Letter Number 4." Undated letter. Buffalo *Express*, 11 December, 2. Reprinted in *ET&S4*, no. 266.

1869ll. "Around the World. Letter Number 5." Undated letter. Buffalo *Express*, 18 December, 2. Reprinted in *ET&S4*, no. 267.

1869mm. "Ye Cuban Patriot." Buffalo *Express*, 25 December, 2.

1870a. Untitled autobiographical reminiscence. MS of thirteen pages, CU-MARK. Published, with omissions, as "The Tennessee Land," in *MTA*, 1:3–7, and, untitled, in *AMT*, 22–24.

1870b. "An Awful—Terrible Medieval Romance." Buffalo *Express*, 1 January, 2. Reprinted in *ET&S4*, no. 276.

1870c. "Around the World. Letter Number 6." Undated letter. Buffalo *Express*, 8 January, 2–3. Reprinted in *ET&S4*, no. 268.

1870d. "A Ghost Story." Buffalo *Express*, 15 January, 2. Reprinted in *ET&S4*, no. 278.

1870e. "Around the World. Letter Number 7." Undated letter. Buffalo *Express*, 22 January, 2. Reprinted in *ET&S4*, no. 269.

1870f. "Around the World. Letter Number 8." Letter dated 20 November 1869. Buffalo *Express*, 29 January, 2. Reprinted in *ET&S4*, no. 270.

1870g. "Post-Mortem Poetry." *Galaxy* 9 (June): 864–65.

1870h. "Unburlesquable Things." *Galaxy* 10 (July): 137–38.

1872. *Roughing It*. Hartford: American Publishing Company.

1874. *The Gilded Age: A Tale of Today*. Charles Dudley Warner, coauthor. Hartford: American Publishing Company.

1875. *Mark Twain's Sketches, New and Old*. Hartford: American Publishing Company.

1876. *The Adventures of Tom Sawyer*. Hartford: American Publishing Company.

1880. *A Tramp Abroad*. Hartford: American Publishing Company.

1884. "Ye Equinoctial Storm." *Wasp* 12 (19 January): 2. Written ca. 19 March–2 April 1868, but first printed in 1884; the present location of the MS is unknown. Reprinted in *ET&S3*, no. 224.

1885. *Adventures of Huckleberry Finn*. New York: Charles L. Webster and Co.

1897. "Villagers of 1840–3." MS of forty-three pages, CU-MARK. Published in *Inds*, 93–108.

1897–98. "My Autobiography. [Random Extracts from it.]" MS of seventy-five pages, CU-MARK. Published, with omissions, as "Early Days" in *MTA*, 1:81–115.

1898. Untitled autobiographical reminiscence. MS of sixteen pages, CU-MARK. Published in part as "Old Lecture Days in Boston" in *MTA*, 1:147–53, and, untitled, in *AMT*, 166–69.

1903. "*As Regards the Company's Benevolences*." TS of four pages, CU-MARK. Published in *HHR*, 533–34.

1906. "Statement of Mr. Samuel L. Clemens." In *Arguments before the Committees on Patents of the Senate and House of Representatives, Conjointly, on the Bills S. 6330 and H. R. 19853. To Amend and Consolidate the Acts Respecting Copyright. December 7, 8, 10, and 11, 1906*. Washington, D.C.: Government Printing Office. A version of this statement, conflated from various texts, can be found in Fatout 1976, 533–39.

1907a. Untitled autobiographical reminiscence dated 10 August. MS of six pages, CU-MARK.

1907b. "Chapters from My Autobiography—XXIV." *North American Review* 186 (November): 327–36. Reprinted in Kiskis, 221–29.

1909. "*Notes*." Autobiographical reminiscence. MS of three pages (numbered 5–7), dated 30 April, appended to unsent four-page letter of 14 May 1887 to Jeannette Gilder, both in CU-MARK. Published in *MTL*, 2:487–88.

Slee, John De La Fletcher.
   1869. "The Coal Question." Letter to the editor dated 19 August. Buffalo *Express*, 20 August, 2.

Smith, Henry Perry, ed.
   1884. *History of the City of Buffalo and Erie County*. 2 vols. Syracuse, N.Y.: D. Mason and Co.

Sobel, Robert, and John Raimo, eds.
   1978. *Biographical Directory of the Governors of the United States, 1789–1978*. 4 vols. Westport, Conn.: Meckler Books.

Steiner, Bernard C.
1914. *Life of Reverdy Johnson*. Baltimore: Norman, Remington Company.

Stevenson, Burton, comp.
1934. *The Home Book of Quotations, Classical and Modern*. New York: Dodd, Mead and Co.

Stowe, Harriet Beecher.
1869. "The True Story of Lady Byron's Life." *Atlantic Monthly* 24 (September): 295–313.

Strong, Leah A.
1966. *Joseph Hopkins Twichell: Mark Twain's Friend and Pastor*. Athens: University of Georgia Press.

Swan, Marshall W. S.
1980. *Town on Sandy Bay, a History of Rockport, Massachusetts*. Canaan, N.H.: Phoenix Publishing.

Swann.
1990. *Autographs, Letters, Photographs, Historic Documents, Signed & Inscribed Books*. Sale no. 1539 (11 October). New York: Swann Galleries.

Sweets, Henry H., III.
1984. *The Hannibal, Missouri, Presbyterian Church: A Sesquicentennial History*. Hannibal: Presbyterian Church of Hannibal.

Tauranac, John.
1979. *Essential New York: A Guide to the History and Architecture of Manhattan's Important Buildings, Parks, and Bridges*. New York: Holt, Rinehart and Winston.

Tennyson, Alfred.
1987. *The Poems of Tennyson*. Edited by Christopher Ricks. 3 vols. 2d ed. Harlow, Eng.: Longman.

Thomas, Jeffrey F.
1975. "The World of Bret Harte's Fiction." 2 vols. Ph.D. diss., University of California, Berkeley.

Thompson, Noyes L.
1873. *The History of Plymouth Church (Henry Ward Beecher) 1847 to 1872*. New York: G. W. Carleton and Co.; London: S. Low, Son and Co.

Thompson, Samuel Chalmers.
[1918–20]. Untitled reminiscences. TS of 224 pages, CU-MARK.

Thurston, George H., comp.
1869. *Directory of Pittsburgh and Allegheny Cities, the Adjacent Boroughs, and Parts of the Adjacent Townships. For 1869–70*. Pittsburgh: Geo. H. Thurston.
1870. *Directory of Pittsburgh and Allegheny Cities, the Adjacent Boroughs, and Parts of the Adjacent Townships. For 1870–71*. Pittsburgh: Geo. H. Thurston.

TIA
1958. *Traveling with the Innocents Abroad: Mark Twain's Original Reports from Europe and the Holy Land*. Edited by Daniel Morley McKeithan. Norman: University of Oklahoma Press.

Toledo Blade History
   n.d. "History." TS of three pages. Microfilm edition of Toledo *Blade*, OTU.

Towner, Ausburn (Ishmael).
   1869a. "Ishmael's Corner." Elmira *Saturday Evening Review*, 24 April, 4.
   1869b. "Ishmael's Corner." Elmira *Saturday Evening Review*, 22 May, 5.
   1869c. "Ishmael's Corner." Elmira *Saturday Evening Review*, 21 August, 5.
   1869d. "Ishmael's Corner." Elmira *Saturday Evening Review*, 28 August, 5.
   1869e. "Ishmael's Corner." Elmira *Saturday Evening Review*, 4 September, 5.
   1869f. "Ishmael's Corner." Elmira *Saturday Evening Review*, 11 September, 5.
   1892. *Our County and Its People: A History of the Valley and County of Chemung from the Closing Years of the Eighteenth Century*. Syracuse, N.Y.: D. Mason and Co.

Train, George Francis.
   1902. *My Life in Many States and Foreign Lands*. New York: D. Appleton and Co.

Trefousse, Hans L.
   1989. *Andrew Johnson: A Biography*. New York and London: W. W. Norton and Co.

Trumbull, James Hammond, ed.
   1886. *The Memorial History of Hartford County, Connecticut, 1633–1884*. 2 vols. Boston: Edward L. Osgood.

Tuckerman, Henry T.
   1867. *Book of the Artists: American Artist Life*. New York: G. P. Putnam and Son.

TxEU   University of Texas at El Paso.

UCCL
   1986. *Union Catalog of Clemens Letters*. Edited by Paul Machlis. Berkeley, Los Angeles, London: University of California Press. [In a few cases, *UCCL* catalog numbers cited in this volume supersede those assigned in 1986 and reflect corrections or additions to the catalog since publication.]

Ulster County Directory
   1871. *Gazetteer and Business Directory of Ulster County, N.Y., for 1871–72*. Syracuse, N.Y.: Hamilton Child.

Utica Directory
   1869. *Utica City Directory, 1869–70*. Utica, N.Y.: John H. Francis.

Vallejo [pseud.].
   1868. "California." Letter dated 7 December. Providence *Journal*, 28 December, Supplement, 1.

Van Deusen, Glyndon G.
   1967. *William Henry Seward*. New York: Oxford University Press.

Vann, Elizabeth C. Denny.
   1964. "William Ritenour Denny, of Winchester, Va. A Pilgrim to Europe in the Summer of 1867." TS in CU-MARK.

Van Why, Joseph S.
1975. *Nook Farm*. Rev. ed. Edited by Earl A. French. Hartford: Stowe-Day Foundation.

ViU   University of Virginia, Charlottesville.

Walker, Franklin.
1969. *San Francisco's Literary Frontier*. Seattle: University of Washington Press.

Wallace, Robert D.
n.d. "A Gentleman of Some Notoriety: Mark Twain Speaks in Illinois." Unpublished TS in CU-MARK.

Wecter, Dixon, ed.
1947a. "The Love Letters of Mark Twain." *Atlantic Monthly* 180 (November): 33–39.

1947b. "The Love Letters of Mark Twain." *Atlantic Monthly* 180 (December): 66–72.

1948. *Mark Twain in Three Moods: Three New Items of Twainiana*. San Marino, Calif.: Friends of the Huntington Library.

Wheat, Carl I., ed.
1930. "The Journals of Charles E. De Long, 1854–1863." *Quarterly of the California Historical Society* 9 (September): 243–87.

White, William Gee.
1980. *Our Colonial Heritage: Plymouth and Jamestown*. Rev. ed. Encino, Calif.: Glencoe Publishing Company.

White's Conspectus
1937. *White's Conspectus of American Biography: A Tabulated Record of American History and Biography*. 2d ed. Compiled by the editorial staff of the National Cyclopædia of American Biography. New York: James T. White and Co.

Whitney, William Dwight, and Benjamin E. Smith, eds.
1913. *The Century Dictionary: An Encyclopedic Lexicon of the English Language*. Rev. and enl. 12 vols. New York: Century Company.

Wilson, Erasmus, ed.
1898. *Standard History of Pittsburg, Pennsylvania*. Chicago: H. R. Cornell and Co.

Wilson, H., comp.
1867. *Trow's New York City Directory*, . . . *Vol. LXXXI. For the Year Ending May 1, 1868*. New York: John F. Trow.

1868. *Trow's New York City Directory*, . . . *Vol. LXXXII. For the Year Ending May 1, 1869*. New York: John F. Trow.

1869. *Trow's New York City Directory*, . . . *Vol. LXXXIII. For the Year Ending May 1, 1870*. New York: John F. Trow.

WIM
1973. *What Is Man? and Other Philosophical Writings*. Edited by Paul Baender.

The Works of Mark Twain. Berkeley, Los Angeles, London: University of California Press.

Wisbey, Herbert A., Jr.
1991. "The Tragic Story of Emma Nye." *Mark Twain Society Bulletin* 14 (July): 1–4.

Wolcott, Ella.
1896. "A Seedling Church." In *Park Church*, 6–9.

Woods, Samuel D.
1910. *Lights and Shadows of Life on the Pacific Coast.* New York and London: Funk and Wagnalls Company.

WU   Memorial Library, University of Wisconsin, Madison.

Young, James Harvey.
1961. *The Toadstool Millionaires: A Social History of Patent Medicines in America before Federal Regulation.* Princeton, N.J.: Princeton University Press.

Index

T HE FOLLOWING have not been indexed: fictional characters, Editorial Signs, Guide to Editorial Practice, and Textual Commentaries. Place names are included when they refer to locations that Clemens lived in, visited, or commented upon, but are excluded when mentioned only in passing.

Alphabetizing is *word-by-word,* except for the following. (1) When persons, places, and things share the same name, they are indexed in that order: thus "Washington, George" precedes "Washington, D.C." (2) Formal titles (Mr., Mrs., Dr., and so forth) may be included with a name, but are ignored when alphabetizing. (3) When the subheading "letters to," "letters by," or "letters from" appears, it *precedes* all other subheadings; when the subheading "mentioned" appears, it *follows* all other subheadings.

Recipients of Clemens's letters are listed in **boldface type;** boldface numbers (**208n2**) designate principal identifications. Numbers linked by an ampersand (39 & 41n6) indicate that the allusion in the letter text is not explicit, and can best be located by reading the note first. Works written by Mark Twain are indexed separately by title *and* under "Clemens, Samuel Langhorne: works," as well as, when appropriate, under the publishing journal. Works written by others are indexed both by title and by author's name. Newspapers are indexed by their location (city or town), other periodicals by title.

Abbey, Henry, 313n5, **315n1***top*, 330, 331n1, 346, 347n1, 353n1
  letter to, 314–15
Abbott, E. L., 415
Abbott, Joseph C., **208n2**
Abd-el-Kader, 200, 200*illus*, **203n3**
Abdul Aziz (sultan of Turkey), 201*illus*, 203*illus*, 203n3, 212, **213n1**
Abdullah Frères, 200–201
Abington, Mass.
  proposed lecture by SLC, 415, 430n3, 485n16
Academy of Music, Pittsburgh, 382n2, 384n9
Acropolis, 187, 188n3, 454, 455
Across the Continent, 407n6
Adams, Edwin, 204, **205n3**, 206n4
The Adventures of Gil Blas of Santillane, 440, 441n5
Adventures of Huckleberry Finn, 441n5
The Adventures of Tom Sawyer, 441n5
The Age of Fable, 39 & 41n6
Akron, Ohio, 39
  lecture by SLC, 2n2, 41n3, 43, 482, 482n1
Alabama, 461, 461n12
Alaska, 462, 462n13
Alba Nueva mine, 370, 373n6
Albany, N.Y.
  lecture by SLC, 416, 486
Albemarle Hotel, New York, 412
Aldrich, Thomas Bailey, 440 & **441n4**
Aleksandr Nikolaevich (Aleksandr II), 187 & **188n2,** 490
Alexandria, 186n2
Alliance, Ohio
  lecture by SLC, 35n5, 86, 87n2, 88–89, 93, 94n2, 95, 97n1, 103–4, 107, 109n2, 123, 483, 483n9
"Allie, the Blue-Eyed Blonde," 319n5
Allyn, Richard J., **208n3**
  envelope, 207, 210, 266
Allyn Hall, Hartford, 407n8
Allyn House, Hartford, 143, 147n1, 158, 204 & 205n2, 208n3, 239
  envelope, 207, 210, 266
Alonzo and Melissa; or, the Unfeeling Father, 176, 177n2

Amenia, N.Y.
  lecture by SLC, 416, 416n1, 486
Amenia *Times*, 416, 416n1
America, 369n5
American Asylum, 232n3
American Literary Bureau, 353n2, 400n1*bottom*, 481
American Phrenological Journal, 318n4
American Publishing Company, 530*caption*. *See also* Bliss, Elisha, Jr.; Bliss, Francis E.; *The Innocents Abroad*
  address, 98n1*letterhead*, 118 & 120n16, 193n2*letterhead*, 214, 223n2, 286n1*letterhead*, 287n1*letterhead*, 292n1*letterhead*
  The Innocents Abroad: xxvi–xxvii, 15nn1–2, 125n3, 142n4, 215, 343n3, 364n4; attempt to break contract, 170–71n5, 293n1; publicity (see *The Innocents Abroad:* publicity)
  officers, xxvii, 15n1, 98n1*letterhead*, 170–71n5, 193n2*letterhead*, 286n1*letterhead*, 287n1*letterhead*, 292–93n1
  other works, 98–99n1, 193n2*letterhead*, 228, 230n5, 284–85, 286n1, 286nn1–2, 293n1
  subsidiaries, 339n8
American Sunday-School Union, 230n4, 288n3
"The American Vandal Abroad," xxv, xxvi, 2–175 *passim*, 185, 214–15, 261n2, 276n1, 286n3, 315–16n1, 474n1
  lecture schedule, 481–83
  reception and reviews: favorable, xxvi, 2–3, 6n2, 8–9n1, 20n2, 24–25, 27nn1–3, 28, 28n1, 29, 30n2, 30–31, 35n2, 40–41n1, 48n2, 51–52, 56n1, 56n5, 68, 68n5, 68n7, 72, 79, 81n7, 81n9, 81, 83n1, 87–88n4, 93, 94n1, 94–95, 98, 104, 105n1, 108, 109n3, 126, 130, 175, 217n3, 384n9, 453–57, 487–93; unfavorable, 35n2, 48n2
"The American Woman," 455n2
Ames, Frank, 433–34, **434n2**
Ames, Henry, 434n2
Ames, Oakes, 433, **434n2**
Ames, Oakes Angier, **434n2**
Ames, Oliver, **434n2**

Andersonville, Ga., prison, 305, 465n20

Andrews, Edward, 185, 187n5
  portrait in *The Innocents Abroad*, 169, 170n4

Andrus, Sylvester G., 244n7

Andrus, Langdon and Company, 244n7

The Angel in the House, 33 & 36n8

Anthracite Coal Association, 119n4, 294n2, 306n3, 334n5

Appletons' Journal of Literature, Science, and Art, 226n6, 236, 238n2

Appomattox, Va., 259n7

Arnold, George H., 362, 363n3

Arnold, Matthew, 233, 235n3

Arnold, Samuel, 465n20

"Around the World" letters, 7n6, 360–61n5, 402n2

"Arthur," 359 & 361n8

Arthur William Patrick Albert (English prince)
  visits Buffalo, 359, **361n8**

Asa's, San Francisco, 383n7

Associated Press, 373n2, 459

Associated Western Literary Societies, 35n5, 481

Astor House, New York, 171

The Asylum; or, Alonzo and Melissa, 177n2

Athens, 48n2, 105n1, 187, 454, 455, 490

Atlantic Monthly, 169, 171n7, 350n7, 378, 382–83n6

Atwater, Andrew, 118 & 120n14, 154, 157n4

Auburn, N.Y.
  proposed lecture by SLC, 94, 94n3, 104, 109n4, 483n10

Aurora (Ill.) *Beacon*
  review of SLC's lecture, 81n7

Aurora (California/Nevada Territory)
  residence of SLC, 373n5

Aurora Leigh, 26, 27–28n5

Austria, 461n11

The Autocrat of the Breakfast-Table, 149, 223, 226n2, 365
  annotated by SLC, 149–50n2, 175, 184n9, 188n1

"An Awful—Terrible Medieval Romance," 402n2

Ayrault, Rose and Company, 205n1

Baker, Miss, 158, 160n2

Baker, G. A., 275n2

Baker, George M., 406*caption*, 408n10, 411*caption*

Baldwin, Alexander W. ("Sandy"), **434n1**

Baldwinsville, N.Y.
  lecture by SLC, 416, 486

Bancroft, Hubert H.
  agent for *The Innocents Abroad*, 355 & 355–56n1

"Banks of the Genessee," 319n5

Barnefield, Thomas Pierce, 415, **416n1**

Barnes, George E., 354n1, 354n2, 354n3, 369n3
  letter to, 354–55

Barstow, Kate D. (Mrs. William H.), 346n6, 431, 432n2, 436
  agent for *The Innocents Abroad*, 339–40, 340n1, **341n3**, 345, 433n6

Barstow, William H., 340, 341n3, 345, 432n2
  job reference by SLC, 431, 433n6, 436, 438n6

Bartlett, William Chauncey, 321n1

Batavia, Ill., 80n2
  letter from, 76–81
  lecture by SLC, 38, 55, 81n7, 483

Batavia Laconian Literary Society, 79 & 81n8

Bateman, Ellen, 414n5

Bateman, Hezekiah, 414n5

Bateman, Kate Josephine, 413, **414n5**

Bates, G. A., 415

Beach, Moses S.
  portrait in *The Innocents Abroad*, 212, 213n1
  Quaker City excursion photographs, 213–14n2

Beard, John Relly, 218n8

Becket, Thomas à, 266n2

Beeber, J. A., 416

Beech, Mr., 107, 108n3

Beecher, Henry Ward, 13n4, 167n1, 205, 206n6, 215, 217n5, 270, 272n1, 292, 389n6, 420n1
  characterizes Olivia Langdon, 270
  sermons: 5 & 7n9, 140, 143n10, 172, 174n3, 232, 232n6, 247 & 249n2, 323

Beecher, Henry Ward (*continued*)
    & 324n5, 344–45 & 346n2; charac-
    terized by SLC, 46; "The Hidden
    Christ," 82, 83n4; "The Love of
    Money," 39, 41n4; "The Nobility of
    Confession," 69 & 72–73n2; "Self-
    Control Possible to All," 49, 51n2
Beecher, James Chaplin, **183n7**
Beecher, Julia Jones (Mrs. Thomas K.),
    240–41, **243–44n6**, 506*illus*
Beecher, Katherine Edes, 431 & 433n5
Beecher, Lyman, 389–90n6, 431, 433n5
Beecher, Olivia Day (Mrs. Thomas K.), 241
    & **243n6**
Beecher, Robert, 390n6
Beecher, Thomas K., **13n4**, 140, 143n10,
    175, 181, 183n7, 222, 223n7, 239,
    243n2, 389n7, 507*illus*
    Byron scandal, 350–51n7
    eulogizes Eunice Ford, 164–65n5
    "Friday Miscellany," 11, 13–14n4, 57n9,
        154, 155–57, 157n5, 183n7, 350–
        51n7
    marital life, 240–41, 243–44n6
    officiates at SLC's wedding, 405, 408n9
    sermons, 46, 48n4, 140, 143n10
    services at Elmira Opera House, 54–55 &
        57n9, 183n7
"Belle Mahone," 23, 24n5
Bement, Edward P., 116, 120n11, 139,
    142n3, 157n3
Bench Street Methodist Church, Galena,
    Ill., 83n1
Benedict, George A., 7n7, 49, 51n3, 69,
    72n1, 85n2, 88*letterhead*, 195, 196n2,
    277n1
Benedict, George S., 7n7, 85n2, 88*let-
    terhead*, 277n1
Bennett, Joseph L., 134, **135n2**
Bennett, Oliver T., 378, 379, 382n5, 383n9,
    383–84n9
Benning, Carrie A., 467
Benton, Joel, 416, **416n1**
Berry, Anna E. (Mrs. Thomas S.), 13n2
Berry, Earl D.
    recalls SLC, **296–97n2,** 306n2
Berry, John W., 416
Berry, Thomas S., 10, 13n2
Bethlehem, 9n2

Beyond the Mississippi, 98n1*letterhead,*
    193n2*letterhead,* 228, 230n5, 284,
    286n1, 407n6
Bible, 26, 28n6, 39, 148n4, 149, 173, 181,
    225, 226n7, 247, 317, 330n2
    quotations and allusions: Acts, 348 &
        350n2; Ecclesiasticus, 133 & 134n10;
        Exodus, 130 & 133n5; Genesis, 257
        & 259n8; Hebrews, 164, 165n6; Isa-
        iah, 13 & 14n7, 68 & 68n6, 269 &
        270n5; James, 220 & 223n3; Jere-
        miah, 299 & 300n5; Kings, 257 &
        259n8, 435n3; Luke, 91 & 93n4, 124
        & 125n6, 173 & 174n7, 290, 291n4,
        372 & 374n11; Matthew, 103 &
        103n2, 123 & 125n4; Peter, 173,
        174n6
    references to characters: Christ, 9n2, 12,
        19, 37n14, 82, 96, 147n4, 173,
        176n6, 225, 381, 384–85n11; Herod,
        319n5; Job, 178; Jonas, 194n2; Lot's
        wife, 330n2; Mark, 190, 191*illus;*
        Matthew, 190, 191*illus;* Moses, 39,
        463; Noah, 313–14n7; Prodigal Son,
        91 & 93n4, 372, 374n11; Rachel,
        299, 300n5; Shem, 312, 314n7
*Biblical Researches in Palestine, Mount Sinai
    and Arabia Petraea,* 365–66n1
Big Trees, Calif., 359
Biglow Papers, 456n4
Billings, Josh. *See* Shaw, Henry Wheeler
"Biography of Samson," 202n2
Bird, Francis W., 431 & **432–33n4**
Birney, Nancy, 469, 469n9
Bixby, Horace E., 277n4
Black, James Wallace, 400n1*top,* 411, 411n3
Blair, Francis Preston, 305, 462, **462n14**
Bliss, Almira, **15n4**
Bliss, Amelia Crosby (Mrs. Elisha, Jr.),
    15n4, 197, 247, 362
Bliss, Elisha, Jr., xxvii, **15n1,** 204, 314n7,
    405. See also *The Innocents Abroad*
    letters to, 98–100, 178–79, 187–88, 192–
        95, 197–98, 199–203, 283–88, 291–
        97, 301–2, 327–28, 329–30, 339–41,
        355–56, 362–64, 442–43, 530–
        31*facsimile,* 540–41*facsimile*
    letters by, 98–99n1, 142n4, 193–94n2,
        286n1, 287n1, 288n3, 292–93n1, 385

characterized by SLC, 246
family, 15n1, 15n4
Hartford residence: 223n6; visits of SLC,
  220, 222, 222–23n2, 236, 237n1,
  246–47
letterhead, 98n1, 193n2, 286n1, 287n1,
  292n1
meets Olivia Langdon, 265, 266n1
notation on SLC letter, 362
subscription agents, 301, 302n3, 339–41,
  345
mentioned, 178n2, 190n1, 198n3, 236,
  283n1, 288n2, 313, 314n8
Bliss, Emma, **15n4**
Bliss, Francis E., **15n1**, 15n4, 98n1, 204,
  362
letters to, 14–15, 84
letters by, 283n1, 492
letterhead, 98n1, 193n2, 286n1, 287n1,
  292n1
meets Olivia Langdon, 265, 266n1
The Innocents Abroad, 15, 15n2, 84, 84n1,
  178, 492
Bliss, Lois (Mrs. Elisha, Jr.), 15n4
Bliss, Walter, **15n4**
Bliss (R. W.) and Company, 339n8
Bloomington, Ill.
  lecture by SLC canceled, 5, 482n3
"The Blush Rose," 319n5, 336, 338–39n6
Boas, John R., 276, 277n3
Bonaparte, Charles Louis Napoleon (em-
  peror of France), 212, **213n1**
"Bonnie Eloise," 336, 339n6
  envelope, 337
Book of Common Prayer, 289 & 291n2
Booth, Edwin, 204, **205n3**, 206n4
Booth, John Wilkes, 465, 465n20
Booth's Theatre, New York, 204, 205n3,
  414n5
Borrows, William B., 273n10
  envelope, 272
Boston, Mass.
  letters from, 386–95, 398–416, 425–39
  lecture by SLC, 216, 282, 324, 324n1,
    333, 387, 389n3, 390, 391, 392,
    394nn1–2, 484
  visits of SLC, 164, 165n7, 169, 172, 173 &
    174n8, 174, 179n1, 199, 199n1,
    261n3, 365n1, 386, 396, 397n2,

  407n6, 408n10, 424, 425, 426,
  428n2, 429n5
mentioned, 283, 440, 485n16
Boston *Advertiser*
  commentary on SLC, 324n1, 437 &
    438n8
  reviews: Griswold's lecture, 324n1; Nas-
    by's lecture, 389n4; SLC's lecture,
    392, 394n2, 394–95n3
Boston *Evening Transcript*
  review of Nasby's lecture, 389n4
Boston *Herald*
  review of SLC's lecture, 395n3
Boston Lyceum Bureau, 106n2, 421n1. *See
  also* Redpath, James; Fall, George L.
  address, 351, 406*envelope*, 410*envelope*,
    415*letterhead*, 418 & 418n1, 425 &
    425n1, 427*envelope*, 433*letterhead*,
    434*envelope*
  advertising circular for SLC, 217n3,
    226n3, 227, 230n8, 422, 422n2,
    457n1, 487–91
  lecturers represented: 466–67; Josh Bill-
    ings, 397n3; Nasby, 199n1, 389nn3–
    4; SLC, 199n1, 389n3, 415–16,
    416n1, 418–20, 420n2, 422, 422n2,
    481
Boston Lyceum Course, 389n3, 397n3
Boston *Post*, 466
Boston Press Club, 386
Bowen, Dennis, 294n2
Bowles, Samuel (father), **267n1**
Bowles, Samuel (son), 513*illus*
  letter to, 267
  Across the Continent, 407n6
  characterized: by Nasby, 405; by Wendell
    Phillips, 407n6; by SLC, 405
  disparages SLC, 405
  meets SLC, **267n1**, 405, 407n6
Boyington, William, 20n1
Boynton, John, 37n12
Brackett, Anna C., 280n2
Bradbury, William B., 184n9
Braddon, Mary Elizabeth, 386
Bradford, William, 119n9
Brennan, James (Jimmie), 300n2
Bridgeport (Conn.) *Standard*
  review of *The Innocents Abroad*, 498, 500
Bridges, Fidelia, 506*caption*

Bridgman, Herbert L., 267n1
Bridgman, William S., 215, 217n4
Briggs, George B., 363n3
Bromley, Isaac Hill, 228 & 230n4, 231 & 232n2, 266, **266n4**
Brooklyn, N.Y., 7n9, 167n2, 206n6, 214n2, 216, 412
  letter from, 417
  lectures by SLC, 166–67, 167n1, 399, 400n2, 400, 413n1, 415, 416n1, 417–21, 484, 484n15, 487, 489
Brooklyn Atheneum, 419–20, 420n4, 489
Brooklyn *Eagle*, 329n1, 420n3, 420n4
  letter to, 417
  reviews of SLC's lectures, 417n2, 487, 489
  staff, 417n1
Brooklyn Library Association, 415, 417n2
Brooklyn *Times*
  review of SLC's lecture, 417n2
Brooklyn *Union*, 420–21n4
Brooks, Fidele (Mrs. Henry), 111, 114n1, 114–15, 121, 140, 204–5, 394n1
  family, 268, 269n2, 270, 274, 299, 300n4
  praises Olivia Langdon, 136–37, 138n1
  residence, 83n2, 115 & 119n3, 206n5, 266 & 267n5, 273, 274, 275*envelope*, 410, 411*envelope*, 411n1, 418n3
  visit to Niagara Falls, 299, 300n4
  visits of Olivia Langdon, 82, 83n2, 85–86n3, 266 & 267n5, 268–69, 270, 273–75, 276, 280, 410, 411n1, 412
  visits of SLC, 115, 119n3, 137 & 138n2, 268–69
Brooks, Henry, 82, 83n2, 85–86n3, 115, 270, 274, 300n4
  residence, 83n2, 115 & 119n3, 206n5, 266 & 267n5, 273, 274, 275*envelope*, 410, 411*envelope*, 411n1, 418n3
Brooks, Noah, 321n1
Brooks, Remsen G., 268 & 269n2, 270, 274, 299, 300n4
Brookville, Pa.
  lecture by SLC, 385, 484, 484n12
Brown, Flavius A., 238n3
Brown, John, 218n8
Brown and Company, 265n2, 278, 278n1
Brown and Gross, 238n3
Browne, Charles Farrar (Artemus Ward), 305

compared to SLC, 438–39n8, 456
  death, 456n4
Browne, J. Ross, 76n2
Browne, Junius Henri
  The Great Metropolis, 99n1, 284 & 286n1, 293n1
  Sights and Sensations in Europe, 285 & 286n2
"Brownie" (lecture reviewer), 29, 453–55
Browning, Elizabeth Barrett
  poetry characterized by SLC, 26 & 27–28n5, 95, 241, 244n9
Browning, Orville H., **458n2,** 466
Browning, Robert, 244n9
Brown's Hall, Rockford, Ill., 8n1
"Browsing Around" letters, 402n2
"The Bucket," 50 & 51n5
Buffalo, N.Y.
  letters from, 289–351, 353–66, 466–72
  coal monopoly controversy, 304 & 306–7n3, 333–34, 334–35n5
  lecture missed by SLC, 482n1
  reading by SLC, 424–25n2
  residence of SLC, 44n7, 326n5, 430, 430n2, 440n1; boardinghouse, 291n4, 318n3, 325, 344; gift of house from Jervis Langdon, 406n1
  visits of SLC, 290n1
  mentioned, 115, 116, 119nn4–5
Buffalo *Commercial Advertiser*, 292, 297n3, 328n1*top*, 335n5, 362
  described, 363n3
  review of *The Innocents Abroad*, 364n4
Buffalo *Courier*, 292, 307n3, 328n1*top*, 333 & 334–35n5, 362
  described, 363n3
  review of *The Innocents Abroad*, 364n4
Buffalo *Express*, 292, 350n6, 395n3
  coal monopoly controversy, 304 & 306–7n3, 333–34, 334–35n5
  ,contributions by SLC: 306n1; "Around the World" letters, 7n6, 360–61n5, 402n2; "Arthur," 359 & 361n8; "An Awful—Terrible Medieval Romance," 402n2; "Browsing Around" letters, 402n2; "The California Pioneers," 372n1; "A Day at Niagara," 300n4, 358 & 359–60n1, 360n2; "English Festivities. And Minor

Matters," 300n4, 358 & 360n1, 360n2; "A Fair Career Closed," 434n1; "The Gates Ajar," 321n1; "A Ghost Story," 402n2; "A Good Letter," 338n4, 402n2; "Inspired Humor," 305, 306n1, 307n6; "Journalism in Tennessee," 358 & 360n1, 360n2; "The Last Words of Great Men," 358 & 360n1, 360nn2–3; "The Monopoly Speaks," 306n3, 334n5; "More Byron Scandal," 350 & 350–51n7; "People and Things," 303 & 306n1, 307n6, 320n7, 329n1, 338–39n6, 345, 346n5, 372n1, 466–70; "Removal of the Capital," 313n4; "Rev. H. W. Beecher. His Private Habits," 338n4, 358 & 360n1, 360n2; "Salutatory," 335 & 337n1, 345, 470–72; "The 'Wild Man.' 'Interviewed,'" 358 & 360n1, 360n2; "Ye Cuban Patriot," 402n2
envelope, 323, 326
front page, 304 & 307n4, 308*illus*, 309*illus*
history and publication frequency, 294n3, 296–97n2, 318n2, 331, 402n2. *See also* Express Printing Company: letterhead
Innocents Abroad advertising supplement, 297n4, 320n6, 327, 328n1*top*, 328n2, 330n2, 339n8, 343n1, 345, 346n3, 359, 361n7, 362, 363n1
letterhead, 364
offices, 303, 306n2, 318n3, 326n3, 480n24
read by Langdon family, 339n10
report of SLC's marriage, 219n3
review of *The Innocents Abroad*, 363–64n4
SLC as editor, 296–97n2, 299, 301, 303–4, 306n2, 317, 320, 323n1, 324, 324n1, 326n1, 327, 328n1*top*, 333, 349, 354, 358, 401, 402n2, 466–72
SLC as owner: xxvii, 261n6, 281n4, 288n2, 290, 290n1, 291n5, 291, 294n2, 295, 297, 298, 300n2, 301, 311, 315, 319n6, 333, 334n4, 360n5, 387 & 389n5, 407n4, 430n2; encouraged to sell, 404, 440
staff, 296–97n2, 300n2, 306n2, 322 & 323n3, 360n2. *See also* Larned, Josephus N.; Selkirk, George H.

Buffalo General Hospital, 307n3
Buffalo *Post*, 328n1*top*
Buffalo *Republic*, 300n2
Buffalo *Republic and Times*, 324n1
Bulfinch, Thomas
    The Age of Fable, 39 & 41n6
Bunyan, John
    The Pilgrim's Progress, 169, 198n2
Burlingame, Anson, 74, 76n2
Burnside, James Oliver Perry, 415, **416n1,** 437
Burtis Opera House, Davenport, Ia., 40n1
Burton, Henry Eugene, 140, **143n11,** 144
Burton, Mary Hooker (Mrs. Henry Eugene), 140, **143n11,** 144, 149, 149n4
Bushnell, Horace, **223n6**
Bushnell Park, Hartford, 221 & 223n6
Byron, George Gordon, 350–51n7, 367n1
Byron letter (SLC's burlesque), 366 & 367n1

C. A. Pease and Company
    envelope, 92
Cadets of Temperance, 202n2
California, 250, 359, 360n5, 368, 369n5. *See also* San Francisco, Calif.
    proposed trip by SLC, 68, 84, 99n1, 100, 101, 106, 117, 124, 127, 135, 136n1, 153, 166, 169, 176, 177, 182, 184, 215, 216n1, 228–29, 245–46, 255, 255n1, 260, 282, 282n1, 319n6, 360n5
    residence of SLC, 320, 370–71, 373nn4–5
California Pioneers
    letter to, 370–74
    "The California Pioneers," 372n1
Californian, 401n1
Calvary Presbyterian Church, San Francisco, 57n6
Calvary Presbyterian Sabbath School, San Francisco, 57n6
Cambridge, N.Y.
    lecture by SLC, 416, 486
Cameron, Simon, 368, **369n3**
Campbell, A. S., 83n1
Canada, 466, 466n1
Canton, Mass., 434n2
    lecture by SLC, 415, 433, 485

Capitol, Washington, D.C., 310
Carpenter, William Henry, 357n1*top*
Carpenter, William P., 357n1*top*, 416, 416n1
    letter to, 356–57
Carpet and Upholstery Trade Review, 294n2
"Carrie, with the Golden Hair," 319n5
Carson, John B., 52, 56n3, 56n5
Carson, Mrs. John B., 52, 56n3, 56n5
Carson City, Nev., 388n1, 434n1
    residence of SLC, 373n6
Case Hall, Cleveland, 17n2, 488
Castilian Days, 66n2
"The Celebrated Jumping Frog of Calaveras County," 392, 425n2*top*
    SLC's opinion, 423
The Celebrated Jumping Frog of Calaveras County, And other Sketches, 232, 232n5, 319n6
    SLC's opinion, 132, 134n9
    edited by Webb, 42n8, 100n1*top*
Central Pacific Railroad, 215 & 217n7, 282n1
Century Club, New York, 341n1*bottom*
Cervantes Saavedra, Miguel de
    Don Quixote, 132
Chalfant, William Lusk, 378, 381, **383n7**
Charlestown, Mass., 485n16
    lecture by SLC, 484
Charlotte, Mich., 455n2
    lecture by SLC, 27n2, 29 & 30n2, 453–55, 482
Charlotte *Republican*
    review of SLC's lecture, 29, 30n2, 453–55
Charlotte *Argus,* 29, 30n2
Chase, William H., 301, 302n3
Chelsea, Mass., 485n16
Chemung River, Elmira, 181, 183n8
Chicago, Ill.
    letters from, 14–21, 45–49
    lectures by SLC, 18, 20n2, 43, 56n2, 482
    mentioned, 17n3, 18, 19, 20n4, 24n6, 32, 36n9, 39, 59, 62
Chicago, Burlington and Quincy Railroad, 20n4
Chicago *Republican,* 487, 491
    contributions by SLC, 373n7, 374n8
Chicago *Times*
    review of SLC's lecture, 20n2, 487, 489

Chicago *Tribune,* 36n9, 37n14, 313n4
    review of SLC's lecture, 52, 56n5, 487, 491
Christian Union, 167n1, 353n2
Christian William Ferdinand Adolphus George (George I, king of Greece), **188n2**
Cincinnati *Commercial,* 403n1
    review of *The Innocents Abroad,* 339n8
Cincinnati *Gazette,* 265n1
    review of *The Innocents Abroad,* 339n8
Cincinnati *Times,* 324n1
Citizen's Mutual Coal Mining, Purchasing and Sale Company, 306n3, 334n5
Civil War, 21n7, 119n2, 160n5, 256–57, 258n6, 259n7, 265n1, 305, 460n9, 461 & 461n12, 463n17, 464–65, 467n2
Clapp, Almon M., **294n3,** 296–97n2
Clapp, Harry H., 294n3
Clark, E., 47n2
Clark, Ida B., 160n6, 233 & 235n1, 299 & 300n4, 349, 350n3, 350n4, 375, 375n2, **450,** 507*illus*
Clark, Jefferson B., 300n4
Clark, Julia (Mrs. Jefferson B.), 300n4
Clayton, Joshua E., 373n5
Clayton's Mill, 370 & 373n5
Clemens, Benjamin L., **448**
Clemens, Clara Langdon, **449,** 529*caption*
Clemens, Henry, 91 & 93n2, **448**
Clemens, Jane Lampton, 46, 91, 134n8
    letters to, 84–86, 120–22, 177–78, 218–19, 259–61, 276–77, 425–26, 532–34*facsimile*
    letter by, 277n4
    birth and death, **448**
    church attendance, 134, 135n2
    financial assistance from SLC, 120, 121n1, 178n2, 219, 219n2, 271–72, 273n7, 276, 277nn3–4, 387, 425, 425–26n2, 429, 430n2, 433
    gift of *The Innocents Abroad,* 292, 311, 313, 313n8
    health, 218, 430
    influence on SLC, 76n3, 205n1, 212
    invitation to SLC's wedding, 311, 430n2, 433
    residences: Fredonia, N.Y., 44n7; St.

Louis, 44n7, 85n1, 219n4, 292. *See also* Moffett, Pamela A.: residences

Tennessee land, 270–72, 272n4, 273n8, 279n1*bottom*, 386–87, 389n2

mentioned, 19, 274, 382n1

Clemens, Jane Lampton (Jean), **449**

Clemens, Jennie, **449**

Clemens, John Marshall, 243n1, **448**

Clemens, Langdon, **449**

Clemens, Margaret L., **448**

Clemens, Mary E. (Mollie; Mrs. Orion)

letter to, 84–86

birth and death, **448**

residence in St. Louis, 44n8, 85n1, 280n2

mentioned, 219, 260, 311, 388

Clemens, Olivia Susan (Susy), **449**

Clemens, Orion, 43, 219, 260, 276, 388

letters to, 84–86, 279–80

letters by, 276, 277n6, 279–80, 388n1, 388–89n2

birth and death, **448**

employment, 177 & 178n1, 388n1

financial assistance from SLC, 386, 387, 393n1

mining investments, 373n4, 373n6, 374n8

Olivia Langdon's sympathy, 271, 272n5, 312, 393n1

residence in St. Louis, 44n8, 85n1, 178n1, 280n2

sense of humor, 189

Tennessee land, 270–72 & 272n4, 277n6, 279, 279–80n1, 386–87, 388–89n2, 393n1, 426n2

Treasury department dispute, 386 & 388n1

Clemens, Pamela Ann. *See* Moffett, Pamela A.

Clemens, Pleasant Hannibal, **448**

CLEMENS, SAMUEL LANGHORNE

appearance and speech, 56n5, 57n9, 86, 129, 149, 212, 306n2, 311–12, 326, 331–32, 392, 455, 457, 491, 493. *See also* photographs

artistic interests

literary references and reading: drama, 12 & 14n6, 132–33, 257 & 259n8; fiction, 16 & 17n5, 104, 105n2, 132–33, 225 & 226n6, 365,

366n2, 413, 414n4, 440, 441n2; history, 26, 39 & 41n5, 116 & 119n9; humor and satire, 132–33, 149, 149–50n2, 160n1, 175, 184n9, 188n1, 223, 226n2, 365; mythology, 39 & 41n6; poetry, 26, 27–28n5, 33 & 36n8, 50 & 51n5, 71 & 73n5, 95, 127 & 128n3, 169, 171n7, 171, 221 & 223n5, 228 & 229n1, 233, 235n1, 241, 244nn8–9, 317 & 318–19n5, 335–36, 338n5, 338–39n6; sermons and religious material, 5, 7n9, 11 & 13–14n4, 39, 41n4, 46, 48n4, 48–49n5, 49, 51n2, 69, 72–73n2, 78, 82, 83n4, 140, 143n10, 154, 155–57, 157n5, 169, 172, 174n3, 198n2, 232, 232n6, 247, 249n2, 289 & 291n2, 323, 324n5, 344–45, 346n2 (*see also* Bible)

music: 23 & 24n5, 50 & 51n5, 106n2, 265 & 266n2, 463; hymns, 181, 183–84n9, 235 & 236n6, 380–81, 384–85n11

painting and sculpture, 181, 274, 275n2

theater, 204, 205n3, 205–6n4, 386

birth and death, 184n9, 413, **448, 450**

character and habits

cardplaying, 181

cribbage, 21, 25, 49–50, 222, 223n7

drinking, 52, 56n5, 90, 202n2, 436, 438n2

profanity, 90, 178, 202n2

reformation, 53, 56n5, 73–75, 76n3, 90

temper, 45, 48n2, 284–85, 334, 352, 395–96, 433–34, 436

tobacco use, 19, 39, 52, 56n5, 76n3, 202n2, 206, 261, 433–34, 491

wanderlust, 74, 75, 359, 360n5

courtship, engagement, and marriage, xxv–xxviii

concern for Olivia Langdon's health, 10 & 13n1, 64, 107, 117–18, 152, 154, 157n3, 206, 212, 221, 239–40, 243n4, 268, 273, 397, 435

discourages activism in Olivia Langdon, 63, 117–18

engagement: formal, xxv, 83n2, 84–85, 86, 87, 90nn3–4, 93n5, 101,

Clemens, Samuel Langhorne (*continued*)
161n7, 196n1, 209, 348, 358, 403 &
407n2; informal, xxv, 81n3, 157n6,
230n8, 438n2; ring, 86, 89, 102,
108 & 109n1, 118, 120, 122,
358–59
indifference to Olivia Langdon's
wealth, 91
introduction to Olivia Langdon: first
meetings, 10, 13n2, 123, 125n3, 132
& 133–34n7, 139, 142n8, 162–63;
sees photograph, 132 & 133–34n7,
291n5, 313n2
letters: calendar and dockets, 7–8n12,
473–80; characterized, xxv–xxviii;
diary format, 381–82n1
marriage, xxv, xxvii, 105–6, 207,
207n1, 225, 271, 297–98, 301, 430;
date, xxv, 219n3, 292, 297, 299, 311,
313n5, 315, 333, 342, 347, 348,
350n1, 358–59, 368, 408n9, 430n2;
guests, 219, 219n3, 311, 358, 374,
394n1, 429, 430n2; officiating clergymen, 405, 408n9; preparations,
391, 406n1, 425, 437n1; proposal,
xxv, 7n10, 7n12, 119n3, 169 &
171n6, 220 & 223n2, 344 & 345n1,
403 & 407n2
need for discretion, 5 & 7–8n12, 22–
23n2, 43 & 44n5, 85n1, 89 & 89n1,
121–22n2, 157 & 157n6, 159 &
160n7, 195 & 196n1, 205n1, 211–12,
244n13
role of Charles Langdon, 7–8n12, 22,
89n1. *See also* Langdon, Charles J.:
transmits courtship letters
role of Harriet Lewis, 21n10, 23–24n2
role of the Twichells, 1n1
SLC's character references, 6n5, 52–
53, 56–57n6, 106n1, 135n3, 162 &
164n1, 320, 355n3, 432n2
SLC's self-assessments for the Langdons, 74, 90–93, 102, 320–21, 321n3
dreams, xxvi, 58, 134n8, 154, 162, 224,
251, 423–24
financial affairs, 404. *See also* income *and*
lectures and speeches: profits and expenses
assistance to mother, 120, 121n1,
178n2, 219, 219n2, 271–72, 273n7,
276, 277nn3–4, 387, 425, 425–26n2,
429, 430n2, 433
Buffalo *Express* purchase. *See* Buffalo
Express: SLC as owner
expenses, 271–72, 276, 277nn2–3,
300n4
indebtedness, 291n5, 294n2, 297, 311,
333, 334n4, 387, 389n5, 393n1,
430n2
life insurance, 387, 389–90n6
Tennessee land, 270–72, 272n4,
273n8, 277n6, 279, 279–80n1, 386–
87, 388–89n2, 426n2
handwriting, 228, 229–30n2
health, 4–5, 45, 64, 81–82, 98n1, 103–4,
220, 239, 243, 245–48, 248–49n1,
251, 397, 423, 425, 426–27, 429n4,
430, 431, 485n16
income, 85, 91–92, 96, 429n6
books, 66n2, 385–86, 440n2
journalism, 150n1, 259, 347, 360n1
lecturing, 30n3, 43, 44n2, 98, 106,
106n2, 214, 259, 261n2, 384n9, 429,
430n2, 438n4
lectures and speeches, 160n1
1866 tour, 106, 106n2, 321, 321n4,
382n5, 401n1
1868 tour, 106, 106–7n2, 261n2, 332,
334n3
1868–69 tour. *See* "The American Vandal Abroad"
1869 California tour. *See* California:
proposed trip by SLC
1869–70 tour: xxvi, xxvii, 375–442 *passim*, 477n13, 478n16, 479n19,
479n22, 480nn23–24; attempt to
cancel, 297–98, 298n1, 299, 301,
315, 317, 324, 330, 333, 342, 347,
351, 351n1, 358; composition of lecture, 215–16, 218n9, 276, 277n5,
279, 280n2, 280–81, 281n3, 360–
61n5, 362, 363n2, 422n2; planning
and publicity, 199, 214–18, 226n3,
227, 227nn1–2, 229, 230n8, 259,
282, 283, 283n1, 333, 348, 351,
351n1, 374, 387, 420, 420n2, 420–
21n4, 422, 422n2, 457n1, 487–91.
See also "Our Fellow Savages of the
Sandwich Islands"
1870–71 season, 347, 347n4

1871–72 tour, 20n2, 347n4
curtain speeches, 87–88n4, 106n2, 126
hardships of lecture circuit, xxvi, 4, 18,
    20n4, 31, 79, 81–82, 84, 88–89,
    103–4, 105, 139–40, 259, 333, 395–
    96, 433–34, 436
hatred of synopses, 379–80, 392
invitations to lecture, 14, 15–16, 16–
    17n1, 17n2, 18, 19, 25, 29, 31, 43, 65,
    67, 86, 121, 139–40, 142n9, 166 &
    167n1, 314–15, 330–31, 331n1, 346–
    47, 351, 356, 357n1, 387, 390, 402,
    403n1, 419–20, 420nn1–2
lecture reputation and style: compared
    to Dickens, 392; compared to A.
    Miner Griswold, 324n1; compared
    to Nasby, 41n1; compared to Arte-
    mus Ward, 438–39n8, 456. *See also*
    "The American Vandal Abroad": re-
    ception and reviews; "Our Fellow
    Savages of the Sandwich Islands":
    reception and reviews
lecturing in churches, 35n2, 107n2*top*,
    414n2
profits and expenses, 30n3, 43, 44n2,
    48n2, 68, 68n5, 72, 87n4, 98, 105,
    106, 106n2, 107, 110n1*top*, 123, 126,
    214, 259, 261n2, 384n9, 420, 429,
    430n2, 436, 438n4
lectures and speeches: locations
    Akron, Ohio, 2n2, 41n3, 43, 482,
        482n1
    Albany, N.Y., 416, 486
    Alliance, Ohio, 35n5, 86, 87n2, 88–89,
        93, 94n2, 95, 97n1, 103–4, 107,
        109n2, 123, 483, 483n9
    Amenia, N.Y., 416, 416n1, 486
    Baldwinsville, N.Y., 416, 486
    Batavia, Ill., 38, 55, 77, 79, 80n2, 81n7,
        483
    Boston, Mass., 216, 282, 324, 324n1,
        333, 387, 389n3, 390, 391, 392,
        394nn1–2, 484
    Brooklyn, N.Y., 400n2, 400, 413n1,
        415, 416n1, 417–21, 417n2, 484,
        484n15, 487, 489
    Brookville, Pa., 385, 484, 484n12
    Buffalo, N.Y., 424–25n2, 482n1
    Cambridge, N.Y., 416, 486
    Canton, Mass., 415, 433, 485

Charlestown, Mass., 484
Charlotte, Mich., 27n2, 29 & 30n2,
    453–55, 482
Chicago, Ill., 18, 20n2, 43, 56n2, 482
Cleveland, Ohio, 16, 17nn1–2, 19, 38,
    43, 47n1, 68, 68n5, 72, 481, 482,
    482n6
Clinton, Mass., 397n2, 484
Cohoes, N.Y., 416, 486
Danvers, Mass., 393n1, 397n2, 484
Davenport, Iowa, 38, 43, 482
Decatur, Ill., 5, 7n11, 25 & 27n3, 43,
    482
Detroit, Mich., 27n2, 482
Elmira, N.Y., 30, 35n1, 481
Fort Plain, N.Y., 136n1, 482
Fort Wayne, Ind., 2–3, 5–6nn1–2, 43,
    482
Franklin, Pa., 47, 49n7, 94, 94n3, 107,
    107–8n2, 109n3, 483
Fredonia, N.Y., 480n24, 486
Freeport, Ill., 38, 55, 81n9, 483
Galena, Ill., 38, 55, 81, 83n1, 483
Galesburg, Ill., 23n1, 43, 482
Geneseo, N.Y., 94, 94n3, 109–11 *pas-
    sim*, 122n3, 123, 130, 133n1, 483
Germantown, Pa., 415, 416n1, 485
Hartford, Conn., 405 & 407–8n8, 484
Holyoke, Mass., 397n2, 484
Hornellsville, N.Y., 486
Hudson, Mass., 415, 434–35n3,
    479n19, 485
Indianapolis, Ind., 20n3, 43, 474n1,
    482
Iowa City, Iowa, 43, 48n2, 482
Jacksonville, Ill., 38, 55, 78 & 81n5,
    84n2, 483
Jamaica Plain, Mass., 399, 400n3,
    438n5, 484
Jamestown, N.Y., 422n2, 486
Johnstown, Pa., 385, 484, 484n12
Lansing, Mich., 27n2, 29 & 30n2, 455–
    56, 482
Lockport, N.Y., 114, 119n2, 121,
    122n3, 126, 133n1, 483, 483n11
Marshall, Mich., 29, 30n3, 38, 55,
    80n1, 483
Meriden, Conn. *See* West Meriden,
    Conn.
Monmouth, Ill., 20n4, 43, 482

Clemens, Samuel Langhorne (*continued*)
  Mount Vernon, N.Y., 415, 416n1, 421n1, 422n2, 478n16, 485
  New Britain, Conn., 415, 422n1, 423, 485
  New Haven, Conn., 416, 485
  New York, N.Y., 230n8
  Newark, N.J., 81n6, 348, 416, 481, 485
  Newtonville, Mass., 412, 414n2, 484
  Newtown, N.Y., 135n1, 164, 174n2, 174, 483
  Norwalk, Ohio, 19, 38, 43, 51n1, 482
  Norwich, Conn., 397n1, 484
  Norwich, N.Y., 481
  Ogdensburg, N.Y., 480, 480n23, 486, 486n19
  Oswego, N.Y., 486
  Ottawa, Ill., 30n1, 30–31, 35n2, 43, 482
  Owego, N.Y., 391n1, 416, 416n1, 485
  Pawtucket, R.I., 415, 416n1, 425, 428nn1–2, 429n4, 485
  Peoria, Ill., 24–25, 27n1, 28, 43, 482
  Philadelphia, Pa., 414n1, 415, 416n1, 485
  Pittsburgh, Pa., 339n9, 366, 382n2, 385, 477n13, 481, 483
  Portland, Maine, 415, 479, 479n19, 485
  Poughkeepsie, N.Y., 400n2, 414n1, 415, 478n16, 484
  Providence, R.I., 387–88, 390, 391n3, 393, 484
  Ravenna, Ohio, 93, 94n1, 94–95, 98, 483
  Rockford, Ill., 8–9n1, 43, 482
  Rockport, Mass., 415, 416n1, 438n4, 485
  Rondout, N.Y., 81n6, 315–16n1, 346, 353n1, 416, 416n1, 481, 486
  Sacramento, Calif., 401n1
  San Francisco, Calif., 261n2, 321, 321n4, 332, 334n3, 382n5
  Scranton, Pa., 482
  Sharon, Pa., 84n2, 142n9, 175, 185, 385, 483, 484, 484n12
  Slatersville, R.I., 436, 438n3, 485, 485n18
  Stuyvesant, N.Y., 109, 112, 114n1, 483

  Tecumseh, Mich., 27n2, 41n2, 482
  Thompsonville, Conn., 412, 484
  Titusville, Pa., 47, 49n4, 94, 94n3, 104, 105n1, 107, 108n3, 108 & 109n3, 483, 483n9
  Toledo, Ohio, xxvi, 31 & 35n4, 43, 51n1, 51–52, 56n1, 68, 68n7, 456–57, 482
  Trenton, N.J., 111n1*bottom*, 114n1, 416, 442n1, 483, 485
  Utica, N.Y., 356 & 357n1*top*, 416, 416n1, 486
  Virginia City, Nev., 106, 106–7n2
  Waltham, Mass., 415, 485
  Warren, Mass., 415, 425, 485
  Washington, D.C., 403n1, 415, 416n1, 421n1, 438–39n8, 485
  Waterloo, Iowa, 38, 55, 81n9, 483
  West Meriden, Conn., 415, 421n1, 424n1, 485
  West Troy, N.Y., 416, 416n1, 479n22, 486
  Wilkes-Barre, Pa., 416, 416n1, 485
  Williamsport, Pa., 391n1, 416, 485
  Worcester, Mass., 385, 386, 484, 484n12
lectures and speeches: subjects and titles
  "The American Vandal Abroad": xxv, xxvi, 2–175 *passim*, 185, 214–15, 261n2, 276n1, 286n3, 315–16n1, 474n1; lecture schedule, 481–83; reception and reviews (favorable), xxvi, 2–3, 6n2, 8–9n1, 20n2, 24–25, 27nn1–3, 28, 28n1, 29, 30n2, 30–31, 35n2, 40–41n1, 48n2, 51–52, 56n1, 56n5, 68, 68n5, 68n7, 72, 79, 81n7, 81n9, 81, 83n1, 87–88n4, 93, 94n1, 94–95, 98, 104, 105n1, 108, 109n3, 126, 130, 175, 217n3, 384n9, 453–57, 487–93; reception and reviews (unfavorable), 35n2, 48n2
  "Curiosities of California," 215–16, 218n9, 276 & 277n5, 279, 280n2, 280–81, 281n3, 360–61n5, 362 & 363n2, 422n2, 491
  "Incorporated Company of Mean Men," 423 & 424n1
  "Mark Twain's Eulogy on the 'Reliable

Contraband,'" 255–58, 258nn2–3, 258n6, 260, 356n1*bottom*
"Moses Who?" 39, 41n2
"M'sieu Gor-r-dong," 332, 334n3
"The Oldest of the Republics, VENICE, Past and Present," 332, 334n3
"Our Fellow Savages of the Sandwich Islands": xxvi, xxvii, 375–442 *passim*, 422n2, 477n13; composition, 277n5, 360n5, 362 & 363n2, 367; lecture schedule, 366–67, 367n2, 415–16, 481, 483–86; reception and reviews (favorable), xxvi, 324, 383–84n9, 391, 392–93, 394n2, 394–95n3, 407–8n8, 414n2, 417n2, 423, 436, 437, 439n8; reception and reviews (unfavorable), 410, 411n2, 429n4, 438n4, 438–39n8
"Pilgrim Life," 106 & 106–7n2
"Roughing It," 20n2
Sandwich Islands lecture (1866–67), 106n2, 230n8, 321, 321n4, 382n5, 401n1, 489
letters, interest defined, 181, 184n10
literary reputation, xxvii, 83n1, 161n7, 196n1, 229, 319n6, 488. See also *The Innocents Abroad:* reception and reviews
"Moralist of the Main," 99n1
political satirist, 148–49, 150 & 151n2, 174, 207 & 208–9n2, 458–66
"Wild Humorist of the Pacific Slope," 42n8
literary style and methods, 92, 98, 181, 184n10, 231, 298–99, 304, 306, 317
notebooks, 121n1, 193n2, 435n3
occupations, xxvii, 298
  interest in newspaper proprietorship: xxv, 81n6, 92, 259; Cleveland *Herald*, xxvi, 4, 7n7, 17n6, 49, 51n3, 69, 72n1, 85, 85n2, 96, 185 & 187n4, 195, 196n2, 212 & 214n3, 260, 261n6, 270, 271, 276, 276–77n1, 281 & 281n4, 287 & 287–88n2, 291n3, 291, 298–99; Hartford *Courant*, xxvi, 96, 97n5, 100, 101, 145 & 148n5, 195–96, 196n3, 225 & 226n10, 229, 261n5, 265–66, 266n3, 404, 407n4, 440; Hartford *Evening*

Post, 229, 266, 268–69; Springfield *Republican*, 267; Toledo *Blade*, 159 & 160n5, 177–78, 178n2. *See also* Buffalo *Express:* SLC as owner
  journalist, 259, 261n1, 343n3, 354n1, 371, 373n7, 374n10. *See also* Buffalo *Express*, Chicago *Republican*, Cleveland *Herald*, Elmira *Advertiser*, *Galaxy*, New York *Herald*, New York *Tribune*, *Packard's Monthly*, San Francisco *Alta California*, San Francisco *Wasp*, *Spirit of the Times*, Virginia City *Territorial Enterprise*, Washington *Morning Chronicle*
  miner and mining investor, 370–71, 373n4, 373n6, 373n7, 373–74n8
  pilot, 76n3, 121n1, 134n8, 277n4
  proposed political appointments, 74–75, 75–76n2
  quartz-mill laborer, 370, 373n5
  secretary to William M. Stewart, 150n1, 438n6, 458n3
  Senate clerk, 458, 458n3, 459, 459n6
philosophy and opinions
  children, 231, 378–79
  copyright, 380, 384n10
  death, 239, 243n1, 358, 360n3
  financial independence, 85, 91–92, 120
  friendship, 52–53, 124, 140–41
  good and bad luck, 123
  hospitality, 433–34
  idealization of marriage: xxvi, 11–12, 25–26, 33, 46, 58–59, 116–17, 348; wife's role, 91–92, 120–21
  indelicacy in literature, 132–33
  indifference to wealth, 91, 101, 120–21
  public vs private lives, 90–91
  sowing wild oats, 131, 153, 157n3
  woman-haters, 39–40
  womanly ideal, xxvi, 63, 117–18, 132–33
photographs, 113*illus*, 114n3, 118, 120n13, 122, 152–53, 158–59, 227, 248*illus*, 249n3, 399*illus*, 400n1, 411*illus*, 411n3, 503*illus*
"The American Humorists," 397n3, 406*illus*, 408n10, 411*illus*
caricature, 186*illus*, 187n5

Clemens, Samuel Langhorne (*continued*)
porcelaintype, ix*illus*, 165*illus*, 166n1, 236, 238n4
poetry and poetry burlesques, 127, 128n3, 335–36, 338n5, 471
obituary poetry, 336 & 339n7
"Ye Equinoctial Storm," 357, 357n2
pseudonym, 161n7, 207, 226n1, 260, 267n1, 343, 359–60n1, 456
religion
character references from clergymen, 56–57n6, 320, 321n2
Christmas sentiment, 8 & 9n2
church attendance, 38–39, 41n2, 72, 95, 101, 103, 134–35, 289–90, 291n4, 378, 380–81
ministerial friendships, 7n6. *See also* Twichell, Joseph H.
religious reformation, xxv–xxvi, 1, 5, 12–13, 18, 20n3, 90, 95–96, 104, 140, 225, 226n7
social and political attitudes
bigotry, 7n6, 192, 237, 426, 428n3
politics and politicians, 207, 207–8n2, 298–99, 305, 458–66
sweethearts, 132, 134n8
travels (major). *See also* lectures and speeches: locations *and* California *and* Nevada
Edinburgh (1873), 314n7
Hawaii (1866), 167n1
San Francisco (1868), 125n3, 293n1, 354 & 354–55n3, 357 & 357nn1–2, 383n7
works. *See also* Clemens, Samuel Langhorne: lectures and speeches, subjects and titles, *and* Chicago *Republican*, Cleveland *Herald*, New York *Tribune*, San Francisco *Alta California*
Adventures of Huckleberry Finn, 441n5
The Adventures of Tom Sawyer, 142n5, 441n5
"Around the World" letters, 7n6, 360–61n5, 402n2
"Arthur," 359 & 361n8
autobiographical writings, 56–57n6, 160n1, 170n5, 182n6, 217–18n8, 249n1

"An Awful—Terrible Medieval Romance," 402n2
"Biography of Samson," 202n2
"Browsing Around" letters, 402n2
Byron letter (burlesque), 366 & 367n1
"The California Pioneers," 372n1
"The Celebrated Jumping Frog of Calaveras County," 392, 423, 425n2*top*
The Celebrated Jumping Frog of Calaveras County, And other Sketches, 42n8, 100n1*top*, 132, 134n9, 232, 232n5, 319n6
"Concerning Gideon's Band," 463n16
"A Day at Niagara," 300n4, 358 & 359–60n1, 360n2
"English Festivities. And Minor Matters," 300n4, 358 & 360n1, 360n2
"The Experience of the McWilliamses with Membranous Croup," 318n3
"The Facts Concerning the Recent Resignation," 459n6
"A Fair Career Closed," 434n1
"The Gates Ajar," 321n1
"A Ghost Story," 402n2
The Gilded Age, 142n5, 170n5, 266n3
"A Good Letter," 338n4, 402n2
"Incorporated Company of Mean Men," 423 & 424n1
"Information Wanted" (1867), 462n13
"Information Wanted" (1868), 145 & 148n6
The Innocents Abroad. See *The Innocents Abroad*
"Inspired Humor," 305, 306n1, 307n6
"Journalism in Tennessee," 358 & 360n1, 360n2
"The Last Words of Great Men," 358 & 360n1, 360nn2–3
L'Homme qui rit (burlesque), 226n6
"Mark Twain's Eulogy on the 'Reliable Contraband,'" 255–58, 258nn2–3, 258n6, 260, 356n1*bottom*
Mark Twain's Sketches, New and Old, 142n5, 230n3, 300n4, 318n3
"Memoranda," 367n1
"The 'Monopoly' Speaks," 306n3, 334n5
"More Byron Scandal," 350 & 350–51n7

"Mr. Beecher and the Clergy," 183n7
"Niagara," 300n4
"Open Letter to Com. Vanderbilt,"
124, 125n8, 144, 176 & 177n1, 215,
223, 226n3, 356n1*bottom*
"An Open Letter to the American
People," 184n10
"Papers of the Adam Family," 314n7
"People and Things," 303 & 306n1,
307n6, 320n7, 329n1, 338–39n6,
345, 346n5, 372n1, 466–70
"Personal Habits of the Siamese
Twins," 228, 230n3, 356n1*bottom*
"Petrified Man," 467n3
"Private Habits of Horace Greeley,"
127, 128n5
"Remarkable Murder Trial," 207 &
207–8n2, 302n1
"Removal of the Capital," 313n4
"Rev. H. W. Beecher. His Private Hab-
its," 338n4, 358 & 360n1, 360n2
Roughing It, 41n2, 66n2, 142n5,
373nn5–7, 374n9, 424n1
"Salutatory," 335, 337n1, 345, 470–72
Shem's diary, 312, 313–14n7
A Tramp Abroad, 142n5
"Villagers of 1840–3," 44n3
"The White House Funeral," 148–49,
150 & 151n2, 174, 458–66
"The 'Wild Man.' 'Interviewed,'" 358
& 360n1, 360n2
"Ye Cuban Patriot," 402n2
"Ye Equinoctial Storm," 357, 357n2
Cleveland, Ohio
letters from, 1–2, 49–51, 61–76, 88–90,
456–57
characterized by SLC, 103
lectures by SLC, 15–16, 16–17n1, 17n2,
19, 38, 43, 44, 46, 47n1, 68, 68n5,
72, 481, 482, 482n6
visits of SLC: xxv, 1, 2n2, 4–5, 8, 17nn3–
4, 18, 21n10, 40, 41n3, 44, 49–50,
51n1, 54, 85n2, 176, 177n3, 260 &
261n6, 281n4, 287n2, 290n1, 344,
476n9; proposed visits of SLC, 124,
169, 176, 184, 185, 196, 212, 268,
269n3, 270, 276, 280–81, 374,
375n1, 398, 399n1
Cleveland *Herald*, 27n2, 28n1, 68n5, 72n1,
87n3, 169n1, 311, 469, 469n9,
486n19
characterized by SLC, 96
contributions by SLC, 8, 9n2, 10, 17n1,
42n8
envelope, 87, 89, 186, 192, 398
letterhead, 88
proposed partnership of SLC: xxvi, 4,
7n7, 17n6, 49, 51n3, 69, 72n1, 85,
85n2, 96, 185 & 187n4, 195, 196n2,
212 & 214n3, 260, 261n6, 270, 271,
276, 276–77n1, 281 & 281n4, 304;
negotiations broken off, 287 & 287–
88n2, 291n3, 291, 299; political editorship offered, 298–99
proprietors. *See* Benedict, George A.;
Benedict, George S.; Fairbanks,
Abel W.
review of *The Innocents Abroad*, 359,
361n7
reviews of SLC's lectures, 88n4, 487, 488,
492, 493
Cleveland *Leader*, 482n1
prints SLC speech, 87–88n4
Cleveland *Plain-Dealer*, 324n1
Cleveland Protestant Orphan Asylum,
47n1, 68, 68n5, 72, 86, 87–88n4,
482n6
letter to, 15–17
letter by, 17n1
Clifton, Harry, 93n3
Clinton, Mass., 396
letters from, 395–97
lecture by SLC, 397n2, 484
Clinton House, Clinton, Mass.
characterized by SLC, 396
Clinton House, Iowa City, 45 & 47–48n2
Codner, Elizabeth, 181 & **183n9**
Coffroth, James W., 370 & 373n3
Cohoes, N.Y.
lecture by SLC, 416, 486
Coit, Benjamin B., 32 & **36n7**
Coit, Eliza Hitchcock. *See* Hitchcock, Eliza
(Lillie)
Coit, Howard, 32, 34, **35–36n7**, 37n14
Colfax, Ellen W. Wade (Mrs. Schuyler),
369n4
Colfax, Evelyn Clark (Mrs. Schuyler), 368
& 369n4

Colfax, Schuyler, 368–69n1, 369nn4–5, 407n6, 421n1, 462n14, 467, 467n4, 515*illus*
letters to, 368–69, 421
Collins, Thomas K., 43, **44n4**
Collyer, Robert, 46 & **48–49n5,** 78
"Columbia, Queen of the Land," 319n5
"Columbia, the Gem of the Ocean," 265 & 266n2
Columbus, Ohio, 86, 87n2
The Complaint, or Night Thoughts on Life, Death, and Immortality, 241, 244n8
Comstock, A. H., 416
"Concerning Gideon's Band," 463n16
Condensed Novels, 160n1
Congressional Committee on Patents, 384n10
Conness, John, 74, 75–76n2
Conrad, Louisa (Lou), 19 & 20n5, 43, 44n6
Constantinople, 200
Continental Life Insurance Company, 389–90n6
Coolidge, E. B., 378, 383n7
Cooper Institute, New York, 489
Corey, Ella J., 214n5, 240, 243n4, 247, 506*caption,* 508*illus*
Corinthian Hall, Titusville, Pa., 105n1
Corry, Pa., 104
Cowles, R. P., 416
Cox, Mathew B., 357n1*bottom,* 369n3
letter to, 357
Cradle Lands, 366n1
Craik, Dinah Maria Mulock
A Life for a Life, 104 & 105n2
Crane, Henry M., 314, 315n1*top,* **315n1***bottom,* 416, 416n1
letters to, 315–16, 330–31, 346–47, 353
Crane, Martha Powley (Mrs. Henry M.), 346, **347n2**
Crane, Susan Langdon (Mrs. Theodore W.), **49n8,** 152, 157n2, 159, 185, 211, 224, 225, 228, 241, 244n7, 406n1, 412
letter to, 179–84
birth and death, **450**
characterized by SLC, 47, 312
health, 182n2, 212, 214n4, 240 & 243n5
visit to the South, 182n2, 212

mentioned, 210, 251, 252, 269
Crane, Theodore W., 180, 211, 240, 390, 507*illus*
letter by, 390
birth and death, **450**
characterized by SLC, 47
partner in J. Langdon and Company, 49n8, 119n4
SLC's opinion, 47
visit to the South, 182n2
mentioned, 210, 242, 244n12, 269, 391n2
Crédit Mobilier, 434n2
Creel, Ella, 134n8
Crittenden, E. H.
letterhead, 103, 107
Crittenden House, Titusville, Pa.
letterhead, 103, 107
Cromwell, Oliver, 39, 41n5
Crossey, Mary (Langdon servant), 162 & 164n2
Crowninshield, Mr., 429n4
"Curiosities of California," 215–16, 218n9, 276 & 277n5, 279, 280n2, 280–81, 281n3, 360–61n5, 362 & 363n2, 422n2, 491
"Cussed be Canaan," 56n1, 258n6, 282n1
praised by SLC, 158 & 159–60n1, 169
Cutter, Bloodgood Haviland, 169, 170n4, 185, 187n5

Dakin, Charlotte Brown (Mrs. George), 119n5
Dakin, George, 115–16 & **119n5**
Dale, George W., 296, 297n5
Daly, John J., 276, 277n3
Daly and Boas, 276, 277n3
Damascus, 246, 249n1
Danvers, Mass., 396
lecture by SLC, 393n1, 397n2, 484
Davenport, Iowa
letters from, 38–44
lecture by SLC, 38, 43, 482
Davenport *Democrat*
review of SLC's lecture, 40–41n1
Davenport Library Association, 40n1
Davis, Jefferson, 465, 465n20
Day, Alice Hooker (Mrs. John Calvin), 79,

81n8, 158, 160n2, 173, 234, 405, 440, 510*illus*
friendship with Charles Langdon, 225, 226n5
friendship with Olivia Langdon, 143n12
wedding, 185, 235n5, 244n13, 253n5, 261n5, 265n2, 266n1, 266n3, 269n4, 270 & 272n1, 276
mentioned, 294n4, 369n2
Day, John Calvin, 79, **81n8,** 158, 160n2, 239, 511*illus*
wedding, 235n5, 261n5, 265n2, 266n1, 266n3, 269n4
Day, Thomas M., 97n5, 407n4
"A Day at Niagara," 300n4, 358 & 359–60n1, 360n2
Dayton, Ohio
lecture by SLC canceled, 482n1
"The Dead Canary," 317, 318–19n5, 335, 336, 337n2, 345
Dean, Elijah, 49n8
Dean, George W., 378, 382n6
Dean, Mary Andrus (Mrs. Elijah), 49n8
Dean, William, 382n6
Decatur, Ill., 25, 27n4
lecture by SLC, 5, 7n11, 25 & 27n3, 43, 482
Decatur *Republican*, 7n11
review of SLC's lecture, 27n3
Decorator and Furnisher, 294n2
Delaware, Lackawanna and Western Railroad Company, 119n4, 119n5
Delmonico, Lorenzo, 373n2
Delmonico's restaurant, New York, 258n3, 373n2
Detroit, Mich.
lecture by SLC, 27n2, 482
Detroit *Advertiser*, 324n1
Detroit *Advertiser and Tribune*
review of SLC's lecture, 487, 489–90
Detroit *Republican*, 487, 489
Deuther, George A., 333–34, 334–35n5
DeVoto, Bernard, 314n7
Dickens, Charles, 408n8, 425n2*top*
Our Mutual Friend, 16 & 17n5
platform style, 392
Dickinson, Anna E., 29, **30n3,** 79, 81n8, 259, 511*illus*

characterized by SLC, 63, 66n2
characterizes SLC, 66n2
Elmira lectures, 66n2, 414
meetings with SLC, 192n2, 261n3
visits Langdon family, 192n2, 261n3, 414n1
Dixon, William Hepworth, **365–66n1**
Doddridge, Philip, **183n9**
Don Quixote, 132
Donald, Robert, 384n10
Doten, Alfred R.
comments on SLC's lecture, **106n2**
Douglass, Frederick, 428n3, 512*illus*
letter by, 428n2
characterized by SLC, 426
escape from slavery, **428n2**
friendship with Langdon family, 428n2
lecture, 428n2
protests segregated school, 428n3
Douglass, Rosetta, **428n3**
Drake, P. H., 24n4
Drake, Sidney, 293n1
characterized by SLC, 170n5
letterhead, 98n1, 193n2, 286n1, 287n1
Du Chaillu, Paul Belloni, 215, **217n1**
Duff, Bradford, 410n3
Duff, Grace Ann Shaw (Mrs. William H.), 409 & 410n3
Duff, William H., 410n3
Duncan, Charles C., 212, 213n1, 215

Eastman, Annis Ford, 243n6
Eclectic Magazine, 394n3, 400n1*top*
Edinburgh, 314n7
Egypt, 200, 215, 359, 365–66n1, 369n5, 453. *See also* Alexandria
El Dorado Saloon and Chop House, Virginia City, 383n7
El Paso, Ill., 24n6
letters from, 24–28, 453–56
Elizabeth (N.J.) *Journal*
review of *The Innocents Abroad,* 498, 499
Ellet, Elizabeth Fries Lummis, 33, **36–37n10**
Elliott, George W., 136n1, 335 & 337n2, 337n3, 338n4
letter to, 135–36

Elliott, George W. (*continued*)
  characterized by SLC, 317 & 318–19n5, 320n7, 335–37, 338–39n6, 345 & 346n4
  poetical works, 318–19n5, 335–37, 338n5, 338–39n6
  "puffs" Mark Twain, 317, 319–20n6
  threatens bad review of *The Innocents Abroad*, 336, 338n4
Ellis, Henry H., 370 & 373n3
Elmira, N.Y.
  letters from, 84–88, 110–11, 176–203, 254–64, 276–88, 352, 366–75
  Langdon family residence, 505*illus*
  lecture by SLC, 30, 35n1, 481
  visits of SLC, xxvii, 7n8, 23n2, 28n6, 35n5, 57n9, 70 & 73n4, 78 & 81n3, 81n6, 82, 83n2, 84, 88–89, 97n1, 99n1, 101, 102, 107, 108, 109, 113–14n1, 121, 122, 124, 125n3, 127, 129, 138n1, 139 & 142n8, 160n6, 169, 170n3, 175, 179n1, 195, 196n1, 205n1, 211, 218, 226n9, 253n7, 258n3, 277n2, 287n2, 290n1, 291, 300n4, 318n1, 323n2, 343n1, 350, 362, 363n2, 385, 391n1, 432n2, 440n1, 474n3, 475n5, 476n9, 477n11, 477n13, 479n21, 482n1
  mentioned, 13n4, 22, 49, 59, 62, 67, 79, 83n2, 85, 90n3, 98, 105, 109n1, 115, 119n4, 122–23, 133n2, 133n3, 139, 142n3, 150n6, 182n2, 183n7, 184n9, 192n2, 214n4, 221, 244n7, 245, 251, 252, 261n4, 267n5, 271, 272, 281n1, 287n1, 293n1, 297n5, 302n1, 307n3, 307n5, 316, 318n3, 324n4, 342, 357, 409, 411n1, 414n1, 421n1, 430n2, 431, 433, 437n1
Elmira *Advertiser*, 208n2
  commentary on SLC, 196n1, 360n5
  contributions by SLC, 183n7
  "Friday Miscellany," 11, 13–14n4, 57n9, 154, 155–57, 157n5, 183n7, 350–51n7
  reviews of *The Innocents Abroad*, 296n1
Elmira College (Elmira Female College), 7n6, 350n3, 361n5, 368
Elmira *Gazette*, 492
  review of *The Innocents Abroad*, 295–96, 297n4, 493

Elmira Opera House, 57n9, 66n2, 175, 183n7, 414n1
Elmira *Saturday Evening Review*, 296n1, 350–51n7, 352
  characterized by SLC, 301
  commentary on SLC, 208n2, 301–2n1, 360n5
  described, 302n2
  reviews of *The Innocents Abroad*, 302n1
Elmira Water Cure, 369n4
The Elms, South Windsor, Conn.
  visits of SLC, 249–51, 253n2
Elsie Venner: A Romance of Destiny, 365, 366n2
England, 359, 369n5
"English Festivities. And Minor Matters," 300n4, 358 & 360n1, 360n2
Ensign, George H., 332, **334n3**
Eothen, 48n2
Erie Canal, 463, 463n16
Erie (Pa.) *Dispatch*, 337, 339n9
Erie Railway, 324n4, 375n1
Esmeralda mining district (California/Nevada Territory)
  residence of SLC, 370, 373n4, 373n5
Etna House, Ravenna, Ohio
  envelope, 92
Eugénie (empress of France), 34 & **37n13**
Evarts, William M., **458n2**
"Even Me," 181, 183–84n9, 235 & 235n6
Everett House, New York, 268, 270, 273n10, 273, 412
  described, 269n1
  envelope, 272
Evers, J. W., 56n4
Every Saturday, 441n4
"The Experience of the McWilliamses with Membranous Croup," 318n3
Express Printing Company, 294n2, 294n3, 360n1, 389n5, 390n6, 402n2
  letterhead, 313, 314, 315, 316, 324, 327, 328, 329, 330, 331, 339, 341, 342, 344, 346, 353, 357, 358, 362

F. A. Hutchinson and Company, 313, 314n8
"The Facts Concerning the Recent Resignation," 459n6
"A Fair Career Closed," 434n1

Fairbanks, Abel W., 2n2, 16, 86, 87n3, 196, 281, 361n7, 509*illus*
  letter to, 298–300
  letter by, 288n2
  characterized by SLC, 16, 88–89
  Cleveland *Herald:* offers political editorship, 299; partnership negotiations with SLC, 7n7, 51n3, 185, 195, 196n2, 214n3, 276–77n1, 281n4, 287 & 287–88n2, 299; proprietor, 7n7, 51n3
  letterhead, 88
  schedules lectures for SLC, 87n2, 88, 93, 95, 107, 276n1
  visits Langdon family, 176
  visits of SLC. *See* Fairbanks, Mary Mason: visits of SLC
  mentioned, 6n5, 17n3, 17n4, 19, 28, 28n1, 42n8, 50, 51n1, 123, 212, 300n1, 337, 359
Fairbanks, Alice Holmes (Allie), 2n2, 8 & **9n3**, 19, 21n9, 49–50 & 51n4, 281 & 281n5
  visits Langdon family, 170n3, 176
  mentioned, 2n2, 42n8, 123
Fairbanks, Charles Mason, 2n2, 281 & **281n5**, 299 & 300n3
  visits Langdon family, 170n3
Fairbanks, Frank, 2n2, 359 & 361n7
Fairbanks, Mary Mason (Mrs. Abel W.), 54, 88, 118, 334n3, 509*illus*
  letters to, 8–9, 15–17, 28, 86–88, 93–94, 107–9, 122–25, 168–71, 176–77, 184–87, 190–92, 195–96, 211–14, 261–62, 280–81, 298–300, 358–61, 398–99, 453–56
  letters by, 16, 17n3, 19, 21n6, 21n8, 108, 123–24, 124n2, 195, 358, 521*facsimile*
  character reference for SLC, 6n5
  characterized by SLC, 18, 40
  characterizes Olivia Langdon, 52
  fires, 86, 87n3, 124n2, 168, 169–70n1, 171, 176, 177n3
  first meets Olivia Langdon, 170n3
  mentor, "mother," censor: 1, 2n2, 16, 17n3, 40, 79, 177n3, 195, 358; advises SLC on propriety, 196n1, 205n1, 211; literary advice, 169,

170n5, 176, 190, 192, 358 & 360nn2–3, 374
  orders engagement ring for SLC, 86, 89, 102, 109n1, 122
  publishes SLC letter, 8, 9n2, 10, 15–16 & 17n1, 42n8
  review of SLC's lecture, 25, 27n2
  visits Langdon family: 170n3; proposed visit to Elmira, 4, 6n5. See also *Quaker City* excursion: reunion
  visits of SLC: xxv, 1, 2n2, 4–5, 8, 17nn3–4, 18, 21n10, 40, 41n3, 44, 49–50, 51n1, 54, 85n2, 176, 177n3, 260 & 261n6, 281n4, 287n2, 290n1, 344, 476n9; proposed visits, 124, 169, 176, 184, 185, 196, 212, 268, 269n3, 270, 276, 280–81, 374, 375n1, 398, 399n1
  mentioned, 9n2, 9n3, 30n1, 41–42n8, 50, 64, 76n3, 78, 93n1, 93n5, 105, 122n4, 127, 166n1, 186n2, 196n2, 202n1, 339n9, 406n1
Fairbanks, Mary Paine (Mollie), 2n2, 42n8, 54, **57n8**, 86, 88n5, 196, 196n5, 281 & 281n5
  visits Langdon family, 170n3
Fairbanks, Benedict & Company, 89*envelope*
Fairbanks family. *See* Fairbanks, Mary Mason *and* Cleveland, Ohio
Fall, George L., **199n1**, 481, 485n16
  envelope, 434
  lecture itineraries for SLC, 385, 415–16, 420n2, 481, 484n12
  letterhead, 415, 433
"Farewell!—But Whenever You Welcome the Hour," 19 & 21n8
Fay, Cyrus W., 129 & 133n3, 149 & 150n6, 159 & 160n6
Fay and Cox, 142n5, 214n2
Fentress County, Tenn., 272n4
Fields, James T., 382–83n6
Fiji Islands, 460n9
First Congregational Church, Ravenna, Ohio, 97n2
First Presbyterian Church, Hannibal, Mo., 135n2
First Unitarian Church, San Francisco, 57n6

Fitch, Thomas, 388n1
Flag of Our Union, 485n16
Ford, Darius R., 162, 164n2, 164n5, 182n6,
      325, 326n5, 350n5, 421n1, 508*illus*
   characterized by SLC, **6–7n6**
   publishes travel letters in Buffalo *Express,*
      360–61n5
   world tour: 7n6, 350n3, 354, 355n4, 357,
      360–61n5, 368, 369n2; itinerary,
      359, 369n5; letters of introduction,
      354, 357, 368, 369n3, 369n5, 421
Ford, Eunice King, 128 & 129n7, 163 &
      164–65n5, 242
Ford (J. B.) and Company, 167n1
Fort Plain, N.Y.
   lecture by SLC, 136n1, 482
Fort Plain *Mohawk Valley Register,* 135,
      136n1, 319n5, 336, 338n6, 492
   commentary on SLC, 319–20n6, 337–
      38n3, 493
   publishes Mark Twain items, 337–
      38nn3–4
   review of *The Innocents Abroad,* 319–
      20n6, 493
Fort Wayne, Ind., 38
   letter from, 2–8
   lecture by SLC, 2–3, 5–6nn1–2, 43, 482
   mentioned, 17n3, 41n3
Fort Wayne *Democrat*
   review of SLC's lecture, 6n2
Fort Wayne *Gazette,* 5–6n1
   review of SLC's lecture, 6n2
France, 194, 369n5, 460n9. *See also* Paris;
      Versailles
Franklin, Pa., 109–10n1, 123, 124
   letters from, 108–10
   lecture by SLC, 47, 49n7, 94, 94n3, 107,
      107–8n2, 109n3, 483
Fredericksburg, Va., 339, 340, 345, 432n2
Fredonia, N.Y.
   lecture by SLC, 480n24, 486
   Moffett/Clemens residence, 44n7, 430n2
Freedmen's Bureau, 464, 465n20
Freeport, Ill., 80
   lecture by SLC, 38, 55, 81n9, 483
"Friday Miscellany," 11, 13–14n4, 57n9,
      154, 155–57, 157n5, 183n7, 350–
      51n7
Frisbie, Eaton N., 115, **119n4**
Frost, G. W., 415

Fry's Hall, Freeport, Ill., 81n9
Fuller, Frank, 230n8
Furbish, H. F., 415
"The Future of the Blacks in America,"
      157n5

Gabrilowitsch, Nina, **449**
Gabrilowitsch, Ossip, **449**
Galaxy
   contributions by SLC, 367n1
Galena, Ill.
   letter from, 81–83
   lecture by SLC, 38, 55, 81, 83n1, 483
   mentioned, 89
Galena *Gazette*
   review of SLC's lecture, 83n1
Galesburg, Ill.
   letter from, 21–24
   lecture by SLC, 23n1, 43, 482
Galilee, Sea of (Gennesaret, Lake of), 335,
      337–38n3, 381, 384–85n11
Gallaudet, Thomas Hopkins, 232n3
The Gates Ajar, 321n1
   review by Bret Harte, 321n1
Gay, H. G., 415, 435n3
"Geer" (hymn), 181, 183n9, 250
General Average, 341n1*bottom*
Genesee College, Lima, N.Y., 131 & 133n6
Genesee Wesleyan Seminary, Lima, N.Y.,
      133n6
Geneseo, N.Y.
   lecture by SLC, 94, 94n3, 109–11, 122n3,
      123, 130, 133n1, 483
   SLC's social activities, 130–31
   mentioned, 126, 129, 133n2, 133n4, 139,
      157n3
Geneseo Academy, 110n1*top*
Geneseo *Genesee Valley Herald*
   publishes letters by SLC, 109–11
Gennesaret, Lake of. *See* Galilee, Sea of
Genoa, 188n1
George (Langdon coachman), 180, 182n4
George, Henry, **401n1,** 402n2, 514*illus*
   letter by, 401
George, Henry, Jr., 401n1
George I (king of Greece), **188n2**
Germantown, Pa.
   lecture by SLC, 415, 416n1, 485
Germany, 359, 369n5

"A Ghost Story," 402n2
Gibson, Susan (Mrs. William)
  characterized by SLC, 185 & 186–87n2
Gibson, William
  characterized by SLC, 185 & 186–87n2
The Gilded Age, 142n5, 170n5, 266n3
Gillette House, Ravenna, Ohio
  envelope, 92
  letterhead, 90, 93, 94, 98, 100, 101, 102
Gloucester (Mass.) *Cape Ann Advertiser*,
  485n17
  review of SLC's lecture, 438n4
Goggin, Pamelia, 447
Gold Hill (Nev.) *Evening News*
  review of SLC's lecture, 106n2
"A Good Letter," 338n4, 402n2
Goodman, Ellen (Mrs. Joseph T.), 431,
  432n2
Goodman, Joseph T.
  letter to, 105–7
  character reference for SLC, 106n1,
    432n2
  employs SLC on *Territorial Enterprise*,
    106n1
  marriage, 432n2
  meets the Langdons, 431, 432n2
  visits East Coast, 431, 432n2, 433, 434n1
Goodrich, William H., 97n5, 407n4
Gough, John Bartholomew, 106–7n2, 259,
  261n3
Gourlie, John H., 341n1*bottom*
Gourlie, John H., Jr., 341n1*bottom*
  letter to, 341
Grand Army of the Republic, 119n2, 126,
  410n2, 437
Grand Army of the Republic Course, 403n1
Grand River Valley Railroad Company
  letterhead, 29
Grant, Ulysses S., 56n5, 148n5, 151n2, 241,
  257 & 259n7, 462n14, 466, 491
Gray, David, **363n3**
  review of *The Innocents Abroad*, 364n4
Gray, Henry Peters, **275n2**
Great Britain, 461, 461n12
The Great Metropolis; A Mirror of New York,
  99n1, 284, 286n1, 293n1
Greatorex, Henry Wellington, 183n9
Greece, 187, 188n3
Greeley, Horace, 154–56, 157n5, 167n1,
  265n1

Greene, Mary (Langdon servant), 162 &
  164n2
Greer, Frederick H.
  portrait in *The Innocents Abroad*, 169 &
    170n4
Greeves, John (*or* Sanford), 14n5, 211n1,
  224, 233–34, 269, 269–70n5
Gregg, William H., 182n6
Griswold, A. Miner (Fat Contributor)
  letter to, 324
  lecture style compared to SLC, **324n1**
Gross, William H., 236, 238n3
Grubb, John, 415
A Guide to Hayti, 218n8
Gulliver's Travels, 132
Gurney and Son, 113, 503*caption*

Haiti, 218n8
Hale and Norcross mine, 371
Hale and Norcross Silver Mining Company,
  373–74n8
Hall, Ezra, 266n4
Hamersly, Lewis Randolph, 415, **416n1**
Hamilton's Hall, Fort Wayne, Ind., 6n2
Hamlet, 12 & 14n6, 127, 128n4, 257 & 259n8
Hannibal, Mo.
  early residence of SLC, 134–35, 202n2
  residents, 43 & 44nn3–4, 85 & 85–86n3
Harper's New Monthly Magazine, 379, 383n8
Harrington's Opera House, Providence,
  R.I., 393
Harris, Stephen R., 370 & 373n3
Hart, Ira F., 416, 416n1
Harte, Francis Bret, 320, 321n1
  Condensed Novels, 160n1
  The Innocents Abroad: review, 356n1*top;*
    unable to get review copy, 355 &
    355–56n1
  "The Luck of Roaring Camp," 321n1
  on California chauvinism, 372n1
  praised by SLC, 321n1
Hartford, Conn., 217n7
  letters from, 135–74, 179–84, 206–49,
    265–67, 403–8, 458–66
  Bushnell Park, 221 & 223n6
  characterized by SLC, 101, 103, 221, 404
  lecture by SLC, 405 & 407–8n8, 484
  Nook Farm, 143, 147n1
  residence of SLC: 253n2, 294n4, 407n3;

Hartford, Conn. (*continued*)
  proposed residence of SLC, 96, 101,
    103, 404–5
  visits of SLC: xxvi–xxvii, 15n2, 15n4,
    56n1, 68, 81n6, 84n1, 98, 100n1*top*,
    100, 101, 109, 109n4, 118, 121, 124,
    126, 129, 131, 138, 143n12, 156,
    166n1, 170n5, 179n1, 180, 193n2,
    196, 197, 205n1, 237, 251, 261n3,
    277n2, 344, 346n1, 385, 402n2, 412,
    439, 440, 440n2, 476n9; Hooker-
    Day wedding, 81n8, 242 & 244n13,
    260, 261n5, 266n1, 270, 276
  mentioned, 116, 125n3, 135, 135n3,
    142n5, 148n6, 159n1, 204, 235n5,
    243n2, 265n2, 286, 292, 303, 327,
    409
Hartford *Courant*, 15n2, 68n7, 217n7, 266–
    67n4
  characterized by SLC, 96
  history and proprietors, 97n5, 230n7,
    266n3, 407n4
  proposed partnership of SLC, xxvi, 96,
    97n5, 100, 101, 145 & 148n5, 195–
    96, 196n3, 225 & 226n10, 229,
    261n5, 265–66, 266n3, 404, 407n4,
    440
  reviews: George Francis Train's lecture,
    148n6; Nasby's lecture, 159n1;
    SLC's lecture, 407–8n8; *The Inno-
    cents Abroad*, 498
Hartford *Evening Post*, 68n7, 266–67n4, 469
  partnership considered by SLC, 229, 266,
    268–69
  proprietors, 228 & 230n4, 231, 266, 266–
    67n4, 269n4
Hartford *Evening Press*, 97n5, 266n3,
    463n16
Hartford National Bank, 217n4
Hartford *Times*, 68n7, 436n16
  reviews: Nasby's lecture, 159n1; *The In-
    nocents Abroad*, 498
Hartford Young Men's Institute, 215 &
    217n4
Hastings, E. G.
  letterhead, 292n1
Hastings, J. W., 415
Hawaii, 167n1, 460n9. *See also* "Our Fellow
    Savages of the Sandwich Islands"
    and Sandwich Islands lecture

Hawley, **Joseph R., 97n5,** 231, 266n3,
    267n1, 431, 432n4, 513*illus*
  letter to, 100
  SLC's partnership proposal, 96, 97n5,
    101, 145 & 148n5, 151n2, 225 &
    226n10, 229, 266n3, 405, 440
Hay, John, 66n2
Heacock, Grosvenor Williams, 291n4
Helmbold, Henry T., 367n1
Helmbold's Extract of Buchu, 366 & 367n1
*Henry Ward Beecher: A Study of His Person-
    ality, Career, and Influence in Public
    Affairs*, 167n1
Herbert, Mary Elizabeth, **365–66n1**
Herculaneum, 197
Hewitt, George M., 363n3
"The Hidden Christ," 82, 83n4
Hilderbrand (*or* Hildebrand), Samuel, 467,
    467n2
Hill, Thomas, 47n2
Hillyer, Edgar W., **434n1**
History of Plimoth Plantation, 119n9
History of the Bible, 98n1*letterhead*,
    193n2*letterhead*
Hitchcock, Charles McPhail, 32 & **35n6,** 33,
    35–36n7, **37n11,** 37n12, 37n14
Hitchcock, Eliza (Lillie), **35n6,** 36n9,
    514*illus*
  characterized by SLC, 32
  described, 33–34, 36n10, 37n14
  marriage, 34, 35–36n7
  rescued by fire department, 34, 37n12
Hitchcock, Martha Hunter, 32 & **35n6,**
    35n7, 37n14
Hobson, M., 93n3
Hoffman, John Thompson, 368, **369n3**
Holmes, John Grier, 378, **383n7**
Holmes, **Oliver Wendell,** 259–60, 261n3,
    512*illus*
  letter to, 364–66
  letter by, 365–66n1
  The Autocrat of the Breakfast-Table: 149;
    SLC's courting book, 149–50n2,
    175, 184n9, 188n1, 223 & 226n2, 365
  Elsie Venner: A Romance of Destiny, 365,
    366n2
  meets SLC, **165n7,** 174
  praise for *The Innocents Abroad*, 365–
    66n1
  visit of SLC and Nasby, 365–66n1

Holy Land, 288n3, 330n2, 338n3, 359, 366n1. *See also* Bethlehem; Damascus; Galilee; Gennesaret; Jaffa; Palestine; Smyrna
The Holy Land, 366n1
Holyoke, Mass.
   letter from, 395–97
   lecture by SLC, 397n2, 484
Hooker, Alice Beecher. *See* Day, Alice Hooker
Hooker, Edward Beecher, 144 & **147n2**, 510*illus*
Hooker, Isabella Beecher (Mrs. John), 143n11, 144, 147n1, 149, 158, 163, 272n1, 440, 442, 510*illus*
   characterizes Olivia Langdon, 159
   gives Jervis Langdon opinion of SLC, 135n3, 136, 138n1, 164n1
   Hartford residence, 147n1, 237n1, 407n3
   SLC visits, 144, 158, 161–62, 172–73, 210, 234, 235n4
   SLC's antipathy, 140–41, 143n12, 163–64, 164n1
   theological views, 173, 174nn6–7
   mentioned, 116 & 120n10, 149, 236
Hooker, John, 144, 510*illus*
   characterized by SLC, 173
   gives Jervis Langdon opinion of SLC, 135n3, 136, 138n1, 164n1
   Hartford residence, 147n1, 237n1, 407n3
   SLC visits, 144, 163–64, 172–73, 234, 235n4, 404
   SLC's antipathy, 140–41, 143n12, 149, 162, 163–64, 164n1
   mentioned, 116 & 120n10, 236
Hooker, Mary. *See* Burton, Mary Hooker
Hornellsville, N.Y.
   lecture by SLC, 486
House, Edward H.
   review of Sandwich Islands lecture, 230n8
"How deep and tranquil is the joy," 183n9
Howard, Edward Tasker, **167n1**
Howard, Ethan H., 363n3
Howard, John R., **167n1**
   letter to, 166–67
Howard, William Neill, 378, **383n7**, 383n9
Howells, William Dean, 378, 441n5
   meets SLC, 382–83n6
   review of *The Innocents Abroad*, **382–83n6**

Hubbard, Stephen A., **97n5**
Hudson, Mass.
   lecture by SLC, 415, 434–35n3, 479n19, 485
Hugo, Victor
   L'Homme qui rit: 225, 226n6, 238n2; SLC's burlesque, 226n6
Humboldt, Alexander von, 366 & **367n1**
Humboldt district, Nevada Territory
   residence of SLC, 370, 373n6
Huntington, Collis P., 282n1
Hutchins, G. L., 416
Hutchinson, Francis A., 313, 314n8
Hutchinson, James S., 57n6
Hutchinson (F. A.) and Company, 314n8

Illman, Thomas, **239n5**
"Incorporated Company of Mean Men," 423 & 424n1
Indianapolis, Ind., 6n1, 14n9, 18, 39
   lecture by SLC, 20n3, 43, 474n1, 482
Indianapolis Journal, 20n1, 28n1
"Information Wanted" (1867), 462n13
"Information Wanted" (1868), 145 & 148n6
Ingham, Prof., 29, 30n2
Inman, Henry, 237, **238–39n5**
The Innocents Abroad, xxv, 149, 205n1, 229, 249n1, 330n2, 335 & 337–38n3, 425n2*top*
   characters drawn from life, 168–69, 170n4, 185, 186*illus*, 186–87n2, 187n5, 212, 213n1, 213*illus*, 332, 334n3
   complimentary copies, 292, 311, 313, 314n8, 327, 365, 365–66n1, 368; inscribed copy to Olivia Langdon, 292, 294n5. *See also* publicity: review copies
   contract, 99n1
   copyright, 287n1
   dispute with *Alta California* over use of letters, 125n3
   illustrations: 98, 99–100n1, 100, 136n1, 139, 142nn4–5, 150, 151n3, 151 & 157n1, 155*illus*, 163, 166n1, 168–69, 172, 187, 188n3, 192, 193n1, 193–94n2, 215, 232, 232n4, 293n1; cost, 215, 218; frontispiece, 168, 170n4, 172, 197, 198n2, 198*illus*, 232n4; Old

The Innocents Abroad (*continued*)
Masters, 169, 190, 191*illus*, 192n1,
192; photographs and portraits,
15n2, 139, 142n6, 169, 170n4, 185,
186*illus*, 187n5, 188n2, 200, 200*illus*,
201*illus*, 202–3n3, 203*illus*, 212,
213n1, 213*illus*, 214n2, 442, 443n2
manuscript and printer's copy: delivered
to American Publishing Company,
xxvi, 15n2, 98n1, 125n3, 293n1;
Harte's revision, 355n1; length,
194, 196, 197, 199–200, 202nn1–2,
262; revision, 15n4, 98, 99–100n1,
139, 159, 187–88, 188n4, 194, 194–
95n1, 196, 197, 199–200, 202n2,
223n2, 225
publication by subscription: 99n1, 215,
230n5, 238n1, 319–20n6, 339–40,
364n4, 442–43, 496; agents, 296,
297n5, 313, 314n8, 339–41, 345, 355
& 355–56n1, 362, 363n3, 429n4,
442–43, 498
publication date: xxvii, 15n2, 135, 136n1,
150, 151n3, 179, 287n1; publication
delays, xxvi–xxvii, 136n1, 151n3,
284–85, 286n1, 287, 292–94n1;
SLC's anger over publication delays,
xxvii, 284–87, 291, 292–94n1
publication process: 14, 15n2, 258n3;
electrotyping, 15n2, 99–100n1, 100,
142n4, 188n2, 210, 225, 228; first
printing, 228, 232, 239, 270; proofs
and proofreading, xxvi–xxvii, 84,
84n1, 98, 99–100n1, 100, 136n1,
139, 142n4, 163, 168, 175, 176, 178,
179, 179n1, 181, 185–86, 187n5,
188, 188n1, 188n2, 190–91*illus*,
192n1, 192, 193, 193n1, 193–94n2,
194n3, 194, 194–95n1, 195, 196,
196n4, 197–98, 198n1, 198n3, 199–
203, 210, 212, 213n1, 215, 218, 225,
226n9, 239, 251–52, 254, 255 &
258n1, 259, 262. *See also* illustrations
publicity: 14, 99n1, 142n6, 292n1, 320n6,
323n1, 327, 328n1*top*, 328n2, 330n3,
340, 342, 362, 363n3, 492; American
Publishing Company circulars,
136n1, 142n6, 283, 283n1, 292,
292n1, 294n7, 301 & 302n5, 320n6,

457n1, 487, 492–500; American
Publishing Company prospectus,
14, 283n1, 286n1, 323n1, 328n1*top*,
328n2, 492; Buffalo *Express* advertising supplement, 297n4, 320n6, 327,
328n1*top*, 328n2, 330n2, 339n8,
343n1, 345, 346n3, 359, 361n7, 362,
363n1; review copies, 286–87,
287n1, 292, 293n1, 295, 301, 303,
303n1, 327, 329, 330n3, 340, 355,
355–56n1, 364n5; *Stray Leaves from
Mark Twain's New Book*, 337n3
publisher's attempt to break contract,
170–71n5, 293n1
reception and reviews: xxvii, 217n6,
288n3, 292, 293n1, 295–96, 296n1,
297n4, 302n1, 302n3, 302n5, 303,
303n1, 319–20n6, 322, 323n1, 327,
328n1*top*, 328n2, 329, 330n2, 330n3,
336, 337, 338n4, 339n8, 340, 341n2,
342, 343n1, 345, 346n3, 355–56n1,
359, 361n7, 362, 363–64n4, 382n6,
492–93, 498–500; irreverence criticized, 288n3, 329, 330n2, 343n1;
private reaction, 66n2, 287, 288n3,
292, 292n1, 335, 355–56n1, 365–
66n1, 374
sales: xxvii, 14, 285, 288n3, 292, 292n1,
342, 343n3, 385–86, 440, 440–41n2,
442–43; earnings, 66n2, 385–86,
440–41n2
SLC's opinion of the book: 194, 215, 291–
92, 374; illustrations, 98, 100, 139,
142nn4–6, 150, 168–69, 170n4, 172,
190, 192n1, 192, 193n1, 193–94n4,
212
title, 15n2, 84n1, 99n1, 135, 150, 151n3,
169, 170n5, 175, 176, 178–79, 193,
193n2, 197, 198n2
"Inspired Humor," 305, 306n1, 307n6
Iowa City, Iowa, 46
lecture by SLC, 43, 48n2, 482
Iowa City *Republican*
review of SLC's lecture, 48n2
Iowa City *State Democratic Press*, 20n1
review of SLC's lecture, 48n2
Irish Melodies, 19 & 21n8
Irwin, Richard B., 369n3
Ishmael. *See* Towner, Ausburn

Ismail Pasha (viceroy of Egypt), 201*illus*, 203*illus*, 203n3, 212, **213n1**
Italy, 490. *See also* Herculaneum; Genoa; Milan; Pompeii; Rome; Venice

"J. B.," 176, 177n1
J. B. Ford and Company, 167n1
J. E. Merriman and Company, 270–71 & 272n4, 279–80n1
J. Langdon
  envelope, 87
  letterhead, 176, 184, 254, 278, 282, 283, 368
J. Langdon and Company, 115
  organization and staff, 49n8, 119n4, 318n3
Jackson, Daniel, 176 & 177n2
Jackson, Mich., 29
Jacksonville, Ill., 89
  letter from, 84
  lecture by SLC, 38, 55, 78 & 81n5, 84n2, 483
Jaffa, 199, 202n2, 214n2
Jamaica Plain, Mass., 409, 436
  lecture by SLC, 399, 400n3, 438n5, 484
James, William E., 212 & 213–14n2
Jamestown, N.Y.
  lecture by SLC, 422n2, 486
Jamestown *Journal*, 422n2
Jefferson, Thomas, 460n8
Jewell, Marshall, 266 & 266n4, 269, **269n4**
Jewett, Elam R., 295 & **297n3**, 331 & 334n2
Joan of Arc, 63
Johns, Mrs. H. O., 5, 7n11
Johnson, Andrew
  burlesque speech, 463–65
  cabinet, 458–66
  drunkenness, 464 & 464n18
  early life, 464n19
  political career, 305, 463–65, 465n20
  "White House Funeral," 151n2, 458–66
Johnson, Jacob, 464n19
Johnson, James M., 363n3
Johnson, Mary McDonough, 464n19
Johnson, Reverdy, 461, **461n12**
Johnson, William H., 322 & 323n3
Johnstown, Pa.
  lecture by SLC, 385, 484, 484n12

"Journalism in Tennessee," 358 & 360n1, 360n2

Kalloch, Isaac Smith, 468, **468n7**
Kane County Gazetteer, 80n2
Kant, Immanuel, 408n8
Kellogg, Edwin P., 166n1, 238n4
Kennett, Thomas A., **294n2**, 294n3, 334n4, 389n5, 472 & 472n2
Keokuk, Iowa, 44n8
Kidd, William, 468
King, Esther (Mrs. Horatio C.), 167n1
King, Horatio C., 167n1, 167n2, 167n3, 419, 420n1
  letter to, 166–67
  letter by, 419
Kinglake, Alexander, 48n2
Kingsley, Charles, 413 & 414n4
Kingston, N.Y., 314 & 315n1*top*, 315, 330
Kinney, Peter, 19, 21n7
Kinsella, Thomas, 417 & **417n1**
Knickerbocker Engine Company No. 5, 34, 37n12
Konstantin Nikolaevich Romanov (grand duke), **188n2**
Ku Klux Klan, 305, 464

La Marmora, Carlo Emanuele Ferrero (prince of Masserano), 187 & **188n1**
Labouchere, Henry, 467–68, **468n5**
Lady Audley's Secret, 386
Lafayette Street Presbyterian Church, Buffalo, 291n4
Laird, John, 461n12
Lane, Augustus H., 378, **383n7**
Langdon (J.)
  envelope, 87
  letterhead, 176, 184, 254, 278, 282, 283, 368
Langdon (J.) and Company, 115
  organization and staff, 49n8, 119n4, 318n3
Langdon, Charles J., 25, 91–92, 153, 170n4, 180, 189, 274, 292, 299 & 300n4
  letters to: 29–30, 158–61; notes to, 27, 47, 141, 147, 149

Langdon, Charles J. (*continued*)
  letters by, 42n8, 50, 51n6, 107, 108n4,
    171, 172, 174n4, 228, 251, 304,
    307n5
  affection for Olivia Langdon, 11 & 13n3,
    121
  assistance to SLC: accounts, 30n1, 133n3,
    160n6, 253n7, 300n4; tailor, 129,
    133n3, 149, 150n6, 160n6
  birth and death, **450**
  business affairs: coal, 119n4; hardware,
    133, 134n11, 204 & 205n1
  characterized by SLC, 163, 207, 349,
    350n5
  drinking problem, 349 & 350n5, 369n2
  engagement and marriage, 159, 160n6,
    235n1, 299, 300n4, 349, 350n4, 375,
    375n2
  friends, 31 & 35n5, 42n8, 225, 226n5
  health, 205n1, 212, 214n4
  horse, 172, 180, 182n3
  introduces SLC to Olivia Langdon, 133–
    34n7, 290, 291n5
  studies, 369n2. *See also* world tour
  transmits courtship letters: 5 & 7–8n12,
    22, 38, 47, 89 & 89n1, 141, 159 &
    160n7; addressee, 19, 40, 47, 51, 60,
    65, 72, 80, 83, 89, 92, 105, 113, 118,
    128, 133, 135, 138, 147, 474n2,
    529*caption*
  visits New York with SLC, 204, 205n1
  world tour: 7n6, 349 & 350n3, 354,
    355n4, 357, 360–61n5, 368, 369n2,
    375n2; itinerary, 359, 369n5; letters
    of introduction, 354, 357, 368,
    369n3, 369n5, 421, 421n1
  mentioned, 28n1, 30n1, 47, 81n8, 127,
    206, 242, 244n12, 269
Langdon, Ida, **451**
Langdon, Jervis, 89, 90n3, 91, 117, 135,
    152, 157n3, 180, 210, 211, 213, 218,
    262, 263, 368, 369n2, 440. *See also*
    Langdon family
  letters to: 3, 6n4, 409, 433; note to, 251–
    52
  letters by: 1, 2n4, 3, 157n2; in support of
    Thomas K. Beecher, 183n7
  affection for Olivia Langdon, 121
  aids Frederick Douglass, 428n2

  assistance to SLC: 106; Buffalo *Express*
    purchase, xxvii, 281n4, 290 &
    291n5, 291 & 294n2, 298, 300n4,
    304, 311, 334n4, 387 & 389n5,
    430n2; proposed newspaper pur-
    chases, 268–69, 270, 276, 281n4,
    288n2, 404; Tennessee land, 270–71,
    272n4, 277n6, 279, 279–80n1, 387,
    388n2, 393n1
  attitude toward SLC and courtship, 3,
    6n4, 46, 57n6, 74, 93n5, 211, 271,
    272–73n6
  birth and death, 6n5, 45 & 48n3, 428n2,
    440n1, **450**
  business affairs and associates: 49n8,
    115–16, 119n4, 120n11, 142n3,
    244n7, 271, 304, 306–7n3, 368 &
    369n3; Memphis investment, 263 &
    264n2, 264 & 265n2, 271, 272n4,
    278, 278–79n1
  characterized by SLC, 46, 120, 278
  described: 307n3; tribute by Frederick
    Douglass, 428n2
  health, 6n5, 116, 325 & 326n6, 361n5,
    387, 440n1
  income and expenses, 260, 261n4, 276
  SLC's character references, 6n5, 52–53,
    56–57n6, 106n1, 135, 135n3, 162,
    164n1, 320, 321n3, 355n3
  supports Thomas K. Beecher, 183n7
  travels: Buffalo, 298, 300n4; Hartford,
    116, 242 & 244n13, 251, 253n5, 260,
    266n1; New York, 13n2, 111, 114n1,
    114–16, 265n2, 266n1, 267n5, 270,
    272n2, 277n2, 406n1, 411n1, 414n1,
    425; Niagara Falls, 288n2, 290n1,
    299; Spencer Springs, 326n6
  mentioned, 22, 47, 69, 85, 92, 127, 129,
    139, 173, 182n4, 189, 219, 242,
    244n12, 273, 342, 391, 421n1
Langdon, Jervis (grandson), **451**
Langdon, John, **182n4**
Langdon, Julia, 180 & 182n4
Langdon, Julia Olivia (Julie), **451**
Langdon, Olivia L. (Livy), 35n5, 89, 262,
    318n3, 402n2
  letters to, 2–8, 10–14, 18–21, 24–28, 30–
    42, 45–66, 69–83, 88–90, 94–97,
    102–5, 111–20, 126–35, 136–50,

151–66, 171–74, 204–11, 219–26, 227–54, 262–64, 265–67, 273–75, 289–91, 303–9, 316–20, 322–24, 325–27, 331–39, 344–46, 348–51, 375–85, 390–97, 399–400, 403–16, 423–25, 426–29, 431–41, 466–72, 516–22*facsimile*, 523–29*facsimile*, 535–39*facsimile*. *See* Appendix C, Calendar of Courtship Letters, 473–80

letters by: 42n8; courtship letter, 2n3, 393n1; joint letter with SLC, 184–87; quoted, 11, 25, 33, 45, 53–55, 63, 69–70, 78–79, 104, 112, 118, 122, 136, 222, 234, 239, 242, 350, 350n3, 369n2, 369n5; spelling, 45, 71, 116, 145, 222, 397; style, 1, 2n3, 67, 71, 73n7

amusements, 25, 181, 222, 223n7, 414n5

appearance and dress, 77–78, 86, 105–6, 123, 173, 275n2

assists SLC: 432n2; gathering articles and reviews, 127, 154, 207, 215, 217n2, 223, 227n1, 229, 326 & 327n8, 345, 346n5, 431 & 432n3; proposed posthumous editor, 345; reading proofs of *The Innocents Abroad*, xxvii, 139, 163, 168, 176, 179n1, 181, 185, 188n1, 210, 225, 226n9, 251–52, 255 & 258n1, 259, 262

birth and death, **448, 450**

birthday, 412–13, 414n3

characterized by friends and relatives, 9n2, 52, 66n2, 136–37

courtship, engagement, and marriage. *See* Clemens, Samuel Langhorne: courtship, engagement, and marriage

dockets love letters, 7–8n12. *See* Appendix C, Calendar of Courtship Letters, 473–80

friends: 14n5, 79 & 81n8, 85–86n3, 121, 136, 141, 143n12, 181 & 182n6, 214n5, 240, 243n4, 244n7, 247, 267n5, 268–69, 269n5, 270, 292 & 294n4, 299, 300n4, 325, 326n5, 404 & 407n3; meets Mrs. Fairbanks, 168 & 170n3

handwriting, 228, 229–30n2

health, 10 & 13n1, 64, 107, 117–18, 137, 140, 152, 154, 157n3, 206, 212, 221, 239–40, 243n4, 268, 273, 397, 435

hymns, 181, 183n9, 250, 253n3, 384–85n11

opinion of Cleveland *Herald*, 276, 276–77n1

philosophy and opinions: economy, 260, 393n1, 427 & 429n6; indifference to wealth, 101, 120–21; married life, 33

portraits and photographs: 5 & 7n10, 13, 14n8, 31, 47, 54, 65*illus*, 112, 114n3, 118, 122–23, 220, 221, 233, 250, 253n4, 504*illus*, 506*illus*; porcelain-types, ix*illus*, 59–60, 60n1, 61–62, 64, 65, 65–66n1, 67, 72, 76–77, 96–97, 166n1, 173 & 174n5, 220, 223n4, 235n2, 250, 253n4, 310, 313n2, 409, 410n1, 504*illus*; SLC first sees photo of Olivia Langdon, 134n7, 291, 313n2

pregnancy, 440n1

reading: Bible, 26, 28n6, 103, 181, 225, 226n7, 247 (*see also* Bible: quotations and allusions); drama, 127, 128n4, 132–33; fiction, 104, 105n2, 132, 365, 366n2; history, 116 & 119n9; humor and satire, 132, 149, 149–50n2, 175, 184n9, 188n1, 223, 226n2, 365; journalism, 350 & 351n7; mythology, 39 & 41n6; poetry, 26, 27–28n5, 33 & 36n8, 95, 97n3, 233, 235n3, 241, 244nn8–9; sermons and religious material, 5 & 7n9, 11, 13–14n4, 39, 41n4, 46, 48n4, 48–49n5, 49, 51n2, 69 & 72–73n2, 78, 82, 83n4, 140 & 143n10, 154, 155–57, 157n5, 172, 174n3, 232, 232n6, 247, 249n2, 323, 324n5, 344–45, 346n2; SLC's works, 132, 134n9, 223 & 226n3, 228, 230n3. *See also* assists SLC: gathering articles and reviews; reading proofs of *The Innocents Abroad*

reforming SLC: xxv–xxvi, 52 & 56n5, 95–96, 140, 225, 226n7, 436, 438n2; gift of Bible, 26, 28n6

sense of humor: 9n2, 118, 223, 228; opinion of humorists, 8, 9n2, 42n8

Langdon, Olivia L. (*continued*)
  studies, 4, 6–7n6, 162, 164n2, 181,
    182n6, 185, 326n5, 350n3
  suitors, 116 & 120n11, 118 & 120n14, 139
    & 142n3, 154 & 157n4
  sympathy for Orion Clemens, 271,
    272n5, 312, 393n1
  travel: Hartford, 242 & 244n13, 251,
    253n5, 266n1, 270, 276; New York,
    13n2, 82, 83n2, 85, 85–86n3, 265n2,
    266n1, 268, 270, 276, 280, 403,
    406n1, 410, 411n1, 412, 413–14n1,
    425, 428n1, 433, 437n1, 478n16; Ni-
    agara Falls, 288n2, 290n1, 299,
    300n4, 476n9
  visits to Fairbanks family proposed, 184,
    185, 196, 212, 398
  mentioned, 7n8, 16, 17n4, 30n1, 35n1,
    35n3, 44n6, 51n6, 57n9, 81n6, 94,
    94n2, 97n7, 100n1*bottom*, 128n4,
    179, 180, 190, 195, 253n7, 292, 298,
    307n5, 326n1, 375, 381n1, 384n10,
    388n2, 391n4, 397n3, 421n1, 428n2,
    430, 432n1, 438n8, 442, 482n1
Langdon, Olivia Lewis (Mrs. Jervis), 3–4,
  23n2, 42n8, 89, 210, 221, 263, 311,
  391, 429. *See also* Langdon family
  letters to: 90–93, 236, 268–70; note to,
    251–52
  letters by, 1, 2n4, 6n5, 93n5, 206, 272–
    73n6, 325–26, 406n1
  affection for Olivia Langdon, 121
  aids Frederick Douglass, 428n2
  attitude toward SLC and courtship: 3, 74,
    93n5, 271, 272–73n6; propriety,
    205n1, 211
  birth and death, **450**
  SLC's character references: 53, 56–57n6,
    92n1, 321n3; requests letter from
    SLC, 90 & 92–93n1, 102; requests
    letter from Mrs. Fairbanks, 6n5
  travels: Hartford, 242 & 244n13, 251,
    253n5, 266n1, 268; New York, 13n2,
    265n2, 266n1, 267n5, 270, 272n2,
    277n2, 406n1, 411n1, 413n1, 425;
    Niagara Falls, 288n2, 290n1, 299;
    Spencer Springs, 326n6
  visit to Fairbanks family proposed, 185,
    196, 212

  mentioned, 1, 2n4, 6n4, 11, 47, 69, 85,
    118, 173, 189, 206, 210, 236, 242,
    244n12, 251, 252, 273, 290, 325, 375,
    421n1
Langdon, Susan. *See* Crane, Susan Langdon
Langdon family, 13n4, 35n1, 184n11, 350n5
  attend Dickinson lecture, 66n2
  attend Hooker-Day wedding, 81n8,
    266n1
  Elmira residence, 505*illus*
  friends, 13n2, 30n3, 83n2, 85n3, 92n1,
    143n12, 170n3, 175, 192n2, 261n3,
    270, 299, 300n4, 369n4, 414n1
  genealogy, 450–51
  pets, 180, 182n4, 242, 244n12
  servants, 162 & 164n2, 180, 182n4, 196
  mentioned, 253n7, 339n10, 350n6
Lansing, Mich., 6n4, 29
  lecture by SLC, 27n2, 29 & 30n2, 455–56,
    482
Lansing *State Republican*, 29, 30n2
  review of SLC's lectures, 455–56
Larned, Anne, **326n3**
Larned, Frances Anne Kemble McCrea
  (Mrs. Josephus N.), **326n3**
Larned, Josephus N., 322, 325, 326n3, 344,
  515*illus*
  Buffalo *Express* owner and editor, 294n3,
    299 & **300n2**, 317, 471 & 471n1
  characterized by SLC, 316, 349, 471 &
    471n1
  collaboration with SLC, 313n4, 317
  review of *The Innocents Abroad*, 363–64n4
  writings: 318n4, 337, 339n10; praised by
    SLC, 337
Larned, Mary, **326n3**
Larned, Sherwood, 326n3
"The Last Words of Great Men," 358 &
  360n1, 360nn2–3
Le Sage, Alain René
  The Adventures of Gil Blas of Santillane,
    440, 441n5
Leigh, Augusta, 351n7, 367n1
Leonardo da Vinci, 190, **192n1**
Lepsius, Karl Richard, **365–66n1**
Lewis, Mr. (brother of Harriet Lewis), 32
Lewis, Mr. (father of Harriet Lewis), 25,
  27n4, 64, 66n4

characterized by SLC, 31, 35n3
Lewis, Mrs. (mother of Harriet Lewis), 31,
    35n3
Lewis, Edward, **129n7**
Lewis, Harriet (Hattie), **23n2**, 32, 118,
    120n13, 129n7, 211, 220 & 223n4,
    221, 304, 381, 504*illus*
  letter to, 21–24
  characterized by SLC, 23, 89 & 90n2,
    137, 180, 210 & 211n4
  characterizes Olivia Langdon, 9n2
  courtship of SLC and Olivia Langdon re-
    called, 23–24n2
  role in courtship, 19, 21n10, 21–24,
    42n8
  teases Olivia Langdon, 23n2, 122, 127–28
  visits Langdon family, 23n2, 163, 212
  mentioned, 24n6, 27n4, 47, 242 &
    244n12, 325, 474n2
Lewis, Olive Barnard (Mrs. Edward), **129n7**
L'Homme qui rit, 238n2
  characterized and burlesqued by SLC,
    225 & 226n6
Library and Lecture Association, Fort
    Wayne, Ind., 3 & 6n2
Library Hall, Chicago, 20n2
A Life for a Life, 104, 105n2
"Lilly Dale," 23, 24n5
Lima, N.Y., 131, 133n6
Lincoln, Abraham, 160n5, 297n2, 305,
    458n2, 459n7, 460, 464n18, 465n20
Lincoln Literary Association, Rondout,
    N.Y., 315n1*bottom*
Lisbon, Ill., 210, 211n4
Locke, David Ross (Petroleum V. Nasby),
    xxvi, 51–52, **56n1**, 56n4, 59, 68, 79,
    81n8, 397n3, 405, 406*illus*, 408n10,
    411*illus*
  letters by, 258n6, 282n1
  characterized by SLC, 158, 160n1
  "Cussed be Canaan": 56n1, 158 & 159–
    60n1, 258n6, 282n1; reviewed and
    discussed by SLC, 160n1, 169
  lecturer: 44n2, 56n1, 259, 261n3, 387,
    389n3, 394n3, 409, 410n2, 456,
    456n4; compared to SLC, 41n1
  meets SLC, 158, 169, 180
  offers SLC position on Toledo *Blade*, 159,
    177–78, 178n2

"The Struggles of a Conservative on (*or*
    with) the Woman Question": 56n1,
    387 & 389n4, 409 & 410n2; discussed
    by SLC, 387
  visits Boston with SLC, 164, 165n7, 169,
    174, 199, 199n1, 365–66n1, 405 &
    407n6
Locke, Martha H. Bodine (Mrs. David
    Ross), 81n8
Lockport, N.Y.
  letters from, 114–25, 134–35
  lecture by SLC, 114, 119n2, 121, 122n3,
    126, 133n1, 483, 483n11
  mentioned, 112, 119n1, 135n2, 139,
    142n9
Logan, James (*or* John; Tahgahjute), 460 &
    460n8
Logan, John, **183n9**
Longfellow, Henry Wadsworth
  Voices of the Night, 221, 223n5
Loomis, Edward Eugene, **451**
"Lord, I hear of showers of blessing," 181 &
    183–84n9, 235 & 235n6
"The Love of Money," 39 & 41n4
"Love's Queen," 169 & 171n7, 171
Lowell, James Russell, 456, 456n4
"The Luck of Roaring Camp," 321n1
Lyceums
  letter to, 351
Lynn, Mass.
  lecture canceled, 485n16
Lyon, Isabel V., 76n3

McAtee, William A., **211n1**
Macaulay, Thomas Babington, 26
McCarthy, Denis E., 401n1
McCulloch, Hugh, **458n2,** 466
McCune, Robert, 56n4
McEwen, Daniel Church, **150n1**
McFarland, Abby Sage, 407n6
McFarland, Daniel, 407n6
McGinley's dining saloon, Pittsburgh,
    382n2
McKeever, Mr., 459, 459n5
McKinney, Glenn Ford, **449**
McNaughton, J. H., 23 & 24n5
McVicker, Mary, 204, **205n3**
McWilliams, Esther Keeler Norton (Mrs.

McWilliams, Esther (*continued*)
John James), 316 & 318n3, 325 & 326n2
McWilliams, John James, 316 & **318n3**, 325 & 326n2
McWilliams, Mary, 318n3
McWilliams, Shirrell, 318n3
Maguire's Opera House, Virginia City, 106n2, 107n2*top*
Mantz, Mary Emily, **449**
Margaret (Moffett family maid), 44n7, 189 & 190n2, 260, 312
letter to, 84–86
"Mark Twain's Eulogy on the 'Reliable Contraband,'" 255–58, 258nn2–3, 258n6, 260, 356n1*bottom*
Mark Twain's Sketches, New and Old, 142n5, 230n3, 300n4, 318n3
Marsellus, John, 415, **416n1**
Marshall, Mich., 29, 77
lecture by SLC, 29, 30n3, 38, 55, 80n1, 483
Mary (Langdon family servant), 162 & 164n2, 180, 182n4, 196
Mary Warner, 414n5
Mason, Edward B., 95, **97n2**
Masserano, prince of, 187 & **188n1**
Massett, Stephen C. (Jeems Pipes), **328–29n1**, 514*illus*
letter to, 328–29
Massey, Atkins, 370 & 373n3
Matthews, Carrie, 467
Matthews, George W., 467, 467n4
Matthews, Hannah Stryker (Mrs. George W.), 467, 467n4
Matthews, James M., 467
Matthews, Mrs. James M., 467
Matthews, James N., 363n3
Matthews, Lucy, 467
Mead's Hall, Lansing, Mich., 455
Medbery, James K., 216 & 218n10, 400n1*bottom*, 481, 512*illus*
letter to, 400
attempt to be SLC's lecture agent, 337 & 339n9, 353, **353n2**
"Memoranda," 367n1
Memphis, Tenn., 264, 271, 278, 279n1*bottom*
street-paving contract, 265n2, 342

Memphis *Appeal*, 278, 278–79n1
Meneely, George Rodney, 416, 416n1
Mercantile Library Association, Peoria, 27n1
Mercantile Library Association, Pittsburgh, 382n2
Meriden, Conn. *See* West Meriden, Conn.
Meriden *Republican*
review of *The Innocents Abroad*, 498, 500
Merriman (J. E.) and Company, 272n4, 279–80n1
Metropolitan Hall, Indianapolis, 20n3
Metropolitan Hall, Iowa City, 48n2
Mexico, 460n9
Milan Cathedral, 192, 193n2
Milburn, William Henry, **83n1**
"Milk and Natral Histry," 397n3
Millport, N.Y., 428n2
Mills, John Harrison, 360n2
recalls SLC's arrival at Buffalo *Express*, **296n2**
Milton, John, 1, 26
Mitchell, Isaac, 177n2
Mitchell, Rob. W. C., 416
Moffett, Anita, **449**
Moffett, Annie E., 147n4, 218, 430, 509*illus*
letter to, 84–86
attends SLC's wedding, 219, 219n3, 394n1, 429, 430n2
birth and death, **449**
mentioned, 44n7, 260, 430n4
Moffett, Francis Clemens, **449**
Moffett, Pamela A., 44n5, 84 & 85n1, 91, 184n10, 279n1*bottom*, 314n7, 389n6. *See also* Moffett/Clemens family
letters to, 43–44, 84–86, 189–90, 270–73, 276–77, 310–14, 386–90, 429–30, 542–47*facsimile*
attends SLC's wedding, 219n3, 394n1, 429, 430n2, 433
birth and death, **448**
Buffalo *Express* subscription, 311
characterized by SLC, 144–45
church attendance, 134, 135n2
health, 218
interest in SLC's religious reformation, 147–48n4
name, 447
plans to relocate to the East, 43, 44n7

residences: Fredonia, N.Y., 44n7; St. Louis, 44n7, 44n8, 85n1, 219n4, 272*envelope*, 273n9, 414n5
Tennessee land, 270–72, 272n4, 277n6, 279n1*bottom*, 386–87, 389n2
mentioned, xxv, 19, 86n4, 274, 326n4, 382n1, 388n1, 430n4, 477n10

Moffett, Samuel E., 147n4, 430, 509*illus*
letter to, 84–86
birth and death, **449**
mentioned, 44n7, 260, 430n4

Moffett, William A., 147n4, 387, 389n6
birth and death, **448**
St. Louis residence, 414n5

Moffett/Clemens family, 44n5
genealogy, 448–49
invitation to SLC's wedding, 311, 313n5
scrapbooks, 438n8
St. Louis residence, 219n4, 272, 273n9, 280n2
visits of SLC: 20n5; proposed visits, 276, 277n4

Monmouth, Ill., 19
lecture by SLC, 20n4, 43, 482

Mono Lake, 216 & 218n9
"The 'Monopoly' Speaks," 306n3, 334n5
Moore, Thomas, 19 & 21n8
"More Byron Scandal," 350 & 350–51n7
Morris, John, 28n1, 30n1, 30n4
letter by, 29
Morris, W. F., 416
"Moses Who?" 39, 41n2
Motley, John Lothrop, 461, **461n11**
"Mr. Beecher and the Clergy," 183n7
"M'sieu Gor-r-dong," 332, 334n3
Mount Vernon, N.Y.
lecture by SLC, 415, 416n1, 421n1, 422n2, 478n16, 485
Mudd, Samuel A., **465n20**
Murphy, John J., 255n1, 282n1
letter to, 254–55
Music Hall, Boston, 324n1, 389n3, 389n4, 397n3, 428n2
My Summer in a Garden, 66n2

Napa Valley Railroad, 34
Napoleon III, **37n13**, 201, 203n3, 212, **213n1**, 241, 332

Nasby, Petroleum V. *See* Locke, David Ross
Nation, 321n1
National Academy of Design, New York, 274, 275n2
Nature and Life: Sermons by Robert Collyer, 46 & 48–49n5, 78
Nettleton and Company, 339n8
Nevada, 359
holdup on the Divide, 106
residence of SLC, 184n10, 341n3, 370–71, 373nn4–5, 373n6, 456
SLC's acquaintances, 208n2, 250, 253n2, 341n3, 378, 383n7, 388n1, 433, 434n1
Nevada territorial legislature, 341n3
Nevius, Abigail Gertrude, **114n2**
Nevius, Elbert, 112, 114, **114n2**
Nevius, Maria Louisa Condict (Mrs. Elbert), **114n2**
New Britain, Conn.
lecture by SLC, 415, 422n1, 423, 485
New Haven, Conn., 435, 441, 442n1
letter from, 439–41
lecture by SLC, 416, 485
New York, N.Y., 399, 433. *See also* Brooklyn, N.Y.
letters from, 204–6, 264–65, 268–75, 418–21, 441–43
lecture by SLC, 230n8
lecture by SLC canceled, 31, 35n5, 43, 47, 49n7, 109n2, 482n1, 483n9
visits of SLC, 13n2, 79, 81n6, 111n1*bottom*, 111–12, 114n1, 119n3, 121, 125n8, 164, 171–72, 174, 174n2, 175, 205n1, 253n7, 265, 266n1, 277n2, 400, 412, 421n1, 428n1, 432n2, 476n7, 479n16
mentioned, 54, 82, 83n2, 85n3, 116, 164, 184n9, 216, 251, 409, 441, 442n1
New York Custom House, 465n20
New York *Evangelist*, 183n7
New York *Evening Express*
review of *The Innocents Abroad*, 323n1
New York *Evening Mail*, 353n2
New York *Evening Post*, 306n3, 353n2
review of *The Innocents Abroad*, 323n1
New York *Evening Telegram*, 208n2, 329n1
New York *Herald*
contributions by SLC, 202n1

New York *Herald* (*continued*)
   review of *Othello*, 205n3
   review of *The Innocents Abroad*, 302n3, 329, 330n2
   staff, 301, 302n3
New York *Independent*, 155, 157n5, 455n2
New York *Leader*
   review of *The Innocents Abroad*, 323n1
New York *Liberal Christian*
   review of *The Innocents Abroad*, 323n1
New York, New Haven & Hartford Railroad, 253n8
New York Press Club
   letter to, 255–59
   speech by SLC, 255–58, 258n3, 260, 261n7
New York *Sun*
   review of *The Innocents Abroad*, 323n1
New York *Times*, 208n2, 373n3, 467n2
   interview of SLC, 384n10
   review of *The Innocents Abroad*, 323n1
   staff, 167n1, 373n2, 384n10
New York *Tribune*, 265n2, 267n1, 278, 278–79n1
   contributions by SLC, 145 & 148n6, 150, 150n1, 151n2, 151n3, 174, 202n1, 202n2, 206n5, 207, 207–8n2, 343n1, 458–66, 459n6, 462n13
   review of *The Innocents Abroad*, 303, 303n1, 342, 343n1
   review of *Othello*, 205n3, 205–6n4
   review of Sandwich Islands lecture, 229, 230n8
   SLC's association, 215, 342, 343n4, 456
   staff, 128n5, 150n1, 228, 230n6, 265n1, 301, 403n1
   mentioned, 20n1, 204–5
New York *World*, 305
   review of *The Innocents Abroad*, 323n1
Newark, N.J., 216
   lecture by SLC, 81n6, 348, 416, 481, 485
Newark *Advertiser*
   review of *The Innocents Abroad*, 323n1
Newark *Courier*
   review of SLC's lecture, 487, 489
Newark Opera House, 489
Newton (Mass.) *Journal*
   review of SLC's lecture, 414n2
Newtonville, Mass.

   lecture by SLC, 412, 414n2, 484
Newtown, N.Y.
   lecture by SLC, 135n1, 164, 174n2, 174, 483
"Niagara," 300n4
Niagara Falls
   visit of SLC, 288n2, 290n1, 299, 300n4, 476n9
Nichols, Henry, 425n2*top*
Nicolson, Samuel, **279n1***top*
Nicolson pavement, 279n1*top*
Night Thoughts. See *The Complaint, or Night Thoughts on Life, Death, and Immortality*
Nightingale, Florence, 240
Nile, 359, 369n5
Norris, Basil, 151n2
North Ophir mine, 371, 373n7
North Pacific Squadron, 383n7
Norton, Dr., 202n2
Norton, Joshua A. (Emperor Norton), 332, **334n3**
Norwalk, Ohio, 46, 66n1
   letter from, 58–60
   lecture by SLC, 19, 38, 43, 51n1, 482
Norwich, Conn., 395, 396, 397n2
   lecture by SLC, 397n1, 484
Norwich, N.Y.
   lecture by SLC, 481
   proposed residence for Moffett/Clemens family, 43, 44n7
Norwich (Conn.) *Advertiser*, 484n13
Norwich (Conn.) *Morning Bulletin*, 266n4
Notes, on the State of Virginia, 460n8
Noyes, Henry Babcock, 244n7
Noyes, Thomas, 244n7
Noyes, William Lord, 241, 242, **244n7**
Nye, Emma, 506*illus*
Nye, James W., 208n2
Nye, Mary, 506*caption*

"O God of Bethel! by whose hand," 183n9
Oakland (Calif.) *Transcript*, 401n1
Occidental Hotel, San Francisco, 32, 368
O'Connell, Daniel, 175
"O'er the Dark Wave of Galilee," 381, 384–85n11

Ogdensburg, N.Y.
lecture by SLC, 480, 480n23, 486, 486n19
Ogdensburg *Journal*, 486n19
"The Oldest of the Republics, VENICE, Past and Present," 332 & 334n3
Olga Konstantinovna (queen of Greece), 187, **188n2**, 212, 213n1
"Open Letter to Com. Vanderbilt," 124, 125n8, 144, 176 & 177n1, 215, 223, 226n3, 356n1*bottom*
"An Open Letter to Mark Twain," 177n1
"An Open Letter to the American People," 184n10
Oswego, N.Y.
lecture by SLC, 486
Othello, 205n3, 205–6n4
SLC's comments, 204
Ottawa, Ill., 25, 27n4, 38, 66n4, 211n4
letters from, 29–37
lecture by SLC, 30n1, 30–31, 35n2, 43, 482
Ottawa *Free Trader*, 482n4
review of SLC's lecture, 35n2
Ottawa *Republican*
review of SLC's lecture, 35n2
"Our Composite Nationality," 428n2
"Our Fellow Savages of the Sandwich Islands," xxvi, xxvii, 375–442 *passim*, 422n2, 477n13
composition, 277n5, 360n5, 362 & 363n2, 367
lecture schedule, 366–67, 367n2, 415–16, 481, 483–86
reception and reviews: favorable, xxvi, 324, 383–84n9, 391, 392–93, 394n2, 394–95n3, 407–8n8, 414n2, 417n2, 423, 436, 437, 439n8; unfavorable, 410, 411n2, 429n4, 438n4, 438–39n8
Our Mutual Friend, 16 & 17n5
Our Young Folks, 441n4
Overland Monthly, 320, 355, 355n1
on California chauvinism, 372n1
praised by SLC, 321n1
review of *The Innocents Abroad*, 356n1*top*
Owego, N.Y.
lecture by SLC, 391n1, 416, 416n1, 485
Owen, Silas, 416

Pacific Mail Steamship Company, 357n1*bottom*, 369n3, 369n5
Packard, Silas S., 125n8, 230n3, 258n2, 258n3, 327, 328n2
letters to, 255–59, 356
Packard's Business College, New York, 125n8
Packard's Monthly: The Young Men's Magazine, 176, 327
contributions by SLC, 124, 125n8, 144, 176 & 177n1, 215, 223, 226n3, 228 & 230n3, 258n2, 258n3, 258n6, 356n1*bottom*
publishes rebuttal to SLC, 177n1
review of *The Innocents Abroad*, 328n2
Paine, Albert Bigelow, 122n2, 219n3
Palestine, 215
Palmer, Henry Wilbur, 416, **416n1**
Palmer, Lorin, 420n1
letter by, 419
"Papers of the Adam Family," 314n7
Paris, 32, 35n6, 201, 361n5, 490
Paris, Ky., 192, 193n1, 194n2
Park Congregational Church, Elmira, 13n4, 183n7, 183n9, 243n6
Park River, Hartford, 223n6
Parker Fraternity Course, 389n4, 428n2
Parsons, James S., 389n6
Parthenon, 48n2
Patch, Sam, 146 & 148n7
Paterson (N.J.) *Guardian*
review of *The Innocents Abroad*, 323n1
Patmore, Coventry
The Angel in the House, 33 & 36n8
Patterson, Ella, 134n8
Pavey, Catharine (Mrs. Jesse H.), 43 & **44n3**
Pavey, Fanny, 44n3
Pavey, Jesse H., **44n3**
Pavey, Julia, 44n3
Pavey, Sarah, 44n3
Pavey, Susan, 44n3
Pawtucket, R.I.
letter from, 426–29
lecture by SLC, 415, 416n1, 425, 428nn1–2, 429n4, 485
Pawtucket *Gazette and Chronicle*
review of SLC's lecture, 429n4
Peabody, George, 468, **468n6**
Pearce, Henry B., 415

Pease (C. A.) and Company
     envelope, 92
Pensacola, 383n7
"People and Things," 303 & 306n1, 307n6,
     320n7, 329n1, 338–39n6, 345,
     346n5, 372n1, 466–70
Peoria, Ill.
     lecture by SLC, 24–25, 27n1, 28, 43, 482
Peoria *National Democrat*
     review of SLC's lecture, 27n1
Perkins, Charles Enoch, **294n4**
Perkins, Lucy Maria (Mrs. Charles Enoch),
     294n4, 405, 407n7
     praises *The Innocents Abroad*, 292
"Personal Habits of the Siamese Twins,"
     228, 230n3, 356n1*bottom*
A Personal History of Ulysses S. Grant, 284,
     286n1, 293n1
     letterhead, 98n1, 193n2
"Petrified Man," 467n3
Phelps, Elizabeth Stuart, 321n1
Philadelphia, Pa.
     lecture by SLC, 414n1, 415, 416n1, 485
Philadelphia *Public Ledger*
     obituary poetry, 336, 339n7
Phillips, Wendell, **175**, 260, 407n6
     visits Langdon home, 261n3
"Pilgrim Life," 106 & 106–7n2
The Pilgrim's Progress, 169, 198n2
Pioneer Women of the West, 37n10
Pitt, William, 41n5
Pittsburgh, Pa., 216, 337, 374
     letter from, 375–85
     lecture by SLC, 339n9, 366, 382n2, 385,
     477n13, 481, 483
Pittsburgh *Commercial*, 378, 379, 382n5,
     383n7
     review of SLC's lecture, 383–84n9
Pittsburgh *Dispatch*, 378, 382n5, 383n7
Pittsburgh *Evening Chronicle*
     review of SLC's lecture, 384n9
Pittsburgh *Gazette*, 385, 484n12
     review of SLC's lecture, 384n9
Pittsburgh Mercantile Library Association,
     383n7
Pittsburgh *Post*, 378, 383n7, 384n9
Pittsburgh *Saturday Visiter*, 382n3
Pittston and Elmira Coal Company, 119n4
Pius IX, 468, 468n6

Plantation Bitters, 24n4
Plymouth Church, Brooklyn, 7n9, 41n4,
     51n2, 72n2, 83n4, 167n1, 205 &
     206n6, 399, 419, 420n1, 420n2
Plymouth Collection of Hymns and Tunes,
     183–84n9, 250, 384n11
Plymouth Pulpit, 5, 7n9, 41n4, 49, 51n2, 69,
     72, 72n2, 83n4, 174n3, 232n6, 346n2
Plymouth Young People's Association, 419,
     420n2
Poe, Edgar Allan, 26
Polhemus, Josephine Griffiths, 268 &
     269n2, 270, 299, 300n4
Pollard, Edward A., **465n20**
Pompeii, 197, 198
Pompey's Pillar, 185, 186n2
Portland, Maine
     lecture by SLC, 415, 479, 479n19, 485
Poughkeepsie, N.Y.
     lecture by SLC, 400n2, 414n1, 415,
     478n16, 484
Prince Edward Island, 466, 466n1
The Princess; A Medley, 26 & 27n5, 71 &
     73n5
"Private Habits of Horace Greeley," 127,
     128n5
Promontory, Utah, 217n7
Providence, R.I.
     lecture by SLC, 387–88, 390, 391n3, 393,
     484
Providence *Journal*, 33, 36n9, 37n14
     review of *The Innocents Abroad*, 323n1
     review of SLC's lecture, 429n4
Providence *Morning Herald*, 394n2
     review of *The Innocents Abroad*, 323n1
     review of SLC's lecture, 393
Pugh, T. B., 415, 416n1
Pym, John, 41n5

Quaker City, 134n7, 177n3, 190, 213n1, 215,
     343n1, 364n4, 442, 490
     illustration in *The Innocents Abroad*, 168,
     170n4, 198*illus*, 198n2
Quaker City excursion, 1, 17n3, 125n3,
     150n1, 183n9, 215, 282n1, 364n4
     Bethlehem recalled, 9n2
     passengers, 2n5, 21n7, 125n8, 170n4,
     185, 186–87n2, 187n5, 217n5, 334n3

photographs, 213–14n2
reunion, 6n5, 31, 35n5, 42n8, 65, 66n5, 127, 128n4, 153, 157n3
SLC in Paris, 32, 35n6
Quaternion Association, 20n4
The Queens of American Society, 33 & 36n10

R. W. Bliss and Company, 339n8
Rahhahman, Abduhl, 237 & 238–39n5, 238*illus*
Ramsdell, Hiram J.
letter to, 402–3
Randall, Alexander W., **458n2,** 466
Randall, Mrs. J. C., 318n3
Ravenna, Ohio, 103–4, 123
letters from, 90–103
lecture by SLC, 93, 94n1, 94–95, 98, 483
Ravenna *Democratic Press,* 483n8
review of SLC's lecture, 94n1
Ravenna *Portage County Democrat*
review of SLC's lecture, 94n1
Reade, Charles
The Cloister and the Hearth: A Tale of the Middle Ages, 413, 414n4
Reconstruction, 464, 465n20
Redpath, James, 283n1, 512*illus*
letters to, 199, 214–18, 282, 297–98, 418–21, 422
letters by: 216–17n1, 385; telegram, 418n3
advertising circular for SLC, 217n3, 226n3, 227, 230n8, 422, 422n2, 457n1, 487–91
career: 217–18n8; lyceum business, **199n1,** 324n1, 389n3, 389n4, 397n3, 410n2, 418n1, 466–67
characterized by SLC, 218n8
letterhead, 415, 433
SLC's lecture agent: 35n2, 199n1, 227, 229, 283, 301 & 302n4, 339n9, 348, 353 & 353n2, 356, 392, 402, 481; SLC tries to cancel tour, 298n1, 301, 316n2, 317, 324, 333, 351
mentioned, 106n2, 282n1, 334n4, 337, 361n5, 408n10, 417n2, 422n1, 435
Redpath Lyceum Bureau, 199n1
Reed, Alfred, 442n1
Reed, Andrew, **183n9**

Reformed Church, Stuyvesant, N.Y., 114n2
Reid, Whitelaw, 265n1, 278–79n1, 279n2, 301, 343n4, 513*illus*
letters to, 264–65, 278–79, 303, 342–43
mentioned, 302n3, 343n1
"Remarkable Murder Trial," 207 & 207–8n2, 302n1
"Removal of the Capital," 313n4
"Rev. H. W. Beecher. His Private Habits," 338n4, 358 & 360n2, 360n1
Richardson, Albert Deane, 405, 407n6
Beyond the Mississippi, 228, 230n5, 284 & 286n1, 407n6
letterhead, 98n1, 193n2
A Personal History of Ulysses S. Grant, 284, 286n1, 293n1
Richmond, Va., 257, 259n7
Richmond *Examiner*
staff, 465n20
Riley, John Henry, 228, **230n6**
Robbins, Nancy Miriam (Myra), 134n8
Roberts, James B., 57n6
Robinson, Edward, **365–66n1**
Rochester, N.Y., 133n1, 340, 341n2, 350n6
letters from, 126–34
Rochester *Chronicle,* 109–10n1
Rochester *Courier,* 428n3
Rochester *North Star,* 428n3
Rockford, Ill., 14n9, 16, 18, 24n6
letters from, 8–14
lecture by SLC, 8–9n1, 43, 482
Rockford *Register*
review of SLC's lecture, 8–9n1
Rockport, Mass., 436, 479n19
lecture by SLC, 415, 416n1, 438n4, 485
Roe, Azel Stevens, 250, 251, **253n2**
Roe, Azel Stevens, Jr., 250, 253n2
Roe, Emma Comfort, 134n8
Roe, Fanny Bartlett (Mrs. Azel Stevens), 250, 253n2
Rogers, Sherman S., 294n2
"Romance in Real Life," 237 & 238–39n5
Romanov, Aleksandr Nikolaevich (Aleksandr II), 187 & **188n2,** 490
Romanov, Konstantin Nikolaevich (grand duke), **188n2**
Romanov, Olga Konstantinovna (queen of Greece), 187, **188n2,** 212, 213n1
Rome, 196

Rondout, N.Y., 315n1*top*
   lecture by SLC, 81n6, 315–16n1, 346,
      353n1, 416, 416n1, 481, 486
Roughing It, 41n2, 66n2, 142n5, 373nn5–7,
      374n9, 424n1
"Roughing It" (lecture), 20n2
Round Table, 353n2
Rouse's Opera House, Peoria, 27n1
Roxbury, Mass., 485n16
Ruffner, Ann Virginia, 134n8
Russell, William, **384n11**
Russia, 359, 361n8, 462n13
Rutland, Vt., 409, 410n2
   lecture by SLC canceled, 484n14
Rutland Opera House, 410n2

Sacramento, Calif.
   lecture by SLC, 401n1
   SLC's acquaintances, 373n3, 401n1
Sacramento, 357n1*bottom*, 357n2
Sacramento *Reporter*, 401n1
St. Cecilia, 137
St. Jerome, 190, 191*illus*, 192n1
St. John (island), 462n13
St. Louis, Mo., 310–11, 313n4
   Moffett/Clemens residences, 44n5, 44n7,
      44n8, 85n1, 86n4, 178n1, 190n2,
      219n4, 272*envelope*, 273n9, 280n2,
      292, 414n5
   residence of SLC, 44n3, 134n8, 246, 248–
      49n1, 414n5
   SLC's reluctance to visit, 184
   visits of SLC: 19, 20n5; proposed visits,
      272, 276, 277n4, 310, 313n3
   mentioned, 30n1, 85n3, 124, 272n4, 274,
      277n3, 314n8, 388n1, 430
St. Louis *Missouri Republican*, 467n2
St. Mark, 190, 191*illus*, 192
St. Matthew, 190, 191*illus*, 192n1
St. Nicholas Hotel, New York, 10, 13n2,
    111, 114n1, 139, 142n1, 205n1, 207,
    212, 255, 264, 265n2, 267n5, 274,
    406n1, 411n1, 412, 413n1, 425
   envelope, 205, 406, 410, 427
   letterhead, 204
St. Peter, 194
St. Peter's Cathedral, 194, 194–95n1
St. Sebastian, 190, 191*illus*

St. Thomas (island), 462, 462n13
Salem, Mass.
   lecture by SLC canceled, 416, 438n3,
      485n18
Salem (N.J.) *National Standard*
   review of *The Innocents Abroad*, 323n1
Salisbury, Guy H., 339n10
Salt Lake City, Utah, 359, 368
"Salutatory," 335, 337n1, 345, 470–72
Samossoud, Jacques Alexander, **449**
San Francisco, Calif.
   lecture by SLC, 261n2, 321, 321n4, 332,
      334n3, 382n5
   residence of SLC, 32, 35n6, 332, 354n3,
      374n8, 374n10, 401n1, 407n6
   SLC's acquaintances, 32, 35n6, 56–57n6,
      250 & 253n2, 321nn1–2, 328–29n1,
      332, 334n3, 354n3, 357n1*bottom*,
      369n3, 373n3, 378, 383n7, 401n1
   visit of SLC in 1868, 125n3, 243n1, 328–
      29n1, 354 & 354–55n3, 357 &
      357nn1–2, 383n7
   mentioned, 124
San Francisco *Alta California*, 255 & 255n1
   contributions by SLC, 20n1, 66n2,
      125n8, 160n1, 177n3, 188n4, 202n1,
      202n2, 226n8, 238n5, 267n1, 321n1,
      431, 432n3, 459n4, 460n9, 461n10,
      462n13
   dispute over use of *Quaker City* letters,
      125n3
   staff, 228, 230n6, 255n1, 282n1
San Francisco *Chronicle*, 401n1
San Francisco *Evening Bulletin*, 174, 373n2
San Francisco *Morning Call*, 328–29n1,
    373n2
   SLC's employment, 32 & 35n6, 354n1,
      354n2, 374n10
San Francisco Stock and Exchange Board,
    36n7
San Francisco *Times*, 401n1
San Francisco *Wasp*
   contributions by SLC, 357, 357n2
Sanborn, John E., 436, 438n4
Sandwich Islands lecture (1866–67), 106n2,
    230n8, 321, 321n4, 382n5, 489
Sandy (Fairbanks family servant), 86, 88n6
Sanford, S. B., 47–48n2
Santana, Henry Shaw, 410n3

Santana, Jose Ventura, 410n3
Santana, Kate Alice Shaw (Mrs. Jose Ventura), 409 & 410n3
Santana, Rosa Grace, 410n3
Sayles, Charles, **76n4**
Sayles, Eleanor, **451**
Sayles, Emma, **76n4**, 506*caption*
  broken engagement, 14n5, 209, 211n1, 224, 233–34, 235n3, 235n5, 269, 269n5
Sayles, Emma Halsey (Mrs. Henry), **76n4**, 299, 300n4, 326n6
Sayles, Guy, **76n4**
Sayles, Henry, 75 & **76n4**, 299, 300n4, 326n6
Sayles, Henry (son), **76n4**
Schofield, John M., **458n2**, 463, 463n17
Schuyler, Montgomery, 305
Scranton, Pa.
  lecture by SLC, 482
Seely, Jonas, 433, **434n1**
Selkirk, George H., 294n3, 401 & 401–2n2
  letter to, 401–2
Selwyn's Theatre, Boston, 386
Severance, Allen, 8 & 9n4
Severance, Emily A. (Mrs. Solon Long), 2n5, 9n4, 107, 107n1, 123, 176
  letter to, 374–75
  mentioned, 42n8, 124n1, 190
Severance, Julia, 8 & 9n4
Severance, Mary Helen, 8 & 9n4
Severance, Solon Long, 2n5, 9n4, 107, 107n1, 374
  mentioned, 4, 8, 185, 190, 375
Seward, Frederick W., 460 & **460n8**
Seward, William H., 150–51n1, **458n2**, 459n7, 460n9, 461n11, 466
  burlesque speech, 459–62
Seward Seminary, Rochester, N.Y., 428n3
Seymour, Horatio, 462, **462n14**
Shakespeare, William, 132, 181, 425n2*top*
  Hamlet, 12 & 14n6, 127, 128n4, 257 & 259n8
  Othello, 204, 205n3, 205–6n4
  sonnets, 228 & 229n1
Sharon, Pa.
  lectures by SLC, 84n2, 142n9, 175, 185, 385, 483, 484, 484n12, 493
Sharon *Herald*

review of SLC's lecture, 492 & 493
Sharon *Times*
  review of SLC's lecture, 492 & 493
Shaw, Charles H., 415
Shaw, David T., 266n2
Shaw, Henry Wheeler (Josh Billings), 394n3, 397, **397n3**, 406*illus*, 408n10, 409, 410n3, 411*illus*, 438n3, 478n15, 485n18
Shaw, Zilpha E. Bradford (Mrs. Henry Wheeler), 410n3
Shem's diary, 312, 313–14n7
Sherman, William Tecumseh, 215, 217n5
Sherman House, Chicago, 15, 18, 20n1
  letterhead, 14, 45
  SLC criticizes, 18, 20n1
Sherwood, Mrs., 357, 357n1*bottom*
Sights and Sensations in Europe, 285 & 286n2
Simonton, James William, 370, **373n2**
Slatersville, R.I.
  lecture by SLC, 436, 438n3, 485, 485n18
Slee, Emma Virginia Underhill (Mrs. John D. F.), 119n4, 406n1
Slee, John D. F., 115, 116, **119n4**, 119n8, 294n2, 304, 306–7n3, 311 & 313n6, 334n4, 406n1, 515*illus*
Slote, Daniel, 125n8, 176, 177n3, 204, 206n5, 276, 327
  portrait in *The Innocents Abroad*, 169, 170n4, 212, 213n1, 443n2
  sells *The Innocents Abroad*, 442–43
Slote, Woodman and Company, 204 & 206n5
  keeps account for SLC, 277nn2–3, 294n2, 425–26n2
Smith, Goldwin, 39, **41n5**
Smith, Horatio G., 406, 408n10, 411
Smollett, Tobias, 441n5
Smyrna, 188n4
Smythe, William C., 378, 382n5
  lecture experiences, 376–77
Snyder, Cornelius, 469
Society of California Pioneers, 372n1
Sons of Temperance, 202n2
South Windsor, Conn., 253n2, 476n7
  letter from, 249–53
Spangler, Edward, 465n20
Sparta, Wis., 47, 49, 52, 53, 57n6, 62, 75
  lecture by SLC canceled, 43, 482n5

Spaulding, Alice, 181, **182n6,** 185, 242, 244n12, 325 & 326n5, 506*caption,* 508*illus*

Spaulding, Clara L., 181, 185, 242, 244n12, 325 & 326n5, 506*caption,* 508*illus*
   characterized by SLC, **182–83n6**

Spaulding, Clara Wisner (Mrs. Henry Clinton), 182n6

Spaulding, Henry Clinton, 182n6

Spencer Springs, N.Y., 326n6

Sperry, H. T., 266n4

Sphinx, 9n1, 48n2, 105n1, 151, 155*illus,* 454, 455, 490, 493

Spirit of the Times
   contributions by SLC, 128n5

Sprague, William, **208n2**

Spring Valley Water Works, 334n3

Springfield, Mass., 422n1
   letters from, 422–25

Springfield *Republican,* 405
   described, 267n1
   review of *The Innocents Abroad,* 323n1
   SLC seeks partnership, 267

Stanchfield, John Barry, **183n6**

Stanton, Edwin M., 464, 465n20

State Deaf and Dumb and Blind Institution, San Francisco, 253n2

Stebbins, Horatio, 321n2
   characterization of SLC, 57n6, 320

Stebbins, J. E.
   History of the Bible, 98n1*letterhead,* 193n2*letterhead*

Stevens, Milo, 363n3

Stewart, William M., 150n1, 434n1, 436, 438n6, 458n3

Stilwell, Charles B., 42n8, 50, 54

Stoddard, Charles Warren, 321n1, 321n4
   letter to, 320–21

The Story of a Bad Boy, 440, 441n4

Stotts, Mary (Mrs. William), 44n8

Stotts, Mary Eleanor (Mollie). *See* Clemens, Mary E.

Stotts, William, 44n8

Stowe, Harriet Beecher, 352n1, 366, 511*illus*
   Byron scandal, 350–51n7, 367n1
   Uncle Tom's Cabin, 440, 441n2

Stray Leaves from Mark Twain's New Book, 337n3

Strong, Mrs. (daughter of Jesse H. Pavey), 43 & 44n3

"A Struggle for Life," 66n2

"The Struggles of a Conservative on (*or* with) the Woman Question," 56n1, 387 & 389n4, 410n2

Stuyvesant, N.Y., 114, 119n1
   letter from, 111–14
   lecture by SLC, 109, 112, 114n1, 483

Surratt, Mary, 465n20

Swain, Clara (Mrs. Robert Bunker), 354–55n3

Swain, Robert Bunker, 354, 354n3
   letter by, 355n3
   provides character reference for SLC, 355n3

"The Sweet Good Night," 319n5

Swift, Jonathan
   Gulliver's Travels, 132

Swisshelm, Jane Grey Cannon, 376, **382n3**

Syracuse University, 133n6

Tahgahjute (James *or* John Logan), 460 & **460n8**

Tahoe, Lake, 216, 218n9, 277n5

Taylor, Ann Elizabeth, 134n8

Taylor, Esther, 134n8

Taylor, John, 416

Taylor, Mary Jane, 134n8

Taylor, R. W., 388n1

Taylor, Tom, 414n5

Taylor, William A., 378, 383n7

Tecumseh, Mich., 39
   lecture by SLC, 27n2, 41n2, 482

Temple Hill Academy, Geneseo, N.Y., 110n1*top*

Tennessee land, 270–72, 272n4, 277n6, 279, 279–80n1, 386–87, 388–89n2, 393n1
   SLC renounces his share, 387, 388n2
   taxes, 272, 273n8, 425, 425–26n2

Tennyson, Alfred; 26 & 27n5, 71 & 73n5

Thackeray, William Makepeace, 425n2*top*

Thatcher, Henry Knox, 378, **383n7**

"There was an old horse," 106n2

Thompson, H. S., 23 & 24n5

Thompsonville, Conn.

lecture by SLC, 412, 484
Thomson, William W., 378, **383n7**
Three English Statesmen, 39 & 41n5
Tifft House, Buffalo, 281n4, 361n8
Tilton, Theodore, 454, **455n2**
Tintoretto, 190, **192n1**
Titian, 190, **192n1**
Titusville, Pa., 108n3
  letters from, 103–8
  lecture by SLC, 47, 49n4, 94, 94n3, 104,
    105n1, 107, 108n3, 108 & 109n3,
    483, 483n9
  mentioned, 104, 105, 107n1, 110n1*top*,
    123
Titusville *Morning Herald*
  review of SLC's lecture, 105n1
Toledo, Ohio
  letter from, 51–57
  lecture by SLC, xxvi, 31 & 35n4, 43,
    51n1, 51–52, 56n1, 68, 68n7, 456–
    57, 482
  mentioned, 40, 56n3, 59, 62, 339n8
Toledo *Blade*, 56n1, 56n4, 456n4
  described, 160n5
  review of SLC's lecture, 56n1, 68n7, 456–
    57, 457n1, 492 & 493
  SLC offered partnership, 159, 160n5,
    177–78, 178n2
Toledo *Commercial*, 56n4
  review of *The Innocents Abroad*, 339n8
  review of SLC's lecture, 68n7, 457, 457n1,
    487, 490–91
Toledo *Deutsche Zeitung*, 56n4
Toledo, Wabash and Western Railway, 56n3
Torbert, G. L., 31 & 35n5, 82 & 83n3,
    481
*Toussaint L'Ouverture: A Biography and Au-
    tobiography*, 218n8
Towner, Ausburn (Ishmael), 350
  letter to, 352
  criticizes Harriet Beecher Stowe, 350–
    51n7, 352n1
  commentary on SLC, **208n2**, 301–2n1,
    351n7
Tracy, Lucilia, 426, 428n3
Train, George Francis, **148n6**
  characterized by SLC, 145
A Tramp Abroad, 142n5
Trenton, N.J., 108, 109, 129n8

lecture by SLC, 111n1*bottom*, 114n1, 416,
    442n1, 483, 485
"The True Story of Lady Byron's Life,"
    350n7
Trumbull, Alice Cogswell Gallaudet (Mrs.
    Henry Clay), 231, **232n3**
Trumbull, Alice Gallaudet, 232n3
Trumbull, Henry Clay, 228, 229, **230n4**,
    231, 232n1, 232n3, 237, 238n5,
    383n8, 511*illus*
  endorses *The Innocents Abroad*, 287,
    288n3, 292n1
Trumbull, James Hammond, **230n4**
Trumbull, Mary Prime, 232n3
Trumbull, Sophie Gallaudet, 232n3
Tuck, J. Warren, 415
Tuileries, 34, 37n13
Twichell, Edward Carrington, 68n1
Twichell, Harmony C. (Mrs. Joseph H.),
    68n1, 71, 173
  attends SLC's wedding, 439
  meets SLC, 1n1
  mentioned, 207, 233, 442
Twichell, Joseph H., 102–3, 135, 135n3,
    207, 209, 405, 412, 413, 439
  letters to, 1–2, 66–68, 101, 441–42, 456–
    57
  characterized by SLC, 31, 35n3, 173
  discussions with SLC, 153, 173
  family, 66–67, 68n1, 71, 139
  meets SLC, 1n1
  officiates at SLC's wedding, 405, 408n9,
    439
  social engagements, 158, 172, 228, 231
  mentioned, 2n3, 30n1, 68n7, 81n6, 97n5,
    138, 233, 404
Twichell, Julia Curtis, 68n1, 71, 139 &
    142n7

Uncle Tom's Cabin
  sales compared to *The Innocents Abroad*,
    440, 441n2
Unidentified
  letter to, 366–67
Union Pacific Railroad, 215 & 217n7, 434n2
United States Congress, 83n1, 311, 458,
    459, 465n20
  Senate, 75n2, 208n2, 459

United States Patent Office, 311
United States Treasury Department, 388n1, 388n2
University Reporter
  review of SLC's lecture, 48n2
Up de Graff, Thaddeus S., **214n4**
Utica, N.Y.
  lecture by SLC, 356 & 357n1*top*, 416, 416n1, 486
Utica Mechanics' Association, 357n1*top*

"Vallejo" (journalist), 36n9
Van Nostrand, John A. (Jack), 212, 213n1, 213*illus*
  portrait in *The Innocents Abroad*, 169, 170n4
Vanderbilt, Cornelius, 125n8
Venice, 48n2, 105n1, 332, 334n3, 454, 455, 490
Veronese, Paul, 190, **192n1**
Versailles, 188n1
Vibbert, George H., 415, 416n1
Victoria (queen of England), 241, 361n8
"Villagers of 1840–3," 44n3
Virginia City, Nev., 253n2, 373n7, 434n1. *See also* Nevada
  lectures by SLC, 106, 106–7n2
Virginia City *Territorial Enterprise*, 106n1
  contributions by SLC, 373n7, 467n3
  review of SLC's lecture, 106n2
  SLC's employment, 341n3, 456
Virginia City *Trespass*
  review of SLC's lecture, 106n2
Voices of the Night, 221, 223n5

Wade, Benjamin F., 369n4
Wadsworth, Charles, 57n6
Waggoner, Clark, **56n4**
Waltham, Mass.
  lecture by SLC, 415, 485
Ward, Artemus. *See* Browne, Charles Farrar
Wardell, Francis, 300n2
Warehouse Point, Conn., 253n8
  envelope, 252
Warner, Charles Dudley, 66n2, **97n5**, 170n5, 407n3, 407n5, 407n8, 513*illus*

considers SLC as partner in Hartford *Courant*, 96, 265–66, 404, 405, 440
  European trip, 101, 195 & 196n3, 229, 230n7
  meets SLC, **266n3**
Warner, H. G., 428n3
Warner, Susan Lee (Mrs. Charles Dudley), 404, **407n3**, 440
Warren, James D., 363n3
Warren, Joseph, 363n3
Warren, Mass., 424, 425n4
  lecture by SLC, 415, 425, 485
Washington, George, 275*illus*, 280, 463
Washington, D.C.
  lecture by SLC, 403n1, 415, 416n1, 421n1, 438–39n8, 485
  moving the capital, 310–11
  residence of SLC, 74–75, 150n1, 230n6, 403n1, 458
  visits of SLC, 421
  mentioned, 145, 228, 297n2, 368
Washington Correspondents' Club
  speech by SLC, 403n1
Washington *Evening Star*
  review of SLC's lecture, 439n8
Washington *Morning Chronicle*
  contributions by SLC, 463n16
  review of SLC's lecture, 437 & 438–39n8
Washington *National Intelligencer and Express*
  review of SLC's lecture, 439n8
Washington *National Republican*
  review of SLC's lecture, 439n8
Wasson, S. E., 415, 416n1, 418 & 418n3, 419, 420, 420n2, 420–21n4
Waterloo, Iowa
  lecture by SLC, 38, 55, 81n9, 483
Waterloo *Courier*, 483n7
Watts, Robert M., 302n2
Waugaman, Asa Lobeus, 378, **383n7**, 383n8
Waugaman, Mrs. Asa Lobeus, 378, 383n8
Webb, Charles Henry, 42n8, 100n1*top*
Webb, Doris, **449**
Webster, Alice Jane (Jean), **449**
Webster, Charles Luther, **449**
Webster, Samuel Charles, **449**
Webster, William Luther, **449**
Wecter, Dixon, 86n4, 128n4

Wedlock; or, The Right Relations of the Sexes, 317, 318n4

Welles, Gideon, **458n2,** 463n16, 465
  burlesque speech, 462–63, 462n14

Wells, Samuel Roberts
  Wedlock; or, The Right Relations of the Sexes, 317 & 318n4

Wermicke, Frederick, 467

West, William F., 420n1
  letter by, 419

West Meriden, Conn.
  lecture by SLC, 415, 421n1, 424n1, 485

West Troy, N.Y.
  lecture by SLC, 416, 416n1, 479n22, 486

Western Union Telegraph Company, 217n7

Westminster Hotel, New York, 413n1

Weston, Edward Payson, 469, **469n8**

Wheeler, Orrin H., 302n2

"While Thee I seek, protecting Power," 183n9

"The White House Funeral," 148–49, 150 & 151n2, 174, 458–66

White's Hall, Toledo, 456, 490

Whittier, John Greenleaf, 66n2

Wide West mine, 370, 373n4

Wilcox, Chester A., 300n2

"The 'Wild Man.' 'Interviewed,' " 358 & 360n1, 360n2

Wilder, Mr., 340, 341n1*top*

Wiley, Clara, 85, 85–86n3

Wiley, Elmira (Mrs. George), 85, 85–86n3, 270, 272n3

Wiley, George, 85, 85–86n3, 270, 272n3

Wilkes-Barre, Pa.
  lecture by SLC, 416, 416n1, 485

Williams, E. Z.
  letterhead, 103, 107

Williams, Helen Maria, **183n9**

Williams, Samuel, 321n1

Williams, True W., 139 & **142n5,** 142n6

Williamsburgh Library Association, 417n2

Williamsport, Pa.

lecture by SLC, 391n1, 416, 485

Winchester, Arthur S., 389n6

Winnemucca mine, 370, 373n4

Winter, William
  "Love's Queen," 169 & 171n7, 171

Wirz, Henry, 465 & 465n20

The Women of the American Revolution, 37n10

Woodward, Calvin M., 280n2

Woodworth, Samuel, 50 & 51n5

Worcester, Mass.
  lecture by SLC, 385, 386, 484, 484n12

Worcester Lyceum and Natural History Association, 386

Wright, Laura M., 134n8

Wright, William (Dan De Quille), 293n1

"Ye Cuban Patriot," 402n2

"Ye Equinoctial Storm," 357, 357n2

Yosemite, 216, 218n9, 359

Young, Edward, 241, 244n8

Young, George, 395n4

Young, James Rankin, 228 & **230n6**

Young, John, 466 & **466n1**

Young, John Russell, 150n1, 151n3, 174, 228, **230n6,** 265n1, 343n4
  letters to, 150–51, 457–66

Young, William, 226n6

Young Men's Association of Geneseo Academy, 133n4

Young Men's Christian Association, 48n2, 429n4

Young Men's Hall, Detroit, 489

Young Men's Library Association, 20n2, 20n3

Young People's Association of Plymouth Church, 167n1

Young's Hotel, Boston, 389n3
  described, 395n4
  envelope, 393, 398, 400, 411, 416, 437

The text of this book is set in Mergenthaler Linotype Plantin. Headings are in Plantin Light. Plantin was originally designed for the Monotype Company by F. H. Pierpont in 1913. The paper is Perkins & Squier High Opaque Offset, acid free, manufactured by the P. H. Glatfelter Company. The book was composed by Wilsted & Taylor Publishing Services of Oakland, California, using Data General Nova 4c and Nova 4x computers, Penta software, and a Linotron 202 typesetter. It was printed and bound by Maple-Vail Book Manufacturing Group in Binghamton, New York.